The Library of Aḥmad Pasha al-Jazzār

Islamic History and Civilization

STUDIES AND TEXTS

VOLUME 219

The titles published in this series are listed at *brill.com/ihc*

The Library of Aḥmad Pasha al-Jazzār

Book Culture in Late Ottoman Palestine

Edited by

Said Aljoumani
Guy Burak
Konrad Hirschler

BRILL

LEIDEN | BOSTON

Cover illustration: The Jazzār Mosque in the early 1920s after the library had undergone a significant revival, photo by Ludwig Preiss, public domain, accessed at https://commons.wikimedia.org/wiki/File:PikiWiki_Israel_51654_the_al_jazar_mosque_in_acre.jpg

The Library of Congress Cataloging-in-Publication Data is available online at https://catalog.loc.gov
LC record available at https://lccn.loc.gov/2024051300

Typeface for the Latin, Greek, and Cyrillic scripts: "Brill". See and download: brill.com/brill-typeface.

ISSN 0929-2403
ISBN 978-90-04-72053-4 (hardback)
ISBN 978-90-04-72052-7 (e-book)
DOI 10.1163/9789004720527

This book is printed on acid-free paper and produced in a sustainable manner.

Contents

Acknowledgements IX
Figures and Tables X
Contributors XIV

Introduction: The City, the Endowment and the Manuscripts 1
Said Aljoumani, Guy Burak and Konrad Hirschler

PART 1
The History of al-Jazzār, His Library and the Inventory

1 Al-Jazzār's Library and Its Ottoman Context 33
Berat Açıl, Nimet İpek and Guy Burak

2 The Inventory: Documentary and Bibliographical Practices in al-Jazzār's Library 52
Said Aljoumani

3 From Whom and for Whom? The Audience and Provenance of al-Jazzār's Manuscripts 71
Boris Liebrenz

4 Historical Representations of al-Jazzār: 'Butcher' or Patron of the Poor? 89
Feras Krimsti

5 Uncovering al-Jazzār's Wealth: Confiscation and Power Struggle 111
Yasin Arslantaş

6 The Library of Abū Nabbūt in Early Nineteenth-century Jaffa 124
Benedikt Reier

7 A (Mostly) Local Story: The Translocations of al-Jazzār's Books in the Nineteenth and Twentieth Centuries 144
Konrad Hirschler

PART 2
The Materiality of al-Jazzār's Manuscripts

8 Notes on Materials: How Brief Descriptions Indicate Substantial Losses 171
Karin Scheper

9 Calligraphic Descriptions 190
Nimet İpek and Guy Burak

10 The Endowment Seals 207
Boris Liebrenz

11 By the Keepers' Hands: Comparing the Inks of Endowment Statements, Mottos and Seals 219
Claudia Colini and Kyle Ann Huskin

PART 3
The Intellectual Profile of al-Jazzār's Library: The Inventory's Sections

12 The Qur'an Section (*maṣāḥif*) 239
Walid A. Saleh

13 A Foreshadowing: The Qur'an Commentary Section (*tafsīr*) 242
Walid A. Saleh

14 The Recitation Section (*qirā'āt*) 260
Shady H. Nasser

15 The *ḥadīth* Section 271
Garrett Davidson

16 The Section on Islamic Law (*fiqh*) 299
Ahmed El Shamsy

17 Books on Islamic Theology (*tawḥīd*) and Sufism (*taṣawwuf*): Rational Verification and Experiential Learning in Ottoman Palestine 315
Hadel Jarada

18 Textbooks of Grammar, Morphology and Lexicography: Cosmopolitan Arabic Philology in Early Nineteenth-century Acre 345
Christopher Bahl

19 Manuals for Manners: Books on *adab* in the Inventory of the Aḥmad Pasha al-Jazzār Library 358
Berat Açıl

20 Logic in the Jazzār Collection (*manṭiq*) 375
Asad Q. Ahmed

21 The Poetry Section (*al-dawāwīn wa-al-qaṣā'id*): Pedagogy and Devotional Piety 382
Khalil Sawan

22 The Pasha's New Clothes: The History Section (*tārīkh*) 400
Dana Sajdi

23 Amassing Medicine (*ṭibb*): Selections from an Ottoman Governor's Medical Collection 427
Deborah Schlein

24 The Occult Sciences 449
Liana Saif

25 A Language-oriented Approach: The Section on Persian and Turkish Books 465
Berat Açıl

Edition of the Inventory 481
Said Aljoumani

Facsimile of the Inventory 561
Index of the Inventory's Book Titles 604
List of Identified al-Jazzār Manuscripts and Their Current Location 621

Acknowledgements

We are grateful to Nada Moumtaz who provided us with a copy of the inventory and sparked the Jazzār Library Project. The Board of Trustees of the Jazzār Mosque in Acre warmly welcomed us and its members, particularly Hussam Tafesh, were wonderful partners throughout the project. We thank all the participants and contributors to the Jazzār Library Project for their efforts, intellectual generosity and enthusiasm. The work on this volume could not have been done without the support of librarians, curators, archivists and digitisers in numerous institutions worldwide. Their assistance has been indispensable. Colleagues who have generously shared their time and knowledge in identifying manuscripts of the Jazzār library distributed across the world include Adel El-Awadi (United Arab Emirates), Al Mahdi Al Rawadieh (University of Jordan), Mohammad Alsorayiea (Qassim University), Ahmed Abd El Baset (Institute of Arabic Manuscripts, Cairo), Bashir Barakat (Jerusalem), Vincent Engelhardt, Samah Hijab (Acre), Lina Jabali (National Library of Israel), Mahmoud Jabr (Cairo), Ahmet Kaylı (Istanbul), Yusuf al-Uzbaki (Masjid al-Aqsa Library) and Mahmoud Zaki (Qatar National Library). The Centre for the Study of Manuscript Cultures (CSMC) at Universität Hamburg has generously supported this project. We thank Maria Luisa Russo and Doreen Schröter for running the safeguarding project at the Jazzār Mosque. Philip Saunders meticulously edited the chapters. The support of Teddi Dols and Mona Saif of Brill was invaluable.

Figures and Tables

Figures

0.1 al-Jazzār's mosque complex in Acre c. 1950 (Library of Congress, G. Eric and Edith Matson Photograph Collection, LC-M305-SL13-B-174) 7

0.2 Courtyard of Jazzār's mosque, general plan (Drawing: D. Sharon; Plan extracted from Corpus Inscriptionum Arabicarum Palaestinae Volume 1 Originally published in 1997 by BRILL (CIAP, 1:48 (pl. 3)) 8

0.3 The facade of the mosque from the north (Adeeb Daoud Naccache Architecture and Urban Studio) 9

0.4 Cross-section of the mosque from the north (Adeeb Daoud Naccache Architecture and Urban Studio) 10

0.5 Cross-section of the mosque from the east (Adeeb Daoud Naccache Architecture and Urban Studio) 11

0.6 The pseudo-coat of arms above the entrance to the prayer hall (photographed by Guy Burak, 31 December 2021) 12

0.7 The scrolled capitals at the prayer hall of al-Jazzār Mosque (photographed by Guy Burak, 31 December 2021) 13

0.8 The niche in the entrance portico in an Ottoman baroque style. Compare to Rüstem, *Ottoman Baroque*, Fig. 59 (photographed by Guy Burak, 31 December 2021) 14

0.9 The prayer niche at the al-Jazzār Mosque (photographed by Guy Burak, 31 December 2021) 15

0.10 The prayer niche at the Nuruosmaniye Mosque, Istanbul (photograph by Ünver Rüstem) 16

0.11 The interior of the mosque of Abū al-Dhahab in Cairo (photographed by Guy Burak, 25 January 2023) 18

0.12 The mosque built by Ẓāhir al-ʿUmar in Tiberias, photograph taken between 1898 and 1946 (Library of Congress, G. Eric and Edith Matson Photograph Collection, LC-M32-51011-X) 19

0.13 Endowment statement of al-Jazzār, Jerusalem, National Library of Israel, AP Ar. 290, fol. 2ª, top right corner (= #416), digitised by the National Library of Israel, Project 'Warraq' 21

0.14 Endowment seal of al-Jazzār, Berlin, Staatsbibliothek, Landberg 9, fol. 1ª 22

0.15 Endowment motto of al-Jazzār (وقف الله تعالى), Berlin, Staatsbibliothek, Landberg 9, fol. 79ª, top of the page 23

0.16 Tampered endowment motto in al-Surūrī, *Sharḥ Gulistān*, fol. 10ᵇ, top of the page, Antiquariat Inlibris, Vienna ('Paris book') 26

1.1 Engraving of the interior of the Ḥamīdiye library in Istanbul. Ignatius Mouradgea d'Ohsson, *Tableau général de l'Empire othoman* (Paris 1787), plate from volume 1 (Library of Congress) 38

1.2 The inscription above the entrance to al-Jazzār's library (photograph by Guy Burak) 42

1.3 The inscription at the entrance to the Enderūn Library (photograph by Nimet İpek) 43

1.4 The inscription at the entrance to Rāğıp Paşa Library (photograph by the Database of Ottoman Inscriptions Project) 43

1.5 The first page of the inventory of the Ayasofya Library (Süleymaniye Library, Yazma Fihrist 25-2) 45

1.6 The first two folios of the inventory of the Rāğıp Paşa Library (Süleymaniye Library, Ragip Paşa 4111) 46

4.1 Al-Jazzār, the ruling tyrant in the European imagination, here gesturing for one of his subjects to be beheaded. Image from: Francis B. Spilsbury. *Picturesque Scenery in the Holy Land and Syria Delineated during the Campaigns of 1799 and 1800*. London: Orme, 1803, image before p. 5 ('Jezzar Pacha

Condemning a Criminal') (Image credit: Kunstbibliothek, Staatliche Museen zu Berlin) 93
4.2 A collection of songs and poems on al-Jazzār. Image credit: Gotha Research Library of the University of Erfurt, Ms. orient. A 2347, fol. 1r. Seetzen himself gave this manuscript the title 'Songs about the invasion of Egypt and Syria by the French' ('Lieder über den Einfall der Franzosen in Egypten und Syrien') 106
6.2 Sketch Plan of the Great Mosque. The courtyard to the west is the one built in 1812. Kana'an, *Waqf, Architecture, and Political Self-Fashioning*, p. 121 (© Ruba Kana'an) 129
6.3 Estate inventory of Shaykh Muḥammad (d. 1807), position with books squared in red. Jaffa, *Sijill al-Maḥkama al-Sharʿiyya* 3, p. 79 132
6.4 Abū Nabbūt's seal which only appears in 1822, after his ousting from Jaffa (MS Gaza, ʿUmarī Mosque 206 [CC BY-NC 4.0]) 136
6.5 ʿUthmān al-Ṭabbāʾ wrote a note below the endowment note of Abū Nabbūt regarding the arrival of this manuscript to Gaza in 1935 (MS Gaza, ʿUmarī Mosque 94 (CC BY-NC 4.0)) 140
7.1 al-Surūrī, *Sharḥ Gulistān*, Antiquariat Inlibris, Vienna ('Paris book', see *Introduction* to this volume) 162
8.1 Leiden University Library Or. 1350 II. Dated 1238 AH/1823 CE, copied in Tunis. A full leather slipcase contemporary with the manuscript it protects, *Kitāb al-ʿIbar*, volume II, by ʿAbd al-Raḥmān b. Muḥammad Ibn Khaldūn 173
8.2 CBL Ar. 3294. The rebound manuscript still has original components, such as the textile doublures and the largest part of the old, tooled leather covering, pasted onto new leather-covered boards 180
8.3 Princeton Garrett 3516Y, exterior. See fig. 8.7 for the binding's interior 182
8.4 Princeton Garrett 3959Y, textblock f. 76a and b, with cut fold-ins indicating rebinding 183
8.5 Leiden University Library Or. 1516 and Or. 1520. Two examples of silver stamped decorated papers, similar to the inner joints covered with silver stamped paper in NL 211508 185
8.6 Leipzig Vollers 118, inner joint showing a distinctive decorative paper 186
8.7 Princeton Garrett 3516Y, interior with silver flecked greenish paper lining and flyleaf with marbled paper 187
9.1 Annotation of the description of the manuscript, including the calligraphic style, in one of the manuscripts in the library from Hamîdiye. *Majmūʿa fī al-Hayʾa*, Süleymaniye Library MS Hamidiye 1450, IIv 195
9.2 Ibn al-Nadīm, *al-Fihrist*, Chester Beatty Library MS Ar. 3315 (10th century), 8v 197
9.3 Muḥammad al-Shibshirī, *al-Jawāhir al-bahiyya fī sharḥ al-Arbaʿīn al-Nawawiyya* Princeton University Library MS Garrett 2996Y (early 18th century), 1v 198
9.4 ʿAbd al-Raḥīm b. al-Ḥasan al-Isnawī, *al-Muhimmāt fī sharḥ al-Rawḍah wa-al-Rāfiʿī*, Jerusalem, National Library of Israel, MS. AP Ar. 290 (late 14th century), 80v–81r 199
9.5 Taqī al-Dīn al-Maqrīzī, *al-Niṣf al-awwal min al-Khiṭaṭ*, Princeton Library MS 3516Y, 1v. (18th century) 200
9.6 Taqī al-Dīn al-Tamīmī, *al-Ṭabaqāt al-saniyya fī tarājim al-sāda al-Ḥanafiyya*, Staatsbibliothek zu Berlin MS Landberg 9 (dated 1633), 1v 201
9.7 Anonymous, *Kitāb jifr*, Süleymaniye Library MS Pertevniyal Valide. Sultan 759 (dated 1475/6), 7v1r–8r2v 202
9.8 al-Mullā ʿAlī al-Qārī, *al-Ḥirz al-thamīn lil-Ḥiṣn al-ḥaṣīn*, National Library of Israel MS. AP. Ar. 258 (16th century), 1r–2v. 202
10.1 Al-Jazzār's nearly circular endowment seal; MS Jerusalem, Isʿāf Nashashibi Library, MS 115, 1r 208
10.2 Al-Jazzār's flat oval endowment seal; MS Doha, QNL 17150, 1r 208
10.3 A seal signed by the same engraver who produced al-Jazzār's nearly circular seal; MS Ann Arbor, University of Michigan, Isl. Ms. 347, 1r 209
10.4 Khalīl b. Qāsim Ṭāshköprü-zāde's seal, dated

879/1475, is the earliest dated endowment seal in the Ottoman tradition; MS Istanbul, Beyazıt Kütüphanesi, Veliyyüddin Efendi 906, 16r 211
10.5 Endowment seal of Fāẓil Aḥmad Pasha Köprülü (d. 1087/1676), dated 1088/1677–1678; MS Istanbul, Köprülü Kütüphanesi, Fazıl Ahmed Paşa 652, 1r 211
10.6 Endowment seal of the şheyhülislām Feyzullah Efendi (d. 1115/1703), dated 1112/1700–1701; MS Istanbul, Millet Kütüphanesi, Feyzullah Efendi 1292, 1r 212
10.7 Endowment seal of ʿAmja-zāde Ḥusayn Pasha (d. 1114/1702), dated 1111/1699–1700; MS Istanbul, Süleymaniye Kütüphanesi, Amcazade Hüseyin 162, 1r 212
10.8 Endowment seal of Çorlulu ʿAlī Pasha (d. 1123/1711), dated 1120/1708–1709; MS Istanbul, Süleymaniye Kütüphanesi, Çorlulu Ali Paşa 278, 1r 212
10.9 Endowment seal of Shahīd ʿAlī Pasha (d. 1128/1716), dated 1130/1718; MS Istanbul, Süleymaniye Kütüphanesi, Şehid Ali Paşa 1835, 1r 212
10.10 Endowment seal of Nevşehirli Dāmād Ibrāhīm Pasha (d. 1143/1730), dated 1132/1720; MS Istanbul, Süleymaniye Kütüphanesi, Damat Ibrahim Paşa 787, 1r 212
10.11 Endowment seal of Ḥakīm-ūğlī ʿAlī Pasha (d. 1171/1758), dated 1146/1733–1734; MS Istanbul, Süleymaniye Kütüphanesi, Hekimoğlu Ali Paşa 168, 1r 213
10.12 Endowment seal of Tiryaki Mehmed Pasha (1680–1751, in office 1746–1747), dated 1160/1747; MS Istanbul, Süleymaniye Kütüphanesi, Fatih 2431, 29r 213
10.13 Endowment seal of Rāghib Pasha (d. 1176/1763), dated 1175/1761–1762; MS Istanbul, Ragıp Paşa Kütüphanesi, Ragıp Paşa 905 213
10.14 Endowment seal of Bashīr Agha (d. 1159/1746), dated 1130/1718; MS Istanbul, Süleymaniye Kütüphanesi, Hacı Beşir Ağa 553, 1r 213
10.15 Endowment seal of raʾīs al-kuttāb Muṣṭafā Efendi (d. 1162/1749), dated 1154/174; MS Istanbul, Süleymaniye Kütüphanesi, Reisulküttab 170, 1r 213
10.16 Endowment seal of Muṣṭafā ʿĀshir Efendi (d. 1219/1804), dated 1161/1748; MS Istanbul, Süleymaniye Kütüphanesi, Aşir Efendi 167, 1r 214
10.17 Endowment seal of Aḥmad b. Nuʿmān Köprülü (1183/1769), dated 1170/1756–1757; MS Istanbul, Köprülü Kütüphanesi, Hacı Ahmed Paşa 337, 240r 214
10.18 Endowment seal of şeyhülislām Veliyüddin Efendi (d. 1182/1768), dated 1175/1761; MS Istanbul, Beyazıt Kütüphanesi, Veliyyüddin Efendi 2035, 1r 214
10.19 Large seal found on the endowed books of Muḥammad Bey Abū al-Dhahab in Egypt; MS Paris, BnF, Arabe 5901, 1r 214
10.20 Endowment seal of Sulaymān Pasha al-ʿAẓm (d. 1156/1743), dated 1150/1738; MS Damascus, al-Majmaʿ al-ʿIlmī 61, 1r 215
10.21 Endowment seal of Asʿad Pasha al-ʿAẓm (d. 1171/1757); MS Damascus, al-Majmaʿ al-ʿIlmī 1070, unfoliated 216
10.22 Endowment seal of Muḥammad Pasha al-ʿAẓm (d. 1197/1783); MS Paris, BnF, Arabe 5828, 1r 217
10.23 Endowment seal of ʿAbd Allāh Pasha al-ʿAẓm (d. 1224/1809), dated 1211/1796–1797; MS Jerusalem, National Library of Israel, MS. Yah. Ar. 308, 1v 217
11.1 Comparison of the chemical composition of iron gall and mixed carbon-iron-gall inks 229
11.2 a) Left, visible light image of Ar. 3315, fol. 1a, with red boxes indicating the location of Dino-Lite micrographs in 2b and 2d, and right, IR light image of the same area using the LWP1510 filter; b) Dino-Lite micrographs from left to right in VIS, UV, and NIR light; c) XRF spectra of the ink and paper, analysed in the same area identified in 2b; d) Dino-Lite micrographs from left to right in VIS, UV, and NIR light 230
11.3 a) Top, visible light image of Ar. 3272, fol. 104b,

with a red box indicating the location of Dino-Lite micrographs in 3[b], and bottom, IR light image of the same area using the LWP1510 filter; b) Dino-Lite micrographs from left to right in VIS, UV, and NIR light; c) XRF spectra of the motto ink and paper, analysed in the same area identified in 3b 231
11.4 a) Top, visible light image of Ar. 3334, fol. 1[a], with a red box indicating the location of Dino-Light micrographs 4b, and bottom, IR light image of the same area using the LWP1510 filter; b) Dino-Lite micrographs from left to right in VIS, UV, and NIR light; c) XRF spectra of the endowment statement ink and paper, analysed in the same area identified in 4b 232
11.5 a) Top, visible light image of Ar. 3342, fol. 1[b], with a red box indicating the location of Dino-Light micrographs in 5[b], and bottom, IR light image of the same area using the LWP1510 filter; b) Dino-Lite micrographs from left to right in VIS, UV, and NIR light; c) XRF spectra of the motto ink and paper, analysed in the same area identified in 5b 233
15.1 Geographical Distribution of Authors 287

Tables

2.1 Approximate thematic distribution of the entirety of the library's holdings in 1218/1803 61
11.1 The Jazzār manuscripts preserved at the Chester Beatty Library 221
11.2 Examples of the various hands writing the mottos and endowment statements in the manuscripts of the Chester Beatty Library 223
11.3 Identification of the ink types according to the protocol. The manuscripts Ar. 3268 and Ar. 3310 were identified as belonging to the Jazzār library months after the analysis were completed, therefore, their inks were not analysed 227
19.1 *al-Balāgha* Works Listed in the Jazzār Library 363
23.1 Libraries and Shared Medical Titles 432
24.1 Thematic distribution of the titles in the Occult Sciences section of the Jazzār library 452

Contributors

Berat Açıl
Boğazici University

Asad Q. Ahmed
University of California, Berkeley

Said Aljoumani
Universität Hamburg

Yasin Arslantaş
Anadolu University

Christopher Bahl
Durham University

Guy Burak
New York University

Claudia Colini
Universität Hamburg

Garrett Davidson
College of Charleston

Konrad Hirschler
Universität Hamburg

Kyle Ann Huskin
Universität Hamburg

Nimet İpek
Sabancı University

Hadel Jarada
Wesleyan University

Feras Krimsti
Gotha Research Library of the University of Erfurt

Boris Liebrenz
The Saxon Academy of Sciences and Humanities in Leipzig

Shady H. Nasser
Harvard University

Benedikt Reier
Universität Hamburg

Liana Saif
University of Amsterdam

Dana Sajdi
Boston College

Walid A. Saleh
University of Toronto

Khalil Sawan
Boston College

Karin Scheper
University Libraries Leiden

Deborah Schlein
Princeton University

Ahmed El Shamsy
University of Chicago

INTRODUCTION

The City, the Endowment and the Manuscripts

Said Aljoumani, Guy Burak and Konrad Hirschler

This book presents for the first time one of the largest Islamic libraries in the history of Palestine and, more broadly, the Arabic-speaking provinces of the Ottoman Empire before the twentieth century, that of the Jazzār Mosque in Acre (modern-day northern Israel).[1] The history of this splendid library of more than 1,800 volumes founded in the late eighteenth century by the Ottoman governor of Bosnian origin, Aḥmad Pasha al-Jazzār (Cezzār Ahmed Paşa, d. 1219/1804), has so far remained unwritten. Even Thomas Philipp's seminal and unmatched monograph on the history of eighteenth-century Acre and the governorship of al-Jazzār has not a single word to say about this library.[2] The one significant exception among the histories of al-Jazzār is the book by Mustafa Güler, who has devoted several pages to the library based on the inventory studied in this volume.[3] That modern scholarship has largely ignored the library goes back to several interlinked factors, chief among them is that the field of West Asian history has only recently discovered book history as a broader field of scholarly investigation,[4] that nineteenth-century Arabic accounts were silent on the governor's bibliographic interest and that the library today is only a shadow of itself, with just fourteen of the originally over 1,800 volumes still in situ.

This book, therefore, has a straightforward aim: putting the Jazzār library onto the map of Palestinian history and Ottoman Palestine onto the map of West Asian book history. This library particularly deserves to be placed on the map as it was a spectacular book collection. We cite but two examples: The *Fihrist* of al-Nadīm (#998, Chapter 19), the most important bio-bibliographical catalogue of the early Islamic period, was on its shelves. The presence of this text by itself is already noteworthy, yet, the Jazzār library held the manuscript that is today one of the centrepieces of the Arabic manuscript collection in the Chester Beatty Library in Dublin. This is one of only two extant early copies of this work, probably going back to late tenth-century Baghdad, and checked against the author's autograph. The second example is the Qurʾan commentary of al-Ṭabarı (#39). As Walid A. Saleh shows in Chapter 13, very few nineteenth-century libraries held a complete copy of this multi-volume work, but the Jazzār library was one of them.

Regarding West Asian book history, this book especially seeks to expand the scope of the study

1 We are grateful to Dana Sajdi and Ruba Kanaʿan for their generous comments and readings of parts of this chapter. The al-Jazzār Library Project and the publication of this book was funded by the Deutsche Forschungsgemeinschaft (DFG, German Research Foundation) under Germany's Excellence Strategy—EXC 2176 'Understanding Written Artefacts: Material, Interaction and Transmission in Manuscript Cultures', project no. 390893796. The project was conducted within the scope of the Centre for the Study of Manuscript Cultures (CSMC) at Universität Hamburg.

2 Philipp, *Acre*.

3 Güler, *Cezzar Ahmed Paşa*, 184–194.

4 Among the studies of libraries and book collections in the Arabic-speaking provinces of the Ottoman Empire: Aljoumani, "Masrad kutub"; Aljoumani, *Makataba madrasiya*; Crecelius, "The Waqf of Muhammad Bey"; Ibrāhīm, "Maktaba ʿUthmāniyya"; Rāʾūf, *Dirāsāt turāthiyya*; Marino, "Engager des livres"; Barakat, *Tārīkh al-maktabāt al-ʿarabīya*; Liebrenz, *Rifāʿiya aus Damaskus*. Among the studies of libraries and book collections in the Turkish-speaking lands of the empire: Erünsal, *Osmanlılarda Kütüphaneler*; Erünsal, *A History of Ottoman Libraries*; Bouquet, "Pour une histoire instrumentale"; Açıl, *Osmanlı Kitap Kültürü*; Necipoğlu et al., *Treasures*; Derin Can, "Manuscript Collections"; Atbaş, "A Grand Collection"; Sezer, "The Architecture of Bibliophilia".

of Ottoman libraries beyond the core, Turkish-speaking lands of the empire. Numerous studies have followed in the footsteps of İsmail Erünsal in the past two decades and explored various aspects of the library culture that has emerged in Anatolia and the Balkans. More specifically, as the late Yavuz Sezer noted, the eighteenth century witnessed the rise of a distinctive library culture in the Ottoman capital.[5] As discussed below, al-Jazzār was aware, to a considerable extent, of the aesthetic and intellectual conventions of the imperial capital and aspired to be an actor on the imperial, and not just the local, scene. This book, thus, also aims at bringing the scholarship of libraries in the Arabic-speaking provinces of the empire into dialogue with the studies of libraries in Anatolia and the Balkans. Such a dialogue, as this volume illustrates, casts new light on the political and intellectual dynamics of the Ottoman domains in the eighteenth century.

The idea to write the history of the Jazzār library goes back to October 2021 when Guy Burak gave an online talk in the *Readings in the Khalidiyya* series at the Center for Palestine Studies, Columbia University. In that talk, he presented the Jazzār library inventory from 1221/1806, at the heart of this volume, and a vivid email exchange ensued between the three editors. It was quickly decided to undertake this project as a collective endeavour with colleagues from a wide variety of disciplinary backgrounds within the framework of what we called the Jazzār Library Project (ALP). This means we have some experts in Ottoman Studies and also contributors whose main research field is elsewhere in terms of region and period. The aim of bringing together these colleagues was to make this volume speak to a broad range of fields, especially the wider book history of West Asia. We also decided to connect the traditionally text-focused disciplines with those interested in the book as a material object (mainly reflected in Part 2 and chapters such as Chapter 2 by Said Aljoumani). The project then also grew well beyond this volume. It led, among others, to the safeguarding initiative *Rescuing the Books of al-Jazzār* under the auspices of the al-Jazzār Mosque endowment board, funded by the ALIPH Foundation and implemented by the Centre for the Study of Manuscript Cultures (CSMC) at Universität Hamburg.[6]

Working on the history of a vanished library entails studying the removal of written artefacts from a library or book collection. This raises legal and ethical questions on legitimate ownership and potential reconstitution. This is particularly the case if the artefacts were moved from Africa and Asia to Europe and the US in (proto)colonial contexts. This removal of artefacts is a process that is still ongoing: The Iraqi and Syrian wars of the twenty-first century have led to the widespread theft and plunder of cultural artefacts, including handwritten books. Attitudes on the ethical and legal status of such removed artefacts have rapidly shifted since the 2010s, as evidenced by the events surrounding the (by now notorious) Schøyen collection.[7] This book sees itself as the historical study of a library's development and its books' trajectories. These two processes cannot be understood with a focus on one specific period (such as the colonial period) or one particular group of historical actors alone. The book's findings, especially on translocations, are meant to contribute to discussions on provenance with a much broader perspective regarding the period and actors. In the ALP, we have worked closely with the endowment board of the Jazzār Mosque in Acre as the crucial stakeholder in the status of these books. Its

5 Sezer, "The Architecture of Bibliophilia".

6 https://www.csmc.uni-hamburg.de/cultural-heritage/akka.html (accessed 5 March 2024).

7 Museum of Cultural History (University of Oslo), *Report with assessment and recommendations concerning objects impounded at Martin Schøyen's residence August 24, 2021*, March 2022 https://www.regjeringen.no/en/dokumenter/report-with-assessment-and-recommendations-concerning-objects-impounded-at-martin-schoyens-residence-august-24-2021/id2903280/ (accessed 3 January 2023). One group of Syrian fragments is discussed in Hirschler, *Saleroom Fiction versus Provenance*.

members demand the reconstitution of al-Jazzār books; members of the ALP differ on this issue. Irrespective of its members' various positions, the project consistently shared all the information on the books' trajectories and their present-day location with our partners in Acre.[8]

1 Setting the Scene: al-Jazzār and Acre

By the time Aḥmad Pasha al-Jazzār consolidated his power in Acre, the city had emerged from 'a fishing village to an important fortified port city'.[9] The envoy of the Moroccan sultan, Muḥammad b. ʿUthmān al-Miknāsī, leaves no doubt in his account of his visit to Acre in 1787 as to whom he deemed to be the driving force behind this transformation: 'This vizier had a great impact on the city. He made it famous and it, in return, made him famous.'[10] The city's rise over the eighteenth century was quite exceptional, given its modest starting point: 'it was a new foundation', Thomas Philipp remarks, 'populated by immigrants in the eighteenth century'.[11] The rise of the city as a major port—indeed, the most important port of the Syrian littoral—and an administrative centre has been attributed to the rise of local power brokers, most notably Ẓāhir al-ʿUmar (d. 1775), within the Ottoman imperial framework and the integration of Syria and Palestine into the Mediterranean economy, primarily through the region's cultivation of silk and raw cotton. As Philipp observes, 'the economic center of gravity moved slowly from inland Syria to the coastal lands of the southwest'.[12] The integration of the city into the Mediterranean trade of the eighteenth century was also coupled with its growing incorporation into its hinterland. Ẓāhir al-ʿUmar's fortification of the city and the construction of its seaport were instrumental in turning Acre into an important node in the eastern Mediterranean.

Local actors across the empire, such as regional governors, consolidated considerable power throughout the eighteenth century, but the Ottoman imperial centre and empire's political framework remained significant.[13] The Ottoman imperial centre was an active player in the Levant both politically and militarily, as al-Jazzār's biography attests. Furthermore, and this is quite significant for writing the library's history, the Ottoman imperial centre was an important cultural and intellectual focal point. At the same time, there were many other intellectual hubs across the Levant, Egypt and North Africa, the Hijaz, and, further east, Iran, Central Asia and South Asia. Al-Jazzār's library, as we shall see throughout this volume, was also a product of these transregional intellectual and political dynamics (see for instance Chapters 17 on Islamic theology (*tawḥīd*) and sufism (*taṣawwuf*) as well as Chapter 20 on logic for the importance of North Africa).

The biography of the renowned Governor of Sidon, Damascus and Acre has been the focus of several studies, and the contributors to this volume will discuss relevant aspects of his biography in due course. Here, suffice it to outline the pasha's career in fairly broad strokes. Aḥmad Pasha al-Jazzār was born in Bosnia in 1135/1722–1723. At some point, he left his hometown Fatnica and moved to the imperial capital, where he struggled to find employment. According to some accounts, he found employment as the barber of some dignitaries close to Ḥekīmoğlu ʿAlī Paşa (d. 1758), the Grand Vizier (and a founder of an impressive library in Istanbul). Consequently, in 1155/1742, the

8 The information on the location of those manuscripts identified so far is available open access at the Research Data Repository of Universität Hamburg where we will keep updating it (https://doi.org/10.25592/uhhfdm.14178).

9 Philipp, *Acre*, 1.

10 Matar, *An Arab Ambassador*, 170.

11 Ibid., 5.

12 Ibid.

13 Barbir, *The Ottoman Rule*; Hathaway, *The Politics of Households*; Khoury, *State and Provincial Society*; Toledano, "The Emergence of Ottoman-Local Elites"; Wilkins, "The Self-Fashioning"; Yaycıoğlu, *Partners of Empire*.

young al-Jazzār decided to leave the capital for Egypt as part of the entourage of Hekīmoğlu, now the Ottoman governor of Egypt.[14] It is worth stressing that al-Jazzār's connections with Ḥekīmoğlu seem unverifiable and may have been a rumour that circulated among contemporaries and later writers. In Egypt, he entered the service of several Mamluk leaders. A brutal retaliation campaign against the Hanadi Bedouins, following the assassination of his master, ʿAbd Allāh Bey, earned him the honorary epithet 'al-Jazzār' (the butcher). In 1183/1167, al-Jazzār joined the troops of ʿAlī Bey al-Kabīr (d. 1773), the powerful governor of Egypt, and was awarded the title Bey. Shortly after that, the relationship with ʿAlī Bey soured when al-Jazzār failed to execute his master's order to assassinate his rival, Ṣāliḥ Bey. In 1183/1769, al-Jazzār fled for his life to Istanbul. From there he continued to Syria, where he entered the service of the Ottoman governor of Damascus, ʿUthmān Pasha al-Miṣrī. In 1184/1770, al-Jazzār joined the governor of Mount Lebanon, Amir Yūsuf al-Shihābī. Three years later, in 1187/1773, al-Shihābī appointed al-Jazzār his governor in Beirut. Al-Jazzār consolidated his power in Beirut and fortified the city. When al-Shihābī called him back, al-Jazzār refused to leave the town. He was ousted from the city, in 1187/1773, after the city was besieged by a coalition formed by al-Shihābī and Ẓāhir al-ʿUmar. Once again, al-Jazzār found refuge in Istanbul.[15]

When Ẓāhir al-ʿUmar was killed in 1190/1775, al-Jazzār was appointed the governor of Sidon. In 1190/1776, al-Jazzār entered the city. The arrival in the city marks a new chapter in al-Jazzār's career; for the next three decades, he became a major actor in the Levant. From Istanbul's perspective, his appointment was an attempt to strengthen the capital's hold on Syria after the rebellious campaigns of Ẓāhir al-ʿUmar and his partner ʿAlī Bey al-Kabīr against the governor of Damascus. As a governor of Sidon, al-Jazzār established his seat in Acre, the district's capital. He also turned against his former master, al-Shihābī, and raided the Shiʿite region of Jabal ʿĀmil. In addition to the position in Sidon, al-Jazzār was also appointed governor of Damascus in 1198/1783. In that capacity, he was also in charge of leading the annual Damascene pilgrimage caravan to Mecca. His appointment in Damascus did not last long, and in 1199/1784, he was removed from this office after several complaints. In the following years, al-Jazzār was repeatedly reappointed as governor of Damascus and shortly before his second tenure as governor of Damascus, in 1213/1799, al-Jazzār successfully warded off the conquest of Acre by Napoleon's troops. He died in Acre in 1219/1804 and was buried in the mosque complex he built in the city.

According to the nineteenth-century biographer ʿAbd al-Razzāq al-Bayṭār (d. 1335/1916), when al-Jazzār was appointed governor of Damascus in 1803 he was granted the title 'vizier'.[16] However, other sources suggest that the governor was granted the vizierate much earlier. Al-Miknāsī, the envoy of the Moroccan sultan, calls al-Jazzār 'the vizier' in his account of his visit to Acre in 1787,[17] and an Ottoman edict dated 1790 refers to al-Jazzār as the sultan's vizier ('my vizier', *vezirim*).[18] The title positioned al-Jazzār among the most senior administrators of the empire (and may have been interpreted as fulfilling prophecies about his career). The title seems particularly significant for interpreting the governor's library as vizierial, comparable to similar libraries built in the imperial capital and elsewhere.

Al-Jazzār was remarkably savvy of the Ottoman administration and his observations in the lengthy report he compiled for the Grand Vizier in Istanbul on the state of affairs in Egypt (*Niẓāmnāme-i Mıṣır*)

14 Câbî, *Câbî Târihi*, I, 84.

15 The outline of al-Jazzār's biography is based on Cohen, *Palestine*; Philipp, *Acre*, 138–147; Safi, "*al-Jazzār, Aḥmad Pasha*"; al-Bayṭār, *Ḥilyat al-bashar*, I, 127–132; Ḥammūd, "Aḥmad Bāshā al-Jazzār"; and Güler, *Cezzar Ahmed Paşa*.

16 al-Bayṭār, *Ḥilyat al-bashar*, I, 129.

17 Maghribi, "Waṣf lil-madīna", 61.

18 Aras, *191 Numaralı Mühimme Defterinin*, 91–92.

in 1785 reflects deep familiarity with the state of affairs in the province and imperial institutions more generally. Stanford Shaw points out in the introduction to the English translation of this report that al-Jazzār's astute recommendations 'were followed almost to the letter in the expedition which landed in Egypt in July of 1786 under the command of the Ottoman Grand Admiral, Gāzī Ḥasan Paşa'.[19] His administrative competence, as Arslantaş points out in Chapter 5, helped al-Jazzār fend off calls for his removal from office due to what the Sublime Porte perceived as his rebellious actions.[20]

The ascendance of Acre as a commercial and political centre led to the concentration of wealth and talent in the city. Al-Jazzār relied on mercenaries and *mamlūks* of diverse backgrounds, including Kurds, Bosnians and Maghrebis. According to Moshe Sharon and 'Alī Ḥammūd, al-Jazzār also employed Greek builders to construct the city's mosque complex (a point we shall return to below).[21] Apparently, al-Jazzār also managed to attract some talent from the core lands of the empire, as the bibliographic practices of at least one of his librarians suggest (see Chapter 1 by Berat Açıl, Nimet İpek and Guy Burak and Chapter 10 by Boris Liebrenz). The accumulation of capital allowed al-Jazzār to carry out the various construction projects and, among other things, amass a significant library.[22]

Al-Jazzār's notorious cruelty is a recurring trope in contemporary and later accounts of his career written in Arabic and European languages (see Chapter 4 by Feras Krimsti). Indeed, much of the historiographical attention has been focused on al-Jazzār's political and administrative ambitions. European travellers and consuls stereotypically portrayed the pasha as the quintessential oriental tyrant. Nevertheless, other contemporary accounts portray al-Jazzār as charitable. The French traveller Olivier, who met him in 1802, remarked that al-Jazzār was 'simple in his manners, [al-Jazzār] becomes popular and sometimes familiar with the inhabitants of Acre. Charitable and compassionate in appearance, he himself administrates to the poor the remedies which he believes to be efficient for their ills.'[23] A similar comment is made by the Moroccan envoy al-Miknāsī: 'The local inhabitants praise him a lot because he succoured the weak and the poor, especially those who were embarrassed to ask for help.'[24] Other European accounts mention the governor's intellectual acumen. Indeed, Philipp argues that 'a conscious effort is needed to break through the various cliches that have been developed for political and entertainment reasons and to reach a more balanced view of the man'.[25]

In addition to the narrative tropes of al-Jazzār's cruelty and cunning, several sources mention prophecies surrounding the governor. The chronicler Cābī Ömer Efendi (d. after 1814), roughly contemporary with al-Jazzār, relates an interesting vignette about an encounter the young al-Jazzār had in Egypt:

> Jazzār Aḥmed Pasha was one of the ağas of the inner court (Enderun) of the deceased honourable formerly [known] as Ḥekīmzāde, the former vizier 'Alī Pasha [...] He arrived in Egypt with the aforementioned Pasha [...] One day, one of the competent [officials], while Ahmed Pasha was in a neighbourhood called him: 'Come over here', three people said: 'Look, my son Ạmed Ağa, you are the *Jim Jim* that the Greatest Shaykh (Ibn al-'Arabī) wrote and alluded to.' One of them held his nose and the other two held their ears, and said: 'This so-called Sublime State [the Ottoman state] is the state of Muḥammad (*Devlet-i Muḥammadiyye*) [...] Whoever betrays this state betrays the Prophet and re-

19 al-Jazzār, *Ottoman Egypt*, 8.

20 Selīm III issued an edict in 1803 denouncing al-Jazzār as a rebel. See Cohen, *Palestine*, 63.

21 Sharon, *Corpus Inscriptionum Arabicarum Palaestinae*. I, 43; Ḥammūd, "Aḥmad Bāshā al-Jazzār".

22 For a detailed account of al-Jazzār's financial administration and his contributions to the imperial treasury, see Cohen, *Palestine*, especially 226–249.

23 Philipp, *Acre*, 59.

24 Matar, *An Arab Ambassador*, 170.

25 Philipp, *Acre*, 60.

ligion and will be quickly punished soon. You are a man of a degree lower than sultans [but] higher than viziers. But be loyal to the Muḥammadan State and do not fear anyone.'[26]

This prophecy, which was most probably written with hindsight, reveals al-Jazzār's unusual status within the Empire, but also stresses his loyalty to the Ottoman dynasty (a loyalty that was also celebrated in the Ottoman Turkish accounts of his career and successful defence of Acre against the French siege). It also suggests that the governor's ambitions were not limited to the accumulation and consolidation of power and wealth, but also carried a theological baggage. From this perspective, the governor was fulfilling a divine plan. Süreya (d. 1909), another late nineteenth-century biographer, also remarks that the pasha was interested in letterist divination (*jafr* or *cifr*, in Turkish), as the 1221/1806 inventory of the library he endowed confirms (see Chapter 24 by Liana Saif).[27]

Al-Bayṭār, in his biography of the governor, mentions another prophecy. According to this account, the leader of the Kurdish troops in the service of al-Jazzār, who was interested in Sufism (*taṣawwuf*), claimed that Ibn al-ʿArabī in his *Meccan Revelations* (*al-Futūḥāt al-Makkiyya*) had foreseen al-Jazzār's appearance (the library held the Greatest Shaykh's work, as Hadel Jarada discusses in Chapter 17). Moreover, the nineteenth-century biographer relates that 'some of the reckless' authored a book in which they claimed that al-Jazzār was the renewer (*mujaddid*) (see Chapter 22 by Dana Sajdi).[28] The attribution of this title was not exclusive to al-Jazzār. The governor's contemporary, the late eighteenth-century Ottoman historian Aḥmed Vāṣif (d. 1806), described Grand Vizier Ḥalīl Paşa (d. 1785) as the 'renewer' (*müceddid*), hoping that 'that the Grand Vizier would return the empire to proper practices and purer religion'.[29]

26 Câbî, *Câbî Târihi*, I, 84.

27 Süreyya Bey, *Sicill-i Osmânî*, I, 277.

28 al-Bayṭār, *Ḥilyat al-bashar*, I, 129–130.

29 Menchinger, *The First of the Modern Ottomans*, 86.

The reports about prophecies associated with the governor cast light on the pasha's intellectual and cultural aspirations and ambitions. Indeed, as Boris Liebrenz in Chapter 3 points out, Acre during al-Jazzār's tenure was an intellectual backwater, and very few scholars from Acre attracted the attention of Damascene chroniclers and authors of biographical dictionaries. Nevertheless, he was clearly as ambitious culturally as he was politically. Being the governor of Sidon, al-Jazzār built on the urban development of Acre that Ẓāhir al-ʿUmar had started. He undertook several large construction projects, including an impressive caravansary (*Khān al-ʿUmdān*), a water fountain, a bazaar, a bathhouse and, most notably for this volume, a mosque complex on the northern side of the city.[30]

2 The Mosque Complex: The Nuruosmaniye and al-Nūr al-Aḥmadī

Al-Jazzār's career trajectory and ambitions are reflected in the construction projects he led in the city he turned into his seat of power. He evidently aspired to build an impressive urban centre that would be recognised as such at the imperial level. Moreover, al-Jazzār sought to project his ambition by employing the visual idioms of the upper echelons of the Ottoman imperial administrative elite. The design of the seals with which the endowed books were stamped, as Boris Liebrenz shows in Chapter 10, is a case in point, as is the impressive mosque complex al-Jazzār founded in Acre. Ghassān Mūsā Muḥaybish has studied the mosque complex thoroughly and the aim here is to build on his authoritative study to situate the complex in the eighteenth-century Ottoman imperial and provincial contexts.[31]

The elevated mosque complex situated on the northern side of Acre, south of the citadel, follows the layout and architectural idiom of similar complexes in the imperial capital (fig. 0.2, 0.3,

30 Ḥammūd, "Aḥmad Bāshā al-Jazzār."

31 Muḥaybish, *Mujammaʿ al-Jazzār*.

FIGURE 0.1 al-Jazzār's mosque complex in Acre c. 1950
LIBRARY OF CONGRESS, G. ERIC AND EDITH MATSON PHOTOGRAPH COLLECTION, LC-M305-SL13-B-174

0.4 and 0.5).[32] The mosque, with its single lead-clad dome and pencil-shaped minaret, stands at the centre of the complex surrounded by the courtyard. Al-Jazzār's mausoleum is adjacent to the mosque to the west. The main entrance, through a domed portico, is across the courtyard from the main, northern entrance to the precinct. It leads along the main thoroughfare to al-Jazzār's mansion and the bathhouse he built (two other entrances are located to the east, from the adjacent market, and the south). The mosque's courtyard is surrounded on its eastern, northern and western sides by domed colonnades preceding vaulted chambers. The *madrasa*, the library and (at least in later decades) the city's *qāḍī* court were located on the row of chambers along the eastern side of the complex. The engraved Qur'anic verse 'it contains upright scriptures' (Qur'an 98:3) framed by decorative tiles marks the entrance to the library.

The mosque complex and the Ottoman-style mosque itself are highly unusual in the architectural landscape of Palestine.[33] Al-Jazzār evidently wanted to draw a connection to the imperial capital. But it was not simply a generic Istanbul mosque that al-Jazzār had in mind. It seems that he aimed to emulate the first sultanic mosque of the eighteenth century, the Nuruosmaniye (*Nūr-i Osmānī* or the *Light of Osman*), which had been inaugurated several decades earlier in 1755.[34] The

32 Sharon, *CIAP*, I, 47–51.

33 There were several complexes and mosques that followed the Ottoman architectural idiom in Damascus. See Kafescioğlu, "'In the Image of Rūm'". Also see Kana'an, "Waqf, Architecture, and Political Self-Fashioning".

34 Rüstem, *Ottoman Baroque*, esp. ch. 3.

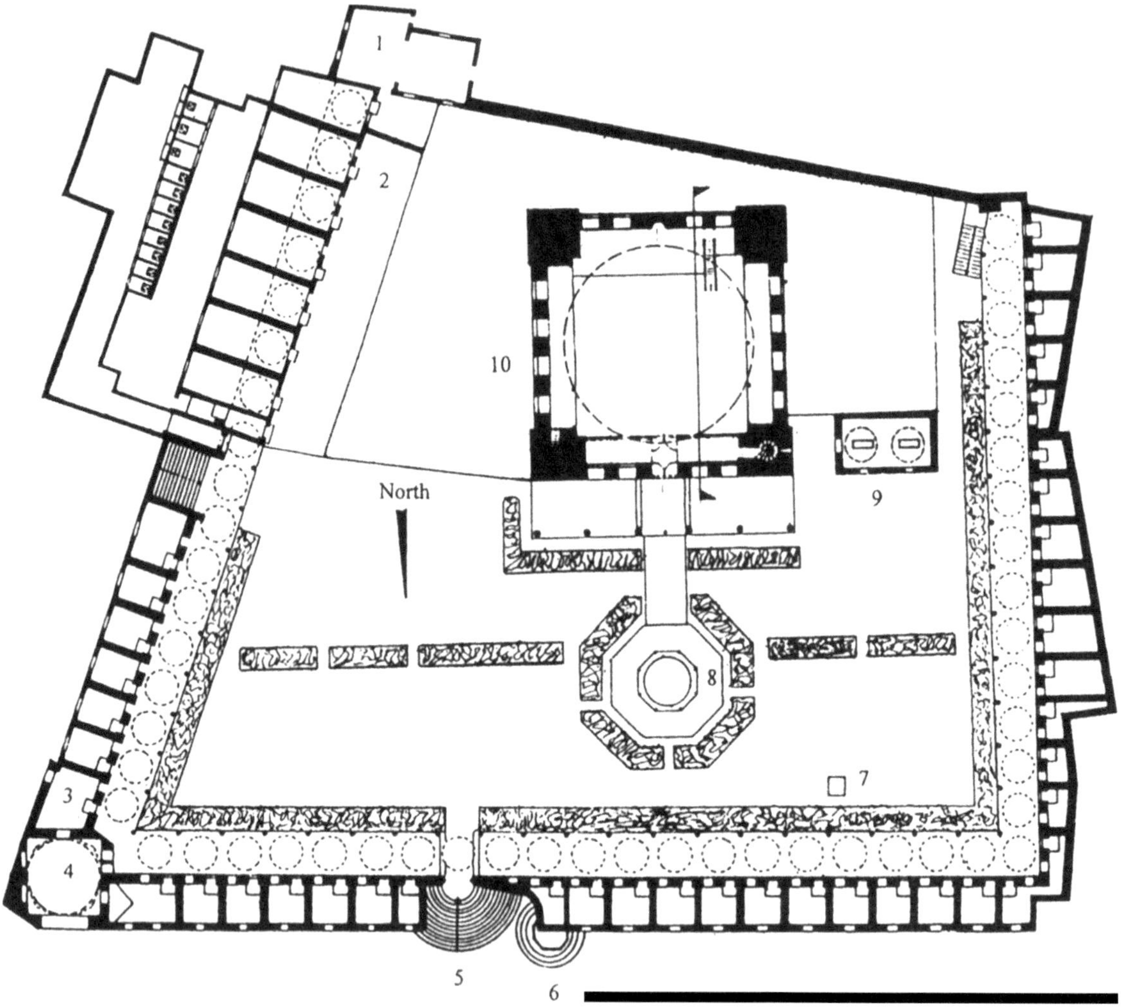

FIGURE 0.2 Courtyard of Jazzār's mosque, general plan
1. Offices; 2. Library today; 3. Jazzār's library (formerly); 4. Shari'ah court; 5. Northern entrance; 6. Sabil; 7. Sundial; 8. Ablution tank; 9. Tombs of Jazzār and Sulayman Pasha; 10. Jazzār's mosque (Moshe Sharon, *CIAP*)
DRAWING: D. SHARON; PLAN EXTRACTED FROM CORPUS INSCRIPTIONUM ARABICARUM PALAESTINAE VOLUME 1 ORIGINALLY PUBLISHED IN 1997 BY BRILL (CIAP, 1:48 (PL. 3)

connection is made quite clear in the name the governor chose for his mosque in Acre, *al-Nūr al-Aḥmadī* (the *Light of Aḥmad*), referring to al-Jazzār's first name Aḥmad. The consecration inscription refers to the mosque as '[...] a holy mosque and a safe house/full of veneration and shimmering lights'.[35] Several years later, in 1786 or 1787, when the sundial was installed in the complex's courtyard, the inscription referred to the mosque as the 'mosque of the lights of Aḥmad'.[36]

35 Sharon, *CIAP*, I, 51–52: *'wa-masjid ḥaram wa-bayt āmin/fīhi al-waqār wa-lāḥat al-anwār'*.

36 Ibid., I, 53–54: *'jāmiʿ al-anwār al-Aḥmadīyya'*. The expression also appears in endowment notes on the endowed manuscripts. The endowment note in the copy of al-Maqrizi's topographical work, currently at the Firestone Library at Princeton, refers to the *Nūr Aḥmadīyya* Mosque. The endowment note was written in 1200/1785 or 1786. Aḥmad ibn ʿAlī al-Maqrīzī, *al-Niṣf al-awwal min al-Khiṭaṭ* [*Mawāʿiẓ wa-al-iʿtibār fī dhikr al-khiṭaṭ wa-al-āthār*], Firestone Library MS Garrett 3516Y.

FIGURE 0.3
The facade of the mosque from the north
ADEEB DAOUD NACCACHE ARCHITECTURE AND URBAN STUDIO

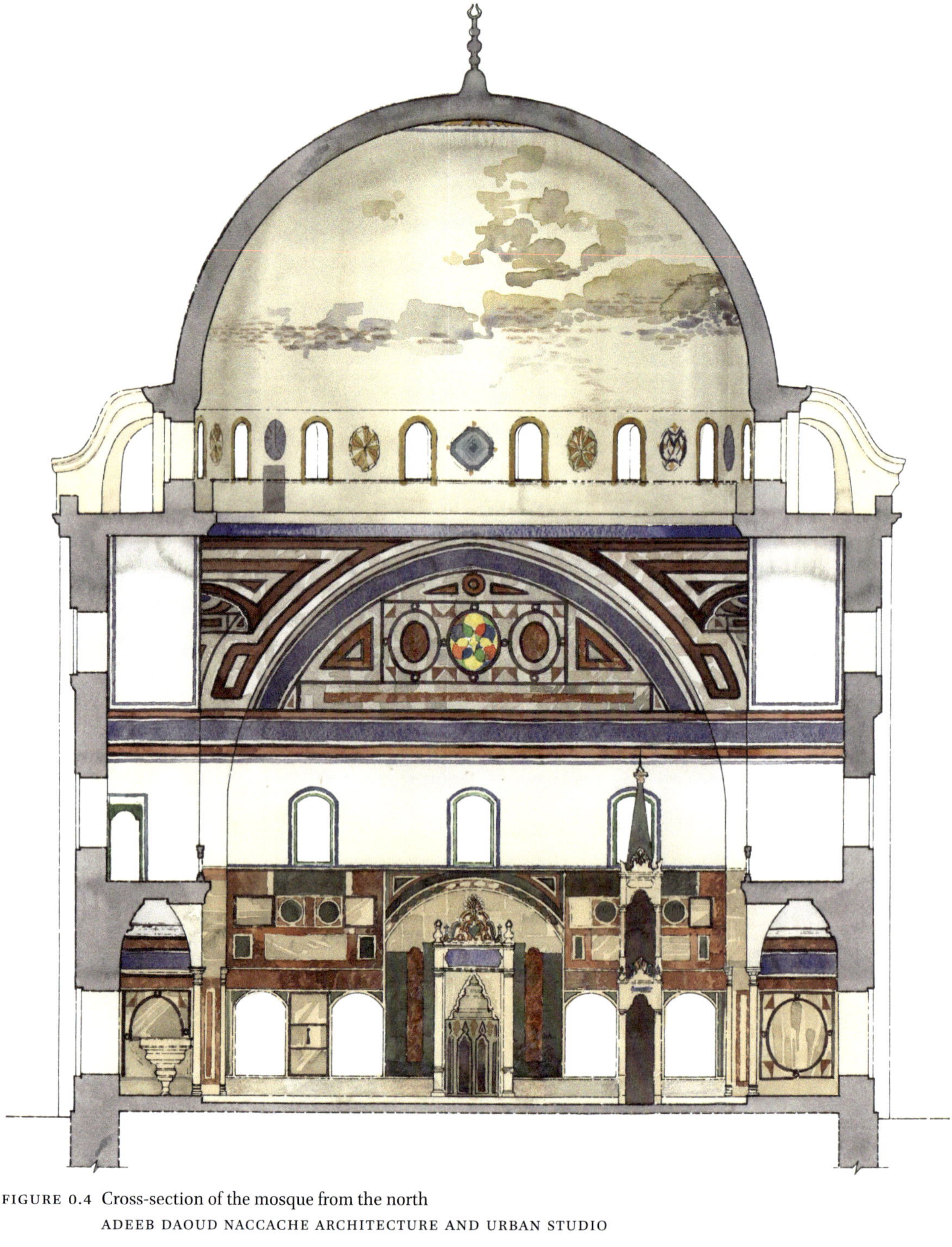

FIGURE 0.4 Cross-section of the mosque from the north
ADEEB DAOUD NACCACHE ARCHITECTURE AND URBAN STUDIO

FIGURE 0.5
Cross-section of the mosque from the east
ADEEB DAOUD NACCACHE ARCHITECTURE AND URBAN STUDIO

FIGURE 0.6
The pseudo-coat of arms above the entrance to the prayer hall
PHOTOGRAPHED BY GUY BURAK, 31 DECEMBER 2021

The mosque's name is not the only allusion to the sultanic mosque in Istanbul. The layout of al-Jazzār's mosque is square, much like that of the Nuruosmaniye's prayer hall and other sultanic mosques, such as the Sulaymāniyya Mosque in Damascus.[37] Moreover, the Qur'anic inscription along the arches, the circumference of the base of the main dome and along the walls of the prayer hall are taken from the Qur'anic Victory Sura (*Surat al-Fatḥ*), which is also inscribed on the wide concave in 'a busy but lucid *thuluth*', circumscribing the main prayer hall of the Nuruosmaniye.[38] Other ornaments, such as the pseudo-coat of arms above the entrance (fig. 0.6), the scroll capitals (fig. 0.7), the prayer niche (*miḥrāb*) and the niche in the portico (figs. 0.8–0.9), also reflect familiarity with the Ottoman baroque idiom. Al-Jazzār's efforts to establish a connection between his mosque and the imperial capital were successful, at least according to one contemporary observer. 'He built one of the finest mosques, following the design of mosques in Constantinople', noted the Moroccan envoy al-Miknāsī, recognising al-Jazzār's aspirations.[39]

Moshe Sharon argues (without reference) that many of the builders employed by al-Jazzār were

37 Thanks to Ruba Kana'an for pointing this out.
38 Rüstem, *Ottoman Baroque*, 144.
39 Matar, *An Arab Ambassador*, 170.

FIGURE 0.7
The scrolled capitals at the prayer hall of al-Jazzār Mosque
PHOTOGRAPHED BY GUY BURAK, 31 DECEMBER 2021

FIGURE 0.8 The niche in the entrance portico in an Ottoman baroque style. Compare to Rüstem, *Ottoman Baroque*, Fig. 59
PHOTOGRAPHED BY GUY BURAK, 31 DECEMBER 2021

FIGURE 0.9 The prayer niche at the al-Jazzār Mosque
PHOTOGRAPHED BY GUY BURAK, 31 DECEMBER 2021

FIGURE 0.10 The prayer niche at the Nuruosmaniye Mosque, Istanbul
PHOTOGRAPH BY ÜNVER RÜSTEM

expert Greek masons.[40] The Greek identity of the builders is intriguing because of the prominence of Greek builders and architects in Istanbul in the eighteenth century, as Ünver Rüstem has shown in the context of the Nuruosmaniye. It is quite possible that the Greek masons in Acre were responsible for the baroque ornaments in the mosque or that some of these decorative elements were transported to the city.[41] It is also possible that al-Jazzār invited calligraphers (or, at least, commissioned the calligraphy) of the inscriptions in the complex. Most of these inscriptions were written in Ottoman *thuluth* script and followed the cartouche layout of inscriptions from the empire's core lands. Several decorative elements, such as the *miḥrāb* (figs. 0.9, 0.10) and the scrolled capitals,[42] may also have been chosen to allude to the Nuruosmaniye.

Al-Jazzār's experimentation with the idiom associated with the imperial capital and particularly with the Ottoman Baroque may have also inspired his *mamlūk*, Muḥammad Aghā Abū Nabbūt, who ruled Jaffa from 1803 to 1819,[43] as is evident in the two water fountains (*sabīl*) the latter built during his tenure (the *Maḥmūdī* and the *Shifāʾ/Abū Nabbūt* fountains). The Maḥmūdī fountain and, to a considerable extent, the later Abū Nabbūt *sabīl*, 'follow the Ottoman baroque architectural style that was common in the second half of the eighteenth century', making references to the Nuruosmaniye Mosque and elements associated with

40 Sharon, *CIAP*, I, 50.
41 Ruba Kanaʿan pointed out that Abū Nabbūṭ imported the marble panels for his fountain in Jaffa from Istanbul (and they were probably carved there). Kanaʿan, "Two Ottoman Sabils in Jaffa", 192.
42 For the scrolled capitals at the Nuruosmaniye, see Rüstem, *Ottoman Baroque*, 146.
43 On his library, see Chapter 6 by Benedikt Reier.

the idiom promoted by the court of the Ottoman Sultan Mahmūd II (r. 1809–1839).[44] It is noteworthy that Abū Nabbūt also emulated his former master in building a splendid library, discussed by Benedikt Reier in Chapter 6.

At the same time, al-Jazzār's mosque reflects the founder's interest in adopting other architectural idioms, mainly from the Levant and Egypt. The large marble discs at the entrance to the mosque and around the *miḥrāb* appear in Mamluk monuments (such as the complex built by Sultan Barqūq in Cairo) and, closer to al-Jazzār's time, in the mosque built in Cairo in 1774 by Muḥammad Bey Abū al-Dhahab (d. 1775), the former *mamlūk* of ʿAlī Bey al-Kabīr and governor of Egypt (fig. 0.11). Abū al-Dhahab, it is worth mentioning, joined forces with Ẓāhir al-ʿUmar against the Ottoman governor of Damascus and later, as the ruler of Egypt, led an expedition to Palestine against Ẓāhir during which he conquered Acre. Similarly, the inlaid stone and marble ornaments in the *miḥrāb* and the circular marble panels allude to local Mamluk and post-Mamluk idioms. Al-Jazzār's mosque can also be read against the mosque that Ẓāhir al-ʿUmar built in Tiberias in 1743. Very similar to al-Jazzār's, ʿUmar's mosque (known as *al-Jāmiʿ al-ʿUmarī*) consists of a square, single-domed prayer hall, preceded by a three-arched vaulted portico. The stonework and marble ornaments of the Tiberias mosque, as well as its minaret, clearly drew on the Mamluk and post-Mamluk architectural and ornamental idioms (fig. 0.12).

The references in al-Jazzār's complex to local, regional and imperial idioms echo the governor's career with his regional and imperial ambitions. The mosque complex and the governor's career path capture the dynamics between the imperial centre, especially Istanbul, and the Greater Syrian provinces. The complex casts light on how al-Jazzār projected this ambition by employing and manipulating the visual idiom of the imperial centre and the Arab-speaking provinces simultaneously. The mosque complex, thus, casts light on the geographical, political and cultural horizons of al-Jazzār, and can, therefore, help interpret the founder's library.

3 The Quest for Manuscripts: Methodological Considerations

The library the pasha assembled in his mosque complex in Acre has mostly vanished. When writing the history of such a vanished library, we face the classical methodological challenge presented by any such library: How do we find the actual books that once sat on its shelves and are scattered in libraries worldwide today? When we started the ALP, we knew of twenty-two al-Jazzār books that Boris Liebrenz had identified in eight libraries around the world, including Princeton, Dublin, Berlin and Acre.[45] In our project, we have expanded this corpus to seventy-eight books in twenty-eight libraries (see *List of Identified al-Jazzār Manuscripts and Their Current Location*), including those in Egypt, Turkey, Saudi Arabia, Qatar, Mauritania and Japan.[46] We know that these books once belonged to the Jazzār library because they carry the Jazzār endowment statement, endowment seal and/or endowment motto (more on these below). This number of seventy-eight has enlarged the known number of al-Jazzār books substantially, but the depressing fact remains that the vast majority of the books that once sat on the shelves of his library remain unaccounted for.

To be more precise, if we take the Jazzār library inventory from 1221/1806, the central document for this book, as a yardstick, the current location of some ninety-five per cent of the inventory's over 1,800 books remains unknown. The situation is worse still because our seventy-eight books

44 Kanaʿan, "Two Ottoman Sabils in Jaffa".

45 Liebrenz, *Rifāʿīya aus Damaskus*, 162.

46 The *List of Identified al-Jazzār Manuscripts and Their Current Location* is also available at the Research Data Repository of Universität Hamburg where we will keep updating it (https://doi.org/10.25592/uhhfdm.14178).

FIGURE 0.11 The interior of the mosque of Abū al-Dhahab in Cairo
PHOTOGRAPHED BY GUY BURAK, 25 JANUARY 2023

FIGURE 0.12 The mosque built by Ẓāhir al-ʿUmar in Tiberias, photograph taken between 1898 and 1946
LIBRARY OF CONGRESS, G. ERIC AND EDITH MATSON PHOTOGRAPH COLLECTION, LC-M32-51011-X

include eighteen not listed in the library inventory. Yet, the presence of the endowment statement, seal and/or motto leaves no doubt that these books once belonged to the pasha's library. Our corpus, thus, consists of seventy-eight al-Jazzār books of which sixty are al-Jazzār inventory books (JIBs) and eighteen are al-Jazzār non-inventory books (JnIBs). The JnIBs must have been in the original library, but extracted before our inventory was written. One possibility regarding when these JnIBs left the library is the upheaval caused by the 1799 siege of Acre by Napoleon, as Said Aljoumani argues in Chapter 2. This is especially likely as this siege had an impact on the overall endowment, as argued by Yasin Arslantaş in Chapter 5.

How did we enlarge the number of identified al-Jazzār books? The method adopted to identify books that once belonged to a library has to be tailored for each case. The provenance traces left on the books can be very different (such as ownership note, endowment seal, reading notes, endowment statement), the trajectories can be radically different (the majority of the historical library's books can be in one modern-day library or the books might be distributed across libraries all over the world), and the available source material other than the books themselves can differ considerably in nature and density (for example, inventory, catalogue, endowment deed, estate record, auction list, court proceedings of a legal dispute).[47] In our case, we focused our search strategy on matching the two main anchor points of the project, the Jazzār library inventory from 1221/1806 and the traces left on the books themselves. The traces relevant for identifying books that had once belonged to the Jazzār library consist of the three main textual elements named already: the endowment statement setting out the stipulations, the endowment seal and the brief endowment motto at the top of many pages.

The endowment statement has a fairly standardised text that states that the book in question is endowed in Acre for the benefit of students and cannot be removed from the endowment. Significantly, the text always highlights that the book is endowed in 'al-Nūr Aḥmadiyya', 'The Light of Aḥmad' Mosque, closely tying al-Jazzār's vision of the endowment complex, and his reference to the imperial centre, to his library. In the case of our example, the legal *Muhimmāt* by al-Isnawī (d. 772/1370–1371) (see Chapter 16), the text of the endowment statement reads:

Al-Ḥājj Aḥmad Pasha al-Jazzār endowed this book as a valid and legal endowment in his Nūr al-Aḥmadiyya Mosque in Acre for the benefit of students and under the condition that it will not be removed from its place, not sold, not pawned and not substituted. Whoever alters it [the endowment's conditions] after he has heard it, the sin is upon those who have altered it. Indeed, God is Hearing and Knowing [Qur'an, al-Baqara, 181]. Written 5 Dhū al-Ḥijja of the year 1196 [1782 CE].

أوقف وحبس وتصدق بهذا الكتاب الحاج
أحمد باشا الجزار في جامعه الذي بعكا النور
الأحمدية على طالب العلم وأنه لا يطلع من محله
وقفا صحيحا شرعيا لا يباع ولا يرهن ولا يبدل
فمن بدله بعدما سمعه فإنما إثمه على الذين
يبدلونه إن الله سميع عليم تحرير في 5 ذ[ي] الحجة سنة 1196

The endowment seal exists in two shapes, one oval and the other more circular.[48] Even though they have different shapes, they carry the same text indicating the importance of the wording. The seals' text reiterates that the book was endowed for the Nūr Aḥmadiyya, but states that the place of endowment is the Nūr Aḥmadiyya *madrasa*, not the Nūr Aḥmadiyya mosque as in the

47 For different methods see D'hulster, *Browsing*; Necipoğlu et al., *Treasures*; Déroche et al., *Livres du sultan*; Hirschler, *Medieval Damascus*; Hirschler, *Monument*; Aljoumani/Hirschler, *Owning Books*.

48 The endowment seal is discussed in more detail in Chapter 10 by Boris Liebrenz.

او قف وحبس وتصدق بهذا الكتاب الحاج
احمد باشا الجزار في جامعه الذي بعكا النور
الاحمديه على طالب العلم وانه لا يطلع من محله
وقفا صحيحا شرعيا لا يباع ولا يرهن ولا يبدل
فمن بدله بعدما سمعه فانما اثمه على الذين
يبدلونه ان الله سميع عليم تحريرا ٥ ذا الحجه

FIGURE 0.13 Endowment statement of al-Jazzār, Jerusalem, National Library of Israel, AP Ar. 290, fol. 2ª, top right corner (= #416), digitised by the National Library of Israel, Project 'Warraq'.

FIGURE 0.14
Endowment seal of al-Jazzār, Berlin, Staatsbibliothek, Landberg 9, fol. 1ª.

statement. We will return to the significance of the term *madrasa* further down. Both seals carry the same date, 1205/1790–1791 and arguably the one seal matrix was produced after the original matrix had been lost. The distribution of the two seals across the corpus does not follow a chronological order, as we can see from dated endowment statements. We, thus, find the oval seal imprint on books endowed in the years 1196,[49] 1197,[50] 1199[51] and 1201.[52] And we find the more circular seal imprint on books endowed in the years 1196,[53] 1197,[54] 1200[55] and 1205.[56] There is no chronological logic to the distribution of the seal imprints, thus, it seems that they were not applied when books entered the library, but rather during a later revision of the library's stock.

Apart from the endowment statement and seal, the third feature to identify al-Jazzār books is the motto 'endowment for God, the exalted' (either *waqf Allāh taʿāla* or *waqf li-llāh taʿāla*). These mottos are discussed in more detail in Chapter 11. This motto is found in the vast majority of al-Jazzār books on top of numerous pages. This motto by itself is not enough to ascribe a given book in a library somewhere in the world to the Jazzār library. Yet, as it turned out, this motto was generally written in quite distinctive hands. It, thus, led us, in some cases, to a closer inspection of the volume and to find remnants of the statement and/or the seal that were obliterated to conceal the book's previous endowment status.

In numerous cases, we find all these three elements in a book, but more often we only find two or even just one element. Linking books to a specific historical library is cumbersome because cataloguing practices during the nineteenth and most of the twentieth centuries paid little heed to such statements, seals and mottos. Many of our present-day catalogues were primarily philology-driven undertakings that show limited interest in the objects' trajectories. A search in most major catalogues of Arabic collections of handwritten books will, thus, not yield any information on these three elements.

In order to compensate for this lack of data, the ALP adopted three main strategies to identify the books from the library scattered throughout numerous collections today. Firstly, entire collections were searched. This is the working method that Boris Liebrenz has adopted for many years in the framework of the Bibliotheca Arabica project in Leipzig, and we benefited greatly from his work and expertise. He has especially covered European and American collections, such as the Bibliothèque Nationale de France in Paris, the Royal Library in Copenhagen, most of the Staatsbibliothek Berlin, other German collections, such as

49 Acre, al-Jazzār Mosque Library, MS 21 (ʿAṭāʾ Allāh, *Fihris ʿAkkā*, 1983); EAP399/1/3.
50 Cairo, Ministry of Awqaf Library, MS 4490.
51 Cairo, Dār al-kutub, Taymur, Muṣṭalaḥ al-ḥadīth 97.
52 Qatar National Library, QNL00017150.
53 Acre, al-Jazzār Mosque Library, MS 6 (ʿAṭāʾ Allāh, *Fihris ʿAkkā*, 1983); EAP399/1/46.
54 Beirut, Université Saint-Joseph, HMML project no. USJ 200214.
55 Princeton University Library, Garrett 3516Y.
56 Istanbul, Süleymaniye Library, Kemankeş 21.

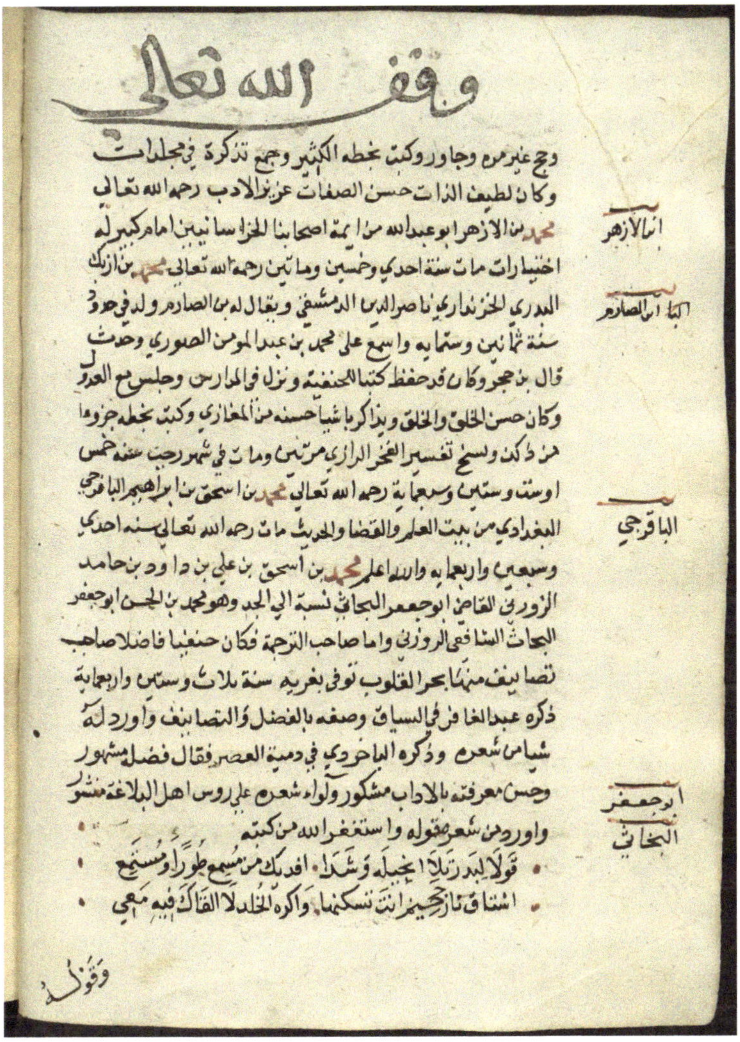

FIGURE 0.15
Endowment motto of al-Jazzār (وقف الله تعالى), Berlin
STAATSBIBLIOTHEK, LANDBERG 9, FOL. 79[A], TOP OF THE PAGE

Gotha and the Tübingen and Leipzig university libraries, as well as parts of the university libraries of Leiden, Cambridge, Columbia, Harvard and Princeton. Collections searched in their entirety in West Asia include: the American University library in Beirut (Boris Liebrenz); al-Majmaʿ al-ʿIlmī (Academy of Sciences) Library in Damascus (Boris Liebrenz/Said Aljoumani); and in Palestine/Israel, the Great Omari Mosque library in Gaza (Benedikt Reier), al-Najah National University library in Nablus (Dana Sajdi/Benedikt Reier), the Khalidi Library in Jerusalem (Said Aljoumani/Boris Liebrenz), the Jazzār library itself (Konrad Hirschler) and the 'Abandoned Property' section of the National Library of Israel in Jerusalem (Vincent Engelhardt, also using the unpublished notes of Efraim Wust).

It is important to note that some searches were conducted based on digitised images, therefore, erased or pasted over seals and notes might have been missed. That other al-Jazzār books are hidden in those collections we have already searched is evident from the case of the Chester Beatty Library. Through the work of Moya Carey, we became aware that the seven known al-Jazzār books in the Chester Beatty Library were part of a purchase of 126 handwritten books in 1928; a purchase that is discussed in more detail in Chapter 7. This corpus of 126 books is today in the Chester Beatty Library classmark range Ar. 3225 to 3341.[57] Once we had this background knowledge, we conducted a more thorough search in this classmark range and this search indeed brought up two books where the al-Jazzār seal had been defaced (Ar. 3310) or pasted over (Ar. 3268)—traces that had been previously missed.

The second strategy to identify al-Jazzār books consisted of automated searches of digitised books using the learning-free Visual-Pattern Detector that Hussein Mohammed (CSMC/Hamburg) has developed.[58] The Visual-Pattern Detector compared samples of the endowment seal of al-Jazzār with a large number of images to suggest possible matches.[59] This strategy has the advantage of speed, but it does not work for those cases where the endowment seal was erased, defaced or pasted over.

The third strategy was to search for exemplars of a specific title mentioned in the Jazzār library inventory. Once an exemplar of such a title was found in a given library, it was checked for possible traces of a Jazzār provenance. This strategy only works for titles for which few handwritten exemplars have survived. The number of handwritten copies of bestsellers, such as al-Buṣīrī's *Qaṣidat al-Burda*, is so high that a targeted search would be too resource-intensive. The same applies to books with generic titles, such as *Sharḥ al-Shāṭibiyya* (for example, #97 in the Jazzār library inventory). In addition to these targeted searches, colleagues who became aware of our project generously shared their knowledge and directed us to many books.

Our efforts to identify al-Jazzār books yielded some results and enlarged the corpus, but the vast majority of the library's books remain unaccounted for. There are two main possible explanations. Firstly, a large corpus of al-Jazzār books might have been moved to a library that we could not search, but where a strong presence of al-Jazzār books is plausible. The difficult-to-access National Library in Cairo (Dār al-Kutub) and the National al-Asad Library in Damascus are strong candidates for this scenario. The second explanation is that searches depended very much on the presence of al-Jazzār's endowment statement, seal or motto. The seal and the statement especially were defaced or removed in many cases, therefore, identifying the book in question positively as a Jazzār book required close examination. One example is the previously mentioned Ar. 3310 in the Chester Beatty Library with a defaced seal and Ar. 3268 in the same library with the seal pasted over. It is unclear who tried to conceal their endowment status. However, the cataloguer was sufficiently concerned when they entered Chester Beatty's possession in 1928 to write: 'the donation [waqf] note might cause discussion should it be known generally'.[60] The brief endowment motto at the top of many pages is less often tampered with. A clumsily attempted example is the 'Paris book', where a book user tried to overwrite the word '*waqf*' (Figure 7.1).[61] That attempt failed spectacularly as the writer created a mess that was surely more likely to draw the attention of subsequent users.

In addition, it is difficult to ascertain how systematically al-Jazzār's endowment statement, endowment seal or endowment motto were put on the books in the library. In their work on the seventeenth-century library of the Moroccan Sultan Mulāy Zaydān, for instance, the editors estimate that less than 20 per cent of all the

57 In addition to Per 140, T 472, Ar 4190, Ar 4201, Ar 4235, and excluding Ar 3237 (email from Moya Carey to Konrad Hirschler, 29 August 2023).

58 https://www.csmc.uni-hamburg.de/publications/software/vdp.html (accessed 3 January 2023).

59 Mohammed et al., "*Pattern Analysis Software Tools* (*PAST*)".

60 Carey, "Real Mine".

61 Offered by Antiquariat Inlibris (Vienna), Catalogue *37th Antiquaria Ludwigsburg* (15–17 June 2023), no. 18: https://inlibris.com/item/bn60713/?catalogue=102466 (accessed 19 June 2023). We call it the 'Paris book' as the catalogue states that this book was 'latterly in a Parisian private collection, kept in the family for several generations over the 20th century and dispersed in 2022'.

manuscripts that once belonged to the palace library carry any traces of ownership, including seals.[62]

4 This Volume's Outline and Main Arguments

This volume has three main parts focused on the library's historical context (Part 1), the materiality of its books (Part 2) and its intellectual profile (Part 3). These three parts reflect three different methodological perspectives simultaneously. Part 1 is based on a wide corpus of sources and, amongst others, places the library and its founder in the context of Ottoman libraries, discusses the perception of its founder, follows the confiscation procedures of al-Jazzār's estate and introduces the 'successor' library founded in Jaffa after al-Jazzār's death. The historical context of the library's foundation is central to the interpretation of its intellectual composition.

Part 2 hones in primarily on the al-Jazzār manuscripts identified so far. Its contributions show the loss of material evidence, discuss the meaning of the library seal and analyse the profile of the inks used for the endowment motto and statement. This part draws heavily on one particular feature of the inventory—its outstandingly rich description of the books' materiality. Part 3 focuses on the inventory itself. Its chapters are based on the fundamental methodological decision to follow the inventory's thematic classification system as it was put to paper in the early eighteenth century. This system often seemed somewhat awkward and surprising compared with the classification systems we are used to today. The prime example of such a rather unwieldy case is the category of *ḥadīth*. Here, we find numerous books that do not fall into contemporary concepts of *ḥadīth* (see Chapter 2 by Said Aljoumani and especially Chapter 15 by Garrett Davidson).

Several chapters in Parts 1 and 2 (Chapters 1, 2, 9, 10) draw attention to the inventory's bibliographic practices that were arguably adopted from the Ottoman core lands and adapted to the local context of Acre. The study of the bibliographic practices of al-Jazzār's librarians compared to those of their colleagues in the Ottoman capital reveals significant differences among the practitioners adhering to a recognisably shared bibliographic tradition. These differences are illuminating and raise questions about how standardised the Ottoman library culture of the eighteenth century actually was.

As a collective endeavour, this volume does not drive home one single argument. Instead, we have numerous argumentative strands in the individual chapters. Yet, some topics repeatedly appear in different places in this volume and these themes also came up in the project's workshop in March 2023 when chapter drafts were discussed. The function of the library and the Shiʿite elements in its collection are just two of these shared topics that we want to sketch briefly here. Beyond doubt, books played an important role in al-Jazzār's career as Dana Sajdi shows in Chapter 22. Four years before he built his endowment complex in Acre, for instance, he ordered the production of two volumes in 1192/1778 that were missing from the *ḥadīth* collection *Ṣaḥīḥ al-Bukhārī*. This particular copy was held in the religiously most significant place in the southern Levant, the Dome of the Rock in Jerusalem. Al-Jazzār ensured his good deeds were appropriately celebrated on the copies with embellished endowment statements.[63] Moreover, many of his patrons and peers, such as the above-mentioned governor of Egypt Abū al-Dhahab, were involved in establishing libraries.

The importance of books in al-Jazzār's career also raises the question of what function the library played in Acre. The endowment seal on the books identified states unequivocally that they were endowed to the '*madrasa*' and the endow-

62 Déroche et al., *Livres du sultan*, 35.

63 *Ṣaḥīḥ al-Bukhārī*, Jerusalem, Al-Budeiri Library, MS 451, vol. 1, fol. 2[a] and vol. 2, fol. 1[a].

FIGURE 0.16
Tampered endowment motto in al-Surūrī, *Sharḥ Gulistān*, fol. 10b, top of the page, Antiquariat Inlibris, Vienna ('Paris book')

ment deed provides salaries for two teachers. So, at first glance, it seems this is a straightforward case of a library founded with an educational function in mind. Yet, narrative sources hardly ever mentioned such a *madrasa* in Acre in the biographies of individuals active in the southern Levant. Even more worrying, we have a register that provides an insight into the endowment's expenditures (see Chapter 2 by Said Aljoumani for more details). These accounts mention salaries paid to the endowment's various position holders, such as the imam, the librarian and the preacher (*khaṭīb*). However, they do not mention any teacher who received a salary. Perhaps the imam or the *khaṭīb* taught in addition to their primary task, but even if that were the case, teaching was a secondary concern at best.

The library's function is also far from being clear when analysing the profile of its contents. It is evident that al-Jazzār aspired to found an 'encyclopaedic' Islamic library, covering most of the Islamic sciences and disciplines, written in the three predominant languages of the Ottoman intellectual elite (Arabic, Persian and Turkish). However, at the level of the individual sections, the contributors to this volume offer different interpretations concerning the intended readers and audience. Asad Ahmed, for example, argues in his chapter on logic (Chapter 20) that the books in this section indicate a pedagogical function of the library. Dana Sajdi, by contrast, posits that the profile of the history section (Chapter 22) reflects al-Jazzār's political ambitions at the Ottoman imperial level. In this reading, the function of the library was primarily a vizierial one, emulating Ottoman libraries in the imperial capital and elsewhere. These different functions are most probably not exclusive, but reflect the various motivations that led al-Jazzār to establish his library.

The question of the curatorial choices that shaped the library is also pertinent to the interpretation of the presence of Shiʿi books in the library's collection. We, thus, find books of Shiʿite authors in the section on Qur'an Commentary (Chapter 13), that has, in contrast to comparable libraries, a considerable number of Shiʿite works. The *ḥadīth* section (Chapter 15) contained forty *ḥadīth* transmitted by the Shiʿite scholar Ḥusayn al-ʿĀmilī (d. 984/1577), and the law section of the library (Chapter 16) held more Shiʿite legal works than Mālikī and Ḥanbalī works combined. How to interpret the inclusion of all these works in the library is a question we cannot resolve. Yet, it is noteworthy that such books could make their way into a library that had a strong Sunni background.[64]

The presence of these books brings up the topic of al-Jazzār plundering or destroying libraries in the Shiʿite Jabal ʿĀmil region, a trope that appears in certain accounts of his career. Boris Liebrenz makes a strong case in Chapter 3 that reports on the destroying and burning of libraries should not be taken at face value. However, there is a high probability that al-Jazzār confiscated libraries in that region, similar to what he did elsewhere, as the case of the three confiscated libraries that Said Aljoumani discusses in Chapter 2 shows. In fact, there are arguably two books in our corpus of seventy-eight identified books that have a distinct link to Jabal ʿĀmil: 1) The JnIB title *Zubdat al-uṣūl* by Bahā' al-ʿĀmilī, today in Cairo, al-Azhar Library, MS 91135, had been owned by Ḥasan ʿAlī Ḥalāwī al-Faqʿānī before its inclusion in the Jazzār library. In his ownership note, Ḥasan states that Jabal ʿĀmil was where he was born and resided. 2) The JIB *al-Kashshāf* by al-Zamakhsharī (#45) is today in Jerusalem (Abu Dis), The Center for Heritage Revival and Islamic Research, 301/2. This book had been owned by Abū al-Ḥasan b. Ḥaydar al-Ḥusaynī al-ʿĀmilī (d. 1195/1781), a well-known scholar of Jabal ʿĀmil (see Chapter 3). Two books from Jabal ʿĀmil constitute a noteworthy proportion within our corpus of seventy-eight identified manuscripts. Suppose we extrapolate this to the overall number of 1,820 entries (obviously an exercise fraught with numerous methodological problems). In that case, we get the number of some forty-seven books from Jabal ʿĀmil that had been in the Jazzār library.

That there were more books from Jabal ʿĀmil beyond our present corpus is made very likely by the story of entry #1342, entitled *al-Rawḍatayn fī akhbār al-dawlatayn* (*The Two Gardens on the Reports on the Two Dynasties*) in the inventory. As we have not yet found the Jazzār manuscript of this dynastic history, the exact identity of this entry's text and author is open to interpretation. The first possibility that comes to mind is the famous *al-Rawḍatayn fī akhbār al-dawlatayn* by Abū Shāma (d. 665/1268) on the Zangid and early Ayyubid dynasties in the Levant of the twelfth century CE. Yet, there is another intriguing possibility, the lost *al-Rawḍatayn fī akhbār banī Būyah wa-al-Ḥamdāniyyīn* on the Shiʿite Buyid and Hamdanid dynasties of the tenth and eleventh centuries. That this is the work meant by entry #1342 is plausible because it was authored by Muḥammad b. Ḥasan b. ʿAlī Āl Shukr al-ʿĀmilī (d. 1207/1792–1793),

64 It is possible that studies of Ottoman Iraqi libraries would reveal similar patterns of inclusion of Shiʿite books into predominantly Sunni collections.

a Shiʿite scholar from Jabal ʿĀmil whom al-Jazzār killed. We not only have reports that al-Jazzār plundered this scholar's library, but also the explicit statement that 'one of his compositions remains in the library of that mosque [the al-Jazzār mosque in Acre] today: *al-Rawḍatayn fī akhbār banī Būyah wa-al-Ḥamdāniyyīn*'.[65] Many reports on al-Jazzār's actions, especially on his plundering libraries in Jabal ʿĀmil, were produced much later and can, thus, not be taken at face value. The report in question is mentioned in al-Amīnī's *Shuhadāʾ al-faḍīla*, first published in Iraq in 1936. Al-Amīnī states that he cites this information 'from *Tārīkh Jabal ʿĀmil* by the Shaykh Muḥammad al-Zayn who transmits from *Nuzhat al-nuẓẓār* by the Shaykh Ḥasan Khātūn and *Tārīkh ʿulamāʾ ʿĀmil* by the Shaykh ʿAlī al-Subaytī'. We could not identify Ḥasan Khātūn, nor the actual texts used. However, Subaytī lived between the years 1236/1821 and 1303/1886, which makes his statement (or that of Ḥasan Khātūn) that 'the copy of the *Rawḍatayn* is now' in the Jazzār library particularly exciting as it would be one of the few statements on the library in the decades after its founder's death.

The multiplicity of possible interpretations of the library's function and the manners in which it was assembled leave a lot of room for additional research. We hope this volume provides ample material and argumentative suggestions to enrich the scholarship on book collections and libraries in Palestine, the Arabic-speaking provinces of the Ottoman Empire, the empire at large and West Asia. Regarding Palestinian book history, the study of al-Jazzār's library and its legacy will have to be matched by a wide range of further cases to complete the picture. To name but a few of the desiderata: The history of the Khalidi Library in Jerusalem can be enlarged with a stronger focus on the manuscript evidence;[66] the former Abū Nabbūt library of Jaffa deserves a complete study based on Benedikt Reier's Chapter 6; the history of late-Ottoman and Mandate Period private Palestinian libraries urgently requires more research based on the 'Abandoned Property' section in the National Library of Israel (see Chapter 7); the potential of the Ottoman court records has to be tapped into;[67] the history of the book collections in the Aqṣā Mosque and the broader Ḥaram al-sharīf complex awaits in-depth study; and the same goes for the library of the Ḥaram al-Ibrāhīmī in Hebron, the ʿUmarī Mosque in Gaza[68] as well as smaller mosque collections, such as that of the Burqayn mosque library near Jenin. This, in turn, will have to be combined with the evidence of Christian and Jewish libraries of Palestine, for which the first steps have been taken for Jerusalem.[69] Similarly, future study of libraries in the Arabic-speaking provinces of the empire can reveal the extent to which the dynamics observed in the library in Acre are part of a broader exchange of bibliographic practices and conventions across the empire and, in this process, nuance some of the categories commonly used to describe libraries across West Asia.

Bibliography

Açıl, Berat (ed.). *Osmanlı Kitap Kültürü: Cârullah Efendi Kütüphanesi ve Derkenar Notlari*. Istanbul, 2020.

Aljoumani, Said. "Masrad kutub madrasat Muḥammad Bāshā al-ʿAẓm: nashr wa-dirāsa." *Majallat Maʿhad al-Makhṭūṭāt al-ʿArabiyya* 61, no. 2 (2017): 10–73.

Aljoumani, Said. *Maktaba madrasiya fī ḥalab nihāyat al-ʿahd al-ʿUthmānī: al-daftar al-mujaddad li-kutub waqf ʿUthmān Bāshā al-Dūrikī*. Beirut, 2019.

65 Al-Amīnī, *Shuhadāʾ al-faḍīla*, 272.

66 Khalidi, *Khalidi Library*.

67 For some examples of such records relevant for Palestinian book and library history, see Ghosheh, *Encyclopædia Palestinnica*, vol. 16: *Manuscripts and libraries in Palestine*. For the value of court records for the reconstruction of book collections in late seventeenth-century Damascus, see Marino, "Engager des livres".

68 The bombardment of the mosque in December 2023 makes it uncertain to what extent, if at all, its manuscript collection is still extant when we are writing these lines in mid-2024.

69 Such as the survey by Mack/Balint, *City of the Book*.

Aljoumani, Said and Konrad Hirschler. *Owning Books and Preserving Documents in Medieval Jerusalem. The Library of Burhan al-Din*. Edinburgh, 2023.

Al-Amīnī al-Najafī. *Shuhadāʾ al-faḍīla*. Beirut, 1983.

Aras, Bekir Uğur. "191 Numaralı Mühimme Defterinin Latin Harflerine Çevirisi ve Değerlendirmesi." Unpublished MA thesis, Kütahya Dumlupınar University, 2018.

Atbaş, Zeynep. "A Grand Collection from the Topkapı Palace Library Treasury: The Library of Ahmed III." In *Proceedings of 16th International Congress of Turkish Art: Ankara*, 3–5 October. 2 vols. 1:161–181. Istanbul, 2023.

Barakat, Bashir. *Tārīkh al-maktabāt al-ʿarabiyya fī Bayt al-Maqdis*. Riyad, 2012.

Barbir, Karl. *Ottoman Rule in Damascus, 1708–1758*. Princeton, 1980.

Al-Bayṭār, ʿAbd al-Razzāq al-Dimashqī. *Ḥilyat al-bashar fī tārīkh al-qarn al-thālith ʿashar*. Edited by Muḥammad Bahjat al-Bayṭār. 3 vols. Damascus, Majmaʿ al-Lugha al-ʿArabiyya, 1961–1963.

Bouquet, Olivier. "Pour une histoire instrumentale des savoirs ottomans: à quoi servaient les «livres tenus en haute estime» et autres précieux manuscrits conservés dans une bibliothèque de madrasa anatolienne (Burdur, seconde moitié du XVIIIe siècle)?" *Arabica* 67, no. 5–6 (2020): 502–559.

Câbî Ömer Efendi. *Câbî Târihi: Târîh-i Sultân-i Selîm-i Sâlis ve Mahmûd-i Sânî: Tahlîl ve Tenkidli Metin*. Edited by Mehmet Ali Beyhan. 2 vols. Ankara, 2003.

Carey, Moya. "'A Real Mine for All Kinds of Research': Abraham Yahuda's Exchanges with Chester Beatty, and the Introduction of Arabic Rare Texts." In *A.S. Yahuda as Cultural Broker. Between Near Eastern Philology and the Manuscript Trade* (working title), edited by Stephanie Luescher, Marina Rustow and Samuel Thrope. Forthcoming.

Cohen, Amnon. *Palestine in the 18th Century: Patterns of Government and Administration*. Jerusalem, 1973.

Crecelius, Daniel. "The Waqf of Muhammad Bey Abu al-Dhahab in Historical Perspective." *International Journal of Middle East Studies* 23 (1991): 57–81.

Derin Can, Elif. "Manuscript Collections of the Chief Harem Eunuchs in the Early Modern Ottoman Empire." MA thesis, Marmara University, 2022.

Déroche, François, Nuria de Castilla and Lbachir Tahali. *Les livres du sultan. Matériaux pour une histoire du livre et de la vie intellectuelle du Maroc saadien (XVIe siècle)*. Paris, 2022.

D'hulster, Kristof. *Browsing through the Sultan's Bookshelves. Towards a Reconstruction of the Library of the Mamluk Sultan Qāniṣawh al-Ghawrī (r. 906–922/1501–1516)*. Göttingen, 2021.

Erünsal, İsmail E. *Osmanlılarda Kütüphaneler ve Kütüphanecilik*. Istanbul, 2015.

Erünsal, İsmail E. *A History of Ottoman Libraries*. Boston, 2022.

Ghosheh, Mohammad H. *Encyclopædia Palestinnica*, Amman, 2019.

Güler, Mustafa. *Cezzar Ahmed Paşa ve Akka Savunması*. Istanbul, 2013.

Ḥammūd, ʿAlī. "Aḥmad Bāshā al-Jazzār: al-Wālī al-khālid li-ʿAkkā wa-Filasṭīn fī al-qarn al-thāmin ʿashar". In *Aḥmad Bāshā al-Jazzār: 200 ʿām ʿalá wafātihi*, edited by Shukrī ʿArrāf and Yaʿqūb Ḥijāzi, 36–56. Muʾassasat al-Aswār, 2004.

Hathaway, Jane. *The Politics of Households in Ottoman Egypt: The Rise of the Qazdağlis*. Cambridge, 1997.

Hirschler, Konrad. *Medieval Damascus: Plurality and Diversity in an Arabic Library. The Ashrafīya Library Catalogue*. Edinburgh, 2016.

Hirschler, Konrad. "Saleroom Fiction versus Provenance. Historicizing Manuscripts via Their Marginal and Material Logic (Schøyen Fragments 1776)." *Journal of Islamic Manuscripts* 13 (2022): 1–54.

Hirschler, Konrad. *A Monument to Medieval Syrian Book Culture. The Library of Ibn ʿAbd al-Hādī*. Edinburgh, 2019.

Ibrāhīm, ʿAbd al-Laṭīf. "Maktaba ʿUthmāniyya: dirāsa naqdiyya wa-nashr li-raṣīd al-maktaba." *Majallat Kuliyyat al-Adab* 20, no. 2 (1958): 1–35.

Al-Jazzār Aḥmad Pasha. *Ottoman Egypt in the Eighteenth Century: The Nizâmnâme-i Misir of Cezzâr Ahmed Pasha*. Edited and translated by Stanford Shaw. Cambridge, MA, Harvard University Press, 1962.

Kafescioğlu, Çiğdem. "'In the Image of Rūm': Ottoman Architectural Patronage in Sixteenth-Century Aleppo and Damascus." *Muqarnas* 16 (1999): 70–96.

Kanaʿan, Ruba. “Two Ottoman Sabils in Jaffa (c. 1810–1815): An Architectural and Epigraphic Analysis.” *Levant* 33, no. 1 (2001): 189–204.

Kanaʿan, Ruba. “Waqf, Architecture, and Political Self-Fashioning: The Construction of the Great Mosque of Jaffa by Muhammad Aga Abu Nabbut.” *Muqarnas* 18 (2001): 120–140.

Khalidi, Walid. *The Khalidi Library in Jerusalem, 1720–2001*. Beirut, 2020.

Khoury, D. Rizk. *State and Provincial Society in the Ottoman Empire: Mosul, 1540–1834*. Cambridge, 1998.

Liebrenz, Boris. *Die Rifāʿīya aus Damaskus. Eine Privatbibliothek im osmanischen Syrien und ihr kulturelles Umfeld*. Leiden, 2016.

Mack, Merav and Benjamin Balint. *Jerusalem, City of the Book*. New Haven/London, 2019.

Maghribi, ʿAbd al-Raḥmān. “Waṣf lil-madīna fī mudhakkirāt diblūmāsī Maghribī zāra al-Sharq”. In *Aḥmad Bāshā al-Jazzār: 200 ʿām ʿalá wafātihi*. Edited by Shukrī ʿArrāf and Yaʿqūb Ḥijāzi. 59–64. Mu'assasat al-Aswār, 2004.

Marino, Brigitte. “Engager des livres à Damas à la fin du XVIIe siècle. La bibliothèque de la famille Ḥamza mise en caisses (1092/1681).” *Studi arabistici in memoria di Anna Pagnini* (2023): 299–364.

Matar, Nabil. *An Arab Ambassador in the Mediterranean World: The Travels of Muhammad ibn ʿUthmān al-Miknāsī, 1779–1788*. Routledge, 2015.

Mehmet Süreyya Bey. *Sicill-i Osmânî, yahut, Tezkire-i Meşâhîr-i Osmâniye*. 4 vols. Matbaa-i Amire, 1891–1899.

Menchinger, Ethan L. *The First of the Modern Ottomans: The Intellectual History of Ahmed Vâsif*. Cambridge, 2017.

Mohammed H.A., Helman-Wazny A., Colini C., Beyer W. and Bosch S. “Pattern Analysis Software Tools (PAST) for Written Artefacts” In *Proceedings 15th IAPR International Workshop, DAS 2022*, edited by S. Uchida, E. Barney and V. Eglin, 214–229. Cham, 2022.

Muḥaybish, Ghassān Mūsā. *Mujammaʿ al-Jazzār al-khayrī fī ʿAkkā*. Mu'assasat al-Aswār, 1993.

Necipoğlu, Gülru, Cemal Kafadar and Cornell H. Fleischer (eds). *Treasures of Knowledge. An Inventory of the Ottoman Palace Library (1502/3–1503/4)*. 2 vols. Leiden, 2019.

Philipp, Thomas. *Acre: The Rise and Fall of a Palestinian City, 1730–1831*. New York, 2001.

Rā'ūf, ʿImād ʿAbd al-Salām. *Dirāsāt turāthiyya fī al-buldān wa-al-tarājim wa-al-adab wa-al-riḥlāt*, 2 vols. Irbil, 2019.

Rüstem, Ünver. *Ottoman Baroque: The Architectural Refashioning of Eighteenth-century Istanbul*. Princeton, 2019.

Safi, Khaled. “al-Jazzār, Aḥmad Pasha.” *Encyclopedia of Islam*, third edition. Leiden.

Sezer, Yavuz. “The Architecture of Bibliophilia: Eighteenth-century Ottoman Libraries.” PhD Dissertation, Massachusetts Institute of Technology, 2016.

Sharon, Moshe. *Corpus Inscriptionum Arabicarum Palaestinae (CIAP)*. Leiden, 1997-

Toledano, Ehud R. “The Emergence of Ottoman-local Elites (1700–1900): A Framework for Research.” In *Middle Eastern Politics and Ideas: A History from Within*, edited by Ilan Pappé and Moshe Maʿoz, 145–162. London, 1997.

Wilkins, Charles L. “The Self-fashioning of an Ottoman Urban Notable: Ahmad Efendi Tahazâde (d. 1773).” *Osmanlı Araştırmaları: Journal of Ottoman Studies* 44 (2014): 393–425.

Yaycıoğlu, Ali. *Partners of Empire: The Crisis of the Ottoman Order in the Age of Revolutions*. Stanford, 2016.

PART 1

The History of al-Jazzār, His Library and the Inventory

CHAPTER 1

Al-Jazzār's Library and Its Ottoman Context

Berat Açıl, Nimet İpek and Guy Burak

Aḥmad Pasha al-Jazzār's biography reveals that his career was entangled with numerous power brokers at both the imperial and provincial levels. Indeed, it is quite evident that al-Jazzār aspired to become an actor on the Ottoman imperial scene, "higher than viziers and lower than sultans", in the words of the prophecy related by the chronicler Cābī.[1] This ambition was translated, among other things, into the library he assembled in Acre. This chapter seeks to situate al-Jazzār's library in its broader imperial context. We aim specifically to examine how the governor and his librarians participated in the distinctive library culture that emerged primarily in the core lands of the empire and especially, though not exclusively, in Istanbul from the late seventeenth century onwards.[2]

The sheer size of al-Jazzār's collection—1,631 volumes in its core collection in addition to three additional smaller collections (seventy-six volumes)—reflects his imperial ambition. Indeed, the library is ranked among one of the largest libraries founded over the long eighteenth century: the books collection of the Grand Vizier Köprülü Fāżıl Aḥmed Paşa (d. 1676), which was posthumously endowed in his name in 1678, consisted of approximately 1,600 volumes;[3] the library collection of the chief imperial mufti, Feyżullāh Efendi (d. 1703) included more than 2,000 books;[4] the library of the jurist and scholar Veliyyüddīn Cārullāh Efendi (d. 1738) held around 2,200 titles;[5] the library endowed by Rāġıp Mehmed Paşa (d. 1763), an influential bureaucrat who eventually served as the Grand Vizier (from 1757 to his death), contained 1,100 titles in 1762;[6] and the Hamidiye Library, which was endowed by Sultan Abdülḥamīd (r. 1774–1789) in 1780, held 1,504 manuscripts.[7] Moreover, al-Jazzār's library collection was considerably larger than many others assembled by eighteenth-century book collectors across the Ottoman Empire: the core collection endowed by ʿUthmān Pasha al-Dūrikī (d. 1747), the collector of the revenues of the imperial estates (*muḥaṣṣil al-amwāl al-miriyya*) in Aleppo comprised 409 titles;[8] Asʿad Pasha al-ʿAẓm (d. 1758), the governor of Damascus, endowed 92 titles (some are multivolume) to the library of the *madrasa* built by his father Ismāʿīl Pasha (d. 1732);[9] his son and successor Muḥammad Pasha al-ʿAẓm (d. 1783) endowed 457 titles (some multivolume) to the library of his *madrasa*;[10] his contemporary, the Governor Ḥalīl Ḥamīd Paşa (d. 1785) endowed 106 books to his library in the Anatolian town of Burdur;[11] the Governor of Egypt Muḥammad Abū al-Dhahab (d. 1775)

1 Câbî Ömer Efendi, *Târîh-i Câbî*, 1, 84.

2 Several individuals seem to have been involved in handling the books over the decades, only one of whom is mentioned by name in the inventory. See Claudia Colini and Kyle Ann Huskin's Chapter 11 in this volume.

3 Sezer, "The Architecture of Bibliophilia", 40–42.

4 Ibid. 46.

5 Açıl, *Osmanlı Kitap Kültürü*.

6 Sievert, "Eavesdropping on the Pasha's Salon".

7 Cunbur, "i. Abdülhamid Vakfiyesi ve Hamidiye Kütüphanesi": 29. On the Hamidiye Library, also see Erünsal, "Hamidiye Kütüphanesi".

8 Aljoumani, *Maktaba madrasiyya*. On ʿUthmān Paşa al-Dūrikī, see al-Murādī, *Silk al-durar*, 3, 151–153; and Aljoumani, *Maktaba madrasiyya*, 33–35.

9 *Kitāb waqf Asʿad Bāshā al-ʿAẓm*.

10 Aljoumani, "Masrad kutub".

11 Bouquet, "Pour une histoire instrumentale des savoirs ottomans". A few libraries in late Ottoman Jerusalem, such as those of the Abū al-Luṭf and the Khālidi, held 1,000–1,300 manuscripts. Many other libraries in the cities, however, held much smaller collections (less than 250 volumes each). Barakāt, *Ta'rikh al-maktabāt al-ʿArabiyya*, 53–54.

initially endowed 1,008 volumes;[12] and the Governor of Baghdad Büyük Süleymān Paşa (or Sulaymān Pasha al-Kabīr, served as governor from 1783–1802), endowed 427 volumes to the library of the *madrasa* adjacent to the "New" Ḥasan Pasha Mosque.[13]

We hope to show in the following pages that the inventory of al-Jazzār's library reflects a considerable degree of familiarity with endowments of comparable size and the function of libraries and their culture in the capital and elsewhere. Moreover, we would suggest that al-Jazzār sought to promote and propagate his prestige, at least in part, within the new library culture. His provincial library can be seen in the broader context of the Ottomanised library culture in the empire's provinces, especially in its Arabic-speaking areas.

1 The Proliferation of Libraries in Eighteenth-century Istanbul

A short survey of the new library culture that emerged over the course of the late seventeenth and eighteenth centuries across the empire, especially in the capital, is in order to understand the imperial context of al-Jazzār's library. Numerous libraries were founded by sultans, viziers, scholars, chief eunuchs and lower-ranked bureaucrats during the long eighteenth century. Library founders in the eighteenth century certainly built on a long tradition of establishing libraries throughout the Islamic world and specifically the Ottoman lands. But the library culture of the eighteenth century was novel in several aspects. Those eighteenth-century libraries, we suggest, served as an important source of inspiration for al-Jazzār when he assembled his own library. Unfortunately, the study of Ottoman(ised) libraries in the provinces is still in its early phases, so, a comprehensive comparison of al-Jazzār's library with those founded by other provincial governors would be difficult. That said, we will allude to eighteenth-century Ottomanised libraries in the provinces when possible. By "Ottomanisation", we aspire to capture the complex dynamics between the imperial centre and the provinces, whereby members of the provincial administrative elites, either natives to the provinces or governors sent from the imperial centre, shared cultural and intellectual sensibilities with and saw themselves part of the imperial elite.

The construction of sultanic libraries predated the late seventeenth century. Meḥmed II (r. 1451–1481) and his son, Bāyezīd II (r. 1481–1512), assembled large libraries as part of their broader patronage of scholars and poets.[14] Murād III (r. 1574–1595), Özgen Felek argues, also recognised the importance of books as a means to gain legitimacy and promote a sultanic image.[15] Others in Murād III's court understood the power of book collections: The first chief harem eunuch, Ḥabeşī Meḥmed Ağa, who served under Murād III, established a library[16] which set an example for later chief eunuchs.[17]

Two members of the influential vizierial family (arguably the de facto rulers of the empire), Köprülü Meḥmed Paşa (d. 1661) and his son Fāżıl Aḥmed Paşa (d. 1676), founded a library in the middle of the seventeenth century where they endowed their manuscripts. Köprülü Meḥmed Paşa intended to establish the library as part of the complex (*külliye*) he was not able to complete due to his death (by the time of his death, he had only completed the *madrasa*, the hammam and the tomb). Fāżıl Aḥmed Paşa built the library,[18] complying

12 Crecelius, "The Waqf of Muhammad Bey".

13 Rā'ūf, *Dirāsāt turāthiyya*, I, 303–350. The books were endowed in 1781.

14 For the libraries of Mehmed II and Bāyezīd II see Erünsal, *A History of Ottoman Libraries*; Necipoğlu and Fleischer, *Treasures of Knowledge*.

15 Felek, *Kitābü'l-Menāmāt*.

16 For the books he endowed to his library see: Açıl, "Habeşi Mehmed Ağa'nın".

17 For the libraries of the chief eunuchs, see Derin Can, "Manuscript Collections".

18 Erünsal, "Köprülü Kütüphanesi". The endowment deed (*waqfiyya*) for the library was prepared by the grandson,

with his father's last request, where he placed ten of his father's manuscripts and endowed his own 1,397 manuscripts.[19] Many manuscripts in the collection were owned, copied and authored by renowned seventeenth-century scholars, such as the great poet Veysī (d. 1037/1628). It is noteworthy that Fāżıl Aḥmed Paşa or his librarians seem to have chosen manuscripts not just for their intellectual content but also for their antiquity, and artistic and aesthetic qualities. İpek and Burak discuss in Chapter 9 in this volume that the librarians were also interested in the calligraphic qualities of the collection.

Another remarkable and quite unusual feature of the Köprülü Library is that its endowment deed (*waqfiyya*) is the only one known which refers to professional copyists (*verrāḳūn*) as designated beneficiaries of the endowment other than the students of the *madrasa*.[20] This stipulation set an important precedent, and copying became a common library function in the following decades.[21] We shall see that the Köprülü Library set an important model for many late seventeenth- and eighteenth-century sultans and viziers in establishing their libraries.

Sultans and viziers started building libraries across the capital in the following decades, with the intention of preserving and making manuscripts more accessible in the imperial centre. Aḥmed III (r. 1703–1730) concentrated the manuscripts preserved in the imperial treasury into a single new library. The *waqfiyya* of the library elaborates on the reasons for its foundation:

> There are numerous illuminated manuscripts that were owned [by the Palace], bought or presented to the treasury of the imperial Palace, which are priceless pearls from the old ages. However, since talented people could not access and use them, those exquisite copies and manuscripts stayed in the dust of oblivion. Thus, people waiting for permission to thoroughly examine them and use them are unhappy [...].[22]

In other words, one of the primary goals of Ahmed III was to make manuscripts more accessible to readers. Eventually, Ahmed III founded two libraries: one in the innermost court of the Palace (*Enderun*) and another in front of Yeni Cami under the name the Turhan Valide Library. The former, for which the aforementioned endowment deed was written, ended up serving the fairly limited circle of palace pages.[23]

Courtiers in the court of Aḥmed III shared the sultan's bibliophilia. Şehīd ʿAlī Paşa (d. 1716), the Grand Vizier during the reign of Aḥmed III (served between 1713 and 1716), was famous for his love of books. His bibliophilia led the Grand Vizier to issue a ban on the export of books to prevent booksellers from selling splendid manuscripts to other countries instead of keeping them in the capital.[24] Şehīd ʿAlī Paşa established three libraries in Istanbul: one in his kiosk in Üskübī neighbourhood; the second in his waterside residence in Kuzguncuk (Üsküdar); and the third, which was built in 1716 and is known today as the Şehid Ali Paşa Library, in Fatih.[25] İsmail Erünsal has argued that Şehīd ʿAlī Paşa intended to prevent the confiscation of his book collection by endowing it to three libraries

Fāżıl Mustafā Paşa (d. 1691), in 1678 after Fāżıl Ahmed Paşa's sudden death in 1676. We made all the translations, unless stated otherwise.

19 Although the narrative about the library suggests that Köpürülü Mehmed Paşa endowed ten manuscripts to the library, only eight of them are currently held there. See Açıl, "Kütüphane Fihristlerinin Tenkitli".

20 Sezer, "The Architecture of Bibliophilia", 42.

21 Later Ottoman libraries chose the word *istinsākh* (copying) and/or istiktāb (commissioning) for this facility in their endowment deeds. The endowment deed of Ebūbekir Efendi b. Meḥmed Ağa (1777) in Sofia, for example, mentions the words "*istiktāb*" and "*istinsākh*" when listing the functions of his library. Similarly, the endowment deed of the Ayasofya Library uses the term *istinsākh*.

22 Erünsal, *Osmanlılarda kütüphaneler*, 181.

23 Erünsal, *Osmanlılarda Kütüphaneler*, 185.

24 Râşid, *Târîh-i Râşid*, IV, 238. Quoted by Erünsal, *Osmanlılarda Kütüphaneler*, 172.

25 Erünsal, *Osmanlılarda Kütüphaneler*, 172–174.

and consolidate them in a single library later on, a plan that did not materialise due to his death.[26] In any case, Şehīd ʿAlī Paşa assembled a sizable collection: According to Tülay Artan, the collection of the Şehīd ʿAlī Paşa Library consists of 2,840 manuscripts (more than 6,000 titles, as some volumes are composite manuscripts consisting of multiple titles).[27]

Fears and concerns about the confiscation of books (and other types of property), while certainly not the only reason for endowing book collections, spurred members of the Ottoman elite to establish endowment libraries in the following decades. This strategy was only partially successful, as *waqf* libraries founded by prominent bureaucrats were confiscated in the eighteenth century and will be discussed below. This common practice in the core lands may correspond with al-Jazzār's decision to endow his books to prevent them from being confiscated.[28]

Grand Vizier Ḥekīmoğlu ʿAlī Paşa (d. 1758) built a library in Istanbul in the mid-1730s.[29] Ḥekīmoğlu ʿAlī Paşa's, part of the complex of the largest vizierial mosque of the eighteenth century, was the first library built in Istanbul which was intended to be accessible to a significantly broader circle of readers (one of the so-called "public" libraries).[30] The number of manuscripts endowed by Ḥekīmoğlu ʿAlī Paşa and the main purpose of the library is not stated in its endowment deed. Erünsal has suggested that the library was intended for teaching classes, a common feature of many libraries established during the reign of Maḥmūd I.[31] Yavuz Sezer agreed that teaching was one of the functions of the library because the complex did not include a *madrasa*. This absence suggests that the library served the complex's teaching space.[32] According to the Grand Vizier's endowment deed, students received stipends from the library.[33] The library as a teaching space also became a feature of other eighteenth-century Istanbulite libraries: Most notably, Maḥmūd I's Ayasofya Library is described in several archival sources as "*kütübkhāne ve derskhāne-i hümāyūn* (imperial library and teaching institution)".[34]

Yavuz Sezer pointed out that Ḥekīmoğlu ʿAlī Paşa's endowment deed employs a metaphor that appears in several earlier *waqfiyya*s, such as those of the mosque complex of Fātih Sultan Mehmed Mosque (originally built between 1463 and 1470) and the Yeni Cami Mosque (composed in 1663), as well as in the deeds of several eighteenth-century libraries, such as those founded by Dāmād İbrāhīm Paşa, Rāğıp Paşa and Murād Molla.[35] The library of Ḥekīmoğlu ʿAlī Paşa is described as "an example of [God's] well-built house (*al-Bayt al-Maʿmūr*), a library replete with light", comparing the library to the Kaʿba,[36] the source of both knowledge and light. We shall return to this metaphor in the context of al-Jazzār's library below.

The reign of Sultan Maḥmūd I (r. 1730–1754), under whom Ḥekīmoğlu ʿAlī Paşa served, stands out as a distinctive era in the history of libraries in the Ottoman capital. The Sultan initiated the re-

26 Ibid., 175.

27 Artan, "On Sekizinci Yüzyil Başinda". Artan has argued that the Paşa started building his library while he was still a sword-bearer of the sultan (*silāḥdār*), and further developed it between 1713 and 1716 after he became Grand Vizier, using the opportunities of having both power and wealth. One reason for this initiative, she has suggested, was the competition with Çorlulu ʿAlī Paşa. Ibid., 39–40.

28 There are a few exceptions to this pattern. Books endowed by el-Ḥāc Tiryākī Meḥmed Paşa (d. 1751), for example, in the libraries of Maḥmūd I, were integrated into the collection with their endowment seals defaced or covered. See, for example, MS Ayasofya 125, 132, 149.

29 Although the library was built in 1734–1735 along with the mosque, its *waqfiyya* was prepared in 1738. Çolak, "Hekimoğlu Ali Paşa Kütüphanesi".

30 Sezer, "The Architecture of Bibliophilia", 54–55.

31 Erünsal, *Osmanlılarda Kütüphaneler*, 191.

32 Sezer, "The Architecture of Bibliophilia", 56.

33 Students, for instance, were also eligible, according to the endowment deeds, to funds distributed during the visit of the Sultan to the library. TS.MA.d.1067.

34 BOA TS.MA.d / 3153.

35 Sezer, "The Architecture of Bibliophilia", 117, 120, 121, 125, 126, 127.

36 Ibid., 112.

organisation of several major libraries, such as the Fatih and Süleymaniye Libraries. In addition, he sought to enrich the collections of previous book endowers in various parts of the Empire.[37] Most notably, he founded the Ayasofya Library in 1740. This library has two distinctive features compared to other contemporary libraries. Firstly, the Sultan created a new position for this library, the instructor of the library (*kütüpkhāne kẖācesi*), who was responsible for the classes organised on a weekly basis within the library.[38] Secondly, a significant part of the collection (almost half) entered the library as gifts, as is evident from copious notes on the manuscripts in the collection.[39] The remaining half of the collection consisted of books selected from the imperial treasury, and confiscated from older and roughly contemporary collections, such as those of the Chief Eunuch Moralı Beşīr Ağa (d. 1752) and Tiryākī el-Hāc Mehmed Paşa (d. 1751).[40]

Although not a sultanic nor a vizierial library, it is worth devoting a few words to the library of Mustafā ʿĀṭıf Efendi, the head treasurer (*defterdār*) of Mahmūd I, which was apparently founded in 1740 (the library's endowment deed was prepared twice, in 1740 and 1741).[41] The eighteenth-century scholar Mustaḳīmzāde (d. 1788) acknowledged the importance of the library as "the model/example for the other libraries [built] by sultans and viziers who, thus, became his imitators" (*sāʾir mülūk ve vüzerā dārü'l-kütüblerine nümūne olup anın muḳallidi olmuşlardır*).[42] Yavuz Sezer argued that it was the first Ottoman library with a book depository separate from the study/reading hall,[43] though the library of Feyżullāh Efendi (d. 1703) has a similar separation. In any case, Mustafā ʿĀṭıf Efendi introduced other novelties. The library had, for instance, a secluded study space. According to Sezer, this feature may be a reflection of the renewed individualised/private practices of reading and studying among the Ottomans.[44] In addition, as Erünsal has proposed, the library's *waqfiyya* seems to attach importance to praying in the library, which is one of the characteristics of later eighteenth-century Ottoman libraries.[45] Ragıp Paşa Library, for instance, has a praying niche within the confines of the reading room.[46]

Sultan Maḥmūd I also initiated the construction of the library (and the mosque complex) of the Nur-ı Osmaniye (or Nuruosmaniye), an important model for Aḥmad Pasha al-Jazzār (see the introduction to this volume). Although the library opened its doors in 1755, during the reign of ʿOthmān III (r. 1754–1757), Maḥmūd I had conceived the project as a monumental symbol of the cultural power in the capital of the Empire. The library building resembles Rome's San Carlo Alle Quattro Fontane (1638–1641), and the reading hall seems like an Ottomanised version of the Roman church's interior.[47] Sezer argued that "the rococo designs carved in relief at the fountains, the mosque, and the library, the Nuruosmaniye stands as the principal rococo landmark of Istanbul".[48]

---

37 The collections he enhanced are located in Belgrade, Vidin, Cairo, Bahçesaray of Crimea and Hios (Sakız). The library on the island of Chios was founded by Aḥmed III, on behalf of his mother Gülnuş Emetullāh Sultan, in 1711. See Erünsal, *Osmanlılarda Kütüphaneler*, 210–212.

38 According to the endowment deed, three tutors are supposed to teach their classes on the specific day prescribed to them: the *ders-i ʿām* (public lecturer) is assigned *tafsīr* classes twice a week, while the *muḥaddith* was to teach a *ḥadīth class* and a *shaykh al-qurrā* was to teach a *tajwīd* class once a week. VGMA 1399, 15ʳ–15ᵛ.

39 The earliest example of this practice may be seen in the establishment process of the library of the Sahn-i Semān *madrasas* in Istanbul during the reign of Meḥmed II. Several scholars may have encouraged the sultan to undertake this initiative. Şen, "The Sultan's Syllabus Revisited", 211–212.

40 TS.MA.d. 10524.002.

41 Erünsal, *Osmanlılarda Kütüphaneler*, 198.

42 Sezer, "The Architecture of Bibliophilia", 73–74.

43 Ibid., 69.

44 Ibid., 71.

45 Erünsal, *Osmanlılarda Kütüphaneler*, 199.

46 The endowment deeds of other libraries, however, do not mention praying at the library, whereas Muṣṭafā ʿĀṭıf Efendi's seems to allude to the practice.

47 Sezer, "The Architecture of Bibliophilia", 176.

48 Ibid., 172.

FIGURE 1.1 Engraving of the interior of the Hamidiye library in Istanbul. Ignatius Mouradgea d'Ohsson, *Tableau général de l'Empire othoman* (Paris 1787), plate from volume 1 (Library of Congress)

In terms of the size of its collection, this library was the most extensive *waqf* library in the empire's history. About 5,030 manuscripts were endowed to the library, most of which were lavishly illustrated or ancient copies of well-known works, such as the tenth-century copy of Abū Yūsuf Yaʿqūb b. Isḥaq Ibn al-Siqqit's (d. 857 or 8) *The Correction of Logic* (*Iṣlāḥ al-Manṭiq*).[49] Sezer points out that "the *waqfiyya* of the library is the earliest case where students are not referred to, and a general readership is defined as its intended users". Moreover, its book depository is adjacent to but separate from the study hall.[50] This was not the first experiment with this layout, since it had already been employed in the Âtıf Efendi library, but it was certainly not a common one. Meanwhile, the declared intention to serve a general readership may not be only associated with Nuruosmaniye, as Ayasofya Library aspired to serve *hevācir* (passengers) and the library of Hacı Beşir Ağa in Baghdad sought to welcome "commoners" (*ʿavāmm*) among its readers.[51]

The last example of the capital's separate libraries of the eighteenth century is the Ragıp Paşa Library, founded in March 1763. According to Giambattista Toderini (d. 1799), when it first began operating, the library housed a collection of 1,173 volumes.[52] Notably, this library initiated several novelties that mark further professionalisation of Ottoman librarianship. Firstly, it provided wages

49 Öngül, "Nuruosmaniye Kütüphanesi".
50 Sezer, "The Architecture of Bibliophilia", 173.
51 SL, MS Yazmafihrist, 25-1, 1v. SL, MS Yazmabağişlar, 2524.
52 Erünsal, "Ragıp Paşa Kütüphanesi".

for two librarians that were generous enough to allow them to dedicate themselves to librarianship without having to work in an additional job, as was the case in earlier libraries. In addition to the two full-time librarians, an apprentice (*kütübkhāne yamağı*) was employed for the first time in the history of Ottoman libraries.

The library of Abdülḥamīd I, the Hamidiye Library (f. 1781), is the last major library to be established in the capital in the eighteenth century. The library was fairly modest, by the standard of earlier sultanic libraries, consisting of 1,552 volumes.[53] The Hamidiye has gained some renown since it was also depicted in Ignatius Mouradgea d'Ohsson's *Tableau général de l'Empire othoman* (see fig. 1.1). This is one of the very few contemporary illustrations of an operating library, and since its size is quite comparable to that of al-Jazzār's library, the depiction may help us imagine how the Palestinian library was set up.

This brief history of establishing libraries in the imperial capital enables us to contextualise al-Jazzār's decision to build a complex with a sizable library. The establishment of new libraries in the eighteenth century was clearly a common practice to gain legitimacy, prestige and political power throughout the capital (and elsewhere across the empire). Unfortunately, the study of Ottoman libraries in the provinces in this period is still in its early stages, but as several provincial libraries, including al-Jazzār's, suggest, the capital's library culture of the eighteenth century served as a model, albeit not an exclusive one, for ambitious library builders in the provinces.

Al-Jazzār's decision to assemble a major collection may have also been informed by libraries founded in the Arabic-speaking provinces of the empire. Such was the library built by the late eighteenth-century Governor of Egypt, Muḥammad Bey Abū al-Dhahab (d. 1775). The library, which was part of a complex he founded in Cairo, held more than 1,000 volumes. In terms of the subjects/disciplines covered, Abū al-Dhahab's library was narrower than al-Jazzār's. The Cairene Library, for instance, did not have sections on medicine and occult sciences and had a very small section on belles-lettres (on the other hand, it had dedicated sections for jurisprudence of each of the four schools of law).[54]

2 Al-Jazzār's Librarians and the Rūmī Bibliographic Tradition

The proliferation of libraries in the capital and the emergence of a distinctive library culture were accompanied by the growing professionalisation of librarianship. As we have seen, this professionalisation is evident in the endowment deeds and library inventories. It also contributed to the development and implementation of new bibliographic practices. Here again, we suggest that the Palestinian library reflects the standardisation and proliferation of bibliographic practices in the capital and across the empire over the course of the eighteenth century.

The systematic compilation and preservation of inventories coincided with the proliferation of libraries across Istanbul and the provinces over the course of the eighteenth century. The earliest known eighteenth-century inventory of the Enderun Library (founded by Sultan Aḥmed III in 1719) marks the beginning of this practice. The inventories were instrumental in the management of the endowed collection and part of the endowment's paper trail. Therefore, they follow the bureaucratic conventions of the imperial register (*defter*).

The bibliographic description of the manuscripts was also gradually standardised over the course of the century. Normally written in a triangular shape, the entries became quite elaborate in the bibliographic information they recorded: title,

53 Erünsal, *Osmanlılarda Kütüphaneler*, 223.

54 Crecelius, "The Waqf of Muhammad Bey Abu al-Dhahab"; Ibrāhīm, "Maktaba 'Uthmaniyya".

author, number of volumes, script, layout/size, and number of folios and lines. Librarians also occasionally documented damage caused to the manuscripts (missing pages and poor condition). These descriptive practices and shared terminology are evident in the inventory of al-Jazzār's library. The Persian word "*köhne*" (worn out), for example, one of the frequently employed adjectives in the Ottoman inventories to describe the condition of the codices, appears six times in the al-Jazzār inventory.[55] Boris Liebrenz shows in his discussion of the al-Jazzār seals Chapter 10 in this volume that the governor's seals must have seemed recognisable to Rūmī bibliophiles.

The Rūmī bibliographic practices circulated across the empire with trained librarians. One Sulaymān Efendi (or Afandī) appears in the concluding paragraph of the register. He is described as the librarian (*nāẓir*[*-i?*] *kutubkhāna al-madhkūra wa-aminuhā*) and the recipient of the books inventoried. The librarian was only *amīn* in other libraries across the Arabic-speaking provinces.[56] The designation *nāẓir* may suggest that he also served as the custodian of the library's endowment. It is unclear when he was appointed to the position. It is possible that he had predecessors, colleagues and assistants, but the register is silent about them. Claudia Colini and Kyle Ann Huskin's Chapter 11 in this volume suggests that there were, indeed, several individuals involved in handling the books. The endowment deed for the complex (from 1776) stipulates a position for a librarian (*ḥāfiẓ lil-kutub wa-al-mudarris khāna*), whose monthly salary was 10 *qurush*, but does not mention assistants or secretaries.[57] It is also unclear how much of the organisation and description practices which are manifest in the library's inventory could be attributed to him. Whether Sulaymān was the sole librarian or had predecessors is less significant for the purpose of this essay. It is important, however, that the inventory reflects bibliographic expertise and, possibly, a sense of professional identity.[58]

The title *Efendi* suggests that Sulaymān was a learned man (or *ʿālim*), but apparently not eminent enough to attract the attention of biographers. Historically, librarianship was one of the career paths available to jurists, members of Sufi networks and scholars for centuries. The list of luminary and less famous figures who served as librarians is quite long, from the scholar and historian Ibn Ḥajar al-ʿAsqalanī (d. 1449), who worked as the librarian of the *madrasa* of Maḥmūd al-Ustādār in Cairo,[59] to Bāyezīd II's librarian ʿAṭūfī to Nedīm (d. 1730), one of the leading poets of the first half of the eighteenth century, who was appointed as the librarian at the library of the Grand Vizier Nevşehirli Dāmād İbrāhīm Paşa (d. 1730).[60] With the proliferation of libraries across the Ottoman lands over the course of the eighteenth century, jurists, poets and scholars were also appointed as librarians in newly founded libraries in the provinces. The profession *ḥāfiz-ı kütüb* or *kitābcı* (librarian) became a new career line among litterateurs of the Ottoman circles, both at the centre and in the provinces. The Damascene Shāfiʿī scholar and linguist ʿAbd al-Raḥmān ibn Aḥmad al-Ṣanādiqī (d. 1750), for example, was appointed as the preacher of the *madrasa* built by Ismāʿīl Paşa al-ʿAẓm (d. 1732) and its librarian (*amīn al-kutub*).[61] And the eighteenth-century poet Zihnī Efendi (d. ?), one of the librarians in the library founded by Rāġıp Paşa was known as "the bookish" (*Kitābī Zihnī Efendi*).[62]

55 To examine a representative example of the Ottoman bibliographic tradition, see Süleymaniye Library, Ragıp Paşa, MS 4111.

56 At the library of ʿUthmān Paşa al-Dūriki, the librarian was referred to as *amin al-kutub*. Aljoumani, *Maktaba madrasiyya*, 71–72.

57 Abū Diya. *Waqfiyyat Aḥmad Bāshā al-Jazzār*, 33.

58 The endowment deed of Asʿad Pasha al-ʿAẓm refers to the "custodian of books" (*khāzin al-kutub*). *Kitāb waqf Asʿad Bāshā al-ʿAẓm*, 22.

59 Behrens-Abouseif, *The Book in Mamluk Egypt and Syria*, 29; Wynter-Stoner, "The Maḥmūdiyah".

60 Sezer, "The Architecture of Bibliophilia", 51.

61 Al-Murādī, *Silk*, II, 281.

62 Aziz-zâde Hüseyin Râmiz, *Âdâb-i Zurefâ*, 219–220; Erünsal, *Osmanlılarda Kütüphaneler*, 215.

The biographical dictionaries regarding the eighteenth and the nineteenth centuries seem to be silent about al-Jazzār's Sulaymān Efendi. This is not unusual for Acre: as Boris Liebrenz has observed, the scholarly scene in the northern Palestinian city did not attract the attention of the biographers who authored the centennial dictionaries.[63] His attribute (*nisba*) is not mentioned, so it is difficult to trace his family or educational background. It is quite possible that Sulaymān is mentioned in other historical sources, but, for the time being, the inventory is the richest source we have on the librarian and, possibly, his colleagues and predecessors. Could his Turkish spelling of the title, *nāẓir[-i?] kutubkhāna*, suggest that he arrived in the Palestinian city from one of the Turkish-speaking parts of the Empire? Moreover, Sulaymān was possibly the latest in a series of librarians about whom there is no information. If they compiled earlier versions of the inventory upon which the extant inventory drew, it is possible that they shared some career paths and bibliographic training with Sulaymān.

Be that as it may, it is clear that the librarian(s) at al-Jazzār's library were familiar with the Rūmī bibliographic and library practices. In the following pages, we will turn to examine several case studies to illustrate this point (as other aspects will be explored in other chapters of this volume). We would particularly like to focus on aspects concerning the administration of the library and the maintenance of its collection.

3 Reading the Introductory Paragraph of al-Jazzār's Inventory in Its Eighteenth-century Context

Similar to many other eighteenth-century (and earlier) inventories, al-Jazzār's opens with a short introduction that summarises the scope of the library and the basic guidelines to maintain the collection.

63 Liebrenz, *Die Rifa'iya aus Damaskus*, 164.

Furthermore, as was the case in other inventories and endowment deeds of eighteenth-century libraries from the core lands of the empire, and specifically from Istanbul,[64] the opening paragraph of the inventory associated the library and its books with light and celebrates "the enlightening books which are concealed in the *madrasa* of the congregational mosque of light of Aḥmad" (*al-kutub al-nūrāniyya al-maknūna bi-madrasat jāmiʿ al-Nūr al-Aḥmadī*).[65] When describing the content of the collection, al-Jazzār quotes the Qur'anic phrase "it contains the correct writings/books" (*fīhā kutub qayyima*, Qur'an 98:3), which appeared in inscriptions in several libraries in Istanbul, such as the Ayasofya Library, the library founded by Rāgıp Paşa and the Enderun Library (and, more than a century later, above the entrance to the Khālidiyya Library in Jerusalem).[66] This phrase was also inscribed above the entrance to the library (see figs. 1.2, 1.3, 1.4).

The opening paragraph of the inventory also refers to the mode of individualised "deep reading" (*muṭālaʿa*) at the library. The term *muṭālaʿa* also had a long, pre-Ottoman history,[67] but several thinkers from the core lands of the empire composed treatises on the nature of such reading in the seventeenth and eighteenth centuries, as Khaled el-Rouayheb has pointed out.[68] Other eighteenth-century inventories and endowment deeds employ

64 Sezer, "The Architecture of Bibliophilia", 112, 119, 128, 212. Also see Khalil Sawan's Chapter 21 in this volume.

65 VGM 1058, 13.

66 The Qur'anic verse *fīhā kutubun qayyima* first appears at the entrance of the Enderun Library of Aḥmed III, as a chronogram of the year the library was founded (1131). The exact phrase was inscribed above the entrances of the subsequent libraries (not as a chronograph). Sezer, "Architecture of Bibliophilia", 103.

67 Wynter-Stoner, "The Maḥmūdiyah", 11–12.

68 El-Rouayheb, *Islamic Intellectual History in the Seventeenth Century*, ch. 3. See also Sezer, "The Architecture of Bibliophilia", 70–71. Münnecimbaşi Aḥmed Efendi's (d. 1702) treatise on *muṭālaʿa* entitled Feyżu'l-Ḥarem shifts the mode of the learning process from a master-student relationship to one in which the student and a text are at the core of the mechanism.

FIGURE 1.2 The inscription above the entrance to al-Jazzār's library
PHOTOGRAPH BY GUY BURAK

this notion of *muṭālaʿa* as well. The endowment deed of Ragıp Paşa Library (founded in 1762), for example, associates the library with several textual practices and modes of reading and copying: The library is said to be a place for "deep reading, copying, and collating" (*muṭālaʿa, istinsākh*, and *muḳābele*).[69] Closer to Acre, the endowment deed of the library of Asʿad Pasha al-ʿAẓm in Damascus also stipulates that the librarian should bring out the book for the reader so that the latter could examine and read according to his need (*murājaʿa wa-muṭālaʿa*).[70]

Finally, al-Jazzār stipulates that the library was part of the complex' *madrasa*, but was intended for the general (or public) benefit/utility (*nafʿ ʿamīm*). As we have seen, the notion that libraries are intended to serve a relatively broad circle of readers, and not the select few, was shared by many eighteenth-century library founders in the capital and elsewhere. Similarly, the Ayasofya Library (founded in 1740) was supposed to serve a broad group of litterateurs (*erbāb-ı ifāde ve aṣḥāb-ı istifāde*);[71] and the endowment deed of the chief eunuch Ḥācī Beşīr Ağa (d. 1746) for the library in the tomb complex of Abū Ḥanīfa in Baghdad also stipulates that "students, dignitaries and commoners" (*ṭullāb, khavāṣṣ ve ʿavāmm*) should be

69 Şeriye Sicilleri, Evkâf-ı Hümâyun Müfettişliği Mahkemesi 171, 1v–6v; Buluş, "15–18. Yüzyıl Kütüphane Vakfiyeleri", 560.

70 *Kitāb waqf Asʿad Bāshā al-ʿAẓm*, 22.

71 Süleymaniye Library, MS Yazma Fihrist 25-1, 1v.

FIGURE 1.3 The inscription at the entrance to the Enderun Library
PHOTOGRAPH BY NIMET IPEK

FIGURE 1.4 The inscription at the entrance to Rāgıp Paşa Library
PHOTOGRAPH BY THE DATABASE OF OTTOMAN INSCRIPTIONS PROJECT

granted access to the collection.[72] Al-Jazzār's Damascene predecessor, Muḥammad Pasha al-ʿAẓm, also stipulated that the endowed books in his *madrasa*'s library should be used by the students and hoped that they would be used for the "general benefit" (*nafʿ ʿamīm*).[73] Taken together, it appears that al-Jazzār, or, at least, the librarian who compiled the inventory for the library, was fairly

72 Süleymaniye Library, MS Yazma Bağişlar 2524, 1ᵛ.

73 Aljoumani, "Masrad kutub".

well-informed about discussions about the emerging institution of the library in the central lands of the empire and, specifically, in the Ottoman capital.

4 The Register (*Defter*)

The inventory of the al-Jazzār library is in the form of an Ottoman register (*defter*). Thirty titles were recorded (three titles on each of the ten lines) on an average page of the elongated register, and the librarian(s) wrote the number of volumes in digits and words at the end of each section. The librarian sums up again the number of volumes in each section of the library's core collection (though the titles of sections differ slightly from the section titles in the body of the inventory) in the concluding paragraph of the inventory. The *defter* form suggests that al-Jazzār's librarians were familiar with the bibliographic and bureaucratic practices of their colleagues in the core lands of the empire. Despite some variations, the inventories of other eighteenth-century libraries, such as those of the Ayasofya and Ragıp Paşa, were written in similar registers (see Fig. 1.5, 1.6).

The inventory of al-Jazzār's library is structured according to disciplines/sciences, as was the case with other contemporary and earlier inventories. This comparison suggests that al-Jazzār aspired to build a comprehensive collection in terms of its disciplinary coverage, with representations of the major Ottoman-Sunni Islamic disciplines (the extent to which he succeeded is debated among the contributors of this volume). The classification of sciences, however, varied from library to library. Berat Açıl has demonstrated the change of the classification of sciences over the course of the fifteenth through to the seventeenth centuries.[74] Variations in the classification of sciences also existed across contemporaneous collections.[75]

Generally speaking, however, the classification of al-Jazzār's librarian(s) seems quite conventional, similar to classifications in other Ottomanised libraries from the Arabic-speaking provinces. The librarians clearly also enjoyed some liberty in developing their own constellation of sciences. As an example, they grouped Sufi (*taṣawwuf*) and theological (which they called *tawḥīd*) works together. This is a fairly uncommon classification in the inventories we have seen.[76] Several chapters in this volume, such as Garrett Davidson's (15) and Berat Açıl's (19), suggest that the scope of the disciplines were not fully stable, and librarians had their own understanding of what titles fell under which discipline.

Since al-Jazzār's library was situated in a predominantly Arabophone part of the empire, the librarian(s), much like his (their) colleagues in other libraries in Greater Syria, created two separate, fairly small sections dedicated to books in Persian and Turkish (containing 22 and 56 titles, respectively). The books in these sections cover different genres in disciplines—law, theology, history and poetry. As is evident from the chapters in this volume, the dominant language in al-Jazzār's library collection was Arabic (some books in Persian and Turkish are dispersed throughout the collection), and the library was home to a large collection of manuscripts dealing with Arabic literature, grammar, poetry and historiography. It is difficult to estimate how many visitors to the library were able to read Persian and Turkish. As several biographies in Muḥammad Khalīl al-Murādī's centennial biographical dictionary of the twelfth *hijri*/eighteenth century indicates, language proficiency in Turkish and Persian was a remarkable biographical fact worth mentioning, suggesting that mastery in

74 Açıl, "Fazıl Ahmed Paşa".

75 Açıl, "Fazıl Ahmed Paşa".

76 Historical catalogues of eighteenth- and nineteenth-century Istanbul libraries listed theology books under sections titled "*kelām*", "*kelām-aqāid*", "*aqāid*" or "*kelām-aqāid-hikma*". The term *tawḥīd* was not applied in Istanbul libraries for these disciplines during the eighteenth century. For a list of library catalogues see, Erünsal, *Osmanlılarda Kütüphaneler ve Kütüphanecilik*, 644–646.

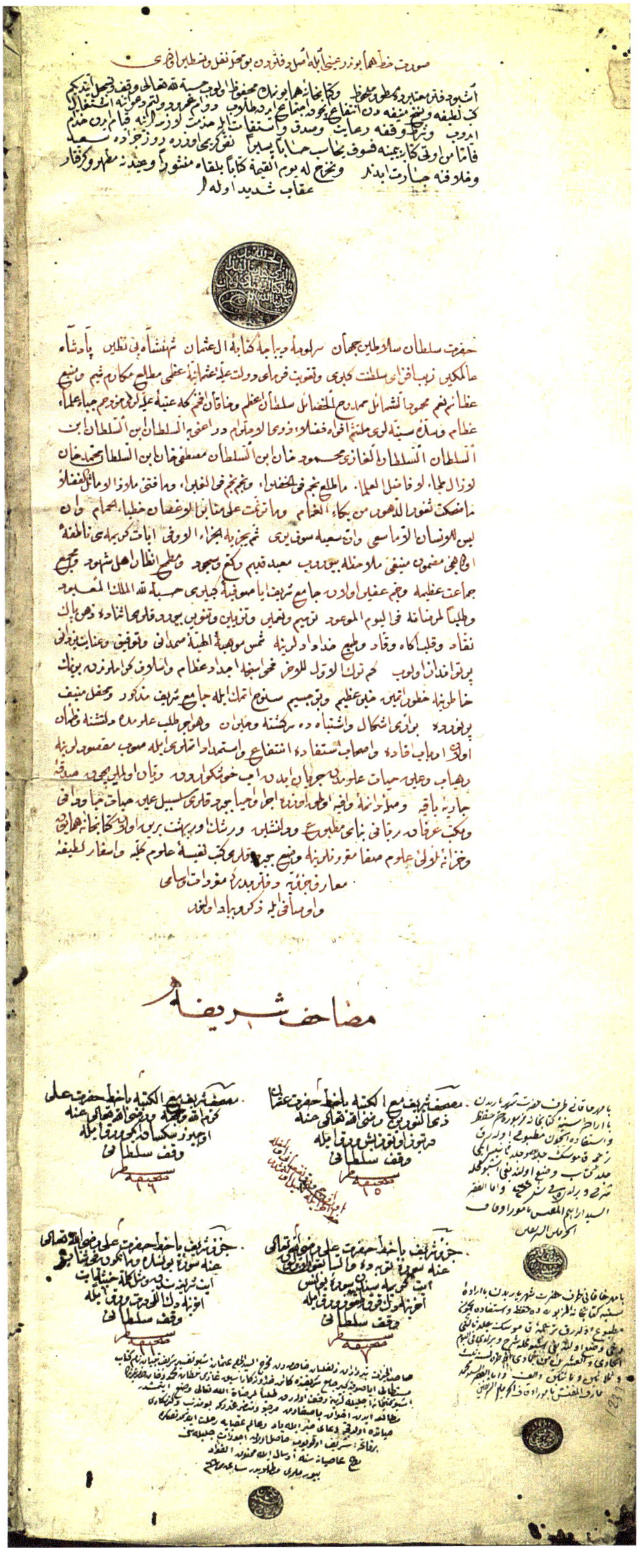

FIGURE 1.5
The first page of the inventory of the Ayasofya Library
SÜLEYMANIYE LIBRARY, MS YAZMA FIHRIST 25-2

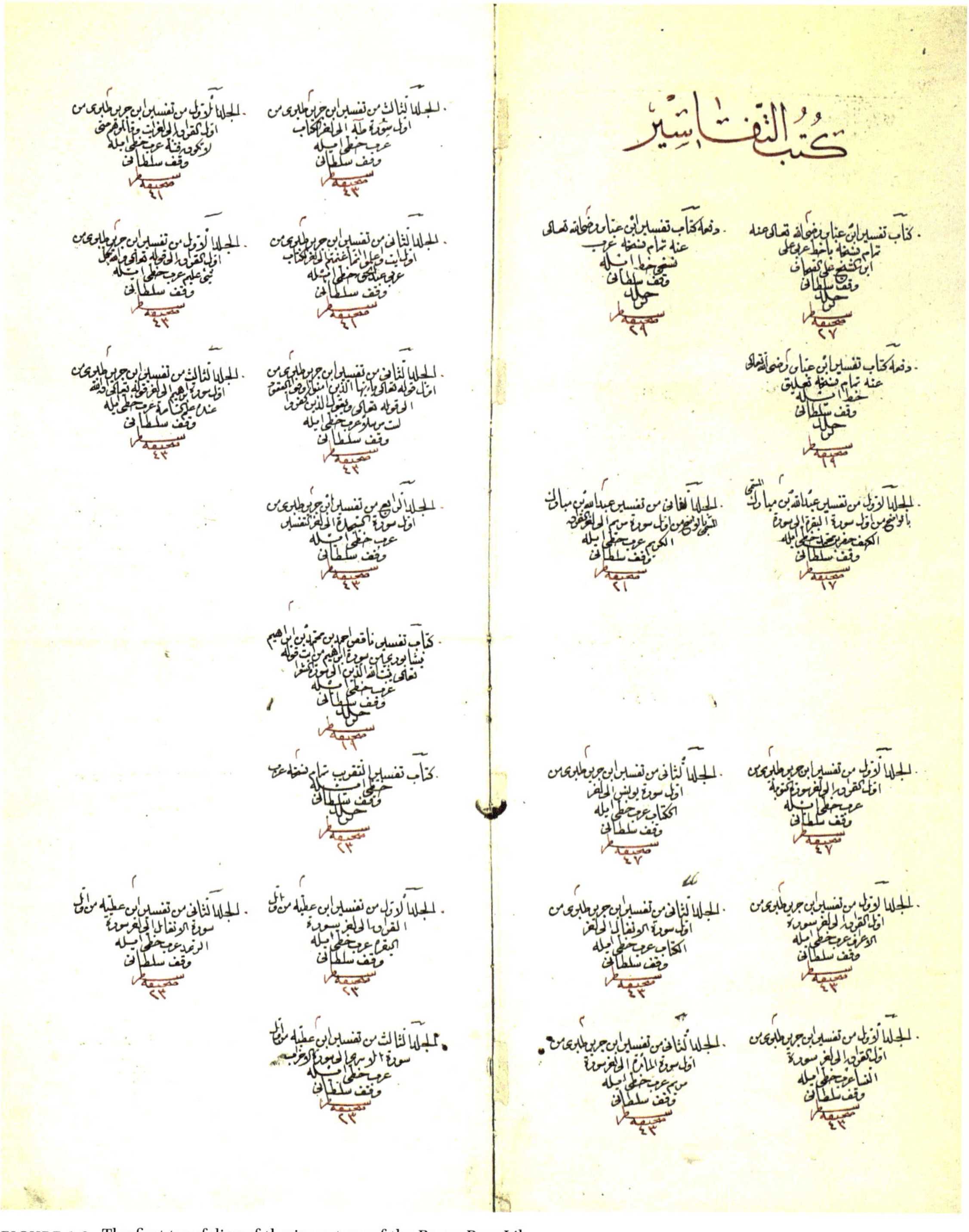

FIGURE 1.6 The first two folios of the inventory of the Ragıp Paşa Library
SÜLEYMANIYE LIBRARY, RAGIP PAŞA 4111

these languages was not very common in the Ottoman province of Damascus. Since it is possible that many of the library's frequent users and visitors had not mastered Turkish and Persian, one could assume that the audience of the Turkish and Persian sections were Turkish- and Persian-reading Ottoman officials and governors sent from the centre to Acre. In any case, the Turkish and Persian sections alluded to a trilingual intellectual/literary linguistic ideal in the context of a predominantly Arabic-speaking province.

Finally, a word is in order on the format of the inventory. The *defter* form suggests that the inventories were intended for administrative purposes. Indeed, many of these registers, including that of al-Jazzār's library, were used to inspect the holdings and the proper administration of the library. The administrative purpose of the registers also explains the archival history of the inventory of al-Jazzār's library and its current location in the General Directorate of Endowments in Ankara (see Chapter 2 by Said Aljoumani).

In some instances, as was apparently the case in al-Jazzār's library, the inspection resulted in a new, clean register. Another example of this practice is the inventory of the library established by Aḥmed III, the Turhān Valide Sultan Library. The inventory does not bear inspection marks.[77] But, in other instances, inspection notes were recorded in the extant inventory, by adding notes on each entry about the existence of the volume and its condition. It appears that, over time, standardised abbreviations evolved. The dashes and the letter mīm, indicating the existence of the volume (*mīm* stands for *mevcūd/mawjūd*), are the most common.[78] Lost or stolen books were also occasionally recorded in these inspections, as was the case in the inventories of the Fazıl Ahmed Paşa[79] and Ragıp Paşa Libraries.[80] The letter *qāf* may suggest that the book was stolen (*qāf* possibly standing for *masrūq*). Similarly, the circled word *lā* in the inventory of Ragıp Paşa Library indicates a non-existent or lost book (*lā* stands for *lā mevcūd/mawjūd*).[81] In other instances, it is difficult to decipher the abbreviation. Certain titles in the inventory of the Enderun Library are marked with the letter *nūn*[82] and, in another inventory of the same library, some titles are marked with the letter *sīn*.[83] The exact meaning of these letters is still unknown. Another set of notations records the physical state of the volume. In the inventory of the library of Ragıp Paşa, for example, the inspector inserted a note that the book "was split up into two volumes" (*iki cilde taḳsīm olunmuşdur*).

5 Circulation

The inventory's opening paragraph stipulates the manner in which the books will be handled and used. They were to be read only at the library, and should be handled with care (*ḥifẓan lahā wa-ṣiyāna*). Importantly, the books were not to be removed from the endowment in exchange, presumably for compensation or other books, as they were God's property.[84] This stipulation, it turns out, was not respected in the following decades and centuries, as most manuscripts were removed from the library.

Doris Behrens-Abouseif argues in her study of Mamluk book and library cultures that book lending was a common practice among Mamluk scholars. Indeed, biographical dictionaries even adopted the individual's willingness to lend books as a criterion for assessing a scholar's ethical stance.[85] In other words, lending his book out stood out as a crucial unwritten rule of etiquette

77 TiEM, 2218.
78 Süleymaniye Library, MS Yazma Bağışlar 2278.
79 Süleymaniye Library, MS Köprülü ilave 38.
80 Süleymaniye Library, MS Ragip Paşa 4111. 4r.
81 Süleymaniye Library, MS Ragıp Paşa 4111, 31v.
82 Süleymaniye Library, MS Yazma Bağışlar 2742, 2v. It is possible to observe this notation scattered throughout the entire inventory.
83 Süleymaniye Library, MS Yazma Bağışlar 2743, 4r.
84 VGM 1058, 13.
85 Behrens-Abouseif, *The Book in Mamluk Egypt and Syria*, 43.

among the litterateurs. However, the situation for the endowment libraries might have differed slightly from what one expects of a private collection. The endowment library created by Maḥmūd Ustādār, known as the Maḥmūdiya Library, for instance, prohibits lending the books out. Against this prohibition, the outstanding Mamluk scholar al-Suyūṭī (d. 911/1505) composed an epistle entitled *Exert Effort on Maḥmūd's Cupboard* (*al-Badhl al-Majhūd fī Khizānat Maḥmūd*), where he criticises the strict rule of the Maḥmūdiyya Library.

Broadly speaking, Ottoman libraries initially allowed their collections to circulate as lending libraries until the first separate libraries appeared at the centre.[86] However, the practice of asking for compensation became a norm during Süleymān's and Selīm II's reigns, extending through to the end of the sixteenth century.[87] As Erünsal argues, library founders increasingly opposed book loans due to the losses over time.[88]

The trend of limiting circulation intensified over the course of the eighteenth century. The Köprülü Library (founded in 1678), for instance, started as a lending/circulating library. However, Nuʿmān Paşa (d. 1719), one of Köprülü Meḥmed Paşa's descendants, imposed a ban in 1698 and changed the status of the library from a lending library to one where books could only be used on-site. In a similar vein, even though the Turhān Valide Sultan (f. 1652, 1663) Library permits taking books out, the harshening conditions to meet expectations of the endowment deed reduced the circulation of the collection dramatically.[89] A few decades later, Maḥmūd I strictly banned lending out manuscript copies from the library he established in Belgrade (founded in 1743). The ban was intended to be quite egalitarian, as the endowment deed specifically mentions that governors, rulers and those with administrative rank should not be exempted.[90] Similarly, Dāmād İbrāhīm Paşa (f. 1720) and Hācı Beşīr Ağa (f. Eyüp 1735, Cağaloğlu 1745) forbade the removal of the books from their rooms, even if the books were only to circulate within the confines of the *madrasa*. In Damascus, Asʿad Pasha al-ʿAẓm and his son Muḥammad also prohibited the circulation of endowed books from their libraries.[91]

It is worth stressing that this ban on the circulation of books was not applied consistently in eighteenth-century libraries in Istanbul, some of which allowed books to circulate, albeit to select readers. In other instances, the stipulations banning the removal of books were not enforced or breached: The administrators of the Turhān Vālide Sultan Library were asked in 1711 to pay the endowment for lost books that had been unlawfully lent out;[92] and in 1892, Şeyhülislām ʿÖmer Lüṭfī Efendi (d. 1897) was asked to return a book he had once borrowed from the non-circulating Ayasofya Library.[93]

Similar to many of their colleagues in the imperial capital, al-Jazzār's librarians prohibited the circulation of the collection and books were not supposed to leave the premises of the library.[94] This, however, does not seem to have been the rule in other libraries in the Arabic-speaking provinces. The early eighteenth-century library of al-Dūrikī was set in a *madrasa* in Aleppo to cater for the students and checking out the library's books continued until 1921 when the circulation of the collection was restricted to on-site use only.[95] Similarly, the library of the complex commissioned by Muḥammad Bey Abū al-Dhahab in Cairo in 1774 did not appear to impose a restriction on book lending.

86 Erünsal, *Osmanlılarda Kütüphaneler*, 447.
87 Ibid., 540.
88 Ibid., 447.
89 Ibid., 455. The eighteenth-century *madrasa* libraries in the imperial capital did not lend out their books. However, some minor mosque libraries continued lending out their holdings.
90 Ibid., 461.
91 Kitāb waqf Asʿad Bāshā al-ʿAẓm, 22; Aljoumani, "Masrad kutub".
92 Süleymaniye Library, MS Turhan Valide 19, 1ʳ.
93 BOA, MF.MKT. 143-16. BOA. MF.iBT. 28–65.
94 VGMA 1626, 5ᵛ.
95 Aljoumani, *Maktaba madrasiyya*, 38, 65.

6 Concluding Remarks

Dedicating a separate chamber to the library was a relatively recent development in the Ottoman capital and the provinces. İsmail Erünsal and, more recently, the late Yavuz Sezer pointed out that the foundation of libraries to house manuscript collections emerged in the late seventeenth century and gained popularity among members of the Ottoman administrative and scholarly elites over the course of the eighteenth century.[96] The rise of Ottoman library building in the eighteenth century, as Sezer convincingly showed, was emblematic of "a major leap in the Ottoman's embrace of books as this particular form of publication found considerable ground and admiration".[97] As this chapter has tried to demonstrate, al-Jazzār and his librarian(s) were familiar with and participated in a Rumi/Ottoman(ised) bibliographic culture. Similar to the sultans and viziers he aspired to emulate, al-Jazzār tried to project his political aspirations on the imperial stage through his library.

Said Aljoumani's Chapter 2 illustrates that these dynamics are evident elsewhere throughout the Arabic-speaking provinces, and it seems that other librarians across the Empire's Arab lands experimented to varying degrees with the Rumi bibliographic practices. Indeed, some classification principles and bibliographic descriptions appear in other eighteenth-century libraries. Al-Dūrikī, for instance, in the endowment he established in Aleppo in the first half of the eighteenth century, also had dedicated sections for Turkish and Persian books, similar to the sections in the inventory of al-Jazzār's library. The 1781 endowment deed of Süleymān Paşa of Baghdad is reminiscent, to some extent at least, of some of the descriptive practices followed by al-Jazzār's librarian. The Baghdadi *waqfiyya*, for instance, is very systematic in the description of the format/layout of the manuscript and the type of binding used (in fact, the description of the types of binding there is more detailed than in the inventory of al-Jazzār's library). However, the endowment deed does not specify the calligraphic style employed.

Moreover, while the Baghdadi endowment deed does not make references to the metaphors used in the imperial capital to discuss libraries (such as the metaphor of light and the comparison to the Kaʿba), the endower was clearly familiar with the eighteenth-century library culture of the core lands. Similar to the case of endowment created by al-Jazzār, the books were endowed to the *madrasa* adjacent to the "new" mosque of Ḥasan Paşa, so that the students and whoever is interested in the books could read (*yuṭāliʿuhā*) and benefit from them, and the endowment deed explicitly forbade the removal of the books from the premises of the library to the mosque and elsewhere.[98] On the other hand, the books in the endowment deed are not classified according to disciplines/subject matters and there are no sections dedicated to books in Turkish and Persian, as was the case with the libraries of al-Dūrikī and al-Jazzār.

Similar to al-Jazzār's librarian(s), the founders of these collections also had to translate the Rumi bibliographic tradition into this linguistic and scholarly context of their respective province and, more broadly, the empire's Arab provinces. Moreover, all these libraries serve as an interesting example of the "Ottomanisation" of the book culture in Palestine (and Greater Syria) and other Arab provinces over the course of the eighteenth century. In this respect, the book collections and the bibliographic practices employed to describe them cast light on the broader Ottomanisation of the Arab provinces of the eighteenth century.[99]

---

96 Erünsal, *Osmanlılarda Kütüphaneler*, 160–264; Sezer, "The Architecture of Bibliophilia".

97 Sezer, "The Architecture of Bibliophilia", 34.

98 Rāʾūf, *Dirāsāt turāthiyya*, I, 312.

99 On the rise of Ottomanised elites in the eighteenth century, see Barbir, *Ottoman Rule in Damascus*; Toledano, "The Emergence of Ottoman-local Elites"; Hathaway, *The Politics of Households*; Khoury, *State and Provincial Society*; Wilkins, "The Self-fashioning of an Ottoman Urban Notable".

Bibliography

Archival Sources

Süleymaniye Library, MS Ayasofya 125, 132, 149; MS Köprülü ilave 38; MS Ragıp Paşa 4111; MS Yazma Bagışlar 2278, 2742, 2743; MS Turhan Valide Sultan 19.

TiEM 2218.

VGMA 1058, 1399, 1626.

BOA TS.MA.d 1067, 3153, 10524-002; BOA, MF.MKT.143-16; BOA. MF.iBT. 28–65.

Primary Sources

Abū Diyya, Mūsā. *Waqfiyyat Aḥmad Bāshā al-Jazzār: Dirāsa wa-taḥqiq*. Nablus, 1998.

Aziz-zâde Hüseyin Râmiz. *Âdâb-i Zurefâ inceleme-Tıpkıbasım-indeks*. Edited by Sadı2k Erdem. Ankara: Türk Tarıh Kurumu Yayınları, 2019.

Câbî Ömer Efendi. *Târîh-i Câbî: Târîh-i Sultân Selîm-i Sâlis ve Mahmûd-i Sânî*. Edited by Mehmed Ali Beyhan. 2 vols. Ankara: Türk Tarih Kurumu, 2003.

Kitāb waqf Asʿad Bāsha al-ʿAzm ḥākim Dimashq 1137 H–1143 H, edited by Ṣalāḥ al-Dīn al-Munajjid. Beirut: Dār al-Kitāb al-Jadīd 1980.

Murādī, Muḥammad Khalīl ibn ʿAlī. *Silk al-durar fī aʿyān al-qarn al-thāni ʿashar*. 4 vols. Beirut: Dār al-Bashāʾir al-Islāmiyya, 1988.

Râşid, Mehmed. *Târîh-i Râşid*, 4 vols. Istanbul 1282.

Secondary Sources

Açıl, Berat. “Habeşi Mehmed Ağa’nın (ö. 1590) Vakfettiği Kitaplar ve Akibetleri.” *International Journal of Turkology* 6 (2020): 67–83.

Açıl, Berat (ed.). *Osmanlı Kitap Kültürü: Cârullah Efendi Kütüphanesi ve Derkenar Notlari*. Istanbul 2020

Açıl, Berat. “Fazıl Ahmed Paşa Koleksiyonu ve ilimler Tasnifi: Karşılaştırmalı Bir Değerlendirme.” *darülfünun ilahiyat*, 34, no. 2 (2023). DOI :10.26650/di.2022.34.2.1324985

Açıl, Berat. “Kütüphane Fihristlerinin Tenkitli Neşirine Doğru: Fazil Ahmed Paşa Koleksiyonuna Ait Defterlerin Mukayesesi.” In *Osmanlı Tarihinde Köprülüler Dönemi (1656–1710): Yeni Kaynaklar, Yeni Yaklaşımlar*, edited by M. Fatih Çalışır, 415–450 Istanbul 2024.

Aljoumani, Said. “Masrad kutub madrasat Muḥammad Bāshā al-ʿAẓm: nashr wa-dirāsa.” *Majallat Maʿhad al-Makhṭūṭāt al-ʿArabiyya* 61, no. 2 (2017): 10–73.

Aljoumani, Said. *Maktaba madrasiya fī Ḥalab nihāyat al-ʿahd al-ʿUthmānī: al-daftar al-mujaddad li-kutub waqf ʿUthmān Bāshā al-Dūrikī*. Beirut, 2019.

Artan, Tülay. “On Sekizinci Yüzyil Başinda Osmanlı Bilgi Üretimi ve Dağilimi: Yazma Eser Koleksiyonları ve Koleksiyonerler Arasında Şehid Ali Paşa’nın Yeri.” *Müteferrika* 58, no. 2 (2020): 5–40.

Barakāt, Bashīr ʿAbd al-Ghanī. *Taʾrīkh al-maktabāt al-ʿArabiyya fi Bayt al-Maqdis*. Riyad, 2012.

Barbir, Karl K. *Ottoman Rule in Damascus, 1708–1758*. Princeton, 1980.

Behrens-Abouseif, Doris. *The Book in Mamluk Egypt and Syria (1250–1517): Scribes, Libraries and Market*. Leiden, 2019.

Bouquet, Olivier. “Pour une histoire instrumentale des savoirs ottomans: à quoi servaient les «livres tenus en haute estime» et autres précieux manuscrits conservés dans une bibliothèque de madrasa anatolienne (Burdur, seconde moitié du XVIIIe siècle)?” *Arabica* 67, no. 5–6 (2020): 502–559.

Çolak, Orhan M. “Hekimoğlu Ali Paşa Kütüphanesi.” *Z Dergisi* 5 (2021): 168–169.

Crecelius, Daniel. “The Waqf of Muhammad Bey Abu al-Dhahab in Historical Perspective.” *International Journal of Middle East Studies* 23 (1991): 57–81.

Cunbur, Müjgân. “I. Abdülhamid Vakfiyesi ve Hamidiye Kütüphanesi.” *Ankara Üniversitesi Dil ve Tarih-Coğrafya Fakültesi Dergisi* 22 (1964): 17–68.

Derin Can, Elif. “Manuscript Collections of the Chief Harem Eunuchs in the Early Modern Ottoman Empire.” MA thesis, Marmara University, 2022.

Erünsal, İsmail E. “Hamidiye Kütüphanesi.” *Türkiye Diyanet Vakfi İslam Ansiklopedisi*.

Erünsal, İsmail E. “Köprülü Kütüphanesi.” *Türkiye Diyanet Vakfi İslam Ansiklopedisi*.

Erünsal, İsmail E. “Ragıp Paşa Kütüphanesi.” *Türkiye Diyanet Vakfi İslam Ansiklopedisi*.

Erünsal, İsmail E. *Osmanlılarda Kütüphaneler ve Kütüphanecilik*. Istanbul 2015.

Erünsal, İsmail E. *A History of Ottoman Libraries*. Boston, 2022.

Felek, Özgen (editor). *Kitābü’l-Menāmāt: Sultan III. Murad’ın Rüya Mektupları*. Istanbul, 2012.

Ibrāhīm, ʿAbd al-Laṭīf. “Maktaba ʿUthmāniyya: dirāsa

naqdiyya wa-nashr li-raṣīd al-maktaba." *Majallat Kuliyyat al-Adab* 20, no. 2 (1958): 1–35.

Hathaway, Jane. *The Politics of Households in Ottoman Egypt: The Rise of the Qazdağlis*. Cambridge, 1997.

Khoury, Dina Rizk. *State and Provincial Society in the Ottoman Empire: Mosul, 1540–1834*. Cambridge, 1998.

Liebrenz, Boris. *Die Rifāʿiya aus Damaskus: Eine Privatbibliothek im osmanischen Syrien und ihr kulturelles Umfeld*. Leiden, 2016.

Necipoğlu, Gūlru Cemal Kafadar and Cornell H. Fleischer (editors). *Treasures of Knowledge: An Inventory of the Ottoman Palace Library (1502/3–1503/4)*. 2 vols. Leiden, 2019.

Öngül, Ali. "Nuruosmaniye Kütüphanesi." *Türklük Araştırmaları Dergisi* 6, (1990).

Rāʾūf, ʿImād ʿAbd al-Salām. *Dirāsāt turāthiyya fī al-buldān wa-al-tarājim wa-al-adab wa-al-riḥlāt*, 2 vols. Irbil, 2019.

El-Rouayheb, Khaled. *Islamic Intellectual History in the Seventeenth Century: Scholarly Currents in the Ottoman Empire and the Maghreb*. New York, 2015.

Şen, Ahmet Tunç. "The Sultan's Syllabus Revisited: Sixteenth Century Ottoman Madrasa Libraries and the Question of Canonization." *Studia Islamica* 116 (2021): 198–235.

Sezer, Yavuz. "The Architecture of Bibliophilia: Eighteenth-century Ottoman Libraries." PhD Dissertation, Massachusetts Institute of Technology, 2016.

Sievert, Henning. "Eavesdropping on the Pasha's Salon: Usual and Unusual Readings of an Eighteenth-century Ottoman Bureaucrat." *Osmanlı Araştırmaları/The Journal of Ottoman Studies* XLI (2013): 159–195.

Toledano, Ehud R. "The Emergence of Ottoman-local Elites (1700–1900): A Framework for Research." In *Middle Eastern Politics and Ideas: A History from Within*, edited by Ilan Pappé and Moshe Maʿoz, 145–162. London, 1997.

Wilkins, Charles L. "The Self-fashioning of an Ottoman Urban Notable: Ahmad Efendi Tahazâde (d. 1773)." *Osmanlı Araştırmaları/The Journal of Ottoman Studies* 44 (2014): 393–425.

Wynter-Stoner, Kyle. "The Maḥmūdiyah: The History of a Library, Its Books, and Its Readers." PhD Dissertation. Chicago University, 2022.

CHAPTER 2

The Inventory: Documentary and Bibliographical Practices in al-Jazzār's Library

Said Aljoumani

This chapter will focus on the booklist that is at the heart of our volume, as this complex document has its own fascinating history that makes it much more than a straightforward window into a collection of books that is no more.[1] The document describes itself as the *Daftar of the Books that Were in the Library of al-Nūr al-Aḥmadī Mosque in Acre*. 'Daftar' was a widely-used term in Ottoman documentary culture and can refer here to all kinds of different booklists, including a catalogue. Yet, what we want to show in this chapter is that we can identify the nature of this *daftar* and its function much more precisely, namely, as an administrative inventory. The chapter will, thus, discuss this document's history, including its genesis and the actors involved in creating it, as well as the purposes it was meant to serve (and not to serve). The chapter will subsequently zoom in on the inventory's contents to discuss the bibliographical strategies of its writer for listing the contents of the books and their materiality. This will provide not only a unique insight into the bibliographical practices in Ottoman Palestine at the turn of the eighteenth century but is an essential element in making our argument that the document's function was that of an inventory with an emphasis on the books' materiality and not that of a catalogue emphasising the books' contents.

This inventory is the central point for our overall project on studying the history of the holdings that belonged to Aḥmad Pasha al-Jazzār's library at his al-Nūr al-Aḥmadī endowment complex in Acre. It is of particular importance as we can correlate some of the titles recorded in this inventory with the actual material books that we have identified in libraries around the world. This affords a privileged insight into the terminology used by the writer of the inventory, as we can compare the terms he used for bibliographical descriptions with the physical books that have survived.

We will particularly show that the library inventory was produced in 1221/1806 after the death of al-Jazzār. This was done, we argue, in the framework of the Ottoman centre's confiscation procedures to establish al-Jazzār's properties and endowments (on the confiscation procedures see Chapter 5 for more detail). Most of our inventory goes back to an earlier inventory written in 1215/1800, which has been lost (or not found yet). This 1215/1800 document, in turn, was written within the framework of an inventory of the library stock nearly twenty years after the library's foundation. It was arguably produced after a portion of the library's manuscripts had gone missing in the aftermath of Napoleon's siege of Acre. Our 1221/1806 inventory, however, is more than a simple copy of the 1215/1800 document. Its writer, instead, merged other documents (again lost or not found yet) with the 1215/1800 document while producing our inventory. Without understanding the story of this inventory's genesis,

1 Translation by Ali Porteous and Joud Nassan Agha. The research for this chapter was funded by the Deutsche Forschungsgemeinschaft (DFG, German Research Foundation) under Germany's Excellence Strategy—EXC 2176 'Understanding Written Artefacts: Material, Interaction and Transmission in Manuscript Cultures', project no. 390893796. The research was conducted within the scope of the Centre for the Study of Manuscript Cultures (CSMC) at Universität Hamburg.

any attempt to interpret its content or to use it for a larger historical argument would border naïve positivism.

1 Philological-material Analysis of the Inventory

Before embarking on a study of the inventory's bibliographical strategies via analysing its text, it is worth dwelling on the document as a material written artefact. This kind of material-philological approach is essential for understanding the complex web of administrative procedures of which it was part and, thus, to avoid a reductionist reading of it as a simple booklist.

The library inventory at the heart of this volume is found in what we call the 'multiple-document manuscript' (MDM) related to the confiscation of al-Jazzār's estate.[2] This undated manuscript (or *daftar*), preserved today in Ankara, comprises three distinct documents that are all related to the endowments of al-Jazzār. Arguably, it was written by the *muhallefat mübaşiri*, a low or mid-ranking official commissioned for the sole purpose of confiscation (see Chapter 5). Our choice of the term MDM alludes to the concept of the 'multiple-text manuscript' and is meant to show the complexity of the Ankara manuscript that was produced, as we argue, within the framework of the confiscation procedures to establish the endowment properties that were not to be subject to confiscation.[3] The three documents were brought together either by copying the text (first and second document) or by adding a formerly stand-alone material object to it (third document).

The first document is a copy of al-Jazzār's endowment deed for the complex he originally constructed in Acre in the year 1196/1781, consisting of a mosque (*masjid*), school (*madrasa*), library (*maktaba*), public drinking-fountain (*sabīl*), shelter (*maljā'*), mausoleum (*ḍarīḥ*), cistern (*ṣihrīj*) and ablution fountain (*shādharwān*).[4] This copy occupies the first seven pages of the Ankara MDM. The deed claims to be an exact copy of an 'original' registered in the court register (*sijill*) of Acre,[5] but regrettably this *sijill* has not reached us. The term 'original' should be used with caution because the text of this deed was entered into the court register on 6 Rajab 1200/1786, that is some five years after the endowment was made. So far, we know of two other exemplars of the endowment deed preserved in Palestine that were used in the 1998-edition of the deed by Mūsā Abū Diyya.[6] One exemplar was copied on 17 Rajab 1271/1855 and is held at the Center for Documentation and Manuscripts at Al-Najah National University in Nablus, while the second exemplar, copied on 12 Shawwāl 1330/1912, is preserved at The Center for Heritage Revival and Islamic Research in Jerusalem. There is no doubt that the history of the deed in the Ankara manuscript is much more complex than just being a copy of *the* original, but this is not our prime concern here.

The second document in the Ankara MDM is our library inventory. It comprises thirty-one leaves (sixty-two pages) and occupies pages 14 to 72 in the Ankara MDM. The text of the inventory is continuous and complete—as the scribe himself confirmed by means of catchwords curiously written at the end of the recto (rather than the customary location at the bottom of the verso). There is a blank page in the middle of the section of books

2 Vakıflar Genel Müdürlüğü (Ankara), Defter 1626.

3 For the term 'multiple-text manuscript', see Friedrich and Schwarke, *One-Volume Libraries*.

4 Muḥaybish, "Mujammaʿ Al-Jazzār al-Khayrī", 23.

5 Vakıflar Genel Müdürlüğü (Ankara), Defter 1626, p. 6.

6 Abū Diyya, *Waqfiyyat Aḥmad Pāshā Al-Jazzār*. A comparative analysis between this version and the Ankara version shows the necessity of republishing the text. Ghassān Muḥaybish published the deed as an appendix to his master's thesis using the copy from The Center for Heritage Revival and Islamic Research in Jerusalem (Muḥaybish, "Mujammaʿ Al-Jazzār al-Khayrī", 163–169). Additionally, Muḥammad Mājid al-Ḥazmāwi conducted an analytical study of this document (Al-Ḥazmāwi, "Waqfiyyat Aḥmad Pāshā al-Jazzār").

on jurisprudence, but the number of volumes on jurisprudence matches the tally given at the end of the inventory. We can, thus, safely assume that the inventory itself is complete and the blank page is merely the result of the scribe accidentally flipping a page.

The inventory's colophon dates it to the year 1215/1800. Yet, the inventory contains several philological and material features that suggest it was penned at a later point. The most evident indicator for this are two additional booklists that we find copied into the text of the inventory. These record the collections of three personal libraries incorporated into the holdings of the Jazzār library in two batches in the years 1216/1801 and 1218/1803. These personal libraries, based on the wording of the inventory, are likely to have been confiscated from their original owners before being incorporated into the library:

Inventory (*bayān*) of the number of books, as enumerated below, taken (*ma'khūdha*) from Sayyid Yaḥyā Efendi, the son of Sayyid Muḥammad al-Ṭībī from Jaffa, on 23 Ṣafar 1218/1803, while a few books have remained with them (*wa-dhālika mawjūd bi-him ba'ḍ al-kutub*).[7]

The word *ma'khūdha* (meaning 'taken' or 'seized'), used in preference to other options such as endowed, purchased, donated or reclaimed, as well as the expression 'while a few books have remained with them', strongly suggests that the books' owner Yaḥyā Efendi fell victim to an act of confiscation of his possessions, including his books.[8] The other booklist is entitled 'Inventory (*bayān*) of the books taken (*ma'khūdha*) from Shaykh 'Alī al-Rashīdī and from Shaykh Muḥammad Wakīlkharaj, on 17 Ṣafar 1216'.[9] That the writer employed the term *ma'khūdh* (taken) for confiscation, rather than the technical term *muṣādara*, probably goes back to the fact that the exact administrative framework for the incorporation of the books into the library did not matter in the context of producing this inventory.

That we are looking at lists of confiscated books is also supported by contextual evidence. A confiscation document from the court register of Jaffa, for instance, records the expropriation of an individual called Ya'qūb Mitrī in 1214/1799 at the hands of al-Jazzār.[10] We find notebooks (*dafātir*), papers (*awrāq*) and pieces of writing (*awrāq makātīb*) among the properties that the latter seized from this individual:

[...] which were found among the [personal] effects removed from the house of Ya'qūb Mitrī following the requisition ordered by His honourable Excellency, Efendi Aḥmad Pasha al-Jazzār—may God give him victory! This took place in the month of Muḥarram, and they [the items] are now kept in the Armenian monastery, comprising of:

7 Vakıflar Genel Müdürlüğü (Ankara), Defter 1626.

8 A certain Yaḥyā Efendi al-Ṭībī, who is said to have co-owned a soap factory in Jaffa, is mentioned in a document dated 1214 AH, and it is possible that the same individual is meant here. This document has been published by Ghosheh in *'Ā'ilat 'Arafāt al-Qudwa-fī-l-Quds*, 57–64. The same name also appears in the dedication to a work titled, *Īḍāḥ al-maqṣūd min ma'nā waḥdat al-wujūd*, copied in 1198/1284 (now part of a manuscript kept at the National Library of Israel, NLI, MS Ar. 438): 'A gift from the poor servant of God the Creator, Muḥammad b. Aḥmad b. Muḥammad al-Atharī al-Ḥanafī al-Bukhārī [d. 1200/1786], may God pardon his sins and forgive his faults (amen!), to our most generous and ever-giving master, Yaḥyā Efendi al-Ṭībī, esteemed and admired among men, may God Almighty and All-glorious preserve him (amen! amen!).' It is possible that this is again the same Yaḥyā al-Ṭībī, though one should bear in mind that this title is not present in the inventory of books prepared for the al-Nūr al-Aḥmadī library in Acre. Since the giver of the book died before the act of confiscation, and the manuscript does not bear any notice of al-Jazzār's ownership, we can only surmise the book had left al-Ṭībī's library before this confiscation.

9 Vakıflar Genel Müdürlüğü (Ankara), Defter 1626, 31–32. Wakīlkharaj is 'a term employed during the Ottoman era to designate an individual responsible for overseeing expenditures and managing the supply logistics within each block or unit of the Janissary army's organization' (Ḥallaq and Ṣabbāgh, *al-Mu'jam*, 231 f.).

10 Jaffa, *Sijill al-Maḥkama al-Shar'iyya*, 1, 57[a].

A green box, inside of which are	Another green box	copper utensils (*ʿan fard al-nuḥās*)
Frankish [... *iyāt*], and otherwise papers,	papers, and pieces of writing	2 kettles, 2 small pans [...]
notebooks and pieces of writing	3 cushions	2 trays, [...], 1 heater (*sakhāna*)
	1 filter (*miṣfāhiyya*), [...]	1 small bucket, 6 old plates (*ṣuhūn kuhnā*)

This [list] was accurately made in the Armenian monastery on 14 Muḥarram in the year 1214.

Significantly, the process of confiscating Mitrī's properties, including written artefacts, is described here with a non-technical term, 'removed' (*mukharraj*), similar to the non-technical term 'taken' that we find in the two booklists. Based on the evidence presented so far, we will, henceforth, call the two incorporated booklists the 'confiscation booklists'.

The materiality of these two confiscation booklists, dated 1216/1801 and 1218/1803, show unequivocally that our inventory must have been written later than the date in its colophon, 1215/1800. Both lists were included in the flow of the original inventory's text and written in the same hand as the rest of the inventory. Their texts were not added as appendices at the end of the original inventory, nor were they stand-alone codicological units glued into the inventory. Thus, the writer of our inventory must have integrated the texts of these booklists into the copy he produced of the 1215/1800 inventory.

The textuality of our inventory gives us further insight into how this writer proceeded: The bibliographical strategies to describe the books, particularly regarding terminology, is strikingly different in the two booklists and the original text of the inventory. The author of the first confiscation list, for instance, concerning Sayyid Yaḥyā Efendi in 1218/1803, used the term *numirū* to indicate the number of volumes (*jild* in the original inventory),[11] the term *rāyiḥ* to indicate a missing or incomplete work (*nāqiṣ* or *makhrūm* in the original inventory)[12] and when attributing a book to a given author, he used the preposition *ilā* (*li-* in the original inventory). His wording of entries such as *Kitāb al-Rūḥ ilā Ibn al-Qayyim numirū 1* and *Kitāb Fiqh ḥanafī ilā Ibrāhīm al-Ḥalabī numirū 1*[13] are miles apart from the formulations used by the writer of the original inventory. Apart from the terminology, the scribe of the Yaḥyā Efendi list also paid scant attention to material features, such as the book format, mentioning the sizes of only five out of ninety-five volumes,[14] never recording whether the book was in a slipcase or not and only mentioning the type of script on one occasion.[15] As discussed below, recording these features was an integral part of the bibliographical practices of the writer of the original inventory.

Turning to the second confiscation list, the inventory of the books taken from ʿAlī al-Rashīdī and Muḥammad Wakīlkharaj in 1216/1801, its author did not make a distinction between the books that had belonged to ʿAlī al-Rashīdī and those that had belonged to Muḥammad Wakīlkharaj. It is, therefore, not possible for us to reconstruct which books originally belonged to whom. The author of this list also did not mention whether the books have a slipcase or not except in three cases (out of a total of seventy-six volumes),[16] and also sometimes employs the term *numirū* rather than *jild*.[17] A particularly striking difference between this list and

11 Inventory book #520.
12 Inventory book #592.
13 Inventory books #551, 553.
14 Inventory books #517, 520, 523, 529, 571.
15 Inventory books #519.
16 Inventory books #1668, 1695, 1696.
17 Inventory books #1651, 1657, 1668, 1673, 1680, 1682, 1694, 1704.

the original inventory is that its writer did not attach any honorifics to the name of Shaykh ʿAbd al-Ghanī al-Nābulusī,[18] whereas the writer of the original inventory consistently wrote *qaddasa Allāh sirrahu* at every mention of al-Nābulusī's name.[19]

There are further striking differences between the original inventory and the two booklists: Firstly, the books of the two confiscation lists are not arranged thematically, in contrast to those in the original inventory. Secondly, the confiscation list from 1216/1801 does not contain a numerical tally of the books at the end. This contrasts with the thematic sections of the original inventory, where the writer first listed all the books of the subject matter in question and then added 'the total of [this section] is [followed by the number given in numerals and words]'.[20]

The observations made so far allow us to suggest the following story for the library inventory as we have it in the Ankara MDM: Within the framework of the confiscation procedures of al-Jazzār's estate, the MDM's writer copied the original 1215/1800 inventory. While producing this copy, he incorporated two independent lists of book confiscations dated 1216/1801 (on ʿAlī al-Rashīdī and Muḥammad Wakīlkharaj) and 1218/1803 (on Yaḥyā Efendi). The writer of the Ankara MDM simply followed the ordering and the logic of the three documents that were before him (the original inventory and two confiscation booklists). It is worth noting that the chronologically later booklist (dated 1218/1803) appears in our copy before the earlier one (dated 1216/1801).

This argument on the genesis of our inventory is supported by another feature: The inventory has an overall tally of the books at its end. This overall tally was written, as a note shows, when a new librarian, Sayyid Sulaymān Efendi, took charge of the library in 1215/1800.[21] The number of books in this tally matches exactly the number of books in the original inventory, but the books of the two confiscation lists are not included in it. Thus, when the writer of the Ankara MDM merged the confiscation booklists with the original inventory, he did not change the numbers of the 1215/1800 tally, but simply copied over the numbers as he found them in the original inventory.

Thus, the year 1215/1800 is clearly not the date when the inventory as we find it in the Ankara MDM was produced. We know that it must have been produced after 1218/1803 when the last confiscation booklist was written. We are fortunate to have a brief statement in Ottoman appended to the inventory that allows us to pinpoint the production of our copy more exactly:

> According to a noble edict saying: 'The supplement of the register of the aforementioned endower that has arrived and been sealed with his seal, should be returned to its [proper] place and recorded as [part] of the account of [the endowment] of the Two Sanctuaries'; it [has been] explained that [it should] be recorded with the same [original document?] and then returned to this place, at the beginning of Muḥarram 1221[/1806].[22]

Therefore, we can presume that the Ankara MDM, and, thus, also the inventory, was written in the year 1221/1806, two years after the death of al-

18 Inventory book #1676.

19 Inventory books #643, 684, 686, 723, 1138, 1139, 1140, 1258, 1259, 1260.

20 The writer made an error in calculating the total number of books on grammar and on poetry and verse. This became apparent due to the discrepancy between the sum total of all the books and the tallies given for each subject at the end of every section.

21 Vakıflar Genel Müdürlüğü (Ankara), Defter 1626, 72.

22 واقف مشار إليهك مهريله ممهور ورود ايدن دفترى ذيلنه حرمين شريفين محاسبه سيكه قيد اولنمه سى محلنه إيصال اولنمق ا چون رد اولنه ديو صادر اولان فرمان شريف موجبنجه عينيله قيد اولنوب رد اولنمغله اش بو محله شرح ويريلدى في غره م سنه ١٢٢١

Vāḳifi muşār ileyhin mührüyle memhūr vurūd eden defteri ẕeylini Ḥaremeyni'şerīfeyn muḥāsebesine ḳayıd olunması maḥalline īṣāl olunmak içün redd oluna diye ṣādır olan fermān-i şerīf mucibince ʿaynıyla ḳayıd olunub redd olunmaġla iş bu maḥalle şerḥ vėrildi fī ġurra mīm [*Muḥarrem*] *sene 1221*. Thanks to Nimet Ipek for transcribing and translating this text.

Jazzār, and that the lost original inventory bore the seal of the endower, that is of al-Jazzār himself, and was returned to its original place (we do not know what this place was) in Acre.

The Ankara MDM includes a third document, a register (*daftar*) recording endowed estates and accounts. In contrast to the MDM's first two documents (the endowment deed and inventory), this third document was not copied into the MDM. Instead, it is a large, single-folded sheet that was first produced as an independent document and subsequently added to the MDM. It was written in Jumādā I 1219/1804, four months after the death of al-Jazzār, and is again the copy of a (lost) original document. We can deduce this from its conclusion written by the Deputy of Acre, the Mufti Muḥammad Abū al-Hudā al-Tājī:

> We have examined the register of properties endowed by [... Aḥmad al-Jazzār] to the noble mosque he constructed in Acre, as well as to the *madrasa*, eminent library, and public drinking fountain. These are the places enumerated in this register. Likewise, we have examined the arrangements made by the aforementioned endower for those holding positions and the *mujāwarīn*, and the arrangements of His Excellency, the noble Vizier ʿAbd al-Qādir Pasha, Grand Admiral of the Navy, for the freedmen of [al-Jazzār]. This has been copied into this register word-for-word without any additions or omissions. The humble servant of the Sublime Porte, Muḥammad Abū al-Hudā al-Tājī, the Deputy of Acre—may his sins be forgiven.[23]

It is clear from the above that all three documents in the Ankara MDM are copies of originals kept in Acre. At least two of them were copied after al-Jazzār's death, which confirms our argument that they were copied within the context of the Ottoman state registering al-Jazzār's possessions. The role of the Ottoman centre as originating the 'copying' process of these documents is also indicated by the role of specific offices (registry office of the Two Holy Sanctuaries) and wordings, such as 'servant of the Sublime Porte'. That the MDM is today in Ankara supports this hypothesis. It was probably held in Istanbul as part of the Ottoman archives and, with the reconfiguration of the archives in the Republic period, this MDM was subsequently incorporated into the holdings of the endowment ministry in Ankara.

2 Why Was the 1215/1800 Inventory Written?

The original 1215/1800 inventory of the Jazzār library was produced, as the colophon of the inventory makes clear, as the end result of a process that involved inventorying the entire contents of the library, and handing it over to a new librarian, Sulaymān Efendi. We know that the library was established in 1196/1781,[24] when the mosque and the *madrasa* were built, and that a large number of books were endowed in that year. It is necessary, therefore, to ask why this inventory was written twenty years after the establishment of the library.

Arguably, the production of this inventory was linked to Napoleon's siege of Acre in the spring of 1213/1799. This siege caused considerable upheaval in the town and it stands to reason that this upheaval also led to theft and plundering, including theft from the library. This argument is supported by a phenomenon that has startled us while working on the Jazzār library: We identified numerous manuscripts in libraries around the world, more precisely seventy-eight, that clearly belonged to the Jazzār library as they carry al-Jazzār's endowment deed, endowment seal and/or his endowment motto. Yet, eighteen of them are not recorded anywhere in our inventory; they are 'al-Jazzār non-inventory books' (JnIBs; on this,

23 Vakıflar Genel Müdürlüğü (Ankara), Defter 1626, 6; Abū Diyya, *Waqfiyyat Aḥmad Pāshā al-Jazzār*, 32.

24 Vakıflar Genel Müdürlüğü (Ankara), Defter 1626, 32.

also see Introduction and Chapter 7). The endowment statement of nine out of these eighteen manuscripts is dated and all of them were endowed in the library between the years 1196/1782 and 1201/1787. Princeton University Library, for example, holds a copy of the *Durar al-farāʾid* by Muḥammad al-Ḥarfūshī (d. 1059/1649; Garrett Islamic Manuscripts 3959y), and a copy of *al-Jawāhir al-bahiyya fī Sharḥ al-Arbaʿīn al-Nawawiyya* (Garrett Islamic Manuscripts 2996y). Both manuscripts were endowed by al-Jazzār in the years 1196/1782 and 1197/1783, respectively. Yet, neither of these two titles appears in our inventory. In other words, the eighteen books had once belonged to the library, but they must have been taken out of it before the inventory was written in 1215/1800.

There is further evidence that indicates that Napoleon's siege of the town in 1213/1799 caused upheaval in the library. One of the teachers in the Jazzār *madrasa* during (and shortly after) the siege was ʿAlī al-Rashīdī[25]—arguably the same person whose books al-Jazzār confiscated in 1216/1801. That ʿAlī al-Rashīdī from the confiscation booklist is identical to the teacher is especially likely as his books entered the library together with those of another holder of a salaried position, Muḥammad Wakīlkharaj. The teaching staff at the Jazzār *madrasa* in Acre consisted of only two teachers, both of whom were entrusted with additional duties within the endowment complex. The endowment deed in the Ankara MDM stipulates that one of them also worked as a preacher (*khaṭīb*) and the other as the keeper of the books (*ḥāfiẓ lil-kutub*): 'The endower stipulated that there should be a keeper of the books and teacher, who is to be given ten *qurūsh* per month.'[26] Given that ʿAlī al-Rashīdī was a teacher at the *madrasa* during and after the siege of Acre, he was possibly also the librarian who lost his job to Sulaymān Efendi in Jumādā I 1215/1800 after the end of the siege. Arguably, ʿAlī al-Rashīdī was dismissed and his possessions confiscated after a portion of the library's holdings had disappeared. The process of confiscating ʿAlī al-Rashīdī's possessions, extracting his books and incorporating them into the library took, as the date of the confiscation list shows, some nine months. That the administration of the endowment appointed the new librarian Sulaymān Efendi after the upheaval of the siege was certainly aimed at conducting a thorough investigation of the library's stock to register its contents before handing responsibility to this new librarian.

As the library and the position of the librarian moved into the focus of the administration's concerns, the position's profile must have been raised. At least, there is evidence that the position of the librarian increased in importance in the long term if we look at its salary. The endowment deed from 1200/1786 refers to this position as 'keeper of the books' and allotted a salary of ten *qurūsh* per month.[27] In the register of estates written almost twenty years later in 1219/1804, the third document in the Ankara MDM, however, the role is referred to as 'distinguished supervisor of the library' (*nāẓir kitābkhāna munīf*). At the same time, the allotted salary had doubled to twenty *qurūsh* per month.[28] Even leaving aside the change in nomenclature, the twofold increase in the librarian's wages is remarkable. It cannot be explained by inflation as, for instance, the salary of the endowment's supervisor decreased from 120 *qurūsh* per month in 1200/1786 to seventy-five *qurūsh* per month in 1219/1804. The substantial pay rise of the librarian must have reflected the growing importance of the position, though it is unknown whether this is because the library had been ex-

25 This is evident from a poem by ʿAbd al-Laṭīf Fatḥallāh, the Mufti of Beirut, in which he reminded ʿAlī al-Rashīdī of an *ijāza* that he had promised him but never issued; see Fatḥallāh, *Dīwān al-Muftī*, I, 152. This means that al-Jazzār confiscated his library within two years (1801 CE). See the final paragraph of the inventory's introduction.

26 Vakıflar Genel Müdürlüğü (Ankara), Defter 1626, 5.

27 Ibid., 5.

28 Ibid., 77.

posed to theft or due to the expansion of the library's holdings.

The original 1215/1800 inventory was written for taking stock of the library after numerous books must have disappeared, therefore, we can be relatively confident that it is a complete reflection of the library's holdings at that point.[29] Sulaymān Efendi, the new librarian, certainly did not undertake this work as this would have left any information about the collection, especially the number of its books, severely exposed to tampering. There is reason to suspect that the two confiscation booklists, by contrast, may not have been a complete record of the books taken from the three personal libraries, especially the list from the year 1216/1801 since it does not provide a final numerical count.

3 Bibliographical Practices I: Describing Contents (Disciplines, Titles and Authors)

After having discussed the history of the Ankara MDM, and especially our inventory, we can now zoom in on the inventory's bibliographical strategies. This discussion, as the following will argue, shows that the logic of the original inventory was closely linked to the fact that it was produced within administrative procedures to hand over the library's holdings to the care of a new librarian. The copy that we have in the Ankara MDM was, furthermore, produced within the framework of assessing al-Jazzār's properties after his death. In the following, we will assume that the scribe of the Ankara MDM had no reason to change the organisation of the original inventory as both were meant to serve broadly comparable administrative purposes. This administrative genesis is crucial to understanding the logic of the inventory as it takes great care to describe the physical aspects of the books and identify them as material objects, facilitating any subsequent inventory of the library's holdings. This genesis is arguably also the reason for the relative lack of importance given to the documentation of authors and titles. The writers of the original inventory and the Ankara MDM both saw no need to provide much detail on them as they were of marginal relevance for the document's administrative function.

Apart from the two confiscation lists, the library inventory is organised thematically. Its subject headings are in terms of visual organisation clearly distinguished from the rest of the text, although they are written in the same script with the same colour of ink. The book entries are uniformly listed beneath each heading: The information given for each book is formatted in the shape of an inverted pyramid, each row consisting of three book entries, and each column of ten entries (except where the columns are interrupted by a new subject heading). A typical page, thus, comprises thirty entries. The scribe provided tallies for the number of books under each subject heading. He forgot to provide such a tally at the end of the section on Qurʾan commentary (*tafsīr*), but compensates for this in the final tally at the end of the inventory. Under the subject headings (and under the headings of the names of Yaḥyā Efendi, ʿAlī al-Rashīdī and Muḥammad Wakīlkharaj in the case of the two confiscation lists), the entries are not arranged in alphabetical order or any other apparent order. In many instances, even entries for different copies of a single work are given in different places, such as the copies of *K. Matn al-Jazariyya*.[30] However, some of the following chapters argue that the order of the titles follows a cultural logic that emerges when studying the respective section in more detail. The writer of the inventory provided a list of eighteen subject headings under which the relevant books are recorded:

29 The production of an inventory after books have disappeared was a common practice in this period, as discussed in Chapter 1 by Berat Açıl, Nimet İpek and Guy Burak.

30 Inventory books #105, 106, and 140.

1. *Maṣāḥif sharīfa* (Exemplars of the Qur'an)
2. *Kutub al-tafsīr al-sharīfa* (Qur'an Commentary)
3. *Kutub ʿilm al-qirāʾāt* (Qur'an Recitation)
4. *Kutub al-ḥadīth al-sharīf* (Prophetic Traditions)
5. *Kutub al-fiqh al-sharīf* (Law)
6. *Kutub al-tawḥīd wa-al-taṣawwuf* (Islamic Theology and Sufism)
7. *Kutub al-naḥw* (Grammar)
8. *Kutub al-maʿānī wa-al-bayān wa-al-ādāb wa-al-uṣūl wa-al-ʿarūḍ* (Rhetoric, *adab*, Rule of Conduct and Prosody)
9. *Kutub ʿilm al-manṭiq* (Logic)
10. *Kutub ʿilm al-ṣarf* (Morphology)
11. *Kutub al-dawāwīn wa-al-qaṣāʾid* (Poetry)
12. *Kutub taʿbīr wa-ruʾya* (Dream Interpretation)
13. *Kutub ʿilm al-tārīkh* (History)
14. *Kutub ʿilm al-lugha* (Lexicography)
15. *Kutub ʿilm al-ṭibb* (Medicine)
16. *Kutub ʿilm al-falak wa-al-hayʾa wa-al-ḥarf wa-al-rūḥānī wa-al-raml wa-al-handasa wa-al-ḥisāb wa-al-kīmīyāʾ* (Occult Sciences)
17. *Kutub al-Fārisī* (Persian Books)
18. *Kutub al-Turkī* (Turkish Books)

Table 2.1 uses this classification scheme to also include the books from the two confiscation lists, so that it reflects the library's probable holdings in 1218/1803. This comes with the important caveat that some books are difficult to identify or classify due to a dearth of bibliographical information. It is also worth noting that several books in the original inventory have been included under a subject heading that is counter-intuitive to current definitions of these disciplines. Therefore, the information contained in the table should be seen only as an approximation of the thematic distribution of the library's holdings. Yet, this table offers a general picture of the bookish life in Acre at the beginning of the thirteenth century/around 1800. It shows that transmitted sciences accounted for 47 % of the library's holdings, works on Arabic language and literature for 28 %, and historical works for 9 %.

The subject classifications show some idiosyncrasies of the writer of the inventory and this topic will be repeatedly taken up in the following chapters on specific sections. This includes that some related disciplines are divided across separate subject headings, so that, for example, books on grammar appear in separate sections from books on morphology and lexicography (see Chapter 18). At the same time, the inventory includes, in other cases, several disciplines under a single heading, such as, most importantly, the section on *Kutub al-maʿānī wa-al-bayān wa-al-ādāb wa-al-uṣūl wa-al-ʿarūḍ*, including rhetoric, *adab*, rule of conduct and prosody. In this section, the writer did not identify which book belongs to which of these disciplines. It is most surprising in the *Kutub al-maʿānī* section that we also find books on *uṣūl al-fiqh* (legal theory), which one would expect in the section on *fiqh* (jurisprudence). The classification of specific books is sometimes difficult to follow. A work on Qur'an commentary, *al-Taysīs li-Ibn al-Jawzī*, for example, is listed in the section on Qur'an recitation.[31] Similarly, *Kitāb Falāḥat al-basātīn* is a work on horticulture, not medicine, as suggested by the writer of the inventory.[32]

The *ʿilm al-ḥadīth* section (Prophetic Traditions), discussed in Chapter 15 by Garrett Davidson, is a particularly intriguing example of a subject classification that is, at first glance, surprising. Apart from the titles that are also today understood to be part of this subject, we find a wide array of titles that do not seem to fit. This includes particularly works that relate to the biography of the Prophet, such as *K. al-Shifāʾ bi-taʿrīf ḥuqūq al-Muṣṭafā* by Qāḍī ʿIyāḍ, *K. al-Shamāʾil al-nabawiyya wa-al-khiṣāl al-muṣṭafawiyya* by al-Tirmidhī, *K. al-Ṭarīqa al-Muḥammadiyya wa-al-sīra al-aḥmadiyya* by Muḥammad al-Birgawī, and *K. al-Mawāhib al-laduniyya fī al-minaḥ al-muḥammadiyya* by Aḥmad al-Qasṭallānī. Tellingly, we find that the inventory affixed the epithet 'noble' (*sharīf*) to many

31 Inventory book #90.
32 Inventory book #1463.

TABLE 2.1 Approximate thematic distribution of the entirety of the library's holdings in 1218/1803

Subject	No. of volumes			
	Original inventory	Two booklists	Total	
			No.	%
Exemplars of the Qur'an	24	16	179	10
Qur'an Commentary	77			
Qur'an Recitation	62			
Prophetic Traditions	231	27	258	14.4
Jurisprudence	203	20	223	12.5
Islamic Theology and Sufism	156	23	177	10
Grammar	196	6	204	11.3
Rhetoric, *adab*, Rule of Conduct and Prosody	132	7	139	7.7
Logic	47	0	47	2.6
Morphology	24	1	25	1.4
Poetry	111	1	112	6.25
Dream Interpretation	5	0	5	0.3
History	150	6	156	8.7
Lexicography	27	5	32	1.7
Medicine	49	7	56	3.1
Occult Sciences	81	20	101	5.6
Persian Books	22	0	22	1.2
Turkish Books	56	0	56	3.1

of these titles, such as *al Shifāʾ al sharīf* or *Shifāʾ sharīf*, *al-shamāʾil al-sharīf* or *shamāʾil sharīf*. Apart from the biographical works, we also find poems in praise of the Prophet under the heading of *ḥadīth*, namely, *Qaṣīdat al-Burda* and *Qaṣīdat Umm al-qurā fī madḥ khayr al-warā* by al-Būṣīrī, as well as commentaries on these poems. The *ḥadīth* section also includes books of prayer and devotion, such as *Dalāʾil al-khayrāt wa-shawāriq al-anwār fī dhikr al-ṣalāh ʿalā al-nabī al-mukhṭār* by Muḥammad al-Jazūlī. Again, the epithet *sharīf* was added, recording the book as *Dalāʾil al-sharīf*. We also find the use of the epithet *sharīf* for 'proper' works of *ḥadīth*, so that they describe *Ṣaḥīḥ al-Bukhārī* as *Bukhārī sharīf*. In other words, all these works receive a status equivalent to the *Ṣaḥīḥ al-Bukhārī* and are treated as related works. What emerges is an understanding of *ḥadīth* that encompasses everything related to the Prophet Muḥammad including his biography, his words and deeds, and his virtues and characteristics.[33]

This broad definition of *ḥadīth* is not unique to the Jazzār inventory, but is part of a general understanding of that period. For this, we can turn to two other booklists that we will repeatedly use in the course of this chapter as they were written in close chronological and spatial proximity. These are the updated register of books endowed by ʿUthmān Pasha al-Dūrikī at the Riḍāʾiyya Madrasa in Aleppo written in 1252/1836[34] and

33 Al-Khaṭīb, *al-Sunna*, 15 f.
34 Aljoumani, *Maktaba madrasiyya fī Ḥalab*.

the register of the books endowed by Muḥammad Ṣanʿallāh b. Khalīl al-Khālidī (d. 1139/1726), his son Muḥammad Ṣanʿallāh b. Muḥammad Ṣanʿallāh al-Khālidī (d. 1205/1781), and his daughter-in-law, Ṭarafanda Hatun bt. Najm al-Dīn al-Khayrī, the wife of Ibrāhīm b. Muḥammad Ṣanʿallāh.[35] A dedicated study of the Khālidiyya register is yet to appear, therefore, we can only shed light on it in summary form. This register is not dated but, based on internal and external evidence, we have been able to date it to a period between the middle of Rabīʿ II and the end of Rajab 1201/1787. There are two references to the year 1201 in the final section, containing accounts and lending notices (folia 34ᵃ), so the register was drafted in or before Rajab 1201/1787. Furthermore, it was almost certainly written shortly after the endowment deed of Muḥammad Ṣanʿallāh b. Muḥammad Ṣanʿallāh and his sister-in-law Ṭarafanda was drafted in the middle of Rabīʿ II 1201/1787.[36] We can infer this because the order of the books listed in the endowment deed corresponds exactly with the list of books in the register. Yet, the register mentions additional books that do not appear in the endowment deed. One can, thus, assume that the register was produced after the endowment deed. Returning to the discussion of subject classifications, the ʿUthmāniyya Riḍāʾiyya register and the Khālidiyya register include a similar wide array of books under the heading of *ḥadīth* and there was clearly a shared understanding of the contours of this subject and the works that fall under it.

The Jazzār library comprised scholarly works in the three principal languages of the Ottoman period: Arabic, Persian and Turkish. The writer of the inventory did not highlight works in Arabic since it was the dominant language of the holdings, whereas he dedicated two sections specifically for books in Persian and Turkish (see Chapter 25). Apart from the subject-based sections, he, thus, brought together diverse disciplines in the two language-based sections of *Kutub al-Fārisī* (Persian Books) and *Kutub al-Turkī* (Turkish Books).[37] However, he did not follow a consistent approach since we repeatedly find books in these languages listed according to subject rather than language, although, in these cases, the writer identified the books as being 'in Persian' or 'in Turkish'.[38] One finds, for example, 'a Persian *tafsīr*' in the section on Qurʾan commentary[39] and '*Manāsik al-ḥajj* by Mulla ʿAlī al-Qārī in Turkish'[40] in the section on jurisprudence.

Comparing the classification system of the Jazzār inventory to those of the ʿUthmāniyya Riḍāʾiyya register and the Khālidiyya register allows us to profile the approach of the writer of the Jazzār inventory more distinctively. With eighteen headings, this inventory makes use of a wider range of subject headings than the ʿUthmāniyya Riḍāʾiyya register with twelve. While the writer of the ʿUthmāniyya Riḍāʾiyya register incorporated *Books related to the magnificent Qurʾan* under a single heading, the Jazzār inventory divided books on the Qurʾan into three distinct headings: exemplars of the Qurʾan, Qurʾan commentary and Qurʾan recitation. Similarly, the writer of the ʿUthmāniyya Riḍāʾiyya registered books on logic into a broader heading, *Books on Logic, Astronomy, Philosophy (ḥikma), Geometry, and Arithmetic* due to the few books owned by the library in these fields. The Jazzār inventory, by contrast, listed books on logic under a separate heading due to the large number of books on this subject (forty-seven volumes). The writer of the ʿUthmāniyya Riḍāʾiyya register did not specify a heading for dream interpretation due to the absence of any holdings on this subject, whereas the Jazzār inventory gave dream interpretation a distinct heading despite the mod-

35 Register of the *Khālidiyya* endowments, Ms. 1126.
36 Jerusalem, *Sijill al-maḥkama al-sharʿiyya*, No. 267, 152–154.

37 In one case, a Turkish book is mistakenly listed in the Persian section (#1569).
38 For the Persian books listed according to subject see #57 and 700, and for the Turkish books see #414, 733, 1379, 1390, 1422, 1443.
39 Inventory book #57.
40 Inventory book #414.

esty of the library's collection on the subject (five volumes).

The Khālidiyya register is divided into two main sections.[41] The first section concerns the endowments of Muḥammad Ṣanʿallāh b. Khalīl al-Khālidī, and lists the library's holdings according to the following headings: *tafsīr* (Commentary); *ḥadīth* (Prophetic Traditions); *tawḥīd* and *taṣawwuf* (Islamic Theology and Sufism); *fiqh*, *uṣūl* and *farāʾid* (Islamic Law); *naḥw* and *manṭiq* (Grammar and Logic); *dawāwīn*, *adab* and *tawārīkh* (Poetry, Literature and History); *ṭibb* (Medicine); and *majāmīʿ* (Multiple-text and Composite Manuscripts). The second section concerns the endowments of his son Muḥammad Ṣanʿallāh and of his daughter-in-law Ṭarafanda. The books are listed under the following headings: *mukarramāt sharīfa* (Exemplars of the Qurʾan); *tafsīr* (Commentary); *ḥadīth* (Prophetic Traditions); *tawḥīd* (Islamic Theology); *taṣawwuf* (Sufism); *fiqh*, *farāʾid*, and *uṣūl* (Islamic Law); *naḥw*, *lugha* and *manṭiq* (Grammar, Language and Logic); *dawāwīn*, *adabiyyāt* and *tawārīkh* (Poetry, Literature and History); *majāmīʿ* and *taʿbīr al-ruʾyā* (Multiple-text, Composite Manuscripts and Dream Interpretation); *rasāʾil* (Epistles); *kutub Turkī* and *Fārisī* (Turkish and Persian Books).

Thus, the Khālidiyya register only employs twelve subject headings compared to the eighteen of the Jazzār inventory. The writer of the Khālidiyya register incorporated Qurʾan Recitation (*al-qirāʾāt*) under *ʿilm al-tafsīr* (Commentary), presumably because of the small number of holdings on this subject. By contrast, the writer of the Jazzār inventory provided a separate heading for works on Qurʾan Recitation, since the library possessed a sizeable collection of sixty-two volumes on this subject. The writer of the Khālidiyya register incorporated books of logic into the broader subject heading, *kutub al-naḥw wa-tawābiʿhi wa-al-manṭiq* (Books on Grammar and Logic), for the same reason. The writer of the Jazzār inventory, as mentioned above, listed books on logic under a separate heading due to the large number of books on the subject. The writer of the Khālidiyya register did not specify a heading for astronomy, arithmetic and alchemy, since the library only owned one volume on arithmetic, one on alchemy, and a handful on astronomy and geomancy. In the case of the Jazzār library, these subjects are listed under the separate heading of *Kutub ʿilm al-falak wa-al-hayʾa wa-al-ḥarf wa-al-rūḥānī wa-al-raml wa-al-handasa wa-al-ḥisāb wa-al-kīmīyāʾ* (Books on Astronomy, Spiritual Sciences, Geomancy, Geometry, Arithmetic and Alchemy).

The writer of the Jazzār inventory chose a variety of bibliographical strategies to reproduce the titles of books in the inventory. However, untitled books are also relatively common in the inventory and the writer repeatedly explained that he was unable to provide the title as a result of missing folia of the manuscript. As an example, we find 'a book of grammar, the beginning and end of which is incomplete'.[42] We identified six main ways of how the writer reproduced titles:

1) *Full titles* are provided for only nine books in the whole inventory.[43]
2) *Abbreviated titles* are the most common form in the inventory. The book *Qurrat al-ʿayn fī al-fatḥ wa-al-imāla bayn al-lafẓayn*, for instance, is listed in the inventory as *Qurrat al-ʿayn*.[44] These abbreviated titles are repeatedly ambiguous and insufficient to identify the book intended. This is particularly common for commentarial texts, such as commentaries (*shurūḥ*), scholia (*ḥawāshī*), summaries (*mukhtāṣarāt*) and appendices (*dhuyūl*).
3) *Alternative titles* are especially applied to commentaries, as these might have their own

41 A third section contains a miscellany of accounts related to the household of Muḥammad Ṣanʿallāh b. Muḥammad Ṣanʿallāh and lending notices of library books.

42 Inventory book #905, 906, 907.

43 Inventory books #81, 83, 88, 109, 119, 209, 396, 634, 841.

44 Inventory book #118.

titles, but can also be referred to as 'commentary on X'. The inventory lists '*Sharḥ Jawharat al-tawḥīd* known as *Hidāya al-murīd*' are an example of this.[45] However, the writer of the inventory did not have a consistent method when referring to commentarial texts.

4) *Differing titles*. The writer of the inventory, for example, identified *K. Anwār al-tanzīl wa-asrār al-ta'wīl* by al-Qāḍī al-Bayḍāwī in two different ways: in one case, he simply wrote *al-Bayḍāwī* and in another, he wrote *Tafsīr al-Bayḍāwī*.[46]
5) An *explanatory title* appears on a single occasion: 'poems in praise of the best of all creation (God bless him and keep him!), and they are the *Badī'iyya* of al-'Umiyyān'.[47]
6) *Corrected titles*. The writer of the inventory only corrected the title of a book on one occasion, pointing out: 'the fourth [part] al-Qasṭallānī's *Sharḥ al-Bukhārī* that is erroneously called *Tafsīr Abī Dharr*'.[48]

A specific challenge for the writer of any book list is the listing of composite and multiple-text manuscripts.[49] The Khālidiyya register took the option to create an extra section '*majāmī'*' for these works, but the writer of the Jazzār inventory slotted them, instead, into the thematic sections. He generally tended towards brevity when describing such manuscripts and did not adhere to a systematic approach in dealing with them. He sometimes neither mentioned the titles to be found in the manuscript collection nor identified their authors, but simply stated that all the texts come under a certain topic.[50] At other times, he identified the author of the texts, but without specifying the individual titles.[51] He might only mention the title of the first work and the total number of texts, without giving us any indication of the authorship.[52] In other cases, he mentioned neither the titles, nor the authors, nor the number of writings.[53]

The writer of the inventory, for instance, listed book #311 simply as *Bushrā al-ka'īb*, so that one might believe that it is a single-text manuscript. Yet, we have been able to find the actual manuscript in Cairo, al-Azhar Library, MS 83318, and this artefact tells a very different story. It contains eight works by Jalāl al-Dīn al-Suyūṭī, the first one being *Bushrā al-ka'īb*. All eight texts were copied by a single scribe in one sitting, in other words, this is a multiple-text manuscript. One could hypothetically argue that the first text was originally a single-text book to which the other works were only added at a later date, after the writing of the inventory, but this argument would only be credible if we were dealing with a composite manuscript, which is clearly not the case here: The colophon of the first work is immediately followed on the same page by the introduction to the second work, and this is the case with all the texts in this manuscript. There remains another remote possibility that the library had acquired two copies of *Bushrā al-ka'īb*, the first being a single-text book and the second contained within a multiple-text manuscript. This would mean that one of the two copies was not included in the inventory and is not very likely.

The inventory shows different bibliographical strategies for providing the author's name. Full Arabic and Islamic names both before and during the Ottoman period consist of a *laqab* (epithet), *kunya* (teknonym), *ism* (given name), *nisba* (relational name) and *nasab* (genealogy). In most cases, the author is not named in the inventory as its writer was clearly not concerned with identifying the authorship of works. This means that, in many cases, it is impossible to identify books in the inventory conclusively. The entry '*Sharḥ al-Shāṭibiyya* in an Egyptian hand [...]'[54] does not pro-

45 Inventory book #603.
46 Inventory books #27, 28, 29, 51.
47 Inventory book #1161.
48 Inventory book #146.
49 For these two types of books, see Aljoumani and Hirschler, *Mu'allafāt Yūsuf Ibn 'Abd al-Hādī*, 19.
50 Inventory book #303.
51 Inventory book #304.
52 Inventory book #305.
53 Inventory books #306, 307.
54 Inventory books #97–100.

vide any indication which of the many commentaries on the *Shāṭibiyya* is meant. We identified two main ways of how the writer of the inventory referred to authors:

1) The standard form used for an author's name are *abbreviated names* by using the part of the name by which an author is commonly known, such as *Iʿrāb al-Qurʾān* by al-ʿAkbarī'.[55]
2) *Differing names* are occasionally found when the same author is named in different ways. Muḥyī al-Dīn Ibn al-ʿArabī, for example, is designated as both 'al-Shaykh al-Akbar'[56] and 'Muḥyī al-Dīn Ibn al-ʿArabī'.[57]

What we do not find in the inventory is the use of full names to identify the author. This is noteworthy as we find the practice in seven other book lists from the Arabic lands that we studied previously within the framework of a larger project.[58] These lists providing full names are *Risālat Asāmī baʿḍ al-kutub* (copied in the 12th century AH), *Fihrist Kutub al-madrasa al-Aḥmadiyya al-qadīma* (copied in 1166 AH), *Fihris Maktabat ʿĀṭif Efendi* (copied in the 12th century AH), *Daftar Asmāʾ kutub jāmiʿ al-ʿUthmāniyya* (the first half copied in 1252 AH), *Taqyīd Kutub khizānat al-Mawlawiyya bi-Fās* (copied in 1289 AH), *Daftar Khizānat kutub Shaykh al-Islām Aḥmad ʿĀrif Ḥikmat* (copied 1297 AH) and *Fihris Khizānat Ibrāhīm Ḥalīm Bāshā bi-al-Qāhira* (copied in the 13th century AH). This list indicates that the full names of authors only appeared in twelfth- and thirteenth-century booklists. The practice was adopted unevenly and a full name appears only once in the *Daftar Asmāʾ kutub jāmiʿ al-ʿUthmāniyya*[59] and in *Taqyīd Kutub khizānat al-Mawlawiyya bi-Fās*, but it is the most common form in *Fihris Khizānat Ibrāhīm Ḥalīm Bāshā bi-al-Qāhira* (copied in the 13th century AH). Our inventory is, thus, an example of a bibliographical practice that had not yet started to adopt this convention.

The inventory's system of unevenly providing the titles and authors of the books, especially in cases where there are various commentaries on a work, ultimately shows that it was not intended to be used as a catalogue or finding aid. The inventory, for example, lists sixteen commentaries on the *Alfiyya*, a work of grammar by Ibn Mālik, but only the authors of three of these are mentioned.[60] One of these copies with the Jazzār endowment statement survives in Cairo, at the Ministry of Islamic Endowments Library, MS 3018. The author of this text is ʿAbd al-Raḥmān b. ʿAlī al-Makkūdī (d. 807/1405), but it is impossible to correlate this manuscript with the exact entry in the inventory because the latter does not provide most of the authors' names. While it is clear that our inventory was not intended for tracing books written by a specific author or a particular title, the ʿUthmāniyya Riḍāʾiyya register showed considerably more concern for recording the titles and authors of the works.

The Jazzār inventory also provides no means to correlate its entries with the location of books on the shelves. The books are not provided with numbers or another system, and there is no indication that the shelves or cases had any such system either.[61] It is possible, of course, that there is a basic relationship between the books in the inventory and the library's shelves, if one assumes that the bookcases were divided according to subject. This would mean that the two supplementary collections of confiscated books must have been allocated two independent spaces among the library's shelves.

55 Inventory book #59.
56 Inventory book #1493.
57 Inventory book #1133.
58 Aljoumani, "al-Fahāris al-Makhṭūṭa".
59 Aljoumani, *Maktaba madrasiyya fī Ḥalab*, 56.
60 Inventory books #755, 761, 769.
61 See the cohesive linking mechanisms employed in the inventory of Ashrafiya library (7th-century copies), a historical compilation (*sijil qadīm*) of the Kairouan Mosque (7th-century copies) and the library's inventory of Ibrāhīm Ḥalīm Pāshā (13th-century copies). Aljoumani, "al-Fahāris al-makhṭūṭa".

4 Bibliographical Practices II: Describing the Materiality

While the information on the contents of the books via identifying titles and authors is limited in the inventory, this is not the case for information on the materiality of the books on the shelves. Here, the inventory provides extraordinary information that indicates to what extent it was meant to function as an administrative document for surveying the stock of the library and checking this stock at a later point. This is particularly evident from the fact that the writer, remarkably so, provided, in many cases, a description of the materiality of all the individual copies of the same work if these existed. This allowed users of the inventory to distinguish each one according to its material features. The scribe deviated from this careful approach only in six cases, and merely states there to be two copies of a given work without providing further information.[62] In the following, we enumerate the main features that the inventory highlighted to identify the actual copy that sat on the shelves of the library. Some of these features will be discussed in more detail in the following chapters, such as Chapter 8 on book sizes, bindings and slipcases, as well as Chapter 9 on scripts. In addition to the terms below, the writer also employed the term *kuhnā* (old or antique in Persian), and the writer stated, for example, '*muṣḥaf qadīm kuhnā*'.[63]

1) *Number of volumes*. This is the material feature that the writer most diligently recorded for every item in the inventory. His interest in recording the number of volumes so precisely is a clear token of the document's function as an inventory. In the same vein, the writer included information on the parts of a book (*juzʾ/ajzāʾ*), indicating any parts missing from a book, and specifying the parts the library possesses.[64] He did the same even for works that have no parts missing, stating their number and confirming that the book is complete.[65]
2) *Type of script*. The writer was also very diligent in recording the different types of scripts. He considered the script to be a material feature that distinguished duplicate copies of the same work. In some cases, two copies are identical in every aspect of their bibliographical description except the script, such as '*al-Muṭawwal in a naskhī* script, half format, bound with a slipcase, one volume' and '*al-Muṭawwal* in an Egyptian script, half format, bound with a slipcase, one volume'.[66] The scribe also sometimes assessed the quality of the script and the skill of the scribe: 'a script of high quality' (*khaṭṭ ʿālin*)[67] or 'a script of average quality' (*khaṭṭ wasaṭ*).[68]

The most important element for describing scripts, however, was the use of regional categories, such as Egyptian script, Istanbul script, Persian (*ʿajam*) script, Maghrebi script, and Turkish script. The categorisation of scripts on a regional basis by writers of booklists has roots extending back at least to the seventh/thirteenth century. This historical trace is evident in the library record of the Kairouan Mosque, dated to 693/1294. The record notes the presence of two volumes in an eastern script (*khaṭṭ sharqī*)[69] and another work in five volumes in Sicilian script (*khaṭṭ Ṣiqillī*).[70] The use of the category 'Egyptian script' is particularly noteworthy. The scribe used this category for approximately eight hundred books, nearly half of the library's entire collection. Interestingly, he did not employ the categories of Levantine or Iraqi script (*khaṭṭ Shāmī* or *khaṭṭ ʿIrāqī*). This absence is particularly intriguing when we look at the books in more detail. The scribe, for instance, described a copy of *Dīwān*

62 Inventory books #105, 345, 380, 394, 600, 612.
63 Inventory book #18.
64 Inventory books #41, 42, 43.
65 Inventory books #26, 30, 39.
66 Inventory books #931, 932.
67 Inventory books #1, 2, 5.
68 Inventory books #7, 8, 9.
69 Shabbūḥ, "Sijill qadīm".
70 Ibid.

al-Dawāwīn as being written in 'Egyptian script'.[71] In this case, we can access the actual manuscript and see that this copy was written by a certain Muḥammad b. Ibrāhīm al-Dakdakjī (d. 1131/1719). This Dakdakjī was of Turkmen origin and born and died in Damascus.[72] He did not have any connection with Egypt. Why, then, was the script labelled as 'Egyptian'? It is plausible that what had previously been called an 'Eastern script' is identical to what the cataloguer of the Jazzār library identified as an 'Egyptian script'. This conjecture gains support from the fact that the manuscripts originating from the Jazzār library described in the book inventory as being in Egyptian script are, in reality, in a variety of Eastern scripts.[73]

The writer of the inventory only provided the name of the copyist in two cases, namely, when they were autographs: '*al-Bayān al-maqbūl fī radd al-sūl* in the hand of its respected author ʿAbd al-Ghanī al-Nābulusī (may God bless him!)',[74] and '*Khulāṣat taḥqīq al-ẓunūn* in the hand of its author Ibn al-Bakrī'.[75]

3) *Book size/format*.[76] The formats of the books is another material feature that the writer consistently included in the inventory, with only a few exceptions, for identifying the specific copies that were part of the library's stock. The main formats the writer used for this purpose were full format, half format, quarter format and eighth format. A further term that we find frequently associated with paper formats is *muḥayyar*. The use of this term in our inventory and the register of the books by Muḥammad Ṣanʿallāh b. Khalīl al-Khālidī in Jerusalem[77] shows that this term aimed to highlight deviations from standard formats. It, thus, translates as 'non-standard full format' (*qaṭʿ kāmil muḥayyar*),[78] 'non-standard half format' (*qaṭʿ al-niṣf muḥayyar*)[79] and 'non-standard quarter format' (*qaṭʿ al-rubʿ muḥayyar*).[80] In those cases, the book did not conform to the precise full, half or quarter format and, thus, occupied an intermediary space—somewhere between the full and the half, or the half and a quarter, or the quarter and an eighth. Two plausible scenarios arise: either the book was initially crafted in a non-standard format or its format was altered during binding or rebinding. In addition to *muḥayyar*, the writer used the terms *talkhīṣ*, *ṭawīl* and *wāsiʿ* to qualify formats. *Talkhīṣ*, which literally means 'outline, summary', is mentioned in entries such as 'half format *al-talkhīṣ*'[81] and 'full format *al-talkhīṣ*',[82] but it has proved impossible to ascertain the meaning of this term because the relevant manuscripts have not yet been found. The terms *ṭawīl* (long) and *wāsiʿ* (broad) appear in phrases such as 'half format long (*ṭawīl*)',[83] 'eighth format broad (*wāsiʿ*)'[84] and 'quarter format long and broad (*ṭawīl wāsiʿ*)'.[85] We have not yet identified manuscripts described with these two terms, but the term *ṭawīl* possibly indicates an elongated book form. We identified only three types of *ṭawīl* formats in the inventory: the half-long format, the quarter-long format and the eighth-long format.
4) *Binding*. The diligence of the inventory writer in recording the binding adds yet another

71 Inventory book #1187. A copy of this manuscript is preserved in the library of al-Imam Muḥammad bin Suʿūd Islamic University, No. (M 1094). The original is from the Rawḍa Khayrī Library in Egypt.
72 Al-Murādī, *Silk al-Durar*, IV, 25–27.
73 Inventory books #81, 91, 150, 186, 193, 221, 276, 311, 416, 438, 492.
74 Inventory book #643.
75 Inventory book #1021.
76 On paper formats, see Aljoumani, "Quṭūʿ al-waraq".
77 Jerusalem, Khalidi Library, Ms. 1126, 15[a].
78 Vakıflar Genel Müdürlüğü (Ankara), Defter 1626, 15.
79 Ibid., 14.
80 Ibid., 14.
81 Inventory book #57.
82 Inventory book #1376.
83 Inventory books #63, 266, 446, 478, 495, 933.
84 Inventory books #10, 11, 17.
85 Inventory book #1518.

thick layer of material identity to the books held in the library. The writer's attention to this matter reveals that the library's holdings in 1215/1800 were all bound, except for a single book: '*Shāṭibiyya* [...] without binding (*bi-lā jīld*)'.[86] The writer's material-focused approach meant that he repeatedly recorded the colour and other specific characteristics of the leather used, such as '*rabʿa sharīfa* [...] with tooled, green-grey binding'.[87]

5) *Slipcases* (*ẓarf*). The writer also recorded the presence or absence of protective book encasements quite consistently in this inventory. He mentioned this feature for over 1,500 volumes, and this is unique among comparable booklists of the region and period.[88] The writer deliberately employed this feature to differentiate between different copies of the same book: We find, for instance, under #634 and #635, two copies of *al-Yawāqīt wa-al-jawāhir fī ʿaqāʾid al-sāda al-akābir*. The writer notes for the first copy that it is 'with slipcase', while the second is recorded as 'without slipcase'.

6) *Gilding*. Another material feature the writer used to identify manuscripts in the inventory is the presence of gilded elements. He did not make use of this category for most books, of course, since only a few of them were actually gilded. Yet, when he did so, he might also specify a particular style of gilding, such as 'gilded according to the western style'[89] or 'Istanbul gilding',[90] and whether both the cover and text of a book were gilded: 'gilded on the outside and the inside'.[91]

7) *Rule-borders*. The inventory writer often referred to the 'rule-border' (*al-jadwala*), that is, the frame that surrounds the written text. He occasionally characterised these rule-borders in more detail, stating, for example, 'with rule-borders in red',[92] 'with rule-borders in red and blue'[93] or 'with decorated rule-borders'.[94] This descriptive category has, indeed, allowed us to identify a specific copy of *al-Itqān fī ʿulūm al-Qurʾān* that is listed in the inventory (#81). Two copies of this work, which were once part of the Jazzār library, are extant. One of them is in the Khālidiyya Library in Jerusalem and the other copy is in the Jazzār library in Acre. The inventory's description of the rule-borders clearly shows that the copy listed in the inventory is the one in the Khālidiyya Library. The writer also referred to a lack of rule-borders as a means to differentiate between different copies of the same work, such as *Maṣḥaf sharīf* [*the Noble Qurʾān*] without rule-borders.[95]

8) *Marginal paracontent*. The writer repeatedly specified that a copy carries writings in the margins of the main text, such as explanatory notes, comments and glosses. The writer of the inventory wrote, for example, 'with *Shifāʾ sharīf* [...] in the margins (*muḥashshā*)'[96] and '*Sharḥ al-shāfiya* [...] in the margins (*muhammash*)'.[97] He used the two terms *hāmish* and *ḥāshiyya* to refer to this phenomenon. We are not certain whether he saw the two terms to be synonymous for the margins on all four sides of the main text, as some modern researchers do, or whether he restricted the term *ḥāshiya*, as others modern researchers do, to the margins directly below the text, and the term *hāmish* to the margins next to and above the text.[98]

86 Inventory book #96.
87 Inventory books #21, 22.
88 See some examples on storage containers for books in Aljoumani, "al-Fahāris al-Makhṭūṭa".
89 Inventory book #3.
90 Inventory book #4.
91 Inventory books #25, 155, 156, 245, 260, 332, 367, 1324, 1327, 1332.
92 Inventory book #10.
93 Inventory book #30.
94 Inventory book #5.
95 Inventory book #12.
96 Inventory book #159.
97 Inventory book #1110.
98 ʿAbd al-Qādir, *Tawthīq*, 221–222.

9) *Incomplete single-volume works*. Another set of material features that allowed the writer to characterise the specific copies held in the Jazzār library are damages.[99] He sometimes specified both the location and extent of a deficiency,[100] occasionally only the location, and every so often he merely stated that there was a missing passage without mentioning either its location or extent.[101]
10) *Print*. In the inventory, we find the early beginnings of the adoption of print in the region. The writer noted in five entries that it is a printed book.[102] The place of publication is only specified for two of these books, both of which were printed in Istanbul.[103]
11) *Writing Support*. The writer of the inventory only mentioned once any detail of the material of the writing support: 'the seventh [part] of *Ṣaḥīḥ al-Bukhārī* [...] on old (*ʿatīq*) paper'.[104] It is probable that paper was the writing support in all the books of the library and it was simply the age of the paper of this particular book that caught his eye. As we have not identified the manuscript in question, it is impossible to understand to what this description refers exactly.

The scribe's particular concern for the physical description of the books was arguably an unprecedented achievement compared to any booklist of an Arabic historical library that has been studied to date. He was remarkably consistent in noting the material features and using these to differentiate between multiple copies of the same work. If we compare the bibliographical strategies of the writer of the Jazzār inventory with the two comparator booklists: the ʿUthmāniyya Riḍāʾiyya register of Aleppo and the Khālidiyya register of Jerusalem, one feature immediately makes the Jazzār inventory stand out: It provides numbers for the overall stock of the library as well as for each subject section. By contrast, neither the ʿUthmāniyya Riḍāʾiyya register nor the Khālidiyya register provides any such numbers. In the same vein, in terms of material description, the information observed and recorded by the Jazzār inventory is much broader than that recorded by the ʿUthmāniyya Riḍāʾiyya register. The latter does not pay any attention to details, such as script types, protective slipcases, gilding, marginal paracontent or rule-borders. The Jazzār inventory's material description of books is also much richer than that of the Khālidiyya register. The latter, for instance, only mentions the script type for 7 out of 577 volumes, and does also not pay any attention to details such as protective slipcases, gilding, marginal paracontent or rule-borders. Both the ʿUthmāniyya Riḍāʾiyya register and the Khālidiyya register simply restrict themselves to listing several copies of the same work with the term 'another' (*ayḍan*). We find, for example, 'another (*ayḍan*) commentary on *al-ʿAqāʾid* by Saʿd'.[105] Consequently, the two registers have much less potential to identify specific copies of a work than the Jazzār inventory.

5 Conclusions

Our analysis of the Jazzār inventory at the heart of the Jazzār Library Project has shown that it should be read as an administrative document that has its own particular history of coming into being. This analysis has shown that we are looking at a booklist that was neither original nor a copy, but is the result of creatively merging three different documents. This, in turn, means that it provides us with a snapshot of the library's holdings around the year 1218/1803, the date of the last of these three documents. We can assume this snapshot to be reasonably complete. However, the fact that so many

99 Inventory book #36.
100 Inventory books #33, 370.
101 Inventory book #377.
102 Inventory books #1392, 1393, 1423, 1490, 1503.
103 Inventory books #1393, 1490.
104 Inventory book #143.
105 Register of the *Khālidiyya* endowments, Ms. 1126, 15^b.

extant manuscripts carry Jazzār endowment statements and/or seals, but are not part of our inventory, clearly alerts us to the fact that any such booklist is always only a snapshot taken at one specific point in history. We suggested that Napoleon's siege led to a considerable drain of manuscripts out of the library and this upheaval was also the reason that the original inventory was written in the first place. The heavy administrative character of our inventory allowed us to explain the writer's bibliographical strategies with his heavy focus on material features and limited concern for the contents of the books on the shelves. This is exactly the opposite of the ʿUthmāniyya Riḍāʾiyya and Khālidiyya registers, which provide much more detail on the contents of the books, but are much less forthcoming on their materiality. It is only against this backdrop of the inventory's history and function that we can appreciate what we have in front of us and can analyse it without falling back on inadequate value judgements on its supposed shortcomings.

Bibliography

Primary Sources

Jaffa, *Sijill al-Maḥkama al-Sharʿiyya*, 1.

Jerusalem, Khālidiyya Library, *Register of the Khālidiyya endowments*, Ms. 1126.

Jerusalem, National Library of Israel, MS AP Ar. 438.

Jerusalem, *Sijill al-maḥkama al-sharʿiyya*, No. 267.

Vakıflar Genel Müdürlüğü (Ankara), Defter 1626.

Secondary Sources

ʿAbd al-Qādir, Muwaffaq b. ʿAbd Allāh. *Tawthīq al-nuṣūṣ wa-ḍabṭuhā ʿinda al-muḥaddithīn*. Mecca, 1993.

Abū Diyya, Mūsā. *Waqfiyyat Aḥmad Pāshā al-Jazzār*. Nablus, 1998.

Abū Diyya, Mūsā. "Waqfiyyat Aḥmad Pāshā Al-Jazzār." In *Aḥmad Pāshā al-Jazzār. 200 ʿām ʿalā wafātihi*, edited by Shukrī ʿArrāf and Yaʿqūb Ḥijāzī, 125–169. Acre, 2004.

Aljoumani, Said. "al-Fahāris al-Makhṭūṭa lil-Maktabāt." *Turāthiyyāt* 7, no. 14 (2009): 9–75.

Aljoumani, Said. *Maktaba madrasiyya fī Ḥalab Nihāyat al-ʿAhd al-ʿUthmānī: al-Daftar al-Mujaddad li-kutub waqf ʿUthmān Bāshā al-Dūrikī*. Beirut, 2019.

Aljoumani, Said. "Quṭūʿ al-waraq al-ʿarabī: Muṣṭalaḥatuhā wa-qīyāsātuhā al-mitriyya." *Majjallat al-uṣūl* (2023): 82–111.

Aljoumani, Said and Konrad Hirschler. *Muʾallafāt Yūsuf Ibn ʿAbd al-Hādī wa-Musāhamatuhu fī Ḥifẓ al-Turāth al-Fikrī*. Leiden, 2021.

Fatḥallāh, ʿAbd al-Laṭīf. *Dīwān al-Muftī ʿAbd al-Laṭīf Fatḥallāh*. Edited by Zuhayr Fatḥallāh. Beirut, 1984.

Friedrich, Michael and Cosima Schwarke (eds). *One-volume Libraries: Composite and Multiple-text Manuscripts*. Berlin, 2016.

Ghosheh, Muḥammad Hāshim. *ʿĀʾilat ʿArafāt al-Qudwa-fī-l-Quds min khilāl al-Wathāʾiq al-ʿUthmaniyya wa-al-Makhṭūṭāt al-ʿarabiyya*. Al-Quds, 1999.

Ḥallaq, Ḥassan and ʿAbbās Ṣabbāgh. *al-Muʿjam al-jāmiʿ fī al-muṣṭalaḥāt al-ayyūbiyya wa-al-mamlūkiyya wa-al-ʿuthmāniyya*. Beirut, 1999.

Al-Ḥazmāwi, Muḥammad Mājid. "Waqfiyyat Aḥmad Pāshā al-Jazzār: Dirasa tāḥlīliyya." In *al-Awqāf fī Bilād al-Shām min al-fāth al-ʿArabī al-Islāmī ila nihāyat al-qarn al-ʿishrīn*, edited by Muḥammad ʿAdnān al-Bakhīt. Amman, 2008.

Al-Khaṭīb, Muḥammad ʿAjāj. *al-Sunna qabla al-tadwīn*. Cairo, 1988.

Muḥaybish, Ghassān. "Mujammaʿ al-Jazzār al-khayrī fī ʿAkkā." Unpublished MA thesis, al-Quds University, 1996.

Al-Murādī, Muḥammad Khalīl. *Silk al-durar fī aʿyān al-qarn al-thānī ʿashar*. Beirut: Dār al-Bashāʾir, 1988.

Shabbūḥ, Ibrāhīm. "Sijill qadīm li-jāmiʿ al-Qayrawān." *Majallat Maʿhad al-Makhṭūṭāt al-ʿarabiyya bil-Qāhira* 2, no. 2 (1956): 339–372.

CHAPTER 3

From Whom and for Whom? The Audience and Provenance of al-Jazzār's Manuscripts

Boris Liebrenz

This chapter will attempt to enter into conversation two very distinct sources in order to tackle two interwoven questions: Who reported on the library of Aḥmad Pasha al-Jazzār and its history and from where did the books that constituted this library come? These seemingly isolated questions are intricately related because the answer to the first presents a narrative that has dominated the political persona of the governor, one of deliberate brutality in the pursuit of power, while the second challenges this narrative, if only regarding the establishment of his library. In the first part, I will let contemporary European visitors speak, then turn to regional historians, who continuously retold and transformed an unstable narrative of oral reports over the past century, before interrogating in the second part the surviving manuscripts themselves. While the methodological difference that comes with these different sets of source materials creates a somewhat sharp divide in the narrative of this chapter, it thus allows for a fuller picture.

1 Visitors

When I tried to write a study on the book culture and libraries of Ottoman Syria previously, I attempted to let the books speak for themselves and put manuscript notes at the centre of my investigation.[1] Naturally, I also poured through local chronicles and biographical collections for any information on books, libraries and bibliophilia in its many forms. But sometimes, it was the reports written by European travellers during their stays in the region that proved to be the immensely rich, diverse and enlightening sources that I was looking for. They provide for us the eyes of the outside observer. That comes with problems, of course, as these visitors cannot always observe with their own eyes, might not understand what they are seeing, are not rarely misinformed or do not have direct linguistic access to the explanations necessary to put what they experienced into context. Nonetheless, they have proved indispensable and often reliable for research on Ottoman Syria. European visitors constitute not only the largest but, in fact, the only documented audience for the library of al-Jazzār in Acre, a group of people that have heard of, seen and even sometimes used the collection.

The first of these witnesses chronologically was Constantin Francois de Chasseboeuf, comte de Volney (1757–1820). The French nobleman-philosopher travelled the region between 1783 and 1785 and formed his own, very pessimistic opinions about the state of culture that he observed. The report in which he published these observations became massively influential and was often translated throughout Europe. About books and libraries in particular, he was of the opinion that there were basically none.

> There are but two libraries throughout Syria, that of Marhanna, of which I have spoken, and that of Djezzar at Acre. […] I shall not speak of the latter as an eye witness; but two persons who have seen it have assured me that it did not contain more than three hundred volumes; yet those are the spoils of all Syria, and, among others, of the Convent of St.

1 Liebrenz, *Die Rifāʿīya aus Damaskus*.

Sauveur, near Saide, and of the Shaik Kairi, Mufti of Ramla.[2]

The first half sentence does not encourage much confidence in Volney's report. The thought that there were only two libraries in all of Syria, however one would understand this term geographically and even if one were to exclude categorically all private book ownership, is blatantly absurd. And yet, if we use this text not for everything that its author apparently does not know, but that which he relates from experience, we actually find Volney playing with open cards, as he limits his report to the one library he saw himself and the other for which he had a reliable source. What strikes the reader used to a narrative tradition of absurdly inflated library sizes is the rather small number of no more than 300 volumes. If it is, thus, much more realistic than what we are used to from narrative sources in Arabic, it is also strikingly smaller than the scope of the collection as we know it from the inventory. This can, of course, easily be explained by the fact that this figure comes from very early in the history of the collection. If his two informants talked to Volney in 1783/1197 or 1784/1198, they must have seen the library before this, perhaps by some days but possibly even by some years and, therefore, before the dates that we see on most of the handwritten endowment notes on the manuscripts, where 1196 does occur several times, but 1197/1783 is most often found, while 1199/1784–1785, 1200/1785–1786 and 1205/1790–1791 are comparatively rare.[3] With this earliest notice of the library, we already see fully formed the motives of plunder and violence that would permeate any writing on al-Jazzār the politician and book collector if we can interpret the phrase 'spoils of all Syria' in this sense.

Only a little later, we encounter a second report, this one by Johan David Åkerblad (1763–1819), a learned secretary and translator in the Swedish diplomatic service in Constantinople, who travelled through Syria and Egypt and acquired some lasting fame for his role in the path towards deciphering the Egyptian hieroglyphs.[4] It is preserved in a letter written in Constantinople, which reads: 'Acre, ancient Ptolemais, is expanding ever since the famous Jezar Pasha chose it as a residence. He has had a beautiful Mosque built, a library etc. and considerably embellished the town.'[5] The Swedish scholar had already used the mosque library in 1786 and reported back on it in a letter to a patron in that year, but the text of his report is not accessible to me beyond that fact. Åkerblad's modern biographer Thomasson sums up the letter thus: 'By 4 December Åkerblad was back in Acre, where he stayed for a fortnight studying in the library of the mosque.'[6] If Thomasson's rendering of Åkerblad's words is accurate, this would be a tremendously rare occasion. Being able to take a quick look into a library room, gathering intelligence about size and contents through Muslim friends, perhaps even finding a contact able and willing to smuggle the odd book out for perusal or purchase, these were all hard enough to achieve for European visitors even in the more liberal atmosphere of Constantinople and until well into the nineteenth and twentieth centuries. Even the book markets were often not directly accessible to them. But outright studying in a mosque library is on a different level of access, a fact that will be discussed later on.

It would take another two decades for the next voice to appear on the record, that of the German

2 Volney, *Travels through Syria and Egypt*, II, 449.

3 The dates of the *waqf* notes show when the respective volumes were registered in the library, not when they entered it. It is very plausible to think of the attachment of these notes as a process that stretched out over a longer period. This is suggested by provenance clusters, such as that of the previous owner Muqbil b. Ḥasan, discussed below, whose manuscripts were registered at different times. The notes of 1196 and 1197, thus, show us a collection as it was already assembled in Acre at this point, but which could have formed over many years.

4 See Thomasson, *The Life of J.D. Åkerblad.*

5 Ibid., 77.

6 Ibid., 79.

scientific traveller Ulrich Jasper Seetzen (1767–1811). Seetzen was not a philologically trained orientalist but an engineer with some foundation in other sciences, such as medicine, yet, he had a curiosity that he applied to Arabic literature and manuscripts which, coupled with a comparatively comfortable budget for the acquisition of such artefacts, allowed him to amass one of the premier such collections in Europe for his patron, the duke of Gotha.[7] Seetzen stayed in Acre in 1806[8] and wrote the following lines in his journal:

Afterwards I visited the new mosque erected by Dschessar Pascha, located next to his Saráï. It is quite a peculiar thing that a Christian is allowed to see this mosque, something that is granted in only very few cities of the Ottoman Empire. [...] Dschessar Pascha gifted his mosque with a small library that can never be sold. Such libraries can be found within all mosques of some stature.[9]

The few lines are marked by Seetzen's sober style, unimpressed yet not arrogant. Unlike Volney, Seetzen knew that institutional libraries such as this could be found in many other places as well, even when he could usually not set foot in them. Still, the description of al-Jazzār's library as small is probably irritating in light of the considerable size of this collection in its regional context and given that by the time he saw it, its growth had already stopped. Did he perhaps not see the whole of it? In my opinion, it is more likely that Seetzen's perception was guided by the fact that his frame of reference was not other mosque libraries (which he could barely have seen) but the European institutional libraries with which he was familiar, such as that of his university in Göttingen. Libraries in the places he visited in Europe at the time were already often prestigious places housed in sumptuous buildings. A small room within a mosque complex filled with some 1,500 volumes could conceivably have seemed small to Seetzen in comparison.

Charles Lewis Meryon (1783–1877) travelled as a physician in the entourage of Lady Hester Stanhope (1776–1839). The courageous and eccentric noblewoman, who spent roughly three decades of her life until her death in the region, occupies a unique space in the history of Western traveling in the Middle East. Not only was she one of the few women to journey and leave a report at the time, the erroneous perception of her as a princess from the British royal family also opened many doors for her, forged friendships with many of the powerful men of the area, and allowed her a conduct that was usually not even allowed for male Europeans, such as riding on horseback. Meryon describes Acre and al-Jazzār's mosque thus in his account of their travels in 1812: 'It has a liberal endowment, and professors of theology have their share in it. It has, besides, a most splendid library, collected by El Gezzàr.'[10] Meryon also published a letter of his employer, Lady Hester, in which she describes to him a visit to al-Jazzār's mosque in 1812 while he was absent from the city: 'I was even admitted', she writes, 'into the library of the famous mosque and fumbled over the books at pleasure—books that no Christian dare to touch, or even cast his eyes upon'.[11] As we have seen, entry into and even use of the books was not as exclusively restricted as Lady Hester flatters herself. But her peculiar status probably could have helped to give her the freedom to 'fumble over the books at pleasure' that is not usually granted to any user in the institutional libraries of the region, not even those scholars and students for whom they were nominally endowed.

7 On the collection see Stein, *Orientalische Buchkunst in Gotha*; Krimsti, "Von Aleppo nach Gotha".
8 An original letter of his written in Acre and describing his stay there is preserved in Uppsala, but it is silent on the library; Uppsala University Library, Erik Wallers autografsamling, Waller Ms de-05342.
9 Seetzen, *Reisen durch Syrien*, II, 82–83.

10 [Meryon], *Travels of Lady Hester Stanhope*, I, 262.
11 Ibid., II, 35.

Those are the five reports I could identify mentioning al-Jazzār's library, written by writers of different backgrounds within 30 years of each other between 1783 and 1812. Their value lies, I would argue, not so much in what their authors have to say (in reality, the texts do not offer spectacular new insights into the history and development of al-Jazzār's library), but in the fact that they could have been written at all. Damascus, Jerusalem, Cairo or Aleppo have seen a far greater number of visitors who dwelled there for much longer periods. The descriptions of these places over the centuries fill volumes, whereas Acre was of very modest interest for European travellers in comparison, at least those among them with learned interests who wrote up their experiences in travelogues and journals. All of these cities also had a much larger number of institutional and private libraries. And yet, no other library of the region has been mentioned and described so often in such a compressed time frame. What was it about this place that allowed such an access to happen?

2 The Demography and Scholarly Life of Acre

One part of the answer could be sought in the demography of the city that gave it a very different atmosphere from some of the major centres of learning and bibliophilia in the region, such as Damascus, Aleppo or Jerusalem. Unlike those places, Acre had a majority of Christian inhabitants until the turn of the nineteenth century, when the number of Muslims was slowly beginning to rise.[12] The travellers are very outspoken about this fact. Domingo Badía y Leblich (1767–1818), who travelled and published under the pseudonym ʿAlī Bey b. ʿUthmān Bey al-ʿAbbāsī, described Acre during his stay there in 1807, just after Seetzen had left: 'Europeans enjoy an extreme liberty, and a great degree of respect at Acre, as well on the part of the government as on that of the people, who are a mixture of Turks and Arabs'.[13] Interestingly, he also gave a detailed description of al-Jazzār's mosque, from its architecture to the antelopes grazing in its garden, however, he failed to mention any library or books. Louis Nicolas Auguste, the comte de Forbin (1777–1841), is also surprised to be able to explore the city in 1817. The French painter, ironically a former member of the court of Napoleon's sister, can even make drawings of its main attractions in 'the greatest tranquillity (*la tranquilité la plus profonde*)': 'Never did the slightest insult, the faintest threat, follow the curiosity that we inspired when we traversed the bezestans (*Jamais la plus petite insulte, la moindre menace, ne suivirent le mouvement de curiosité que nous inspirions en parcourant les bezestans*).'[14] These experiences resonate with Seetzen's observation that entering a mosque, like he could do here, was forbidden in most other cities.

Beyond the testimony of European travellers, there are a number of contemporary Arabic letters that show Christian merchants whose centres of operation were in Jerusalem, Damascus and on the Egyptian coast frequented Acre in the years of al-Jazzār's reign.[15] One of the younger family members is sent to the city to apprentice with a European physician, something that could not be done in many other places in Syria.[16] This fact points to another peculiarity of the city's demography,

12 Philipp, *Acre*, 23.

13 Ali Bey (= Domingo Badía y Leblich). *Travels of Ali Bey*, II, 287.

14 De Forbin, *Voyage dans le Levant*, 74. The results of his work can be seen in the folio atlas volume of the travelogue's first edition and are accessible on https://eng.travelogues.gr/collection.php?view=517.

15 Liebrenz, *Arab Traders in Their Own Words*, 44–45.

16 The doctor was the Neapolitan Adamo Monghelly, see Seetzen, *Reisen*, II, 103–104, 108, 131; Liebrenz, *Arab Traders*, 530–539. Another European doctor, the French surgeon Chaboçeau/Chabacon, was present for many decades in Damascus, but nothing is known about his taking apprentices and he is said to have been the only European living permanently in the city apart from the Spanish monks of the Franciscan monastery; see Liebrenz, "The Social History of Surgery".

namely, the strong presence of a European merchant community. As al-Jazzār tried to reorient the economy of his province towards the production of cash-crops for export to Europe, he also wanted to establish his favoured city and its harbour as a centre for these mercantile networks. Consequently, it was certainly favourable for those with an interest in access to these cash-crops to be present close to the governor, even though this fact alone does not explain why social interactions were apparently more relaxed than in previous centres of European commercial presence, such as Aleppo in the seventeenth century. While the public perception of al-Jazzār is dominated by his successful antagonism towards the French army under Napoleon Bonaparte, the governor had a real interest in keeping European economic actors, among them those from France, in his city placated and comfortable.

What can we say about scholarly life in Acre? Seetzen was able to observe a teaching session in the mosque that housed the library, but had no information to give on its participants or contents. Biographical dictionaries of the time, written in the large centres of scholarship, mainly Damascus, Aleppo and Jerusalem, were very myopic when it came to the peripheries of their scholarly world, which is evidently where we have to place Acre. The city and its newly founded institutions of learning and devotion are not mentioned as the place where anyone studied, taught or lived. The vast biographical compendium *Silk al-durar* by the Damascene scholar Muḥammad Khalīl al-Murādī registers a meagre two biographees with connections to Acre. The first is ʿAbd al-Ḥalīm b. ʿAbd Allāh al-Shāfiʿī al-Nābulusī, who grew up around Jerusalem, studied at the Azhar in Egypt, then died in the city in 1185/1771–1772, after having taught there for years during the reign of Ẓāhir al-ʿUmar.[17] There is not much more to say about the second, one Aḥmad b. Bakr Baṭḥīshī al-ʿAkkī al-Ḥanafī (born in 1095/1684), other than that he was mufti of the city.[18] Unfortunately, Murādī's successors in Damascus in the nineteenth century, al-Shaṭṭī and al-Bayṭār, had a much stricter focus on their home town. The scholars who could have profited from the positions created in al-Jazzār's endowment, of whom Seetzen and Meryon both speak in general terms, and who would have been entered in a collection of biographies of the nineteenth century, are invisible to us because no comparable literature has been written in or survived from Acre in this period.

Manuscript notes have very little to add to the picture. We do know of occasional books that were copied in Acre or belonged to people from that city. However, apart from its small overall size, not many volumes from this corpus can be securely placed in Acre during the time of al-Jazzār as opposed to thousands from other centres, such as Cairo or Damascus. One of the very few, a volume today found in Beirut (AUB, MS 610 I131maA), was copied in the city in 1788 by a Christian doctor, Rustam walad Sulaymān known as Ṣawān. The profile of the copyists and owners of these volumes is distinctly Christian and occasional connections to the nearby Monastery of St Savior (Dayr al-Mukhalliṣ) in Ṣaydā are apparent, such as with a copy of the *Dīwān* of Niqūlā al-Ṣāyigh that was copied by a monk from that monastery, albeit in Alexandria in 1797, but was bought in Acre in 1816 (MS Tübingen, MA VI 47). Overall, the material we have does not speak to any discernible book culture in the city before the nineteenth century.

This assessment leads to two fundamental questions. The first is: Why would one want to build up a major library in Acre? This could be explained, infusing the explanation of historical processes with the usual ingredients of speculative psychological interpretation, as the intention to create from scratch rather than serve an existing scholarly environment. Al-Jazzār's power in Acre was relatively stable, while his reach to Damascus was feeble. Had he erected an institution in his name there,

17 Al-Murādī, *Silk*, II, 256–260.

18 Ibid., I, 151–153.

it would have been one among many and also exposed to the envy of rivalling strongmen. The second, more fundamental question is: How to build up a major library in Acre? After all, there were, according to both narrative sources and the manuscript record, probably no large private libraries available in the city and there could not have been but a very small book market. This state of affairs lends credence to sources that have previously been employed[19] to highlight the broad historical development of the Nūr Aḥmadiyya and which stress forceful translocations of whole libraries to Acre from outside the city.

3 Provenance: The Making of the Library

This small number of regional narrative sources, based presumably on oral accounts usually far removed in time from the events or, in other words, rumours, does, nonetheless, offer some hints that we need to investigate seriously.

There is a strong tradition that ascribes the growth of Acre's mosque library to its founder's looting sprees within the region, particularly the Lebanese coast and the mountains of the Jabal ʿĀmil. As can be seen above, Volney had already been exposed to these accounts and used them when he described the library's make-up as one of spoils, specifying the latter to be "of the Convent of St. Sauveur, near Saide, and of the Shaik Kairi, Mufti of Ramla".[20] The first source he names is the monastery called Dayr al-Mukhalliṣ close to Ṣaydā, a convent of the Basilian order of the Greek-Catholic church. We do not know much of the library of this institution, which, at the time, was not yet eighty years old and might not be expected to have amassed a large stock of books grown over centuries. There are occasional finds in the manuscript collections I could survey that point to this early phase in the eighteenth century: In 1740, Ḥannā Warde endowed MS Paris, BnF Arabe 6165, a copy made by the famous Maronite bishop and grammarian Jabrīl Farḥāt (Germanos Farhat, 1670–1732), to the Basilian monks of Dayr al-Mukhalliṣ. Whatever al-Jazzār did to the convent's library, such stock-building activities are also documented under his reign. The monk Samʿān al-Ṣabbāgh owned MS Paris, BnF 5782 and donated Beirut, AUB MS 349.1767 S564kA, which he had bought in Damascus, to the monastery in 1800. The monastery and some of its monks who copied manuscripts in other places[21] have, thus, left a small but discernible mark on the book culture of the region. However, most of the books I can connect to Dayr al-Mukhalliṣ were produced or came there later in the nineteenth century,[22] long after al-Jazzār was said to have taken the convent's books for his own foundation. And none of the earlier specimens bear any sign of having at any point been in the Nūr Aḥmadiyya in Acre.

Volney's second concrete piece of evidence, 'Kairi, the Mufti of Ramla', should be understood as the Frenchman's clumsy rendition of a man from the al-Khayrī family. The fact that the traveller Muṣṭafā al-Bakrī (d. 1162/1749)[23] visited al-Ramla in 1148/1736 and lodged with the town's mufti Muḥammad al-Khayrī[24] lends credibility to this identification and suggests that either this man was the one whose library was allegedly seized by al-Jazzār or that this family held the post of mufti for several generations, which is not uncommon. I could find only two volumes that once belonged

19 See Liebrenz, *Die Rifāʿīya*, 159–162.

20 Volney, *Travels through Syria and Egypt*, II, 449.

21 The volume MS Tübingen, MA VI 47 was copied in 1797 by Mīkhāʾīl Ḥamawī, a monk in the Dayr al-Mukhalliṣ monastery, but in Iskandarīya. By 1816, it was found in Acre, where it was purchased by another Christian.

22 Dayr al-Mukhalliṣ and its library had a hard time building up its stock undisturbed. In 1860, it was thoroughly looted again, this time by local Druze in the context of the massacres against Christians in 1860; see Liebrenz, "From Leipzig to Damascus", 337–338.

23 Elger, *Muṣṭafā al-Bakrī*.

24 Al-Bakrī, "Riḥla ilā Diyār al-Rūm" (I used the text as available via https://shamela.ws/book/29674/60939#p1). I owe this reference to Ahmed El Shamsy.

to one Muḥammad Khayrī (MS Paris, BnF Arabe 5942; MS Vienna, ÖNB N.F. 185), who could conceivably be this man. Again, no signs of al-Jazzār's library (like the destruction of a large seal, a long endowment note or the secondary endowment statements throughout the book) can be found on the manuscripts owned by anyone from the al-Khayrī family, nor are men of this name found on the volumes so far identified from the Jazzār manuscript corpus. Volney's report has even been cited by Kāmil al-ʿAsalī to show that the library of the great legal scholar Khayr al-Dīn al-Ramlī (993/1585–1081/1670) was integrated into the Nūr Aḥmadiyya.[25] This point is most unlikely. While Khayr al-Dīn was probably a forefather and namesake to the mufti mentioned by al-Bakrī and Volney, the famous scholar lived many generations before the creation of the Jazzār library and the continued existence of his book collection is not to be expected, as such private collections generally dissolved pretty quickly after their owner's death and even endowed libraries often did not fare much better. Furthermore, we can actually identify many of Khayr al-Dīn al-Ramlī's books in other libraries well before they were allegedly taken by al-Jazzār, yet, none so far in the Nūr Aḥmadiyya itself.

Finally, there are the reports of violent clashes between the Shiite families of the Jabal ʿĀmil region in Lebanon and al Jazzār in which enormous numbers of books are said to have fallen prey to the governor and been transported back to his residence in Acre. These reports were written down long after the fact, more than a century as far as I can tell, and presumably transmitted as family lore and stories of regional and communal resistance. The most pertinent and, in terms of usable information for our purposes, most detailed among them, see al-Jazzār facing off in battle against a coalition of Shiite families in a place called variably either Yārūn, Bārūn or Mārūn.[26] The sources disagree about the date of that battle to no small degree, placing it either in 1195/1781 or 1209/1794–1795. After a resounding victory, the rich libraries of his foes were allegedly sacked by the governor. The library of Mahdī al-Khātūn from one of the foremost families of the Jabal ʿĀmil, which alone supposedly numbered more than 4,000 volumes, was named as the richest among them, though only one of many.[27] In light of the size of eminent libraries even in the greatest urban centres of the Ottoman Empire, this number is no more than pure fantasy.[28] And yet, the specificity of the charge with a concrete name applied to the collection makes it a promising target to investigate. I have found very few traces of the Khātūn family in the manuscripts I have seen: Firstly, one Muḥammad b. ʿAlī al-shahīr bi-Ibn Khātūn al-ʿĀmilī owned two books in the first half of the seventeenth century (those are Leiden Or. 1323 in 1019/1610–1611 and Leiden Or. 1317 in 1034/1624–1625); then, ʿAlī b. Ḥasan b. ʿAlī al-Khātūnī or al-shahīr bi-Ibn Khātūn is attested more than a century later, close to the period of al-Jazzār's rule (he owned MS Damascus,

25 Al-ʿAsalī, "Al-Maktabāt al-filisṭīnīya", 289.

26 Ẓāhir, "Ṣilat al-ʿilm", has Bārūn, which I could not identify, in this early piece; then, several decades later, the same author writes of Yārūn ("Wathāʾiq"), which is a village in the south of Lebanon very close to the modern border with Israel and also to Acre itself. However, Āl Ṣafā, *Tārīkh Jabal ʿĀmil*, 239, names the village Mārūn in the South of Lebanon, which can probably be identified with the modern village Mārūn al-Raʾs.

27 Ẓāhir, "Ṣilat al-ʿilm"; Āl Ṣafā, *Tārīkh Jabal ʿĀmil*, 239 (I owe this reference to Said Aljoumani); Dī Ṭarrāzī, *Khazāʾin al-kutub fī al-khāfiqayn*, III, 1033. Dī Ṭarrāzī (1865–1956) names the oral account of Aḥmad ʿĀrif al-Zayn, owner of the journal *al-ʿIrfān*, a man who lived several generations after the events, as his source. Al-Zayn himself might have relayed orally the gist of the article by Aḥmad Riḍā, "Al-Matāwila aw al-shīʿa fī Jabal ʿĀmil", published in his journal, in which the author also talks about the libraries of the al-Khātūn family, but does not single out Mahdī Khātūn.

28 Where we know of the actual size of libraries, whether through concrete documentary evidence or the continued existence of endowed collections, most of all in Istanbul, the numbers are usually well below 4,000. The size of great libraries in classical narrative sources was usually expressed by not only inflated but also highly symbolic numbers, based most of all on 4 and 7, which, in this case, makes the number 4,000 additionally suspicious; see Hirschler, *The Written Word*, 128–129.

al-Majmaʿ al-ʿIlmī 140 in 1160/1650).[29] But, so far, no man of this name has turned up in the Jazzār manuscript corpus.

Other of the reputedly many ʿĀmilī libraries are equally hard to find in Acre. One of Jazzār's books now in the Azhar Library bears an undated ownership note of one Ḥasan ʿAlī Ḥalāwī al-Faqʿānī *nasaban* al-ʿĀmilī *mawlidan wa-mawṭinan* (MS Azhar 91135). Al-Jazzār endowed this book in 1197 and we do not know whether the man who, according to his own testimony was born and lived in the Jabal ʿĀmil, owned it prior to al-Jazzār or after it had left the Nūr Aḥmadiyya. This is different for MS Jaffa 52,[30] which was owned by Abī al-Ḥasan Mūsā b. Ḥaydar al-Ḥusaynī (d. 1194/1780), an eminent Shiite scholar who taught in the thriving *madrasa* in Shaqrāʾ in the Jabal ʿĀmil, where he also died.[31] It is, of course, tempting to posit a connection between this man's book turning up in the Nūr Aḥmadiyya and the battle of Yārūn/Mārūn in 1195/1780, especially since the biographer Muḥammad Jābir Āl Ṣafā (1870–1945) positions al-Ḥusaynī's death in the same year and talks about the battle on the same page of his account. Other sources, however, convincingly date al-Ḥusaynī's death to Muḥarram of 1194/January 1780,[32] long before these clashes. It is not reported that al-Jazzār took possession of al-Ḥusaynī's books, but the sources do speak of him transporting building material, such as marble, from the scholar's tomb, which the political leader of the region's Shiites, Nāṣīf al-Naṣṣār, had ordered to be built but had not yet been completed when al-Naṣṣār was defeated by al-Jazzār and lost his life in 1195/1780. On that occasion, the governor could also have ordered the transport of whatever books were still available at the grave and *madrasa* of al-Ḥusaynī in Shaqrāʾ. Be that as it may, two possible previous owners with a definitive connection to the Jabal ʿĀmil in our Jazzār manuscript corpus is not a whole lot since people with the *nisba* al-ʿĀmilī or biographical connections to these areas can of course be found in many other collections as well. But it shows, at least, that the Lebanese Mountains as a provenance are indeed generally, if rarely, attested in al-Jazzār's books.

Next to the mythical number of 4,000 volumes given for Mahdī al-Khātūn's library, the report also offers a handy explanation for why the books cannot be found today: So great was the volume of the papery loot, we are told, that, after only a small number from among them had been chosen for the Nūr Aḥmadīya, the rest kept Acre's ovens running for several days or even a week.[33] The efficacy of books as fuel is very questionable to begin with, but the claim that looted libraries kept baths and bakeries warm for long stretches of time is simply a worn trope.[34] Assuming that numbers large enough to keep them burning for a long time even existed, transporting such numbers through the mountains to Acre would probably have consumed more resources than whatever use a bit of paper could have served in this capacity. It might

29 There is also a whole collection, endowed by one Muḥammad Ibn Khātūn al-ʿĀmilī in the seventeenth century in Mashhad, that is currently being investigated by Fatima al-Bazzal in the context of the *Bibliotheca Arabica* project at the *Saxon Academy of Sciences and Humanities* in Leipzig. But this collection is an Iranian one and had never been in Lebanon.

30 Due to its lively history, this has now become MS Jerusalem (Abu Dis), The Center for Heritage Revival and Islamic Research, 301/2 (see ʿAfāna et al., *Fihris makhṭūṭāt Filasṭīn al-muṣawwara*, v, 72; formerly Jaffa: MS 52).

31 Āl Ṣafā, *Tārīkh Jabal ʿĀmil*, 239 (Thanks to Said Aljoumani for this reference).

32 Al-Amīn, *Aʿyān al-Shīʿa*, x, 182. Contemporary chronograms are among the convincing sources for a death date in 1194 cited here.

33 Āl Ṣafā, *Tārīkh Jabal ʿĀmil*, 239, does not mention a specific time frame but states generally that after the battle of Mārūn, 'the libraries were pillaged and most of it burned in the ovens of ʿAkkā'. Again, the author writes without sources more than a century after the events (he lived 1870–1945).

34 On books and fires, see Al-Ḥazīmī, *Ḥaraq al-kutub fī al-turāth al-ʿArabī*. For further accounts of bookburning, see Mez, *Die Renaissance des Islâms*, 167; Bergé, "Justification d'un autodafé des livres"; Rosenthal, "'Of Making Many Books There is No End'," 39, 51; Morris, "An Arab Macchiavelli?".

be that these stories grew out of the real experience of violence, experiences that conceivably could have included fires. The biographies of Shiite scholars of the Jabal ʿĀmil region contain accounts of the burning of whole libraries as a means of cultural destruction more than a part of looting. In one such account, the eminent scholar Zayn b. Khalīl al-ʿĀmilī was killed in 1211/1796–1797 in the village of Tibnīn close to Ṣūr (Tyre) by al-Jazzār, who then proceeded to burn not only the scholar's corpse but also his library of allegedly more than 3,000 volumes.[35] Again, the number is far removed from the realm of credibility. In the biography of Muḥammad b. Ḥasan b. ʿAlī Āl Shukr al-ʿĀmilī, on the other hand, al-Jazzār's killing of this scholar in 1207/1792–1793 and the confiscation of his library resulted in the burning of only some of the books, namely, those that were 'in conflict with his creed' (*mā kāna yukhālif madhhabahu*), while the rest were incorporated into the Nūr Aḥmadiyya.[36] If, however, the book-burning was part of a sorting process, it is hard to imagine that the library of a Shiite scholar would have contained too much that would have been utterly unacceptable to the Sunni readers of the region. As the *Introduction* to this volume points out, even a work of one of the aforementioned Shiite victims of al-Jazzār found a place in the Nūr Aḥmadiyya. Other works of Shīʿī authors, such as Bahāʾ al Dīn al ʿĀmilī's (953/1546–1031/1622) *Zubdat al-uṣūl* (Cairo, Azhar MS 91135) and Muḥammad b. ʿAlī Aʿtham al-Kūfī's (d. ca. 314/926) report on the early Islamic conquests (*al-Futūḥ*, MS Dublin, CBL Ar 3272), are similarly attested in al-Jazzār's own library. As we find more Shīʿī literature in the Chapters by Garrett Davidson (15), Ahmed El Shamsy (16), Dana Sajdi (22) and Walid Saleh (13), we may ask whether the numbers encountered there are significantly larger than one would expect in the region or the Ottoman context as a whole and, thus, point to different sources either by sheer proximity or through violence, but it is certainly clear that, just like they could be encountered in other libraries of the region, these works were not ostracised in al-Jazzār's collection either. What is not attested in the corpus of surviving Jazzār manuscripts are the families whose libraries the sources see vanishing into the Nūr Aḥmadiyya.

The number of accounts that speak of book-looting and the many different libraries that are described as being burned either in situ or after having been transported to Acre makes it very hard to dismiss them. If half a dozen Mamluk historians had told us about a certain event from different angles with fluctuating actors and numbers, we would probably deem those accounts basically true and chisel away at the discrepancies between them. Recent scholarship on the Shiites of Lebanon has reproduced these accounts of burnt libraries and al-Jazzār's role in their destruction, even when they diagnosed exaggerations in them.[37] And yet, there are serious considerations for why these stories could be entirely fabricated. The first is that they were put to paper very late and we do not find any such stories in the contemporary chronicles. The earliest could be the article "al-Matāwila" on the Shiites in the Jabal ʿĀmil in the journal *al-ʿIrfān*, published in 1910.[38] By 1929, the Shiite intellectual Sulaymān Ẓāhir repeated it in his article on the intellectual connections between Damascus and the Jabal ʿĀmil.[39] Muḥammad Jābir Āl Ṣafāʾ in his *Tārīkh Jabal ʿĀmil*, although published only posthumously, must have

35 Al-Amīnī al-Najafī, *Shuhadāʾ al-faḍīla*, 274. The first edition of this book appeared in 1936 in Najaf.

36 Ibid., 272.

37 Jaber, "Pouvoir et société au Jabal Amil," I, 53; Winter, *The Shiites of Lebanon*, 139. Most recently, Fatima Al-Bazzal, who researches the libraries of Jabal ʿĀmil, repeated the story on the research blog of the Orient Institut Beirut (https://oib.hypotheses.org/1420), stating: 'According to a popular narrative distributed among the people of Jabal Amil Region, today's Southern Lebanon, Ahmad Pasha al-Jazzar, the Ottoman governor of Acre confiscated all the Amili manuscripts and ordered them to be burned in the incinerators of Acre. These incinerators kept ignited for days.'

38 Riḍā, "Al-Matāwila".

39 Ẓāhir, "Ṣilat al-ʿilm".

been writing around this time as well, as he lived from 1870 to 1945. ʿAbd al-Ḥusayn al-Amīnī, in his 1936 book *Shuhadāʾ al-faḍīla*, speaks of concrete libraries but without sources.[40] Fīlīb Dī Ṭarrāzī (Philippe de Tarrazi), who included a small section on al-Jazzār's raids and his burning of Shiite libraries in his sweeping history of libraries in the Arab world that appeared between 1947 and 1951, gives the editor of *al-ʿIrfān* as his source, that is not Aḥmad Riḍā's article published in the journal but an oral report that consequently deviates slightly from the written text.[41] It was again Sulaymān Ẓāhir who published a contemporary document in 1950, but his remarks on the burning of books in Acre's ovens is found in his own commentary to that document and is again not referenced with any source.[42] The internal discrepancies of these reports make it likely that they were not copies of each other but that such stories circulated orally, were retold, grew and transformed over the century since the events they portrayed and even after they were first published. This is why we find discrepancies in the time through which the ovens of Acre purportedly burnt on these books, ranging from three days to a week or just a long time; the date of the battle that led to the loss of these libraries either in 1195/1780 or 1197/1782 or 1209/1794; the name of the place where it was fought either in Yārūn[43] or Bārūn or Mārūn; or the owners of those libraries themselves. In Riḍā's account in 1910, the library of the Khātūn family contained 5,000 volumes, was burned in Acre, and a particular battle or date was not specified.[44] Then, talking of the many libraries of the region that were confiscated, the "ovens of Acre" are said to have been fuelled by them 'for an entire week' (*usbūʿan kāmilan*).[45] The story as told by the journal's editor, Aḥmad ʿĀrif al-Zayn, to Fīlīb Dī Ṭarrāzī was that the confiscation happened in 1209/1794, Mahdī al-Khātūn's books numbered 4,000 and those al-Jazzār did not include in his library fired up Acre's ovens for three days.[46] Other writers, such as Āl Ṣafāʾ in the early twentieth century and Sulaymān Ẓāhir in 1950, who dates the burning to 1195, do not specify the time that Acre's ovens stayed burning on books.[47] Many speakers at a recent conference on the Jabal ʿĀmil during al-Jazzār's reign, conducted in 2014, refer to the plundering and Acre's ovens as a historical fact.[48] One of the more embellished retellings assures us that the books of the region were transported on camel-back to Acre, where they were distributed to the ovens, while some were kept and others gifted to dignitaries and sultans. Others, however, were stolen by the people of Acre and resold to the ʿĀmilīs who had just lost them.[49] Another contribution has the libraries of Jabal ʿĀmil burn in Acre's ovens for a whole week again, 'according to some narrators and historians' (*ʿalā mā yaqūlu baʿḍ al-ruwāt wa-al-muʾarrikhīn*).[50] It is easy to see these stories, apart from the thorny question of their veracity, as building blocks of a shared mythology of suffering, as a means for communal identity-building and, at the same time, a handy explanation for the fact that the many incredibly large libraries that had reportedly been collected in the Jabal ʿĀmil regions were, in fact, nowhere to be found.

These incendiary stories are generally, thus, widely accepted. But they are not corroborated in the surviving manuscript corpus. If we take what surviving manuscripts we have discovered so far as a representative sample, then, at least, the foundational nature of these violent lootings for al-

40 Al-Amīnī al-Najafī, *Shuhadāʾ al-faḍīla*, 272, 274.

41 Dī Ṭarrāzī, *Khazāʾin al-kutub fī al-khāfiqayn*, III, 1033.

42 Ẓāhir, "Wathāʾiq".

43 This name in Ẓāhir, "Wathāʾiq"; Al-Zayn, *Fuṣūl min tārīkh al-shīʿa*.

44 Riḍā, "Al-Matāwila".

45 Riḍā. "Al-Matāwila".

46 Dī Ṭarrāzī, *Khazāʾin al-kutub fī al-khāfiqayn*, III, 1033.

47 Āl Ṣafāʾ, *Tārīkh Jabal ʿĀmil*, 239; Ẓāhir, "Wathāʾiq".

48 *Jabal ʿĀmil wa-ʿahd al-Jazzār*.

49 Raʿd, "Kalimat rāʿī al-muʾtamar," 14.

50 Al-Zayn, "Al-ʿAwāmil". The same facts are presented again in Bizzī, "Al-Khasāʾir," here with the interesting addition that the stories are relayed by "old people from the region" who tell them "from the mouth of their fathers and grandfathers."

Jazzār's library needs to be questioned. Still, being mindful of the maxim that an absence of evidence is not an evidence of absence, we could not rule out the possibility that these stories of looting and translocation hold a kernel of truth.

What evidence we find instead, though, points us in other directions. Another rumour, written down much closer to the time in which it was said to have occurred, sets us on the right path. It reports of an incident that did not end a library but, curiously, rather led to the opening of one. Al-Jazzār's role in it, however, is no less tyrannical. The tragic hero of the story is Aḥmad al-Rabbāṭ (d. about 1254/1838),[51] a poet and himself a successful storyteller who sometime at the end of the eighteenth century, probably by 1202/1799, had migrated from Aleppo to Damascus. After his death, the Prussian consul in the city, Johann Gottfried Wetzstein (1815–1905), would buy a great number of books from his locally famous library that al-Rabbāṭ had used as a business by lending them out for money. But it had not always been this way. As Wetzstein was told, the young al-Rabbāṭ was brought out of a "considerable fortune" (*bedeutenden Vermögens*) by the governor al-Jazzār in an unspecified way. As he was, thus, reduced to poverty and wondered how to feed his family, he fell back on his books and decided to establish the lending library with them.[52] Notably, in this anecdote, the rapacious governor did not take away any of those books (so we are not looking for Aḥmad al-Rabbāṭ in the Jazzār manuscript corpus) but presumably everything else. Yet, it shows the reach of his demand and the appeal of a city that was also Syria's main centre of books.

Indeed, this is reflected in the prominent place of Damascus in the history of the books we have been so far able to identify and which emerges from an analysis of their manuscript notes. Judging by these notes, the city seems to have been a major source for the Jazzār library well before he attained the power of governor there. He was first appointed to the post only in 1199/1785. By contrast, many of the handwritten endowment notes that are dated to 1196 and 1197—that is, the absolute majority of all endowment dates found so far—are on books that clearly came from Damascus. There are no less than three volumes formerly in the possession of Taqī al-Dīn al-Ḥiṣnī al-Ḥusaynī (1053/1643–1129/1717),[53] two of them with a short form of al-Jazzār's endowment note dated 1197 (Khalidi Library MS 1125; MS Berlin, Landberg 9), yet one (MS London, BL or. 4706) with a long form note dated only in 1199. There are also at least two volumes with ownership notes by ʿAbd al-Raḥmān al-ʿImādī:[54] MS Dublin, CBL Ar 3342, part of Abū Ḥayyān al-Andalusī's (654/1256–745/1344) massive work of philology *al-Tadhyīl wa-al-takmīl fī sharḥ Kitāb al-Tashīl*, was owned by him in 1173/1759–1760 and then endowed to the Nūr Aḥmadiyya already in 1196. This volume has a longer and continuous Damascene history, having been in the possession, firstly, of Ḥasan b. al-Muzallaq al-Anṣārī al-Shāfiʿī (d. 965/1557–1558),[55] then of a man whose last name, al-ʿAkkārī, can still be read and to whom ʿAbd al-Raḥmān al-ʿImādī relates himself as his great-grandson. The other volume from al-ʿImādī's books is MS London, BL or. 1206, a copy of *Dīwān Jarīr* in Maghribi script. This one bears an endowment statement dated in 1197, but also again the destroyed ownership note of

51 See Liebrenz, "The Library of Aḥmad al-Rabbāṭ"; Liebrenz, *Die Rifāʿīya*, 228–235; Akel, "Ahmad al-Rabbât al-Halabî".

52 Wetzstein, *Bruchstück eines wissenschaftl. Katalogs*, 113–114; see Liebrenz, *Die Rifāʿīya*, 228.

53 Ibn Kannān, *Al-Ḥawādith al-yawmīya*, 277; Murādī, *Silk*, II, 6–7; al-Ziriklī, *Al-Aʿlām*, II, 86.

54 He is probably not the ʿAbd al-Raḥmān b. ʿAlī b. ʿAbd al-Raḥmān b. ʿAlī al-ʿImādī al-Ḥanafī who died in 1223 as mentioned by al-Shaṭṭī, *Aʿyān Dimashq*, 167.

55 The note is not visible to the naked eye and only appeared on a photograph taken by Claudia Collini and Kyle Ann Huskin with infrared reflectography. Even then, the central part with the owner's name is scratched out beyond the overall destruction and only identified by me because of the very peculiar handwriting of Ibn al-Muzallaq. On his biography, see Al-Būrīnī, *Tarājim al-aʿyān*, II, 68; Al-Ghazzī, *Al-Kawākib al-sāʾira*, II, 137, no. 944.

al-ʿImādī's great-grandfather al-ʿAkkārī. Al-ʿImādī's ownership notes in both cases are destroyed, but that is usually the case on volumes that did not end up in the Jazzār library, therefore, this destruction should not be misinterpreted as a sign of unlawful transactions. The interesting thing about these two purchases is that the books' owner was apparently still alive when they were endowed in Acre, as some of his ownership marks elsewhere are dated as late as 1200.[56]

MS Princeton, Garrett 3415Y, a volume of Ibn Khallikān's biographical dictionary *Wafayāt al-aʿyān*, was copied in 1165/1752 by Darwīsh Muḥammad, a grandson of the former Governor of Damascus, Ḥasan Shūrbaza Pasha, then in 1172/1758–1759 passed to Muṣṭafā b. ʿAlī efendī al-Ḥamawī, a former *daftardār* of Damascus and, at that time, *aghā* of the local Janissary unit there. A copy of ʿAbd al-Ghanī al-Nābulusī's (1050/1641–1143/1731) *Dīwān* (MS Rawḍat Khayrī 1094) was produced at the beginning of the twelfth/eighteenth century by his servant, the Damascene scholar Muḥammad b. Ibrāhīm al-Dakdakjī (1080/1669-70-1131/1719). Another volume probably from Damascus is MS Dublin, CBL Ar 3294. Although this commentary on a famous biography of the prophet Muḥammad was produced in 731/1331 in northern Syria for a judge of al-Fūʿa and Maʿarrat Miṣrīn, in the sixteenth century we find it among the books of the Damascene scholar ʿAbd al-Bāsiṭ b. Mūsā al-ʿAlmawī (907/1502–981/1573).[57] Furthermore, MS Jerusalem, Khalidi 700 was probably produced in Damascus in 808/1405[58] and still found there at the end of the sixteenth century when it was owned by Abū Bakr b. Aḥmad al-Akhnāʾī (d. 1030/1620–1621), a notary witness (*aḥad al-shuhūd*) at al-Kubrā court.[59] Finally, MS Beirut, USJ, BO 214 comes from the library of the great Damascene bibliophile Sulaymān b. Aḥmad al-Maḥāsinī (1139/1726-27-1189/1775),[60] who dated his ownership to 1175/1761–1762.

The volume MS Cairo, Azhar 83318 might have been found closer to its new home in Acre: It was copied by Muḥammad b. Ḥammād *al-shahīr bi-*Ibn Maʿn, whose name lets one think about the Druze Maʿn family that ruled large parts of the Lebanese mountains in the sixteenth and seventeenth centuries.

Jerusalem was the closest major centre of libraries to Acre. But the city appears very few times in comparison with Damascus. We could point to MS London, BL or. 1183, that was owned by ʿAbd al-Raḥmān b. Sulaymān al-Ḥusaynī al-Jaʿfarī al-Ḥanbalī, who was an imam at the Aqṣā Mosque, in 1079/1668–1669. MS Princeton, Garrett 3959Y was copied by a man from Jerusalem (Muḥammad al-Maqdisī *waṭanan*) in 1090/1679, but was then immediately in the hands of owners from Damascus.

Another surprisingly strong subset of books came to Acre from much farther away: Istanbul. Though surprising only in light of the picture the narrative sources had painted. In fact, it should only be expected that the great book market of the Ottoman capital, which attracted books from all over its vast domains, was also a source for the empire's regional libraries. The title page of a volume of Walī al-Dīn al-ʿIrāqī's (d. 826/1433) *ḥadīth* work *al-Bayān wa-al-tawḍīḥ*, written by himself in 789/1387 and now in the American Uni-

56 MSS Berlin, Wetzstein II 1233 in 1200, Wetzstein II 1764 in 1199; Princeton, Garrett 227Y in 1198. But there are the puzzling instances of MS Damascus, al-Majmaʿ al-ʿIlmī 443 and MS Berlin, Wetzstein II 1391, both owned by what appears to be this man's son, ʿImād al-Dīn, and who calls his father deceased/*al-marḥūm* in 1198 and 1200, respectively. Is this a case of post facto note-taking that records the dates the possession actually happened even when it was written down at a later time after the father's death?

57 Al-Ghazzī, *Al-Kawākib*, II, 249, no. 1171.

58 The catalogue erroneously reads the date as 708/1308–1309; the copying in Damascus is suggested by notes penned next to two of the volume's colophons (85^{r} and 93^{v}) that speak of *al-sabīl al-ʿuthmānī* known as *sabʿ al-maṣṣāṣa* at the foot of Jabal Qāsyūn. However, their precise meaning in relation to the production of the book remains enigmatic.

59 Al-Ghazzī, *Lutf al-samar*, I, 246, no. 80.

60 Al-Murādī, *Silk*, II, 161–165; see Liebrenz, *Die Rifāʿīya*, 73, 239–240.

versity of Beirut (MS 920.05 I65bA), assembles an illustrious line of Constantinopolitan bibliophilia: Firstly, ʿAlī b. Amr Allāh b. Muḥammad, better known as Qīnālī-zāde or Kınālızāde (916/1510–979/1571),[61] whose immense library was in no small part brought together on his many sojourns as a judge in the Arab provinces, as he usually notes in his ownership statements. He bought this particular volume in 975/1567–1568 in Cairo. Next, the unmistakable seal of Muḥammad b. Muḥammad Juwī-zāde (d. 995/1587) shows that the volume stayed in Constantinople.[62] Then there is Abū Bakr b. Rustam al-Shirwānī (d. 1135/1723), one of the most fervent bibliophiles of Constantinople at the end of the seventeenth and the beginning of the eighteenth century.[63] Finally, the owner Muḥammad Wāṣif al-Murādī Ibn Ḥasan *al-mutaṭabbib* could let one think of the famous Damascene al-Murādī family, yet, he is also attested in other manuscripts, many also previously owned by al-Shirwānī, that stayed in Constantinople (e.g. MSS Dublin, CBL Ar 3714, dated 1139/1726–1727; Istanbul, Fatih 4709; Istanbul, Hekimoğlu 579; Paris, BnF Arabe 3313), thus, he constitutes no Damascene hinge between the centre and the province. There is even a second volume of ʿAlī b. Amr Allāh, this one now in Damascus (al-Majmaʿ al-ʿIlmī 44). However, it appears to have taken a curious detour through the Iranian city of Ṭūs, where one Muqbil b. Ḥasan is said to have bought it in 1190/1776. Only seven years later, it was found all the way over on the Mediterranean coast in the mosque library of Acre. Though, as we shall discuss below, this does not speak to such a great reach of al-Jazzār's acquisition project, since we can connect Muqbil to Damascus like so many other previous owners. MS Princeton, Garrett 3516 bears the ownership note of the important yet understudied Ottoman bibliophile ʿIffatī,[64] dated 1151/1738–1739. And while MS Dublin, CBL Ar 3310 was made for the library (*li-khizāna*) of a Mamluk emir, it must have been in Constantinople at the end of the tenth/sixteenth or beginning of the eleventh/seventeenth century, as attested by its owner Asʿad b. Saʿd al-Dīn b. Ḥasan Jān al-Tabrīzī (d. 1034/1625), a native of Constantinople who was also the teacher of the Ottoman sultan Murād and a judge in his hometown. Al-Jazzār's own biography, namely, the start of his career in Constantinople, could not explain such a mass of material from that city's book market. But connections to the capital always needed to be maintained and the provincial governors had their agents and patrons in Istanbul to influence crucial decisions, not least about their own regular nominal appointments and reappointments, in their favour. It could be through such political agents that cultural matters were also dealt with, especially since the erection of a library and charitable complex as that of the Jazzār mosque-*madrasa*-library was a highly political affair as well. Of course, the precise pathways of these volumes' migration are ultimately impossible to determine: the books from Istanbul could also reasonably have been found on the market in Damascus.

There are books with an Egyptian history in the Nūr Aḥmadiyya, but it is, nonetheless, difficult to establish the country as a direct source of any major consequence for the library. It clearly was not in the case of MS Berlin, Landberg 9, even though this book indeed has several ownership notes of Egyptian scholars on it. The first among them is Madyan al-ṭabīb, who is none other than the famous physician Madyan al-Qūṣūnī (969/1562–

61 Ibn Ayyūb al-Anṣārī, *Kitāb al-Rawḍ al-ʿāṭir*, 35; Pfeifer, *Empire of Salons*, 185–189.

62 Al-Ghazzī, *Kawākib*, III, 24–26, no. 1223. The seal does, in fact, identify its owner simply as 'Muḥammad b. shaykh Muḥammad'. But this man's identity was apparently well-known among Ottoman scholars and bibliophiles and several handwritten notes identify him as Juwī-zāde where the seal impression was found.

63 See Süreyya, *Sicill-i ʿosmānī*, II, 430–431; Sayyid, "Les marques de possession"; Liebrenz, "The History and Provenance".

64 See the short notice in Richard, "Lecteurs ottomans". Bauden, "Maqriziana X". According to Bauden, ʿIffatī died in 27.1.1139/24.9.1726, yet I found notes of his with dates ranging from 1131 to 1165.

after 1044/1634),[65] and who had ordered the copy made (*mālikuhū istiktāban*) in Jumādā I 1043/1633. Then, in 1094/1683, it was among the books of Ibrāhīm al-Ḥusaynī naqīb Miṣr, who also spells out that he bought it in Cairo. By the time the volume was acquired for al-Jazzār, it had already travelled to Damascus, where Taqī al-Dīn al-Ḥiṣnī owned it in 1120/1708. One of the collection's most famous and important manuscripts, the very old fragment of al-Nadīm's (d. 385/995) *Fihrist* in Dublin (CBL Ar 3315), has an equally strong Egyptian prehistory. Most notably, we see a note by the famous historian of Cairo, Aḥmad b. ʿAlī al-Maqrīzī (764/1364–845/1442),[66] stating that he read the book in 824/1421. Another man, also named Aḥmad b. ʿAlī, but not to be mistaken for al-Maqrīzī, then bought the volume in the following year, and writes that this was done in Damascus. However, this does not mean that the *Fihrist* went to a Syrian library, since in 837/1433–1434 we find the same Aḥmad b. ʿAlī in Cairo, where he buys MS Ayasofya 4241 (not in the Jazzār library). The next owner, Yaḥyā b. Ḥijjī al-Shāfiʿī (838/1435–888/1483),[67] although he was born in Damascus, had long since moved to Cairo when he bought the volume at the end of his life in 885/1480–1481. But this Egyptian history is purely a Mamluk one. Where the book was found after the fifteenth century, in the Ottoman period, is not accessible to us and it could have come to Acre through many plausible routes. A volume that was still found in Egypt during the Ottoman period is MS Princeton Garrett 4691Y. Its first part was copied in 792/1390 by Aḥmad b. Naṣr Allāh b. Aḥmad al-Baghdādī al-Ḥanbalī (765/1363-64-844/1440–1441), who had been born in Bagdad, but became one of Egypt's leading scholars of law and *ḥadīth*. In the sixteenth century, precisely in 954/1547, MS Garrett 4691Y was owned, partly copied and collated by the Egyptian philologist and jurist ʿAlī b. Ghānim al-Maqdisī (d. 1004/1596). Here again, the trail of this item subsequently gets cold until it resurfaces in Acre more than two centuries later. No less than five volumes came to Acre from one source, the Muqbil b. Ḥasan mentioned previously,[68] which, given the small size of the sample corpus, is a remarkably large number. He bought his books as far in the East as Karbalāʾ[69] in Iraq and, as mentioned above, Ṭūs in Iran. But this does not indicate that his library was actually located in any of these places, if indeed we can imagine it to be a stable entity in one locale, since this man Muqbil simply appears to have travelled back and forth widely and we also find him buying three volumes in Damascus, just as much as he bought in Karbalāʾ. Two of them, now in Mecca and Jerusalem (al-Ḥaram al-Makkī, MS 1499; NLI AP Ar. 410), were bought there in Rabīʿ I 1188/1774. The chronologically last of his acquisitions (Garrett 3959) was bought by Muqbil still in Rajab 1195/1781, just as he was heading out of Damascus. It had previously been in the possession of the city's great biographer and littérateur Amīn al-Muḥibbī (1062/1658-9-1111/1699), who had bought it, also in Damascus, in 1093/1682. Its endowment to the Nūr Aḥmadiyya was already registered in Dhū al-Ḥijja 1196/1782, seventeen months after Muqbil's purchase. This fact seems to demonstrate, once again, the importance of Damascus for al-Jazzār's library, even for volumes that appear to have a back story much farther away.

65 Al-Muḥibbī, *Khulāṣat al-athar*, IV, 325–327, no. 1157; Al-Ziriklī, *Aʿlām*, VII, 198; for the relations among the members of the family, see Veselý, "Neues zur Familie al-Qūṣūnī"; Bonmariage, "Un nouvel élément".

66 On him, see the many contributions by Frédéric Bauden in a series of articles called "Maqriziana", most recently and with a focus on Maqrīzī's reading and books, see Bauden, "Maqriziana XVI"; Rabbat, *Writing Egypt*.

67 Ibn Iyās, *Badāʾiʿ al-zuhūr*, III, 200–201, 203; al-Sakhāwī, *Al-Ḍawʾ al-lāmiʿ*, X, 252–254, no. 1030.

68 MS Mecca, al-Ḥaram al-Makkī, MS 1499 (Rabīʿ I 1188 in Damascus); MS Jerusalem, NLI, AP Ar. 410 (Rabīʿ I 1188 in Damascus); MS Jaffa, MS 86 (Rajab 1189 in Karbalāʾ); MS Damascus, al-Majmaʿ al-ʿIlmī 44 (1190 in Ṭūs); MS Princeton, Garrett 3959Y (Rajab 1195 on the way from Damascus to the village al-Ḥawsīya).

69 Besides the volume in the Jazzār corpus, he also bought there: MS Damascus, al-Majmaʿ al-ʿIlmī 8 (in 1190) and MS Leiden, UL Or. 1450 (in Rajab 1188).

Seeing as the alleged provenance from the monastery Dayr al-Mukhalliṣ was a central piece of information in our sources, the complete absence of any manuscripts from this place or, in fact, the scarce representation of Christians in general is remarkable. At the end of 1197/1783, when the library of the Nūr Aḥmadiyya was already taking shape, a Christian scribe finished MS QNL 17150 for *al-muʿallim* Mīkhāʾīl b. Ḥannā, known as al-Sakrūj (d. 1795).[70] This man and his brother Buṭrus, not merely Acre's wealthiest merchants during the reign of al-Jazzār but also his secretaries, would later be executed by the governor. However, such violence does not explain the fate of this item. Four years after its completion, in 1201/1786–1787, with its owner still very much alive, the volume ended up in al-Jazzār's mosque.

The odd one out, in many regards, is MS Istanbul, Kemankeş 21. The endowment note of the Jazzār library is of a distinctly different wording than throughout the rest of the corpus. Al-Jazzār himself is here unusually called not Aḥmad bāshā al-Jazzār but 'Aḥmad known as Jazzār, the governor of Sidon (*Aḥmad al-mushtahir bi-Jazzār wālī Ṣaydā*)'. This could probably be explained by the fact that the note bears the latest date of any of the manuscripts recovered so far, namely, 1205/1790–1791, similar to the endowment seals themselves. The person responsible for writing the endowment notes might have changed by then. Additionally, this note is written not on the actual title page but on a strip of paper, which was then loosely pasted over an older endowment note, this latter one in Persian.[71] The date of this older note, unfortunately, could not be read, nor was I able to make out the name of a place or institution to which the volume was given. The endower was Muḥammad Dāwūd Ibn ʿInāyat Allāh called (*mukhāṭab bi-*) Taqarrub Khān. The fact that the writer uses the phrase *mukhāṭab bi-* instead of *al-shahīr bi-* or *al-mushtahir bi-* clearly points to a background in the Eastern Persian-speaking world. Indeed, this person is found in a collection of biographies from the Moghul court in India.[72] According to this biography, Muḥammad Dāwūd was a greatly acclaimed physician at the court of Shāh ʿAbbās I in Safavid Iran, but fell out of favour with this ruler's successors and surreptitiously retreated to the Mughal court of Shāh Jahān, where he was held in the highest esteem. It is important for the dating and location of the note on al-Jazzār's book that Muḥammad Dāwūd received the honorific Taqarrub Khān only three years into his time as the court physician of Shāh Jahān in 1056/1646. He died in 1073/1662 after a stellar career in the service of the Moghul court. How the book then made its way out of its designated endowment, presumably in Mughal India, into another one on the Syrian coast remains unclear for the moment.

4 Conclusion

In the first part of this chapter, a cluster of interdependent narratives on al-Jazzār and his books gave the prodigiously and influential impression of a library that was brought together by violent means in the immediate vicinity of Acre. The manuscripts, on the other hand, interrogated in the second part, overwhelmingly tell the distinctly different story of legal acquisitions from the regional centres of Ottoman book culture, with some possible outreach to Constantinople. With several clusters of contemporaneous and immediately previous Damascene owners (two volumes from ʿAbd al-Raḥīm al-ʿImādī, three from Taqī al-Dīn al-Ḥiṣnī and five from Muqbil b. Ḥasan), this city emerges as the main source of the Nūr Aḥmadīya, and that happened well before al-Jazzār attained any political power there.

70 Philipp, *Acre*, 117, 118, 120, 160–161.

71 I was able to read the older Persian note only thanks to new photographs made and generously shared by Nimet İpek.

72 Shāh Nawāz Khān and Shāh Nawāz Khān, *The Maāthir-ul-Umarā*, II, 922–925. I thank Christopher Bahl for this reference.

A careful analysis of the manuscripts has shown how al-Jazzār or the agents responsible for building up his splendid library were casting a broader net than the narrative sources tell us. This review allowed us to recalibrate the importance of violent acquisitions, previously thought to have been the central feature of the governor's book collection. While it does not deny or downplay the possibility of destructive episodes for cultural heritage in the context of constant regional warfare, this contribution has put into question the foundational myths associated with them for the creation of the Nūr Aḥmadiyya. We could also see that no strong scholarly and book culture existed in the immediate region around Acre that would have allowed the build-up of a major library from it. Al-Jazzār's efforts to change that created one of the richest places of literature in all of Syria and the coast of the Eastern Mediterranean, but proved ultimately short-lived, with its success hard to measure.

Bibliography

Āl Ṣafā', Muḥammad Jābir. *Tārīkh Jabal ʿĀmil*. Beirut, 1981.

ʿAfāna, Ḥusām al-Dīn et al., *Fihris makhṭūṭāt Filasṭīn al-muṣawwara*. Jerusalem, 2000.

Akel, Ibrahim. "Ahmad al-Rabbât al-Halabî: sa bibliothèque et son rôle dans la réception, diffusion et enrichissement des Mille et une nuits." PhD diss., Institut National des Langues et Civilisations Orientales, 2016.

Ali Bey (= Domingo Badía y Leblich). *Travels of Ali Bey, in Morocco, Tripoli, Cyprus, Egypt, Arabia, Syria, and Turkey. Between the Years 1803 and 1807*. 2 vols. Philadelphia, 1816.

Al-Amīn, Muḥsin. *Aʿyān al-Shīʿa*. Vol. 10. Beirut, 1983.

Al-Amīnī al-Najafī, ʿAbd al-Ḥusayn. *Shuhadāʾ al-faḍīla*. Beirut, 1983.

Al-ʿAsalī, Kāmil. "Al-Maktabāt al-Filisṭīniyya mundhu al-fatḥ al-ʿArabī al-Islāmī ḥattā sana 1985." In *al-Mawsūʿa al-Filisṭīniyya. Al-Qism al-thānī: Al-Dirāsāt al-khāṣṣa*, vol. 3: *Dirāsāt al-ḥaḍāra*. Beirut, 1990.

Al-Bakrī, Muṣṭafā; edited by Sāmiḥ al-Khālidī. "Riḥla ilā Diyār al-Rūm." *Majallat al-Risāla* 946 (1951): 33–41.

Bauden, Frédéric. "Maqriziana X: al-Maqrīzī and His al-Tārīḫ al-Kabīr al-Muqaffā li-Miṣr. Part 2: The Fortunes of the Work and Its Copies." *Quaderni di Studi Arabi* 15 (2020): 194–269.

Bauden, Frédéric. "Maqriziana XVI: al-Maqrīzī as a Reader." In *Authors as Readers in the Mamlūk Period and Beyond*, edited by Élise Franssen, 195–266. Venice, 2022.

Bergé, Marc. "Justification d'un autodafé des livres. Lettre d'Abū Ḥayyān al-Tawḥīdī au Qāḍī Abū Sahl ʿAlī ibn Muḥammad." *Annales Islamologiques* 9 (1970): 65–85.

Bizzī, Muṣṭafā. "Al-Khasāʾir allatī muniya bi-hā Jabal ʿĀmil jarrāʾ ḥukm al-Jazzār," in *Jabal ʿĀmil wa-ʿahd al-Jazzār bayna al-nakba wa-al-nahḍa. 1190h 1781m–1219h 1804m*. Beirut, 2014, 73–111.

Bonmariage, Cécile. "Un nouvel élément à propos des Qūṣūnī." *Arabica* 56 (2009): 269–273.

Al-Būrīnī, al-Ḥasan. *Tarājim al-aʿyān min abnāʾ al-zamān*. Edited by Ṣalāḥ al-Dīn al-Munajjid. 2 vols. Damascus, 1959–1963.

De Forbin, Auguste. *Voyage dans le Levant en 1817 et 1818*. Paris, 1819.

Dī Ṭarrāzī, Fīlīb (de Tarrazi, Philippe). *Khazāʾin al-kutub fī al-khāfiqayn*. 4 vols. Beirut, 1947–1951.

Elger, Ralf. *Muṣṭafā al-Bakrī. Zur Selbstdarstellung eines syrischen Gelehrten, Sufis und Dichters des 18. Jahrhunderts*. Schenefeld, 2004.

Al-Ghazzī, Najm al-Dīn Muḥammad. *Luṭf al-samar wa-qaṭf al-thamar. Min tarājim aʿyān al-ṭabaqa al-ūlā min al-qarn al-ḥādī ʿashar*. Edited by Maḥmūdal-Shaykh. 2 vols. Damascus, 1981–1982.

Al-Ghazzī, Najm al-Dīn Muḥammad. *Al-Kawākib al-sāʾira bi-aʿyān al-miʾa al-ʿāshira*. Edited by Khalīl al-Manṣūr. 3 vols. Beirut, 1997.

Al-Ḥazīmī, Nāṣir. *Ḥaraq al-kutub fī al-turāth al-ʿarabī*. Cologne, 2003.

Hirschler, Konrad. *The Written Word in the Medieval Arabic Lands. A Social and Cultural History of Reading Practices*. Edinburgh, 2012.

Ibn Ayyūb al-Anṣārī, Sharaf al-Dīn Mūsā. *Kitāb al-Rawḍ al-ʿāṭir*. Partial edition by Ahmet Halil Güneş as *Das Kitāb ar-rauḍ al-ʿāṭir des Ibn Aiyūb. Damaszener Bi-*

ographien des 10. / 16. Jh. Beschreibung und Edition. Berlin, 1981.

Ibn Iyās, Muḥammad. *Badāʾiʿ al-zuhūr fī waqāʾiʿ al-duhūr*. Edited by Muḥammad Muṣṭafā. 6 vols. Beirut, 2010.

Ibn Kannān, Muḥammad b. ʿĪsā. *Al-Ḥawādith al-yawmiyya min tārīkh aḥad ʿashar wa-alf wa-miʾa*. Edited by Akram al-ʿUlabī. Damascus, 1994.

Jabal ʿĀmil wa-ʿahd al-Jazzār bayna al-nakba wa-al-nahḍa. 1190h 1781m–1219h 1804m. Beirut, 2014.

Jaber, Mounzer. "Pouvoir et société au Jabal Amil de 1749 à 1920 dans la conscience des chroniqueurs shiites." PhD diss., Sorbonne-Paris IV, 1978.

Krimsti, Feras. "Von Aleppo nach Gotha: Der Aleppiner Buchmarkt des 18. Jahrhunderts im Spiegel der von Ulrich Jasper Seetzen erworbenen Gothaer Handschriften." In *Bücher bewegen. 375 Jahre Forschungsbibliothek Gotha, Katalog zur Jubiläumsausstellung auf Schloss Friedenstein Gotha*, edited by Kathrin Paasch, 56–63. Gotha, 2022.

Liebrenz, Boris. "The Library of Aḥmad al-Rabbāṭ. Books and Their Audience in 12th to 13th / 18th to 19th Century Syria." In *Marginal Perspectives on Early Modern Ottoman Book Culture. Missionaries, Travelers, Booksellers*, edited by Ralf Elger and Ute Pietruschka, 17–59. Halle, 2013.

Liebrenz, Boris. "The Social History of Surgery in Ottoman Syria: Documentary Evidence from Eighteenth-century Hamah." *Turkish Historical Review* 5 (2014): 32–58.

Liebrenz, Boris. *Die Rifāʿīya aus Damaskus. Eine Privatbibliothek im osmanischen Syrien und ihr kulturelles Umfeld*. Leiden, 2016.

Liebrenz, Boris. "From Leipzig to Damascus. Wetzstein as a Broker of Arabic Prints in Syria." In *Manuscripts, Politics and Oriental Studies. Life and Collections of Johann Gottfried Wetzstein (1815–1905) in Context*, edited by Boris Liebrenz and Christoph Rauch, 323–345. Leiden, 2019.

Liebrenz, Boris. "The History and Provenance of the Unique *Dustūr al-munağğimīn* Manuscript, BnF Arabe 5968." *Journal of Islamic Manuscripts* 11 (2020): 28–42.

Liebrenz, Boris. *Arab Traders in Their Own Words. Merchant Letters from the Eastern Mediterranean around 1800*. Leiden, 2022.

[Meryon, Charles Lewis]. *Travels of Lady Hester Stanhope*. 2 vols. London, 1846.

Mez, Adam. *Die Renaissance des Islâms*. Heidelberg, 1922.

Morris, James. "An Arab Macchiavelli? Rhetoric, Philosophy, and Politics in Ibn Khaldun's Critic of Sufism." *Harvard Middle Eastern and Islamic Review* 8 (2009): 242–291.

Al-Muḥibbī, Muḥammad Amīn. *Khulāṣat al-athar fī aʿyān al-qarn al-ḥādī ʿashar*, edited by Muḥammad Ḥasan Muḥammad Ḥasan Ismāʿīl. 4 vols. Beirut, 2006.

Al-Murādī, Muḥammad Khalīl. *Silk al-durar fī aʿyān al-qarn al-thānī ʿashar*, Edited by Muḥammad ʿAbd al-Qādir Shāhīn. 4 vols. Beirut, 1997.

Pfeifer, Helen. *Empire of Salons. Conquest and Community in Early Modern Ottoman Lands*. Princeton, 2022.

Philipp, Thomas. *Acre. The Rise and Fall of a Palestinian City, 1730–1831*. New York, 2001

Rabbat, Nasser. *Writing Egypt. Al-Maqrīzī and His Historical Project*. Edinburgh, 2022.

Raʿd, Muḥammad. "Kalimat rāʿī al-muʾtamar," in *Jabal ʿĀmil wa-ʿahd al-Jazzār bayna al-nakba wa-al-nahḍa. 1190h 1781m–1219h 1804m*. Beirut, 2014, 11–17.

Richard, Francis. "Lecteurs ottomans de manuscrits persans du XVIe au XVIIIe siècle." *Revue des mondes musulmans et de la Méditerranée* 87–88 (1999): 79–83.

Riḍā, Aḥmad. "Al-Matāwila aw al-shīʿa fī Jabal ʿĀmil." *Al-ʿIrfān* 8, no. 2 (1910): 381–392.

Rosenthal, Franz. "'Of Making Many Books There is No End': The Classical Muslim View." In *The Book in the Islamic World*, edited by George N. Atiya, 33–55. Albany, 1995.

Al-Sakhāwī, Muḥammad. *Al-Ḍawʾ al-lāmiʿ li-ahl al-qarn al-tāsiʿ*. 12 vols. Beirut, 1992.

Sayyid, Ayman Fuʾād. "Les marques de possession sur les manuscrits et la reconstitution des anciens fonds des manuscrits arabes." *Manuscripta Orientalia* 9 (2003): 14–23.

Seetzen, Ulrich Jasper. *Reisen durch Syrien, Palästina, Phönicien, die Transjordanländer, Arabia Petraea und Unter-Aegypten*, edited by Fr. Kruse. 4 vols. Berlin, 1854–1859.

Shāh Nawāz Khān, Nawwāb Ṣamṣām-ud-Daula and ʿAbdul Ḥayy Shāh Nawāz Khān. *The Maāthir-ul-Umarā*.

Being Biographies of the Muḥammadan and Hindu Officers of the Timurid Sovereigns of India from 1500 to about 1780 A.D. Translated by H. Beveridge, revised, annotated and completed by Baini Prashad. Calcutta, 1952.

Al-Shaṭṭī, Muḥammad Jamīl. *Aʿyān Dimashq fī al-qarn al-thālith ʿashar wa-niṣf al-qarn al-rābiʿ ʿashar, 1201–1350 h.* S.l., 1976.

Stein, Hans (ed.). *Orientalische Buchkunst in Gotha: Austellung zum 350 jährigen Jubliäum der Forschungs- und Landesbibliothek Gotha.* Gotha, 1997.

Süreyya, Mehmed. *Sicill-i ʿoṯmānī.* 6 vols. Istanbul, 1996.

Thomasson, Fredrik. *The Life of J.D. Åkerblad. Egyptian Decipherment and Orientalism in Revolutionary Times.* Leiden, 2013.

Veselý, Rudolf. "Neues zur Familie al-Qūṣūnī. Ein Beitrag zur Genealogie einer ägyptischen Ärzte- und Gelehrtenfamilie." *Oriens* 33 (1992): 437–440.

Volney, Constantin Francois. *Travels through Syria and Egypt in the Years 1783, 1784, and 1785.* 2 vols. London, 1788.

Wetzstein, Johann Gottfried. *Bruchstück eines wissenschaftl. Katalogs der arab. HSS. der Bibl. Wetzst. II von N. 314 bis 418,* MS Berlin, Staatsbibliothek, Hs. or. sim. 8943.

Winter, Stefan. *The Shiites of Lebanon under Ottoman Rule, 1516–1788.* Cambridge, 2010.

Ẓāhir, Sulaymān. "Ṣilat al-ʿilm bayna Dimashq wa-Jabal ʿĀmil." *Majallat al-Majmaʿ al-ʿIlmī al-ʿArabī* 9 (1929): 269–279.

Ẓāhir, Sulaymān. "Wathāʾiq." *Al-ʿIrfān* 37, no. 4 (1950): 377–380.

Al-Zayn, ʿAlī. *Fuṣūl min tārīkh al-shīʿa fī Lubnān.* Beirut, 1979.

Al-Zayn, ʿAlī. "Al-ʿAwāmil allatī addat ilā suqūṭ Jabal ʿĀmil bi-yad al-Jazzār," in *Jabal ʿĀmil wa-ʿahd al-Jazzār bayna al-nakba wa-al-nahḍa. 1190h 1781m–1219h 1804m.* Beirut, 2014, 35–56.

Al-Ziriklī, Khayr al-Dīn. *Al-Aʿlām. Qāmūs tarājim li-ashhar al-rijāl wa-al-nisāʾ min al-ʿarab wa-al-mustaʿribīn wa-al-mustashriqīn.* 8 vols. Beirut, 2002.

CHAPTER 4

Historical Representations of al-Jazzār: 'Butcher' or Patron of the Poor?

Feras Krimsti

The well-known Jordanian historian Muḥammad 'Adnān al-Bakhīt reflects on the image of Aḥmad Pasha al-Jazzār in his preface to the catalogue of the remnants of the Aḥmadiyya Library in Acre:

> The image of Aḥmad Pasha al-Jazzār (d. 1219/1804) that is painted and anchored in the spirits is that of a butcher who finds joy in bloodshed and in the confiscation of the possessions of others, whether these others are his opponents or the wealthy. This is not the place to discuss this image, but the way I see it, the time has come to re-evaluate Aḥmad Pasha al-Jazzār, the man who took charge of protecting the existence of the Ottoman state, the precise execution of the *sunna* and the main school of the state. He did this because a major section of the local leaders on the coasts of the *vilayet*s of Syria were diverging from the *sunna*, and because of the movements of Arab tribes, especially those from whom emerged a new call, namely the Islamic Salafi movement, which is known as Wahhabism. In addition to this, the intervention of foreign states in affairs of the Ottoman state intensified, and the number of those who profited from the advantages of *berats* increased. It is clear to us that Aḥmad Pasha tried to save the state from the destruction that was approaching.[1]

Al-Bakhīt calls for re-envisioning Aḥmad Pasha al-Jazzār: he defends al-Jazzār against the accusation that he was a butcher who revelled in bloodshed and argues that he protected the Ottoman state and Islam, the *sunna*, against inner and outer foes. Al-Bakhīt does not explain how he thinks al-Jazzār's political role related to his library and bibliophilia, but the context of his reflections—a library catalogue—suggests that al-Jazzār the collector and owner of books can only be better understood once the profile of al-Jazzār the politician emerges more clearly through the haze of what al-Bakhīt sees as misconceptions.

The American Lebanese intellectual and writer Amīn al-Rayḥānī (1876–1940) in his book *al-Nakabāt* ('Calamities'), by contrast, found the political player al-Jazzār and the bibliophile irredeemably at odds. The book deals with a number of historical disasters and crises that happened in Syria, al-Jazzār being described as one of them.[2] Al-Rayḥānī paints a dark picture of al-Jazzār, with one important exception: al-Rayḥānī had the opportunity to visit the Grand Mosque in Acre where he saw the Jazzār library. He finds al-Jazzār's personality incompatible with his bibliophilia and is puzzled at the apparent paradox: 'Is it not really strange that this man was so fond of books and collected them eagerly!'[3] The contradictions between al-Jazzār's character as a ruler and his love of books probably left many contemporary and modern historians somewhat baffled—a fact that may explain why the library was barely ever mentioned.

1 'Aṭā' Allāh, *Fihris*, pp. alif-bā'. Unless otherwise specified, all translations from Arabic, German and French into English are my own.

2 Al-Rayḥānī, *Al-Nakabāt*, 98–101 (ch. 16). Also see the comment on al-Rayḥānī's statement in Ghannām, *Al-Muqāṭa'āt al-lubnāniyya*, 41–42.

3 Al-Rayḥānī, *Al-Nakabāt*, 100.

This article examines a variety of different historical representations of al-Jazzār and shows that these images have often more to do with those who developed and cultivated them than with the historical al-Jazzār. The latter's representations have been shaped by the beliefs and convictions, the economic agenda and wealth (or lack of wealth), the kinship ties and group memberships, and the political goals of those who wrote about him. I argue that the starkly contrasting representations of al-Jazzār captured in historical sources do not only suggest a complex and multifaceted historical figure. Instead, they also point to a complex discursive world in which the rhetoric around this political agent served very real identarian, communal, political, social and economic purposes. I focus on three important trends in the representation of al-Jazzār. The first is his depiction as a tyrant, often motivated by political rivalries and/or shaped by confessional agendas. A second tendency in the representation of al-Jazzār is constituted by reports about his financial extortions and upsetting of social hierarchies in the framework of his competition with notables in trade, especially Damascene personages. The third image is organically connected to the second one: it is that of a patron and benefactor of the urban poor, an image that al-Jazzār was able to cultivate especially in Beirut, but also beyond. This specific trend in writing emerges from what I call 'popular literature', that is, epics and songs, which give a voice to parts of the population which are normally poorly represented in historiography. In each of the three sections, I first offer an overview of the individuals who stand for a certain trend in representation and sketch their background and commitments before I turn to each of them individually and discuss their specific views on al-Jazzār. What emerges from a study of the historical representations of al-Jazzār is the complex picture of a man despised and loathed by some, but also celebrated by others, for reasons having to do with their place in society.

A quick glance at the historical literature that mentions al-Jazzār shows that a negative image of him prevailed. This should not automatically be taken as evidence that the historical al-Jazzār was in fact the extraordinarily cruel tyrant and extortionist that so many contemporaries depict—the quantity of surviving negative reports is probably misleading. It does not necessarily suggest that more contemporaries agreed that he was brutal and ruthless; it may simply point to an imbalance in the degree to which these individuals were able to voice their opinions, grievances or endorsement. Those who were al-Jazzār's opponents clearly had much more powerful voices than those who were firmly on his side. 'As ruler of the eyalet of Sidon, his unwavering championship of the Ottoman cause, which was the cause of Islam, probably secured for him some popularity among the lower Muslim classes of the coastal towns', Kamal Salibi observed. 'Whatever the extent of this popularity was, it has remained unrecorded, because the accounts of his regime available were not written by his supporters but by the Christians, the foreigners and the Muslim notables who, as communities and sometimes possibly as individuals, had suffered at his hands and were unanimous in branding him as a bloodthirsty tyrant.'[4] We already know that important parts of urban populations, especially the lower classes, were muted in the biographies of other eminent political figures of the period.[5] Taking Salibi's observation as a point of departure, this article also sets out to trace the voice of subaltern groups that went unheard. Sometimes that voice can be recovered by reading between the lines of historical representations of more vocal (and more elite) contemporaries. In other cases, popular songs and epic poems have survived. Such non-elite popular compositions have been shown to treat political events

4 Salibi, "Al-Djazzār Pasha", 269.

5 The Janissary leader 'Abdallāh Bābinsī (1780s–1850) is one such figure about whom very little is known—despite the tremendous amount of power that he held in Aleppo during his career, because his power base was the 'unruly' Eastern quarters of the city. See Krimsti, "The Last Janissary Leader", especially 76.

perceived as vital—the genres of panegyric and elegy were especially used to express such experiences.[6]

Al-Jazzār was both an agent of the Porte and an autonomous force in the Levant. Despite his political importance, scholarly publications about him are few. An important exception is Thomas Philipp's study of Ottoman Acre, which dedicates significant space to al-Jazzār.[7] Before Philipp's seminal work, Abdul Latif Tibawi approached al-Jazzār in the framework of a history of modern Syria.[8] Amnon Cohen focused on al-Jazzār by studying the relations of rulers of Palestine to the centre of the Ottoman Empire and other local power holders.[9] Linda Schatkowski Schilcher also discussed al-Jazzār in a brief chapter of her work on Damascene families and factional politics.[10] Antoine Abdel Nour (1949–1982) argued, in a chapter dedicated to al-Jazzār, that French perspectives on him were skewed because he intervened in trade and manipulated it.[11] An aspect of al-Jazzār's political role for which he became infamous, namely his association with violence, was highlighted by Dick Douwes. According to him, al-Jazzār's rule 'can be seen as illustrative of the painful change from premodern to modern realities in the Middle East' since it reflected a tendency towards fragmentation of the military and increased use of violence.[12] His monograph, *The Ottomans in Syria*, analyses al-Jazzār's politics in the framework of an Ottoman policy of coercion which characterised the administration of Syria in the period between 1785 and 1841.[13] More recently, Ali Yacioglu has taken up this focus by studying al-Jazzār as a notable who governed in a time of crisis of empire.[14] Scholarship in the Arab world attempting to revisit the Ottoman era, depicted for a long time as characterised by political, moral and intellectual decline, started to be produced in the 1980s. This scholarship does not, however, focus on al-Jazzār.[15] No biographies of al-Jazzār have been written either. Philipp has suggested that a reason for this might be the overwhelmingly negative perceptions of al-Jazzār: 'The early reports on him had drawn such an ambivalent or straight-out negative picture that no national historiography cared to claim him.'[16] This is confirmed by the doubts expressed by the participants in a conference and collected volume on the occasion of the 200th anniversary of al-Jazzār's death whether it was acceptable to honour him at all.[17] The situation is different where individuals on the political scene before and after al-Jazzār are concerned: both Ẓāhir (Ḍāhir) al-ʿUmar (d. 1775) and Sulaymān Pasha (d. 1819), the successor to al-Jazzār in Acre, have received more scholarly and popular attention recently.[18] This article dedicated to al-Jazzār is accordingly also a contribution towards a better understanding of a major political player in the region.

6 Kilpatrick, "Poetry and Political Events".

7 See Philipp, *Acre*, 48–78. Al-Jazzār is also mentioned repeatedly in Reilly's study of the Ottoman cities of Lebanon: Reilly, *The Ottoman Cities*, *passim*.

8 See Tibawi, *A Modern History*, 19–39.

9 See Cohen, *Palestine*, 19–29, 53–77, and *passim*. The study focuses on Palestine on the eve of Napoleon's failed invasion. Cohen has also written about the siege of Acre. See Cohen, "Napoleon and Jezzar". On the topic of the invasion, see, more recently, Zeʿevi, "Ottoman Intelligence Gathering". He discusses intelligence gathering for the sultan during the invasion, based on letters written by locals and al-Jazzār.

10 See Schatkowski Schilcher, *Families*, 36–40 (especially 36–39).

11 See ʿAbd al-Nūr, *Tijārat Ṣaydā*, 56–63.

12 Douwes, "Reorganizing Violence", 116–119.

13 Douwes, *The Ottomans in Syria*, especially 52–59, 91–99, and *passim*.

14 See Yacioglu, *Partners*, 65–115.

15 See, for example, al-Shinnāwī, *Al-Dawla*.

16 Philipp, *Acre*, 49.

17 Abū al-Fahd, "Al-Mughāmir", 24. Most of the contributions in the collected volume focused on the impact of al-Jazzār's architectural interventions in urban space rather than his policies.

18 See, for example, the comments on Ẓāhir (Ḍāhir) al-ʿUmar in Sajdi, "Review".

1 Al-Jazzār the Tyrant, or the Lens of Political Allegiance and Confessional Self-Affirmation

The strongest and most pervasive representation of al-Jazzār in historical works is the image of the tyrant. Al-Jazzār was depicted by countless contemporaries as an absolute evil-doer, a representation that continues to influence modern historiography and even fiction. Such an image was inaugurated and perpetuated, in the first place, by Europeans, notably French travellers who stayed in or passed through the region. Thomas Philipp has characterised this group of texts dealing with al-Jazzār as the French 'school of biographical interpretation'.[19] This genre of literature had a tendency to stress the outrageous. Given that al-Jazzār was able to successfully defend the fortress of Acre during Napoleon's siege and stop his advance in 1799, he served particularly well as an anti-hero. French travellers extended the political discourse on Ottoman despotism to al-Jazzār. He accordingly came to be seen not only as Napoleon's formidable enemy but as the incarnation of oriental decay and weakness.[20] Ideas of al-Jazzār's cruel despotism even shaped the European pictorial representation of him, as seen in a drawing included in Francis Spilsbury's (1756–1823) *Picturesque Scenery in the Holy Land and Syria* (originally published in 1803) (see fig. 4.1).

The first section of this essay argues that some contemporaries who authored historical works in Arabic also saw al-Jazzār as a tyrant and despot—especially those who were allied to or moved in the circles of his political adversaries. In these cases, al-Jazzār was used as an anti-model and an instructive example of the abuse of political authority, his rule was a lesson on the absence of moral consciousness. Ḥaydar Aḥmad Shihāb (1761–1835),[21] a prince, statesman and family historian from Mount Lebanon who was a cousin of al-Jazzār's opponent Amīr Bashīr (Bashīr Shihāb II, 1789–1840), devoted to al-Jazzār a very well-known and widely diffused account titled *Tārīkh Aḥmad Bāshā al-Jazzār*.[22] The work complements another one which is dedicated to the history of the Shihāb family.[23] The intention behind the two works is clear: one praises the noble deeds of the Shihāb family, the other one highlights al-Jazzār's anti-model. Al-Jazzār's political adversaries—Catholic Christians figuring prominently among them—often adopted the discourse on al-Jazzār's tyrannical rule for purposes of political legitimisation. Ḥaydar Aḥmad Shihāb belonged to the section of the Shihāb family that had openly converted to Maronite Christianity. Amīr Bashīr was also Maronite, although his religious allegiance remained more ambiguous. Another example of a Christian who helped forge the image of al-Jazzār the tyrant was Mikhā'īl Mishāqa (1800–1888), who converted from Catholicism to Protestantism. In the memoirs that he composed at the age of 73, he reflected on the numerous interactions of his grandfather Ibrāhīm and his father Jirjis with al-Jazzār, under whose rule they engaged in tax-farming and trade.[24] The Mishāqas were not only working under al-Jazzār, but also under Amīr Bashīr, who again emerges as the positive and exemplary counterpart to the tyrant. Another example is the account of the Catholic Mīkhā'īl Niqūlā al-Ṣabbāgh (d. 1816 in Paris). He was the grandson of Ibrāhīm al-Ṣabbāgh, the treasurer of Ẓāhir al-ʿUmar. His account is primarily intended as an apology for his grandfather who was blamed to have caused, with his greed, the downfall of his own master. The sections dedicated to al-Jazzār that the account includes are steeped in stereotypes issuing from European discourses[25]—a reason being that al-Ṣabbāgh wrote his account when he was staying in Paris where he absorbed some of these ideas. In all

19 Philipp, *Acre*, 49.
20 Philipp, *Acre*, 54.
21 On Ḥaydar Aḥmad Shihāb (or: Shihābī) as a chronicler, see Bualuan, *Lebanese Historical Thought*, 31–37.
22 See Shihāb, *Tārīkh*.
23 See Shihābī, *Lubnān*.
24 See Thackston, *Murder, Mayhem, Pillage*.
25 On al-Jazzār, see al-Ṣabbāgh, *Tārīkh*, 114–121.

JEZZAR PACHA Condemning A CRIMINAL.

FIGURE 4.1 Al-Jazzār, the ruling tyrant in the European imagination, here gesturing for one of his subjects to be beheaded. Image from: Francis B. Spilsbury. *Picturesque Scenery in the Holy Land and Syria Delineated during the Campaigns of 1799 and 1800*. London: Orme, 1803, image before p. 5 ('Jezzar Pacha Condemning a Criminal')
IMAGE CREDIT: KUNSTBIBLIOTHEK, STAATLICHE MUSEEN ZU BERLIN

these cases, a coalescence of discourses prevalent among French contemporaries and those of al-Jazzār's political enemies, especially Catholic and Maronite Christians, can be observed.

By contrast, Greek Orthodox representations of al-Jazzār, though often also relatively bleak, are more nuanced, for example, those of ʿAbdallāh ibn Mīkhāʾīl Ṭarrād al-Bayrūtī (fl. beginning of the nineteenth century) and Mikhāʾīl Burayk al-Dimashqī (fl. second half of the 18th century). These two Greek Orthodox historians commented on al-Jazzār's rule in Beirut and Damascus, respectively. They did not subscribe to the stark image painted, especially by Catholic historians, but their image of al-Jazzār also depends on political frameworks and is shaped by inner-Christian struggles.

After this brief overview of key voices who helped shape the image of al-Jazzār the tyrant, some comments on their specific arguments are in order. Ḥaydar Aḥmad Shihāb's *Tārīkh Aḥmad Bāshā al-Jazzār* has been preserved in many manuscript copies, some of them even in Karshūnī (Arabic written in Syriac script), a fact that points to the tremendous popularity and influence of the account. The narration was instrumental in diffusing the negative image of al-Jazzār in Lebanon. Ḥaydar Aḥmad Shihāb, who belonged to the party of Amīr Bashīr, al-Jazzār's opponent, does not even make an attempt to point out any redeeming qualities in his political opponent. He casts aspersions on his character wherever he can. He recounts how al-Jazzār once returned from pilgrimage and, hypocrite that he was, henceforth abstained from drinking wine and committing sodomy (*liwāṭ*), making sure to pray the five daily prayers.[26] This of course implies that al-Jazzār committed all these offences before, which serves to depict him as essentially non-Islamic.

A more nuanced view does not even emerge regarding events throughout al-Jazzār's career that Ḥaydar Aḥmad Shihāb could have condoned. When recounting al-Jazzār's victory over the French during the siege of Acre, he writes that the English General Smith (Sir William Sidney Smith, 1764–1840) had, in fact, been the one to defeat Napoleon.[27] He describes the celebrations after al-Jazzār's death,[28] and mentions that individuals who had long disappeared returned from prisons. He includes three poems in praise of al-Jazzār's death by 'some poets':[29]

O people in the land of al-Shām,
Give good tidings: the one who committed evil deeds perished and was torn apart—
The faithless traitor, the butcher who shed blood,
The one who abandoned himself in the killing of souls.
Acre calls out: 'Mercy, our Lord! Save us from this oppressor. How much blood did he spill!'
[…]
I recited verses full of joy on the day that has come,
When that butcher Aḥmad has perished![30]

It is noteworthy that some of the stories narrated about al-Jazzār stem from a repertoire of discourses and tropes shared with French travelogues. One such story included in Shihāb's *Tārīkh* is the following one: While al-Jazzār was on pilgrimage, women in his harem were involved in a plot with his Mamluks/slaves. Al-Jazzār is said to have punished them atrociously for their act of rebellion.[31] Ḥaydar Aḥmad Shihāb concludes his narration by stating that 'after this event, he became like an unbridled beast.'[32]

The story is widespread in historical accounts of al-Jazzār, but it is not told everywhere with the same degree of graphic detail and horrifying brutality.[33] French travellers especially dwell on it extensively, as Thomas Philipp observed; al-Jazzār's deeds became ever 'bloodier, more cruel, and, indeed, pornographic as time went by'.[34] An example is the account of the physician Guillaume Antoine Olivier (1756–1814), who travelled through North Africa and the Levant between 1792 and 1798:

When Dgézar [al-Jazzār] learned after the revolt of the Mamluks […] of the outrage that was done to him when his harem was penetrated, he had a fit of jealousy, and in that moment the most violent rage came over him. […] All of his wives were marked and different forms of torture specified for them. The less pretty and older ones were thrown into boats, driven out to the middle of the sea, and drowned. Other ones were thrown in leather sacks into the Gulf of Acre; those whose suffering he wanted to extend had to undergo a thousand torments before they were buried alive in a deep cistern, the tomb of several of his main officers from which stinking vapours emanated; the youngest and most pretty women were mutilated and eviscerated by his own hand.[35]

26 Shihāb, *Tārīkh*, 109.
27 Ibid., 133.
28 Ibid., 167.
29 Ibid., 169–170.
30 Ibid., 170.
31 Ibid., 92–95.
32 Ibid., 95.
33 For example, cf. the episode as al-Jabartī tells it: 'On one occasion, he became suspicious of certain of his concubines and mamluks. He murdered those he suspected strongly and burned their bodies; the rest he exiled, first cutting off their noses, both men and women, leaving them to wander, and making it known that his wrath would descend on anyone who took them in and gave them protection […].' Philipp et al., *History of Egypt*, vol. 3, 494. In al-Jabartī's description, the cruel punishment is meted out in a calculated way and clearly functions as a deterrent.
34 Philipp, *Acre*, 55–56 (quotation 55).
35 Olivier, *Voyage*, vol. 2, 265–266. I would like to thank

Versions of the story also ended up in English accounts, for example, in the 1797 memoirs of the Irish politician, libertine, and gambler Thomas 'Buck' Whaley, published posthumously.[36] From contemporary reports, the harem episode and related narratives were passed on to later historiography in English, French and even Russian. A noteworthy example is the account of the Russian consul of Beirut, Konstantin Mikhailovich Bazili (1809–1884). He writes that al-Jazzār 'put eunuchs, servant girls, and even his pregnant wives to the sword'.[37] The episode became legendary to a degree that it even entered modern fiction. It figured prominently in a 1960 theatre play titled *Warīth al-Jazzār* ('Al-Jazzār's Heir') by Salīm Khūrī (1934–1991).[38] In the play, al-Jazzār appears as the evil anti-hero right from the first scene of the first act in which he is presiding over an unfair tribunal. The harem scene figures in the fifth scene of the second act: al-Jazzār threatens the women in dramatic dialogue, a sword in his hand, and announces that he is going to kill them. He, thus, attempts to quell a rebellion for freedom among the Arabs. In the same scene, he orders their corpses to be burned.[39]

Turning to Mikhā'īl Mishāqa's memoirs and his views of al-Jazzār, we find the harem episode known from Shihāb's *Tārīkh*. It is recounted in gruesome, and new, detail:[40]

> After Salīm Pasha set off with his troops and comrades from al-Jazzār's *mamlūk*s and had arrived at Ḥārat Ṣaydā with his troops, news reached him that, when al-Jazzār returned from the pilgrimage, someone had reported to him that his *mamlūk*s had acted perfidiously and had been having relations with his harem during his absence. 'Therefore', [Salīm Pasha was told,] 'he has sent you from him in order to do away with you. After your departure from Acre, he murdered everyone in his house, except for a young slave girl eight years old, by grilling their faces. He locked the door of the house from within, the eunuchs with him, lit a great pile of coal in the courtyard, seized each woman by the hair and held her face down on the coals with his foot until she died. In this horrible operation he killed thirty-seven women.'[41]

In numerous other contexts, Mishāqa describes random instances in which a raging al-Jazzār mutilated, tortured and killed individuals.[42] His reasons for doing so emerge quite clearly from the account: The struggle for power in Mount Lebanon is intimately connected with the fate of Mishāqa's family. He describes in great detail how his father Jirjis inherited his grandfather's tax-farms, and the subsequent extortions by al-Jazzār which almost led to the family's financial ruin.[43] Jirjis is only saved when Amīr Bashīr provides him with employment.[44]

The coalescence of Lebanese Christian and European representations of al-Jazzār goes beyond the episode just discussed. It is obvious in the ac-

Dana Sajdi for the observation that this account reflects a 'Shahrayarisation' of al-Jazzār. He is turned into a veritable Shahrayar, another version of a king betrayed and fearing betrayal who exacted indiscriminate vengeance on all his wives. This coalescence of al-Jazzār's description with the tales of *One Thousand and One Nights* tales is all the more intriguing as the *Nights* themselves reflected an *imaginaire* jointly elaborated by Levantine Christians and French scholars.

36 Whaley, *Memoirs*, 169–170.

37 Basīlī, *Sūriyā*, 73.

38 I am grateful to Anton Shammas for drawing my attention to Salīm Khūrī's theatre play and sending me an electronic copy of the play.

39 Khūrī, *Warīth al-Jazzār*, 72, 74.

40 See Thackston, *Murder, Mayhem, Pillage*, 39–41 (section 'Al-Jazzār Returns and Murders the Women of his Harem; the Mamlūks Revolt against Him and Plunder Ṣūr').

41 Thackston, *Murder, Mayhem, Pillage*, 39–40.

42 Ibid., 28–30 (section 'Al-Jazzār Slaughters Two Hundred and Thirty Human Beings for No Reason'), 30–31 (section 'Forty Innocent Prisoners Are Killed for their Chains'), 50 (the fate of the Jewish superintendent of the treasury of Acre, Muʿallim Ḥāyīm: 'Once in anger he had his nose cut off, another time his right ear, and another time he had his right eye plucked out'), and so on.

43 Ibid., especially 32–36.

44 Ibid., 42.

count of Mīkhāʾīl Niqūlā al-Ṣabbāgh, the grandson of Ibrāhīm al-Ṣabbāgh, Ẓāhir al-ʿUmar's treasurer. Given that Mīkhāʾīl al-Ṣabbāgh was enthusiastic about Napoleon's campaign and even included laudatory poetry praising Napoleon, it is not surprising that his image of al-Jazzār is no less bleak than that of Ḥaydar Aḥmad Shihāb. In contrast to most chroniclers, who state that al-Jazzār was a Bosnian Christian who converted to Islam, he presents an alternative story regarding al-Jazzār's origins. He claims that al-Jazzār's father was the well-known Ottoman governor Hekīmoğlu ʿAlī Pasha (1689–1758), who had an affair with a Jewish woman named Rīnā.[45] Because of his parents, al-Jazzār wavered between Islam and Judaism before he went to Istanbul and was sold there. We see how in this account, antisemitic stereotypes, probably assimilated from French political discourse of the time, were employed to denigrate al-Jazzār.

The image of al-Jazzār conveyed by Mīkhāʾīl Niqūlā al-Ṣabbāgh is one forged in accordance with the image to be found in European political discourse, but it is also constructed to articulate inner-Christian rivalries and ruptures. This is especially visible when Mīkhāʾīl al-Ṣabbāgh blames Orthodox Christians employed by al-Jazzār to have incited him to do evil.[46] The image of al-Jazzār seems to have served as a discursive instrument in communal self-affirmation, intercommunal polemics and in the expression of political allegiance. Al-Jazzār became a trope in sectarian politics before the age of sectarianism.

Greek Orthodox historians, by contrast, seem to have had a somewhat more nuanced perspective on al-Jazzār, as suggested by Mikhāʾīl Burayk's references to him. Burayk mentions al-Jazzār only three times in his *Tārīkh*: He holds al-Jazzār responsible for an episode of unrest in Beirut in 1776 during which his troops plundered the city and left it in ruins.[47] In 1777, he blames him for plundering the land of the Druze and the Biqāʿa, and for the rape and kidnapping of women, who ended up being sold, together with children, in Damascus.[48] In 1780, however, his perspective shifted noticeably:

In this year, the above-mentioned Vizier Aḥmad Pasha al-Jazzār, the *vali* of Sidon who lives in the city of Acre, displayed justice and impartiality towards the entire community (*ṭāʾifa*) of the Christians in this land (with cunning and duplicity). He made a campaign against the Mountain of the Druze (al-Shūf), dominated them, and humiliated them. Peace and security reigned without and within. Then he made a campaign against the land of the Mitwālīs [Lebanese Shiite Muslims, FK], and God let him defeat them. He killed their shaykh Nāṣīf, took possession of the forts and the land, and humiliated the rebels. The wolf was now with the sheep. The name of al-Jazzār was extolled, and justice, security and safety spread throughout this land.[49]

Al-Jazzār emerges as a somewhat ambiguous figure in this description but for all his political cunning, he is seen as a protector of the Christians. ʿAbdallāh ibn Mīkhāʾīl Ṭarrād al-Bayrūtī also praises al-Jazzār for his fairness towards Beirut's Christians, especially for protecting the city's Christian merchants:

All that time, when al-Jazzār was in Beirut, he established peace and safety for the Christians. When the prominent Christians went to greet him, he comforted them and calmed their fears that their possessions would be safe and that they would be able to continue buying and selling, taking and giving, and that they should continue to

45 Al-Ṣabbāgh, *Tārīkh*, 115.
46 Ibid., 119.
47 Burayk, *Tārīkh*, 106.
48 Ibid., 108. In this context, al-Jazzār's army is said to have plundered *khazāʾin jazīla*, probably a reference to the looting of libraries. This episode is particularly interesting since the content of the Jazzār library reflects a certain Shii presence. See Chapter 16 by Ahmed El Shamsy and Chapter 13 by Walid Saleh in this volume.
49 Ibid., 112.

ask for Yūnus Niqūlās's [the Greek Orthodox customs officer, FK] long life because the town was his and not al-Jazzār's. Such were his good deeds (*maḥāsinuhū*).[50]

Ṭarrād also reports that interconfessional tensions arose at the time of Napoleon's campaign. Beirut's Muslims started to attack Christians because they presumed that the latter sided with the French. Al-Jazzār thereupon sent orders that the Christians were not to be bothered, since they were loyal subjects of the Sultan. Whoever attacked them should be held accountable before al-Jazzār.[51]

The image of al-Jazzār that emerges from these reports by Orthodox historians could not be any more different from the image painted by the contemporaries that were discussed above. To what degree this image took shape in response to the representations of al-Jazzār by Levantine Catholics can best be gleaned when Ṭarrād describes a sudden change in al-Jazzār: at some point before the French campaign, al-Jazzār started accepting bribes. It was then that he became brutal, cut off noses and extorted Beirut's inhabitants. This narrative of a shift affecting al-Jazzār's character accompanies statements on the hardship Greek Orthodox Christians now suffered.[52] We can perhaps glean some of the author's motivations in his discussion of al-Jazzār when we learn that a Catholic, Fāris al-Dahhān, had now been appointed to the post of overseer of customs and duties, a position that had been in Greek Orthodox hands before. Even when manipulating al-Jazzār's image in light of day-to-day politics that had an impact on the struggles between different Christian communities, however, Ṭarrād does not completely betray his generally positive perspective on al-Jazzār. He eventually concludes that al-Jazzār coerced no one in matters of religion.

What emerges from these entangled elite historiographies is the fact that al-Jazzār's rule was seen as the tyranny of a butcher who acted like an oriental despot, reflecting a coalescence of European, especially French, discourses and ideas with those of Maronite Christian notables. Al-Jazzār posed a threat to these Christians' social and financial security. Orthodox Christians adopted a somewhat ambiguous attitude towards al-Jazzār because of the intermittent periods in which they were favoured by him. 'Al-Jazzār the tyrant' is a representation that emerged as a result of his involvement in sectarian politics and in a framework of inner-Christian differentiation and communal self-affirmation.

2 Al-Jazzār the Extortionist Who Upset Social Hierarchies—the Elite View from Damascus

Another prominent image of al-Jazzār which is intimately connected with the one just sketched, the representation of al-Jazzār as a tyrant, is that of the extortionist and manipulator of the market who disrespected his opponents, thus, upsetting social hierarchies and deliberately turning them on their head. Historiographical accounts of the different periods during which al-Jazzār held the post of *vali* of Damascus (1784–1785, 1790–1795, 1799–1803) especially develop and perpetuate this image. These accounts were authored by individuals belonging to very different factions and groups of Damascene society; the common denominator is that the individuals in question were members of urban elites. Virtually nothing is known about Mikhā'īl al-Dimashqī (fl. 1841) except that he was Catholic and resided in Damascus during the period covered by his chronicle (1782–1841). Economic and social grievances are also expressed by Ruslān ibn Yaḥyā al-Qārī al-Shāghūrī (fl. late 18th century). He was a Muslim, probably a Janissary Aghā. The same holds true for Ḥasan Aghā (fl. late 18th/ early 19th century), whose chronicle covers the period between 1186/1772 and 1241/1825 and who is the last individual to be discussed below in this section. We are confronted in these ac-

50 Ṭarrād, *Mukhtaṣar*, 106.
51 Ibid., 141.
52 Ibid., 114.

counts with a Damascene urban representation of al-Jazzār and his tenure of office in Damascus that is strongly shaped by a number of recurring elite concerns, especially of an economic nature.

The Catholic Mikhā'īl al-Dimashqī is anything but nuanced in his appraisal of al-Jazzār's personality. According to him, al-Jazzār 'hated mankind (*jins al-bashar*) very much, he was not to be trusted, and no one served him and came out unscathed—they would either lose their money or their life'.[53] The misdeeds he lists are, first and foremost, economic grievances: al-Jazzār is said to have extorted money, to have been responsible for a devaluation of money and to have contributed to the rise of prices for goods in the market.[54]

Besides blaming al-Jazzār for economic developments, Mikhā'īl al-Dimashqī also accuses him of having poisoned the grandson of Asʿad Pasha al-ʿAẓm (d. 1758).[55] The ʿAẓms were an influential family whose members, over several generations, held the office of governor appointed by the Porte in the city; they can be understood as direct contenders of al-Jazzār for control of the politics of the city and its economic resources. Mikhā'īl al-Dimashqī furthermore reports that al-Jazzār killed a member of the influential Murādī family—one of the families of notables who shaped Damascene politics, as was the case elsewhere in Syria[56]—as though the individual from this family belonged to the 'common people' (*ʿāmma*), meaning that al-Jazzār went against the dictates of social hierarchy in his political interventions.[57] The *muftī* ʿAbdallāh ibn Ṭāhir al-Murādī belonged to a family close to the ʿAẓm family, and he was hanged by al-Jazzār in the citadel in 1797 or 1798.[58] As Douwes observed, *muftī*s were 'prime targets' of al-Jazzār's repressions in Damascus because they came from influential notable families, were sometimes affiliated with the ʿAẓms and they were also those who voiced the population's grievances against him.[59] Other notables and *aghās* did not fare any better. What lingers behind the accusations above is a threatened urban mercantile elite who felt that al-Jazzār's tenure of office was destroying the prevailing social order.

Mikhā'īl al-Dimashqī's social grievances are confirmed by Ruslān ibn Yaḥyā al-Qārī al-Shāghūrī, who expresses his hate of al-Jazzār in unequivocal terms. To him, al-Jazzār was 'an evil-doer, depraved, and he manipulated food (prices)'.[60] Whereas the first two accusations are rather general, the last one has an economic dimension. He effectively enumerates the same economic grievances as Mikhā'īl al-Dimashqī.[61]

The Janissary Ḥasan Aghā describes a regime of terror in Damascus: al-Jazzār started executing and mutilating people during his second term of office in Damascus.[62] While Ḥasan Aghā does not extensively deal with al-Jazzār's economic misdeeds, he too mentions the death of the al-Murādī family member.[63] Similar to Mikhā'īl al-Dimashqī, he accuses al-Jazzār of not respecting social hierarchies, though in a different context.[64]

Not even al-Jazzār's victory over the French was sufficient reason for Ḥasan Aghā, who was deeply suspicious of Europeans, to celebrate al-Jazzār. He relativises al-Jazzār's triumph by stating that he only won because of the support of the English.[65] Upon hearing the news of al-Jazzār's death in 1804, he wrote that 'all creatures were happy about his

53 Al-Dimashqī, *Tārīkh*, 80–81.
54 Ibid., 75.
55 Ibid., 77–78.
56 See especially Hourani, "Ottoman Reform" and Schatkowski Schilcher, *Families*. See also Meriwether, "Urban Notables", and *The Kin who Count*, with a focus on notable families in Aleppo.
57 Al-Dimashqī, *Tārīkh*, 92–93.
58 Schatkowski Schilcher, *Families*, 38.
59 Douwes, *Ottomans in Syria*, 92–93. Also see 167 on al-Jazzār's lack of respect for the religious establishment, which was perceived by Damascene society as outrageous.
60 Al-Qārī al-Shāghūrī, "Al-Wuzarā'," 85.
61 Al-Qārī al-Shāghūrī, "Al-Wuzarā'", 88–89.
62 Ḥasan Aghā, *Tārīkh*, 23.
63 Ibid., 89.
64 Ibid., 24.
65 Ibid., 52.

death'.[66] A reference to revolts by al-Jazzār's followers, who are called 'the Kurds' (*al-akrād*) and effectively identified as his henchmen, seems significant.[67] Al-Jazzār is, thus, associated with lowly classes of the population, since the designation *al-akrād* was often used to designate 'the rabble'. Very significantly, in his historical account Ḥasan Aghā included poems celebrating al-Jazzār's death that Ḥasan Aghā himself claims to have composed.[68] One of these poems in particular sheds further light on al-Jazzār's association with the most lowly and unruly strata of society. The opening verses are as follows:

He is Aḥmad, whose deeds should not be praised
[a word play: *hūwa-Aḥmadun lā tuḥmadu fa'āluhū*]!
The Butcher of the people of Damascus suppressed them with fear.
And he sent Kurds to Damascus
Whose leader dwells in the fortress of Acre.
Sheikh Ṭāhā is his name, and he became
Infamous for the outrage he committed and his error.
His brother-in-law came to Damascus as financial officer,
'Abd al-Wahhāb—he now dwells in hell.
Of Kurdish origin, worse, Yazīdī. He came
From the seed of a lowly people, more lowly than cows.[69]

A very negative image of the group designated as *al-akrād* emerges from this poem. They are depicted as al-Jazzār's henchmen. The poem particularly demonises a figure said to have been the head of the Kurds in Acre, Ṭāhā al-Kurdī, a torturer and gangster brought to Damascus by al-Jazzār. The subsequent verses describe the terror to which the people of Damascus are subjected by al-Jazzār's Kurds in graphic detail.

The poem points to a situation in which Damascus was torn between two factions that vied for control, as Schatkowski Schilcher has argued: one faction was connected to the 'Aẓm family, oriented towards the imperial centre, and consisted of merchants of the northern quarters; the rivalling faction consisted of the men of the Maydān quarter, southern aghās, and poorer, semi-urbanised elements.[70] The poem describes how al-Jazzār had lost some of his previous power and the support of merchants of the Maydān quarter and, therefore, ruled through a splinter Kurdish faction in Damascus. Upon al-Jazzār's death in 1804, a mob attacked these Kurdish collaborators of al-Jazzār.[71]

Al-Jazzār appears in the accounts of Damascene Catholic merchants and those of Janissaries, all of them connected to the rivalling faction in the city, as an extortionist whose nefarious deeds destroyed the delicate balance of the market and society. The accounts depict him as the cold-blooded murderer of urban elites and the head of a lowly pack of henchmen of dubious ethnic background labelled 'Kurds'. Urban elite anxieties about economic status linger in the background of this historical representation of al-Jazzār. As the historian al-Jabartī observed in his necrology on al-Jazzār, 'He dispossessed many wealthy men of their fortunes and uprooted their wealth.'[72] Al-Jazzār managed to gain control of the trade via Sidon and Acre, especially the trade in cotton. His conflict with the Janissary aghās goes back to his obtaining the position of commander of the pilgrimage (*amīr al-ḥajj*); in this position, he also started to infringe on the overland trade in grain and the production of livestock.[73]

It is interesting to confront the views of Damascene urban elites with al-Jazzār's self-representation, albeit mediated through an unknown number of intermediary accounts in Ottoman historiography. The nineteenth-century historian Nawfal Ni'matallāh Nawfal (1812–1887) used Ottoman

66 Ibid., 107.
67 Ibid., 107–113.
68 Ibid., 113–116.
69 Ibid., 114.

70 Schatkowski Schilcher, *Families*, 58.
71 Ibid., 38.
72 Philipp et al., *History of Egypt*, vol. 3, 494.
73 Schatkowski Schilcher, *Families*, 36–37.

source texts for his history of Lebanon, and he quoted them in excerpts. He particularly includes the fragment of a letter written by al-Jazzār and addressed to one *kethüda* Pasha in Istanbul, probably the deputy of the Grand Vizier:

He [al-Jazzār] sent a note to the *kethüda* Pasha in which he said: 'The state of Damascus, Jerusalem and of the Muslim pilgrims are known to the Porte (*al-dawla*). If you will, remove the *vali* of Damascus and the one who guides the pilgrimage (*amīr 'alā al-ḥajj*). I shall accept this in addition to the *eyalet* of Sidon. I will pay to the public kitchen (*maṭbakh*) of our benefactor the Sultan four hundred *kese* and two hundred more to the required places. If things stay as they are, it is your decision. I swear by the Qur'an and by the spirituality of His Eminence the owner of this letter that the position is not what I am aiming for. But I heard that the poor and the destitute have become displeased (*munkassirī al-khāṭir*) with our Master the Sultan, so I am worried and impatient, and I cannot bear this. End.'[74]

We do not know whether these are the actual words of al-Jazzār, and to what degree the wording has been edited. The general direction of this fragment of a letter to the Ottoman bureaucracy in Istanbul is still noteworthy. The al-Jazzār emerging from this letter describes himself as a protector of the poor and the destitute. He claims to apply for the position of the *vali* of Damascus only out of worry because of their displeasure with the Sultan, not simply out of greed and longing for influence and positions. This is in keeping with the image of a governor who could potentially undermine the striving for financial betterment among urban elites. We will see in the next section that the final representation of al-Jazzār to be discussed here, the image of a patron of the poor, seems compatible with the image of the socially subversive extortionist that urban elites came to dread.

74 Nawfal, *Kashf al-lithām*, 211.

3 Al-Jazzār the Just, Patron of the Poor

The images of al-Jazzār as a tyrant and extortionist have left a strong imprint not only on the collective memory, as reflected by poems, but have also shaped later historiography and fictional literature. The recurring reports about cruel punishments meted out by al-Jazzār are too often repeated to be dismissed as literary fictions. Contemporaries who claim to have seen mutilated individuals who had come to experience al-Jazzār's 'justice' are unlikely to have fabricated such accounts.[75] Despite the likelihood that al-Jazzār was indeed a volatile ruler who was quick to punish, other texts shed an altogether different light on him. In these texts, al-Jazzār emerges as a ruler aware of the principles of just governance and, more particularly, as a patron of the poor. The first text to be examined is an account by al-Jazzār himself, the *Niẓāmnāme-i Mıṣır*. He wrote it at the request of the imperial *divan* during his tenure of office as governor of Damascus. The account, which was sent to Istanbul in 1199/1785 and which describes Ottoman Egypt in terms of its geography and social fabric to prepare a military intervention,[76] is not autobiographical in the least, but it subtly sheds light on al-Jazzār's understanding of just rule. Kemp suggested, somewhat hesitantly, that the 'qualified, experienced, and determined Governor' described in the *Niẓāmnāme* may be al-

75 See, for example, the comment in Seetzen, *Reisen*, vol. 2, 137: 'In Acre, many people can still be seen whose noses and ears were cut off or who lost one eye because of Dschessar Pascha [al-Jazzār]. He did this occasionally himself, with much dexterity and apparent joy.'

76 A unique copy has been preserved in the Topkapı Saray in Istanbul, Bağdad Koşk Ms. 288. It was edited and translated by Stanford Shaw in *Ottoman Egypt*. For an analysis of the *Niẓāmnāme-i Mıṣır*, see Kemp "An Eighteenth-Century Turkish Intelligence Report". Uriel Heyd has questioned Shaw's dating of the *Niẓāmnāme-i Mıṣır*. Despite some disagreements with Shaw's analysis, he considers it 'quite possible that this work was written by Cezzār'. Heyd, "Review of Stanford J. Shaw", 188.

Jazzār himself.[77] Without any doubt, this is the case; the *Niẓāmnāme* has all the features of an 'application letter' for the position of governor of Egypt. Read in this way, the documentary report suggests that al-Jazzār knew how to gain favour among the masses by alleviating financial burdens.

A number of scattered historical reports by contemporary chroniclers confirm al-Jazzār's ideas regarding lower segments of society, albeit in complex ways and mostly in passing. They stem from the Greek Catholic historian Ḥanānyā al-Munayyir (1756–1823)[78] and from the Greek Orthodox historian and chronicler ʿAbdallāh ibn Mikhāʾīl Ṭarrād al-Bayrūtī introduced above. We will see in the following that al-Jazzār's vision of the just ruler and his contemporaries' assessment of his tenure of office converge in some interesting points.

We are also in the fortunate position to know some of the popular songs sung and epic poems recited in praise of al-Jazzār that were circulating at the time of his victory over Napoleon and al-Jazzār's death. The natural scholar and traveller Ulrich Jasper Seetzen (1767–1811) collected such popular literature eagerly.[79] Besides these songs, we will see that poetry composed by the religious scholar and *muftī* of Beirut ʿAbd al-Laṭīf Fatḥallāh (1766–1844) in praise of him also perpetuates the image of al-Jazzār as a generous benefactor who protected and supported the destitute[80]—those who usually remain without voice in the historiography of urban notables and elites. They are given a voice in these songs and epics.

Al-Jazzār repeatedly emphasises in the *Niẓāmnāme* that the 'tyranny' of the Mamluk rulers of Egypt prepares the ground for the defection of influential political agents to the Ottoman side. When reflecting on the religious establishment and their influence on the common people, for example, he points out:

> If there should come to Egypt an able Governor in whom they [the two highest religious dignitaries, FK] have confidence, and if they understand that he will conquer the tyrants, that he will not be negligent in inflicting proper punishment on them, and that he will restore and complete the *Vaqfs* and other revenues established for them since olden times, they will cooperate with him and will do all in their power to overcome and annihilate these tyrants. And their efforts will be of use because of all the *ʿUlemâ* of the Azhâr, the *Imâms* and the *Ḥâṭîbs*, the *Ḥâfiẓes*, the poor of the city, the *Rûm Ôṣâğî*, and the North African merchants follow them and never contradict their words. In sum, they have the ability to assemble in a single day a powerful military regiment of at least seventy or eighty thousand men who are docile and loyal to them, and in this way they can assist the Governor.[81]

Al-Jazzār sees the religious elites and the masses of Cairo as crucial groups in the population who must be won over to consolidate political power—he emerges as a studious political strategist. We are confronted here with a political strategy that al-Jazzār employed throughout his career. Nowhere does this become more tangible than in the architectural landscape of Acre, which he shaped decisively. It is not by coincidence that he built a mosque and a fountain (*sabīl*), dedicating significant resources to shaping the religious infrastructure of the city.

In contrast to what the merchants from Damascus, who complained about al-Jazzār's extortions, suggest, al-Jazzār was acutely aware of the importance of not putting unbearable financial burdens on his subjects. He suggests in the *Niẓāmnāme* that an imperial order be read upon the Ottoman conquest of Cairo. Among other points, it includes the following message:

77 Kemp, "An Eighteenth-Century Turkish Intelligence Report", 505.

78 On Ḥanānyā al-Munayyir as a chronicler, see Bualuan, *Lebanese Historical Thought*, 19–26.

79 See Gotha, Gotha Research Library of the University of Erfurt, Ms. orient. A 2189; Ms. orient. A 2222; Ms. orient. A 2347; Ms. orient. A 2840.

80 See Fatḥ Allāh, *Dīwān*.

81 Shaw, *Ottoman Egypt*, 23.

[…] therefore, it is ordered that an experienced and faithful scribe be appointed especially from the Sublime Porte, that he make a full survey under the supervision of the Governor and *Qâḍî* of Egypt, and that the tax be apportioned anew according to the capacity of each, so that the poor subjects will be spared from the injustice of giving too much or too little […].[82]

Al-Jazzār was a financially savvy politician and saw himself as a good administrator, just like the one he suggested the Porte send to Egypt in 1785. The *Niẓāmnāme* shows that he was fully aware of the negative sides of his image among political and mercantile elites in southern Bilād al-Shām. In concluding his report, he emphasises:

First of all, the most important thing is that the Governor who is appointed to carry it out must be a man who is extremely rightly guided and wise, a good administrator with great capacity and dignity who is reliable and faithful. Once such a reliable man, trusting in God, is sent, no attention should be paid to all sorts of useless nothings which will be said about him by the people.[83]

Al-Jazzār knew that he was infamous among his contemporaries. Yet, he was not overly worried about it, since in his eyes other qualities made a good governor and administrator. The *Niẓāmnāme* here clearly reflects al-Jazzār's engagement with intellectual debates about violence and charity in just rule, which are also represented in his library, namely, in the collection of 'Mirrors for Princes'. The history section of al-Jazzār's library more generally can be seen as a site of al-Jazzār's self-positioning as a just ruler in a long-standing Islamic tradition.[84]

What al-Jazzār suggests to the Porte in the *Niẓāmnāme* is to send a model ruler, one embodied by himself. Some of the features appearing in the description of this model ruler, among them the ability to strike and punish ruthlessly and swiftly, the ability to gain the favour of the religious establishment and the masses, especially the poor, and financial even-handedness, also emerge from some accounts by his contemporaries in descriptions of al-Jazzār. One of the more ambiguous of these accounts regarding the historical image of al-Jazzār is found in the works of the Greek Catholic Lebanese historian and litterateur Ḥanānyā al-Munayyir.[85]

Al-Munayyir generally paints a dark picture of al-Jazzār, but he is also critical of the other political agents in Mount Lebanon, adopting a negative perspective on them as well. An example is his description of the Battle of Zahla (1792), which he claims to have experienced first-hand.[86] On this occasion, al-Jazzār and his army, consisting of Dalātiyya, Maghāriba, Arnā'ūṭ elements and 'strangers', clashed with the 'people of the land'—by which the author means Druze and Christians, unified in their fight.[87] The people of Mount Lebanon won this battle.[88] Surprisingly, when discussing the responsibility of the parties involved, al-Munayyir insists that the war was not al-Jazzār's responsibility, but that all those in power in Mount Lebanon were to be blamed. In his eyes, those in charge had acted only out of self-interest, ignoring the needs of the people and the land.

This measured criticism of al-Jazzār is a characteristic of al-Munayyir's historical account. His balanced view allows him to admit that al-Jazzār was not hated by all. Notably, when writing about al-Jazzār's death, al-Munayyir not only includes laudatory poetry and expresses his own relief and joy. Instead, he admits that the people of Beirut were saddened by his passing and deplored his death:

82 Ibid., 37.
83 Ibid., 49.
84 See Dana Sajdi's Chapter 22 in this volume.

85 Al-Munayyir, *Waqāʾiʿ al-Durūz* and *al-Durr al-marṣūf*.
86 Al-Munayyir, *Waqāʾiʿ al-Durūz*, 134–141.
87 On the unity of the people of Mount Lebanon, see ibid., 135.
88 Ibid., 140.

There was joy everywhere when al-Jazzār died, except among the Muslims of Beirut (*illā islām Bayrūt*). A great sadness descended on them, and they were very worried because he loved them immeasurably (*yuḥibbuhum maḥabbatan tafūqu al-qiyās*), and he cared about them more than any other people.[89]

Al-Munayyir makes it sound as though al-Jazzār's popularity among Sunni Muslims in Beirut were an exception, but a passage in his *al-Durr al-marṣūf* suggests that this popularity was not limited to Beirut. When writing in 1775 about al-Jazzār's time as the governor of Sidon, he clearly states that he was popular with the city's Muslim populace, especially with the poor:

And around this time, al-Jazzār was accepted by the Porte and his words were heard, and he achieved his goals. The Sultan graced him with the governorship of Sidon, so Acre also came under his rule. He came as sovereign to this land and made Acre his dwelling-place. He erected buildings and created gardens there and drew plenty of water to them. He fortified the walls and spent a lot of money on them. Every creature was afraid of him in their heart. He dominated the Mitwālīs, took their land, defeated their rulers, scattered them, and confiscated their land and possessions. He also stretched out his hand to the city of Beirut which had been in the hand of the princes of the house of Shihāb and under their rule. After that he was appointed governor of Damascus, in addition to the governorship of Sidon. He directed the pilgrims and brought them back safely three or four years. He subdued the rebels and terrorised those who diverged. He sent to the Sultan money in vast quantities. He extended his rule from Jerusalem to Homs, collected gold and silver—it is impossible to say how much. He became stronger and stronger. He was smart (*ṣāḥib fiṭna*) and an experienced governor (*tadbīr muḥannak*) in all areas. *He loved the poor with contentment and ethics*, except he was unreliable and there was no relying on him because he betrayed many [emphasis mine, FK].[90]

Al-Munayyir clearly stresses al-Jazzār's popularity with Sidon's poor, and his benevolence towards them. This benevolence is manifest in interventions in the urban architectural landscape.[91]

The comments al-Munayyir made in passing, and almost despite himself, are confirmed by the historical accounts of Greek Orthodox chroniclers and historians discussed above. ʿAbdallāh ibn Mīkhāʾīl Ṭarrād, who lived in Beirut, confirms al-Munayyir's claims in his *Mukhtaṣar*. Ṭarrād conveys a very positive image of al-Jazzār, thereby adopting the diametrically opposite perspective of Catholic historians, as discussed above. He does not deny the darker aspects of al-Jazzār's rule. He admits, for example, that his North African (Maghāriba) soldiers caused a lot of destruction when al-Jazzār first arrived in Beirut.[92] He also thinks that al-Jazzār was responsible for preventing the Christians from returning to Beirut after the city was bombarded by the Russian forces in 1773.[93] Such criticisms notwithstanding, Ṭar-

89 Ibid., 241.

90 Al-Munayyir, *Al-Durr al-marṣūf*, 20.

91 To what degree urban space was characterised by al-Jazzār's interventions emerges, for example, from contemporary reports about Acre, especially those of travellers such as Ulrich Jasper Seetzen. See Seetzen, *Reisen*, vol. 2, 74–78, 82–83 (in the context of a description of al-Jazzār's Mosque, Seetzen also mentions his library). The Moroccan traveller Muḥammad ibn ʿAbd al-Wahhāb al-Miknāsī (d. 1799) was also full of praise of Acre during a stay described in his travelogue. Mentioning al-Jazzār by name, he compares the splendour of the mosques and bath houses of Acre to those of Constantinople. He also mentions that the weak and poor were taken care of. See al-Miknāsī, *Riḥla*, 288–290. A century later, the historian Asad Rustum (1897–1965) makes similar observations on urban space and al-Jazzār's impact; Rustum, "Akka". Acre's architecture is also the focal point of ʿArrāf and Ḥijāzī, *Aḥmad Bāshā al-Jazzār*. More than half of the contributions are dedicated to this topic.

92 Ṭarrād, *Mukhtaṣar*, 95.

93 Ibid., 103.

rād claims that al-Jazzār governed Beirut with justice.[94] He reports that people in Beirut prayed that he may have a long life, and he praises al-Jazzār's 'beautiful rulership' (*siyāsa ḥasana*).[95] He describes how, in a conflict that opposed al-Jazzār and Ottoman troops from Istanbul, the people of Beirut displayed loyalty to him.[96] These references are likely references to the Muslim population of Beirut.

Despite their scarcity, some of the articulations of religious scholars and of the lower strata of society in cities under al-Jazzār's rule have been preserved—precisely those groups of the population who stood to profit from his policies, as suggested above. Al-Jazzār's ties to the religious elite were certainly peculiar, as demonstrated by the odd reports that al-Jazzār claimed to be the expected *mahdī*, a claim he wanted scholars to bolster with esoteric speculations. It seems that some religious scholars embraced this idea,[97] while others were not too accommodating in their scepticism.[98] This somewhat odd story notwithstanding, al-Jazzār certainly had some religious scholars firmly on his side. The *muftī* of Beirut ʿAbd al-Laṭīf Fatḥallāh, for example, included two poems in praise of al-Jazzār in his *Dīwān*. One was a laudatory poem praising his victory over Napoleon's army and the other one was an elegy on the occasion of his death that expresses utter desperation at his passing.[99] The background of the praise poem is the Battle of Acre in the Napoleonic campaign. Besides deploying conventional imagery, such as the depiction of al-Jazzār as a 'lion' in war, the *muftī* also depicts al-Jazzār's generosity. While generosity is regularly described in panegyric poetry, the particular brand of generosity that emerges from the poem is noteworthy:

> You never drove away the one who asked,
> Even though the mortals before you became many.
> And when good news were not forthcoming to them,
> Their bodies and hearts were revived in your generosity (*jūd*).[100]

More than the generous patron, al-Jazzār emerges from the poem as the benefactor of the destitute who came to him to ask for charity. In addition, he appears as the protector of Islam whose *jihād* was rejected only by those who erred or were envious. The people with whom al-Jazzār enjoyed popularity are explicitly identified once again as 'the people of Beirut':

> O pride of Acre in the land—
> Acre is the crown of the land, and its walls and its pillars.
> Within them, you guarded religion (*al-dīn*), the religion of Muḥammad,
> And you destroyed what the unbelievers have built.
> You are the one to protect our possessions, our land,
> Our blood, the earth, and the children.

94 Ibid., 100.

95 Ibid., 106.

96 Ibid., 110.

97 We learn from al-Jabartī that the Hanafi religious scholar Murtaḍā al-Ḥusaynī al-Zabīdī (1145/1732–1205/1790), the author of the *Tāj al-ʿarūs*, believed al-Jazzār's messianic claims: 'Once he sent a letter to Aḥmad Pasha al-Jazzār in which he mentioned that he was the awaited Mahdī and that he would attain great importance. He was moved to believe it because of the tendency of souls towards their desires.' Philipp et al., *History of Egypt*, vol. 2, 334.

98 The Moroccan scholar Abū al-Qāsim al-Zayyānī (d. 1249/1833) calls al-Jazzār an 'idiot' (*aḥmaq*) because of his attempt to sell himself as a saviour figure; al-Zayyānī, *al-Turjumāna*, 258. Al-Jabartī considers it all 'nonsense'; Philipp et al., *History of Egypt*, vol. 3, 495. The issue of al-Jazzār's messianic claims and esoteric speculations is discussed at greater length in Chapter 22 by Dana Sajdi and Chapter 24 by Liana Saif in this volume.

99 Fatḥallāh, *Dīwān*, vol. 1, 235–237 (no. 282) = *Madīḥ Aḥmad al-Jazzār*; vol. 1, 325–326 (no. 407) = *Qism min Rithāʾ Aḥmad al-Jazzār*.

100 Ibid., 235.

Woe to those who refuse to acknowledge you, out of ignorance,
Transgression is ignorance and error is obstinacy!
When they deny what you did—
The denial of your favours in this world is heresy.
[...]
I am a man from among those who love (*yuḥibbūna*) whom
You love and who become adversaries (*yuʿādū*) of the one you hate.
And I am one of those who talk about thanking you,
And loudly proclaim it and repeat it.
They are the people of Beirut whose necks you adorned
With the pearl of your presents.
Their natural disposition and their love (*widād*) are reliably yours,
They do not harbour love (*widād*) for anyone except you.[101]

The enormous popularity of al-Jazzār that emerges from this poem by a religious scholar from Beirut resonates with numerous popular songs (*aghānī*, sg. *ghināʾ*) and epic poems (*siyar*, sg. *sīra*) that were sung and recited by the people of different cities. Ulrich Jasper Seetzen, who travelled the area two years after al-Jazzār's death, collected such popular expressions.[102]

101 Ibid., 236–237.

102 They were for Seetzen primarily an instrument to learn Arabic. He had locals pen them down on his behalf, and orthographical mistakes, dialectal elements and unsteady handwriting suggest that these locals did not have a high degree of literacy. The songs and poems they wrote down were no prestigious poetic compositions; they were circulating orally. Despite their low literary prestige, they enjoyed tremendous popularity. Palestinian historians recognised their importance in the twentieth century. A noteworthy example is Iḥsān al-Nimr (1905–1985) who observed that they combined the language of the Bedouin with the structure of epics like the *Sīrat Banī Hilāl*. See al-Nimr, *Tārīkh Jabal Nābulus*, vol. 2, 24–29.

'The Arabs, city-dwellers as well as peasants and nomads, enjoy stories [epic poems, FK] very much, which are often full of humour, vividly narrated and have an impeccable moral,' Seetzen relates in 1806 in Acre, when discussing one poem about Napoleon's unsuccessful siege.[103] 'Some of them deal with the heroic deeds of their ancestors—one could compare them to our chivalric romance. The stories of Antar, of the Beni Helál, el Daher and others are especially appreciated.'[104] He mentions in his travelogue that such songs and epic poems were recited on the occasion of important political events.[105]

Many of the songs and epic poems concerning al-Jazzār were composed in the aftermath of his victory over the French.[106] Al-Jazzār emerges from these popular expressions as an epic hero. The people venerated him; he is addressed as 'Abū Ḥamda,' a *nom de guerre*, which is cognate with his first name Aḥmad.[107] He is seen as a religious warrior (*mujāhid*):

This is the *mujāhid* Aḥmad—
His courage equals that of a lion.

103 On Napoleon's invasion of Palestine and the Siege of Acre, see in detail Cohen, "Napoleon and Jezzar", and Zeʿevi, "Ottoman Intelligence Gathering".

104 Seetzen, "Beyträge", 129. The text that he discusses is now preserved in Gotha, Gotha Research Library of the University of Erfurt, Ms. orient. A 2222.

105 Seetzen, *Reisen*, vol. 2, 79–80.

106 For example, Gotha, Gotha Research Library of the University of Erfurt, Ms. orient. A 2347 and Ms. orient. A 2840, fol. 175 and fol. 176. As seen in fig. 4.2, a local hand opens one such collection of songs on al-Jazzār with the following words: 'We shall write about the songs that appeared in the year of the French (*fa-l-naktub mā kharaja ghinā fī sanat al-Faransāwī*).' Gotha, Gotha Research Library of the University of Erfurt, Ms. orient. A 2347, fol. 1^{r}. Seetzen also mentions that in al-Ṣalt, he was gifted a long, pro-Napoleonic song on the occupation of Egypt by the French. It was composed and put into writing by a Greek Orthodox *shammās* who was also able to recite it from memory. See Seetzen, "Beyträge", 128–129.

107 Gotha, Gotha Research Library of the University of Erfurt, Ms. orient. A 2347, fol. 2^{r}.

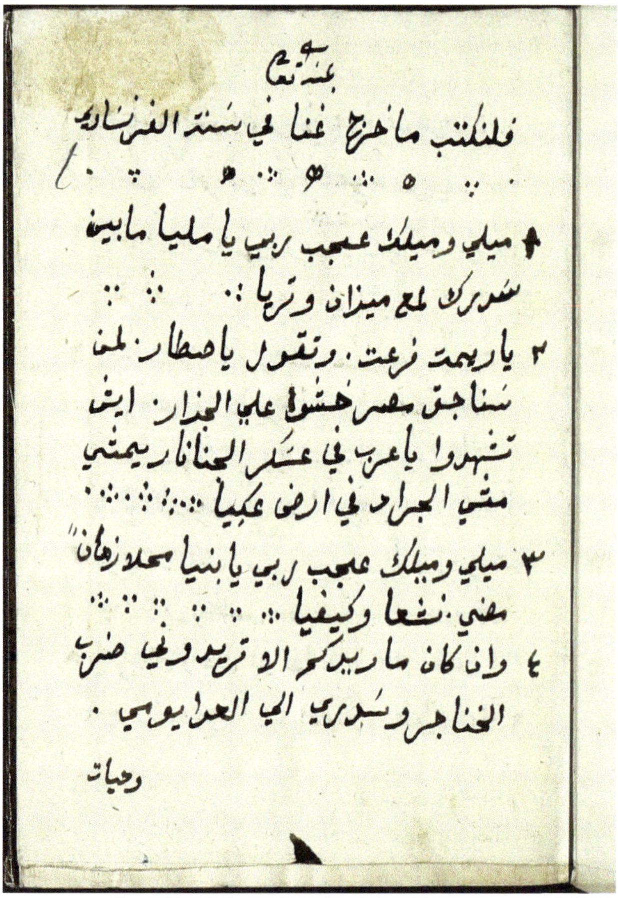

FIGURE 4.2
A collection of songs and poems on al-Jazzār. Seetzen himself gave this manuscript the title 'Songs about the invasion of Egypt and Syria by the French' ('Lieder über den Einfall der Franzosen in Egypten und Syrien')
IMAGE CREDIT: GOTHA RESEARCH LIBRARY OF THE UNIVERSITY OF ERFURT, MS. ORIENT. A 2347, FOL. 1R

He killed numerous Frenchmen,
  On account of that, his epic story is told with praise (*ḥumidat bi-dhālika sīratuhū*).[108]

We can learn more about the social composition of those who fought with al-Jazzār by examining one particularly important popular epic, known as *Rajjat al-dunyā* ('The World Was Trembling').[109] *Rajjat al-dunyā* deals with the Battle of Acre in 124 verses. It is characterised by graphic imagery and rhetoric (e.g. beheadings, blood flowing, attacks on women). The composition opens with a reference to the Napoleonic wars in Europe and Napoleon's arrival in Egypt. Throughout the text, two groups are depicted in constant confrontation: the unbelievers (*kuffār*), Europeans (*ifranj*), dogs of the Greeks (*kalb al-rūm*), Christians (*naṣāra*), and associators (*ahl al-shirk*) on Napoleon's side are opposed by the Muslims (*islām*), the people of monotheism (*ahl al-tawḥīd*), and religious warriors (*mujāhidūn*) on al-Jazzār's side. Al-Jazzār himself is depicted as the 'Sultan of War' (*sulṭān al-nufūr*).[110]

It is noteworthy that although al-Jazzār and his men represent the 'good side', the composition is quite ambiguous about the social composition of

108 Gotha, Gotha Research Library of the University of Erfurt, Ms. orient. A 2347, fol. 13v.

109 The text of this epic poem has been preserved twice as a loose paper in Gotha, Gotha Research Library of the University of Erfurt, Ms. orient. A 2840, fols. 175 and 176 (the latter one is in a better state of preservation).

110 Ms. orient. A 2840, fol. 175/176, v. 43.

his army. Among them are the ignorant (*juhhāl*), men without experience who cannot distinguish *ḥalāl* and *ḥarām*, who only destroy and drink alcohol, tyrannise the poor and deny the reckoning on Judgment Day.[111] Despite their lowliness, these men become defenders of the people of Acre:

'Where are the people of Acre, a wall protecting the women?
O *sekmen*, hurry, I don't want to hear excuses!'
They pounced on them like numerous lions,
The Arnā'ūṭ and Kurds, their breasts boiling.
They drew their swords like lions,
To gain the reward of palaces and *ḥūrī*s (in paradise).
They made religion (*al-dīn*) triumph, their faces pale,
Selling their souls for a reward (in the next world).[112]

The image of al-Jazzār in the texts discussed in this section is, unsurprisingly, very different from the representation of him in historiographical works by historians who were allied to his enemies or with whom he was in economic competition. Al-Jazzār's correspondence with the Porte, comments made in passing by historians and popular compositions all suggest that a representation of al-Jazzār existed that has been mostly forgotten. It was the image of al-Jazzār as a patron of the poor and vanquisher of the French cultivated by wide segments of lower-class urban populations who gained rather than lost under his rule as well as by some elite authors who were conscious of this side of al-Jazzār.

4 Conclusion

Representations of al-Jazzār, this chapter suggests, are projections that reflect those to whom they can be traced more than the 'historical al-Jazzār'. They are crystallisations of individual aspirations, processes of communal-building, economic interests and political alliances. They point to the divergence of historical perceptions articulated by different groups in the societies of regions and urban centres ruled by al-Jazzār during his career, notably Mount Lebanon, Damascus and Beirut. These representations even point to al-Jazzār's deployment as a trope in politics along confessional lines before the age of sectarianism.

Al-Jazzār was demonised by the Maronites of Mount Lebanon, whose interests clashed with his, but intersected with those of the French. Accordingly, representations of al-Jazzār among the French coalesced with theirs. The Greek Orthodox maintained a more ambiguous position vis-à-vis 'al-Jazzār the tyrant', presumably because they received more merciful treatment under his rule. The image of 'the extortionist al-Jazzār', a man who ignored social hierarchies, executed notables belonging to the upper echelons of the religious establishment and manipulated the market, is a clear reflection of the interests of Muslim elite politics in Damascus. Al-Jazzār threatened the monopolies and status of these elites. Nevertheless, al-Jazzār was not only seen as a tyrant and an extortionist. Some historical sources suggest that al-Jazzār found favour among the poor. Such scattered references are corroborated by popular songs and epic tales about al-Jazzār, gathered by the German traveller Ulrich Jasper Seetzen at the beginning of the nineteenth century. An engagement with subaltern historical perceptions allows for the reconstitution of an image of al-Jazzār that is mostly absent from the accounts of elite historiographers and scholars. The 'patron of the poor' positioned himself and was perceived as a protector of the destitute.

It is interesting that the different historical views of al-Jazzār are not incompatible—quite the opposite, actually. They seem to fit together well. The image of the tyrant demonised by Catholic notable historians from Mount Lebanon who were allied with his enemies (Lebanese contenders for

111 Ms. orient. A 2840, fol. 175/176, vv. 23–25.
112 Ms. orient. A 2840, fol. 175/176, vv. 46–49.

power, foreign powers) ties in well with the image of the extortionist who was unpopular with urban elites in cities such as Damascus because of the fierce economic competition he represented. Both reflect threats to different social elites. Al-Jazzār's portrayal as an extortionist of urban mercantile elites, in turn, ties in well with his representation as a patron of the urban poor who knew how to gain popularity among the masses. Meting out violence and giving charity were the two strategies he used to establish what he perceived as just rule.

It is difficult to pierce through the representations of al-Jazzār to the political power broker and economic stakeholder, but perhaps one can go so far as to say that the clearest image of the unattainable 'historical' al-Jazzār emerges at the intersection of all these representations. Al-Jazzār was neither the tyrant of his detractors nor the ideal ruler of his supporters. The foundation of the library that baffled his later detractors is, thus, a strong reminder of the many facets of this strongman of the late eighteenth and early nineteenth centuries. However, the fact that the library was virtually forgotten among Arabic readers also raises the question regarding how successful the Jazzār library was in creating and promoting the image of the ruler that he himself wanted to project.

Bibliography

Manuscripts

Gotha, Gotha Research Library of the University of Erfurt, Ms. orient. A 2189.

Gotha, Gotha Research Library of the University of Erfurt, Ms. orient. A 2222.

Gotha, Gotha Research Library of the University of Erfurt, Ms. orient. A 2347.

Gotha, Gotha Research Library of the University of Erfurt, Ms. orient. A 2840.

Printed works

ʿAbd al-Nūr, Anṭwān [Abdel-Nour, Antoine]. *Tijārat Ṣaydā maʿa al-gharb: Min muntaṣaf al-qarn al-sābiʿ ʿashar ilā awākhir al-qarn al-thāmin ʿashar* [*Le Commerce de Saïda avec l'occident: Du milieu du XVIIe siècle jusqu'à la fin du XVIIIe siècle*]. Beirut, 1987.

Abū al-Fahd, ʿUmar al-Shaykh Muḥammad. "Al-Mughāmir al-jabbār Aḥmad Bāshā al-Jazzār." In *Aḥmad Bāshā al-Jazzār (200 ʿām ʿalā wafātihi)*, edited by Shukrī ʿArrāf and Yaʿqūb Ḥijāzī, 24–35. Acre, 2004.

ʿArrāf, Shukrī, and Yaʿqūb Ḥijāzī (eds). *Aḥmad Bāshā al-Jazzār (200 ʿām ʿalā wafātihi)*. Acre, 2004.

ʿAṭāʾ Allāh, ʿAlī Maḥmūd. *Fihris makhṭūṭāt al-Maktaba al-Aḥmadiyya fī ʿAkkā*. Amman, 1983 [1403 AH].

Basīlī, Qusṭanṭīn. *Sūriyā wa-Filisṭīn taḥta al-ḥukm al-ʿuthmānī*. Translated by Ṭāriq Maʿṣrānī. Moscow, 1989 (Russian original published in 1962).

Bualuan, Hayat El Eid. *Lebanese Historical Thought in the Eighteenth Century*. New York/Abingdon, 2023.

Burayk, Mikhāʾīl. *Tārīkh al-Shām (1720–1782)*. Edited by Qusṭanṭīn al-Bāshā. Ḥarīṣā, 1930.

Cohen, Amnon. *Palestine in the 18th Century: Patterns of Government and Administration*. Jerusalem, 1973.

Cohen, Amnon. "Napoleon and Jezzar: A Local Perspective." In *Napoleon and the French in Egypt and the Holy Land: Articles Presented at the 2nd International Congress of Napoleonic Studies*, edited by Aryeh Shmuelevitz, 79–86. Piscataway, NJ, 2010.

Al-Dimashqī, Mikhāʾīl. *Tārīkh ḥawādith jarrat bi-al-Shām wa-sawāḥil barr al-Shām wa-al-jabal*. Edited by Muḥammad ʿAbd al-Karīm Muḥāfaẓa. Amman, 2004.

Douwes, Dick. "Reorganizing Violence: Traditional Recruitment Patterns and Resistance against Conscription in Ottoman Syria." In *Arming the State: Military Conscription in the Middle East and Central Asia. 1775–1925*, edited by Erik J. Zürcher, 111–127. London/New York, 1999.

Douwes, Dick. *The Ottomans in Syria: A History of Justice and Oppression*. London/New York, 2000.

Fatḥallāh, ʿAbdallaṭīf. *Dīwān*. Edited as: *Der Dīwān des ʿAbd al-Laṭīf Fatḥallāh*, vol. 1. Edited by Zuhair Fatḥallāh and Muḥammad al-Ḥujayrī. Beirut, 1984.

Ghannām, Riyāḍ. *Al-Muqāṭaʿāt al-lubnāniyya fī ẓill ḥukm al-amīr Bashīr al-Shihābī al-thānī wa-niẓām al-qaʾimqāmiyyatayn 1788–1861*. Beirut, 1998.

Ḥasan Aghā. *Tārīkh Ḥasan Aghā al-ʿabd. Qiṭʿa minhu. Ḥawādith sanat 1186 ilā sanat 1241 h*. Edited by Yūsuf Jamīl Nuʿaysa. Damascus, 1979.

Heyd, Uriel. Review of Stanford J. Shaw (ed. and trans.), Ottoman Egypt in the Eighteenth Century. *Bulletin of the School of Oriental and African Studies* 26, no. 1 (1963): 187–188.

Hourani, Albert. "Ottoman Reform and the Politics of Notables." In *Beginnings of Modernization in the Middle East: The Nineteenth Century*, edited by William R. Polk and Richard L. Chambers, 41–68. Chicago, 1968.

Kemp, Percy. "An Eighteenth-Century Turkish Intelligence Report." *International Journal of Middle East Studies* 16 (1984): 497–506.

Khūrī, Salīm. *Warīth al-Jazzār*. Acre, 1960.

Kilpatrick, Hilary. "Poetry and Political Events in the Mamluk and Early Ottoman Periods." In *A Festschrift for Nadia Anghelescu*, edited by Andrei A. Avram, Anca Focşeneanu and George Grigore, 297–305. Bucharest, 2011.

Krimsti, Feras. "The Last Janissary Leader of Aleppo: ʿAbdallah Babinsi (1780s–1850), a Notable between Urban and Rural Spheres." In *From the Household to the Wider World*, edited by Yuval Ben-Bassat and Johann Buessow, 67–78. Tuebingen, 2022.

Meriwether, Margaret L. "Urban Notables and Rural Resources in Aleppo, 1770–1830." *International Journal of Turkish Studies* 4 (1987): 55–73.

Meriwether, Margaret L. *The Kin Who Count: Family and Society in Ottoman Aleppo, 1770–1840*. Austin, 1999.

al-Miknāsī, Muḥammad ibn ʿAbd al-Wahhāb. *Riḥlat al-Miknāsī: Iḥrāz al-muʿallā wa-al-raqīb fī ḥajj Bayt Allāh al-Ḥarām wa-ziyārat al-Quds al-Sharīf wa-al-Khalīl wa-al-tabarruk bi-qabr al-Ḥabīb, 1785*. Edited by Muḥammad Būkabūṭ. Abu Dhabi/Beirut, 2003.

al-Munayyir, Ḥanānyā. *Al-Durr al-marṣūf fī tārīkh al-Shūf*. Edited by Aghnāṭiyūs Sarkīs. Beirut, 1984.

al-Munayyir, Ḥanānyā. *Waqāʾiʿ al-Durūz maʿa Aḥmad Bāshā al-Jazzār 1697–1809m. Ḥawliyyāt majhūla*. Edited by Mundhir al-Ḥāyik. Damascus/Dubai, 2018.

Nawfal, Nawfal Niʿmatallāh. *Kashf al-lithām ʿan maḥyā al-ḥukūma wa-al-aḥkām fī iqlīmayy Miṣr wa-barr al-Shām*. Edited by Mīshāl Abī Fāḍil and Jān Nakhkhūl. Tripoli, 1990.

al-Nimr, Iḥsān. *Tārīkh Jabal Nābulus wa-al-Balqāʾ*, vol. 2. Nābulus, 1961.

Olivier, Guillaume Antoine. *Voyage dans l'Empire othoman, l'Égypte et la Perse, fait par ordre du gouvernement, pendant les six premières années de la République*, vol. 2. Paris, 1804.

Philipp, Thomas. *Acre: The Rise and Fall of a Palestinian City, 1730–1831*. New York, 2001.

Philipp, Thomas, Moshe Perlmann and Guido Schwald (ed. and trans.). *ʿAbd al-Raḥmān al-Jabartī's History of Egypt: ʿAjāʾib al-Āthār fī ʾl-Tarājim wa-al-Akhbār*. 4 vols. in 2. Stuttgart, 1994.

Al-Qārī al-Shāghūrī, Ruslān ibn Yaḥyā. "Al-Wuzarāʾ alladhīna ḥakamū Dimashq." In *Wulāt Dimashq fī al-ʿahd al-ʿuthmānī*, edited by Ṣalāh al-Dīn al-Munajjid, 71–90. Damascus, 1949.

Al-Rayḥānī, Amīn. *Al-Nakabāt aw khulāṣat tārīkh Sūriya mundhu al-ʿahd al-awwal baʿda al-ṭawafān ilā ʿahd al-jumhūriyya bi-Lubnān*. Beirut, 1928.

Reilly, James A. *The Ottoman Cities of Lebanon: Historical Legacy and Identity in the Modern Middle East*. London, 2016.

Rustum, Asad J. "Akka (Acre) and its Defences." *Palestine Exploration Quarterly* 58, no. 3 (1926): 143–157.

al-Ṣabbāgh, Mīkhāʾīl Niqūlā. *Tārīkh al-shaykh Ẓāhir al-ʿUmar al-Zaydānī*. Edited by Aḥmad Ḥasan Jawda. Amman, 2019.

Sajdi, Dana. "Review of *Revolt in Palestine in the Eighteenth Century: The Era of Shaykh Zahir al-ʿUmar*, by Ahmad Hasan Joudah." *Journal of Palestine Studies* 44, no. 3 (2015): 58–60.

Salibi, Kamal S. "Al-Djazzār Pasha." In *Encyclopaedia of Islam Second Edition*, vol. 12, *Supplement*, edited by P.J. Bearman et al., 268–269. Leiden, 2004.

Schatkowski Schilcher, Linda. *Families in Politics: Damascene Factions and Estates of the 18th and 19th Centuries*. Stuttgart, 1985.

Seetzen, Ulrich Jasper. "Beyträge zur Kenntnis der arabischen Stämme in Syrien und im wüsten und peträischen Arabien." *Monatliche Correspondenz zur Beförderung der Erd- und Himmelskunde* (February 1809): 105–133.

Seetzen, Ulrich Jasper. *Ulrich Jasper Seetzen's Reisen durch Syrien, Palästina, Phönicien, die Transjordan - Länder, Arabia Petrata und Unter-Aegypten*, vol. 2. Edited by Friedrich Kruse. Berlin, 1854.

Shaw, Stanford J. *Ottoman Egypt in the Eighteenth Cen-*

tury: The Nizamname-i Misir of Cezzar Ahmed Pasha. Cambridge, 1962.

Shihāb, Ḥaydar Aḥmad. *Tārīkh Aḥmad Bāshā al-Jazzār*. Edited by Anṭūniyūs Shiblī and Aghnāṭiyūs ʿAbduh Khalīfa. Beirut, 1955.

Shihābī, Ḥaydar Aḥmad. *Lubnān fī ʿahd al-umarāʾ al-shihābiyyīn*, 3 vols. Edited by Asad Rustum and Fuʾād Afrām al-Bustānī. Beirut, 1933.

Al-Shinnāwī, ʿAbd al-ʿAzīz [El-Shennawy, Abdel Aziz]. *Al-Dawla al-ʿuthmāniyya: Dawla islāmiyya muftarā ʿalayhā* [The Ottoman Empire: An Islamic Maligned State]. 4 vols. Cairo, 1980–1986.

Spilsbury. Francis B. *Picturesque Scenery in the Holy Land and Syria Delineated during the Campaigns of 1799 and 1800*. London, 1803.

Ṭarrād, ʿAbdallāh ibn Mīkhāʾīl. *Mukhtaṣar Tārīkh al-asāqifa alladhīna raqqū martabat riʾāsat al-kahanūt al-jalīla fī madīnat Bayrūt*. Edited by Nāʾila Qāʾidbayh. Beirut, 2002.

Thackston, W.M. (trans.). *Murder, Mayhem, Pillage, and Plunder: The History of the Lebanon in the 18th and 19th Centuries by Mikhāyil Mishāqa*. Albany, 1988.

Tibawi, Abdul Latif. *A Modern History of Syria Including Lebanon and Palestine*. Edinburgh, 1969.

Whaley, Buck. *Buck Whaley's Memoirs Including His Journey to Jerusalem: Written by Himself in 1797 and Now First Published from the Recently Discovered Manuscript*. Edited by Edward Sullivan. London, 1906.

Yacioglu, Ali. *Partners of the Empire: The Crisis of the Ottoman Order in the Age of Revolutions*. Stanford, 2016.

al-Zayyānī, Abū al-Qāsim Muḥammad. *Al-Turjumāna al-kubrā fī akhbār al-maʿmūr barran wa-baḥran*. Edited by ʿAbd al-Karīm al-Fīlālī. Rabat, 1991.

Zeʿevi, Dror. "Ottoman Intelligence Gathering during Napoleon's Invasion of Egypt and Palestine." In *The Ottoman Middle East: Studies in Honor of Amnon Cohen*, edited by Eyal Ginio and Elie Podeh, 45–54. Leiden/Boston, 2014.

CHAPTER 5

Uncovering al-Jazzār's Wealth: Confiscation and Power Struggle

Yasin Arslantaş

The confiscation of assets from officials who were dismissed, executed or died of natural causes, known as *müsādere*, was a common practice in the Ottoman Empire from the second half of the fifteenth century through the early nineteenth century. The term *müsādere* originates from the Arabic word *muṣādara*, meaning 'to wrest'.[1] While earlier Muslim polities employed *müsādere* as a punitive measure, it was in the Ottoman Empire that this practice became highly institutionalised. Despite the wide use of the term *müsādere* in modern Ottoman historiography, archival documents often referred to it as *'zabt'*, using expressions such as *'mīrīden/mīrīye/mīrīce zabt'*, translating to 'seizure by the state'. However, in line with the convention in modern historiography, I will use the terms *müsādere* or confiscation throughout this chapter to refer to the state's seizure of wealth.

The revenue-generating aspect of *müsādere*, especially during fiscal distress, is undeniable, but it fails to capture the whole complexity of the practice. It is held that the Ottoman political regime considered wealth acquired through public offices as state property, prohibiting its transfer to heirs. Consequently, post-mortem confiscation of inheritance was perceived as the state reclaiming what rightfully belonged to it.[2] Whereas this principle guided many earlier confiscations, *müsādere* also served as a tool for the central state to reassume its authority, especially in response to the influence of local figures and the resulting erosion of its control over fiscal resources in the eighteenth century.[3] The flexible and selective enforcement of confiscations in the eighteenth century, however, highlights that the state's power to confiscate was far from absolute.[4] Therefore, it is not easy to provide a universal definition of Ottoman *müsādere* applicable throughout its four centuries of existence.

The primary focus of the study of *müsādere* has been on the long eighteenth century due to the heightened frequency of confiscations during this time. Confiscation cases rose notably in the last quarter of the century, coinciding with the peak of power and wealth of the *ayan* (local elites), which the central government sought to curb by confiscating their inheritances. During this period, *müsādere* functioned to impede the transfer of wealth across generations and prevent the rise of a landed aristocracy in Ottoman provinces, where patrimonial families were consolidating their influence. *Müsādere* which was often a supplementary punishment to political execution (*siyāseten katl*), sometimes faced either violent or non-violent resistance from the family and associates of the deceased. Managing such opposition, often with the help of local governors, constituted a crucial task for the *muhallefat mübāşiri* (confiscator, usually a low or mid-ranking official commissioned for the sole purpose of confiscation). However, opposition to confiscation should not be viewed solely as an attempt to safeguard wealth, as it also represented resistance to the transfer of power. This is why confiscation records offer valuable insights into not only the composition of the elite's wealth but also the dynamics of domestic politics in eighteenth-century Ottoman provinces.

1 Tomar, *Müsadere*.
2 For legal aspects of *müsādere*, see Kalıpçı, "Klasik Osmanlı".
3 Arslantaş, "Making Sense of Müsadere Practice".
4 For an analysis of these constraints, see Arslantaş, "Confiscation by the Ruler".

This chapter delves into the extensive process of uncovering the inheritance of al-Jazzār, the Ottoman governor of Bosnian origin who held significant offices in Ottoman Syria, including the governorships of Damascus and Sidon, for many years, while accumulating a substantial fortune. His primary source of income as a governor came from tax collection on behalf of the central state. His annual income was reported to amount to an astounding 20,000 bags of akçe. Despite gaining a reputation for successfully defending the fortress of Acre against Napoleon, al-Jazzār was a controversial figure plagued by allegations of mistreating people, unjustly collecting taxes, monopolising domestic trade and misusing state resources for personal gain. Previous research on al-Jazzār has focused primarily on his political and military endeavours, but this chapter delves into his wealth and the seizure of his inheritance. The following section examines his involvement in confiscating the riches of others. Section III is dedicated to the confiscation proceedings of his own inheritance. Section IV assesses the magnitude of his fortune, offering a comprehensive analysis of an inventory containing some of his belongings. In light of the evidence presented, Section V presents some remarks regarding al-Jazzār's endowment and books listed in the Library inventory written in 1221/1806, and section VI concludes the chapter.

1 Al-Jazzār's Role in Confiscating the Wealth of Others

We need to explore al-Jazzār's relationship with the central state in order to understand his involvement in confiscating the wealth of others. Al-Jazzār rose to prominence through his military and political endeavours. Initially serving under Osmān Pasha, the guardian of Damascus, he garnered recognition for effectively suppressing rebellious tribes in Syria, which resulted in his appointment as the district governor of Karahisar. In no hurry to assume his new position, al-Jazzār suppressed a rebellion in Damascus before ultimately being granted the governorship of Sidon in 1775, which he held until he died in 1804, a remarkable span that exceeded twenty-nine years. Al-Jazzār's long reign can be attributed to his maintaining a delicate balance between insurgent tribes (notably the Druze) and the local elite, while showing a reasonable degree of loyalty to Istanbul.[5] In 1792, for instance, he promptly returned to Damascus from Hejaz upon hearing about a rebellion that had started there. After he had suppressed the rebellion, he sent eighty-one severed heads of rebels to Istanbul from both the Druze and Qizilbash communities as a symbol of preserving the Sultan's authority against disobedience.[6]

However, a few months later, al-Jazzār himself faced accusations from the central government. A harsh decree listed his crimes (quote from the document: 'which have been customary for him') of looting wealth, abducting children and violating the dignity of the people in Damascus. The decree ordered his dismissal and replacement by al-Haj Mehmed Pasha, referencing a *ḥadīth*: 'whoever gives up obedience and separates from the Muslim community and then dies has died a death like that of the pre-Islamic era of ignorance',[7] and stating that it was now the duty of the recipient of the order to catch and kill al-Jazzār. Those who spilled his and his troops' blood would be rewarded, and the failure to act accordingly would be punished severely, the decree continued.[8] He was pardoned, though, and even kept his post as the governor of Damascus until 1795.[9]

The central state often sought assistance from provincial officials in the area where a person died or was dismissed because of the frequent post-

5 Güner, "Cezzar Ahmed Paşa".
6 HAT.1400/56405.
7 *Sahih Muslim*, Book 33, Hadith 83.
8 C.DH.74/3652. I thank Said Aljoumani for the translation of two documents written in Arabic.
9 While he uninterruptedly held the governorship of Sidon from 1775 to 1804, he held the governorship of Damascus for relatively shorter periods between 1785 and 1786, 1790 and 1795, 1799 and 1800 and, finally, 1802 and 1804. Güner, "Cezzar Ahmed Paşa".

confiscation resistance from the deceased's family or entourage and potential looting. Al-Jazzār was involved in such confiscations.[10] In one instance, when Feyzullah Efendi, the financial directorate of Damascus, died in 1785, al-Jazzār, serving as the governor of Damascus, was ordered to help confiscate his inheritance. However, upon discovering its insignificance and the poverty of the heirs, the Sultan ordered al-Jazzār and the local judge to leave it to the family instead.[11] A year later, al-Jazzār was ordered to collaborate with an appointed official for Giridi Ahmed's confiscation (the chief of staff, *vezīrler kethüdāsı*). In this case, the decision was to confiscate the deceased's substantial wealth (200 bags of akçe in cash, 100 bags of akçe worth of goods and assets, and seventy-eight bags of akçe worth of houses). While a certain Davud seized these properties and assets, al-Jazzār was ordered to oversee and document the entire estate, including lands, farms, belongings and possessions. According to the order, he was supposed to hand them over to the confiscator appointed, who would send them to Istanbul, where some pieces would be distributed to the heirs, and the rest would be auctioned off.[12] Confirming whether al-Jazzār used to buy items from such auctions would require examining numerous inventories of individuals whose wealth was confiscated in the region. It was also important if he illegally took any property before the central state intervened. Local governors, such as al-Jazzār, were often responsible for reporting a potential confiscation case to the imperial centre, after which, they would usually be instructed to seal it and await the arrival of the confiscator. To determine how effectively they complied with these expectations before the confiscator's arrival is beyond what historians can ascertain unless a letter of complaint about their misuse of authority exists. Aside from his potential involvement in confiscations by the central government, there is another form of confiscation in which he was probably involved, that is, the confiscation of books while creating his library, which we shall discuss below.

2 Confiscation and the Change of Power in Sidon

Al-Jazzār was known to suffer from a chronic illness that sometimes worsened, confining him to bed. The Moroccan traveller and envoy Muḥammad b. ʿUthmān al-Miknāsī reports that al-Jazzār told him about the pain the latter was experiencing when they met in 1787. In 1791, Selim III responded to a rumour: 'Kāim-i Makām Paşa, hopefully, the news of Jazzār Pasha's passing is false. It should be verified, and if true, the property should be confiscated [...].'[13] An anonymous letter received in Istanbul in 1796 claimed that al-Jazzār had not left his house for a long time, which opponents interpreted as a sign of death.[14] The central government expected provincial governors to write such letters, reporting the terminal illness or death of other officials or notables. These letters served various motivations, one being to ensure that the central government was prepared for an upcoming confiscation. Upon receiving this anonymous letter, the government immediately issued an order to local governors in the region, instructing them to seize the properties of al-Jazzār if he were to die.[15] However, he lived for another eight years. In 1804, a letter arrived in Istanbul from Aleppo informing Selīm III (r. 1789–1807) of al-Jazzār's desperate illness. The sultan responded to the Grand Vizier's question regarding how they should proceed if al-Jazzār were to pass away: 'Act accordingly to what we have spoken in our meeting today', which probably meant issuing orders to the governors of the region concerning confiscating al-Jazzār's wealth. Additionally, the document includes a story shared

10 Also see Güler, *Cezzar Ahmed Paşa*, 14–15.
11 AE.SABH.I.237/15811.
12 C.ML.731/29862.
13 Güler, *Cezzar Ahmed Paşa*, 42.
14 Ibid., 8.
15 Ibid., 14.

by the Grand Vizier during his encounter with al-Jazzār some time ago, expressing the former's desire that al-Jazzār's fortunes be bestowed upon the imperial treasury. The document does not mention how al-Jazzār responded to this wish, but it could be argued that the Vizier would only have mentioned it if al-Jazzār had objected to his request. We do not know whether al-Jazzār approved or remained silent. What we know is that office-holders were often aware of the high price they (or their families, for that matter) had to pay after their death for the many privileges they enjoyed during their lifetime.

Indeed, after al-Jazzār's death in Acre in May of 1804, the central government faced two concerns: confiscating his fortunes and appointing a new governor for Sidon. İbrahim Pasha, the former governor of Aleppo, was immediately granted the provincial governorships of Damascus and Tripoli.[16] The first document that pertains to the confiscation (dated 31 May 1804) is an order addressed to İbrahim Pasha and to Mehmed Rāgıb Efendi (the head of the gunpowder factory), who were both tasked with seizing al-Jazzār's inheritance.[17] The order begins by explaining why al-Jazzār's inheritance was being confiscated. To make the point, it portrays al-Jazzār as an exceptionally wealthy governor (incomparable to other viziers), followed by a list of revenue sources he controlled, such as the collection of *jizya* and *avarız* taxes, tax-farming rights of Acre, Haifa and Beirut, among others, along with the salaries of janissaries and revenues from inns, stores, and estates in Acre and other places. It then accuses al-Jazzār of embezzling a significant portion of the annual revenues despite it being about 20,000 bags of akçe.[18] As far as this document is concerned, he was known for establishing monopolies in markets (particularly in the cotton, silk and grain trade), collecting unjust taxes and using state-owned munitions for his personal affairs.[19] When it came to funding wars against the enemy, however, al-Jazzār is reported to have allegedly abstained from spending any money. The Siege of Acre in 1799 by Napoleon was presented as an exception, where he supposedly spent more than usual, although there are claims that he extracted two or three times what he actually spent.[20] The document concludes with a warning to İbrahim Pasha and Rāgıb that they would be punished if they failed to accurately record al-Jazzār's assets [without leaving even a tiny item behind] or attempted to profit from it.[21] One might wonder why these accusations had not led to the punishment of al-Jazzār (in the form of capital punishment, dismissal or confiscation of assets) before his natural death. The answer probably lies in his networks, military power,[22] the distance between the region and Istanbul, and his local know-how, especially regarding the organisation of pilgrimage. Although there was once an attempt to send him to Erzurum to hamper his power consolidation in Palestine, he successfully justified his staying in Acre.[23] Therefore, even though al-Jazzār's authority and autonomy in the region

16 Ibid., 15.

17 C.ML.312/12780. An order asking for his military support, if needed, was sent to Mehmed Pasha the governor of Aleppo and son of İbrahim Pasha. C.DH.78/3899.

18 This amount was merely an estimation. A separate document, dated eight months later, provides a revised estimate of al-Jazzār's annual revenues, which were reported to be around 30,000–40,000 bags of akçe after additional information was submitted by the confiscators. C.ML.269/11044.

19 Emecen, "Suriye Bölgesinde", 5.

20 Another letter sent to Mehmed Ragıb also demonstrates the centre's mistrust of al-Jazzār. In this letter, Mehmed Ragıb was instructed to inspect the accuracy of the revenue from the tax units that had been farmed out to al-Jazzār. The central government suspected that the revenues were actually eight to ten times higher than what had been reported. C.ML.21/960.

21 This warning refers to the corruption that was often involved in confiscations. It was not uncommon for governors and confiscators to strike bargains with the family members to benefit by intentionally underestimating the value of the assets confiscated.

22 He is said to have had some thirty thousand armed men at the time of his death. Güler, *Cezzar Ahmed Paşa*, 9.

23 Yaycıoğlu, *Partners of the Empire*, 82.

were not necessarily welcomed by the Ottoman central government, precisely because of this authority and autonomy, they probably approached him with caution while he was alive. Chapter 4 by Feras Krimsti in this book discusses the conflicting representations of al-Jazzār, which is also evident from the shifting tone in Ottoman state documents following his death.

After al-Jazzār's death, the state attempted to take control of Acre. İsmāʿīl Pasha, who had been appointed deputy governor by al-Jazzār, anticipated that he would be given Acre and, consequently, the Sidon province. In his letter, he assured that he would diligently document and forward the inheritance to the central government, emphasising his qualifications for serving as governor of Sidon due to his long-standing residence in the region along with his family and troops.[24] Rüşdī Efendi, formerly a gatekeeper of al-Jazzār, similarly wrote a letter endorsing İsmail Pasha as governor of Sidon and himself the latter's gatekeeper.[25] When consulted about these proposals, Rāgıb voiced support for Süleymān Pasha, a *mamlūk* (manumitted slave soldier) and a close associate of al-Jazzār. Not surprisingly, in a confidential letter, Süleyman Pasha is seen to have asked for Rāgıb's support, pledging to improve the management and successfully enforce the Sultan's order to confiscate al-Jazzār's inheritance should he be appointed the governor of Sidon. In the letter, Süleymān Pasha also mentions that İbrahim Pasha would not be able to accomplish this mission to deliver the riches of al-Jazzār due to disobedience from soldiers, poor management and disloyalty from the people.[26] In a similar vein, in a letter dated September 1804, Rāgıb complained about İbrahim Pasha's insistence for a permanent appointment as the governor, stating that, unlike others such as İbrahim Pasha, he prioritised state objectives but had become exhausted from all he had been through in the last months.[27] One factor contributing to his stated exhaustion was İsmail Pasha, who had seized the inheritance without permission.[28] Eventually, Süleymān Pasha was granted the province of Sidon partially because the hajj was approaching, and he had been successful as the previous year's commander of the pilgrimage caravan. The Sultan ordered the forced deportation of İsmail Pasha from Acre with a certain Kasım Ağa assigned for this task.[29]

Ragıb finally returned to Istanbul in October 1805. Although his efforts were appreciated, the whole process was largely unsuccessful.[30] Rāgıb was ridiculed in a popular tale circulating in Istanbul at that time, for attempting to locate al-Jazzār's hidden treasures using magical methods and talismans. He even enlisted the help of skilled experts in digging and dredging from Istanbul to assist in the search in Palestine. Despite his efforts, the outcome was far from satisfactory; Ragıb could not locate the silver and gold coins believed to be buried in different locations in Acre and Sidon. The collection of what they owed from those who were purportedly indebted to al-Jazzār also proved fruitless.[31] As a result, a significant portion of al-Jazzār's wealth remained unconfiscated. Reminders about the amounts needed to be sent to the central government continued even decades after his death.

3 The Confiscation Inventory

The correspondence contains references that strongly suggest the existence of an initial (and apparently very detailed) inventory brought to Istanbul by Ragıb. However, I have been unable to locate this specific inventory. Nevertheless, multiple inventories exist recorded for various purposes.

24 Güler, *Cezzar Ahmed Paşa*, 11.
25 HAT.101/4029A.
26 HAT.101/4029.
27 HAT.102/4040.
28 HAT.105/4154.
29 C.ML.98/4363.
30 HAT.106/4192.
31 Yaycıoğlu, *Partners of the Empire*, 110.

A particularly comprehensive one is a twenty-page document in the *Maliyeden Müdevver Defterler* collection in the Ottoman State Archives.[32] This document is essentially a list of items found in his house in Acre, with their respective values.[33] The first two pages of the inventory provide a good representation of the rest of its content.

Confiscation Inventory (Muhallefat) of Aḥmad Pasha Al-Jazzār[34]

The register of Ebū-Bekir Efendi, the minister of Harameyn in 1805	
Piasters	
1430	Coloured belt
0380	Velvet
0230	Coloured belt
0360	Ornate belt
0500	Muslin
0080	Wool muslin
0350	White solid fabric
0290	White solid fabric
0265	Black solid fabric
0400	White belt
0400	White belt
1400	Silk fabric
0150	Regular towel
0140	Yellow towel
0060	Kaftan
0145	Hook lock
0700	Muslin
0910	Muslin
0330	Muslin
11137	[Total]

32 MAD.d.23879.

33 Mustafa Güler writes that his properties in Damascus and Tripoli can be found in another inventory. MAD.d.9571 (pages 274–279). Güler, *Cezzar Ahmed Paşa*, 16.

34 The translation omits any irrelevant financial transaction details.

(*cont.*)

Confiscation Inventory (Muhallefat) of Aḥmad Pasha Al-Jazzār

The register of Sinān Pashalu Ahmed Ağa.	
Piasters	
140	Muslin
330	Coloured [...]
901	Coloured fur
040	Setrâh Serâser?
1431	[Total]
The register of Şakir Kıbrısi.	
Piasters	
422	Muslin
701	Muslin
1123	[Total]
The register of Kumaşçı Tekfur.	
Piasters	
1004	Crested yellow gun
The register of Sinān Ahmed, cash delivered to İrād-ı Cedīd treasury.[35]	
Piasters	
276	Der-Saʿādet
The register of Hācı ʿAlī, charged to İrād-ı Cedīd	
Piasters	
231	Muslin
The register of ...	
Piasters	
0800	Crested scarf
0700	Pants fabric 12
0845	Double hook
6750	Coloured scarf and pants fabric 27
9095	[Total]
0720	Wired solid fabric 2
1300	Brocade
1170	Wired red brocaded needlework

35 *Irād-i Cedīd* was a new treasury established by Selīm III (r. 1789–1807) within the context of his *nizam-ı cedid* (new order) reforms.

(*cont.*)

Confiscation Inventory (Muhallefat) of Aḥmad Pasha Al-Jazzār

1900	Wired fabric
1001	Two muslins, wired pants cloth
15226	[General total]
The register of …	
Piasters	
0252	Sable fur 1
1320	Fur (worn by the Sultan at the time of granting the vizier title) 6
0370	Fur (worn by the Sultan at the time of granting the vizier title) 5
0301	Fur scarf 5
0300	Coloured scarf 5
1001	Belt with two wings 1 Three-sided needlework 15
3994	[Total]
1860	Coloured scarf 24
2410	Coloured scarf 11
0800	White fabric
0136	Scarf needlework
0050	Brocaded 1
0219	Wired fabric 3
9469	[Total]
0130	Silk pants cloth 2
0261	Minākārı Topluk
0101	Artistic needlework belt 1
0421	Muslin number of units: 14
0590	Muslin number of units: 18
0400	Muslin number of units: 10
1030	Muslin number of units: 17
12402	[General total]
The register of Dervīş Yeniçeri Kethüdāsı	
Piasters	
340	Coloured brocade 10
300	Silk brocade 10
257	White brocade 10
250	White belt 10
370	Muslin 81
580	Muslin 20

(*cont.*)

Confiscation Inventory (Muhallefat) of Aḥmad Pasha Al-Jazzār

600	Coloured burqa
260	Bloomy velvet 5
2957	
The register of El-Seyyid Ahmed Efendi.	
Piasters	
61	Wired prayer rug number of units: 1
25	Maraş macramé number of units: 1
86	[Total]
The register of Kethüdā-yı Yeniçeriyān.	
Piasters	
350	Coloured burqa
The register of Ahmed Ağa.	
Piasters	
361	White solid fabric number of units: 10
The register of Hācı Hüseyin Ağa.	
Piasters	
030	Mohair fabric
055	Mardin bed tie 2
040	Mardin towel 1
650	Muslin 20
775	[Total]
The register of Silāhdār Ağası Pir Murād.	
Piasters	
460	Muslin number of units: 10
290	Belt number of units: 10
109	Yellow muslin number of units: 30
700	Brocaded muslin number of units: 12
221	Coloured belt number of units: 10
1780	[Total]
0503	White turban number of units: 15
0181	Coloured turban number of units: 7
0250	Wired regular
1410	Wired bolted belt
1100	Wired white bolted belt
5224	[Total]

(*cont.*)

Confiscation Inventory (Muhallefat) of Aḥmad Pasha Al-Jazzār	
0800	Wired brocaded
0361	Muslin roll: 1
0261	Regular muslin roll: 6
0120	Wired French 3
0710	Muslin number of units: 20
7476	[Total]
0735	Muslin 20
0600	Muslin 20
0290	Coloured burqa 9
0360	Coloured scarf
9461	[General total]

Source: MAD.d.23879

Based on my calculations, the value of this inventory is 250,641 piasters. Of this, cash amounts to only 1,416, while items wholly or partly made of precious metals are worth 89,285 piasters.[36] Therefore, only 36 per cent of the total value (90,701 piasters) consists of cash and items made of precious metals. The remaining 64 per cent includes less valuable items, such as household appliances, clothing and accessories, and military gear, such as rifles and swords. I have yet to find the initial inventory recorded by Rāgıb Efendi. One document says: '[…] in the previous inventory, there were 60,000 pieces of golden sent on one occasion, and an additional 1,950 bags of akçe sent separately, with more expected […]'.[37] In response to the Grand Vizier, Selīm III stated that the total value of al-Jazzār's inheritance was some 40,000 bags of akçe.[38] If this was the estimation of Rāgıp in the first inventory, we need a little calculation to get a rough idea about the magnitude of the inheritance.

1 bag of akçe: 50,000 akçes (in 1786)[39]
1 piaster = 120 akçes (fixed rate)[40]
1 bag of akçe = 50,000/120 = 416.66 piasters
40,000 bags of akçe = 16,666,400 piasters

This is such an enormous sum that could only have been amassed by a select few during that time. According to the calculation above, the value of the inventory examined represents only one and a half percent of al-Jazzār's wealth, as estimated by Mehmed Rāgıb. It is important to be cautious here as this estimation was based on Rāgıb's observations and the testimonies gathered. Following the preparation of inventories, a complex process would begin, involving selling goods on-site or sending them directly to Istanbul, collecting debts from debtors, and settling debts with creditors. This process proved to be particularly challenging for the confiscation of al-Jazzār's inheritance. Although the central state had ordered the collection of the amount stated in Rāgıb's initial inventory, Süleymān Pasha, the new governor, disputed al-Jazzār's alleged wealth. He pointed out that the province's finances would be harmed if a large amount were demanded and suggested that a revised inventory be prepared to ascertain its true value.[41] Rāgıb also subsequently acknowledged errors in his initial inventory book and concurred with creating a new one.[42] Mustafa Güler raised an interesting point regarding why Ragıb might have exaggerated the value of the inventory. Al-Jazzār accused Hasan Ağa, Mehmed Rāgıb's brother and the Deputy Treasurer of Damascus, of corruption in a letter dated 1799. Al-Jazzār proposed appointing Mehmed Rāgıb (Hasan's patron in Istanbul) to a distant province to resolve this issue. Hasan was later killed by al-Jazzār, while Ragıb ended up

36 The inventory lists two items of exceptional value: an aigrette adorned with diamonds and emeralds (worth 19,000 piasters) and a sword adorned with the same precious stones (worth 35,000 piasters). It is worth noting that the combined value of these two items exceeded the worth of many confiscated estates during that period.

37 HAT.174/7550.

38 HAT.114/4570.

39 Çakır, *Kese*.

40 Pamuk, *Kuruş*.

41 HAT.4022.

42 HAT.4026E.

in Amasya. According to Güler, this indicates that Rāgıb had a personal issue with al-Jazzār, which may have influenced his recording of the inventory.[43] However, there are some problems with this argument. Firstly, we cannot ascertain how much Rāgıb exaggerated the inheritance value, as Süleymān Pasha and others were probably concealing certain pieces of the inheritance. Secondly, if Rāgıb had indeed exaggerated, he would have had a stronger motivation than his personal grievance for doing so, namely, obtaining a higher commission for his services.[44] In any case, the value assigned by Ragıb in his initial investigation was never transferred to Istanbul. While certain goods, such as those listed in the inventory mentioned above, were sent to Istanbul on various occasions, their combined value was arguably far from reaching millions of piasters.

4 The Confiscation and Fate of the *Waqf* Properties

Several questions concern us here. First and foremost is the purpose or context behind the compilation of the library inventory dated 1806. Could this document have been generated within the context of confiscation proceedings? It is important to note that the confiscation of endowment properties, including books, was an exceptional occurrence given the sacred and inviolable status typically accorded to such assets, though not unprecedented.

There is convincing evidence that the Jazzār library was no exception, meaning the properties he endowed, including the books, were not confiscated. Ottoman *waqfs* can be divided into three categories: charitable, family and semi-family.[45] Into which category did his *waqf* fall? Analysis of the endowment deed written in 1786 reveals that the surplus income from al-Jazzār's *waqf* was designated for himself during his lifetime and, after his death, for his surviving or future sons and daughters.[46] Services open to public use, such as foundations, mosques and libraries, can easily be considered charitable acts. However, the allocation of the endowment's net income to al-Jazzār and his family, even to his odalisques after his death, indicates a semi-family nature of the endowment, a characteristic shared by seventy-five per cent of *waqfs* founded within the Ottoman Empire during the eighteenth century.[47]

What motivated al-Jazzār to establish this semi-family *waqf*? Some economic historians contend that the primary motivation behind the establishment of *waqfs*, particularly when it comes to family *waqfs*, was the protection of assets from *müsādere*, for it functioned as a means of intergenerational transfer of wealth.[48] However, Yediyıldız's analysis of eighteenth-century Ottoman *waqfs* presents a more nuanced perspective, indicating that alongside factors such as sensitivity, benevolence and sociability (the religious dimension of these senses cannot be denied either), protection from political pressures and the cultivation of a benevolent image also played significant roles.[49] Given that two-thirds of the endowments in the eighteenth-century Ottoman Empire were founded by the members of the military-administrative (*askerî*)

43 Güler, *Cezzar Ahmed Paşa*, 20.

44 Yaycıoğlu, *Partners of the Empire*, 110.

45 Endowments belonging to members of the imperial family and the pashas in the Ottoman Empire were administered by the Harameyn Evkāf Nezāreti. This endowment was, thus, under the supervision of the Chief Harem Eunuch (Darüssaade Ağası), who received a share of the endowment's income (two hundred and fifty piasters annually). Güler, *Cezzar Ahmed Paşa*, 206.

46 Although there is a controversy about the legality of this practice in Islamic law, there are numerous examples of it throughout Ottoman history, indicating that the Ottomans generally aligned with the view of Abu Yusuf that justified it. Akgündüz, *İslam Hukukunda*, 252.

47 While family endowments constituted seven percent of the overall total, only eighteen percent of established endowments were dedicated exclusively to charitable activities. Yediyıldız, *Türkiye'de Vakıf Müessesesi*, 15.

48 Kuran, "Provision of Public Goods".

49 Yediyıldız, *Türkiye'de Vakıf Müessesesi*, 55–85.

class, the motivation to gain public favour via charitable acts should not be underestimated, as these acts contributed to the creation of public consent necessary for the collection of taxes from the populace, which was the primary source of revenue of this class.[50] In the case of al-Jazzār's endowment, the role of these factors appears evident, as the endowment served charitable purposes (in addition to providing a source of income for himself and his retinue), possibly helping to mitigate negative perceptions associated with his name.

Speaking of his family, an ambiguity arises from the statement in the endowment deed, indicating that the net income would pass to al-Jazzār's living or future children. As emphasised by other scholars, there is no other evidence of the existence of his children. If he, indeed, did not have any children (and if he did, one would expect to see their names mentioned in the confiscation records), this statement could be interpreted as either a generic statement or a reflection of al-Jazzār, in his mid-sixties in 1786, maintaining hope for having children in the future.[51] Regardless, considering al-Jazzār's anticipation (or even knowledge) of potential confiscation of his assets after (or even before) death, establishing a semi-family semi-charitable endowment seems a reasonable move to secure benefits in both this world and the afterlife.

Although the endowment was established in 1786, subsequent additions were made to its assets, notably after Napoleon's siege of Acre. Al-Jazzār incorporated properties abandoned by the non-Muslim population that had assisted Napoleon, expanding the endowment's holdings.[52] The last two pages of the Vakıflar Genel Müdürlüğü (Ankara), Defter 1626, also allude to al-Jazzār appropriating properties of certain individuals unjustly, presented as publicly known information. The document requests the central government to remove the houses, shops and stores of these individuals, who were allegedly in a distressed situation, from the endowment register and return them to their rightful owners.[53] The list of these properties is followed by a section stating that the estates, lands and gardens of Ẓāhir al-ʿUmar (the preceding governor of Sidon), seized by al-Jazzār after the former's death, were granted to the latter as a life-term tax farm (*ber vech-i malikane*). The document clearly expresses that these were state-owned properties registered in tax farming books, and no other estates or lands belonging to al-Jazzār than these and those mentioned in his endowment book could be detected.[54]

This section concludes with the expression '*fermān men lehü'l-emr hazretlerinindir*' (the rest is at His Majesty's command), commonly used when referring to the Grand Vizier or high-ranked government officials. Combined with another expression in the previous section, '*irāde-i ʿāliyye ve müsāʿade-i seniyye*', it becomes clear that the document was intended for the central government, specifically for the office of the Grand Vizier. The accompanying date, 19 Ramadan 1219 (22 December 1804), not only specifies the document's date of production but also suggests it was probably prepared by Süleyman Pasha shortly after he as-

50 Ibid., 159.

51 Güler, *Cezzar Ahmed Paşa*, 206–207.

52 This is explicitly mentioned on the last two pages of the Vakıflar Genel Müdürlüğü (Ankara), Defter 1626, 74–75: '*Fransalu üzerine sefer-i hümayun esnası asker üzerine tesallutı hengamında bazı hanelerden sahipleri mahal-ı ahire nakilleri hasebiyle merhum-ı müşarünileyhin zabt idüb vakf-ı mezkûr defterine kayd ve idhal eylediği hane ve mağaza beyanıdır.*'

53 '*Balada mezkur mağaza ve hane ve dekakinin bazıları köhne ve harab ve bazıları derununda asakir iskan etmiş olup nıfsı miktarında elhalet hazihi müstacirin iskan eylediğinden zikr olunan mahiyelerin nıfsı miktarı tahsil olunmakda ise dahi bazılarının sahibleri hayatda ve bazılarının varisleri olduğundan derun-ı memlekette ve civarında birer mahalde iskan ve perişan-ül ahval olduklarını inha ederek müşarünileyhin bigayrı hakkın zabt ve defter-i vakfa idhal eylediğini cümle şehadetiyle redd ve defter-i vakıfdan terkın olunması istida ve niyazda olub ashaplarına reddiyle defter-i vakfdan terkini idare-i aliyye ve müsaade-i seniyyeye menut olduğundan merbut vakfi ifraz ve zikr olunan mazbutat-ı ahali iş bu mahale başkaca terkim ve işaret olundu.*' Ibid.

54 Ibid.

sumed the role of Sidon governor on 5 Receb 1219 (10 October 1804).[55] Given that Süleymān Pasha had promised to resolve the confiscation issue if granted the governorship, it can be concluded that he promptly paid attention to it upon taking office, and the document is associated with the confiscation process. However, this is not an association to mean that the *waqf* properties were confiscated. This document must have been prepared most probably by Süleymān Pasha for either one or both of the following purposes: (1) segregating the endowment's assets from personal properties subject to confiscation and (2) providing an update on the status of the endowment's sources of revenue after the death of al-Jazzār.

Regarding the second purpose, it must be acknowledged that the *waqf* inventories underwent periodic updates in the Ottoman Empire. İsmail Erünsal suggests for *waqf* libraries that it was common practice to create a new catalogue whenever there was a new trustee or librarian or when necessary.[56] An update was probably prompted by the need to clarify which items were part of the endowment. As is understood from the last two pages of the Vakıflar Genel Müdürlüğü (Ankara), Defter 1626, al-Jazzār previously seized properties from people who were arguably unable to object during his lifetime. With his passing, these individuals in all likelihood came forward seeking the return of their possessions, necessitating a new inventory to accurately reflect the *waqf*'s ownership of items. Beside staff changes and ownership disputes, inventories were crucial for seeing the current status of the *waqf* properties. In the case of libraries, a new inventory was needed to manage book losses that occurred for several reasons. Borrowers could neglect to return materials, or books were sometimes changed with low-quality copies.[57] When the library reclaimed these books, they were often documented with terms such as 'found' or 'received'. Thus, the very function of this inventory could be to ensure that it reflects the current status of the library's collection and the *waqf* properties.

A broader question arises at this point: How did al-Jazzār accumulate such an extensive library? In Chapter 2, Said Aljoumani compellingly points to the confiscation of books from three individuals named Sayyid Yaḥyā Efendi, Shaykh ʿAlī al-Rashīdī and Shaykh Muḥammad Wakīlkharaj. He demonstrates that one hundred and seventy books from these individuals found their way into the Jazzār library. This finding aligns with the fact mentioned previously that the Defter 1626 mentions al-Jazzār's unlawful acquisition of non-book *waqf* properties. It also coincides with regional narratives, based on oral accounts, claiming that the collection was largely built through confiscation.[58] Mustafa Güler stands on the other end of the spectrum, attributing the acquisition of books solely to legal means. Boris Liebrenz argues in his Chapter 3, without denying the possibility of book confiscation, that legal acquisitions played a significant role, with the Damascus book market being a primary source.

We shall now return to our initial question and conclude by presenting additional considerations: Did the central government confiscate the Jazzār library after his death?[59] This is a viable question because it was not uncommon for books, being rare and valuable items, to be confiscated after

55 HAT.102/4041.

56 In fact, al-Jazzār was not the trustee of the endowment. He had appointed a certain Süleymān Ağa as the trustee. The trusteeship duty would pass to Süleyman Ağa's children in the event of his death, or if the lineage ceased, to someone appointed by the judge of Acre. Güler, *Cezzar Ahmed Paşa*, 206.

57 Erünsal, *Ottoman Libraries*.

58 Güler, *Cezzar Ahmed Paşa*, 184.

59 The inventory mentioned above contains only three books, probably those found in his house. The first one, recorded by Kasım Ağa as 'Sim Kalemü'l Sunūhī, 1 volume', was worth forty-three piasters. The second one was recorded as 'Eczā-ı Şerīf, Volume 1' by Mustafa Ağa and valued at 151 piasters. Lastly, there was a copy of the Qur'an, worth 260 piasters. As discussed above, most of the remaining items in the inventory are household items.

someone's passing.[60] The absence of books from this inventory per se is not enough evidence to determine whether his library was confiscated. For one thing, the correspondence documents refer to the existence of another inventory prepared by Mehmed Ragıb, and, for whatever reason, we have not yet been able to find it. In addition to the evidence presented above, however, several documents written long after his death mention the existence of the library in Acre. A document from 1855, for example, mentions repairing three damaged structures at the 'al-Nūr al-Aḥmadī endowment complex' in Acre, specifically the mosque, fountain and library, suggesting that the library was still standing at that time.[61] Moreover, the fact that Ragıb returned to Istanbul in October 1805 reduces the likelihood of him producing such an inventory in 1806. Considering that even the most valuable belongings of al-Jazzār did not end up in Istanbul, the possibility of the *waqf* library being confiscated does not appear to be very high. All in all, we can conclude, with a reasonable degree of confidence, that the Ottoman central state did not confiscate al-Jazzār's books.

5 Conclusion

This chapter examined how the Ottoman central state attempted to seize the assets of Ahmed Pasha al-Jazzār, a prominent political figure in the Ottoman Middle East during the last quarter of the eighteenth century, and what happened to the properties of his *waqf*. Debates on this confiscation in the imperial centre started as early as 1786 and continued until long after his death. The findings presented here show that the state largely failed in its tremendous efforts to confiscate al-Jazzār's enormous wealth. Two-thirds of the goods recorded in the inventory examined above and sold in Istanbul were relatively insignificant household items. The evidence also strongly indicates that the books were not part of the confiscation. Thus, his books were probably dispersed to various parts of the world from his *waqf* in Acre later rather than via Istanbul. The *waqf* inventory was probably prepared in association with the confiscation process. However, this is not to say that the *waqf* properties were confiscated. Instead, the inventory was arguably made as part of an attempt to take out the *waqf* properties of those properties to be seized.

60 İsmail Erünsal examined the case of the confiscation of Şehid Ali Pasha's library. He notes that Ali Pasha (d. 1716) had also endowed his books before his death. However, the state tried to legally justify the confiscation of these books for the palace library. There was even a fatwa-issued by Şeyhülislām İsmāʿīl Efendi, legitimising the confiscation of Pasha's books. However, it is possible that the confiscation of the majority of Ali Pasha's endowed books was an exceptional case, as it required such a fatwa. Confiscating books endowed to a *waqf* in a distant province was much less likely to occur. Erünsal, "Şehit Ali Paşa'nın İstanbul'da Kurduğu Kütüphane".

61 A.MKT.MHM.65/12.

Bibliography

Archival Sources

Ali Emiri I. Abdülhamid (AE.SABH.I): 237/15811
Cevdet Maliye (C.ML.): 731/29862, 312/12780, 98/4363, 21/960, 269/11044
Cevdet Dahiliyye (C.DH): 74/3652, 78/3899
Hatt-ı Humayun (HAT): 1400/56405, 105/4154, 101/4029, 102/4040, 114/4570, 174/7550, 106/4192, 4022, 4026E
Maliyeden Müdevver Defterler (MAD): 23879, 9571
Topkapı Sarayı Müzesi Arşivi (TS.MA): 787/7, 787/8
Saderet Mektubi Kalemi Mühimme Evrakı/Dahiliyye Nezareti Mektubi Kalemi (A.MKT.MHM): 65/12
Vakıflar Genel Müdürlüğü Arşivi (VGM): Defter no: 1626

Secondary Sources

Akgündüz, Ahmet. *İslam Hukukunda ve Osmanlı Tatbikatında Vakıf Müessesesi*. İstanbul, 1996.
Arslantaş, Yasin. "Confiscation by the Ruler: A Study of the Ottoman Practice of Müsadere, 1700s–1839." PhD Diss., London School of Economics and Political Science, 2017.

Arslantaş, Yasin. "Making Sense of Müsadere Practice, State Confiscation of Elite Wealth, in the Ottoman Empire, circa 1453–1839." *History Compass* 17 (2019): e12548.

Çakır, Baki. "Kese." in *TDV İslam Ansiklopedisi*, 42–43. İstanbul, 2019.

Emecen, Ayşe. "Suriye Bölgesinde Bir Osmanlı Valisi ve İmajı: Cezzar Ahmed Paşa (TSMA, nr. E. 4079'daki Takrir ve Nizam-name-i Mısr Adlı İki Raporun Neşir ve Tahlil Denemesi)." Master's Thesis, Marmara University, 1994.

Erünsal, İsmail. "Şehit Ali Paşa'nın İstanbul'da Kurduğu Kütüphane ve Müsadere Edilen Kitapları." *İstanbul Üniversitesi Edebiyat Fakültesi Kütüphanecilik Dergisi*, no: 1, 79–88.

Erünsal, İsmail. *The Ottoman Libraries: A Survey of the History, Development and Organization of Ottoman Foundation Libraries*. Harvard University, 2008.

Güler, Mustafa. *Cezzar Ahmed Paşa ve Akka Savunması*. İstanbul, 2013.

Güner, Selda. "Cezzar Ahmed Paşa (Ö. 1804) Hakkında Bir Takrir Münasebetiyle Suriye'de İktidar Oyunları." *Belleten* 79, no. 284 (2015): 163–198.

Kalıpçı, Mahmud Esad. "Klasik Osmanlı Hukukunda Müsadere Kurumu." Master's Thesis, İstanbul University, 2013.

Kuran, Timur. "The Provision of Public Goods under Islamic Law: Origins, Impact and Limitations of the Waqf System." *Law & Socicty Rcvicw*. 35, no. 4 (2001): 841–898.

Pamuk, Şevket. "Kuruş." In *TDV İslam Ansiklopedisi*, 458–459. İstanbul, 2002.

Sahih Muslim, Book 33. Sunnah.com. https://sunnah.com/muslim:1848a

Tomar, Cengiz. "Müsadere." In *TDV İslam Ansiklopedisi*, 65–67. İstanbul, 2007.

Yaycıoğlu, Ali. *Partners of the Empire: The Crisis of the Ottoman Order in the Age of Revolutions*. Stanford, 2016.

Yediyıldız, *Bahaeddin. XVIII. Yüzyılda Türkiye'de Vakıf Müessesesi: Bir Sosyal Tarih İncelemesi*. Ankara, 2003.

CHAPTER 6

The Library of Abū Nabbūt in Early Nineteenth-century Jaffa

Benedikt Reier

The history of libraries in Ottoman Palestine is faced with two main issues, lack of attention and a biased coverage of Jerusalem.[1] This is surprising given the wealth of sources to reconstruct Palestinian book culture. Several catalogues of historic book collections are mere handlists and await detailed cataloguing.[2] Furthermore, the modern whereabouts of these collections are not always clear and the political situation in the region frequently prevents a suitable research atmosphere. Hence, books and libraries have not been seriously taken up as study objects in research on Ottoman (and post Ottoman) Palestine. The book culture of this region in the existing literature on the social, cultural and political landscape of Greater Syria is mostly described as insignificant if at all, especially for the Muslim majority population.[3] This is in stark contrast to neighbouring Syrian and Egyptian societies, which are well-known to have produced many private book collections, libraries and a vivid culture around the written word. The most recent survey of the various holdings in different Palestinian cities suggests that many libraries await in-depth studies.[4]

Jerusalem is comparatively well represented in not only historical research on Palestine generally but also the meagre existing literature on libraries and books. This is not only thanks to the increasing number of detailed catalogues that are continuously being published.[5] The last few years have witnessed notable digitalisation projects and the holdings of some libraries, especially from Jerusalem, are now accessible online. Exciting source material, hitherto unused for the history of libraries in the Ottoman realm, such as the guest books of the Khālidiyya library, are available and await dedicated research. In comparison to Jerusalem, other towns lag behind and this volume on the library of al-Jazzār in Acre is a first attempt to broaden the scope.

In this chapter, we will leave Acre and turn south. A little more than a hundred kilometres down the Mediterranean coast, in the ancient town of Jaffa, a *mamlūk* of Aḥmad Pasha al-Jazzār (d. 1219/1804) by the name of Muḥammad Aghā (d. ca. 1833–1834), better known as Abū Nabbūt, embarked on an urban development project including striking parallels to what his master, al-Jazzār, did in Acre. Abū Nabbūt was the deputy governor (*mutasallim*) of Jaffa in the early nineteenth century, and invested time and money in the economic and military infrastructure of his place of residence. His urbanisation project changed the townscape of Jaffa decisively and elevated the place into a regional hub, a centre of trade for the produce of the fertile hills of Nablus. Abū Nabbūt fostered Jaffa's role as the major entry point of seafaring pilgrims and visitors for Jerusalem and some of his buildings still stand today.

1 The research for this chapter was funded by the Deutsche Forschungsgemeinschaft (DFG, German Research Foundation) under Germany's Excellence Strategy—EXC 2176 'Understanding Written Artefacts: Material, Interaction and Transmission in Manuscript Cultures', project no. 390893796. The research was conducted within the scope of the Centre for the Study of Manuscript Cultures (CSMC) at Universität Hamburg.

2 See the various *fahāris* published by Maḥmūd ʿAṭāʾ Allāh for libraries in Nablus, Hebron, Akka and Jaffa.

3 Büssow, *Hamidian Palestine*, 465–467; Pohl, "Führer Durch Die Bibliothek Palästinas"; For a heavily politicised account, see Schidorsky, "Libraries in Late Ottoman Palestine".

4 Conrad and Salameh, "Palestine".

5 See most recently Barakāt, *al-Maktabat al-Budayriyya*; Barakāt, *Maktabat Dār Isʿāf al-Nashāshībī*.

Similar to al-Jazzār's urban project and certainly inspired by it, Abū Nabbūt resorted to the time-tested strategy of creating a large endowment complex to fund his enterprise and extend his influence in the social fabric of the town. The endowment complex involved *khāns*, markets and several fountains. It also included a mosque, the Great Mosque (also known as the Maḥmūdiyya or Maḥmūdī Mosque), the largest religious building in Jaffa at that time. Abū Nabbūt built a *madrasa* as an essential component of the Great Mosque, and founded a library in this educational facility. This chapter will explore the history of Abū Nabbūt's library, based mostly on the endowment statements on its books.

The history of Abū Nabbūt's library can be examined based on various documentary and material evidence, not all of which can be used exhaustively in this chapter. The endowment documents prove particularly helpful for the endowment complex of Abū Nabbūt in its larger context. These texts provide an insight into the financial substructure of the endowed institutions and Abū Nabbūt's vision about how they should function. It is important to note from the outset that we are not dealing with the initial endowment deeds but transcriptions of various endowment-related documents which survive in two different forms. Firstly, we have a composite-document manuscript, containing transmediations of various documents concerning Abū Nabbūt's endowment complex.[6] This manuscript[7] has been transcribed and analysed in depth by Ruba Kana'an in her 1998 PhD dissertation, which remains the prime study on Jaffa under the rulership of Abū Nabbūt.[8] Each transmediated document is provided in duplicate in this composite-document manuscript: once in Arabic, as registered in the Islamic court register (*sijill*) of Jerusalem, and once in Ottoman Turkish, as registered in Istanbul (*dār al-salṭana al-ʿāliyya*). Many questions concerning the history of this important manuscript remain unanswered. We do not know, for example, exactly by whom and for what purpose it was produced. The Ottoman government was collecting copies of endowment deeds in different parts of the empire[9] in the late nineteenth century to enable a more effective management, and our composite-document manuscript may very well have been produced in this context. Its producer was knowledgeable in Arabic and Ottoman Turkish and had access to the documents in both languages, indicating that he was probably tasked by a higher authority.

The court registers of the Islamic Court of Jaffa and the Islamic Court of Jerusalem are a second source for the history of the library. Similar to most cities of the Arab provinces of the Ottoman empire, the records from Jaffa are incomplete. Jaffa was subject to a devastating occupation by Napoleon in 1799, taken over by Egyptian forces in 1831, and ravaged by the tremendous changes of the twentieth century. There are no register volumes from the period before 1799; apparently the earlier volumes got destroyed in a fire. Be that as it may, the surviving volumes allow important insights as Abū Nabbūt's endowment complex left many traces in the court registers of early nineteenth-century Palestine.[10]

An inventory of books that was drawn up in the first third of Dhū al-Ḥijja 1228/November–December 1813 in the court registers of the Islamic Court of Jaffa is specifically interesting regarding Abū Nabbūt's library. Ruba Kana'an reproduced it in her PhD thesis in 1998 and Fatima al-Wahsh

6 For composite-document manuscripts and transmediation, see Reier, "Books as Archives".

7 Jaffa, al-Maktaba al-Islāmiyya, MS 162, (accessed via Nablus, https://manuscripts.najah.edu/node/234, 25 October 2023).

8 Kana'an, "Jaffa and the Waqf", I, 95–101; For the manuscript, see ʿAṭāʾ Allāh, *Fihris Makhṭūṭāt Yāfā*, 233.

9 Gerber, *Ottoman Rule*, 184.

10 Yazbak, *Madīnat al-Burtuqāl*, 4; Qaṭnānī, "al-Awqāf fī qaḍāʾ Yāfā", 281–282; for an overview of the court records in Jaffa, see Layish, "The *Sijill* of Jaffa and Nazareth Sharīʿa Courts"; for an overview of court records from Palestine and their importance for the writing of history, see Doumani, "Palestinian Islamic Court Records."

published an article in 2011 based on this inventory.[11] Abū Nabbūt's books are listed on three pages under twelve thematical categories. The inventory provides two names of people involved in the affairs of the library, gives a total number of books in stock (538) and reveals the existence of a dedicated library catalogue in the possession of its librarian. The available reproduction of this inventory is rather challenging to work with and poses several challenges. The listed books, for example, do not add up to the 538 books declared that were apparently housed in the library at the time of its production, even if we consider that more than one copy of some books was in stock.

Finally, next to these two main sources that have, to some extent, already been used in research on the library of Abū Nabbūt, are those objects that, more than anything else, define a library, the books themselves. Compared to similar libraries, not least the Jazzār library in Acre, a sizable number of manuscripts that were once part of the library in the Great Mosque of Jaffa are identifiable today. What enables us to identify them with certainty are the endowment statements they carry on their title pages (or later fly pages). I have been able to track down 146 books so far. I will call this corpus in the following the Abū Nabbūt manuscript corpus and aim to publish it in full in the future. If we take the number 538 from the inventory in the court record of Jaffa in 1813 as a yardstick, the Abū Nabbūt manuscript corpus is certainly only a sample of the library's former holdings. However, with roughly twenty-five per cent, this sample can be regarded as fairly representative, and some conclusions, however tentative, can be drawn.

This chapter argues that the library of the Great Mosque of Jaffa was an integral element of Abū Nabbūt's urban programme. Furthermore, he used the books of the library to make his political allegiances and ambitions known. Based on the endowment notes, I advance the argument that for Abū Nabbūt, his affiliation to al-Jazzār was a highly important and meaningful condition, and that he utilised his books to proclaim this in his attempt to obtain a promotion within the Ottoman hierarchy. But before we explore what these books tell us about the history of the library, we will introduce its founder and his endowment project to later connect these dots to his bookish endeavour.

1 Abū Nabbūt

Little is known about Abū Nabbūt before he became the deputy governor of Jaffa in the early nineteenth century, and even less about his life before he came to Acre. It is only known that he served as a customs officer (*gümrük emini*) in Acre and, for a brief period, as deputy governor of Damascus under Aḥmad Pasha al-Jazzār.[12] What allowed Abū Nabbūt to rise to such positions was his membership of al-Jazzār's household, that is, the extended group of dependents held together by various forms of social, economic and personal ties. The innermost circle of the household was, at least in its early years, a group with a pronounced loyalty, a feature often described as typical for such a social formation. Al-Jazzār himself set an example: The reason that he initially fled Egypt in 1768 was his refusal to take part in a plot against his former master.[13] His worldview must have been heavily shaken when in May 1789, after he himself grew to be the master of a household, his own *mamlūk*s started a rebellion. Although al-Jazzār eventually weathered the insurrection, the effects of the disloyal behaviour of his *mamlūk*s have been profound. After the rebellion, he was described as paranoid and constantly on guard. Still, in 1802, he

11 Kana'an, "Jaffa and the Waqf", II, 120–122; al-Waḥsh, "Dirāsat."

12 About Ottoman *mamlūk* households, see Hathaway, *The Politics of Houselholds*, 17–31; about Abū Nabbūt's early career, see Kana'an, "Jaffa and the Waqf", I, 65–66; about al-Jazzār's household, see Philipp, "The Last Mamluk Household", 326–329; Philipp, *Acre*, 142–147.

13 Philipp, "The Last Mamluk Household", 319; Philipp, *Acre*, 50–52.

readopted at least one of the *mamlūk*s who took part in the rebellion against him, a certain Sulaymān.[14] When al-Jazzār died in 1219/1804, Sulaymān eventually assumed power and became the governor of Sidon. Under Sulaymān Pasha (r. 1804–1818), Abū Nabbūt further advanced his career and left his imprint on Jaffa and its environs.

Abū Nabbūt's stellar career was enabled by a change of policy. Although Sulaymān followed al-Jazzār in keeping Acre the official residence of the governorate of Sidon, his politics were decisively different. He loosened the reins on the monopoly on cotton and other agricultural produce that made his predecessors al-Jazzār and Ẓāhir al-ʿUmar (ca. 1690–1775) such prosperous rulers. This involved laxer taxation for the peasants and artisans who were seriously afflicted by al-Jazzār's policy.[15] In terms of manpower, Sulaymān Pasha maintained a much smaller regiment than his predecessor. This style of leadership earned him the appellation 'the just' (*al-ʿādil*) and stood in self-evident contrast to al-Jazzār ('the butcher'). Under Sulaymān Pasha's decentralised rule, his deputies were able to act more independently in their regions and virtually establish lordships, such as Muṣṭafā Barbar in Tripolis and Abū Nabbūt in Jaffa and southern Palestine.[16]

When exactly Abū Nabbūt assumed his position in Jaffa is contested. Al-Jazzār integrated the town into his district in 1803—before, it was officially part of the *sanjak* Damascus—and appointed Abū Nabbūt his deputy governor (*mutasallim*) around that time. Abū Nabbūt's early tenure in Jaffa was shortly interrupted by Abū Maraq, a local from Gaza who had already ruled Jaffa from 1801 until 1803 and who returned briefly to rule the town in 1804. Al-Jazzār's successor Sulaymān the Just sent Abū Nabbūt to oust Abū Maraq for good, and reappointed Abū Nabbūt, who was, in theory, of equal rank to his former *mamlūk* comrade. Jaffa was badly afflicted not only during Abū Nabbūt's siege but also with previous military attempts to capture the town. Egyptian forces under ʿAlī Bey al-Kabīr and Abū Dhahab lay Jaffa under siege in the early 1770s. Though the subsequent Siege of Jaffa under Napoleon in 1799 was much shorter, the accompanying massacre and the following outbreak of the bubonic plague were far more devastating. After he captured the town, Abū Nabbūt held the position of deputy governor until he was eventually ousted in 1819.

In his position as deputy governor, Abū Nabbūt's domains include Jaffa, Gaza, Ramla and Lid. He asserted various military and administrative tasks in this southernmost region of Ottoman Greater Syria. His main responsibilities were maintaining security and collecting various forms of taxes, including the customs of the port, for his superior in Acre. His role gave him some leverage concerning trade, which, in turn, helped him to turn Jaffa into a port city of transregional importance. In addition, he was the administrator of the sultanic endowment (*mutawallī al-waqf al-sharīf*) in his region, *silaḥshūr khāṣṣa* (commander in chief) and port director (*ḍābiṭ iskila Yāfā*).[17] With these official titles behind him, Abū Nabbūt was an ambitious ruler who did not simply use the existing structures in the region for his personal profit but initiated a large-scale rebuilding project in and around Jaffa. In his efforts to develop the town into a proper port city, he resorted to the well-established practice of creating an endowment complex by acquiring and subsequently endowing property to ensure the continuous financing of his projects. The composite-document manuscript mentioned above enables an in-depth look into his various infrastructural projects taking place mostly between 1812 and 1816.[18]

14 Philipp, "The Last Mamluk Household", 326–331; Philipp, *Acre*, 143–147.

15 Doumani, *Rediscovering Palestine*, 100–102; More critically, Philipp, *Acre*, 123–126.

16 About the relationship between Sulaymān Pasha and Abū Nabbūt, see Saʿīd, *Yāfā*, 57–59.

17 Kana'an, "Jaffa and the Waqf", I, 66–70.

18 Kana'an, "Jaffa and the Waqf", I, 94–126; Qaṭnānī, "al-Awqāf fī qaḍāʾ Yāfā", 290–299; Yazbak, "al-Waqf al-islāmī fī Yāfā", 311 ff.

FIGURE 6.1 The cemetery can be seen in this painting of Jaffa by David Roberts from 1813. (Jaffa, formerly Joppa, looking south). Coloured lithograph by Louis Haghe after David Roberts, 1843
WELLCOME COLLECTION. PUBLIC DOMAIN MARK. SOURCE: WELLCOME COLLECTION

Abū Nabbūt took care of the fortification of the city to foster security and, importantly, create a haven for himself and his retinue. He initiated the refurbishment of the land walls including the digging of a moat.[19] He bought land outside the city to move the cemetery outside the city walls (see fig. 6.1) and make space for more buildings. He built two new markets with thirty-six and eleven shops, respectively, to encourage trade and, thus, income. In addition, he built two new *khāns*.[20] The two fountains built at Abū Nabbūt's behest are most famous among his buildings, one outside the city on the way to Jerusalem and one within the town annexed to the Great Mosque, both of which still stand today.[21] He attempted to build a sea wall late in his tenure in Jaffa, but this last project was not realised.

Abū Nabbūt was brought down in the summer of 1819 through a scheme plotted by Ḥaim Farḥī, the secretary and financial administrator of Sulaymān Pasha, ʿAbd Allāh Pasha and Samʿān al-Ṣāliḥ, a scribe at the Court of Jaffa. His attempt to obtain the official status of Pasha and gain a degree of independence from his superior Sulaymān had not only failed but triggered his opponents to eventually remove him. Upon returning from Gaza, Abū Nabbūt was denied access to Jaffa, and he was never to enter his former seat of power again. After a brief interlude in Cairo, where Abū Nabbūt is said to have arrived with an entourage of about 500

19 Yazbak, *Madīnat al-Burtuqāl*, 133–141.
20 Kana'an, "Jaffa and the Waqf", I, 38–44; Yazbak, *Madīnat al-Burtuqāl*, 126–130.
21 Kana'an, "Two Ottoman *Sabils*".

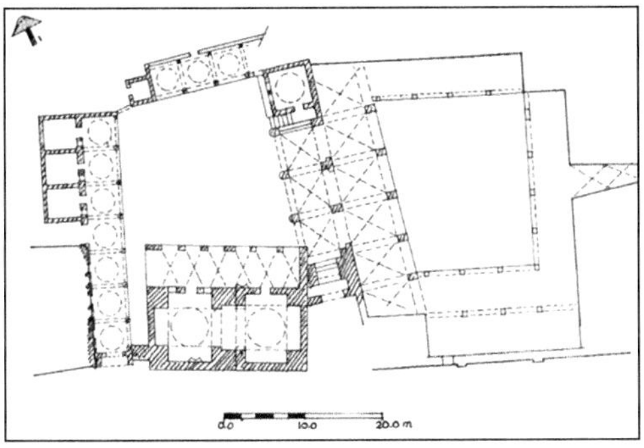

FIGURE 6.2
Sketch Plan of the Great Mosque. The courtyard to the west is the one built in 1812. Kana'an, *Waqf, Architecture, and Political Self-Fashioning*, p. 121
© RUBA KANA'AN

people as a guest of Egypt's strongman Muḥammad ʿAlī,[22] he later held other high-ranking positions, such as that of the *wālī* of Salonika in 1821 and later also the *wālī* of Diyar Bakir (1826).[23]

2 Building a Library in Early Nineteenth-century Palestine

The Great Mosque was the religious signature project of Abū Nabbūt's endowment complex in Jaffa. It stood on the remains of an earlier, ruinous mosque, built in the eighteenth century by a certain Muḥammad al-Bībī.[24] After the devastating period of the late eighteenth and early nineteenth century, the mosque lay in ruins. Abū Nabbūt decided to rebuild it and the construction phase concluded in 1812.[25] The new building was enlarged and equipped with running water, carpets and several employees. A *madrasa* was attached to the mosque to serve local educational needs and attract scholars (see fig. 6.2). This *madrasa* housed a library (*kitābkhāne*), located in the north-east corner of the Great Mosque.[26] The Great Mosque and Abū Nabbūt's fountains have gained some scholarly attention, most notably by Ruba Kana'an and, more recently, by Mahmud Yazbak. Only one dedicated article has been written on the library by Fatima al-Wahsh, who based her research on the inventory from the Jaffa court records described above, but unfortunately missed one entire page of it in her analysis.[27] For the first time, the present chapter includes the books that once lay (or stood) on the shelves of the library, which enable us to add another layer to its history.

The Abū Nabbūt manuscript corpus as it stands today comprises 146 books. These books are identifiable as formerly belonging to Abū Nabbūt's library thanks to the endowment statements they carry. The largest bulk of books (124 manuscripts) I have been able to find so far are manuscripts that have remained in Jaffa for at least a century and in 1923, became part of the newly established Islamic Library in Jaffa. Pictures of these manuscripts can be found today on the website of the al-Najah National University Library in Nablus. These pictures are reproductions of microfilms, presumably those produced by Maḥmūd ʿAṭā Allāh (d. 2002) in 1984 when the latter produced a catalogue for the Islamic Library and, in its course, microfilmed some 339 manuscripts.[28] I will cite these manuscripts by their Islamic Library in Jaffa class mark and provide links to the al-Najah library website. Unfortunately, I was not able to track down the current

22 al-Jabartī, *ʿAjāʾib al-āthār*, IV, 469, 473.
23 For his career after he left Jaffa, see Kana'an, "Jaffa and the Waqf", I, 89–90; Saʿīd, *Yāfā*, 84–88; Yazbak, *Madīnat al-Burtuqāl*, 152–154.
24 Qaṭnānī, "al-Awqāf fī qaḍāʾ Yāfā", 286.
25 Yazbak, *Madīnat al-Burtuqāl*, 106–107; Sharon, *Corpus Inscriptionum Arabicarum Palaestinae 6—J (1)*, VI, 78–79.
26 Kana'an, "Jaffa and the Waqf", I, 103–109; Kana'an, "Waqf, Architecture, and Political Self-fashioning".
27 al-Waḥsh, "Dirāsat".
28 ʿAṭāʾ Allāh, *Fihris Makhṭūṭāt Yāfā*, 3–4.

whereabouts of most of these 124 manuscripts and, thus, had to work with the uploaded pictures of varying quality.

Some 19 of those 124 manuscripts uploaded on the al-Najah National University Library's website appear in the 5 published catalogues of the Center for Heritage Revival and Islamic Research (*Mu'assasat Iḥyā' al-Turāth wa-al-Buḥūth al-Islāmiyya*) in Abu Dis next to Jerusalem, where they are also kept today.[29] This institution was set up by the Palestinian Ministry of Endowments and Religious Affairs in 1983 to safeguard the written heritage of Muslim Palestine. It holds (at least) another eight manuscripts formerly owned by Abū Nabbūt, making the total number of books formerly part of Abū Nabbūt's library there twenty-seven (for now). The role of the Center for Heritage Revival and Islamic Research in the more recent history of books and libraries in Palestine is certainly highly relevant and awaits dedicated research.

A further thirteen manuscripts in the Abū Nabbūt manuscript corpus are today in the ʿUmarī Mosque in Gaza. They have been digitised in a collective effort by Muneer Elbaz from the University College of Applied Sciences in Gaza within the framework of the Endangered Archives Programme of the British Library (EAP1285/1) in cooperation with the Hill Museum & Manuscript Library. A total of 211 manuscripts have been digitized and uploaded online. It is not clear whether these are all the manuscripts kept in the ʿUmarī Mosque or only a sample. The catalogue of the ʿUmarī Mosque library published in 2016, for example, speaks of only 187 manuscripts.[30] Should there be more manuscripts in the ʿUmarī Mosque than those uploaded, there may also be more manuscripts formerly kept in the library of Abū Nabbūt.

A single manuscript in the Abū Nabbūt manuscript corpus is today part of the National Library of Israel in Jerusalem. Unfortunately, the manuscript itself is very sparse in terms of information about its own history: besides the endowment note of Abū Nabbūt, the only other paratextual clues are the stamp and the shelf number of the National Library. The manuscript in question, Ms Ar. 266, was, according to the inventory book of the 'Ar. Stock', bought from a certain Dr. Goldstein on 14 December 1955.[31] I will come back to some of the institutions named in the preceding paragraphs in the last part of this chapter.

The corpus of 146 identified books, though not the sum total of the library's former stock, allows a corpus-based approach to the history of the library and, thus, an important addition to the documents at hand. In the meantime, additional manuscripts are expected to be found in the region and, maybe, around the world. Any quantitative detail and argument based on quantitative data in this chapter must, thus, be treated with reasonable caution. The corpus I have built (so far) and on which this chapter is based is, in many regards, indebted to the digitalisation efforts of different institutions and individuals, but, at the same time, it is based on their selection criteria, which are not always clearly stated. We can read in Konrad Hirschler's chapter on the translocation of al-Jazzār's manuscripts (Chapter 7) that the al-Najah Library's website only hints at from where they got their manuscripts ("established families of Nablus known for their famous scholars, litterateurs and poets"), but provides neither details of single manuscripts, their current class marks, nor information about which manuscripts are actually part of their library today and for which they only have digital reproductions. Though we can detect a most welcomed reappraisal of historical Palestinian book collections in recent years, the references to actual manuscripts in this chapter will show that the situation is not always satisfactory. Nevertheless, it is my conviction that we should

29 ʿAfāna et al., *Fihris Makhṭūṭāt Filasṭīn al-Musawwara, al-Fiqh wa-uṣūl*.

30 Abū Hāshim, *Fihris Makhṭūṭāt Maktaba al-Jāmiʿ al-ʿUmarī al-Kabīr*, 13. The lower number might be the result of the *dasht* section which is digitised and uploaded but not catalogued by Abū Hāshim.

31 I am grateful to Samuel Thrope for this information.

not wait until the research situation is fully satisfying, with each and every manuscript clearly locatable and digitised according to the most recent state-of-the-art.

Before we come to the books and their endowment statements, I will briefly outline some key points about the library based on the other sources at hand. We know from the endowment document in the composite-document manuscript that Abū Nabbūt conceived the library to be a part of the *madrasa* and not an independent institution. He added seven shops, a *khān* and a house to the already existing endowment to secure the financial maintenance. He deployed a staff for the whole mosque complex of, among others, himself as the administrator of the endowment (*mutawallī*), a preacher (*khaṭīb*), an imam, a person spreading the prayer carpets, a sweeper, an unknown number of servants (*khudām dākhil wa-khārij*) and two muezzins. Regarding the *madrasa*, Abū Nabbūt allocated stipends for thirteen non-resident students of three different stipend brackets and another category for students living in the mosque. These students were taught by two teachers (sg. *ʿālim mudarris*),[32] each of which was given a teaching assistant (*muqrī*ʾ).[33] Finally, a librarian (*amīn kutubkhāne*) was designated for the upkeep of the library.[34]

The inventory in the Islamic Court of Jaffa mentioned above is a major source for the number of books in Abū Nabbūt's library, though its interpretation is not straightforward and the number of books a library holds is usually fluid. The entry was drawn up on the first day of Dhū al-Ḥijja 1228/25 November 1813, that is, approximately a year and a half after the foundation was registered in court.[35] In its surviving form, it consists of a preamble, twelve thematic sections and a closing formula from which the number 538 derives. As we will see, Abū Nabbūt endowed books over time, well beyond the production of the inventory. The number 538 can, thus, only be seen as a snapshot of the holdings for that particular date. Be that as it may, the fact that the number of books had reached 538 after only one and a half years of the library's foundation is significant. It suggests that either Abū Nabbūt had started acquiring books long before he founded the library or he was able to acquire such a huge number of books in such a short time. This, in turn, would mean that books were available in the early nineteenth century by the hundreds. Can we get any closer to the origins of the books in his library?

The provenance of books in libraries endowed by political and military rulers are sometimes shrouded in myth. Politically motivated confiscation, shifty means or even violent looting are sometimes go-to explanations for how high-calibre men built their libraries, and Abū Nabbūt's leadership style is sometimes described as rather harsh, including occasional looting.[36] These stories about the appropriation of books by dubious practices can be true, as Kyle Wynter-Stoner has recently shown for the Maḥmūdiyya library in fifteenth-century Cairo.[37] Other times, they are bloated narratives meant to speak ill of certain figures. The recurring narrative of al-Jazzār plundering libraries, among others in Jabal ʿĀmil, to stock his library in Acre is as persistent as it is dubious. The credibility of this narrative is highly doubtful as we can read in Chapter 3 of this volume. What can we say about the previous life of the books in Abū Nabbūt's library?

Firstly, it is telling to note that, so far, no conclusive evidence has emerged that Abū Nabbūt's library housed a single book formerly held in the Jazzār library in Acre. Not a single endowment statement of Aḥmad Pasha al-Jazzār can be found, nor any of his endowment seals, among the Abū Nab-

32 For teachers at the school in the late nineteenth century, see al-Ṭarāwana, "Qaḍāʾ Yāfā", 492–493.

33 Kana'an, "Jaffa and the Waqf", II, 61, 65.

34 For the title "*amīn kutubkhāne*", see Chapter 1.

35 For black and white reproductions of the microfilmed entry, see Kana'an, "Jaffa and the Waqf", II, 120–122.; also see al-Waḥsh, "Dirāsat", missing one page.

36 See, for example, Mannāʿ, *Taʾrīkh Filasṭīn*, 123.

37 Wynter-Stoner, "Books, Corruption, and an Emir's Downfall"; Wynter-Stoner, "The Maḥmūdīyah", 42–44.

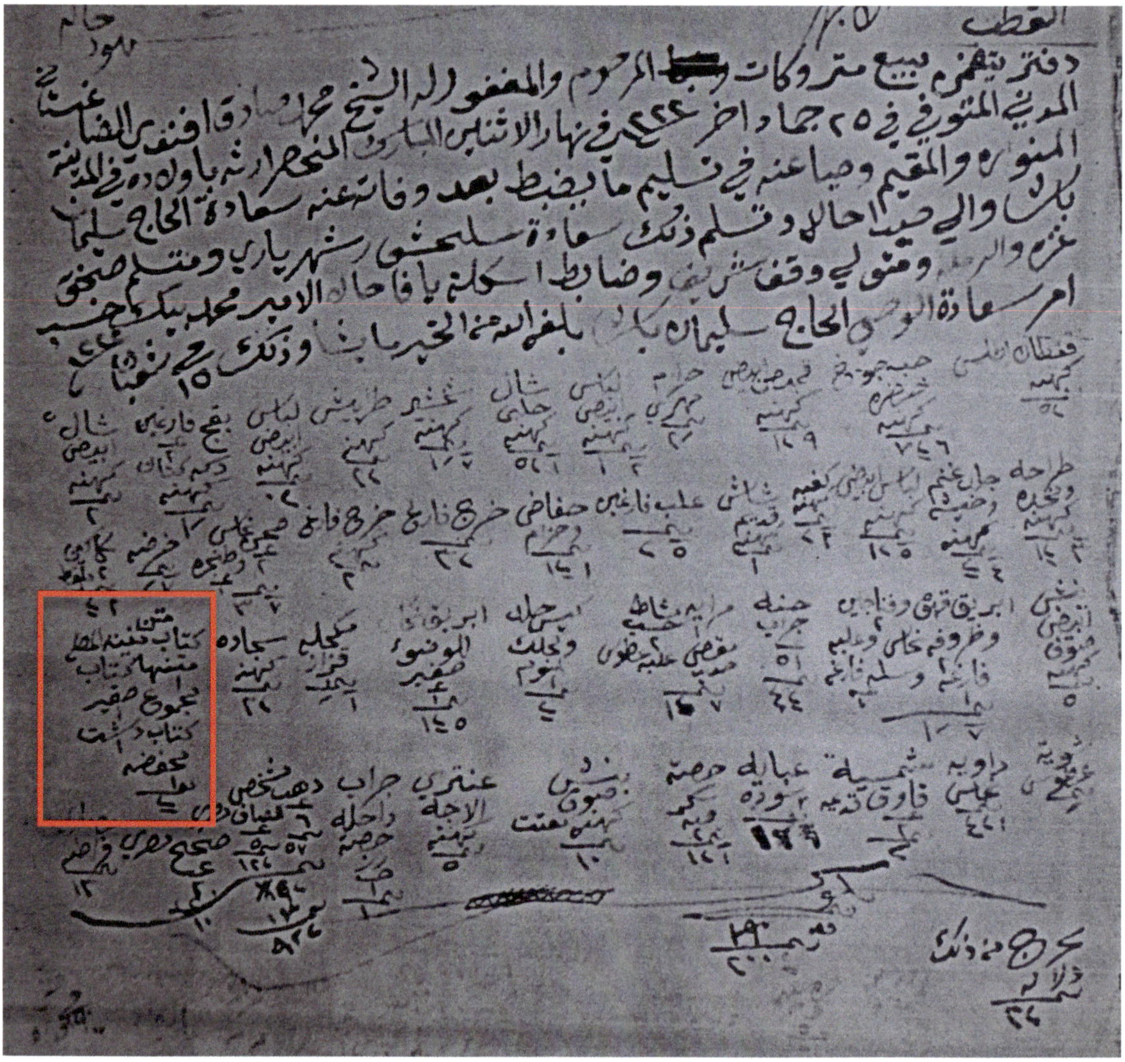

FIGURE 6.3 Estate inventory of Shaykh Muḥammad (d. 1807), position with books squared in red. Jaffa, *Sijill al-Maḥkama al-Sharʿiyya* 3, p. 79.

būt manuscript corpus. The book market of early nineteenth century southern Greater Syria was, apparently, sufficiently saturated to enable the establishment of more than one library created by an emir. On the other hand, the absence of books previously owned/endowed by al-Jazzār from Abū Nabbūt's library suggests that, at least until the latter's career in Jaffa ended, al-Jazzār's books were quite secure in their place. From where, then, did Abū Nabbūt get his books?

There has been only one indication so far that his books were, at least partially, acquired from the selling of estates. Estate inventories are one type of document we find repeatedly in Ottoman court registers and Bashīr Barakāt has pioneered their study for book ownership in Ottoman Jerusalem. Mohammad Ghosheh's publication of facsimiles of book-related estate inventories, again from Jerusalem, shows that there is much more work to be done on this rich material.[38] In con-

38 Barakāt, *Taʾrīkh al-maktabat*; Ghosheh, *Encyclopaedia Palestinnica: Manuscripts.*

trast to Jerusalem, in the court register of Jaffa I was able to see, estate inventories are not only rarer, but books appear less often. In fact, I have found only one estate inventory containing books in the Jaffa court registers from 1215/1800 to 1223/1810 (see fig. 6.3).

This inventory lists the estate of a certain Shaykh Muḥammad Ṣādiq Efendī (al-Ḍāghistānī) al-Madanī, who died in 1222/1807. One of the last positions in the inventory enumerates the following items: *Kitāb* (*matn*) *munyat al-muṣallī matnhā kitāb 1, majmūʿ ṣaghīr 1, kitāb dasht 1, maḥfaẓa*. From these four items, only one title is clearly identifiable, *Kitāb munyat al-muṣallī*, a book on prayer by Sadīd al-Dīn al-Kāshgharī (d. 705/1305), the others being an unspecified small collection of multiple texts (*majmūʿ*), one book of fragmentary material (*dasht*) and one folder. The governor of the province of Sidon, Sulaymān Pasha, became the official legal guardian of the deceased's estate because the legal heirs of Shaykh Muḥammad were in Medina and, thus, out of reach. Being equally far away in Acre, Abū Nabbūt assumed the role of the trustee of the inheritance.

As the trustee of the estate, Abū Nabbūt was in pole position and could very well have bought Shaykh Muḥammad's copy of the book (as well as the other items in that position). And indeed, one copy of the *Munyat al muṣallī* can bc found among Abū Nabbūt's books.[39] Matching titles from estate inventories to actual books, however, is not an easy task, and this case is no exception. There is no clear evidence that Abū Nabbūt's copy of the *Munyat al-muṣallī* is actually the one formerly owned by Shaykh Muḥammad; an ownership statement from the latter is missing. What speaks for the fact that we have the very same copy is the date of the endowment statement by Abū Nabbūt (here Abū Labbūt)–1238/1822–1823—that is, *after* the death of Shaykh Muḥammad.

How often Abū Nabbūt was lucky enough to acquire books in Jaffa, the other towns in his domain or the wider region is not clear; the case of Shaykh Muḥammad is, to date, an exceptional find. Furthermore, as we have seen in the contribution of Said Aljoumani in Chapter 2, some 95 books of one particularly fervent book collector from Jaffa, al-Sayyid Yaḥyā Efendī b. al-Sayyid Muḥammad al-Ṭībī, were integrated into the Jazzār library in 1218/1803, that is, a couple of years before Abū Nabbūt founded his library. Jaffa was a small town and certainly not famous for scholarship. It can be assumed that not too many inhabitants collected books and their scant appearance in estate inventories reflects this state.

Another hint regarding from where he got his books appears on (so far) twelve books in the Abū Nabbūt manuscript corpus. All of these twelve manuscripts carry an undated ownership statement by a certain Ḥāfiẓ ʿUthmān (b. Ibrāhīm). Ḥāfiẓ ʿUthmān was also the copyist for one manuscript in the corpus, a commentary on the famous *Dalāʾil al-khayrāt* by al-Jamal al-ʿUjaylī (d. 1204/1790) with the title *al-Minaḥ al-ilāhiyyāt*. The dated colophon (1218/1803)[40] gives one point in time allowing us to estimate when this book collector was alive. Strikingly, all of the twelve manuscripts with an ownership statement of Ḥāfiẓ ʿUthmān were endowed in 1234/1818–1819, after Abū Nabbūt's ousting from Jaffa. This makes it probable that Ḥāfiẓ ʿUthmān's books ended up in Abū Nabbūt's library and not vice versa. Unfortunately, I have not been able to find out anything about Ḥāfiẓ ʿUthmān so far. Having reached the Abū Nabbūt's manuscripts themselves, we will now interrogate them more thoroughly to see what they can add to our knowledge of the library and its endower.

One element on Abū Nabbūt's books that helps us to reconstruct some details of the library's history are the endowment statements. In the following, we will rely on these endowment state-

39 Jaffa, al-Maktaba al-Islāmiyya, MS 1656 (accessed via Nablus, https://manuscripts.najah.edu/node/172, 25 October 2023).

40 Jaffa, al-Maktaba al-Islāmiyya, MS 1286, fol. 187[a], (accessed via Nablus, https://manuscripts.najah.edu/node/191, 25 October 2023).

ments to look at the formation of Abū Nabbūt's library, the endower's vision and the library's afterlife. This chapter argues implicitly that a detailed study of endowment statements can add an essential layer to the history of libraries not mentioned in other sources. I argue more explicitly that the endowment statements and endowment notes on the books of Abū Nabbūt's library were perceived of and used as a form of 'public text'. By linking subtle changes in these short texts to leaps in his career, we will see how Abū Nabbūt utilised the books to make public (and perpetuate) his various positions of power, openly display his allegiance to al-Jazzār and insert himself into a political genealogy. Before delving into the argument, I will briefly introduce some of the irks and quirks of the endowment statements.

While on the books of the Jazzār library, we have one endowment statement with only minor variations,[41] Abū Nabbūt's books have a host of different endowment statements which vary in length and the range of information they provide. For one, there are long statements that contain the well-known elements such as the *waqf* formula (*waqafa wa-ḥabbasa* [...]), specification of the endowed object, name of the endower, the beneficiaries (*ahl al-ʿilm al-qāṭinīn bi-iskila Yāfā*), the conditions (*lā yubāʿu wa-lā yurhanu wa-lā yubaddalu* [...]) and the exact date of the endowment act. On the other hand, there are shorter endowment statements that only consist of the declaration '*waqf*', the endower's name, a date and a seal. I will call these shorter texts endowment 'notes' in the following. Overall, we can detect (so far) fifteen different statements, which, in each case, cluster around a certain period, each written in a different hand. The various hands and formulations of the endowment statements and notes show that various people were involved in the maintenance of the library over time. This variety made it initially more complicated to gather the Abū Nabbūt manuscript corpus, but eventually provides some fascinating insights into the history of the library. Before coming to the specifics of these insights, we will briefly ascertain the function of these endowment statements.

We can read about one way in which the political/military elite used their books in Dana Sajdi's chapter on the history section of the Jazzār library inventory (Chapter 22). Accordingly, a wayfaring Moroccan scholar met al-Jazzār on the pilgrimage, who showed him a book containing a riddle the scholar was asked to solve. This is an all too rare report about how a ruler, al-Jazzār, brought his books into action. It is a case of blatant (but failed) self-promotion, but revealing regarding the instrumentalisation of books by the political/military elite. Why books? As a local governor you could not mint coins. You had to produce other 'public' texts, such as public announcements or inscriptions on buildings, to make yourself, your name and whatever you wanted to convey known. Another form to make your message public was to utilise the endowment statement on your books which, as the preceding anecdote has shown, were not only meant to be seen by the odd library user but, at times, rubbed in a scholar's face in an event as prominent as the annual pilgrimage. How, then, did Abū Nabbūt utilise his books to spread his name publicly, and what were the messages he tried to convey?

The first notable point regarding Abū Nabbūt's endowment statements is how he used them to emphatically proclaim his allegiance to his former master, Aḥmad Pasha al-Jazzār. We can find his affiliation to al-Jazzār on fifty books (so far), in formulations such as '[...] the manumitted slave of the late (the pardoned) the Mecca Pilgrim, Aḥmad Pasha al-Jazzār' (*maʿtūq/ʿatīq al-marḥūm (al-maghfūr) al-Ḥajj Aḥmad Pasha al-Jazzār*). This suffix to his own name appears on the very first batch of (to date) fifteen books Abū Nabbūt endowed in various months of 1226/1811–1812, that is, right when he established his library and some seven years after al-Jazzār had passed away. The association to his former master was apparently so mean-

41 The endowment statements on the Maḥmūdiyya Library books are also quite consistent, see Wynter-Stoner, "Books, Corruption, and an Emir's Downfall".

ingful to him that he made sure to have it spread across the town, carved in stone: of the surviving monuments built by Abū Nabbūt, we can find the affiliation to al-Jazzār on the inscription on the Great Mosque, the *khān al-Maḥmūdiyya* and on two fountains.[42] In the inscription on one fountain, he even calls himself the 'successor of al-Jazzār' (*khalīfat al-Jazzār*).

Abū Nabbūt's proximity to al-Jazzār went beyond bluntly stating it in various public texts. It can also be seen in his emulation of the architectural style of the Aḥmadī Mosque in his Great Mosque in Jaffa.[43] As suggested in the Introduction to this volume, the Aḥmadī Mosque in Acre was itself an imitation of the imperial Ottoman style, diverting from the regional Syrian mosque tradition and meant to echo the more recent style of mosques built in the Ottoman capital. Abū Nabbūt's adoption of this architectural style, in turn, can be seen not only as an emulation of his former master, but equally shows him displaying his claim to power within the Ottoman hierarchy. It is interesting that the endowment statements on his books starting in 1228/1813–1814 lack the affiliation to al-Jazzār and it reappears only in 1234/1818 when Abū Nabbūt was forcibly exiled from Jaffa. What are we to make out of the later reappearance?

Being from the same *mamlūk* household, Abū Nabbūt saw himself as equal in rank to Sulaymān Pasha. Upon the death of Sulaymān's deputy, ʿAlī Pasha (d. 1230/1815), Abū Nabbūt was stepping up his efforts to obtain the title of Pasha. He saw himself the most suitable contender, but, much to his disappointment, Sulaymān's choice fell on another candidate, the son of the deceased ʿAlī Pasha.[44] Towards the end of the following year (1231/1816), Abū Nabbūt is said to have changed his approach towards reaching his career ambitions. He tried to pull strings directly in Istanbul, again without success. He now aimed to further enhance the fortification of Jaffa, to build a sea wall to eventually break away from the district of Sidon, in order to have a better basis for negotiations.[45] It is arguably against this background that he decided to have his affiliation to al-Jazzār put back on his books, aiming to promote his status as an equal to Sulaymān Pasha and emphasise his claim for his own realm.

We can read yet another feature on Abū Nabbūt's books as a reference to al-Jazzār. Starting in 1238/1822 (that is, after his ousting from Jaffa), the endowment notes on his books come with a seal impression (see fig. 6.4). The appearance of the seal itself is not as impressive as al-Jazzār's larger (almost identical) ones, which, as Boris Liebrenz argues in Chapter 10, al-Jazzār's used as an 'element of emulation and ambition' of Ottoman imperial book culture. In al-Jazzār's case, this emulation is based on the form and size of the seal. It could be argued that Abū Nabbūt's seal is an emulation of al-Jazzār's seal based not on its grandiose appearance but on the motto, both read '*wa-mā tawfīqī illā bi-llāh*'. It should be noted, however, that this was a common phrase on seals and also used by other owners.

The affiliation to al-Jazzār is dropped once again in the endowment notes of books that entered the library in 1238/1822–1823. Along the same line as above, this can be explained by his eventual promotion in the Ottoman hierarchy. Abū Nabbūt finally rose in the hierarchy in 1821, becoming the *wālī* of Salonica, where he would become infamous in the Massacre of Naoussa. He again became the *wālī* in 1242/1826, this time in Diyarbekir.[46] These positions finally put him on an equal footing with not only Sulaymān (who was already dead), but also his former master, al-Jazzār.

42 Sharon, *Corpus Inscriptionum Arabicarum Palaestinae 6—J (1)*, Great Mosque 6, 79, *khān* 6, 81, fountain (*al-sabīl al-Maḥmūdī*) 6, 76, fountain (*sabīl al-shifāʾ*) 6, 102.

43 Kana'an, "Jaffa and the Waqf", I, 155; Yazbak, *Madīnat al-Burtuqāl*, 109.

44 Kana'an, "Jaffa and the Waqf", I, 79–80.

45 His wish for independence was noticed by the French painter and traveller De Forbin, who had met him personally, see *Travels*, 155.

46 Kana'an, "Jaffa and the Waqf", I, 90.

FIGURE 6.4
Abū Nabbūt's seal which only appears in 1822, after his ousting from Jaffa
MS GAZA, ʿUMARĪ MOSQUE 206 [CC BY-NC 4.0]

Accordingly, his name was from now on given as 'the vizier, the warrior champion, Muḥammad Pasha al-Wazīr al-Ghāzī Muḥammad Pasha Abū Labbūt'. The affiliation to his former master al-Jazzār apparently lost its function. It was now he who served as an affiliation in the names of some of his former *mamlūks* who started to provide their names with the addition *maʿtūq al-wazīr Muḥammad Amīn Pasha*.[47]

A second point we can glean from his name on the endowment notes relates to how he was addressed. We can detect a change in the notes starting in 1234/1818. For one, his name in the early statements tends to be much longer than the later ones. The higher he rose in rank, the shorter his name on these statements and notes became. In the earlier statements, for example, he is often addressed with a firework of honorifics, such as 'glory of the grand emirs, prime of the senior-ranking nobles, authorised carrier of the stately responsibility, commander in chief, governor of the district of Gaza, Ramla, administrator of the Sultanic endowment, acting officer of the harbour of Jaffa, the emir Muḥammad Aghā' (*iftikhār al-umarāʾ al-fakhām wa-zubdat al-kubrā al-kirām wa-muʿtamad al-wizr al-ʿiẓām silaḥshūr khāṣṣa wa-mutasallim liwāʾ Ghazza wa-al-Ramla wa-mutawallī waqf sharīf wa-ḍābiṭ iskila Yāfā ḥālan al-Amīr Muḥammad Aghā*). In the later notes, his name is severely abbreviated, and he is mostly addressed simply as vizier and warrior champion (*ghāzī*).

More crucially, he is no longer addressed as Muḥammas Aghā in these later notes but by his moniker, Abū Nabbūt, 'father of the cudgel'. It is not always easy to get to the heart of monikers. Al-Jazzār, 'the butcher', got his after killing a large number of Bedouins in Egypt and in his case this '[...] certainly was meant as a term of respect and did not reflect a perception of general cruelty of character'.[48] That behind al-Jazzār's moniker lurks a complex and nuanced perception by different historians can be read in Chapter 4 of this volume by Feras Krimsti. Abū Nabbūt, similarly, earned his moniker for his rough style of leadership. There are, for example, entries in the Jaffa court records of two men who stole from a shop run by a Christian and who were beaten to death by Abū Nabbūt during the interrogation. Abū Nabbūt continued to be remembered as a stern ruler in stories circulating among the peasants in the vicinity of Jaffa, though in contexts in which he eventually dispersed justice. In one rather amusing story, Abū Nabbūt is said to have beaten the door of a house that got robbed until the door revealed the thief.[49]

47 Ibid., 89–90.

48 Philipp, *Acre*, 50.

49 Concerning the two thieves, see Kana'an, "Jaffa and the Waqf", I, 53–54; regarding the door, see Macalister, "Some Miscellaneous Tales"; also see Meryon, *Travels of Lady Hester Stanhope*, I, 197.

He certainly got the image of a ruler who did not shun violent measures and he should live up to his moniker in his tenure in Salonica.

To bring the comparison to a close, al-Jazzār evidently used his moniker himself, probably with some pride, as can be seen, among others, in his usage of it in his seal(s). Not so Abū Nabbūt. We cannot find him addressed by his moniker in his inscriptions, his seal, or the books he endowed during his tenure in Jaffa. Regarding the court records of Jaffa, he is never referred to as Abū Nabbūt either, but always as Muḥammad Aghā, with the usual shower of honorifics. According to Mahmoud Yazbak, his moniker appears in the court records only in 1241/1826.[50] It is only after he was exiled that we find this moniker in one of its derivatives, Abū Labbūt or Abū Labbūṭ (this is how he became known in Salonica). There is no clear answer as to why this change took place. Perhaps whoever was responsible for the endowment notes felt that Abū Nabbūt was at a safe distance and, thus, no repercussions could be expected.

The third main insight we can gain from the endowment statements and notes relates to the building of the library's stock, namely, that its stocking was a continuous effort. Based on the dates provided in the endowment statements and notes, a detailed timeline can be reconstructed.[51] The different dates show that Abū Nabbūt endowed books over a period of one-and-a-half decades, gradually enlarging his library. A first batch of books entered the library in 1226/1811, while a last batch of the corpus was added in 1238/1822–1823. There are two years, 1231/1816 and 1234/1818, in which the library received large numbers of books, but smaller supplies entered the library in between. There were several occasions of additions to the library's stock in some years. In 1232/1817, for example, books were added in three months (Jumādā I, Jumādā II and Shaʿbān).[52] The absence of one particular date with a massive number of books entering the library suggests that there was no looting or acquisition of a single large library involved but that the books were collected from different sources on various occasions. This can also be seen in the different hands of the endowment statements and notes, suggesting, furthermore, several different people involved in running the library over the years of its increasing stock.

It is striking, and probably telling, that Abū Nabbūt continued endowing books as late as 1238/1822–1823. As we have seen above, at this date he was no longer deputy governor of Jaffa nor residing in the town. Four years after his ousting, he was apparently still hoping to return to Jaffa or, at least, to exert influence. This is also supported by his continued acquisitions of property in the city. For this matter, Abū ʿAbduh al-Bannā al-Nāblusī, who previously worked for him as an architect/builder (*miʿmār*), was acting as his legal trustee who took care of his foundation complex in Jaffa.[53]

A fourth point the endowment statements on these manuscripts reveal is that Abū Nabbūt was not the only person responsible for stocking the library. The endowment statements of two manuscripts[54] in the Abū Nabbūt manuscript corpus—and here we see that this label has its limits—reveal that a *mamlūk*, ʿUthmān Aghā (d. 1229/1814), brother-in-law and the emir of the treasury (*khaz-*

50 Yazbak, *Madīnat al-Burtuqāl*, 93–94.

51 There are several undated endowment statements and notes in the Abū Nabbūt manuscript corpus which can, however, be easily matched to a date thanks to the used formulation and the handwriting.

52 Jaffa, al-Maktaba al-Islāmiyya, MS 509 (accessed via Nablus, https://manuscripts.najah.edu/node/72, 25 October 2023), Jaffa, al-Maktaba al-Islāmiyya, MS 470 (accessed via Nablus, https://manuscripts.najah.edu/node/169, 25 October 2023), Jaffa, al-Maktaba al-Islāmiyya, MS 1661 (accessed via Nablus, https://manuscripts.najah.edu/node/79, 25 October 2023).

53 Yazbak, *Madīnat al-Burtuqāl*, 153.

54 Jaffa, al-Maktaba al-Islāmiyya, MS 426 (accessed via Nablus, https://manuscripts.najah.edu/node/191, 25 October 2023) and Jaffa, al-Maktaba al-Islāmiyya, MS 428 (accessed via Nablus https://manuscripts.najah.edu/node/96, 25 October 2023).

īna al-ʿāmira) of Abū Nabbūt, endowed the books in 1229/1814[55] from the money of the deceased Aḥmad Aghā al-Alfī, another member of Abū Nabbūt's household.[56] The (so far) comparatively low number of books endowed by others than Abū Nabbūt himself suggests that these two books are outliers and that Abū Nabbūt himself was indeed the main driving force providing the financial means to stock his library.

3 The Afterlife of Abū Nabbūt's Books—Regional Dispersal

The library landscape of Palestine and the wider region went through changes in the late nineteenth century. This period particularly saw the opening of an increasing number of what we today call family and public libraries. These developments were accompanied with massive reshuffling of books.[57] Abū Nabbūt's library in the Great Mosque of Jaffa was to some extent a phased-out model, being one of the last libraries founded by a non-local ruler, a type of library with an uncertain future in times of increasing efforts to centralise what became treated as 'cultural heritage'. Abū Nabbūt was certainly not the last local governor of Jaffa to endow books. But instead of founding a new library or adding to the existing library in the Great Mosque, his successors Muṣṭafā al-Saʿīd Aghā (d. ca. 1260/1844) endowed books to the library of Ḥusayn Efendī al-Dajānī (d. 1274/1857–1858), mufti of Jaffa.[58] Abū Nabbūt's library was, thus, most probably never as well-stocked as it was back in 1238/1822–1823, the last date he endowed books to the existing stock.

What happened to his books right after this date is mostly obscure. We, therefore, have to zoom out a bit and see the library in the context of its associated *madrasa*. The court records of Jaffa reveal some names of scholars with teaching positions in the *madrasa* of the Great Mosque, at least until 1909.[59] For some, their affiliation to the school was apparently meaningful. Abū Rabbāḥ ʿAbd al-Qādir al-Dajānī (d. 1290/1873–1874), a Sufi scholar of some fame and cousin of the mufti Ḥusayn al-Dajānī mentioned above, reveals on one of his manuscripts that he had a teaching position in the *madrasa* of the Great Mosque (*khādim al-ʿilm fī madrasa jāmiʿ Yāfā*) in 1270/1853–1854.[60] The latter was, thus, functioning at least until the early twentieth century. The library, as part of the *madrasa*, was also still functioning in one way or another. According to the official Ottoman *Yearbook* (*sālnāmeh*) from 1318/1900, however, the number of its books had shrunk to 263 and, thus, half as many as in its heyday.[61]

Two decades later, the 1920s are a particularly significant period for the history of libraries in Palestine in general. Several new libraries were founded in this period and older collections were being reshuffled. The *Supreme Muslim Council*, after finishing their work on the *ḥaram al-sharīf* in Jerusalem, including opening the al-Aqṣā Mosque Library and the Islamic Museum, now concentrated on other towns and asked local dignitaries to help establish more libraries across the country.[62] The Supreme Muslim Council (*al-Majlis al-*

55 The date of the endowment statement on Jaffa, al-Maktaba al-Islāmiyya, MS 428 is wrong, and most certainly missing the decade (*ʿishrīn*). The library did not even exist yet on the date given (1209/1794).

56 On ʿUthmān Agha, see Yazbak, *Madīnat al-Burtuqāl*, 98, 100–101, 209. On Aḥmad Agha al-Alfī, see ibid., 100.

57 For the fate of Damascene libraries in this period, see Hirschler, *A Monument*, 64–66.

58 Jaffa, al-Maktaba al-Islāmiyya, MS 424 (accessed via Nablus, https://manuscripts.najah.edu/node/166, 25 October 2023) and Jaffa, al-Maktaba al-Islāmiyya MS 84, (accessed via Nablus, https://manuscripts.najah.edu/node/128, 25 October 2023).

59 al-Ṭarāwana, "Qaḍāʾ Yāfā", 492; See also al-ʿAsalī, Kāmil, "al-Taʿlīm fī Filasṭīn", 22; al-Dabbāgh, *Bilādunā Filasṭīn*, IV, 165.

60 Jerusalem, National Library of Israel, Ms. AP Ar. 254, fol. 1ª. On al-Dajānī, see Sālim, *Aʿlām min madīnat Yāfā*, 30–31; Bayṭār, *Ḥilyat al-bashar*, I, 71–72.

61 al-Ṭarāwana, "Qaḍāʾ Yāfā", 493.

62 Kupferschmidt, *The Supreme Muslim Council*, 144; Roberts, *Islam under the Palestine Mandate*, 128–129.

sharʿī al-islāmī al-ʿalā) founded the Islamic Library in Jaffa (*al-Maktabat al-Islāmiyya—Yāfā*) in 1923 as part of a large-scale effort to establish educational facilities and libraries across Palestinian cities, such as Gaza, Hebron and Acre. A substantial part of Abū Nabbūt's books ended up in the Islamic Library in Jaffa, which was built next to the Great Mosque and equipped with a proper reading room including working desks, proper lighting and lockable bookshelves.[63] How many of the 263 books mentioned in the *Yearbook* in 1900 made it to the newly established Islamic Library is not known. The same goes for their fate over the next 60 years, a period with substantial disruptions in the region.

It is only in the 1980s that we can recover their scent. Nablus-born historian Maḥmūd ʿAṭāʾ Allāh published a catalogue in 1984 with the somewhat misleading title *Manuscript Catalogue of The Islamic Library in Jaffa*. The catalogue contains 288 shelf marks (339 titles) of books ʿAṭāʾ Allāh found in the al-Nuzha Mosque in Jaffa, books that were formerly part of the Islamic Library in Jaffa. Unfortunately, he had nothing to say about how the books came to the al-Nuzha Mosque, that once the Islamic Library in Jaffa had more manuscripts than listed in the catalogue, and that a large portion of the Islamic Library in Jaffa manuscripts were once part of Abū Nabbūt's library.[64] Fortunately, though, ʿAṭāʾ Allāh produced microfilms which, according to his short introduction, he deposited in the Islamic Club in Jaffa (*al-Nādī al-Islāmī fī Yāfā*) and copies of which are at the al-Najah University Library in Nablus and the Centre for Archives and Manuscripts of the University of Jordan in Amman.[65] The history of the Islamic Library in Jaffa, thus, remains largely obscure and awaits further research. According to Muḥammad Kurd ʿAlī (d. 1953), it existed simultaneously with Abū Nabbūt's library.[66]

When we set sail and turn further south, the library of the ʿUmarī Mosque in Gaza complicates the story further. Here, we find the (so far) second biggest batch of the Abū Nabbūt manuscript corpus—thirteen manuscripts. The ʿUmarī Mosque library has a long history going back to the rule of the Mamluk sultan Baybars (r. 1260–1277). How far this genealogy is fictional remains to be studied in detail. The more recent history of the library after World War I was largely influenced by ʿUthmān al-Ṭabbāʾ (1882–1950), who held various positions in the mosque, among others serving as the director of its library. When he became the librarian, he called upon fellow scholars and book collectors to donate books to the recently reopened library.[67] In this effort, manuscripts formerly situated in Jaffa came to Gaza, for example, some books previously owned by the mufti of Jaffa, ʿAlī b. al-Mawāhib al-Dajānī.[68] The al-ʿUmari Mosque was severely damaged as a result of an Israeli attack in December 2023. It is unclear what has happened to its library.

Al-Ṭabbāʾ was an active librarian who, when newly donated books entered the library, wrote what we can call acquisition notes on some of their title pages. The lower note on fig. 6.5 shows such a note on a copy of the second volume of al-Suyūṭī's *Jāmiʿ al-ṣaghīr*. From the thirteen manuscripts of the Abū Nabbūt manuscript corpus that are today in Gaza, eight carry such an acquisition note, dated between 4 Muḥarram 1354/8 April 1935 and 25 Rabīʿ I 1354/18 June 1935. Who was responsible for their translocation to Gaza, if they were taken from the Great Mosque of Jaffa or the Islamic

63 For pictures, see "Bayān al-majlis al-sharʿī al-islāmī al-aʿlā fī Filasṭīn sanat 1341/2 (1923/4)", between 32 and 33.

64 For a very short description of the opening, see ʿAṭāʾ Allāh, *Fihris Makhṭūṭāt Yāfā*, 3–4.

65 Conrad and Salameh, "Palestine", 572–573.

66 Kurd ʿAlī, *Khiṭaṭ*, VI, 197.

67 al-Ṭabbāʿ, *Itḥāf al-aʿizza*, II, 116–126; also see Mubayyaḍ and Kullāb, *Maktabat al-Jāmiʿ al-ʿUmarī al-Kabīr*, 48–50.

68 Abū Hāshim, *Fihris Makhṭūṭāt Maktaba al-Jāmiʿ al-ʿUmarī al-Kabīr*, 13–14; Mannāʿ, *Aʿlām Filasṭīn*, 172; Bayṭār, *Ḥilyat al-bashar*, I, 69–70; Mubayyaḍ and Kullāb, *Maktabat al-Jāmiʿ al-ʿUmarī al-Kabīr*, 73–77.

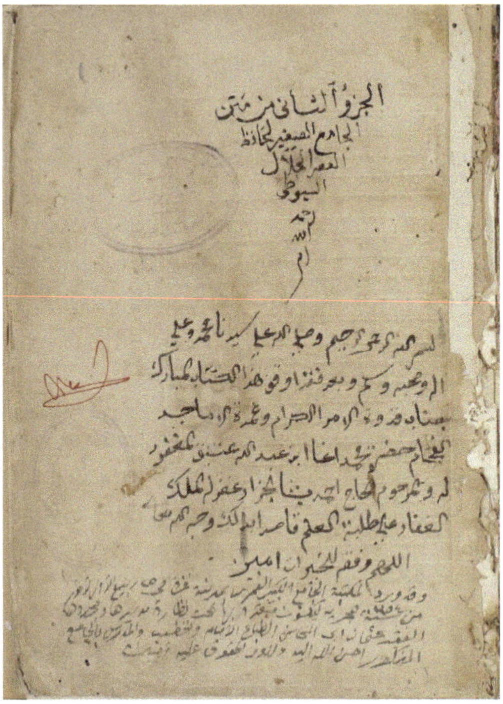

FIGURE 6.5
'Uthmān al-Ṭabbā' wrote a note below the endowment note of Abū Nabbūt regarding the arrival of this manuscript to Gaza in 1935
MS GAZA, 'UMARĪ MOSQUE 94 (CC BY-NC 4.0)

Library in Jaffa is currently unknown. The wording of al-Ṭabbā's notes, 'came to the library of the Great 'Umarī mosque' ([…] *qad warada li-maktabat al-jāmiʿ al-kabīr al-ʿumarī* […]) are not revealing in this regard. Al-Ṭabbā' only mentions that he was 'repeatedly successful in taking books from a library in Jaffa' (*wa-tawaffaqnā li-akhdh al-mukarrar min maktabat Yāfā*).[69]

What we can say, apart from all open questions, is that not all the books of Abū Nabbūt's library were transferred to the Islamic Library in Jaffa, even though this library was only some metres away from their original place in the Great Mosque. The books that ended up in Gaza (and a single book in Jerusalem) were most probably taken out of the Mosque library before the Islamic Library in Jaffa was founded in 1923—they miss the seal imprint of the 1923 library. Furthermore, their arrival in Gaza on two different dates may suggest that they came from two different sources.

Moreover, we have concentrated in the preceding paragraphs solely on two institutions that played a fundamental role in the afterlife of Abū Nabbūt's books. Based on a detailed study of ownership statements on the books, private individuals may be brought to light who took possession of books in the decades between the early nineteenth and the early twentieth century.

4 Conclusion

In this chapter, we have left al-Jazzār's Acre and turned to Jaffa to explore what one of his former *mamlūk*s did in yet another harbour town on the Mediterranean coast. Inspired by the accomplishments of his former master, Abū Nabbūt embarked on quite a similar project in his seat of power, securing the town against potential threats, developing an infrastructure for trade, and building a mosque with a *madrasa* and a library. A library was apparently an essential element in Abū Nabbūt's vision of what a ruler such as himself needed.

69 al-Ṭabbāʿ, *Itḥāf al-aʿizza*, II, 121.

To materialise all this, he followed al-Jazzār, and indeed many rulers before him, and established an endowment complex to enable the continuous funding of his project. This chapter has argued that Abū Nabbūt used the endowment statements on his books strategically to make himself and his ambitions known to the users of the library. He used his books as a public text to proclaim his affiliation to al-Jazzār, display his status as an equal to his superior Sulaymān Pasha, and ultimately in order to influence decision makers to promote him and to give him his own realm.

The library built by Abū Nabbūt was one of the last of its kind. Few, if any, local governors of non-local descent after him built a comparable institution in the Arab provinces of the Ottoman realm. In contrast to some of the major Palestinian family libraries, mostly in Jerusalem, Abū Nabbūt's books did not stay together, but the library witnessed an increasing drop in its stock. And although Jaffa witnessed an uneasy history in the period after Abū Nabbūt with the Egyptian occupation (1831–1840), the British Mandate (1919–1948) and the founding of Israel in 1948, a major portion of the books survived in close proximity to or in the region of the Great Mosque, with the Islamic Library in Jaffa and the ʿUmarī Mosque in Gaza as the two main sites so far.

Zooming out, what can Abū Nabbūt's library contribute to the history of books and libraries of the Ottoman Arab provinces in the early nineteenth century? The continuous additions to the library in the Great Mosque of Jaffa suggest that a substantial number of handwritten books were available for and within reach of a local governor of a minor town such as Jaffa. Furthermore, the spatial extent of the Abū Nabbūt manuscript corpus as it stands now is remarkably local, with not a single manuscript found in the major European and American manuscript collections to date. In this, the afterlife of Abū Nabbūt's library resembled the Jazzār library, as will be discussed by Konrad Hirschler in the following chapter.

Bibliography

Abū Hāshim, ʿAbd al-Lāṭīf. *Fihris Makhṭūṭāt Maktaba al-Jāmiʿ al-ʿUmarī al-Kabīr bi-Madīnat Ghazza—Filasṭīn*. London, 2016.

ʿAfāna, Ḥusām al-Dīn, Muḥammad al-Ṣafadī, Intiṣār Muḥammad al-Ṣāliḥ and Muḥammad Rizq Jaffāl. *Fihris makhṭūṭāt Filasṭīn al-muṣawwara*. 5 vols. Jerusalem, 2000–2012.

Al-ʿAsalī, Kāmil. "al-Taʿlīm fī Filasṭīn min al-fatḥ al-islāmī ḥatta bidāya al-ʿasr al-ḥadīth." In *al-Mawsūʿa al-Filasṭīniyya*, edited by Aḥmad al-Marʿashlī and ʿAbd al-Hādī Hāshim Vol. 3. Beirut, 1990.

ʿAṭāʾ Allāh, Maḥmūd ʿAlī. *Fihris makhṭūṭāt al-Maktaba al-Islamiyya fī Yāfā*, 1984.

Barakāt, Bashīr. *Taʾrīkh al-maktabāt al-ʿarabiyya fī Bayt al-Maqdis*. Riyad, 2012.

Barakāt, Bashīr. *al-Fahrasa al-ḥisbiyya li-makhṭūṭāt al-Maktabat al-Budayriyya*. Jerusalem, 2023.

Barakāt, Bashīr. *Fihris makhṭūṭāt Maktabat Dār Isʿāf al-Nashāshībī*. Jerusalem, 2023.

"Bayān al-majlis al-sharʿī al-islāmī al-aʿlā fī Filasṭīn sanat 1341/2 (1923/4)." *Maṭbaʿat madrasat al-aytām al-Islāmiyya*, 1343 (1924), 33.

Bayṭār, ʿAbd al-Razzāq. *Ḥilyat al-bashar fī taʾrīkh al-qarn al-thālith ʿashar*, edited by Muḥammad Bahjat Bayṭar. 3 vols. Damascus, 1961.

Büssow, Johann. *Hamidian Palestine: Politics and Society in the District of Jerusalem 1872–1908*. Leiden, 2011.

Conrad, Lawrence, and Khader Salameh. "Palestine." In *World Survey of Islamic Manuscripts*, edited by Geoffrey Roper, 563–600. London, 1992.

Al-Dabbāgh, Muṣṭafā Murād. *Bilādunā Filasṭīn*. Vol. 4, n.d.

De Forbin, Louis Philippe Auguste. *Travels in Greece, Turkey, and the Holy Land, in 1817–1818*. London, 1819.

Doumani, Beshara. "Palestinian Islamic Court Records: A Source for Socioeconomic History." *MESA Bulletin* 19, no. 2 (1985).

Doumani, Beshara. *Rediscovering Palestine: Merchants and Peasants in Jabal Nablus, 1700–1900*. Berkeley, 1995.

Gerber, Haim. *Ottoman Rule in Jerusalem, 1890–1914*. Berlin, 1985.

Ghosheh, Mohammad. *Encyclopaedia Palestinnica: Manuscripts and Libraries in Palestine 1516–1918*. Vol. 16. 24 vols. Amman, 2019.

Hathaway, Jane. *The Politics of Households in Ottoman Egypt: The Rise of the Qazdağlis*. New York, 1997.

Hirschler, Konrad. *A Monument to Medieval Syrian Book Culture—The Library of Ibn ʿAbd al-Hādī*. Edinburgh, 2019.

Al-Jabartī, ʿAbd al-Raḥmān b. Ḥasan. *ʿAjāʾib al-āthār fī tarājim al-akhbār*, edited by ʿAbd al-Raḥmān ʿAbd al-Raḥīm. 4 vols. Maṭbaʿat Dār al-Kutub al-Miṣriyya, 1997.

Kana'an, Ruba. "Jaffa and the Waqf of Muḥammad Aġā Abū Nabbūt (1799–1821): A Study in the Urban History of an East Mediterranean City." PhD Dissertation, University of Oxford, 1998.

Kana'an, Ruba. "Two Ottoman *Sabils* in Jaffa (c. 1810–1815): An Architectural and Epigraphic Analysis." *Levant* 33, no. 1 (2001): 189–204.

Kana'an, Ruba. "Waqf, Architecture, and Political Self-fashioning: The Construction of the Great Mosque of Jaffa by Muhammad Aga Abu Nabbut." *Muqarnas* 18 (2001): 120–140.

Kupferschmidt, Uri M. *The Supreme Muslim Council: Islam under the British Mandate for Palestine*. Leiden, 1987.

Kurd ʿAlī, Muḥammad. *Khiṭaṭ al-Shām*. 2nd ed. 6 vols. Damascus, n.d.

Layish, Aharon. "The *Sijill* of Jaffa and Nazareth Sharīʿa Courts as a Source for the Political and Social History of Ottoman Palestine." In *Studies on Palestine during the Ottoman Period*, edited by Moshe Ma'oz, 525–532. Jerusalem, 1975.

Macalister, R.A. Stewart. "Some Miscellaneous Tales of the Fellahin." *Palestine Exploration Quarterly* 41, no. 3 (1909): 219–227.

Mannāʿ, Ādil. *Aʿlām Filasṭīn fī awākhir al-ʿahd al-ʿuthmānī (1800–1918)*. Beirut, 1995.

Mannāʿ, Ādil. *Taʾrīkh Filasṭīn fī awākhir al-ʿahd al-ʿuthmānī 1700–1918: Qirāʾa jadīda*. 3rd ed. Beirut, 2003.

[Meryon, Charles Lewis]. *Travels of Lady Hester Stanhope; Forming the Completion of Her Memoirs*. 3 vols. London, 1846.

Mubayyaḍ, Salīm, and Muḥammad Khālid Kullāb. *Maktabat al-Jāmiʿ al-ʿUmarī al-Kabīr bi-Ghazza wa-juhūd al-Shaykh ʿUthmān al-Ṭabbāʿa fī Iʿmārihā*. Amman, 2013.

Philipp, Thomas. *Acre: The Rise and Fall of a Palestinian City, 1730–1831*. New York, 2001.

Philipp, Thomas. "The Last Mamluk Household." In *The Mamluks in Egyptian and Syrian Politics and Society*, edited by Michael Winter and Amalia Levanoni, 317–338. Leiden, 2004.

Pohl, Johannes. "Führer Durch Die Bibliothek Palästinas." *Zentralblatt Für Bibliothekswesen* 55, no. 1 (1938): 55–64.

Qaṭnānī, ʿAbīr. "al-Awqāf fī qaḍāʾ Yāfā khilāl al-mudda (1214h/1799m–1282/1864m)." In *al-Awqāf fī Bilād al-Shām mundhu al-fatḥ al-ʿarbī al-islāmī ilā nihāya al-qarn al-ʿishrīn: al-Mujallad al-thālith "Filasṭīn"*, edited by Muḥammad ʿAdnān al-Bakhīt, 3: 281–302. ʿAmmān: Jordan University Press, 2008.

Reier, Benedikt. "Books as Archives." In *Material Aspects of Archiving*, edited by Markus Friedrich. De Gruyter, forthcoming.

Roberts, Nicholas E. *Islam under the Palestine Mandate: Colonialism and the Supreme Muslim Council*. London, 2017.

Sālim, Fu'ad ʿĪsā Saʿd. *Aʿlām min madīnat Yāfā*. Beirut, 2019.

Saʿīd, Ḥasan Ibrāhīm. *Yāfā min al-ghazū al-Nābulīyūnī ilā ḥamlat Ibrāhīm Bāshā (1799–1831)*. 2nd ed. Beirut, 2008.

Schidorsky, Dov. "Libraries in Late Ottoman Palestine between the Orient and the Occident." *Libraries & Culture* 33, no. 3 (1998): 260–276.

Sharon, Moshe. *Corpus Inscriptionum Arabicarum Palaestinae*. Leiden, 2017.

Al-Ṭabbāʿ, ʿUthmān Muṣṭafā. *Itḥāf al-aʿizza fī taʾrīkh Ghazza*, edited by ʿAbd al-Laṭīf Zakī Abū Hāshim. 4 vols. Gaza, 1999.

Al-Ṭarāwana, Muḥammad. "Qaḍāʾ Yāfā fī al-ʿahd al-ʿUthmānī 1281–1333h/1864–1914." PhD Dissertation, Jordan University, 1997.

Al-Waḥsh, Fāṭima Muḥammad. "Dirāsat taʾṣīliyya tarbawiyya li-maktabat jāmiʿ Yāfā al-kabīr min khilāl al-sijillāt al-ʿuthmāniyya li-maḥkamat Yāfā al-sharʿiyya fī al-qarn al-tāsiʿ ʿashr." *al-Manāra* 18, no. 2 (2012): 231–256.

Wynter-Stoner, Kyle. "Books, Corruption, and an Emir's

Downfall: The Founding of the Maḥmūdīyah Library in Mamluk Cairo." *Journal of Near Eastern Studies* 81, no. 2 (2022): 335–362.

Wynter-Stoner, Kyle. "The Maḥmūdīyah: The History of a Library, Its Books, and Its Readers." PhD Dissertation, The University of Chicago, 2022.

Yazbak, Mahmoud. "al-Waqf al-islāmī fī Yāfā min al-dawla al-ʿuthmāniyya ilā dawla al-ʿibriyya." In *al-Awqāf fī Bilād al-Shām mundhu al-fatḥ al-ʿarbī al-islāmī ilā nihāya al-qarn al-ʿishrīn: al-Mujallad al-thālith "Filasṭīn"*, edited by Muḥammad ʿAdnān al-Bakhīt, 303–334. Amman, 2008.

Yazbak, Mahmoud. *Madīnat al-Burtuqāl Yāfa: Ḥaḍāra wa-mujtamʿa 1700–1840*. Beirut: Institute for Palestine Studies, 2018.

Yazbak, Mahmoud. "A Mamluk Household in Jaffa: The Case of Abu Nabbut (1805–1819)." In *From the Household to the Wider World: Local Perspectives on Urban Institutions in Late Ottoman Bilad al-Sham*, edited by Yuval Ben-Bassat and Johann Büssow, 35–45. Tübingen, 2022.

CHAPTER 7

A (Mostly) Local Story: The Translocations of al-Jazzār's Books in the Nineteenth and Twentieth Centuries

Konrad Hirschler

The manuscripts described [in this catalogue] do not constitute the original al-Jazzār library. Rather, what was identified only represents a small fraction, because many of the [original library's] manuscripts have been lost for one reason or another.[1]

This statement by Maḥmūd ʿAlī ʿAṭā' Allāh, the great twentieth-century cataloguer of Palestinian book collections, in the introduction to his catalogue of the Jazzār library in 1983, throws up this chapter's core questions: Where have all the books gone that once constituted al-Jazzār's splendid library in Acre and how did these translocations happen?[2] How can we, in other words, write the history of the process that ʿAṭā' Allāh described with the opaque phrase 'many of the [original library's] manuscripts have been lost for one reason or another'? The loss of handwritten books from Acre has been massive: When the inventory was written in 1221/1806 the library held 1,820 volumes, in 1983 ʿAṭā' Allāh listed, as our analysis shows, just fourteen of them.[3] This chapter, thus, explores the fate of the 1,806 volumes that are no longer in Acre and their possible trajectories between the year 1806 and the present day. The development of the library over the last 200 years, including the translocations of almost all of its handwritten books, has been unchartered territory so far. Yet, it is possible to shine a light on some periods, and among them, is a story entirely untold to date, namely, the revival of the Jazzār *madrasa* and, hence, its library in the early twentieth century.

This chapter has two main argumentative axes: Firstly, it argues that the extraction of books from the Jazzār library was a prolonged and multifaceted process stretching most likely from the 1820s to around 1900. As is the case with many other historical libraries, dissolution cannot be pinned to one particular moment that saw all the books of the Jazzār library move into the possession of new owners. Nor was there a dramatic point of destruction that saw the library's books perish in fire or warfare. Rather than looking for one such spectacular turning point, we have to reconstitute a lengthy process that led to the gradual dismantlement of the library. In that sense, the post-al-Jazzār development of the library is quite similar to how it was built. As Boris Liebrenz argues in Chapter 3, the stocking of the library was probably not the result of spectacular raids, plunder and warfare but rather a protracted process involving multiple strategies, including purchasing books.

1 ʿAṭā' Allāh, *Fihris ʿAkkā*, 1983, p. ج. The research for this chapter was funded by the Deutsche Forschungsgemeinschaft (DFG, German Research Foundation) under Germany's Excellence Strategy—EXC 2176 'Understanding Written Artefacts: Material, Interaction and Transmission in Manuscript Cultures', project no. 390893796. The research was conducted within the scope of the Centre for the Study of Manuscript Cultures (CSMC) at Universität Hamburg.

2 This chapter will use the term 'book' for handwritten codices and where pertinent, 'printed book'. 'Manuscripts', by contrast, refers to all handwritten artefacts and is not used here (see Lorusso, *Definition*, 2015).

3 ʿAṭā' Allāh also described sixty-four additional handwritten books. These were, as argued below, added to the collection from the late nineteenth-century onwards.

As is the case for many other historical libraries, the dismantlement of the Jazzār library and the translocation of its books cannot be deduced from external sources, such as reports in chronicles, travel reports and newspapers; these sources are simply silent on the library for most of the nineteenth century.[4] Nor do we have any internal sources from the Jazzār library itself, such as further inventories written in the course of the nineteenth century. Instead, the translocation of the library's books has to be primarily reconstructed from the books themselves by following the textual and material traces they carry. These traces show us a multitude of individual trajectories with numerous individuals taking ownership of books from the library at different points in time.

That we are looking at a gradual and lengthy process is indicated by those books providing firm dates for when they left the library. The earliest definite date we have is a book that is in the Khalidi Library in Jerusalem today. In 1245/1829–1830, some twenty-five years after al-Jazzār's death, a new owner, a certain Ibrāhīm ʿAbd al-Muʿṭī, proudly inscribed his ownership of Ibn al-ʿArabī's *Futūḥāt al-Makkiyya* on the book's title page.[5] Another former al-Jazzār book, today in the National Library of Israel, went into the possession of a new owner, ʿAbd al-Qādir al-Dajānī, in 1268/1851–1852.[6] In contrast to these early departures, we have books that stayed in the library for many more decades and we even have those fourteen books that are still in Acre today.

The argument that the process of extracting books was a gradual one is supported by the fact that the library was not dismantled right after the death of al-Jazzār. An endowment is particularly vulnerable upon its founder's death. This was particularly true in the case of al-Jazzār, as his succession was contentious and as the Ottoman centre started confiscation proceedings straight after his death (see Chapter 5 by Yasin Arslantaş). However, there are no notes in the books themselves, nor narrative reports or other documentary evidence that indicate a massive extraction of books in the years after his death in 1804. At the same time, reports from European travellers, discussed by Boris Liebrenz in Chapter 3, describe a fully functioning library in the years after al-Jazzār's death. Charles Lewis Meryon (1783–1877), for instance, visited the Acre Mosque in 1810, six years after al-Jazzār's death, and described the library as 'most splendid'.[7]

That the Jazzār library was not dismantled immediately after his death is corroborated by two striking absences. Firstly, if the books had been confiscated by the Ottoman centre, we would probably have found a large number of them in libraries in Istanbul, yet, there are only three al-Jazzār books known so far that have made their way to Istanbul. Secondly, if the Ottoman centre had confiscated the books but did not take them to Istanbul, they would have flooded the book markets of southern Greater Syria (Bilād al-Shām). That this was not so is evident from cases that include that of Muḥammad Aghā Abū Nabbūt (d. ca. 1833–1834). This former *mamlūk* and deputy of al-Jazzār built a large library in southern Greater Syria, in Jaffa, in the years after al-Jazzār's

4 The only evidence known so far is a document dated 1855 that mentions the repair of damaged structures at the Jazzār complex, including the library (see Chapter 5). This does not give any insight into the number of books in the library, but shows that there was, at least, still a dedicated library space.

5 Jerusalem, Khalidi Library, MS 1060, fol. 1ª: (cf. https://www.vhmml.org/readingRoom/view/509558) [accessed 3 January 2023]

دخل في نوبة الفقير إليه تعالى / إبراهيم عبد المعطي المروزي / وقد [كلام مطموس] [خمس وأربعين] ومايتين وألف 1245

6 Jerusalem, National Library of Israel, AP Ar. 258, fol. 1ª (with seal dated to 1268):

هذا الكتاب من من ذي المن دام مَنُّه على الفقير إليه سبحانه السيد عبد القادر أبو رباح الدجاني الحنفي الأحمدي الخلوتي القادري الرفاعي الدسوقي خادم العلم والطريق بمدينة يافا عفى عنه بمنه آمين.

7 Meryon, *Travels of Lady Hester Stanhope*, I, 262.

death, as discussed in Chapter 6 by Benedikt Reier. Among almost 150 handwritten books from this library that Benedikt Reier has identified, we were not able to identify a single one that had previously been in al-Jazzār's ownership. That al-Jazzār's books were seemingly not available in the local book market when Abū Nabbūt built up his library in the 1810s and 1820s indicates an impressive stability of the Jazzār library after its founder's death.

The second argumentative strand of this chapter is that the main actors deciding the fate of the Jazzār library were individuals situated in Greater Syria. Their agency is evident from looking at the identity of the respective first owner after a book left the Jazzār library: As we will see in the following, individuals situated within Greater Syria constitute the vast majority, while individuals or institutions situated in Egypt, Istanbul or Europe did not play a salient role in extracting books from the library. It was not only individuals based in Greater Syria who extracted a lot of books from the library, we also find those who strove to rebuild the library in the late nineteenth and early twentieth centuries. These rebuilding efforts were part of the reconfiguration and revival of the region's libraries during that period. They are often little-known individuals whose contribution to developing a 'modern' topography of libraries in the region is underacknowledged to date. Most importantly for this chapter, they were the driving force in 're-endowing' al-Jazzār books that had been translocated. They returned these books into an endowment context in either their original library in Acre or a new endowment library in cities such as Jerusalem.

1 Looking beyond Istanbul and Europe

Regarding books that were removed from a library in the Arabic lands in the nineteenth and early twentieth century, two main sets of historical actors who might have driven this development come to mind: institutions or individuals based in the Ottoman centre in Istanbul and those linked with European colonial expansion. After the incorporation of Greater Syria and Egypt into the Ottoman Empire in the early sixteenth century, vast numbers of books did indeed make their way to Istanbul, a veritable book drain. At some points, this might have been an act of military force,[8] but more often, the movement of books to Istanbul was a more complex process where trade, economic wealth and geographies of scholarship were important factors.[9] Berat Açıl showed this with the example of the Cârullah Efendi collection from the late seventeenth and early eighteenth centuries, currently housed in the Süleymaniye Library in Istanbul.[10] In the same vein, almost all known books of the Damascene Ashrafiyya library, which was dissolved in the early sixteenth century, are today in Istanbul.[11] Yet, there are very few al-Jazzār books in the libraries of Istanbul, just three to be precise.[12] It seems that by the nineteenth century, the centripetal movement of books to the city had come to an end as the Ottoman centre ceased to attract large numbers of books from the provinces. The Jazzār library might even indicate a more far-reaching change in the relationship between centre and province regarding the movement of books: As Boris Liebrenz shows in Chapter 3, Istanbul was one of the main places from where al-Jazzār bought books to build up his library. Rather than books moving from the provinces to the centre, the Jazzār library indicates a process of books moving from the centre to the provinces.[13] In the

8 Aleppo inventory: Bağcı/Yürekli, "Book-Picking"; D'hulster, *Browsing through the Sultan's Bookshelves*.

9 For some preliminary remarks see Hirschler, *Plurality and Diversity in an Arabic Library*, 51–53.

10 Acıl, *Osmanlı kitap kültürü*.

11 Hirschler, *Plurality and Diversity in an Arabic Library*.

12 Istanbul, Süleymaniye Library, Yazma Bağışlar 766, Pertevniyal V. Sultan 759 and Kemankes 21.

13 The fact that members of the Khalidi family bought many books in the eighteenth century in Istanbul indicates the same trend. This research has not been published yet and my statement is based on the notes retrieved by Boris Liebrenz and Said Aljoumani.

process of building up his local polity, al-Jazzār not only made references to the material topography of Istanbul (see the *Introduction* to this volume), but also appropriated moveable artefacts from the centre.

Do we, thus, have to turn to European institutions and actors to understand the movement of al-Jazzār's books? Ahmed El Shamsy spoke, for instance, of a massive 'book drain' to conceptualise the movement of Arabic handwritten books to Europe, especially in the course of the nineteenth century.[14] Yet, among the seventy-eight al-Jazzār books identified so far only twenty-two moved to European or US American libraries. A ratio of twenty-eight per cent is substantial, but it does not sustain the impression of a massive movement of books. What is more, this ratio is arguably misleading, owing to selection bias, and should be lower still: It is calculated based on our current corpus of seventy-eight identified al-Jazzār books, which is relatively small and—more importantly—arguably includes an overproportionate number of European and US American collections. The holdings of libraries in Europe and the US are relatively easy to access (online or in person) and they are, thus, much better represented in research corpora such as ours. The possibility that we have simply missed a large corpus of al-Jazzār books in one of these libraries is, therefore, comparatively low, while it is very likely for libraries in West Asia and North Africa. This is especially true for our corpus, as Boris Liebrenz focused in particular on European and US American libraries in his many years of work gathering notes from handwritten books (see *Introduction* to this volume). As a result, his original corpus of twenty-two al-Jazzār books mostly came from Princeton, Dublin, London, Berlin and Leipzig libraries. The ratio of al-Jazzār books in European and US American libraries was sixty-eight per cent in Boris Liebrenz' corpus, and it is telling that this ratio dropped to twenty-eight per cent just by enlarging the corpus to seventy-eight books. I am, thus, convinced that the growing size of the Jazzār corpus will push in coming years the ratio of such books in European and US American collections down even further.

There is no doubt that we need a lot more scholarship to understand how written artefacts moved to Europe and the US in the nineteenth and early twentieth centuries. However, this does not mean that we have to focus on this trajectory exclusively. Based on the Jazzār library as a case study, this chapter suggests that the translocation of books in the nineteenth and early twentieth centuries is not predominantly the story of a (proto)colonial book drain, but at least as much one of local book circulation driven by local actors. The main aim of this chapter is, therefore, to show that an a priori fixation on European colonialism and European actors when studying the movements of North African and Western Asian artefacts in the nineteenth and twentieth centuries carries the danger of marginalising the deeds and life stories of individuals who lived through this period. As shown in other cases, these actors disposed of substantial agency in determining where books moved—irrespective of whether we see them as heroes saving cultural heritage or as villains appropriating endowment books.[15]

Most of the seventy-eight al-Jazzār books known are today in regional libraries in Acre, Nablus, Jerusalem, Damascus, Beirut and so on. Numerous institutions and individuals in southern Greater Syria, especially in Palestine, took a great interest in collecting al-Jazzār books after they left the library in Acre. This chapter uses the neutral term of 'translocation' (rather than theft, plunder, decline, drain and so forth) in recognition of the multiple trajectories of the books that were once part of the Jazzār library—and, thus, also the multitude of contexts in which these movements took place.

14 El Shamsy, *Rediscovering the Islamic Classics*.

15 Erbay/Hirschler, "Middle Eastern Agency".

2 Acre and the Reconfiguration of Late Ottoman Libraries

The present-day library of the Jazzār endowment in Acre is the obvious starting point to mount a search for al-Jazzār books. Yet, the number of handwritten books in this library today is very small, well below one hundred, and the vast majority of these books have no link with the historical Jazzār library at all. Only fourteen books in the present-day library can be linked to the historical Jazzār library, each of these original books carrying at least one of the Jazzār provenance elements: the endowment statement, the endowment seal and/or the endowment motto (on these elements, see the *Introduction* to this volume).[16] The other 'new' handwritten books were added to the library at a later point, especially in the early twentieth century. A large corpus of almost twenty new books, for instance, most of them written well after al-Jazzār's death in the course of the nineteenth century, was endowed to the Jazzār library in memory of ʿAlī Mīrī, the former mufti of Acre, by his two sons Rashīd and Aḥmad.[17]

Any statement on the number of original or new al-Jazzār handwritten books in Acre comes with a major methodological caveat as the library's stock has never really stabilised. The holdings of this library have been highly dynamic and, until the present day, the books have not even acquired stable class marks. The volatility of the library is exemplified by the short period of 1983–2022, for which we have three reliable datasets: Maḥmūd ʿAlī ʿAṭāʾ Allāh published his catalogue of the library mentioned above in 1983; between 2010 and 2012, the British Library *Endangered Archives Project* digitised the library's handwritten books; and in 2021, Samah Hijab conducted an unpublished survey of the holdings.[18] These datasets show that more than two dozen (original and new) handwritten books that ʿAṭāʾ Allāh had catalogued in 1983 were no longer in the library in 2010.[19] A further seven handwritten books disappeared between 2012, when the British Library concluded its digitisation project, and 2021.[20] Yet, we also have additions, that is, books that do not appear in the 1983 catalogue but are part of the *Endangered Archives Project* between 2010 and 2012,[21] as well as books that appear neither in the 1983 catalogue nor in the *Endangered Archives Project*, but in the 2021 handlist.[22] This is certainly not the end of the story: During the sorting of archival material in the Acre mosque in 2023 within the framework of the Jazzār Mosque endowment board-ALIPH foundation-CSMC Hamburg *Rescuing the Books of al-Jazzār* project, for instance, a handwritten Koran exemplar was found.[23]

We have no similarly comprehensive datasets for the decades prior to 1983, but anecdotal evidence shows that the library's holdings were also highly volatile before this point. Isaac Hasson, for instance, submitted his MA thesis on al-Wāsiṭī's work on the *Merits of Jerusalem* (*Faḍāʾil al-Bayt al-Muqaddas*) at the Hebrew University in 1969.[24] He

16 Acre, al-Jazzār Mosque Library, MS 1, MS 2, MS 6, MS 9, MS 21, MS 25, MS 33, MS 34, MS 37, MS 40/1, MS 47 MS 51, MS 64 and MS 67 (ʿAṭāʾ Allāh, *Fihris ʿAkkā*, 1983).

17 Acre, al-Jazzār Mosque Library, MS 36, MS 43, MS 44, MS 46, MS 48, MS 49, MS 53, MS 59, MS 60, MS 62, MS 63, MS 68, MS 69, MS 71, MS 72, MS 73, MS 76, MS 77 (ʿAṭāʾ Allāh, *Fihris ʿAkkā*, 1983).

18 We greatly thank Samah Hijab for her generosity in sharing this list with us.

19 Acre, al-Jazzār Mosque Library, MS 9, MS 13, MS 16–20, MS 22–24, MS 26–30, MS 33, MS 35, MS 38, MS 40–42, MS 42, MS 43, MS 50–52, MS 56–58, MS 74 and MS 80 (ʿAṭāʾ Allāh, *Fihris ʿAkkā*, 1983).

20 Acre, al-Jazzār Mosque Library, MS 8, MS 43–43, MS 59–52, MS 61–63 and MS 68–62 (ʿAṭāʾ Allāh, *Fihris ʿAkkā*, 1983).

21 Endangered Archives Project, numbers 11, 21 and 28; https://eap.bl.uk/collection/EAP399-1 [accessed 2 January 2023].

22 Handlist Samah Hijab, numbers 56 (Koran) and 57 (*Ijāzat al-Rifāʿī*, a scroll of several metres in length).

23 https://www.csmc.uni-hamburg.de/cultural-heritage/akka.html (accessed 5 March 2024). My thanks go to Maria Luisa Russo (CSMC, Hamburg) for drawing my attention to this find.

24 Al-Wāsiṭī, *Faḍāʾil al-Bayt al-Muqaddas*, ed. Hasson.

states in the introduction to his edition of the text that he used the unicum exemplar from the Jazzār library in Acre for this thesis and he thanks his supervisor M.J. Kister for 'putting it under my disposition'.[25] Oral testimony shows that he did, in fact, use images taken in Acre by Yaakov Yehoshua, an official in the Ministry of Religious Affairs, who, in turn, gave a copy of the photostat to M.J. Kister.[26] This photostat is now held in the National Library of Israel.[27] Yet, the actual exemplar must have disappeared from the library in Acre after the photos had been taken: It no longer appears in the 1983 catalogue (nor in the *Endangered Archives Project* or the 2021 handlist).

If we go further back to the early twentieth century, the impression of a highly volatile situation persists. This is exemplified by the grammatical commentary *al-Tadhyīl wa-takmīl* by Abū Ḥayyān (d. 745/1344), #750 in the Jazzār library inventory. Volumes one, three, four and seven of this work are today in Cairo in the National Library carrying al-Jazzār's endowment statement, endowment seal and endowment motto.[28] The fourth volume carries a note dated to 1906 stating that the book was at that point in the mosque of Nazareth from where it was returned to Acre. Thus, we have an object that was originally in Acre in the Jazzār library, was translocated to Nazareth, returned to Acre in 1906 and then translocated to Cairo at some point before 1944.[29]

If we zoom in on the fourteen original handwritten books that belonged to the historical Jazzār library and are in Acre today, we are immediately reminded that the library was also far from stable during al-Jazzār's lifetime. Eight of these books are al-Jazzār inventory books (JIB), that is books that carry (some of the) three provenance elements (endowment statement/seal/motto) and are listed in the 1221/1806 library inventory.[30] Yet, six of the books in Acre are al-Jazzār non-inventory books (JnIB), that is books that carry provenance elements, but are not listed in the 1221/1806 library inventory. These JnIBs probably left the library during the Napoleonic siege of 1799 and were returned at some point after the inventory was written.[31] Even the eight JIBs tell tales of volatility. As they were in the library in 1806 when the inventory was written, and are also in the library today, one might be tempted to see them as unproblematic cases of linear continuity. Yet, their stories are more complex and they clearly need to be included in any discussion of the local trajectories of this library's books: The legal work *Jāmiʿ al-kabīr* by al-Subkī, for instance, appeared in the 1221/1806 library inventory and it is in the library today. However, this book had a spell outside the library, as it carries an early twentieth-century note saying that it was returned (and, thus, re-endowed) to the library after being in private ownership.[32]

25 Al-Wāsiṭī, *Faḍāʾil al-Bayt al-Muqaddas*, ed. Hasson, 38.

26 Email by Sam Thrope (National Library of Jerusalem) to Konrad Hirschler, 8 June 2023, on the basis of his conversation with I. Hasson.

27 Shelfmark PH AR 452. Another reproduction of the work is held by the Maʿhad al-makhṭūṭāt al-ʿArabiyya in Cairo (see https://archive.org/details/ahmad_20140615 [accessed 8 January 2024]). These photos were taken in 1932 when the book was taken to Cairo to be photographed in the National Library (Dār al-kutub) (al-Wāsiṭī, *Faḍāʾil al-Bayt al-Muqaddas*, ed. Abū al-Mundhir, 7/8).

28 Cairo, Dar al-kutub, 6016h. The fifth volume is in Dublin, Chester Beatty Library, Ar. MS 3342.

29 This title is not recorded in the 1944 inventory of the library: Jerusalem (Abu Dis), The Center for Heritage Revival and Islamic Research, MD/70/33: *Lāʾiḥa bi-asmāʾ al-kutub maʿa ʿadadihā al-mawjūda fī al-maktaba al-Aḥmadiyya al-ʿilmiyya al-Jazzāriyya*, 4 April 1944. I thank Samah Hijab for sharing reproductions of this list.

30 The JIB are: Acre, al-Jazzār Mosque Library, MS 1, MS 2, MS 6, MS 9, MS 34, MS 40/1, MS 51 and MS 64 (ʿAṭāʾ Allāh, *Fihris ʿAkkā*, 1983).

31 The JnIB are: Acre, al-Jazzār Mosque Library, MS 21, MS 25, MS 33, MS 37, MS 47 and MS 67 (ʿAṭāʾ Allāh, *Fihris ʿAkkā*, 1983).

32 Acre, al-Jazzār Mosque Library, MS 2 (ʿAṭāʾ Allāh, *Fihris ʿAkkā*, 1983), fol. 1[a]:

هذا الكتاب المسمى بالجامع الكبير من الأوقاف الجزارية كما عُلم
من ختم الجزار الذي كان على ظهره قبل التجليد وقد أُعيد إلى

The practice of endowing new and re-endowing original al-Jazzār handwritten books to the library in Acre is not only important in terms of methodology to show the volatility and movability of the library's holdings. Much more significantly, it shows that the library's history after the death of al-Jazzār has not just been one of dispersal and decline, but also includes episodes of rebuilding and growth. The most visible episode of this is the early twentieth century when the practice of endowing and re-endowing al-Jazzār handwritten books was particularly intensive. In this period, various actors returned books to their original site and—as seen by the example of Rashīd and Aḥmad, the sons of the mufti of Acre—endowed new handwritten books to the library.

The revival of the Jazzār library in the early twentieth century was part of the wider reconfiguration of libraries in West Asia and North Africa from the late nineteenth century onwards. This reconfiguration in Greater Syria included the foundation of the new Ottoman Public Library (*al-maktaba al-ʿumūmīya*) in Damascus in the 1880s, in which the books of all the 'old' endowment libraries of the city were, henceforth, to be housed.[33] The transformation of the Khalidi family libraries in Jerusalem into one public family library in the following years was part of the same process. The Supreme Muslim Council continued this process in Mandate Palestine in the 1920s by founding the Aqṣā library on the Ḥaram al-sharīf (Temple Mount) in Jerusalem in 1922. Shortly afterwards, it opened the Islamic Library in Jaffa in 1923. The ʿUmarī Mosque library in Gaza was also substantially enlarged with ʿUthmān al-Ṭabbāʿ (d. 1950/1) playing a central role in this process.[34] These new (or renewed) libraries not only preserved handwritten books, but also made printed books available, often including those in European languages as part of a new 'Arabic textual economy,' where print technology furthered new modes of textual production and dissemination.[35]

The history of the late Ottoman reconfiguration of libraries in Greater Syria still needs to be written, but it is clear that it was a development driven by regional and local actors on the ground. Ṭāhir al-Jazāʾirī (1852–1920), a driving force in the late Ottoman reconfiguration of libraries throughout Greater Syria,[36] belonged most famously to these regional actors, and also individuals such as ʿUthmān al-Ṭabbāʿ in Gaza. Individuals who are undeservedly much less well-known to date, such as Muḥammad al-Ḥabbāl from Beirut (fl. 1320/1902), were also among these actors. We see from extant printed and handwritten books that al-Ḥabbāl was engaged in a wide variety of activities linked to writerly culture, including copying books[37] and commissioning handwritten books.[38] He wrote for newspapers, such as *al-Ittiḥād al-ʿUthmānī*[39] and the weekly *Thamarāt al-funūn*, founded in Beirut in 1875,[40] and also used the newspaper's network to distribute a print edition that he commissioned in 1902.[41] Most importantly for our purposes, he catalogued the handwritten books in the Khalidi Library of Jerusalem and published its first printed catalogue in 1900.[42] Al-Ḥabbāl was closely connected with Ṭāhir al-Jazāʾirī: They worked together in the Khalidi Library and al-Jazāʾirī was the editor of the book that al-Ḥabbāl commissioned in 1902.

محله مكتبة المدرسة الأحمدية الجزارية بواسطة صاحب الفضل
والفضيلة فضيلتلو الشيخ يوسف أفندي النبهاني وكان استحصاله
من يد الحاج محمد يحيى العرابي.

33 Hirschler, *Monument*, 64–67.

34 Al-Mubayyaḍ/Kullāb, *Maktabat*.

35 Wallach, *City in Fragments*, 46.

36 On him, see El Shamsy, *Rediscovering the Islamic Classics*, 158–170.

37 Damascus, National al-Asad Library, MS 5580, 5644 and 8144.

38 Damascus, National al-Asad Library, MS 5615.

39 See, for instance, his note on Acre, al-Jazzār Mosque Library, MS 4 (ʿAṭāʾ Allāh, *Fihris ʿAkkā*, 1983), fol. 1[a] where he describes himself as *ʿwakīl jarīdat al-Ittiḥād al-ʿUthmānī*'.

40 Ṭarrāzī, *Tārīkh al-ṣaḥāfa al-ʿarabīya*, 25.

41 Ibn al-Zubayr al-Aswānī, *Umnīyat al-almaʿī*.

42 Al-Ḥabbāl, *Barnāmaj al-Maktaba al-khālidiyya al-ʿumūmiyya*.

The close connection between this wider reconfiguration of libraries in Greater Syria and the revival of the Jazzār library in Acre is primarily evident from notes on the books. We see the same protagonists appearing in handwritten books still in Acre, such as Ṭāhir al-Jazā'irī, who endowed a new handwritten book to the Jazzār library and presented himself in the endowment note as responsible for the 'libraries of Syria'.[43] He mentions in his personal notebooks that he saw books endowed by al-Jazzār when he was in Acre in 1316/1898.[44] Al-Ḥabbāl was also among those contributing to rebuilding the Jazzār library, and we read on one of the title pages of a Jazzār manuscript: 'It was returned to its place in the library of the Aḥmadiyya Madrasa [al-Jazzār library] by the littérateur Muḥammad Efendi b. Maḥmūd al-Ḥabbāl, correspondent of the *Ottoman Unity* [*al-Ittiḥād al-ʿUthmānī*] newspaper.'[45] On the grammatical commentary mentioned above, now in Cairo, he states: 'For several years I have been aware of this fourth volume (and the seventh volume, too) of the *Tashīl* [...] I returned these two volumes from the Mosque of Nazareth to their place [in Acre]. [...] The writer of these words is Muḥammad b. Maḥmūd al-Ḥabbāl, inhabitant of Beirut.'[46]

Another regional actor who participated in the revival of the Jazzār library and is evident from the notes in the books was the late Ottoman Palestinian scholar Yūsuf al-Nabhānī (1849–1832). He was born in the village of Ijzim (near Haifa, some forty kilometres from Acre). After an education in Cairo at al-Azhar, he settled in Acre in 1872 to teach in the town, probably in al-Jazzār's *madrasa*. In 1876 he moved to Istanbul where he edited a newspaper and subsequently had a short stint as a judge in Mosul in northern Iraq. From 1883, he held positions in the judiciary across Greater Syria, most notably in Beirut for some twenty years.[47] Notes in Acre show that he re-endowed books of the original Jazzār library, probably in the early twentieth century.[48] He declared, for instance, on the title page of volume three of the *Jamʿ al-jawāmiʿ* by al-Subkī: 'This book is part of the Jazzār endowment as is evident from al-Jazzār's seal that was on the back before it was bound. It was returned to the library of al-Jazzār's Aḥmadiyya Madrasa by the honourable Shaykh Yūsuf Efendi al-Nabhānī. It was retrieved from the hands of al-Ḥājj Muḥammad Yaḥyā al-ʿUrābī.'[49] I have not been able to identify al-ʿUrābī, but we do, at least, know that he bought another handwritten book that is in Acre in 1291/1874[50] and that in 1301/1883–1884, he copied a book that is today held in Damascus.[51]

Individuals such as al-Jazā'irī, al-Ḥabbāl and al-Nabhānī are the very same actors who were instrumental in changing the landscape of books and libraries in Greater Syria, including Acre. These in-

43 Acre, al-Jazzār Mosque Library, MS 55 ('Aṭā' Allāh, *Fihris ʿAkkā*, 1983)/EAP 5, fol. 1[a] (JnIB).

44 Al-Jazā'irī, *Tadhkira*, fol. 4[b].

45 Acre, al-Jazzār Mosque Library, MS 4 ('Aṭā' Allāh, *Fihris ʿAkkā*, 1983)/EAP 50, fol. 1[a] (JnIB):

أعيد لمقره مكتبة المدرسة الأحمدية بواسطة الاديب الكامل محمد
أفندي بن محمود الحبال وكيل جريدة الاتحاد العثماني.

46 Cairo, Dar al-kutub, 6016h (= #750). Al-Ḥabbāl's note is dated 1324/1906.

47 See his biography in the introduction to al-Nabhanī, *al-Sharaf al-mu'abbad*.

48 The suggested date is based on the dated endowment deed (1323/1906) on a printed book that al-Nabhānī endowed to the Jazzār library. I thank Samah Hijab for sharing this information.

49 Acre, al-Jazzār Mosque Library, MS 1 ('Aṭā' Allāh, *Fihris ʿAkkā*, 1983), fol. 1[a]:

هذا الكتاب من أوقاف الجزار كما عُلم من ختم الجزار الذي
كان على ظهره قبل التجليد وقد أرجع |أعيدا| إلى محله مكتبة
المدرسة الأحمدية الجزارية بواسطة الفاضل فضيلتلو الشيخ
يوسف أفندي النبهاني وكان استحصاله من يد الحاج محمد يحيى
العرابي.

A similar note is on Acre, al-Jazzār Mosque Library, MS 2 ('Aṭā' Allāh, *Fihris ʿAkkā*, 1983), fol. 1[a].

50 Acre, al-Jazzār Mosque Library, MS 4 ('Aṭā' Allāh, *Fihris ʿAkkā*, 1983)/EAP 50, fol. 256[b].

51 Damascus, Maktabat al-Majmaʿ al-ʿilmī, MS 811. I thank Boris Liebrenz for sharing this information with me.

dividuals were deeply committed to safeguarding written heritage, but we do not know how exactly they got hold of the books that they (re)endowed. We know, at least, that at some points, the re-endowment of original al-Jazzār books went hand in hand with rebinding them, as we see from the Jazzār books held in Acre, such as the *Mukhtaṣar tanbīh al-anām*.[52]

The notes left on handwritten books not only show to what extent the revival of the Acre library was embedded in the wider late Ottoman reconfiguration of books and libraries, they also show the contribution of decisively local actors to this process. The central local figure in this regard was ʿAbd Allāh al-Jazzār (1855–1939), no descendant of the library's founder, who was the teacher in the Jazzār *madrasa*, imam of the mosque and judge of Acre.[53] ʿAbd Allāh al-Jazzār has received hardly any attention in scholarship to date, but clearly deserves to be put on the map. He was born and schooled in Acre, from where he went to Cairo to study at al-Azhar. Upon his return to Acre, he became the teacher in the Jazzār *madrasa*, the imam of the mosque, the mufti of the town and finally its judge.[54] Under his leadership, the *madrasa* experienced an important upsurge that went hand in hand with that of the library. This link between him and the revival of the library is evident from the new library seal that some of the Jazzār books carry. This new seal is dated 1323/1905–1906 and proudly describes the library as a 'renewed' library: 'Endowment of the renewed Aḥmadiyya Madrasa library in the mosque of al-Jazzār Pāshā'.[55] Notes ascribe the foundation of this new library unequivocally to ʿAbd Allāh al-Jazzār: 'I endow […] this book to the library of Aḥmad Pasha al-Jazzār in Akka [Acre], which was renewed and rebuilt by his honour the mufti ʿAbd Allāh Efendi al-Jazzār […]'.[56]

In addition to ʿAbd Allāh al-Jazzār, we find other local actors, such as the two sons of ʿAlī Mīrī mentioned previously, who added almost twenty new handwritten books to the library. A certain Ḥasan Saʿīd al-Qawwās al-Ṣaydāwī identifies himself as a primary school teacher in Acre and he endowed a new handwritten book to the Jazzār library in 1323/1905.[57] These local actors are often difficult to identify, but it is possible to discern a systematic effort by these late Ottoman library builders to retrieve endowed handwritten books from private ownership. We, thus, find a certain Rafīq ʿAbd al-Malik contributing to this process in a note on an original al-Jazzār book where an owner states: 'I gave this book to Shaykh Muḥammad Rafīq ʿAbd al-Malik al-Shaʿbī [?] so that he returns it to al-

52 Acre, al-Jazzār Mosque Library, MS 67 (ʿAṭāʾ Allāh, *Fihris ʿAkkā*, 1983), fol. 1[a]:

هذا كتاب وقف جزار باشا كما عُلم من ختمه الذي كان على ورقة قد أُعدمت من تجديد تجـ[ـليده] وقد أُعيد بالشراء إلى هذه المكتبة

53 Muḥaybish, "Mujammaʿ al-Jazzār al-khayrī fī ʿAkkā".

54 This information is based on contemporaneous newspaper articles, especially Kurd ʿAlī, "Baḍʿat ayyām fī al-Jalīl (1912)"; Yūsuf Ḥasan, "al-Madrasa al-Aḥmadiyya fī ʿAkkā (1943)"; in addition to Mannāʿ, *Aʿlām Filasṭīn*, 83.

55 Acre, al-Jazzār Mosque Library, MS 1, fol. 1[a] and 239[b]:

وقف مكتبة المدرسة الأحمدية في جامع أحمد باشا الجزار في عكا المجددة سنة 1323.

The same seal is also on Acre, al-Jazzār Mosque Library, MS 2, MS 21, MS 34 and MS 67.

56 Acre, al-Jazzār Mosque Library, MS 39 (ʿAṭāʾ Allāh, *Fihris ʿAkkā*, 1983)/EAP 7, fol. 1[a]:

وقفت وحبست لله تعالى هذا الكتاب على أن يكون مقره مكتبة أحمد باشا [الجـ]ـزار بعكا المجدد إنشاؤها من قبل فضيلة مفتيها الحاج الفاضل الشيخ عبد الله أفندي الجزار …

57 Acre, al-Jazzār Mosque Library, MS 39 (ʿAṭāʾ Allāh, *Fihris ʿAkkā*, 1983)/EAP 7, fol. 1[a]:

وقفت وحبست لله تعالى هذا الكتاب على أن يكون مقره مكتبة أحمد باشا [الجـ]ـزار بعكا المجدد إنشاؤها من قبل فضيلة مفتيها الحاج الفاضل الشيخ عبد الله أفندي الجزار شرطت أن لا يخرج منها بوجه من الوجوه تحريرا في 4 ذي القعدة سنة 1323 الفقير معلم مكتب عكا حسن سعيد القواس الصيداوي.

Jazzār's library in the Jazzār Mosque in Acre in the year 1324/1906.'[58] We also see a certain ʿAbd al-Wāḥid al-Khaṭīb from Haifa[59] and probably ʿAfīfa, an otherwise unknown woman,[60] adding to the library stock. In other cases, the actors remain entirely anonymous: 'This book is an endowment of al-Jazzār Pasha, as is evident from al-Jazzār's seal on a page that was lost because of its rebinding. It was returned to this library by purchase.'[61]

The revival of the Jazzār library in the early twentieth century was not limited to re-endowing original handwritten books or adding new ones, the library was also enlarged by numerous printed books. These printed books are still in the Jazzār library today and constitute an important insight into intellectual life in late Ottoman Palestine. They have not yet been studied in depth, but Samah Hijab has taken a first step by examining them with a focus on the endowment notes. The large number of these notes shows wonderfully the extent to which local actors also drove the expansion of the library's print collection. The vast majority of the notes date to the first decade of the twentieth century, when the development of the library gained pace. Here, we see dozens of notables of early twentieth-century Acre who endowed printed books to the library, including scholars, administrators, judges, officials and officers. In addition, individuals from nearby towns and villages, such as Haifa, Ṣafad, Umm al-Faḥm and Samakh (close to Tiberias), also actively contributed to the build-up of the library. Among those endowing printed books are also those who re-endowed original handwritten books or endowed new ones, such as Rashīd and Aḥmad, Ṭāhir al-Jazāʾirī and Yūsuf al-Nabhānī.[62]

An inventory of the Jazzār library from 1927 shows the success of the library-building process as it held an impressive 1,200 printed books at that point. The number of handwritten books is, by contrast, astonishingly low, a mere fifty, and this might represent only part of the collection.[63] Another inventory from 1944, discussed below, gives the number of 148 for handwritten books in the Jazzār library, and this indicates that we are clearly looking at a very low number of handwritten books in the Jazzār library in the first half of the twentieth century. That we have somewhere between 50 and 150 handwritten books in the library after so many of them had been re-endowed and so many new ones had been added means that the Jazzār library must have been practically devoid of any handwritten books in the late nineteenth century.

The revival of the Jazzār library in the late Ottoman period within the framework of the relaunch of the *madrasa* was, thus, clearly a success, and late Ottoman library builders, such as ʿAbd Allāh al-Jazzār, put this library back on the cultural map of Palestine. Amīn al-Rayḥānī (1876–1940), for instance, published his Arab nationalist Syrian history in 1928, in which al-Jazzār is framed as a non-Arab tyrant. Al-Rayḥānī, therefore, had nothing positive to say about al-Jazzār except 'one good deed of which I saw the traces

58 Acre, al-Jazzār Mosque Library, MS 40/1 (ʿAṭāʾ Allāh, *Fihris ʿAkkā*, 1983), fol. 1a.

59 Acre, al-Jazzār Mosque Library, MS 32 (ʿAṭāʾ Allāh, *Fihris ʿAkkā*, 1983)/EAP 49, fol. 1a.

60 Acre, al-Jazzār Mosque Library, MS 78 (ʿAṭāʾ Allāh, *Fihris ʿAkkā*, 1983)/EAP 20, fol. 1a (ʿAfīfa bt. ʿAlī Pasha). Though in her case the Jazzār library is not explicitly named as the place of endowment.

61 Acre, al-Jazzār Mosque Library, MS 67 (ʿAṭāʾ Allāh, *Fihris ʿAkkā*, 1983), fol. 1a:

هذا كتاب وقف جزار باشا كما عُلم من ختمه الذي كان على ورقة قد أُعدمت من تجديد تجـ[ـليده] وقد أُعيد بالشراء إلى هذه المكتبة

Other anonymous endowers appear on Acre, al-Jazzār Mosque Library, MS 12, MS 21, MS 41 and MS 79 (ʿAṭāʾ Allāh, *Fihris ʿAkkā*, 1983).

62 Rashīd and Aḥmad in 1324/1906–1907, al-Jazāʾirī in 1323/1906 and al-Nabhānī in 1323/1906. I thank Samah Hijab for sharing this information.

63 Jerusalem (Abu Dis), The Center for Heritage Revival and Islamic Research, T-MS/2–230/325: *Bayyān asmāʾ al-kutub al-mawjūda bi-al-Maktaba al-Aḥmadīya*, 17 January 1927.

when I visited the Jazzār Mosque in Acre. In it is a library with books, most of them handwritten.'[64] Considering the massive influx of printed books, al-Rayḥānī's statement that the majority of books in the library in the 1920s were handwritten is highly unlikely. However, the library must have made quite an impression on him to grudgingly concede that this tyrant has, at least, one good deed to his name. The library must have stayed in good shape well into the 1930s when Johannes Pohl included the library in his overview article on the libraries of Palestine, stating that it 'encompasses c. 1,000 volumes, mostly Arabic manuscripts and books'.[65]

The library continued to function well into the 1940s. ʿAbd Allāh Mukhliṣ, for instance, the scholar and former director of the Supreme Muslim Council's General Endowment Administration (*Idārat al-Awqāf al-ʿĀmma*), borrowed three handwritten books from the Jazzār library to publish them in articles in 1946 and 1947 (#977, #982 and #1241 in the Jazzār library inventory).[66] Documents kept today in Jerusalem (Abu Dis) at *The Center for Heritage Revival and Islamic Research* show a substantial amount of paperwork produced by the General Endowment Administration, ʿAbd Allāh Mukhliṣ and the (anonymous) librarian of the Jazzār library on the return of these three books to the library in 1944.[67] The discussions around the three books were part of a wider interest of the General Endowment Administration in the affairs of the library and the interest of a local *Committee of the Aḥmadiyya Library in Acre* that was founded in 1943 by local notables.[68] The General Endowment Administration particularly demanded that the Jazzār librarian carried out a full revision of the library's stock, including information on any books currently on loan. The librarian did indeed produce a list that provides a wonderful snapshot of the state of the library in 1944 with 1,377 printed books and 148 handwritten books.[69]

The three ʿAbd Allāh Mukhliṣ books must have been extracted from the library at some point after 1944, as they are not listed in ʿAṭā' Allāh's 1983 catalogue. On account of such losses, the library's importance waned, and it started to fade from the map of well-known Palestinian libraries. Ṭarrāzī's survey of Arabic libraries published in the late 1940s/early 1950s, for instance, has a section specifically dedicated to Palestinian libraries. While the Aqṣā Mosque library and the Khalidi Library are discussed, the Acre library is absent.[70] When al-Munajjid published his work on Arabic handwritten books in Palestine in 1982 he lists some fifteen libraries, but again the Jazzār library is not among them.[71]

This overview of the development of the Jazzār library has shown that we are looking at a gradual and long-term process during which books left the library over the course of the nineteenth century. This process did not start before the 1820s, as indicated by the Abū Nabbūt library, and the library must have been practically devoid of handwritten books by the late nineteenth century. While we have some books that allow us to see individual trajectories, we do not yet have the data to really see the larger picture of how this library was dismantled. By contrast, there is ample evidence to trace the revival of the library and influx of

64 Al-Rayḥānī, *al-Nakabāt*, 100. See also Chapter 4 by Feras Krimsti in this volume on al-Rayḥānī.

65 Pohl, *Bibliotheken Palästinas*, 52.

66 Mukhliṣ, "Majmūʿat ashʿār" (= #1241), Mukhliṣ, "Kitāb Rawḍat al-faṣāḥa" (= #977) and Mukhliṣ, "Kitāb Taḥrīr al-taḥbīr" (= #982).

67 Jerusalem (Abu Dis), The Center for Heritage Revival and Islamic Research, MD/70/33: Letter by ʿAbd Allāh Mukhliṣ to the General Endowment Administration in Jerusalem, 1 July 1944, and letter by the Endowment Administration in Jerusalem to ʿAbd Allāh Mukhliṣ, 13 October 1944. I thank Samah Hijab for sharing reproductions of these letters.

68 On this committee see Muḥaybish, *al-Madrasa al-Aḥmadīya*, 174–175.

69 Jerusalem (Abu Dis), The Center for Heritage Revival and Islamic Research, MD/70/33: *Lāʾiḥa bi-asmaʾ al-kutub maʿa ʿadadihā al-mawjūda fī al-maktaba al-Aḥmadiyya al-ʿilmiyya al-Jazzāriyya*, 4 April 1944.

70 Ṭarrāzī, *Khazāʾin al-kutub al-ʿArabiyya*, I, 141–143.

71 Al-Munajjid, *al-Makhṭūṭāt al-ʿArabiyya fī Filasṭīn*.

handwritten books in the early twentieth century. The 'post-revival' period from the 1940s onwards is again rather difficult to describe in conceptual terms. Handwritten books were clearly extracted until very recently, but we have insufficient data to understand the nuts and bolts of this process. The immediate impact of the violence of 1948 and the foundation of the state of Israel on the collection is, for instance, entirely unclear.

3 Translocation within Southern Greater Syria beyond Acre

Even though the library was practically devoid of handwritten books by the late nineteenth century, the late Ottoman revival of the Acre library was possible because a substantive number of original al-Jazzār books had remained in the region and could, thus, be returned to the library. Individuals such as Yūsuf al-Nabhānī, Rafīq ʿAbd al-Malik, al-Ḥabbāl and ʿAbd Allāh al-Jazzār played a crucial role in preserving the book heritage in Acre and, thereby, contributing to shaping a new library topography in the region. This preservation of al-Jazzār books within this new topography was a much wider phenomenon that is visible in libraries well beyond Acre. A total of twenty-three of the overall corpus of seventy-eight al-Jazzār handwritten books, that is almost thirty per cent, are today in libraries in southern Greater Syria beyond Acre, including Damascus (National Asad Library and al-Majmaʿ al-ʿilmī), Beirut (American University of Beirut, Université Saint-Joseph, Zuhayr al-Shāwīsh), Jerusalem (Khalidi, Isʿāf al-Nashāshībī, 'Abandoned Property' (AP) collections in the National Library of Israel and *The Center for Heritage Revival and Islamic Research*) and Nablus (al-Najah University Library). All of them carry at least one of the Jazzār provenance elements—endowment statement, endowment seal, endowment motto—and/or can be linked to the Jazzār library inventory from 1221/1806.

Many of the books that left Acre went into the region's private libraries. Four of them are today in the Khalidi Library in Jerusalem.[72] In one case, it is evident that this happened before the Khalidi Library became a public library in 1900 and this is probably also true for the other three books. We find the statement at the end of *al-Ishrāf bi-faḍl al-ashrāf* that '[t]he loose pages of this book had become separated in the *dasht* [the section of the library with unbound books and loose papers]. Ḥusayn Ḥusnī b. ʿAlī al-Khālidī assembled them and organised them in their original way in 1309[/1891].'[73] Ḥusayn's name appears in numerous books in the Khalidi Library with such notes typically dated to the years before 1900. He must have played an important role in the years leading up to the transformation of this private library into a public library. Lawrence Conrad argued that 'there was already a nascent institution in place more than a decade earlier [than 1900]',[74] and Ḥusayn arguably played an important role in this nascent institution. Yet, his role as a late Ottoman library builder has not been acknowledged in scholarship so far, in contrast to that of Rāghib al-Khālidī (1858–1951).[75] The fact that Ḥusayn reconstituted and rebound so many handwritten books, among them this Jazzār book, links him closely to his contemporaries, such as al-Nabhānī, who displayed similar rebinding efforts when they revived and renewed the library of Acre.

That al-Jazzār books were translocated from Acre to Palestinian private libraries is also evident from the five handwritten books within the 'AP'

72 Jerusalem, Khalidi Library, MS 73 (JIB), 966 (JIB), 1060 (JnIB) and 1699 (JIB).

73 Jerusalem, Khalidi Library, MS 1699, fol. 146^b: (cf. https://w3id.org/vhmml/readingRoom/view/510065) [accessed 3 January 2023]:

جامع أوراق هذا الكتاب بعد شتاتها وتفرقها بين الدشت
ومرجعه لأصله كما كان راجي عفو مولاه المنان الفقير حسين
حسني ابن المرحوم الحاج علي أفندي الخالدي يرجو من طالع
فيه أن يدعو له بالغفران محرم سنة 1309.

74 Conrad, "The Khalidi Library", 198.

75 Conrad, "The Khalidi Library"; Khālidī, *al-Maktaba al-Khālidīya*.

section in the National Library of Israel.[76] Among the library's holdings of Arabic handwritten books, those with an AP class mark constitute a substantial corpus of some 700 books so far. Little research has been done yet on the history of these handwritten artefacts that were appropriated from Palestinian homes in 1948. The printed AP books in the library, by contrast, have garnered some interest and research has started to show what catastrophic consequences dismantling such libraries had on Palestinian cultural life.[77] My comments here are very much indebted to Vincent Engelhardt, who has worked on this collection in preparation for his thesis under the supervision of Samuel Thrope (National Library of Israel) and with support from Lina Jabali. More specifically, the role of Efraim Wust has to be highlighted, as it is he who catalogued the Arabic AP handwritten books, along with the rest of the National Library's Islamic handwritten book collection, including many ownership marks. While Wust's work has not been published, it is accessible in the online cataloguing records of the National Library along with digitised copies of the AP handwritten book collection.[78] This newly completed digitisation is part of the Library's efforts over the past decade to make the AP collection and its history more accessible. Nevertheless, it is still mostly unclear from which Palestinian libraries the AP handwritten books were removed. Hidden beyond the blank AP class marks are stories of book collections owned by individuals, families and institutions that are yet to be uncovered.

Two al-Jazzār books in the AP section do, however, carry a clear indication as to their pre-1948 location and trajectory. Ms. AP Ar. 177 carries not only a defaced endowment seal of al-Jazzār, but also the note that '[i]t entered the ownership of Ḥusayn Ṭāhā al-Dāwūdī on the 15th Ramadan 1290[/1873]'.[79] The Dāwūdīs, or al-Dajānīs, were among the important Palestinian families during the Ottoman period.[80] The family held the role of guardians of the Tomb of the Prophet David in Jerusalem from the early sixteenth century onwards and Ḥusayn underlines in other ownership notes that he holds this position.[81] Ḥusayn was a very active library builder and there are more than fifty handwritten books in the AP section alone that carry his ownership notes from the late nineteenth century.[82] While Ḥusayn died well before 1948, the high number of his books in the AP section makes it very likely that his library was preserved, probably within the family, until it became 'AP'.

Ḥusayn's library was part of a wider topography of al-Dajānī libraries, and the court register of Jerusalem from this period shows the number of books that circulated within various households of that family.[83] The second al-Jazzār book in the AP section carrying an indication as to its pre-1948 location brings us to one other such library within that large family, namely, to the Jaffa branch of the Dijānīs. This book carries not only another defaced al-Jazzār seal, but also an ownership note naming ʿAbd al-Qādir al-Dijānī (1809–1877) with a seal dated to 1268/1851–1852.[84] The AP section in the National Library of Israel has again a large cor-

76 Jerusalem, National Library of Israel, AP Ar. 177 (JIB), AP Ar. 258 (JIB), AP Ar. 261 (JnIB), AP Ar. 290 (JIB) and AP Ar. 410 (JIB).

77 Amit, "*Salvage or Plunder*".

78 https://www.nli.org.il/he/discover/manuscripts/warraq [accessed 29 November 2023]. I thank Samuel Thrope for his advice on this section.

79 Jerusalem, National Library of Israel, AP Ar. 177, fol. 1[a].

80 Mannāʿ, "al-Nukhba al-Maqdisiyya".

81 For instance, Jerusalem, National Library of Israel, AP Ar. 185, fol. 1[a].

82 I thank Vincent Engelhardt who generously shared this information.

83 See the reproduction of one document in Ghosheh, *Encyclopædia Palestinnica*, XVI, 228 as well as Barakat, *Tārīkh al-maktabāt al-ʿarabīya*, 88.

84 Jerusalem, National Library of Israel, AP Ar. 258, fol. 1[a]:
هذا الكتاب من من ذي المن دام مَنُّه على الفقير إليه سبحانه السيد عبد القادر أبو رباح الدجاني الحنفي الأحمدي الخلوتي القادري الرفاعي الدسوقي خادم العلم والطريق بمدينة يافا عفى عنه بمنه آمين.

pus of handwritten books by ʿAbd al-Qādir, around fifty, so that his library was also probably preserved within the family until 1948.

The other handwritten books preserved in Palestinian libraries do not carry any notes providing insight into their trajectory between the early nineteenth century and their current location. In the case of the two al-Jazzār handwritten books in al-Najah University Library in Nablus, it is their very presence in this library that indicates a trajectory involving Palestinian family libraries.[85] The library's webpage profiles its holdings of handwritten books as follows: 'The libraries of al-Najah National University hold a large collection of old and important handwritten books. These were collected from the established families of Nablus known for their famous scholars, litterateurs and poets.'[86] There is no conclusive evidence that the Jazzār books in this library have a provenance going back to family libraries. The prominent role of such libraries in the trajectories of the other Palestinian handwritten books previously discussed makes it very likely.

We have two handwritten Jazzār books that are (or were) part of the Jaffa collection.[87] I use the imprecise term 'Jaffa collection' to refer to the books of the Islamic Library (*al-Maktaba al-Islāmiyya*) that the Supreme Muslim Council founded in 1923 in dedicated premises and that included the remnants of the Abū Nabbūt library mentioned previously. The fate of this library after 1948 is unclear, but the presence of bi-scriptural Arabic/Hebrew seals on the books shows that the library continued to exist beyond 1948. When ʿAṭāʾ Allāh wrote the catalogue of this collection in the early 1980s, the Islamic Library had ceased to exist, and what was left of the collection was stored in the town's al-Nuzha Mosque. After ʿAṭāʾ Allāh catalogued the books, they became part of the library of a club called al-Nādī al-Islāmī.[88] We accessed microfilm copies (probably produced by ʿAṭāʾ Allāh himself) of the two al-Jazzār handwritten books that ʿAṭāʾ Allāh catalogued via the Najah University Library website.[89] One of the two books has since moved to *The Center for Heritage Revival and Islamic Research* in Jerusalem (Abu Dis)[90] and we have not been able to verify the whereabouts of the second book. There are no indications as to the trajectories of these books between the writing of the library inventory in 1221/1806 and the foundation of the Islamic Library in Jaffa. The opening of the library in 1923 by the Supreme Muslim Council is described as a civic event in which 'a large number of the town's grandees' participated. This description also stresses that the library was intensively used not only for reading purposes but also for numerous public lectures and other events.[91] It is, thus, possible that the library's stock was built up, at least in part, by donations from the town's family libraries.[92]

When we move beyond modern-day Palestine and Israel to Damascus, the role of family libraries in hosting translocated al-Jazzār books in southern Greater Syria is again visible. Among the five

---

85 Nablus, al-Najah University Library, NL 211508 and NL 250213 (barcode numbers).

86 https://manuscripts.najah.edu/ [accessed 16 August 2022]:

تحوي مكتبات جامعة النجاح الوطنية مجموعة كبيرة من المخطوطات القديمة الهامة التي تم جمعها من البيوت النابلسية العريقة التي تميزت بعلمائها وادبائها وشعرائها المشهورين [...].

87 ʿAṭāʾ Allāh, *Fihrist Yāfā*, no. 52 (pp. 623): *al-Kashshāf ʿan ḥaqāʾiq al-tanzīl* by al-Zamakhsharī and Ibid., no. 86 (p. 96): *Kitāb Sībawayhi*.

88 Ibid., 34.

89 Ibid., no. 52: https://manuscripts.najah.edu/node/217; Ibid., no. 86: https://manuscripts.najah.edu/node/140 [both accessed 3 January 2023].

90 Jerusalem (Abu Dis), The Center for Heritage Revival and Islamic Research, 301/2 (Afaneh et al., *Fihris makhṭūṭāt Filasṭīn al-muṣawwara*, V, 72; formerly Jaffa, MS 52 (ʿAṭāʾ Allāh, *Fihrist Yāfā*, 1984): al-Zamakhsharī, *al-Kashshāf ʿan ḥaqāʾiq al-tanzīl*).

91 *Bayān al-majlis al-sharʿī al-Islāmī al-aʿlā fī Filasṭīn sanat 1341/2 (1923/4)*, Jerusalem: Maṭbaʿat madrasat al-aytām al-Islāmiyya, 1343/1924, 33.

92 Al-Dajānī, *Madīnat Yāfā*, 258.

handwritten books in Damascus, no. 44 in the Majmaʿ al-ʿilmī Library carries a seal showing that this book entered the ownership of the great Damascene *ḥadīth* scholar Muḥammad Badr al-Dīn al-Ḥasanī (1267/1850–1354/1935).[93] Al-Ḥasanī systematically purchased handwritten books that had been taken out of endowment libraries, such as the eighteenth-century Damascene book endowment by Mollah ʿUthmān al-Kurdī. His stipulation that these books should be returned to the status of endowed books was only implemented many decades after his death in 1975, when his grandson Muḥammad Fakhr al-Dīn al-Ḥasanī endowed some of his books.[94]

The final handwritten book of relevance for this section on southern Greater Syria might seem somewhat surprising at first glance: #1267 in a library inventory that is today in Tokyo in the Daiber collection of the University Library.[95] This collection was bought from Hans Daiber in two batches, one in 1986–1987 and the second in 1994. The Jazzār book #1267 belongs to the second batch and Hans Daiber states that he, in turn, bought this handwritten book in Damascus at some point between the years 1986 and 1992 from a souvenir shop owner called Abū Aḥmad near the Umayyad Mosque.[96] In other words, this book stayed in southern Greater Syria for almost 200 years after al-Jazzār's death and was, until very recently, part of Damascene book culture. Regrettably, the book does not carry any ownership notes that would offer an insight into its trajectory in the nineteenth and twentieth centuries.

In sum, it is evident that almost fifty per cent of the known al-Jazzār books stayed in southern Greater Syria, including Acre (in addition to the manuscript that only recently moved to Tokyo). That these thirty-seven handwritten books remained in the region indicates that the dispersal of the books and their preservation in new libraries was very much driven by local actors who extracted books from and sometimes returned them to the library. Their translocation to other libraries in the region repeatedly also took place with the aim of returning the books to endowed status, even if their new home was not the Jazzār library itself. The extraction of handwritten books from the Jazzār library and their subsequent trajectories was, thus, at least on the basis of the current small corpus, to a large extent, a local story involving local actors.

4 Translocations in West Asia and North Africa beyond Greater Syria

If we now move beyond Greater Syria to consider the trajectories of al-Jazzār books to libraries in the wider West Asian and North African region, one phenomenon, as mentioned above, is particularly striking: the low number of books in Istanbul. There are only three al-Jazzār handwritten books in Istanbul today (bearing at least one of the three Jazzār provenance elements). They are all in the Süleymaniye Library, which has increasingly become the central library of handwritten books in Turkey since the late nineteenth century.[97] The Süleymaniye's system of class marks thankfully preserves the name of the historical library where the book was held before its integration into the Süleymaniye Library. The three al-Jazzār books did not come from one of the grand libraries that had

93 Damascus, Maktabat al-Majmaʿ al-ʿilmī, MS 44, fol. 1[a]:

تنفيذا لوصية المحدث الأكبر السيد محمد بدر الدين الحسني أعاد هذا الكتاب إلى الوقف حفيده السيد محمد فخر الدين ابن محمد عصام غفر الله لهم سنة 1395 هـ

We have not been able to access three other Damascene handwritten books in the National al-Asad Library (MS 44, 219 and 11144).

94 Aljoumani, "Tārīkh maktabat al-Mullā ʿUthmān al-Kurdī", 244–247.

95 Tokyo, University Library, Daiber Collection II, 76.

96 Email Hans Daiber to Konrad Hirschler, 25 January 2023.

97 Istanbul, Süleymaniye Library, Yazma Bağışlar 766, Pertevniyal V. Sultan 759 and Kemankes 21.

been established in Istanbul in the previous centuries, such as the Ayasofya (Hagia Sofia) or Fatih libraries. Instead, one of them came into the Süleymaniye Library via a library that was established in the course of the later nineteenth century, Pertevniyal Valide Sultan. Another book is in the residual 'Donations' class mark (Yazma Bağışlar), which was set up after the Süleymaniye started to function as a de facto central library of handwritten books.

Cairo, with nine handwritten books, is more important than Istanbul as a destination of al-Jazzār books. As mentioned in the *Introduction* to this volume, the actual number of al-Jazzār books in Cairo is most certainly significantly higher because the holdings of the National Library, the largest collection of handwritten books in the Arabic world, could not be systematically searched within the framework of the Jazzār Library Project. Private libraries of the late nineteenth and early twentieth century that were subsequently integrated into the National Library would be prime locations to search for al-Jazzār handwritten books in the future. Aḥmad Pasha Taymūr (1871–1930), for instance, had over 8,000 handwritten books in his library, parts of which he acquired in Damascus where he was a member of the Arabic Academy of Sciences.[98] One of the two known al-Jazzār books in the National Library is indeed from the Taymūr subcollection (carrying al-Jazzār's endowment statement, seal and motto), thus, indicating that the role of private collectors went beyond Greater Syria.[99] Four other books are in the second largest library in Cairo, al-Azhar Library (all carrying at least the Jazzār endowment motto).[100] The higher number compared to the National Library is probably only due to the fact that al-Azhar is a much more welcoming place for researchers and the Jazzār books are, thus, easier to identify. One of these handwritten books, #1166 in the Jazzār library inventory, was in the private library of the Egyptian legal scholar Ḥasan Jalāl al-Ḥusaynī (1271/1855–1336/1918) who bequeathed his books to al-Azhar Library.[101]

Three further handwritten books in Cairo are held in the Central Library of Islamic Manuscripts of the Egyptian Ministry of Endowments.[102] From the early 2000s, this library has brought together handwritten books that had been previously held in endowed mosques such as Masjid al-imām Ḥusayn and Masjid al-Sayyida Zaynab.[103] Regrettably, the new class marks in the Central Library do not provide any insights into the books' previous library. However, there are traces on the books themselves that offer an insight into their place prior to their present-day location. One of the Central Library's handwritten books is entitled *Waqf al-Malik al-Ashraf*, referring to the massive endowments of the Mamluk Sultan al-Malik al-Ashraf Barsbay (d. 841/1438). At first glance, it seems self-evident that the medieval text of a Cairene endowment deed is in the Ministry of Endowments in Cairo today. Yet, this is de facto a JIB that was in Acre in 1806 bearing an [effaced] endowment seal and the motto. There is no indication when this codex was written and how al-Jazzār got hold of it (or perhaps even had it produced for his library?). This codex is the summary version of a larger manuscript that is, in turn, kept in the Ministry of Endowments' archive with the number 880. This larger 'original' deed conserves the texts of the endowment deeds in more detail and has probably been in Cairo continuously since it was first produced.[104] The summary *Waqf al-Malik al-Ashraf* came into the holdings of the Ministry

98 Sayyid, *Dār al-kutub al-miṣrīya*, 74–76.

99 Cairo, Dar al-kutub, Taymūr, Muṣṭalaḥ al-ḥadīth 97.

100 Cairo, al-Azhar Library, MS 22783, MS 83318, MS 85307 and MS 91135.

101 Cairo, al-Azhar Library, MS 22783. On him, see the biography in *al-Manār* 10/20 (1918): 441–444.

102 Cairo, Ministry of Islamic Endowments Library, MS 3018, MS 2398/209 and MS 4490.

103 According to the memorial plate on the building, the Central Library was opened 26 June 2004.

104 Darrāj, *L'Acte de waqf de Barsbay*. Darrāj bases his edition on the codex Cairo, Dār al-kutub, *ta'rīkh* 3390 that has the same text as that in the Jazzār/Ministry of endowment manuscript.

of Endowments from 'Maktabat Ḥusayn', probably the library of the Ḥusayn Mosque in Cairo close to al-Azhar.[105]

Another Central Library book, no. 4490, that had been part of the Jazzār library (bearing the endowment seal, statement and motto) brings us back to the importance of family libraries and the complicated post-al-Jazzār endowment trajectories of many books. Before coming to the Cairo ministry, this book had been part of the library of the Directorate of Alexandrian Endowments (*Mudīrīyat al-Awqāf al-Iskandarīya*) and had moved there from the library of the Mursī Abū al-ʿAbbās Mosque in Alexandria. The book endowment in the Mursī Abū al-ʿAbbās Mosque, in turn, goes back to a merger of Alexandrian family libraries in 1903. Our al-Jazzār book must have become part of one of these family libraries in the course of the nineteenth century.[106] The third Central Library book with a Jazzār provenance, no. 3018 (bearing the endowment seal), came into the ministry from the library in the Dardīr Mosque/Mausoleum in Cairo, which goes back to the Cairene scholar Aḥmad al-Dardīr (d. 1201/1786).[107]

The importance of family libraries in the trajectories of al-Jazzār books is also evident from entry #1187 that is today in Riyadh, Imam Muhammad Ibn Saud Islamic University, MS 1094. This JIB became part of the library of Aḥmad Khayrī Bey (1907–1967) in the Buḥayra Governate in Lower Egypt. This library was constituted as an endowment and seemingly contained some 16,000 volumes of printed or manuscript books by 1960. Despite the founder's intentions, the library was sold after his death via the book trader Muḥammad b. Aḥmad Ṣādiq to the Cairene publisher and book trader Ra'ūf Nuʿmān, who, in turn, sold most of the books to the Imam Muhammad Ibn Saud Islamic University in Riyadh. At least, the books retained an independent identity in this collection and are labelled as going back to the 'Maktabat Aḥmad Khayrī'.[108]

Two handwritten books are today in Qatar in the National Library and they are the only al-Jazzār artefacts that have a clear trajectory beyond Arabic/Muslim contexts. They are a medical work[109] (carrying the endowment seal, the [effaced] motto and the statement) and an Arab translation (via Pahlavi) of Kassiano's Greek work on agriculture (carrying seal, statement and motto).[110] While neither book carries any subsequent ownership notes that would have indicated their post-al-Jazzār library trajectory, they carry very rich paracontent referring to the text as well as guest content.[111] The agricultural work has scribbles, lines and numerous other doodles on virtually every page, including some animals. These are all drawn in pencil and do not reveal anything about the identity of the former owner. The owner of the medical work—probably the same person—engaged in the margins in an equally vivid manner with the text of the book. However, in the case of this book, we find numerous commentaries, notes and *nota bene* marks in addition to the doodles (which include a human being, a flower and many crowns).[112] These marginalia are written in Western Armenian, suggesting that this al-Jazzār book had found a private owner (perhaps in Jerusalem) well beyond the Muslim community, who also adorned the margins with a cross. The fact that these two books have a

105 Cairo, Ministry of Islamic Endowments Library, MS 209/2398 (#1372 in the Jazzār library inventory). Zaydān, *Tārīkh ādāb al-lugha al-ʿarabīya*, IV, 123.

106 Cairo, Ministry of Islamic Endowments Library, MS 4490.

107 Cairo, Ministry of Islamic Endowments Library, MS 3018. On this library see Zaydān, *Tārīkh ādāb al-lugha al-ʿarabīya*, IV, 118.

108 Ḥamāda, *ʿĀshiq al-kutub*.

109 Doha, Qatar National Library HC.MS.00211 (#1431 in the Jazzār library inventory).

110 Doha, Qatar National Library QNL00017150. On Kassiano's work see Ullmann, *Natur- und Geheimwissenschaften im Islam*, 434–435.

111 For paracontent and guest content cf. Ciotti et al., *Definition of Paracontent*.

112 I thank Meliné Pehlivanian (Staatsbibliothek Berlin) for generously sharing her readings of the marginalia with me.

shared trajectory towards Qatar, both are thematically not linked to Islamic fields of knowledge and they share similar vivid marginalia makes it very likely that they were both in the possession of the same Armenian-writing owner.

In total, there are, thus, nineteen handwritten books, twenty-four per cent, in the libraries of Western Asia and North Africa beyond southern Greater Syria.[113] They indicate again that the translocation of al-Jazzār books is not so much a phenomenon that has to be understood with reference to the Ottoman centre or European (proto)colonial intrusion. Rather, it was a gradual and multifaceted process that involved a large number of mostly nineteenth-century local and regional individuals and their private libraries.

5 Translocations to Europe and the US

A number of twenty-two al-Jazzār books in European and US-American libraries, twenty-eight per cent, is significant. Yet, this is clearly not a large enough number to see the translocation of books to Europe and the US as the main factor in the demise of the Jazzār library. In addition, even in the case of these departures to Europe and the US, we repeatedly see the role of local actors who first extracted these books from the Jazzār library in the course of the nineteenth century. This is particularly evident in those cases where the books had been in local private libraries after they left the Jazzār library and before they went into the ownership of European or US-American libraries. This is, for instance, the case for the only al-Jazzār handwritten book in Leipzig (carrying the Jazzār seal), which was formerly part of the Rifāʿiyya library.[114] The Rifāʿiyya was a Damascene private library sold in 1853 via the Prussian consul Johann Gottfried Wetzstein (1815–1905). The owner of this private library was, as Boris Liebrenz has argued, ʿUmar al-Ḥarīrī al-Rifāʿī, a leading member of the Rifāʿiyya order.[115] Yet, even al-Rifāʿī was not the first owner of the book after its extraction from the Jazzār library. Rather, prior to its incorporation into the Rifāʿiyya library, the book had already been in the ownership of another Damascene book owner, a chancery secretary named Muṣṭafā b. Muḥammad Saʿīd Efendī al-Būsnawī.[116]

The role of consuls in translocating al-Jazzār books to Europe goes well beyond Wetzstein. The three books that are today in the British Library (they all carry the Jazzār seal and endowment motto) originate from the same milieu. Two of them were sold to the library in 1872 by the scholar and consul Auguste de Jaba (1801–1894) as is evident from the books' final flyleaves. De Jaba lived in Erzurum as the Russian consul from 1848 to 1866 and subsequently in Smyrna/Izmir.[117] The third book, #221 in the Jazzār library inventory, was sold to the British Library in 1893 by the art and book dealer Joseph-Ange Durighello (1863–1924), the son of the French vice-consul in Sidon.[118] The

113 To this number belong the books Mecca, al-Ḥaram al-Makkī Library, MS 1499 and Riyadh, King Faisal Center for Research and Islamic Studies, MS 100, that do not carry indications on their post-al-Jazzār trajectory, as well as the book Shinqit (Mauritania), Collection of Ahl Ḥabat, MS 9/96 (according to Baffioni, *Catalogue des Manuscrits*, 227) for which we were not able to access reproductions.

114 Universitätsbibliothek Leipzig, Vollers 118: https://www.refaiya.uni-leipzig.de/receive/DE15Book_manuscript_00015338 [accessed 3 January 2023].

115 Liebrenz, *Rifāʿīya aus Damaskus*.

116 Universitätsbibliothek Leipzig, Vollers 118, fol. 1^v, ed. Boris Liebrenz: https://www.refaiya.uni-leipzig.de/receive/DE15SecEntry_secentry_00000604 see also https://www.refaiya.uni-leipzig.de/receive/MyMssPerson_agent_00005532 [both accessed 3 January 2023].

117 London, British Library, Or. 1183 and Or. 1206. My thanks go to Daniel Lowe (British Library) for providing crucial support on this matter. On de Jaba, see Conermann/Kemper, *Soviet Oriental Studies*, 87–88.

118 London, British Library, Or. 4706. British Library Corporate Archives, BLCA/S81/02 (British Museum, Department of Oriental Printed Books and Manuscripts, Registers of Oriental Manuscripts, Or.3481–Or.90340, 1887–1921) and BLCA/S74/01 (British Museum, Department of

FIGURE 7.1 al-Surūrī, *Sharḥ Gulistān*, Antiquariat Inlibris, Vienna ('Paris book', see *Introduction* to this volume)

case of the 'Paris book' that was offered up for sale in June 2023 (#1561 or #1562 in the Jazzār library inventory) is strikingly similar. Its last identifiable owner, the French scholar Frédéric Macler, had received it from the French consul of Damascus, Paul Savoye, in 1901.[119] In contrast to the Wetzstein case, there is no indication where and when De Jaba, Durighello and Savoye acquired their al-Jazzār books. Yet it is striking that they all owned only small numbers of al-Jazzār books, which suggests that they were not able to extract books directly from the library. Instead, they probably bought them from previous owners long after the books had left the library. They must, thus, have been part of the constant trickle of books out of the library into local ownership over the course of the nineteenth century.

Extraction by a local nineteenth-century actor with a trajectory through a local private library is also possible in the case of the Jazzār handwritten book that is today in Staatsbibliothek Berlin and bears al-Jazzār's endowment seal, motto and statement. In Berlin, it is part of the Landberg subcollection of over 1,000 handwritten books that the library acquired in 1884 from Carlo Landberg who, in turn, had bought parts of the collection from the Egyptian scholar and book trader Amīn b. Ḥasan al-Ḥulwānī al-Madanī. The latter had travelled to Europe to sell his collection of some 3,000 handwritten books that were subsequently to also enlarge the collections of Leiden and

Oriental Printed Books and Manuscripts: Acquisition Invoices, 1892–1896). My thanks go to Victoria Ogunsanya (British Library) for providing this information.

119 Book note in hand of F. Macler on a paper slip pasted onto the inner front cover: 'Ce manuscrit m'a été donné à Damas en 1901, par M.P. Savoye, consul de France. F. Macler'. Also see Dussaud, "Rapport"; Dussaud, "Missions".

Princeton.[120] He had acquired the books from numerous private owners in the Hijaz, Damascus and Cairo, as Garret Davidson has shown.[121] It is, thus, possible that the Jazzār book in Berlin had also been in private ownership (or part of a private library) before it came into al-Madanī's ownership and before he sold it to Landberg.

The role of local actors in extracting al-Jazzār books that are today in European and US-American libraries is beyond doubt in the case of the largest sub-corpus. Almost all of the fifteen handwritten books held in Princeton's Garrett collection (six) and the Chester Beatty library in Dublin (nine) carry the endowment seal and most of them, the endowment motto and/or statement. The Princeton Garrett collection and the Chester Beatty library constitute a single corpus in terms of provenance of their Islamicate handwritten books. Many books in both collections were sold to the respective new owners, the American collector Robert S. Garrett (1875–1961) and the Irish-American collector Alfred Chester Beatty (1875–1968), by the same book trader and collector, Abraham Shalom Yahuda (1877–1951). Yahuda was in Acre in 1929 and described the Jazzār library in a letter to Alfred Chester Beatty, with whom he worked closely from 1927 onwards.[122] In this letter, Yahuda informed Chester Beatty that 'the last important [handwritten books] still left there [in the Jazzār library] I hope to get through a scholar there soon'.[123] We have no idea who this 'scholar' might have been and whether Yahuda did actually extract books from this library.

However, Yahuda must have been aware of the Jazzār library as he had sold a group of 126 handwritten books to Chester Beatty the previous year, 1928. As Moya Carey has shown, such acquisitions were recorded in the ART notebooks kept in Chester Beatty's collection. Here, the 126 books are recorded as coming from a 'very big old library'.[124] Among them are nine al-Jazzār books and they include some of the most spectacular that al-Jazzār had in his library, among them the *Fihrist* (*Catalogue*) of Ibn al-Nadīm (d. c. 380/990).[125] This is not only one of the most important sources for the intellectual and book history of the early Islamic period, but the Jazzār exemplar is one of the two earliest copies of this work and certainly ranks among the most spectacular early Arabic handwritten books in general. That one of the best-known Egyptian historians of the late medieval period, al-Maqrīzī (d. 845/1442), left a reader's note on it bears testament to its importance.[126] That it ended up in the ownership of Chester Beatty certainly reflects his interest in particularly old and valuable books.

The six Princeton books arguably come from the same 'very big old library'. In parallel to selling outstanding handwritten books to Chester Beatty, Yahuda built up his own research collection of rather less spectacular pieces. Yahuda sold his collection in 1942 to Robert S. Garrett, who, in turn, donated it to Princeton University Library.[127] It is, thus, probable that Yahuda split the books that he bought from the 'very big old library' into two groups, with the 126 more spectacular items going to Chester Beatty and the others staying in his private collection. The six Princeton al-Jazzār books are indeed less outstanding than their peers in Dublin.

From where did Yahuda buy the fifteen books that are today in Dublin and Princeton? The only information we have on the provenance of these

120 Rauch, "Wettkampfe", 123–127.

121 Davidson, "History of the Princeton University Library Collection", 425–434. On al-Madanī see Schwartz, "Eastern scholar's engagement".

122 Carey, "Real Mine".

123 Yahuda to Beatty, 15 May 1929, National Library of Israel Archives, MS. Var. Yah 38 01 217: Beatty A Chester.; quoted in Davidson, "History of the Princeton University Library Collection", 456.

124 ART C notebook as discussed and quoted by Carey, "Real Mine".

125 #998 in the Jazzār library inventory, today Chester Beatty Ar. 3315.

126 Dublin, Chester Beatty Library, Ar. 3315, fol. 1[a].

127 Davidson, "History of the Princeton University Library Collection".

books is the reference to the unidentified 'big old library' in the ART notebook. It is very unlikely that this refers to the Jazzār library: The nine Chester Beatty library books definitely belong to the larger corpus of 126 books that come from this library. As discussed in the *Introduction* to this volume, we have checked all of these 126 books regarding possible provenance from the Jazzār library and 117 of them have no link to it whatsoever. Yahuda probably bought these books from intermediary dealers. As Lina Jabali shows in her ongoing work on the Yahuda collection in the National Library of Israel, Yahuda relied on a wide network of dealers, especially in Cairo, such as al-Khānjī, ʿAbd al-Ghanī al-Shihābī, Yūsuf Tūmā al-Bustānī (*Maktabt al-ʿArab*), Zaydān (*Maktabt Zaydān al-ʿUmūmiyya*) and Yūsuf Eliān Sarkīs libraries, as well as al-Hilāl press. Yahuda's connection with the Khānjī library is particularly well-documented, as is also shown in the work by Garrett Davidson. A slip in the hand of Sāmī Amīn al-Khānjī that is now in the Yahuda archive in Jerusalem shows that their dealings involved books from the Jazzār library. Here, al-Khānjī wrote: 'The *Dīwān* of [...] Ibn al-Muʿtazz, a fine copy, a rare manuscript [...] from the endowment of the Jazzār library in Akka.'[128] This book is indeed listed in the Jazzār library inventory (#1195) and is no longer in Akka. Such slips were typical for the books that Yahuda acquired from al-Khānjī, but Yahuda must have sold it to another customer as we have not been able to identify this manuscript in Dublin, Princeton or the National Library of Israel.

The manuscripts that went through the hands of Yahuda are, thus, another case of books from the Jazzār library initially moving into local or regional ownership and subsequently being purchased for the European/US-American market. The scenario might be different for the Princeton books (or some of them) as we cannot be certain that all of them go back to the same 'big old library' as those in Dublin. Yahuda plainly states his intention in the 1929 letter from Acre to directly remove books from the Jazzār library. Considering his success in navigating difficult purchases,[129] it is possible that this happened here and that at least some of the six Princeton books were directly removed from the Jazzār library.

6 Conclusion

The initial question posed in this chapter, where have all the books gone, is still, to a large extent, an open question, as the current whereabouts of the vast majority of the Jazzār handwritten books remain unknown. It can only be hoped that this book leads to increased awareness of the Jazzār collection and that more will be identified in the future. However, even based on the small corpus identified so far and a consideration of their trajectories, it can be argued that the demise of the Jazzār library was a gradual and protracted process over the course of the nineteenth century. This was not a linear process of decline; the early twentieth century witnessed a remarkable renewal of the library driven by individuals such as ʿAbd Allāh al-Jazzār that was part of a much wider development in which libraries in Greater Syria were reconfigured and rebuilt by individuals such as Muḥammad al-Ḥabbāl. This renewal was arguably also a reaction to the fact that the Jazzār library, and other libraries, had lost so many books in the course of the nineteenth century.

Yet, there is no indication that European traders had direct access to the library during the nineteenth century. Instead, all books that show any evidence of having left the library during this period went into local private libraries first and were then either re-endowed or sold to new owners, non-European or European. In contrast to what one might have assumed, this is, to a large extent, a

128 A.S. Yahuda Archive, National Library of Israel Archives. I am grateful to Lina Jabali who made a reproduction of this slip available and provided me with the contextual information.

129 Carey, "Real Mine".

local and regional story driven by scholars, librarians and notables in the region—and not a story driven by outside statesmen, consuls and traders. The story of the translocation of written artefacts from West Asia and North Africa to Europe and the US in this period seems to be different for non-Muslim books that were much more in the focus of European and US-American scholarship. Regarding Christian handwritten books from the Sinai, for instance, and Jewish material from the Cairo Geniza corpus, there is a much stronger role of non-local and non-regional actors.[130] Yet, the trajectory of written artefacts from collections such as the Jazzār library or the Damascene Qubbat al-Khazna was clearly a very different story.[131]

Bibliography

Acıl, Berat (ed.). *Osmanlı kitap kültürü: Carullah Efendi kütüphanesi ve derkenar notları*. Istanbul, 2015.

Afaneh, Hosam El Din (ʿAfāna, Ḥusām al-Dīn) et al. *Fihris makhṭūṭāt Filasṭīn al-muṣawwara*. 5 vols. Jerusalem, 2000–2012.

Aljoumani, Said. "Tārīkh maktabat al-Mullā ʿUthmān al-Kurdī bi-Dimashq iʿtimādan ʿalā khawārij makhṭūṭātihā." *Journal of the Institute of Arabic Manuscripts* 65, no. 1 (2021): 210–260.

Aljoumani, Said, Burak, Guy and Hirschler, Konrad. *List of Identified al-Jazzār Manuscripts and Their Current Location*, Research Data Repository of Universität Hamburg, https://doi.org/10.25592/uhhfdm.14178.

Amit, Gish. "Salvage or Plunder? Israel's 'Collection' of Private Palestinian Libraries in West Jerusalem." *Journal of Palestine Studies* 40, no. 4 (2011): 6–23.

ʿAṭāʾ Allāh, Maḥmūd ʿAlī. *Fihris makhṭūṭāt al-Maktaba al-Aḥmadiyya fī ʿAkkā*. 1983.

ʿAṭāʾ Allāh, Maḥmūd ʿAlī. *Fihris makhṭūṭāt al-Maktaba al-Islamiyya fī Yāfā*. 1984.

Baffioni, Carmela. *Fondation Sidi Mohamed Ould Habott. Bibliothèque des manuscrits*. Siena/Chinguetti, 2006.

Bağcı, Serpil and Zeynep Yürekli. "Book-Picking in a Conquered Citadel." In *Crafting History: Essays on the Ottoman World and Beyond in Honor of Cemal Kafadar*, edited by R. Goshgarian, I. Khouri-Makdisi and A. Yaycıoğlu, 77–103. Boston, MA, 2023.

Barakat, Bashir. *Tārīkh al-maktabāt al-ʿArabiyya fī Bayt al-Maqdis*. Riyadh, 2012.

Carey, Moya. "'A Real Mine for All Kinds of Research': Abraham Yahuda's Exchanges with Chester Beatty, and the Introduction of Arabic Rare Texts." In *A.S. Yahuda as Cultural Broker. Between Near Eastern Philology and the Manuscript Trade* (working title), edited by Stephanie Luescher, Marina Rustow and Samuel Thrope. Forthcoming.

Ciotti, Giovanni, Michael Kohs, Eva Wilden and Hanna Wimmer. *Definition of Paracontent*, CSMC Occasional Paper No. 6, Hamburg, 2018.

Conermann, Stephan and Michael Kemper. *The Heritage of Soviet Oriental Studies*. Abingdon, Oxfordshire, 2011.

Conrad, Lawrence I. "The Khalidi Library." In *Ottoman Jerusalem: The Living City: 1517–1917*, edited by Sylvia Auld and Robert Hillenbrand, 191–209. London, 2000.

Conrad, Lawrence I. "Ibn Aʿtham and His History." *al-ʿUṣūr al-Wusṭā* 23 (2015): 87–125

Al-Dajānī, Aḥmad Zakī. *Madīnat Yāfā fī dhākirat al-taʾrīkh*. N.p., n.d.

Darrāj, Aḥmad. *L'Acte de waqf de Barsbay* (*Ḥujjat waqf Barsbay*). Cairo, 1963.

Davidson, Garret. "On the History of the Princeton University Library Collection of Islamic Manuscripts." *Journal of Islamic Manuscripts* 13 (2022): 421–479.

D'hulster, Kristof. *Browsing through the Sultan's Bookshelves. Towards a Reconstruction of the Library of the Mamluk Sultan Qāniṣawh al-Ghawrī* (*r.* *906–922/1501–1516*). Göttingen, 2021. Dussaud, René. "Rapport à M. le Secrétaire perpétuel sur une mission dans le désert de Syrie." *Comptes rendus des séances de*

130 See for instance Jefferson, "Trade in Cairo Genizah fragments"; Peter Tarras. "A Blog Dedicated to the Dispersed Manuscript Heritage of Saint Catherine's Monastery", April 2023 https://medisi.hypotheses.org/5 (accessed 1 September 2023).

131 Erbay/Hirschler, "Middle Eastern Agency".

l'Académie des Inscriptions et Belles-Lettres Année 46, no. 3 (1902): 251–264.

Dussaud, René. "Missions de la Ville de Paris." *Annuaires de l'École pratique des hautes études* (1902): 90–111.

El Shamsy, Ahmed. *Rediscovering the Islamic Classics. How Editors and Print Culture Transformed an Intellectual Tradition*. Princeton, 2020.

Erbay, Cüneyd and Konrad Hirschler. "Writing Middle Eastern Agency into the History of the Qubbat al-khazna. The Late Ottoman State and Manuscripts as Historical Artefacts." In *The Damascus Fragments: Towards a History of the Qubbat al-khazna Corpus of Manuscripts and Documents*, edited by Arianna D'Ottone Rambach, Konrad Hirschler and Ronny Vollandt, 151–178. Beirut, 2020.

Ghosheh, Mohammad H. *Encyclopædia Palestinnica*, vol. 16: *Manuscripts and libraries in Palestine (1516–1918)*. Amman, 2019.

Al-Ḥabbāl, Muḥammad b. Maḥmūd. *Barnāmaj al-Maktaba al-Khālidiyya al-ʿumūmiyya*. Jerusalem, 1900.

Ḥamāda, Jalāl Muḥammad. *ʿĀshiq al-kutub. Aḥmad Khayrī Bek, sīrat shakhṣ wa-masīrat maktaba*. Amman, 2023.

Hirschler, Konrad. *Medieval Damascus: Plurality and Diversity in an Arabic Library. The Ashrafīya Library Catalogue*. Edinburgh, 2016.

Hirschler, Konrad. *A Monument to Medieval Syrian Book Culture. The Library of Ibn ʿAbd al-Hādī*. Edinburgh, 2020.

Ibn al-Zubayr al-Aswānī. *Umnīyat al-almaʿī wa-manīyat al-muddaʿī*. Edited by Ṭ. Al-Jazāʾirī. Jerusalem, 1900.

Al-Jazāʾirī, Ṭāhir. *Al-Tadhkira*. Damascus, National al-Asad Library, MS 11728.

Jefferson, Rebecca J.W. "The Trade in Cairo Genizah Fragments in and out of Palestine in the Late 19th and Early 20th Centuries." *Journal of Ancient Judaism* 14 (2023): 1–30.

Khālidī, Walīd. *al-Maktaba al-Khālidiyya fī al-Quds: 1720–2001*. Beirut, 2002.

Kurd ʿAlī, Muḥammad. "Baḍʿat ayyām fī al-Jalīl." *al-Muqtabas* 76 (1912): 373.

Liebrenz, Boris. *Die Rifāʿīya aus Damaskus. Eine Privatbibliothek im osmanischen Syrien und ihr kulturelles Umfeld*. Leiden, 2016.

Lorusso, Vito. *Searching for a Definition of "Manuscript"*. CSMC Occasional Paper no. 1, 2015. http://doi.org/10.25592/uhhfdm.9796.

Mannāʿ, ʿĀdil. "al-Nukhba al-Maqdisiyya ʿulamāʾ al-madīna wa-aʿyānuhā." *Ḥawliyat al-Quds* 5 (2007): 5–46.

Mannāʿ, ʿĀdil. *Aʿlām Filasṭīn fī awākhir al-ʿahd al-ʿuthmānī, 1800–1918*. Beirut, 1995.

Meryon, Charles Lewis. *Travels of Lady Hester Stanhope*. 2 vols. London, 1846.

Al-Mubayyaḍ, Salīm ʿArafāt, Muḥammad Khālid Kullāb. *Maktabat al-Jāmiʿ al-ʿUmarī al-Kabīr bi-madīnat Ghazza*. Amman 2013.

Muḥaybish, Ghassān. "Mujammaʿ al-Jazzār al-khayrī fī ʿAkkā." unpubl. MA thesis, al-Quds University, 1996.

Muḥaybish, Ghasān. "*Al-Madrasa al-Aḥmadiyya wa-al-maktaba al-Aḥmadiyya fī ʿAkkā*." In *Aḥmad Pāshā al-Jazzār. 200 ʿām ʿalā wafātihi*, edited by Shukrī ʿArrāf and Yaʿqūb Ḥijāzī, 170–776, ʿAkkā, 2004.

Mukhliṣ, ʿAbd Allāh. "Kitāb Rawḍat al-faṣāḥa." *Majallat al-Majmaʿ al-ʿIlmī al-ʿArabī* 22.9–10 (September 1947): 418–426.

Mukhliṣ, ʿAbd Allāh. "Kitāb Taḥrīr al-taḥbīr fī ʿilm al-badīʿ." *Majallat al-Majmaʿ al-ʿIlmī al-ʿArabī* 22.11–12 (October 1947): 524–531.

Mukhliṣ, ʿAbd Allāh. "Majmūʿat ashʿār." *Majallat al-Majmaʿ al-ʿIlmī al-ʿArabī* 21.11–12 (October 1946): 544–547.

Al-Munajjid, Ṣalāḥ al-Dīn. *al-Makhṭūṭāt al-ʿArabiyya fī Filasṭīn*. Beirut, 1982.

Al-Nabhanī, Yūsuf b. Ismāʿīl. *al-Sharaf al-muʿabbad li-Āl-Muḥammad ṣallā allāh alayhī wa-sallama*. 2015.

Pohl, Joh. *Führer durch die Bibliotheken Palästinas*. 1938.

Rauch, Christoph. "‚Im Wettkampfe mit den Bibliotheken anderer Nationen': Die Königliche Bibliothek zu Berlin und der Erwerb arabischer Handschriftensammlungen zwischen 1850 und 1900." In *Sammler—Bibliothekare—Forscher: Beiträge zur Geschichte der Orientalischen Sammlungen an der Staatsbibliothek zu Berlin*, edited by Sabine Mangold-Will, Christoph Rauch and Siegfried Schmitt, 87–150. Frankfurt/M., 2022.

Al-Rayḥānī, Amīn. *Al-Nakabāt. Khulāṣat taʾrīkh Sūriyya mundhu al-ʿahd al-awwal baʿd al-ṭūfān ilā ʿahd al-jumhūriyya bi-Lubnān*. Beirut, 1948.

Sayyid, A.F. *Dār al-Kutub al-Miṣrīya: ta'rīkhuhā wa-taṭawwuruhā*, Cairo, 1996.

Schwartz, Kathryn. "An Eastern Scholar's Engagement with the European Study of the East: Amin al-Madani and the Sixth Oriental Congress Leiden, 1883." In *The Muslim Reception of European Orientalism: Reversing the Gaze*, edited by Susanah Heschel and Umar Ryad, 39–60. Philadelphia, 2020.

Ṭarrāzī, Fīlīb Dī. *Tārīkh al-ṣaḥāfa al-ʿarabīya*. Beirut, 1913.

Ṭarrāzī, Fīlīb Dī. *Khazā'in al-kutub al-ʿarabiyya fī al-khāfiqayn*, Beirut, 1947–1951.

Ullmann, Manfred. *Die Natur- und Geheimwissenschaften im Islam*, Leiden, 1972.

Wallach, Yair. *A City in Fragments. Urban Text in Modern Jerusalem*. Stanford, CA, 2020.

Al-Wāsiṭī, Muḥammad b. Aḥmad. *Faḍā'il al-Bayt al-Muqaddas*. Edited by Isaac Hasson. Jerusalem, 1979.

Al-Wāsiṭī, Muḥammad b. Aḥmad. *Faḍā'il al-Bayt al-Muqaddas*. Edited by Abū al-Munzir. Nicosia, 2010.

Yūsuf Ḥasan, Aḥmad. "al-Madrasa al-Aḥmadiyya fī ʿAkkā." *al-Muntadī* 1 (1943): 16.

Zaydān, Jurjī. *Tārīkh ādāb al-lugha al-ʿarabīya*. Cairo, 1911–1914.

PART 2

The Materiality of al-Jazzār's Manuscripts

CHAPTER 8

Notes on Materials: How Brief Descriptions Indicate Substantial Losses

Karin Scheper

One of the marvels of the library inventory of Aḥmad Pasha al-Jazzār's library is the consistent inclusion of remarks on the physical appearance of the manuscripts. The entries include notes on whether the volumes are bound (most of them are), what formats the manuscripts have (the large majority falls in the 'quarter' category, a size after 'full' and 'half' and before 'eighth'), and there is often a remark on the type or colour of the leather, or the presence of gold in the decoration. In addition, the inventory states which volumes had a protective enclosure: *ẓarf*, a slipcase. Compared to today's standard cataloguing, this is more information than anyone could expect.[1] Compared with other inventories of manuscript libraries of the time, the extent of material information provided is also noteworthy, although brief physical descriptions are not uncommon. For reasons of recognition or more precise identification, it was necessary to note the physical appearance of a volume in such a manner that two similar titles could be distinguished from each other.[2] The level of detail in the inventory, however, is exceptional, and the recording of the presence or absence of the slipcase is remarkable. No other historical inventories are known in which the protective enclosures are recorded.

The generous provision of all this information can be studied in two ways. We can aim to understand the exact usage of the inventory at the time; the book list served a purpose, and these entries fulfilled a requirement.[3] We can also compare the notes on materiality with the physical characteristics of the surviving volumes that have been identified in the various collections. When two entries, for example, with similar titles match with one specific volume, the material specifics might help to exclude one or the other. The additional benefit of this approach is that, with the help of the physical items, we may answer questions about the meaning and translation of certain terms. Language is a fluid system, characterised by local variants, and historical terminology to describe objects has proven to be exceptionally diverse and untidy. We may question the clarity and usefulness of the terms used; it is, therefore, good to keep in mind that the material descriptions were not written for us. The notes must have had a clear meaning at the time, and the terminology chosen must have sufficed for the inventory's purpose. They were never meant to be meaningful to a wide audience 200 years after the inventory's compilation. Therefore, some terms seem vague to us without context, and we cannot fully understand the original meaning or value of these descriptions. Exploring the material descriptions in relation to the physical volumes in our corpus, thus, helps us to understand the language. This understanding, in turn, may help us to comprehend how the inventory functioned.

1 Nowadays, the focus on bibliographical details is prevalent, and item-specific details concerning the materiality are often lacking. This is especially true for historical enclosures, which apparently are not often considered to be part of the item and may go unrecorded. Practices vary between institutions.

2 Erünsal, *A History of Ottoman Libraries*, 143–154.

3 See Chapter 2 (Aljoumani, *Bibliographical Practices*).

DOI:10.1163/9789004720527_010

Exploring the material features of the volumes in our corpus is also an end in itself. The physical characteristics of manuscripts tell a story of their making and use, of how they were valued and how perhaps our perception of what is of value changes over time. These individual stories may not necessarily have much to say about the library in al-Jazzār's time or answer questions about the dispersion of the books. On the other hand, characteristics might be identified (such as a specific type of repair material) that can possibly help to ascertain the identity of yet unknown al-Jazzār manuscripts. In any case, highlighting certain observations and findings will illustrate how we may need features or components that are easily overlooked, to get a better understanding of the full story. This chapter focuses on the material aspects of the manuscripts identified that could be accessed either digitally or physically.[4] In doing so, it also makes visible what we have lost.

1 Some Thoughts on the Physical Location

The Jazzār library was, of course, an actual place that could be visited and where the books would be retrieved from their shelves, cabinets or other storage spaces when they were needed. We have no documents on how exactly this was arranged, or how the manuscripts were stored. However, the inventory is organised by subject, and this suggests that the physical collection was also divided into subject categories, as this would certainly ease the use of the library. Since the inventory also mentions the volumes' formats, would the librarian then further have arranged the manuscripts according to their formats, as a practical subdivision, when he placed the volumes? If the inventory represents the physical reality, this does not seem to be the case. In the list, the largest, 'full formats' are not necessarily found at the beginning of the entries under a new subject heading, and the four different formats appear haphazardly throughout the inventory. Even when we think of the inventory as a description of a collection at a certain point in time, which began to be assembled a few decades previously and must have accumulated volumes in different sizes, then the list does not indicate that the first acquisitions were arranged according to formats within the different subject categories. However, we cannot be sure that the inventory represents the physical order of the collection in the library.

Pictorial evidence suggests that at the time the Jazzār library was built and stocked, most manuscript collections in the Middle East were still stored horizontally, usually with either head or tail of the volumes towards the room.[5] There is no reason to assume that things were any different with this particular collection. It usually meant that several volumes were stacked on top of each other, and that items that needed to be retrieved had to be identified by an abbreviated title or author's name on the head or tail edge of the textblock, written in ink.[6] Or, alternatively, as the same pictorial evidence shows, the title could be written on a paper label pasted onto the short end of the slipcase in which the manuscript was kept.[7] Slipcases, thus, seem to have had two functions. The first and most important was their protective capacity, the second was their practical ability to easily be the carrier of the manuscript's identifier.

4 I am grateful for all the observations made and images and notes taken by the team members who accessed certain items in person. Special thanks to colleagues who answered some of my queries by accessing the items in their institutions: Annabel Teh Gallop, Daniël Lowe, Sam Thrope, Vincent Engelhardt, Kristine Rose Beers.

5 See, for example, D'Ohsson, *Tableau Général de l'Empire Othoman*, Plate 39.

6 This tradition-specific phenomenon explains why the spines of bound manuscripts in the Islamic world are not embellished nor provided with titles or other indications of the content.

7 In a study on the use and development of slipcases, the term 'cartouche' was used for this paper label as it was usually decoratively cut into the shape of a scroll or oval. Plummer et al., "Between Bag and Box", 495, 498. An abundance of surviving slipcases illustrates the practice of using cartouche labels on the closing flap.

FIGURE 8.1 Leiden University Library Or. 1350 II. Dated 1238 AH/1823 CE, copied in Tunis. A full leather slipcase contemporary with the manuscript it protects, *Kitāb al-ʿIbar*, volume II, by ʿAbd al-Raḥmān b. Muḥammad Ibn Khaldūn

The tradition of keeping valuable manuscripts within a protective enclosure has a long history in the Islamic world. Documentary sources as early as the eleventh and thirteenth century mention the use of chests for Qur'ans, and the making of 'sleeve-cases' and boxes.[8] We can see the use of bags, presumably made of textile, in manuscript paintings dating to the late fifteenth century.[9] The tradition continued into the nineteenth century, although the type of enclosures developed and changed over the centuries and regions. The slipcase became the predominant type of enclosure in the Ottoman world. They were custom-made for a volume, ensuring a perfect fit and optimal economic use of storage space. We do not know who exactly made these slipcases. There may have been specialised craftsmen, but they may also have been produced by bookbinders. The materials that constitute a slipcase—pasteboard, leather and decorated paper, sometimes cloth—are similar to the materials used to bind books, and there are several examples of bound volumes with associated slipcases of similar design and materials, which surely suggests contemporary production in one and the same workshop.[10] However, many slipcases were made to protect already existing manuscripts, often much older than the enclosure itself. In theory, it is feasible that a slipcase-maker visited the collection venue, measured the manuscripts in situ, then conducted his slipcase-making business in his workshop. The cartouche labels probably re-

8 Gacek, "Arabic bookmaking and terminology"; part 16 and 17 of 20 unnumbered chapters concern the making of sleeve-cases and boxes, 106, 110; Gacek, *Arabic Manuscripts*, 254–255.

9 Scheper, "Bindings, Bags and Boxes", 147–148.

10 Plummer et al., "Between Bag and Box", 515.

mained blank for the librarian to fill in. This means that the loss of the Jazzār slipcases is another piece of lost information: it would have been interesting to examine the hand and the ink(s) in which these titles were copied. Would this have been the same for most manuscripts? And how would these titles compare to the inventory entries?

A question that remains unanswered but may be connected to the layout of the library and manner of storage of the physical items is why the inventory has no slipcases listed for the manuscripts in the Qur'an section. While not all the manuscripts in the other sections necessarily have a slipcase, many of the entries actually make mention of the absence of a slipcase when a manuscript goes without. The omission of any reference to a protective container for the Qur'an manuscripts, whether present or absent, is, therefore, noteworthy and appears to be intentional. This is especially remarkable since it has been stated that

> In the Ottoman world, small-format Qur'ans were provided with 'a close-fitting envelope made from two pieces of paper pasteboard lined with leather and held together on three sides by cloth accordion gusset; a fore-edge flap [...] allowed the box to be sealed shut once the manuscript was replaced, and a cloth pull was fixed inside the case so that it could be slid out easily'.[11]

However, it is possible that the library was furnished with Qur'an cabinets, or chests, that could be locked and may have been the preferred choice of storage—a solution not uncommon in Ottoman times.[12] The use of such specially made storage space would explain the absence of slipcases, because the Qur'ans would then have no use for them.

11 Gacek, *Arabic Manuscripts*, 50. Gacek quotes François Déroche, whose description clearly points to a slipcase, although 'cloth' should be leather, and the term 'gusset' is what we (Plummer et al.) have called side-and-bottom strip in our slipcase terminology.

12 Gacek, *Arabic Manuscripts*, 254–255.

2 Historical Terminology and Its Use

A broadly accepted vocabulary is a necessary tool to talk, or write, about manuscripts in a meaningful way. Although we may (or may not) agree on terminology in the current codicological field, when we work with historical sources, we realise that the vocabulary does not conform to the accepted terminology. The terms used will have to be interpreted and explained, and we often only have tentative explanations—more studies may be needed to confirm or disprove these interpretations. When we examine the Jazzār inventory, descriptions seem cursory and not very descriptive at all. The obvious conclusion is that these notes on the materiality are not intended as stylistic descriptions, they do not classify the volumes. It is noteworthy that subjective qualifications such as 'beautiful', 'costly' or 'high quality' are lacking. In a similar vein, we find no references to specific cultural origins. In fact, most of the bindings are not actually described. Only a small percentage have distinctive features mentioned, such as 'gilded' or gold-tooling, a colour (green or red) or a specific type of skin ('Egyptian leather'). The qualification 'old' may describe either the textblock or the binding. While we accept that these descriptions were meaningful and, therefore, that those bindings are somehow noteworthy and stand out from the rest of the collection, it is difficult to understand what these indicators mean exactly. Unfortunately, the number of surviving bindings in our corpus of identified manuscripts is small, relative to the total, and none of these belongs to the select group of explicitly mentioned bound volumes.

Since the description of bindings is not very elaborate and explicit descriptions are used sparingly, we may wonder how these brief notations were useful. They will not have been used to locate a volume; you do not go looking for a green leather binding when only two such bindings occur in a collection of about 1800 items. Instead, these descriptions will have served to identify the items during regular checks of stock and completeness of the collections. More specifically, as the more notable items may have represented a certain value, such descriptions could help prevent the replacement of these items by a similar text, yet bound in a more modest, cheaper binding. An early example of this fraudulent practice occurred in 1560.[13] Records show that a practice developed in which libraries created inventories that described the appearance of each volume, including the paper type or colour, and binding, for reasons of identifying the volumes.[14]

3 Formats, in Theory and Practice

With some exceptions, the formats of the books are consistently included. The large majority of the manuscripts, nearly 70 per cent, has a so-called 'quarter format', the third size of the categories. Fewer than a tenth of all entries is 'full format', and an equally small group is 'eighth format', which indicates they are the smallest size. The remaining volumes are in between the quarter and largest format, so-called 'half'. When we compare these qualifications with the physical manuscripts that could be measured, we can equate 'full format' to an average of 29.7×19.8 cm; 'half format' equates to 24.7×16.7, 'quarter format' to 21.1×14.9, and the smallest format, denoted as 'eighth', measures 18.0×13.5 cm.

Apart from the categories 'full', 'half', 'quarter' and 'eighth', additional remarks were used to denote item-specific qualities. Of course, terms such as 'broad', 'long' or 'elongated' are always subjective. They depend on a specific collection or the reference framework of the given individual who uses the qualification, and they merely indicate a characteristic deviation from the most common, the norm, the ordinary. 'Broad', thus, means broader than average, or than expected, although it remains unclear what the ratio of the exception is when this is not specified. As a result, we cannot be certain what these qualifications signify. They denote, we must assume, a divergent format significant enough to help identify this volume. In order to understand the meaning of the qualifications used at the time, and in the context of al-Jazzār's library, we have to return to the corpus of identified manuscripts. Unfortunately, as we will see below, the limited number of manuscripts does not provide much explanation.

A first case in point is the term 'broad'. While fifty manuscripts in the inventory are described as broad, only one item is described as such in our corpus. It concerns Chester Beatty Ar. 3334 (#492), described as 'broad' quarter format. Since we cannot study several 'broad' manuscripts comparatively, for lack of multiple specimens, we will have to compare the format with the 'average' to understand 'broad'. One way to make this comparison is to use the ratio of width to height. Our four standard groups have ratios varying between 0.66 and 0.75. The physical 'broad' manuscript, Chester Beatty Ar. 3334, measures 24.5×16.5 cm, which gives a ratio of 0.67, which is, therefore, not out of the ordinary and renders the qualification puzzling. In fact, the measurements are very close to the average size of a half format. Why then was it qualified as a quarter? The ratio of a textblock format, however, could change with rebinding, when a textblock could be trimmed to smoothen and even out its edges. Although this textblock was rebound, presumably after its transfer to the Chester Beatty Library (CBL), the material evidence indicates that the treatment did not include trimming, as the textblock edges remain tattered and, most importantly, the prominently rounded corners bare clear signs of extensive use. Could the qualification 'broad' perhaps relate to the text panel, which is, indeed, taking up much space on the page, leaving only a small fore-edge margin, certainly in comparison with many other manuscripts? Without other items with which to compare this theory that could shed light on the meaning of 'broad', it is impossible to verify the rationale for this term. The other deviating format, 'long', is found in many of the subcategories of the

13 Erünsal, *A History of Ottoman Libraries*, 139.
14 Ibid., 143–154.

inventory and occurs 34 times, yet none of these entries matches the manuscripts in our corpus.

The group 'non-standard' in the inventory is exceptionally large with 198 counts (which in itself can be questioned), and is also well-represented, by nine or ten manuscripts, in our corpus. How does 'non-standard' deviate from 'long' and 'broad' as used in the inventory? When we tentatively set the 'standard' ratio between 0.66 and 0.75, and consider the volumes that are denoted as 'non-standard', there are only two items that fall outside those standard measures. The most prominent is Shinqit, Mauritania, MS 9/96 (either #816 or #828).[15] We do not have images of this manuscript but the volume measures 24×13 cm, which gives a ratio of 0.54. The other one is Chester Beatty Ar. 3316 (#438), whose format equates with 0.55. This means that both these manuscripts are more elongated than average, so, one of the questions is: why are they not denoted as 'long format' instead? And how are the other manuscripts different from the standard when the ratio meets the requirements? Perhaps the 'non-standard' should be explained as the manuscript falling somewhere between the half and the quarter categories. We currently have too few manuscripts to work with and analyse the data.

Let us also briefly consider the paper used to copy these manuscripts. It is perhaps too often thought that the paper substrate can be a key to unlock the secrets. Yet, though it is certainly useful to examine the paper for individual manuscript studies, because it may provide a time frame in which the paper was made or point to a region where it was produced, it can hardly ever do much more. The list of things we do not yet know about papermaking in the Islamic world, throughout the ages, and about the paper trade and distribution of European paper ever since the fourteenth century, is long. We find manuscripts on a wide variety of paper in a collection as mixed as the Jazzār library: on Islamic paper from well before the introduction of papermaking techniques in Europe, on paper from the Islamic world that coincides with European paper, and on European paper. We even find European paper from the industrial period in some of the manuscripts.

By contrast, the English terminology concerning book formats is based on the production of western printed books, printed solely on European paper. The terms 'folio', 'quarto' and 'octavo' refer to the number of times a full sheet of paper was folded to form a gathering, and, as a consequence of the folding, such gatherings have an even number of pages. These terms do not relate to the manuscript tradition, which is not only centuries older than the printing industry but also much more flexible when it comes to the composition of gatherings. Quinions, gatherings consisting of five bifolios, are most commonly encountered in the Islamic world.[16] There is no correlation between the manner in which the scribe assembled their paper (or parchment) sheets and compiled the necessary gatherings, and the processing of paper and producing gatherings in the world of printing that developed much later.

Although we cannot fully explain the indication of the formats 'full', 'half' and 'quarter' as used in the inventory, they do not seem to have a relationship to the way the original paper sheet was folded. If these terms indicated such a relationship, we would expect consistency in the position of the grain of the paper (the laid lines and chain lines) for each format. When the paper was folded only once for the 'full format', the laid lines would be horizontal, and the chain lines vertical—following the formation of the paper sheet on the mould. When the paper was folded once more, to form the 'half format', the laid lines should be vertical and the chain lines horizontal. The next 'quarter format' should have the laid lines horizontal again when it was formed by folding the 'half format' once more. However, the manuscripts show that

15 While #828 has 'non-standard' in its description, #816 does not, which may suggest that this is the more likely entry for this manuscript.

16 Déroche, *Islamic Codicology*, 84.

this is not consistently the case. The original paper size (formats could vary significantly, depending on the origin of the paper production and preferred size of the papermaker's mould), therefore, seems to bear no relation to the format indications per se. Mathematically, the measurements do not indicate such a relation either; the format categories are too close together to result from simple folding.

4 Notes on Material Characteristics in General

The Islamic bookbinding tradition developed over the first few centuries of Islam, into what became its archetypal format and structure as it was still used in the time of al-Jazzār, and long after that, in some regions well into the twentieth century. Perhaps the most important material innovation took place in the early centuries. The art of papermaking had dispersed from China along the Silk Roads and was introduced into the Middle East around 750, which had an enormous impact on manuscript making. Until then, texts were copied onto parchment, which was durable and beautiful, but difficult to obtain in large quantities of consistent quality. When paper became abundant, there was almost no limit to the number of manuscripts that could be produced. The typical Islamic book structure, with a relatively simple unsupported link-stitch sewing on two stations only, which contributed to the speed with which books could be produced, came into practice with the implementation of paper as a substrate. Parchment, a heavier and sturdier material that would respond to changes in temperature and humidity, had required a more intensive sewing method. Using paper also resulted in compact and lightweight textblocks that could sufficiently be protected with a binding made with paper-laminate pasteboards. Such bindings were covered in full leather, sometimes in part leather combined with costly textiles. Gradually, in the course of the fifteenth and sixteenth centuries, we see an increase of the partial leather binding when decorated papers started to be used as a covering material, as an economic substitute. Leather continued to be used for the flexible and heavily charged binding parts, such as the spine and fore-edge flap.

Regional and temporal variations in the tradition can be explained given the expanse of the Islamic world, yet, the bookbinding tradition was also remarkably consistent. The structure, in essence, never changed much, but region-specific materials and local variants of techniques or methods may characterise the appearance of manuscripts. Examples of identifiable features can be found in manuscripts from South-East and Central Asia, Indonesia, Yemen and North-Africa.[17] While the use of certain materials or cross-influences illustrate the spread of the craft, other practices remained fairly local and perhaps indicate a particularly isolated tradition. Since the study of developments in Islamic bookbinding techniques is relatively young, there are still many gaps in our knowledge of these developments, and every well-preserved manuscript collection may offer unique information about regional bookbinding practices, the availability of materials or users' preferences. We hoped that the manuscripts from the Jazzār library would provide such new insights.

However, we also know that a library such as this, assembled in a short period, will, out of necessity, include many older items from multiple regions, bound either in original bindings or previous rebindings, which themselves may derive from other locales than the textblocks. Such volumes contain regional-specific materials and were made according to fashions that cannot be explained by the period of the library's creation. The majority of the older volumes, therefore, will not inform us about the state of the bookbinding art at the end of the eighteenth century in Palestine.

17 Scheper, *Technique*, 69–78, 149–152, 353–358; Scheper/Vrolijk, "From the eyries of Yemen", 498–513; Rose-Beers et al., "Islamic Bindings", 37–44.

5 What Is Lost, What Has Survived?

So far as the actual manuscripts could be accessed and examined, either 'in the flesh' or from digitised images, we can verify that the number of traditional structures and bindings in the total corpus of al-Jazzār manuscripts identified is nineteen.[18] This does not yet mean that these bindings are the original ones, but they were certainly made by local craftsmen working in the classic tradition. A relatively high number of these, twelve, are still in the Middle East. Only seven volumes of the twenty-one al-Jazzār manuscripts that moved to European (or American and Japanese) libraries retained their local binding.[19] Five of these are in Princeton University Library, one is in Leipzig and one is in the CBL in Dublin.[20] Five manuscripts in the CBL have been resewn by western bookbinders who retained parts of the former binding; in this process, the books were given western structures.[21] Although these binders may have incorporated some of the original materials, the structures were thoroughly altered and changed into hybrid objects, no longer allowing the study of the traditional features. The remaining three manuscripts in the CBL,[22] the sixth volume in Princeton, and those in London and Berlin have been rebound by western bookbinders. It is important to note that these new, western bindings have boards that are larger than the original boards—Islamic bindings traditionally have boards flush with the textblock, unlike the European binding tradition in which the boards extend beyond the textblock edges. As a result, had slipcases been preserved, they would no longer have fitted these rebound (enlarged) items. This obviously made the slipcases redundant and their preservation unlikely.

There are another nine or ten of the fifty-two al-Jazzār manuscripts that remained in the Middle East, that appear to have a traditional binding, judging from what can currently be seen in the photographs, but we cannot be sure because the range of images does not include photographs of the exterior. This omission is understandable

18 The digitised copies vary in usefulness when it comes to material characteristics. I acknowledge the primal goal of digitisation: the accessibility of the text. However, it appears that often even basic features can hardly be deduced from good quality images made according to modern standards. The Princeton digital images, for example, display the manuscripts in individual pages. The gutters of the gatherings including the central spinefold are obscured, due to the imaging of the separate rectos and versos of the manuscript, which hampers the visibility of the sewing structure. Some institutions choose to photograph only one of the boards, or only the interior and not the exterior of the boards, or the back-board was imaged but not the fore-edge and envelope flap. The images presented in other institutions were cropped so much that the edges of the paper margins were no longer visible. This results in a decidedly unsatisfying image of the original manuscript that is bare of any clues as to its condition, binding and three-dimensionality. Some institutions present images of the edges of the textblock, which is commendable because then the endbands are included, and it is possible to see the thickness of the boards. This may seem trivial to some, but being able to distinguish between limp covers and solid pasteboard covers means a lot to material researchers like me.

19 The local binding may include local mends of both textblock and covering.

20 Princeton Garrett 2996Y, Garrett 3415Y, Garrett 3516Y, Garrett 3959Y, Garrett 4691Y (a much-repaired binding), Leipzig Vollers 118, CBL Ar. 3272 (with local repairs of spine and corners).

21 CBL Ar. 3236, Ar. 3268, Ar. 3294, Ar. 3310, Ar. 3316. Except for the latter, which has partial leather covers, probably dating to after the sixteenth century, it concerns full leather bindings that were contemporary to the fourteenth- and fifteenth-century manuscripts. Of these, Ar. 3268 is fairly well-preserved: the original boards and envelope flap were included in the new structure. As for the others, only the original, beautifully tooled leather parts that covered the outside boards were retained; these pieces were reattached to completely new boards.

22 Ar. 3334 and Ar. 3342 now have a plain library binding, while Ar. 3315, the *Fihrist* (*Kitāb al-fihrist lil-Nadīm*) was bound in a 'historicising' full leather binding with an envelope flap, with simple blind-tooling. It is unknown whether this new binding was inspired by the binding that this tenth-century manuscript had when it arrived in the CBL, or if it is a rather neutral version of the predominant binding type that the manuscript could have had.

from the point of view that the manuscript's importance is its textual content. From the point of view of those who want to understand the manuscripts in their historical context and as material objects, such an omission is certainly regrettable. The manuscripts that *can* be studied as material objects are in Cairo, Qatar, Beirut and Jerusalem. Some of these do not retain the binding they had in al-Jazzār's time, but were rebound in the late nineteenth or early twentieth century. One manuscript in the Jazzār Mosque belongs to this group of post-al-Jazzār bindings: (#902). This early rebinding led to the loss of a binding that contained marbled paper doublures, which can only just be gleaned from a few black and white images taken prior to that rebinding.[23] The most depressing news is that the other al-Jazzār manuscripts in Acre have only very recently been rebound, in 2008 and 2009. These manuscripts were digitised for the Endangered Archives Programme, run by the British Library, and the rebinding of these volumes is probably connected to this digitisation project.[24] It is extremely sad that a project aiming to preserve cultural heritage, as a by-product may lead to the substantial loss of material evidence of said cultural heritage.

None of the slipcases that, according to the inventory, accompanied the manuscripts seem to have survived.[25] As explained above, it seems logical that the slipcases for those manuscripts that were rebound in European-format binding structures with so-called square boards, larger than the original boards, were discarded. As slipcases were made to have a perfect fit, they lost their functionality with the rebinding process. They may have been repurposed for another book or other objects,[26] but the relation to the associated manuscript would be permanently lost, and the slipcases can be considered orphaned. It was not only the manuscripts that were traded to the west that were subjected to this fate of rebinding in European format, but also several manuscripts that were probably rebound in the early twentieth century, in Mecca, in the Khalidi library in Jerusalem, and the group of manuscripts in Acre that were very recently rebound. There is still a possibility that one of the slipcases belonging to the other manuscripts that remained in the Middle East surfaces at some point, for not all of the institutions involved have had the opportunity to search the shelves.

6 Manuscript Bindings, Local Repairs, and Traces of Use

Among the manuscripts that retained their original bindings are a few that date back to the fifteenth century. The manuscript in the library of the University Saint-Joseph, Beirut (#189), is not dated (other than described to date to 1500–1600), but the full leather binding has a decorative design made with small tools in a layout that very much resembles a binding in the Topkapı Palace Library, dating to 1480.[27] The binding is heavily repaired

23 Akka MS 64 (microfilm reproduction, probably early 1980s, held at the Center for Documents, Manuscripts and Bilad al-Sham Studies, University of Jordan, Amman).

24 Konrad Hirschler established that most manuscripts in Acre underwent this fate, including those not formerly part of the Jazzār collection. Documentation of their condition prior to rebinding seems to be lacking. A sparse reference is found in Abu Harb, "Digitisation of Islamic manuscripts", 396: 'The manuscripts are tightly bound and have been damaged through constant use.'

25 We do not know precisely what the number is because not all the manuscripts can be related to an entry in the inventory. Based on the entries that we have, thirty manuscripts had a slipcase, and seven manuscripts were described not to have a slipcase.

26 Five slipcases in the University of Cambridge Library, for example, no longer contain the original manuscript but were repurposed as a protective container for specimens of calligraphy, notes, letters and an oblong-shaped manuscript containing poetry; materials formerly belonging to the Swiss explorer John Lewis Burkhardt (1784–1817). University of Cambridge Library Add 274; Add 275; Add 276; Add 277; Add 281. See Plummer et al., "Between Bag and Box", 514.

27 Described by Raby/Tanındı. *Turkish Bookbinding in the 15th Century.*, 24–25.

FIGURE 8.2 CBL Ar. 3294. The rebound manuscript still has original components, such as the textile doublures and the largest part of the old, tooled leather covering, pasted onto new leather-covered boards

with leather strips on the spine and board edges, but the covering stems from the Mamluk tradition. Parts of the original leather covering were integrated in the new bindings in three bindings in the Chester Beatty CBL: Ar. 3294 (#276), dated 731/1331, CBL Ar. 3236 (#718), dated 856/1452, and CBL Ar. 3310 (#1148), undated but late eighth/fourteenth century. The tooling represents the liking for central designs, one with a lobbed circular ornament and another with a six-pointed star, and intricately tooled borders, with blind and gold-tooling. Ar. 3294 must once have been an especially stunning and special binding, as the original boards were lined with indigo blue and crème-coloured striped cloth (probably silk) doublures. Although we may assume that these doublures were the original ones, or at least the ones that lined the former original boards when the manuscript arrived in the Chester Beatty collection, the rebinding campaign and absence of sound documentation of that intervention render this manuscript a difficult object for material examination.

Other manuscripts have traces that point to a former binding from the Mamluk period, despite the absence of the original. The first example is Jerusalem NLI Ms. AP Ar. 290 (#416). At the back of the manuscript, we can see a brown geometric pattern in the last two leaves of the textblock, a mirror pattern caused by the block-stamped leather doublure that once covered the inside of the original binding. The manuscript dates to 775/1374, which could well fit with the date of that lost binding. The manuscript's current leather binding is a modest binding from the Ottoman period. Due to severe water damage and mechanical stress, the textblock is now loose in its cover and the leather has shrunk. A similar brownish pattern on the folio can be seen in Acre MS 21 EAP399/1/3, a manuscript dating to 833/1429. Despite the total loss of the former regional binding, this is a clear material trace of the manuscript's original binding, and the block-stamped leather doublures themselves point to Mamluk Egypt or Syria.[28]

28 These regions are most often mentioned, but block-stamped doublures are also found in manuscripts from the Persian-Turkish region, the Maghrib and South Arabia. Bosch, "Medieval Islamic Bookbinding", 221. Also see Otha, *Covering the Book*, 297–311.

Garrett 4691Y, a composite volume, shows the same phenomenon but in a more complex situation. The discoloration of the paper sheds light on the previous lives of the separate codicological entities. Folio 13^b, the reverse of the colophon of the volume's second text, has a mirror pattern of a block-stamped leather doublure, the feature associated with Mamluk bindings from the thirteenth to fifteenth centuries. The first folio of this text shows many paper patches and stains that do not match the condition of the preceding folio 4^b, the last page of the first text, nor does it reveal traces of a leather doublure, which may indicate that this text was formerly part of a different collective volume and had another preceding text, or it was a separate single entity and had a different material that did not leave stains or discolouration facing what is now folio 5^a. The third and fourth texts in this volume have distinctive traces of some sort of water damage, leaving a clear diagonal brown stain in the upper inner corner of each leaf from about folio 100 onwards. Remarkably, the fifth, thin text in this volume does not share this discoloured pattern with the previous text, yet, the two endleaves at the back of the volume do. This indicates that the fifth text was inserted or added to the volume after the calamity took place that caused the staining of the paper.[29] The pinkish paper lining the left board does not have the brown water stain either, suggesting that the binding—which shows multiple repairs and interventions—was applied after the current compilation of the manuscript. The binding itself shows so many patches of different materials that it is no longer possible to deduce which materials may have belonged to a former binding, or whether all layers were taken from different sources. The manner in which the leather pieces have been sewn onto the paper boards is not uncommon, but it is not a bookbinder's manner to bind a volume. Instead, this is a lovely example of domestic repair.

Princeton Garrett 3516Y represents a fine Ottoman binding, fully covered in a dark red goat leather with gold-tooling, and though the fore-edge and envelope flap are now missing, the damage to the small edge of the backboard is evidence of the former presence of these flaps. As the manuscript dates before 1786, this binding could well be its original, and textblock repairs could not be found. The silver flecked, greenish paper lining of the boards, and the marbled paper used as flyleaves conform to this dating as well.

Two other manuscripts with Ottoman bindings are the ones in Nablus. NL 211508 (#150) is in good condition. It has a full leather binding, with a central stamp and pendants that include paper onlays, that does not appear to have been tampered with. This binding is discussed below. The other, NL 250213 (#1291/1290), has paper repairs signifying resewing. This could mean that the partial leather binding is not the manuscript's first binding. The light blue cloth spine-lining, the yellow paper stubbed doublures and partial leather binding are exemplary of typical, relatively low-cost users' bindings.

The two manuscripts now in Qatar National Library, ANL00017150 and HC.MS.00211 (#1431) are well-preserved full leather bindings with a few interesting elements. Though the latter has to be a later binding, judging by the abundant paper repairs in the fold-lines, the former appears to be original to the textblock. The central and corner stamps with green paper onlays have a simplicity that resembles other bindings from the Arabian Peninsula. The block-printed decorative paper (in three colours) lining the boards may be an Italian paper.[30] Some of the other preserved manuscripts in our corpus are non-descriptive full

29 This physical change matches with a discrepancy between the 'table of content' on folio 1^b that lists a different text than the current *Kāfī ūlī al-ʿuqūl fī al-ḥādith*, and a sixth text on *Faḍāʾil* which is not present. Thanks to Konrad Hirschler for the textual clarification.

30 Block-printed papers were widely used and although it must be possible to retrace the use of specific designs to production in certain workshops, a lot of the research into the history of these papers still needs to be done.

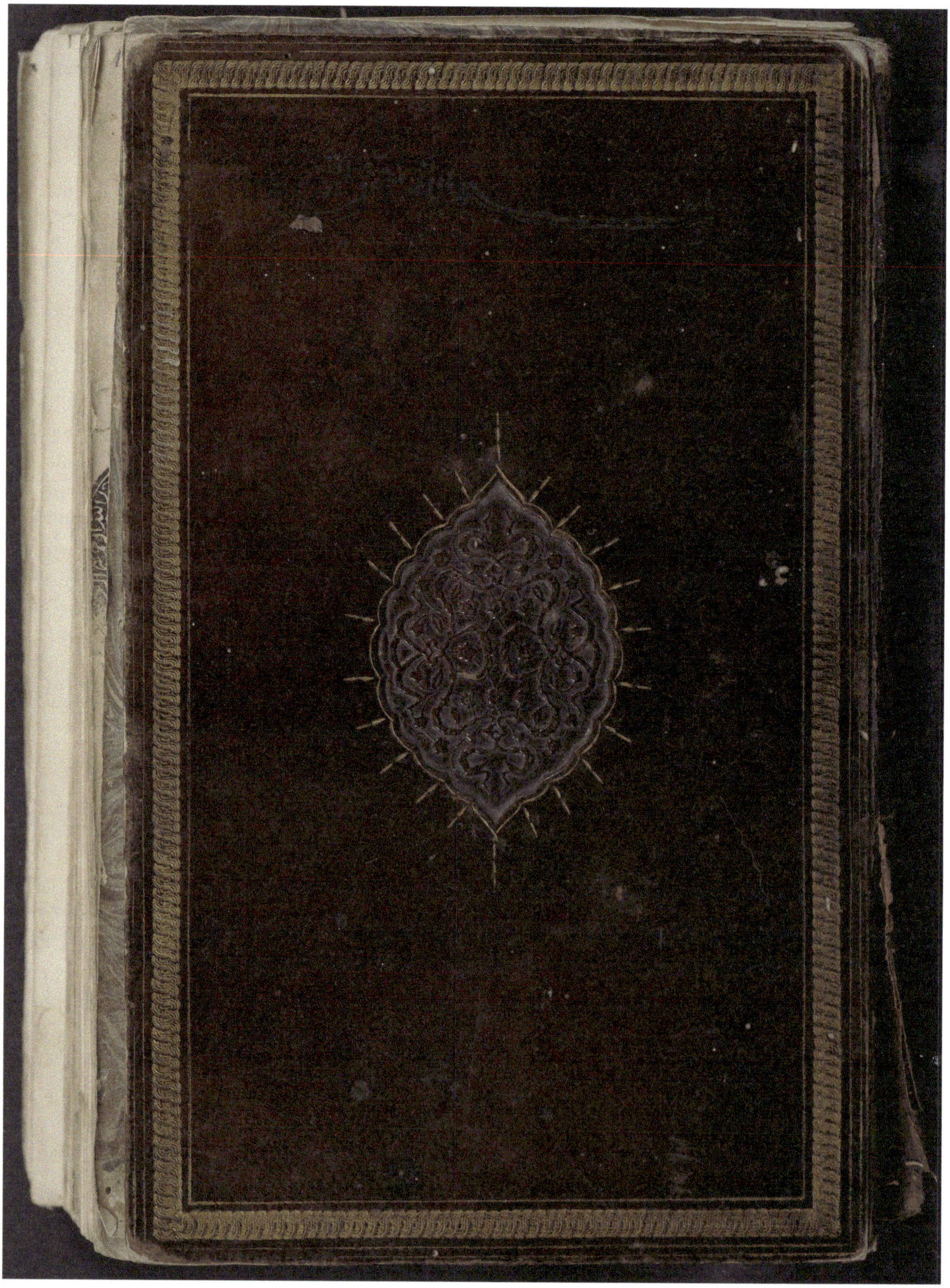

FIGURE 8.3 Princeton Garrett 3516Y, exterior. See fig. 8.7 for the binding's interior

FIGURE 8.4 Princeton Garrett 3959Y, textblock f. 76[a] and [b], with cut fold-ins indicating rebinding

leather or partial leather bindings. They lack specific decorative tooling or other remarkable features that can help to date or localise these volumes. Though rather useless for individual codicological study, these bindings represent an important part of the manuscript culture. Indeed, many manuscripts were made for owners with a small budget, or for libraries where usability and functionality were much more important than a fashionable binding.

Princeton Garrett 3959Y represents a specific bookbinder's practice from the Islamic world. In order to safeguard paratexts in the margins, bookbinders used to cut the paper perpendicular to the edge, so that the paper containing comments or annotations could be folded inwards. When the edges of the textblock then would be trimmed after sewing (with the aim to smooth the textblock's edges, especially for reused and resewn manuscripts) these bits of text would be preserved.

In this case, the combination of the manuscript's fine condition yet very wide fold-ins of the fore-edge, to spare or preserve annotations during the trimming of the textblock, are intriguing. The manuscripts' size is 20.0 × 11.9 cm. Given these dimensions and the measurements of the fold-ins, we can deduce that the width of the paper when the manuscript was copied must have been at least 14 cm. The widest fold-out/fold-in with paratext is about 3 cm wide (f. 76) and there are others: f. 18[a], f. 30 (though cut off). The manuscript dates to 1090/1679. The textblock is hardly damaged and may not have required repair, but the full leather binding has been provided with a new spine. Supposedly, damage to the original structure and spine warranted the rebinding, which then also instigated the trimming of the textblock. The question remains why the second bookbinder cut so much width off the textblock. What would a binder do with such wide strips of paper? He could certainly have found a good use for good-quality paper strips for paper repairs, or for the making of inner hinges. Another option—though we know very little of this practice from the Islamic world—is that off-cuts were sold to a paper maker.[31] The discoloration on f. 76 also very clearly shows the size/width of the envelope flap, which must have been tucked in there for some time. The width of the present envelope flap corresponds with the discoloration, the slightly wider outer flap hinge gives the flap the flexibility to be tucked in at this position, perhaps marking the marginal annotation.[32]

The Princeton manuscript Garrett 2996Y gives us some insight into the frequency of use and subsequent mechanical damage of a manuscript. It is a composite volume, consisting of five texts that date to 1125–1126/1713–1714. The first letter of the *waqf* statement on f. 1ª, which is dated 1197/1783, is copied onto a paper repair strip in the spine-fold, close to the upper edge and no doubt meant to strengthen the paper where it was damaged from a previous primary endband sewing. This repair strip was needed to allow the sewing of a new endband structure. The binding also shows signs of repair; the paper covering of the board panels is pasted over other leather—presumably the former full leather boards. This indicates that the repair and resewing of this manuscript was required when the manuscript was merely 70 years old.

7 Remarkable Decorative Papers

One of the materials used in a volume now in Nablus, NL 211508 (#150) that may give a lead is a small strip of paper used to cover the manuscript's inner joints. The use of paper as a hinge between the textblock and the inner boards is nothing special in itself, nor is the fact that a decorative paper was used for the purpose. In some cases, the decorative papers can be a clue for dating the making or repair of a manuscript, although the use of such papers was widespread, and the history of their making is not neatly recorded. In our case, the type of decorated paper is very specific: a silver paint was used to stamp a pattern on a monochrome dyed paper surface. It is a rather inconspicuous material and could easily be mistaken for a sprinkled or dirty paper, especially given its small size in the current manuscript. However, it is an uncommon type of paper; marbled papers, sprinkled papers (as used for the flyleaf of Nablus UL NL 211508) or block-printed papers were much more common. Because of this, the presence of this type of decorated paper caught my eye during the survey I conducted in the Leiden University oriental collection. Ten manuscripts have been identified for which similar paper was used. None of these is exactly the same, but the similarities are too obvious to not think that these papers were made in the same workshop or locality. The paper in the volume now in Nablus has its silver pattern stamped on a yellow-orange ground, the papers in the volumes in Leiden use pink, a petrol-blue and yellow surfaces. Various patterns of the block-stamped decoration were used, most are geometric, one has a flowing floral pattern.

Three manuscripts in this 'set' arrived in the library around 1970, and unfortunately their origin cannot be verified.[33] The other seven belong to a group of manuscripts which arrived in the

31 For western handmade paper production this is a known custom; paper could be repulped.

32 It has been suggested that the flap was commonly used as a reading aid, but this is not confirmed by material evidence. The joints are often small, and the rigid fore-edge flap covers the width of the textblock. This then prevented the placement of the envelope flap anywhere but under the front board. In this manner, the fore-edge and envelope flap fulfil their primal function: they protect the textblock from dust and dirt and keep the volume closed.

33 It concerns UBL Or. 11.938 and UBL Or. 12.105, manuscripts said to originate from private collections in Anatolia, and UBL Or. 14.098, purchased from an Iraqi scholar, without notes on provenance.

FIGURE 8.5 Leiden University Library Or. 1516 and Or. 1520. Two examples of silver stamped decorated papers, similar to the inner joints covered with silver stamped paper in NL 211508

library in April 1839, as part of the Testa collection.[34] Which member of the Testa family exactly assembled the collection is not known, and it is not certain where the Arabic and Turkish manuscripts were collected.[35] The arrival date, nonetheless, may be significant. The manuscripts themselves date to various periods, stretching several centuries, yet the bindings display remarkable similarities and characteristics, and they all appear to have been made around the same time, in the same workshop.[36] It is feasible that Testa upon purchasing the manuscripts had them rebound by a local bookbinder, thus, physically and materially uniting these very diverse manuscripts. This suggests the availability of this type of decorative paper in the first few decades of the nineteenth century. It is also important to note that I have not seen this decorated paper used in other books than the Middle Eastern volumes mentioned above. It places the making of Nablus UL NL 211508 around the time of the Jazzār library.

Another example that includes a small piece of a very specific decorative paper is Leipzig Vollers 118 (#212). The manuscript dates to 972/1565, but the stratification of paper repairs in the gatherings indicate that it was resewn at least once. The manuscript has a trajectory of private ownership after leaving Acre, and it is probable that its current appearance is due to an intervention during that period. The flyleaves appear to consist of a machine-made dyed paper, the endbands and overall structure are clearly traditional, as are the local paper repairs. The current binding may actually date to the period around when this manuscript was acquired in Damascus, 1853. The decorated paper (not mentioned in the Leipzig catalogue or in the inventory)—seems to belong to a second rebinding campaign (there are two layers of paper repairs in the spine-folds, plus traces of a former sewing, with a shorter link-stitch thread in fold-line than the current sewing, located between folios 16 and 17). Had this decorative paper occurred in other al-Jazzār manuscripts, then the rebinding could have been retraced to Acre and an earlier date.

34 Witkam, *Inventory of the Oriental Manuscripts*, II, 162–163. UBL Or. 1516, Or. 1520, Or. 1524, Or. 1529, Or. 1530, Or. 1538, Or. 1546. The total collection was registered in 1837 and in April 1839, containing 83 manuscripts.

35 Schmidt, *Catalogue*, 80–81. Schmidt suggests Syria as the origin of the collection.

36 Apart from the decorated paper and the blank paper lining the boards, a remarkable feature can be found in the inside of the boards. There is a 'ghost stamp' in the shape of a mandorla in these boards that points to the reuse of pasteboards. These boards appear to have been stripped of the original (leather) covering material and were then used inside out.

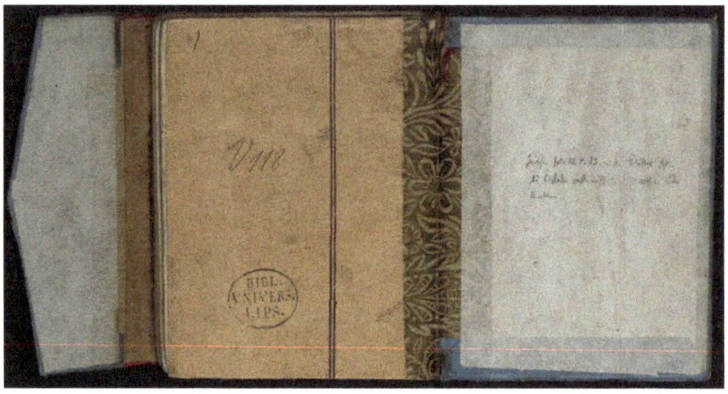

FIGURE 8.6
Leipzig Vollers 118, inner joint showing a distinctive decorative paper

8 Other Traces of a Post-al-Jazzār Time

One of the manuscripts, now in the Jerusalem AP section, NLI-MsAP Ar 177 (#1493), has traces of use that date from after leaving the Jazzār library. The manuscript 'entered the ownership of Ḥusayn Ṭāhā al-Dāwūdī on the 15th Ramadan 1290 [1873]'.[37] The current appearance of the volume shows a fairly modern machine-made paper and a leather rebacking, over boards that were formerly covered in full leather, and of which the front board shows a remarkable set of vertical holes along the long sides. These holes were clearly made intentionally but not for the purpose of a rebinding; they signal the pasteboard's previous function as a *misṭara*—a ruling board. Since these manuscripts in the AP section have received little attention and treatment so far, we can be certain that the paper covering and leather rebacking were added to this volume before 1948, but, given the nature of the materials, surely after 1880 or thereabouts, when it entered the ownership of Ḥusayn Ṭāhā al-Dāwūdī. The question remains when the ruling-board became part of the binding. Did this happen in Acre? Or even well before the manuscript was added to the Jazzār library?

Equally interesting is NLI-Ms AP Ar 258 (#215), at first glance a very modestly bound volume, with a dark red leather spine with traditional tabbed ends at the head and tail,[38] and a brownish paper covering the boards and their edges. The boards are lined with stubbed blue paper doublures. Upon closer examination it is, however, clear that the binding was quite possibly once a full leather binding with gold decoration along the edges of the board. Remnants of this gold painting or tooling are only just visible below the damaged paper covering.[39] It remains a possibility that a set of boards, once belonging to a different manuscript, were repurposed to fit NLI-MsAp Ar 258, but it is equally feasible that the current binding, with its new leather spine, paper covering and damages actually reveal the original appearance of this item. The quite prominent paper repairs as well as the new-looking endbands probably date to the rebinding. Though these endbands with a chevron pattern were made in the traditional manner, it is noteworthy that the endband at the head is made with red and pale-yellow threads, whereas the tail shows a green and pale-yellow chevron. Did the binder-repairer run out of one of these colours? Did he not mind? Given the condition of the paper repairs and these endbands, it seems likely that the intervention dates to the pe-

37 See Chapter 7 (Hirschler, *Translocations*).

38 The extending leather at head and tail of the spine is a characteristic feature of Islamic bookbinding, see Scheper, *Technique*, 106V11.

39 I am grateful that Konrad Hirschler was granted the opportunity to take multiple images of the manuscript as an object, which provided more information than the standard digital images of this volume could.

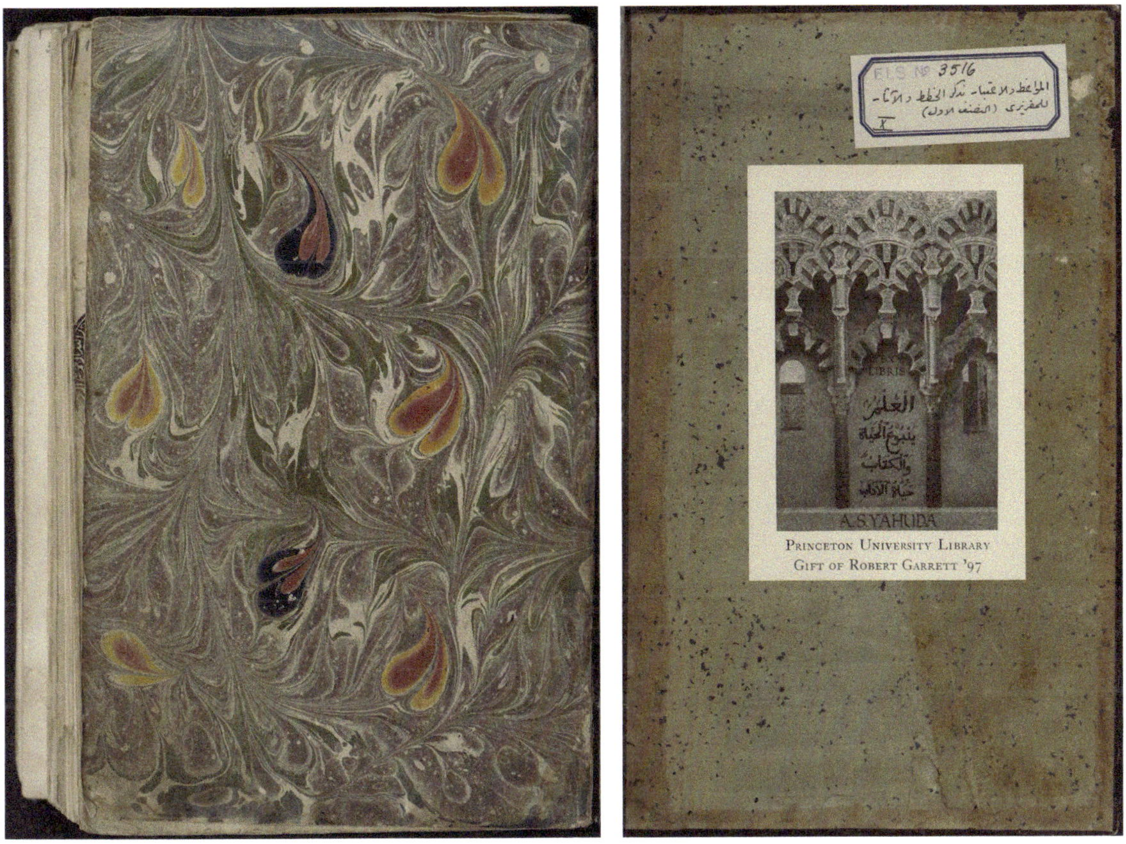

FIGURE 8.7 Princeton Garrett 3516Y, interior with silver flecked greenish paper lining and flyleaf with marbled paper

riod when the manuscript was in the possession of the Dajānī family; ʿAbd al-Qādir's seal is dated 1268/1851–1852.[40]

9 Insect Damage and Slipcases, Again

One aspect that catches the eye when examining the items in our corpus is the profound insect damage to some of the manuscripts. The damage to the manuscripts that remained in Palestine are most prominent. Other items, now housed elsewhere, show that the infestation did not necessarily take place during their time in the Jazzār library. Garrett 3516Y, for example, an attractive volume, with Ottoman marbled paper flyleaves and silver flecked, greenish-blue dyed paper lining the boards, is an almost pristine copy—it has some water stains in the lower margin but no insect damage, neither to the textblock nor to the binding. This specimen also shows no traces of local mends. The mild water damage could have occurred anywhere, and it is significant, it seems, that the volume left the Middle East without biological damage.

An even more striking example may be Ms. AP Ar. 410, dated 762/1361. It has only a few traces of worm holes in the middle of the manuscript (around ff. 70–80), so it was, at some point, inhabited by an insect but cleaned in time to prevent further damage. This manuscript never left the Middle East, and it survived several hundreds of years in 'traditional' circumstances (prior to modern library standards and conditions). While the climate must have posed challenges for the safeguarding

40 See Chapter 7 (Hirschler, *Translocations*).

and preservation of paper and book collections, the evidence shows that it was possible to protect collections.

Historical deeds that stipulate the tasks of an endowment library's librarian or administrator, mention annual checking and cleaning of the volumes. Any damage should be addressed without delay.[41] The sources also mention the upkeep of cleanliness in the library and, in some cases, the frequency of airing and cleaning the books was even set at three times a year.[42] This practice, to thoroughly clean the books at regular intervals, must have prevented insect damages to a certain—possibly large—extent, as infestations may have been noticed in their early stages. Good housekeeping and the overall hygiene in a library, which means that dusty corners with ample food for insects and rodents were limited, also contributed to the preservation of the collection. By the same token, the regular use of manuscripts in a library is to be preferred over collections stowed away and hardly accessed, since usage keeps the volumes within view.

The slipcases probably played an important role in the preservation strategies. These enclosures kept the manuscripts neatly closed, protected and not immediately accessible to insects that were looking for a nesting space. Examples of manuscripts that retained their associated slipcase elsewhere show that worm infestation of the slipcase may be severe while the manuscript itself remained almost unscathed.[43] When the slipcases indeed took the brunt of the insect infestation, this further explains their poor survival rate. Slipcases may have been replaced more often than we realise and discarded when they no longer fulfilled their purpose.

41 Erünsal, *Ottoman Libraries*, 111.

42 Ibid, 183.

43 UBL Or. 11.073 is a good example; see also Plummer et al., "Between Bag and Box", 518.

10 Concluding Thoughts

It is clear that since the copying of the inventory, many manuscripts were taken out of the library, and there is only a very small percentage of those that we can localise and study. The physical features of the majority of this regrettably very select group of manuscripts have changed as well, and only around twenty manuscripts still conform to the inventory's material description. The condition and appearance of the larger part of our corpus has been altered by interventive repairs or rebinding. Since these interventions predate the developments in conservation that dictate the documentation of treatments, there are no records available in which an account is given of why the changes were made and what was removed or replaced.

In addition, none of the slipcases survived according to our current knowledge. Though their disappearance may seem less of a deficiency than the replacement of original bindings, their loss is a setback for material studies and our understanding of library and bookbinding practices. Especially since the inventory includes physical characteristics and qualifications, such as 'ancient' and 'new', it would have been incredibly valuable to have been able to compare these descriptions with the physical items.

All these losses amount to a substantial drain of information, and it is only fair to say that the surviving items cannot give us a good picture of what the library looked like in al-Jazzār's time. The very reduced library in Acre has not only thinned in content, but also in cultural representativeness in a much wider sense. The losses are also painful for the scholarly field of codicology and the understanding of materiality. The scant survivors provide no basis to fully understand the terminology used in the inventory, and the absence of the slipcases prevents any in-depth study of this particular Ottoman practice. At best, we can use the individual material characteristics of each volume to explore the use and whereabouts of these manuscripts, before and after their placement in the Jazzār library in Acre.

Bibliography

Abu Harb, Qasem. “Digitisation of Islamic Manuscripts and Periodicals in Jerusalem and Acre.” In *From Dust to Digital: Ten Years of the Endangered Archives Programme*, edited by Maja Kominko, 376–415. Cambridge, UK, 2015.

Bosch, Gulnar K. “Medieval Islamic Bookbinding: Doublures as a Dating Factor.” In *Proceedings of the 26th Art Congress* Or. 1964, 4 (1970): 217–221.

Déroche, François. *Islamic Codicology: An Introduction to the Study of Manuscripts in Arabic Script* [translation of Déroche 2000 by Deke Dusinberre and David Radzinowicz, edited by Muhammad Isa Waley]. London, 2006.

Erünsal, İsmail E. *Ottoman Libraries. A Survey of the History, Development and Organization of Ottoman Foundation Libraries*. Cambridge, Mass., 2008.

Erünsal, İsmail E. *A History of Ottoman Libraries*. Boston, Mass, 2022.

Gacek, Adam. “Arabic Bookmaking and Terminology as Portrayed by Bakr al-Ishbili in His Kitab al-taysir fi sinaʿat al-tasfir.” *Manuscripts of the Middle East* 5 (1990–1991): 106–113.

Gacek, Adam. *Arabic Manuscripts. A Vademecum for Readers*. Leiden, 2009.

D’Ohsson, Ignatius Mouradgea. *Tableau Général de l’Empire Othoman*. Vol. 1. Paris, 1790.

Otha, Alison. “Covering the Book: Bindings of the Mamluk Period, 1250 v 1516 CE.” PhD diss., SOAS, University of London, 2012.

Plummer, David, Paul Hepworth and Karin Scheper. “Between Bag and Box. Characteristics and Conservation Issues of the Islamic Slipcase.” In *Suave Mechanicals. Essays on the History of Bookbinding*, vol. 8, edited by Julia Miller, 476–528. Ann Arbor, MI, 2023.

Raby, Julian, and Zeren Tanındı. *Turkish Bookbinding in the 15th Century. The Foundation of an Ottoman Court Style*. London, 1993.

Rose-Beers, Kristine, Amélie Couvrat Desvergnes, Karin Scheper and Nil Baydar. “Islamic Bindings”. In *Conservation of Books. Routledge Series in Conservation and Museology*, edited by Abigail Bainbridge. London, 2023.

Scheper, Karin. *The Technique of Islamic Bookbinding: Methods, Materials and Regional Varieties* [revised 2nd ed], Leiden/Boston, 2019.

Scheper, Karin, and Around Vrolijk. “From the Eyries of Yemen to the Pastures of Holland. The Acquisition and Preservation of Yemeni Manuscripts at Leiden University Library.” In *Yemeni Manuscript Cultures in Peril*. Gorgias Handbook 49, edited by Hassan Ansari and Sabine Schmidtke, 485–515. Piscataway, NJ, 2022.

Scheper, Karin. “Bindings, Bags and Boxes: Sewn and Unsewn Manuscript Formats in the Islamic World”. In *Tied and Bound: A Comparative View on Manuscript Binding. Studies in Manuscript Cultures*, edited by Allesandro Bausi and Michael Friedrich, 121–154. Berlin, 2023.

Schmidt, Jan. *Catalogue of Turkish Manuscripts in the Library of Leiden University and Other Collections in the Netherlands* Vol. 2. Leiden, 2002.

Witkam, Jan Just. *Inventory of the Oriental Manuscripts of the Library of the University of Leiden* Volume 2, Leiden, 2007.

CHAPTER 9

Calligraphic Descriptions

Nimet İpek and Guy Burak

The librarian at the library of Aḥmad Pasha al-Jazzār paid a remarkable amount of attention to the calligraphic scripts in which the works were copied and applied this description practice consistently across the inventory's sections of the library's main collection (excluding the appendices for the three confiscated libraries).[1] This chapter explores the descriptive practices of the scripts/calligraphic styles employed by the Jazzār librarian and situates them in the broader imperial context. It also intends to examine how the descriptive calligraphic terminology was applied in Acre by comparing the description of extant manuscripts from the Jazzār library to their description in the inventory. The chapter will demonstrate that the application of the calligraphic terminology was not always systematic and consistent. However, this is also the case with the application of descriptive terms in other bibliographic traditions. In other words, our aim is to emphasise this ambiguity and inconsistency not as a particular feature of Ottoman bibliographic practices but of bibliographic taxonomies and classifications more generally.

The terminology which the Jazzār librarian employed reveals a fairly nuanced familiarity with calligraphic hands. They used around fifteen terms to denote different calligraphic styles, along with additional adjectives to describe the quality and characteristics of the hand. Three of the fifteen calligraphic hands are relatively well-known: *naskh, taʿlīq*, and *rayḥānī*. It is more challenging, however, to identify the other scripts precisely, such as the Egyptian (*khaṭṭ Miṣrī*), Istanbulite (*khaṭṭ Islāmbūl*), Arab (*khaṭṭ ʿArabī*), Persian (*khaṭṭ ʿAjam*), Turkish *naskh* (*naskh Turkī*) and Maghribi scripts (*khaṭṭ Maghribī*).[2] It is important that many of these scripts are not mentioned in Mamluk and Ottoman treatises and other works dealing with calligraphy.[3]

The practice of mentioning the script or the calligraphic hand in which a manuscript was written was apparently quite uncommon in the Arabic-speaking lands of the empire, including Bilād al-Shām. The endowment deed of the library of the Governor of Egypt Muḥammad Abū al-Dhahab in Cairo (dated 1770) does not provide any information about the scripts in which the manuscripts were written. Similarly, the appendix of the 1781 endowment deed of the book endowment made by the governor of Baghdad Süleymān Paşa does not specify the calligraphic style (although the deed occasionally mentions the quality of the hand). Nor does the inventory of the early eighteenth-

1 It is understood that there may have been more than one librarian involved sequentially or consecutively in the Jazzār library, however, we have used the singular throughout for the sake of simplicity. Chapter 11 by Claudia Colina and Kyle Ann Huskin in this volume suggests that several individuals handled the manuscripts over the years. It is unclear, however, how many individuals were involved in the bibliographic description of the collection.

2 In some instances, the librarians failed to record the script. This is the case, for example, with the description of the copy of Abū Ḥāmid al-Ghazālī's (d. 1111) *The Precious Pearl on the Revelation of the Sciences of the Future Life* (*al-Durra al-fākhira fī kashf ʿulūm al-ākhira*), currently in Leipzig, (Universitätsbibliothek Leipzig MS Vollers 118). For the entry in the inventory see VGM 1058, 19.

3 Gacek, "Arabic Scripts", 144–149; Blair, *Islamic Calligraphy*. Also see Karen Scheper's Chapter 8 in this volume. Most scripts mentioned in the inventory do not appear in seminal works on calligraphy by Rumi authors. See, for instance: Müstakîmzâde Süleymân Sadeddîn, *Tuhfe-i Hattâtîn*; Nefeszâde İsmâîl, *Gülzâr-ı Savâb*; Yaman, "Hat Sanatı"; Akın-Kıvanç, *Mustafa Âli's Epic Deeds of Artists*.

century library which was founded by ʿUthmān Pasha al-Dūrikī in Aleppo provide any calligraphic description of the books.[4] At the same time, the practice of specifying the script employed was more common, though perhaps not particularly ubiquitous, in the core lands of the empire and imperial capital. Other eighteenth-century library catalogues and inventories—such as those of the Ayasofya (documenting the endowment of Sultan Maḥmūd I) and the library of Rāğıp Paşa, to mention two salient examples—do mention the script in which the manuscript was copied. In addition to library inventories, mentions of the calligraphic styles may appear in lists of manuscripts enclosed in endowment deeds and in bibliographic notes on the flyleaves of the manuscripts. The book lists attached to the endowment deeds of İsmihān Sultān (d. 1585) and Rüstem Paşa (d. 1561), for example, provide calligraphic information. In other words, we would like to suggest in the following pages that al-Jazzār's librarian seems to have been familiar and tried to engage with the descriptive practices of scripts that had gained popularity and evolved in the core lands of the empire over the course of the eighteenth century.

1 Calligraphy in the Inventories of the Ottoman Core Lands

Library inventories compiled in the Ottoman core lands from the sixteenth through to the eighteenth century apply various descriptive practices to ascertain that a copy mentioned in the inventory is the same as the extant copy. While some of the library inventories from the Ottoman centre provide a detailed description for each copy, others tend to list book titles along with other minor identifying details. Our examination of the descriptive practices in Ottoman libraries focuses on the Ottoman centre since its library culture is studied better. It is important to stress, however, that the inventories and other forms of bibliographic descriptive practices from the empire's core lands varied considerably. Put differently, while it is perhaps possible to speak about shared Rūmī bibliographic/descriptive practices, it was not a fully standardised bibliographic tradition.

The origins of the eighteenth-century bibliographic practices in the core lands of the empire can be traced back to the sixteenth century, if not earlier. The inventory of the manuscripts endowed by Sultan Meḥmed II and several eminent scholars, such as the sixteenth-century Çelebīzāde and Şehzāde, to the Saḥn-ı S̱emān Madrasas (dated 968/1561),[5] mentions the books' titles, the names of their authors, information on the completeness of the manuscripts, the ruling, the type of paper, binding, page count and other distinctive features of the copies. Consider, as an example, the following, quite typical entry: "*The Ḥamāsa* by Abū Tammām, complete, Damascene, folded green paper in folio, pasteboard covers, written on flyleaf *Kitāb al-Ḥamāsa* in *thuluth* script. It is a lucid copy. 183 folios" (*Kitābu Metni'l-Hamāse li-Ebī Temmām. Tamām. Dımaşḳī. Tamāmından kıvrılmış yeşil kağıd. Mukavvā cildle. Mektūbun fī żahrihi Kitābu'l-Hamāse bi-ḳalemi's-s̱ülüs̱. Ve hüve nüskhatun vâzıḥatun. Yüz seksen üç varaḳ*).[6] Interestingly, the compilers of this inventory did not regularly mention the script in their description of manuscripts. In some instances, however, the inventory comments on the quality of the script by employing adjectives such as *vāżıḥ* (Ar. lucid), *ḫūb* (Per. pleasant), *ḫurde* (Per. minute) and *eyü* (Tur. fine). Therefore, it may be fair to argue that, for the most part, the mention of the script in this inventory was selectively utilised to highlight distinctive aesthetic features of the copy at hand.

4 Crecelius, "The Waqfīyah of Muḥammad Bey Abū al-Dhahab II"; Aljoumani, *Maktaba madrasiyya*, 69–178; Rā'ūf, *Dirāsāt turāthiyya*, I, 303–350.

5 BOA, TS.MA.d 9559. For a recent study of this inventory see Şen. "The Sultan's Syllabus Revisited". Şen and Abdurrahman Atcıl are currently preparing an edition of this inventory.

6 BOA, TS.MA.d 9559, f. 82v.

ʿAṭūfī, the early sixteenth-century palace librarian of Bāyezīd II, did not dwell on the calligraphic style in the inventory he compiled.[7] The difference between the inventory of Meḥmed II and that of the Palace Library may stem from the manner in which the collections were used: access to the palace library was more limited and more strictly regulated, whereas the library of the *madrasa* served a much larger audience. Moreover, the inventories fulfilled different bureaucratic purposes: the inventory of the palace library was intended to monitor (or inventory) the holdings of the library, whereas that of the *madrasa* was intended to regulate an endowment. It is quite likely that the function and location of the collections informed the different descriptive practices of their librarians.

To our knowledge, there are no extant library inventories from the late decades of the sixteenth century and the first half of the seventeenth. However, it is possible to trace the descriptions of scripts during this time period from book lists attached to endowment deeds. Consider, for example, the library of Rüstem Paşa's *madrasa* (f. 1561), which was adjacent to the namesake complex.[8] The endowment deed of this humble library of 120 volumes set for the *madrasa*'s students applies an elaborate description for each copy. The entries mention not only generic information, such as book titles and authors, but also the script, type of binding and the number of lines. The list of scripts employed to describe the manuscripts is slightly more elaborate than the six canonical Ottoman hands and includes "Arab" and "Maghribī" scripts (these latter scripts, however, appear quite rarely in the list and are commonly added as an adjective to the more common script *naskh*).[9]

Librarians in other sixteenth-century libraries, on the other hand, opted for a much more concise description. Such was the case, for instance, in the endowment deed of the library established by the chief eunuch to Murād III, Ḥabeşī Meḥmed Ağa (d. 1590), which only provides basic information for each title (title, author and number of volumes).[10] It is hard, therefore, to speak about a canonised or standardised set of descriptive bibliographical practices in the sixteenth century.

Library inventories in the core lands of the empire had developed more standardised distinctive features by the late seventeenth century, as İsmail Erünsal has argued, while not fully eliminating variations.[11] The emergence of the detailed inventory coincided with the proliferation of libraries in the core lands and elsewhere across the empire over the course of the long eighteenth century (see Chapter 1). The inventories varied in terms of the bibliographic details they recorded, as was the case with the sixteenth-century endowment deeds. In some cases, the inventories described the holdings of the library succinctly, whereas other inventories listed the books along with a more detailed description. Such, for example, was the inventory of the Turḫān Vālide Sulṭān Library.[12]

The variation is also evident in the manner different inventories treat the script in which the manuscripts were copied. The entries in the inventory of the library established by Fāżıl Aḥmed Paşa (d. 1676), the first to establish a stand-alone library in the seventeenth century, does not regularly mention scripts.[13] There are a few instances where the compiler chose to record the calligraphic hand, usually when there were multiple copies of the same work in the library: when describing the commentaries on the *ḥadīth* compilation of al-Bukhārī, for instance, the librarian inserted "*bi-ḫaṭṭ-ı taʿlīḳ*"

7 Necipoğlu et al., *Treasures of Knowledge*. On calligraphy in the inventory of the palace library, see Burak, "*The Section*" and Burak, "Alphabets and 'Calligraphy'".

8 Erünsal, *Osmanlılarda Kütüphaneler*, 131.

9 VGMA 635, 73–82.

10 Açıl, "Habeşî Mehmed Ağa'nın", 67–83.

11 Erünsal, *Osmanlılarda Kütüphaneler*, 412–413.

12 TIEM, MS 2218. The entries in this inventory mentioned the size of the copy and the ruled border.

13 Süleymaniye Library, MS Köprülü İlave 19. The inventory under consideration bears two seal impressions of Fāżıl Ahmed Paşa, which are the endowment seal and his personal seal. Hence, this book list is probably the inventory compiled as part of the foundation process.

in the entry of the commentary of Osmān Hanefī, probably to emphasise the distinctive features of this copy.[14]

The inventory of the library established by Aḥmed III (founded in 1719), which was situated in the palace's innermost court (*Enderūn*), seems to be the first in the long eighteenth century to record scripts systematically.[15] The gallery of scripts in the inventory includes *nesẖ, ta'līḳ, ruḳ'a, Özbek* and *'Arab* (the script was normally mentioned in Persian). When the copy was an autograph, the compiler of the inventory stated it (*muṣannifihi*) explicitly. Importantly, the scripts in the inventory apart from the six canonical Ottoman scripts (*aḳlām-i sitte*)[16] are "the Arab script" (*ẖaṭṭ-ı 'Arab*) and "the Uzbek script" (*ẖaṭṭ-ı Özbek*), possibly indicating the provenance of the copy in the Arabic-speaking lands or Central Asia, respectively. The inventory also specifies the quality of the script (with the Arabic adjective *ḥasen*, "beautiful").

Similarly, the inventory of the Ayasofya Library of Maḥmūd I (f. 1740) diligently records the script employed in each copy.[17] One of the most salient features of the Ayasofya inventory is the fairly extensive list of scripts mentioned, well beyond the six canonical calligraphic styles. Among the additional scripts are the Maghribī and Arab scripts. Moreover, the inventory refers to a particular Mamluk *naskh* style (*nesẖ-i Memlūk, Memlūk, nesẖ-i Memlūk-i Ḳayıtbāy-ı 'Arab*). In addition, rich terminology is used to indicate the quality of the hand: *'ālī* (Ar. high), *ḥasen* (Ar. fine), *ẖurde* (Per. minute), *laṭīf* (Ar. delicate), *'atīḳ* (Ar. ancient) and *ẖūb* (Per. fine).

The inventory of Rāgıp Paşa's (f. 1763) library[18] reflects a similar interest in the calligraphic hand in which the manuscripts were copied. Here, too, the list of scripts is more elaborate than the canonical scripts and includes *Baghdād, Akrād, 'Acem, Mıṣr(ī), 'Arab* and *Mağribī* scripts. The geographical adjectives were occasionally attached as qualifiers to other scripts, such as *naskh* and *ta'līḳ* (*ẖaṭṭ-ı nesẖ-i 'Arab*, for example). In addition, other adjectives further qualified the description. One entry in the inventory, for instance, states that the manuscript was written in "old Baghdādī hand" (*ẖaṭṭ-i ḳadīm-i Bağdād*).[19]

The descriptions in the inventory of the Rāğıp Paşa Library draw on the most extensive gallery of scripts. Reading the list (Appendix 1) against Rāğıp Paşa's career (d. 1763) raises interesting questions about the relationship between the description of the script and the manuscripts' provenance. Over the course of his lifetime, Rāğıp Paşa assumed various positions across the empire: He served in the eastern provinces/Iran (1727–1730), Baghdad (1730–1735), Istanbul (1735–1744), Cairo (1744–1748), Aydın (1748–1750), Raqqa (1751–1755), Aleppo (1755–1757) and Istanbul (1757–1763).[20] Building on Henning Sievert's observations, it is possible that, as Grand Vizier, Rāğıp Paşa maintained his relationship with the provinces he had served in before his appointment to the vizierate in 1757. Rāğıp Paşa's interregional network encompassed individ-

14 Ibid., f. 2r.

15 Topkapı Library, MS III. Ahmed 3679. Here is a sample entry: "Ḥāşiye-i Beyżāvī li'l-'Aṭūfī bā-ẖaṭṭ-ı nesẖ cild bir" (Ḥāshiyat al-Bayḍāwī by al-'Aṭūfī, in *naskh* script, one volume). Ibid., 4r.

16 The canonical calligraphic hands are *tavqī', ruq'a, muḥaqqaq, rayḥānī, thuluth* and *naskh*. Welch, *Calligraphy in the Arts of the Muslim World*; Blair, *Islamic Calligraphy*.

17 Süleymaniye Library, MS Yazma Fihrist 25-1. A representative entry reads as follows: "*Kitābu tefsīru'l-vecīz* tamām nüsẖa 'Arab ẖaṭṭı ile bir cild ṣaṭr-ı ṣaḥīfe 21" (*Kitāb tafsīr al-wajīz*, complete copy, in *Arab* script, one volume, 21 lines per page), Ibid., 4v.

18 Süleymaniye Library, MS Rāgıp Paşa 4111. Sievert, "Eavesdropping on the Pasha's Salon". A sample entry reads as follows: "*Tefsīr-i Neysābūrī bā-khaṭṭ-ta'līḳ ḳırḳ bir saṭr ḳit'a-i kāmile der-cild-i vāḥid müzehheb ve muḥallā*" (*Tafsīr al-Naysābūrī*, in *ta'līq* script, forty-one lines, complete copy, in one volume, illuminated and ornamented).

19 The range of adjectives used in the inventory to refer to the quality of the script is not as rich as in the Ayasofya inventory and the compiler(s) merely use the adjective *ḥusn* (fine) throughout the inventory.

20 Sievert, *Zwischen arabischer Provinz und Hoher Pforte*, 560.

uals from different locales such as Diyarbakır, Ruha (Urfa), Baghdad, Damascus, Aleppo, Cairo, Mosul, Bağçesaray and Medina.[21] It is possible that Rāgıp Paşa's familiarity with the provinces, through service and personal connections with individuals, informed his bibliographic knowledge and calligraphic sensibilities. Indeed, the inventory of his library employs a rich and nuanced calligraphic vocabulary: in addition to the canonical scripts of *nesẖ*, *ruḳa*, *reyḥānī* and *ta'līḳ*, the gallery of scripts includes "Egyptian" (Mıṣr(ī)), "Baghdadi" (Bağdād), "Persian" ('Acem), "Arab" ('Arab), "Kurdish" (Akrād) and "Maghribī" (Mağrib).[22] Some of these calligraphic/styles presumably prevailed in places where Rāğıp Paşa spent extended periods of time, and it is possible that he even acquired the manuscripts during his tenure in those places or through connections he maintained after he had left.

The case of Rāğıp Paşa also illustrates how knowledge about different calligraphic styles circulated throughout the Ottoman lands and reached the imperial capital (as well as other provinces). Indeed, as we have seen earlier, sixteenth-century endowment deeds which were compiled in Istanbul, such as Rüstem Paşa's, demonstrate familiarity with calligraphic styles associated with the "Arab" or "Persian" lands.[23] As we will discuss below, the geographical qualification of the calligraphic style may not point to a markedly different script. A manuscript from the library of Rāğıp Paşa (Rāgıp Paşa 645), for instance, is described as written in "Baghdadi *ta'līḳ*", but is not markedly different from other manuscripts in the library written in *ta'līḳ* script. It seems that the geographical qualification was intended to indicate the manuscript's provenance (the province of Baghdad in this case).[24]

As we have already mentioned, in addition to endowment deeds and library inventories, descriptions of scripts also appear in annotations on the front pages of manuscripts, as was the case in the library founded by Sultan Abdülḥamīd I (d. 1789) (fig. 9.1).[25] The librarian there wrote short bibliographic notes on the front folios of the manuscripts held at the library. The notes, which may have corresponded to entries in a lost inventory, also include a description of the script. Most manuscripts are described as written in *nesẖ* and *ta'liḳ* scripts, but, in some instances, the script is described as 'Arab'.

This brief survey of the descriptive practices of the calligraphic hands suggests that a fairly standardised bibliographic tradition emerged in the imperial capital over the course of the long eighteenth century. This tradition paid a great deal of attention to scripts in bibliographic descriptions of manuscripts. Some of the terms, it appears, gained greater currency in the intellectual circles of Istanbul (and, possibly, elsewhere across the empire). The late eighteenth-century Ottoman intellectual and contemporary of al-Jazzār, Aḥmed Vāṣıf Efendi (d. 1806), for instance, recorded his impressions of his visit to the library of El Escorial Monastery in 1787–1788 and observed that he "saw some ten Qur'ans in the collection and a great many works of jurisprudence, traditions, and theology, some of them written in Egyptian script and some in Maghrebi."[26]

Similar to the remarks Aḥmed Vāṣıf Efendi made, archival documents also suggest that familiarity with calligraphic styles beyond the six scripts existed in broader intellectual circles. The confiscation list of the former belongings of the deceased

21 For a list of these political clienteles, see ibid., 561.

22 Süleymaniye Library, M Rāğıp Paşa 4111.

23 See, for instance, VGMA 635, 73–82.

24 Süleymaniye Kütüphanesi, MS Rāgıp Paşa 4111. Instances of the Baghdadi script in the Rāğıp Paşa Library, such as numbers 645 and 846, appear to us like *naskh* script. Yet, a copy of the Selîmnâme from the Enderūn Library of Aḥmed III, which is described on the flyleaf as written in the "Baghdādī script", appears like a version of *ta'līq*. See *Şahnâme-i Selîm Şâh*, Topkapı Library, MS III. Ahmed 3595.

25 For instance, Süleymaniye Library, MS Hamidiye 1450. One of the front pages displays bibliographic details in red ink. The script is *ta'līq*.

26 Menchinger, *The First of the Modern Ottomans*, 126.

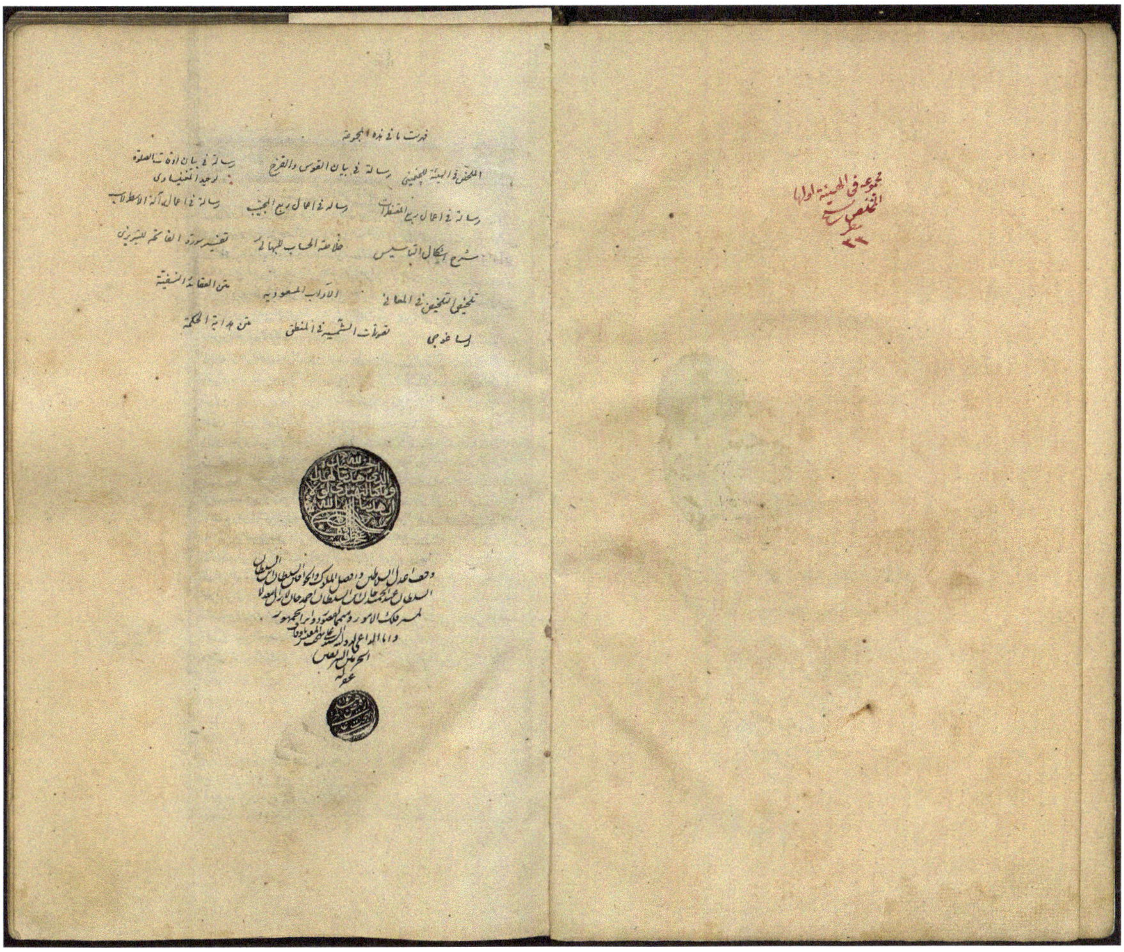

FIGURE 9.1 Annotation of the description of the manuscript, including the calligraphic style, in one of the manuscripts in the library from Hamîdiye. *Majmūʿa fī al-Hayʾa*, Süleymaniye Library MS Hamidiye 1450, 11ᵛ.

Custodian of Ganja, Vezir Ḥācī Muṣṭafā Paşa, in 1142/1730, mentions two *muṣḥaf*s copied in *ʿAcem* script and *Rūmī* script (the calligraphic styles of the other books on the list are not mentioned).[27] Another example is the inventory listing the manuscript holdings of the former Grand Vizier Aḥmed Paşa (d. 1742), which were subsequently relocated to the Enderūn Treasury. Among the many Qur'an manuscripts he held, one manuscript is described as written in "Arab script" and the other as written in "ʿAjam script."[28]

The sensibility regarding calligraphy in the eighteenth-century library inventories (and other sources) may be interpreted as an indicator of the growing awareness among bibliophiles in the core lands of the diverse calligraphic landscape of the empire. In particular, a growing sense of regional calligraphic styles is evident: the endowment deed of the Ayasofya elementary school (*ṣıbyān mektebi*), dated 1753, for example, stipulates that the students should learn to write according to the regional custom (*ʿādet-i belde üzere* [...] *meşḳ u taʿlīm*).[29] This stipulation may reflect a sense of

27 BOA.C.ML. 112/4981.
28 TS.MA.d 2386, 2^{a}. 1155 Safer.

29 VGMA, 1399, 32^{b}–33^{a}.

a fairly canonised local calligraphic style. At the same time, since the inventories vary in terms of relation to the scripts to which they refer, it seems that librarians enjoyed a considerable extent of liberty in developing their own taxonomies beyond the six conventional scripts.

2 Describing Scripts in the Inventory of al-Jazzār's Library: Exemplarily, Miṣrī/Egyptian Script

This brief survey of the descriptive practices of scripts in the imperial core lands and Arab provinces suggests that the al-Jazzār librarian was familiar with this Rūmī bibliographic tradition. The considerable variation across inventories in terms of the description of calligraphic scripts begs the question: How did specific librarians interpret and describe the calligraphic styles in which manuscripts in their library were copied? Concretely, how did al-Jazzār's librarian employ the calligraphic categories in his descriptions?

An examination of the extant manuscripts from al-Jazzār's library may help us in gaining a better understanding of the manners in which the librarian implemented the calligraphic classification. The vast majority of the extant copies that are represented in the inventory were written in the Egyptian script and a few were written in *naskh, taʿlīq* and *rayḥānī*. Unfortunately, other scripts listed in the inventory are not represented in this corpus of manuscripts.

The "Egyptian script" is the most frequently mentioned in the inventory. Fortunately, it is possible to identify several manuscripts from al-Jazzār's library described in the inventory as written in this script. The extant manuscripts were copied over centuries and considerable geographical distances, from the tenth to the eighteenth centuries and from Iraq to Egypt. Despite the fact that al-Jazzār's librarian identified the script in all these manuscripts as Egyptian script, and while the scripts in a significant number of these manuscripts bear close stylistic similarities, the manuscripts in the cluster written in "Egyptian script" are quite diverse (for example, see figs. 9.2, 9.3, 9.4). This stylistic diversity suggests that "Egyptian script" covered a range of calligraphic styles for the librarian who worked in the service of al-Jazzār.

As we have already seen, Miṣrī script also features in the inventory of the library of Rāgıp Paşa. There, too, the script is among the most frequently mentioned and was used to copy books in a wide range of sciences, from Qurʾānic exegesis (*tafsīr*) to philosophy. As opposed to al-Jazzār's library, however, the description "*ḫaṭṭ-i Miṣrī*" is applied quite consistently.[30] The comparison of the two libraries may be interpreted as evidence of the lack of a consistent definition of the script and, possibly, as an example of regional variations across the Ottoman lands based on local calligraphic sensibilities.

Returning to the library of al-Jazzār, a similar diversity can be found within the cluster of extant manuscripts the librarian identified as written in *naskh* script. Much like the cluster of manuscripts written in Egyptian script, the *naskh* manuscripts were copied over several centuries from the late fifteenth through to the eighteenth centuries. There is some stylistic coherence within the *naskh* cluster, but there are a few outliers (figs. 9.5, 9.6, 9.7. 9.8).

3 Comparing Notes

The fact that several manuscripts from al-Jazzār's library ended up in libraries in which Western bibliographical and codicological descriptive practices are followed provides a fairly unique opportunity to examine the description of the same manu-

30 As an illustration, see: MS Rāgıp Paşa 489, 518, 510, 542, 1333, 884, 1052, 1134, 1220, and 1141. They are all described as being copied in *Ḫaṭṭ-ı Mıṣrī* in the inventory of the Rāgıp Paşa Library.

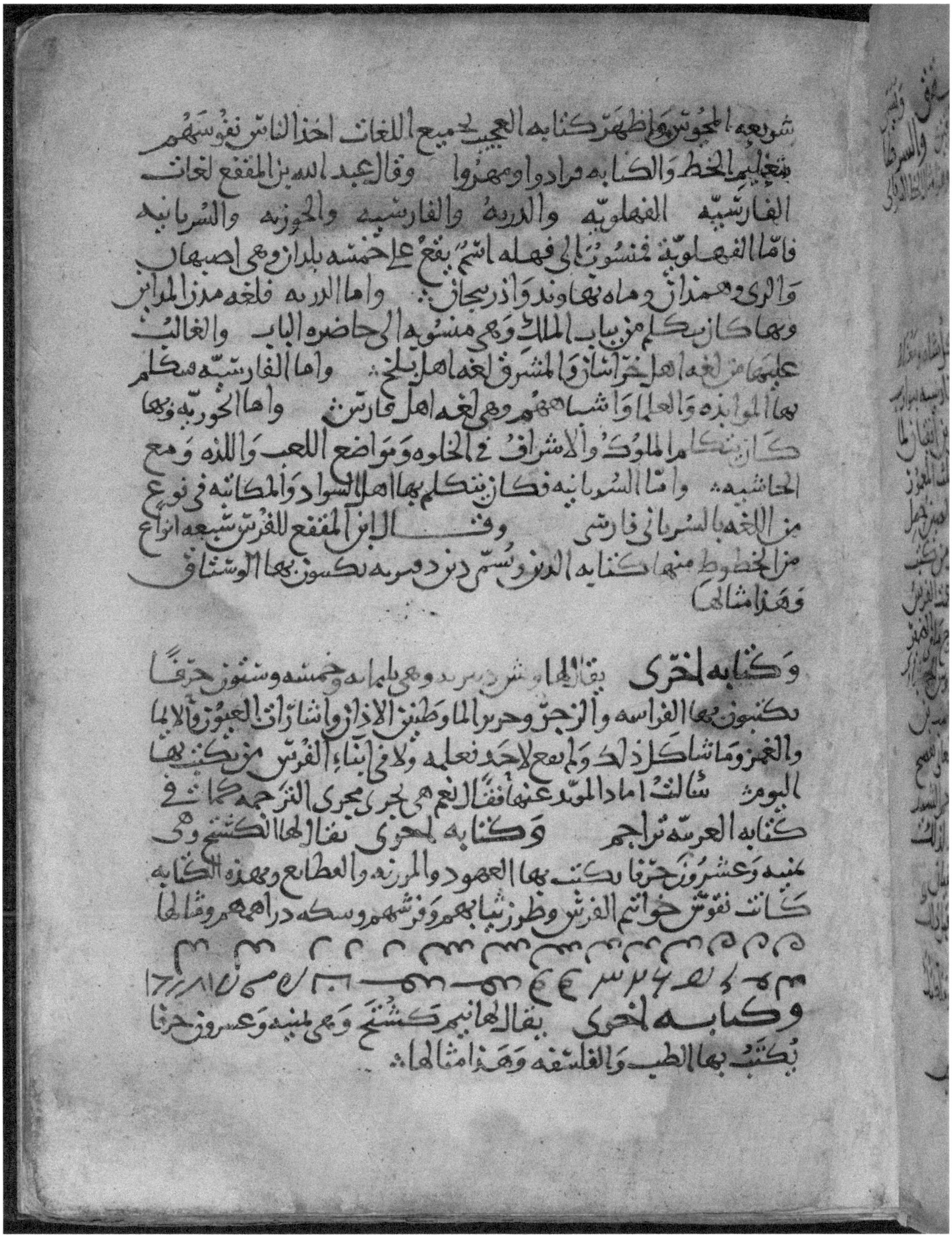

FIGURE 9.2 Ibn al-Nadīm, *al-Fihrist*, Chester Beatty Library MS Ar. 3315 (10th century), 6[r]

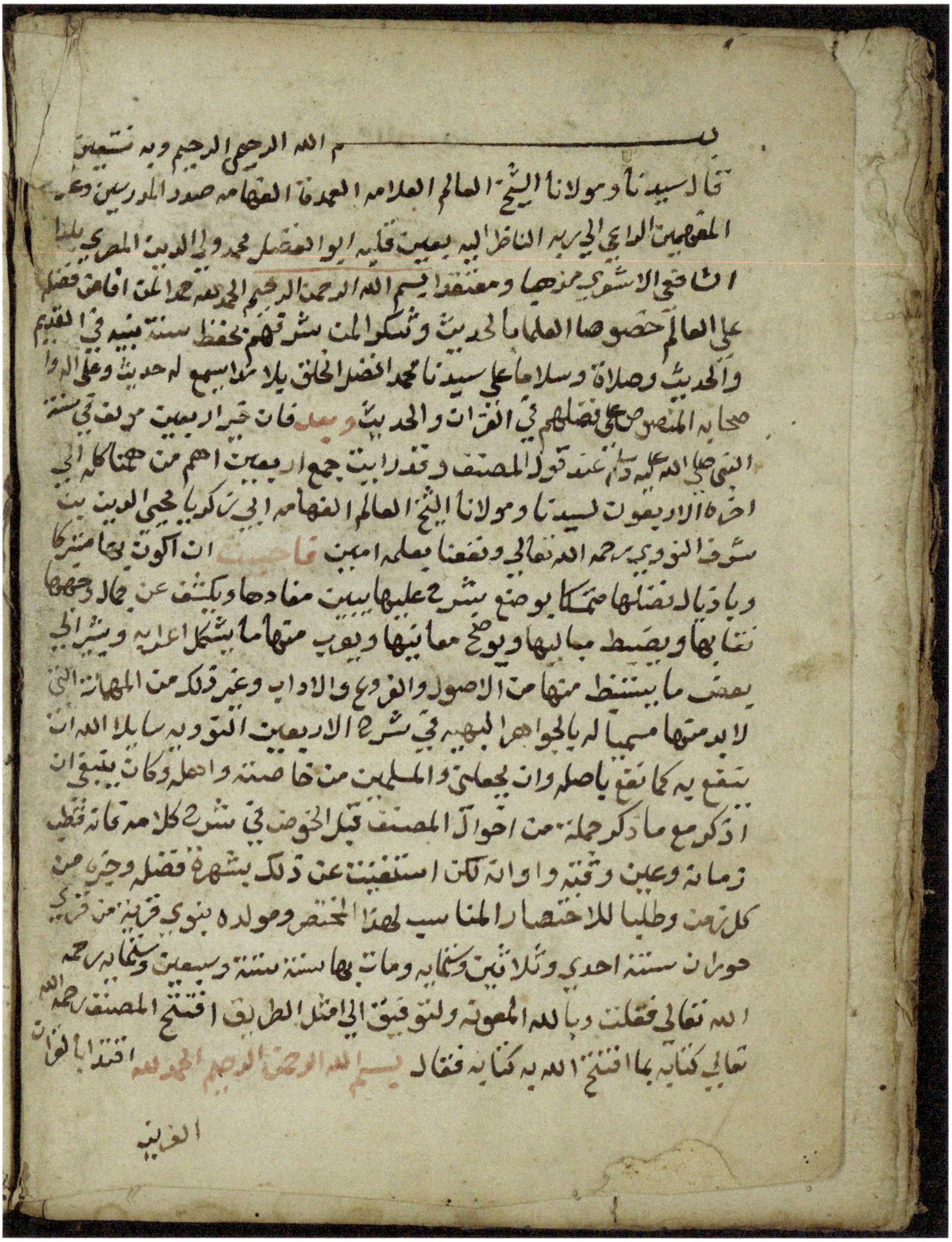
بسم الله الرحمن الرحيم وبه نستعين
قال سيدنا ومولانا الشيخ العالم العلامة المحدث الفهامة صدر المدرسين [illegible]
المفيدين الداعي الى ربه الناظر اليه بعين قلبه ابو الفضل محمد ولي الدين المصري بلدا
الشافعي الاشعري مذهبا ومعتقدا بسم الله الرحمن الرحيم الحمد لله حمدا لمن افاض فضله
على العالم خصوصا العلما بالحديث ونشكر [illegible] حفظ سنة نبيه في القديم
والحديث وصلاة وسلاما على سيدنا محمد افضل الخلق [illegible] له حديث وعلى اله
واصحابه المنصوص على فضلهم في القرآن والحديث وبعد فان خير اربعين مؤلف في سنة
النبي صلى الله عليه وسلم عند قول المصنف وقد رأيت جمع اربعين اهم من هذا كله الى
اخره الاربعون لسيدنا ومولانا الشيخ العالم الفهامة ابي زكريا يحيى الدين بن
شرف النووي رحمه الله تعالى ونفعنا بعلمه امين فاحببت ان اكون بها متبركا
[illegible] بفضلها [illegible] بوضع شرح عليها يبين مفادها ويكشف عن [illegible]
[illegible] ويوضح معانيها ويقرب منها ما يشكل اعرابه ويشير الى
بعض ما يستنبط منها من الاصول والفروع والاداب وغير ذلك من المهمات التي
لابد منها مسميا له بالجواهر البهية في شرح الاربعين النووية سايلا الله ان
ينفع به كما نفع باصله وان يجعله [illegible] والمسلمين من خاصته واهله وكان ينبغي ان
اذكر مع ما ذكر جملة من احوال المصنف قبل الخوض في شرح كلامه [illegible]
زمانه [illegible] لكن استغنيت عن ذلك بشهرة فضله [illegible]
[illegible] وطلبا للاختصار المناسب لهذا المختصر ومولده بنوى قرية من قرى
حوران سنة احدى وثلاثين وستمائة ومات بها سنة ست وسبعين وستمائة رحمه
الله تعالى فقلت وبالله المعونة والتوفيق الى امثل الطريق افتتح المصنف رحمه الله
تعالى كتابه بما افتتح الله به كتابه فقال بسم الله الرحمن الرحيم الحمد لله اقتداء بالقرآن
[illegible]

FIGURE 9.3 Muḥammad al-Shibshirī, *al-Jawāhir al-bahiyya fī sharḥ al-Arbaʿīn al-Nawawiyya* Princeton University Library MS Garrett 2996Y (early 18th century), 1v

FIGURE 9.4
ʿAbd al-Raḥīm b. al-Ḥasan al-Isnawī, *al-Muhimmāt fī sharḥ al-Rawḍah wa-al-Rāfiʿī*, Jerusalem, National Library of Israel, MS. AP Ar. 290 (late 14th century), 80v–81r

script across bibliographical traditions. Consider, for instance, two manuscripts that are identified in the inventory as copied in the Egyptian script: A copy of Jalāl al-Dīn al-Suyūṭī's (d. 1505) exegesis, *The Perfect Guide to the Sciences of the Qur'an* (*al-Itqān fī ʿulūm al-Qurʾān*), which was probably copied in Egypt or Syria and is currently at the Khalidiyya Library in Jerusalem, and a tenth-century copy of Ibn al-Nadīm's (d. 995) *Catalog* (*Fihrist*), which was probably copied in Iraq, currently at the Chester Beatty Library in Dublin. Both manuscripts are classified in the inventory as written in the Miṣrī script, significant calligraphic variations notwithstanding. Their modern/Western cataloguers, on the other hand, described the script as *naskh*. Similarly, Arthur J. Arberry (d. 1969) defines the script used in copying a copy of Ibn Aʿtham's (d. after 819) *Conquests* (*al-Futūḥ*) by al-Kūfī as "clear *naskh*".[31] But what appeared like "clear" *naskh* to a trained modern/Western eye was recognised as Egyptian script by al-Jazzār's librarian.

Indeed, modern interpreters/classifiers of scripts tend to loosely apply *naskh* to a varied range of calligraphic hands. Similarly, al-Jazzār's copy of *Guiding Seekers to the Ranks of Practising Scholars* (*Irshād al-ṭālibīn ilā marātib al-ʿulamā al-ʿāmilīn*) by ʿAbd al-Wahhāb b. Aḥmad al-Shaʿrānī (d. 1565), currently in the Daiber Collection at Tokyo University, is described in the Japanese catalogue as copied in the *muḥaqqaq* script.[32] al-Jazzār's librarian, however, identified the script as Egyptian. While al-Jazzār's librarian employed a nuanced calligraphic taxonomy, perhaps alluding to the manuscript's provenance, his modern counterparts decided to limit their descriptions to the six canonical Ottoman scripts.

At the same time, there are instances where al-Jazzār's librarian and his modern counterparts agree on the script's description: the eighteenth-century librarian describes the script used in the copy of al-Maqrīzī's topographical chronicle, titled *Homilies and Consideration by Mentioning Plans*

31 Chester Beatty Library, MS Ar. 3272. Arberry, *Chester Beatty Library*, 9.

32 Tokyo University MS Daiber 76. http://ricasdb.ioc.u-tokyo.ac.jp/daiber/fra_daiber_I_II.php?vol=2&ms=Ms.76&txtno=2147 (accessed 24 February 2023). Moreover, the entry states that "Paper, script and front cover point to a Mamluk origin, perhaps the 8th/14th century".

FIGURE 9.5 Taqī al-Dīn al-Maqrīzī, *al-Niṣf al-awwal min al-Khiṭaṭ*, Princeton Library MS 3516Y, 1v. (18th century)

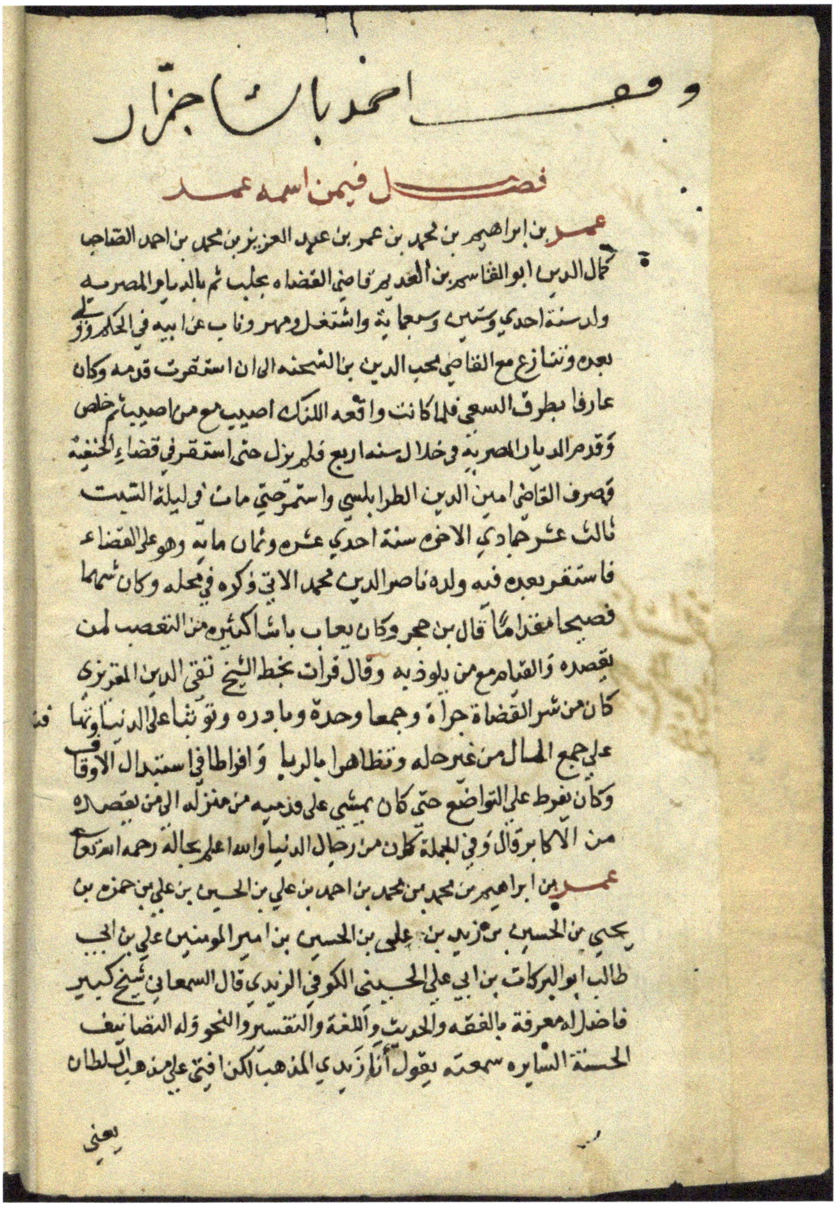

FIGURE 9.6 Taqī al-Dīn al-Tamīmī, *al-Ṭabaqāt al-saniyya fī tarājim al-sāda al-Ḥanafiyya*, Staatsbibliothek zu Berlin MS Landberg 9 (dated 1633), 1v

and Monuments (*al-Mawāʿiẓ wa-al-iʿtibār fī dhikr al-khiṭaṭ wa-al-āthār*) as *naskh* and the cataloguer at Princeton concurred.[33] But even in these instances of agreement, al-Jazzār's librarian and the modern cataloguers may disagree on the quality of the scripts. The copy titled *Revelation and Perfection as Commentary on Facilitating Book* (*al-Tanzīl wa-al-takmīl fī sharḥ kitāb al-tashīl*) by Abū Ḥayyān al-Andalusī (d. 1344), currently held at the Chester Beatty Library (MS Ar. 3342), is identified as *naskh* by both the eighteenth-century librarian and the Chester Beatty cataloguer. But what seemed to al-

33 We believe that Firestone Library MS Garrett 3516Y is the copy referred to in the inventory. VGMA 1058, 56.

FIGURE 9.7 Anonymous, *Kitāb jifr*, Süleymaniye Library MS Pertevniyal Valide Sultan 759 (dated 1475/6), 7ᵛ1ʳ–8ʳ2ᵛ

FIGURE 9.8 al-Mullā ʿAlī al-Qārī, *al-Ḥirz al-thamīn lil-Ḥiṣn al-ḥaṣīn*, National Library of Israel MS. AP. Ar. 258 (16th century), 1ʳ–2ᵛ.

Jazzār's librarian to be "*naskh qadīm*" (old *naskh*), appeared to his twentieth-century counterpart Arberry as "fine naskh" (*al-naskh al-jayyid* in the Arabic translation).[34]

To conclude, the reading of the al-Jazzār inventory and other inventories from the core lands of the empire along with the modern catalogues illustrates the complexity of classification and uniform terminology. The richer gallery of script found in these documents is indeed fascinating and perplexing, as the exact application of the calligraphic terms is not always clear or systematic. Such a comparison for cataloguers and codicologists trained in one of the Western bibliographic traditions can be a rare and stimulating opportunity to compare notes, literally and figuratively, with eighteenth-century colleagues who struggled to describe the same manuscripts. Moreover, as we have seen, many of the scripts mentioned in the al-Jazzār and other eighteenth-century (and earlier) inventories are not mentioned in modern scholarly works on the history of Ottoman and "Islamic" calligraphy.[35] Since most modern studies tend to follow the manuals on calligraphy, they, too, concentrate on the six canonical scripts. But the library inventories, including that of the al-Jazzār library, offer a glimpse into the taxonomies favoured by communities of practice and bibliophiles, and allow a more nuanced understanding of thc history of "Islamic calligraphy".

Appendix 1

The list below has been created to show the scripts in the Rāğıp Paşa and Jazzār libraries. The data for the Rāğıp Paşa Library is taken from the inventory (Süleymaniye Library MS Rāgıp Paşa 4111) and for Jazzār is taken from the inventory of the library (VGMA 1626).

34 Ibid., 41. There are also instances where the description of al-Jazzār's librarian does not have a parallel in the modern catalogues. *The Abridgment of the Marvelous Correspondences on What is Written on the Ordinances/Topics of Sharīʿa* (*Mukhtaṣar al-Mukātabāt al-badīʿa fī mā yuktab min umūr al-sharīʿa*) by Muḥammad b. ʿAbd al-Raḥmān b. al-Ṣayrafī (d. ?) is described by the eighteenth-century librarian as copied in *rayḥānī* script. The catalogue of the Khālidiyya Library by Hill Manuscript Museum and Library (HMML), however, does not attribute a script to this manuscript. al-Juʿbah, *Catalog of Manuscripts in al-Khālidiyyah Library*, 451.

35 Derman, *İslam Kültür*; Yazır, *Medeniyet Alеminde Yazı*. Serin, *Hat Sanatı ve Meşhur Hattatlar*; Welch, *Calligraphy*; Blair, *Islamic Calligraphy*.

Rāgıp Paşa Collection	Vol.	Al-Jazzār Collection	Vol.
Nesẖ	305	Naskh	438
Ḥüsn-i ẖaṭṭ-ı nesẖ	31	Naskh ʿāl	14
Nesẖ-i müẕehheb	4	Naskh jadīd	5
Taʿlīḳ	327	Naskh kadīm/ʿatīk	7
Taʿlīḳ-i müẕehheb	4	Naskh mamhūw	1
Taʿlīḳ-i ḳadīm	1	Taʿlīq	161
Ṭālū-yı(?) taʿlīḳ	1	Taʿlīq ʿaẓīm	1
Ḥüsn-i ẖaṭṭ-ı taʿlīḳ	29	Taʿlīq ʿāl	8
Mıṣr(ī)	229	Taʿlīq ʿatīq	3
Taʿlīḳ-i Mıṣr	1	Miṣrī	754
Nesẖ-i Mıṣr	3	Miṣrī ʿatīq	21
Ḫuṭūṭ-ı muẖtelife-i Mıṣriyye	5	Miṣrī ʿāl	1
Ḥüṣn-i ẖaṭṭ-ı Mıṣr	5	Miṣrī jadīd	3
Bağdād	117	Miṣrī Naskh/Naskh Miṣrī	11
Nesẖ-i Bağdād	14	Taʿlīq Misrī	1
Ḳadīm Bağdād	7	Turkī	8
Ḳadīm Bağdād Taʿlīḳ	1	Ruqʿa al-Turkī	1
Ḥüsn-i ẖaṭṭ-ı Baġdād	1	Naskh Turkī	5
Ḥüsn-i ẖaṭṭ-ı nesẖ-i Baġdād	2	Taʿlīq Turkī	4
Ḫuṭuṭ-ı muẖtelife-i Baġdād	1	Istānbūl ʿāl	4
ʿAcem	1	ʿAjam	1
Nesẖ-i ʿAcem	13	Fārisī Taʿlīq	1
Taʿlīḳ-i ʿAcem	4	ʿArabī	1
Ḥüsn-i ẖaṭṭ-ı taʿlīḳ-i ʿAcem	3	Rayḥānī	39
Ḥüsn-i ẖaṭṭ-ı taʿlīḳ-i ʿAcem-i müẕehheb	2	Rayḥānī kadīm/ʿatīq	3
Ḥüsn-i ẖaṭṭ-ı nesẖ-i ʿAcem	1	Naskh rayhānī	1
Ḥüsn-i ẖaṭṭ-ı nesẖ-i Acem-i müẕehheb	1	Maghribī	9
ʿArab	3	Maghribī ʿatīq	1
ʿArab-ı Nesẖ	2	Shattā/mukhtalifa/khutūt/mushakkala	8
Akrād	12	Muʾallifihi	1
Mağrib	1	Ṭabʿ	2
Ruḳʿa	1	Ṭabʿ Istānbūl/Turkī	3
Reyḥānī	1		
Buḳāʿī/Biḳāʿī	1		
Ḳadīm	1		
Zerrīn-ḳalem	1		
Ḫuṭūṭ-ı muẖtelife/mütenevviʿa	6		
Muṣannifihi/Müʾellifihi/Mütercimihi	2		
Matbūʿ	3		

Bibliography

Archival Documents

Vakıflar Genel Müdürlüğü Arşivi 635, 1058, 1399.

Başkanlık Osmanlı Arşivi, TS.MA.d 9559; TS.MA.d 2386 (Safer); C.ML. 112/4981.

Manuscripts

Dublin, Chester Beatty Library, Ar. 3272.

Istanbul, Süleymaniye Library, Hamidiye 1450; Köprülü İlave 19; Rāgıp Paşa 489, 518, 510, 542, 645, 846, 884, 1333, 1052, 1134, 1220, 1141, 4111; Yazma Fihrist 25-1.

Istanbul, Topkapı Library, III. Ahmed 3595, 3679.

Istanbul, Türk-İslam Eserleri Müzesi 2218.

Leipzig, Universitätsbibliothek, Vollers 118.

Princeton, Firestone Library, Garrett 3516Y.

Tokyo, University Library, Daiber Collection 76. http://ricasdb.ioc.u-tokyo.ac.jp/daiber/fra_daiber_I_II.php?vol=2&ms=Ms.76&txtno=2147 (accessed 24 February 2023)

Secondary Sources

Açıl, Berat. "Habeşî Mehmed Ağa'nın (ö. 1590) Vakfettiği Kitaplar ve Akıbetleri." *International Journal of Turcology* 6 (2020): 67–83.

Akın-Kıvanç, Esra. *Mustafa Âli's Epic Deeds of Artists: A Critical Edition of the Earliest Ottoman Text about the Calligraphers and Painters of the Islamic World.* Leiden, 2011.

Aljoumani, Said. *Maktabah madrasiyyah fī ḥalab nihāyat al-ʿahd al-ʿUthmānī: al-daftar al-mujaddad li-kutub waqf ʿUthmān Bāshā al-Dūrikī.* Beirut, 2019.

Arberry, Arthur J. *The Chester Beatty Library: A Handlist of the Arabic Manuscripts.* 8 vols. Dublin, 1955.

Blair, Sheila. *Islamic Calligraphy.* Edinburgh, 2008.

Burak, Guy. "The Section on Prayers, Invocations, Unique Qualities of the Qur'an, and Magic Squares in the Palace Library Inventory." In *Treasures of Knowledge: An Inventory of the Ottoman Palace Library (1502/3–1503/4)*, edited by Gülru Necipoğlu, Cemal Kafadar and Cornell H. Fleischer. Leiden, 2019.

Burak, Guy. "Alphabets and 'Calligraphy' in the Section on Prayers, Special Characteristics of the Quran and Magic Squares in the Inventory of Sultan Bayezid II's Palace Library." *Journal of Material Cultures in the Muslim World* 2 (2021): 32–54.

Crecelius, Daniel. "The Waqfiyah of Muḥammad Bey Abū al-Dhahab II." *Journal of the American Research Center in Egypt* 16 (1979): 125–146.

Derman, Uğur. *İslam Kültür Mirasında Hat Sanatı.* Istanbul, 1992.

Erünsal, İsmail. *Osmanlılarda Kütüphaneler ve Kütüphanecilik.* Istanbul, 2015.

Gacek, Adam. "Arabic Scripts and Their Characteristics as Seen through the Eyes of Mamluk Authors." *Manuscripts of the Middle East* 4 (1989): 144–149.

al-Juʿbah, Nazmi. *Catalogue of Manuscripts in al-Khālidiyyah Library.* London, 2006.

Menchinger, Ethan L. *The First of the Modern Ottomans: The Intellectual History of Ahmed Vasif.* Cambridge/New York, 2017.

Necipoğlu, Gülru, Cemal Kafadar and Cornell H. Fleischer (eds). *Treasures of Knowledge: An Inventory of the Ottoman Palace Library (1502/3–1503/4).* 2 vols. Leiden, 2019.

Nefeszâde İsmâîl, *Gülzâr-ı Savâb*, edited by Kilisli Muallim Rifat. Istanbul, 1939.

Müstakîmzâde Süleymân Sadeddîn. *Tuhfe-i Hattâtîn*, edited by Mustafa Koç. Istanbul, 2014.

Raʾūf, ʿImād ʿAbd al-Salām. *Dirāsāt turāthiyya fī al-buldān wa-al-tarājim wa-al-adab wa-al-riḥlāt.* 2 vols. Irbil, 2019.

Serin, Muhittin. *Hat Sanatı ve Meşhur Hattatlar.* İstanbul, 1999.

Sievert, Henning. *Zwischen arabischer Provinz und Hoher Pforte: Beziehungen, Bildung und Politik des osmanischen Bürokraten Rāgıp Meḥmed Paşa (st. 1763).* Würzburg, 2008.

Sievert, Henning, "Eavesdropping on the Pasha's Salon: Usual and Unusual Readings of an Eighteenth-century Ottoman Bureaucrat." *Osmanlı Araştırmaları* 41 (2013): 159–195.

Şen, Ahmet Tunç. "The Sultan's Syllabus Revisited: Sixteenth-century Ottoman Madrasa Libraries and the Question of Canonization." *Studia Islamica* 116 (2021): 198–235.

Yaman, Ayşe Peyman. "Hat Sanatı İçin Devhatü'l Küttab Kaynak İncelemeli Metin Çevirisi." M.A. thesis, Marmara University, 2003.

Welch, Anthony. *Calligraphy in the Arts of the Muslim World*. New York, 1979.
Yazır, Mahmud Bedreddin. *Medeniyet Aleminde Yazı ve İslam Medeniyetinde Kalem Güzeli*, edited by Hüseyin Gündüz and Faruk Taşkale. Ankara, 2023.

CHAPTER 10

The Endowment Seals

Boris Liebrenz

Impressions of the large oval endowment seal, even when badly damaged, were a crucial help and often the only clue for the central task of matching the library catalogue's records with existing manuscript volumes and identifying the remnants of al-Jazzār's once splendid library. Therefore, the seal itself was usually regarded as a mere means to an end. Of course, this was also in line with the seal's intended main purpose, announcing the fact that a specific book belonged to the library of the Nūr Aḥmadīya-Mosque in Acre. Through this utilitarian approach, it might be missed that the seal itself has more to tell than the text it contains. More subtly, but probably not obscured to many contemporaries with a penchant for books, its design and form could be read as a statement legible against a tradition of sealing manuscripts in Islamicate book cultures, and particularly the practice of large institutional endowment libraries in the centre of the Ottoman empire.

When we discuss al-Jazzār's library seal, the most basic observation is also the most puzzling. The fact that not one but two seals existed for this library is in itself not unheard of. Many individual book owners had a great number of different seals and some institutions also changed theirs over time, especially when new books came into the collection after the original founder's death. However, in al-Jazzār's case, both seals are not only inscribed with exactly the same text and a near identical layout, albeit with one of them having a more circular and the other a flatter oval aspect. Crucially, they also bear the same date, 1205/1790–1791. This is hard to make sense of since they do not appear to represent two distinct phases in the collection's history or its cataloguing, and the year 1205/1790–1791 does not hold any immediately recognisable significance for the history of al-Jazzār, the endowment of his mosque or the city of Acre as a whole.

The text of the seals reads as follows:

In the name of God, the Compassionate, the Merciful.
There is no success for me but with God. This is the endowment
of the pilgrim Muḥammad Pasha al-Jazzār
to his *madrasa* al-Nūr Aḥmadīya
in 1205.

بسم الله الرحمن الرحيم
وما توفيقي الا بالله هذا
وقف
الحاج محمد باشا الجزار
بمدرسته النور احمدية
1205

Should we question the veracity of the date itself? Maybe one of the seals was meant to replace the other when the first was damaged or destroyed? It could then have mimicked the older seal completely, including the date, with the slight altering of the layout as a result of practical necessities of craftsmanship. But such a hypothesis is not supported by the reality of the manuscript record. Both seal types are found on volumes that have the long-form endowment statements with early dates such as 1197/1783.[1] Therefore, we are not seeing a later seal being used on later additions to the collection.

If, indeed, two seals were produced in the same year and in use since then, we may think about a shared responsibility of collection care. If,

1 A *waqf* statement dated 1197 together with the flat oval type is found on MS Cairo, Azhar 22783, with the more circular type on MS Berlin, Landberg 9. A *waqf* dated 1196 with the flat oval type is found on MS Dublin, CBL Ar 3342 and with the more circular type on MS Akka, EAP 399/1/46.

 DOI:10.1163/9789004720527_012

FIGURE 10.1
Al-Jazzār's nearly circular endowment seal; MS Jerusalem, Isʿāf Nashashibi Library, MS 115, 1r.

FIGURE 10.2
Al-Jazzār's flat oval endowment seal; MS Doha, QNL 17150, 1r.

in 1205/1790–1791, two people were charged with stamping all the books in the library, then each could have been issued with a seal of their own. Although only one actual librarian (*ḥāfiẓ al-kutub*) is mentioned in the endowment deeds, other personnel of the endowment could have been conscripted or allowed to help with the task, be they from the teaching personnel of the *madrasa* or lower-level assistants to the librarian. It is also possible that the governor al-Jazzār himself took enough interest in his books to maintain one seal for himself.

Another explanation appears to be out of the question, namely, the possibility of the collection being stored in two distinct locations. Both seals explicitly mention the Nūr Aḥmadiyya Mosque, and volumes bearing both seal types also have handwritten inscriptions that show that the books were already in this institution many years earlier, therefore, did not come together from two distinct collections in 1205/1790–1791.

Thus, there appears to be no meaningful correlation between the different seals and the development of the library stock or any material criteria. But there is, at this point, a significant, if not categorically explicable, discrepancy in the frequency of the respective seal's application. Where they can be distinguished, despite the often severe damage, I count 17 impressions of the flat oval seal type, but precisely twice as many instances, that is, 34, of its rounder sibling. Despite the small size of our corpus of identified manuscripts relative to the overall size of the library, this discrepancy appears to be too large to be a mere accident at this point. These preliminary observations cannot be explained at the moment, but they foster the hope that a larger corpus could reveal correlations that would point to a better understanding of the history of the collection and the work of its custodians.

One thing we can postulate with certainty is that, even if both seals were made at the same time, they were not produced by the same craftsman. We can say this with certainty because of a minute detail that usually only the very best seal impressions reveal and that is, consequently, often overlooked. On many seals, especially in the twelfth/eighteenth century and onwards, and probably more in the centre of the Ottoman Empire than anywhere else, the signature of an engraver can be found. These extremely small and delicate traces are very often illegible, destroyed and easily missed. What they mean precisely is also

FIGURE 10.3
A seal signed by the same engraver who produced al-Jazzār's nearly circular seal; MS Ann Arbor, University of Michigan, Isl. Ms. 347, 1r

not straightforward. Unlike craftsmen's signatures on other objects of art, for example metalwork or paintings, the single word we find is not accompanied by any explanatory term such as *ʿamal* (work of). Do they refer to an individual craftsman or a workshop? Many seals are entirely void of any such signature. Only one of al-Jazzār's seals, namely, the more circular type, has such a mark, directly next to the date: حطى, which could probably be read as khaṭṭī or ḥaẓẓī. There are a number of engravers of seals whose work could, thus, be documented over decades and with rather large dossiers of specimens that they signed. Ḥaẓẓī is a bit more obscure, but I could find another one of his works, this one dated in 1185/1771–1772, two decades prior to the seal this person or workshop produced for al-Jazzār's library. The text on this earlier specimen is in Turkish and the seal belongs to one Muḥammad Yumnī b. Muḥammad b. ʿAlī, whom I have not yet been able to identify.

Furthermore, Nimet İpek has alerted me to another seal, also dated 1185/1771–1772, signed by Ḥaẓẓī, this one inscribed with a Persian text and the name of Bahjat ʿAlī, the Ottoman overseer of the *awqāf al-ḥaramayn*, the endowments for Mecca and Medina.[2] This officer was also stationed in Constantinople. The signature of the engraver of the seal could, therefore, point to the Ottoman centre and the second version of al-Jazzār's seal, the one without the signature, to its possible local production. Alas, any certainty in these matters still eludes us.

1 Historical Context

Sealing things has tremendously deep roots going back millennia in the economic and administrative practices of the Middle East. Such practices were continued, also in the sphere of the written word, with the advent of the Islamic empire, and personal seals with names, pious formulas or images impressed on clay can be seen on early Arabic papyrus documents.[3] After the establishment of the Mongol reign of the Ilkhanids in the seventh/thirteenth century, seal impressions with ink are preserved as a diplomatic practice in the correspondence with foreign powers. The Eastern influence of this practice is obvious in the rectangular shape of the seals and their placement over the folds of scrolls, especially as many of the seals used by the Ilkhanids were not engraved with Arabic but Chinese characters.[4]

2 See this seal on https://muhur.yek.gov.tr/muhur/yekmu0145.

3 See Sijpesteijn, "Seals and Papyri from Early Islamic Egypt"; Sijpesteijn, "Expressing New Rule".

4 Yokkaichi, "Chinese Seals"; Yokkaichi, "Four Seals"; Matsui, "Six Seals". For diplomatic correspondence, we could point to the Letter of Güyük Khan to Pope Innocence IV, datable to 1246–1248, preserved at the Vatican, and the letter

Impressing seals with ink on books, on the other hand, is a relatively late development within a sophisticated tradition of handwritten notes to mark the legal status or use of a volume. These notes usually remained handwritten even after seals had made their first shy appearance on the pages of manuscripts. The first Arabic script seal we know of that was used for documentation in books was, in fact, an endowment seal. It was introduced by the Ilkhanid vizier Rashīd al-Dīn Faḍl Allāh Hamadānī (d. 718/1318)[5] to mark the volumes preserved in the library of his endowed complex Rabʿ-i Rashīdī in Tabrīz.[6] It was of an elongated, rectangular shape with a square kufic text more akin to those of monumental inscriptions in stone, and placed not on the title page, but in the margins of the text throughout a volume, and, where those books have survived, is usually destroyed today. It would also remain the only one of its kind for a long time and, in size, script and shape, a complete outlier that probably took its inspiration from Chinese documentary traditions rather than from that of Islamic antecedents. At the time of al-Jazzār's endowment seal, a similar form had not been seen for half a millennium.

Designing purpose-made seals for book endowments and whole libraries, on the other hand, had become standard by the eighteenth century. Within the traditions of book culture as practiced within the Ottoman empire and by that empire's elite in particular, the many large libraries endowed by the latter routinely employed customised seals. Throughout the seventeenth to nineteenth centuries, these seals often contained much or all of the elements that the more complete handwritten texts had previously displayed: the name of the donor, beneficiaries, institution and standard stipulations, such as the ban on lending out books beyond the premises of the library. As can easily be imagined, such texts, despite the compact measurements of their carriers, were occasionally quite long. Al-Jazzār's seals, which mention the name of the donor, the institution to which the book was endowed and the city in which this institution was situated, can be considered a standard middle ground.

This can easily be seen as a decision governed by an economy of time, alleviating the burden on the librarian of repeating the same endowment inscription hundreds and thousands of times. Even more economical was the possibility of repeating an impression of the exact same text throughout the book, as was often practiced. Previously, regarding handwritten endowment notes, a long-form endowment note on the title page was often followed by very rudimentary notes throughout the book, often consisting of only the word *waqf*, sometimes supplemented with a short form of the endower's name or that of the institution. With the help of seals, applying a large number of endowment notes actually became easier than erasing all of them. This reasoning appears to have worked: so often, when a volume slipped out of the library in which it was meant to remain for eternity, we can see the endowment seal meticulously destroyed dozens of times, but it only takes one oversight or one sloppy job of erasure to give away the original source. Additionally, since a seal reproduces exactly the same image with every single impression, even such small decorative features as a flower bud or knot at the right place can help to identify seals with certainty.

Nevertheless, *waqf* seal impressions were sometimes also accompanied by a long handwritten text or short-form handwritten notes throughout a volume. We can see that on many of al-Jazzār's books as well, where the seal supplements such earlier notes and probably replaces them altogether after 1205/1790–1791 since no notes with a later date have surfaced so far. However, the librarians of al-Jazzār's mosque usually do not repeat the seal impression and are content with placing it on the ti-

of Arghūn to Philip Le Bel, dated 1289, preserved in Paris, Archives Nationales.

5 Kamola, *Making Mongol History*.

6 On the Rabʿ-i Rashīdī, see Hoffmann, "In Pursuit of *Memoria* and Salvation"; Ben Azzouna, *Aux origins du classicisme*, 359–363. On the seal, see Richard, "Muhr-i kitābkhāna-yi Rashīd al-Dīn"; Richard, "Stamps", 345; Özgüdenli, "Nuskha-i az Tārīkh Waṣṣāf".

FIGURE 10.4
Khalīl b. Qāsim Ṭāshköprü-zāde's seal, dated 879/1475, is the earliest dated endowment seal in the Ottoman tradition; MS Istanbul, Beyazıt Kütüphanesi, Veliyyüddin Efendi 906, 16r

FIGURE 10.5
Endowment seal of Fāẓil Aḥmad Pasha Köprülü (d. 1087/1676), dated 1088/1677–1678; MS Istanbul, Köprülü Kütüphanesi, Fazıl Ahmed Paşa 652, 1r

tle page or a convenient place in the margin of an early page.

It is based on this background of historical development that the endowment seals impressed on the books of Aḥmad Pasha al-Jazzār become readable as an element of emulation and ambition. These aspects will become clearer as we take a look at the specific form of al-Jazzār's seal and where we can position it within the historical development of the medium. The oldest dated seal in the Ottoman tradition of which I am aware is actually an endowment seal. It was used by Khalīl b. Qāsim b. ḥājjī Ṣafā', that is, Ṭāshköprü-zāde (d. 879/1475), and is inscribed 879/1475, the year in which its owner died.[7]

This seal is of a small circular shape. Most other seals from that era, however, do not have a specific role inscribed on them. This is also true for the seals used by the Ottoman sultans on the books that they either put in the palace treasury or endowed to public institutions, such as the *madrasas* they founded. In all of those cases, the early sultans used small pointed oval seals with only their *ṭughrā* inscribed on them.[8] It is unclear whether these were meant particularly for books or had other documentary functions as well. However, the Ottoman sultans had, by the eighteenth century, additionally developed particular seals designated for their endowments. Since they were technically not endowment seals, lacking the necessary information in their inscriptions, they are usually found next to a handwritten endowment note. Designed to a uniform circular shape with the same Qur'anic motto (الحمد لله الذي هدانا لهذا وما كنا لنهتدي لولا ان هدانا الله) followed by the sultan's individual *ṭughrā*, this particular design was reserved for the sovereign. But the form of a large oval, to which al-Jazzār resorted, was encountered on the endowed books of many from the political elite of Constantinople.

The second half of the seventeenth and the eighteenth century can be considered the heyday of public-facing library institutions set up by grand viziers, chief muftis, chief eunuchs and other high functionaries in Constantinople.[9] A review of the most important among them in the century before al-Jazzār's creation will show his seals to stand conceptually in line with those used in the capital. The library endowed by the Grand Vizier Fāḍil Aḥmad Pasha from the Köprülü family (d. 1087/1676) played a crucial role in this development. By accident more than design, it became the first standalone library institution in the Ottoman Empire.[10] Its founder, a highly cultured intellectual who had harboured scholarly ambitions earlier in life, also chose to use a large oval seal very different from those his peers and other members of his family had used before him. It is dated 1088/1677. The

7 The seal can be found in the seal database of the Türkiye Yazma Eserler Kurumu Başkanlığı: https://muhur.yek.gov.tr/muhur/yekmu0766.

8 Kut/Bayraktar, *Yazma eserlerde vakıf mühürleri*, contains many, but not all of these sultanic seals, and they are now accessible via https://muhur.yek.gov.tr.

9 For a general overview, see Erünsal, *Ottoman Libraries*; Erünsal, *A History of Ottoman Libraries*.

10 See, for example, Erünsal, *Ottoman Libraries*, 43–44.

FIGURE 10.6
Endowment seal of the şheyhülislām Feyzullah Efendi (d. 1115/1703), dated 1112/1700–1701; MS Istanbul, Millet Kütüphanesi, Feyzullah Efendi 1292, 1r

FIGURE 10.7
Endowment seal of ʿAmja-zāde Ḥusayn Pasha (d. 1114/1702), dated 1111/1699–1700; MS Istanbul, Süleymaniye Kütüphanesi, Amcazade Hüseyin 162, 1r

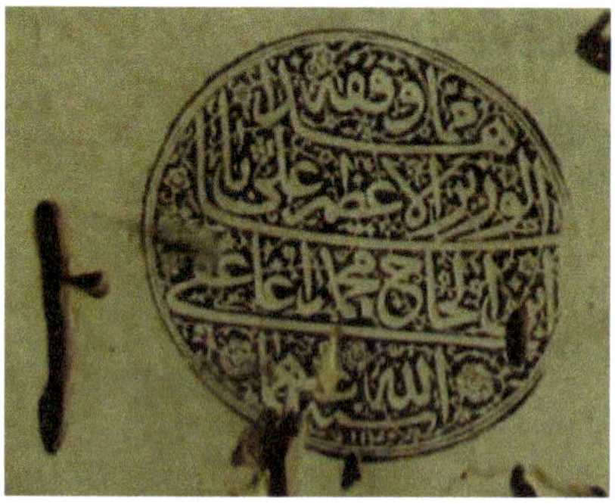

FIGURE 10.8
Endowment seal of Çorlulu ʿAlī Pasha (d. 1123/1711), dated 1120/1708–1709; MS Istanbul, Süleymaniye Kütüphanesi, Çorlulu Ali Paşa 278, 1r

FIGURE 10.9
Endowment seal of Shahīd ʿAlī Pasha (d. 1128/1716), dated 1130/1718; MS Istanbul, Süleymaniye Kütüphanesi, Şehid Ali Paşa 1835, 1r

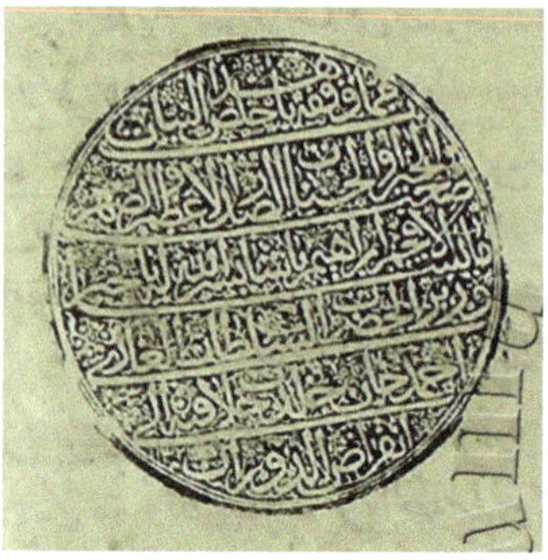

FIGURE 10.10
Endowment seal of Nevşehirli Dāmād Ibrāhīm Pasha (d. 1143/1730), dated 1132/1720; MS Istanbul, Süleymaniye Kütüphanesi, Damat Ibrahim Paşa 787, 1r

next great library builder, the *şeyhülislam* Feyzullah Efendi (d. 1115/1703),[11] followed him in this regard when his seal was produced a quarter of a century later, in 1112/1700–1701. These two were the most visible, accessible and precious non-sultanic libraries in the city at the turn of the eighteenth century. They still were when al-Jazzār dwelled in the city later in the century, even though it is more than unlikely that he would have looked at them at all or with the intention of emulating their sealing practice. In the meantime, many more similar institutions had also sprung up.

A look at the line of Ottoman grand viziers who established endowment libraries shows many similarities between their seals. I have identified those of seven of these officers, engraved between the years 1111/1699–1700 and 1175/1761–1762. The three earliest of them are oval and three later ones more or less circular. The Grand Vizier Muḥammad Pasha (Tiryaki Mehmed Pasha) chose a highly unusual upright oval format in 1160/1747. But it could hardly ever be seen because his library appears to have been sequestered and the traces of his seal systematically destroyed, although with the right knowledge they can be identified dispersed in many collections in Istanbul. Early on, Damad Ibrāhīm Pasha's large circular seal contains the most amount of text, in 1132/1719–1720, while Hekīmoğlu ʿAlī Pasha's equally circular seal is the smallest in this group in 1146/1733–1734. Rāghib Pasha's (d. 1176/1763)[12] is more circular than oval, but shares with al-Jazzār's seals the spacing of the lines within cartouches separated by double lines,

11 Abou-El-Haj, *The 1703 Rebellion*; Nizri, *Ottoman High Politics*.

12 Sievert, *Zwischen arabischer Provinz und Hoher Pforte*.

FIGURE 10.11
Endowment seal of Ḥakīm-ūġlī ʿAlī Pasha (d. 1171/1758), dated 1146/1733–1734; MS Istanbul, Süleymaniye Kütüphanesi, Hekimoğlu Ali Paşa 168, 1r

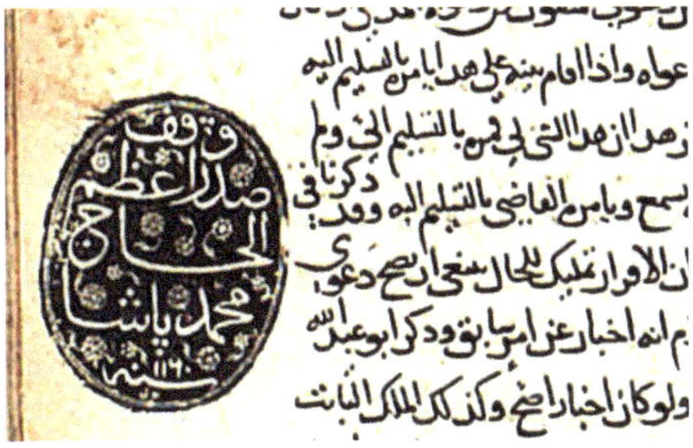

FIGURE 10.12
Endowment seal of Tiryaki Mehmed Pasha (1680–1751, in office 1746–1747), dated 1160/1747; MS Istanbul, Süleymaniye Kütüphanesi, Fatih 2431, 29r

FIGURE 10.13
Endowment seal of Rāghib Pasha (d. 1176/1763), dated 1175/1761–1762; MS Istanbul, Ragıp Paşa Kütüphanesi, Ragıp Paşa 905

FIGURE 10.14
Endowment seal of Bashīr Agha (d. 1159/1746), dated 1130/1718; MS Istanbul, Süleymaniye Kütüphanesi, Hacı Beşir Ağa 553, 1r

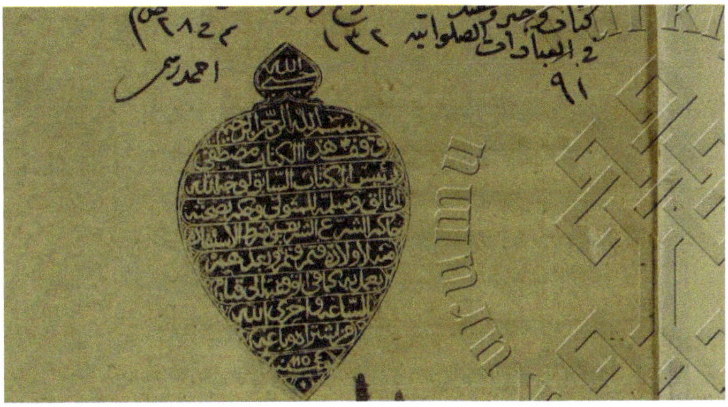

FIGURE 10.15
Endowment seal of raʾīs al-kuttāb Muṣṭafā Efendi (d. 1162/1749), dated 1154/174; MS Istanbul, Süleymaniye Kütüphanesi, Reisulküttab 170, 1r

that is, lines that are not formed by elongated letters.

Of course, there are extravagant exceptions in the city's great libraries, especially when we look at the level below the grand viziers. We can find an innovative design like that of Muṣṭafā, the *raʾīs al-kuttāb*, whose seal in 1154/1741–1742 opted for something like a crowned drop shape. Bešīr Aghā's seal, while oval, has a very different internal layout, with four cartouches grouped around a central round field, than the other examples that shared this outward shape. However, the seal of the *şeyhülislām* Veliyüddin Efendi, still in 1175/1761–1762, is strikingly similar in shape, layout and script to that of his predecessor Feyzullah Efendi at the beginning of that century. One of the later Köprülüs, the vizier Aḥmad b. Nuʿmān, also used a very similar seal in 1170/1756–1757.

There was clearly not a single normative way prescribed for what an endowment seal should look like in the period. But the prevalent ideas, especially on the level of the vizierate, coalesced around an oval, round or circular shape of rather large proportions, even though many other forms were available at the time for personal seals. What al-Jazzār had designed for his book endowment,

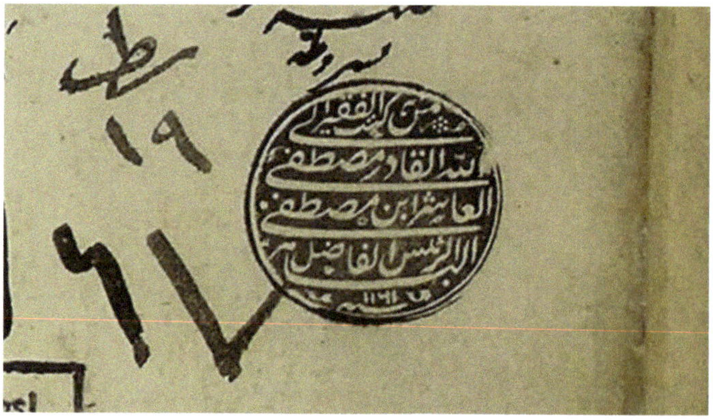

FIGURE 10.16
Endowment seal of Muṣṭafā ʿĀshir Efendi (d. 1219/1804), dated 1161/1748; MS Istanbul, Süleymaniye Kütüphanesi, Aşir Efendi 167, 1r

FIGURE 10.17
Endowment seal of Aḥmad b. Nuʿmān Köprülü (1183/1769), dated 1170/1756–1757; MS Istanbul, Köprülü Kütüphanesi, Hacı Ahmed Paşa 337, 240r

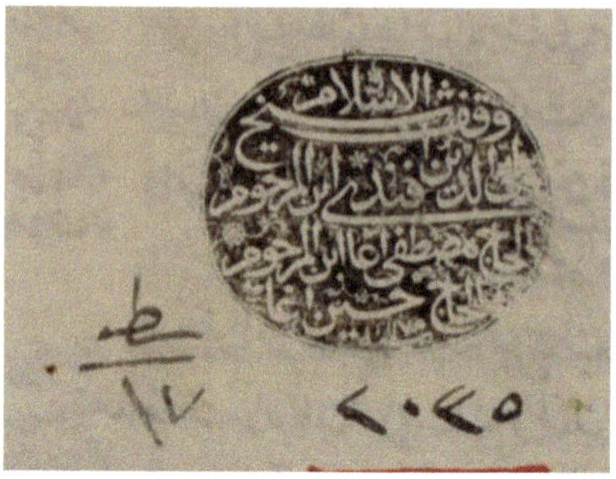

FIGURE 10.18
Endowment seal of şeyhülislām Veliyüddin Efendi (d. 1182/1768), dated 1175/1761; MS Istanbul, Beyazıt Kütüphanesi, Veliyyüddin Efendi 2035, 1r

FIGURE 10.19
Large seal found on the endowed books of Muḥammad Bey Abū al-Dhahab in Egypt; MS Paris, BnF, Arabe 5901, 1r

then, was totally conventional by the standards of Ottoman elite libraries in the centre of the empire throughout the eighteenth century.

However, at the same time, it was quite out of place within its specific environment, the Arabic provinces of Syria and Egypt. This is apparent when we take a look at the other large book endowments set up there by governors throughout the eighteenth century. The endowment notes of the great library of Muḥammad Bey Abū al-Dhahab (d. 1189/1775)[13] in Egypt were accompanied by the impression of a large circular seal that bore nothing but the name Muḥammad. This represents an idiosyncratic solution without a real precedent in Cairo, and ensures an easy recognition. It should be noted that most of the endowments by Egypt's powerful Mamluk emirs, especially those made for the existing libraries within the Azhar mosque, were actually done completely without a seal. So, although al-Jazzār had spent considerable time in Egypt in the entourage of Mamluk emirs, and even if, unexpectedly, he might have spent his time in the country's libraries, he could not have found any inspiration for his later sealing practice on the shores of the Nile.

A more instructive comparison can be sought closer to Acre with al-Jazzār's most enduring rivals on a provincial level, the ʿAẓm family in Damascus.[14] Established within 60 years from each other,

13 Ḥājjī Khalīfa, *Kashf al-ẓunūn*, VII, 3–22; Paton, *A History of the Egyptian Revolution*, II, 247; Crecelius, "The Waqf of Muhammad Bey Abu al-Dhahab"; Liebrenz, *Die Rifāʿīya*, 152–153.

14 For their libraries and books, see Liebrenz, *Die Rifāʿīya*, 168–176.

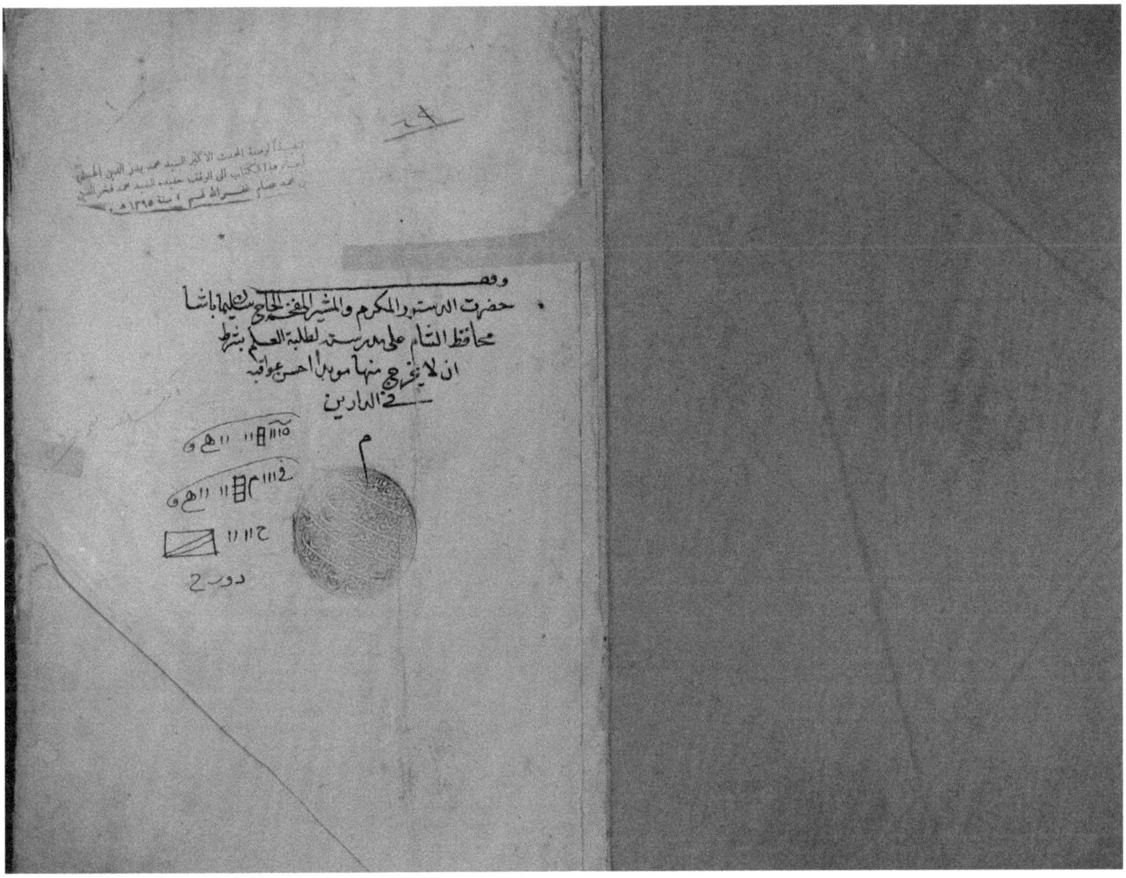

FIGURE 10.20 Endowment seal of Sulaymān Pasha al-ʿAẓm (d. 1156/1743), dated 1150/1738; MS Damascus, al-Majmaʿ al-ʿIlmī 61, 1r

their endowments shaped the library landscape of Syria's most bookish city for three generations, making them the natural contenders for the intellectual reputation for which the erection of a library aims. The family brought forth five governors in the city, four of whom did, on different scales, put their names on book endowments. First in this line was Sulaymān Pasha (d. 1156/1743), who founded a *madrasa* in 1150/1738,[15] the date that is also found on his large oval-to-circular endowment seal.

Sulaymān was followed as governor by his nephew Asʿad Pasha al-ʿAẓm (d. 1171/1757).[16] Asʿad was responsible for some of the most memorable buildings of Ottoman Damascus, such as the Khān Asʿad Pasha. But he chose the *madrasa* that his father Ismāʿīl had erected as the appropriate place to receive his book endowment. He used a small octagonal seal with, relatively, a lot of information densely packed into it to mark his endowed books.

Muḥammad Pasha al-ʿAẓm (d. 1197/1783)[17] served as governor in the 1770s, but was said to have been quite devout and prone to studying. His octagonal seal looks very similar to that of Asʿad, but I could not accurately decipher the date inscribed on it.

15 Marino, "Les investissement", 217; Badrān, *Munādamat al-aṭlāl*, 266.

16 *Kitāb waqf Asʿad bāshā al-ʿAẓm*.

17 Rafeq, *The Province of Damascus*, 286–319; al-Murādī, *Silk al-durar*, IV, 111–116; Seetzen, *Reisen durch Syrien*, I, 281.

FIGURE 10.21 Endowment seal of Asʿad Pasha al-ʿAẓm (d. 1171/1757); MS Damascus, al-Majmaʿ al-ʿIlmī 1070, unfoliated

Closest in time to al-Jazzār was ʿAbd Allāh Pasha (d. 1224/1809), son of Muḥammad Pasha. He was appointed governor of Damascus intermittently with al-Jazzār, had to flee the region altogether when al-Jazzār assumed the governorship of Damascus in 1799, and only returned when his rival had died. His *madrasa* with an integrated book endowment had already been erected in 1193/1779.[18] The small circular seal that belonged to it is dated 1211/1796–1797 and, therefore, several years after that of the Nūr Aḥmadiyya. Although it deviates in shape, the text of the seal is precisely the one used on that of his father Muḥammad's.

Among the four seals used on the endowed books of several governors from the al-ʿAẓm family in Damascus, only that of Sulaymān Pasha in 1150, with its large size and circular shape, conformed to the sealing practices en vogue among the political elite in Constantinople. This stylistic orientation towards the centre was apparently not an obvious choice for a governor in the Arabic provinces, if they used endowment seals at all. Like the name of the institution written on the seal, al-Nūr Aḥmadiyya, a clear reference to the Nūr ʿUthmāniyya (Nuruosmaniye) in Constantinople, the seal as a whole can probably be seen as an attempt to take the capital and not the province as its point of reference, maybe even a conscious decision to emulate Ottoman imperial book culture and claim its place within it.

18 Al-ʿUlabī, *Khiṭaṭ Dimashq*, 273–275.

FIGURE 10.22
Endowment seal of Muḥammad Pasha al-ʿAẓm (d. 1197/1783); MS Paris, BnF, Arabe 5828, 1r

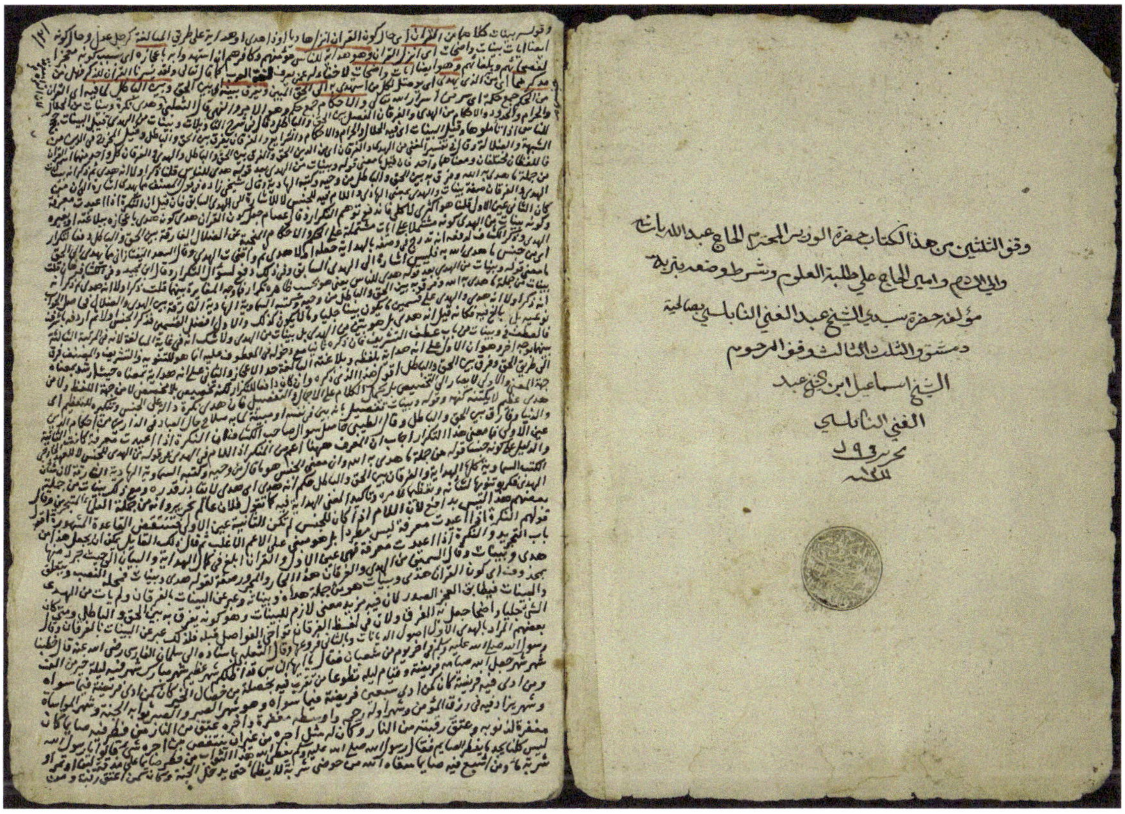

FIGURE 10.23 Endowment seal of ʿAbd Allāh Pasha al-ʿAẓm (d. 1224/1809), dated 1211/1796–1797; MS Jerusalem, National Library of Israel, MS. Yah. Ar. 308, 1v

Bibliography

Abou-El-Haj, Rifaʿat Ali. *The 1703 Rebellion and the Structure of Ottoman Politics*. Istanbul, 1984.

Badrān, ʿAbd al-Qādir. *Munādamat al-aṭlāl wa-musāmarat al-khayāl*, edited by M.Z. al-Shāwīsh. Damascus, 1960.

Ben Azzouna, Nourane. *Aux origins du classicisme. Calligraphes et bibliophies au temps des dynasties mongoles*. Leiden, 2018.

Crecelius, Daniel. "The Waqf of Muhammad Bey Abu al-Dhahab in Historical Perspective." *International Journal of Middle East Studies* 23 (1991): 57–81.

Erünsal, İsmail E. *Ottoman Libraries. A Survey of the History, Development and Organization of Ottoman Foundation Libraries*. Cambridge, Mass., 2008.

Erünsal, İsmail E. *A History of Ottoman Libraries*. Boston, 2022.

Ḥājjī Khalīfa, Muṣṭafā b. ʿAbdallāh known as. *Kashf al-ẓunūn ʿan asāmī al-kutub wa-al-funūn*, edited by Gustav Flügel. 7 vols. Leipzig/London, 1835–1858.

Hoffmann, Birgitt. "In Pursuit of *Memoria* and Salvation: Rashīd al-Dīn and His Rabʿ-ı Rashīdī." In *Politics, Patronage, and the Transmission of Knowledge in 13th–15th Century Tabriz*, edited by Judith Pfeiffer, 171–185. Leiden, 2014.

Kamola, Stefan. *Making Mongol History. Rashid al-Din and the Jamiʿ al-Tawarikh*. Edinburgh, 2019.

Kitāb waqf Asʿad bāshā al-ʿAẓm. Edited by Ṣalāḥ al-Dīn al-Munajjid. Damascus, 1953.

Kut, Günay and Nimet Bayraktar. *Yazma eserlerde vakıf mühürleri*. Istanbul, 2021.

Liebrenz, Boris. *Die Rifāʿīya aus Damaskus. Eine Privatbibliothek im osmanischen Syrien und ihr kulturelles Umfeld*. Leiden, 2016.

Marino, Brigitte. "Les investissement de Sulaymān Pacha al-ʿAẓm à Damas." *Annales Islamologiques* 34 (2000): 209–226.

Matsui, Dai. "Six Seals on the Verso of Čoban's Decree of 726 AH/1326 CE." *Orient* 50 (2015): 35–39.

Al-Murādī, Muḥammad Khalīl. *Silk al-durar fī aʿyān al-qarn al-thānī ʿashar*, edited by Muḥammad ʿAbd al-Qādir Shāhīn. 4 vols. Beirut, 1997.

Nizri, Michael. *Ottoman High Politics and the Ulema Household*. Basingstoke, 2014.

Özgüdenli, Osman Ghazi. "Nuskha-i az Tārīkh Waṣṣāf be khaṭṭ muʾallif wa-muhr Kitābkhāna-i Rabʿ-i Rashīdī." *Nāma-i Bahāristān* 4 (1382): 63–73.

Paton, Andrew Archibald. *A History of the Egyptian Revolution, from the Period of the Mamelukes to the Death of Mohammed Ali*. London, 1863.

Rafeq, Abdul-Karim. *The Province of Damascus, 1723–1783*. Beirut, 1966.

Richard, Francis. "Muhr-i kitābkhāna-yi Rashīd al-Dīn Faḍlallāh Hamadhānī."*Ayāndah* 8/6 (1982): 343–346.

Richard, Francis. "Stamps." In *Islamic Codicology. An Introduction to the Study of Manuscripts in Arabic Script*, edited by François Déroche, 335–344. London, 2005.

Seetzen, Ulrich Jasper. *Reisen durch Syrien, Palästina, Phönicien, die Transjordanländer, Arabia Petraea und Unter-Aegypten*, edited by Fr. Kruse. 4 vols. Berlin, 1854–1859.

Sievert, Henning. *Zwischen arabischer Provinz und Hoher Pforte. Beziehungen, Bildung und Politik des osmanischen Bürokraten Rāġıb Meḥmed Paşa (st. 1763)*. Würzburg, 2008.

Sijpesteijn, Petra M. "Seals and Papyri from Early Islamic Egypt." In *Seals and Sealing Practices in the Near East*, edited by Ilona Regulsji, Kim Duistermaat and Peter Verkinderen, 163–174 Leuven, 2012.

Sijpesteijn, Petra M. "Expressing New Rule: Seals from Early Islamic Egypt and Syria, 600–800 CE." In *Seals. Making and Marking Connections Across the Medieval World*, edited by Brigitte Bedos-Rezak and Carol Symes, 99–148. Amsterdam, 2019.

Al-ʿUlabī, Akram Ḥusayn. *Khiṭaṭ Dimashq. Dirāsa tārīkhiyya shāmila*. Damascus, 1989.

Yokkaichi, Yasuhiro. "Chinese Seals in the Mongol Official Documents in Iran: Re-examination of the Sphragistic System in the Il-Khanid and Yuan Dynasties." *Journal of the Dunhuang and Turfan Studies* (2010): 215–230.

Yokkaichi, Yasuhiro. "Four Seals in `Phags-pa and Arabic Scripts on Amīr Čoban's Decree of 726 AH/1326 CE." *Orient* 50 (2015): 25–33.

CHAPTER 11

By the Keepers' Hands: Comparing the Inks of Endowment Statements, Mottos and Seals

Claudia Colini and Kyle Ann Huskin

The library of Aḥmad Pasha al-Jazzār (d. 1219/1804) contained over 1,800 volumes, according to the library inventory copied in 1221/1806.[1] In order to protect the collection and assure its permanence after his death, he included the library in the Nūr al-Aḥmadī complex, established in Acre in 1196/1781. The salary for a librarian is recorded in the endowment deed dating 1200/1786, but the list of the volumes is not provided; thus, other strategies to identify the books as part of the collection and prevent their loss and active removal needed to be set in place.

Some of them can be encountered directly in the pages of the manuscripts belonging to this collection: al-Jazzār's seal was stamped with black ink at the beginning of the volumes; the handwritten endowment statement can often be found in the same place; short versions of the endowment statement—from now on referred to as mottos—were, instead, annotated throughout the pages, with varying frequency. Seals and annotations are not present in all the surviving books of the library; often only some can be found on a single volume. Additionally, there are two matrices of al-Jazzār's seal, and the writing styles and hands of the annotations—particularly of the mottos—are clearly different. We believe that the books were annotated on different occasions by multiple writers, perhaps depending on the acquisition date of the volumes or based on periodic checking of the collection's content.

Different occasions may result in changes to the inks and tools employed to mark the books, changes that can be identified through the application of scientific analytical methods. If the same material features are shared by groups of writing, we can conclude that those writings were made during the same instance or period of time. In order to verify this hypothesis, a small corpus of al-Jazzār's manuscripts was selected as a pilot project for analysis: it consists of seven manuscripts preserved at the Chester Beatty Library (CBL), sporting various combinations of seals, endowment statements and mottos, from various and recurring matrices, hands, and dates.[2] The CBL's collection has two crucial advantages for this study: firstly, it houses the largest collection of al-Jazzār manu-

1 Library inventory, Vakıflar Genel Müdürlüğü (Ankara), Daftar 1626. The authors would like to thank Said Aljoumani for having shared the palaeographic assessment of the various hands annotating the book with us. Without his notes, the evaluation of the data would have been much more difficult and incomplete. We also thank Astrid Meyer, Karin Scheper, Boris Liebrenz and the editors for their contribution in improving the first draft. And, last but not least, our thanks go to Moya Carey and Kristine Rose-Beers, who welcomed and hosted us at the Chester Beatty Library, facilitating our work in all ways possible.

The research for this chapter was funded by the Deutsche Forschungsgemeinschaft (DFG, German Research Foundation) under Germany's Excellence Strategy—EXC 2176 'Understanding Written Artefacts: Material, Interaction and Transmission in Manuscript Cultures', project no. 390893796. The research was conducted within the scope of the Centre for the Study of Manuscript Cultures (CSMC) at Universität Hamburg.

2 The CBL actually houses a total of nine al-Jazzār manuscripts, but our present corpus omits two (Ar. 3268 and Ar. 3310) whose connection to al-Jazzār was not known at the time of the analysis. The authors are grateful to curator Moya Carey and Said Aljoumani for identifying the two additional manuscripts.

 | DOI:10.1163/9789004720527_013

scripts in the European Union, which is logistically important for transporting equipment with X-ray components and an infrared (IR) camera, and secondly, the manuscripts have a wide range of features.

The comparison of the inks was conducted according to the standard protocol for the characterisation of writing materials in use at the Centre for the Study of Manuscript Cultures (CSMC) in Hamburg, including ultra-violet (UV) visible (VIS) near-infrared (NIR) microscopy, short wave IR reflectography (IRR) and X-ray fluorescence (XRF).[3] These methods allow us to differentiate between ink classes and compare inks that belong to the same class but have a different elemental composition.

1 Corpus

The seventy-eight manuscripts that currently comprise the Jazzār corpus are scattered around the world but are identifiable by three means of library annotation: endowment statements, endowment seals and short endowment mottos (on these elements, see the *Introduction* to this volume). The first chronologically datable activity in the Jazzār corpus was the annotation of the endowment statement at the beginning of the volumes. The statements are dated between 1196/1782 and 1205/1791, with a striking majority written in the years 1196/1782–1197/1783 by the same hand. While the layout and number of lines can vary, the wording is standardised, although a few variants have been noticed. The second datable marking method consists of seal impressions. They can be found at the beginning of the volumes, either on the first folios or on the recto (corresponding to side a) prior to the beginning of the text. The black-inked impressions were left by one of two different matrices, one circular and one oval, both dated 1205/1790–1791, as can be seen in the lower margin of the impression.[4] It is possible, however, that the seals were used beyond this date.[5] The third method, the annotation of mottos, is not dated. This extremely short version of the endowment statement can be found on the margins of several pages throughout the book. If there are only two textual variants for the mottos—A) وقف الله تعالى, which is the most frequent, and B) وقف لله تعالى—everything else differs greatly: the location in the page and their frequency throughout the book, the writing implements and inks used, and, even more surprisingly, the writing hands and styles. Multiple series of mottos by different hands were observed in the same volume (Ar. 3272, for instance), but they can also be completely omitted (as in Ar. 3316). Said Aljoumani's preliminary palaeographic assessment identifies around twenty-five distinct hands and subtypes of hands that penned mottos and endowment statements in the manuscripts identified so far.[6] Additionally, in this case, one hand—from now on referred to as Hand no. 1—is found more frequently and corresponds to the same one that wrote most of the endowment statements from 1196/1782 to 1197/1783, suggesting that it might belong to the first librarian. Finally, single occurrences of mottos were also found: they are often incomplete, shorter versions of the usual formula and are sometimes written by unskilled hands. For this reason, they might be errors, pen trials or writing exercises.

A subset of nine al-Jazzār manuscripts are preserved at the CBL, all identifiable from the library inventory written in 1221/1806.[7] As has been

3 Rabin et al., "Identification and Classification"; Rabin, "Instrumental Analysis"; Colini et al., "New Standard Protocol."

4 The date of the seal on Ar. 3342 is illegible due to some abrasions and damages that occurred to the paper, but the comparison with other oval impressions leaves no doubt as to its identification.

5 See Chapter 10 on seals by Boris Liebrenz.

6 The authors are extremely grateful to Said Aljoumani for sharing the results of his preliminary palaeographic description. The assessment is still incomplete due to limited access to the manuscripts and images.

7 Library inventory, Vakıflar Genel Müdürlüğü (Ankara), Daftar 1626.

TABLE 11.1 The Jazzār manuscripts preserved at the Chester Beatty Library

Shelf-mark	Title	Author	Al-Jazzār Library inventory nr.	Seal	Endowment statement	Mottos
Ar. 3236	تذكرة الإعداد ليوم المعاد Tadhkirat al-iʿdād li-yawm al-miʿād	الصنهاجي al-Ṣinhājī	718	Oval, fol. 1ª	Absent	Mottos A (Hand no. 7) and Mottos B (Hands no. 6 and U1)
Ar. 3268	معالم التنزيل Maʿālim al-tanzīl	البغوي al-Baghawī	44	Absent	Absent	Motto A (Hands no. 1 and 10) Motto B (Hand no. 12)
Ar. 3272	الفتوح al-Futūḥ	ابن أعثم الكوفي Ibn Aʿtham al-Kūfī	1366	Circular, fol. 1ª	25 Ṣafar 1197 / 30 January 1783, fol. 1ª, Hand no. 1, triangular shape	Motto A (Hands no. 1 and 5) Motto B (Hand no. 4) Incomplete: U2 and U3
Ar. 3294	الروض الأنف الباسم al-Rawḍ al-unuf al-bāsim	عبد الرحمن السهيلي ʿAbd al-Raḥmān al-Suhaylī	276	Circular, fol. 2ª	Absent	Absent
Ar. 3310	أهنى المنائح في أسنى المدائح Ahnā ʾl-Manāʾiḥ fī asnā al-Madāʾiḥ	ابن فهد Ibn Fahd	1148	Circular, fol. 1ª	Absent	Motto A (Hand no. 11)
Ar. 3315	الفهرست al-Fihrist	النديم al-Nadīm	998	Circular, fol. 1ª	Undated, fol. 1ª, Hand no. 3, rect-angular shape	Motto A (Hands no. 3 and 8)
Ar. 3316	شرح الجامع الصغير Sharḥ al-jāmiʿ al-ṣaghīr	علي بن مكي الرازي ʿAlī b. Makī al-Rāzī	438	Circular, fol. 2ª	Absent	Absent
Ar. 3334	الوجوه والنظائر al-Wujūh wa-al-naẓāʾir	هارون بن موسى الأزدي الأعور Hārūn b. Mūsā al-Azdī al-Aʿwar	492	Circular, fol. 1ª	1197/1783, fol. 1ª, Hand no. 2, rect-angular shape, shorter version of text	Motto B (Hand no. 9)
Ar. 3342	التذييل والتكميل في شرح كتاب التسهيل Manaj al-al-Tadhyīl wa-al-takmīl fī sharḥ kitāb al-tashīl	أبو حيان الأندلسي Abu Ḥayyān	750	Oval, fol. 1ª	5 Dhū al-Ḥijja 1196 / 11 November 1782, fol. 1ª, Hand no. 1, rect-angular shape	Motto A (Hand no. 10)

mentioned previously, seven manuscripts were analysed for this paper because the other two were unknown to us at the time. The most important characteristics of the manuscripts, particularly referring to the three marking methods, are summarised in table 11.1.

Two manuscripts of the CBL corpus—Ar. 3342 and Ar. 3272—present the standard endowment statement, written by the most frequent hand (Hand no. 1) and dated 1196/1782 and 1197/1783, respectively. During the year 1197/1783, a different hand (Hand no. 2) penned a shorter version of the endowment statement on Ar. 3334. A third, different hand (Hand no. 3) wrote the standard version of the endowment statement on Ar. 3315; the annotation is undated, but it overlaps the seal impressions, suggesting it was written after the seal was stamped. Five of the manuscripts do not present any endowment statements.

The seal impression is visible on eight of the CBL manuscripts, although in one case (Ar. 3310), it was partially erased in an attempt to mask the provenance of the book. The circular matrix was mostly used to mark these manuscripts, with the oval seal appearing in only two of them (Ar. 3236 and Ar. 3342).

Several hands penned the mottos in the CBL manuscripts. Hand no. 1 appears in two manuscripts, showing slightly different writing styles on the upper margins of Ar. 3268 and on the upper and fore margins of Ar. 3272. In both cases the variant A of the motto is repeated on several folios throughout the books, at almost regular intervals (on average, every 20 and 30 folios, respectively). Both books, however, also show mottos written by other hands. In addition to two incomplete mottos (U2 and U3), two sets of mottos were left by Hand no. 4 (motto B) and Hand no. 5 (motto A) in Ar. 3272. They occur at more irregular intervals than Hand no. 1, but with a certain frequency. On the contrary, Hands no. 10 and 12 only added two (motto A) and one annotation, respectively, to Ar. 3268. Hand no. 10, which shares some palaeographical characteristics with Hand no. 1, wrote variant A mottos on the upper margins of fols 1^{b}–2^{a} in Ar. 3342. The person (Hand no. 3) who wrote the endowment statement on fol. 1^{a} of Ar. 3315 also added a motto (variant A) on the same folio, between the decorative cartouche and the statement. Another hand (no. 8) added mottos on the upper margins of several pages of the same volume, at irregular intervals. Hand no. 7 penned mottos (variant A) on the upper margins on the verso (side b) of several folios of Ar. 3236, also at irregular intervals, while the motto (variant B) left by Hand no. 6 and an incomplete one (U1) are visible on the fore margin of fol. 1^{a}. Ar. 3334 sports only a series of mottos on the upper margin made by Hand no. 9, while Hand no. 11 wrote two mottos (variant A) on the upper margin of fol. 30^{b} and lower margin of fol. 31^{a} in Ar. 3310.

We provide a summary of the writing hands encountered in the CBL corpus with examples of their writings in table 11.2.

2 Ink Classes and Scientific Analysis

Black inks can be grouped into four main classes: carbon, plant, iron-gall and mixed inks.[8] Carbon inks are obtained by mixing charcoal or soot with a water-soluble binder in a water-based solvent. Several precursors were used to obtain the carbonaceous material in the Islamic world: lamp oils were the most appreciated, due to the fine particles of the soot obtained, although the burnt material collected from ovens and pots was also used because of its abundance and convenience, despite being of a lower quality. Gum arabic is normally used as a binder dissolved in simple fresh water or enriched with some perfumes, such as rosewater. Carbon inks can sometimes contain metallic impurities, such as traces of iron, copper or lead, probably contaminants from the tools used to prepare or store the ink (such as bronze or lead inkwells) or from the water. Such elements are present in a more consistent amount in rare cases, suggesting an intentional addition rather than an occasional contamination. We refer to the latter as carbon-based inks with metallic admixtures, and they are sometimes included in the class of mixed inks.[9]

It is possible to obtain tannins, which are the main components of plant inks, by cooking or macerating various vegetal materials, such as bark, fruits or flowers. There are only a few Arabic reci-

8 Rabin, "Building a Bridge", 315. For the information specifically related to Arabic inks provided in the following paragraphs, see Colini, "From Recipes to Material Analysis", 15–19, 39–40, 106–108.

9 Rabin, "Building a Bridge," 315–318.

TABLE 11.2 Examples of the various hands writing the mottos and endowment statements in the manuscripts of the Chester Beatty Library

Hand no.	Shelf mark	Writing	Location	Example
1	Ar. 3272	Endowment statement	fol. 1ᵃ	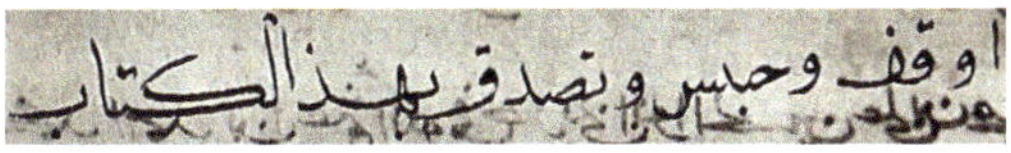
1	Ar. 3342	Endowment statement	fol. 1ᵃ	
1	Ar. 3272	Motto A	fol. 1ᵃ, above and below the endowment statement; fols 11ᵇ–12ᵃ; 38ᵇ–39ᵃ; 72ᵇ–73ᵃ, 104ᵇ–105ᵃ, 142ᵇ–143ᵃ, 169ᵇ–170ᵃ, 209ᵇ–210ᵃ, 239ᵇ–240ᵃ, 270ᵇ–271ᵃ, 303ᵇ–304ᵃ, 360ᵇ–361ᵃ, in pairs, upper margin on the verso (b), fore margin on the recto (a)	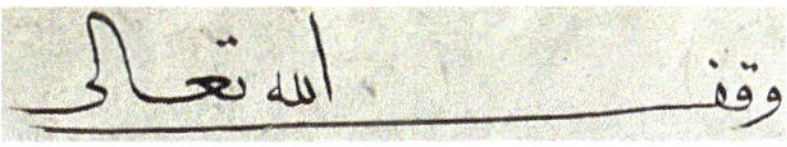 fol. 210ᵃ 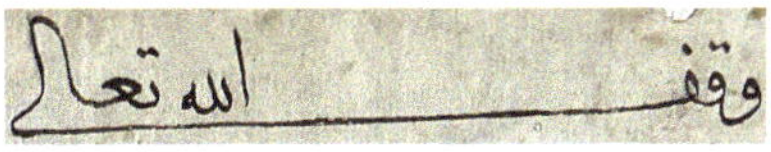 fol. 361ᵃ
1	Ar. 3268	Motto A	fols 10ᵇ–11ᵃ, 20ᵇ–21ᵃ, 35ᵇ–36ᵃ, 50ᵇ–51ᵃ, 70ᵇ–71ᵃ, 93ᵇ–94ᵃ, 114ᵇ–115ᵃ, 133ᵇ–134ᵃ, 152ᵇ–153ᵃ, 175ᵇ–176ᵃ, 179ᵇ–180ᵃ; in pairs, upper margins	 fol. 11ᵃ
2	Ar. 3334	Endowment statement	fol. 1ᵃ	
3	Ar. 3315	Endowment statement	fol. 1ᵃ	
3	Ar. 3315	Motto A	fol. 1ᵃ, above the endowment statement	
4	Ar. 3272	Motto B	fols 30ᵇ–31ᵃ, 68ᵇ–69ᵃ, 107ᵇ–108ᵃ, 122ᵇ–123ᵃ, 186ᵇ–187ᵃ, 228ᵇ–229ᵃ, 258ᵇ–259ᵃ, 287ᵇ–288ᵃ, in pairs, upper margins	 fol. 186ᵇ
5	Ar. 3272	Motto A	fols 14ᵇ, 49ᵇ, 90ᵇ, 118ᵇ, 154ᵇ, 180ᵇ, 222ᵇ, 247ᵇ, 273ᵇ, 297ᵇ, 329ᵇ, upper margin	 fol. 90ᵇ
6	Ar. 3236	Motto B	fol. 2ᵃ, lower fore margin	
7	Ar. 3236	Motto A	fols 1ᵇ, 4ᵇ, 17ᵇ, 37ᵇ, 52ᵇ, 92ᵇ, 126ᵇ, 170ᵇ; upper margin	 fol. 52ᵇ

TABLE 11.2 Examples of the various hands writing the mottos and endowment statements (*cont.*)

Hand no.	Shelf mark	Writing	Location	Example
8	Ar. 3315	Motto A	fols 2^a, 91^a, 94^a, 99^b, upper margin; fols 16^b–17^a, 17^b–18^a, 30^b–31^a, 42^b–43^a, 62^b–63^a, 76^b–77^a, 101^b–102^a, in pairs, upper margins	 fol. 2^a 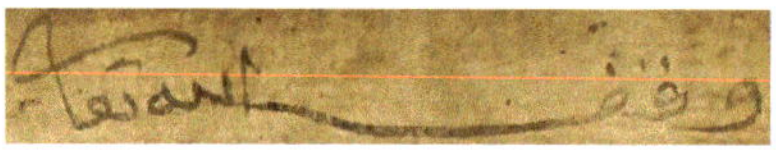 fol. 43^a
9	Ar. 3334	Motto B	fols 4^b–5^a, 9^b–(10^a), 15^b–16^a, 23^b–24^a, 28^b–29^a, 42^b–43^a, in pairs, upper margin	 fol. 42^b
10	Ar. 3342	Motto A	fols 1^b–2^a; in pairs, upper margins	 fol. 2^a
10	Ar. 3268	Motto A	fols 57^a, 100^a; upper margin	 fol. 57^a
11	Ar. 3310	Motto A	fols 30^b–31^a; in pairs, upper margin on the verso (b), lower margin on the recto (a)	 fol. 30^b
12	Ar. 3268		fol. 29^b, upper margin	
U1	Ar. 3236	Motto B	fol. 2^a, upper fore margin	
U2	Ar. 3272	Motto B (short)	fol. 315^b, upper margin	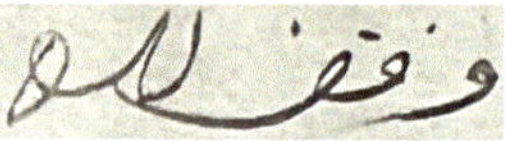
U3	Ar. 3272	Motto (short)	fol. 1^a, lower margin	

pes for plant inks, and they were rarely employed, probably because the final product is not black but rather light to dark brown. Tannins, particularly hydrolysable ones, are also among the main components of iron-gall inks. The latter are obtained by the reaction between iron ions (Fe^{2+}) and gallic acid in a water-based solvent, with the addition of a binder (gum arabic).[10] Arabic recipes mention gall nuts as the best source for gallic acid, but a variety of plant parts (for example, tree bark, leaves and fruit) can be used as substitutes. The most common and appreciated source of iron is vitriol (a mixture of hydrated metallic sulphates, often including copper and zinc). Filings, slag, nails and pieces of iron were used in a small number of Arabic recipes, resulting in inks without metallic impurities, although the extraction of iron ions and the consequent reaction are more difficult to obtain.[11]

The class of mixed inks comprises the inks resulting from blending together inks or ingredients from the previous classes. Several mentions of these preparations can be found in Arabic treatises. This class consists of two subtypes: mixed carbon-plant inks, when tannins are added to carbon inks, and mixed carbon-iron-gall inks. The latter include inks with different ratios of carbon to iron because they can be formulated by either adding small amounts of carbonaceous material to an iron-gall ink or including some vitriol and tannins in a carbon ink. Such inks are attested for the first time in Arabic recipes dating between the ninth and thirteenth centuries and have continued to be used until recent times.

In order to differentiate the inks, we exploit the distinct optical properties that their ingredients have in IR light: carbonaceous materials remain opaque throughout the IR regions, unbound tannins appear transparent at around 940 nm, while the iron-gallotannic complex, characteristic of iron-gall inks, loses opacity more slowly and become completely transparent between 1200 and 1500 nm.[12] We can observe the presence of tannins in UV light, as they have the ability to quench the fluorescence from the writing material, thus, enhancing the contrast between the ink strokes and the background. This behaviour is readily apparent in pure plant and iron-gall inks. In mixed ink, however, it can be difficult to notice because the carbonaceous materials are opaque in UV light and can, therefore, mask the enhancement of the tannins unless the amount of carbon particles is negligible, the writing is damaged or the tannins spread into the writing support around the stroke.

The XRF spectrometry is used to identify the elemental composition of the inks. Semi-quantitative measurements can also be used to differentiate inks, especially of the iron-gall type, based on the various ratios of the vitriolic impurities (copper, zinc and the like) to iron (the main component).[13] This method was successfully applied to discriminate mediaeval European iron-gall inks,[14] but it can also be effectively employed to differentiate mixed carbon-iron-gall inks when vitriol was used. It is also possible with XRF to carry out a qualitative evaluation of the impurities or the addition of metallic admixture in carbon-based inks.[15]

10 Krekel, "Chemistry of Historical Iron Gall Inks".

11 Colini, "'I tried it'", 146–148.

12 Mrusek et al., "Spektrale Fenster", 72; Colini et al., "New Standard Protocol", 163, 172.

13 The model is designed to also take into consideration the impurities of the paper; Hahn et al., "Characterization of Iron-gall Inks".

14 Hahn et al., "Erfurt Hebrew Giant Bible"; Geissbühler et al., "Advanced Codicological Studies".

15 Concerning the identification of impurities in carbon inks, see Hahn, "Analyses of Iron Gall and Carbon Inks". Carbon inks containing copper or lead have been reported in several works: Nir-El/Broshi, "Black Ink"; Brun et al., "Revealing Metallic Ink"; Christiansen et al., "Nature"; Christiansen et al., "Insights"; Colini et al., "Quest for the Mixed Inks"; Rabin et al., "Ink Characterisation"; Cohen, *Composition Analysis*; Ghigo, "Coptic Inks"; Ghigo et al., "Black Egyptian Inks"; Nehring et al., "Missing Link"; Bonnerot/Mascia, "Scribes and Writing Practices". The differentiation between a mixed carbon-iron-gall ink and a carbon-based ink with an admixture of iron or copper, however, is not possible to ascertain with non-destructive methods alone. Additionally,

3 Analytical Protocol and Equipment

The inks have been studied according to the standard protocol for the characterisation of writing materials in use at the CSMC at Universität Hamburg.[16] This protocol consists of a visual examination of the writing substances with a microscope in visible light, followed by a primary screening performed with NIR and UV reflectography at two specific wavelengths. IR reflectography is then used to capture images in the short wave IR region (900–1700 nm), while the elemental composition of the inks is determined with XRF. Additional in-depth analysis conducted with various spectroscopic methods can be added to the protocol but were not applied in this case.

The visual examination of the inks and the primary screening is conducted with a miniature, handheld Dino-Lite USB microscope. The microscope has built-in LED illumination at 395 nm (UV) and 940 nm (NIR), and a customised external white light (VIS) source functioning as a stand. In VIS light we observe the feature of the inks—that is, the distribution of the writing matter and the presence of particles, halos, cracks, bleeding or of other alterations of the writing due to damage, loss or retouching. By comparing the change of opacity of the writing between the visible and the IR micrograph, it is possible to differentiate the pure classes of black inks. Additionally, the presence of tannins can be detected in many cases by examining the micrograph captured under UV light: tannins have the ability to quench fluorescence, thus enhancing the contrast between inks with tannins and a fluorescent background under UV light. In the case of tannins spreading in the writing support beyond the limits of the ink stroke, it is even possible to observe that its dimensions appear larger in the UV micrograph compared to the VIS image.

OPUS Instruments APOLLO Infrared Reflectography Imaging System is used to ascertain the presence of carbon in the inks and allow for the discrimination of pure iron-gall inks and mixed inks. The regular short-wave IR sensing range (900–1700 nm) of the 128 × 128 pixel scanning InGaAs sensor can be reduced by the following filters: short wave pass filter (SWP1250, range 900–1250 nm), band pass filter (BPF1250–1510, range 1250–1510 nm) and long wave pass filter (LWP1510, range 1510–1700 nm). Each filter is mounted in front of the IR lens (150 mm, f/5.6–45). The working distance between the sensor and the object for this analysis was set to 74 cm with an aperture of f/11 and exposure time of 50 ms per tile. Two 20 W halogen lamps provide broadband illumination. In order to carry out this study, we used the long wave pass filter to limit the range of IR light to the portion of the spectrum where iron-gall inks become completely transparent.

Elio Bruker Nano GmbH (formerly XG Lab) is used for the identification of the elemental composition of the inks and was obtained through this compact X-ray spectrometer. It features a 4 W low-power rhodium tube and adjustable excitation parameters. It has a 17 mm^2 silicon drift detector (SDD) with energy resolution < 140 eV for Mn Kα. The beam size is roughly 1 mm, compatible with the size of the ink strokes we selected for the analysis. The measurements were performed on single spots at 40 kV and 80 μA, with an acquisition time of 2 min. At least three spectra for each different writing were acquired. Bruker's SPEKTRA software was used for the peak fitting and the semi-quantitative data evaluation.

4 Results and Discussion

The results of the analysis on endowment statements and mottos are summarised in table 11.3.

As shown in this table, different classes of inks were identified, although the majority of them

none of the methods applied so far can unequivocally identify the presence of tannins in the ink; see Rabin, "Instrumental Analysis", 30; Colini et al., "New Standard Protocol", 165.

16 Rabin et al., "Identification and Classification"; Colini et al., "New Standard Protocol".

TABLE 11.3 Identification of the ink types according to the protocol. The manuscripts Ar. 3268 and Ar. 3310 were identified as belonging to the Jazzār library months after the analysis were completed, therefore, their inks were not analysed.

Shelf-mark	Writing	Hand no.	Ink type	Visual examination (microscopy)	NIR/UV Reflectography	XRF Qualitative analysis
Ar. 3236	Motto A	7	Carbon with metallic admixture? Mixed?	Dark brown, surface characterised by the presence of black/grey crystals or salts (like a crust)	Little opacity changes in IR, little enhancement in UV	Traces of metallic elements, including Hg and Pb
Ar. 3236	Motto B	6	Mixed carbon-iron-gall	Dark brown, coffee-ring effect	Opacity changes in IR, enhancement in UV	Presence of Fe, Cu, Zn
Ar. 3236	Motto B	U1	Mixed carbon-iron-gall	Dark brown, coffee-ring effect	Opacity changes in IR, enhancement in UV	Presence of Fe, Cu, Zn
Ar. 3272	Endowment statement	1	Carbon	Dark black, thick, glossy surface with cracks	No opacity changes in IR, no enhancement in UV	Traces of Fe and Pb
Ar. 3272	Motto A	1	Carbon	Dark black, thick, glossy surface with cracks	No opacity changes in IR, no enhancement in UV	Traces of Fe and Pb
Ar. 3272	Motto (short)	U3	Mixed carbon-plant? Carbon?	Dark brown, thin ink	No opacity changes in IR, little enhancement in UV?	Traces of Fe
Ar. 3272	Motto A	5	Carbon? Mixed carbon-plant?	Black with brown hue, coffee-ring effect, black particles on the surface	No opacity changes in IR, no enhancement in UV	Traces of Fe
Ar. 3272	Motto B	4	Mixed carbon-iron-gall	Dark brown, coffee-ring effect on occasions	Little opacity changes in IR, enhancement in UV	Presence of Fe, Cu and Zn
Ar. 3272	Motto B (short)	U2 = 4	Mixed carbon-iron-gall	Dark brown	Little opacity changes in IR, enhancement in UV	Traces of Fe, Cu and Zn
Ar. 3315	Endowment statement	3	Iron-gall	Severely damaged: loss of material especially in the centre of the stokes; retouched with carbon ink	Clear opacity changes in IR, clear enhancement in UV	Presence of Fe and Cu
Ar. 3315	Motto A	3	Iron-gall	Severely damaged: loss of material especially in the centre of the stokes; retouched with carbon ink	Clear opacity changes in IR, clear enhancement in UV	Presence of Fe and Cu
Ar. 3315	Motto A	8	Carbon (watered down)	Brown grey with grey particles, thin	No opacity changes in IR, no enhancement in UV	No additional elements
Ar. 3334	Endowment statement	2	Mixed carbon-iron-gall	Black with brown hue, thick surfaces with some gaps and losses	Clear opacity changes in IR, enhancement in UV	Presence of Fe, Cu and Zn
Ar. 3334	Motto B	9	Mixed carbon-iron-gall	Grey with brown hue, grey particles, coffee ring effect	Opacity changes in IR, enhancement in UV	Presence of Fe, Cu and Zn
Ar. 3342	Endowment statement	1	Carbon	Dark black, thick, glossy surface with cracks	No opacity changes in IR, no enhancement in UV	Traces of Fe and Pb
Ar. 3342	Motto A	10	Mixed carbon-iron-gall	Dark black with brown hue, think, glossy surface	Opacity changes in IR, clear enhancement in UV	Presence of Fe, Cu, Zn, Pb

belong to those of pure carbon inks and mixed carbon-iron-gall inks with a prevalence of the carbonaceous component. We observed a pure iron-gall ink only in the endowment statement and motto written by Hand no. 3 on the first folio of Ar. 3315. We tentatively assigned the inks to the classes of mixed carbon-plant ink in two cases and to the subclass of carbon-based ink with metallic admixture in one case. The dubious identifications are marked with a question mark in table 11.3. Such uncertainty arises from the impossibility of detecting the organic component of the ink with the methods applied.[17] Additionally, the manuscripts were subjected to heavy restorations in the past. The application of aqueous treatments, splitting and lamination, and pigment retouching have caused the migration of ions (including iron ions) from the original inks to the paper and the introduction of external materials and elements. This made the evaluation of XRF data particularly complicated, especially when dealing with elements detected as traces in carbon-based and mixed inks, because the high amount and heterogeneity of the same elements in the writing support makes it hard to discern whether they are impurities in the inks or a contribution of the writing support.

Despite these difficulties in analysis, we can, nevertheless, observe that inks belonging to the same class are also very different due to their optical properties, elemental composition and, for mixed inks, the ratio of carbon to iron-gall. The latter can only be qualitatively appreciated in the VIS and IR images. The distribution of mixed carbon-iron-gall and pure iron-gall inks depending on their elemental composition is shown in fig. 11.1. The graph displays the percentage of iron, copper and zinc detected in the strokes normalised to their total.[18] It is possible to observe three subgroups, which suggests the use of different vitriols for the ink preparation. The first subgroup is characterised by a high amount of iron (65–90%) and a low amount of copper (10–35%) with no or just traces of zinc (0–12%), corresponding to the inks used by Hand no. 2 to write the endowment statement on Ar. 3334 and by Hand no. 3 for both the endowment statements and motto on Ar. 3315 (highlighted by the light blue circle in fig. 11.1). The second subgroup is characterised by a high amount of iron (60–75%), a low amount of copper (25–40%) and zinc (13–25%), corresponding to the inks used by Hand no. 9 to write the mottos on Ar. 3334 (highlighted by the light green hexagon with a dashed line in fig. 11.1). Finally, the third subgroup is characterised by a medium amount of iron (35–60%) and copper (25–45%) and a low amount of zinc (0–12%), corresponding to the inks used by Hand no. 4 and Hand no. 10 to write the mottos on Ar. 3272 and Ar. 3342, respectively (highlighted by the yellow hexagon with a solid line in fig. 11.1). The ratio obtained for the spots analysed on the partial motto named U2, written on Ar. 3272 by an unknown hand, falls exactly in the same area occupied by results of the Hand no. 10, suggesting that it was written with the same ink. A closer palaeographical examination confirms that it was probably penned by Hand no. 10 and left incomplete perhaps for aesthetic reasons or for an erroneous positioning in the book (see table 11.2 for comparison). The ink used by Hand no. 6 and that of the motto U1 from an unknown hand, both penned on the fore-edge of Ar. 3236, show a broad fluctuation in the elemental content and cannot be assigned to any of the subgroups. As has been clarified previously, such inhomogeneity is probably caused by the spreading of metallic elements in the writing support during conservation treatment.

The only pure iron-gall ink was used by Hand no. 3 for both the endowment statement and the motto on fol. 1ª of Ar. 3315. Interestingly, this is the only hand that can be surely dated to after

17 Rabin et al., "Identification and Classification"; Rabin "Instrumental Analysis"; Colini et al., "New Standard Protocol".

18 We used this normalisation instead of the normalisation to iron usually employed for the comparison of iron-gall inks as it captures the variability of the samples better.

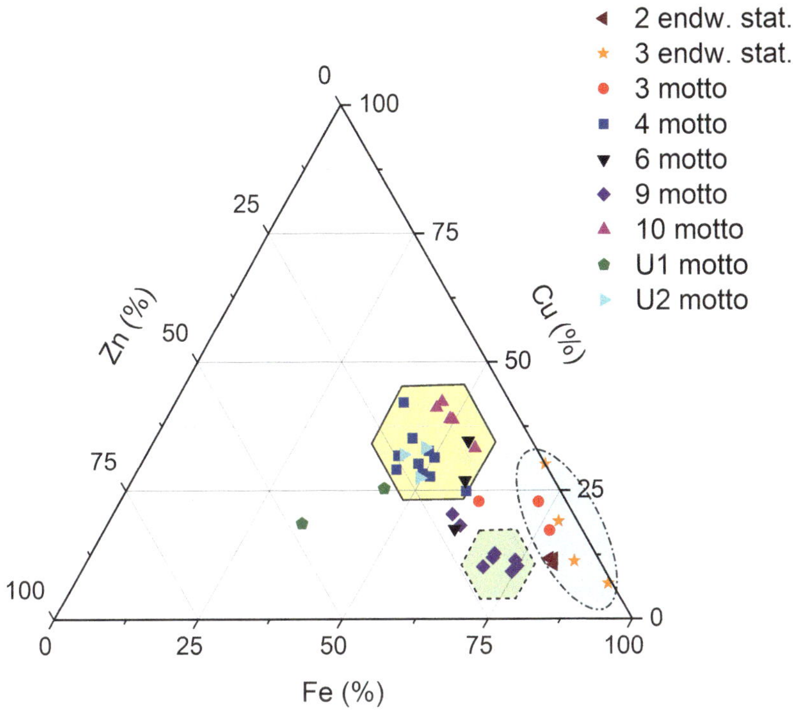

FIGURE 11.1
Comparison of the chemical composition of iron-gall and mixed carbon-iron-gall inks.

1205/1790–1791, as it overlaps the seal impression. The identification of its class is based on optical properties in both IR and UV light (fig. 11.2a–b): the ink clearly changes opacity at 940 nm and becomes transparent above 1510 nm, and the presence of tannins makes it homogeneously dark in UV. The increased intensity of the peaks of iron, copper, zinc and sulphur in the XRF spectra of the ink with respect to those of paper confirms the identification as a vitriolic iron-gall ink (fig. 11.2c). Probably due to the damages that this ink suffered, the writing was retouched with a carbon-based ink in some places. This intervention is clearly visible in the images taken in IR light, as the overlapping ink does not change opacity (figs. 11.2a and 11.2d). As seen on fig. 11.1, the elemental composition of the ink used by Hand no. 3 is similar to the one used by Hand no. 2 in the endowment statement on Ar. 3334. That statement, however, was written at least eight years before the one penned by Hand no. 3, suggesting that a same source of vitriol was available on the market for a longer period of time and that perhaps other sources were available as well.

Based on the class identification and the semi-quantitative evaluation of the XRF data, it appears that none of the writings attributed to different hands share the same characteristics, discarding the hypothesis that the apposition of endowment statements and mottos was a collegial operation of people working together and sharing the same materials. The results seem, instead, to suggest a very personal ink usage, although we were able to analyse more than one note type penned by the same person on two different manuscripts only in the case of Hand no. 1. According to the abundance of this handwriting compared to the others, we provisionally identify Hand no. 1 as the handwriting of the first librarian. He used a glossy, deep black ink for both the endowment statement and a series of mottos on Ar. 3272 and the endowment statement on Ar. 3342. As an example, we show in fig. 11.3 the results of the motto on Ar. 3272, fol. 104^b, identifying the ink as carbon: there is no change of opacity and intensity in either the IR or UV images (fig. 11.3a–b), and only traces of iron and lead are detected with XRF (fig. 11.3c). Due to the aforemen-

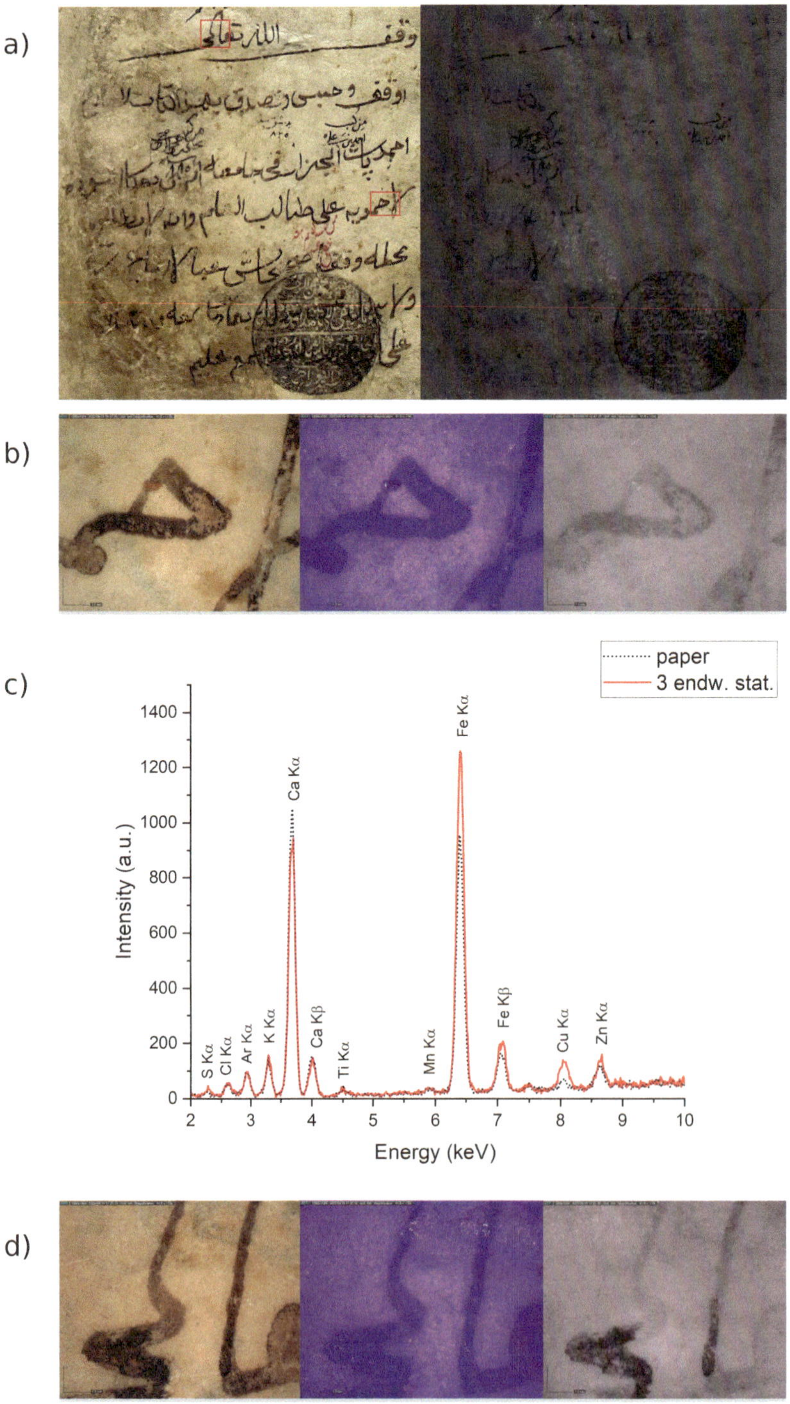

FIGURE 11.2 a) Left, visible light image of Ar. 3315, fol. 1^{a}, with red boxes indicating the location of Dino-Lite micrographs in 2b and 2d, and right, IR light image of the same area using the LWP1510 filter; b) Dino-Lite micrographs from left to right in VIS, UV, and NIR light; c) XRF spectra of the ink and paper, analysed in the same area identified in 2b; d) Dino-Lite micrographs from left to right in VIS, UV, and NIR light.

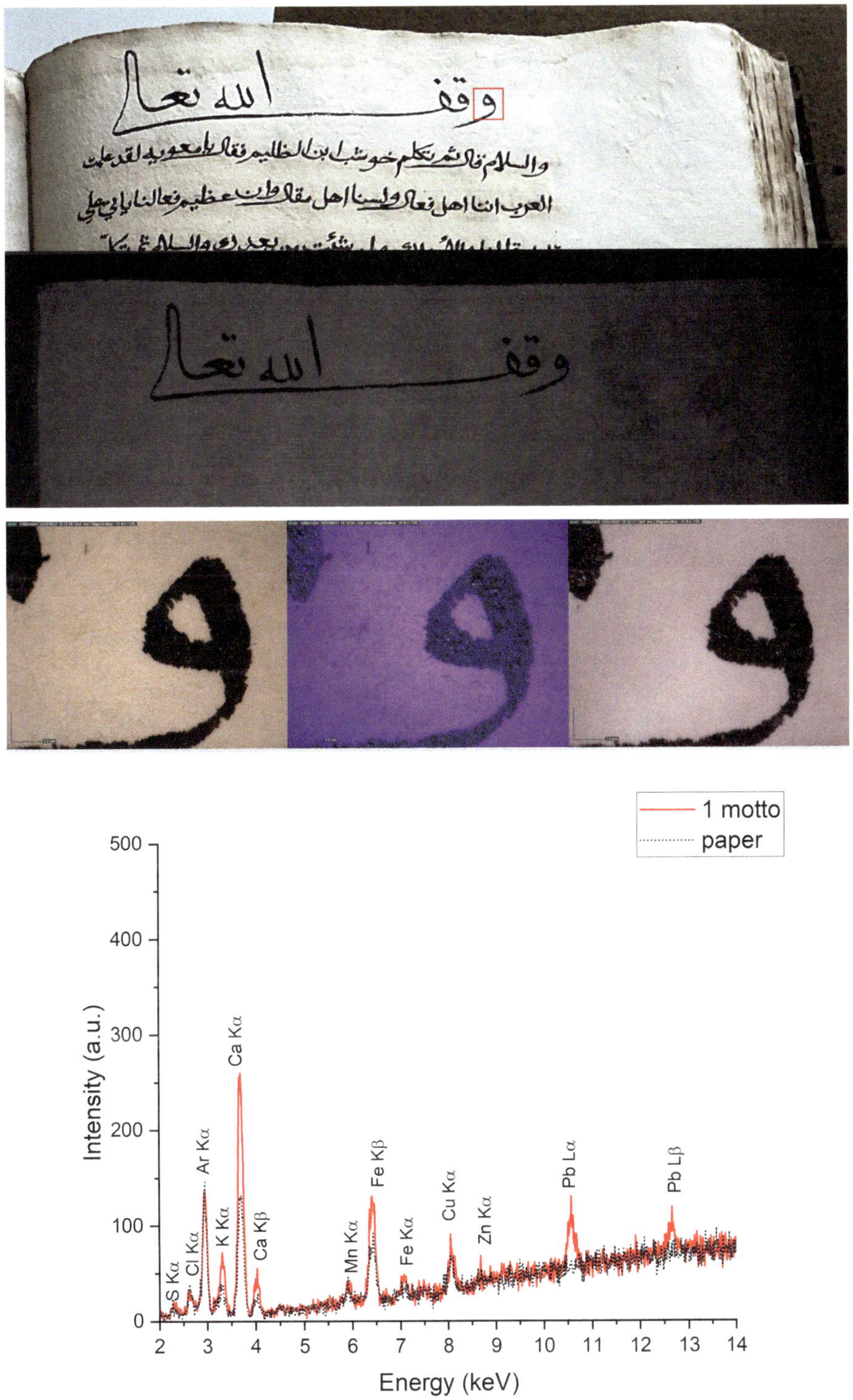

FIGURE 11.3 a) Top, visible light image of Ar. 3272, fol. 104[b], with a red box indicating the location of Dino-Lite micrographs in 3b, and bottom, IR light image of the same area using the LWP1510 filter; b) Dino-Lite micrographs from left to right in VIS, UV, and NIR light; c) XRF spectra of the motto ink and paper, analysed in the same area identified in 3b.

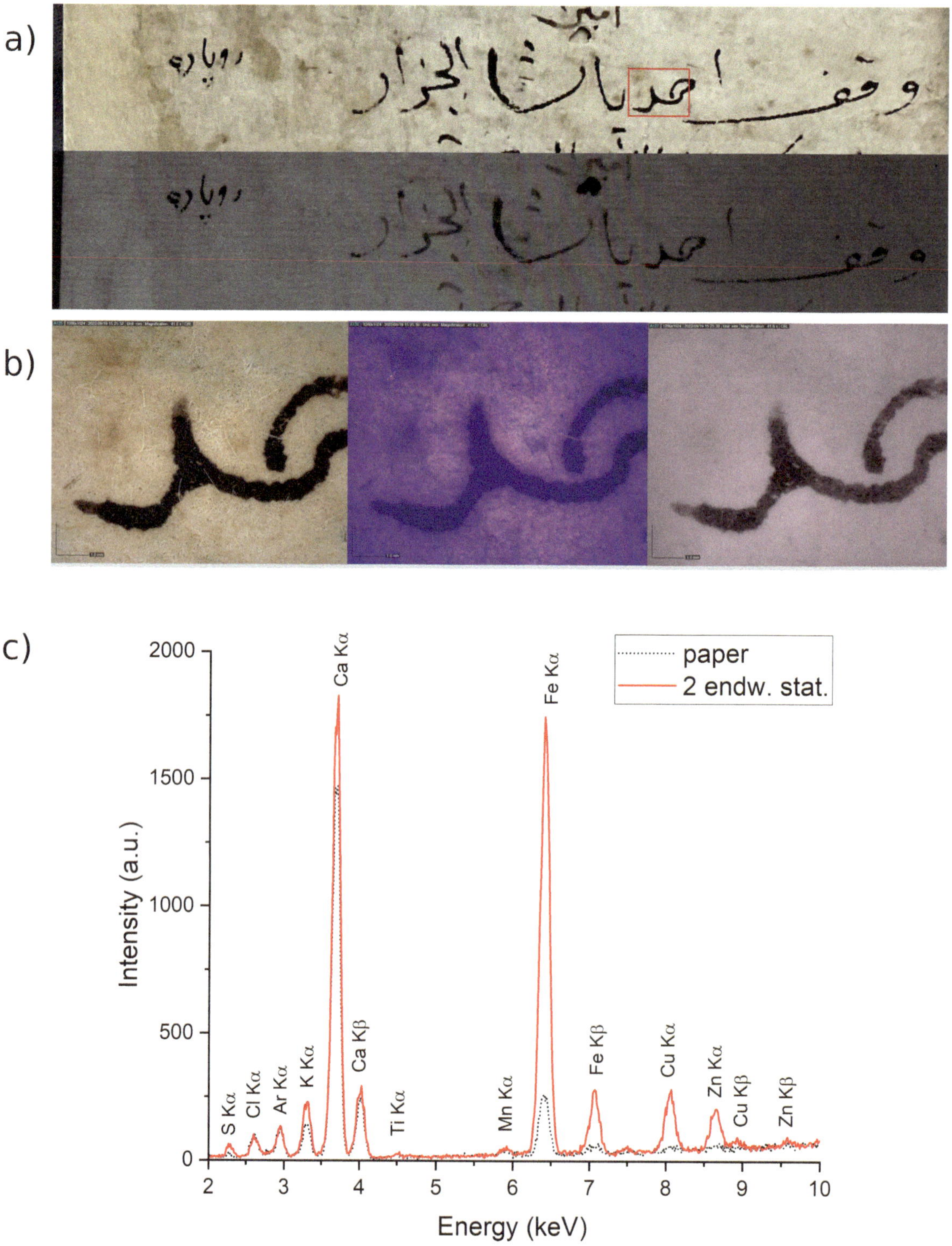

FIGURE 11.4 a) Top, visible light image of Ar. 3334, fol. 1^{a}, with a red box indicating the location of Dino-Light micrographs in 4b, and bottom, IR light image of the same area using the LWP1510 filter; b) Dino-Lite micrographs from left to right in VIS, UV, and NIR light; c) XRF spectra of the endowment statement ink and paper, analysed in the same area identified in 4b.

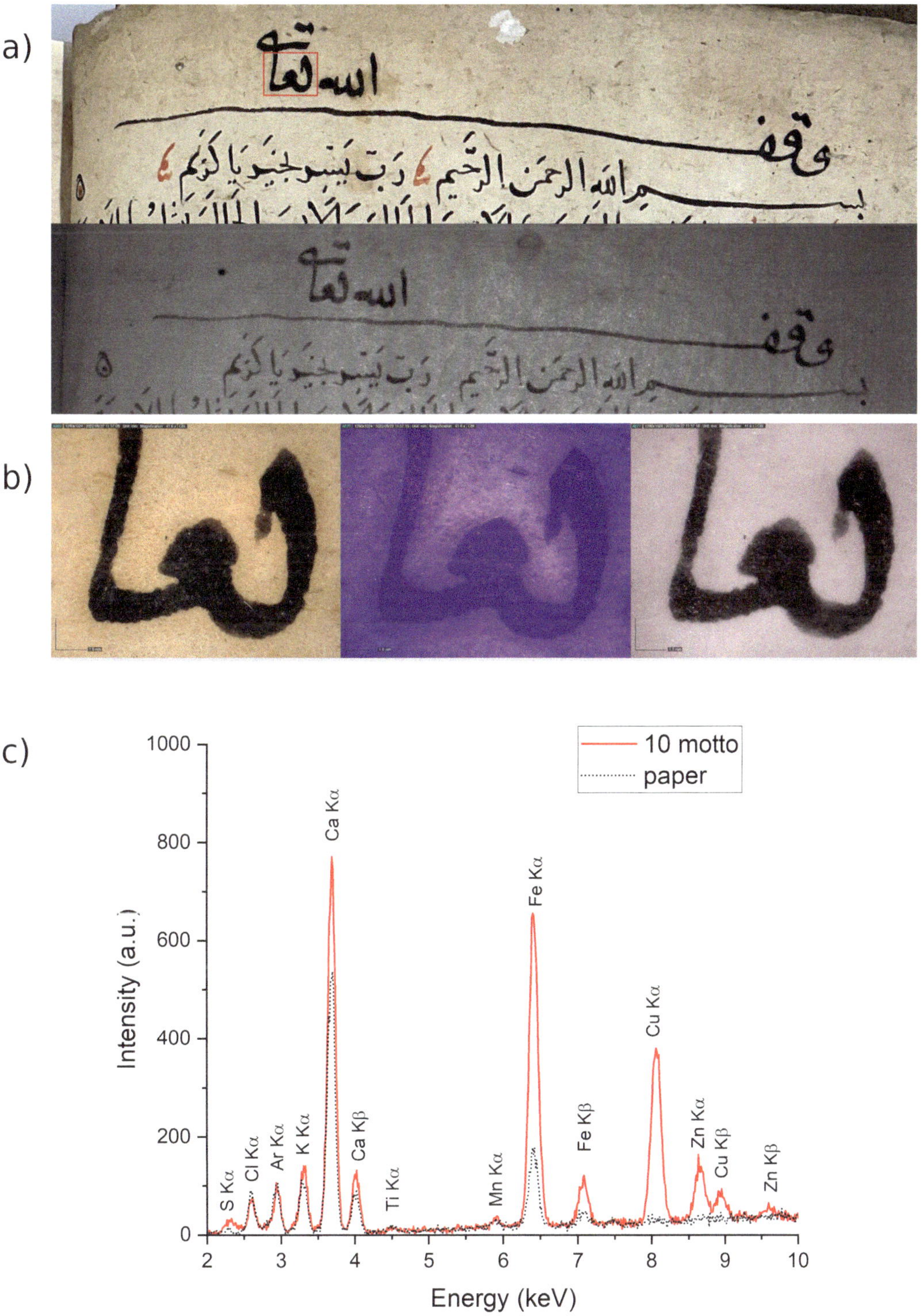

FIGURE 11.5 a) Top, visible light image of Ar. 3342, fol. 1^{b}, with a red box indicating the location of Dino-Light micrographs in 5b, and bottom, IR light image of the same area using the LWP1510 filter; b) Dino-Lite micrographs from left to right in VIS, UV, and NIR light; c) XRF spectra of the motto ink and paper, analysed in the same area identified in 5b.

tioned limitations, it is not possible to unequivocally confirm that the two endowment statements and the series of mottos were written with exactly the same ink, however, the scribe clearly wrote them with inks of the same class, the same optical characteristics and a very similar elemental composition. Additionally, the endowment statements were written within a three months interval, highly suggesting the ink is, indeed, the same.

In 1197/1783, Hand no. 2 penned the endowment statement on Ar. 3334 with a mixed carbon-iron-gall ink (fig. 11.4), and a mixed carbon-iron-gall ink was also used for the three mottos written by Hand no. 10 on Ar. 3342 (fig. 11.5), although the ink has a different elemental ratio compared to that of Hand no. 2 (fig. 11.1). We do not know if these mottos were penned in 1197/1783 at the same time as the endowment statement by Hand no. 1 or later. The abundance of ink classes and recipes detected, even during the same time span, reinforce the idea that different inks were available contemporaneously, either premade and sold on the market or prepared by the scribes themselves, and that the latter were using their own inks to write on al-Jazzār's books.

Finally, all the inks used for the seals are carbon-based and, unsurprisingly, do not correspond to any of the inks used for the handwritten annotations. In some cases, it is possible to observe a small increase in the iron and lead peaks in the area around the seals compared to the paper, but the amounts are too low and heterogeneously distributed depending on the point of analysis to exclude the possibility that they may be merely impurities found in the writing support. Additionally, no clear correlation was noticed between the impurities in the inks and the seals stamped with the two matrices. It is, therefore, impossible to determine whether two different inks were used or if the matrices were made of different materials that left specific trace elements while stamping.

5 Conclusions

Overall, the observations suggest that a multitude of people had access to and responsibility over the books of the Jazzār library—challenging the assumption, based on the statement in the endowment deed, that only one position of librarian was envisaged for the complex. It is possible, for reasons unknown to us, that several people alternated in this position during the institution's active years, or that users of the library and school had a more proactive role than we expect. It is also possible that some of the annotations were added during the revision of the library's possessions that led to the production of the library inventory in 1215/1800.[19] Extending the palaeographical analysis to other manuscripts from the collection might prove instrumental to defining each actor's contribution to the annotation of the books. The application of the Handwriting Analysis Tool (HAT) developed by Hussein Mohammad (CSMC, Universität Hamburg) could be of help in the identification and attribution of hands.[20] Enlarging the pool of handwriting analysed with archaeometric methods could answer additional questions concerning scribal habits and preferences, and perhaps clarify the temporal distribution or the order of the annotations.

As expected, the inks employed for stamping do not correspond to the inks used for the annotations. It was not possible, however, to discriminate the carbon-based inks of the seals, or clearly define the presence of metallic elements in some of the annotations, as it is unclear whether the trace elements are truly present in the inks—an impurity from the production process of the ink, or a contamination from the metallic seal matrix or the inkwell could have occurred—or are due to the contribution of the writing supports. Such an open question can only be answered through the future application of XRF mapping.[21]

19 See Said Aljoumani's Chapter 2 in this volume.
20 Mohammed, "Handwriting Analysis Tool v3.5".
21 Nehring et al., "Missing Link."

Bibliography

Bonnerot, Olivier and Leah Mascia. "Scribes and Writing Practices in Egypt's *ala Veterana Gallica*: A Preliminary Study of Inks from a Military Roll." In *2023 IMEKO TC-4 International Conference on Metrology for Archaeology and Cultural Heritage: Rome, Italy, October 19–21, 2023*, 845–850. http://dx.doi.org/10.21014/tc4-ARC-2023.157

Brun, Emmanuel, Marine Cotte, Jonathan Wright, Marie Ruat, Pieter Tack, Laszlo Vincze, Claudio Ferrero, Daniel Delattre and Vito Mocella. "Revealing Metallic Ink in Herculaneum Papyri." *Proceedings of the National Academy of Science* 113, no. 14 (March 2016): 3751–3754. https://doi.org/10.1073/pnas.1519958113.

Christiansen, Thomas, Marine Cotte, Wout de Nolf, Elouan Mouro, Juan Reyes-Herrera, Steven de Meyer, Frederik Vanmeert, Nati Salvadó, Victor Gonzalez, Poul Erik Lindelof, Kell Mortensen, Kim Ryholt, Koen Janssens and Sine Larsen. "Insights into the Composition of Ancient Egyptian Red and Black Inks on Papyri Achieved by Synchrotron-based Microanalyses." *Proceedings of the National Academy of Science* 117, no. 45 (October 2020): 27825-35. https://doi.org/10.1073/pnas.2004534117.

Christiansen, Thomas, Marine Cotte, René Loredo-Portales, Poul Erik Lindelof, Kell Mortensen, Kim Ryholt, and Sine Larsen. "The Nature of Ancient Egyptian Copper-containing Carbon Inks Is Revealed by Synchrotron Radiation Based X-ray Microscopy." *Scientific Reports* 7 (2017): 15346. https://doi.org/10.1038/s41598-017-15652-7.

Cohen, Zina. *Composition Analysis of Writing Materials in Cairo Genizah Documents*. Leiden/Boston, 2022.

Colini, Claudia. "From Recipes to Material Analysis: The Arabic Tradition of Black Inks and Paper Coatings (9th to 20th Century)." PhD diss., Universität Hamburg, 2018.

Colini, Claudia. "'I tried it and it is really good': Replicating Recipes of Arabic Black Inks." In *Traces of Inks: Experiences of Philology and Replication*, edited by Lucia Raggetti, 131–153. Leiden, 2021. https://doi.org/10.1163/9789004444805

Colini, Claudia, Oliver Hahn, Olivier Bonnerot, Simon Steger, Zina Cohen, Tea Ghigo, Thomas Christiansen, Marina Bicchieri, Paola Biocca, Myriam Krutzsch and Ira Rabin. "The Quest for the Mixed Inks." *manuscript cultures* 11 (2018): 41–48.

Colini, Claudia, Ivan Shevchuk, Kyle Ann Huskin, Ira Rabin and Oliver Hahn. "A New Standard Protocol for Identification of Writing Media." In *Exploring Written Artefacts: Objects, Methods, and Concepts*, edited by Jörg B. Quenzer, 161–182. Berlin/Boston: 2021. https://doi.org/10.1515/9783110753301-009.

Geissbühler, Mirjam, Georg Dietz, Oliver Hahn and Ira Rabin. "Advanced Codicological Studies of Cod. germ. 6 (Hamburg, Staats- und Universitätsbibliothek): Part 2." *manuscript cultures* 11 (2018): 133–139.

Ghigo, Tea. "A Systematic Scientific Study of Coptic Inks from the Late Roman Period to the Middle Ages." PhD diss., Universität Hamburg and La Sapienza (Rome) University, 2020.

Ghigo, Tea, Ira Rabin and Paola Buzi. "Black Egyptian Inks in Late Antiquity: New Insights on Their Manufacture and Use." *Archaeological and Anthropological Sciences* 12 (February 2020): 70. https://doi.org/10.1007/s12520-019-00977-3.

Hahn, Oliver. "Analyses of Iron Gall and Carbon Inks by Means of X-ray Fluorescence Analysis: A Non-destructive Approach in the Field of Archaeometry and Conservation Science." *Restaurator: International Journal for the Preservation of Library and Archival Material* 31, no. 1 (2010): 41–64. https://doi.org/10.1515/rest.2010.003

Hahn, Oliver, Wolfgang Malzer, Birgit Kanngiesser and Burkhard Beckhoff. "Characterization of Iron-gall Inks in Historical Manuscripts and Music Compositions Using X-ray Fluorescence Spectrometry." *X-Ray Spectrometry* 33, no. 4 (February 2004): 234–239. https://doi.org/10.1002/xrs.677

Hahn, Oliver, Timo Wolff, Hartmut-Ortwien Feistel, Ira Rabin and Malachi Beit-Arié. "The Erfurt Hebrew Giant Bible and the Experimental XRF Analysis of Ink and Plummet Composition." *Gazette du livre médiéval* 51 (Fall 2007): 16–29. https://doi.org/10.3406/galim.2007.1754

Krekel, Christoph. "The Chemistry of Historical Iron Gall Inks: Understanding the Chemistry of Writing Inks Used to Prepare Historical Documents." *Inter-*

national Journal of Forensic Document Examiners 5 (December/January 1999): 54–58.

Mohammed, Hussein. "Handwriting Analysis Tool v3.5 (HAT3.5)" (Version 3.5.0), May 21, 2021. https://doi.org/10.25592/uhhfdm.900

Mrusek, Ralf, Robert Fuchs and Doris Oltrogge. "Spektrale Fenster zur Vergangenheit: Ein neues Reflektographieverfahren zur Untersuchung von Buchmalerei und historischem Schriftgut." *Naturwissenschaften* 82 (February 1995): 68–79. https://doi.org/10.1007/BF01140144

Nehring, Grzegorz, Olivier Bonnerot, Marius Gerhardt, Myriam Krutzsch and Ira Rabin. "Looking for the Missing Link in the Evolution of Black Inks." *Archaeological and Anthropological Sciences* 13 (March 2021): 71. https://doi.org/10.1007/s12520-021-01320-5

Nir-El, Yoram and Magen Broshi. "The Black Ink of the Qumran scrolls." *Dead Sea Discoveries* 3, no. 2 (July 1996): 157–167.

Rabin, Ira. "Instrumental Analysis in Manuscript Studies." In *Comparative Oriental Manuscript Studies: An Introduction*, edited by Alessandro Bausi, Pier Giorgio Borbone, Françoise Briquel-Chatonnet, Paola Buzi, Jost Gippert, Caroline Macé, Marilena Maniaci, Zisis Melissakis, Laura E. Parodi and Witold Witakowski, 27–30. Hamburg, 2015. http://dx.doi.org/10.5281/zenodo.46784

Rabin, Ira. "Building a Bridge from the Dead Sea Scrolls to Mediaeval Hebrew Manuscripts." In *Jewish Manuscript Cultures: New Perspectives*, edited by Irina Wandrey, 309–322. Berlin/Boston, 2017. https://doi.org/10.1515/9783110546422-012

Rabin, Ira, Roman Schütz, Anka Kohl, Timo Wolff, Roald Tagle, Simone Pentzien, Oliver Hahn and Stephen Emmel. "Identification and Classification of Historical Writing Inks in Spectroscopy: A Methodological Overview." *Comparative Oriental Manuscript Studies Newsletter* 3 (January 2012): 26–30. https://doi.org/10.25592/uhhfdm.508

Rabin, Ira, Carsten Wintermann and Oliver Hahn. "Ink Characterisation Performed in Biblioteca Medicea Laurenziana (September 2018)." *Analecta Papyrologica* 31 (2019): 301–313.

PART 3

The Intellectual Profile of al-Jazzār's Library: The Inventory's Sections

CHAPTER 12

The Qur'an Section (*maṣāḥif*)

Walid A. Saleh

The introduction to the library inventory is a Qur'anically infused preamble. It is unusual in this respect. The writer of the inventory, adept at referencing all the Qur'anic verses that deal with books, quotes no less than five verses from the Qur'an. The preamble starts with the Qur'anic verse Q. 27:30 ('It is from Solomon [this letter] and it starts with: In the Name of God the Merciful the Compassionate'), a verse that is reporting about a royal missive from Solomon to Queen of Sheba. This is already a clever allusion to al-Jazzār as a latter-day King Solomon. The preamble also uses Q. 98:3, 'in it [are] precious books', to refer to the collection, thus, daring to compare the content of the library to holy scripture. The introduction finishes by conflating the theft or damage to any of the library books with the crime of tampering with divine scripture (Q. 2:181). Indeed, the introduction, by its Qur'anic structure, is hinting at the list of the Qur'ans that follows. The writer is not without literary sensibility; he is certainly adroit at flattery of the highest kind.

That the library inventory started with the enumeration of the Qur'an manuscripts in the collection is, thus, not surprising, all Islamic book inventories and catalogues do.[1] It is the sheer number of Qur'an entries in the inventory that is surprising, twenty-four individual items in total.[2] The number of volumes, however, is much higher, since three entries (#21, #22, #23) refer to *rabʿah*, consisting of thirty volumes each, and a fourth copy (#24) consists of ten volumes. The writer of the inventory used two systems of volume naming in this section. He utilised the normal *jild* (volume) for the individual complete copies of the Qur'an, and *juzʾ* (division) for the multivolume copies. When he tallied the total number, he used another term, *qiṭaʿan*, pieces, to indicate that these are not the volumes but the individual discreet Qur'ans; and gave the number as twenty-four. The total number of volumes, however, in this section is 120. The use of the term *juzʾ* when referring to multivolume Qur'ans reflects the traditional Muslim division of the Qur'an into equal parts, that uses the same term (whether thirty, which was the predominant division, seven or ten).

We can see that al-Jazzār was making a statement with the large number of copies of Qur'ans in his collection (twenty-four copies) by comparing this with a similar contemporaneous collection, that of the Governor of Egypt Muḥammad Bey Abū al-Dhahab (d. 1189/1755) in Cairo. We find only five copies in the Dhahab collection (two individual Qur'an copies and three *rabʿah*, two of them in thirty volumes each; the third in ten volumes, consisting of seventy-two volumes).[3] Why such a high number, is a question that needs to be asked. The answer depends on how we see the function of this collection. I think that this collection was not a mere *madrasa* library, this was also a palace-like library; it reflects the power and the prestige of the donor.[4] The abundance of Qur'an copies pointed

1 See the remarks of Tanindi, "Arts of the Book", I, 213.

2 If you add the copy #1668 from the library from Sheikh ʿAlī al-Rashīdī and Sheikh Mūḥammad, military supplies manager (*wakīl kharāj*), we have twenty-five in total. #1640 is a copy of Sura 6 (Surat al-Anʿām); copying Sura 6 as a standalone booklet was an Ottoman tradition; see Rettig, *The Rise of the Enʿam*, 185–212.

3 For details about this collection, see the entry on Qur'an commentary.

4 In this sense it has Istanbul as the model and not the Levant or Cairo at this moment of history. See the Sultan Bayezid inventory, both the introduction and the list

to the ambition of creating not only a centre of learning out of nothing but also a pious presence, which only the Qur'ans could bestow.

Since we have not been able to locate any copies of the Qur'ans from the al-Jazzār library anywhere, we are dealing with a phantom list that is both revealing and completely inaccessible. As uniquely individually handwritten artefacts, it is impossible to analyse them without inspection. As works of art, we have no access to these codices, only a description that can reveal merely a skeletal outline. We can only appreciate the loss of this collection by comparing it with another regional collection that is still preserved, the one which is housed in al-Ḥaram al-Sharīf Islamic Museum in Jerusalem (al-Quds).[5] The stunning beauty and artistry of the al-Ḥaram al-Sharīf's collection evokes what is inaccessible of the Jazzār collection.

One of the main features of the inventory description of the Qur'ans is the listing of the script in which each was written. Each of the twenty-four listed entries names the script. This is infrequent among Islamic inventories and catalogues, and not even the Bāyezīd inventory of Istanbul names the script—apart from naming the Kufi script Qur'ans.[6] The writer of the Jazzār inventory was clearly a professional scribe and few other book lists are as meticulous, if at all, in recording the scripts of the books in their collection. He names six scripts in total: *Islambūlī*[7] (#1, #4, #21), *ʿajam* (#2), *rayḥānī*[8] (#3, #6, #23), *naskh*[9] (#5, #7, #8, #9, #10, #11, #12, #13, #16, #20, #22), *maṣrī* (#15, #17, #19, #24), *qadīm kuhnā* (#18). There is one entry that did not have a script named (#14), probably an oversight since the script is described as of average quality. That the writer of the inventory is a professional scribe can be seen by the judgements he issued on each of these scripts; some were *ʿāl* (high quality, for example, #1 and #4), others *wasaṭ* (average quality, for example, #7, #8, and #14), while others were *qadīm* or *ʿatīq* (archaic, for example #20, #23). I do think that #18, described as *qadīm kuhnā* (doubly archaic, *kuhnā* is archaic in Farsi), is an appellation for Kufic script, or an archaic script with which the writer was not familiar.

The question of why script identification is central to the shaping of the inventory is, thus, essential to our assessment of the native curatorial approach to the collection (see Chapter 9 by Nimet Ipek and Guy Burak in this volume on scripts in the inventory). Why such inordinate attention is paid to script, to the degree that one can speak of script as the unifying quality that grids the description of the collection? This is not a mere scholar, the one describing the collection, this is an expert on scripts and their quality, an assessor who knows the mettle of a script—and does not shy from downgrading a work by describing its script as average (*wasaṭ*). When describing #18, the one that I think is a Kufic Qur'an, the writer of the inventory states that it is written with different scripts (*bi-khuṭūṭ mukhtalifah*), he had leafed through every volume and inspected them like a professional librarian. He also knows whether the same script is archaic (that is, old style) or just regular, thus, some of the *rayḥānī* script manuscripts are described as archaic *rayḥānī* (#23). I think that al-Jazzār was not going to pay for books whose value he could not

of Qur'ans in Necipoğlu, "The Spatial Organization", II, 11–17 (the facsimile edition). See also the remarks of Zeren Tanindi, "Arts of the Book", I, 213.

5 Salameh, *The Qur'ān Manuscripts*.

6 Necipoğlu, "The Spatial Organization", II, 13 (pagination of the facsimile).

7 This script is attested as the script of a Qur'an given as a gift to the Mosque of Muhammad Ali in the Citadel of Cairo, see Mubārak, *al-Khiṭaṭ al-Tawfīqiyya al-Jadīda* V, 87 (*muṣḥaf bi-khaṭṭ Islāmbūlī*). He also mentions a copy of *Dalāʾil al-khayrāt* in the same script (*wa-nuskhat Dalāʾil bi-al-khaṭṭ al-Islāmbūlī*). The editors of the Journal *al-Muqtaṭaf* spoke of a manuscript as resembling the *Islāmbūlī* script that is in use now (*wa-khaṭṭuhā qarīb min al-khaṭṭ al-Islāmbūlī al-mustaʿmal al-ān*), see *al-Muqtaṭaf* 20 (1896), 294. We find a mention of this script in an article in the journal *al-ʿIrfān* as being developed in Istanbul, see *al-ʿIrfān* 5 (1332/1914), 182.

8 On this script, see Blair, *Islamic Calligraphy*, 678 (index for *rayḥān* script).

9 On the development of the *naskh* script in the Ottoman period, see ibid. 476–533.

determine. This was a collection created by a professional scholar-scribe, or at least a committee or team with various expertise. Each volume was inspected and assessed. The codex #7 which is characterized as *qadīm* (an ancient copy) is described as written in average quality *naskh* script, and we are informed that it has variant readings (*qirā'āt*) on the margins.

Not all Qur'ans are the same, although most were written in one volume; some cathedral, or mosque and *madrasa* Qur'ans, however, also came in multivolume sets, called *rabʿah*.[10] The copy was called *rabʿah* after the name given to the ornate wooden cabinet that holds the volumes. The Jazzār Qur'an collection has the usual one-volume Qur'ans (the first seventeen listed), a Qur'an in two volumes (#18), then two incomplete copies originally in four volumes (#19, #20). Then we have three *rabʿah* (named as such in the inventory), each in thirty volumes. Unfortunately, the writer of the inventory said nothing about the cabinets, and they must have had such cabinets. The last listed Qur'an #24 is a *rabʿah* of ten volumes.

This must have been an impressive collection of Qur'ans: four *rabʿahs*, seventeen individually complete, and three multivolume copies. We are not aware if there was a reading chair in the mosque, but clearly al-Jazzār did not spare money to supply his collection with a dignified number of Qur'ans that pointed to his piety. I also think these were public Qur'ans, that is, I do not think they were at the disposal of any but professional paid readers. By the eighteenth century, copies of the Qur'an were cheap enough for a learned reader to have their own copies.

10 On the term *rabʿah*, see Gacek, *The Arabic Manuscript Tradition*, 52.

Bibliography

Blair, Sheila S. *Islamic Calligraphy*. Edinburgh, 2006.

Gacek, Adam. *The Arabic Manuscript Tradition: A Glossary of Technical Terms and Bibliography*. Leiden, 2001.

Mubārak, ʿAlī. *al-Khiṭaṭ al-Tawfīqiyya al-Jadīda*. Cairo, 1886.

Necipoğlu, Gülru. "The Spatial Organization of Knowledge in the Ottoman Palace Library: An Encyclopedic Collection and Its Inventory." In *Treasures of Knowledge: An Inventory of the Ottoman Palace Library (1502/3–1503/4)*, edited by Gülru Necipoğlu, Cemal Kafadar and Cornell H. Fleischer, II, 1–77. Leiden, 2019.

Rettig, Simon. "The Rise of the Enʿam: Manuscripts of Selections of Suras in the Early Sixteenth-century Ottoman Empire," In *The Word Illuminated: Form and Function of Qur'anic Manuscripts from the Seventh to the Seventeenth Century*, edited by Simon Rettig and Sana Mirza, 185–212. Washington, DC, 2023.

Salameh, Khader. *The Qur'ān Manuscripts in the al-Haram al-Sharif Islamic Museum, Jerusalem*. Reading, 2001.

Tanindi, Zeren. "Arts of the Book: The Illustrated and Illuminated Manuscripts Listed in ʿAtufi's Inventory." In *Treasures of Knowledge: An Inventory of the Ottoman Palace Library (1502/3–1503/4)*, edited by Gülru Necipoğlu, Cemal Kafadar and Cornell H. Fleischer, I, 213–239. Leiden, 2019.

CHAPTER 13

A Foreshadowing: The Qur'an Commentary Section (*tafsīr*)

Walid A. Saleh

Almost a century after the death of al-Jazzār, Arab intellectuals in Cairo were frantically looking for a complete manuscript copy of al-Ṭabarī's Qur'an commentary to print. The world had changed radically by then—Europe had arrived fully on the Eastern shores of the Mediterranean, forcing a new world-view, gone was the indirect 'penetrated system' of the previous centuries.[1] Egypt was under indirect British rule and Arabic printing in the Arab Ottoman provinces had been introduced since the 1820s for use by the Muslims.[2] One of the leading Arab Cairene publishers, Muṣṭafā Ibn Muḥammad al-Bābī al-Ḥalabī, the owner of the famed al-Maymaniyya publishing company, was lamenting Muslims' disinterest in al-Ṭabarī's work, while European scholars, called 'Orientalists' (*mustashriq*), were searching everywhere for a fragment of this work.[3] The personal reflections of Muṣṭafā which appeared in the index volume of the first ever Cairene edition of al-Ṭabarī's Qur'an commentary are worth quoting in full because they capture the complex intellectual atmosphere in Cairo at this juncture:

For long I have seen Christian western scholars obsessively searching for early Islamic books (*al-kutub al-Islāmiyya al-qadīmat al-ʿahd*) and eager to acquire what is in them from knowledge—one calls such scholars 'Orientalist' because they are always searching after Oriental books. One of the most sought after works that they were rummaging for was the Qur'an commentary of Muḥammad Ibn Jarīr al-Ṭabarī, so much so that when one of them would hear that a fragment of the work is available in one of the libraries, he would do anything to see it and copy it, with no concern for how much time or money it costs him to do that.[4] I used to melt of shame and die of sorrow when I would see Arabic books first published by Europeans and we have no access to these works but through their effort; with the added humiliation that we only have a belated access to these works after they had appeared in Europe. Now it behooves us to have been the ones who are publishing these works. But this sad state is but the result of the negligence of Muslims in shouldering their duties. I want to thank European scholars who continue to search for Islamic works and who recognise the significance of Muslim scholars and are busy publishing these Muslim scholars' works. Now since I have been able to publish Islamic works before, I decided to publish the Qur'an commentary of Muḥammad Ibn Jarīr al-Ṭabarī, who died almost 1011 years ago. I published this work because I wanted to spread its benefits and for fear that Europeans will beat us to publish it first and make it public, as they did with many of the Islamic masterpieces.[5]

1 On the use and meaning of this phrase 'penetrated system', see Philipp, *Acre*, 68.

2 On the introduction of printing to Egypt, see El Shamsy, *Rediscovering*, 63–92.

3 On Muṣṭafā al-Bābī al-Ḥalabī, see Ṣābāt, *Tārīkh al-ṭibāʿah*, 200, 236 and 261.

4 This must be clearly a reference to the activities of Otto Loth, who visited Cairo looking for manuscripts of the commentary, see his "Ṭabarî's Korancommentar". Loth was one of the editors of the Leiden edition of the history of al-Ṭabarī. For the trouble European orientalists went to get copies of this history, see Vrolijk, "The Leiden Edition", 319–336.

5 Al-Ṭabarī, *Jāmiʿ al-Bayān*, Index volume (*Fihrist*, v. 31), 2. This index volume is not numbered in the edition and is simply called 'catalogue'.

Muṣṭafā al-Bābī al-Ḥalabī then described the state of the manuscripts of al-Ṭabarī's Qur'an commentary: manuscript copies of this work were very rare and hard to locate (*wa-lammā kānat nusakhuh ʿazīza jiddan*).[6] He did not elaborate why this was the case. It is not, however, difficult to explain this situation. There were several reasons why it was hard to find an exemplar copy of al-Ṭabarī's commentary to use for printing. This was a multivolume work and, therefore, prone to be dispersed easily, such that no accessible library seems to have had a complete set of its volumes. Moreover, the work had ceased to be important for a long time and, hence, there was no demand for its copies or for copying it.[7] To print it one needed to gather manuscript volumes from more than one collection in order to constitute a complete copy. The copy in Cairo in the Royal Egyptian library (known then as al-Kutubkhānah al-Khudaywiyya) was incomplete.[8] To fill the gap, Muṣṭafā al-Ḥalabī managed to borrow a copy from Hail, the capital of the Āl al-Rashīd principality in Najd, as well as the copy in the famed Aḥmadiyya Library in Aleppo.[9] Apart from a handful of libraries in Istanbul, few libraries in the Muslim world had a complete copy of al-Ṭabarī. However, the Jazzār library did have one, 'eight volumes complete' as the cataloguer stated (#39).

I began this article with the history of the first publication of the Qur'an commentary of al-Ṭabarī, which was finalised in Jumādā al-Ūlā 1321/August 1903, in order to emphasise the significance of al-Jazzār's collection.[10] Not even Cairo had a complete manuscript copy of this work.[11] But even more perplexing is that few Muslims were interested in this work in the late eighteenth century, the time al-Jazzār's collection was put together, and to go through the trouble of obtaining a complete copy is remarkable when the work had been all but forgotten by then. This is no slender work; the copy that was housed in the Jazzār library was eight volumes—al-Ṭabarī's is among the most voluminous of Qur'an commentaries, an encyclopaedic commentary.[12] Whoever was curating the collection in Acre, and we know little about how this collection was gathered, must have been deeply and intimately knowledgeable about the history of Qur'an commentary to insist on having a complete copy of this work. This collection, I would like to emphasise, was the result of autochthonous expertise, before the encounter with European orientalism and their rediscovery of al-Ṭabarī.[13] While the presence of the copy of Cairo in 1903 is a historical accident, a remanent of the great Mamluk collections, its presence in Acre was a deliberate act of deep significance.[14] The discovery of al-Ṭabarī in early twentieth-century Cairo was reflective of the awareness of Muslim intellectuals of the European orientalist project; the place of al-Ṭabarī's commentary in the Jazzār collection reflected, I believe, a different conception of Islamic intellectual history.[15] Only Istanbul had multiple complete copies of al-Ṭabarī and I am almost certain that al-Jazzār's copy was commis-

6 Ibid.

7 See Saleh, "Marginalia and Peripheries", 298–299, for the checkered history of al-Ṭabarī's Qur'an commentary.

8 The earliest description of this copy is in Loth's article, "Ṭabarī's Korancommentar", 591–593.

9 I failed to find any information about the Āl al-Rashīd library. The name of Prince Ḥammūd Ibn ʿUbayd al-Rasīd appears in the first volume of the edition, *Jamiʿ al-Bayān*, I, 1.

10 The story of the successive publications of al-Ṭabarī's Qur'an commentary has yet to be written. I am preparing a history of its publication history and its relationship to European orientalism.

11 See the evaluation of Loth of the copy in Egypt, see footnote 8 above.

12 On Encyclopaedic commentaries, see Saleh, "Preliminary Remarks", 20.

13 For the discovery of al-Ṭabarī in Europe, see the introduction of Rosenthal, *General Introduction*, 135–147.

14 On the Mamluk provenance of the Cairene copy, see Loth, "Ṭabarī's Korancommentar", 591–592; the date on the manuscript is 714–715 H. (1314–1315).

15 European scholars were, in addition to producing a critical edition of his history between 1879 and 1901, toying with the idea of an edition of his Qur'an commentary. See Bosworth, "al-Ṭabarī", X, 13.

sioned or obtained from Istanbul.[16] The cataloguer of the Jazzār library describes the script of this copy as *'miṣrī'* (Egyptian). I am not sure what he meant by this description.[17] As it happens, a lone volume of the al-Jazzār copy is currently preserved in Saudi Arabia.[18] The script is deliberative, clear, uncluttered, dotted and extremely readable. This is what you want from a script used for a very functional purpose. This is most probably the script that was used to copy works for *madrasa* libraries, I would call it Ottoman Arabic *madrasa* script (see Chapter 9 by Nimet Ipek and Guy Burak in this volume on scripts in the inventory).

1 The Qur'an Commentary Collection in the Jazzār Library: A Unique Provincial Collection?

The Qur'an commentary collection in the Jazzār library is remarkably rich and unique. It is a provincial collection that reflects an ambitious rivalry with imperial Ottoman collections. Its content not only mirrors the consensus in Islamic scholarship dominant in Ottoman lands, but also shows signs of different regional sensibilities in Arab provinces. What I find most significant about this collection is that it does not contain the usual books we expect from libraries of this period only in the *madrasa* curriculum. Instead, it has a depth that is surprising. I will argue that this depth is not accidental—it could not be so; and having a complete copy of al-Ṭabarī's commentary is a prime example of the deliberative curatorial nature of the collection.

The cataloguer of the Jazzār library starts his enumeration of the list of commentaries with the Qur'an commentary of Ibn ʿAbbās (#25)—this is supposedly the first and oldest of Qur'an commentaries ever written in the genre.[19] This work was an Ottoman popular slim Ottoman work—used, if at all, as a primer for novice students of the art of commentary. It was, however, long overtaken by a series of new works, the latest of which was that of al-Suyūṭī (d. 911/1505) *Tafsīr al-Jalālayn*, of which the Jazzār library had three copies (#32, #33 and #594). That there was only one exemplar of Ibn ʿAbbās's commentary points to the unique function of this work in the collection. Ibn ʿAbbās was seen as the father and founder of the Qur'an commentary tradition; having at least one copy of the work attributed to him gave the collection both gravitas and *barakah* (the blessings one accrued from being pious). By then, this work was hardly consulted and seldom used. It was, however, turned into an object of veneration and art by the Ottoman collectors.[20] If Muslims wanted a short (*wajīz*) Qur'an commentary, *al-Jalālayn* (already mentioned) was the go-to commentary. The presence of Ibn ʿAbbās' work reflects an abundance of means for the one curating the collection, for they are gathering works that were non-functional. The copy was fully described by the cataloguer: it was written in elegant *naskh* script (calligraphic quality) on full format (*qaṭʿ kāmil*), gilded on both the title pages and all through (although it is not clear what was in gold, probably ornamentations). This was not a cheap copy, and its talismanic quality should not be overlooked. It has the nature of a trophy.[21]

16 For the manuscripts of *Jāmiʿ al-bayān*, see *al-Fihris al-shāmil*, 60–77.

17 Most of the works in the collection are described as *'Miṣrī'* (Egyptian).

18 Saudi Arabia, Markaz al-Malik Fayṣal lil-Buḥūth wa-al-Dirāsāt al-Islāmiyya, *tafsīr* 100.

19 On this Qur'an commentary, see Rippin, "Tafsīr Ibn ʿAbbās", see especially Appendix I (copies consulted), 75–76.

20 Most of the copies available of this work are late, and most of them are housed in Ottoman imperial collections. See *al-Fihris al-shāmil* (2nd edition, 1989), I, 11–14.

21 For an example of such ornate Ottoman late copies, see the two manuscripts in Chester Beatty Library nos. Ar. 4224 and Ar. 5465. Kristine Rose-Beers (Cambridge), described the gilded copies stating 'the gold is sprinkled shell gold (paint) and gold leaf. It is very luxurious' (personal correspondence).

The second title on the list is *al-Durr al-manthūr* (#26) by al-Suyūṭī (d. 911/1505).[22] This author is amply represented in the collection with his aforementioned one-volume commentary al-Jalālayn (#32, #33 and #594)—one of the most ubiquitous Qur'an commentaries in the history of Islam.[23] Al-Suyūṭī was also the author of one of the most authoritative of glosses (*ḥāshiyah*) on the Qur'an commentary of al-Bayḍāwī (d. 719/1319)—which is not represented in the collection. *Al-Durr al-manthūr* (#26), the third Qur'an commentary written by al-Suyūṭī, as popular as it was, was not as ubiquitous as the other two. Its rise to fame and centrality is the product of a transformation in the Islamic tradition that started around the time of al-Jazzār and was only complete by the middle of the twentieth century. To place *al-Durr al-manthūr* as the second entry is, thus, not an innocent gesture. If Ibn 'Abbās' work can naturally fall into the first rank—by whatever cataloguing principles one wishes to follow, *al-Durr al-manthūr* is a rather odd title to place second, unless you know what you are doing. Al-Suyūṭī was a ubiquitous author, though this work was not a central text for the discipline of *tafsīr*. It is not clear why the curator chose this of his commentary works when he had authored two more popular works. The only possible explanation that I can offer is that the curator—who influenced the cataloguer—knew the history of *tafsīr* all too intimately and knew that *al-Durr al-manthūr* was a partisan work that attempted to gather all the early phases of Qur'an commentary, the tradition-based material.[24] As such, although authored very late in the timeline of Islam, it represented the early phase of *tafsīr*, and was second to Ibn 'Abbās' work conceptually. These two titles ensures that the collection has covered the early phase of the genre in a way that makes it unique. It is important to note that *al-Durr al-manthūr* is an extensive commentary—the recent edition is in seventeen volumes.[25] It is also remarkable that the Jazzār library has a complete set of the work. The cataloguer stated that this was a complete copy in four volumes written in full format (*qaṭʿ kāmil*) and described the script as 'Egyptian' (*bi-khaṭṭ Miṣrī*). As I stated previously, the only reasonable explanation for 'Egyptian' when used to describe the script is that it is a professional functional script employed when copying scholarly works that need care when copied with a script that prevented the misreading of words.

I have described this collection as unique for the fact that it has copies of these three works: Ibn 'Abbās', al-Ṭabarī's and al-Suyūṭī's *al-Durr*. Each on its own would have been interesting but not unusual, the three together beg for an explanation. If we add #54 to them, which is described as a commentary work by Ibn al-Jawzī (d. 597/1201), then we have another indication that this collection was not haphazard. The cataloguer did not name the work, but it could only be his *Zād al-masīr fī 'ilm al-tafsīr*.[26] This was an outlier of a work when it was written, a harkening back to al-Ṭabarī when his authority was all but forgotten. *Zād al-masīr* (#54) was an obscure work with a connoisseur audience, a Hanbalite audience.[27] Ibn Taymiyya, the great excavator of things Hanbalite, was a great admirer of Ibn al-Jawzī and read his works.[28] The copy was a high-end copy, written in artistic *naskh* script, with a gilded front page. The cataloguer knew that this was the second part of a two-volume set for he de-

22 First published in six volumes in Cairo 1314/1897 by the previously mentioned al-Maṭbaʿa al-Maymaniyya. For the critical edition, see al-Suyūṭī, *al-Durr al-manthūr*.
23 The collection has the other famed work by al-Suyūṭī on the study of the Qur'an, the classical *al-Itqān fī 'ulūm al-Qur'ān*, see #81 which starts the third subheading in the catalogue: *'ulūm al-qirā'āt* (variant readings of the Qur'an).
24 See the dissertation of Ally, "Culmination".
25 See note 22 above.
26 This is the only Qur'an commentary work of this author to survive. The work was late in being published, appearing in Damascus in 1964 in nine volumes, Ibn al-Jawzī, *Zād al-masīr*. A new edition has been issued from Qatar. On this work, see Holzman, "Ibn al-Jawzī".
27 See the analysis of *Zād al-masīr* in Geissinger, "Female Figures", 151–178.
28 As mentioned by Holzman, "Ibn al-Jawzī".

scribed this volume as the second half of the work (*al-niṣf al-akhīr*). The work is not widely attested in the manuscript collections in the world, a clear indication that this was a specifically sought-after title by the curator of this collection.[29]

The mystery, however, is compounded with title #90 from the Variant Readings section of the catalogue discussed in Chapter 14 by Shady Nasser. The title given is *al-Taysīr li-Ibn al-Jawzī*. Although this work is attested as a title of his, no manuscript has survived. There is no evidence of this title surviving, and no such title is available in *al-Fihris al-Shāmil*.[30] *Kashf al-ẓunūn* does not mention such a title.[31] This could not be the only surviving unicum of the work in the world.[32] Most probably it is another copy of *Zād al-masīr*, and the title was misread (*taysīr* and *masīr* could be easily corrupted to one another). #54 and #90 have the same paper size (*qaṭʿ al-rubʿ*). In any case, it is not clear why a Qur'an commentary work ended up in this section. To accept this title as truly a copy of this lost work is too convenient and cannot be justified since it will make this collection a depository of unicums; I am inclined to see it as just a second volume of #54. Whoever was curating this collection wanted the works of this Hanbalite scholar.

These four titles are remarkable together. These are peripheral works to the discipline of *tafsīr* as it was conceived then (and till recently), yet, when compared to the other volumes in the *tafsīr* collection, they stand out in the expenditure laid out for them. Al-Ṭabarī's Qur'an commentary at eight volumes is undoubtedly the most expensive and extensive of all the titles in the collection. One of the surviving volumes of this set is preserved in Saudi Arabia, as I mentioned.[33] It has 335 folios; if we take this as the average of the eight volumes, then we had a work of 2680 folios. This set dwarfs all the other works in the Qur'an commentary section. The second most voluminous work in the collection is al-Suyūṭī's *al-Durr al-manthūr* in four volumes. We do not have any volume of this set surviving, but comparable manuscripts are available, and they run from 2265 to 2782 folios.[34] Al-Jazzār's Qur'an commentary collection has nothing comparable to these two works. Of the three titles in four volumes in the collection, two constitute the Qur'an commentary of al-Bayḍāwī (#30 and #31), but these are not full folio paper but rather quarter paper. Usually al-Bayḍāwī's work is written in one volume.

The other title in four volumes is al-Khaṭīb al-Shirbīnī's (d. 977/1570; #58) *al-Sirāj al-Munīr*.[35] This voluminous Qur'an commentary belongs to the scholastic Asharite *tafsīr* tradition, although it was not as popular as al-Bayḍāwī's *Anwār al-tanzīl*. But even as voluminous as it is, with 2118 pages in the printed Bulaq format edition, it is only half the size of *al-Durr al-manthūr*, and as a ubiquitous work, its presence in the collection is to be expected.[36]

One could assess the significance of these four titles in a different way. They represent 18 percent of the volume number of the collection of *tafsīr* (14 out of 77 volumes in total), and at thirty-nine discreet titles they represent 10 per cent of the titles (4 out of 39). If we remove the slender authorless insignificant titles (#49, #50, #57, #67–69, #73,

29 Most of the copies are in Ottoman collections or Ottoman established collections (such as the Maḥmūdiyya of Medina). Only Cairo has a sizable number of copies. For copies, see *al-Fihris al-shāmil*, I, 210–212.

30 See *al-Fihris al-shāmil*, II, 1147–1148.

31 Ḥājī Khalīfah, *Kashf al-ẓunūn ʿan asmā'*, IX, 173.

32 Granted that al-ʿAlwajī in his book *Muʾallafāt Ibn al-Jawzī*, 116–117, mentions a unicum in a private library in Baghdad.

33 See footnote 18 above.

34 See *al-Fihris al-shāmil*, I, 531 (for the Indian four-volume copy of 2265 folios), and I, 533 (for the al-Ḥaram al-Makkī six-volume copy of 2782 folios). See also ms 111 of Dār al-Kutub in Cairo made up of two large volumes with thirty-seven lines per page, with a total of 1430 folios. For information on ms 111, see al-Suyūṭī, *al-Durr al-manthūr*, I, 79–81.

35 On al-Khaṭīb al-Shirbīnī see Brockelmann, *GAL* II, 320, *Suppl.* II, 441.

36 Although first published in 1285/1868, I am using the Cairo edition of 1311/1894. This edition in four volumes consists of 2118 pages or 1059 folios.

#75, #77–80) and then all the Shiite titles, which one presumes were looted from Jabal ʿĀmil (#40–42, #56, #64 and #72) and the only Persian Qur'an commentary work (#57,) then we end up with only twenty significant Sunni titles in the collection. The percentage of the four titles goes up to 20 per cent. Suddenly the significance of these four titles to the collection becomes irrefutable. But even by sheer folio number, the four titles could easily equal all the rest. I will return to these four titles at the end of the article to give another reason why I think they foreshadow the history of *tafsīr* in peculiar ways.

2 The *Madrasa* Curriculum in the *Tafsīr* Collection

The discussion above should not obscure the function of the *tafsīr* collection in the Jazzār library. This was a *madrasa* library, and it had *Anwār al-tanzīl* of al-Bayḍāwī, the central textbook for the teaching of Qur'an commentary in the Ottoman *madrasa* curriculum. The third to the seventh books listed in the catalogue (#27–31) are none other than the Qur'an commentary of al-Bayḍāwī, *Anwār al-tanzīl* (a title that was rarely used). One simply knew if one mentioned al-Bayḍāwī in the context of Qur'an commentary that one was talking about this specific work. The cataloguer simply states al-Bayḍāwī or Bayḍāwī, knowing all too well that there will be no confusion as to what he was referring. Placing it so early and so prominently in the enumeration leaves no doubt what was at the heart of this collection. #51 in the list is also another copy of this work. It is not clear why it is separated from the first five copies. #523 is also a copy of the Qur'an commentary of al-Bayḍāwī. We have a total of seven copies of the work in the catalogue. This is the most attested work in the collection. Two of the copies are in four-volume set each (#30 and #31). But one usually had the work copied in one volume (#27–29, #51 and #523)—one of the many advantages of this work is that it could be copied in one volume and, as such, obviated the need to carry or consult multivolume works. As the most attested title in the collection, it is clear that this was central to the discipline.

The Qur'an commentary of al-Bayḍāwī was never read in a vacuum; it came with a long rich history of glossing. The Jazzār library has at least one of the most famous of the glosses on al-Bayḍāwī (#62), that of Shaykh-Zādah (d. 951/1544). This was and remains one of the most acclaimed Ottoman works in *tafsīr*. Unfortunately, the cataloguer does not state if this was a complete copy, but one volume of this gloss is not the complete gloss given the massive size of the work and the fact that it is impossible to copy into one volume.[37] Two other glosses on al-Bayḍāwī are also listed. The second gloss (#63) is authored by ʿIṣām al-Asfarāyīnī (d. 945/1538); this was one of the most popular glosses in the Ottoman lands being dedicated to no other than the Sultan Suleiman the Magnificent.[38] The third gloss (#518), titled *Rafʿ al-kisāʾ*, is most probably the work by ʿAbd al-Ghanī al-Nābulusī (d. 1143/1731).[39] The glosses of al-Bayḍāwī in this collection are all Ottoman bestsellers.

3 The Shiite *Tafsīr* Works in al-Jazzār's Collection

The fourth gloss (#64) on al-Bayḍāwī listed in the catalogue is a genuine surprise. This is a gloss written by Bahāʾ al-Dīn al-ʿĀmilī (d. 1031/1622). He is not only one of the leading luminaries of Shiite scholarship but also one who lived and resided in

37 The printed first edition is a massive four-volume print. For the history of its publication, see Saleh, "The Qur'an Commentary of al-Bayḍāwī", 94. This printed copy has 2303 pages.

38 See *al-Fihris al-shāmil*, I, 569–576 (260 copies of this work). See Mujammaʿ al-Malik ʿAbd al-ʿAzīz lil-Maktabāt al-Waqfiyya, ms. AB013072 (from the al-Shifāʾ School waqf in Medina), fol. 2ᵃ. for the name of Sulayman the Magnificent.

39 See *al-Fihris al-shāmil*, II, 756. The complete title is *Rafʿ al-kisāʾ ʿan ʿibārat al-Bayḍāwī fī sūrat al-Nisāʾ*.

Safavid Iran.[40] The work itself is an intriguing instance of the universal dominance of al-Bayḍāwī's commentary, when even Shiite scholars were reading and studying it, and some wrote glosses on it. Sunnis were not generous readers of Shiite scholarship, and few Shiite works are preserved in Sunni libraries. The presence of this work in this collection is, thus, an aberration.

Al-Jazzār's collection has, moreover, two other Shiite Qur'an commentaries. There are four listings for *Majmaʿ al-bayān* of al-Ṭabrisī (d. 548/1153), these are #40–42 and #72. This is one of the most important of Twelver Shiite Qur'an commentaries.[41] Its presence in the collection is nothing short of remarkable. The cataloguer claims that #40 is a complete copy—although in one volume. I doubt this could be the case, since this work is voluminous, and I would attribute the confusion to the absence of familiarity with Shiite works. Finally, the work *Ghurar al-fawā'id* by al-Sharīf al-Murtaḍā (d. 436/1044) is also available in the collection (#56).[42]

#124 in the Variant Readings (*qirā'āt*) section of the catalogue is another remarkable work and a surprise. The title given is *Zubdat al-bayān*, but no author is given. There is no such work in *qirā'āt* works, and the only work that fits Qur'anic studies is *Zubdat al-bayān fi barāhīn aḥkām al-Qur'ān* of al-Muḥaqqiq al-Ardabīlī (d. 993/1585).[43] The manuscripts of this work are only available in Shiite libraries, and only outside the Arab and Ottoman world.[44] #57, simply titled Persian Commentary (*tafsīr fārisī*), is also out of place in the collection. If one was to make a guess, this work must be from a bilingual Shiite scholar from Jabal ʿĀmil in southern Lebanon. The presence of four Shiite works and a Persian work adds to the uniqueness of this collection. There is a preponderance of evidence that these works are related to the campaigns of al-Jazzār in the mountain areas of Metwali (Shiite) and acquired then.[45]

4 The Other Textbooks of *Tafsīr*: *al-Kashshāf* of al-Zamakhsharī and *al-Jalālayn* of al-Suyūṭī

There were three Qur'an commentaries that were used to teach *tafsīr* in the *madrasa* across the centuries. The first to become the universally acknowledged textbook was *al-Kashshāf* of al-Zamakhsharī. This work was used for over three centuries across the Islamic world, and tens of glosses were written on it by professors who taught it.[46] The supremacy of *al-Kashshāf* was eventually replaced by al-Bayḍāwī's commentary, a process that saw its completion in the Ottoman curriculum.[47] Most professors teaching al-Bayḍāwī continued to consult the glosses on *al-Kashshāf*, since al-Bayḍāwī was based on it and, as such, a lot of the insights of the glosses on *al-Kashshāf* could be used for al-Bayḍāwī.[48] Thus, although disused in the teaching of *tafsīr*, *al-Kashshāf* was always consulted and the glosses on it always read by professors teaching al-Bayḍāwī. One would expect to have both *al-Kashshāf* and some glosses on it in

40 For manuscripts of this work, see *al-Fihris al-shāmil*, II, 672–675.

41 For al-Ṭabrisī, see Fudge, *Qur'anic Hermeneutics*. See the edition al-Ṭabrisī, *Majmaʿ al-bayān*.

42 The work has been edited, see al-Sharīf al-Murtaḍā, *Ghurar al-fawā'id* (also known as *Amālī al-Murtaḍā*).

43 On Ardabīlī, see the article written by W. Madelung in *Encyclopædia Iranica*, II, 368–370. The Qur'an commentary has been published recently, see al-Ardabīlī, *Zubdat al-bayān*.

44 See *al-Fihris al-Shāmil*, I, 639–641. No copy is in a Sunni collection.

45 On his campaigns, see Philipp, *Acre*, 65.

46 For a list of the glosses on *al-Kashshāf*, see Lane, *Traditional Muʿtazilite*, 300–328. For the most famous of the glosses, see Saleh, "The Gloss as Intellectual History", 217–259.

47 See Gunasti, "Political Patronage", 335–357. For a different view as to why al-Bayḍāwī replaced al-Zamakhsharī, see Saleh, "The Qur'an Commentary of al-Bayḍāwī".

48 See the classic remarks of al-Suyūṭī in *Nawāhid al-abkār*, I, 18, where he states clearly that one needs to read the glosses on *al-Kashshāf* to write a gloss on *Anwār*.

any Ottoman library. The Jazzār library has two copies of *al-Kashshāf* and a rather miniscule number of its glosses. There is a copy of *al-Kashshāf* in two volumes (#45 and #46) and a copy of the second half of the work (#47). Al-Kashshāf usually came in two volumes, and it is, thus, usually divided into two equal parts. I am inclined to see the anonymous volume #48 as the second part of #47 given the proximity of the two entries and, thus, forming the second copy in the collection.

The presence of two anonymous glosses on *al-Kashshāf* (#65 and #71) and another anonymous gloss on the preamble of the work (#66) are but a shadow of the gloss literature on *al-Kashshāf*.[49] The only gloss with a title available in the collection is #70, an obscure author and title.[50] There is information that this author, al-Fāḍil al-Yamanī (d. 750/1349), authored two glosses on *al-Kashshāf*, the most ubiquitous is, however, *Tuḥfat al-ashrāf*.[51] Another work that should be considered as part of the gloss apparatus on *al-Kashshāf* is #216 (*Aḥādīth al-Kashshāf*), which is an inventory of the prophetic *ḥadīths* in this Qur'an commentary.[52] The low number of glosses on *al-Kashshāf* is not a surprising state because there had been a continuous decline in the connection between the gloss literature of the two works: al-Bayḍāwī was becoming increasingly independent, and the more glosses written on it, the less the need for the glosses on *al-Kashshāf*. Only imperial collections managed to keep an inventory of the rich glosses on *al-Kashshāf*. More unexpectedly, the glosses of al-Bayḍāwī themselves are not well represented in the Jazzār library. One can argue that since *tafsīr* was not a central discipline in the hierarchy of religious sciences in Islam, the *tafsīr* selection in the Jazzār library did the bare minimum to provide the basic texts. *Fiqh*, *ḥadīth* and recitation were far more important—thus, there are as many recitation volumes in the collection (66 volumes) as there were *tafsīr* volumes (77), which might appear unusual for us, but is normal for the hierarchy of sciences at that time.

The other work used to teach *tafsīr*, though to a far lesser degree, was the concise Qur'an commentary known as *Tafsīr al-Jalālayn*. Al-Jazzār had three copies (#32, #33 and #594). This was one of the handiest and most accessible of commentaries on the Qur'an. It was based on *al-Wajīz* of al-Wāḥidī (d. 468/1076) and was as popular as al-Bayḍāwī's commentary.[53] #32 is described as written in *naskh* calligraphic script, gilded and with a gilded leather case. Again, I think the curator of the collection had striven to have high-end copies of the major works he wanted to obtain. #33 is less valuable with some missing material in its middle (an indication, incidentally, that each volume was closely inspected). #594 is only the second volume of a two-volume set. Two works (#533 and #539) titled *Tafsīr al-Jalīlī* are most probably also copies of this work. There is no attested work of this title or an author with this name.

5 The Inheritors of the Nishapuri School of *Tafsīr* and Works on Grammar and Rare Words

The dominant school of commentary before the rise of *al-Kashshāf* by al-Zamakhsharī, its writing was an event that transformed the genre and set the tone for the coming six centuries, was what I have termed as the Nishapuri school of *tafsīr*.[54] The collection has what one can call the second manifestation of this school, thus, a complete copy in two volumes (#521: the work is named here as

49 The glosses run into the hundreds. See note 46 above.
50 It is most probably *Tuḥfat al-ashrāf fī kashf ghawāmiḍ al-Kashshāf*, see *al-Fihris al-Shāmil*, I, 408.
51 For references on the two works, see Lane, *Traditional Muʿtazilite*, 303–304.
52 On this kind of work, see Saleh, *The Formation*, 210, footnote 22. This work can be one of two, either a work by Ibn Ḥajar, *al-Kāfī al-shāfī* or by al-Zayʿalī, *Takhrīj al-aḥādīth*.
53 On al-Wāḥidī and his al-Wajīz, see Saleh, "The Last of the Nishapuri School", 238.
54 See Saleh, "Nishapuri School of Quranic Exegesis".

Maʿālim al-tanzīl) of al-Baghawī's Qur'an commentary and two incomplete copies (#43 and #44, both attributed to al-Baghawī). This is the famous work, *Maʿālim al-tanzīl*.[55] #43 is half the commentary; #44 only covers up to the end of Sura 6. Al-Baghawī (d. 516/1122) was a leading luminary in the Sunni revival tradition and his reworking of al-Thaʿlabī's (d. 427/1035) Qur'an commentary *al-Kashf wa-al-bayān* became the most copied work in the history of Qur'an commentary.[56] *Maʿālim al-tanzīl* is available in every manuscript collection, and its presence here is to be expected.

The other representative of this school is the Qur'an commentary of al-Khāzin (d. 741/1341), *Lubāb al-taʾwīl fī maʿānī al-tanzīl* (#38), which is a summary and updating of al-Baghawī's *Maʿālim*.[57] This work was as popular as its model, and they all depend on *al-Kashf* of al-Thaʿlabī. These two works were always present in the landscape of Sunni *tafsīr* and represent the safest works in the tradition, works that all Sunni currents seemed to accept.

The collection has a few titles that are part of the specialised literature on the Qur'anic language, these are works dedicated to the obscure words in the Qur'an (*gharīb*) and the grammatical parsing of its phrases (*iʿrāb*). #53 is a work from this genre with the title *Tafsīr Gharīb al-Qur'ān*, a work on the obscure words in the Qur'an. #75 similarly is an anonymous work in this genre. Available works with this title are numerous and it is not clear who was meant by this work.[58] #59 is given as *Iʿrāb al-Qur'ān* by al-ʿUkbarī (d. 616/1219). This is his famous *al-Tibyān fī iʿrāb al-Qur'ān* (first published under a different title *Imlāʾ mā mann bihi al-raḥmān*).[59] Actually, #1683 gives the correct title of this work as *al-Tibyān fī iʿrāb al-Qur'ān*. The other work from the genre of obscure words of the Qur'an is #61, *Iʿrāb al-Qur'ān* and the author is given as Ibn al-Naḥḥās (d. 338/949, referred to as al-Naḥḥās in the editions of this work).[60] Finally, #537 titled *Nuzhat al-Qulūb* was a bestseller in this genre; this is none other than the work of al-Sijistānī (d. 330/941).[61] We can add to this group two works, #512 and #525, which deal with the occasions of revelations; this was a genre of works dedicated to historicising the suras' original moment of revelation, why this chapter was revealed, where and about what.[62] #512 is anonymous, while #525 is attributed to al-Suyūṭī.[63]

That this collection is Ottoman is unmistakable. The centrality of al-Bayḍāwī and the presence of Shaykh Zadeh's gloss on it are not only culturally specific to the Ottoman curriculum, but also reflect the dominance of the Ottoman curriculum all over the empire.[64] It is, however, the presence of the Qur'an commentary of Abū al-Suʿūd (d. 982/1574), the Sheikh al-Islām of Süleyman the Magnificent, that firmly places this collection in its Ottoman milieu. His Qur'an commentary comes as the fifth-ranked work in the collection at the very top of it, thus, after Ibn ʿAbbās, al-Suyūṭī, al-Bayḍāwī, al-Suyūṭī again, then Abū al-Suʿūd. If we remove the two commentaries that were ideological (that is, the first two), we have Abū al-Suʿūd third in the hierarchy. The work is rightly a celebrated work; it was seen as the coming of age of the Ottoman scholastic tradition, now capable of producing a

55 The work was published early and repeatedly for its publication. See the introduction in al-Baghawī, *Maʿālim al-tanzīl*, I, 20.

56 See Saleh, *Formation*, 208–209.

57 Brockelmann, *GAL* II: 109; *SII* 135. Al-Khāzin clearly states in his introduction that he is updating al-Baghawī's. for this, see Saleh, *Formation*, 209.

58 See Ḥājī Khalīfah, *Kashf al-ẓunūn*, IX, 400 (13 authors for the same title); also see *al-Fihris al-shāmil*, (2nd edition), II, 1134, 1211, (31 authors with the same title).

59 See the introduction to the edition of the work, al-ʿUkbarī, *al-Tibyān*, Ḥ for a discussion of the title and why *Imlāʾ* is not the title of the work.

60 Al-Naḥḥās, *Iʿrāb al-Qur'ān*.

61 On this title, see *al-Fihris al-shāmil*, I, 42–48.

62 On this genre, see Rippin, "The Function of asbāb", 1–20.

63 The title of #525 is *Lubāb al-nuqūl fī asbāb al-nuzūl*, Dimashq 1961.

64 For the centrality of *Anwār al-tanzīl* of al-Bayḍāwī in the Ottoman curriculum, see Gunasti, "Political Patronage", 335–357.

commentary on its own and of equal rank to any before it.[65] That we have three complete copies of the work (#34 and #35 are each a complete one-volume copy, and #36 and #37 constitute the third copy in two volumes) indicates the value given to this commentary. Only al-Bayḍāwī has more copies (six). If we add the Shaykh Zadeh copy (#62), then the Ottoman school has a formidable presence in the collection. The Ottoman presence is, thus, the third pillar of this collection. We have the Salaf-oriented cluster, the Bayḍāwī cluster and the Ottoman cluster.

The collection has at least five titles that are dedicated to the merits and benefits of the Qur'an.[66] This was one of the major uses of the Qur'an on the ritual level, its use for salvific, healing, apotropaic or incantatory purposes. The Qur'an was seen as a source of wealth, in so far that its reading brought good luck and averted misfortunes. Specialised works that were dedicated to the powers of the Qur'an became popular and part of the commentary scholarly tradition. There are five titles that belong to the genre of merits of the Qur'an: #60 (refers to two copies of the same work), #74, #76, #77 and #1702. Two (#60 × 2 and #74) are called *Khawāṣ al-Qur'ān*. These, I believe, are nothing but the famous work attributed to al-Ghazālī (d. 505/1111), also known as *al-Dhahab al-ibrīz*.[67] This was a popular work that included incantation formulas, magical squares and described the powers of each Sura. The other title, #76, *al-Durr al-naẓīm*, can be only one of two works, both of which derive from the pseudo-al-Ghazālī's work and from one another and repeat the same material.[68] #77 is a *majmūʿ*, a volume that has various short epistles and writings bound together. This catalogue does not give us the content of these types of volumes and only mentions the first epistle. The first epistle here is entitled *Faḍā'il al-Qur'ān*, the merits of the Qur'an. This is a very ubiquitous title, and it could be any number of works.[69] #1702 is an epistle on the benefits of the Qur'an (*Manāfiʿ al-Qur'ān*), these were a subgenre of works on the use of the Qur'an that culled from bigger works the 'benefits' of reading or using the Qur'an for various purposes.[70] Finally, #595, titled *Aḥwāl al-Qur'ān* and described as constituted of 560 chapters, is impossible to identify. This is clearly in the same genre as the merit of Sura works. *Al-Fihris al-shāmil* has a ninety-eight folios epistle attributed to al-Ghazālī with such a title, but I doubt this is the same work.[71]

The collective title of #78, *Ḥamā'il*, indicates that these were collections of amulets that used Qur'anic verses as the main apotropaic text. Other Ottoman libraries included such items as part of their inventory and their presence here should not be surprising. Guy Burak has studied this aspect of Qur'anic use in Islamic culture, and he has shown that the *ḥamā'il* were part of library collections.[72]

There are a few anonymous items (some with titles, others untitled) that are clearly remnants from previous collections that were collected without existing documentation of authorship or sometimes titles. #49, #50, #55, #65, #67–69, #73, #75, #78, #80 and #571 are all without title; they are also short works (except for #571), and one

65 On the status of this work in the Ottoman scholarly tradition, see Naguib, "Guiding the Sound Mind", 1–52.

66 Afsaruddin, "The Excellence of the Qur'ān", 1–24. See also Saleh, *Formation*, 103–108.

67 See al-Badawī, *Mu'allafāt al-Ghazālī*, 283. It is not clear why the title *Khawāṣ* became the more used instead of the formal title.

68 It is most probably authored by Ibn al-Khashshāb (d. 567/1172), see *al-Fihris al-shāmil*, I, 251–252, since this is the work most available in the manuscript collections. This was based on the pseudo-al-Ghazālī's work and was the basis of the second work by the same title by al-Yāfiʿī (d. 768/1367); for the statement that it is an abridgment of the above see Ibid., I, 252, for the copies of the manuscripts see I, 419–420.

69 On works with this title, see *al-Fihris al-shāmil*, II, 1215–1216.

70 On works with this title, see *al-Fihris al-shāmil*, II, 1239–1240. For an example of such a work, see Abū Bakr b. Ḥasan al-Wattād, *Manāfiʿ al-Qur'ān*.

71 *Al-Fihris al-shāmil*, I, 127. Such a title is not mentioned in al-Badawī's catalogue of the works of al-Ghazālī.

72 Burak, "The Section on Prayers", I, 341–366. Also see Burak, "Alphabets and 'Calligraphy'", 32–54.

doubts of any significance. Five of them are called *ḥāshiyah* (#65, #67–69 and #73), a title of sorts one might argue, but still unhelpful. By then, many epistles were written on the interpretations of single verses, a mode of writing that became popular in late Ottoman scholastic tradition (#50, #79 and #80).[73] The problem with the short epistles is that they could easily become anonymous because of the nature of copying small works, for example, no title pages and/or grouped together in *majāmīʿ* (collected epistles volumes). Short works, moreover, provide fewer clues that one can use to guess their authorship if the title or author is not mentioned. Many of these works were also not supposed to be officially published (*ibrāz*); however, they were preserved as archival material of the scholarly Nachlass of authors that made its way into library collections. One can add anonymous titled works to this group; these were works with titles but no author. Examples of titled works are #52, #53, #77 and #79; at present, it is impossible to identify the authors.

6 A Comparison with the Qur'an Commentary Books in the *Madrasa* of Muḥammad Bey Abū al-Dhahab (d. 1189/1775)[74]

The Egyptian governor Muḥammad Bey Abū al-Dhahab established his mosque and library in Cairo in 1774.[75] This means that the two collections are not only geographically close but also contemporaneous. The endowment copy has been preserved and the Qur'an commentary section is internally divided into three parts: Part A *tafsīr* proper (13 works), Part B obscure words works (*gharīb*, 5 works) and Part C glosses (*ḥawāshī*, 6 works). A total of twenty-four titles in the *tafsīr* section were given for this Cairene collection. A comparison between the two lists of works helps to shed light on al-Jazzār's list and its significance. It shows, without doubt, that Acre was more in the sphere of the Ottoman *madrasa* tradition than that of the Mamluk Egyptian curriculum. The two collections have nine titles in common (the first number refers to the Jazzār catalogue number):

#25 (Qur'an commentary of Ibn ʿAbbās, no. 8 in the *tafsīr* Part A of the Cairo collection, one copy called the commentary of al-Kalbī).
#26 (Qur'an commentary of al-Suyūṭī, *al-Durr al-manthūr*, no. 3 in Part A of the Cairo collection, one copy).
#27–31, #51 and #523 (the Qur'an commentary of al-Bayḍāwī, no. 6 in Part A; the Cairo collection has six complete copies of this work. The Jazzār library has one copy more than the Cairo collection.)
#32, #33 and #594 (the Qur'an commentary *Tafsīr Jalālayn* of al-Suyūṭī, no. 7 in Part A; the Cairo collection has four copies of this work).
#34–37 (the Qur'an commentary of Abū al-Suʿūd, no. 11 in Part A; the Cairo collection has one copy. The Jazzār collection has three copies, clearly a homage to the Ottomans by Acre.)
#38 (Qur'an commentary of al-Khāzin, no. 9 in Part A; the Cairo collection has five copies of this work).
#43, #44 and #521 (Qur'an commentary of al-Baghawī, no. 10 in Part A; the Cairo collection has one copy).
#58 (Qur'an commentary of al-Khaṭīb al-Sharbīnī, no. 12 in Part A; the Cairo collection has one copy).
#81 (which is technically not in the *tafsīr* section but the first in the Variant Readings section, this is the famous *al-Itqān* of al-Suyūṭī, no. 1 in Part B; the Cairo collection has one copy)

There is, thus, a remarkable congruence between the two collections: both have al-Bayḍāwī as the

73 For an example of such works, see Ibn Kamāl Bāshā, *Tafsīr surat al-Mulk*.

74 For the list of books in Arabic, see ʿAbd al-Laṭīf, "Maktabah ʿUthmāniyya", 19–20. An English translation with no commentary or dates or identification of books was published by Crecelius, "Waqfiyah", 135–136.

75 For the establishment of the endowment complex, see Crecelius, "Waqf", 57–81.

central work (and the most attested in both collections). However, they share none of the glosses; they have Abū al-Suʿūd in common (which was, indeed, universally acknowledged as a masterpiece); both have works from the Nishapuri school, and both have *Tafsīr al-Jalālayn*. Al-Suyūṭī was, by then, the most important post-classical author and his *Itqān* was in every library. What is remarkable is that the Cairo collection has not one copy or a gloss on *al-Kashshāf* of al-Zamakhsharī. Acre was intellectually still mirroring the Ottoman *madrasa* which did not fully abandon *al-Kashshāf*. More telling is that although both focus on al-Bayḍāwī, the glosses they chose are not the same. Cairo has the Arab Cairene glossers (Shaykh al-Islām Zakarīyā al-Anṣārī and al-Shihāb), while the glosses in al-Jazzār's collection are Ottoman and eastern Iranian. The Cairo collection is also far more scholastic: it knows how to divide the discipline and the division is squarely *madrasa*-based. Al-Jazzār's collection shows what I call an ideological trajectory that is remarkable. The presence of al-Ṭabarī remains the most indicative sign of an echo to the rise of restrictive understanding of hermeneutics. The Jazzār collection, by its peripheral nature, was able to scramble the hierarchies in a frightening foreshadowing. The governor of Egypt was wealthier, the resources for his endowments far superior to any al-Jazzār could muster, and yet, they did not care to have a copy of al-Ṭabarī. Had they wanted they could have. Al-Jazzār's collection remains, as such, unique in the Arab provinces.

Thomas Philipp's work on Acre remains a milestone in scholarship on the city at its zenith, which coincides with the formation of the Jazzār library. Philipp stated that the city 'developed quite literally ex nihilo'; a city made up of immigrants and exclusively oriented to trading with Europe based on 'one major cash crop'.[76] Despite the abundance of political and economic sources, somehow there is almost no information about the social structures or social groups, and as Philipp stated 'our information [about the Acre society] remains maddeningly sporadic and anecdotal'.[77] Philipp described the city as unique in the Arab Ottoman provinces: an entirely immigrant city, with no local elites and very shallow social structures.[78] He concluded his book by asking several questions, the most provocative being if in the history of Acre in the eighteenth and early nineteenth century one can 'trace the beginnings of modernity here, or do we recognize only variations of traditional patterns?'.[79] One can ask the same about the Qur'an commentary collection: is it a typical Ottoman collection or was it a harbinger of things to come in the Islamic religious tradition?

Or to ask the basic question of who was reading this collection, or its opposite: who gathered it? It was not a strictly *madrasa* scholastic collection—al-Ṭabarī and all—it was not yet a Wahhābī collection—al-Bayḍāwī and all. One can only speculate—or to paraphrase Philipp again—there is maddeningly little we can go by here. I am still, however, inclined to see a general provincial upheaval in the Arab Ottoman East; it is not that only Wahhābism was seeking a puritan Islam, but rather this *ad fontis* was in the air in the late eighteenth century, and one should go after the harbingers everywhere. I have already detailed the transformation in the modern Qur'an commentary historiography of the field.[80] The rise of the notion of tradition-based commentary (*al-tafsīr bi-al-ma'thūr*) meant that the pre-nineteenth century hierarchy was completely reversed, and the Bayḍāwī-gloss tradition was completely forgotten.[81] The hierarchy shown in placing Ibn ʿAbbās and al-Suyūṭī's *al-Durr* as the first two titles shows a unique sense of prioritising the Salaf period despite the *madrasa* nature of the collection. This hi-

76 Philipp, *Acre*, 170–171.

77 Ibid., 178.
78 Ibid., 181.
79 Ibid., 187.
80 Saleh, "Preliminary Remarks", 6–40.
81 Saleh, "The Qur'an Commentary of al-Bayḍāwī".

erarchy will look familiar after 1940 in the Arab and Islamic worlds, and, as such, Acre was, in this case, all too modern.

Bibliography

References to *al-Fihris al-Shāmil lil-turāth al-ʿArabī al-makhṭūṭ, ʿulūm al-Qurʾān, makhṭūṭāt al-Tafsīr*, 2 vols., Jordan: al-Majmaʿ al-Malakī li-Buḥūth al-Ḥaḍārah al-Islāmiyyah, 2nd Edition 1989, is *al-Fihris al-Shāmil.*

ʿAbd al-Ḥamīd al-ʿAlwajī. *Muʾallafāt Ibn al-Jawzī*. Kuwait, 1992.

ʿAbd al-Laṭīf Ibrāhīm. "Maktabah ʿUthmāniyya: Dirāsah naqdiyya wa-nashr li-raṣīd al-maktabah." *Majallat Kullīyat al-Ādāb: Jāmiʿat al-Qāhira* 20 (1958): 19–20.

ʿAbd al-Raḥmān al-Badawī. *Muʾallafāt al-Ghazālī*. Kuwait, 1977.

Abū Bakr b. Ḥasan al-Wattād. *Manāfiʿ al-Qurʾān*, edited by ʿAbd al-Ghanī al-Fāsī. Beirut, 2004.

Afsaruddin, Asma. "The Excellences of the Qurʾān: Textual Sacrality and the Organization of Early Islamic Society." *Journal of the American Oriental Society* 122 (2002): 1–24.

Ally, Shabir. "The Culmination of Tradition-based Tafsīr The Qurʾān Exegesis 'al-Durr al-manthūr' of al-Suyūtī (d. 911/1505)." PhD Thesis, University of Toronto. 2012.

al-Ardabīlī. *Zubdat al-bayān fī barāhīn aḥkām al-Qurʾān*, edited by Riḍā al-Ustādī. Qumm, 2000.

al-Baghawī. *Maʿālim al-tanzīl*, edited by Muḥammad Nimr et. al., 8 vols. Riyadh, 1993.

Bosworth, C.E. "al-Ṭabarī." in: *Encyclopaedia of Islam*, Second Edition. x, 10–15. Leiden, 2012.

Brockelmann, Carl. *Geschichte der arabischen Litteratur*. Leiden 2012.

Burak, Guy. "The Section on Prayers, Invocations, Unique Qualities of the Qurʾan, and Magic Squares in the Palace Library Inventory." In *Treasures of Knowledge: An Inventory of the Ottoman Palace Library (1502/3–1503/4)*, edited by Gülru Necipoğlu, Cemal Kafadar and Cornell H. Fleischer, 341–366. Leiden, 2019.

Burak, Guy. "Alphabets and 'Calligraphy' in the Section on Prayers, Special Characteristics of the Quran and Magic Squares in the Inventory of Sultan Bayezid II's Palace Library." *Journal of Material Cultures in the Muslim World* 2 (2021): 32–54.

Crecelius, Daniel. "The Waqfīyah of Muḥammad Bey Abū al-Dhahab." *Journal of the American Research Center in Egypt* 16 (1979): 125–146.

Crecelius, Daniel. "The Waqf of Muhammad Bey Abu al-Dhahab in Historical Perspective." *International Journal of Middle East Studies* 23 (1991): 57–81.

El Shamsy, Ahmed. *Rediscovering the Islamic Classics: How Editors and Print Culture Transformed an Intellectual Tradition*. Princeton, NJ, 2020.

Fihris al-makhṭūṭāt fī Markaz al-Malik Fayṣal lil-buḥūth wa-al-dirāsāt al-islāmiyya, 8 vols. 1994.

al-Fihris al-shāmil lil-turāth al-ʿarabī al-makhṭūṭ: ʿulūm al-Qurʾān: Makhṭūṭāt al-tafsīr, 2 vols. ʿAmmān: Muʾassasat Āl al-Bayt 1987.

Fudge, Bruce. *Qurʾānic Hermeneutics: al-Ṭabrisī and the Craft of Commentary*. London, 2011.

Geissinger, Aisha. "Female Figures, Marginality, and Qurʾanic Exegesis in Ibn al-Jawzī's Ṣifat al-ṣafwa." In *Islamic Interpretive Tradition and Gender Justice: Processes of Canonization Subversion and Change*, edited by Nevin Reda and Yasmin Amin, 151–178. Montreal/Kingston, 2020.

Gunasti, Susan. "Political Patronage and the Writing of Quran Commentaries among the Ottoman Turks." *Journal of Islamic Studies* 24 (2013): 335–357.

Ḥājī Khalīfah. *Kashf al-ẓunūn ʿan asmāʾ al-kutub wa-al-funūn*, edited by Akmal al-Dīn Iḥsān Ughlī et al., 10 vols. London, 2021.

Holzman, Livnat. "Ibn al-Jawzī (d. 597/1201)." In *Handbook of Qurʾanic Hermeneutics*, edited by Georges Tamer. Berlin, forthcoming.

Ibn al-Jawzī. *Zād al-masīr fī ʿilm al-tafsīr*, edited by Muḥammad Zuhayr al-Shāwīsh. Damascus, 1964.

Ibn Ḥajar. *al-Kāfī al-shāfī fī takhrīj aḥādīth al-Kashshāf*. Beirut, 1997.

Ibn Kamāl Bāshā. *Tafsīr surat al-Mulk* (Q. 67), edited by Ḥasan ʿItr. Beirut, 1986.

Lane, Andrew J. *A Traditional Muʿtazilite Qurʾān Commentary: The Kashshāf of Jār Allāh Al-Zamakhsharī*. Leiden, 2006.

Loth, Otto. "Ṭabarî's Korancommentar." *Zeitschrift der*

Deutschen Morgenländischen Gesellschaft 35 (1881): 588–628.

Madelung, W. "Ardabīlī." In *Encyclopaedia Iranica*, edited by Ehsan Yarshater, II, 368–370. London, 1987.

Motzki, Harald. "Dating the So-called Tafsīr Ibn ʿAbbās: Some Additional Remarks." *Jerusalem Studies in Arabic and Islam* 31 (2006): 147–163.

Mujammaʿ al-Malik ʿAbd al-ʿAzīz lil-Maktabāt al-Waqfiyya, ms. AB013072 (from the al-Shifāʾ School waqf in Medina), fol. 2ª.

Naguib, Shuruq. "Guiding the Sound Mind: Ebu's-suʿūd's *tafsīr* and Rhetorical Interpretation of the Qur'an in the Post-classical Period." *The Journal of Ottoman Studies* 42 (2013): 1–52.

Al-Naḥḥās. *Iʿrāb al-Qurʾān*, edited by Zuhayr Zāhid. 5 vols. Baghdad, 1985.

Philipp, Thomas. *Acre: The Rise and Fall of a Palestinian City, 1730–1831*. New York, 2002.

Rettig, Simon. "The Rise of the Enʿam: Manuscripts of Selections of Suras in the Early Sixteenth-century Ottoman Empire." In *The Word Illuminated: Form and Function of Qur'anic Manuscripts from the Seventh to Seventeenth Centuries*, edited by Simon Rettig and Sana Mirza, 185–212. Washington, D.C., 2022.

Rippin, Andrew. "The Function of asbāb al-nuzūl in Qurʾānic Exegesis." *Bulletin of the School of Oriental and African Studies* 51 (1988): 1–20.

Rippin, Andrew. "Tafsīr Ibn ʿAbbās and Criteria for Dating Early tafsīr Texts." *Jerusalem Studies in Arabic and Islam* 18 (1994): 38–83.

Rosenthal, Franz. *General Introduction, and, From the Creation to the Flood*. (History of al-Ṭabarī, volume 1). Albany, 1989.

Ṣābāt, Khalīl. *Tārīkh al-ṭibāʿa fī al-sharq al-ʿarabī*. Cairo, 1966.

Saleh, Walid S. "Nishapuri School of Quranic Exegesis." In *Encyclopaedia Iranica*, edited by Ehsan Yarshater. New York, 2000.

Saleh, Walid A. *The Formation of Classical Tafsīr Tradition: The Qurʾān Commentary of Al-Thaʿlabī (d. 427/1035)*. Leiden, 2004.

Saleh, Walid A. "The Last of the Nishapuri School of Tafsīr: Al-Wāḥidī (d. 468/1076) and His Significance in the History of Qur'anic Exegesis." *Journal of the American Oriental Society* 126 (2006): 223–243.

Saleh, Walid A. "Preliminary Remarks on the Historiography of *tafsīr* in Arabic: A History of the Book Approach." *Journal of Qur'anic Studies* 12 (2010): 6–40.

Saleh, Walid A. "Marginalia and Peripheries: A Tunisian Historian and the History of Qur'anic Exegesis: Cultural Memory and Islam." *Numen* 58 (2011): 284–313.

Saleh, Walid A. "The Gloss as Intellectual History: The Ḥāshiyahs on al-Kashshāf." *Oriens* 41 (2013): 217–259.

Saleh, Walid A. "The Qur'an Commentary of al-Bayḍāwī: A History of Anwār al-tanzīl." *Journal of Qur'anic Studies* 23 (2021): 71–102.

al-Sharīf al-Murtaḍā. *Ghurar al-fawāʾid wa-durar al-qalāʾid* (also known as *Amālī al-Murtaḍā*), edited by Muḥammad Abū al-Faḍl Ibrāhīm, 2 vols. Cairo, 1954.

al-Suyūṭī. *al-Durr al-manthūr fī al-tafsīr bi-al-maʾthūr*, edited by ʿAbd Allāh al-Turkī, 17 vols. Cairo, 2003.

al-Suyūṭī. *Nawāhid al-abkār wa-shawārid al-afkār*, edited by Māhir Adīb Ḥabbūsh, 10 vols. Istanbul, 2022.

al-Ṭabarī. *General Introduction and From the Creation to the Flood*. Albany, 1989.

al-Ṭabarī. *Jāmiʿ al-bayān fī tafsīr al-Qurʾān*, edited by Muḥammad al-Ghamrāwī, 30 vols. Cairo, 1321/1903.

al-Ṭabrisī. *Majmaʿ al-bayān fī tafsīr al-Qurāʾn*, edited by Hāshim al-Maḥallātī et al., 10 vols. Beirut, 1986.

al-ʿUkbarī. *al-Tibyān fī Iʿrāb al-Qurʾān*, edited by Muḥammad al-Bajāwī. Cairo, 1976.

Vrolijk, Arnoud. "The Leiden Edition of al-Ṭabarī's Annals: The Search for the Istanbul Manuscripts." In *Al-Ṭabarī: A Medieval Muslim Historian and His Work*, edited by Hugh Kennedy, 319–336. Princeton, NJ 2008.

al-Zayʿalī. *Takhrīj al-aḥādīth wa-al-āthār al-wāqiʿa fī tafsīr al-Kashshāf lil-Zamkhsharī*. al-Riyāḍ, 1414.

The Noble Qur'an Commentary Books

[25] ***Tafsīr Ibn ʿAbbās**, Al-Wāḍiḥ fī tafsīr al-Qurʾān al-karīm*, AUTHOR: Ibn ʿAbbās (d. ca. 68/687), EDITION: Edited by Aḥmad Farīd, 2 vols. Beirut: Dār al-Kutub al-ʿIlmiyya 2003, STUDY: Motzki, "Dating the so-called Tafsīr Ibn ʿAbbās", 147–163.

[26] ***al-Durr al-manthūr** fī al-tafsīr bi-al-maʾthūr*, AUTHOR: Jalāl al-Dīn al-Suyūṭī (d. 911/1505), EDITION: Edited by ʿAbd Allāh al-Turkī, 17 vols. Cairo: Markaz Hajar lil-Buḥūth wa-al-Dirāsāt

al-ʿArabiyya wa-al-Islāmiyya 2003, STUDY: Ally, *Culmination.*

[27] ***al-Bayḍāwī***, AUTHOR: al-Bayḍāwī (d. 719/1319), EDITION: *Tafsīr al-Qāḍī al-Bayḍāwī al-musmmā Anwār al-tanzīl wa-asrār al-taʾwīl (wa-maʿahu Ḥāshiyat al-ʿallāma al-Suyūṭī)*, edited by Māhir Ḥabbūsh, 10 vols. Istanbul: Maktabat al-Irshād 2022.

[28] ***Bayḍāwī***, see #27.

[29] ***Bayḍāwī***, see #27.

[30] *min **al-Bayḍāwī***, see #27.

[31] *min **al-Bayḍāwī***, see #27.

[32] *Tafsīr al-**Jalālayn***, AUTHORS: Jalāl al-Dīn al-Maḥallī (d. 864/1460) and Jalāl al-Dīn al-Suyūṭī (d. 911/1505), EDITION: *al-Mufaṣṣal fī tafsīr al-Qurʾān al-karīm al-mashhūr bi-Tafsīr al-Jalālayn*, edited by Fakhr al-Dīn Qabāwa. Beirut: Maktabat Lubnān 2008.

[33] *Tafsīr al-**Jalālayn***, see #32.

[34] ***Abū al-Suʿūd,*** *Irshād al-ʿaql al-salīm ilā mazāyā al-kitāb al-karīm*, AUTHOR: Abū al-Suʿūd Afandī (d. 982/1574), EDITION: Edited by Muḥammad Būyāliq et al., 9 vols. Istanbul: ISAM 2021.

[35] ***Abū al-Suʿūd***, see #34.

[36] ***Abū al-Suʿūd,*** *nāqiṣ min al-awwal ilā ākhir, Sūrat Hūd (Sura 11)*, see #34.

[37] ***Abū al-Suʿūd,*** *nāqiṣ min Sūrat Yūsuf (Sura 12) ila al-ākhir*, see #34.

[38] ***al-Khāzin,*** *Lubāb al-taʾwīl fī maʿānī al-tanzīl*, AUTHOR: ʿAlāʾ al-Dīn, ʿAlī b. Muḥammad al-Khāzin (d. 725/1324), EDITION: Edited by ʿAbd al-Salām Shāhīn, 4 vols. Beirut: Dār al-Kutub al-ʿIlmiyya 1995.

[39] ***Tafsīr al-Ṭabarī,*** *Jāmiʿ al-bayān ʿan taʾwīl āyi al-Qurʾān*, AUTHOR: Ibn Jarīr al-Ṭabarī (d. 310/923), EDITION: Edited by ʿAbd Allāh al-Turkī, 26 vols. Cairo: Markaz Hajar lil-Buḥūth wa-al-Dirāsāt al-ʿArabiyya wa-al-Islāmiyya 2001. MANUSCRIPT: Riyadh, King Faisal Center for Research and Islamic Studies, MS 100 (Q. 6:74 to Q. 10:56); Ms. 101, starts Q. 6:75 ends Q. 27:93. Copied on Wed. end of month Shawwāl, 1147; 552 fols.

[40] ***Majmaʿ al-bayān*** *fī tafsīr al-Qurʾān*, AUTHOR: al-Ṭabrisī, al-Faḍl b. al-Ḥasan (d. 548/1153), EDITION: Edited by Hāshim al-Maḥallātī, 10 vols. Beirut: Dār al-Maʿrifa 1986, STUDY: Fudge, *Qurʾānic Hermeneutics.*

[41] *al-awwal wa-al-Thānī min* ***Majmaʿ al-bayān***, see #40

[42] al-*Khāmis min* ***Majmaʿ al-bayān*** see #40

[43] *al-Niṣf al-awwal min* ***al-Baghawī***, Maʿālim al-tanzīl of al-Baghawī, AUTHOR: al-Baghawī, al-Ḥusayn b. Masʿūd (d. 516/1122), EDITION: Tafsīr al-Baghawī, Maʿālim al-tanzīl, edited by Muḥammad al-Nimr and ʿUthmān Ḍamīriyya, 8 vols. al-Riyāḍ: Dār Ṭība 1989.

[44] *min* ***al-Baghawī,*** *juzʾān al-awwal Tafsīr Sūrat al-Baqara (Sura 2), wa-al-Thani Āl ʿUmrān (Sura 3) ilā ākhir al-Anʿām (Sura 6)*. See #43. MANUSCRIPT: Dublin, Chester Beatty Library, Ar. 3268.

[45] *al-Niṣf al-awwal min* ***al-Kashshāf*** *ʿan ḥaqāʾiq al-tanzīl*, AUTHOR: al-Zamakhsharī, Jār Allāh (d. 538/1144), EDITION: Māhir Adīb Ḥabbūsh, 10 vols. Istanbul: Dār al-Irshād 2021. MANUSCRIPT: Jerusalem (Abu Dis), The Center for Heritage Revival and Islamic Research, 301/2 (Afaneh et al., *Fihris makhṭūṭāt Filasṭīn al-muṣawwara*, V, 72 (formerly Jaffa: MS 52 (ʿAṭāʾ Allāh, *Fihris Yāfā* 1984)).

[46] *al-Niṣf al-thānī min* ***al-Kashshāf***, see #45.

[47] *al-Niṣf al-thānī min* ***al-Kashshāf***, see #45.

[48] ***Tafsīr*** *al-Niṣf al-awwal [of al-Kashshāf?]*, see #45.

[49] ***Tafsīr Sūrat Yāsīn*** (Sura 36), and with it *Sharḥ al-istighfār*. There are two titles in this entry, *Tafsīr Surat Yāsīn*, a title that is attested in the catalogues of libraries. It is, however, not clear which one is meant here. For examples of such works, see *al-Fihris al-Shāmil*, II, 1131. Many individual suras became the subject of commentary—that is, instead of writing a whole commentary on the Qurʾan, some scholars chose a particular sura upon which to comment. Such attention was given to salvific potent suras, Sura 36 happens to be one of the most beloved in the Islamic tradition. The other title given in this entry is *Sharḥ al-Istighfār*, probably an epistle by Ibn Taymiyya (d. 728/1328), for this work see: *Jāmiʿ al-masāʾil*, EDITION: Muḥammad Shams, Makka 2001, I, 157–162.

[50] ***Tafsīr 'inna awwala baytin'***. Commentary on the verse that starts with the phrase 'The First house' (Q. 3:96) ***wa-yalih Risala***. This is clearly an epistle on a Qur'anic verse, such works were common. For examples of such epistles see *al-Fihris al-Shāmil*, II, 1138–1141.

[51] ***Tafsīr al-Bayḍāwī***, *Anwār al-Tanzīl*, see #27.

[52] ***Tafsīr Mā' al-ḥayāt***. I was not able to identify this commentary. The similarity with the title of Ibn Ẓafar al-Makkī's (d. 565/1170) Qur'an commentary, *Yanbūʿ al-ḥayāt*, raises the possibility that this is a copy of that work. For manuscripts of Ibn Zafar's work, see *al-Fihris al-shāmil*, I, 205. Also see al-Dāwūdī, *Ṭabaqāt al-mufassirīn*, EDITION: 'Alī 'Umar. Cairo: Maktabat Wahba 1994, II, 167–168.

[53] ***Tafsīr Gharīb al-Qur'ān***. There are at least 17 works by different authors with such a title. There is no indication to which of them this one corresponds. For manuscripts of works with the same title, see *al-Fihris al-shāmil*, II, 1134.

[54] *Tafsīr al-Niṣf al-ākhir li-**Ibn al-Jawzī***; *Zād al-masīr fī 'ilm al-tafsīr*, AUTHOR: Ibn al-Jawzī, Abū al-Faraj, 'Abd al-Raḥmān b. 'Alī (d. 597/1200), EDITION: 15 vols. Doḥah: Wizārat al-Awqāf wa-al-Shu'ūn al-Islāmiyya 2021.

[55] ***Tafsīr al-Fātiḥa*** (Q.1) ***wa-al-Baqara*** (Q.2), ***wa-niṣf Āl 'Imrān*** (Q. 3). This is one of several anonymous works in this section; for anonymous works, see #50, #52, #53, #65, #67–69, #73, #75, #77–80 and #571.

[56] ***Ghurar al-fawā'id*** wa-durar al-qalā'id, AUTHOR: al-Sharīf al-Murtaḍā (d. 436/1044), (also known as *Amālī al-Murtaḍā*), EDITION: Muḥammad Abū al-Faḍl Ibrāhīm, 2 vols. Cairo: 'Īsā al-Bābī al-Ḥalabī 1954.

[57] ***Tafsīr Fārisī***. This is the only non-Arabic title in this section. This is probably the manuscript Istanbul, Süleymaniye Library, Kemankes 21.

[58] min ***al-Sirāj al-munīr*** *fī al-i'āna 'alā ma'rifat ba'ḍ ma'ānī kalām rabbinā al-ḥakīm al-khabīr*, AUTHOR: al-Khaṭīb al-Shirbīnī (d. 977/1570), EDITION: Edited by Muḥammad al-Asyūṭī, 4 vols. Cairo: al-Maṭba'a al-Khayriyya 1311/1894.

[59] *al-Tibyān fī **i'rāb al-Qur'ān lil-'Ukbarī***, AUTHOR: **al-'Ukbarī**, Abū al-Baqā' (d. 616/1219), EDITION: Edited by Muḥammad al-Bajāwī. Cairo: Maktabat 'Īsā al-Bābī al-Ḥalabī 1976.

[60] ***Khawāṣṣ al-Qur'ān***, *al-Dhahab al-ibrīz fī asrār **khawāṣṣ** kitāb Allāh al-'azīz*. AUTHOR: Pseudo-Ghazālī, EDITION: 'Abd al-Ḥamīd Ḥamdān. Cairo: Maktabat al-Kullīyāt al-Azhariyya, n.d.

[61] ***I'rāb al-Qur'ān li-Ibn al-Naḥḥās***, AUTHOR: al-Naḥḥās (or Ibn al-Naḥḥās) Abū Ja'far (d. 338/949), EDITION: Zuhayr Zāhid, 5 vols. Baghdad: Maktabat al-Nahḍa al-'Arabiyya 1985.

[62] ***Ḥāshiyat Shaykhī Zādah 'alā al-Bayḍāwī***, AUTHOR: Shaykh Zadah, Muḥyī al-Dīn (d. 951/1544), EDITION: 4 vols. Istanbul: al-Maṭba'a al-Sulṭāniyya 1283/1866.

[63] ***Ḥāshiyat 'Iṣām 'alā al-Bayḍāwī***, AUTHOR: 'Iṣām al-Dīn al-Isfarāyīnī (d. 945/1538); for manuscripts of this work see *al-Fihris al-shāmil*, I, 569–576.

[64] ***Ḥāshiyat Bahā' al-Dīn al-'Āmilī 'alā al-Bayḍāwī***, AUTHOR: Bahā' al-Dīn al-'Āmilī (d. 1031/1622); for manuscripts of this work see *al-Fihris al-shāmil*, II, 672–675.

[65] ***Ḥāshiya 'alā al-Kashshāf***. This is the usual title for glosses on *al-Kashshāf*, and there are no clues as to who the author is.

[66] ***Ḥāshiya 'alā khuṭbat al-Kashshāf lil-Zamakhsharī***. I was unable to identify this work. There is an anonymous work with a title that approaches it, *Ḥāshiyah 'alā awā'il al-Kashshāf*, though I doubt it is the same work. See *al-Fihris al-shāmil*, II, 997 (no. 67). The other possibility is a work by al-Fayrūzābādī (d. 817/1414), *Nughbat al-rushāf min khuṭbat al-Kashshāf*, for manuscripts of this work see *al-Fihris al-shāmil*, I, 448–449.

[67] ***Ḥāshiya 'alā tafsīr sūrat al-a'rāf*** (Sura 7). This title presents an interesting window on the craft of glossing in *tafsīr*. This is clearly a gloss on a commentary, and most probably, if not certainly, it is on *Anwār al-tanzīl* of al-Bayḍāwī. It was either independently written on this Sura only (Sura 7), or it is most probably from a larger complete gloss on the whole commentary, selected and copied into a booklet. For a work

with a similar title see the work of al-Lakhnawī, Ghulām Naqshband b. ʿAṭāʾ Allāh (d. 1126/1714), titled: *Ḥāshiya ʿalā tafsīr sūrat al-aʿrāf*, see *al-Fihris al-shāmil*, II, 747.

[68] ***Ḥāshiyat taqdīm al-basmala ʿalā al-ḥamdala.*** There is no indication who the author is; for works with similar titles see *al-Fihris al-shāmil*, II, 1204–1205 (under *Sharḥ al-basmalah*).

[69] ***Ḥāshiya ʿalā tafsīr sūrat al-nabaʾ***, *Ḥāshiya ʿalā al-juzʾ al-thalāthīn* (Sura 78), AUTHOR: al-Anṭākī, Muṣṭafā b. Ḥasan (d. 1100/1689). For other copies, see *al-Fihris al-shāmil*, II, 734. MANUSCRIPT: This copy has survived and is available in the Library of the Ministry of Awqāf (Maktabat Wizārat al-Awqāf, Egypt) ms 3018.

[70] *al-juzʾ al-awwal min* ***Ḥāshiyat al-ʿImād ʿalā al-Kashshāf***, *Tuḥfat al-ashrāf fī kashf ghawāmiḍ al-Kashshāf*, AUTHOR: al-Fāḍil al-Yamanī, ʿImād al-Dīn (d. after 750/1349). For manuscript copies of this work, see *al-Fihris al-shāmil*, I, 408.

[71] ***Ḥāshiya ʿalā juzʾ thālith min talkhīṣ al-Kashshāf***, unidentified.

[72] *juzʾ ʿāshir min* ***tafsīr Majmaʿ al-bayān***, see #40.

[73] ***Ḥāshiya ʿalā tafsīr sūrat al-munāfiqūn*** (Sura 63), unidentified.

[74] ***Khawāṣṣ al-Qurʾan***, see #60.

[75] ***Mukhtaṣar fī iʿrāb baʿḍ suwar al-Qurʾān al-ʿaẓīm.*** There is a work with the same title in the National Library of Syria, Damascus, number 7430.

[76] ***al-Durr al-naẓīm fī faḍl al-Qurʾān al-ʿaẓīm.*** There are two works with such a title, both could be candidates. This could not be the work of al-Suyūṭī by the same name, since this is an obscure work of his. 1) Ibn al-Khashshāb, *al-Durr al-naẓīm fī faḍāʾil khawāṣṣ al-Qurʾan al-ʿaẓīm*; for manuscripts of this work see *al-Fihris al-shāmil*, I, 251–252 (38 manuscripts listed). 2) al-Yāfiʿī, ʿAfīf al-Dīn (d. 768/1367), Title: *al-Durr al-naẓīm fī khawāṣṣ al-Qurʾān al-ʿaẓīm*, EDITION: *al-Durr al-naẓīm fī khawāṣṣ al-Qurʾān al-ʿaẓīm*, edited by Muḥsin ʿAqīl. Beirut: Dār al-Rasūl al-Akram 1999; for manuscripts of this work see *al-Fihris al-shāmil*, I, 419–420 (30 manuscripts listed)

[77] *Majmūʿa awwaluhā* ***Faḍāʾil al-Qurʾān.*** The title of this epistle is a very common title. For manuscripts with the same title, see *al-Fihris al-shāmil*, II, 1215–1216.

[78] ***Ḥamāʾil.*** These are amulets and incantations that use verses and suras from the Qurʾan. For a discussion, see Guy Burak's articles in the bibliography. It is interesting that the cataloguer did not state that these were bound.

[79] ***Dhahāb layl al-shukūk fī maʿnā qawlihi taʿālā ʿinna al-mulūkʾ***, see #50. I was unable to identify this work. This is an epistle on verse Q. 27:34

[80] ***Sharḥ Āyat al-Isrāʾ.*** This epistle is a commentary of the beginning of Sura 17:1 which is unusual; there are usually works that tell the story of Ascension (*Isrāʾ*). The title is, thus, unusual and there are no similar works in any catalogue. There are works with titles *Tafsīr Surat al-Isrāʾ*—this might be what we have here. For works with such titles, see *al-Fihris al-shāmil*, II, 1123.

Works of tafsīr *from the provenanced sections of the inventory*

Works taken from the library of al-Sayyid Yaḥyā Efendī b. al-Sayyid Muḥammad al-Ṭībī of Jaffa in 1218/1803

[512] ***Kitāb sabab nuzūl al-Qurʾān***, see #525. This work is most probably the work by AUTHOR: al-Wāḥidī (d. 468/1076), *Asbāb nuzūl al-Qurʾān*, EDITION: Al-Sayyid Aḥmad Ṣaqr. Cairo: Dār al-Kitāb al-Jadīd 1969.

[518] ***Kitāb Rafʿ al-kisāʾ***, AUTHOR: ʿAbd al-Ghanī al-Nābulusī (d. 1143/1731). TITLE: *Rafʿ al-kisāʾ ʿan ʿibārat al-Bayḍāwī fī sūrat al-Nisāʾ*. See *al-Fihris al-shāmil*, II, 756.

[521] ***Kitāb Maʿālim al-tanzīl fī tafsīr al-Qurʾān***, see #43.

[523] ***Kitāb Tafsīr al-Bayḍāwī***, see #27.

[525] *Fī Nuzūl al-Qurʾān*, AUTHOR: Jalāl al-Dīn al-Suyūṭī (d. 911/1505), TITLE: *Lubāb al-nuqūl fī asbāb al-nuzūl.* EDITION: Dimashq: Maṭbaʿat al-Mallāḥ 1961.

[533] ***Kitāb tafsīr al-Qurān al-Jalīlī.*** Most probably *Tafsīr al-Jalālayn*. See #32.

[537] ***Kitāb Nuzhat al-qulūb.*** AUTHOR: al-Sijistānī (d. 330/941). TITLE: *Nuzhat al-qulūb wa-farḥat al-makrūb fī tafsīr kalām ʿallām al-ghuyūb*. See *al-Fihris al-shāmil*, I, 42–48. EDITION: *Nuzhat al-qulūb fī tafsīr al-Qurʾān al-ʿazīz*, edited by Yūsuf al-Marʿashlī. Beirut: Dār al-Maʿrifa 1990.

[539] ***Tafsīr al-Jalīlī.*** Most probably *Tafsīr al-Jalālayn*. See #32, #537.

[571] ***Kitāb Tafsīr al-Qurʾān.*** Anonymous work, starts from Sura 34 onwards.

[594] ***Tafsīr al-Jalālayn***, see #32. Second volume only.

[595] ***Kitāb fī aḥwāl al-Qurʾān.*** Anonymous work. Could be related to an obscure work by al-Ghazālī. See *al-Fihris al-shāmil*, I, 127.

Works taken from the libraries of al-Shaykh ʿAlī al-Rashīdī and al-Shaykh Muḥammad Wakīlkharaj in 1216/1801

[1640] **Anʿām Sharīf.** This is a stand-alone copy of Sura 6 of the Qur'an. This was a new Ottoman tradition. For details about this kind of booklet, see Rettig, "The Rise of the Enʿam", 185–212.

[1668] ***Qurʾan*** codex.

[1683] ***Kitāb al-Tibyān fī iʿrāb al-Qurʾān***, see #59.

[1702] ***Risālat manāfiʿ al-Qurʾān.*** Anonymous work. For works with this title, see *al-Fihris al-shāmil*, II, 1239–1240. For an example of such a work, see Abū Bakr b. Ḥasan al-Wattād. *Manāfiʿ al-Qurʾān*, edited by ʿAbd al Ghanī al-Fāsī. Beirut: Dār al-Kutub al-ʿIlmiyya 2004.

CHAPTER 14

The Recitation Section (*qirāʾāt*)

Shady H. Nasser

Most of the collection of the works on recitation in the Jazzār inventory reflects the standardised manuals of *Qirāʾāt* used throughout the Muslim world for the past eight hundred years. Unsurprisingly, the collection is dominated by three works and their derivatives: commentaries, excerpts and summaries. These works are al-Shāṭibī's (d. 589/1194) *Ḥirz al-amānī* (*al-Shāṭibiyya*), Ibn al-Jazarī's (d. 833/1429) *al-Nashr/al-Durra* and the latter's short manual on *tajwīd*, *al-Muqaddima al-Jazariyya*. Any student of Islamic religious sciences who embarks upon memorising the Qurʾān according to one system of recitation (*Qirāʾa*) would do so based on *al-Shāṭibiyya* accompanied by Ibn al-Jazarī's *tajwīd* manual. Students of Qurʾānic recitation who memorise the Qurʾān in the seven canonical readings would do so almost exclusively based on *al-Shāṭibiyya*. Those who go further and specialise in the ten readings would do so almost exclusively based on Ibn al-Jazarī's *al-Durra*/*Ṭayyibat al-Nashr* (a versified form of *al-Nashr*). Other works in this collection are specialised short manuals that focus on specific technical aspects of Qurʾānic recitation (most of which are already part of the *al-Shāṭibiyya* or *al-Nashr*), such as when and how to pause during recitation, the different ways of saying the phrase '*Allāhu akbar*' in between the *sūras*, the correct articulation of Arabic letters and Qurʾānic orthography. Some advanced works on *Qirāʾāt* made their way into the collection. They target specialists and advanced students in the field. A few unusual works of *Qirāʾāt* that did not enjoy popularity or circulation are also part of this collection. These titles will be discussed in more detail below, with some speculation towards the end concerning their inclusion in the library.

1 *Qirāʾāt* and *Tajwīd*

The discipline of Qurʾānic recitation comprises two main categories. The smaller one is *tajwīd*, mainly concerned with correctly reciting the Qurʾān. This includes the proper way of articulating the letters (*makhārij al-ḥurūf*) as well as learning when and how to apply different recitational techniques, such as lengthening of vowels (*madd*), assimilation (*idghām*) and nasality (*ghunna*). The larger category is that of *Qirāʾāt* (variant readings), mainly concerned with the different ways, both textual and phonetic, the Qurʾān was read, understood and recited. Individual textual variants of the Qurʾān are referred to as *farsh*. Certain words are read differently due to different assignments of dots and diacritics on the consonantal outline (*rasm*), for example, فىٮٮوا is read as فتثبتوا and فتبينوا, or يغل is read as يَغُلّ and يُغَلّ.[1] Phonetic or recitational variants are referred to as *uṣūl* (principles). They are recitational techniques followed systematically throughout the Qurʾān. These techniques vary from one eponymous reader to another. Ibn Kathīr, the Meccan, for instance, would vowel the *mīm* of the third person masculine plural with a long *ḍamma* or *wāw*, for example, *ʿalayhimū*. Other readers would perform an a>e vowel shift (*imāla*), for example, *al-nās* → *al-nēs*.[2] While *tajwīd* could be considered a subcategory of the *uṣūl*, it specialises in the articulation of letters and identifying their characteristics.[3]

1 Abū Shāma, *Ibrāz al-maʿānī*, 401, 420.
2 Ibid., 73–74, 203, 237.
3 The phonology of letters and the correct way of articulating them are occasionally added as a supplement or conclusion to the *Qirāʾāt* manual, including works like *al-Shāṭibiyya*; ibid., 743.

2 *Ḥirz al-amānī* or *al-Shāṭibiyya* and Its Derivatives

Variant readings of the Qur'ān (*Qirāʾāt*) underwent a long journey until a canonised body was officially institutionalised. Many recitational systems were used throughout the Muslim world until the third/ninth century, although some were more popular and widespread than others. In the first quarter of the fourth/tenth century, Ibn Mujāhid (d. 324/936) selected seven readings as the representative, authoritative systems in Medina, Mecca, Damascus, Baṣra and Kūfa. Ibn Mujāhid's work became the prototype for later works on *Qirāʾāt*.[4] Due to its length and detailed nature that deter beginners from studying it, al-Dānī (d. 444/1052–1053) wrote a digest manual for students, titled *al-Taysīr*, in which he simplified and summarised the variants for each of the seven eponymous readers: Nāfiʿ, Ibn Kathīr, Ibn ʿĀmir, Abū ʿAmr b. al-ʿAlāʾ, ʿĀṣim, Ḥamza and al-Kisāʾī. The popularity of *al-Taysīr* drove al-Shāṭibī (d. 589/1194) to render it in verse as a didactic poem titled *Ḥirz al-amānī*, also known as *al-Shāṭibiyya*.[5] The latter marked a new era in the discipline of *Qirāʾāt* literature throughout the Muslim world. It became the leading text which has been studied and memorised by all students and scholars of the Qur'ān until today.[6] It is said that by the ninth/fifteenth century, people would spend a fortune to own a good copy of *al-Shāṭibiyya* and that any student of knowledge would have owned at least one copy of it.[7]

Unsurprisingly, the inventory of the Jazzār library has five copies of *al-Shāṭibiyya* (#92–96) alongside five commentaries. *Al-Shāṭibiyya*'s fame and wide circulation made it subject to many commentaries,[8] thus, it is difficult to determine the identity of these five works in the inventory (#97–101). The works by al-Sakhāwī (d. 643/1245),[9] Abū Shāma al-Maqdisī (d. 665/1267) and Ibn al-Qāṣiḥ (d. 801/1399)[10] are among the commentaries most well-known and used. That being said, there is one copy of *Inshād al-sharīd fī ḍawāll al-qaṣīd* (#131) by Ibn Ghāzī al-Miknāsī of Fez (d. 919/1513), a prolific Maghribī scholar in different disciplines including *Qirāʾāt*, which is a commentary on *al-Shāṭibiyya*. *Inshād al-sharīd* enjoyed limited circulation in the *maghrib* among specialised scholars who were teaching *al-Shāṭibiyya*.[11]

Before the 'viral' spread of *al-Shāṭibiyya*, *al-ʿUnwān fī al-Qirāʾāt al-sabʿ* by Abū Ṭāhir al-Andalusī (d. 455/1063) enjoyed some popularity and scholarly attention. It is said that Egyptians used to memorise *al-ʿUnwān* before the emergence of *al-Shāṭibiyya*.[12] One copy of *al-ʿUnwān* (#116) is found in the inventory[13] as well as a manual written by Ibn al-Jazarī titled *Tuḥfat al-Ikhwān* (#104) in which he explained the differences between *al-Shāṭibiyya* and *al-ʿUnwān*.[14] Both works target a more specialised audience of *Qirāʾāt*, similar to *Ḥiṣn al-qāriʾ* (#138) by Hāshim al-Maghribī (d. after 1179/1765), which tracks the different variants documented in *al-Shāṭibiyya* through other sources and chains of transmissions (*wujūh* or *taḥrīrāt*).[15]

4 Nasser, *The Second Canonization of the Qurʾān*, 5–9; Melchert, "Ibn Mujāhid", 22.
5 Nasser, "Canonizations", 100–105.
6 Nöldeke, *Geschichte des Qorâns*, III, 220–227; Neuwirth, "al-Shāṭibī".
7 Ibn al-Jazarī, *Ghāyat al-nihāya fī ṭabaqāt al-qurrāʾ*, II, 21–22.
8 According to bibliographic sources, at least one hundred and sixty classical commentaries were written on *al-Shāṭibiyya*; Ḥamītū, *Zaʿīm al-madrasa al-athariyya*, 145–212.
9 al-Sakhāwī, *Fatḥ al-waṣīd fī sharḥ al-qaṣīd*.
10 Ibn al-Qāṣiḥ, *Sirāj al-qāriʾ*.
11 al-Wāfī, *al-Dirāsāt al-Qurʾāniyya bi-al-Maghrib*, 38. The work was edited as part of a master's thesis at the Faculty of Arts and Sciences in Rabat; ibid., 38, footnote #59. An online record shows an MA thesis at Dār al-Ḥadīth al-Ḥasaniyya in Rabat by al-Ḥasan al-ʿAlamī: http://thesis.mandumah.com/Record/130858.
12 al-Qasṭallānī, *Laṭāʾif al-ishārāt li-funūn al-Qirāʾāt*, I, 89.
13 Abū Ṭāhir al-Andalusī, *al-ʿUnwān fī al-qirāʾāt al-sabʿ*.
14 Ibn al-Jazarī, *Tuḥfat al-ikhwān*.
15 al-Maghribī, *Ḥiṣn al-qāriʾ fī ikhtilāf al-maqāriʾ*. A similar work in the inventory is titled *maʾākhidh (or maʾkhadh) al-khilāf min al-Shāṭibiyya* (#103). It is difficult to iden-

The inclusion of a treatise dedicated to the reading of Ḥafṣ *ʿan* ʿĀṣim[16] (#102) suggests that the audience of the library were practitioners of the reading of Ḥafṣ, which became the official system of the recitation of the Qurʾān during and after the Ottoman period.[17]

3 *Al-Nashr* and Its Derivatives

The popularity of *al-Shāṭibiyya* almost made it the exclusive reference for the variant readings of the Qurʾān, where people almost ignored other works of *Qirāʾāt*. The perception of what was Qurʾānic and what was not became closely associated with the content of *al-Shāṭibiyya*. While scholars applauded the greatness of the work and its positive influence on the discipline, they also lamented the fact that people were ignoring other authentic readings of the Qurʾān and dismissing them as non-canonical simply because they were not mentioned in *al-Shāṭibiyya*.[18] These efforts culminated in Ibn al-Jazarī's (d. 833/1429) publication of *al-Durra al-muḍiyya* that systematised three additional systems of recitation: Abū Jaʿfar from Medina, Yaʿqūb from Baṣra, and Khalaf from Baghdād/Kūfa. Building on the popularity of *al-Shāṭibiyya*, Ibn al-Jazarī composed his didactic poem in the same metrical style and made it as a supplement. One copy of *al-Durra* (#122) is noted in the inventory.[19] Ibn al-Jazarī then wrote his monumental work, *al-Nashr fī al-qirāʾāt al-ʿashr*, in which he collected the systems of the recitations of the ten readers from different sources and chains of transmissions. Similar to *al-Shāṭibiyya*, *al-Nashr* and its versified version, *Ṭayyibat al-Nashr*, enjoyed tremendous popularity and scholarly attention. One copy of *al-Nashr* (#89) and its abridged version, *Taqrīb al-Nashr* (#88), are part of the inventory.[20] Since this section of the inventory is related to *Qirāʾāt*, the *tafsīr* work attributed to Ibn al-Jawzī is either misplaced or misspelled: Ibn al-Jazarī's *al-Nashr* (النشر لابن الجزري) could have been easily misread as Ibn al-Jawzī's *al-Taysīr* (التيسير لابن الجوزي) (#90).[21] The inventory also contains a copy of the commentary on *Ṭayyibat al-Nashr* (#119) by the chief Qurʾān reciter in Ottoman core lands during his time, al-Manṣūrī (d. 1134/1722).[22]

4 *Al-Jazariyya* and Its Derivatives

Al-Muqaddima al-Jazariyya is another didactic poem on the rules of *tajwīd* and the proper articulation of letters. It became the central manual studied and memorised by students and scholars of the Qurʾān. Some scholars would not even grant their students a certificate (*ijāza*) in Qurʾānic recitation unless they had memorised *al-Jazariyya*

tify the work precisely, but it follows the same genre of tracking differences in the transmission of variants between *al-Shāṭibiyya* and other manuals of *Qirāʾāt*.

16 It is not easy to determine the exact identity of the work. There are several treatises written on the same topic. They often extract the recitation system of an eponymous reader from the more comprehensive works of *Qirāʾāt*, such as *al-Shāṭibiyya* or *al-Nashr*. Another unclear title in the inventory is *al-Shamʿa* (#114). It could be *al-Shamʿa al-muntakhaba min al-sabʿa*, a work dedicated to the reading of ʿĀṣim; *Fihris kutub al-qirāʾāt al-qurʾāniyya fī al-Jāmiʿa al-Islāmiyya bi-al-Madīna*, 201. It could also be the work by al-Ṭablāwī, *al-Shamʿa al-muḍiyya bi-nashr qirāʾāt al-sabʿa al-marḍiyya*.

17 Nasser, "Canonizations," 106–107; Blachère, *Introduction au Coran*, 134–135. The Ottomans naturally adopted a Kufan reading instead of the Baṣran Reading of Abū ʿAmr b. al-ʿAlāʾ, that dominated the Eastern Islamic lands for centuries. The Medinan Reading (both Warsh and Qālūn) has been the dominant system of recitation in the Maghrib for over a millennium. The Reading of Abū ʿAmr b. al-ʿAlāʾ is still used today in some African countries, such as Somalia and Sudan.

18 Nasser, "Canonizations," 16–20; Ibn al-Jazarī, *Munjid al-muqriʾīn*, 102–104.

19 *Matn fī takmilat al-ʿashara* accompanied by Ibn al-Jazarī's *tajwīd* manual; al-Ḍabbāʿ/Ibn al-Jazarī, *al-Bahja al-marḍiyya*.

20 Ibn al-Jazarī, *al-Nashr fī al-qirāʾāt al-ʿashr*; *Taqrīb al-Nashr fī al-qirāʾāt al-ʿashr*.

21 Cf. Walid Saleh's note on the work in Chapter 13, 246.

22 al-Manṣūrī, *Irshād al-ṭalaba ilā shawāhid al-Ṭayyiba*.

by heart.[23] The library inventory lists five copies of this poem (two copies of #105, #106, #122 and #140), as well as two commentaries on it: one by Ibn al-Jazarī's student Burhān al-Dīn al-Anṣārī (d. 893/1488) (#108)[24] and another by a Damascene *Qirā'āt* scholar, al-Masʿadī (d. 1017/1608) (#109).[25] Other works on *tajwīd* in the inventory include *Bughyat al-mustafīd* (#117), a short manual for beginners by the Damascene Ḥanbalī jurist Ibn Balbān (d. 1083/1672),[26] and *al-Qawāʿid al-muqarrara wa-al-fawā'id al-muḥarrara* (#123) by the Egyptian scholar Muḥammad b. Qāsim al-Baqarī (d. 1111/1699). Al-Baqarī was the chief Qur'ān reciter in al-Azhar and a prolific figure in several disciplines. *Al-Qawāʿid al-Baqariyya* is a student manual targeting students and beginners in the discipline of *Qirā'āt*. It simplifies and summarises the recitation principles for each of the seven eponymous readers. The book has been used in teaching until today.[27]

5 Specialised Works on *Qirā'āt*

After Ibn al-Jazarī, most works on *Qirā'āt* revolved around *al-Nashr* and its contents. Tracking the variants of the ten readings in different sources and transmissions (*taḥrīr al-qirā'āt*) became the subject of several important books written in the discipline.

- *ʿUmdat al-ʿIrfān fī taḥrīr awjuh al-Qur'ān* (#121) and its larger version *Badā'iʿ al-burhān* (#85): A technical work for specialists written by Muṣṭafā al-Izmīrī (d. 1155/1742), probably the most celebrated *Qirā'āt* scholar after Ibn al-Jazarī. His works on tracking and documenting different transmissions of the ten canonical readings from multiple sources (*taḥrīrāt*) have been authoritative among *Qirā'āt* scholars until today.[28] *ʿUmdat al-ʿIrfān* is a shorter version of his more comprehensive work *Badā'iʿ al-burhān*, in which he provided valuable insights and corrections to earlier sources and transmissions.[29]
- *Al-Durar al-Lawāmiʿ fī aṣl maqra' al-Imām Nāfiʿ* (#135) is a didactic poem by Ibn Barrī al-Tāzī (d. 730/1330), mostly known for this work in which he condensed the fundamentals of Nāfiʿ's reading through his two transmitters Warsh and Qālūn. Since Nāfiʿ's reading was the primary system of recitation used in the *maghrib*, the poem received a lot of scholarly attention, including several commentaries. The poem concludes with another didactic poem on *tajwīd* composed as an appendix. The work is listed in the inventory as an independent title *Risāla fī naẓm makhārij al-ḥurūf* (#139). It is probably the concluding section of *al-Durar al-Lawāmiʿ* often studied in tandem but also independent of one another.[30]
- *Sharḥ urjūzat mushkilāt al-Qur'ān* (#137) is a didactic poem by the Damascene Shāfiʿī judge Zayn al-Dīn al-Ṭībī (d. after 870/1466) written in response to another didactic poem by Ibn al-Jazarī titled *Arbaʿūn mas'ala min al-masā'il al-mushkila fī al-Qirā'āt*. Ibn al-Jazarī selected forty complex problems in the *Qirā'āt* litera-

23 al-Faḍālī, *al-Jawāhir al-muḍiyya ʿalā al-muqaddima al-Jazariyya*, 12.

24 al-Anṣārī, *Tuḥfat al-murīd li-muqaddimat al-tajwīd*.

25 al-Masʿadī, *al-Fawā'id al-Masʿadiyya fī ḥall al-Jazariyya*. One Treatise is simply titled "*tajwīd*" (#133). It is difficult to identify the work, which could be a commentary or a simplified guide based on *al-Jazariyya*.

26 Ibn Balbān al-Ḥanbalī, *Bughyat al-mustafīd fī ʿilm al-tajwīd*, 9–16.

27 al-Baqarī, *al-Qawāʿid al-muqarrara*, 98.

28 al-Barmāwī, *Imtāʿ al-fuḍalā'*, II, 390–391.

29 al-Izmīrī, *Itḥāf al-barara*, 20–21. The *ʿUmda* and the *Badā'iʿ* are already edited and published, although very poorly. The *ʿUmada* was edited by Muḥammad Muḥammad Jābir and published in Egypt, Maṭbaʿat al-Jundī. It was republished by Dār al-kutub al-ʿIlmiyya, Beirut, in 2008, probably as a pirated copy. The editor of *Itḥāf al-barara* mentioned in his introduction that he finished an edition of the *Badā'iʿ*. Eren Pilgir, a PhD student at Marmara University, Turkey, is currently working on a proper edition of the *Badā'i* as part of his PhD dissertation.

30 al-Mārghanī and Ibn Barrī, *al-Nujūm al-ṭawāliʿ*, 3–4, 155.

ture and put them in verse in the form of riddles—the work is also known as *al-alghāz al-Jazariyya*. Several scholars solved Ibn al-Jazarī's riddles and wrote their responses in verse form as well.[31] A similar work in the inventory is titled *al-masāʾil wa-al-ajwiba* (#112), probably a work by al-Asqāṭī (d. 1159/1746), in which he answered problematic *Qirāʾāt*-related questions asked by one of his students.[32]

- *Al-Luʾluʾ al-maknūn fī jamʿ al-awjuh* (#120): A work by Sayf al-Dīn Abū al-Futūḥ al-Faḍālī (d. 1020/1611), chief Qurʾān reciter of Egypt during his time. Al-Faḍālī is mainly known for *al-Jawāhir al-muḍiyya*, an extensive commentary on Ibn al-Jazarī's *tajwīd* manual. *Al-Luʾluʾ al-maknūn* is a relatively unfamiliar *Qirāʾāt* work that did not seem to have been widely circulated among scholars or students of the discipline.[33]
- *Qurrat al-ʿayn fī al-fatḥ wa-al-imāla bayn al-lafẓayn* (#118): A work by the renowned *Qirāʾāt* scholar, Ibn al-Qāṣiḥ (d. 801/1399), dedicated to the rules of *imāla* in the Qurʾān (a>e vowel shift). It is a less well-known work than his *Sirāj al-qāriʾ al-mubtadiʾ*, one of the authoritative commentaries on *al-Shāṭibiyya*.[34]
- *Al-Tatimma fī qirāʾat al-thalātha al-aʾimma* (#115) by Ṣadaqa b. Salāma al-Mashharāʾī (d. 825/1422), a Damascene scholar of *Qirāʾāt*. Similar to *al-Nashr*, *al-Tatimma* collected three additional readings to the seven, but it did not enjoy the same circulation and popularity as Ibn al-Jazarī's works.[35]
- *Muntahā al-Amānī wa-al-masarrāt* (#83), also known by the title *Itḥāf fuḍalāʾ al-bashar*, by the renowned *Qirāʾāt* scholar Aḥmad al-Bannā al-Dimyāṭī (d. 1117/1705). It is a detailed and technical work on the ten readings and their different transmissions (*wujūh* and *taḥrīrāt*), as well as four additional Readings by al-Ḥasan al-Baṣrī and his fellow Baṣran al-Yazīdī, the Meccan Ibn Muḥayṣin, and the Kūfan al-Aʿmash. These four additional Readings were never elevated to the seven or ten Readings' Canonical status. They have always been relegated to the non-canonical status (*shawādhdh*), despite the efforts of some scholars to recognise their legitimacy over the centuries.[36]
- *Laṭāʾif al-ishārat* by al-Qasṭallānī (d. 923/1517) (#84, #86) is an encyclopaedic compendium on *Qirāʾāt* targeting experts in the field. It gathers data from previous *Qirāʾāt* works and summarises the opinions of grammarians concerning the grammatical aspects of the different readings of the same word.[37]
- *Awjuh al-takbīr*: Four generic titles (#127, #128, #130 and #134) on the *takbīr* formula. They could be independent short treatises or excerpts from more significant works of *Qirāʾāt*.
- *Wuqūf al-Qurʾān*: Knowing when to pause during the recitation of the Qurʾān is a subcategory of the *Qirāʾāt* discipline. Pausing at specific locations may change the meaning of the verse. Thus, scholars developed several categories for *waqf*, such as when it is allowed, recommended or forbidden. Additionally, the eponymous readers developed unique techniques for pausing on certain forms, such as nouns that contain the glottal stop *hamza* or end with feminine *tāʾ*. The inventory contains one anonymous work on *wuqūf* (#87) and another by Zakariyyā al-Anṣārī (d. 926/1520) (#113).[38] One specialised treatise is dedicated to a unique technique developed by the two eponymous readers Ḥamza and Ibn ʿĀmir → Hishām (#111) when they pause

31 Including al-Biqāʿī, *al-Ajwiba al-sirriyya ʿan al-alghāz al-Jazariyya*.
32 al-Asqāṭī (d. 1159/1746), *Ajwibat al-masāʾil al-mushkilāt fī ʿilm al-qirāʾāt*.
33 Al-Faḍālī, *Jawāhir*, 57–64.
34 Ibn al-Qāṣiḥ, *Qurrat al-ʿayn*, 11–31.
35 al-Mashharāʾī, *al-Tatimma*.
36 al-Dimyāṭī himself acknowledged the non-canonicity of these additional four Readings; al-Dimyāṭī, *Itḥāf fuḍalāʾ*, I, 65.
37 al-Qasṭallānī, *Laṭāʾif al-ishārāt li-funūn al-Qirāʾāt*.
38 al-Anṣārī, *al-Maqṣad li-talkhīṣ*.

on words that contain *hamzas*.[39] The knowledge of orthography that affects the recitation of the words is related to pausing techniques, for example, if words are written with a final *tāʾ* or *hāʾ*. One such work is noted in the inventory (#110).[40] Finally, there is an index or concordance of the Qurʾān by Maḥmūd al-Wārdārī (d. 1061/1651), written in both Arabic and Ottoman Turkish, where the vocabulary of the Qurʾān is arranged alphabetically (#91).[41]

- Miscellaneous: A copy of al-Suyūṭī's *Itqān* (#81) is probably a general reference work since it contains rich information on Qurʾānic recitation, the history of the codices, orthography and even technical discussions on recitational techniques.[42]

6 Concluding remarks

The *Qirāʾāt* section of the Jazzār library inventory contains an impressive collection of *Qirāʾāt* titles that range from student manuals to advanced works written for scholars and specialists in the field. Multiple copies of *al-Shāṭibiyya*, *al-Jazariyya*, *al-Nashr* and their commentaries—the three works that have been dominating the discipline of *Qirāʾāt* until today—are indicative of their popularity and simultaneous use by multiple individuals. Furthermore, the inclusion of advanced works of *wujūh* and *taḥrīrāt*, such as those by al-Bannā and al-Izmīrī, indicate their use by advanced scholars in the field, possibly professors and higher authorities in *Qirāʾāt*. If one may speculate, some teaching activity was taking place with this collection. Indeed, the existence of three certificates (*ijāzas*) in *Qirāʾāt* (#126, #132 and #136) as well as four short manuals on performing the *takbīr* formula, often done during sessions of complete auditions of the Qurʾān, may point to students and teacher(s) of *Qirāʾāt* who frequently accessed the collection. A few relatively arcane works on *Qirāʾāt* could have been used for advanced 'research projects'. The existence of *al-ʿUnwān* by Abū Ṭāhir, for example, alongside Ibn al-Jazarī's work on tracking the differences between *al-ʿUnwān* and *al-Shāṭibiyya* highly suggests that the same individual(s) was consulting and studying both works.

The existence of one work only on Qurʾānic orthography may indicate a lack of interest in the subject matter, especially with the stabilisation of Qurʾānic orthography in the past few centuries. One might have expected a copy of al-Shāṭibī's second didactic poem on Qurʾānic orthography, *ʿaqīlat atrāb al-qaṣāʾid*, which was as famous and popular as *Ḥirz al-amānī*, to the extent that it was nicknamed as *al-Shāṭibiyya* minor.[43] There are no works dedicated to the non-canonical (*shawādhdh*) literature, except for the two works by al-Naḥḥās and al-ʿUkbarī in the *tafsīr* section (#59 and #61), which are meant as reference works on the grammar and syntax of the Qurʾān as a whole. In sum, the recitation collection of the Jazzār library reflects a period where Qurʾānic recitation in both of its subfields, *Qirāʾāt* and *tajwīd*, had been already fixed, standardised, and institutionalised through specific manuals that students and scholars alike have been memorising and studying until today.

39 There are several treatises written on the subject and it is difficult to identify this particular work. A short treatise by the same title, *muqaddima fī waqf Ḥamza wa-Hishām*, by Aḥmad al-Rashīdī is listed in King Faisal Center for Research and Islamic Studies: https://library.kfcris.com/cgi-bin/koha/opac-detail.pl?biblionumber=972734.

40 The title of the treatise is *al-badīʿ fīmā rusima fī maʿrifat al-tāʾ wa-al-hāʾ wa-al-wāw wa-al-yāʾ fī al-muṣḥaf*. It could be by Ibn Muʿādh al-Juhanī, *al-Badīʿ fī maʿrifat mā rusima fī muṣḥaf ʿUthmān*.

41 al-Khaymī, *Fihris Makhṭūṭāt dār al-kutub al-Ẓāhiriyya*, I, 328–329.

42 al-Suyūṭī, *al-Itqān fī ʿulūm al-Qurʾān*, 377, 458, 483, 491, 539, 583, 599.

43 Ḥamītū, *Abū al-Qāsim al-Shāṭibī*, 56–79.

Bibliography

Abū Shāma (al-Maqdisī), Shihāb al-Dīn. *Ibrāz al-ma'ānī min Ḥirz al-amānī fī al-qirā'āt al-sab'*. Edited by Ibrāhīm 'Aṭwa-'Awaḍ. Beirut: Dār al-kutub al-'ilmiyya, 1982.

al-Anṣārī, Burhān al-Dīn. *Tuḥfat al-murīd li-muqaddimat al-tajwīd*. Edited by 'Imād Ḥusayn. Amman: Amwāj lil-ṭibā'a wa-al-nashr, 2014.

al-Anṣārī, Zakariyyā. *al-Maqṣad li-talkhīṣ mā fī al-Murshid fī al-waqf wa-al-ibtidā'*. Cairo: Dār al-muṣḥāf, 1985.

al-Asqāṭī, Aḥmad b. 'Umar. *Ajwibat al-masā'il al-mushkilāt fī 'ilm al-qirā'āt*. Edited by Amīn al-Shinqīṭī. Riyadh: Kunūz Ishbīliyyā, 2008.

Ibn Balbān al-Ḥanbalī, Muḥammad. *Bughyat al-mustafīd fī 'ilm al-tajwīd*. Edited by Ramzī Sa'd al-Dīn Dimashqiyya. Beirut: Dār al-bashā'ir al-islāmiyya, 2001.

al-Baqarī, Muḥammad b. Qāsim. *al-Qawā'id al-muqarrara wa-al-fawā'id al-muḥarrara*. Edited by Muḥammad al-Mashhadānī. Riyadh: Maktabat al-Rushd, 2005.

al-Barmāwī, Ilyās. *Imtā' al-fuḍalā' bi-tarājim al-qurrā'*. Medina, 2000.

al-Biqā'ī, Burhān al-Dīn. *al-Ajwiba al-sirriyya 'an al-alghāz al-Jazariyya*. Edited by Jamāl Rifā'ī al-Shāyib. Cairo: Maktabat awlād al-shaykh lil-turāth, 2005.

Blachère, Régis. *Introduction au Coran*. Paris, 1959.

al-Ḍabbā', 'Alī Muḥammad and Ibn al-Jazarī. *Al-Bahja al-marḍiyya sharḥ al-Durra al-muḍiyya*. Cairo, 2002.

al-Dimyāṭī, Shihāb al-Dīn. *Itḥāf fuḍalā' al-bashar fī al-qirā'āt al-arba'ata 'ashar*. Edited by Sha'bān Muḥammad Ismā'īl. 2 vols. Beirut: 'Ālam al-kutub, 1987.

al-Faḍālī, Sayf al-Dīn Abū al-Futūḥ. *al-Jawāhir al-muḍiyya 'alā al-muqaddima al-Jazariyya*. Edited by 'Azza bint Hāshim Mu'īnī. Riyadh: Maktabat al-Rushd, 2005.

Fihris kutub al-qirā'āt al-qur'āniyya fi al-Jāmi'a al-Islāmiyya bi-al-Madīna (Medina: 1994).

Ḥamītū, 'Abd al-Hādī 'Abd Allāh. *Za'īm al-madrasa al-athariyya fī al-qirā'āt wa-shaykh qurrā' al-maghrib wa-al-mashriq al-imām Abū al-Qāsim al-Shāṭibī*. Riyadh: Aḍwā' al-salaf, 2005.

Ismā'īl b. Khalaf, Abū Ṭāhir al-Andalusī. *al-'Unwān fī al-qirā'āt al-sab'*. Edited by 'Iṣām Fārūq Imām. Cairo: Mu'assasat al-'alyā' lil-nashr wa-al-tawzī', 2010.

al-Izmīrī, Muṣṭafā. *Itḥāf al-barara bi-mā sakata 'anhu Nashr al-'ashara*. Edited by Khālid Ḥasan Abū al-Jūd. Riyadh: Dār aḍwā' al-salaf, 2007.

Ibn al-Jazarī, Abū al-Khayr. *al-Nashr fī al-qirā'āt al-'ashr*. Edited by 'Alī Muḥammad al-Ḍabbā'. 2 vols. Beirut: Dār al-kutub al-'ilmiyya.

Ibn al-Jazarī, Abū al-Khayr. *Ghāyat al-nihāya fī ṭabaqāt al-qurrā'*. Edited by Gotthelf Bergsträsser. 2 vols. Beirut: Dār al-kutub al-'ilmiyya, 2006.

Ibn al-Jazarī, Abū al-Khayr. *Munjid al-muqri'īn wa-murshid al-ṭālibīn*. Edited by 'Alī b. Muḥammad al-'Imrān. Mecca: Dār al-fawā'id, 1998.

Ibn al-Jazarī, Abū al-Khayr. *Taqrīb al-Nashr fī al-qirā'āt al-'ashr*. Edited by 'Ādil Ibrāhīm Rifā'ī. Riyadh: Mujamma' al-malik Fahd, 2012.

Ibn al-Jazarī, Abū al-Khayr. *Tuḥfat al-ikhwān fī al-khulf bayn al-Shāṭibiyya wa-al-'Unwān*. Edited by Aḥmad al-Ruwaythī. Riyadh: Dār kunūz Ishbīliyyā, 2009.

al-Juhanī, Ibn Mu'ādh. *al-Badī' fī ma'rifat mā rusima fī muṣḥaf 'Uthmān*. Edited by Ghānim Qaddūrī al-Ḥamad. Amman: Dār 'Ammār, 2000.

al-Khaymī, Ṣalāḥ Muḥammad. *Fihris Makhṭūṭāt dār al-kutub al-Ẓāhiriyya: 'ulūm al-Qur'ān al-karīm*. Damascus, 1983.

al-Maghribī, Hāshim b. Muḥammad. *Ḥiṣn al-qāri' fī ikhtilāf al-maqāri'*. Edited by Ḥabīb al-Sulamī. Damascus: Dār al-Aḥbāb, 2018.

al-Manṣūrī, 'Alī Sulaymān. *Irshād al-ṭalaba ilā shawāhid al-Ṭayyiba*. Edited by Jamāl al-Dīn Sharaf. Cairo: Dār al-ṣaḥāba lil-turāth, 2004.

al-Mārghanī, Ibrāhīm and Abū al-Ḥasan Ibn Barrī, *al-Nujūm al-ṭawāli' 'alā al-Durar al-lawāmi' fī aṣl maqra' al-imām Nāfi'*. Beirut: Dār al-fikr, 1995.

al-Mas'adī, 'Umar b. Ibrāhīm. *al-Fawā'id al-Mas'adiyya fī ḥall al-Jazariyya*. Edited by Jamāl al-Sayyid Rifā'ī. Cairo: Maktabat awlād al-Shaykh lil-turāth, 2005.

al-Masharā'ī, Ṣadaqa b. Salāma. *Al-Tatimma fī qirā'at al-thalātha al-a'imma*. Edited by al-Sālim al-Jakanī. Medina: Dār Ṭība, 2017.

Melchert, Christopher. "Ibn Mujāhid and the Establishment of Seven Qur'anic Readings." *Studia Islamica* 91 (2000): 5–22.

Nasser, Shady Hekmat. "The Canonizations of the

Qurʾan: Political Decrees or Community Practices?" In *Non Sola Scriptura: Essays on the Qurʾan and Islam in Honour of William A. Graham*, edited by Bruce Fudge, Kambiz GhaneaBassiri, Christian Lange and Sarah Bowen Savant, 93–107. London: Routledge, 2022.

Nasser, Shady Hekmat. *The Second Canonization of the Qurʾān (324/936): Ibn Mujāhid and the Founding of the Seven Readings*. Leiden, 2020.

Neuwirth, Angelika. "al-Shāṭibī." In *Encyclopaedia of Islam, Second Edition*. Published electronically 2012. DOI: 10.1163/1573–3912_islam_SIM_6866.

Nöldeke, Theodor, Gotthelf Bergsträsser and Friedrich Schwally. *Geschichte des Qorâns*. 3 vols. Leipzig: Dieterich'sche Verlagsbuchhandlung, 2006 reprint.

Ibn al-Qāṣiḥ, Abū al-Baqāʾ. *Qurrat al-ʿayn fī al-fatḥ wa-al-imāla bayn al-lafẓayn*. Edited by Ibrāhīm al-Jarmī. Amman: Dār ʿAmmār, 2005.

Ibn al-Qāṣiḥ, Abū al-Baqāʾ. *Sirāj al-qāriʾ al-mubtadī wa-tidhkār al-muqriʾ al-muntahī*. Edited by ʿAlī Muḥammad al-Ḍabbāʿ. Cairo: Muṣṭafā al-Bābī al-Ḥalabī, 1954.

al-Qasṭallānī, Shihāb al-Dīn. *Laṭāʾif al-ishārāt li-funūn al-Qirāʾāt*. Edited by ʿĀmir al-Sayyid ʿUthmān and ʿAbd al-Ṣabūr Shāhīn. Cairo: Lajnat iḥyāʾ al-turāth al-islāmī, 1972.

al-Sakhāwī, ʿAlam al-Dīn. *Fatḥ al-waṣīd fī sharḥ al-qaṣīd*. Edited by Muḥammad al-Idrīsī al-Ṭāhirī. 2 vols. Riyadh: Maktabat al-rushd, 2002.

al-Suyūṭī, Jalāl al-Dīn. *al-Itqān fī ʿulūm al-Qurʾān*. Edited by Markaz al-dirāsāt al-qurʾāniyya. Medina: Mujammaʿ al-malik Fahd li-ṭibāʿat al-muṣḥaf al-sharīf, 2005.

al-Wāfī, Ibrāhīm. *al-Dirāsāt al-Qurʾāniyya bi-al-Maghrib fī al-qarn al-rābiʿ ʿashar al-Hijrī*. Casablanca: Maṭbaʿat al-najāḥ al-jadīda, 1999.

The Recitation Books

[81] ***al-Itqān fī ʿulūm al-Qurʾān***, AUTHOR: Jalāl al-Dīn al-Suyūṭī (d. 911/1505), EDITION: edited by Markaz al-dirāsāt al-qurʾāniyya, Medina: Mujammaʿ al-malik Fahd li-ṭibāʿat al-muṣḥaf al-sharīf, 2005. MANUSCRIPT: This particular copy is kept in al-Khālidiyyah Library, Jerusalem MS #586 (https://www.vhmml.org/readingRoom/view/508759)

[82] ***Ḥujaj al-Qurʾān***, AUTHOR: Abū al-Faḍāʾil Ibn al-Muẓaffar al-Rāzī (d. after 637/1239), EDITION: edited by Aḥmad ʿUmar al-Maḥmaṣānī, Cairo: Maṭbaʿat al-mawsūʿāt, 1903.
This book is a work on theology and not related to *Qirāʾāt*. It is either misplaced in this section or misattributed. There is a work of Qurʾānic recitation and etiquette by another scholar named Abū al-Faḍl al-Rāzī (d. 454/1062), edited by ʿĀmir Ḥasan Ṣabrī, Beirut: Dār al-bashāʾir al-islāmiyya, 1994. It is possible that the two works and authors were confused.

[83] ***Muntahā al-amānī wa-al-masarrāt fī ʿulūm al-Qirāʾāt***, also known as *Itḥāf fuḍalāʾ al-bashar fī al-qirāʾāt al-arbaʿata ʿashar*, AUTHOR: Shihāb al-Dīn al-Dimyāṭī (d. 1117/1705), EDITION: edited by Shaʿbān Muḥammad Ismāʿīl, 2 vols, Beirut: ʿĀlam al-kutub, 1987.

[84] ***Laṭāʾif al-ishārāt** li-funūn al-Qirāʾāt*, AUTHOR: Shihāb al-Dīn al-Qasṭallānī (d. 923/1517), EDITION: edited by ʿĀmir al-Sayyid ʿUthmān and ʿAbd al-Ṣabūr Shāhīn, Cairo: Lajnat iḥyāʾ al-turāth al-islāmī, 1972.

[85] ***Badāʾiʿ al-burhān fī ʿulūm al-Qurʾān***, *Badāʾiʿ al-burhān sharḥ ʿUmadat al-ʿirfān*, AUTHOR: Muṣṭafā al-Izmīrī (d. 1155/1742), EDITION: edited by Maryam Jandalī, Beirut: Dār al-kutub al-ʿilmiyya, 2008.

[86] ***Laṭāʾif al-ishārāt***, see #84

[87] ***Dhikr wuqūfāt al-Qurʾān***: There are many works written on the rules of pausing and resuming the recitation (*al-waqf wa-al-ibtidāʾ*). It is difficult to know if this is an independent treatise or a section taken from larger works on *Qirāʾāt*.

[88] ***Taqrīb al-Nashr fī al-qirāʾāt al-ʿashr***, AUTHOR: Abū al-Khayr Ibn al-Jazarī (d. 833/1429), EDITION: edited by ʿĀdil Ibrāhīm Rifāʿī, Riyadh: Mujammaʿal-malik Fahd, 2012.

[89] ***al-Nashr fī al-qirāʾāt al-ʿashr***, AUTHOR: Abū al-Khayr Ibn al-Jazarī (d. 833/1429), EDITION: edited by ʿAlī Muḥammad al-Ḍabbāʿ, 2 vols, Beirut: Dār al-kutub al-ʿilmiyya, [1960?]

[90] ***al-Taysīr by Ibn al-Jawzī***. This is probably a corruption in copying the title of the work: *al-Nashr* by Ibn al-Jazarī instead of *al-Taysīr* by Ibn al-Jazwzī. See #89

[91] ***Tartīb Zība***, AUTHOR: Maḥmūd al-Wārdārī (d. 1061/1651). This is a tabulated index work of Qurʾānic verses and their arrangements. The manuscript is also mentioned in the Ẓāhiriyya manuscript collection: Ṣalāḥ Muḥammad al-Khaymī, *Fihris Makhṭūṭāt dār al-kutub al-Ẓāhiriyya: ʿulūm al-Qurʾān al-karīm*, Damascus: Maṭbūʿāt majmaʿ al-lugha al-ʿarabiyya, 1983, 1: 328–329. This particular copy is kept in *al-Maktaba al-Azhariyya* #874. Also see *Fihris al-Maktaba al-Azhariyya*, edited by Abū al-Wafā al-Marāghī, 1: 146.

[92] ***Shāṭibiyya***, also known as *Ḥirz al-amānī wa-wajh al-tahānī*, AUTHOR: Abū al-Qāsim al-Shāṭibī's (d. 589/1194), EDITION: edited by Muḥammad Tamīm al-Zuʿbī, Damascus: Dār al-Ghawthānī, 2005

[93] ***Shāṭibiyya***, see #92

[94] ***Shāṭibiyya***, see #92

[95] ***Shāṭibiyya***, see #92

[96] ***Shāṭibiyya***, see #92

[97] ***Sharḥ al-Shāṭibiyya***: There are numerous commentaries on *al-Shāṭibiyya*, and it is difficult to determine which one is meant here. The most popular commentaries were by ʿAlam al-Dīn al-Sakhāwī (d. 643/1245), *Fatḥ al-waṣīd fī sharḥ al-qaṣīd*, edited by Muḥammad al-Idrīsī al-Ṭāhirī, 2 vols, Riyadh: Maktabat al-rushd, 2002; Abū al-Baqāʾ Ibn al-Qāṣiḥ (d. 801/1399), *Sirāj al-qāriʾ al-mubtadī wa-tidhkār al-muqriʾ al-muntahī*, edited by ʿAlī Muḥammad al-Ḍabbāʿ, Cairo: Muṣṭafā al-Bābī al-Ḥalabī, 1954; Shihāb al-Dīn Abū Shāma al-Maqdisī (d. 665/1267), *Ibrāz al-maʿānī min Ḥirz al-amānī fī al-qirāʾāt al-sabʿ*, edited by Ibrāhīm ʿAṭwa-ʿAwaḍ, Beirut: Dār al-kutub al-ʿilmiyya, 1982.

[98] ***Sharḥ al-Shāṭibiyya***, see #97

[99] ***Sharḥ al-Shāṭibiyya***, see #97

[100] ***Sharḥ al-Shāṭibiyya***, see #97

[101] ***Sharḥ al-Shāṭibiyya***, see #97

[102] ***Qirāʾat Ḥafṣ min ṭarīq al-Shāṭibiyya***: There are many short treatises and short manuals that single out the system of recitation of one eponymous reading, for example, a treatise by Abū al-Mawāhib al-Ḥanbalī (d. 1126/1714), *Risāla fī qāʿidat qirāʾat Ḥafṣ*, edited by ʿAbd Allāh al-Mighlāj, Dubai, Jāʾizat Dubayy al-duwaliyya lil-Qurʾān al-karīm, 2017.

[103] ***Maʾākhidh al-khilāf min Shāṭibiyya***: A treatise that lists the differences between *al-Shāṭibiyya* and other manuals of *Qirāʾāt*. It is difficult to determine the identity of the work with certainty. See #104

[104] ***al-Tuḥfa fī ḥall Mushkilāt al-Shāṭibiyya***, *Tuḥfat al-ikhwān fī al-khulf bayn al-Shāṭibiyya wa-al-ʿUnwān*, AUTHOR: Abū al-Khayr Ibn al-Jazarī (d. 833/1429), EDITION: edited by Aḥmad al-Ruwaythī, Riyadh: Dār kunūz Ishbīliyyā, 2009.

[105] ***Matn al-Jazariyya***: Also known as *al-Muqaddima al-Jazariyya*, AUTHOR: Abū al-Khayr Ibn al-Jazarī (d. 833/1429), EDITION: edited by Ayman Suwayd, Jedda: Dār nūr al-maktabāt, 2006.

[106] ***Matn al-Jazariyya***: See #105

[107] ***Majmūʿ adillat Matn al-Jazariyya***: This could be another copy of *al-Jazariyya* (#105) or a commentary (See #108)

[108] ***Sharḥ al-Jazariyya***: *Tuḥfat al-murīd li-muqaddimat al-tajwīd*, AUTHOR: Burhān al-Dīn al-Anṣārī (d. 893/1488), EDITION, edited by ʿImād Ḥusayn, Amman: Amwāj lil-ṭibāʿa wa-al-nashr, 2014.

[109] ***Al-Fawāʾid al-Masʿadiyya fī ḥall al-Muqaddima al-Jazariyya***, AUTHOR: ʿUmar b. Ibrāhīm al-Masʿadī (d. 1017/1608), EDITION: edited by Jamāl al-Sayyid Rifāʿī, Cairo: Maktabat awlād al-Shaykh lil-turāth, 2005.

[110] ***Al-Badīʿ fī ma rusim fī maʿrifat al-tāʾ wa-al-hāʾ wa-al-wāw wa-al-yāʾ fī al-muṣḥaf***: There is a work by Ibn Muʿādh al-Juhanī (d. 442/1050) titled *al-Badīʿ fī maʿrifat mā rusima fī muṣḥaf ʿUthmān*, edited by Ghānim Qaddūrī al-Ḥamad, Amman: Dār ʿAmmār, 2000. However, this treatise deals with a very limited subject, namely, the orthography of four specific letters, whereas al-Juhanī's work is a more comprehensive work on Qurʾānic orthography and its history.

[111] ***Muqaddima fī waqf Ḥamza wa-Hishām***: There are several treatises that deal with the technique of Ḥamza and Hishām when they paused on particular words that contain the *hamza* glottal stop, for example, Abū al-Baqāʾ Ibn al-Qāṣiḥ (d. 801/1399), *Tuḥfat al-anām fī al-waqf ʿalā al-*

hamz li-Ḥamza wa-Hishām, *Fihris Makhṭūṭāt Khizānat al-turāth*, VI, 736.

[112] ***al-Masāʾil wa-al-ajwiba***: *Ajwibat al-masāʾil al-mushkilāt fī ʿilm al-qirāʾāt*, AUTHOR: Aḥmad b. ʿUmar al-Asqāṭī (d. 1159/1746), EDITION: edited by Amīn al-Shinqīṭī, Riyadh: Kunūz Ishbīliyyā, 2008.

[113] ***Al-Maqṣad li-talkhīṣ*** *mā fī* ***al-Murshid*** *fī al-waqf wa-al-ibtidāʾ*, AUTHOR: Zakariyyā al-Anṣārī (d. 926/1520), EDITION: Cairo: Dār al-muṣḥaf, 1985.

[114] ***Kitāb Al-Shamʿa***: It is difficult to identify this work. It could be *al-Shamʿa al-muntakhaba min al-sabʿa*, see: *Fihris kutub al-qirāʾāt al-qurʾāniyya fī al-Jāmiʿa al-Islāmiyya bi-al-Madīna*: Medina, 1994, 201. It could also be the work by Abū al-Saʿd al-Ṭablāwī (d. 1014/1603), *al-Shamʿa al-muḍiyya bi-nashr qirāʾāt al-sabʿa al-marḍiyya*, edited by ʿAlī Sayyid Jaʿfar, Riyadh: Maktabat al-rushd, 2003.

[115] ***Kitāb al-Tatimma*** *fī qirāʾat al-thalātha al-aʾimma*, AUTHOR: Ṣadaqa b. Salāma al-Masḥarāʾī (d. 825/1422), EDITION: edited by al-Sālim al-Jakanī, Medina: Dār Ṭība, 2017.

[116] ***al-ʿUnwān*** *fī al-qirāʾāt al-sabʿ*, AUTHOR: Abū Ṭāhir Ismāʿīl b. Khalaf (d. 455/1063), EDITION: edited by ʿIṣām Fārūq Imām, Cairo: Muʾassasat al-ʿalyāʾ lil-nashr wa-al-tawzīʿ, 2010.

[117] ***Bughyat al-mustafīd*** *fī ʿilm al tajwīd*, AUTHOR: Muḥammad Ibn Balbān al-Ḥanbalī (d. 1083/1672), EDITION: edited by Ramzī Saʿd al-Dīn Dimashqiyya, Beirut: Dār al-bashāʾir al-islāmiyya, 2001.

[118] ***Qurrat al-ʿayn*** *fī al-fatḥ wa-al-imāla bayn al-lafẓayn*, AUTHOR: Abū al-Baqāʾ Ibn al-Qāṣiḥ (d. 801/1399), EDITION: edited by Ibrāhīm al-Jarmī, Amman: Dār ʿAmmār, 2005.

[119] ***Irshād al-ṭalaba ilā shawāhid al-Ṭayyiba***, AUTHOR: ʿAlī Sulaymān al-Manṣūrī (d. 1134/1722), EDITION: edited by Jamāl al-Dīn Sharaf, Cairo, Dār al-ṣaḥāba lil-turāth, 2004, MANUSCRIPT: Riyadh, Imam Mohammad Ibn Saud Islamic University, MS 979.

[120] ***Al-Luʾluʾ al-maknūn*** *fī jamʿ al-awjuh*, AUTHOR: Sayf al-Dīn Abū al-Futūḥ al-Faḍālī (d. 1020/1611). See: *Kashf al-ẓunūn*, II, 1570.

[121] ***ʿUmdat al-ʿIrfān*** *fī taḥrīr awjuh al-Qurʾān*, AUTHOR: Muṣṭafā al-Izmīrī (d. 1155/1742), EDITION: edited by Muḥammad Muḥammad Jābir and ʿAbd al-ʿAzīz al-Zayyāt, Cairo: Maktabat al-Jundī.

[122] ***Matn fī takmilat al-ʿashara*** and ***al-Jazariyya***, also known as *al-Durra al-muḍiyya*, AUTHOR: Abū al-Khayr Ibn al-Jazarī (d. 833/1429), EDITION: edited by Muḥammad al-Zuʿbī, Jedda: Maktabat al-hudā. Also see #105.

[123] ***Tajwīd al-Qawāʿid al-muqarrara*** *wa-al-fawāʾid al-muḥarrara*, AUTHOR: Muḥammad b. Qāsim al-Baqarī (d. 1111/1699), EDITION: edited by Muḥammad al-Mashhadānī, Riyadh: Maktabat al-rushd, 2005.

[124] ***Zubdat al-bayān***: The identity of this book is difficult to determine. No popular work of *Qirāʾāt* has this title. A work by the Shīʿī scholar al-Muḥaqqiq al-Ardabīlī (d. 993/1585) carries the title of *Zubdat al-bayān fī barāhīn aḥkām al-Qurʾān*, but it is work on Qurʾānic verses that deal with legal rulings.

[125] ***Kitāb al-tanbīh***: There are many works that have this title. A work by Ḥamza b. al-Ḥasan al-Iṣfahānī (d. 360/971), titled *al-Tanbīh ʿalā ḥudūth al-taṣḥīf*, deals with scribal errors and variants in the Qurʾān, poetry and *Ḥadīth*.

[126] ***Risāla Ijāza fī ʿilm al-qirāʾāt***: a personal certificate awarded to one who memorised the Qurʾān in different systems of recitation.

[127] ***Risāla fī jamʿ awjuh al-takbīr***: a generic title on the *takbir* (*Allāh akbar*) formula. It could be an independent short treatise or an excerpt from a larger work of *Qirāʾāt*, such as *al-Shāṭibiyya*.

[128] ***Risāla fī jamʿ awjuh al-takbīr***, see #127.

[129] ***Risāla fī bayān taṣḥīḥ al-muʿtamad***: The title is not clear. There are many works titled *al-muʿtamad*, but they are mostly legal works.

[130] ***Risālat awjuh al-takbīr***, see #127.

[131] ***Inshād al-sharīd*** *fī ḍawāll al-qaṣīd*, AUTHOR: Ibn Ghāzī al-Miknāsī (d. 919/1513), EDITION: The work was edited as part of a master's thesis at the Faculty of Arts and Sciences in Rabat by al-Ḥasan al-ʿAlamī, http://thesis.mandumah.com/Record/130858.

[132] ***Ijāza fī al-qirāʾāt***, see #126.

[133] ***Risāla fī ʿilm al-tajwīd***: A generic work on Qurʾānic recitation.

[134] ***Risāla fī jamʿ awjuh al-takbīr***, see #127.

[135] ***al-Durar al-lawāmiʿ*** *fī aṣl maqraʾ al-imām Nāfiʿ*, AUTHOR: Abū al-Ḥasan Ibn Barrī (d. 730/1330), EDITION: Beirut: Dār al-fikr, 1995.

[136] ***Ijāza fī al-qirāʾāt***, see #126.

[137] ***Sharḥ Urjūzat Mushkilāt al-Qurʾān***, see #112.

[138] ***Ḥiṣn al-qāriʾ*** *fī ikhtilāf al-maqāriʾ*, AUTHOR: Hāshim b. Muḥammad al-Maghribī (d. after 1179/1765), EDITION: edited by Ḥabīb al-Sulamī, Damascus: Dār al-aḥbāb, 2018.

[139] ***Risāla fī naẓm makhārij al-ḥurūf***, an appendix to *al-Durar al-Lawāmiʿ*, see #135.

[140] ***Matn al-Jazariyya***, see #105.

CHAPTER 15

The *ḥadīth* Section

Garrett Davidson

The *'Kutub al-ḥadīth al-sharīf'* section is the third largest part of the Jazzār library inventory. This section of the 1221/1806 inventory consists of 189 entries and 230 volumes.[1] Thirteen of the 189 entries are titles with multiple copies (thirty-two codices in total), thus, there are 157 distinct titles in this section.[2] The section is, therefore, a fairly large sample of the books that were thought to fit under the rubric of *al-ḥadīth al-sharīf*. Unfortunately, we do not know who the author of this inventory was, nor do we fully understand the circumstances that led to its composition.[3] Yet, despite these issues, the relatively large size of the inventory provides us with a unique reflection of how the category of *al-ḥadīth al-sharīf* was conceived in this period, as well as the concerns and interests that shaped the concept.

Historically, the discipline of *ḥadīth* is, of course, one of the most productive disciplines of Islamic thought and it is not surprising to find a relatively large number of books in the section. It will be shown, however, that this section, in part, owes its size to the expansive and eclectic conception of *al-ḥadīth al-sharīf* that informed the selection of its titles. It encompasses works spanning a wide range of disciplines produced across a millennium in virtually all regions of Dār al-Islām. It includes some of the foundational works of the discipline of *ḥadīth*, and those written in its service, as well a number of fields and genres outside traditional conceptions of the discipline. Definitions of the discipline of *ḥadīth* produced by its practitioners, revolve around the words and actions attributed to the Prophet, and the branches of knowledge that emerged to serve their preservation, transmission and interpretation.[4] This definition is partially reflected in this section of the inventory, but the concept of *ḥadīth* that shaped it was much broader than that. It would seem this notion of *al-ḥadīth al-sharīf* revolved not only around the reports attributed to the Prophet, but also encompassed devotion to him and his family, his benediction, his praise and more. This section, thus, contains *ḥadīth* collections and their commentaries, as well as litanies of blessings on the Prophet, panegyric poems, odes commemorating his birth, works on the merits of his descendants, and numerous other related genres and topics.

As remarkable as the collection's diversity and breadth are, what it does not contain is equally remarkable. One of its most conspicuous gaps is that it contains only a fraction of the *ḥadīth* canon. Of the six books of the *ḥadīth* canon, only *Ṣaḥīḥ al-Bukhārī* and the *Sunan* of al-Tirmidhī exist in complete copies (#141, #142, #143 and #162). Remarkably, it does not contain a complete copy of *Ṣaḥīḥ Muslim*, the second ranking book in the hierarchy of the *ḥadīth* canon. More precisely, it would seem the entire first half of *Ṣaḥīḥ Muslim*, and probably more, is absent from the inventory, with only two copies of the second volume of the multivolume work mentioned (#152 and #153). Significantly, the other works of the canon are entirely absent, as are many other foundational *ḥadīth* collections, such as those of the *musnad* and *sunan* genres.

1 According to the endowment statement found in many volumes of the library, it was established in 1197/1783.

2 Library inventory, Vakıflar Genel Müdürlüğü (Ankara), Defter 1626.

3 The Chapters of Yasin Arslantaş (5) and Said Aljomani (2) in this volume offer insights on the possible circumstances that may have led to the creation of this document.

4 Ibn al-Ṣalāḥ, *'Ulūm al-ḥadīth*, 6–11.

DOI:10.1163/9789004720527_017

The genre of the vast tradition of commentary on the *ḥadīth* canon is present in the inventory, but only very partially so. The inventory only contains commentaries on al-Bukhārī's *Ṣaḥīḥ*, and those are mostly incomplete.[5]

What emerges as the most popular subject in this section is also quite noteworthy. The biography of the Prophet, which is sometimes not considered part of the discipline of *ḥadīth*, is the single most popular subject in the collection. There are a total of fifteen titles of *sīra* in some thirty volumes. Indeed, al-Qāḍī ʿIyāḍ's famous biography of the Prophet, *al-Shifāʾ*, is the most popular title in the inventory with six copies (#155–160). The *Sīra* of Burhān al-Dīn al-Ḥalabī is also among the most popular works in the inventory with four copies (#179–182).

The popularity of various books of invocations, prayers for the Prophet and their commentary are another striking feature of this section of the inventory. The collection of prophetic invocations of al-Nawawī, *al-Adhkār*, is the second most popular book in the collection, with five copies. Al-Fāsī's commentary on the *Dalāʾil al-khayrāt*, *Maṭāliʿ al-musarrāt* exists in four copies, making it one of the most popular books in the collection. The *mawlid* genre is also quite popular as are the genres of panegyrics and odes dedicated to the Prophet; in all, there are some twelve titles belonging to these genres, or roughly 6 per cent of the section.

Taken as a whole, while the *al-ḥadīth al-sharīf* section of the inventory has certain notable gaps, it contains much of the common core of *ḥadīth* works found in the *ḥadīth* sections of many libraries. It is, however, somewhat distinct in its pronounced devotional nature. In addition to the works of poetry, prayers and benedictions already noted, the section holds a number of works informed by a kind of Muḥammad-centric piety. It contains, for example, two copies of al-Birgivī's popular *al-Ṭarīqa al-Muḥammadiyya*.[6] It might also be noted that one of the two copies of the *Ṣaḥīḥ* is also divided into thirty parts for devotional purposes. It also has a number of works of the forty *ḥadīth* genres that often had devotional uses. Indeed, even a list of the names of the people involved in the Battle of Badr, that could be categorised as belonging to the genre of *ḥadīth*-based biography, could also be used for devotional purposes and recited as a litany.[7]

While we can speculate about certain orientations that seem to inform the inventory, it is also important to note that it appears random in places both in the selection of titles and in terms of their organisation. The organisational principle of the first entries in the section is rather easy to comprehend. After the entries on *al-Shifāʾ*, however, any organisational scheme seems to fade away and the remaining entries appear to be more or less random. There are also a number of books in this section that seem to have been included by accident or mistake.[8]

Imposing order on a list of books that is seemingly random is challenging. To organise this material, I have chosen to, firstly, treat the books that were positioned at the beginning of the inventory. I begin with these works because their placement at the top of the list seems to have been quite deliberate and, furthermore, because they are some of the most numerous books in the inventory. I next study those books that appear in multiple copies throughout this section of the inventory in the order of their quantity. I then discuss the works of authors who have multiple books in the inventory.

5 Ahmed El Shamsy notes in Chapter 16 in this volume that the inventory's section on law contains similar noteworthy gaps.

6 It is worth noting that the inventory includes commentaries on al-Birgivī's *al-Ṭarīqa al-Muḥammadiyya*; they are, however, found in the section on poetry treated by Khalil Sawan in Chapter 21.

7 Al-Shāmī, *al-Duʿā*.

8 This section is not alone in the seeming randomness of its organisational scheme, nor is it the only section to contain titles that were included by mistake. Dana Sajdi, in Chapter 22 in this volume, presents a quite novel theory to explain these seeming mistakes and randomness in the history section of the inventory.

Finally, I will write about the common genres and subgenres that can be identified in the contents of the inventory.

1 Ṣaḥīḥ Works

Not surprisingly, pride of place in the *'kutub al-ḥadīth al-sharīf'* section of the inventory goes to the *Ṣaḥīḥ* of Muḥammad b. Ismāʿīl al-Bukhārī (d. 256/870). The vast majority of scholars, of course, considered the *Ṣaḥīḥ* to be the most authoritative and esteemed of all *ḥadīth* collections. Due to its premier position in the hierarchy of *ḥadīth* collections, it was standard to begin inventories of *ḥadīth* works with the *Ṣaḥīḥ*.[9] Our inventory contains three copies of 'Bukhārī sharīf', the first of these is described as a complete copy of the *Ṣaḥīḥ* in thirty volumes in a box with a table of contents (*fihrist*) (#141). It was fairly common for the *Ṣaḥīḥ* to be divided into thirty parts to facilitate the ritual reading of the text over the course of a month, the month of Ramaḍān being particularly popular for this type of ritual reading.[10] The following manuscript of the *Ṣaḥīḥ* seems to have been a luxury copy: it is described as a complete copy, written in 'an Egyptian hand of high quality (*khaṭṭ Miṣrī ʿāl*)', on large format paper, with a gold embossed leather binding and a slipcase (#142). The third *Ṣaḥīḥ* manuscript is described as incomplete, consisting of only the seventh volume of an ancient copy (*ʿatīq al-waraq wa-jild*; #143).

Immediately following the main entry on the *Ṣaḥīḥ* come the entries for two commentaries on the collection. The first of these is al-Qasṭallānī's (d. 923/1517) multivolume commentary *Irshād al-ṣārī*. Significantly, the description of these manuscripts of *Irshād al-ṣārī* would seem to indicate that all three were incomplete. The first manuscript is described as consisting of the first volume but missing the introduction (#144), the second manuscript is described as comprising the first and third volumes (#145), and the third manuscript is described as consisting of the fourth volume (#146). It is unclear to what extent these four volumes constituted the entirety of al-Qasṭallānī's commentary, however, it is a rather large work and manuscript copies can consist of ten or twelve volumes. It is, thus, quite possible that these manuscripts together contained only a small portion of the whole commentary.[11]

The inventory mentions four incomplete manuscripts of Ibn Ḥajar's commentary on the *Ṣaḥīḥ*, *Fatḥ al-bārī*. The first manuscript is described as the second volume of a manuscript (#147), next comes the fifth volume of a manuscript (#148), the third manuscript is another of a second volume (#149), the fourth copy is of the fourteenth volume of a manuscript (#150). Unfortunately, none of the descriptions specify how of many total volumes each manuscript originally consisted, but *Fatḥ al-bārī* is a massive work, and manuscripts of the work vary, some in as many as ten volumes,[12] but there can be little doubt that these manuscripts together contained only a fraction of the whole text. That a total of eight volumes of the commentaries of *Irshād al-ṣārī* and *Fatḥ al-bārī* are listed in the inventory, making them among the most popular works therein, is noteworthy. It is interesting to compare this to the inventory of the Bāyezīd library from the sixteenth century, as, according to Göktaş, longer detailed commentaries such as *Fatḥ* were generally not popular among Ottoman scholars, who preferred shorter, more accessible ones.[13] These are not the only commentaries on the *Ṣaḥīḥ* present in the inventory; it also contains the first volume of al-Kirmānī's (d. 786/1384) commentary (#154) as well as one volume of al-Ajhūrī's

9 Works of the *fihrist* genre employ this organisation from as early as the sixth/twelfth century.

10 Davidson, *Carrying on the Tradition*, 87.

11 For examples of ten and twelve volume manuscripts, see the Süleymaniye Library, Murad Molla 486, Laleli 538, Yazma Bağışlar 1563; al-Azhar University Library, MS 3147 Ḥadīth.

12 National Library of Tunis MS 5799, for instance, consists of ten volumes.

13 Göktaş, "On the Hadith Collection", 311.

(d. 1066/1656) commentary on Ibn Abī Jamra's (d. 675/1276) abridgment of the *Ṣaḥīḥ* (#151).[14] As a whole, it can be said that the library provided users with a fair number of reference works on the *Ṣaḥīḥ*, yet, the fact that the library does not seem to have contained a single complete commentary on the *Ṣaḥīḥ*, considered to be the most authoritative collection of the Sunni *ḥadīth* canon, is also quite remarkable.

The *Ṣaḥīḥ* of Muslim b. al-Ḥajjāj (d. 261/875), of course, comes second only to al-Bukhārī in the hierarchy of the *ḥadīth* canon and traditionally follows it in lists and inventories of *ḥadīth* works. The two partial manuscripts of Muslim's *Ṣaḥīḥ* in our inventory follow the commentaries on al-Bukhārī. Both manuscripts are described as the second volume of the work, but neither notes the total number of volumes of which the manuscripts consisted. Manuscripts of the book vary considerably in size. Both manuscripts, however, are described as being composed in quarto format, which would almost certainly mean they were both quite incomplete copies of the text. That the second work in the hierarchy of *ḥadīth* collections is apparently only very partially represented in the library is remarkable. Moreover, commentary on Muslim's *Ṣaḥīḥ* is entirely absent from the inventory. The ritual status of *Bukhārī* in comparison to *Muslim* might partially explain the discrepancy. Bukhārī's *Ṣaḥīḥ* had a variety of ritual usages: as was noted above, it was ritually read during the month of Ramaḍān, it was also read to alleviate various communal tribulations, including drought and the plague.[15] Likewise, it was commonly publicly read for the general *baraka* its reading was believed to bring. Muslim's *Ṣaḥīḥ* never achieved the same ritual status.

1.1 *Al-Shifāʾ*

Six copies of al-Qāḍī ʿIyāḍ's (d. 544/1150) *al-Shifāʾ fī ḥuqūq al-Muṣṭafā* appear in the inventory, making it the single most numerous work in this section. These six manuscripts of the *al-Shifāʾ* are significantly given priority of place and listed immediately after the two *Ṣaḥīḥs*. That such a relatively large number of copies of the *al-Shifāʾ* occurs in the inventory and that they are given priority of place is not very surprising. *Al-Shifāʾ* was one of the most popular and esteemed biographies of the Prophet in the history of Islamic civilisations. According to the Ilm Database, which contains entries for 1.7 million manuscripts held in libraries around the world, there are 2386 manuscripts of the text held in libraries worldwide, making it among the top five books in terms of copies produced.[16] Perhaps one of the factors of the general popularity of *al-Shifāʾ* is its brevity, which allowed it to be relatively easily read and copied, and the inventory gives no indication that any of the copies in the library were incomplete. The presence of six copies of the text is reflective of the particularly esteemed place it had in Ottoman culture contemporary to the formation of the Jazzār library. The place of *al-Shifāʾ* in the book culture of the period is quite literally illustrated in an 1803 portrait of Selīm III (r. 1789–1807), where it conspicuously appears among ten other books on a shelf behind the Sultan.[17]

Although some purists considered *sīra* a discipline distinct from *ḥadīth*, *sīra* books were regularly included in lists and inventories of *ḥadīth* books.[18] The *al-Shifāʾ*, perhaps more than many *sīra* works, fits well into the category of '*kutub al-ḥadīth al-sharīf*'. Individual *ḥadīth* make up the bulk of the work and the author cites *ḥadīth* from a wide range of collections. In some cases, he presents his personal chains of transmission for

14 It is worth noting that according to Gōktas, al-Kirmānī was generally one of the most popular commentaries in the Ottoman context. The Bāyezīd library, for example, contains ten copies. He attributes the popularity of al-Kirmānī, over works like *Fatḥ al-bārī*, to the concise nature of the former work. Göktaş, "On the Hadith Collection", 312.

15 Davidson, *Carrying on the Tradition*, 85.

16 Ilm Database, Cairo, Egypt. Last accessed 23 October 2022.

17 Şen, *Making Sense of History*, 24.

18 Brown, *Muhammad's Legacy*, 13.

the *ḥadīth* he cites,[19] in others, he cites an abbreviated chain of transmission with only the first link.

From the perspective of organisation, the position of the *al-Shifāʾ* within the inventory makes sense, it is one of the premier books in the hierarchy of *sīra* works and it immediately follows the most revered books in the hierarchy of *ḥadīth* collections. Thus, up to and including *al-Shifāʾ*, the inventory proceeds with a fairly clear logic, however, after it, the organisation of the inventory breaks down almost completely. There are occasional groupings that seem to have some internal logic, such as a cluster of works on Prophetic medicine (#299–302), or a group of *mawlid* works (#201–203), but, on the whole, the entries seem to proceed in an essentially random manner. For the purposes of organising this chapter, these remaining entries are organised and treated, firstly, according to the number of copies of each book noted in the inventory. Secondly, the entries are organised and discussed for those authors who have multiple books in the inventory. Thirdly, the remaining books are discussed according to their disciplines.

1.2 *Works in Multiple Copies*

As was noted above, the inventory contains five copies of al-Nawawī's (d. 676/1277) *al-Adhkār*, making it the second most numerous work in the inventory after *al-Shifāʾ*. Four of these manuscripts are grouped together under the title *al-Adhkār* (#194–197). The fifth manuscript is listed separately under the full title of the work, *Ḥilyat al-abrār*. The placement of the fifth manuscript separately may indicate that whoever composed the inventory did not recognise the work by its full title (#150). Al-Nawawī is, of course, a giant of Islamic thought and spirituality, and requires little introduction. His *al-Adhkār* is a topically organised collection of supplications attributed to the Prophet taken primarily from the *ḥadīth* canon. Historically, *al-Adhkār* is one of the most enduringly popular books in terms of manuscript production; some 450 manuscripts exist in libraries across the world.[20] The considerable success of the work can partially be attributed to the easy access it gave the reader to various prophetic prayers or supplications for virtually any occasion. This ability to easily find a supplication believed to have been uttered by the Prophet for a vast range of daily activities made the *al-Adhkār* a powerful devotional tool, enabling the user to imbue almost every act of their daily life with the remembrance of God and a sense of connection to the Prophet. As will be seen, similar collections of supplications are generally well represented in this inventory.

The inventory notes four copies of the biography of the Prophet titled *Insān al-ʿUyūn bi-sīrat al-Amīn al-Maʾmūn*, commonly known as *al-Sīra al-Ḥalabiyya*, by the Egyptian scholar Burhān al-Dīn ʿAlī b. Ibrāhīm al-Ḥalabī (d. 1044/1635).[21] As his name suggests, al-Ḥalabī's family was originally from Aleppo, but had immigrated to Cairo, before al-Ḥalabī was born in 975/1568. As a student, he trained extensively with the famous scholar Shams al-Dīn al-Ramlī (d. 1005/1596) among others. He then became one of the most prominent scholars of his age, authoring on a wide range of subjects, and attracting a large and diverse body of students.[22] Al-Ḥalabī composed his *Sīra* when he was already well into his sixties and died soon after completing the text. However, according to al-Muḥibbī, it was not long before the *Sīra* 'became extremely famous and well-accepted among the scholars of the age'.[23] The *Sīra's* popularity continued in following generations and it was copied and transmitted extensively, as is witnessed by the at least 350 manuscripts held in libraries globally.[24]

19 Al-Qāḍī ʿIyāḍ, *al-Shifāʾ*, 181.

20 Ilm Database, Cairo, Egypt. Last accessed 23 October 2022.

21 He has a short biography in al-Ghazī, *Diwān al-Islām*, II, 173.

22 Al-Muḥibbi, *Khulaṣat al-āthar*, III, 123.

23 Ibn Sayyid al-Nas's interest in the verification of *ḥadīth*, for example, is entirely absent in al-Ḥalabī's work. See Mayeur-Joauen, "There Is Matter for Thought", 116.

24 Ilm Database, Cairo, Egypt. Last accessed 23 October 2022.

Al-Ḥalabī drew heavily on previous *sīra* works, however, the work is more than a simple compendium and creatively expands on the works from which it draws to create a *sīra* that is markedly different in tone and spirit and serves a variety of readerships.[25] Al-Ḥalabī notes in the introduction to his *Sīra* that the extensive work of previous authors of *sīra* works in establishing the veracity of their *ḥadīth* allowed him to forgo entirely the citation of full chains of transmission to focus on creating a more streamlined and accessible narrative.[26] Ḥalabī effectively synthesised his sources to create a devotional approach to the events of the Prophet's life.[27] Where there are contradictory accounts of an event, for instance, al-Ḥalabī often presents a devotional take on the event, transcending the apparent contradiction and citing relevant verses from the poetry of al-Būṣīrī (d. 696/1294) and al-Subkī (d. 771/1370).[28]

The inventory lists four copies of *Maṭāliʿ al-musarrāt bi-jalāʾ Dalāʾil al-khayrāt*, Muḥammad al-Mahdī b. Aḥmad al-Fāsī's (d. 1109/1698) commentary on al-Jazūlī's (c. 869/1465) famous devotional collection of blessings on the Prophet.[29] Al-Fāsī (d. 1109/1698) was born in al-Qaṣr al-Kabīr, Morocco, in 1033/1624 into a prominent family of Sufi scholars originally from al-Andalus.[30] His great grandfather, Abū al-Maḥāsin Yūsuf (d. 1013/1605), founded a prominent Sufi lodge in Fez that traced its initiatic chain of transmission through al-Jazūlī, and al-Jazūlī's work and legacy were a primary focus of Muḥammad al-Mahdī's scholarship.[31] In addition to *Maṭāliʿ al-masarrāt*, he composed three other commentaries on al-Jazūlī's *Dalāʾil al-khayrāt*. He also wrote hagiographical works on al-Jazūlī and his Sufi order.[32]

Maṭāliʿ al-musarrāt is by far al-Fāsī's most popular work. It achieved widespread popularity and was copied and distributed extensively, as is witnessed by the more than four hundred extant manuscript copies held in world libraries.[33] The popularity of *Maṭāliʿ al-masarrāt* is, of course, a product of the popularity of al-Jazūlī's *Dalāʾil al-khayrāt*, which, by the eighteenth century, had become immensely popular in almost all parts of the Islamic world, ultimately becoming one of the most copied texts of all time, existing in thousands of manuscript copies in libraries worldwide. *Maṭāliʿ al-musarrāt* is distinguished as being the all-time most popular of the many commentaries on the *Dālāʾil*.[34] One of the primary factors in the popularity of al-Fāsī's commentary is that it provided a systematic collation of the multiple versions of the text that were in circulation.[35] Furthermore, it made the text's often obscure vocabulary and esoteric concepts accessible for the many who devotionally read or recited the *Dalāʾil* on a daily

25 As Mayeur-Joauen has shown, he depends heavily on the works of Ibn Sayyid al-Nās (d. 734/1334) and al-Shāmī al-Ṣāliḥī (d. 942/1536), also regularly citing al-Qāḍī ʿIyāḍ, al-Būṣīrī, Ibn Ḥajar, al-Qasṭalānī, al-Suyūṭī, al-Shaʿrānī and others; Mayeur-Joauen, "There Is Matter for Thought".

26 Ibid., 116.

27 Ibid., 118–119.

28 Mayeur-Joauen speculates that al-Ḥalabī's approach to the Sira was intended to reconcile contradictory approaches current in the Ottoman empire, and was, in part, a response to the fundamentalist approach of the Qadızādeli; Ibid.

29 Al-Fāsī, *Maṭāliʿ al-masarrāt*. For a study of the text, see Burak, "Collating The Signs". For a study of *Dalāʾil al-khayrāt*, see Cornell, *Realm of the Saint*.

30 ʿAbd al-Majīd al-Khayālī's introduction to his edition of al-Fāsī, *al-Ilmāʾ*, 7–15 has a useful biography of al-Fāsī.

31 A total of twenty works are attributed to al-Fāsī, four of which are published. A bibliography of his works can be found in al-ʿUwayna's introduction to al-Fāsī, *al-Nabdha*, 31–39.

32 The most important of these consists of the biographies of al-Jazūlī and his primary disciple ʿAbd al-ʿAzīz al-Tabbāʿ (d. 904/1499), and their disciples in al-Fāsī, *Mumtiʿ*. Al-Fāsī later wrote an addendum to this (al-Fāsī, *al-Ilmāʾ*).

33 Ilm Database, Cairo, Egypt. Last accessed 23 October 2022.

34 Al-Fāsī himself produced three, of which *Maṭāliʿ al-masarrāt* is the shorter, the other two, one of which is a multivolume work, remain unedited (Al-Fāsī, *al-Nabdha*, 34).

35 Burak, "Collating The Signs", 139.

basis and, as a result, can be found in almost every library of any size.[36]

Three copies of al-Sharīf al-Raḍī's (d. 406/1015) work *Nahj al-balāgha* are listed in the inventory, as well as one commentary (#314–318). The presence of three copies of *Nahj al-Balāgha* in the inventory is not particularly surprising. It is, of course, a quite famous and popular work; the Ilm database contains entries for some 125 copies of the *Nahj* from all over the world.[37] The work is essentially an anthology of sermons, epistles, prayers, aphorisms and other sayings attributed to the fourth caliph and Shiite imam ʿAlī b. Abī Ṭālib (d. 40/661). According to a traditional, or perhaps conservative, definition of *ḥadīth* most of this material would not fall under the category of *ḥadīth*.[38] It would seem, however, that for the author of the inventory, the *Nahj* fit into a conception of '*ḥadīth*' encompassing not just material attributed to the Prophet but material generally related to him; thus, the material in the *Nahj* attributed to ʿAlī could be seen as an extension of that attributed to the Prophet by virtue to their unique relationship. It is worth noting that the author of the inventory was not the first to consider categorising the *Nahj* as a *ḥadīth* work. As Konrad Hirschler has shown, al-Anṣārī, the compiler of the inventory of the Ashrafiyya library in thirteenth-century Damascus, also originally categorised it as a *ḥadīth* work. He, however, for reasons that are not clear, eventually decided to move the work to the category of works that defied categorisation.[39] It should also be observed that although the *Nahj* is not a particularly voluminous work, all three of the manuscripts in the inventory are noted as incomplete.

Three copies of Muḥammad b. ʿAbd al-Rasūl al-Barzanjī's (d. 1103/1691) apocalyptic work *al-Ishāʿa li-ashrāṭ al-sāʿa* are listed in the inventory (#175, #176 and #191). In addition to these complete copies, there seems to be an extract from the work on the apocalyptic return of Jesus (#327). Born in Sharazūr in 1040/1630, al-Barzanjī hailed from a prominent family of Kurdish scholars. He received his primary education with his father, and then travelled widely in the pursuit of knowledge, studying with numerous scholars in Aleppo, Baghdad, Damascus, Cairo, Hamedan, Istanbul and Yemen. He eventually settled in Medina, where he became the disciple of the famous Sufi master Ṣafī al-Dīn Aḥmad al-Qushāshī (d. 1071/1661).[40] He ultimately became a prominent teacher in the Prophet's Mosque, and authored some twenty works on a wide range of subjects.[41]

Based on the colophons, al-Barzinjī completed *al-Ishāʿa* in Medina in 1076/1666.[42] As Cook has noted, al-Barzanjī's production of *al-Ishāʿa* took place in a context of increased apocalyptic and messianic thinking, in part, tied to the passing of the first millennium of the Islamic calendar.[43] His writing of the *al-Ishāʿa* coincides more specifically with a number of astronomical events, including meteorites and comets, and solar and lunar eclipses that were widely observed in the region in 1665 and seen by many as signs of the imminence of the apocalypse.[44] Al-Barzanjī's completion of the *al-Ishāʿa* also closely coincides with the appearance of the Jewish Messianic figure Shabbetai Zvi in Istanbul in 1666.[45]

The context of al-Barzanjī's authoring of the *al-Ishāʿa* aside, the content of the work provides a broad overview of the progression of Islamic his-

36 The commentary ranges from short glosses of vocabulary to several hundred-word-long discussions of concepts.

37 Ilm Database, Cairo, Egypt. Last accessed 23 October 2022.

38 It is also worth noting that, historically, there is considerable debate over the attribution of the material within the work to ʿAlī.

39 Hirschler, *Medieval Damascus*.

40 Al-Murādī, *Silk al-durar*, IV, 65.

41 For a list of his works, see the Introduction in al-Barzinjī, *al-Ishāʿa*.

42 According to a manuscript note, he later read the text with students and commented on it in 1100/1698; al-Barzinjī, *al-Ishāʿa*, 346.

43 Cook, "Messianism", 269–270.

44 Ibid., 269.

45 Ibid.

tory through an apocalyptic lens. The *ḥadīth* are a major source from which al-Barzanjī draws in the work, and he notes in the introduction the main *ḥadīth* collections from which he drew his *ḥadīth*. Furthermore, he notes that one of the aims of the work is the preservation of *ḥadīth* on the topic.[46] The relative quantity of *ḥadīth* cited in each section is dependent on the topic. The first section treating historical events cites relatively few *ḥadīth*. The second section, however, contains a larger number of *ḥadīth*; he, in fact begins the section with a list of *ḥadīth* and follows it with a subsection he titles 'mention of *ḥadīth* related to the topic'.[47] The third section similarly includes a relatively large number of *ḥadīth*. The work generally consists of a sufficient portion of *ḥadīth* for its placement in the *ḥadīth sharīf* section to be unsurprising.

The work's presence in multiple copies is also unsurprising; it was generally quite popular. Al-Barzanjī notes in the introduction to the work that one of his aims in composing it was to make 'the common folk (*al-ʿawāmm*)' more aware of the coming apocalypse.[48] It is unclear to what extent 'the common folk' read the work, but it did gain considerable popularity; some eighty manuscript copies are found in libraries worldwide. It was also the subject of several commentaries.

The inventory lists two copies of Mehmed Birgivī's (d. 981/1573) famous manual of ethics, *al-Ṭarīqa al-muḥammadiyya* (#238 and #282). Birgivī was one of the most influential scholars of the Ottoman period.[49] He is well-known for his criticism of what he perceived as the decadence of both scholars and Sufis of his time and his call for a return to a more conservative approach to Islam. The book contains a large percentage of *ḥadīth* and easily fits under the rubric of *ḥadīth*. The book was highly influential in the Ottoman realm and beyond. Hundreds of copies of the work are held in libraries today, and it is not surprising to find more than one copy in the inventory.[50]

In addition to his commentary on *al-Bukhārī*'s *Ṣaḥīḥ*, the inventory notes two complete copies, and perhaps two more partial copies,[51] of the Egyptian scholar al-Qasṭallānī's *al-Mawāhib al-ladūniyya bi-al-minaḥ al-Muḥammadiyya*. The latter is a devotional work on the nature of the Prophet and his characteristics, consisting of ten chapters treating various aspects of the Prophet intended to inspire reverence.[52] Naturally, *ḥadīth* are cited extensively in the treatment of each of these topics. Since it was authored in tenth/sixteenth century Cairo, the work gained considerable popularity and was copied widely. Some 300 manuscripts are known to be held in libraries globally.[53] The work was also the subject of an extensive commentary by al-Zurqānī (d. 1121/1710) that was also quite popular. All this is to say that *al-Mawāhib al-ladūniyya* fits quite well under the rubric of *al-ḥadīth al-sharīf* in the inventory.

There at least two copies of Ibn Ḥajar al-Haythamī's refutation of Twelver Shiism, *al-Ṣawāʾiq al-muḥriqa ʿalā ahl al-rafḍ wa-ḍalāl wa-al-zindaqa* in the inventory. Al-Haythamī notes that he authored this book while in Mecca in reaction

46 Al-Barzanjī, *al-Ishāʿa*, 28.

47 Ibid., 170.

48 Ibid., 26.

49 For more on the text, see Ivanyi, *Virtue, Piety, and the Law*. For more on Birgivī and his context, see Yaycıoğlu, "Guarding Traditions and Laws".

50 It is worth noting that the inventory includes commentaries on al-Birgivī's *al-Ṭarīqa al-Muḥammadiyya*, they are, however, found in the section on poetry treated by Khalil Sawan in Chapter 21.

51 #117 in the inventory is described as '*Nafaḥāt al-ʿawārif*, being a portion of *al-Mawāhib*'. This is probably a portion of al-Qasṭallānī's *al-Mawāhib*, although other works share the title *al-Mawāhib* and we cannot be entirely sure. Similarly, entry #121 is a composite manuscript containing "*Aqīla*, wa-*Ḥamziyya*, wa-*Mawāhib*'. It is reasonable to assume this is *al-Mawāhib al-ladūniyya*, although it is impossible to verify.

52 These ten sections are: 1) the primordial perfection of the Prophet; 2) his many names and their meanings; 3) his virtues; 4) his miracles; 5) the *miʿrāj*; 6) mention of him in the Qu'ran; 7) the necessity of loving him; 8) his medicine; 9) his worship of God; and 10) on his death.

53 Ilm Database, Cairo, Egypt. Last accessed 23 October 2022.

to the large number of Shiite pilgrims who were visiting the city at the time. He was, of course, among other things, a *ḥadīth* expert and much of this work consists of his citing of *ḥadīth* as evidence of Shiite heterodoxy. Al-Haythamī's status as a prominent *ḥadīth* scholar and the considerable *ḥadīth* content make the *al-ḥadīth al-sharīf* section a logical place to organise *al-Ṣāwāʾiq al-muḥriqa*.

2 Authors with Multiple Works

There are seven authors with multiple works in the inventory; there are a total of thirty-one titles attributed to these authors. The prolific ninth/fifteenth-century Egyptian polymath Jalāl al-Dīn al-Suyūṭī (d. 911/1505) is by far the most popular author in the inventory, with a total of seventeen distinct titles. The titles range from a work on the names of the Prophet to a book of Prophetic medicine. Most of these titles can fit fairly conveniently under the rubric of 'al-*ḥadīth al-sharīf*', however, others, while they contain some *ḥadīth*, could easily be classified under another discipline. One can only speculate why these works were categorised as *al-ḥadīth al-sharīf*, perhaps it is because *ḥadīth* was one of al-Suyūṭī's main fields of interest.

3 Al-Suyūṭī's Works in the Inventory

Al-Jāmiʿ al-ṣaghīr	*Ḥadīth* compilation
Al-Shamāʾil al-sharīfa	*Sīra*
Al-Riyāḍ al-anīqa fī sharḥ asmāʾ khayr al-khalīqa	*Sīra*
Al-Wasāʾil ilā maʿrifat al-awāʾil	History
Bushrā al-kaʾīb fī liqāʾ al-ḥabīb	Eschatology
Al-Manjam fī al-muʿjam	Post-canonical *ḥadīth*
Al-Durr al-munaẓẓam fī ism Allāh al-aʿẓam	Sufism
Al-Raḥma fī al-ṭibb wa-al-ḥikma	Prophetic medicine
Faḍl al-jalad bi-wafāt al-walad	On the loss of loved ones
Marāṣid al-maṭāliʿ	*Tafsīr*
Al-Lubāb	Genealogy
Muntahā al-ʿuqūl	Cosmology
Al-Araj fī al-faraj	Patience
Al-Budūr al-sāfira	Eschatology
Al-Fawz al-ʿaẓīm	Eschatology
Ḥuṣūl al-rifq	Advice

In addition to his *Fatḥ al-bārī*, mentioned above, the inventory lists three other works by the ninth/fifteenth-century Egyptian scholar, Ibn Ḥajar al-ʿAsqalānī. They are his investigation into the *ḥadīth* found in the important Ḥanafī *fiqh* manual of al-Marghinānī, *al-Dirāya fī takhrīj aḥādīth al-hidāya*, his work on the technical vocabulary of *ḥadīth* scholars *Sharḥ Nukhbat al-fikr* and his biographical dictionary of the companions of the Prophet, *al-Iṣāba*. All three works by Ibn Ḥajar fit squarely in the category of *ḥadīth*. All three works were also quite popular and exist in many manuscript copies.

Besides his *al-Ṣawāʿiq*, there are three other works by Ibn Ḥajar al-Haythamī in the inventory. There is one manuscript of his *ḥadīth*-based work treating major sins, *al-Zawājir* (#205), a work simply described as a '*mawlid*' (#202), and two copies of his commentary on al-Būṣīrī's famous poem *al-Hamziyya* (#218 and #219). All three works can easily fit under an expansive definition of *ḥadīth*.

The inventory includes three works by the renowned fifth-/eleventh-century scholar Abū Ḥāmid al-Ghazālī (d. 505/1111). They are his manual of Sufism, *Iḥyāʾ ʿulūm al-Dīn*, his *Kimyāʾ al-saʿāda*, and his eschatological work, *al-Durra al-fākhira fī ʿulūm al-ākhira*. *Ḥadīth* might not be the most obvious category for these books; Sufism is arguably a much better fit. All three of the works contain varying portions of *ḥadīth*, yet, in all cases, it is a relatively small portion of the total, and certainly not the primary focus of any of them. Nevertheless, in the case of *Iḥyāʾ*, the author of the inventory was not alone in this categorisation. The author of the inventory of the library of the Mosque of the Egyptian governor Muḥammad Bey Abū al-Dhahab, which was built in Cairo roughly a decade before the Jazzār library, also put al-Ghazālī's *Iḥyā'* in the *ḥadīth* section.[54] The author of the inventory of the Jazzār library also placed an abridgment of the *Iḥyā'* in this section (#250).

In addition to his *al-Adhkār* mentioned above, the inventory notes two other titles by al-Nawawī. One of these is his *ḥadīth*-based manual of proper Muslim practice and belief, *Riyāḍ al-ṣāliḥīn*. The other is his famous collection of forty *ḥadīth*. Both of these works obviously fit into the category of *al-ḥadīth al-sharīf*, were extremely popular and copied widely, and exist in virtually every library of any size.

Two titles are attributed to the Egyptian scholar al-Samhūdī (d. 911/1505): one manuscript of his work on the virtue of the descendants of the Prophet, *al-Ishrāf fī faḍā'il al-ashrāf* and another manuscript on the legal rulings regarding Islamic greetings, *Ṭīb al-kalām fī aḥkām al-salām*.

4 Disciplines, Genres, and Subgenres

The sections above treat those works in the inventory that exist in multiple copies, as well as those works by authors who have multiple titles in the inventory. Together these works make up forty-six of 142 titles, or some 32 percent of the total. Twenty-nine of the remaining ninety-six are not identifiable due to the ambiguity of the titles given in the inventory. There are also nine composite or multiple-text manuscripts that are impossible to identify due to ambiguity, thus, leaving eighty-four titles. In what follows, these remaining titles will be examined through the lenses of genre and discipline. These remaining titles are organised in four categories: those titles that squarely fit in the category of *ḥadīth* (55); those that seem to have been included in the '*al-ḥadīth al-sharīf*' section because *ḥadīth* makes up a substantial portion of their content (10); books whose subjects can be seen as closely related to the Prophet (14); and those titles that do not have a substantial *ḥadīth* content and were included for reasons that are not clear (5).

As noted, some fifty-five titles in the inventory fit into disciplines and genres that easily fit into a broad definition of *ḥadīth* and its various subgenres. In other words, the primary focus of these works is either directly related to *ḥadīth* or an ancillary discipline. As can be seen in the table below, these works can be categorised in fourteen *ḥadīth*-focused genres:

Discipline/Genre	Number of titles
Sīra	13
Ḥadīth Commentary	9
Forty *Ḥadīth*	7
Ḥadīth Compilations	3
Post-canonical *Ḥadīth* Transmission	4
Takhrīj	2
Uṣūl al-ḥadīth	2
Biography and Transmitter Criticism	5
Extra Canonical	1
Gharīb al-ḥadīth	1
Musnad	1
Prophetic Invocations	2
Prophetic Medicine	4
Sunan	1
Total	55

Sīra is the single most popular genre in the *al-ḥadīth al-sharīf* section of the inventory. A number of these *sīra* works have already been discussed, it was noted above that there are six copies of *al-Shifā'*, four copies of *al-Sīra al-Ḥalabiyya*, and two or four copies of *al-Mawāhib al-Ladūniyya*. In addition to these works, the inventory lists thirteen other works that neatly fit under the rubric of *sīra*. These works are quite diverse in their style, as well as their geography and chronology. The earliest work is the *sīra* of the Persian *ḥadīth* scholar al-Bayhaqī's (d. 458/1066) *Dālā'il al-nubuwwa*-(#237). Next comes the *sīra* of the Sicil-

54 Crecelius, "Waqf", 69.

ian scholar Ibn Ẓafar al-Siqillī (d. 567/1172) (#248). Al-Siqillī's *sīra* is closely followed by the Andalusian scholar al-Suhaylī's (d. 581/1114) commentary on the renowned third-/ninth-century *Sīra* of Ibn Hishām (d. 218/833) (#276).

The Prophet's miraculous night journey to Jerusalem and the heavens, *al-Isrāʾ wa-al-miʿrāj* is one of the most popular episodes of his biography and was the subject of numerous independent works. The inventory lists three works on the *Isrāʾ wa-miʿrāj*. Chronologically, the first is the popular work of the Egyptian scholar Najm al-Dīn al-Ghayṭī's (d. 981/1573) *work on the miʿrāj* (#329.).[55] Next, al-Ajhūrī's work on the *miʿrāj*, is noted to have been part of a composite volume (#298.).[56] One work is referred to only as *Miʿrāj al-Nabī* and is, thus, impossible to identify (#328).

As has been noted above, the inventory contains a total of seventeen works by the ninth-/fifteenth-century Egyptian polymath al-Suyūṭī, and among these, there are two works that can be categorised as *sīra*: his work on the description of the Prophet *al-Shamāʾil al-sharīfa* and his work on the names of the Prophet *al-Riyāḍ al-anīqa fī sharḥ asmāʾ khayr al-khalīqa* (#280). Al-Suyūṭī's contemporary, Muʿīn al-Dīn al-Miskīn's (d. 907/1501) popular work *Maʿārij al-nubuwwa-wa-madārij al-futuwwa-* is another *sīra* work in the inventory (#277). Two *sīra* works date to the eleventh/seventeenth century, the *Khulāṣat al-akhbār fī aḥwāl al-nabī al-mukhtār* by Maḥmūd al-Uskudārī of Istanbul (d. 1038/1626) (#189) and the Algerian scholar al-Sijilmāsī's (d. 1057/1647) *al-Durra al-munīfa* (#322). Finally, there is a work that is only identified by the very generic title, *Sīrat al-Nabī* (#204).

Commentary is the second most popular genre in the inventory. As has been discussed above, the inventory includes a total of nine copies of the commentaries on al-Bukhārī's *Ṣaḥīḥ* by al-Kirmānī, Ibn Ḥajar and al-Qasṭallānī. In addition to these, the inventory lists nine other works of commentary. The earliest of these would seem to be the book identified as *Mushkil al-Ṣaḥīḥayn*, which may be Ibn al-Jawzī's (d. 597/1116) work on the problematic *ḥadīth* in the *Ṣaḥīḥ*s of al-Bukhārī and Muslim, *Kashf al-mushkil min al-Ṣaḥīḥayn* (#283). As has been noted above, a copy of al-Ajhūrī's (d. 1066/1656) commentary on Ibn Abī Jamra's (d. 675/1277) abridgment of the *Ṣaḥīḥ* is also listed in the inventory (#230). The inventory similarly includes a commentary on al-Qāḍī ʿIyāḍ's *al-Shifāʾ* (#184).[57] Burhān al-Dīn al-Ḥalabī's commentary on al-Mundhirī's collection of *ḥadīth* encouraging good works and discouraging wicked deeds, *al-Targhīb wa-al-tarhīb* is also noted in the inventory (#221). In contrast to the commentaries on collections of *ḥadīth*, the inventory also notes a copy of Ibn Rajab al-Ḥanbalī's (d. 795/1393) commentary on a single *ḥadīth*, *al-Ikhtiyār al-ulā fī sharḥ ḥadīth ikhtiṣam al-malaʾ al-aʿlā* (#233).

The ambiguity of the titles given in the inventory prevents us from identifying several works of commentary. The inventory contains one copy of a commentary on al-Qaḍī ʿIyāḍ's *Mashāriq al-anwār*, however, the work is identified only as a *sharḥ*, and is, thus, too vague to identify further (#173). Another work is described as a commentary on al-Jazarī's collection of prophetic invocations, *al-Ḥuṣn al-ḥaṣīn* (#215). One work is described only with the very ambiguous *Kitāb fī bayān aḥādīth* (Book explaining *ḥadīth*) (#227). Three works are described as commentary on unidentified forty *ḥadīth* collections (#198–200). Only one of these three provides any further information to help us to identify the text; interestingly, it would seem that this collection, described as the forty *ḥadīth* of al-ʿĀmilī, is probably the collection of the Shiite scholar Ḥusayn al-ʿĀmilī (d. 984/1577) (#200).[58]

55 There are some 252 copies worldwide.

56 The title is given only as *Miʿrāj al-Ajhūrī*, this would seem to be al-Ajhūrī's *Nūr al-Wahhāj fī al-Isrāʾ wa-al-miʿrāj*.

57 This may be *Muzīl al-khafāʾ ʿan alfāẓ al-Shifāʾ* by Aḥmad b. Muḥammad al-Shumunnī (d. 872/1468).

58 Shiite works appear in other sections of the inventory as well. See the chapters of Walid Saleh (13), Ahmed El Shamsy (16) and Dana Sajdi (22) in this volume.

The forty *ḥadīth* genre was one of the most popular genres of *ḥadīth* literature and enjoyed popularity from the fourth/tenth century onwards. Inspired by the *ḥadīth* 'whosoever preserves forty of my *ḥadīth*, I will be his witness and intercessor on the day of judgement', scholars produced forty *ḥadīth* collections on a vast number of themes in numerous subgenres. Its brief nature was an important factor in the popularity of the genre, because forty *ḥadīth* works could be quickly copied. This brevity also meant that they could be quickly read or transmitted. It is, therefore, quite expected that in addition to the three commentaries on forty *ḥadīth* mentioned above, there are seven collections of forty *ḥadīth* in the inventory. Unfortunately, the author of the inventory did not identify most of these collections beyond 'forty *ḥadīth*'. One collection, however, is identified as the Forty *Ḥadīth* of al-Nawawī (#324), as noted above. Due to their brevity, forty *ḥadīth* works are often found in composite manuscripts, and one of the forty *ḥadīth* works in the inventory is an example of this. This work is described as being in a composite manuscript along with an abridgment of al-Bukhārī's *Ṣaḥīḥ* and an unspecified commentary on Ibn al-Jazarī's didactic poem on the rules of *tajwīd* (#168).

Works on the biographies of *ḥadīth* transmitters have been part of the discipline of *ḥadīth* since the third/ninth century and five works of this genre are found in the inventory. As has already been mentioned, Ibn Ḥajar's popular biographical dictionary of the companions of the Prophet, *al-Iṣāba*, is one of these (#207). Al-Ḥāfiẓ al-ʿIrāqī's work on the biographies of *ḥadīth* transmitters, *al-Bayān wa-al-tawḍīḥ*, is another (#193).[59] The inventory also includes a work only given the title 'A book on the names of transmitters', that almost certainly belongs to this genre (#234). In addition to these three works that fit squarely into the category of biography and transmitter criticism, there are two other works that partially fit the genre. The first of these is a list of the names of those companions of the Prophet who were present at the Battle of Badr (#260). Although the names of the Muslim participants in the battle of Badr were recited as a form of supplication, and this work may be of this devotional variety and not a work of biography.[60] The other work is al-ʿImādī's (d. 1171/1758) *al-Durr al-mustaṭāb*, which is primarily a treatment of the occasions on which revelation agreed with the opinions of Abū Bakr, ʿUmar and ʿAlī, however, it also includes biographies of these three caliphs.

There are four works in the inventory that can be categorised as *ḥadīth* compilations. In other words, these collections are digests that bring together *ḥadīth* from various other collections. Digests of the *ḥadīth* canon were of great utility as they provided access to the primary texts of the *ḥadīth* canon in one place and without the bulk and burden of their chains of transmission. As a result, *ḥadīth* compilations were one of the most successful of *ḥadīth* genres. Al-Baghāwī's (d. 516/1122) *Maṣābīḥ al-sunna* is the earliest of the compilations in the inventory. The *Maṣābīḥ* essentially compiles the texts (chains of transmission are omitted) of some four thousand *ḥadīth* taken from the canonical *ḥadīth* collections. Al-Suyūṭī's compilation of some ten thousand *ḥadīth*, *al-Jāmiʿ al-ṣaghīr* also occurs in the inventory. Together, these two books were among the most well-known and successful works of the genre. Some eight hundred and fifty manuscripts of *Maṣābīḥ* are known, and about nine hundred copies of *al-Jāmiʿ al-ṣaghīr*.[61] It is, thus, quite natural to find these works particularly in the *al-ḥadīth al-sharīf* section of the library. ʿAbd al-ʿAzīz b. Riḍwān al-Ḥanbalī's compilation of *ḥadīth* from

59 It is worth noting that this copy *al-Bayān wa-al-tawḍīḥ*, now held at the American University in Beirut Library, is an autograph and quite a rare work, with only a few known copies.

60 As is noted above, the various invocations use the names of the People of Badr, and they continue to be used for devotional purposes.

61 Ilm Database, Cairo, Egypt. Last accessed 23 October 2022.

the *Ṣaḥīḥ*s of al-Bukhārī and Muslim, *Maṭlaʿ al-nayyirayn* is also listed in the inventory (#266). In contrast to the two compilations mentioned previously, *Maṭlaʿ al-nayyirayn* is a more obscure book, with only fourteen known manuscripts.[62] What seems to be a compilation of *qudsī ḥadīth* is also found in the inventory (#325).

The various genres of post-canonical *ḥadīth* literature that scholars developed, after the emergence of the *ḥadīth* canon, to serve the joint aims of the preservation and cultivation of the chain of transmission, reflect an important aspect of the culture of *ḥadīth* scholars after the fourth/tenth century.[63] There are four works in the inventory belonging to various genres of post-canonical *ḥadīth* transmission. In essence, these works present the authors' personal chains of transmission across the generations back to the Prophet. These works served both devotional and social purposes. They were a means for scholars to preserve the community's chains of transmission to the Prophet. These chains of transmission were believed to function as channels connecting the community to the Prophet's blessings and spiritual charisma. They were also a means for scholars to express their status as the heirs of the Prophet through the presentation of their chains of transmission linking them to him.

The inventory lists six works of the *thabat/fihrist* genre. Works of this genre essentially function as catalogues mapping and delineating their author's personal connections to the books of *ḥadīth* and the wider Islamic intellectual tradition, as well as to the generations of men and women who transmitted them. Al-Suyūṭī's al-*Manjam fī al-muʿjam* cataloguing the three generations of transmitters from whom he took *ḥadīth* is the earliest of these works in the inventory (#224). Next in chronology is the *thabat of* ʿAbd al-Baqī b. ʿAbd al-Baqī al-Baʿlī's (d. 1071/1661) *Riyāḍ al-janna fī āthār ahl al-sunna*, which seems to occur twice in the inventory (#247 and #251). Al-Baʿlī's work is followed chronologically by the *thabat* of the Meccan scholar Ibn ʿAqīla (d. 1150/1738), which is noted to be the first text in an anthology of Ibn ʿAqīla's works (#304). The inventory also includes the *thabat of* Muḥammad Ibn al-Ṭayyib al-Madanī (d. 1170/1756) titled *Irsāl al-asānīd wa-iṣāl al-muṣannafāt wa-al-masānīd* (#281). The inventory mentions a fourth work described only as *aḥādīth sharīfa wa-ijāzat ṣarīḥa*, although the author is not mentioned, the title indicates that the work was a collection of the *ḥadīth* and *ijāza*s the unknown author had gathered over the course of his career (#239). The genre of forty *ḥadīth* works was often used by scholars as a means for scholars to communicate the various concerns of post-canonical *ḥadīth* culture. It is possible that some of the unidentifiable forty *ḥadīth* works noted above were of this type. Even if this were the case, however, the inventory would still contain a notably small number of post-canonical *ḥadīth* works.

The inventory contains just two works belonging to the *takhrīj* subgenre of *ḥadīth* literature. *Takhrīj* works, in essence, identify and provide citations for the *ḥadīth* used as evidence in the works of other disciplines. The two works of the genre listed in the inventory are the *al-Dirāya fī takhrīj aḥādīth al hidāya* by Ibn Ḥajar al-ʿAsqalānī (already noted) providing the references to the *ḥadīth* cited in al-Marghinānī's important work of Ḥanafī fiqh, *al-Hidāya* (#210), and al-Zaylaʿī's (d. 762/1362) work on the *ḥadīth* cited in al-Zamakhsharī's commentary on the Qur'an, *al-Kashshāf* (#216).

Works on the protocols and technical vocabulary of *ḥadīth* scholarship (*uṣūl al-ḥadīth*) are an essential part of the discipline of *ḥadīth* and it would be surprising to find a collection of *ḥadīth* manuscripts of any size that did not contain some works of the genre and the inventory does include works of this genre, however, only two. The first of these works chronologically is one of the all-time most popular works of the genre, Ibn Ḥajar's commentary on his own work *Nukhbat al-fikr*.

62 Ibid.
63 For a study of post-canonical *ḥadīth* culture, see Davidson, *Carrying on the Tradition*.

The second work is the considerably less popular work *al-Khulāṣa fī maʿrifat al-ḥadīth*, by Sharaf al-Dīn al-Ṭībī (d. 734/1334) (#189). Considering the essential role the *Uṣūl al-ḥadīth* genre plays in the larger discipline of *ḥadīth*, it is quite noteworthy that the Jazzār inventory holds only these two works.

There are four works in this section of the inventory that belong to the genre of Prophetic Medicine (*Ṭibb Nabawī*).[64] Unfortunately, only two of these works are identifiable: the first is ʿAlī b. ʿAbd al-Karīm al-Ḥamawī's (d. 720/1320), *Al-Aḥkām al-nabawiyya fī al-ṣināʿa al-ṭibbiyya* (#299), and the second is al-Suyūṭī's *Al-Raḥma fī ṭibb wa-ḥikma* (#302). The other two works are both described with the generic *'Kitāb ṭibb nabawī'* (#300 and #301).

Although *gharīb* and *musnad* works are both foundational genres of the discipline of *ḥadīth*, the inventory includes only one book of the *gharīb al-ḥadīth* genre and one of the *musnad* genre. Because *ḥadīth* collections contain extensive rare vocabulary, lexical works on *ḥadīth* emerged quite early in the history of the discipline. The only example of this genre in the inventory is Ibn Athīr's popular book on the unusual lexical items found in the primary books of *ḥadīth al-Nihāya fī gharīb al-ḥadīth* (#178). The *musnad* genre is another of the earliest and most important genres of *ḥadīth* literature, but, interestingly, the only *musnad* work in the inventory is the prominent Persian *ḥadīth* scholar Abū Nuʿaym's collection of *ḥadīth* transmitted by the founder of the eponymous school of law, Abū Ḥanīfa (#206).

Two or perhaps three works belonging to the genre of invocations attributed to the prophet are found in the inventory. Works of this genre contain invocations taken from the *ḥadīth* and are designed to make a wide range of prayers accessible for the believer to be said in a variety of activities and life events. One of these works, al-Nawawī's *al-Adhkār*, is arguably the all-time most popular work of the genre, and has already been discussed above. Another of these works al-Jazarī's *al-Ḥiṣn al-ḥaṣīn* (#214), is also among the most popular works of the genre. However, the third work would appear to be obscure and is identified only as *'Kitāb Adʿiya wa-aḥādīth'* (#222).

A total of fourteen works in the inventory belong to genres that, while not *ḥadīth* literature, are essentially about the Prophet, or subjects closely related to him, and seem to have been included in this section due to their focus on the Prophet. The *mawlid* genre, consisting of poetry in praise of the Prophet, is among the enduringly most successful genres of Arabic literature, and is well represented in this section of the inventory.[65] The inventory includes six works that, although the ambiguity of their titles makes it impossible to fully identify them, clearly belong to the genre. Most of these works are identified only with different variations of *'Mawlid sharīf'* (#201–203, #318 and #326). In addition to these works of the *mawlid* genre, there are also two commentaries on al-Būṣīrī's famous panegyric, commonly known as the *Burda* (#236 and #279). Although these works contain very little *ḥadīth*, it would seem that they were included in the *al-ḥadīth al-sharīf* section because their content is directly related to the Prophet, and they, thus, fit into an expansive definition of the discipline.

In addition to these *mawlid* works, the inventory includes four works of blessings and prayers for the Prophet. The most famous of these is the renown *Dalāʾil al-khayrāt* of al-Jazūlī (d. 870/1465) (#284). The popular prayer book of Muṣṭafā al-Bakrī (d. 1162/1748) is another (#235). A third work is described only as 'phrases of blessings on the Prophet' (#254). A fourth work is only given the ambiguous title 'the benefits of blessings on the Prophet' (#273).

64 In addition to these there are four other works on Prophetic medicine in the section of the inventory dedicated to *ʿilm al-ṭibb*. For more on these works, see Deborah Schlein's Chapter 23 in this volume.

65 For more on the genre, see Katz, *Birth of the Prophet Muhammad*.

Two works in the inventory treat the subject of the merits of the descendants of the Prophet. Unfortunately, in both cases, the titles are too ambiguous to be further identified and we can only speculate what percentage of their content may have included *ḥadīth*. It is quite possible that they included a substantial percentage of *ḥadīth*, as there are, indeed, many *ḥadīth* on the merits of the Prophet's family. It also seems possible that these works were included in the *al-ḥadīth al-sharīf* section because, similar to the *mawlid* genre, the topic of the Prophet's descendants was considered an extension of the Prophet himself. One work in the inventory clearly treats the subject of the Prophet's genealogy, unfortunately, however, it is only given the ambiguous title '*Shajarat nasab al-Nabī*' (#241).

The *ḥadīth* are, of course, one of the two primary sources of Islamic thought, and as a result are employed as evidence in virtually all the religious disciplines. There are a number of works in the inventory that clearly belong to disciplines other than *ḥadīth*, but do, however, cite some substantial portion of *ḥadīth*. Substantial is, of course, not a very exact term, and the relative quantity of *ḥadīth* these works contain varies considerably. What the works seem to have in common is that *ḥadīth* makes up much of the evidence they employ, and they were perhaps included in this section for that reason. On the other hand, these works might have simply been included by mistake. One also wonders whether some of these titles might have been included in the *ḥadīth* section because they did not easily fit elsewhere in the inventory. In other cases though, such as al-Ghazālī's *Iḥyā'* and *al-Durra al-fākhira*, they would arguably make more sense in another section of the inventory. As can be seen in the table below, these works span a vast range of disciplines and topics from ethics to works on the death of loved ones. As has already been suggested, some of these works may have been included due to their authors' close association with the discipline of *ḥadīth*.

Title	Author	Subject
Shira'at al-Islām ilā dār al-salām	Muḥammad b. Abū Bakr Imām Zāda (d. 573/1178)	Ritual Law and Ethics
Al-Baraka fī faḍl al-sa'ī wa-al-ḥaraka	Muḥammad b. 'Abd al-Raḥmān al-Ḥubayshī (d. 782)	Ethics
Al-Majālisa al-Shāmiyya fī al-mawā'iẓ al-Rūmiyya	'Abd al-Ghanī al-Nābulusī (d. 1143/1731)	Sermons
Kitāb al-Rūḥ	Ibn Qayyim al-Jawziyya (d. 751/1351)	Eschatology
Al-Tadhkār fī afḍal al-adhkār	Al-Qurṭubī (d. 671/1273)	Quranic Studies
Salwān al-muṣāb bi-firqat al-aḥbāb	Mar'ī b. Yūsuf al-Karmī (d. 1033/1624)	On the Death of Loved Ones
Taṣliyat al-ḥazīn bi-mawt al-banīn	Muṣṭafā al-Dahanī	On the Death of Loved Ones
Iḥyā' 'ulūm al-dīn	Al-Ghazālī (d. 505/1111)	Sufism
'Ayn al-'Ilm mukhtaṣar al-Iḥyā'	'Alī al-Qārī (d. 1014/1605)	Sufism
Al-Durra al-fākhira fī 'ulūm al-ākhira	Al-Ghazālī	Eschatology
Al-Faraj ba'd al-shidda	Al-Tanūkhī	Patience
Rabī' al-abrār	Al-Zamakhsharī	Anthology

There are a handful of titles in this section whose presence is difficult to explain. They neither fit into the discipline of *ḥadīth*, nor contain a significant number of *ḥadīth*. Al-Idrīsī's famous work of geography, *Nuzhat al-mushtāq* is a prime example (#253). Another example is al-Ghazālī's *Kimiyā' al-sa'āda*; it is not related to the discipline of *ḥadīth*, and it employs very few *ḥadīth* as evidence (#288). Ibn Sīnā's *Kanz al-asrār*, which deals with cosmology, is another work whose presence in this category is very difficult to explain (#262). I have not included in this category titles that were impossible to identify due to their ambiguity, but whose subject seems rather removed from the discipline of *ḥadīth*, such as the title 'Book on Horsemanship' (#246).

5 The Addendums

It is important to note that there are two addendums to the main body of the inventory of the Jazzār library consisting of two further lists of small collections that seem to have been confiscated from their original owners.[66] These two lists consist of inventories for three libraries. Two small collections were added to the original al-Jazzār library in 1216/1801: the first of these was owned by one ʿAlī Rashīdī the second by one Muḥammad Wakīlkharaj. These two collections consist of a total of seventy-five manuscripts. A third small collection, consisting of ninety-six manuscripts, previously belonging to one Yaḥyā b. Muḥammad al-Tībī was added in 1218/1803. These three collections contain a total of twenty-six books that could be classified under the rubric of '*al-ḥadīth al-sharīf*'. Because these lists comprise such a relatively small addition to the main inventory, they do little to change its profile and many of the titles are duplicates of those in the main body of the inventory. However, these lists do enrich the library and contain some works not found in the main body.

The repetitions of the books in the main body of the inventory primarily consist of popular works of *ḥadīth* including *Ṣaḥīḥ al-Bukhārī* (#520), al-Nawawī's *al-Adhkār* and three commentaries on al-Nawawī's collection of forty *ḥadīth* (#540, #558 and #1674). Ibn Ḥajar's *Nukhbat al-fikr* and Ibn Qayyim al-Jawziyya's, *Kitāb al-rūḥ* (#1673) are also repeated. Although much of the content in these lists is repetitive, there are some noteworthy additions. The lists, for instance, contain one work of post-canonical *ḥadīth* literature: al-Hamdānī's collection of *ḥadīth* he could transmit with only seven links separating him from the Prophet (#546). Similarly, the library of Yaḥyā al-Ṭībī is noted to have contained the geographical work *Ghāyat al-rishād fī aḥādīth al-bilād* (#552). The list of al-Ṭībī's library also contains Ibn Rajab's work on the virtues of the months of the Islamic year *Laṭāʾif al-maʿārif* (#530). Similar to the main body of the inventory, works consisting of prayers for the Prophet and litanies are well represented; they contain, for example, an abridgment of Ibn Mashshīsh's famous litany (#1694), al-Qasṭallānī's *Masālik al-ḥunafā fī al-ṣalāt ʿalā al-Muṣṭafā* (#572) and Tāj al-Dīn al-Subkī's *Wird al-ṣabāḥ* (#565). As in the main inventory, there are also a number of ambiguous titles, such as 'book related to *ḥadīth*' (#1652), and 'book on the description of the Prophet' (#1653).

6 Conclusions, and Comparisons with Contemporaneous Libraries

The preceding analysis suggests that the conception of *al-ḥadīth al-sharīf* that informed the curation of the Jazzār inventory was expansive and eclectic. There was also probably an element of randomness, error or false identification involved in its organisation. The result is an inventory of *ḥadīth* books with some remarkable contrasts and juxtapositions. It includes two copies of an anti-Shiite polemic and a commentary on a Shiite scholar's forty *ḥadīth* collection. Three copies of an eighteenth-century eschatological work alongside a twelfth-century work of world geography. The works listed in the inventory are also remarkable in their geographical diversity. It contains works produced by authors hailing from Morocco, Egypt, Syria, Iraq, Iran, Sicily, Central Asia, the Hijaz, Yemen and India. The breadth of its chronology is also noteworthy, containing works produced in the third/ninth century up to the decade before the formation of the collection.

66 For more on these lists, see Said Aljoumani's Chapter 2 in this volume.

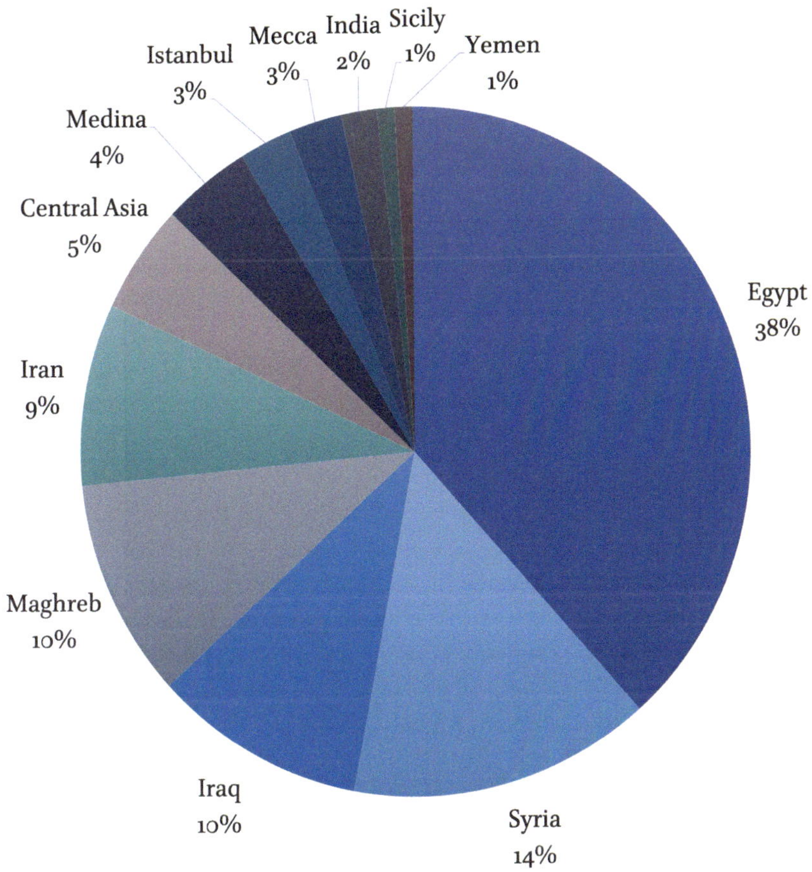

FIGURE 15.1
Geographical Distribution of Authors

Any general conclusions about the *al-ḥadīth al-sharīf* section of the Jazzār library should, however, be tempered by the fact that much about the formation of the library is unknown to us. We have essentially no information about how the collection was curated nor about how the inventory was composed. We are further disadvantaged by the fact that the inventory was composed some twenty years after the library was founded. It is significant that during the process of researching this book, our team of authors randomly discovered several *ḥadīth* works that bear the endowment statement of 1197/1783 and the endowment seal but are not included in the inventory. These 'orphan' manuscripts appear to have been removed in the period of instability between the founding of the library and the composition of the inventory. This, of course, means that the inventory is not a complete account of the original library's holdings but is missing an unknown number of manuscripts from the original *ḥadīth* holdings. There is, for instance, a copy of Zakariyyā al Anṣārī's commentary on al-Bukhārī with the Jazzār stamp and endowment notice, now held in the Süleymaniye, that is not listed in the inventory. It is, therefore, quite possible that certain books that are noted as incomplete in the inventory were originally complete. The size of the *al-ḥadīth al-sharīf* section of the inventory would suggest that it is not missing a very large percentage of the original *ḥadīth* manuscripts, yet, we cannot be sure.

We are fortunate to have the inventories of several roughly contemporaneous collections to provide a useful backdrop against which to view the *ḥadīth* holdings of the Jazzār inventory. The closest of these inventories chronologically is that of the library of the *madrasa-takiyya* built by the Egyptian Mamluk Amīr, Muḥammad Bey Abū al-

Dhahab (d. 1189/1775), in Cairo. Completed in 1774, the complex was undertaken by Abū al-Dhahab, while serving as the Ottoman governor of Egypt from 1773–1775.[67] Situated next to the main entrance of al-Azhar Mosque and overlooking al-Ḥusayn Square, the complex inhabits prime Cairo real estate and was the major project of Abū al-Dhahab's career. The endowment document for the complex is some 110 pages long and includes what seems to be a complete inventory of the library endowed to the complex. It is worth noting that al-Jazzār and Abū al-Dhahab were part of the same cultural network and are connected in various ways. Perhaps most significantly, they were both mamluks of ʿAlī Bey and would have had a similar educational and cultural background. They are also united by their interactions with the renown *ḥadīth* scholar and lexicographer Murtaḍa al-Zabīdī (d. 1205/1791). Abū al-Dhahab famously purchased a copy of al-Zābīdī's *Tāj al-ʿArūs* for his library for 100,000 silver dirhams.[68] Al-Jazzār is noted to have been extraordinarily devoted to al-Zābīdī. According to al-Bayṭar, al-Jazzār wore a letter that al-Zābīdī sent him around his neck as an amulet. Al-Bayṭar also notes that whenever al-Jazzār received a visitor from Egypt, he would ask them about al-Zabīdī, if they responded positively, he would bring them closer and honour them generously. If, on the other hand, they spoke ill of al-Zabīdī, he would distance them and exclude them from his court and its generosity.[69]

The Abū al-Dhahab inventory, with 498 titles and 1004 volumes, is markedly smaller than the Jazzār collection, with the section on *ḥadīth* in the inventory containing entries for 97 titles in some 212 volumes. In spite of their difference in size, the two collections have much in common, including many of the same particularities and seem to have been based on a quite similar understanding of the boundaries of the discipline of *ḥadīth*. The inventories are, however, different in some significant ways. The Abū al-Dhahab inventory is a strikingly more complete collection of primary *ḥadīth* books. It is also less diverse in some ways. Upon comparison, one of the first similarities is that the two inventories both begin with the *ḥadīth* canon. *Ṣāḥīḥ al-Bukhārī* is the first book mentioned in the Abū Dhahab inventory, but, in contrast to the Jazzār inventory, it is followed by the remainder of the Six Books including Ibn Majah. The extent to which the copies of the canonical works in Abū Dhahab's inventory are complete is also noteworthy. There are five complete copies of Bukhārī in ten volumes and the other five canonical books are all present in one complete copy. After the entries on the canon, the Abū Dhahab inventory catalogues six complete copies of *al-Jāmiʿ al-ṣaghīr*, then its three copies of *al-Shifāʾ*. In the Jazzār inventory, its six copies of *al-Shifāʾ* come first, then its single copies of al-Tirmidhī's *Sunan* and *Shamāʾil*, and then al-Suyūṭī's *al-Jāmiʿ al-ṣaghīr*. The contrast between the complete and incomplete statuses of the Abū Dhahab and al-Jazzār sections dedicated to the *ḥadīth* canon causes one to wonder if the Jazzār holdings on the *ḥadīth* canon would have been similarly complete when it was originally established.

The similarities in the organisation of the two inventories breaks down after the entries on *al-Shifāʾ*. One conspicuous difference is that the Abū al-Dhahab inventory is significantly more organised than al-Jazzār's with most of the books belonging to a genre or subdiscipline listed together. Following the entries on *al-Shifāʾ*, for instance, the Abū al-Dhahab inventory lists a cluster of various other *sīra* books together. The majority of the *ḥadīth* commentaries are also listed together, although a group of another four commentaries are haphazardly attached to the end of the list. In terms of content, *ḥadīth* commentary is noticeably better represented in Abū al-Dhahab's inventory. While the al-Jazzār inventory has only partial commentaries on Bukhārī and Muslim, the Abū al-Dhahab inventory lists six complete commentaries on al-Bukhārī, two on Muslim, one on al-

67 ʿAlī Bāshā al-Mubārak, *al-Khiṭaṭ*, v, 237–246.
68 Crecelius, "Waqf", 69.
69 Al-Bayṭār, *Ḥilyat al-bashar*, 1504.

Tirmidhī, and various others. The genre of *Uṣūl al-ḥadīth* is also much better represented in the Abū al-Dhahab inventory. The Jazzār inventory has only two works of the genre, while Abū al-Dhahab has six. One interesting further point of contrast between the two inventories is that while the Jazzār inventory includes five *mawlid*s, Abū al-Dhahab has none. Books of prayers and invocations are also noticeably absent from the *ḥadīth* section of Abū al-Dhahab's inventory. Another striking point of contrast is the absence of *Dalāʾil al-khayrāt* and its commentaries from the Abū al-Dhahab inventory. This is significant because, as noted above, the *Dalāʾil* is one of the most popular works in the Jazzār inventory, containing one copy of the *Dalāʾil* and four copies al-Fāsī's commentary *Maṭāliʿ al-masarrāt*. Forty *ḥadīth* works are another interesting point of comparison between the two inventories. Al-Jazzār's inventory has seven forty *ḥadīth* collections, and three commentaries on forty *ḥadīth* collections. The Abū al-Dhahab inventory has a number of commentaries on forty *ḥadīth* collections, for example, it has nine copies of Ibn Ḥajar's commentary on an unspecified forty *ḥadīth* collection but does not list any forty *ḥadīth* collection independent of commentary.[70] Other works of post-canonical *ḥadīth* literature are similarly absent from the Abū al-Dhahab inventory, but as has been seen above, such works are represented in the Jazzār inventory.

Their differences aside, the two inventories have much in common. *Sīra* literature is quite popular in both. The Abū al-Dhahab inventory has six copies of *al-Sīra al-Ḥalabiyya*, while Jazzār has four. There are four copies of *al-Mawāhib al-Ladūniyya* in the Abū al-Dhahab inventory, and two in the Jazzār inventory. The Abū al-Dhahab inventory has much more extensive holdings in *ḥadīth* commentary, but there is a considerable overlap between the two. Devotional poems in praise of the Prophet are popular in both collections. Ibn Marzūq's commentary on the *Burda*, is present in both, as is Ibn Ḥajar al-Haythami's commentary on the Hamziyyah. Interestingly, both inventories include al-Ghazālī's *Iḥyāʾ* in the *ḥadīth* section. The *ḥadīth* section of Abū al-Dhahab's inventory, similar to the Jazzār inventory, includes some fairly eclectic titles, such as al-Būnī's (d. 622/1225) famous occult work, *Shams al-maʿārif*. The two inventories are generally similar in many regards, their contours, however, noticeably diverge in a number of areas. The Jazzār inventory is, on the whole, more eclectic and diverse, and has more unique and somewhat rare titles, while the Abū al-Dhahab inventory seems more carefully curated and organised, with a focus on primary works of *ḥadīth*, including the *ḥadīth* canon, *sīra* literature, *uṣūl al-ḥadīth* and their commentaries.

There are other inventories that can be used to provide further perspective. The inventory of the Rāgıb Paşa library, composed in 1209/1795, is generally quite similar to the Jazzār library inventory. Although, similar to the Abū al-Dhahab inventory, it is conspicuously more focused on primary *ḥadīth* works, and its coverage of commentary literature is much more complete. It is also much less diverse than the Jazzār inventory. The inventory of the library that the Amīr of Mecca, Sharīf ʿAbd al-Muṭṭallib b. Ghālib (d. 1303/1886), endowed to the Ḥaram of Mecca in 1278/1862 provides another useful point of comparison.[71] A rough comparison of this inventory, consisting of ninety-four entries composed some fifty years after the Jazzār inventory, yields results not very different than the comparison to the Abū al-Dhahab inventory. It has slightly better coverage of the *ḥadīth* canon than the Jazzār inventory but is also missing the *sunan*s of Abū Dāwūd and al-Nasāʾī. It has a better coverage of extra-canonical works with an incomplete copy of the *Musnad* of Aḥmad b. Ḥanbal and a copy of the *Muwaṭṭāʾ*.[72] It has a number of works of devotional poetry in praise of the Prophet, including an unspecified commentary on the *Burda*,

70 It is also not entirely clear which Ibn Ḥajar is meant.

71 Ḥāfiẓ, *Kutub al-Sharīf ʿAbd al-Muṭṭallib*.

72 Ibid., 64.

as well as commentaries on *al-Hamziyya*.[73] Akin to the Jazzār inventory, it has one copy of a *mawlid*, as well as the prayer booklet, *al-Ḥiṣn al-ḥaṣīn*.[74] Additionally, much the same as the Jazzār inventory, various genres of post-canonical literature are represented.[75] One fundamental difference between the two inventories is that no part of the Sharīf ʿAbd al-Muṭṭallib inventory follows any organisational scheme.

In sum, the Jazzār inventory is quite similar to roughly contemporaneous inventories of *ḥadīth* books and does not go very far outside the general outlines of comparable collections. Yet, it does differ in a number of fairly conspicuous ways and seems to have been based on slightly different concerns. By comparison, it emerges as slightly less focused on the *ḥadīth* canon, more devotional and somewhat more eclectic. We can only speculate, but some of the differences, especially regarding its diversity, may be partially explained by the fact that it is roughly twice the size of the other inventories. It is also not entirely clear how the discovery of further 'orphaned' manuscripts might change any conclusions about the contours of the Jazzār inventory. Of the seventy manuscripts that have been found, some 17 (roughly 25 per cent) are not in the inventory. Seventy manuscripts are a small sample, but if this was true for the entirety of the library, then the section might look considerably different. Nevertheless, the inventory provides a fascinating reflection, if fractured, of what the contours of a collection of *al-ḥadīth al-sharīf* could look like in this period.

Bibliography

Al-Barzinjī. *Al-Ishāʿa*, edited by Ḥusayn Muḥammad ʿAlī Shukrī. Jedda: Dār al-Minhāj, 1426/2005.

ʿAlī Bāshā al-Mubārak. *Al-Khiṭaṭ al-tawfiqiyya al-jadīda*. Cairo, 2014.

Al-Bayṭār. *Ḥilyat al-bashar fī tārīkh al-qarn al-thālith ʿashar*, edited by Muḥammad al-Bayṭār. Damascus, 1961.

Brown, Jonathan. *Hadith: Muhammad's Legacy in the Medieval and Modern World*. Oxford, 2009.

Burak, Guy. "Collating The Signs of Benevolent Deeds: Muḥammad Mahdī al-Fāsī's Commentary on Muḥammad al-Jazūlī's Dalā'il al-Khayrāt and Its Ottoman Readers." *Philological Encounters* 4 (2019): 135–157.

Cook, David. "Messianism in the Mid-11th/17th Century as Exemplified by al-Barzanjī (1040–1103/1630/1691)." *Jerusalem Studies in Arabic and Islam* 33 (2007): 261–278.

Cornell, Vincent J. *Realm of the Saint*. Austin, 1998.

Crecelius, David. "The Waqf of Muhammad Bey Abu Al-Dhahab in Historical Perspective." *International Journal of Middle East Studies* 23, no. 1 (1991): 57–81.

Davidson, Garrett. *Carrying on the Tradition. A Social and Intellectual History of Hadith Transmission Across a Thousand Years*. Leiden, 2020.

Al-Fāsī, Muḥammad al-Mahdī. *Maṭāliʿ al-masarrāt bi-jalāʾ Dalāʾil al-khayrāt*, edited by Aḥmad ʿAbd al-ʿĀl. Casablanca, 2005.

Al-Fāsī, Muḥammad al-Mahdī. *Al-Ilmāʾ bi-baʿḍ man lam yudhkar fī mumtiʿ al-asmāʾ*, edited by ʿAbd al-Majīd al-Khayālī. Beirut, 1432/2011.

Al-Fāsī, Muḥammad al-Mahdī. *Mumtiʿ al-asmāʾ fī dhikr al-Jazūlī wa-al-Tibāʿ wa-mā lahumā min al-atbāʿ*. Fez, 1313/1895.

Al-Fāsī, Muḥammad al-Mahdī. *Al-Nabdha al-yasīra wa-al-khaṭīra fī masʾala khalq afʿāl al-ʿibād al-shahīra*, edited by Maḥjūba al-ʿUwayna. Tunis, 1442/2021.

Al-Ghazī, Muḥammad b. ʿAbd al-Raḥmān. *Diwān al-Islām*, edited by Ḥasan Sayyid Kasrawī. Beirut, 1411/1990.

Göktaş, Recep Gürkan. "On the Hadith Collection of Bayezid II's Palace Library." In *Treasures of Knowledge: An Inventory of the Ottoman Palace Library (1502/3–1503/4)*, edited by Gülru Necipoğlu, Cemal Kafadar and Cornell Fleischer, 309–340. Leiden, 2019.

Ḥāfiẓ, Al-Ḥājj Muḥammad. *Kutub al-Sharīf ʿAbd al-Muṭṭallib b. Ghālib allatī waqafahā ʿalā maktabat al-Ḥaram al-Makkī*, edited by Al-Sharīf Ibrāhīm b. Manṣūr al-Hāshimī al-Amīr. Beirut, 1443/2022.

73 Ibid., 70.
74 Ibid., 82, 72.
75 Ibid., 73, 74, 83.

Ḥajjī Khalīfa, Muṣṭafā b. ʿAbd Allāh. *Kashf al-ẓunūn*, edited by Ekmeleddin İhsanoğlu/Bashshār ʿAwwāf Maʿrūf. London, 1443/2021.

Hirschler, Konrad. *Medieval Damascus: Plurality and Diversity in an Arabic Library Catalogue*. Edinburgh, 2016.

Ibn al-Ṣalāḥ. *ʿUlūm al-ḥadīth*, edited by Nūr al-Dīn ʿItr. Damascus, 1425/2004.

Ivanyi, Katharina Anna. *Virtue, Piety, and the Law: A Study of Birgivi Meḥmed Efendi's Al-Ṭarīqa al-Muḥammadiyya*. Leiden, 2020.

Katz, Marion. *The Birth of the Prophet Muhammad: Devotional Piety in Sunni Islam*. London, 2009.

Mayeur-Joauen, Catherine. "There Is Matter for Thought." In *The Presence of the Prophet in Early Modern and Contemporary Islam*, edited by Denis Gril, Stefan Reichmuth and Dilek Sarmis, 115–150. Leiden, 2021.

Al-Muḥibbī, Muḥammad Amīn b. Faḍl Allāh. *Khulaṣạt al-āthar fī aʿyān al-qaran al-ḥādī ʿashar*, edited by Muṣṭafā Wahbī. Cairo, 1284/1867.

Al-Murādī, Muḥammad Khalīl. *Silk al-durar fī aʿyān al qarn al-thānī ʿashar*. Beirut, 1408/1988.

Al-Qāḍī ʿIyāḍ b. Mūsā. *al-Shifāʾ fī ḥuqūq al*-Muṣṭafā, edited by ʿAbduh ʿAlī Kūshak. Damascus.

Şen, Gül. *Making Sense of History: Narrativity and Literariness in the Ottoman Chronicle of Naima*. Leiden, 2022.

Al-Shāmī, ʿAbd al-Laṭīf. *al-Duʿā bi-asmāʾ Ahl al Badr*. Cairo, 2017/1439.

Yaycıoğlu, Ali. "Guarding Traditions and Laws. Disciplining Bodies and Souls: Tradition, Science, and Religion in the Age of Ottoman Reform." *Modern Asian Studies* 52, no. 5 (2018): 1542–603.

The Noble Ḥadīth Books

[141] ***Bukhārī sharīf*** (complete in 30 volumes), AUTHOR: Muḥammad b. Ismāʿīl al-Bukhārī (d. 256/870), EDITION: Cairo: al-Maṭbaʿa al-Amīriyya 1313/1895.

[142] ***Bukhārī sharīf*** (Complete), see #141.

[143] *The Seventh Volume of Ṣaḥīḥ al-Bukhārī*. Obviously the same as the two above, it is, however, interesting that he calls this incomplete volume *Ṣaḥīḥ al-Bukhārī* as opposed to *Bukhārī sharīf*.

[144] ***Irshād al-ṣārī***, AUTHOR: Aḥmad b. Muḥammad al-Qasṭallānī (d. 923/1517), EDITION: Ibrāhīm b. ʿAbd al-Ghaffār Dusūqī, Cairo: al-Maṭbaʿa al-Amīriyya, 1284/1868.

[145] ***Irshād al-ṣārī*, see #144**

[146] ***Irshād al-ṣārī*, see #144.**

[147] ***Fatḥ al-bārī***, AUTHOR: Ibn Ḥajar al-ʿAsqalānī (d. 852/1449), EDITION: Cairo: Maktabat wa-Maṭbaʿat Muṣṭafā al-Bābī al-Ḥalabī, 1378/1959.

[148] ***Fatḥ al-bārī***, see #147.

[149] ***Fatḥ al-bārī***, see #147.

[150] ***Fatḥ al-bārī***, AUTHOR: Same as #147. MANUSCRIPT: Based on the description and the presence of the Jazzār stamp, it appears that this manuscript is housed in the Library of Najāḥ University in Nablus, MS, NL 211508.

[151] ***Sharḥ Mukhtaṣar al-Bukhārī lil-Ajhūrī***, AUTHOR: Nūr al-Dīn al-Ajhūrī (d. 1066/1656). This is al-Ajhūrī's commentary on Ibn Abī Jamra's (d. 675/1277) abridgment of the *Ṣaḥīḥ*. The work does not seem to be published. There are numerous extant manuscripts.

[152] ***Ṣaḥīḥ Muslim*** (second volume), AUTHOR: Muslim b. al-Ḥajjāj (d. 261/875), EDITION: Istanbul; al-Maṭbaʿa al-ʿĀmira, 1329–1334/1911–1916.

[153] ***Ṣaḥīḥ Muslim*** (second volume), AUTHOR: Same as #152.

[154] ***Sharḥ al-Bukhārī lil-Kirmānī*** (second volume), AUTHOR: Muḥammad b. Yūsuf al-Kirmānī (d. 786/1384), EDITION: *al-Kawākib al-darārī fī sharḥ Ṣaḥīḥ al-Bukhārī*, Cairo: Al-Maṭbaʿa al-Bahiyya al-Miṣriyya, 1356/1937.

[155] ***Shifāʾ sharīf***, AUTHOR: al-Qāḍī ʿIyāḍ (d. 544/1149), EDITION: *al-Shifā fī ḥuqūq al-muṣṭafā*, ʿAbduh ʿAlī Kūshak, Damascus: Dār al-Fayhāʾ, 1442/2021.

[156] ***Shifāʾ sharīf***, see #155.

[157] ***Shifāʾ sharīf***, see #155.

[158] ***Shifāʾ sharīf***, see #155.

[159] ***Shifāʾ sharīf***, see #155.

[160] ***Shifāʾ sharīf***, see #155.

[161] ***Shamāʾil sharīfa***, AUTHOR: Probably Jalāl al-Dīn al-Suyūṭī (d. 911/1505). The title is ambiguous, but al-Suyūṭī's *al-Jāmiʿ al-ṣaghīr* has a section with this title that was sometimes copied as a

separate text. Given the popularity of al-Suyuṭī's works in this inventory, it seems a definite possibility.

[162] ***Jāmiʿ al-ḥāfiẓ al-Tirmidhī***, AUTHOR: Muḥammad b. ʿĪsā al-Tirmidhī (d. 279/892). Also commonly known as *Sunan al-Tirmidhī*, EDITION: ʿAbd al-Wahhāb ʿAbd al-Laṭīf, ʿUthmān ʿAbd al-Raḥmān Muḥammad, Medina: al-Maktaba al-Salafiyya, 1384/1965.

[163] ***Al-Jāmiʿ al-ṣaghīr***, AUTHOR: Jalāl al-Dīn al-Suyūṭī, (d. 911/1505), EDITION: ʿAbbās Aḥmad Ṣaqr, Aḥmad ʿAbd al-Jawwād, Damascus: Dār al-Fikr, 1994/1414.

[164] ***Arbaʿīn ḥadīth***, unidentified. The title 'Forty *ḥadīth*' is too generic to identify.

[165] ***Arbaʿīn ḥadīth***, unidentified. The title 'Forty *ḥadīth*' is too generic to identify.

[166] ***Arbaʿīn ḥadīth***, unidentified. The title 'Forty *ḥadīth*' is too generic to identify.

[167] ***Arbaʿīn ḥadīth***, unidentified. The title 'Forty *ḥadīth*' is too generic to identify.

[168] ***Arbaʿīn ḥadīth***, unidentified. The title 'Forty *ḥadīth*' is too generic to identify.

[169] ***Arbaʿīn ḥadīth***, unidentified. The title 'Forty *ḥadīth*' is too generic to identify.

[170] ***Al-Mawāhib al-ladūniyya***, AUTHOR: al-Qasṭallānī (d. 923/1517), EDITION: *al-Mawāhib al-ladūniyya bi-al-minaḥ al-muḥammadiya*, Ṭāhā ʿAbd al-Raʾūf Saʿd, Saʿd Ḥasan Muḥammad ʿAlī, Cairo: al-Maktaba al-Azhariyya, 1438/2017.

[171] ***Al-Mawāhib al-ladūniyya*** (first volume), see #170.

[172] ***al-Maṣābīḥ***, AUTHOR: al-Ḥusayn b. Masʿūd al-Baghāwī (d. 516/1122), EDITION: Yūsuf al-Marʿashlī, Muḥammad Salīm Samāra, Jamāl Ḥamdī al-Dhahabī, Beirut: Dār al-Maʿrifa, 1408/1987.

[173] ***Sharḥ al-Mashāriq***, unidentified. This may be a commentary on al-Qaḍī ʿIyāḍ's compilation of *ḥadīth Mashāriq al-anwār*, however, without any further information is impossible to identify.

[174] ***Shiraʿat al-Islām*** *ilā dār al-salām*, AUTHOR: Muḥammad b. Abū Bakr Imām Zāda (d. 573/1177), EDITION: Muḥammad Nāẓim Nadawī, Beirut: Dār al-Bashāʾir al-Islāmiyya, 1428/2007.

[175] ***Al-Ishāʿa*** *fī ashrāṭ al-sāʿa*, AUTHOR: Muḥammad b. ʿAbd al-Rasūl al-Barzanjī al-Ḥusaynī (d. 1103/1691), EDITION: Ḥasan Muḥammad ʿAlī Shukrī, Jedda: Dār al-Minhāj, 1426/2005.

[176] ***Al-Ishāʿa*** *fī ashrāṭ al-sāʿa*, see #175.

[177] ***Al-Ṣāwāʿiq al-muḥriqa***, AUTHOR: Ibn Ḥajar al-Haythamī (d. 974/1566), EDITION: *Al-Ṣāwāʿiq al-muḥriqa ʿalā ahl al-rafḍ wa-ḍalāl wa-zandaqa*, edited by ʿAbd al-Raḥmān b. ʿAbd Allāh al-Turkī, Kāmil Muḥammad al-Kharrāṭ, Beirut: Muʾassasat al-Risāla, 1418/1998.

[178] ***Al-Nihāya fī gharīb al-ḥadīth***, AUTHOR: Ibn Athīr (d. 606/1210), EDITION: Ṭāhir Aḥmad Zāwī; Maḥmūd Muḥammad Ṭanāḥī, Cairo: Dār Ihyā al-Kutub al-ʿArabiyya, 1383/1963.

[179] ***Sīrat al-Ḥalabī*** (two volumes), AUTHOR: Burhān al-Dīn ʿAlī b. Ibrāhīm al-Ḥalabī (d. 1044/1634), EDITION: *Insān al-ʿUyūn bi-sīrat al-Amīn al-Maʾmūn*, edited by Aḥmad Zaynī Dahlān, Cairo: al-Maṭbaʿa al-ʿĀmira, 1296/1875.

[180] ***Sīrat al-Ḥalabī***, (two volumes).

[181] ***Sīrat al-Ḥalabī***, (two volumes).

[182] ***Sīrat al-Ḥalabī***, (A part of).

[183] ***Al-Ṣāwāʿiq al-muḥriqa***, see #177.

[184] ***Tawḍīḥ mā khafā min alfāẓ al-Shifāʾ***, AUTHOR: Shams al-Dīn Muḥammad b. Muḥammad al-Ḥijāzī (d. 894/1489).

[185] ***Khulāṣat al-akhbār fī dhikr al-Nabī al-mukhtār***, AUTHOR: Maḥmūd al-Uskudārī (d. 1038/1626). There is a slight variation in the title, but this would seem to be the *Khulāṣat al-akhbār fī aḥwāl al-nabī al-mukhtār*.

[186] ***Al-Ishrāf fī faḍāʾil al-ashrāf***, AUTHOR: ʿAlī b. Aḥmad al-Samhūdī (d. 911/1505), EDITION: Ḥusayn Muḥammad ʿAlī Shukrī, Beirut: Dār al-Kutub al-ʿIlmiyya, 1440/2019, MANUSCRIPT: Khālidī Library in Jerusalem, MS 1125.

[187] ***Maṭāliʿ al-masarrāt***, AUTHOR: Muḥammad al-Mahdī b. Aḥmad al-Fāsī (d. 1109/1698), EDITION: *Maṭāliʿ al-masarrāt bi-jalāʾ Dalāʾil al-khayrāt*, edited by Abū al-Saʿūd Effendi, Cairo: Maṭbaʿat Wādī al-Nīl, 1289/1872.

[188] ***Maṭāliʿ al-masarrāt***, see #187.

[189] ***Al-Khulāṣa fī maʿrifat al-ḥadīth***, AUTHOR: Sharaf al-Dīn-Ṭībī (d. 734/1334), EDITION: Abū

ʿĀṣim al-Shawāmī al-Atharī, Cairo: Al-Maktaba al-Islāmiyya, 1430/2009, MANUSCRIPT: Library of Université Saint-Jospeh in Beirut, MS USJ 2 00214.

[190] ***Maṭāliʿ al-masarrāt***, see #187.

[191] ***Al-Ishāʿa fī ashrāṭ al-sāʿa***, see #175.

[192] ***Al-Tadhkār bī aṭyab al-adhkār***, AUTHOR: Al-Qurṭubī (d. 671/1273), EDITION: *Al-Tadhkār fī afḍal al-adhkār*, edited by Muḥammad Amīn al-Khānjī, Cairo: Maktabat al-Khānjī, 1355/1936.

[193] ***Al-Bayān wa-tawḍīḥ tarājim rijāl al-ḥadīth***, AUTHOR: Aḥmad b. ʿAbd al-Raḥīm al-ʿIrāqī's (d. 806/1403). This would seem to be al-ʿIrāqī's (d. 806/1403) *al-Bayān wa-tawḍīḥ li-man ukhrija lahu fī al-Ṣaḥīḥ wa-qad muss bi-ḍarb min al-tajrīh*. EDITION: Kamāl Yūsuf Ḥūt, Beirut: Dār al-Jinān, 1410/1990. MANUSCRIPT: Library of the American University of Beirut, MS 920.05.

[194] ***Al-Adhkār***, AUTHOR: Al-Nawawī (d. 676/1277), EDITION: Jedda: Dār al-Minhāj, 1442/2021.

[195] ***Al-Adhkār***, see #194.

[196] ***Al-Adhkār***, see #194.

[197] ***Al-Adhkār***, see #194.

[198] ***Sharḥ al-Arbaʿīn lil-Miṣrī***, unidentified. The title 'commentary of forty *ḥadīth*' and the author, 'the Egyptian' are far too generic to identify this work.

[199] ***Sharḥ al-Arbaʿīn***, unidentified. The title 'commentary of forty *ḥadīth*' is too generic to identify this work.

[200] ***Sharḥ al-Arbaʿīn* lil-ʿĀmilī**. This is a fairly generic title, but it may be a commentary on the forty *ḥadīth* of the Shiite scholar Bahāʾ al-Dīn Muḥammad b. Ḥusayn al-ʿĀmilī (d. 1031/1622).

[201] ***Mawlid sharīf***, unidentified. The title is too generic to identify this work.

[202] ***Mawlid sharīf li-Ibn Ḥajar***, AUTHOR: Ibn Ḥajar al-Haythamī (d. 974/1566).

[203] ***Mawlid sharīf wa-yalihi rasāʾil***, unidentified. The title is too generic to identify this work.

[204] ***Sīrat al-Nabī***, unidentified. The title is too generic to identify this work.

[205] ***al-Zawājir***, AUTHOR: Ibn Ḥajar al-Haythamī (d. 974/1567), EDITION: *al-Zawājir ʿan ʿuqubat ahl al-kabāʾir*, Cairo: al-Maṭbaʿa al-Wahhābiyya, 1291/1875.

[206] ***Musnad Abī Nuʿaym***, AUTHOR: Abū Nuʿaym al-Isfahānī (d. 430/1038). It is not entirely clear from the title, but this would seem to be Abū Nuʿaym's *Musnad al-Imām Abī Ḥanīfa*. EDITION: Naẓar Muḥammad al-Fariyābī, Riyadh: Maktabat Kawthar, 1415/1994.

[207] ***Al-Iṣāba fī asmāʾ al-ṣaḥāba***, AUTHOR: Ibn Ḥajar al-ʿAsqalānī (d. 852/1449), EDITION: *Al-Iṣāba fī tamyīz al-ṣaḥāba*, edited by Ikrām Allāh Imdād al-Ḥaqq, Beirut: Dār al-Bashāʾir al-Islāmiyya, 1416/1996.

[208] ***al-Iḥyāʾ lil-Ghazālī***, AUTHOR: Abū Ḥāmid al-Ghazālī (d. 505/1111). EDITION: *Iḥyāʾ ʿUlūm al-Dīn*, Jedda: Dār al-Minhāj, 1436/2015.

[209] ***Sharḥ Nukhbat al-fikr***, AUTHOR: Ibn Ḥajar al-ʿAsqalānī (d. 852/1449), EDITION: *Nuzhat al-naẓar fī tawḍīḥ Nukhbat al-fikr*, edited by Ṭāriq b. ʿIwaḍ Allāh Muḥammad, Cairo: Dār al-Māʾthūr, 1432/2011.

[210] ***Al-Dirāya fī al-ḥadīth***. This might be Ibn Ḥajar's *al-Dirāya fī aḥādīth al-Hidāya*, EDITION: ʿAbd Allāh Hāshim al-Madanī, Beirut: Dār al-Maʿrifa, 1408/1988.

[211] ***Al-Budūr al-sāfira***, AUTHOR: Al-Suyūṭī (d. 911/1505), EDITION: *al-Budūr al-sāfira fī aḥwāl al-ākhīra*, edited by Muḥammad Ḥasan Muḥammad, Beirut: Dār al-Kutub al-ʿIlmiyya, 1416/1996.

[212] ***Al-Durra al-fākhira fī ʿulūm al-ākhira***, AUTHOR: Abū Ḥāmid al-Ghazālī (d. 505/1111), EDITION: *Al-Durra al-fākhira fī kashf ʿulūm al-ākhira*, edited by Lucian Gauthier, Beirut: Al-Maktaba al-Thaqāfiyya, 1417/1997, MANUSCRIPT: Leipzig, Universitätsbibliothek, Vollers 118.

[213] ***Maṭāliʿ al-masarrāt***, see #187.

[214] ***Al-Ḥiṣn al-ḥaṣīn***, AUTHOR: al-Jazarī (d. 833/1429), EDITION: Cairo: n.p., 1862.

[215] ***Sharḥ al-Ḥiṣn al-ḥaṣīn***, AUTHOR: ʿAlī al-Qārī (d. 1014/1605), EDITION: Mecca: al-Maṭbaʿa al-Mīriyya, 1305/1886, MANUSCRIPT: National Library of Israel, MS. AP Ar. 258.

[216] ***Aḥādīth al-Kashāf***, AUTHOR: Jamāl al-Dīn al-Zaylaʿī (d. 762/1361). This would seem to be al-Zaylaʿī's *takhrīj* of al-Zamakhsharī's *al-Kashshāf*.

[217] ***Rabīʿ al-abrār lil-Zamakhsharī***, AUTHOR: Maḥmūd b. ʿUmar al-Zamakhsharī (d. 583/1188), EDITION: ʿAbd al-Majīd Diyāb, Ramaḍān ʿAbd

al-Tawwāb; Muḥammad ʿAlī Qurna, Cairo: al-Hay'ah al-Miṣrīyah al-ʿĀmmah lil-Kitāb, 1412/1992.

[218] ***Sharḥ al-Ḥamziyya li-Ibn Ḥajar***, AUTHOR: Ibn Ḥajar al-Haythamī (d. 974/1566), EDITION: *al-Minaḥ al-Makkiyya Sharḥ fī al-Ḥamziyya*, edited by Bassām Muḥammad Bārūd, Abu Dhabi: al-Mujammaʿ al-Thaqāfī, 1418/1998, MANUSCRIPT: Jerusalem, National Library of Israel, Ms. Temp. Ar. 186.1.

[219] ***Sharḥ al-Ḥamziyya li-Ibn Ḥajar***, see #218.

[220] ***Sharḥ al-maḥyā***, unidentified. I was unable to find a title matching this.

[221] ***Ḥashiya ʿalā al-Targhīb lil-Burhān* al-Dīn**, AUTHOR: Burhān al-Dīn al-Ḥalabī (d. 1044/1634), MANUSCRIPT: most probably British Library, MS Or. 4706.

[222] ***Kitāb Adʿiya wa-aḥādīth***, unidentified. The title is too generic to identify.

[223] ***Kitāb al-Muʿjizāt al-bāhira***. This would seem to be *al-Muʿjizāt al-bāhira wa-al-kamālāt al-ẓāhira* of Mūsā b. Muḥammad al-Ghawṭī (d. 1118/1706).

[224] ***Al-Manjam fi al-muʿjam lil-Suyūṭī***, AUTHOR: al-Suyūṭī (d. 911/1505), EDITION: Ibrāhīm Bājis ʿAbd al-Majīd, Beirut: Dār Ibn Ḥazm, 1415/1995.

[225] ***Al-Majālisa al-Shāmiyya fī al-mawāʿiẓ al-Rūmiyya***, AUTHOR: ʿAbd al-Ghanī al-Nābulusī (d. 1143/1731).

[226] ***Faḍā'il Āl al-Bayt***, unidentified. The title is too generic to identify

[227] ***Kitāb fi Bayān al-aḥādīth***, unidentified. The title is too generic to identify.

[228] ***Al-fawz al-ʿaẓīm***, AUTHOR: Jalāl al-Dīn al-Suyūṭī (d. 911/1505), EDITION: Masʿad ʿAbd al-Ḥamīd al-Saʿdanī, Muḥammad Fāris, Beirut: Dār al-Kutub al-ʿIlmiyya, 1414/1994.

[229] ***Sidrat al-muntahā***, The title is ambiguous and there are a number of titles beginning with *Sidrat al-muntahā*. However, *Kashf al-ẓunūn* includes a work identified only as *Sidrat al-muntahā fī al-ḥadīth*, and this may be the same work (Ḥajjī Khalīfa, *Kashf al-ẓunūn*, 4:321).

[230] ***Bahjat al-nufūs***, AUTHOR: Ibn Abī Jamra (d. 675/1277), EDITION: Tawfīq Maḥmūd Takla, Amman: Dār al-Rayāḥīn, 1444/2023.

[231] ***Ṣafḥat al-bayt***, unidentified. I was unable to find a match for this title.

[232] ***Kitāb nawʿ min al-aḥādīth***, unidentified. I was unable to find a match for this title.

[233] ***Ikhtiyār al-ulā fī sharḥ ḥadīth ikhtaṣam al-malā' al-ʿalā***, AUTHOR: Ibn Rajab al-Ḥanbalī (d. 795/1393), EDITION: Bashīr Muḥammad ʿUyūn, Damascus: Dār al-Bayān, 1405/1985.

[234] ***Kitāb asmā' al-ruwāt***, unidentified. The title is too generic to identify.

[235] ***Kitāb Wird al-saḥar wa-ṣalawāt al-Bakrī***, AUTHOR: Muṣṭafā al-Bakrī (d. 1162/1748).

[236] ***Sharḥ al-Barā' li-Ibn Marzūq***, This would seem to be the *Iẓhār ṣidq al-muwada fi sharḥ Qasidat al-Burda* of Muḥammad b. Aḥmad al-Marzūq (d. 842/1349), Edition: Bilāl Muḥammad Ḥatim al-Saqā, Damascus: Dār al-Taqwā, 1442/2021.

[237] ***Dalā'il al-nubuwwa***, AUTHOR: Abū Bakr al-Bayhaqī (d. 458/1066), EDITION: ʿAbd al-Muʿṭī Qalaʿjī, Beirut: Dār al-Kutub al-ʿIlmiyya, 1408/1988.

[238] ***Al-Ṭarīqa al-muḥammadiyya***, AUTHOR: Mehmed Birgivī (d. 981/1573), EDITION: Muḥammad Raḥmat Allāh Ḥāfiẓ Muḥammad Nāẓim al-Nadawī, Damascus: Dār al-Qalam, 1432/2011.

[239] ***Aḥādīth sharīfa wa-ijāzāt ṣarīḥa***, unidentified. The title is too generic to identify.

[240] ***Kitāb al-nafahāt al-saniyya***, unidentified.

[241] ***Kitāb shajarat nasab al-Nabī***, unidentified. The title is too generic to identify.

[242] ***Kitāb al-rūḥ***, AUTHOR: Ibn Qayim al-Jawziyya (d. 751/1351), EDITION: Muḥammad Ajmal Ayūb al-Iṣlāḥī, Kamāl Muḥammad Qālamī, Mecca: Dār ʿĀlam al-Fawā'id, 1432/2011.

[243] ***Al-Baraka fī faḍl al-saʿī wa-al-ḥaraka***, AUTHOR: Muḥammad b. ʿAbd al-Raḥmān al-Ḥubayshī (d. 782/1381), EDITION: Cairo: Maktabat al-Khānjī, 1353/1935.

[244] ***Al-Luṭf***, unidentified. The title is too generic to identify.

[245] ***Kitāb al-ʿUẓma***. Both Abū al-Shaykh al-Iṣbahānī (d. 369/979) and Ibn al-ʿArabi (d. 638/1240) have books by this title.

[246] ***Kitāb taʿallum al-furūsiyya***, unidentified. The title is too generic to identify.

[247] ***Riyāḍ al-janna***. This seems to be the *Riyāḍ al-janna fī āthār ahl al-sunna* of ʿAbd al-Baqī b. ʿAbd al-Baqī al-Baʿlī (d. 1071/1661), EDITION: An abridgement of this work was published by Yāsīn al-Fadānī, Damascus: Dār al-Baṣā'ir, 1405/1985.

[248] ***Khayr al-bishar***, AUTHOR: Ibn Ẓafar al-Siqillī (d. 567/1172), EDITION: Cairo: n.p. 1863.

[249] ***Al-Fawā'id fī ṣilat al-ʿawā'id***. This would seem to be Shihāb al-Dīn al-Sharajī's (d. 893/1448) *al-Fawā'id wa-al-ṣilat wa-al-ʿawā'id*, EDITION: Cairo: al-Maṭbaʿa al-ʿĀmira al-Malījyya, 1330/1911.

[250] ***ʿAyn al-ʿilm mukhtaṣar al-Iḥyā'***, AUTHOR: Muḥammad b. ʿUthmān al-Balkhī (d. 830/1426), EDITION: Istanbul: n.p. 1291/1874.

[251] ***Riyāḍ ahl al-janna***. This would seem to be an alternate title of #247 above.

[252] ***Riyāḍ al-ṣāliḥīn***, AUTHOR: Al-Nawawī (d. 676/1277), EDITION: Shuʿayb al-Arna'ūṭ, Beirut: Mu'assasat al-Risāla, 1419/1998.

[253] ***Nuzhat al-mushtāq***, AUTHOR: Muḥammad b. ʿAbd Allāh al-Idrīsī (d. 560/1166), EDITION: *Nuzhat al-mushtāq wa-ikhtirāq al-āfāq*, Cairo; Maktabat al-Thaqāfa al-Dīniyya, 2002/1422.

[254] ***Ṣiyagh ṣalawāt***, unidentified. The title is too generic to identify.

[255] ***Ḥayat al-qulūb***, unidentified. The title is too generic to identify. Both Muḥammad b. al Ḥusayn al-Isnawī (d. 764/1363) and ʿAbd al-Bārī b. Ṭurkhān al-Sunūnī (d. 936/1530) have works by this title.

[256] ***Ḥalīat al-Khafqānī***, unidentified. I was unable to find a close match for this title.

[257] ***Nafahāt al-ʿawārif***. unidentified. I was unable to find a close match for this title.

[258] ***Al-Durr al-munaẓẓam***, AUTHOR: Al-Suyūṭī (d. 911/1505), EDITION: *Al-Durr al-munaẓẓam fī ism Allāh al-Aʿẓam*, edited by ʿĀṭif Ismāʿīl Muḥsin, Cairo: Burṣat al-Kutub, 1434/2013.

[259] ***Salwat al-ka'īb bi-wafat al-ḥabīb***, AUTHOR: Ibn Nāṣir al-Dimashqī (d. 842/1439), EDITION: Ṣāliḥ Yūsuf Maʿtūq, Cairo: Dār al-Buḥūth, 1421/2001.

[260] ***Asmā' ahl al-Badr***, unidentified. The title is too generic to identify.

[261] ***ʿAqīla wa-Ḥamziyya wa-mawāhib wa-rasā'il***. This is a composite text consisting of works by multiple authors; the *Ḥamziyya* mentioned is well-known poem by al-Būṣīrī's (d. 696/1294), *al-Mawāhib* is probably *al-Mawāhib al-ladūniyya* of al-Qasṭallānī (d. 923/1517).

[262] ***Kanz al-asrār***, AUTHOR: Ibn Sīnā (d. 427/1037). It would seem this is Ibn Sīnā's *Kanz asrār fī istiḥḍār al-jinn wa-ṣarf al-ʿamār*, EDITION: Farīdī Abū Salāfa, Beirut: al-Maktaba al-ʿIlmiyya al-Falakyya, 2002.

[263] ***Rawḍat al-ʿulamā'***, unidentified. The title is too generic to identify with certainty. Both al-Ḥusayn b. Yaḥyā al-Zandawaystī (d. 400/1009) and Aḥmad b. Maḥmūd al-Ghaznawī (d. 593/1197) have works by this title.

[264] ***Al-lubāb lil-Suyūṭī***, AUTHOR: Al-Suyūṭī (d. 911/1505), EDITION: *Lub al-lubbāb fī taḥrīr al-ansāb*, edited by Pieter Jahannes Veth, Baghdad: Maktabat al-Muthanā, 1383/1964.

[265] ***Al-Durr al-mustaṭāb***, AUTHOR: al-ʿImādī (d. 1171/1758), EDITION: *Al-Durr al-mustaṭāb fī muwāfaqāt ʿUmar b. al-Khaṭṭāb wa-Abī Bakr wa-ʿAlī Abī Turāb*, edited by Muṣṭafā ʿUthmān, Beirut: Dār al-Kutub al-ʿIlmiyya, 1417/1996.

[266] ***Maṭlaʿ al-nayrayn***. This would seem to be the *Maṭlaʿ al-nayrayn al-mukhtaṣar min al-ṣaḥīḥayn* of ʿAbd al-ʿAzīz b. Raḍwān al-Ḥanbalī.

[267] ***Kitāb fī madḥ al-Nabī***, unidentified. The title is too generic to identify.

[268] ***Kitāb fī faḍl Āl al-Bayt wa-al-ṣaḥāba***, unidentified. The title is too generic to identify.

[269] ***Kanz al-adkhār***, unidentified. I was unable to find a close match for this title

[270] ***Ḥuṣūl al-rifq***, AUTHOR: Al-Suyūṭī (d. 911/1505), EDITION: *Ḥuṣūl al-rifq bi-uṣūl al-rifq*, edited by ʿAbd al-Qādir Aḥmad ʿAbd al-Qādir, Damascus: Dār al-Wathā'iq lil-Dirāsāt wa-al-Ṭabʿ wa-al-Nashr wa-al-Tawzīʿ, 1429/2008.

[271] ***Muntahā al-ʿuqūl***, AUTHOR: Al-Suyūṭī (d. 911/1505), EDITION: *Munhtahā al-ʿuqūl fī muntahā al-naqūl*, Cairo: n.p., 1276/1860.

[272] ***Taṣliyat al-ḥazīn bi-mawt al-banīn***, AUTHOR: Muṣṭafā al-Dahanī, this does not seem to have been published.

[273] ***Fawāʾid al-ṣalat ʿalā al-nabī***, unidentified. The title is too generic to identify.

[274] ***Al-Fawāʾid fī ṣilat al-ʿawāʾid***, unidentified. I was unable to find a close match for this title.

[275] ***Nuzhat al-abṣār***. A number of titles begin with the *Nuzhat al-abṣār*. Ḥājjī Khalīfa (*Kashf al-ẓunūn*, 7:393) notes one work with this title on the subject of *ḥadīth* (*fī al-ḥadīth*) by one Abū ʿAbd Allāh Muḥammad b. Muḥammad al-Faḍāʾilī; I was unable to find an extant copy.

[276] ***Al-Rawḍ al-unuf***, AUTHOR: ʿAbd al-Raḥmān al-Suhaylī (d. 581/1114), EDITION: *Al-Rawḍ al-unuf fī tafsīr ma ashtamal ʿalayhi al-Sīra al-nabawiyya li-Ibn Hishām*, edited by ʿAbd al-Salām b. Sahqrūn, Cairo: Maṭbaʿa al-Jamāliya, 1331/1913, MANUSCRIPT: Dublin, Chester Beatty Library, Ar. 3294.

[277] ***Maʿārij al-nubuwwa***, AUTHOR: Mullā Miskīn Muʿīn al-Dīn al-Farāhī (d. 907/1501), EDITION: *Maʿārij al-nubuwwa-wa-madārij al-futuwwa*, Kanpur, India: Munshī Nawal Kishūr, 1887.

[278] ***Faḍl al-jalad bi-wafāt al-walad***, AUTHOR: al-Suyūṭī (d. 911/1505), EDITION: ʿAbd al-Qādir Aḥmad ʿAbd al-Qādir, Kuwait: Maktabat al-Sundus, 1409/1989.

[279] ***Sharḥ al-baraʿ***. This may be the same spelling error that is found in #236 above, in which case, this would be a commentary on the Burda.

[280] ***Al-Riyāḍ al-anīqa***, AUTHOR: al-Suyūṭī (d. 911/1505), EDITION: *Al-Riyāḍ al-anīqa fi sharḥ asmāʾ khayr al-khalīqa*, edited by Muḥammad Saʿīd b. Basyūni Zaghlūl, Beirut: Dār al-Kutub al-ʿIlmiyya, 1405/1985.

[281] ***Thabat Muḥammad b. al-Ṭayyib al-Madanī lil-aḥādīth al-musalsala***, AUTHOR: Muḥammad b. al-Ṭayyib al-Madanī (d. 1170/1756). This would seem to be his *Irsāl al-asānīd wa-iṣāl al-muṣannafāt wa-al-masānīd*. There are two known manuscripts of this work, Mecca MS 735 and Medina MS 538.

[282] ***Al-Ṭarīqa al-Muḥammadiyya***, see #238.

[283] ***Mushkil al-Ṣaḥīḥayn***, AUTHOR: Ibn al-Jawzī's (d. 597/1116). This is most probably the Iraqī scholar Ibn al-Jawzī's (d. 597/1116) work on the problematic *ḥadīth* in the *Ṣaḥīḥ*s of al-Bukhārī and Muslim, *Kashf al-mushkil min al-Ṣaḥīḥayn*, EDITION: ʿAlī Ḥusayn Bawwāb, Riyadh: Dār Waṭan, 1417/1997.

[284] ***Dalāʾil al-khayrāt***, AUTHOR: Muḥammad al-Jazūli (c. 869/1465).

[285] ***Al-Araj fī al-faraj***, AUTHOR: al-Suyūṭī (d. 911/1505), EDITION: Aḥmad ʿUbayd, Damascus: al-Maktaba al-ʿArabiyya, 1350/1932.

[286] ***Fawāʾid al-āyāt***, unidentified. The title is too generic to identify.

[287] ***Al-Wasāʾil ilā maʿrifat al-awāʾil***. This would seem to be al-Suyūṭī's *al-Wasāʾil ilā musāmirat al-awāʾil*, EDITION: Asʿad Ṭalas, Baghdad: Maṭbaʿat al-Najāḥ, 1369/1950.

[288] ***Kimiyāʾ al-saʿada***, AUTHOR: Al-Ghazālī (d. 505/1111), EDITION: Muḥyī al-Dīn Ṣabrī al-Kurdī, Cairo: Maṭbaʿat al-Saʿāda, 1924.

[289] ***Al-Faraj***, AUTHOR: Abū ʿAlī al-Tanūkhī (d. 384/394). The title given is ambiguous, but this might be al-Tanūkhī's *al-Faraj baʿd al-shidda*.

[290] ***Ḥilyat al-abrār***, AUTHOR: Al-Nawawī (d. 676/1277). This is al-Nawawī's collection of prophetic supplications commonly known as *al-Adhkār*, see entries #194–197 above.

[291] ***Marāṣid al-maṭāliʿ***, AUTHOR: al-Suyūṭī (d. 911/1505), EDITION: *Marāṣid al-maṭāliʿ fī tanāsab al-maqāṭiʿ*, edited by ʿAbd al-Muḥsin b. ʿAbd al-ʿAzīz al-ʿAskar, Jedda: Dār al-Minhāj, 1426/2005.

[292] ***Salwān al-maṣāb bi-firqat al-aḥbāb***, AUTHOR: Marʿī b. Yūsuf al-Karmī (d. 1033/1624), EDITION: Ibrāhīm Ismāʿīl al-Qāḍī, Cairo: Dār al-Ḥaramayn, 1420/1999.

[293] ***Kitāb ṭīb al-kalām***, AUTHOR: al-Samhūdī (d. 911/1505), EDITION: *Ṭīb al-kalām bi-fawāʾid al-salām*, edited by Abū Ḥamza Anwar b. Abī Bakr al-Shaykī al-Dāghistānī, Jedda: Dār al-Minhāj, 1430/2009.

[294] ***Kitāb al-mahrajān***, unidentified. I was unable to find a close match for this title.

[295] ***Wasiyat Yazīd b. al-Ḥakam***, unidentified, I was unable to find a close match for this title.

[296] ***Kitāb Faḍāʾil al-shuhūr***, unidentified. The title is too generic to identify.

[297] ***Al-Risāla al-wajīza***, unidentified. The title is too generic to identify.

[298] *Kitāb lil-ʿAynī wa-Miʿrāj al-Ajhūrī*. The first title in this composite volume, 'Kitāb lil-ʿAynī', is too generic to identify. The title in the volume would seem to be al-Ajhūrī's al-*Nūr al-Wahhāj fī al-kalām ʿalā al-Isrāʾ wa-al-miʿrāj*, EDITION: Beirut: Dār al-Kutub al-ʿIlmiyya, 1424/2003.

[299] ***Al-Aḥkām al-nabawwiyya fī al-ṣināʿa al-ṭibbiyya***, AUTHOR: ʿAlī b. ʿAbd al-Karīm al-Ḥamawī (d. 720/1320), EDITION: Cairo: Maṭbaʿat Muṣṭafā al-Bābī al-Ḥalabī wa-awlāduhu, 1374/1955.

[300] ***Kitāb Ṭibb Nabawwī***, unidentified. The title is too generic to identify.

[301] ***Kitāb Ṭibb Nabawwī***, unidentified. The title is too generic to identify.

[302] ***Al-Raḥma fī ṭibb wa-al-ḥikma***, AUTHOR: Al-Suyūṭī (d. 911/1505), EDITION: Cairo: Maṭbaʿat Muṣṭafā al-Bābī al-Ḥalabī wa-awlāduhu, n.d.

[303] ***Majmūʿ ḥadīth***, unidentified. The title is too generic to identify.

[304] ***Majmūʿ rasāʾil li-al-ʿallāma al-Atharī al-maʿrūf bi-Ibn ʿAqīla al-Makkī***. This is a composite manuscript consisting of works composed by Muḥammad b. Aḥmad Ibn ʿAqīla (d. 1150/1738).

[305] ***Majmūʿ fīhi Kashf al-asrār wa-rasāʾil thalātha***, unidentified. The title is too generic to identify.

[306] ***Majmūʿ rasāʾil***, unidentified. The title is too generic to identify.

[307] ***Majmūʿ fawāʾid wa-rasāʾil***, unidentified. The title is too generic to identify.

[308] ***Majmūʿ faḍāʾil al-shuhūr***, unidentified. The title is too generic to identify.

[309] ***Majmūʿ fawāʾid***, unidentified. The title is too generic to identify.

[310] ***Majmūʿ yashtamal ʿalā thalātha rasāʾil al-waṣf al-dhamīm wa-al-qawl al-sadīd wa-faḍl al-kilālb***. Composite manuscript consisting of three titles. 1. *al-Waṣf al-dhamīm, which is likely the al-Waṣf al-dhamīm fī fiʿl al-laʾīm* of Shams al-Dīn al-Anṣārī al-Ḥanafī; 2. ***Al-Qawl al-sadīd*** may be ʿAlī b. Aḥmad al-Manīnī's catalogue of personal chains of transmission, *al-Qawl al-sadīd fī ittiṣāl al-asānīd*; 3. ***Faḍl al-Kilāb***. This would seem to be *Faḍl al-kilāb ʿalā kathīr min man labis al-thiyāb* of Muḥammad b. Khalf al-Marzabān (d. 309/902).

[311] ***Bushrā al-kaʾīb fī liqāʾ al-ḥabīb***, AUTHOR: Al-Suyūṭī (d. 911/1505), EDITION: ʿAbd al-Ḥamīd Muḥammad Darwīsh, Damascus: Dār Yaʿrab, 1425/2003. MANUSCRIPT: al-Azhar Library, MS 83318.

[312] ***Kitāb adʿiʾa wa-adhkār***, unidentified. The title is too generic to identify.

[313] ***Sīrat al-anbiyaʾ li-ʿAbd al-ʿAzīz***, unidentified. The title is too generic to identify.

[314] ***Nahj al-balāgha***, AUTHOR: al-Sharīf al-Raḍī (d. 406/1015), EDITION: Tabriz: n.p. 1248/1832.

[315] ***Nahj al-balāgha***, see #314.

[316] ***Sharḥ Nahj al-balāgha***. This is too ambiguous to identify with any certainty, but may by the commentary of Ibn Abī al-Ḥadīd (d. 656/1258).

[317] ***Nahj al-balāgha***, see #314.

[318] ***Mawlid al-Nabī***, unidentified. The title is too generic to identify.

[319] ***Ḥamāʾil sharīf***, unidentified. The title is too generic to identify.

[320] ***Al-Burhān fī ʿalāmāt mahdī ākhar al-zamān***, AUTHOR: ʿAlī b. Ḥusām al-Dīn al-Muttaqī al-Hindī (d. 975/1567), EDITION: ʿAlī Akbar al-Ghaffārī, Qom: Maṭbaʿat al-Khiyyām, 1399/1979.

[321] ***Masāʾil ʿAbd Allāh b. al-Salām***, unidentified. The title is too generic to identify. There are a number of works that narrate the questions that ʿAbd al-Salām reportedly asked the Prophet, but it is impossible to know which one this is.

[322] ***Al-Durra al-munīfa fī al-sīra al-sharīfa***, AUTHOR: ʿAlī b. ʿAbd al-Wāḥid al-Sijilmāsī (d. 1057/1647).

[323] ***Masāʾil al-rāḥib wa-al-raḥbān***, unidentified. The title is too generic to identify.

[324] ***Al-Arbaʿīn ḥadīthā lil-Nawawī***, AUTHOR: al-Nawawī (d. 676/1277), EDITION: Maḥmūd al-Arnāʾūṭ, ʿAbd al-Qādir al-Arnāʾūṭ, Beirut: Dār Ibn Kathīr, 1986/1406.

[325] ***Al-Nafḥa al-saniyya min baʿd al-aḥādīth al-qudsiyya***, unidentified. I could not find a close match for this title.

[326] ***Mawlid al-Nabī***, unidentified. The title is too generic to identify.

[327] ***Muqaddima fī nuzūl sayyidina ʿĪsā***, unidentified. The title is too generic to identify.

[328] ***Miʿrāj al-Nabī***, unidentified. The title is too generic to identify.

[329] ***Miʿrāj al-Nabī***, AUTHOR: Najm al-Dīn al-Ghayṭī (d. 983/1575) Cairo: al-Maktaba al-Tijāriyya al-Kubra, 1356/1937.

[330] ***Ashraf al-wasāʾil fī ajwabat al-sāʾil***, unidentified. I could not find a close match for this title.

CHAPTER 16

The Section on Islamic Law (*fiqh*)

Ahmed El Shamsy

A library is the product of a process of collection. When we lack direct information about the aims and methods that guided this process, we can attempt to infer them by analysing the contents of the library and speculatively tracing them back to identifiable principles of collection. Delving into the history of a particular library in this manner, we might expect to discern something like one of these simplified logics undergirding its collection: (1) the logic of availability, giving rise to a library that contains whatever materials were available via purchase or through other modes of acquisition, such as requisition or looting; (2) the logic of demand, yielding a collection dictated by the needs of its intended audience, such as introductory texts for use by students of a *madrasa* beginning their studies; and (3) the logic of curation, in which works were chosen for inclusion because of their perceived value, whether artistic, historical, intellectual or religious. Each logic entails a higher degree of purposefulness than its predecessor in the list. All three are ideal types; the actual process of collection in any given case is likely to have involved a mixture of two or even all three of them.

The section entitled *Fiqh* (Islamic law) in the handwritten inventory of the holdings of the Jazzār library in Acre is, with its more than two hundred entries, the second largest category. This is not particularly surprising. Law has been a key field of Islamic scholarship since the second/eighth century. It has dominated instruction in *madrasa*s since the institution's inception in the fifth/eleventh century,[1] and is abundantly represented in Muslim bibliographic works[2] and the holdings of other Muslim libraries through the ages.[3]

Almost none of the actual manuscripts of legal works from the Jazzār library have been located so far. One volume of a work on Shāfiʿī law is now in the National Library of Israel.[4] Another work, a Ḥanafī commentary, is held in the Chester Beatty Library in Dublin.[5] A third manuscript, still held in the Jazzār library, was identified as belonging to the law section but is, in fact, a work on *ḥadīth* rather than law.[6] Finally, a manuscript of a legal work that is today held in the Azhar library in Cairo contains the Jazzār library's endowment statement but is not mentioned in the inventory.[7]

Ninety-one of the legal works listed can be identified as belonging to the tradition of the Ḥanafī school of law. Another fifty-one are Shāfiʿī works, while the other two Sunnī schools, those of Mālik and Aḥmad b. Ḥanbal, are represented by seven works and a single work, respectively. Eleven works in the list reflect the Imāmī school of law; the collection, thus, contained more Shīʿī legal works than it did Mālikī and Ḥanbalī works combined. Thirty-nine works, accounting for twenty percent of the

1 See, for example, Makdisi, *The Rise of Colleges*.

2 See Ibn al-Nadīm, *al-Fihrist*; Ḥājjī Khalīfa, *Kashf al-ẓunūn*.

3 See Hirschler, *A Monument to Medieval Syrian Book Culture*, ch. 5; Hirschler, *Medieval Damascus*; El Shamsy, "Islamic Book Culture"; Taşkömür, "Books on Islamic Jurisprudence"; Bedir, "Books on Islamic Legal Theory".

4 ʿAbd al-Raḥīm al-Isnawī, *Muhimmāt* (#416 in the inventory), MS NLI 990034841250205171.

5 Ḥusām al-Dīn al-Rāzī, *Sharḥ al-Jāmiʿ al-ṣaghīr* (#438): Dublin, Chester Beatty Library, Ar. 3316.

6 *Jamʿ al-jawāmiʿ*, MS 1 (ʿAṭāʾ Allāh, *Fihris ʿAkkā*, 1983) = #377. This is not al-Subkī's famous work on legal theory but rather al-Suyūṭī's work on *ḥadīth*, also known as *al-Jāmiʿ al-kabīr*.

7 Bahāʾ al-Dīn al-ʿĀmilī, *Zubdat al-uṣūl*, MS Azhar 91135.

DOI:10.1163/9789004720527_018

law collection, remain unidentified, either because they lack titles or because their titles cannot be matched to known works. The following sections, corresponding to groups of works, describe the contents of the law collection as portrayed in the inventory.

1 Ḥanafī Law

The largest single group of works in the collection consisted of 'general' works on Ḥanafī law, by which I mean books that cover the full range of the usual topics addressed by the genre of *fiqh*: ritual law, interpersonal law, penal law, law of warfare and so on. Eleven of these works are all based on the single-volume compendium *Kanz al-daqāʾiq* authored by the Central Asian jurist Abū al-Barakāt al-Nasafī (d. ca. 710/1310). Two are copies of the base text (#336 and #337 in the inventory), and the other nine are commentaries on it (#338–342, #348, #444, #575 and #1637). Eight entries refer to works closely connected to al-Marghinānī's (d. 593/1197) *Hidāya*, the most important and authoritative Ḥanafī manual of the post-classical period: one complete copy, one incomplete copy and three incomplete commentaries (#332–335 and #343). In addition, the list contains a copy of an abridgement of the *Hidāya*, al-Maḥbūbī's (d. 673/1273–1274) *Wiqāyat al-riwāya fī masāʾil al-riwāya* (#353), and a gloss on a commentary on that text (#354), as well as what was probably a collection of the *ḥadīth* found in the *Hidāya*, *Naṣb al-rāya li-aḥādīth al-Hidāya* (#470). Four of the works listed are connected to al-Shurunbulālī's (d. 1069/1659) primer *Nūr al-īḍāḥ*; three consist of the base text and one is an eighteenth-century commentary (##355, #356, #358 and #361).

The oldest self-standing legal texts in the inventory are two copies of the *Mukhtaṣar* of al-Qudūrī (d. 428/1037) (#359 and #360). The collection also contained two copies of the work of Ibn al-Sāʿātī (d. 694/1294–1295) (#349 and #350), which draws on al-Qudūrī as one of its two main sources. Two texts are related to one of the founders of the Ḥanafī school, al-Shaybānī (d. 187/805): an abridgement of his *al-Jāmiʿ al-kabīr* by al-Khallāṭī (d. 652/1254) (#454 and #490) and a commentary on his *al-Jāmiʿ al-ṣaghīr* by Ḥusām al-Dīn al-Rāzī (d. 598/1201–1202) (#438). Characteristically Anatolian Ottoman (*Rūmī*) Ḥanafī works are almost absent from the collection. There is only one copy of Mullā Husrev's (d. 885/1480) famous *al-Durar wa-al-ghurar* (#331), and no copy of Badr al-Dīn Simawnā's (d. 823/1421) *Jāmiʿ al-fuṣūlayn*.[8]

Many of the collection's works covered only part of the range of *fiqh* topics. The *Muqaddima* of Aḥmad al-Ghaznawī (d. 593/1197) treats ritual law (*ʿibādāt*) (#420, #453 and #538). There is a cluster of works around al-Kāshgharī's (d. 705/1305–1306) *Munyat al-muṣallī*, which focuses on the law of prayer (#362–370 and #524); the cluster includes two copies of the basic teaching pamphlet of about a dozen folios and eight commentaries on the text. Two books cover Ḥanafī inheritance law: Maḥāsin al-Qaysarī's (fl. eighth/fourteenth century) versified *Jāmiʿ al-durar* (#462) and Yūnus al-Rashīdī's (fl. 1010/1601) *al-Maqāṣid al-saniyya* (#491), both based on Sirāj al-Dīn al-Sijāwandī's (d. ca. 600/1204) *al-Sirājiyya*. Several works address the details of the pilgrimage. The list includes one copy of Raḥmat Allāh al-Sindī's (d. 993/1585) *Jamʿ al-manāsik*, the longest of his treatises on pilgrimage (#489), and five copies of Mullā ʿAlī al-Qārī's (d. 1014/1605–1606) *al-Maslak al-mutaqassiṭ* (#411–414 and #507), which is a commentary on al-Sindī's mid-length work on pilgrimage (*Lubāb al-manāsik*); one of these five copies is a Turkish translation. Another work, entitled *Aḥkām al-awqāf* and probably written by Abū Bakr al-Khaṣṣāf (d. 261/874) (#408), delves into the details of religious endowments, while two works survey Ḥanafī procedural law: ʿAlāʾ al-Dīn al-Ṭarabulsī's (d. 844/1440 or 1) *Muʿīn al-ḥukkām* (#468) and Muḥyī al-Dīn al-Kāfiyajī's (d. 879/1474) *Sayf al-quḍā ʿalā al-bughā* (#455).

8 Taşkömür, "Books on Islamic Jurisprudence", 395.

The inventory also features a work on legal maxims, with the characteristic title *al-Ashbāh wa-al-naẓāʾir* (#352), probably written by the Ḥanafī Ibn Nujaym (d. 970/1563). A work belonging to the related but more playful genre of legal riddles (*alghāz*), aimed at scholarly entertainment, is Ibn al-Shiḥna's (d. 921/1515) *al-Dhakhāʾir al-ashrafiyya* (#371). Two works are monographs focusing on specific subjects: a book by ʿAbd al-Ghanī al-Nabulsī (d. 1143/1731), *Kitāb Īḍāḥ al-dalālāt fī samāʿ al-ālāt* (#474), addresses the permissibility of musical instruments, and ʿAlī b. Ghānim al-Maqdisī's (d. 1004/1596) *Radʿ al-rāghib ʿan al-jamʿ fī ṣalāt al-raghāʾib* (#396) argues that the popular 'prayer of great rewards' performed at the onset of the month of Rajab has no precedent in prophetic practice and is, therefore, a blameworthy innovation.[9]

Finally, some of the books listed are connected to the Ḥanafī tradition but not legal in terms of their content. These include the purported testament (*waṣiyya*) of the school's eponym, Abū Ḥanīfa (d. 150/767)—a pseudepigraphic work containing a creedal statement (#500); another work that, in spite of a misspelled title, is probably the *Kitāb al-Kasb* of Abū Ḥanīfa's student al-Shaybānī (#393), which discusses the ethical dimensions of earning a livelihood;[10] and two defences of Abū Ḥanīfa, one written by al-Malik al-Muʿaẓẓam Sharaf al-Dīn al-Ayyūbī (d. 624/1227), the Ayyubid ruler of Damascus and nephew of Saladin (#405),[11] and another whose author is uncertain (#397).[12]

9 On this phenomenon, see Talmon-Heller/Ukeles, "The Lure of a Controversial Prayer".

10 Bonner, "The *Kitāb al-Kasb* Attributed to al-Shaybānī".

11 The book specifically challenges the criticisms of Abū Ḥanīfa that al-Khaṭīb al-Baghdādī (d. 463/1071) had collected in his *Tārīkh Baghdād*.

12 The inventory appears to name al-Ghazālī as the work's author, but Abū Ḥāmid al-Ghazālī is not known to have written such a work, nor is it conceivable that he would have done so. The work could be ʿAbd al-Nabī al-Kankūhī's (d. 991/1583) *Radd ṭaʿn al-Qaffāl al-Marwazī ʿalā al-imām Abī Ḥanīfa*.

2 Shāfiʿī Law

The legal school with the second largest representation is the Shāfiʿī school, with almost sixty entries. The most extensive works found in the inventory—though the library, in fact, held only parts of them—are al-Māwardī's (d. 450/1058) *al-Ḥāwī sharḥ mukhtaṣar al-Muzanī* (#465), of which the library had only a single volume,[13] and al-Isnawī's (d. 772/1370–1371) *Muhimmāt* (#415 and #416),[14] of which three volumes are listed (the published edition contains ten volumes). The inventory also includes a part of al-Shīrāzī's (d. 476/1083) *al-Muhadhdhab* (#423) and a volume of al-Ghazālī's (d. 505/1111) mid-length commentary on the *Muhadhhab, al-Wasīṭ* (#437).

Many of the Shāfiʿī works named in the inventory are teaching texts and commentaries on such texts. The most common Shāfiʿī work on the list—represented by two complete and three incomplete copies—is al-Nawawī's *Minhāj al-ṭālibīn* (#383–386 and #401) a single-volume text that became the most authoritative Shāfiʿī manual of the post-classical period;[15] the list also includes four fragments of commentaries on or abridgements of this work (#387, #388, #418 and #1667). A text of similar authority, a single-volume commentary by Zakariyyā al-Anṣārī (d. 926/1520) on his own work, *Tuḥfat al-ṭullāb bi-sharḥ Taḥrīr tanqīḥ al-lubāb*, appears once (#477). The second most common text is the experimental pedagogical work of Ibn al-Muqriʾ (d. 837/1433), *ʿUnwān al-sharaf* (#372–374 and #501), 'a basic teaching text on law that—when read in columns rather than across lines—contains four other discrete texts on poetic metre, poetic rhyme, history, and grammar'.[16] Three works are connected to the bare-bones teaching

13 However, the list mentions only a work titled *al-Ḥāwī*, so this could also be the Ḥanbalī work of the same name by al-ʿAbdalyānī (d. 684/1285).

14 A commentary on al-Nawawī's *Rawḍat al-ṭālibīn* and al-Rāfiʿī's *Fatḥ al-ʿazīz*.

15 El Shamsy, "The *Ḥāshiya* in Islamic Law".

16 El Shamsy, *Rediscovering the Islamic Classics*, 38–39.

text of Abū Shujāʿ's (fl. fifth/eleventh century) *al-Ghāya wa-al-taqrīb*; one is a complete commentary (*al-Iqnāʿ*) and two are fragments of commentaries (#409, #452 and #1642). Two entries refer to *Sittīn masʾala* by Aḥmad al-Zāhid al-Miṣrī (d. 819/1416), a pamphlet of just a few pages that covers the basics of Islamic ritual law, and a further entry is devoted to a commentary on this work (#450, #505 and #506). A similarly basic work is *al-Zubad* by Aḥmad b. Raslān (d. 844/1440), a versified primer on Shāfiʿī law with a short creedal introduction and a conclusion on Sufism (#449 and #450). The inventory also includes the short Shāfiʿī text *Shubbāk al-munāsakhāt* by Aḥmad b. al-Hāʾim (d. 815/1412) (#1660).

More specialised Shāfiʿī works in the collection include commentaries on the didactic poem of 176 lines on inheritance law by Muḥammad al-Raḥbī al-Mutaqanna (d. 577/1182) entitled *al-Raḥbiyya* (#504, #493 and #1677); a work on legal maxims, *Qawāʿid al-aḥkām* (#410), written by the Shāfiʿī scholar ʿIzz al-Dīn b. ʿAbd al-Salām (d. 660/1262—though this could also be a general work on Imāmī law by al-ʿAllāma al-Ḥillī; see below); and at least five works on legal theory, of which at least four were authored by Shāfiʿīs. These are a fragment of al-Ghazālī's *Mustaṣfā*[17] (#480); al-Ghazālī's less known early work *al-Mankhūl* (the entry incorrectly reads *al-Mutaḥawwil*) (#469); Tāj al-Dīn al-Subkī's basic teaching text on legal theory, entitled *Jamʿ al-jawāmiʿ* (#499); ʿAḍud al-Dīn al-Ījī's (d. 756/1355) commentary on Ibn al-Ḥājib's (d. 646/1249) *Sharḥ muntahā al-sūl* (#497); and a 'text on legal theory' without a title or the author's name.

17 In the entry only the title is given, so this work could also be Abū al-Barakāt al-Nasafī's Ḥanafī law commentary *al-Mustaṣfā fī sharḥ al-Nāfiʿ*, published in three volumes in the edition of Ḥasan Özer and Muḥammad Jābā (Istanbul: Maktabat al-Irshād, 2017).

3 Mālikī Law

The general Mālikī works recorded in the inventory consist of a basic teaching text by Muḥammad al-Bashshār (fl. 1161/1748), *Ashal al-masālik* (#498); the popular pamphlet *al-ʿAshmāwiyya* (#508), which lays out the basics of ritual law; and a short commentary on *al-ʿAshmāwiyya*[18] (#483). The inventory also mentions two works on Mālikī inheritance law, Sirāj al-Dīn al-Mālikī's (d. 842/1438–1439) *Tuḥfat al-rāʾiḍ fī al-farāʾiḍ* (#494) and what is probably Abū al-Barakāt al-Daljimūnī al-Wafāʾī's (fl. 1079/1668) *Jāmiʿ al-ṭuruqāt* (#1670). Finally, it lists Abū Ṭālib al-Ṭarṭūshī's (d. 608/1211) *Taḥrīr al-maqāl*, which addresses the law pertaining to persons with reduced legal capacity (#452).

4 Ḥanbalī Law

The only confirmed Ḥanbalī legal work in the inventory is Shams al-Dīn Muḥammad b. Yūsuf al-Qūnawī's (d. 788/1386) *Durar al-biḥār* (#422). A further work identified as Ḥanbalī, *Muntahā al-maṭlab* (#502), is probably a miscategorised Shīʿī work (see below), and another entry, *al-Ḥāwī* (#465), probably refers not to the Ḥanbalī work of al-ʿAbdalyānī (d. 684/1285) but to the Shāfiʿī work of al-Māwardī (see above). The sparse representation of Ḥanbalism in the library's collection is surprising in view of the strong Ḥanbalī presence not just in Damascus but in Palestine itself, exemplified, for example, by the Palestinian Ḥanbalī jurist Muḥammad al-Saffārīnī, who was born in Saffarin near Tulkarm and died in Nablus in 1188/1774.

5 Imāmī Law

The Imāmī Shīʿī works mentioned in the Jazzār inventory are the following:

- al-ʿAllāma al-Ḥillī (d. 726/1325), *Irshād al-adhhān* (#421)

18 Aḥmad b. al-Turkī's *al-Jawāhir al-zakiyya*.

- al-Shahīd al-Thānī (d. 965/1557), *Rawḍ al-jinān fī sharḥ Irshād al-adhhān* (not *azmān*) (#486)
- al-ʿAllāma al-Ḥillī, *Taḥrīr al-aḥkām* (#417)
- al-ʿAllāma al-Ḥillī, *Qawāʿid al-aḥkām fī maʿrifat al-ḥalāl wa-al-ḥarām* (#404)
- possibly a second copy of al-ʿAllāma al-Ḥillī's *Qawāʿid al-aḥkām* (though this is more likely to be the Shāfiʿī work of ʿIzz al-Dīn b. ʿAbd al-Salām; see above)
- possibly volume 2 of al-Karakī's (d. d. 940/1533–1534) *Jāmiʿ al-maqāṣid*, a commentary on al-ʿAllāma al-Ḥillī's *Qawāʿid al-aḥkām* (#479)
- probably al-ʿAllāma al-Ḥillī, *Muntahā al-maṭlab fī taḥqīq al-madhhab* (rather than a Ḥanbalī work, as the entry suggests), volume 2 (#502)
- al-Shahīd al-Awwal (d. 786/1384), *Ghāyat al-murād fī sharḥ Nukat al-irshād* (#456)
- probably the *Fatāwā* of al-Shaykh Najm al-Dīn al-Aṭrāwī al-ʿĀmilī (fl. mid-eighth/fourteenth century) (#568)
- al-Shahīd al-Thānī, *al-Rawḍa al-bahiyya fī sharḥ al-Lumʿa al-dimashqiyya* (a commentary on al-Shahīd al-Awwal's *al-Lumʿa al-dimashqiyya*) (#488)
- the first three volumes of Muḥammad b. ʿAlī al-Mūsawī al-ʿĀmilī (d. 1009/1600), *Madārik al-aḥkām fī sharḥ Sharāʾiʿ al-islām* (#482)
- probably Sulaymān al-Baḥrānī (d. 1121/1709), *al-ʿAshara al-kāmila fī ʿasharat masāʾil min uṣūl al-fiqh* (#424)

In addition, an Imāmī teaching text on legal theory by Bahāʾ al-Dīn al-ʿĀmilī (d. 1030/1621), *Zubdat al-uṣūl*, is not mentioned in the inventory, but, as noted earlier, the surviving manuscript of the work contains the Jazzār library's endowment note.

6 Other Legal Works

As noted earlier, many works included in the inventory are described in such a general way as to make identification of the title, author or legal school impossible. Such works include, for example, two books on inheritance law, for which no further information is given, and a work carrying the title *Mukhtaṣar ʿUnwān al-adilla lil-aʾimma al-arbaʿa* (#467) by an unknown author. A special case is al-Shaʿrānī's (d. 973/1565) *al-Mizān*[19] (#375). Although the author belonged to the Shāfiʿī school, the work is one of comparative law and has a distinctive Sufi bent.

7 Non-legal or Miscatalogued Works

Works listed under *fiqh* in the inventory that, in fact, have little or no connection to Islamic law include the following:

- a Turkish-language book on the major sins (*kabāʾir*), entitled *Sharḥ al-kabāʾir*, by the Ottoman scholar İsmail Hakkı Bursevi (d. 1137/1725) (#478)
- a *waqf* document written for Maḥmūd b. Muḥammad al-Naqshbandī al-Urmawī (#503)[20]
- Muḥammad b. Budayr's (d. 1220/1805) commentary, entitled *Bughyat al-albāb*, on his own poem, *Ghunyat al-ṭullāb*, which covers a smorgasbord of religious topics (#457)[21]
- the Sufi work *al-Dirāya li-aḥkām al-riʿāya*, whose title appears to have misled the inventory's compiler to suppose legal content (#473)
- a book entitled *al-Wujūh wa-al-naẓāʾir*, which is probably a *tafsīr* text but, like the preceding work, carries a misleading title, in this case, pointing toward legal maxims (a genre that often features the title *al-Ashbāh wa-al-naẓāʾir*) (#492)
- another misidentified work, *Jamʿ al-jawāmiʿ*, which is described as a book on legal theory but is, in fact, about *ḥadīth*[22]

19 On this work, see my discussion in El Shamsy, *Rediscovering the Islamic Classics*, 50.

20 His work, *Kazīd fī ʿilm al-tajwīd*, is preserved in manuscript form: Damascus, Ẓāhiriyya 334, and Medina, Maḥmūdiyya 2831.

21 For other copies of the work, see the Āl Budayrī library in Jerusalem, MSS 273, 480, 481, and an uncatalogued manuscript under HMML Proj. Num. ABLJ 01178.

22 See footnote 6 above.

8 Tentative Conclusions

If we now return to the three ideal types of collection logic outlined in the beginning of this survey, the preceding analysis indicates, firstly, that the Jazzār library's *fiqh* collection is not the product of a deliberate attempt at curation. For one thing, a fifth (20%) of the library's law holdings are identified in such a generic a manner ('a book on Ḥanafī law') as to render any identification impossible. What could have been a discerning collector's motive to acquire such works? For another thing, the majority of the works identified are basic curriculum texts, often mere pamphlets, or commentaries on such basic texts. The library held few multivolume texts in their entirety and contained even fewer extensive works on law (*mutawwalāt*) running to a dozen or more volumes—the kinds of works that someone interested in the details of a legal tradition would want to collect. The few lengthy legal works present in the inventory (such al-Māwardī's *al-Ḥāwī*) appear only as isolated volumes, never in toto. Had there been a conscious effort to assemble a library on law, the acquisition of these kinds of essential reference works would have been prioritised and an effort would have been made to complete the partial sets by copying the missing volumes from endowed libraries in the Levant or elsewhere.

Secondly, there is some evidence that the collection could have been shaped by the demands of its audience, at least to some degree. The works listed could plausibly be seen to constitute a set of foundational readings for a *madrasa* that taught Ḥanafī, Shāfiʿī and/or Imāmī Shīʿī law. By contrast, the inventory features too few Mālikī or Ḥanbalī texts to sustain the teaching of either school.[23] That the library's holdings might have reflected the needs of instruction is further supported by the *waqfiyya* of the Jazzār complex, which specifies the salary for a teacher (thirty *qurūsh* per month) and funds for forty students, each of whom would receive free lodging and a monthly stipend of three *qurūsh*.[24] Remarkably, the *waqfiyya* does not specify the subjects to be taught, but two pieces of information allow us to draw some speculative conclusions about the nature of the teaching activity at the complex. Firstly, the salary assigned to the teacher was relatively modest. It was higher than those paid to less prestigious employees at the complex—the two imams who took turns to lead the daily prayers (twenty *qurūsh* each per month) and the head muezzin who performed the call to prayer on Thursdays and Fridays (fifteen *qurūsh* per month)—but not so much higher as to suggest full-time employment. Perhaps the teacher taught classes only on Fridays after delivering the sermon. And secondly, the position of the teacher was hereditary and was initially granted to mufti ʿAbd Allāh Amīn, who was explicitly permitted to delegate the task, probably paying his replacement even less. Taken together, this information does not point to an intensive academic life in the Jazzār complex, although the students did, no doubt, make use of the law collection. However, there is little chance that the Imāmī legal works would have been taught to Sunnī students, nor that Imāmī students would have travelled to Acre to study; nor do we have any reason to think that the mufti of Acre would had any particular use for these books.[25]

This brings us to the third possible logic, that of simple availability. That the *fiqh* collection ended up containing mostly whatever legal works happened to be available is supported by several features of the data available, such as the presence of a significant number of Imāmī Shīʿī legal texts authored by Levantine scholars from the Jabal ʿĀmil

23 Ahmed Fekry Ibrahim has argued that the maintenance and teaching of the doctrines of all four of the Sunnī schools of law in the period under consideration served to provide society with the 'the least stringent juristic opinion'. However, the Jazzār library does not contain enough literature pertaining to the Ḥanbalī and Mālikī schools to fulfill this role. See Ibrahim, *Pragmatism in Islamic Law*, chs. 2 and 3.

24 *Waqfiyyat Aḥmad Bāshā al-Jazzār*, 32–33.

25 Ibid.

area, arguably the most important centre of Shīʿī thought in the Mamluk and early Ottoman periods. It is tempting to connect the inclusion of these otherwise seemingly out-of-place books in the Jazzār collection to the accounts of al-Jazzār's raids on Jabal ʿĀmil and the reports that he confiscated libraries there.[26] Other reports of wholesale acquisition and confiscation, together with the later addenda to the inventory, give additional support to this hypothesis. However, the total number of Imāmī works in the list is relatively small, suggesting either that the confiscations were modest in scale or that the loot was dispersed and did not all end up in the library.

If the logic of availability indeed played a large role in shaping the law library, we may wonder whether the collection (beyond the books taken by force) simply represents the sum total of books available on the commercial book market of the time, whether obtained through booksellers or bought directly from scholars and their descendants selling entire private libraries. Although the idea of such indiscriminate accumulation may seem farfetched, it is not unreasonable in view of the relatively limited number of books that were likely to have been on offer on the Levantine market at any given moment. It gains support from reports about the German traveller Ulrich Jasper Seetzen (1767–1811), who apparently bought any and all books he came across[27] during his year-and-a-half stay in Aleppo; by the end he managed to acquire 660 manuscripts. Over the following two years, which he spent in other parts of the Levant (including Damascus and Jerusalem), he added several hundred more to amass a total collection of nearly a thousand manuscripts.[28] There is no evidence that al-Jazzār or his employees had books copied specifically for the library, as opposed to simply acquiring whatever books were available on the market. A *fiqh* collection of about two hundred books, like that of al-Jazzār, could, thus, have contained a majority of the legal works that happened to be offered for sale.

The hypothesis of more or less 'blind' acquisition of books for the Jazzār library explains the predominance of basic curricular texts and their presence in multiple copies, the otherwise surprising inclusion of Levantine Shīʿī texts, and the fragmentary and seemingly random occurrence of a few rarer and older works in the inventory. The *fiqh* collection can be described as provincial in several ways. Its textual scope is limited: most of the books are related to a handful of texts, forming clusters comprising basic primers and their abridgements, commentaries and/or versifications. They also overwhelmingly reflect the schools of law present in the Levant—the imperial Ḥanafī school of law as well as its rival, the Shāfiʿī school, and the localised Imāmī minority. But the Ḥanafism represented in the collection has a distinctly Arab rather than Anatolian Ottoman slant: the inventory lacks many of the Ottoman *madrasa* mainstays, while closely matching the contents of the personal libraries of nineteenth-century scholars at al-Azhar in Egypt.[29] Finally, a significant percentage of the works listed were written by authors from the region. In view of the collection's generally provincial character, the low representation of the Ḥanbalī school constitutes a puzzle, given the Ḥanbalī presence in the Levant, in general, and in Palestine, in particular.

The person who compiled the inventory provides a few final clues. In a revealing note, he refers to one manuscript as ancient (*ʿatīq*), even though the work in question had been written by al-Shurunbulālī (d. 1069/1659) and the manuscript could have been no more than 150 years old at the time of his writing. This suggests either that the cataloguer knew little about scripts or that the works he catalogued were overwhelmingly recent copies, making this one seem old by comparison. More significantly, the large number of miscat-

26 See Chapter 3 by Boris Liebrenz in this volume.

27 Pertsch, *Die orientalischen Handschriften*, pt. 3, I, x.

28 Krimsti, "Von Aleppo nach Gotha", 59; Seetzen, *Verzeichniss*.

29 See El Shamsy, "Islamic Book Culture".

egorisations (*Jamʿ al-jawāmiʿ*, *al-Dirāya li-aḥkām al-riʿāya*, *al-Wujūh wa-al-naẓāʾir*) and misspellings in the titles of older and less known legal works (al-Shaybānī's *Kitāb al-Kasb* is listed as *Kashb*; al-Ghazālī's *Mankhūl* is listed as *Mutaḥawwal*) indicate that the compiler had limited familiarity with the literature of Islamic law and simply opened each codex, looked for a title and an author, decided (sometimes perhaps on the basis of little more than a guess) whether the book was legal in nature, copied the title as well as he could, and if the volume at hand was a fragment, added the title of the first chapter (for example, 'Ṣayd wa-dhabāʾiḥ').

Therefore, it seems reasonable to conclude that this was neither the specialised library of a connoisseur nor primarily an active legal teaching collection. Instead, the holdings catalogued under Islamic law offer a snapshot of the legal literature that was available on the Levantine open market at the beginning of the nineteenth century, as well as Shīʿī literature seized by the Jazzār government.

Bibliography

al-ʿĀmilī, Muḥsin. *Aʿyān al-Shīʿa*, edited by Ḥasan al-Amīn. 12 vols. N.p., 1983.

al-Baghdādī, Ismāʿīl Bāshā. *Hidāyat al-ʿārifīn*. 2 vols. Istanbul, 1951–1955.

Bedir, Mürteza. "Books on Islamic Legal Theory (*Uṣūl al-Fiqh*)." In *Treasures of Knowledge: An Inventory of the Ottoman Palace Library (1502/3–1503/4)*, edited by Gülru Necipoğlu, Cemal Kafadar and Cornell H. Fleischer, I, 423–438. Leiden, 2019.

Bonner, Michael. "The *Kitāb al-Kasb* Attributed to al-Shaybānī: Poverty, Surplus, and the Circulation of Wealth." *Journal of the American Oriental Society* 121, no. 3 (2001): 410–427.

El Shamsy, Ahmed. "The *Ḥāshiya* in Islamic Law: A Sketch of the Shāfiʿī Literature." *Oriens* 41, no. 3–4 (2013): 289–315.

El Shamsy, Ahmed. "Islamic Book Culture through the Lens of Two Private Libraries, 1850–1940." *Intellectual History of the Islamicate World* 4 (2016): 61–81.

El Shamsy, Ahmed. *Rediscovering the Islamic Classics: How Editors and Print Culture Transformed an Intellectual Tradition*. Princeton, NJ, 2020.

Ḥājjī Khalīfa. *Kashf al-ẓunūn*, edited by Muḥammad Sharaf al-Dīn Yaltaqāyā and Rifʿat al-Kilīsī. 2 vols. Istanbul, 1941–1943.

Hirschler, Konrad. *Medieval Damascus: Plurality and Diversity in an Arabic Library; The Ashrafiya Library Catalogue*. Edinburgh, 2016.

Hirschler, Konrad. *A Monument to Medieval Syrian Book Culture: The Library of Ibn ʿAbd al-Hādī*. Edinburgh, 2020.

Ibn al-Nadīm. *al-Fihrist*, edited by Ayman Fuʾād Sayyid. 4 vols. in 2. London, 2009.

Ibrahim, Ahmed Fekry. *Pragmatism in Islamic Law*. Syracuse, NY, 2015.

Krimsti, Feras. "Von Aleppo nach Gotha: Der Aleppiner Buchmarkt des 18. Jahrhunderts im Spiegel der von Ulrich Jasper Seetzen erworbenen Gothaer Handschriften." In *Bücher bewegen: 375 Jahre Forschungsbibliothek Gotha*, edited by Kathrin Paasch, 56–63. Gotha, 2022.

Makdisi, George. *The Rise of Colleges*. Edinburgh, 1981.

Pertsch, Wilhelm. *Die orientalischen Handschriften der Herzoglichen Bibliothek zu Gotha*. Gotha, 1878.

Seetzen, Ulrich Jasper. *Verzeichniss der für die orientalische Sammlung in Gotha zu Damask, Jerusalem u.s.w. angekauften orientalischen Manuscripte und gedruckten Werke, Kunst- und Naturprodukte u.s.w.* Leipzig, 1810.

al-Ṭālibī, ʿAbd al-Ḥayy. *al-Iʿlām bi-man fī tārīkh al-Hind min al-aʿlām*. 8 vols. Beirut, 1999.

Talmon-Heller, Daniella, and Raquel Ukeles. "The Lure of a Controversial Prayer: Salat al-Ragha'ib (the Prayer of Great Rewards) in Medieval Arabic Texts and from a Socio-legal Perspective." *Der Islam* 89, no. 1/2 (2012): 141–166.

Taşkömür, Himmet. "Books on Islamic Jurisprudence, Schools of Law, and Biographies of Imams from the Hanafi School." In *Treasures of Knowledge: An Inventory of the Ottoman Palace Library (1502/3–1503/4)*, edited by Gülru Necipoğlu, Cemal Kafadar and Cornell H. Fleischer, I, 389–422. Leiden, 2019.

Waqfiyyat Aḥmad Bāshā al-Jazzār, edited by Mūsā Abū Diyya. Nablus, 1998.

The Law Books

NB. Related works are grouped together in clusters, and the number of the first work in a cluster is marked in **bold.** Well-known works that have been edited and published repeatedly are simply identified as 'published'.

Ḥanafī law

[331] *al-Durar wa-al-ghurar*, AUTHOR: **Mullā Husrev** (d. 885/1480), published.

[**332**] *al-Hidāya*, AUTHOR: **al-Marghinānī** (d. 593/1197), published.

[333] *al-Hidāya*, part 2, AUTHOR: **al-Marghinānī** (d. 593/1197), published.

[334] ***Sharḥ*** (commentary on) ***al-Hidāya*** of al-Marghinānī, part 8, AUTHOR: unknown.

[335] ***Sharḥ*** (commentary on) ***al-Hidāya*** of al-Marghinānī, parts 1–4, AUTHOR: unknown.

[343] ***Sharḥ*** (commentary on) ***al-Hidāya*** of al-Marghinānī, part 1, AUTHOR: unknown

[353] ***Wiqāyat*** *al-riwāya fī masā'il al-riwāya*, abridgement of *al-Hidāya* of al-Marghinānī, AUTHOR: Maḥmūd al-Maḥbūbī (d. 673/1273–1274), published; MANUSCRIPT: Damascus, al-Asad National Library, MS 219.

[354] ***Sharḥ al-Wiqāya*** = *al-Īḍāḥ fī sharḥ al-iṣlāḥ*, gloss on commentary by Ubayd Allāh b. Mas'ūd al-Maḥbūbī (d. 747/1346) on abridgement (*Wiqāya*) by Maḥmūd al-Maḥbūbī on *al-Hidāya* of al-Marghinānī, AUTHOR: Ibn Kamāl Pasha (d. 940/1534), published.

[470] ***Naṣb al-rāya li-aḥādīth al-Hidāya***, (probably) a compilation of the *ḥadīth* in *al-Hidāya* of al-Marghinānī, AUTHOR: unknown, published.

[**336**] ***Kanz al-daqā'iq***, AUTHOR: Abū al-Barakāt al-Nasafī (d. ca. 710/1310), published.

[337] ***Kanz al-daqā'iq***, AUTHOR: Abū al-Barakāt al-Nasafī (d. ca. 710/1310), published.

[338] ***Sharḥ*** (commentary on) ***Kanz*** *al-daqā'iq* of al-Nasafī, AUTHOR: **Mullā Miskīn** (d. after 811/1408), published.

[339] ***Sharḥ*** (commentary on) ***Kanz al-daqā'iq*** of al-Nasafī, AUTHOR: **Mullā Miskīn** (d. after 811/1408), published.

[340] *Ramz al-ḥaqā'iq*, ***Sharḥ*** (commentary) on ***Kanz*** *al-daqā'iq* of al-Nasafī, AUTHOR: Badr al-Dīn **al-'Aynī** (d. 855/1451), published.

[341] *al-Baḥr al-rā'iq*, ***Sharḥ*** (commentary) on ***Kanz*** *al-daqā'iq* of al-Nasafī, AUTHOR: **Ibn Nujaym** (d. 970/1562), published.

[342] *al-Baḥr al-rā'iq*, six parts (in two volumes) of ***Sharḥ*** (commentary) on ***Kanz*** *al-daqā'iq* of al-Nasafī, AUTHOR: **Ibn Nujaym** (d. 970/1562), published, MANUSCRIPT: Acre, al-Jazzār Mosque Library, MS 9 ('Aṭā Allāh, *Fihris 'Akkā*, 1983).

[444] ***Takmilat al-Baḥr al-rā'iq***, continuation of *al-Baḥr al-rā'iq* of Ibn Nujaym, commentary on *Kanz al-daqā'iq* of al-Nasafī, AUTHOR: **Muḥammad al-Ṭūrī al-Qādirī** (d. 1138/1726), EDITION: published with Ibn Nujaym, *al-Baḥr al-rā'iq sharḥ Kanz al-daqā'iq*, 8 vols., Cairo: Dār al-Kitāb al-Islāmī, 1975.

[348] ***Tabyīn al-ḥaqā'iq***, commentary on *Kanz al-daqā'iq* of al-Nasafī, AUTHOR: **Fakhr al-Dīn al-Zayla'ī** (d. 743/1343), EDITION: Bulaq, 1314 [1896–1897].

[575] ***Mustakhlaṣ al-ḥaqā'iq***, commentary on *Kanz al-daqā'iq* of al-Nasafī, AUTHOR: **Abū al-Qāsim al-Samarqandī** (d. 907/1501), published.

[1637] ***Mustakhlaṣ al-ḥaqā'iq***, part 2 of commentary on *Kanz al-daqā'iq* of al-Nasafī, AUTHOR: **Abū al-Qāsim al-Samarqandī** (d. 907/1501), published.

[**344**] ***Multaqā al-abhur***, AUTHOR: Ibrāhīm al-Ḥalabī (d. 956/1549–1550), EDITION: Istanbul: n.p., 1848.

[345] ***Multaqā al-abhur***, two copies, AUTHOR: Ibrāhīm al-Ḥalabī (d. 956/1549–1550), EDITION: Istanbul: n.p., 1848.

[346] ***Multaqā al-abhur***, fragment, AUTHOR: Ibrāhīm al-Ḥalabī (d. 956/1549–1550), EDITION: Istanbul: n.p., 1848.

[553] ***Multaqā al-abhur***, AUTHOR: Ibrāhīm al-Ḥalabī (d. 956/1549–1550), EDITION: Istanbul: n.p., 1848.

[347] ***Tanwīr al-abṣār*** *wa-jāmi' al-biḥār*, AUTHOR: Shams al-Dīn al-Khaṭīb al-Timurtāshī (d. 1004/1596), EDITION: 'Abd al-Raḥmān al-Kharasī, Damascus: Dār al-Minhāj al-Qawmī, 2021.

[**349**] ***Majma' al-baḥrayn*** *wa-multaqā al-nayrayn*, AUTHOR: Ibn al-Sā'ātī (d. 694/1295), EDITION: Ilyās Qablān, Beirut: Dār al-Kutub al-'Ilmiyya, 2005.

[350] ***Sharḥ*** (commentary on) ***Majmaʿ al-baḥrayn wa-multaqā al-nayyirayn*** of Ibn al-Sāʿātī, AUTHOR: unknown.

[351] ***Sharḥ*** (commentary on) *al-Manẓūma* ***al-Wahbāniyya*** = *Manẓūmat Ibn Wahbān* of Ibn Wahbān (d. 768/1367), AUTHOR: possibly Ibn al-Shiḥna, MS: Damascus, Ẓāhiriyya, no. 9159 (another manuscript).

[382] ***Sharḥ*** (commentary on) *al-Manẓūma* ***al-Wahbāniyya*** = *Manẓūmat Ibn Wahbān* of Ibn Wahbān (d. 768/1367), AUTHOR: unknown.

[352] ***al-Ashbāh wa-al-naẓāʾir***, AUTHOR: (probably) Ibn Nujaym (d. 970/1562), EDITION: Calcutta: n.p., 1826.

[355] ***Nūr al-īḍāḥ***, AUTHOR: **al-Shurunbulālī** (d. 1069/1659), published.

[356] ***Nūr al-īḍāḥ***, AUTHOR: **al-Shurunbulālī** (d. 1069/1659), published.

[358] ***Nūr al-īḍāḥ***, AUTHOR: al-Shurunbulālī (d. 1069/1659), published.

[361] ***Ḍaw' al-miṣbāḥ sharḥ Nūr al-īḍāḥ***, commentary on *Nūr al-īḍāḥ* of al-Shurunbulālī, AUTHOR: **Abū al-Suʿūd** (d. 1172/1759), EDITION: 2 vols., Beirut: Dār Ibn Ḥazm, 2021.

[359] *Mukhtaṣar*, AUTHOR: **al-Qudūrī** (d. 428/1037), EDITION: Kāmil ʿUwayḍa, Beirut: Dār al-Kutub al-ʿIlmiyya, 1997.

[360] *Mukhtaṣar*, AUTHOR: **al-Qudūrī** (d. 428/1037), EDITION: Kāmil ʿUwayḍa, Beirut: Dār al-Kutub al-ʿIlmiyya, 1997.

[362] ***Munyat al-muṣallī***, AUTHOR: al-Kāshgharī (d. 705/1305–1306), MS: Umm al-Qurā University, King ʿAbd al-ʿAzīz Library, nos. 1201, 1213 (other manuscripts).

[363] ***Munyat al-muṣallī***, AUTHOR: al-Kāshgharī (d. 705/1305–1306), MS: Umm al-Qurā University, King ʿAbd al-ʿAzīz Library, nos. 1201, 1213 (other manuscripts).

[364] ***Sharḥ*** (commentary on) ***Munyat al-muṣallī*** of al-Kāshgharī, AUTHOR: unknown.

[365] ***Sharḥ*** (commentary on) ***Munyat al-muṣallī*** of al-Kāshgharī, AUTHOR: unknown.

[366] *Ghunyat al-mutamallī fī* ***sharḥ Munyat al-muṣallī***, commentary on *Munyat al-muṣallī* of al-Kāshgharī, AUTHOR: Ibrāhīm **al-Ḥalabī** (d. 956/1549–1550), EDITION: Istanbul: Ali Bey Matbaası, 1295 [1879].

[367] ***Sharḥ*** (commentary on) ***Munyat al-muṣallī*** of al-Kāshgharī, in two volumes, AUTHOR: unknown.

[368] ***Sharḥ*** (commentary on) ***Munyat al-muṣallī*** of al-Kāshgharī, AUTHOR: unknown.

[369] *Ghunyat al-mutamallī fī* ***sharḥ Munyat al-muṣallī***, commentary on *Munyat al-muṣallī* of al-Kāshgharī, AUTHOR: **Ibrāhīm al-Ḥalabī** (d. 956/1549–1550), EDITION: Istanbul: Ali Bey Matbaası, 1295 [1879].

[370] ***Sharḥ*** (commentary on) ***Munyat al-muṣallī*** of al-Kāshgharī (beginning missing), AUTHOR: unknown.

[524] ***Sharḥ*** (commentary on) ***Munyat al-muṣallī*** of al-Kāshgharī, AUTHOR: unknown.

[371] ***al-Dhakhāʾir al-ashrafiyya***, AUTHOR: Ibn al-Shiḥna (d. 921/1515), EDITION: Fāṭima Shihāb, as *Alghāz al-Ḥanafiyya li-Ibn al-Shiḥna al-musammā al-Dhakhāʾir al-ashrafiyya*, Cairo: al-Maktaba al-Azhariyya, 2014.

[390] ***Muqaddima***, AUTHOR: **Abū al-Layth** al-Samarqandī (d. 373/984), EDITION: published with Muṣliḥ al-Dīn al-Qaramānī, *al-Tawḍīḥ sharḥ al-Muqaddima al-fiqhiyya*, edited by ʿAbd al-Muḥsin ʿAbbādī, Kirkuk: Maktabat Amīr, 2018.

[391] ***Sharḥ*** (commentary on) ***Muqaddima*** of Abū al-Layth al-Samarqandī, AUTHOR: unknown.

[466] ***al-Tawḍīḥ*** *sharḥ al-Muqaddima al-fiqhiyya*, one part of a commentary on *Muqaddima* of Abū al-Layth al-Samarqandī, AUTHOR: **Muṣliḥ al-Dīn al-Qaramānī** (d. 809/1406), EDITION: ʿAbd al-Muḥsin ʿAbbādī, Kirkuk: Maktabat Amīr, 2018.

[396] ***Radʿ al-rāghib ʿan al-jamʿ fī ṣalāt al-raghāʾib***, AUTHOR: ʿAlī b. Ghānim al-Maqdisī (d. 1004/1596), EDITION: Muḥammad al-Mubārakī, Amman: Dār al-Fatḥ, 2008.

[399] Autocommentary on ***al-Durra al-munīfa*** *ʿalā madhhab al-imām Abī Ḥanīfa*, AUTHOR: **ʿUmar al-Zuhrī al-Azharī** (d. 1079/1668–1669).

[403] ***al-Wāfī*** *fī al-fiqh ʿalā madhhab al-imām al-aʿẓam Abī Ḥanīfa al-Nuʿmān*, part 2, AUTHOR: Abū al-Barakāt al-Nasafī (d. 710/1310), EDITION: Muḥammad Naẓẓār Tamīm, 3 vols., Damascus: Dār al-Risāla al-ʿĀlamiyya, 2022.

[408] ***Aḥkām al-awqāf***, AUTHOR: (probably) Abū Bakr al-Khaṣṣāf (d. 261/874), EDITION: Cairo: Maṭbaʿat Dīwān ʿUmūm al-Awqāf al-Miṣriyya, 1904.

[411] *al-Maslak al-mutaqassiṭ*, commentary on *Lubāb* ***al-manāsik*** of Raḥmat Allāh al-Sindī, AUTHOR: Mullā ʿAlī al-Qārī (d. 1014/1605–1606), EDITION: Mecca: Maṭbaʿat al-Taraqqī, 1327 [1909].

[412] *al-Maslak al-mutaqassiṭ*, commentary on *Lubāb* ***al-manāsik*** of Raḥmat Allāh al-Sindī, AUTHOR: Mullā ʿAlī al-Qārī (d. 1014/1605–1606), EDITION: Mecca: Maṭbaʿat al-Taraqqī, 1327 [1909].

[413] *al-Maslak al-mutaqassiṭ*, commentary on *Lubāb* ***al-manāsik*** of Raḥmat Allāh al-Sindī, AUTHOR: Mullā ʿAlī al-Qārī (d. 1014/1605–1606), EDITION: Mecca: Maṭbaʿat al-Taraqqī, 1327 [1909].

[414] *al-Maslak al-mutaqassiṭ*, on *Lubāb* ***al-manāsik*** of Raḥmat Allāh al-Sindī, in Turkish, AUTHOR: **Mullā ʿAlī al-Qārī** (d. 1014/1605–1606).

[507] *al-Maslak al-mutaqassiṭ*, commentary on *Lubāb* ***al-manāsik*** of Raḥmat Allāh al-Sindī, AUTHOR: **Mullā ʿAlī al-Qārī** (d. 1014/1605–1606), EDITION: Mecca: Maṭbaʿat al-Taraqqī, 1327 [1909].

[420] *Muqaddima*, AUTHOR: Aḥmad **al-Ghaznawī** (d. 593/1197), EDITION: al-Yamānī al-Fakhrānī and Khālid Duwaydār, Amman: Dār al-Nūr, 2023.

[453] *Muqaddima*, AUTHOR: Aḥmad **al-Ghaznawī** (d. 593/1197), EDITION: al-Yamānī al-Fakhrānī and Khālid Duwaydār, Amman: Dār al Nūr, 2023.

[538] *Muqaddima*, AUTHOR: Aḥmad **al-Ghaznawī** (d. 593/1197), EDITION: al-Yamānī al-Fakhrānī and Khālid Duwaydār, Amman: Dār al-Nūr, 2023.

[430] ***al-Mukhtār*** *lil-fatwā*, AUTHOR: Abū al-Faḍl ʿAbd Allāh al-Baldijī al-Mawṣilī (d. 683/1284), EDITION: Sāʾid Bikdāsh, Beirut: Dār al-Bashāʾir al-Islamiyya, 2012.

[433] ***Khulāṣat al-fatāwā***, AUTHOR: Iftikhār al-Dīn al-Bukhārī (d. 542/1147), MS: Istanbul, Süleymaniye Library, Fatih 2318 (another manuscript), EDITION: ʿAbd Allāh al-Saʿdūn, Master's thesis, Islamic University of Baghdad, 2009 (partial).

[435] ***Fatāwā***, AUTHOR: **ʿAlī Efendi** Çatalcalı (d. 1103/1692), EDITION: 2 vols., Istanbul: Dār Saʿādat, [1866–1867].

[436] ***Fatāwā***, AUTHOR: Muḥammad **al-Badr al-Rashīd** (d. 768/1366).

[438] ***Sharḥ*** (commentary on) ***al-Jāmiʿ al-ṣaghīr*** of al-Shaybānī, AUTHOR: Ḥusām al-Dīn **al-Rāzī** (d. 598/1201–1202), MANUSCRIPT: Dublin, Chester Beatty Library, Ar. 3316, EDITION: ʿAlī al-Ḥājī, PhD diss., Omdurman University, 2015.

[454] ***Talkhīṣ*** (abridgement of) ***al-Jāmiʿ al-kabīr*** of al-Shaybānī (d. 187/805), AUTHOR: al-Khallāṭī (d. 652/1254), MS: Istanbul, Süleymaniye Library, Feyzullah Efendi 696 (another manuscript).

[490] ***Tuḥfat al-ḥarīṣ fī sharḥ al-Talkhīṣ***, two parts of a commentary on al-Khallāṭī's abridgement of *al-Jāmiʿ al-kabīr* of al-Shaybānī (d. 187/805), AUTHOR: ʿAlāʾ al-Dīn al-Fārisī (d. 739/1339), EDITION: Sāliḥ al-Saʿūd, PhD diss., Islamic University of Medina, 2015.

[455] ***Sayf al-quḍā ʿalā al-bughā***, AUTHOR: Muḥyī al-Dīn al-Kāfiyajī (d. 879/1474), EDITION: Ilyās Qablān, Beirut: Dār al-Kutub al-ʿIlmiyya, 2005.

[460] ***al-Jawāhir*** *min fiqh al-Ḥanafiyya wa-mukhtaṣar fī al-ʿaqīda wa-al-sulūk*, AUTHOR: (probably) Ṭāhir al-Khawarizmī (fl. eighth/fourteenth century), EDITION: Muḥammad Ayman al-Jamāl, Istanbul: Maktabat Dār al-Samān, 2019.

[462] ***Jāmiʿ al-durar***, AUTHOR: Maḥāsin al-Qaysarī (fl. eighth/fourteenth century), MS: autocommentary *Sharḥ Jāmiʿ al-durar*, Istanbul: Diyanet Işleri Başkanları, no. 3055.

[464] ***Sharḥ al-Nuqāyā***, AUTHOR: (probably) Mullā ʿAlī al-Qārī (d. 1014/1605–1606), EDITION: Muḥammad Tamīm and Haytham Tamīm, *Fatḥ bāb al-ʿināya bi-sharḥ al-Nuqāyā*, 3 vols., Beirut: Dār al-Arqam, 1997.

[468] ***Muʿīn al-ḥukkām***, AUTHOR: ʿAlāʾ al-Dīn al-Ṭarabulsī (d. 844/1440–1441), EDITION: Bulaq, 1300/1883.

[474] *Kitāb* ***Īḍāḥ al-dalālāt*** *fī samāʿ al-ālāt*, AUTHOR: ʿAbd al-Ghanī al-Nabulsī (d. 1143/1731), EDITION: Damascus: al-Maṭbaʿa al-Ḥifniyya, 1884–1885.

[476] *Jāmiʿ* ***aḥkām al-ṣighār***, AUTHOR: Muḥammad b. Maḥmūd al-Ustarūshanī (d. 632/1234), EDITION: Muḥammad Saʿīd Badrī and Maḥmūd ʿAbd al-Munʿim, Cairo: Dār al-Faḍīla, 1994.

[481] ***Sharḥ*** (commentary on) *al-Muntakhab al-Ḥusāmī* of Ḥusām al-Dīn **al-Akhsīkathī** (d. 644/1247), AUTHOR: unknown.

[489] ***Jam' al-manāsik***, AUTHOR: Raḥmat Allāh al-Sindī (d. 993/1585), EDITION: ʿAbd Allāh Āl Ṭāhā, PhD diss., Umm al-Qurā University, 2012.

[491] ***al-Maqāṣid al-saniyya*** *bi-sharḥ al-Sirājiyya lil-Ḥanafiyya*, AUTHOR: Yūnus al-Rashīdī (d. 1020/1611); see Ḥājjī Khalīfa, *Kashf al-ẓunūn*, II, 1249.

[519] *al-Fawā'id al-samiyya fī* ***sharḥ al-Farā'id al-saniyya***, AUTHOR: Muḥammad al-Kawākibī (d. 1096/1685), published.

[596] ***al-Fatāwā al-Muḥammadiyya fī fiqh al-Ḥanafiyya***, AUTHOR: Ibn Abī al-Luṭf (fl. twelfth/eighteenth century), MS: Cairo, Azhar Library, no. 328017 (another manuscript).

[1646] *Mughnī al-mustaftī ʿan su'āl al-muftī =* ***al-Fatāwā al-Ḥāmidiyya***, AUTHOR: Ḥāmid b. ʿAlī al-ʿImādī (d. 1171/1758), EDITION: Ibn ʿĀbidīn, *al-ʿUqūd al-durriyya fī tanqīḥ al-Fatāwā al-Ḥāmidiyya*, Beirut: Dār al-Kutub al-ʿIlmiyya, 2008 (abridgement).

[1696] ***Kitāb Minḥat al-sulūk fī sharḥ Tuḥfat al-mulūk***, AUTHOR: **Badr al-Dīn al-ʿAynī** (d. 855/1451), EDITION: Aḥmad al-Kubaysī, Doha: Wizārat al-Awqāf, 2007.

Shafiʿī law

[372] ***ʿUnwān al-sharaf***, AUTHOR: **Ibn al-Muqri'** (d. 837/1433), published.

[373] ***ʿUnwān al-sharaf***, AUTHOR: Ibn al-Muqri' (d. 837/1433), published.

[374] ***ʿUnwān al-sharaf***, AUTHOR: Ibn al-Muqri' (d. 837/1433), published.

[501] ***ʿUnwān al-sharaf***, AUTHOR: Ibn al-Muqri' (d. 837/1433), published.

[383] ***Minhāj*** *al-ṭālibīn*, AUTHOR: Sharaf al-Dīn al-Nawawī (d. 676/1277), published.

[384] ***Minhāj*** *al-ṭālibīn*, AUTHOR: Sharaf al-Dīn al-Nawawī (d. 676/1277), published.

[385] ***Minhāj*** *al-ṭālibīn*, incomplete, AUTHOR: Sharaf al-Dīn al-Nawawī (d. 676/1277), published.

[386] ***Minhāj*** *al-ṭālibīn*, incomplete, AUTHOR: Sharaf al-Dīn al-Nawawī (d. 676/1277), published.

[387] ***Sharḥ*** (commentary on) ***Minhāj al-ṭālibīn*** of al-Nawawī, part 3, AUTHOR: unknown.

[388] ***Sharḥ*** (commentary on) ***Minhāj al-ṭālibīn*** of al-Nawawī, part 3, AUTHOR: unknown.

[401] ***Minhāj*** *al-ṭālibīn*, part 1, AUTHOR: Sharaf al-Dīn al-Nawawī (d. 676/1277), published.

[418] *Nihāyat al-muḥtāj*, commentary on *Minhāj al-ṭālibīn* of al-Nawawī, parts 1–3, AUTHOR: Shams al-Dīn **al-Ramlī** (d. 1004/1596), EDITION: 8 vols., Beirut: Dār al-Kutub al-ʿIlmiyya, 2003.

[1667] ***Manhaj al-ṭullāb***, abridgement of *Minhāj al-ṭālibīn* of al-Nawawī, chapter on purity, AUTHOR: **Zakariyyā al-Anṣārī** (d. 926/1520), published.

[409] *al-Iqnāʿ fī ḥall* ***Abī Shujāʿ***, commentary on *al-Ghāya wa-al-taqrīb* of Abū Shujāʿ (fl. fifth/eleventh century), part 2, AUTHOR: **al-Khaṭīb al-Shirbīnī** (d. 977/1570), EDITION: 2 vols., Bulaq, 1876.

[451] ***al-Iqnāʿ*** *fī ḥall Abī Shujāʿ*, commentary on *al-Ghāya wa-al-taqrīb* of Abū Shujāʿ (fl. fifth/eleventh century), part 2, AUTHOR: **al-Khaṭīb al-Shirbīnī** (d. 977/1570), EDITION: 2 vols., Bulaq, 1876.

[487] ***Ḥāshiyat al-Birmāwī***, a gloss either on Ibn Qāsim al-Ghazzī's (d. 918/1512) commentary on Abū Shujāʿ's *al-Ghāya wa-al-taqrīb*, or on Zakariyyā al-Anṣārī's commentary on al-Nawawī's *Minhāj al-ṭālibīn*, or on Sibṭ al-Mardīnī's commentary on Muḥammad al-Raḥbī's *al-Raḥbiyya*, AUTHOR: Ibrāhīm **al-Birmāwī** (d. 1106/1694).

[1642] ***Sharḥ*** (commentary on) *al-Ghāya wa-al-taqrīb* of **Abū Shujāʿ** (fl. fifth/eleventh century), part 2, AUTHOR: unknown.

[410] ***Qawāʿid al-aḥkām***, AUTHOR: (probably) ʿIzz al-Dīn b. ʿAbd al-Salām (d. 660/1262) [or, alternatively, al-ʿAllāma al-Ḥillī (d. 726/1325)], EDITION: Nazīd Ḥammād and ʿUthmān Dumayriyya, as *al-Qawāʿid al-kubrā al-mawsūm bi-Qawāʿid al-aḥkām fī iṣlāḥ al-anām*, 2 vols., Damascus: Dār al-Qalam, 2000.

[415] ***Muhimmāt***, commentary on *Rawḍat al-ṭālibīn* of al-Nawawī and *Fatḥ al-ʿazīz* of al-Rāfiʿī, parts 1 and 2, AUTHOR: ʿAbd al-Raḥīm al-Isnawī (d. 772/1370–1371), EDITION: Abū al-Faḍl al-Dumyāṭī and Aḥmad b. ʿAlī, 10 vols., Beirut: Dār Ibn Ḥazm, 2009.

[416] ***Muhimmāt***, commentary on *Rawḍat al-ṭālibīn* of al-Nawawī and *Fatḥ al-ʿazīz* of al-Rāfiʿī, part 4,

AUTHOR: ʿAbd al-Raḥīm al-Isnawī (d. 772/1370–1371), MANUSCRIPT: Jerusalem, National Library of Israel, Ms. AP Ar. 290.

[423] ***al-Muhadhdhab***, fragment, AUTHOR: Abū Isḥāq **al-Shīrāzī** (d. 476/1083), published.

[437] *al-Wasīṭ*, part 2 of commentary on ***al-Muhadhdhab*** of al-Shīrāzī, AUTHOR: Abū Ḥāmid al-Ghazālī (d. 505/1111), published.

[428] ***Manẓūmat Ibn al-ʿImād*** *fī al-maʿfuwāt*, AUTHOR: Shihāb al-Dīn **Ibn al-ʿImād** al-Aqfahsī (d. 808/1405), EDITION: Quṣayy al-Ḥallāq, Beirut: Dār al-Minhāj, 2015.

[449] *al-Zubad*, AUTHOR: Aḥmad b. Raslān (d. 844/1440), EDITION: Mecca: Maktabat al-Thaqāfa, 1984.

[450a] ***al-Zubad***, AUTHOR: **Aḥmad b. Raslān** (d. 844/1440), EDITION: Mecca: Maktabat al-Thaqāfa, 1984.

[465] *al-Ḥāwī, sharḥ* (commentary on) *Mukhtaṣar* al-Muzanī (d. 264/877), part 2, AUTHOR: (probably) Abū al-Ḥasan al-Māwardī (d. 450/1058), EDITION: 20 vols., Beirut: Dār al-Kutub al-ʿIlmiyya, 1994–1996.

[471] *Tashnīf al-asmāʿ bi-ḥukm al-ḥaraka fī al-dhikr wa-al-samāʿ*, AUTHOR: ʿAbd al-Salām b. Ziyād al-Yamānī (d. 975/1567).

[475] *al-Ghurar al-bahiyya fī* ***sharḥ al-Bahja*** *al-wardiyya*, commentary on *al-Bahja al-wardiyya* of Ibn al-Wardī (d. 749/1349), AUTHOR: **Zakariyyā al-Anṣārī** (d. 926/1520), EDITION: Cairo: al-Maṭbaʿa al-Maymaniyya, 1900.

[477] ***Tuḥfat al-ṭullāb***, autocommentary on ***Taḥrīr tanqīḥ al-lubāb***, AUTHOR: **Zakariyyā al-Anṣārī** (d. 926/1520), EDITION: Cairo: Maktabat al-Īmān, 2019.

[450b] ***al-Sittīn mas'ala***, AUTHOR: **Aḥmad al-Zāhid al-Miṣrī** (d. 819/1416), EDITION: published with Shams al-Dīn al-Ramlī, *Sharḥ al-Sittīn mas'ala*, Bulaq, 1875.

[505] ***al-Sittīn mas'ala***, AUTHOR: **Aḥmad al-Zāhid al-Miṣrī** (d. 819/1416), EDITION: published with Shams al-Dīn al-Ramlī, *Sharḥ al-Sittīn mas'ala*, Bulaq, 1875.

[506] ***Sharḥ*** (commentary on) ***al-Sittīn mas'ala*** of Aḥmad al-Zāhid al-Miṣrī, AUTHOR: **Shams al-Dīn al-Ramlī** (d. 957/1550), EDITION: Bulaq, 1875.

[493] ***al-Minḥa al-biqāʿiyya***, commentary on *al-Tuḥfa al-qudsiyya* of Aḥmad b. al-Hā'im (d. 815/1412), an abridgement *al-Raḥbiyya* of Muḥammad al-Raḥbī al-Mutaqanna (d. 577/1182), AUTHOR: **ʿUrfa b. Muḥammad al-Urmawī** (d. ca. 931/1524).

[504] ***Sharḥ*** (commentary on) ***al-Raḥbiyya*** of Muḥammad al-Raḥbī al-Mutaqanna (d. 577/1182), AUTHOR: unknown.

[1677] ***al-Lumʿa al-shamsiyya***, commentary on *al-Tuḥfa al-qudsiyya* by Aḥmad b. al-Hā'im (d. 815/1412), an abridgement *al-Raḥbiyya* of Muḥammad al-Raḥbī al-Mutaqanna (d. 577/1182), AUTHOR: **Sibṭ al-Mārdīnī** (d. 912/1506); see Ḥājjī Khalīfa, *Kashf al-ẓunūn*, I, 372.

[496] ***Sharḥ*** (commentary on) ***al-Ījāz fī al-farā'iḍ*** of Abū al-Ḥusayn al-Faraḍī (d. 403/1012–1013), AUTHOR: **al-Kirmānī** (?).

[1660] *Shubbāk* ***al-munāsakhāt***, AUTHOR: Aḥmad **b. al-Hā'im** (d. 815/1412), EDITION: Yūsuf al-ʿĀṣim, Doha: Wizārat al-Awqāf, 2011.

Mālikī law

[452] ***Taḥrīr al-maqāl***, AUTHOR: Abū Ṭālib al-Ṭarṭūshī (d. 608/1211), EDITION: Muṣṭafā Bājū, 2 vols., Abu Dhabi: Dār al-Imām Mālik, n.d.

[494] ***Tuḥfat al-rā'iḍ fī al-farā'iḍ***, AUTHOR: Sirāj al-Dīn al-Mālikī (d. 842/1438–1439); see Ḥājjī Khalīfa, *Kashf al-ẓunūn*, I, 366.

[498] *Ashal* ***al-masālik***, fragment, AUTHOR: (probably) Muḥammad al-Bashshār (fl. 1161/1748).

[508] ***Matn al-ʿAshmāwiyya***, AUTHOR: Abū al-Najā al-ʿAshmāwī (fl. tenth/sixteenth century), published.

[483] ***al-Jawāhir al-zakiyya***, commentary on *Matn al-ʿAshmāwiyya* of al-ʿAshmāwī, AUTHOR: **Aḥmad b. al-Turkī** (d. 998/1590), EDITION: Bulaq, 1864.

[1670] ***Jāmiʿat al-ṭuruqāt fī qismat al-muḥāṣāt***, AUTHOR: (probably) Abū al-Barakāt al-Daljimūnī al-Wafā'ī (fl. 1079/1668), MS: Damascus, Ẓāhiriyya, no. 1383 (another manuscript).

Ḥanbalī law

[422] ***Durar al-biḥār*** *al-mutaḍammina ilā majmaʿ al-baḥrayn fī bayān madhhab* ***Aḥmad b. Ḥanbal***, AUTHOR: Shams al-Dīn Muḥammad b. Yūsuf

al-Qūnawī (d. 788/1386), MS: Istanbul, Süleymaniye Library, Ayasofya, no. 2244 (another manuscript).

Imāmī law

[404] *Qawāʿid* ***al-aḥkām fī maʿrifat al-ḥalāl wa-al-ḥarām***, AUTHOR: al-ʿAllāma al-Ḥillī (d. 726/1325), EDITION: Ismāʿīl al-Jīlānī al-Shafatī, 2 vols., n.p.: n.p., 1329 [1911].

[479] *Jāmiʿ al-maqāṣid, **sharḥ*** (commentary on) ***Qawāʿid al-aḥkām*** of al-ʿAllāma al-Ḥillī, part 2, AUTHOR: (possibly) al-Karakī (d. 940/1533–1534), EDITION: 14 vols., Qum: Muʾassasat Āl al-Bayt, 1987.

[417] ***Taḥrīr al-aḥkām***, AUTHOR: al-ʿAllāma al-Ḥillī (d. 726/1325), published.

[421] ***Irshād al-adhhān fī aḥkām*** *al-aymān*, AUTHOR: al-ʿAllāma al-Ḥillī (d. 726/1325), EDITION: Fāris al-Ḥassūn, 2 vols., Qum: Muʾassasat al-Nashr al-Islāmī, 1410 [1989].

[486] *Rawḍ al-jinān fī sharḥ Irshād al-adhhān* (not *al-azmān*), ***Ḥāshiyat*** (gloss on) *Irshād al-adhhān fī aḥkām al-aymān* of al-ʿAllāma al-Ḥillī, AUTHOR: al-Shahīd al-Thānī (d. 965/1557), EDITION: 2 vols., Qum: Bustān-i Kitāb, 2001–2002.

[424] ***al-ʿAshara*** *al-kāmila fī ʿasharat masāʾil min uṣūl al-fiqh*, AUTHOR: (probably) Sulaymān al-Baḥrānī (d. 1121/1709); see al-Baghdādī, *Hidāyat al-ʿārifīn*, I, 405.

[456] ***Ghāyat al-murād***, commentary on *Nukat al-irshād* of al-Shahīd al-Awwal (d. 786/1384), AUTHOR: **al-Shahīd al-Thānī** (d. 965/1557), EDITION: Qum: Markaz al-Abḥāth wa-al-Dirāsāt al-Islāmiyya, 1414 [1993–1994].

[482] ***Madārik al-aḥkām***, commentary on *Sharāʾiʿ al-islām* of al-Muḥaqqiq al-Ḥillī (d. 676/1277), parts 1–3, AUTHOR: Muḥammad b. ʿAlī al-Mūsawī al-ʿĀmilī (d. 1009/1600), EDITION: 9 vols., Qum: Muʾassasat Āl al-Bayt, 1989.

[488] *al-Rawḍa al-bahiyya* (***ḥāshiyat al-Lumʿa***), commentary on *al-Lumʿa al-dimashqiyya* of al-Shahīd al-Awwal (d. 786/1384), AUTHOR: al-Shahīd al-Thānī (d. 965/1557), published.

[502] ***Muntahā al-maṭlab*** *fī taḥqīq al-madhhab*, part 2, AUTHOR: (probably) al-ʿAllāma al-Ḥillī (d. 726/1325), EDITION: 15 vols., Mashhad: Majmaʿ al-Buḥūth al-Islāmiyya, 1993.

[568] ***al-Fatāwā***, AUTHOR: (probably) al-Shaykh **Najm al-Dīn** al-Aṭrāwī al-ʿĀmilī (fl. mid-eighth/fourteenth century); see al-ʿĀmilī, *Aʿyān al-Shīʿa*, III, 523.

Legal theory (*uṣūl al-fiqh*)

[379] ***al-Mughnī fī uṣūl al-fiqh***, AUTHOR: Jalāl al-Dīn al-Khabbāzī al-Khūjandī (d. 691/1292), EDITION: Muḥammad Baqā, Mecca: Jāmiʿat Umm al-Qurā, 1982–1983.

[469] ***al-Mankhūl***, AUTHOR: Abū Ḥāmid al-Ghazālī (d. 505/1111), published.

[480] ***al-Mustaṣfā***, part 2, AUTHOR: Abū Ḥāmid al-Ghazālī (d. 505/1111), published.

[497] ***Sharḥ*** (commentary on) *Sharḥ muntahā al-sūl* of **Ibn al-Ḥājib** (d. 646/1249), AUTHOR: ʿAḍud al-Dīn al-Ījī (d. 756/1355).

[499] ***Sharḥ*** (commentary on) ***Jamʿ al-jawāmiʿ*** of Tāj al-Dīn al-Subkī (d. 771/1370), AUTHOR: unknown.

[378] ***Sharḥ*** (commentary on) ***Jamʿ al-jawāmiʿ*** of Tāj al-Dīn al-Subkī (d. 771/1370), AUTHOR: al-ʿAynī (?).

Comparative law

[375] ***al-Mīzān***, AUTHOR: ʿAbd al-Wahhāb al-Shaʿrānī (d. 973/1565), published.

Unidentifiable but seemingly law-related titles

[357] Unknown work, AUTHOR: **Ṣadr al-Sharīʿa**

[389] ***al-Ṣayd wa-al-dhabāʾiḥ***

[392] ***Asās al-ṣāliḥīn***

[394] ***Taʿlīqāt muhimma***, two copies

[395] ***al-Iḥrām fī rafʿ al-yadayn ʿinda takbīrat al-iḥrām***

[400] ***Khulāṣat al-madhhab***

[402] ***al-Buyūʿ wa-al-rahāʾin***

[406] Five fragments (*ajzāʾ*) on Shāfiʿī law

[407] ***Aḥkām min al-fiqh al-shāfiʿī***

[419] ***Fiqh shāfiʿī***

[425] ***Fiqh shāfiʿī***

[426] ***al-Aḥkām fī fiqh al-Shāfiʿī***

[427] ***al-Masāʾil al-laṭīfa fī al-khilāf bayn al-Shāfiʿī wa-Abī Ḥanīfa***
[429] ***al-Irshād wa-al-naẓarayn*** (?)
[431] ***al-Nahy ʿan irtikāb al-maḥārim***
[432] ***Min al-fiqh al-shāfiʿī***
[434] ***Khulāṣat al-fatāwā***, AUTHOR: **al-Rāfiʿī** (?)
[439] ***Fiqh ḥanafī***
[440] Two fragments on Ḥanafī *fiqh*
[441] ***Kitāb fiqh ḥanafī***
[442] ***Fiqh ḥanafī***
[443] ***Fiqh ḥanafī***, incomplete
[445] ***Fiqh ḥanafī***, fragment
[446] ***Kitāb min uṣūl al-fiqh***
[447] ***Min al-fiqh al-shāfiʿī***
[448] ***Alfāẓ al-kufr*** (Numerous works carry this title. For a collection of such works, see *al-Jāmiʿ fī alfāẓ al-kufr*, edited by Muḥammad al-Khamīs, Kuwait City: Dār Īlāf al-Dawla, 1999.)
[458] ***al-Farāʾiḍ wa-al-waṣāyā***
[459] ***Shurūṭ al-ṣalāh***
[461] ***Shurūṭ al-ṣalāh***
[463] ***Kitāb fiqh ʿalā madhhab al-Imām al-aʿẓam*** [Ḥanafī law]
[467] ***Mukhtaṣar ʿUnwān al-adilla lil-aʾimma al-arbaʿa***
[472] ***al-Mukhtaṣar fī al-aḥkām***
[485] Collected epistles containing sermons, *fiqh*, inheritance rules
[495] ***Kitāb fī al-farāʾiḍ***
[561] ***Fatāwā Shaykh al-Islām***, MANUSCRIPT: arguably Jerusalem, Isʿāf al-Nashāshībī Library, MS 115.
[592] ***Kitāb fiqh***
[1651] ***Kitāb fiqh***, fragment
[1662] ***Masāʾil fiqhiyya***
[1678] ***Kitāb fiqh shāfiʿī***

Non-legal works

[376] ***Shirʿat al-islām***, AUTHOR: **Muḥammad b. Abī Bakr al-Sharghī al-Bukhārī Imām Zāda** (d. 573/1177–1178), EDITION: ʿAlī Sawāʿid and Mājid Ḥassūna, 2 vols., Master's thesis, University of Gaza, 2000.

[377] ***Jamʿ al-jawāmiʿ***, AUTHOR: al-Suyūṭī (d. 911/1505), not **al-Subkī**, MANUSCRIPT: Acre, al-Jazzār Mosque Library, MS 1 (ʿAṭā Allāh, *Fihris ʿAkkā*, 1983) (= EAP399/1/52), EDITION: 4 vols., Cairo: al-Azhar, Majmaʿ al-Buḥūth al-Islāmiyya, 1970.

[380] ***al-Mukhtār***, two copies, possibly an abridgement of *Faḍāʾil al-aʿmāl* of Diyāʾ al-Dīn al-Maqdisī (d. 643/1245), or alternatively another copy of ʿAbd Allāh al-Baldijī al-Mawṣilī's Ḥanafī teaching text *al-Mukhtār lil-fatwā* (see #430 above).

[381] ***al-Mukhtār ʿalā Faḍāʾil al-aʿmāl***, possibly an abridgement of *Faḍāʾil al-aʿmāl* of Diyāʾ al-Dīn al-Maqdisī (d. 643/1245).

[393] ***Kitāb al-Kasb***, AUTHOR: **Muḥammad b. al-Ḥasan al-Shaybānī**, EDITION: ʿAbd al-Fattāḥ Abū Ghudda, Aleppo: Maktab al-Maṭbūʿāt al-Islāmiyya, 1997; *The Book of Earning a Livelihood (Kitab al-Kasb)*, trans. Adi Setia, Kuala Lumpur: Islamic Banking & Finance Institute Malaysia, 2011.

[397] ***al-Radd al-ṭāʿin li-Abī Ḥanīfa*** [possibly *Risāla fī radd ṭaʿn al-Qaffāl al-Marwazī ʿalā al-Imām Abī Ḥanīfa* of ʿAbd al-Nabī al-Kankūhī (d. 991/1583)], AUTHOR: **al-Ghazālī** (?); see al-Ṭālibī, *al-Iʿlām*, IV, 380.

[398] ***al-Ifṣāḥ fī asmāʾ al-nikāḥ***, AUTHOR: al-Suyūṭī (d. 911/1505); see Ḥājjī Khalīfa, *Kashf al-ẓunūn*, I, 81.

[405] ***al-Radd ʿalā Abī Bakr al-Khaṭīb fī-mā dhakara fī tārīkhihi fī tarjamat al-imām sirāj al-umma Abī Ḥanīfa raḍiya Allāh ʿanhu***, AUTHOR: al-Malik al-Muʿaẓẓam Sharaf al-Dīn al-Ayyūbī (d. 624/1227), EDITION: Cairo: Maṭbaʿat al-Saʿāda, 1932.

[457] ***Bughyat al-albāb***, AUTHOR: **Muḥammad b. Budayr** (d. 1220/1805), MSS: Jerusalem, Āl Budayrī Library, nos. 273, 480 and 481; uncatalogued manuscript, HMML Proj. Num. ABLJ 01178.

[473] ***al-Dirāya li-aḥkām al-riʿāya***, AUTHOR: **Sharaf al-Dīn al-Ḥamawī** (d. 738/1338), EDITION: Anas al-ʿUmr, Istanbul: Dār al-Samān, 2020.

[478] ***Sharḥ al-kabāʾir***, in Turkish, AUTHOR: İsmail Hakkı Bursevi (d. 1137/1725), EDITION: Istanbul: Maṭbaʿat Ḥazrat Sirr ʿAskariyya, 1257 [1841].

[492] ***al-Wujūh wa-al-naẓāʾir***; MANUSCRIPT: Dublin, Chester Beatty Library, Ar. 3334.

[500] ***Waṣiyya***, AUTHOR: **Abū Ḥanīfa**, EDITION: Abū Muʿādh ʿUwayna, Beirut: Dār Ibn Ḥazm, 1997.

[484] Commentary on ***Waṣiyya*** of **Abū Ḥanīfa**

[503] ***Waqf*** document written for **Maḥmūd b. Muḥammad al-Naqshbandī al-Urmawī** (d. unknown); his work *Kazīd fī ʿilm al-tajwīd* is preserved in MSS Damascus, Ẓāhiriyya 334, and Medina, Maḥmūdiyya 2831.

CHAPTER 17

Books on Islamic Theology (*tawḥīd*) and Sufism (*taṣawwuf*): Rational Verification and Experiential Learning in Ottoman Palestine

Hadel Jarada

The inventory of the library established by the Ottoman governor of Acre, Aḥmad Pasha al-Jazzār (d. 1219/1804), provides an image of a collection suspended in time. Compiled in 1221/1806—only two years after Jazzār's death—the inventory contains a selection of books on *tawḥīd* and *taṣawwuf*, terms that typically denote the fields of Islamic theology and Islamic mysticism, respectively. A total of 140 entries are listed, containing at least thirty-three distinct titles on *tawḥīd*, and seventy-two distinct titles on *taṣawwuf*, with significant repetition and overlap in between. The inventory invites readers to question what was presumed to be a book of *tawḥīd* during this period, as opposed to a book of *taṣawwuf*. It also invites readers to reflect on why these two fields were catalogued together, given their disparate aims.

As the present chapter demonstrates, *tawḥīd* was a term that underpinned any engagement with broadly theological matters. Like theologians, Sufis were also deeply enmeshed in theological inquiries, and many considered their contributions to fall within the broad domain of *tawḥīd*, a term that signifies the concept of divine unity. This term is frequently invoked in reference to the field of Islamic theology, which aims to articulate and defend fundamental presuppositions of Islamic belief, including the existence of God and His attributes. The most widely used appellation for this field in the premodern period was *ʿilm al-kalām*. *Tawḥīd* is a less technical term that came to signify a domain of knowledge distilled into a set of creedal doctrines, often understood more broadly as the 'Islamic creed'. On the one hand, the term functions as a synonym for *kalām*, and on the other, it is broader and more encompassing of alternative theologies.[1] The purpose of *tawḥīd* works was to articulate the primary theological doctrines that form the framework and foundation of Islamic belief. While these works also often explore the arguments undergirding the creed, introductory *tawḥīd* texts typically focus on outlining the orthodox creed without delving into the underlying argumentative framework.[2] As the Jazzār collection attests, *tawḥīd* is a project in which even Sufis considered themselves engaged. Many of the explicitly Sufi works in this collection laid claim to *tawḥīd* as their central project. Analogous to other highly prized banners in Islam, *tawḥīd*, or the affirmation of God's unity, became a project coveted by all.

The writings on *tawḥīd* and *taṣawwuf* featured in the collection likely found their way into the library through two primary channels: the Egyptian market and the Syrian market.[3] Egypt served

1 *Tawḥīd* has a long-documented history of usage and carries multiple semantic meanings. In the Ottoman period, the term underwent a conceptual evolution, acquiring new connotations while shedding others. Given the semantic complexity of the term, examining its history and usage during this period are beyond the scope of this article. For more on the concept, see Dastagir/Ramzy, "Tawḥīd", 687–690.

2 For more on what is typically understood to be the orthodox creed, see Watt, "ʿAḳīda".

3 By Egyptian and Syrian market, I do not mean that manuscripts were composed by Egyptian or Syrian scribes, or were exclusively sourced from Egypt and Syria. Rather, I mean that the books in this particular section largely derived from an intellectual tradition flourishing in two main hotspots: North Africa (including Egypt) and Syria. Only

DOI:10.1163/9789004720527_019

as the source of a significant portion of texts explicitly aligned with Ashʿarī theology. These works were predominantly studied in educational institutions across North Africa and the Levant. Some writings on *taṣawwuf* also trace their origins to North Africa. Another subset of works likely derived from a more local economy, their authors being mystics or theologians (or mystically inclined theologians) from greater Syria. Many of these works were oriented towards the school of Ibn al-ʿArabī (d. 638/1240) and the controversial doctrine of *waḥdat al-wujūd*. But not all mystics featured in the collection subscribed to this doctrine. Others endorsed *taṣawwuf* only insofar as it cohered with orthodox Ashʿarī theology. A clear vacuum in these writings is the Māturīdī theological tradition. There are no Māturīdī works in the collection,[4] an interesting lacuna given the Ottomans' endorsement of Ḥanafism as official state doctrine.[5] Notably, only rarely do we find an advanced work of theology or mysticism in the collection. The impression one leaves with is that these books were mainly intended for beginner students just embarking on their religious studies.[6] It is also noteworthy that the items in this section are neither rare nor particularly advanced. This accords with the fact that the library was founded by a provincial governor of the Ottoman state rather than a wealthy sultan or a scholar with requirements for a more sophisticated and extensive collection.

In what follows, I begin with an analysis of works in the collection explicitly oriented towards Ashʿarī theology, which form a cornerstone of the library's holdings. I then delve into the works of the Greatest Shaykh (*al-shaykh al-akbar*) Ibn al-ʿArabī (d. 638/1240), whose writings, substantial in themselves, color much of what follows. I then turn to works of proponents of the doctrine of *waḥdat al-wujūd*, before returning once again to Ashʿarism and what I call *kalām*-compliant mysticism. My aim is to demonstrate how these works and their inclusion in the collection mirror the intellectual currents prevalent during the late Ottoman era.

1 Ashʿarī Theology

One of the most prominent works featured in the Jazzār collection is a creed composed by the North African theologian Muḥammad b. Yūsuf al-Sanūsī (d. 895/1490), from the city of Tlemcen in present-day Algeria.[7] Sanūsī wrote extensively on theology and logic, specifically from an Ashʿarī perspective.[8] The inventory features five copies of his short creed *al-ʿAqīda al-ṣughra*, also known as *Umm al-barāhīn* (The Mother of Proofs) and *al-Sanūsiyya* (Sanūsī's Creed) (#605, #607, #608, #734 and #737). Sanūsī's succinct creed served as an essential primer on Islamic theology, thus establishing itself as a 'cornerstone in educational institutions across both the east and west'.[9] Not only does the Jazzār library feature five copies of the base text, but it also boasts four commentaries on the work (#606, #616, #641 and #738) and one epitome (#735), making it one of the most heavily represented works in the collection. While Sanūsī

rarely do we find works that fall outside the confines of the discourse that is happening in these two intellectual hubs. My analysis in what follows will hone in on this central contention. For more on the cataloguer's specification of various calligraphic scripts, see Said Aljoumani's Chapter 2 in this volume. For the difficult-to-ascertain derivation of works directly from Egypt, see Liebrenz's Chapter 3 in this volume.

4 A possible exception may be Taftazānī's commentary on Nasafī's creed (#611 and #614). While the base text is a Māturīdī creed, Taftāzānī was Ashʿarī and glossed over explicitly Māturīdī positions, such as *takwīn*.

5 On which, see Burak, *Second Formation*.

6 It is worth noting that the Jazzār library was attached to Jazzār's endowed mosque, and the books in the collection were intended for the study of the religious sciences. The vast majority of works within this section are introductory or geared towards practical application, suggesting that the collection was curated to serve students just embarking on their religious studies. On the inventory list, see Abū Diyyah, *Waqfiyyat Aḥmad Bāshā al-Jazzār*, 32.

7 For more on his life, see the biography composed by his student al-Mallālī, *al-Mawāhib al-qudsiyya*.

8 See El-Rouayheb, *Development of Arabic Logic*, 130–135.

9 Belhāj, "Muḥammad b. Yūsuf al-Sanūsī", 217.

famously composed versions of his creed in different lengths and levels of difficulty,[10] only his short creed appears in the Jazzār library. Sanūsī's creed was widely read in Egypt and North Africa, but the inventory signals that its popularity also extended to the Levant, where options for theological study were more abundant. The Damascene scholar ʿAbd al-Ghanī al-Nābulusī (1050–1143/1641–1731) notes in his account of his travels to Jerusalem that a fellow intellectual luminary by the name of Badrān al-Khalīlī, presumably from Hebron, put Sanūsī's short creed to verse and asked him to comment on it.[11] The same Khalīlī asked Nābulusī, known for his mystical monism and adherence to the controversial doctrine of *waḥdat al-wujūd*, to comment on key theological problems, such as the faith of Pharaoh, found within such works. Sanūsī's creed was one entryway into these discussions. As Katip Çelebi notes, the work was popular because it contained all creedal doctrines (*jamīʿ ʿaqāʾid al-tawḥīd*) that a practicing Muslim was expected to believe in order to rationally verify his faith.[12] Dozens of commentaries were written on the base text,[13] the inventory listing four such commentaries, without specifying their author. Notably, Sanūsī's project was to distil his creed into smaller and smaller units, while also elaborating on the creed through commentaries that would serve more advanced students. It is therefore not unlikely, given how predominant his name is on the inventory list,[14] that these entries refer to his own commentaries.

Another entryway into the study of theology was the Egyptian scholar Ibrāhīm al-Laqānī's (d. 1041/1631) *Jawharat al-tawḥīd*, a didactic poem which similarly elucidates the main theological doctrines that a believing Muslim was expected to uphold. Like Sanūsī, Laqānī wrote a commentary on his work which was commonly read alongside it, titled *Hidāyat al-murīd* (#603).[15] His son ʿAbd al-Salām al-Laqānī (d. 1078/1668) also wrote a commentary on his father's work, titled *Itḥāf al-murīd bi-sharḥ jawharat al-tawḥīd* (#601). The work was perhaps even more popular than the creed composed by his father, and it was commonly read alongside Laqānī's *Jawhara* once a student had put the poem to memory. The inventory features five copies of the *Jawharat al-tawḥīd* and its commentaries (#600–603 and #640).[16] The importance of these works as mnemonic guides cannot be overstated. Once a student had memorised the base text of the creed—in this case, the didactic poem of the *Jawhara*—they would be in a better position to understand the full composition by studying explications of its principles found in the commentary tradition. As a further testament to Ashʿarī influence, the library also contains two copies of a commentary on the Egyptian scholar Abū al-Irshād ʿAlī b. Muḥammad al-Ajhūrī's (d. 1066/1655) Ashʿarī creed (listed as *Sharḥ ʿaqīdat al-ajhūrī*, #613 and #615).

While the North African theological tradition reigns supreme in the library's holdings, certain 'universal' works also permeate the collection. One author who was almost universally popular in the Islamic world and who makes several appearances on the library's inventory is the well-known mystic and Ashʿarī theologian 'the Proof of Islam', Abū Ḥāmid al-Ghazālī (d. 505/1111). Ghazālī was known not only as a *mutakallim* but also a mystic who

10 His creeds have been edited and published in a five-volume set by al-Sharfāwī, *al-Silsila*.

11 Nābulusī, *al-Haḍra al-unsiyya*, 281.

12 Katip Çelebi, *Kashf al-ẓunūn*, I, 170.

13 Several commentaries have been printed in Sanūsī, *Majmūʿ umm al-barāhīn*.

14 Sanūsī is also the author of a widely read work on logic titled *al-Mukhtaṣar al-manṭīqī* which appears in the logic section of the Jazzār library. See Asad Ahmed's Chapter 20 in this volume.

15 The *Hidāyat al-murīd* was Lāqānī's short commentary on his didactic poem, the *Jawḥarat al-tawḥīd*. Laqānī also wrote a middle commentary titled *Talkhīs al-tajrīd li-ʿumdat al-murīd sharḥ jawharat al-tawḥīd*, and a long commentary titled *ʿUmdat al-murīd*. Both works were likely part of the collection, as indicated in #600 and #602.

16 A further entry #707 lists a work titled *Zād al-murīd*, which may be a commentary on the *Jawharat al-tawḥīd*.

eventually abandoned rational theology in pursuit of a higher experiential mysticism which he discusses in his autobiography *al-Munqidh min al-ḍalāl*. The *Munqidh* appears twice on the inventory list (#620 and #629), although instead of *ḍalāl*, the cataloguer transcribes *ḍalāla*, a minute change which nevertheless indicates that the work may have been known by a slightly different title.[17] A 'Treatise on Theology' (*Risāla fī al-tawḥīd*) is also listed thrice and attributed to Ghazālī (#625, #626 and #660), which likely alludes to a short creed Ghazālī composed as part of his voluminous *Iḥyāʾ ʿulūm al-dīn* (The Revivification of the Religious Sciences). The creed came to be known by the twin names *Qawāʿid al-ʿaqāʾid* (The Principles of the Creed) and *al-Risāla al-qudsiyya* (The Jerusalem Treatise), the latter in reference to the fact that it was reportedly composed while Ghazālī was in Jerusalem.[18] In one entry, the cataloguer explicitly transcribes *al-Risāla al-qudsiyya* (#660). Interestingly, the fact that the treatise appears in three singular manuscripts detached from the broader context of the *Iḥyāʾ* signals that the treatise was read and circulated as an independent creedal work rather than as part of the *Iḥyāʾ*. Perhaps the fact that the treatise was written, according to the biographer Murtaḍā al-Zabīdī (d. 1205/1790), for the sake of the people of Jerusalem, accounts for its popularity in centres of Palestinian learning such as Acre.[19] In connection, one also finds a commentary on Ghazālī's creed by the prominent Moroccan mystic of the Shādhilī order and committed Ashʿarī, Aḥmad Zarrūq al-Fāsī (d. 899/1493), titled *Ightinām al-fawāʾid bi-sharḥ qawāʿid al-ʿaqāʾid* (#676).[20]

2 Theological Works from the East

As the above titles show, the theology section of the Jazzār library contains works that were part of a general 'western' milieu: works that were popular in North Africa, Egypt and the Levant. Up to this point, all listed works have been Ashʿarī creeds, suggesting a centripetal influence from Egypt and North Africa, where Ashʿarism was predominant. But the library also contains works stemming from the eastern Islamic realm, extending from Iraq to Iran and Central Asia. The inventory features one copy of the summa of philosophy and theology *al-Ṣaḥāʾif al-ilāhiyya* (#619) by the Central Asian scholar Shams al-Dīn al-Samarqandī (d. 722/1322), whose works on philosophy, theology, and logic were popular among the Ottoman scholarly class. In particular, Samarqandī's *Ṣaḥāʾif* and its commentary *al-Maʿārif fī sharḥ al-ṣaḥāʾif* are attested in dozens of library collections throughout the region. One also finds a copy of the summa of theology and philosophy, the *Tajrīd al-ʿaqāʾid* (#612), by the Mongol-era Shīʿī philosopher Naṣīr al-Dīn al-Ṭūsī (d. 672/1274), which is one of the more advanced works of philosophical theology in the collection. Notably, these are the only two works in the collection that may be regarded as touching upon *falsafa*. Another popular theological manual arising out of the Central Asian tradition and featured in the library's holdings is the commentary on Nasafī's creed by the major Timurid the-

17 This alternate title is evinced in dozens of works from this period and region, indicating that the work was likely known as *al-Munqidh min al-ḍalāla*, rather than *al-ḍalāl*, in areas of the Levant. See, for example, the following authors who cite Ghazālī's work as *al-Munqidh min al-ḍalāla*: al-Kafawī, *Kitāb aʿlām al-akhyār*, I, 257; Ibn ʿĀbidīn, *Majmūʿat rasāʾil Ibn ʿĀbidīn*, I, 300; Ibn Ḥajar al-Haytamī, *al-Fatāwā al-ḥadīthiyya*, 512; Zaynī Daḥlān, *al-Sīra al-nabawiyya*, I, 133. Ghazālī's *Munqidh* was also translated into Turkish, also with the alternative title *al-Munqidh min al-ḍalāla*. For the Turkish translation, see al-Baghdādī, *Hadiyyat al-ʿĀrifīn*, II, 400.

18 In the *Iḥyāʾ*, Ghazālī states that he has named the work (*samaynāhu*) *al-Risāla al-qudsiyya fī qawāʿid al-ʿaqāʾid* (I, 180). The two parts of the name were separated out and used synonymously to refer to the one work. On *al-Risāla al-qudsiyya*, see Badawī, *Muʾallafāt al-Ghazālī*, 89–92.

19 al-Zabīdī, *Itḥāf al-sāda*, I, 57.

20 On Zarrūq, see the introduction by Nizār Ḥammādī in Zarrūq, *Ightinām al-fawāʾid* and Kugle, *Rebel between Spirit and Law*.

ologian Saʿd al-Dīn al-Taftāzānī (d. 793/1390) (#611 and #614). Taftāzānī's works were a core part of the *madrasa* curriculum in the Ottoman empire.[21] And despite first circulating in far-flung Central Asia, his works on philosophy, theology, rhetoric, jurisprudence and logic were known and studied as far as Egypt possibly within his own lifetime.[22] The Jazzār library features a supercommentary on Taftāzānī's commentary on Nasafī's creed by the Kurdish scholar Ilyās al-Kūrānī (d. 1138/1725) (#638, and possibly also #639), who had travelled to Jerusalem from Damascus after studying in the Kurdish areas of southeastern Anatolia, where he was originally from. A Shāfiʿī scholar with mystical leanings, Kūrānī wrote commentaries on works of logic and theology, illustrating that scholars who were practicing Sufis during this period were also reading and thinking about theology and the rational sciences.[23] Kūrānī's supercommentary was not particularly influential, and its inclusion in the library's inventory suggests that it may have been procured on the heels of Kūrānī's stay in Palestine, reflecting a local economy of works on theology.

Yet, the inclusion of works by eastern authors does not detract from the fact that the Jazzār collection was mainly a representation of the North African theological tradition. *Madrasa* students in Palestine would often travel to Egypt to continue their studies, where they undoubtedly procured works from the Egyptian book market. Some of these students were trained by Maghrebi scholars, and many of them were initiated into Sufi orders popular in various parts of North Africa, such as the Shādhiliyya. Although the collection predominantly features works of Sufism written with the priorities of the Naqshbandiyya and Khalwatiyya in mind, it also contains a distinct subset of writings by North African Shādhilī mystics who fused aspects of Islamic theology with Sufism. A notable figure in this category is the Moroccan mystic Aḥmad Zarrūq al-Fāsī (d. 899/1493). However, it is undoubtedly the 'Greatest Shaykh' (*al-shaykh al-akbar*) Muḥyī al-Dīn Ibn al-ʿArabī who features most prominently on Jazzār's list. The latter's interest in Ibn al-ʿArabī is echoed in the account of the Ottoman chronicler Cābī (d. after 1229/1814), who relates that Jazzār's rise was prophesied by Ibn al-ʿArabī, Jazzār being 'the Jim Jim that the Greatest Shaykh wrote and alluded to [in his *al-Shajara al-nuʿmāniyya*]'.[24]

3 The Works of the 'Greatest Shaykh' (*al-shaykh al-akbar*) Muḥyī al-Dīn Ibn al-ʿArabī (d. 638/1240)

As the ideal of verification permeates the library's holdings on theology, exemplified in creedal works like Sanūsī's *Umm al-barāhīn*, it similarly permeates the library's holdings on mysticism. The Jazzār library features at least seventy-two distinct works of *taṣawwuf*, encompassing a wide range that includes classical Sufi literature, devotional ethics and prayer manuals, and works rooted in the tradition of ontological monism associated with the school of Muḥyī al-Dīn Ibn al-ʿArabī. Eight of the seventy-two *taṣawwuf* works housed in the Jazzār library were penned by Ibn al-ʿArabī himself, constituting eleven per cent of the library's holdings on mysticism. A substantial portion of the remaining works belong to Ibn al-ʿArabī's school, penned by authors who self-identify as Sufi proponents of ideas stemming from the tradition of commentary on his works.

21 On the prominence of Taftāzānī during the post-classical period, see El-Rouayheb, "Rethinking the Canons". On his inclusion in the *madrasa* curriculum, see Subtelny and Khalidov, "The Curriculum of Islamic Higher Learning".

22 See Ibn Khaldūn, *The Muqaddimah*, III, 117.

23 On Ilyās al-Kūrānī, see Murādī, *Silk al-durar*, I, 309–312; Akkach, *Intimate Invocations*, 224; Dumairieh, *Intellectual Life*, 126–127. On the role of Kurdish scholars in the transmission of the rational sciences, see El-Rouayheb, *Islamic Intellectual History*, 13–59.

24 Cābī, *Tārihi*, I, 84. I am grateful to Guy Burak for this reference and translation.

Ibn al-ʿArabī was a prolific writer with an estimated output exceeding three hundred works.[25] Among the eight works featured in the Jazzār library, one finds three copies of his voluminous *al-Futūḥāt al-makkiyya* (#651–653),[26] a vast philosophical compendium and mystical encyclopaedia whose pages number in the thousands, being Ibn al-ʿArabī's longest work. Alongside his shorter compendium *Fuṣūṣ al-ḥikam*, the *Futūḥāt* stands out as possibly Ibn al-ʿArabī's most popular work. The complexity of the *Futūḥāt* defies simple classification: It is not simply a Sufi manual or a philosophical compendium, but addresses a wide range of topics, including metaphysics, cosmology, spiritual psychology and anthropology. Its popularity endured well into the Ottoman period. According to the Mamluk historian Ṣalāḥ al-Dīn al-Ṣafadī (d. 764/1363), the work contains 'precise, strange, and wonderous things not present in anyone else's idiom'.[27] Importantly, Ṣafadī observed that the work aligns with the creed of al-Ashʿarī, noting that 'Ibn al-ʿArabī presents his theology in the first volume of the *Futūḥāt*, and I saw that from its beginning to its end, it is identical to the creed of the Shaykh Abū al-Ḥasan al-Ashʿarī. There is nothing in it that diverges from his thought'.[28] Such interpretations about the coherence between Ibn al-ʿArabī's thought as presented in the *Futūḥāt*, and Ashʿarī theology were widespread. Orthodox Ashʿarīs were inclined to embrace the *Futūḥāt* as a theologically compelling compendium while rejecting the views of the *waḥdat al-wujūd* monists who increasingly pushed for interpretations incompatible with orthodox theological dogma. The *Futūḥāt* served as a gateway into Ibn al-ʿArabī's mystical philosophy among students who, by the late Ottoman period, were simultaneously studying introductory creedal handbooks such as the *Umm al-barāhīn* and the *Jawharat al-tawḥīd*.

While the Jazzār library contains three copies of the *Futūḥāt*, there are no copies of the base text of Ibn al-ʿArabī's *Fuṣūṣ al-ḥikam*, a short but extremely influential compendium that delves into the particular divine wisdom revealed to each of the prophets.[29] However, the library contains three commentaries on the work (#642c, #648 and #649). Both the *Futūḥāt* and the *Fuṣūṣ* were highly sought after, with over one hundred commentaries documented on the *Fuṣūṣ* alone.[30] The work was often a medium through which the philosophy of *waḥdat al-wujūd* was propagated. The absence of copies of the base text of the *Fuṣūṣ* may suggest that the library's holdings on *taṣawwuf* were primarily curated to align with Ashʿarī theology. Another possibility is that the *Fuṣūṣ* was typically studied in conjunction with a commentary, seldom in isolation, and therefore Ibn al-ʿArabī's ideas were accessed through commentaries on his work. As noted, the Jazzār library includes three copies of a 'commentary on the *Fuṣūṣ al-ḥikam*'. In all three cases, the author is not mentioned. Given that the library contains many local productions—works by scholars traveling to or living in the area of Ottoman Palestine—one might be inclined to presume that these entries refer to the commentary of ʿAbd al-Ghanī al-Nābulusī (d. 1143/1731), a mystic who travelled widely and who wrote the first major commentary on the *Fuṣūṣ* by an Arab scholar. But in all but one case, Nābulusī is explicitly mentioned by Jazzār's cataloguer as the author of the work in question. One must therefore look elsewhere for the authors of these commentaries

25 The Ottoman era bibliographer Ṭāşköprīzāde notes that Ibn al-ʿArabī was an incredibly prolific scholar, having produced a multitude of works that defy enumeration (*taṣānīfuhu lā tuḥṣā*) (*Miftāh al-saʿāda*, I, 214). On different accounts of the number of Ibn al-ʿArabī's works, see the editor's remarks in *al-Futūḥāt al-makkiyya*, I, 32.

26 Entry #653 is currently held in the Khālidī Library in Jerusalem under call number AKDI 01060/1026 (Formerly MS 1981).

27 Ṣafadī, *al-Wāfī bi-al-wafāyāt*, IV, 125.

28 Ibid.

29 For more on the *Futūḥāt* and the *Fuṣūṣ* and what they endeavour to do, see Nasr, *Three Muslim Sages*, 98–99.

30 See Yahya, *Historie et classification*, 241–255.

on the *Fuṣūṣ*. The most renowned commentaries were by scholars linked directly to Ibn al-ʿArabī through a master-disciple relationship. They include Ṣadr al-Dīn al-Qūnāwī (d. 673/1274) (his son-in-law and main vehicle for the interpretation of his ideas), Muʾayyad al-Dīn al-Jandī (d. 700/1300), ʿAbd al-Razzāq al-Qāshānī (d. 730–736/1329–1335) and Dāwūd al-Qayṣarī (d. 751/1350). The inventory may be pointing in the direction of one of these commentaries. Importantly, the library contains one copy of a commentary on the divine names by Qūnawī, whose works were the most important vehicle for the invigoration and elaboration of the doctrine of *waḥdat al-wujūd* (#674).[31]

As noted, the reception of the *Fuṣūṣ* was much more contentious compared to the *Futūḥāt*. Many scholars associated the work with the more elaborate ontological monism that the school of Ibn al-ʿArabī became famous for. According to Ṣafadī, 'the *Fuṣūṣ* displays many things that do not reflect reality nor accord with God's revelation', which he explained away by reasoning that perhaps Ibn al-ʿArabī was in an ecstatic state when writing the work and could not find the right language to communicate what he was experiencing. Later scholars associated the *Fuṣūṣ* with the ontological monism famously encapsulated by the formula 'the unity of existence' (*waḥdat al-wujūd*), which in its most basic sense connotes the idea that existence belongs solely to God, that God *is* existence, and therefore, that existence is one and divine.[32] Many thought that this idea descended into pantheism: insofar as existence is one, everything could be worshipped as part of God's efflorescence. While the *Fuṣūṣ* does not make a solo appearance in the Jazzār library, in other libraries contemporaneously established in Ottoman Palestine, both the *matn* of the work, as well as commentaries on the work, abound. We find the base text of the *Fuṣūṣ*, for example, in the endowment document of the books of Ḥasan ʿAbd al-Laṭīf al-Ḥusaynī (dated 1201/1787), along with two copies of the *Futūḥāt*, demonstrating that these works were widely read and studied by scholars interested in Sufism in this region.[33] Moreover, the extensive presence of these works not only in al-Jazzār's collection but also in other libraries suggests their pivotal role as primary sources for the dissemination of mystical philosophy. As a case in point, the Jazzār library boasts an extremely influential work by ʿAbd al-Karīm al-Jīlī (d. 826/1422), titled *al-Insān al-kāmil fī maʿrifat al-awākhir wa-al-awāʾil* (#655), a compendium of Sufi metaphysics which centrally engages with Ibn al-ʿArabī's idea of the perfect man.[34]

Ibn al-ʿArabī's widespread readership can also be gleaned from several other works he composed which are featured in the library's inventory. These include his *al-Tadbīrāt al-ilāhiyya fī iṣlāḥ al-mamlaka al-insāniyya* (#682), a short piece that allegorically represents the human being as a kingdom; his *Mashāhid al-asrār al-qudsiyya wa-maṭāliʿ al-anwār al-ilāhiyya* (#687), which takes the form of dialogues with God manifest in fourteen visions or contemplations; his *Kitāb al-waṣāya* (#688), a work which features an alternate edition of the last chapter of the *Futūḥāt*; a compilation of Ibn al-ʿArabī's letters appropriately titled *Rasāʾil Ibn al-ʿArabī* (#650); and his *ʿAnqāʾ mughrib fī maʿrifat khatm al-awliyāʾ wa-shams al-maghrib* (#740), a work on Islamic sainthood. In total, eight works in the collection belong to Ibn al-ʿArabī, making him one of the most prominently featured mystical authors in the inventory list. But the existence of these works is not the only attestation of the popularity of his thought. The library contains dozens of works by proponents of his mystical philosophy, to which we now turn.

31 The library also contains three other commentaries on the divine names (#673, #680, #699 and #700), one notably in Persian (#700).

32 On the concept of *waḥdat al-wūjud*, see Chittick, "Rūmī and Waḥdat al-Wujūd".

33 Al-Bakhīt, "Al-Maktabāt fī al-Quds al-Sharīf", 448.

34 Parts of the work were translated by Burckhardt in *Universal Man*. For a study of Jīlī and his work, see Morrissey, *Sufism and the Scriptures* and Morris, "Ibn ʿArabi and His Interpreters", 108–110.

4 Proponents of the Akbarī[35] Way in the Jazzār Library

The true significance of Ibn al-ʿArabī's *Futūḥāt* emerges through the commentaries, abridgments and studies authored by scholars who relied on its content. As previously noted, the *Futūḥāt* was often understood as aligning with, rather than conflicting with, orthodox Ashʿarī theology. In the context of the fifteenth and sixteenth centuries, there was a tradition of Sufi commentary, particularly robust in Egypt and the Levant, which venerated Ibn al-ʿArabī as a saint—specifically on the basis of readings of the *Futūḥāt*—while expressing reservations about the later ontological monism expounded by commentators on the *Fuṣūṣ*. Khaled El-Rouayheb, for example, has demonstrated that the reimagining of Ibn al-ʿArabī as a Sufi saint was intimately tied to the interpretation of the *Futūḥāt*.[36]

One author whose works reflect this trend is the Egyptian scholar ʿAbd al-Wahhāb al-Shaʿrānī (d. 973/1565), the second most represented figure in the section on Sufism after Ibn al-ʿArabī himself. Shaʿrānī negotiated the difficult and often frayed relationship between acceptable Sufism and ontological monism. As Leila Hudson has shown with respect to late Ottoman Syria, Shaʿrānī was one of the most widely read scholars from this period whose works were regarded as adeptly treading the fine line between orthodoxy and heterodoxy.[37] The library features seven works by Shaʿrānī, one of which is an abridgment of the *Futūḥāt* titled *Lawāqiḥ al-anwār al-qudsiyya al-muntaqāt min al-futūḥāt al-makkiyya* (#717).

What explains Shaʿrānī's popularity during this period, as evinced on the inventory list? The argument so far has been that the Jazzār collection attests to an increasing trend among scholars to selectively embrace aspects of Ibn al-ʿArabī's thought, while discarding elements deemed theologically problematic, particularly those inherited from the commentary tradition. Shaʿrānī played a pivotal role in reinterpreting Ibn al-ʿArabī to accord with prevailing theological sentiment. His works reconceptualized Ibn al-ʿArabī as a revered Sufi saint, a transformation facilitated primarily through the lens of the *Futūḥāt*.

In the *Lawāqiḥ* (#717), Shaʿrānī presents a case for understanding the *Futūḥāt* in a manner consistent with orthodox theology, thereby painting Ibn al-ʿArabī as a figure unburdened by the later interpretations of the proponents of *waḥdat al-wujūd*. In an even more condensed abridgement of the *Futūḥāt* titled *al-Kibrīt al-aḥmar fī bayān ʿulūm al-shaykh al-akbar*, also featured on the inventory list (#672), Shaʿrānī explores Ibn al-ʿArabī's programmatic for the spiritual life, once again trying to detach his mystical philosophy from the interpretations of the proponents of *waḥdat al-wujūd*. These works in the Jazzār collection demonstrate the centrality of the person of Shaʿrānī to the reimagining of Ibn al-ʿArabī as a Sufi saint during this period.

The library also houses two copies of Shaʿrānī's largest theological work, which contains his most elaborate defence of Ibn al-ʿArabī (#634 and #635), titled *al-Yawāqīt wa-al-jawāhir fī bayān ʿaqāʾid al-akābir*. In this work, Shaʿrānī explicitly notes that his aim is to 'reconcile the creed of the people of Unveiling (i.e. the Sufis) and the people of ratiocination (i.e. the rational theologians)',[38] demonstrating the compatibility of Ibn al-ʿArabī's ideas with Ashʿarī theology. Further works by Shaʿrānī include two copies of his *Kashf al-ḥijāb wa-al-rān ʿan wajh asʾilat al-jān* (#663 and #664), a book that provides answers to eighty questions, mostly of a theological nature, directed at Shaʿrānī by a group of believing jinn (*al-jān*).[39] In another work featured in the library's inventory list titled *Laṭāʾif al-minan*

35 Many of Ibn al-ʿArabī's later followers came to be known as Akbarīs, deriving from Ibn al-ʿArabī's honorific title, *al-Shaykh al-akbar*.

36 El-Rouayheb, *Islamic Intellectual History*, 237.

37 See Hudson, "Reading al-Shaʿrānī".

38 This translation comes from El-Rouayheb, *Islamic Intellectual History*, 238.

39 See the introductory passage in Shaʿrānī, *Kashf al-ḥijāb*, 6.

wa-al-akhlāq fī wujūb al-taḥadduth bi-niʿmat Al-lāh ʿalā al-iṭlāq (otherwise known as *al-Minan al-kubrā*) (#656), Shaʿrānī presents his autobiography, detailing the stages of his initiation into Sufism and the manifold ethical qualities he cultivated along the way, which aims to communicate to his followers the ethics that are demanded of Sufi initiates. In a further work titled *al-Jawāhir wa-al-durar* (#720), Shaʿrānī outlines the main teachings and axioms he learned from his eminent shaykh, a certain ʿAlī al-Khawwāṣṣ al-Burulsī (d. 949/1542). And finally, in a work titled *Mawāzīn al-rijāl al-qāṣirīn* (#662), Shaʿrānī rebukes the Sufis of his era, highlighting the inadequacies of their behavior and explaining what steps they need to take to improve their condition. A theme during this period, Shaʿrāni is one of several prominent mystical scholars who wrote works bemoaning the state of Sufism and the Sufis.[40]

But not all works were explicitly trying to explain away the more problematic aspects of *waḥdat al-wujūd*. Many scholars writing in the Levant during this period in fact embraced the interpretations of the commentators (specifically on the *Fuṣūṣ al-ḥikam*). These include prominent mystics like ʿAbd al-Ghanī al-Nābulusī (d. 1143/1731), Muṣṭafā al-Bakrī (d. 1172/1749) and Qāsim al-Khānī (d. 1109/1697)—all of whom lived in Syria but spent substantial time in Palestine.

The Jazzār library features five (or possibly six) works by the Damascene mystic and scholar ʿAbd al-Ghanī al-Nābulusī (d. 1143/1731), previously mentioned as the first Arab scholar to write a major commentary on Ibn al-ʿArabī's *Fuṣūṣ*. A prolific author with over two hundred works to his name, Nābulusī was heavily influenced by Ibn al-ʿArabī and a prominent advocate of his views. Unlike Shaʿrānī, he explicitly endorsed the more ecstatic elements deriving from the commentary tradition, most importantly the profession of the 'unity of existence' (*waḥdat al-wujūd*). Despite the often-frayed relationship between individuals identifying as orthodox theologians and ontological monists promoting such doctrines, Nābulusī walked a tightrope, garnering considerable praise for his expertise in the traditional Islamic sciences (including law, *ḥadīth* and Qurʾanic exegesis) and eventually earning the esteemed position of Ḥanafi Mufti of Damascus. In addition to his scholarly oeuvre, Nābulusī was well-travelled, and through his own travel accounts, we know that he visited parts of Ottoman Palestine, spending considerable time in Jerusalem and other important locales.[41] The library features five (possibly six) works by Nābulusī, including two commentaries on self-styled creedal works (or *Rasāʾil fī al-tawḥīd*). While described as being on *tawḥīd*, typically associated with theology, both of his commentaries evince a Sufi frame of mind, demonstrating that *tawḥīd* was a flexible term that did not necessarily singularly apply to orthodox Ashʿarī or Māturīdī theology. The first of these works (#684) is a commentary on a creed titled *al-Risāla al-raslāniyya* by Arsalān al-Dimashqī, a highly regarded thirteenth century mystic from Damascus.[42] Nābulusī would often visit Arsalān's grave in the suburbs of Damascus,[43] and also documented teaching his creed at al-Madrasa al-

40 On Muṣṭafā al-Bakrī's critique, see Radtke, "Sufism in the Eighteenth Century," 341.

41 Nābulusī travelled widely in Ottoman Turkey, Egypt and the Hejaz, spending considerable time in Palestine. He wrote testimonies of his travels to Palestine in a work titled *al-Ḥadra al-unsiyya fī al-riḥla al-qudsiyya*, which recounts a trip that lasted a month and a half, seventeen days of which were spent in Jerusalem. Another work, titled *al-Ḥaqīqa wa-al-majāz fī riḥlat Bilād al-Shām wa-Miṣr wa-al-Ḥijāz*, significantly longer than the first, narrates Nābulusī's journey to Syria and Egypt over the course of 388 days, a good portion of which records his time in Palestine. For more on his travel accounts, specifically to Palestine, see Sirriyyah, "The Journeys of ʿAbd al-Ghanī al-Nābulusī". For his life and works, see Sirriyeh, *Sufi Visionary of Ottoman Damascus*.

42 On whom, see Kaḥḥāla, *Muʿjam al-muʾallifīn*, II, 224. The title of Nābulusī's commentary is *Khamrat al-ḥān wa-rannat al-alḥān sharḥ risālat shaykh arsalān*.

43 Nābulusī, *Kashf al-nūr*, 13.

Sulṭāniyya.[44] He notes, in particular, that he was asked by a group of elite students to relay Arsalān's creed, described as being 'on the science of gnostic theology (*fī ʿilm al-tawḥīd al-ʿirfānī*) and the taste of spiritual existence (*dhawq al-wijdān al-rawḥānī*)'.[45] The second of these works (#686) is a commentary on the creed of Aḥmad b. ʿAlī al-Shinnāwī (d. 1028/1619), titled *Taḥrīk al-iqlīd fī fatḥ bāb al-tawḥīd*. The work addresses the topics of existence, annihilation, sainthood and the Sufi path, all as circumscribed within an explicitly Sufi metaphysics. Nābulusī also deals with more 'theological' questions, such as God's names and attributes, His essence and actions, and other related topics. While a seemingly arbitrary choice to write a commentary on, Shinnāwī was in fact the shaykh of Nābulusī's own shaykh, Shihāb al-Dīn Aḥmad b. Aḥmad al-Ḥanafī al-Miṣrī, otherwise known as al-Khaṭīb al-Shawbarī (d. 1066/1656), or even more grandly, 'Abū Ḥanīfa al-Ṣaghīr'. In connection to another figure on the inventory list, Nābulusī notes in his introduction that he composed the work at the request of Ilyās al-Kūrānī (d. 1138/1726)—a prominent Kurdish scholar whose supercommentary on Taftāzānī's commentary on Nasafī's creed is also featured in the Jazzār library (#638). The inventory further mentions a work titled *al-Fatḥ al-rabbānī wa-al-fayḍ al-raḥmānī* (#683), but without attribution. Nābulusī authored a work bearing the same title, drawing inspiration from his distant shaykh, ʿAbd al-Qādir al-Jīlānī (d. 561/1165), eponym of the Qādirī order into which Nābulusī was initiated, and the first to introduce this title.[46] The proximity of this entry to another entry for a work by Nābulusī where his name is specified (*al-Risāla al-raslāniyya li-sayyidī al-shaykh ʿAbd al-Ghanī al-Nābulusī*, #684) suggests that this entry also refers to Nābulusī's *Fatḥ*. This would raise his count in the Jazzār repository to six. Regardless of whose work this entry specifies, Nābulusī would indeed be honoured to be confused with the great Jīlānī, eponym of the Sufi order to which he belonged, and saint of giant proportions.[47]

It is worth noting that Nābulusī stands out as one of the few authors explicitly mentioned by name in the catalogue. In all but one of five entries, the cataloguer specifies that the work belongs to '*Sayyidī* ʿAbd al-Ghanī al-Nābulusī' (#643, #684 and #686), accompanied by the prayer 'may his spirit be sanctified' (*quddisa sirruhu*) and to the '*Shaykh* ʿAbd al-Ghanī al-Nābulusī' (#723), once again followed by the prayer 'may his spirit be sanctified'—an indication that the cataloguer was both familiar with and had a high regard for Nābulūsī's person.[48]

Another prominent advocate of Ibn al-ʿArabī's views listed in the Jazzār inventory is the scholar Qāsim al-Khānī (d. 1109/1697), originally from Aleppo.[49] With Khānī, we get a more explicit invocation and explication of the practice of Sufism. Khanī's manual of Sufi practice was a classic of the period.[50] The Jazzār library features two copies of the work, titled *al-Sayr wa-al-sulūk ilā malik al-mulūk* (#708 and #739). The work explores the seven stages of the mystical path from the perspective of the Khalwatiyya, which was making headway during this period and eventually became the most widespread Sufi brotherhood in the Ottoman world.[51]

44 Nābulusī, *al-Ḥaḍra al-unsiyya*, 172.
45 Ibid.
46 al-Jīlānī, *al-Fatḥ al-rabbānī*.
47 On whom, see Malik, *The Grey Falcon*.
48 The only other author to be honoured in this manner is Ibn al-ʿArabī, but only in one entry from among his eight: #687 (*al-mashāhid al-qudsiyya li-sayyidī muḥyī al-dīn* [*ibn al-*] *ʿarabī quddisa sirruhu*). Said Aljoumani has appealed to the honorific applied to Nābulusī to show that the original inventory of the Jazzār library was penned by a different scribe. See his Chapter 2 in this volume.
49 For Khānī's biography, see Murādī, *Silk al-durar*, IV, 13–14. For his place in and contribution to Sufism during this period, see Radtke, "Sufism in the Eighteenth Century", 330–331 and El-Rouayheb, *Islamic Intellectual History in the Seventeenth Century*, 235–236.
50 For more on Khānī's manual of Sufi practice *al-Sayr wa-al-sulūk*, see Chih, "Le livre pour guide" and Giordani, "Le metamorfosi dell'anima".
51 On the prominence of the Khalwatiyya, see Chih, *Sufism in Ottoman Egypt*, 28–32.

In addition to Khanī's manual, the library features three works on more 'practical' dimensions of Sufi thought by the mystic and prominent Khalwatī shaykh Muṣṭafā b. Kamāl al-Dīn al-Bakrī (d. 1172/1749). Bakrī was also from greater Syria, specifically Damascus. Like Nābulusī and Khānī, he embraced the doctrine of *waḥdat al-wujūd*, eventually forcing himself into self-exile in Jerusalem due to the unsavoury reception of his views in his native Damascus. Bakrī studied under ʿAbd al-Ghanī al-Nābulusī and Ilyās al-Kūrānī, both featured in the Jazzār library. Like Bakrī, Nābulusī and Kūrānī spent significant time in Palestine, and the fact that their works are well-represented in the library's inventory points to a local economy of books.[52] The library's holdings on Sufism show the process by which Ottoman Palestine was pulled into the network of greater Syria by virtue of its geographical proximity and importance of its religious sites, being a gateway to the holy sites of Jerusalem, Hebron, Mecca and Medina, and to the intellectual and cultural capital that was Cairo.

5 Devotional Ethics: The *Awrād, Adʿiyya, Aḥzāb and Adhkār*

One notable emphasis in Muṣṭafā al-Bakrī's teachings was his focus on the recitation of ritual litanies, called *wird* (pl. *awrād*). *Wird* is a term referring to a litany that is designed to complement the five obligatory daily prayers. It is specifically intended to be repeated at designated times throughout the day or week, often at specific locations.[53] In contrast to a *ḥizb*, which is also a prayer focused on the recitation of a *duʿāʾ*, the *awrād* encompass a diverse range of material. They may include prayers of supplication, invocations of the Divine Names, and excerpts from the Qurʾan. For example, the collection contains an *awrād* compilation which is described as being attached to seven verses of the Qurʾan. When recited, these verses would bring salvation to the supplicant (*al-Munjiyyāt al-sabʿ maʿ awrād*, #698).

The *awrād* were often linked to specific Sufi orders and composed by important personalities within those orders. They often included various invocations for God's blessings and pleas for forgiveness, each *wird* having its own unique content. Some *awrād* were particularly celebrated.[54] Bakrī, being the founder of a branch of the Khalwatī order, authored a celebrated *wird* which was, in view of its name, to be recited 'before the sight of dawn'.[55] The Jazzār library contains both the base text of his litany—known as *Wird al-saḥar* (#727)—along with one of the several commentaries he composed on the prayer (*Sharḥ wird al-saḥar*, #728).[56] The library also contains Bakrī's commentary on another reputed *wird* composed by the seventh/thirteenth century scholar Muḥyī al-Dīn al-Nawawī (d. 676/1277) (#730), primarily recognised for his contributions to Shāfiʿī jurisprudence and *ḥadīth*, but who is featured on the inventory list as author of a number of works on ethics.

One of the notable features of this section is the plethora of works on devotional ethics, containing not only *awrād* prayers but varieties on *awrād*, including *aḥzāb* (sing. *ḥizb*), *adʿiyya* (sing. *duʿāʾ*) and *adhkār* (sing. *dhikr*).[57] While the *awrād* are prayers

52 On Kūrānī's travels, see Murādī, *Silk al-durar*, I, 308.

53 For an example of one such schedule for the recitation of these prayers, see Waugh, *Visionaries of Silence*, 70–76; and in farflung Jam, another itinerary in Mahendrarajah, *The Sufi Saint of Jam*, 203.

54 For a study of Ottoman era prayer compositions, see Burak, "Prayers"; on the *awrād* more generally, see Denny, "Wird".

55 On Bakrī's *Wird al-saḥar* in its historical context, see Levtzion, "The Role of *Sharīʿa*-oriented Sufi *Ṭuruq*".

56 The full title is *al-Fatḥ al-qudsī wa-al-kashf al-unsī wa-al-manhaj al-qarīb ilā liqāʾ al-ḥabīb*, the *qudsī* in the title being in recognition of the fact that the work was composed while Bakrī was in Jerusalem (*al-quds*). The shorter title *Wird al-saḥar* indicates when the litany should be recited. For more on Bakrī's *Wird al-saḥar*, including a translation of his prayer for forgiveness, see Chih, *Sufism in Ottoman Egypt*, 69.

57 For more on Sufi prayer and prayer manuals, see Padwick, *Muslim Devotions*; Abun-Nasr, *Muslim Commu-*

composed by a shaykh to be repeated by his disciples or followers at designated times and places, the *aḥzāb* pertained specifically to the repetition of particular sacrosanct statements,[58] called *du'aʿ* (pl. *adʿiyya*), understood to be the actual text of the prayer. The Sufi brotherhoods, in particular, pioneered the recitation of prayers on the Prophet. Many of the *aḥzāb* thus became known as *ṣalāt*, the act of sending prayers upon the Prophet.[59] Unlike the *awrād* and *aḥzāb*, a *du'āʿ* is not conditioned on repetition. There are seventeen works in total on these various aspects of Islamic devotion and prayer in the Jazzār collection, making it the largest subcategory of works within this section. Of note is that these works are not only catalogued in the section on *tawḥīd* and *taṣawwuf* here examined, but are also found in the section on *ḥadīth*, where *adhkār* works and other prayer manuals are listed (such as the popular *Dalā'il al-khayrāt*), distinct insofar as they contain supplications taken specifically from the *ḥadīth* corpus.[60]

These prayers were believed to possess protective qualities akin to talismans; when recited, they were thought to repel evil from the one invoking them. Much like the practice of visiting holy gravesites, reciting prayers crafted by revered individuals was understood to invite grace and blessings (*baraka*) upon the supplicant. The plethora of prayer manuals and guides in the collection alludes to the influence of the Sufi brotherhoods, which typically adopted a specific *wird* composed by a respected shaykh of the order, requiring initiates to invoke the prayer at specific times of the day. Examples include not only the previously mentioned Khalwatī shaykh Muṣṭafā al-Bakrī, who authored a widely read *wird* called *Wird al-saḥar*, but also the *awrād* of Jalāl al-Dīn al-Rūmī, eponym of the Mevlevī order (#724), the *wird* of ʿAbd al-Ghanī al-Nābulusī, esteemed Naqshbandī shaykh (#723), and the *awrād* of ʿAlī al-Qārī, a renowned Ḥanafī scholar (#726). That some of these entries invoke the plural of the term (that is, *awrād*) rather than the singular indicates that the respective author composed more than one *wird*, and that the manuscript in question contains the collation of the various *awrād* composed by the scholar. Many of these *awrād* works are listed anonymously (for example, #698, #710, #721, #729 and #733). But the inventory also mentions specific personalities. Given the prominence of Ibn al-ʿArabī in the collection, it is no wonder that his *al-Dawr al-aʿlā*, a prayer composition also known as *Ḥizb al-wiqāya* or 'The Prayer of Protection', is well-represented: three copies of a commentary on the prayer are listed (#725, #731 and #732), by the scholar Muḥammad b. Maḥmūd al-Dāmūnī (fl. 1208/1794).[61] Importantly, the prayer is invoked as a *ḥizb* rather than a *wird*, indicating that it was not necessarily meant to be regularly repeated as part of a daily spiritual regimen. The Jazzār collection also contains a further work that testifies to the Turkification of the Ottoman empire, and the increasing use of vernacular: a prayer in Turkish (*Duʿā' bi-al-turkī*, #733).

Another prayer that was predominantly prized in Shīʿī circles also appears in the collection: the *Duʿā' al-jawshan* (#722). This prayer began to show up in Shīʿī works beginning in the fifteenth century.[62] It was believed to have two manifestations: a smaller *jawshan* attributed to the seventh Imām Abū al-Ḥasan Mūsā ibn Jaʿfar al-Kāẓim (d. 183/799), and a greater *jawshan* attributed to the Prophet.

nities of Grace, 188–194; Trimingham, *The Sufi Orders*, 194–217.

58 The term *ḥizb* (pl. *aḥzāb*) also refers to a division (one-sixteenth) of the Qur'an.

59 One noteworthy example is *al-Ṣalāt al-mashīshiyya*, attributed to Ibn Mashīsh (d. 622/1225), the teacher of al-Shādhilī, namesake of the Shādhilī order. The prayer was subject to numerous commentaries (one by Nābulusī), and achieved widespread renown throughout the Islamic world.

60 See Garrett Davidson's Chapter 15 in this volume.

61 For more on Ibn al-ʿArabī's *al-Dawr al-aʿlā*, see Taji-Farouki, *Prayer for Spiritual Elevation*; Ibn al-ʿArabī, *Seven Days of the Heart*.

62 For more on the history of this prayer's transmission, see Aydını, "Prayer of *Jawshan*"; Toprak, "Cevşen [Jawshan]".

Although highly regarded in Shīʿī circles, the prayer also held significance in non-Shīʿī contexts. This may explain why, despite Jazzār's anti-Shīʿī sentiment and his reported destruction of the intellectual heritage of Jabal ʿĀmil—including the confiscation of thousands of books—the work found its way into the collection, possibly as part of Jazzār's campaign, or independently. Jazzār famously conquered Jābil ʿĀmil, historically a stronghold of the Imāmī Shīʿīs, subjecting the area to Ottoman rule and confiscating thousands of books in the process.[63] While several sources relay that whole libraries were transferred to Acre and summarily burned,[64] further evidence supporting these claims can be found in this section of the inventory: apart from the *Duʿāʾ al-jawshan*, there are no works of a Shīʿī nature present in the collection. This either confirms the destruction of scholarly books from Jabal ʿĀmil or, more cautiously, casts doubt on these testimonies. Put differently, had Jazzār merely confiscated these books without burning them, they would likely be present, especially in this section on *tawḥīd*, considering the Shīʿī tradition's extensive history of commentary on theological matters.

6 Kalām-compliant Mysticism

Many of the works listed in the previous section were not palatable to theological audiences. This includes, in particular, works by proponents of the controversial doctrine of *waḥdat al-wujūd*. Nevertheless, not all Sufi works faced criticism from orthodox theological circles. In fact, there are several works in the collection that enjoyed almost universal admiration, being regarded as classics of the genre. These works predominantly originated from the pre-Ottoman period. Their authors did not explicitly subscribe to the Akbarī lens, but instead fostered a more 'moderate' form of mystical practice that resonated with some Ashʿarī theologians. Representative figures of this trend include the Moroccan mystic and staunch Ashʿarī Aḥmad Zarrūq al-Fāsī (d. 899/1493), and the Egyptian mystic, author of famous axioms, Ibn ʿAṭāʾ Allāh al-Iskandarī (d. 709/1309).

Among the earliest universally celebrated Sufi authors that appear on the inventory list is Abū al-Qāsim ʿAbd al-Karīm al-Qushayrī (d. 465/1072), often referred to as 'author of the treatise' (*ṣāḥib al-risāla*)[65] or 'author of the treatise to the Sufis' (*ṣāḥib al-risāla ilā al-ṣūfiyya*).[66] Qushayrī wrote a work which came to be known simply as *al-Risāla al-qushariyya*, or Qushayrī's Epistle, which one author has described as 'the most popular Sufi manual ever'.[67] The work was absorbed as a classic of Islamic culture early on, being notorious for 'circulating in all regions of the world' (*sāʾira fī aqṭār al-arḍ*).[68] The eminent Ottoman bibliographer Ṭāşköprīzāde transmits the same praise lauded on Qushayrī by an early biographer: that 'Qushayrī is the author of the Epistle that was notorious in both west and east, through which his person became like a star, illuminated'.[69] His treatise was so well-

63 On Jazzār's confiscation of books from Jabal ʿĀmil and elsewhere, see the Introduction, Said Aljoumani's Chapter 2 and Boris Liebrenz's Chapter 3 in this volume.

64 In particular, 5,000 books were reportedly burned from the Āl Khātūn library. See al-Subḥānī, *Tadhkirat al-aʿyān*, II, 174–175. Confirmation of this report comes from al-Ṣadr, *Takmilat amal al-āmil*, 383. Both sources note that Jazzār confiscated thousands of books and carried them off to Acre, where they were subsequently destroyed.

65 al-Subkī, *Ṭabaqāt al-shāfiʿiyya al-kubrā*, V, 153.

66 Ibn Ṣalāḥ, *Ṭabaqāt al-fuqahāʾ al-shāfiʿiyya*, 562 (entry #211).

67 Qushayrī, *Al-Qushayrī's Epistle on Sufism*, xxiv. There have been numerous translations of the work into English, including Barbara von Schlegell (1990) Rabia Harris (2002) and Alexander Knysh (2007).

68 Ibn Ṣalāḥ, *Ṭabaqāt al-fuqahāʾ al-shāfiʿiyya*, 562. The work made its way to North Africa, which was embroiled in controversy over Abū Ḥāmid al-Ghazālī (d. 505/1111). When a *fatwā* was issued that dismissed Ghazālī's and the Sufis' position on a particular matter, Qushayrī was exempted as a moderate of the tradition. See Griffel, *Al-Ghazālī's Philosophical Theology*, 67.

69 Ṭāşköprīzāde, *Miftāḥ al-saʿāda*, II, 296, copied from Subkī, *Ṭabaqāt al-shāfiʿiyya al-kubrā*, V, 153 (entry #471).

known that no further specification was necessary: he was simply the author of the Epistle. One factor that contributed to its widespread circulation and acceptance as a standard of Sufi practice was that Qushayrī adhered to Ashʿarī principles. His work sought not only to reconcile but also to unite the Sufi path with Ashʿarī theology. Two copies of the work exist in the Jazzār library (#658 and #659), testifying to its continued popularity well into the Ottoman period.

A scholar with a similar project as Qushayrī in his endeavor to reconcile Ashʿarism with Sufism was the eminent figure, the 'Proof of Islam' Abū Ḥāmid al-Ghazālī (d. 505/1111), already mentioned as author of several works on theology housed in Jazzār's repository in Acre. Ghazālī became a household name as far as Spain and into Christian Europe, known for different facets of his scholarship in different places. In Spain, he was known as the author of a work on the doctrines of the philosophers (*Maqāṣid al-falāsifa*), which students of philosophy would initiate the study of philosophy with. He was also embroiled in various controversies in North Africa, and there were pockets of opposition to his writings. But generally speaking, Ghazālī achieved almost universal repute for his confrontation with the Islamic philosophers, his work on Islamic law (*al-Muṣtaṣfā fī ʿilm al-uṣūl*), his intellectual and personal biography documenting his transition and journey into Sufism at the end of his life (catalogued in the Jazzār library as *al-Munqidh min al-ḍalāla*, #620 and #629), and his major work on all aspects of Islamic spirituality, the *Iḥyāʾ ʿulūm al-dīn*. The Jazzār library boasts an epitome of the *Iḥyāʾ* (#654), likely by Shams al-Dīn al-ʿAjlūnī al-Bilālī (d. 820/1417), who wrote the most important epitome of the work and who lived in nearby Egypt. This manuscript is appended to a further work of ethics by the Sicilian scholar Ibn Ẓafar al-Ṣiqillī (d. 565/1169), titled *Sulwān al-mutāʿ fī ʿudwān al-atbāʿ* (#654). Siqillī's work is not the only work in the collection that reached Acre from the Mediterranean: the library contains a work of polemics, responding specifically to Christian claims, by the Christian convert to Islam ʿAbdallāh al-Tarjumān al-Māyūrqī (d. 832/1428) (#705). A manual of Sufi practice titled *Minhāj al-ʿābidīn ilā jannat rabb al-ʿālimīn* is also featured in the Jazzār library (#677), a work that has been widely attributed to Ghazālī.[70]

The Jazzār repository further houses several works by the renowned *ḥadīth* specialist and Shāfiʿī jurisprudent, Muḥyī al-Dīn Abū Zakariyyā Yaḥyā b. Sharaf al-Nawawī (631–676/1233–1277).[71] Nawawī was primarily known for his contributions to Shāfiʿī jurisprudence and the science of *ḥadīth*, and his works in this section address ethical questions using the framework of *ḥadīth*. Many of his most popular compilations condensed the *ḥadīth* corpus in an effort to make it more accessible to a wider audience. This partly accounts for the fact that his compilation of forty *ḥadīth* (*al-Arbaʿūn al-nawawiyya*) became one of the most widely read works in Islamic history.[72] While seemingly miscatalogued, Nawawī's works in this section employ the *ḥadīth* as a means to explore broader topics within the field of Islamic ethics. One work, titled *Riyāḍ al-ṣāliḥīn min kalām sayyid al-mursalīn* (#665), comprises a collection of prophetic statements about piety. Another work, titled *Bustān al-ʿārifīn wa-sabīl al-zāhidīn* (#669 and #670), presents an anthology of statements taken not only from the *ḥadīth* corpus, but from the Qur'an and other sources, endeavouring to explain asceticism, abstinence and the rejection of worldly materialism, all aspects of what is broadly known as Sufism.

70 The attribution has been questioned by al-ʿAllāf, "Kutub al-Imām al-Ghazālī". In his study of the works of Ghazālī, ʿAbd al-Raḥmān Badawī also casts doubt on the attribution (giving the alternate title *Minhāj al-qāṣidīn*). See Badawī, *Muʾallafāt al-Ghazālī*, 56. The work has been translated into English by Faghfoory, *Path of Worshippers*.

71 On Nawawī, see Halim, *Legal Authority*.

72 See Garrett Davidson's Chapter 15 in this volume which mentions Nawawī's collection of forty *ḥadīth* and his *al-Adhkār al-nabawiyya*, described as 'arguably the all-time most-popular work of the genre'.

We thus get a sense of the logic behind the inclusion of these works in this section on *tawḥīd* and *taṣawwuf*: insofar as the latter represents the mystical dimension of Islam, which is understood to be intrinsically concerned with ethical comport and cultivation, these works were thought to cohere with that telos more fully, being primarily on ethics, and only secondarily on *ḥadīth* as a vehicle for the cultivation of the human person.

As the writings of Qushayrī, Ghazālī and Nawawī demonstrate, many works in the field of Sufism were believed to align with Ashʿarī theology. In fact, all three authors embraced the Ashʿarī creed, indicating that Sufism found acceptance among a distinct subset of orthodox theologians. These authors were early pre-Ottoman proponents of the potential confluence between Sufism and theology. In later periods, particularly in North Africa, other figures also contributed to the demand for Sufi literature that would be compliant with the precepts of Ashʿarī theology. Such figures include the renowned Egyptian mystic Ibn ʿAṭāʾ Allāh al-Iskandarī (d. 709/1309), acclaimed for his *Ḥikam* and early contributions to Shādhilī doctrine.[73] The library boasts four copies of Iskandarī's *al-Tanwīr fī isqāṭ al-tadbīr* (#666–668 and #711), a work that probes the question of reliance on God through the lens of the concept of *tadbīr*.[74] The fact that the library houses four copies of this work points to a wide readership and underscores its significance among readers in the Levant. The collection also features what appears to be a commentary on Iskandarī's highly reputed axioms (#675), as well as a third work titled *Miftāḥ al-falāḥ* (#623). Another figure is the Moroccan mystic Aḥmad Zarrūq al-Fāsī (d. 899/1493), a Sufi who was staunchly committed to Ashʿarī theology, seeing mysticism as legitimate only insofar as it coheres with the injunctions of the law. Zarrūq penned two favourable commentaries on Ghazali's *Qawāʾid al-ʿaqāʾid* (#625, #626 and #660), one of which is preserved in the Jazzār collection (*Ightinām al-fawāʾid fī sharḥ qawāʾid al-ʿaqāʾid*, #676). Zarrūq also penned a manual of Sufi practice titled *Qawāʾid al-taṣawwuf wa-shawāhid al-taʿarruf* (#636),[75] which is directed at all categories of wayfarers, including theologians and jurisprudents, serving as a guide towards a greater understanding of the three pillars of faith: *islām*, *iḥsān* and *īmān*.

As a further testament to the interlinking between Sufi doctrine and theological exploration, the library houses *Qawānīn ḥikam al-ishrāq ilā kāfat al-ṣūfiyya bi-jamīʿ al-āfāq* (#681), a work by the Shādhilī mystic Abū al-Mawāhib (d. 882/1478), on Sufi notions of illumination, particularly as sieved through Shādhilī doctrine.[76] Although affiliated with the Shādhilī order, Abū al-Mawāhib was profoundly influenced by Ibn al-ʿArabī, suggesting the presence of diverse manifestations of mystical thought and practice rather than a singular, uniform model of Sufism.

7 Neither *Tawḥīd* nor *Taṣawwuf*: Misplaced Works

Several works catalogued in this section fall outside the scope of theology and mysticism. Ironically, one of these works is the only manuscript in this section which is extant today: Taftāzānī's gloss on Ījī's commentary on Ibn Ḥājib's *Mukhtaṣar muntaḥā al-uṣūlī* (#637), a work on Islamic legal theory and dialectics.[77] The misplacement of this work likely stems from the perception of Taftāzānī as a theologian, possibly due to his commen-

73 See Mackeen, "The Rise of al-Shādhilī", 485.

74 For the English translation, see Ibn ʿAṭāʾ Allāh al-Iskandarī, *The Book of Illumination*.

75 The full title of the work is *Taʾsīs al-qawāʾid wa-al-uṣūl wa-taḥṣīl al-fawāʾid li-dhawī al-wuṣūl fī umūr aʿammuhā al-taṣawwuf wa-mā fīhi min wujūh al-taʿarruf*.

76 On which, see Jurji, *Illumination*.

77 This manuscript from the Jazzār collection is today preserved in Saudi Arabia: Maktabat al-Ḥaram al-Makkī, #1499. I am grateful to Said Aljoumani for this information.

tary on Nasafī's creed, which had a large audience throughout the Islamic world. This is not the only legal manual catalogued under *tawḥīd* and *taṣawwuf*: we further have another legal work by Yūsuf b. Ḥusayn al-Kirmāstī (d. 906/1500), titled *Zubdat al-wuṣūl ilā ʿumdat al-uṣūl* (#671). Given the play on words in this title and the explicit use of *uṣūl* (typically in reference to *uṣūl al-fiqh*), there is little justification for the misplacement of this work in this section. Another prominent theologian whose work is miscatalogued is Muḥammad b. ʿAbd al-Karīm al-Shahrastānī (d. 548/1153), author of the well-known theological manual *Nihāyat al-aqdām fī ʿilm al-kalām*. Even more famously, Shahrastānī penned a doxography considered one of the earliest systematic studies of religion and widely used as a source for the reconstruction of religious doctrine in Islam. The Jazzār library boasts two copies of the work (*al-Milal wa-al-nihal*, #631 and #632) and one copy of another doxography titled *al-Firaq al-ḍāla wa-al-nājiyya* (#703) by the scholar Muḥammad Amīn b. Ṣadr al-Dīn al-Shirwānī (d. 1036/1626). In the field of Qur'anic exegesis, the library features a work titled *Khulāṣat baḥr al-ḥaqā'iq*, a commentary on the Qur'an by Ibn al-Sāwajī (active 732/1332). The work is an epitome of the exegesis *Bahr al-ḥaqā'iq* by the influential mystic Najm al-Dīn Kubrā (d. 618/1221), under whom Ibn al-Sāwajī likely studied. Despite being an exegesis (*tafsīr*) of the Qur'an, it appears that the work is listed in this section because it is specifically a mystical exegesis of the Qur'an (*tafsīr ʿirfānī*) and therefore was thought to accord more fully with *taṣawwuf*. We are also presented with the *thabat* of the Syrian *ḥadīth* specialist ʿImād al-Dīn al-ʿAjlūnī (d. 1162/1749), titled *Ḥilyat ahl al-faḍl wa-al-kamāl bi-ittiṣāl al-asānīd bi-kamāl al-rijāl* (#679). Given that the title does not mention *ḥadīth*, and in fact appears to be a work on mysticism citing perfection and connection, it is perhaps understandable that the library's curator placed the work in the section on Sufism. We further find a work by the premier litterateur of the Islamic East: al-Qāsim b. ʿAlī al-Ḥarīrī (d. 516/1122), widely praised for his *Maqāmāt*. The collection features Ḥarīrī's compilation of common mistakes in language construction, titled *Durrat al-ghawwāṣ fī awhām al-khawāṣṣ* (#715).

8 Concluding Remarks

The Jazzār library features an eclectic mix of books on *tawḥīd* and *taṣawwuf*. The library's inclusion of various Sufi works which claim to be on *tawḥīd* illustrates that *tawḥīd* was a flexible term that encompassed a wide range of works addressing theological matters. In connection, *taṣawwuf* was also a complicated term with multilevel meanings. The unifying thread of all mystical writings held in the collection is the orientation towards inner cultivation, but much of the underlying theology of such works differed. Some Sufi authors were prominent advocates of Akbarī mystical philosophy and the doctrine of *waḥdat al-wujūd*. Others wholly rejected that orientation, instead accepting mysticism only insofar as it cohered with orthodox theology. While a significant portion of the collection stemmed from the tradition of commentary on Ibn al-ʿArabī, another substantial segment was rooted in the North African tradition of Ashʿarī theology. Both in works of theology and mysticism, there is a clear orientation towards and acceptance of Sufi practice. The library illustrates the complicated discourses at play in the late Ottoman world of Palestine, showing its nexus on the map between Syria and North Africa. While established by an ascending overlord of the Ottoman state and governor of Damascus and Sidon, the library remains on the whole provincial, featuring works accessible to a wide range of readers, and not necessarily of immense interest to more specialised audiences.[78]

78 Sincere thanks to Younes Ajoun, Said Aljoumani, Mohamad Jarada, Tanvir Ahmed, Guy Burak and Konrad Hirschler for their comments on this chapter.

Bibliography

Abū Diyyah, Mūsā. *Waqfiyyat Aḥmad Bāshā al-Jazzār*. Nablus, 1998.

Abun-Nasr, Jamil. *Muslim Communities of Grace: The Sufi Brotherhoods in Islamic Religious Life*. New York, 2007.

Akkach, Samer. *Intimate Invocations: al-Ghazzī's Biography of ʿAbd al-Ghanī al-Nābulusī (1641–1731)*. Leiden, 2012.

al-ʿAllāf, Mashhad. "Kutub al-Imām al-Ghazālī al-thābit minhā wa-al-manḥūl." N.p., 2002.

Aydını, Abdullah. "The Prayer of *Jawshan*: A Study of Its Sources." *Ilahiyat Studies* (2011): 47–68.

Badawī, ʿAbd al-Raḥmān. *Muʾallafāt al-Ghazālī*. Kuwait, 1977.

al-Baghdādī, Ismāʿīl Bāsha. *Hadiyyat al-ʿĀrifīn*. Istanbul, 1955.

al-Bakhīt, Muḥammad ʿAdnān. "Al-Maktabāt fī al-Quds al-Sharīf, mundhu al-Fatḥ al-Ṣalāḥī sanat 583/1187 ilā sanat 1367/1948." In *Buḥūth wa-Dirāsāt muhdāt ilā Īrāj Afshār*, edited by Ibrāhīm Shabbūḥ and François Déroche, 409–526. London: Muʾassasat al-Furqān lil-Turāth al-Islāmī, 2018.

Belhāj, Jalūl. "Muḥammad b. Yūsuf al-Sanūsī wa-mawqifuhu min al-taṣawwuf wa-ṣūfiyyat zamānihi." *Al-Shihāb* 5/2 (2019): 415–446.

Burak, Guy. "Prayers, Commentaries, and the Edification of the Ottoman Supplicant." In *Historicizing Sunni Islam in the Ottoman Empire, c. 1450–1750*, edited by Tijana Krstić and Derin Terzioğlu, 232–252. Leiden: Brill, 2021.

Burak, Guy. *The Second Formation of Islamic Law: The Hanafi School in the Early Modern Ottoman Empire*. Cambridge, 2015.

Burckhardt, Titus. *Universal Man*. Gloucestershire, U.K., 1983.

Cābī Ömer Efendi. *Cābī Tārihi: Tārīh-i Sultān Selīm-i Sālis ve Mahmūd-i Sānī: tahlīl ve tenkidli metin*, edited by Mehmet Ali Beyhan. Ankara: Türk Tarih Kurumu Basımevi, 2003.

Chih, Rachida. "Le livre pour guide: éthique (*adab*) et cheminement spirituel (sulūk) dans trois manuels soufis d'époque ottomane (*Al-Sayr wa-l- sulūk* de Qāsim al-Khānī m. 1697, *Tuḥfat al-sālikīn* de Muḥammad al-Samanūdī m. 1785 et *Tuḥfat al-ikhwān* d'Aḥmad al-Dardīr m. 1786)." In *Ethics and Spirituality in Islam*, edited by Francesco Chiabotti, Eve Feuillebois-Pierunek, Catherine Mayeur-Jaouen and Luca Patrizi, 520–544. Leiden: Brill, 2017.

Chih, Rachida. *Sufism in Ottoman Egypt*. New York, 2019.

Chittick, William. "Rūmī and Waḥdat al-Wujūd." In *Poetry and Mysticism in Islam: The Heritage of Rūmī*, edited by A. Banani, R. Hovannisian and G. Sabagh, 70–111. Cambridge: Cambridge University Press, 1994.

Dastagir, Golam and Ismath Ramzy. "Tawḥīd." In *Islam, Judaism, and Zoroastrianism*, edited by Zayn Kassam, Yudit Kornberg Greenberg and Jehan Bagli, 687–690. Dordrecht: Springer, 2018.

Denny, F.M. "Wird." In *Encyclopaedia of Islam, Second Edition Online*, edited by P. Bearman. https://doi.org/10.1163/1573-3912_islam_SIM_7914 Web.

Dumairieh, Nasser. *Intellectual Life in the Ḥijāz before Wahhabism: Ibrāhīm al-Kūrānī's (d. 1101/1690) Theology of Sufism*. Leiden, 2022.

El-Rouayheb, Khaled. "Rethinking the Canons of Islamic Intellectual History." In *Near and Middle Eastern Studies at the Institute for Advanced Study, Princeton: 1935–2018*, edited by Sabine Schmidtke, 154–163. Piscataway, NJ, 2017.

El-Rouayheb, Khaled. *Islamic Intellectual History in the Seventeenth Century: Scholarly Currents in the Ottoman Empire and the Maghreb*. Cambridge, 2015.

El-Rouayheb, Khaled. *The Development of Arabic Logic*. Basel, 2019.

Faghfoory, Mohammad. *The Path of Worshippers to the Paradise of the Lord of the Worlds*. Lanham, 2012.

Giordani, Demetrio. "Le metamorfosi dell'anima e gli stadi della via spirituale: considerazioni intorno a '*Al-Sayr wa-al-sulūk ilā maliki-l-mulūk*' dello 'shaykh' Qāsim ibn Ṣalāḥ al-Dīn al-Khānī di Aleppo (1619–1697)." *Divus Thomas* (2007): 117–134.

Griffel, Frank. *Al-Ghazālī's Philosophical Theology*. Oxford, 2009.

Halim, Azmi. *Legal Authority in Premodern Islam: Yaḥyā b. Sharaf al-Nawawī in the Shāfiʿī School of Law*. New York, 2015.

Hudson, Leila. "Reading al-Shaʿrānī: The Sufi Genealogy of Islamic Modernism in Late Ottoman Damascus." *Journal of Islamic Studies* 15/1 (2004): 39–68.

Ibn ʿĀbidīn. *Majmūʿat rasāʾil Ibn ʿĀbidīn*. Istanbul, 1325/1907.

Ibn al-ʿArabī, Muḥyī al-Dīn. *The Seven Days of the Heart: Prayers for the Nights and Days of the Week*. Translated by Pablo Beneito and Stephen Hirtenstein. Oxford: Anqa Publishing, 2000.

Ibn al-ʿArabī, Muḥyī al-Dīn. *al-Futūḥāt al-makiyya*, edited by ʿAbd al-ʿAzīz Sulṭān al-Manṣūb. Tarim: Wizārat al-Thaqāfa, 2010.

Ibn Ḥajar al-Haytamī. *al-Fatāwā al-ḥadīthiyya*, edited by Muḥammad ʿAbd al-Salām Shāhīn. Beirut: Dār al-Kutub al-ʿIlmiyya, 2013.

Ibn Khaldūn. *The Muqaddimah*. Translated by Franz Rosenthal. Princeton, NJ: Princeton University Press, 1958.

Ibn Ṣalāḥ. *Ṭabaqāt al-fuqaḥāʾ al-shāfiʿiyya*, edited by ʿAlī Najīb. Beirut: Dār al-Bashāʾir al-Islāmiyya, 1996.

al-Iskandarī, Ibn ʿAṭāʾ Allāh. *The Book of Illumination*. Translated by Scott Kugle. Louisville, KY: Fons Vitae, 2005.

al-Jīlānī, ʿAbd al-Qādir. *al-Fatḥ al-rabbānī wa-al-fayḍ al-raḥmānī*, edited by Antonious Shiblī al-Lubnānī. Beirut: al-Maṭbaʿa al-Kāthuluqiyya, 1960.

Jurji, Edward Jabra. *Illumination in Islamic Mysticism*. Princeton, 1938.

al-Kafawī, Maḥmūd b. Sulaymān. *Kitāb aʿlām al-akhyār min fuqahāʾ madhhab al-nuʿmān al-mukhtār*, edited by ʿAbd al-Laṭīf ʿAbd al-Raḥmān. Beirut: Dār al-Kutub al-ʿIlmiyya, 2019.

Kaḥḥāla, ʿUmar. *Muʿjam al-muʾallifīn*. Beirut, 1376/1957.

Katip Çelebi. *Kashf al-ẓunūn ʿan asāmī al-kutub wa-al-funūn*. Beirut, n.d.

Kugle, Scott. *Rebel between Spirit and Law: Ahmad Zarruq, Sainthood and Authority in Islam*. Bloomington, 2006.

Levtzion, Nehemia. “The Role of *Sharīʿa*-oriented Sufi *Ṭuruq* in the Renewal and Reform Movements of the 18th and 19th Centuries.” In *El Sufismo y las normas del Islam: Trabajos del IV Congreso Internacional de Estudios Jurídicos Islámicos: Derecho y sufismo (Murcia, 7–10 mayo 2003) = Papers presented at the IV International Conference on Islamic Legal Studies: Law and Sufism (Murcia, 7–10 May 2003)*, edited by Alfonso Carmona, 377–408. Murcia: Editora Regional de Murcia, 2006.

Mackeen, A.M. Mohamed. “The Rise of al-Shādhilī (d. 656/1258).” *Journal of the American Oriental Society* 91/4 (1971): 477–486.

Mahendrarajah, Shivan. *The Sufi Saint of Jam: History, Religion, and Politics of a Sunni Shrine in Shiʿi Iran*. Cambridge, 2021.

Malik, Hamza. *The Grey Falcon: The Life and Teaching of Shaykh ʿAbd al-Qādir al-Jīlānī*. Leiden, 2019.

al-Mallālī, Muḥammad. *al-Mawāhib al-qudsiyya fī al-manāqib al-sanūsiyya*, edited by Allāl Būrbīq. Bū Saʿāda, Algeria: Dār al-Kardāda, 2011.

Morris, James Winston. “Ibn ʿArabi and His Interpreters Part II (Conclusion).” *Journal of the American Oriental Society* 10/1 (1987): 101–119.

Morrissey, Fitzroy. *Sufism and the Scriptures: Metaphysics and Sacred History in the Thought of ʿAbd al-Karīm al-Jīlī*. London: I.B. Tauris, 2021.

Murādī, Muḥammad Khalīl. *Silk al-durar fī aʿyān al-qarn al-thānī ʿashr*, edited by Akram Ḥasan al-ʿUlbī. Beirut: Dār Ṣādir, 2001.

Nābulusī, ʿAbd al-Ghanī. *Kashf al-nūr ʿan aṣḥāb al-qubūr*. Istanbul, 1986.

Nābulusī, ʿAbd al-Ghanī. *al-Ḥaḍra al-unsiyya fī al-riḥla al-qudsiyya*, edited by Akram Ḥasan al-ʿUlbī. Beirut: al-Maṣādir, 1990.

Nasr, Seyyed Hossein. *Three Muslim Sages: Avicenna, Suhrawardi, Ibn ʿArabi*. Delmar, NY, 1997.

Padwick, Constance. *Muslim Devotions: A Study in Prayer-Manuals in Common Use*. London, 1961.

Qushayrī, Abū al-Qāsim ʿAbd al-Karīm. *Principles of Sufism*. Translated by Barbara von Schlegell, introduced by Hamid Algar. Berkeley: Mizan Press, 1990.

Qushayrī, Abū al-Qāsim ʿAbd al-Karīm. *The Risalah: Principles of Sufism*. Translated by Rabia Harris. Chicago: Kazi Publications, 2002.

Qushayrī, Abū al-Qāsim ʿAbd al-Karīm. *Al-Qushayrī's Epistle on Sufism*. Translated by Alexander Knysh. UK: Garnet Publishing, 2007.

Radtke, Bernd. “Sufism in the Eighteenth Century: An Attempt at a Provisional Repraissal.” *Die Welt des Islams* 36 (1996): 326–364.

al-Ṣadr, Ḥasan. *Takmilat amal al-āmil*. edited by Aḥmad al-Ḥusaynī. Qum: Maktabat Āyatollāh al-Marʿashī, 1985.

Ṣafadī, Ṣalāh al-Dīn Khalīl b. Aybak. *al-Wāfī bi-al-*

wafāyāt, edited by Aḥmad al-Arnāʾūṭ and Turkī Muṣṭafā. Beirut: Dār Iḥyāʾ al-Turāth, 2000.

Sanūsī, Muḥammad b. Yūsuf, et al. *Majmūʿ umm al-barāhīn al-ʿaqīda al-ṣughrā lil-sanūsī*, edited by Māhir ʿAdnān ʿUthmān. Istanbul: Dār Taḥqīq al-Kitāb, 2021.

Shaʿrānī, ʿAbd al-Wahhāb. *Kashf al-ḥijāb wa-al-rān ʿan wajh asʾilat al-jān*, edited by Muḥammad ʿAbdallāh ʿAbd al-Razzāq. Cairo: Maṭbaʿat Ḥijāzī, 1928.

al-Sharfāwī, Anas. *al-Silsila al-ʿaqadiyya al-sanūsiyya*. Damascus, 1441/2019.

Sirriyeh, Elizabeth. *Sufi Visionary of Ottoman Damascus: ʿAbd al-Ghani al-Nabulusi, 1641–1731*. London/New York, 2005.

Sirriyyah, Elizabeth. "The Journeys of ʿAbd al-Ghanī al-Nābulusī in Palestine (1101/1690 and 1105/1693)." *Journal of Semitic Studies* 24/1 (1979): 55–69.

al-Subḥānī, Āyatollāh Jaʿfar. *Tadhkirat al-aʿyān*. Qum, 1419/1998.

al-Subkī, Tāj al-Dīn. *Ṭabaqāt al-shāfiʿiyya al-kubrā*, edited by Maḥmūd Muḥammad al-Ṭanāḥī and ʿAbd al-Fattāḥ Muḥammad al-Ḥilū. Cairo: Dār Iḥyāʾ al-Kutub al-ʿArabiyya, 1964.

Subtelny, Maria Eva and Anas B. Khalidov. "The Curriculum of Islamic Higher Learning in Timurid Iran in the Light of the Sunni Revival under Shāh-Rukh." *Journal of the American Oriental Society* 115/2 (1995): 210–236.

Taji-Farouki, Suha (trans.). *A Prayer for Spiritual Elevation and Perfection*. Oxford, 2006.

Ṭāşköprīzāde. *Miftāḥ al-saʿāda wa-miṣbāh al-siyāda*. Beirut, 1405/1985.

Toprak, Mehmet. "Cevşen [Jawshan]." *Türkiye Diyanet Vakfi İslâm Ansiklopedisi* (DIA) [Turkish Religious Foundation Encyclopedia of Islam], VII, 464.

Trimingham, J. Spencer. *The Sufi Orders in Islam*. Oxford, 1971.

Watt, W. Montgomery. "ʿAḳīda." In *Encyclopaedia of Islam, Second Edition Online*, edited by P. Bearman. https://doi.org/10.1163/1573-3912_islam_COM_0037 Web.

Waugh, Earle. *Visionaries of Silence: The Reformist Sufi Order of the Demirdashiya al-Khalwatiya in Cairo*. Cairo, 2007.

Yahya, Osman. *Historie et classification de l'oeuve d'Ibn ʿArabī*. Damas, 1964.

al-Zabīdī, Murtaḍa. *Itḥāf al-sāda al-muttaqīn bi-sharḥ iḥyāʾ ʿulūm al-dīn*. Beirut, 2005.

Zarrūq, Aḥmad. *Ightinām al-fawāʾid fī sharḥ qawāʾid al-ʿaqāʾid*, edited by Nizār Ḥammādī. Kuwait: Dār al-Ḍiyāʾ, 2022.

Zaynī Daḥlān, Aḥmad. *al-Sīra al-nabawiyya wa-al-āthār al-muḥammadiyya*. Cairo, 1875.

Books on Tawḥīd and Taṣawwuf

[600] *Talkhīs al-tajrīd li-ʿumdat al-murīd* ***sharḥ jawharat al-tawḥīd***, AUTHOR: Burhān al-Dīn Ibrāhīm b. Ibrāhīm al-Laqānī (d. 1041/1631), EDITION: 3 vols, Beirut: Dār Ibn Ḥazm, 2022. Unlike later entries, this manuscript is noted as being in two volumes (*mujalladayn*), which means it might be referring to one of Ibrāhīm al-Laqānī's longer commentaries on his creedal poem. I have here noted his middle commentary, the *Talkhīṣ al-tajrīd*.

[601] *Itḥāf al-murīd bi-**Sharḥ al-jawhara*** [*Sharḥ jawharat al-tawḥīd*], AUTHOR: **ʿAbd al-Salām** b. Ibrāhīm b. Ibrāhīm al-Laqānī (971/1563–1078/1668), EDITION: Miṣr: al-Maktaba al-Tijāriyya al-Kubrā, 1955.

[602] ***al-Awwal min sharḥ jawharat al-tawḥīd al-kabīr*** (*Umdat al-murīd*), AUTHOR: Burhān al-Dīn Ibrāhīm b. Ibrāhīm al-Laqānī (d. 1041/1631), EDITION: ʿAbd al-Mannān Aḥmad al-Idrīsī and Jād Allāh Bassām Ṣāliḥ, Cairo: Dar al-Nur al-Mubīn lil-Nashr wa-al-Tawzīʿ, 2016.

[603] ***Sharḥ jawharat al-tawḥīd al-musammā bi-Hidāyat al-murīd***, AUTHOR: Burhān al-Dīn Ibrāhīm b. Ibrāhīm al-Laqānī (d. 1041/1631), EDITION: Muḥammad ʿAlāʾ al-Dīn Zaynū, Damascus: Dār Ḍiyāʾ al-Shām/Dār Jalīs al-Zamān, 2018.

[604] ***Kitāb uṣūl al-tawḥīd***, AUTHOR: Abū Qāsim al-Ṣaffār (d. 336/947), EDITION: Akram Muḥammad Ismāʿīl Abū ʿAwwād, Cairo: Dār al-Nūr al-Mubīn, 2022.

[605] ***Umm al-barāhīn*** (= *matn al-sanūsiyya*), AUTHOR: Muḥammad b. Yūsuf al-Sanūsī al-Tilimsānī (d. 895/1490), EDITION: Anas Muḥammad ʿAdnān al-Sharfāwī. Dimashq: Dār al-Taqwā, 2019.

[606] ***Sharḥ umm al-barāhīn***. AUTHOR: None speci-

fied, EDITION: Māhir ʿAdnān ʿUthmān. Istanbul: Dār Taḥqīq al-Kitāb, 2021.

[607] ***al-Sanūsiyya wa-maʿhā ghayrhā*** (= *Umm al-barāhīn*), see #605.

[608] ***Matn al-sanūsiyya*** (= *Umm al-barāhīn*), see #605.

[609] ***Sharḥ al-ʿaqāʾid lil-naysābūrī***. Unidentified.

[610] ***Sharḥ ʿaqīdat al-shaybānī***, AUTHOR: Najm al-Dīn Ibn Qāḍī ʿAjlūn (d. 876/1471), *Badīʿ al-maʿānī fī sharḥ ʿaqīdat al-shaybānī*. Baghdad: Maṭbaʿat al-Furāt, 1922; or ʿUlwān Ibn ʿAṭiyya al-Ḥusaynī al-Ḥamawī (d. 936/1529). *Bayān al-maʿānī fī sharḥ ʿaqīdat al-shaybānī*. Beirut: al-Maṭbaʿa al-Adabiyya, 1324/1906. This creed is attributed to Abū ʿAbdallāh Muḥammad b. Ḥasan al-Shaybānī (d. 189/804), the disciple of Abū Ḥanīfa. It is unlikely that it is an authentic work of Shaybānī. Two commentaries on the creed were written at roughly the same time in the same geographical region, and this entry may refer to either one of them. Both are listed here.

[611] ***Sharḥ al-ʿaqāʾid*** *al-nasafiyya*, AUTHOR: Saʿd al-Dīn al-Taftāzānī (d. 793/1390), EDITION: Claude Salāma. Damascus: Manshūrāt Wizārat al-Thaqāfa wa-al-Irshād al-Qawmī, 1974.

[612] ***Tajrīd al-ʿaqāʾid***, AUTHOR: Abū Jaʿfar Muḥammad b. Muḥammad b. al-Ḥasan Naṣīr al-Dīn al-Ṭūsī (d. 672/1274), EDITION: Muḥammad Jawād al-Ḥusaynī al-Jalālī. Qum: Markaz al-Nashr Maktab al-Iʿlām al-Islāmī, 1407/1986.

[613] ***Sharḥ ʿaqīdat al-ajhūrī***, AUTHOR: Abū al-Irshād ʿAlī b. Muḥammad al-Ajhūrī (d. 1066/1655), EDITION: Maḥmūd ʿAbd al-Ṣādiq al-Ḥassānī. Cairo: Dār al-Ṣāliḥ, 2020.

[614] ***Sharḥ al-ʿaqāʾid*** *al-nasafiyya*, see #611.

[615] ***Sharḥ ʿaqīdat al-ajhūrī***, see #613.

[616] ***Sharḥ al-sanūsiyya***, see #606.

[617] ***Sharḥ al-sanūsiyya***, AUTHOR: Muḥammad b. Yūsuf al-Sanūsī **al-Tilimsānī** (d. 895/1490), EDITION: Anas Muḥammad ʿAdnān al-Sharfāwī. Dimashq: Dār al-Taqwā, 2019.

[618] *al-Kawākib al-saniyya* ***sharḥ al-qaṣīda al-maqqariyya***, AUTHOR: Aḥmad b. Ṣāliḥ al-Adhamī al-Ṭarābulsī (d. 1159/1746), EDITION: Master's Thesis, ʿĀʾisha bint Dālish b. Ḥāmid al-ʿAnzī, Saudi Arabia: Jāmiʿat al-Imām Muḥammad b. Saʿūd al-Islāmiyya, 1430/2008.

[619] ***al-Ṣuḥuf al-ilāhiyya***, AUTHOR: Shams al-Dīn Muḥammad b. Ashraf al-Samarqandī (d. 722/1322), EDITION: Aḥmad ʿAbd al-Raḥmān al-Sharīf. Kuwait, 1985.

[620] ***al-Munqidh min al-ḍalāla***, AUTHOR: Abū Ḥāmid al-Ghazālī (d. 505/1111), EDITION: Farid Jabre. Beirut: Commission libanaise pour la traduction des chefs-d'œvre, 1969.

[621] ***Iḍāʾat al-dujunna***, AUTHOR: Shihāb al-Dīn Aḥmad al-Maqqarī al-Tilimsānī (d. 1041/1631), EDITION: Abū al-Faḍl ʿAbdallāh Muḥammad al-Ṣiddīq al-Ghumārī. Cairo: Maktabat al-Qāhira, 1952.

[622] ***Kitāb fī al-tawḥīd***. Unidentified.

[623] ***Miftāḥ al-falāḥ***, AUTHOR: Tāj al-Dīn Aḥmad b. Muḥammad Ibn ʿAṭāʾ Allāh al-Iskandarī (d. 709/1309), EDITION: Miṣr: Muṣṭafā al-Bābī al-Ḥalabī, 1961. The work has also been attributed to a certain Shams al-Dīn al-Barshīnī. See the discussion in Khalid Zahrī, *Tartīb al-sulūk wa-yalīhā Risāla fī adab al-ʿilm* (Beirut, Dār al-Kutub al-ʿIlmiyya, 2004), 11.

[624] ***Khulāṣat baḥr al-ḥaqāʾiq***, AUTHOR: Abū al-Maḥāsin Muḥammad b. Saʿīd b. Muḥammad al-Nakhjawānī Ibn al-Sāwajī (active 732/1332), MANUSCRIPT: *Khulāṣat baḥr al-ḥaqāʾiq wa-al-maʿānī fī tafsīr al-sabʿ al-mathānī*. Istanbul: Rāghib Bāshā, 95. The work is an epitome of the exegesis *Bahr al-ḥaqāʾiq* by the influential mystic Najm al-Dīn Kubrā (d. 618/1221), under whom Ibn al-Sāwajī likely studied. The work is listed in the inventory as a single volume work, and thus cannot refer to Najm al-Dīn's complete exegesis which is in several volumes. Both the exegesis and the epitome by Ibn al-Sāwajī remain unedited. Despite being a exegesis (*tafsīr*) of the Qurʾan, the work is listed in the *taṣawwuf* section because it is specifically a mystical exegesis (*tafsīr ʿirfānī*).

[625] ***Risāla fī al-tawḥīd*** (*Qawāʿid al-ʿaqāʾid* = *al-Risāla al-qudsiyya*), AUTHOR: Abū Ḥāmid **al-Ghazālī** (d. 505/1111), EDITION: Raʾūf Shalabī

and Mūsā Muḥammad ʿAlī. Cairo, Al-Azhar: Majmūʿ al-Buḥūth al-Islāmiyya, 1970.

[626] ***Risāla fī al-tawḥīd***, AUTHOR: Abū Ḥāmid **al-Ghazālī** (d. 505/1111), see #625.

[627] ***ʿUnwān al-taḥqīq***, AUTHOR: ʿAbd al-Ghanī al-Nābulusī (1050–1143/1641–1731), EDITION: *Wasāʾil al-taḥqīq wa-rasāʾil al-tawfīq*, in Samer Akkach, *Letters of a Sufi Scholar: The Correspondence of ʿAbd al-Ghanī al-Nābulusī (1641–1731)*. Leiden: Brill, 2010.

[628] ***al-Muʿāwana wa-al-muẓāhara***, AUTHOR: ʿAfīf al-Dīn ʿAbdallāh b. ʿAlawī b. Muḥammad al-Ḥaddād (1044–1132/1634–1720), EDITION: *Risālat al-muʿāwana wa-al-muẓāhara wa-al-muwāzara lil-rāghibīn min al-muʾminīn fī sulūk ṭarīq al-ākhira*. Cairo: al-Maṭbaʿa al-ʿĀmira, 1309/1891.

[629] ***al-Munqidh min al-ḍalāla***, see #620.

[630] ***al-Sayf al-maslūl*** *ʿalā man sabba al-rasūl* ***wa-maʿhu risāla***, AUTHOR: Taqī al-Dīn al-Subkī (d. 756/1355), EDITION: Īyād Aḥmad al-Ghawj, Amman: Dār al-Fatḥ, 2000. The title of the treatise (*risāla*) attached to this work has not been disclosed.

[631] ***al-Milal wa-al-nihal***, AUTHOR: Abū al-Fatḥ Muḥammad b. ʿAbd al-Karīm al-Shahrastānī (d. 548/1153), EDITION: 3 vols, ʿAbd al-ʿAzīz Muḥammad al-Wakīl, Cairo: Muʾassasat al-Ḥalabī, 1968.

[632] ***al-Milal wa-al-nihal***, see #631.

[633] ***Tashyīd al-arkān*** *fī laysa fī al imkān abdaʿ mimmā kān* ***wa-maʿhu risālatayn***, AUTHOR: Jalāl al-Dīn al-Suyūṭī (d. 911/1505), EDITION: Aleppo: Dār al-Kitāb al-Islāmī, 1998. The titles of the two treatises (*risālatayn*) attached to this work have not been disclosed.

[634] ***al-Yawāqīt wa-al-jawāhir*** *fī bayān* ***ʿaqāʾid al-sādat al-akābir***, AUTHOR: ʿAbd al-Wahhāb al-Shaʿrānī (d. 973/1565), EDITION: Cairo, n.p., 1860.

[635] ***al-Yawāqīt wa-al-jawāhir*** *fī bayān ʿaqāʾid al-akābir*, see #634.

[636] ***Taʾsīs al-qawāʿid*** *wa-al-uṣūl wa-taḥṣīl al-fawāʾid li-dhawī al-wuṣūl fī umūr aʿammuhā al-taṣawwuf wa-mā fīhi min wujūh al-taʿarruf* (= *Qawāʾid al-taṣawwuf wa-shawāhid al-taʿarruf*), AUTHOR: Aḥmad Zarrūq al-Fāsī (d. 899/1493), EDITION: Nizār Ḥammādī, Kuwait: Dār al-Ḍiyāʾ lil-Nashr wa-al-Tawzīʿ, 2018.

[637] *Ḥāshiyyat* ***Saʿd al-Dīn*** *ʿalā sharḥ* ***ʿAḍud*** *al-Dīn al-Ījī li-mukhtaṣar al-muntahā al-uṣūlī*, AUTHOR: Saʿd al-Dīn al-Taftāzānī (d. 793/1390), EDITION: Cairo: al-Maṭbaʿa al-Amīriyya bi-Būlāq, 1316/1898. MANUSCRIPT: This manuscript from the Jazzār collection is today preserved in Saudi Arabia, Maktabat al-Ḥaram al-Makkī, #1499.

[638] ***Ḥāshiyyat Ilyas*** *ʿala sharḥ al-Taftāzānī* ***ʿalā al-ʿaqāʾid*** *al-nasafiyya*, AUTHOR: Ilyās b. Ibrāhīm al-Kurdī al-Kūrānī (d. 1138/1725), EDITION: Bashīr Barmān, Beirut: Dār al-Kutub al-ʿIlmiyya, 2017.

[639] ***Ḥāshiyya fī al-ʿaqāʾid***. Unidentified. Likely refers to a supercommentary either on Taftāzānī's commentary on the Nasafī creed or Dawānī's commentary on the creed of ʿAḍud al-Dīn al-Ījī.

[640] ***Ḥāshiyya ʿalā al-jawhara*** (*jawharat al-tawḥīd*), AUTHOR: not disclosed, numerous possibilties. EDITION: See the collection of commentaries on the *Jawharat al-tawḥīd* in *Majmūʿ jawharat al-tawḥīd*, edited by Māhir Muḥammad ʿAdnān ʿUthmān, 2 vols, Istanbul: Dār Taḥqīq al-Kitāb lil-Ṭibāʿa wa-al-Nashr wa-al-Tawzīʿ, 2021.

[641] ***Ḥāshiyya ʿalā umm al-barāhīn***, see #606.

[642] ***Ḥāshiyyat al-Jurjānī***, AUTHOR: al-Sayyid al-Sharīf ʿAlī b. Muḥammad **al-Jurjānī** (d. 816/1413). Unidentified.

[642[a]] ***Sharḥ al-qaṣīda al-maqqariyya***, see #618.

[642[b]] ***al-Risāla al-qadariyya***. Unidentified.

[642[c]] ***Sharḥ fuṣūṣ al-ḥikam***, AUTHOR: Unidentified. The literature attests to over one hundred commentaries on Ibn al-ʿArabī's *Fuṣūṣ al-ḥikam*. No indication of which commentary this entry represents.

[643] ***al-Bayān al-maqbūl fī radd al-sūl***, AUTHOR: **ʿAbd al-Ghanī al-Nābulusī** (d. 1143/1731). Work unidentified. This entry includes the statement that this is an autograph manuscript (*bi-khaṭṭi sayyidī muʾallifihi*). This work is not mentioned in the list of works by Nābulusī in the biographical collections, but it might be an alternative title for his *Jamʿ al-asrār fī manʿ al-ashrār ʿan al-ṭaʿn fī al-ṣūfiyya al-akhyār ahl al-tawājud fī al-adhkār*. In a description of a manuscript of the *Jamʿ al-asrār*, the cataloguer notes

that Nābulusī ends his work with the statement *'hādhā miqdar mā yassarahu Allāhu lanā min **al-bayān al-maqbūl***', which might be a direct allusion to the work listed in this entry. See the descriptive catalogue of manuscripts held by the American University of Beirut compiled by Yūsuf Khūrī, *Al-Makhṭūṭāt al-ʿarabiyya al-mawjūda fī maktabat al-jāmiʿa al-amrīkiyya fī bayrūt*. Beirut: Markaz al-dirāsāt al-ʿarabiyya wa-dirāsāt al-sharq al-awsaṭ, al-Jāmiʿa al-Amrīkiyya fī Bayrūt, 1985, 119 (entry #313).

[644] ***al-ʿAqd wa-al-tawḥīd wa-kitāb al-kāfī***. Unidentified.

[645] ***Majmūʿ fī al-tawḥīd***. Unidentified.

[646] ***al-Kashf wa-al-tabyīn fī ghurūr al-khalq ajmaʿīn wa-maʿhu ghayruhu***, AUTHOR: Abū Ḥāmid al-Ghazālī (d. 505/1111), EDITION: ʿAbd al-Laṭīf ʿĀshūr, Cairo: Maktabat al-Qurʾān.

[647] ***al-Kashf wa-al-bayān***, see #646.

[648] ***Sharḥ fuṣūṣ** al-ḥikam li-Ibn al-ʿArabī*, see #642c.

[649] ***Sharḥ fuṣūṣ** al-ḥikam li-Ibn al-ʿArabī*, see #642c.

[650] ***Rasāʾil al-Shaykh Muḥyī al-Dīn*** [*Ibn al-ʿArabī*], AUTHOR: Muḥyī al-Dīn Ibn al-ʿArabī (d. 638/1240), EDITION: 7 vols, Saʿīd ʿAbd al-Fattāḥ, Qāsim Muḥammad ʿAbbās, Saḥbān Aḥmad Marawwa, Beirut: Muʾassasat al-Intishār al-ʿArabī, 2001–2006. The name appears as Yaḥyā al-Dīn in the inventory, likely a typographical error for Muḥyī al-Dīn, in reference to Muḥyī al-Dīn Ibn al-ʿArabī (d. 638/1240). We do not know how many or what treatises were included in this manuscript of Ibn al-ʿArabī's treatises. In the printed edition of Ibn al-ʿArabī's treatises cited here, all treatises that are either attributed to or confirmed to be by Ibn al-ʿArabī are printed.

[651] ***al-Futūḥāt al-makkiyya***, AUTHOR: Muḥyī al-Dīn Ibn al-ʿArabī (d. 638/1240), EDITION: 14 vols, ʿUthmān Yaḥyā, Cairo: al-Hayʾa al-Miṣriyya al-ʿĀmma lil-Kitāb, 1972. ʿUthmān Yaḥyā's edition is incomplete, but remains the most dependable. Other editions of the work include: 4 vols, al-Amīr Muḥyī al-Dīn ʿAbd al-Qādir al-Jazāʾirī (reviewed), Cairo: Būlāq, 1269/1852; 13 vols, ʿAbd al-ʿAzīz Sulṭān al-Manṣūb, Tarim: Wizārat al-Thaqāfa, 2010; 17 vols, Muḥammad Khājavī, Qum: Intishārāt Mawlā, 2020.

[652] ***al-Futūḥāt al-makiyya***, see #651.

[653] ***Qiṭʿa min al-futūḥāt al-makkiyya***, AUTHOR: Muḥyī al-Dīn Ibn al-ʿArabī (d. 638/1240), MANUSCRIPT: Jerusalem, Khālidī Library, AKDI 01060/1026 (Formerly MS 1981).
Digitised online: https://w3id.org/vhmml/readingRoom/view/509558.

[654] ***Mukhtaṣar iḥyāʾ*** *ʿulūm al-dīn*, AUTHOR: Shams al-Dīn Muḥammad b. ʿAlī b. Jaʿfar al-ʿAjlūnī al-Bilālī (d. 820/1417), EDITION: Muḥammad Muṣʿab Kalthūm. Amman: Dār al-Fatḥ lil-Dirāsāt wa-al-Nashr, 2022. ***Wa-Sulwān al-muṭāʿ*** *fī ʿudwān al-atbāʿ*, AUTHOR: Ibn Ẓafar al-Ṣiqillī (d. 565/1169), EDITION: Ayman ʿAbd al-Jābir al-Buḥayrī, Cairo: Dār al-Āfāq al-ʿArabiyya, 2001.

[655] ***al-Insān al-kāmil*** *fī maʿrifat al-awākhir wa-al-awāʾil*, AUTHOR: ʿAbd al-Karīm al-Jīlī (d. 826/1422), EDITION: Cairo: Muṣṭafā Bābī al-Ḥalabī, 1970; Cairo: Būlāq, 1293/1876.

[656] *Laṭāʾif **al-minan** wa-al-akhlāq fī wujūb al-taḥadduth bi-niʿmat Allāh ʿalā al-iṭlāq*, AUTHOR: ʿAbd al-Wahhāb **al-Shaʿrānī** (d. 973/1565), EDITION: Muʿādh ʿAbd al-Raḥmān al-Hawwāsh, Dimashq: Dār al-Taqwā, 1440/2019.

[657] ***Maqāmāt al-khawwāṣṣ***. Unidentified.

[658] ***al-Risāla al-qushayriyya***, AUTHOR: Abū al-Qāsim ʿAbd al-Karīm al-Qushayrī (d. 465/1072), EDITION: Anas Muḥammad ʿAdnān al-Sharfāwī, Jeddah: Dār al-Minhāj lil-Nashr wa-al-Tawzīʿ, 1441/2020.

[659] ***al-Risāla al-qushayriyya***, see #658.

[660] ***al-Risāla al-qudsiyya***, see #625.

[661] *Kitāb fī al-**taṣawwuf***. Unidentified. Generic title for a work on *taṣawwuf*.

[662] ***Mawāzīn al-rijāl*** *al-qāṣirīn*, AUTHOR: ʿAbd al-Wahhāb al-Shaʿrānī (d. 973/1565), EDITION: Haṣṣān ʿAbdallāh al-Sarūjī Qinānī, Beirut: Dār al-Imām Yūsuf al-Nabhānī, 2021.

[663] ***Kashf al-ḥijāb wa-al-rān*** *ʿan wajh asʾilat al-jān*, AUTHOR: ʿAbd al-Wahhāb al-Shaʿrānī (d. 973/1565), EDITION: Muḥammad ʿAbdallāh ʿAbd al-Razzāq, Cairo: Maṭbaʿat Ḥijāzī, 1928.

[664] ***Kashf al-ḥijāb wa-al-rān*** *ʿan wajh asʾilat al-jān*, see #663.

[665] ***Riyāḍ al-ṣāliḥīn*** *min kalām sayyid al-mursalīn*, AUTHOR: Muḥyī al-Dīn Abū Zakariyyā Yaḥyā b. Sharaf al-Nawawī (631–676/1233–1277), EDITION: ʿAbd al-ʿAzīz Rabbāḥ, Aḥmad Sharīf al-Daqqāq, and Shuʿayb al-Arnaʾūṭ, Dimashq: Dār al-Maʾmūn lil-Turāth, 1409/1989.

[666] ***al-Tanwīr fī isqāṭ al-tadbīr***, AUTHOR: Ibn ʿAṭāʾ Allāh al-Iskandarī (d. 709/1309), EDITION: Cairo: Muṣṭafā al-Bābī al-Ḥalabī, 1903.

[667] ***al-Tanwīr fī isqāṭ al-tadbīr***, see #666.

[668] ***al-Tanwīr fī isqāṭ al-tadbīr***, see #666.

[669] ***Bustān al-ʿārifīn*** *wa-sabīl al-zāhidīn*, AUTHOR: Muḥyī al-Dīn Abū Zakariyyā Yaḥyā b. Sharaf al-Nawawī (631–676/1233–1277), EDITION: Muḥammad Saʿīd al-ʿUrfī, Cairo: Idārat al-Ṭibāʿa al-Munīriyya, 1348/1929.

[670] ***Bustān al-zāhidīn***, likely #669.

[671] ***Zubdat al-wuṣūl*** *ilā ʿumdat al-uṣūl*, AUTHOR: Yūsuf b. Ḥusayn al-Kirmāstī (d. 906/1500), EDITION: ʿAbd al-Raḥmān Hujqalī, Beirut: Dār Ṣādir, 2008.

[672] ***al-Kibrīt al-aḥmar*** *fī bayān ʿulūm al-shaykh al-akbar*, AUTHOR: ʿAbd al-Wahhāb **al-Shaʿrānī** (d. 973/1565), EDITION: Ḥasan al-ʿAnānī, Cairo, 1277/1861.

[673] ***Sharḥ asmāʾ Allāh al-ḥusnā wa-maʿhu rasāʾil thalātha***. Unidentified. There are two main approaches to commenting on the divine names in the Islamic tradition. One approach focuses on the theological insights that can be gleaned from the divine names, exemplified in the works of Rāzī (d. 606/1210), Ghazālī (d. 505/1111) and Bayhaqī (d. 458/1066). Another approach is to examine God's names from the perspective of Islamic mysticism, the aim being to specify the qualities that are unique to each name (*khaṣāʾiṣ al-asmāʾ*). Some authors amalgamated both approaches. Given the plethora of books dedicated to elucidating and commenting on the divine names in the Islamic tradition, identifying the specific work referenced in this entry proves challenging.

[674] ***Sharḥ asmāʾ Allāh al-ḥusnā***, AUTHOR: Ṣadr al-Dīn Muḥammad b. Isḥāq b. Yūsuf **al-Qūnawī** (d. 673/1274), EDITION: Qāsim al-Ṭihrānī, Beirut: Dār wa-Maktabat al-Hilāl lil-Ṭibāʿa wa-al-Nashr, 2008.

[675] ***Sharḥ al-ḥikam*** *al-ʿaṭāʾiyya*. Unidentified. The term *ḥikam* is very probably a reference to the wisdom sayings of the thirteenth-century sage Ibn ʿAṭāʾ Allāh al-Iskandarī (d. 709/1309), although it is unclear who wrote the commentary (*sharḥ*) on the work referenced here.

[676] ***Ightinām al-fawāʾid*** *fī sharḥ qawāʿid al-ʿaqāʾid*, AUTHOR: Aḥmad Zarrūq al-Fāsī (d. 899/1493), EDITION: Nizār Ḥammādī, Tunis: Dār Ibn ʿArafa, Kuwayt: Dār al-Ḍiyāʾ lil-Nashr wa-al-Tawzīʿ, 1436/2015.

[677] ***Minhāj al-ʿabidīn*** *ilā jannat rabb al-ʿālimīn*, AUTHOR: Abū Ḥāmid al-Ghazālī (d. 505/1111), EDITION: Cairo: Maktabat Muṣṭafā al-Bābī al-Ḥalabī, 1337/1918.

[678] ***Bahjat al-rasāʾil***. Unidentified.

[679] ***Ḥilyat ahl al-faḍl wa-al-kamāl*** *bi-ittiṣāl al-asānīd bi-kamāl al-rijāl*, AUTHOR: Ismāʿīl b. Muḥammad al-ʿAjlūnī (d. 1162/1749), EDITION: Muḥammad Ibrāhīm al-Ḥusayn, Amman: Dār al-Fatḥ lil-Dirāsāt wa-al-Nashr, 2009.

[680] ***Khawāṣṣ al-dumyāṭiyya*** *fī asmāʾ Allāh al-husnā*, AUTHOR: Aḥmad Zarrūq al-Fāsī (d. 899/1493), EDITION: Yūsuf Aḥmad, Beirut: Dār al-Kutub al-ʿIlmiyya, 2007.

[681] ***Qawānīn ḥikam al-ishrāq*** *ilā kāfat al-ṣūfiyya bi-jamīʿ al-āfāq*, AUTHOR: Abū al-Mawāhib al-Shādhilī (d. 882/1478), EDITION: ʿAbd al-Raḥmān Muḥammad Rashīd al-Shaʿʿār, Cairo: Dār al-Iḥsān lil-Nashr wa-al-Tawzīʿ, 2021.

[682] ***al-Tadbīrāt al-ilāhiyya*** *fī iṣlāḥ al-mamlaka al-insāniyya*, AUTHOR: Muḥyī al-Dīn Ibn al-ʿArabī (d. 638/1240), EDITION: H.S. Nyberg, Leiden: Brill, 1919.

[683] ***al-Fatḥ al-rabbānī*** *wa-al-fayḍ al-raḥmānī*, AUTHOR: ʿAbd al-Qādir al-Jīlānī (d. 561/1165), EDITION: Antonious Shiblī al-Lubnānī, Beirut: al-Maṭbaʿa al-Kāthuluqiyya, 1960; or ʿAbd al-Ghanī al-Nābulusī (d. 1143/1731), EDITION: Muḥammad ʿAbd al-Qādir ʿAṭā, Beirut: Dār al-Kutub al-ʿIlmiyya, 1985.

[684] ***al-Risāla al-raslāniyya***, AUTHOR: **ʿAbd al-Ghanī**

al-Nābulusī (d. 1143/1731), EDITION: Dimashq: Maṭbaʿat al-ʿAlam, 1389/1969.

[685] ***Majmūʿ rasāʾil taṣawwuf***. Unidentified.

[686] ***Sharḥ al-risāla al-shinnāwiyya***, AUTHOR: **ʿAbd al-Ghanī al-Nābulusī** (d. 1143/1731), EDITION: Al-Sayyid Yūsuf Aḥmad, Beirut: Dār al-Kutub al-ʿIlmiyya, 2012.

[687] ***Mashāhid** al-asrār **al-qudsiyya** wa-maṭāliʿ al-anwār al-ilāhiyya*, AUTHOR: **Muḥyī al-Dīn** Ibn al-**ʿArabī** (d. 638/1240), EDITION: Suad Hakim and Pablo Beneito, Murcie: Editora regional de Murcia, 2003.

[688] *Kitāb **al-waṣāyā***, AUTHOR: **al-Shaykh al-Akbar** Muḥyī al-Dīn Ibn al-ʿArabī (d. 638/1240), EDITION: Ayman Ḥamdī al-Akbarī and ʿAlī Jumʿa, Cairo: Muʾassasat Ibn al-ʿArabī lil-Buḥūth wa-al-Nashr, 2023.

[689] ***Ijāzāt ahl al-ṭarīq***. Unidentified.

[690] *Duʿāʾ **kanz al-ʿarsh***, AUTHOR: Unidentified, MANUSCRIPT: National Library of Israel, Ar. 213 (probably not the al-Jazzār manuscript).

[691] ***al-Manhaj al-ḥanīf** fī maʿnā ismihi taʿālā al-laṭīf wa-mā qīla fīhi min al-khawāṣṣ wa-al-taṣrīf*, AUTHOR: Abū Bakr b. Ṣāliḥ al-Kutāmī (d. 1051/1641), EDITION: ʿAmmār b. al-Niyya al-Ḥusnā, al-Jazāʾir, al-Maktaba al-Falsafiyya al-Ṣūfiyya, 2016.

[692] ***Risālat al-naqshbandiyya***. Unidentified.

[693] ***Mafātīḥ al-kunūz** wa-ḥall al-rumūz* [or *Ḥall al-rumūz wa-**mafātīḥ al-kunūz***], AUTHOR: ʿIzz al-Dīn ʿAbd al-Salām b. Aḥmad Ibn Ghānim al-Maqdisī (d. 678/1280), EDITION: Maḥmūd Muḥammad Sayyid al-Jamal, Cairo: Dār al-Imām al-Rāzī, 2018; Aḥmad ʿAlī al-Shādhilī and Ḥusayn Fahmī, Cairo: Maṭbaʿat Jarīdat al-Islām, 1317/1899 (printed with Zakariyya al-Anṣārī's commentary on *al-Risāla al-raslāniyya fī ʿilm al-tawḥīd*, titled *Fatḥ al-raḥmān bi-sharḥ risālat al-walī raslān*).

[694] ***Tadhkirat al-sāʾil***, AUTHOR: Muḥammad b. ʿUmar al-Hawārī (d. 843/1439), MANUSCRIPT: unavailable. The inventory edition transcribes *Tadkhirat al-sāʾir*, but the more probable title is *Tadkhirat al-sāʾil*, which is a work by the Algerian scholar Muḥammad b. ʿUmar al-Hawārī. For more on this work, see Muḥammad b. Yūsuf al-Zayyānī, *Dalīl al-ḥayrān wa-anīs al-sahrān fī akhbār madīnat wahrān*, edited by al-Mahdī al-Būʿabdalī (Algiers: al-Sharaka al-Waṭaniyya lil-Nashr wa-al-Tawzīʿ, 1979), 38. The work has not been published nor was I able to locate an extant manuscript.

[695] ***Dalāʾil al-taḥqīq** li-bayān ghālib shurūṭ al-ṭarīq*, AUTHOR: Saʿd al-Dīn Muḥammad b. ʿUmar b. Muḥammad al-Maqdisī (d. 1038/1628), MANUSCRIPT: Alexandria, Abu'l Abbas Almorsi Library, #203/hadith. For this manuscript, see Youssef Ziedan, *Catalogue of Manuscripts in Abu'l'Abbas Almorsi Library* (Alexandria: al-Hayʾat al-ʿĀmma li-Maktabat al-Iskandariyya, 1997), 189–190.

[696] ***Ṭahārat al-qulūb** wa-al-khuḍūʿ li-ʿallām al-ghuyūb*, AUTHOR: Ḍiyāʾ al-Dīn ʿAbd al-ʿAzīz b. Aḥmad b. Saʿīd al-Dīrīnī (d. 696/1297), EDITION: Maḥmūd ʿAlī Ibrāhīm Dāwūd, Cairo: Maktabat Muṣṭafā al-Bābī al-Ḥalabī, 1380/1960.

[697] ***Risāla fī ʿilm al-nafs***: Unidentified.

[698] ***al-Munjiyyāt al-sabʿ maʿ awrād***. Unidentified. Seven verses that are intended to save (*munjī*) the believer when they are recited, paired together with other litanies (*awrād*). No indication of which verses are listed in this particular manuscript.

[699] ***Sharḥ asmāʾ** Allāh **al-ḥusnā***, see #673.

[700] ***Maʿānī asmāʾ Allāh al-ḥusnā bi-al-lugha al-fārisiyya***, see #673.

[701] ***Nūr al-ʿayn***. Unidentified.

[702] ***Qamʿ al-nufūs** wa-ruqyat al-maʾyūs*, AUTHOR: Taqī al-Dīn Abū Bakr b. Muḥammad b. ʿAbd al-Muʾmin al-Ḥiṣnī (d. 829/1425), EDITION: ʿAlāʾ Ibrāhīm al-Azharī, Beirut: Dār al-Kutub al-ʿIlmiyya, 2003.

[703] ***al-Firaq al-ḍāla wa-al-nājiyya***, AUTHOR: Muḥammad Amīn b. Ṣadr al-Dīn al-Shirwānī (d. 1036/ 1626), MANUSCRIPT: Iran: Marʿashī Library, #30–31; Kuwait: Jāmiʿat al-Kuwayt, Maktabat al-Makhṭūṭāt, #525.

[704] ***al-Qawl al-jalī fī dhikr al-ʿalī***. Unidentified.

[705] ***Tuḥfat al-arīb fī al-radd ʿalā ahl al-ṣalīb***, AU-

THOR: ʿAbdallāh b. ʿAbdallāh al-Tarjumān al-Māyūrqī (Latinised: Anselm Turmeda) (d. 832/1428), EDITION: Miguel de Epalza, Roma: Accademia Nazionale dei Lincei, 1971.

[706] ***al-Rawḍ al-fāʾiq*** *fī al-mawāʿiẓ wa-al-raqāʾiq*, AUTHOR: Shuʿayb b. ʿAbdallāh al-Ḥurayfīsh (d. 810/1407), EDITION: Khālid ʿAbd al-Raḥmān al-ʿAkk, Beirut: Dār Ṣādir, Dimashq: Dār al-Bashāʾir lil-Ṭibāʿa wa-al-Nashr wa-al-Tawzīʿ, 2004.

[707] ***Zād al-murīd***. Unidentified. While I could not locate a work from this period with the title *Zād al-murīd*, the entry may be alluding to a commentary on the creedal poem *Jawharat al-tawḥīd*, as the title shares a rhyme with the title of the poem.

[708] ***al-Sayr wa-al-sulūk*** *ilā malik al-mulūk*, AUTHOR: Qāsim b. Ṣalāḥ al-Dīn al-Khānī (d. 1109/1697), EDITION: Saʿīd ʿAbd al-Fattāḥ, Cairo: Maktabat al-Thaqāfa al-Dīniyya, 2008.

[709] ***al-Fiqh al-akbar***, AUTHOR: Abū Ḥanīfa al-Nuʿmān (d. 150/767), EDITION: Muḥammad Zāhid al-Kawtharī, Cairo, 1368/1949. For more on this work's complicated transmission history, see Ulrich Rudolph, *Al-Māturīdī and the Development of Sunni Theology in Samarqand* (Leiden: Brill, 2014), 53–71.

[710] ***al-Mawārid al-ilāhiyya wa-maʿhā rasāʾil***. Unidentified.

[711] ***al-Tanwīr*** *fī isqāṭ al-tadbīr*, see #666.

[712] *Risāla fī tadwīn* ***ʿilm al-kumūn wa-al-burūz***, AUTHOR: Shams al-Dīn Muḥammad b. ʿAlī b. Aḥmad Ibn Ṭūlūn (d. 953/1546), MANUSCRIPT (Autograph): Germany, Staatsbibliothek zu Berlin, Landberg 704.

[713] ***Muṣṭalaḥāt al-qawm***. Unidentified.

[714] ***Kitāb al-nuzha al-fikriyya***. Unidentified.

[715] ***Durrat al-ghawwāṣ fī awhām al-khawāṣṣ***, AUTHOR: Abū Muḥammad al-Qāsim b. ʿAlī al-Ḥarīrī (d. 516/1122), EDITION: Heinrich Thorbecke, Leipzig: Verlag von F.C.W. Vogel, 1871; ʿAbd al-Ḥafīẓ Farghālī ʿAlī al-Qarnī, Cairo: Maktabat al-Turāth al-Islāmī, Beirut: Dār al-Jīl, 1417/1996.

[716] ***Asrār al-surūr*** *bi-al-wuṣūl ilā ʿayn al-nūr*, AUTHOR: Ibrāhīm b. Isḥāq al-Sayrūzī (d. 673/1274), MANUSCRIPT: Turkey, Raghib Basha 1469.

[717] ***Lawāqiḥ al-anwār*** *al-qudsiyya al-muntaqāt min al-futūḥāt al-makiyya*, AUTHOR: ʿAbd al-Wahhāb al-Shaʿrānī (d. 973/1565), EDITION: Cairo: Dār al-Iḥsān lil-Nashr wa-al-Tawzīʿ, 2016. This work is attributed to Muḥyī al-Dīn Ibn al-ʿArabī (d. 638/1240) (***lawāqiḥ al-anwār lil-shaykh al-akbar***) on the inventory list. But the work is actually an abridgement of Ibn al-ʿArabī's *Futūḥāt* by the Egyptian scholar ʿAbd al-Wahhāb al-Shaʿrānī (d. 973/1565).

[718] ***Tadhkirat al-iʿdād li-yawm al-miʿād***, AUTHOR: Abū al-Khayr Khalīl b. Hārūn b. Mahdī al-Ṣanhājī (d. 826/1423), MANUSCRIPT: Dublin, Chester Beatty Library, Ar. 3236. See Arthur Arberry, *A Handlist of Arabic Manuscripts, Volume 1. MSS. 3001 to 3250* (Dublin, 1955), 100.

[719] ***Muḥāḍarat al-awāʾil*** *wa-musāmarat al-awākhir*, AUTHOR: ʿAlāʾ al-Dīn al-Busnawī (d. 1007/1598), EDITION: Cairo: Būlāq, 1300/1882.

[720] ***al-Jawāhir*** *wa-al-durar al-kubrā wa-al-wusṭā wa-al-ṣughrā*, AUTHOR: ʿAbd al-Wahhāb **al-Shaʿrānī** (d. 973/1565), EDITION: Aḥmad Farīd al-Mazīdī, Cairo: Dār al-Āfāq al-ʿArabiyya, 2011.

[721] ***Majmūʿat adʿiyya wa-awrād***. Unidentified.

[722] ***Duʿāʾ al-jawshan***, EDITION: Taqī al-Dīn Ibrāhīm ibn ʿAlī al-Kafʿamī, *al-Miṣbāḥ* (*Miṣbāḥ al-Kafʿamī*) (Beirut: Muʾassasat al-Nuʿmān, 1992), 287–299. *Duʿāʾ al-jawshan* is an Islamic prayer that is particularly prized among the Shīʿa. The prayer first surfaced in the works of the fifteenth-century Shīʿī scholar Taqī al-Dīn Ibrāhīm ibn ʿAlī al-Kafʿamī (d. 905/1499). For more on the history of this prayer's transmission, see Aydını, "Prayer of *Jawshan*" and Toprak, "Cevşen [Jawshan]".

[723] ***Wird al-shaykh ʿAbd al-Ghanī al-Nābulusī***, AUTHOR: **ʿAbd al-Ghanī al-Nābulusī** (d. 1143/1731). EDITION: ʿAbd al-Salām Shaṭṭī, Dimashq: al-Maṭbaʿah al-Dūmāniyya, 1281/1864.

[724] ***Awrād mawlāna***, AUTHOR: Jalāl al-Dīn al-Rūmī (d. 672/1273), EDITION: Bosnavî Elhac Muharrem Efendi Matbaası, 1866. MANUSCRIPT: Kuwait, Jāmiʿat Kuwayt, Maktabat al-Makhṭūṭāt, #597.

[725] *al-Durr al-thamīn li-**sharḥ al-dawr al-aʿlā*** *li-sayyidī Muḥyī al-Dīn*, AUTHOR: Muḥammad

b. Maḥmūd al-Dāmūnī (fl. 1208/1794), MANUSCRIPT: Nablus, Palestine, Al-Najah National University, NL212423. Digitised online: https://manuscripts.najah.edu/node/605?page=1.

[726] ***Awrād li-Munlā ʿAlī al-Qārī***, AUTHOR: **Mulla ʿAlī Qārī** b. Sulṭān b. Muḥammad al-Harawī (d. 1014/1605), EDITION: (1) *al-Ḥizb al-aʿẓam wa-al-wird al-afkham*, edited by Muḥammad al-Ṭayyib b. Bahāʾ al-Dīn al-Hindī, Dimashq: Dār al-Farfūr, 1427/2006. (2) *al-Qawl al-ṣādiq fī munājāt al-khāliq: adʿiyya maʾthūra bi-ʿaddad ayyām al-usbūʿ*, Cairo: Maktabat al-Jundī, 1380/1960.

[727] *al-Fatḥ al-qudsī wa-al-kashf al-unsī wa-al-manhaj al-qarīb ilā liqāʾ al-ḥabīb al-musammā bi-* ***Wird al-saḥar***, AUTHOR: Muṣṭafā b. Kamāl al-Dīn al-Bakrī (1099–1162/1688–1749), EDITION: Aleppo: Maṭbaʿat al-Saʿd, after 1348/1929, 5–17.

[728] ***Sharh wird al-saḥar***: (1) *al-Ḍiyāʾ al-shamsī ʿalā al-fatḥ al-qudsī*, AUTHOR: Muṣṭafā b. Kamāl al-Dīn al-Bakrī (1099–1162/1688–1749), EDITION: Aḥmad Farīd al-Mazīdī, Beirut: Dār al-Kutub al-ʿIlmiyya, 2013; or (2) *al-Fayḍ al-ʿarshī ʿalā al-fatḥ al-qudsī fī* ***Sharḥ wird al-saḥar***, AUTHOR: ʿAbdallāh b. Ḥijāzī al-Sharqāwī (1150–1227/1737–1812), EDITION: ʿĀsim Ibrāhīm al-Kayyālī, Beirut: Dār al-Kutub al-ʿIlmiyya, 2021.

[729] ***Adʿiyya wa-awrād***. Unidentified.

[730] *al-Maṭlab al-tāmm al-sawī* ***sharḥ ḥizb*** *al-imām* ***al-nawawī***, AUTHOR: Muṣṭafā b. Kamāl al-Dīn al-Bakrī (1099–1162/1688–1749), EDITION: Muḥammad ʿAbd al-Qādir Naṣṣār, Cairo: Dār al-Karaz, 1429/2008.

[731] *al-Durr al-thamīn li-* ***sharḥ al-dawr al-aʿlā*** *li-sayyidī muḥyī al-dīn*, see #725.

[732] *al-Durr al-thamīn li-* ***sharḥ al-dawr al-aʿlā*** *li-sayyidī muḥyī al-dīn*, see #725.

[733] ***Duʿāʾ bi-al-turkī***. Unidentified.

[734] ***Matn al-sanūsiyya***, see #605.

[735] ***Mukhtaṣar umm al-barāhīn*** (*Mukhtaṣar al-sanūsiyya*). Unidentified, possibly referring to #605 or #606.

[736] ***Naẓm al-ʿaqīda***. Unidentified.

[737] ***Matn al-sanūsiyya***, see #605.

[738] ***Sharḥ umm al-barāhīn***, see #606.

[739] ***al-Sayr wa-al-sulūk*** *ilā malik al-mulūk*, see #708.

[740] ***ʿAnqāʾ mughrib fī maʿrifat khatm al-awliyāʾ wa-shams al-maghrib***, AUTHOR: Muḥyī al-Dīn Ibn al-ʿArabī (d. 638/1240), EDITION: Khālid Shibl Abū Sulaymān, Cairo: Maktabat ʿĀlam al-Fikr, 1418/1997.

قائمة المؤلفات

كُتُب التوحيد والتصوّف

كُتب التوحيد

1. إتحاف المريد بشرح جوهرة التوحيد، تأليف عبد السلام اللقاني (ت.1078هـ/1667م) [601]
2. إضاءة الدجنّة في عقائد أهل السنّة، تأليف شهاب الدين المقّري (ت.1041هـ/1631م) [621]
3. اغتنام الفوائد في شرح قواعد العقائد، تأليف أحمد زرّوق الفاسي (ت.899هـ/1493م) [676]
4. أمّ البراهين = السنوسية، تأليف محمد بن يوسف السنوسي التلمساني (ت.895هـ/1490م) [605، 607م، 608، 734، 737]
5. بديع المعاني في شرح عقيدة الشيباني، تأليف ابن قاضي عجلون (ت.876هـ/1471م)، أو تأليف علوان بن عطية الحسيني الحموي (ت.936هـ/1529م) [610]
6. تجريد العقائد، تأليف نصير الدين الطوسي (ت.672هـ/1274م) [612أ، 612ب]
7. تحفة الأريب في الردّ على أهل الصليب، تأليف عبد الله الترجمان المايورقي (ت.832هـ/1428م) [705]
8. تشييد الأركان في ليس في الإمكان أبدع مما كان، تأليف جلال الدين السيوطي (ت.911هـ/1505م) [633م]
9. تلخيص التجريد لعمدة المريد شرح جوهرة التوحيد، تأليف إبراهيم اللقاني (ت.1041هـ/1631م) [600أ، 600ب]
10. حاشية على أمّ البراهين، تأليف (؟) [641]
11. حاشية على جوهرة التوحيد، تأليف (؟) [640]
12. حاشية على شرح التفتازاني للعقائد النسفية، تأليف الملّا إلياس الكوراني (ت.1138هـ/1725م) [638]
13. حاشية في العقائد، تأليف (؟) [639]
14. السيف المسلول على من سبّ الرسول، تأليف تقي الدين السبكي (ت.756هـ/1355م) [630م]
15. شرح العقائد النسفية، تأليف سعد الدين التفتازاني (ت.793هـ/1390م) [611، 614]
16. شرح العقائد للنيسابوري ، تأليف (؟) [609]
17. شرح أمّ البراهين، تأليف محمد بن يوسف السنوسي التلمساني (ت.895هـ/1490م) [606، 616، 617، 738]
18. شرح نظم الأجهوري في العقائد، تأليف أبي الإرشاد الأجهوري (ت.1066هـ/1655م) [613، 615]
19. الصحائف الإلهية، تأليف شمس الدين السمرقندي (ت.722هـ/1322م) [619]
20. العقد والتوحيد، تأليف (؟) [644م]
21. عمدة المريد شرح جوهرة التوحيد = الشرح الكبير على جوهرة التوحيد، **الجزء الأول**، تأليف إبراهيم اللقاني (ت.1041هـ/1631م) [602]
22. الفرق الضالة والناجية، تأليف محمد أمين بن صدر الدين الشرواني (ت.1036هـ/1626م) [703]
23. الفقه الأكبر، تأليف أبي حنيفة النعمان (ت.150هـ/767م) [709]
24. قواعد العقائد = الرسالة القدسيّة، تأليف أبي حامد الغزالي (ت.505هـ/1111م) [625، 626، 660]
25. كتاب أصول التوحيد، تأليف أبي قاسم الصفّار (ت.336هـ/947م) [604]
26. كتاب في التوحيد، تأليف (؟) [622]
27. الكواكب السنية شرح القصيدة المقريّة، تأليف أحمد بن صالح الأدهمي الطرابلسي (ت.1159هـ/1746م) [618]
28. مجموع في التوحيد، تأليف (؟) [645]
29. مختصر أمّ البراهين = مختصر السنوسية، تأليف (؟) [735]
30. الملل والنحل، تأليف أبي الفتح الشهرستاني (ت.548هـ/1153م) [631، 632]

31. المنقذ من الضلال والموصل إلى ذي العزّة والجلال، تأليف أبي حامد الغزالي (ت.505هـ/1111م) [620، 629]
32. نظم العقيدة، تأليف (؟) [736]
33. هداية المريد إلى شرح جوهرة التوحيد، تأليف برهان الدين اللقاني (ت.1041هـ/1631م) [603]

كُتب التصوّف

1. إجازات أهل الطريق، تأليف (؟) [689]
2. أدعية وأوراد [698م، 721، 729]
3. أسرار السرور بالوصول إلى عين النور، تأليف إبراهيم بن إسحاق السيروزي (ت.673هـ/1274م) [716]
4. الإنسان الكامل في معرفة الأواخر والأوائل، تأليف عبد الكريم الجيلي (ت.826هـ/1422م) [655]
5. أوراد منلا علي القاري (ت.1014هـ/1606م) [726]
6. أوراد مولانا (= جلال الدين الرومي) (ت.672هـ/1273م) [724]
7. بستان العارفين وسبيل الزاهدين، تأليف محيي الدين النووي (ت.676هـ/1277م) [670، 669]
8. بهجة الرسائل، تأليف (؟) [678]
9. البيان المقبول في رد السول، تأليف عبد الغني النابلسي (ت.1143هـ/1730م) [643]
10. تأسيس القواعد والأصول وتحصيل الفوائد لذوي الوصول في أمورٍ أعمّها التصوّف وما فيه من وجوه التعرّف = قواعد التصوّف وشواهد التعرّف، تأليف أحمد زرّوق الفاسي (ت.899هـ/1493م) [636]
11. التدبيرات الإلهية في إصلاح المملكة الإنسانية، تأليف محيي الدين ابن عربي (ت.638هـ/1240م) [682]
12. تذكرة الإعداد ليوم المعاد، تأليف خليل بن هارون الصنهاجي (ت.826هـ/1422م) [718]
13. تذكرة السائر = تذكرة السائل، تأليف محمد بن عمر الهواري (ت.843هـ/1439م) [694]
14. التنوير في إسقاط التدبير، ابن عطاء الله السكندري (ت.709هـ/1309م) [666، 667، 668، 711]
15. الجواهر والدرر، تأليف عبد الوهاب الشعراني (ت.973هـ/1565م) [720]
16. خواصّ الدمياطيّة في أسماء الله الحسنى، تأليف أحمد زرّوق الفاسي (ت.899هـ/1493م) [680]
17. دعاء (بالتركيّة) [733]
18. دعاء الجوشن[722]
19. دلائل التحقيق لبيان غالب شروط الطريق، تأليف سعد الدين محمد بن عمر بن محمد المقدسي (ت.1038هـ/1628م) [695]
20. رسائل الشيخ محيي الدين، تأليف محيي الدين ابن عربي (ت.638هـ/1240م) [650]
21. الرسالة الرسلانية، تأليف عبد الغني النابلسي (ت.1143هـ/1731م) [684]
22. الرسالة القشيرية، تأليف أبي القاسم القشيري (ت.465هـ/1072م) [658، 659]
23. رسالة المعاونة والمظاهرة والمؤازرة للراغبين من المؤمنين في سلوك طريق الآخرة، تأليف عفيف الدين عبد الله بن علوي بن محمد الحدّاد (ت.1132هـ/1720م) [628]
24. رسالة النقشبنديّة، تأليف (؟) [692]
25. رسالة في علم النفس، تأليف (؟) [697]
26. الروض الفائق في المواعظ والرقائق، تأليف شعيب الحريفيش (ت.810هـ/1407م) [706]
27. زاد المريد، تأليف (؟) [707]
28. السير والسلوك إلى ملك الملوك، تأليف قاسم بن صلاح الدين الخاني (ت.1109هـ/1697م) [708، 739]
29. شرح أسماء الله الحسنى، تأليف (؟) [673م]
30. شرح أسماء الله الحسنى، تأليف (؟) [699]

31. شرح أسماء الله الحسنى، تأليف صدر الدين القونوي (ت.673هـ/1274م) [674]
32. شرح الحكم العطائية، تأليف (؟) [675]
33. شرح الرسالة الشنّاويّة، تأليف عبد الغني النابلسي (ت.1143هـ/1731م) [686]
34. شرح حزب الدور الأعلى لابن عربي = الدر الثمين لشرح الدور الأعلى لسيدي محيي الدين، تأليف محمد بن محمود الداموني (ت.1208هـ/1794م) [725، 731، 732]
35. شرح فصوص الحكم لابن عربي، تأليف (؟) [649, 648, 642c]
36. شرح ورد السَّحَر للبكري ،**إمّا أن يكون** :الضياء الشمسي على الفتح القدسي، تأليف مصطفى بن كمال الدين البكري (ت.1162هـ/1749م)، **وإمّا أن يكون** :الفيض العرشي على الفتح القدسي في شرح ورد السَّحَر، تأليف عبدالله الحجازي الشرقاوي (ت. 1227هـ/1812م)[728]
37. طهارة القلوب والخضوع لعلّام الغيوب، تأليف ضياء الدين الديريني (ت.696هـ/1297م) [696]
38. علم الكمون والبروز، تأليف محمد بن علي ابن طولون (ت.953هـ/1546م) [712]
39. عنقاء مغرب في معرفة ختم الأولياء وشمس المغرب، تأليف محيي الدين ابن عربي (ت.638هـ/1240م) [740]
40. الفتح الرباني والفيض الرحماني، تأليف عبد القادر الجيلاني (ت.561هـ/1165م) [683]
41. الفتوحات المكيّة، تأليف محيي الدين ابن عربي (ت.638هـ/1240م) [651، 652، 653]
42. قمع النفوس ورقية المأيوس، تأليف تقي الدين الحصني (ت.829هـ/1425م) [702]
43. قوانين حكم الإشراق إلى كافة الصوفية بجميع الآفاق، تأليف أبي المواهب الشاذلي (ت.882هـ/1478م) [681]
44. القول الجلي في ذكر العلي، تأليف (؟) [704]
45. الكبريت الأحمر في بيان علوم الشيخ الأكبر، تأليف عبد الوهاب الشعراني (ت.973هـ/1565م) [672]
46. كتاب الوصايا، تأليف محيي الدين ابن عربي (ت.638هـ/1240م) [688]
47. كتاب في التصوف، تأليف (؟) [661]
48. كتاب مقامات الخواص، تأليف (؟) [657]
49. كشف الحجاب والرّان عن وجه أسئلة الجان، تأليف عبد الوهاب الشعراني (ت.973هـ/1565م) [663، 664]
50. الكشف والتبيين في غرور الخلق أجمعين، تأليف أبي حامد الغزالي (ت.505هـ/1111م) [646م، 647]
51. كنز العرش، تأليف (؟) [690]
52. لواقح الأنوار القدسية المنتقاة من الفتوحات المكية، تأليف عبد الوهاب الشعراني (ت.973هـ/1565م) [717]
53. مجموع رسائل في التصوّف، تأليف (؟) [685]
54. محاضرة الأوائل ومسامرة الأواخر، تأليف علاء الدين البوسنوي (ت.1007هـ/1598م) [719]
55. مختصر إحياء علوم الدين، تأليف شمس الدين محمد العجلوني البلالي (ت.820هـ/1417م) [654]
56. مشاهد الأسرار القدسيّة ومطالع الأنوار الإلهية، تأليف محيي الدين ابن عربي (ت.638هـ/1240م) [687]
57. مصطلحات القوم، تأليف (؟) [713]
58. المطلب التام السوي شرح حزب الإمام النووي، تأليف مصطفى البكري (ت.1162هـ/1749م) [730]
59. معاني أسماء الله الحسنى (بالفارسية)، تأليف (؟) [700]
60. مفاتيح الكنوز وحل الرموز = حل الرموز ومفاتيح الكنوز، تأليف ابن غانم المقدسي (ت.678هـ/1280م) [693]
61. مفتاح الفلاح ومصباح الأرواح في ذكر الله الكريم الفتّاح، تأليف ابن عطاء الله السكندري (ت.709هـ/1309م) [623]
62. المنجيات السبع [698م]
63. المنن الكبرى = لطائف المنن والأخلاق في وجوب التحدّث

بنعمة الله على الإطلاق، تأليف عبد الوهاب الشعراني (ت.973هـ/1565م) [656]

64. منهاج العابدين إلى جنّة ربّ العالمين، تأليف أبي حامد الغزالي (ت.505هـ/1111م) [677]

65. المنهج الحنيف في معنى اسمه تعالى اللطيف، تأليف أبي بكر الكّامي (ت.1051هـ/1641م) [691]

66. الموارد الإلهية، تأليف (؟) [710م]

67. موازين الرجال القاصرين، تأليف عبد الوهاب الشعراني (ت.973هـ/1565م) [662]

68. نور العين، تأليف (؟) [701]

69. وِرد السَّحَر، تأليف مصطفى البكري (ت.1162هـ/1749م) [727]

70. وِرد الشيخ عبد الغني النابلسي (ت.1143هـ/1731م) [723]

71. وسائل التحقيق ورسائل التوفيق، تأليف عبد الغني النابلسي (ت.1143هـ/1731م) [627]

72. اليواقيت والجواهر في بيان عقائد الأكابر، تأليف عبد الوهاب الشعراني (ت.973هـ/1565م) [634، 635]

كُتب لا يُعرف مضمونها

1. حاشية الجرجاني (= السيد الشريف علي بن محمد الجرجاني] ([ت.816هـ/1413م]) [642]

2. كتاب الكافي [644م]

3. كتاب النزهة الفكريّة[714]

كُتب ضمن مجاميع لا يُعرف مضمونها

تسع مؤلَّفات لا تُعرف عناوينها ولا مؤلّفوها: [607م، 630م، 633م.أ، 633م.ب، 646م، 673م.أ، 673م.ب، 673م.ج، 710م]

كُتُب فُهرست في غير محلّها

1. حاشيةً على شرح عضد الدين الإيجي لمختصر المنتهى الأصولي لابن الحاجب، تأليف سعد الدين التفتازاني (ت.793هـ/1390م) [637]

2. حلية أهل الفضل والكمال باتصال الأسانيد بكمّل الرجال، تأليف عماد الدين العجلوني (ت.1162هـ/1749م) [679]

3. خلاصة بحر الحقائق = مختصر بحر الحقائق والمعاني في تفسير السبع المثاني، تأليف شمس الدين محمد الساوجي (كان حيا 732هـ/1332م) [624]

4. درة الغوّاص في أوهام الخواص، تأليف القاسم بن علي الحريري (ت.516هـ/1122م) [715]

5. رياض الصالحين من كلام سيد المرسلين، تأليف محيي الدين النووي (ت.676هـ/1277م) [665]

6. زبدة الوصول إلى عمدة الأصول، تأليف يوسف بن حسين الكرماستي (ت.906هـ/1500م) [671]

7. سلوان المطاع في عدوان الأتباع، تأليف ابن ظفر الصقلي (ت.565هـ/1169م) [654م]

CHAPTER 18

Textbooks of Grammar, Morphology and Lexicography: Cosmopolitan Arabic Philology in Early Nineteenth-century Acre

Christopher Bahl

Al-Jazzār's endowed library offered a broad range of definitive textbooks in Arabic philology for study purposes, but it had also accumulated more specialist commentary traditions and, thus, can be considered a well-stocked scholarly collection.[1] The following aims to show the diachronic breadth and diversity of commentarial traditions as a crucial marker of the Arabic philological books in the Jazzār library. However, the study of the intellectual history of the Arabic philological tradition for the eighteenth and nineteenth centuries is, in many aspects, not developed enough to hypothesise here in any serious way about possible relationships between different parts of the corpus and how various commentarial traditions might relate to one another. It is also beyond the scope of this chapter to do so.

Grouping syntax, morphology and lexicography in one section makes sense, since those three fields of inquiry are often joined together as 'auxiliary disciplines'.[2] They offer guidance in the philological exegesis of Islamic transmitted texts and knowledge, such as *ḥadīth* and Qur'an. At the same time, each field also constitutes a scholarly discipline in its own right. The composer of the inventory listed the works of the three disciplines separately. Grammar, morphology and lexicography each boasted a range of standard textbooks or definitive texts by the early nineteenth century that have become central in the continued transmission of the respective discipline. Moreover, they include several layers of commentarial elaborations which refer back to those standard works. I will use the term 'Arabic philology' when referring to all three disciplines in the following. A total of 189 codicological units are recorded in the list of grammar books, twenty-three for morphology and twenty-six for lexicography. Fourteen additional codicological units, listed in other sections of the inventory, can also be assigned to those three fields.

The inventory's sections on *ʿilm al-naḥw, ʿilm al-ṣarf and ʿilm al-lugha* in the Jazzār library contained multiple copies of the same textbooks and often from different branches of commentarial elaboration. They establish its philological section as a participant in the cosmopolitan Arabic philological tradition prevalent across many learned centres of the early modern period, from Northern Africa to the Arab lands and further east to South Asia. The *Ajurrūmīya*, for example, named after its author Muḥammad b. Ajurrūm and its commentaries (#909–922 and #926–929), the *Mughnī al-Labīb* (#741–746) by Ibn Hishām, *al-Kāfiya* by Ibn al-Ḥājib (#811–831) and its commentaries by Mullā Jāmī (#878–885 and #887) and his disciples, for those regions of the world, respectively, constitute widely acknowledged and acclaimed books of Arabic grammatical investigation as early as the thirteenth century (CE). And it seems that they remained central to the discipline up until the

1 I thank the participants at the workshop held in Hamburg in February 2023 for their comments, and particularly Asad Ahmed for his constructive critique and feedback. I am also grateful to Konrad Hirschler and Said Aljoumani for their comments, suggestions, and corrections to this chapter. Said Aljoumani was able to identify several titles that I could not, and I am thankful for his input. Mistakes and errors remain mine alone.

2 The auxiliary disciplines also usually included the field *ʿilm al-balāgha* and *ʿilm al-maʿānī wa-al-bayān*. See, for example, Ghorbal, "Ideas and Movements in Islamic History".

DOI:10.1163/9789004720527_020

early nineteenth century in the Eastern Mediterranean.

The library also preserved and made available to readers a selection of treatises and commentaries from different periods. Thus, we find what can only be Sībawayhi's (d. 180/796) work *al-Kitāb* (See #905–909), which is one of the earliest works to systematise Arabic grammar, in several versions, al-Fārisī's (d. 319/987) *ʿAwāmil* (#814 and #872), the works *al-Kāfiya* and *al-Shāfiya* on syntax and morphology, respectively, by Ibn al-Ḥājib (d. 646/1249), Ibn ʿAqīl's (d. 769/1367) commentary on the *Alfiya*, and al-Aynī's (d. 855/1451) *Shawāhid* but also al-Suyūṭī's (d. 911/1505) commentary on Ibn Mālik's *al-Alfiyya* as well as Birgivī Mehmet Efendi's (d. 980/1573) commentary on the *ʿAwāmil*.

The works listed in the inventory can be split up into roughly two types, a profile which, for now, seems to be further underscored by the cataloguing practices in the library inventory. On the one hand, there are a couple of 'repeat-titles', that is, treatises and commentaries which were preserved in larger numbers, such as the *Ajurrūmiyya*, the *Mughni al-labīb*, the *Kāfiya* and the *Alfiyya*, as well as their commentarial genealogies. This underlines the manuscripts' textbook character and suggests their availability for reading circles and possible studies *in situ*. On the other hand, there is a broad range of singular copies of other commentaries, which offer additional commentarial elaborations on the previous treatises or represent less widespread and very specific commentarial responses to Arabic philological learning.

Regarding the first category, several Arabic philological texts come in multiple versions. Those groups of texts—treatises, commentaries and summaries—qualify as teaching materials. Tahera Qutbuddin has pointed to a similar 'pedagogical function' in the 'clustering of Arabic philology and literature titles' as part of ʿAtūfī's inventory of Sultan Bāyezīd II's palace library in early sixteenth-century Istanbul.[3] From Bāyezīd II's corpus of philological works, she deduced 'a readership interested in learning language-based skills from preferred commentaries on specific texts by a handful of favourite authors'.[4] Similarly, some clusters of Arabic philological texts in the Jazzār library probably served similar functions. Qutbuddin's 'language-based skills' refer to a wide range and high level of linguistic expertise. Those philological textbooks presume a thorough knowledge of Arabic, which could be further refined through the exegesis of commentaries that dissected foundational treatises.

The Jazzār corpus holds a cosmopolitan collection of Arabic philology. Here, the term 'cosmopolitan' refers to 'placeless' texts as set out by Brinkley Messick and Sheldon Pollock in their separate studies of transregional cultural formations and their workings.[5] An essential characteristic of 'placeless' texts is that they become accepted beyond their immediate social and intellectual circles of composition and are transmitted widely among reading communities. They seem to grasp the intellectual engagement with a topic or field in an appealing manner and circulated among scholarly networks in a way conducive to their transgenerational transmission. Such texts are the *Alfiyya* (five entries: #751–754 and #756) a grammatical treatise by Ibn Mālik (672/1274); the *Ajurrūmiyya* (two entries), a succinct grammatical textbook by Ibn Ajjurrūm (d. 723/1323); the *Kāfiya* (five entries), a treatise on Arabic syntax by Ibn al-Ḥājib (646/1249); the *Shāfiya* (one entry), a treatise on Arabic morphology by the same author; and the *Qāmūs* (seven entries), a lexicographical encyclopaedia by al-Fīrūzābādī (817/1415).

Those 'cosmopolitan' philological texts had circulated widely by the beginning of the nineteenth century. Manuscript copies can be found across major and minor collections around the globe. Manuscript collections in the South Asian subcontinent, for example, preserve a huge amount of

3 Qutbuddin, "Books on Arabic Philology and Literature", 607.

4 Ibid.

5 Messick, *Sharia Scripts*, 20–30; Pollock, *The Language of the Gods*, 10–29.

manuscript versions of the *Alfiyya*, the *Kāfiya*, the *Shāfiya* and the *Qāmūs*.[6] Similarly, crucial collections in Cairo and Istanbul also hold those works.[7] Yet, what allowed those 'cosmopolitan' texts to spread even further were the commentaries and supra-commentaries that emerged over the following centuries on the syntactical and morphological treatises. Al-Jazzār's corpus mirrors this canonisation through commentarial elaboration. The endowment, for example, held five versions of *Alfiyya* and fourteen versions of *Sharḥ al-Alfiyya* (partly by different authors). Nineteen commentaries or supra-commentaries (#816–828, #829–831, #879 and #880–883), again by various authors, are linked to the five versions of the *Kāfiya*. Readers of the two copies of the *Ajurrūmiyya* could find fifteen copies of commentaries by different authors, all titled *Sharḥ al-Ajurrūmiyya* (#911–923). As far as the lexicographical works are concerned, there is no similar commentarial tradition, apart from one commentary on the *Qāmūs* (#1403 and #1404) and a selective summary of the *Ṣiḥāḥ* (#1407). There are no further elaborations for *al-Sāmī fī al-asāmī* (#1411 and #1412).

Such groups of commentaries, summaries and further elaborations on a treatise refer to 'definitive texts' in a field of philological/scholarly enquiry.[8] The commentarial genealogy continues to refer back to the initial treatise. Later commentaries might have been read and studied much more intensively than the earlier treatises, but this study also always included the engagement with the initial treatise that prompted the later commentaries. Those commentaries usually contained the text of the initial treatise as part of the hypertextual elaboration and often marked in a separate colour of ink. The *Kāfiya* is the definitive text with the most diverse commentarial tradition in al-Jazzār's library.

Ibn Hishām's *Mughnī al-labīb* (#741–746) was another one of those 'definitive texts' that the library held in several copies, even more than other grammar treatises. A fourteenth-century text, the *Mughnī al-labīb*, constituted an elaborate grammar treatise which scholars held in high esteem over the following decades and even centuries. Gully argued 'that Ibn Hishām was possibly reviving a long-standing tradition of hermeneutics, but through the eyes of a grammarian'.[9] Ibn Hishām's two main aims were 'to correct errors of interpretation' and 'instruct students of Arabic on how to reach the most acceptable interpretation of the language based on the application of sound grammatical and semantic principles' and these were elaborated through the use of Qur'anic and poetic references.[10]

The inventory of al-Jazzār's library holds a corpus of Arabic philological texts which, in some respects, differed from the collections held by many scholarly institutions in the Ottoman capital Istanbul. Ibn Hishām's treatise elicited several commentaries over the centuries. One of them was a lexicographical elaboration and explanation by the Egyptian scholar Muḥammad al-Damāmīnī (d. 827/1424), who composed it during his travels in search for courtly patronage in the South Asian subcontinent in the second half of his life.[11] He had initially composed an elaborate scholarly commentary in Egypt which dealt with different canonical authors famous in the Eastern Mediterranean. The commentary that he wrote in South Asia constituted a lexicographical explanation adapted to the learned environment of the scholarly audiences that he encountered while *en route* in Gujarat and the Deccan. This commentary, entitled *Tuḥfat al-gharīb*, travelled widely and by the seventeenth century, could be found in many mosques and *madrasas* of Ottoman Istanbul. I discovered at least twenty-six copies of this commentary in the collections of the Süleymaniye Library, Istanbul.[12] Presumably, the *Tuḥfa* represented a

6 Bahl, *Histories of Circulation*, Introduction and Appendix.
7 Ibid.; Bahl, "Arabic Grammar Books".
8 See Bahl, *Histories of Circulation*, chapter 5.

9 Gully, *Grammar and Semantics*, 4.
10 Ibid., 14–15.
11 See Bahl, "Arabic Grammar Books", 68–70.
12 Bahl, *Histories of circulation*, 169f.

very accessible 'placeless' grammar commentary that offered a clear lexicographical pathway for the study of Ibn Hishām's *Mughnī al-labīb*.[13] However, the *Tuḥfa* cannot be found in the inventory of the Jāzzār library. This absence is a first indication of a difference in the cosmopolitan Arabic philological cultures that both Istanbul and Acre harboured; Istanbul seemed to have become linked up with different scholarly networks over the early modern period, or, at least, different from the ones that Acre could access.

What else is surprisingly missing and which other gaps in this philological corpus can be explained based on comparisons with other library collections from this period in the Ottoman Empire and beyond? The Mughal courtier 'Abd al-Ḥakīm b. Shams al-Dīn al-Siyālkūtī's (d. 1067/1657) gloss on 'Abd al-Ghafūr al-Lārī's commentary of al-Jāmī's *al-Fawā'id al-ḍiyā'iyya* (Mullā Jāmī's commentary on Ibn al-Ḥājib's *al-Kāfiya*), for example, circulated widely in Ottoman Istanbul by the eighteenth century.[14] However, his commentary cannot be identified in the inventory of al-Jazzār's library. Thus, again, the cosmopolitan culture of the Ottoman capital had a profile different from the Ottoman provinces in the Eastern Mediterranean. But perhaps it is worth considering a variety of cosmopolitan cultures of Arabic learning, which partly overlapped but also developed distinguishing features.

A closer look at the eighteenth-century Ottoman library of the Grand Vizier Rāghip Pasha (d. 1763) further underscores that the Jazzār library was intended to serve as a site for teaching and learning. The catalogue of Raghip Pasha's library lists 95 codicological units for the section on grammar and morphology and 51 for the section on lexicography, compared with 212 for grammar and lexicography (189 and 23, respectively) and twenty-six codicological units in lexicography in al-Jazzār's inventory.[15] While Raghip Pasha's library also housed the standard textbooks of grammar, morphology and lexicography, for example, the *Mughnī al-labīb*, the *Sharḥ al-Shāfiya* and the *Qāmūs al-muḥiṭ*, the number of codicological units are much lower. Rāghip Pasha's library usually holds only one or two copies of such standard works, while al-Jazzār's library provided for six and more copies of the same standard works. A further comparison of the titles demonstrates many similarities. However, the Jazzār library can boast a greater variety of specialised commentaries and treatises (more on those below).

The second category are those singular copies of other commentaries, which offer additional commentarial elaborations on the previous treatises or represent less widespread and very specific commentarial responses to Arabic philological learning. The Jazzār library housed a broad range of singular copies of commentaries, which offer additional commentarial elaborations on the previous treatises or represent rarer and very specific commentarial responses to Arabic philological learning. While such titles do not often come in multiple versions, they suggest that collectors for the library, be they librarians or scholarly groups working *in situ*, tried to build up an expansive range of titles that could serve a scholarly community. The library, for example, holds a copy of Ibn Hishām's *al-Alghāz al-naḥwiyya* (#844), which deals with selected grammatical difficulties and which Ibn Hishām had dedicated to the Mamlūk Sultan al-Malik al-Kāmil (d. 757/1356).[16] While it is not possible at this stage to identify the authors of the *Sharḥ natīja Ibn al-Ḥājib* (#837) and *I'rāb dībāja al-Miṣbāḥ* (#845), those titles seem to be referring to commentaries that served similar specific scholarly purposes.

Judging from the recording practices of the inventory's compiler, they probably encountered a

13 Ibid., 170–171.

14 This statement is based on a search for the commentaries in the online catalogue of the Süleymaniye collections.

15 MS Rāghip Pasha Defter, Ragıp Pasa 4111, Süleymaniye Library, Istanbul, fol. 20^{v}.–24^{r}.

16 Fleisch, "Ibn Hishām", Encyclopedia of Islam, Second Edition. Leiden: Brill Online.

relatively well-structured book collection. Texts of the same title are generally placed next to each other. Commentaries on a particular treatise are often placed next to that treatise, therefore, books were grouped according to intertextual relationships within this section. However, neither an alphabetical nor a chronological nor a geographical order are discernible. Additionally, different texts by the same author are not grouped together. Compared with Chapter 13 by Walid Saleh and Chapter 22 by Dana Sajdi in this volume, who both detected a meaningful ordering of books in their sections on Qur'anic commentary and history, respectively, I am unable to discern an overarching narrative for the arrangement of the books. Commentaries seem to be loosely grouped close to their initial treatise. However, some titles were clearly out of order, for whatever reason. The text *al-Alghāz al-naḥwiyya*, for example, appears as #844 and then again as #926. At the same time, commentarial traditions are not always placed in proximity to each other. Several versions of glosses on *Kāfiya* appear in #880–882, however, the treatise *al-Kāfiya* and its initial commentaries are listed much earlier in #811–831. In cases where no additional authorial identifiers are given and no manuscript has been identified, it is impossible to clearly state to which commentary the listed item is referring. This begs the question: Why was the title of a work more important in the inventory than identifying its author? The only possible rational explanation at this point would be that, according to the local and common knowledge of the inventory's compiler, some texts, no matter how commonplace their titles appeared to be, would have been clearly identified by a scholarly audience.

The inventory's compiler used authorial identifiers in cases where different authors had used the same formalised title. This was a practice common to the disciplines of grammar and morphology. The composer of the inventory added a shorthand of the author's name to the title of the work. For example, among the works of morphology, the title *Jārabardī* (#1120) refers to the commentary on Ibn al-Ḥājib's *Shāfiya* by Aḥmad b. al-Ḥusayn al-Jārabardī (d. 746/1346). Ibn Ajurrūm's *al-Ajurrūmiyya* (#926–928), a title which also remained in titles of later commentaries, is very famous in this context.

There is a diverse and diachronic range of commentaries and elaborations on a treatise in several cases. It suggests collecting practices which aimed at providing a relatively exhaustive corpus of commentaries on a specific treatise, even if those different commentarial branches did not necessarily end up sitting next to each other on the shelves. The commentarial branches of the *Kāfiya* are the most elaborate in this case. Apart from the initial treatise *al-Kāfiya* by Ibn al-Ḥājib, the inventory lists several versions of a commentary, *Sharḥ al-Kāfiya*, anonymously, thus, making it impossible at this stage to identify its author. The Jazzār library also held Mullā Jāmī's famous commentary, *al-Fawā'id al-Ḍiyā'iyya*, as well as later supra-commentaries and the *ḥawāshī* (sg. *ḥāshiya*), which again are not clearly identifiable.

There is a significant overlap of al-Jazzār's Arabic philological corpus with that of Bāyezīd's palace library.[17] The major canonical treatises and commentaries, such as Ibn al-Ḥājib's *al-Kāfiya* and *al-Shāfiya*, can be found in both library inventories, as well as al-Muṭarrizī's *al-Miṣbāḥ*, al-Fārisī's *al-'Awāmil* and Ibn Mālik's *al-Alfiyya*. At the same time, both libraries also housed a similar collection of lexicographical works, including the *Tāj al-lugha* and the *Qāmūs al-muḥīṭ*. The fact that almost three hundred years had elapsed between the establishment of the two libraries suggests that al-Jazzār's selection of philological works, in a very general way, is based on a similarly foundational understanding of canonical texts: mainly those commentary traditions from the thirteenth to the fifteenth centuries.

There are crucial similarities in the number of commentaries available in both libraries. The numbers for al-Jazzār's and Bāyezīd's libraries are respectively: Ibn al-Ḥājib's *al-Kāfiya* (5/10) and

17 For this comparison see Qutbuddin, "Books on Arabic Philology and Literature", 627–634.

al-Shāfiya (1/4), al-Muṭarrizī *al-Miṣbāḥ* (3/2) and al-Fārisī's *al-ʿAwāmil* (3/4). The point is not that both libraries had identical numbers regarding the manuscript versions available, but that both libraries preserved multiple versions of the definitive and foundational textual traditions in Arabic philology. It emphasises the perception of the Jazzār library as a site for scholarly inquiry and study, similar to the palace library. At the same time, the difference between the Jazzār library collection and the Süleymaniye collections in Istanbul, as well as the similarity between the former and Ottoman palatial collections, could also hint at diverging worlds of courtly and scholarly libraries.

The project team have managed to identify several manuscripts from the Arabic philological sections. So far, colleagues have identified the manuscript copy of #750, a commentary on Ibn Mālik's *Tashīl al-fawāʾid wa-takmīl al-maqāṣid* entitled *al-Tadhyīl wa-takmīl* by Abū Ḥayyān al-Andalūsī. Another multivolume manuscript of grammar survives in the Dār al-kutub collections in Cairo, and this again contains Ibn Mālik's *Tashīl al-fawāʾid* (MS Dār al-kutub 6016h), with a provenance history that includes the city of Beirut. Moreover, they have located the copy of the *Sharḥ al-Alfiyya* copied in 873/1469 by a certain Muḥammad b. Yūsuf b. Muḥammad b. Ḥasan al-ʿImadī, held currently in the Ministry of Awqāf in Cairo (corresponding to #759 or one of the following entries). There are also manuscript copies linked to #902, glosses on the *Alfiyya* by al-ʿUthmānī (MS 64, al-Jazzār Mosque Library, Acre), and #777, a commentary on the *Lubāb fī ʿilm al-iʿrāb* by al-Sīrāfī (Ms. AP Ar. 410, NLI, Jerusalem). Since we do not have a significant sample yet (and might never have it), we can only use the diverse profile of the few surviving manuscripts to indicate the Jazzār library as a site of recycled, earlier and often older manuscript versions, reaching as far back as the fifteenth century (see *Sharḥ al-Alfiyya* copied in 873/1469).

Given the small number of manuscript copies identified from the Jazzār library, it is impossible at this stage to differentiate between collecting practices specific to singular copies, on the one hand, and to titles which are repeated, on the other. Moreover, I could not identify specific reading, note-taking or collating practices which could be specific to the Jazzār library or Acre at this period. Overall, it is impossible at this stage to generalise particular features of Arabic philological manuscripts based on the manuscript copies identified.

Bibliography

Bahl, Christopher. "Histories of Circulation—Sharing Arabic Manuscripts across the Western Indian Ocean, 1400–1700." Unpublished PhD Dissertation, SOAS, University of London, 2018.

Bahl, Christopher. "Arabic Grammar Books in Ottoman Istanbul—The South Asian Connection." In *A Handbook and Reader of Ottoman Arabic*, edited by Esther-Miriam Wagner, 65–86. Cambridge, UK, 2021.

Fleisch, H. "Ibn Hishām." *Encyclopaedia of Islam, Second Edition*, edited by: P. Bearman, Th. Bianquis, C.E. Bosworth, E. van Donzel and W.P. Heinrichs. Consulted online on 20 February 2023 http://dx.doi.org.ezphost.dur.ac.uk/10.1163/1573-3912_islam_COM_0326

Ghorbal, S. "Ideas and Movements in Islamic History." In *Islam—The Straight Path: Islam Interpreted by Muslims*, edited by K.W. Morgan, 42–86. New York, 1958.

Gully, Adrian. *Grammar and Semantics in Medieval Arabic: A Study of Ibn-Hisham's 'Mughni L'labib'*. Richmond (Surrey), 1995.

Messick, Brinkley. *Shariʿa Scripts: A Historical Anthropology*. New York, 2018.

Pollock, Sheldon. *The Language of the Gods in the World of Men Sanskrit, Culture, and Power in Premodern India*. Berkeley, 2006.

Qutbuddin, Tahera. "Books on Arabic Philology and Literature. A Teaching Collection Focused on Religious Learning and the State Chancery." Magyar Tudományos Akadémia. Könyvtár és Információs Központ. Keleti Gyűjtemény. In *Treasures of Knowledge: An Inventory of the Ottoman Palace Library (1502/3–1503/4)*, edited by Gülru Necipoğlu, Cemal

Kafadar and Cornell H. Fleischer, 607–634. Leiden/Boston, 2019.

MS Raghip Pasha Defter, Ragip Pasa 4111, Süleymaniye Library, Istanbul.

The Grammar (naḥw) Books

[741] ***Mughnī al-labīb***, AUTHOR: Jamāl al-Dīn Abū Muḥammad ʿAbd Allāh b. Yūsuf, known as Ibn Hishām al-Naḥwī (d. 761/1360). Undoubtedly the famous grammar commentary by Ibn Hishām entitled *Mughnī al-labīb ʿan kutub al-aʿārīb*. EDITION: not identified—several editions of subsequent commentaries and summaries. See, for example, Sāmūlī, Muḥammad Ibn ʿAbd Al-Majīd. *Dīwān al-arīb mukhtaṣar mughnī al-labīb*, edited by ʿAbd Allāh Zakariyā Muḥammad. Madīnat Naṣr, al-Qāhirah: Dār al-Yusr, 2017.

[742] ***Mughnī al-labīb***, see #741.

[743] ***Mughnī al-labīb***, see #741.

[744] ***Mughnī al-labīb***, see #741.

[745] ***Mughnī al-labīb***, see #741.

[746] ***Mughnī al-labīb***, see #741.

[747] ***al-Taṣrīḥ sharḥ al-tawḍīḥ***, AUTHOR: Khālid b. ʿAbd Allāh al-Azharī (Brockelmann, II, 410). This is probably the commentary *Sharḥ al-Taṣrīḥ* on the commentary of Ibn Hishām *al-tawḍīḥ*, on the famous *al-Alfiyya* of Ibn Mālik. Identified through the handlist of the TSGOML, Hyderabad, India. EDITION: Khālid b. ʿAbdallāh al-Azharī, *Sharḥ al-Taṣrīḥ ʿalā al-tawḍīḥ* al-Alfiyya Ibn Mālik, Cairo: Būlāq, 1877.

[748] ***al-Taṣrīḥ sharḥ al-tawḍīḥ***, see #747.

[749] ***al-Taṣrīḥ sharḥ al-tawḍīḥ***, see #749.

[750] ***al-Tashīl li-Abī Ḥayyān***. Corrected by editor: *Al-Tadhyīl wa-takmīl fī sharḥ al-tashīl*. Probably the commentary of al-ʿAllāma Athīr al-Dīn Abū Ḥayyān Muḥammad b. Yūsuf al-Andalūsī (d. 745/1344) on the *Tashīl al-fawāʾid wa-takmīl al-maqāṣid* of Ibn Mālik al-Ṭāʾī (d. 672/1274). Abū Ḥayyān also wrote an abridgement of his commentary, entitled *al-Takhyīl*. See HK, I, 406. AUTHOR: al-ʿAllāma Athīr al-Dīn Abū Ḥayyān Muḥammad b. Yūsuf al-Andalūsī. MANUSCRIPT: Volume 5: Dublin, Chester Beatty Library, Ar. 3342. Volumes 1, 3, 4, and 7 are currently housed in the library of Dār al-Kutub in Cairo, catalogued under the number (6016 AH).

[751] ***Matn al-Alfiyya***. Without doubt the famous grammar treatise, fully entitled *al-Khulāṣa al-Alfiyya*. AUTHOR: Abū ʿAbd Allāh Jamāl al-Dīn Muḥammad b. ʿAbd Allāh b. Mālik al-Ṭāʾī al-Jayyān, commonly known as Ibn Mālik (d. 672/1274). EDITION: Ibn Malik, Muḥammad ibn ʿAbd Allāh and A.I. Baron Silvestre de Sacy. *Alfiyya: Ou, La Quintessence De La Grammaire Arabe*. Paris: Oriental Translation Fund of Great Britain and Ireland, 1833.

[752] ***Matn al-Alfiyya***, see #751.

[753] ***Matn al-Alfiyya***, see #751. According to the inventory, this seems to be a very old (*ʿatīq*) manuscript version of the *Alfiyya*.

[754] ***Matn al-Alfiyya***, see #751.

[755] ***Sharḥ al-Alfiyya li-Ibn ʿAqīl***. Commentary on Ibn Mālik's *Alfīya*. AUTHOR: ʿAbd Allāh b. ʿAbd al-Raḥmān b. ʿAbd Allāh Bahāʾ al-Dīn al-Hāshimī, known as Ibn ʿAqīl (d. 769/1367), EDITION: Ibn ʿAqīl, ʿAbd Allāh b. ʿAbd al-Rahmān and Muḥammad Muḥyī al-Dīn ʿAbd al-Ḥamīd. *Sharḥ Ibn ʿAqīl*. Beirut: Iḥyāʾ al-Turāth al-ʿArabī, 1990.

[756] ***al-Khulāṣa al-Alfiyya***. This is the full title of Ibn Mālik's grammar treatise commonly called *Alfiyya*. See #751.

[757] ***Sharḥ Khulāṣa al-Alfiyya lil-Kurdī***. Possibly a commentary by AUTHOR: Taqī al-Dīn Abū ʿAmr ʿUthmān b. ʿAbd al-Raḥmān al-Kurdī al-Shahrazūrī, known as Ibn al-Ṣalāḥ.

[758] ***Sharḥ al-Alfiyya***. Presumably the same as previous. See #757.

[759] ***Sharḥ al-Alfiyya***, AUTHOR: ʿAbd al-Raḥmān al-Makkūdī (d. 808/1405), EDITION: Al-Khattāb. *A Critical Study and Edition of Sharḥ al-Makkūdī al-Alfiyyat Ibn Mālik by Abū Zaid al-Makkūdī* (d 807 AH–1405 CE), edited by Al-Maktoum Institute, Dundee Scotland (March 2007). MANUSCRIPT: Ms. 4490, Ministry of Islamic Endowments Library, Cairo. It is not possible to determine whether the manuscript corresponds to this entry or one of the following entries with the same title, but without author.

[760] ***Sharḥ al-Alfīyya***, see #759.

[761] ***Sharḥ al-Alfiyya li-Ibn al-Niẓām*** Author: Ibn Mālik (d. 672/1274). See #751. MANUSCRIPT: Ms. 51, al-Jazzār Mosque Library, Acre.

[762] ***Sharḥ al-Alfiyya***, see #759.

[763] ***Sharḥ al-Alfiyya***, see #759.

[764] ***Sharḥ al-Alfiyya***, see #759.

[765] ***Sharḥ al-Alfiyya***, see #759.

[766] ***Sharḥ al-Alfiyya***, see #759.

[767] ***Sharḥ al-Alfiyya***, see #759.

[768] ***Sharḥ al-Alfiyya***, see #759.

[769] ***Sharḥ al-Alfiyya lil-Suyūṭī.*** Commentary on Ibn Mālik's *Alfiyya* by AUTHOR: Jalāl al-Dīn al-Suyūṭī (d. 911/1505).

[770] ***Sharḥ al-Alfiyya***, see #759.

[771] ***Sharḥ al-Alfiyya***, see #759.

[772] ***Ḥall mushkilāt al-Alfiyya.*** Unidentified.

[773] ***I'rāb al-Alfiyya lil-Shaykh Khālid.*** Possibly the *Tamrīn al-ṭullāb fī ṣinā'at al-i'rāb*, AUTHOR: Khālid b. 'Abdallāh al-Azharī (d. 905/1499), EDITION: Al-Azharī, *Tamrīn al-ṭullāb fī ṣinā'at al-i'rāb*, Edited by Nasīm Bal'īd al-Jazā'irī. Dār taḥqīq al-Kitāb.

[774] ***I'rāb al-Alfiyya***, see #773.

[775] ***Sharḥ al-lubāb***, AUTHOR: possibly by Muḥammad al-Quṭb al-Fālī (d. 721/1321), whose commentary is the most 'recent,' but there are several other texts with the same title. The other possibility is Muḥammad b. Mas'ūd al-Sīrāfī, who has been identified as the author of the manuscript copy for #777.

[776] ***Sharḥ al-lubāb***, see #775.

[777] ***Sharḥ al-lubāb***, see #775. MANUSCRIPT: Ms. AP Ar. 410, NLI, Jerusalem.

[778] ***Lubb al-lubāb fī 'ilm al-i'rāb***, AUTHOR: 'Abd Allāh b. 'Umar al-Bayḍāwī (685/1286).

[779] ***Sharḥ al-Khulāṣa.*** Possibly see #757.

[780] ***Khulāṣa al-I'rāb***, AUTHOR: Sulaymān b. Dā'ūd b. Ḥaydar al-Ḥillī (d. 1211/1796). See Kaḥḥāla, *Mu'jam al-Mu'allifīn*, vol. 1, 789.

[781] ***Sharḥ al-shawāhid.*** Several commentaries were written on the *shawāhid* (for the following, see Gilliot, *Shawāhid*, EI²). The most frequent commentaries were written on Ibn Mālik's *Alfiyya* and Ibn al-Ḥājib's *al-Kāfiya* and *al-Shāfiya*. It is, thus, impossible to precisely identify the various titles of *Sharḥ al-shawāhid* in this inventory.

[782] ***Sharḥ al-shawāhid***, see #781.

[783] ***al-Shawāhid lil-'Aynī.*** *al-Maqāṣid al-naḥwiyya fī sharḥ shawāhid shurūḥ al-Alfiyya*, AUTHOR: Abū Muḥammad Maḥmūd b. Aḥmad al-'Aynī (d. 855/1451), EDITION: in the margins of al-Baghdādī, *Khizānat al-Adab*, Cairo: Būlāq 1882.

[784] ***Sharḥ al-shawāhid***, see #781.

[785] ***Sharḥ al-shawāhid lil-'Aynī***, AUTHOR: Badr al-Dīn Maḥmūd b. Aḥmad b. Mūsā al-'Aynī (d. 855/1451), EDITION: edited by Muḥammad Fākhar, Aḥmad Muḥammad Tawfīq al-Sūdānī and 'Abd al-'Azīz Muḥammad Fākhar. Cairo: Dar al-salām, 2010.

[786] ***Sharḥ al-shawāhid***, see #785.

[787] ***Shawāhid al-Qaṭr***, AUTHOR: Ṣādiq b. 'Alī al-A'rajī (d. 855/1415).

[788] ***Sharḥ al-lubāb***, AUTHOR: Either Sayyid 'Abd Allāh, al-Zazānī (d. 1093), al-Fālī (see #775) or an anonymous version.

[789] ***al-Durra al-muḍī' sharḥ al-Alfiyya.*** Possibly the *Sharḥ al-khulāṣat al-Alfiyya* or *al-Durra al-muḍīya fī sharḥ al-Alfiyya*, AUTHOR: Ibn Mālik (d. 686/1287).

[790] ***Sharḥ al-qawā'id.*** Possibly the *Sharḥ qawā'id al-I'rāb li-Ibn Hishām*, AUTHOR: Muḥyī al-Dīn al-Kafayjī (d. 879/1474), EDITION: Dār al-Salām.

[791] ***al-I'rāb 'an qawā'id al-i'rāb***, AUTHOR: Ibn Hishām al-Anṣārī, EDITION: edited by 'Alī Fawda Nīl. Riyāḍ. Jāmi'at Riyāḍ. 1401/1981.

[792] ***Majmū' qawā'id al-i'rāb.*** Unidentified.

[793] ***al-Murshid sharḥ al-Irshād***, AUTHOR: Shams al-Dīn Muḥammad b. Muḥammad b. Maḥmūd al-Bukhārī (d. 869/1465). This Commentary is blended with the text of *al-Irshād* of Sa'd al-Taftāzānī. EDITION: edited by Zāhir al-Makkī, Istanbul: Dār al-Majāl, 2023.

[794] ***al-Basīṭ wa-al-jāmi' al-muḥīṭ.*** Unidentified.

[795] ***Muwaṣṣil al-ṭullāb ilā qawā'id al-i'rāb***, AUTHOR: Khālid b. 'Abd Allāh al-Azharī (d. 905/1499), EDITION: Maktaba al-Adab, 2011.

[796] ***Muwaṣṣil al-ṭullāb ilā qawā'id al-i'rāb***, see #795.

[797] ***Sharḥ al-qawā'id.*** Possibly the same as previous.

[798] ***al-Shudhūr li-Ibn Hishām***, AUTHOR: Jamāl al-Dīn Abū Muḥammad Yūsuf al-Naḥwī, known as Ibn Hishām (d. 761/1360) EDITION: *Shudhūr al-dhahab wa-sharh shudhūr al-dhahab*. ʿAbd al-Mutaʿāl al-Ṣaʿīdī. Cairo, 1962.

[799] ***al-Shudhūr***, see #798.

[800] ***Sharḥ al-shudhūr***. Probably Ibn Hishām's commentary on his own *Shudhūr al-dhahab*. See #798.

[801] ***Sharḥ al-shudhūr***, see #800.

[802] ***Sharḥ qaṭr al-nadā***, AUTHOR: Ibn Hishām, who wrote the *Qaṭr al-nadā wa-ball al-ṣadā* and then its commentary.

[803] ***Sharḥ al-qaṭr lil-Fākihī***, AUTHOR: ʿAbd Allāh b. Aḥmad ʿAbd Allāh al-Fākihī (d. 972/1564). *Mujīb al-nidā ʿalā sharḥ qaṭr al-nadā*.

[804] ***Sharḥ al-qaṭr***, see #803.

[805] ***Sharḥ al-qaṭr***, see #803.

[806] ***Sharḥ al-qaṭr***, see #803.

[807] ***Sharḥ al-qaṭr***, see #803.

[808] ***Sharḥ al-qaṭr***, see #803.

[809] ***Sharḥ al-qaṭr li-Ibn Hishām***, see #802.

[810] ***Sharḥ al-qaṭr li-Ibn Hishām***, see #802.

[811] ***Matn al-Kāfiya wa-al-Shāfiya***. Ibn al-Ḥājib (d. 646/1249). Both are separate treatises on syntax and morphology, respectively.

[812] ***Kāfiya***, see #811.

[813] ***Matn al-Kāfiya***, see #811.

[814] ***Matn al-Kāfiya wa-ʿAwāmil***. For the *Kāfiya*, see #811. The *ʿAwāmil* is a grammar treatise with the full title *Mukhtaṣar ʿawāmil al-iʿrāb* by Abū ʿAlī al-Ḥasan b. ʿAlī al-Fārisī (d. 319/987) and has been shortened to *al-ʿAwāmil al-miʾa* by the biographer Ibn Khallikān. See *ʿAwāmil* in *EI*[2].

[815] ***Matn al-Kāfiya***, see #811.

[816] ***Sharḥ al-Kāfiya***. There are numerous commentaries on Ibn al-Ḥājib's *al-Kāfiya*, making it difficult to identify this version.

[817] ***Sharḥ al-Kāfiya***, see #816.

[818] ***Sharḥ al-Kāfiya***, see #816.

[819] ***Sharḥ al-Kāfiya***, see #816.

[820] ***Sharḥ al-Kāfiya***, see #816.

[821] ***Sharḥ al-Kāfiya***, see #816.

[822] ***Sharḥ al-Kāfiya***, see #816.

[823] ***Sharḥ al-Kāfiya***, see #816.

[824] ***Sharḥ al-Kāfiya li-Mullā Jāmī***. Mawlanā Nūr al-Dīn ʿAbd al-Raḥmān Jāmī (d. 898/1492). *Al-Fawāʾid al-Ḍiyāʾiyya*.

[825] ***Sharḥ al-Kāfiya***, presumably #824.

[826] ***Sharḥ al-Kāfiya***, see #824.

[827] ***Sharḥ al-Kāfiya***, see #824.

[828] ***Sharḥ al-Kāfiya***, see #824.

[829] ***Ḥall mushkilāt al-Kāfiya***, AUTHOR: Mawlanā Nūr al-Dīn ʿAbd al-Raḥmān Jāmī (d. 898/1492). Alternative title: *Al-Fawāʾid al-Ḍiyāʾiyya fī ḥall mushkilāt al-kāfiya*.

[830] ***Ḥall mushkilāt al-Kāfiya***, see #829.

[831] ***al-Fawāʿid al-wāfiya fī ḥall al-Kāfiya***, see #829.

[832] ***al-Miṣbāḥ fī al-naḥw***, AUTHOR: Nāṣir b. ʿAbd al-Sayyid al-Muṭarrizī (d. 609/1213).

[833] ***al-Miṣbāḥ fī al-naḥw***, see #832.

[834] ***al-Miṣbāḥ wa-al-ḍawʾ***, see #832, The *Ḍawʾ fī al-naḥw* is a commentary on al-Muṭarrizī's *al-Miṣbāḥ*.

[835] ***Sharḥ al-Miṣbāḥ***. Unidentified.

[836] ***Asrār al-ʿArabiyya***, AUTHOR: Ibn al-Anbārī, EDITION: Ibn al-Anbārī, *Asrār al-ʿarabiyya*, edited by C.F. Seybold, Leiden, 1886.

[837] ***Sharḥ natīja Ibn al-Ḥājib***. Probably a commentarial elaboration by the author of *al-Kāfiya*, Ibn al-Ḥājib.

[838] ***Fawāʾid Ḥasan al-Kirmānī***. Unidentified.

[839] ***al-Unmūdhaj***. Probably the *Sharḥ al-Unmūdhaj* linked to al-Zamakhsharī's *al-Mufaṣṣal*. See Qutbuddin, *Books on Arabic Philology and Literature*, 629.

[840] ***al-Fawāʾid al-ilahiyya***. Unidentified.

[841] ***Sharḥ al-Iẓhār al-musammā bi-natāʾij al-afkār***, AUTHOR: Aṭalī (d. after 1085/1674). Al-Ziriklī, *al-Aʿlām*, vol. 7, 232.

[842] ***Sharḥ al-Shamsiyya fī al-naḥw***. Unidentified.

[843] ***Sharḥ al-kalām***. Unidentified.

[844] ***Alghāz naḥwiyya***, AUTHOR: Presumably by Ibn Hishām (d. 761/1360).

[845] ***Iʿrāb dībāja al-Miṣbāḥ***. The authorship of the *Dībāja* is not clear, but it is a commentary on the introduction of al-Muṭarrizī's *Miṣbāḥ*.

[846] ***Sharḥ al-qaṭr lil-Ḥarīrī. Dalīl al-Huda Sharḥ mujīb al-nidā***, AUTHOR: Muḥammad b. ʿAlī al-Ḥarīrī al-Ḥarfūshī (d. 1059/1649).

[847] ***Tawjīh al-lumaʿ***, AUTHOR: Aḥmad b. al-Ḥusayn b. al-Khabbāz (d. 639/1241). MANUSCRIPT: Ms. 34, al-Jazzār Mosque Library, Acre.

[848] ***al-Muʿarrab/al-Muʿarrib fī al-naḥw***, AUTHOR: Niʿmat Allāh b. ʿAbd Allāh al-Ḥusaynī al-Jazāʾirī. MANUSCRIPT: Ms. 34, al-Jazzār Mosque Library, Acre. Additionally, a reproduction of this manuscript can be found in the British Library, where it is labelled with the number: EAP399/1/2, https://eap.bl.uk/archive-file/EAP399-1-2.

[849] ***Muṣannafāt Ibn Hishām***. Possibly a *majmūʿa* containing treatises by Ibn Hishām. See #741.

[850] ***al-Intiṣāf***. Possibly the *Taṣḥīf li-kitāb al-Inṣāf fī masāʾil al-khilāf*, AUTHOR: ʿAbd al-Raḥmān b. Muḥammad (d. 577/1181).

[851] ***al-Ṭawāliʿ***. Unidentified.

[852] ***Sharḥ kabīr mutawassiṭ***. Possibly *Kitāb al-Wāfiya fi sharḥ al-Kafiyya* known as *al-Mutawassiṭ* by AUTHOR: Rukn al-Dīn al-Ḥasan b. Muḥammad al-Astarābādhī (d. 714/1315).

[853] ***Sharḥ al-waraqāt wa-ghayruhu***. Possibly Abū ʿAlī Jalāl al-Dīn Muḥammad al-Maḥallī's (d. 864/1459) commentary on al-Juwaynī's *al-Waraqāt fī uṣūl al-Dīn*. See Pellat, "al-Maḥallī", *EI*².

[854] ***Qilāda al-jawhariyya***. Unidentified.

[855] ***Ṣanʿat al-iʿrāb***. Possibly the *Mufaṣṣal fī ṣinaʿat al-Iʿrāb*, AUTHOR: Muḥammad b. ʿUmar al-Zamakhsharī (d. 538/1144).

[856] ***al-Sirāj al-munīr*** *bi-sharḥ al-jāmiʿ al-ṣaghīr li-Ibn Hishām*, AUTHOR: Ismāʿīl b. Ibrāhīm al-Zubaydī (d. 932/1526).

[857] ***Tuḥfat al-Ikhwān***, AUTHOR: Muṣṭafā b. Ibrāhīm al-Ghalībulī (d. 1176/1762).

[858] *al-Sifr al-awwal min* ***iʿrāb shiʿr***. Possibly the *Kitāb Iʿrāb shiʿr al-ḥamāsa*. AUTHOR: possibly Abī al-Biqāʾ ʿAbd Allāh b. al-Ḥusayn al-ʿAkbarī (d. 616/1219).

[859] ***Iʿrāb al-Alfiyya***, see #773.

[860] ***Majmūʿat kutub fi ʿilm al-ʿArabiyya***. Unidentified.

[861] ***al-Iftitāḥ fī ʿilm al-naḥw***. Or *al-Iftitāḥ fī sharḥ al-miṣbāḥ li-Muṭarrizī*. AUTHOR: Ḥasan b. al-Aswad (d. 1025/1616).

[862] ***Kitāb al-Ḍawʾ***. Possibly the *Ḍawʾ fī al-naḥw*, a commentary on al-Muṭarrizī's *al-Miṣbāḥ*.

[863] ***Sharḥ al-wasīṭ***. Unidentified.

[864] ***Sharḥ al-Irshād***. Possibly a commentary on Shihāb al-Dīn Aḥmad b. Shams al-Dīn al-Hindī al-Dawlatābādī's (d. 848/1445) grammar commentary *al-Irshād fī al-naḥw*.

[865] ***Kitāb al-Tahdhīb***, AUTHOR: Abū Manṣūr al-Azharī, EDITION: *Kitāb al-Tahdhīb fī al-lugha*, Cairo, 1964.

[866] ***Sharḥ al-Muqaddima***. Possibly a commentary on *al-Muqaddima al-Azhariyya fī ʿilm al-ʿArabiyya* by the same author, Khālid al-Azharī (see #773) (ed. Būlāḳ 1252).

[867] ***Thimār al-qulūb fi al-muḍāf wa-al-mansūb***, AUTHOR: al-Thaʿālibī, ʿAbd al-Malik b. Muḥammad (d. 429/1038), EDITION: Cairo: Maṭbaʿat al-Zahir, 1908.

[868] ***Milḥat al-Iʿrāb***, AUTHOR: al-Qāsim b. ʿAlī al-Ḥarīrī (d. 516/1112).

[869] ***Muʿarrab al-Awāmil al-jadīda***, AUTHOR: Muṣṭafā b. Muḥammad al-Ḥaṣṣārī, known as Yāzījīzādeh (d. 1215/1800).

[870] ***Sharḥ al-Azhariyya lil-Shaykh Khālid***. Possibly *Farāʾid al-ʿuqūd al-ʿalawiyya fī ḥall alfāẓ sharḥ al-azhārīya*, AUTHOR: Nūr al-Dīn ʿAlī b. Ibrāhīm al-Ḥalabī (d. 1044/1635) or another commentary on the *Tamrīn al-ṭullāb fī ṣināʿat al-iʿrāb* by Khālid b. ʿAbdallāh al-Azharī (d. 905/1499). EDITION: Al-Azharī, *Tamrīn al-ṭullāb fī ṣināʿat al-iʿrāb*, edited by Nasīm Balʿīd al-Jazāʾirī. Dār taḥqīq al-Kitāb.

[871] ***Sharḥ al-Azhariyya***, see #870.

[872] *Mukhtaṣar* ***ʿawāmil*** *al-iʿrāb*, AUTHOR: Abū ʿAlī al-Ḥasan b. ʿAlī al-Fārisī (d. 319/987).

[873] ***al-ʿAwāmil al-jadīda***, AUTHOR: Birgivī Mehmet Efendi (d. 980/1573), EDITION: *Sharḥ ʿAwāmil jadīd al-Birgivī*, edited by Muṣṭafā b. Ibrāhīm. Constantinople, 1220/1805.

[874] ***Sharḥ al-awāmil***, AUTHOR: al-Barkāwī. Or *Lamḥ al-Masāʾil al-naḥwiyya fī sharḥ al-ʿAwāmil al-Barkawīya*, AUTHOR: Yaḥyā b. Bakhshī (d. 1000/1600).

[875] ***ʿAwāmil***. Possibly the same as #872.

[876] ***Ḥāshiya ʿalā sharḥ al-Alfiyya***. Unidentified.

[877] ***Ḥāshiya ʿalā al-Ashmūnī lil-Ḥafnāwī*** *al-juzʾ al-thānī*. A commentary on Ibn Mālik's *Al-*

fiya. AUTHOR: Muḥammad b. Sālim al-Ḥafnāwī (d. 1181/1767).

[878] ***Ḥāshiya ʿalā sharḥ Mullā Jāmī.*** This is a gloss on al-Jāmī's *al-Fawāʾid al-ḍiyāʾiyya*.

[879] ***Ḥāshiya fī ʿilm al-naḥw.*** Unidentified.

[880] ***Ḥāshiya ʿalā al-Kāfiya.*** Unidentified.

[881] ***Ḥāshiya ʿalā al-Kāfiya.*** Unidentified.

[882] ***Ḥāshiya ʿalā al-Kāfiya.*** Unidentified.

[883] ***Ḥāshiya ʿIṣām ʿalā Mullā Jāmī***, AUTHOR: ʿIṣām al-Dīn Ibrāhīm b. Muḥammad al-Isfarāʾinī (d. 943/1536).

[884] ***Ḥāshiya al-Shaykh ʿAbd al-Muʿṭī.*** Unidentified.

[885] ***Ḥāshiya al-Shinwānī ʿalā al-Qaṭr***, AUTHOR: Abū Bakr b. Ismāʿīl al-Shinwānī. An alternative title is *Hidāya mujīb al-nidā ilā sharḥ qaṭr al-nidā*.

[886] ***Ḥāshiya ʿalā sharḥ al-Maṭāliʿ.*** Unidentified.

[887] ***Ḥāshiya ʿIṣām ʿalā Mullā Jāmī***, see #883.

[888] ***Ḥāshiya al-Zurqānī***, AUTHOR: Aḥmad b. Muḥammad al-Zurqānī al-Mālikī (alive in 965/1558). Possibly the commentary entitled *Ḥāshiya ʿalā qawāʿid al-Iʿrāb li-Ibn Ḥishām*.

[889] ***Ḥāshiya fī al-Ishtiqāq.*** Unidentified.

[890] ***Kitāb fī ʿilm al-ʿarabīya.*** Unidentified.

[891] ***Kitāb naḥw li-Abī Ḥayyān wa-huwa-sharḥ al-Milḥa.*** Possibly related to #867.

[892] ***Kitāb fī ʿilm al-naḥw.*** Unidentified.

[893] ***Kitāb fī ʿilm al-naḥw wa-huwa-sharḥ al-shudhūr.*** Unidentified.

[894] ***Ḥāshiya ʿalā sharḥ al-khulāṣa.*** Possibly *al-Durar al-sunniya ʿalā sharḥ al-Alfiyya or Ḥāshiya ʿalā sharḥ al-Alfiyya*, AUTHOR: Zakariyā b. Muḥammad al-Anṣārī, known as Ibn al-Niẓām (d. 926/1521).

[895] ***Ḥāshiya fī ʿilm al-naḥw.*** Unidentified.

[896] ***Majmūʿ ḥawāshī li-Ibn ʿAbd al-Barr.***

[897] ***Majmūʿ fī ʿilm al-naḥw.*** Unidentified.

[898] ***Kitāb al-naḥw.*** Unidentified.

[899] ***Kitāb fī al-naḥw lil-Sayyid ʿAlī.***

[900] ***Kitāb fī al-naḥw.*** Unidentified.

[901] ***al-Juzʾ al-awwal min ḥāshiya al-ḥafnāwī ʿalā al-ashmūnī.*** Related to #877.

[902] ***Ḥāshiya ʿalā al-Alfiyya***, AUTHOR: Muḥammad b. Aḥmad b. ʿĀrī al-ʿUthmānī, MANUSCRIPT: MS 64, al-Jazzār Mosque Library, Acre.

[903] ***Kitāb fī al-naḥw.*** Impossible to identify at this stage.

[904] ***Kitāb naḥw.*** Possibly Sībawayhi's *Kitāb*, AUTHOR: Abū Bishr ʿAmr b. ʿUthmān (d. 180/796), EDITION: *Kitāb Sībawayhi*, 5 vols, edited by ʿAbd al-Salām Muḥammad Hārūn, Cairo 1968–1977, 2nd ed. 1977.

[905] ***Kitāb naḥw***, see #904.

[906] ***Kitāb naḥw***, see #904.

[907] ***Kitāb naḥw***, see #904.

[908] ***Kitāb naḥw***, see #904.

[909] ***Matn al-Ajurrūmiyya wa-sharḥ al-Azhariyya.*** For the former, AUTHOR: Abū ʿAbd Allāh Muḥammad b. Muḥammad al-Sanhājī, known as Ibn Ajurrūm (d. 723/1323). For the latter, see #773.

[910] ***Iʿrāb al-Ajurrūmiyya***, AUTHOR: Khālid b. ʿAbd Allāh (d. 905/1499).

[911] ***Sharḥ al-Ajurrūmiyya.*** Possibly AUTHOR: ʿAlī b. ʿAbd Allāh al-Sanhūrī's (d. 889/1484) *Sharḥ al-Ajurrūmiyya fī ʿilm al-ʿArabiyya*, EDITION: edited by Sanhūrī, ʿAlī b. ʿAbd Allāh b. ʿAlī, and Muḥammad Khalīl ʿAbd al-ʿAzīz Sharaf. *Sharḥ al-Ajurrūmiyya fī ʿilm al-ʿArabiyya*. Beirut: Dār al-Salām, 2006.

[912] ***Sharḥ al-Ajurrūmiyya***, see #911.

[913] ***Sharḥ al-Ajurrūmiyya***, see #911.

[914] ***Sharḥ al-Ajurrūmiyya***, see #911.

[915] ***Sharḥ al-Ajurrūmiyya***, see #911.

[916] ***Sharḥ al-Ajurrūmiyya***, see #911.

[917] ***Sharḥ al-Ajurrūmiyya***, see #911.

[918] ***Sharḥ al-Ajurrūmiyya lil-Shinwānī***, AUTHOR: Abū Bakr b. Ismāʿīl b. Shihāb al-Dīn ʿAmr b. ʿAlī al-Shinwānī (d. 1019/1611).

[919] ***Sharḥ al-Ajurrūmiyya***, see #918.

[920] ***Sharḥ al-Ajurrūmiyya***, see #918.

[921] ***Sharḥ al-Ajurrūmiyya lil-Ḥarīrī.*** Possibly *al-Lāliʾ al-sunniya fī sharḥ al-Ajurrūmīya*, AUTHOR: Muḥammad b. ʿAlī al-Ḥarīrī al-Ḥarfūshī (d. 1059/1649).

[922] ***Sharḥ al-Ajurrūmiyya***, see #921.

[923] ***Alfiyyat Ibn Mālik***, see #751.

[924] ***Sharḥ al-Shawāhid al-kubrā lil-ʿAynī***, see #783.

[925] ***al-Alghāz al-naḥwiyya***, see #844.

[926] ***Matn al-Ajurrūmiyya***, see #909.

[927] ***Matn al-Ajurrūmiyya***, see #909.

[928] ***Sharḥ al-Ajurrūmiyya lil-Shaykh Khālid***, AUTHOR: Khālid b. ʿAbdallāh al-Azharī (d. 905/1499).

[929] ***Sharḥ al-Ajurrūmiyya***, see #928.

The Morphology Books

[1109] ***al-Shāfiya***, AUTHOR: Ibn al-Ḥājib (d. 646/1249).

[1110] ***Sharḥ al-Shāfiya***, AUTHOR: al-Jārabardī, Aḥmad b. al-Ḥusayn (d. 746/1346), MANUSCRIPT: Ms. 51, al-Jazzār Mosque Library, Acre.

[1111] ***Sharḥ al-Shāfiya***, see #1110.

[1112] ***al-Miftāḥ***. Possibly *Al-Miftāḥ fī al-ṣarf*, AUTHOR: ʿAbd al-Qāhir b. ʿAbd al-Raḥmān (d. 471/1078).

[1113] ***Sharḥ al-ʿIzzī***. Possibly Saʿd al-Dīn al-Taftāzānī's (d. 792/1390) *Sharḥ al-ʿIzzī*, a commentary on al-Zanjānī's *al-ʿIzzī*.

[1114] ***Sharḥ al-Marāḥ***, AUTHOR: Yūsuf b. ʿAbd al-Malik (n.d.). *Rawāḥ al-arwāḥ fī sharḥ al-Marāḥ*. This is the possible title of the commentary on Ibn Masʿūd's *Marāḥ al-arwāḥ*.

[1115] ***Sharḥ al-Maqṣūd li-Saʿd al-Dīn***. Probable title: *Sharḥ al-maqāṣid*. Probably referring to al-Taftāzānī (see below).

[1116] ***Sharḥ al-Maqṣūd lil-Taftāzānī***, see #1115.

[1117] ***Sharḥ al-Maqṣūd lil-Taftāzānī***, see #1115.

[1118] ***Amthilat Ṣarf***. Unidentified.

[1119] ***al-Manāhij al-Kāfiya***. Possibly *al-Manāhij al-kāfiya fī sharḥ al-shāfiya*. AUTHOR: Zakariyā b. Muḥammad al-Anṣārī (d. 926/1520).

[1120] ***Jārabardī***, AUTHOR: Aḥmad b. al-Ḥusayn (d. 746/1346). *Sharḥ al-Shāfiya*.

[1121] ***Kitāb fī ʿilm al-ṣarf***. Unidentified.

[1122] ***Kitāb al-ʿUyūn wa-ʿIzzī***. For the latter, see #1113.

[1123] ***Majmuʿ fī ʿilm al-ṣarf***. Possibly the same as #1125.

[1124] ***Kitāb fī ʿilm al-taṣrīf***. Possibly the same as #1125.

[1125] ***Kitāb fī al-taṣrīf***. Possibly *Kitāb al-Taṣrīf* by AUTHOR: Abū ʿUthmān Bakr b. Muḥammad al-Māzinī (d. 248/862).

[1126] ***Kitāb taṣrīf***. Possibly ʿIzz al-Dīn ʿAbd al-Wahhāb b. Ibrāhīm al-Zanjānī's *al-ʿIzzī*.

[1127] ***Kitāb taṣrīf***, see #1127.

[1128] ***Risāla fī al-taṣrīf***. Unidentified.

[1129] ***Kitāb ṣarf***. Unidentified.

[1130] ***Kitāb fī al-ṣarf***. Unidentified.

[1131] ***Taṣrīf al-ʿIzzī wa-Talkhīṣ al-Miftāḥ***, see #1113 and #1112, respectively.

[1132] ***Amthila***. Unidentified.

The Lexicography Books

[1396] ***Qāmūs***, AUTHOR: Muḥammad b. Yaʿqūb al-Fīrūzābādī (d. 817/1415). *Al-Qāmūs al-muḥīṭ wa-al-qābūs al-wasīṭ al-jāmiʿ li-mā dhahaba min al-ʿarab shamaṭīṭ*, commonly abbreviated to *al-Qāmūs al-muḥīṭ*, EDITION: Fīrūzābādī, M. *Al-Qāmūs al-muḥīṭ*. 3 vols, edited by Naṣr Hūrīnī. Būlāq, [Cairo]: Al-Maṭbaʿa al-Mīriyya, 1884.

[1397] ***Qāmūs***, see #1396.

[1398] ***Qāmūs***, see #1396.

[1399] ***Qāmūs***, see #1396.

[1400] ***Qāmūs***, see #1396.

[1401] ***Qāmūs***, see #1396.

[1402] ***Qāmūs***, see #1396.

[1403] ***Min sharḥ al-Qāmūs*** *al-juzʾ al-awwal* ***lil-Manāwī***. Possibly the *Sharḥ al-Qāmūs al-muḥīṭ*, AUTHOR: Muḥammad b. ʿAbd al-Raʾūf al-Manāwī (d. 1031/1622).

[1404] ***Min sharḥ al-Qāmūs*** *juzʾ thānī*. Unidentified.

[1405] ***al-Ṣiḥāḥ***. *Tāj al-lugha wa-ṣiḥāḥ al-ʿarabiyya*, also known as *Ṣiḥāḥ al-Jawharī*, AUTHOR: Ismāʿīl b. Ḥammād (d. 393/1003), EDITION: Beirut: Dār al-Fikr, 1998.

[1406] ***al-Ṣiḥāḥ***, see #1405.

[1407] ***Mukhtār al-Ṣiḥāḥ***. Or possibly *Mukhtār min al-Ṣiḥāḥ*, AUTHOR: Muḥammad b. Abī Bakr al-Rāzī (d. 666/1268).

[1408] ***al-Tawqīf ʿalā muhimmāt al-taʿrīf***, AUTHOR: Muḥammad ʿAbd al-Raʾūf al-Manāwī. Probable title: *al-Taʿārīf/al-Tawqīf ʿalā muhimmāt al-taʿrīf*, EDITION: edited by Muḥammad Riḍwān al-Dāya. Dimashq: Dār al-Fikr, 1410/1989.

[1409] ***al-Niẓām al-gharīb***. Anonymous.

[1410] ***al-Muḍāʿaf min al-lugha***. Unidentified.

[1411] ***al-Sāmī fī al-asāmī***, AUTHOR: Aḥmad b. Muḥammad al-Maydānī (d. 518/1124).

[1412] ***al-Sāmī ii al-asāmī***, see #1411.

[1413] ***al-Durr al-nathīr***. Unidentified.

[1414] ***al-Wajīz***. Unidentified.

[1415] ***al-Muʿarrab ʿalā ḥurūf al-muʿjam***. Unidentified.

[1416] ***Fiqh al-lugha***. Impossible to identify.

[1417] ***Sharḥ al-Kāfiya fī al-lugha***. Unidentified.

[1418] *al-thānī min* ***al-Nihāya***. Presumably the second part of *al-Nihāya fī gharīb al-ḥadīth wa-al-āthār*. AUTHOR: Majd al-Dīn Ibn al-Athīr (d. 660/1210).

[1419] *Qiṭʿa min* ***al-Qurṭubī fī al-lugha***. Possibly *al-Irshād fī al-lugha*, AUTHOR: Ibn ʿAbd Rabih Aḥmad b. Muḥammad al-Qurṭubī (d. 328/940).

[1420] *al-thānī min* ***Lisān al-ʿarab lugha***. *Lisān al-ʿarab*, AUTHOR: Muḥammad b. Mukarram, known as Ibn Manẓūr (d. 711/1312), EDITION: edited by Muḥammad ibn Mukarram Ibn Manẓūr. *Lisān al-ʿarab*. Beirut: Dār Ṣādir, 1997.

[1421] ***Kitāb min al-lugha***. Unidentified.

[1422] ***Kitāb muntakhab fī ʿilm al-lugha Turkī***. Unidentified.

Works from the provenanced sections of the inventory

Works taken from the library of al-Sayyid Yaḥyā Efendī b. al-Sayyid Muḥammad al-Ṭībī of Jaffa in 1218/1803

[517] ***Kitāb al-Ṣiḥāḥ bi-al-lugha***, Author: Ismāʿīl b. Ḥammād al-Jawharī (d. 393/1003). Alternative title: *Tāj al-lugha wa-ṣiḥāḥ al-ʿarabiyya*, EDITION: Beirut: Dār al-Fikr, 1998.

[522] ***Kitāb al-lugha*** *mudhahhab*.

[527] ***Kitāb Tāj al-lugha bi-al-ʿArabiyya***, see #517.

[569] ***Kitāb Sharḥ al-Alfiyya li-Ibn Hishām***, AUTHOR: ʿAbd Allāh b. Yūsuf Ibn Hishām (d. 761/1361). Alternative title: *al-Tawḍīḥ ʿalā al-alfiyya*.

Works taken from the libraries of al-Shaykh ʿAlī al-Rashīdī and al-Shaykh Muḥammad Wakīlkharaj in 1216/1801

[1638] *ʿan* ***Kitāb Sharḥ Maqṣūd min al-ṣarf***. Unidentified.

[1647] *ʿan* ***Sharḥ Iʿrāb***. Unidentified.

[1648] *ʿan* ***Kitāb Shaykh Khālid ʿalā al-Ajurrūmiyya***, AUTHOR: Khālid b. ʿAbdallāh al-Azharī (d. 905/1499).

[1661] ***ʿIlm al-Iʿrāb***. Unidentified.

[1665] ***Kitāb bi-ʿilm al-istiʿārāt***. Unidentified.

[1666] ***Sharḥ al-Alfiyya li-Ibn Mālik***. Unidentified.

[1671] ***Risāla ʿalā naḥw***. Unidentified.

[1682] ***Ḥāshiya al-Shaykh al-Imām al-Shirbīnī***. Unidentified.

[1689] ***Kitāb Zahr al-rabīʿ fī shawāhid al-badīʿ***. Possibly *Zahr al-rabīʿ fī shawāhid al-badīʿ*, AUTHOR: Shaykh Nāṣir al-Dīn Muḥammad b. ʿAbd Allāh b. Qarqmāsh (d. 883/1478).

[1704] ***Risāla fī al-ṣarf***. Unidentified.

CHAPTER 19

Manuals for Manners: Books on *adab* in the Inventory of the Aḥmad Pasha al-Jazzār Library

Berat Açıl

The inventory of Aḥmad Pasha al-Jazzār's Library itemises books on the art of disputation (*ādāb al-baḥth*), embellishment (*badīʿ*), anthology, rhetoric (*khiṭāba*), rational theology (*kalām*), commentary on the Qurʾān (*tafsīr*) and philosophy under the title of '*kutub al-maʿānī wa-al-bayān wa-al-ādāb wa-al-uṣūl wa-al-ʿarūḍ*'.[1] At first glance, it is not easy to understand why the scribe of the inventory classifies 132 manuscripts about distinct fields of knowledge under the same title. Therefore, the first question to be answered should be: Why did the scribe list all those different fields of knowledge under the same section? Which concept or concepts are keys to understanding the scribe's aim in classifying them under the same title?

In the eighteenth century, when the Jazzār Library was established, many libraries were built in distinct places of the Ottoman Empire. Yavuz Sezer relates this tendency to create new libraries to the '*adabization*' movement at the time. Though it is arguable whether there was a movement that could be called *adabization* or not, beginning from the seventeenth century, manuscripts about narrative-related sciences, such as *ḥadīth*, literature, poetry and *taṣawwuf*, were more visible than in previous centuries, at least in the core lands of the empire.[2] Sezer quoted a passage from Penāh Efendi, one of the secretaries of the Imperial Council, who argued that there were enough libraries in the capital, Istanbul, in 1778. Thus, the ruling class should enlarge their charity works, such as library buildings, to the peripheries, specifically to the cities populated by Arabs. Penāh Efendi argues that the 'near absence of contact with the Ottomans left them [the peripheries] devoid of *adab* and rules of conduct; they were not different from American tribes'.[3] Although it is unknown whether a member of the ruling class followed Penāh Efendi's problematic advice, using the terms '*adab* and rule of conduct' together is of importance for the sake of this chapter. This section of the inventory seems to contain titles related to *al-ādāb* and *al-uṣūl*, which may be understood as '*adab* and rule of conduct' in the modern sense of the terms. Then the question is: What ideas about good learning did the Jazzār library reflect? The '*adab* and rule of conduct' of what fields of knowledge should audiences know? The purpose of the founder of the library, al-Jazzār, and the scribe of the inventory may arguably be the same in classifying and ordering manuscripts. A close examination of the manuscripts or better-known titles is needed to reveal the underlying goal of the scribe in clustering them together.

The bulk of entries in the section *kutub al-maʿānī wa-al-bayān wa-al-ādāb wa-al-uṣūl wa-al-*

1 I am indebted to the editors of this volume for their insightful recommendations, comments and corrections. Specifically, Said Aljoumani facilitated writing this chapter by providing a comprehensive library inventory. I am also thankful to Tuncay Azar for his support in searching for titles regarding *al-balāgha*. The first version of this chapter was presented in Deutscher Orientalistentag in 2022 at Freie Universität. I am grateful to the Alexander von Humboldt Association and Judith Pfeiffer for their support. They invited me to Bonn University to contribute to the Islamic Intellectual History Project, which facilitated the presentation and first draft of this paper. I frequently searched the titles using the database supplied by ISAM, 'Türkiye Kütüphaneleri Veri Tabanı Toplu' (http://ktp.isam.org.tr), and the website of Türkiye Yazma Eserler Kurumu Başkanlığı (https://portal.yek.gov.tr). These resources were invaluable for this chapter.

2 Açıl, "Fazıl Ahmed Paşa Koleksiyonu ve İlimler Tasnifi", 150.

3 Sezer, *The Architecture of Bibliophilia*, 214.

ʿarūḍ of the Jazzār library deal with eloquence (*balāgha*). Although the title of the section does not contain *balāgha*, the sciences of semantics (*al-maʿānī*) and figures of speech (*al-bayān*) are two well-established subsections of *balāgha* from the very beginning of the history of the science. The scribe did not use the third subsection of *balāgha*, embellishment (*al-badīʿ*), in the title. It is debatable whether the science of embellishment (*ʿilm al-badīʿ*) is a necessary part of *balāgha* according to classical *balāgha* theory. Ottoman *madrasas*, however, seem to have accepted *badīʿ* as part of *balāgha* in the curriculum.[4] Thus, what makes this discussion even more important in terms of this library is looking at the history of *badīʿ*, because using *badīʿ* might be a distinctive feature of classical Ottoman literature which distinguishes it from Arabic literature, since Ottoman eloquence seems to follow the Sakkākī path that added *badīʿ* as the third chapter of eloquence into his *Miftāḥ al-ʿulūm*.

But is this the case for the content of that section in the Jazzār library? Does the inventory contain texts about *badīʿ*? Searching this part of the inventory regarding the titles of the works, it appears that the inventory includes at least four titles about *badīʿ*: *Taḥrīr al-taḥbīr fī ʿilm al-badīʿ ṣināʿat al-shiʿr wa-al-nathr wa-bayān iʿjāz al-Qurʾān* by Ibn Ebī Iṣbaʿ (d. 654/1256, #982); *Sharḥ Kāfī al-badīʿ al-musammā bi-al-natāʾij* [*al natāʾij al-ilāhiyya fī Sharḥ Kāfiyat al-badīʿiyya*] by Abū al-Maḥāsin Ṣafī al-Dīn ʿAbd al-Azīz b. Sarāyā b. ʿAlī al-Ḥillī (d. 749/1348, #991) is a work penned to praise the Prophet Muḥammad, making especially use of *badīʿ*; similarly, *Mukhtaṣar al-Mukātabāt al-badīʿa* [*fīmā yuktab min umūr sharīʿa*], by Muḥammad b. ʿAbd al-Raḥmān Ibn al-Ṣayrafī (d. 13th century, #1003); and *al-Shifāʾ fī al-badīʿ al-iktifā*, by Shams al-Dīn Muḥammad b. Ḥasan b. ʿAlī b. ʿUthmān al-Nawājī al-Qāhirī (d. 859/1455, #1004).

The terms used in the title, for instance, *maʿānī*, *bayān* and *ʿarūḍ*, denote *balāgha* and poetry-related sciences, except for *ādāb* and *uṣūl*. The definition and borders of terms such as *maʿānī* and *bayān*, which are the first two branches of *balāgha*, and *ʿarūḍ*, which is a branch of classical poetry, are slightly more straightforward than the terms *ādāb* and *uṣūl*, which have more complicated and debatable definitions. The books on topics such as the art of disputation, anthology, rhetoric, rational theology, commentary on the Qurʾān and philosophy, have something to do with *ādāb* and *uṣūl* rather than the other terms used in the title related to *balāgha* and poetry. Thus, it is necessary to examine their history to reveal the linkage or resemblance points of the two concepts.

Beginning from the Abbasid courts, the meaning of *adab* included codes of conduct and chancery for the growing administrative needs. Those needs resulted in manuals, monographs and various sorts of guidelines for the secretarial profession. It was then enlarged by works such as the histories of ancient rulers, manuals to teach a ruler how to conduct himself and books on ethics.[5] The word *adab* had a more significant sense in the eighteenth century than in today's literature because it might consist of ethics, mysticism, history and even international relations.[6] The entries regarding *adab* demonstrate how it has been an evolving term throughout history. Jaakko Hämeen-Anttila shows how the term's meaning changed from the pre-Islamic ages and argues it may be defined as 'suitable things to know and to act upon'.[7]

The other term used in the title by the scribe of the inventory of the Jazzār library was *uṣūl*. The

4 One of the primary *balāgha* texts (if not the most used) employed in the Ottoman *madrasas* is *al-Talkhīs al-Miftāḥ* by al-Qazwīnī (d. 739/1338), a commentary on the third part of *Miftāḥ al-ʿUlūm* by Sakkākī (d. 626/1229), which is about *balagha* and includes *al-badīʿ* as the third section after *al-maʿānī* and *al-bayān*. See Kızılkaya, "From Means to Goal".

5 Pellat, "ADAB II Adab in Arabic Literature".

6 Arıcı, "Başlangıçtan 19", 108. Açıl argues that the first usage of the term *edebiyāt* was in the sixteenth century when the terms *al-adab* and *edebiyāt* began to denote different meanings from each other; see Açıl, "Akl-ı Selimden Zevk-i Selime".

7 Hämeen-Anttila, "Adab a) Arabic, early developments".

term *al-uṣūl* traditionally denotes the principle of jurisprudence, which is used as the methodology of all religious sciences that has nothing to do with the *balāgha* or literature in its traditional usage. In the inventory, *uṣūl* means method, besides its conventional sense. Therefore, *adab* and *uṣūl* have the same meaning for the section: manual or guide to do any science appropriately.

Examining the titles of the Jazzār inventory according to the sequence of sciences and finding a logical connection between them takes considerable effort. That is to say that the scribe did not list the manuscripts according to any criteria regarding the order, be it a classification of sciences or an accumulation of religious knowledge according to a hierarchy to reach the ability to comment on the Qur'ān, which is the ultimate science according to the traditional approach, as the famous scholar Saçaklızade (d. 1145/1732) argues when he put the sciences to be learned in a *madrasa* in order.[8] Consequently, I argue that the hidden rationale for bringing those sciences together under the same title is to use those two terms: *ādāb* and *uṣūl*. Thus, the linkage between *ādāb* and *uṣūl*, which is the manual for manners, is the main reason for gathering all sciences under the same title: *kutub al-maʿānī wa-al-bayān wa-al-ādāb wa-al-uṣūl wa-al-ʿarūḍ*.

1 Is the Inventory a Representative One?

What are the overall characteristics of that part of the inventory? Does it serve the general goals (if any) of the founder, al-Jazzār? Was it established considering the needs of potential readers? Assuming that the *al-maʿānī wa-al-bayān wa-al-ādāb wa-al-uṣūl wa-al-ʿarūḍ* section of the inventory was deliberately established and every single title has the task of bringing the addressee to a certain level of knowledge, what was the expectation of the founder of the library in establishing this section? Furthermore, did the order of the sciences in that section have a meaning? Or were the titles randomly placed in this section? Though the answers to these questions would be hypothetical, I will examine the order and potential connections between the sciences in this section to determine whether there are any logical or pedagogical relations between them.

As has been mentioned above, the section contains 132 titles. The actual manuscripts that were once in the Jazzār Library have not yet been identified, except in a few cases, such as *al-Fihrist* by al-Nadīm (#998)[9] and *Mukhtaṣar al-Mukātabāt al-badīʿah* by al-Ṣayrafī (#1003).[10] Thus, the inquiry regarding these titles is bibliographic in nature. In many cases, it was only possible to identify the author for some titles. In other instances, a title may have more than one potential author because the scribe recorded the titles so generically that it is impossible to decide accurately on the author.

Bearing all these questions and possibilities in mind, one has to recognise that it is impossible to determine the genre of some titles because they are unidentifiable for the time being. Ten titles out of 132 are unidentifiable: *Maʿānī al-akhlāq* (#981), *Ghurar al-dalāʾil wa-al-āyāt* (#993), *Barāʿat al-tawassul* (#994), *Mā yuktab maqṣūran wa-mamdūdan* (#995), *al-Maqālāt al-muhdhiba* (#1002), *Kitāb Nuzhat al-wajīzah* (#1009), *Mukhtār Qalāʾid al-ʿaqīm* (#1016), *Musḥaf al-kashf* (#1022), *Ḥāshiyya ʿalā al-Tahdhīb* (#1039) and *Jāmiʿ al-Tadqīq* (#1051).

The section begins with titles related to *balāgha*, which is the main bulk of the section. I take the term *balāgha* to include all the discipline's sub-branches, such as *maʿānī, bayān* and *badīʿ*. There are thirty-nine *balāgha* works in the section. They are not listed one after another, resulting in the non-sequence of order-

8 Burak, "On the Order of the Sciences", 41.

9 The manuscript is preserved in Dublin, Chester Beatty Library, Ar. 3315.

10 The manuscript is preserved in the Khalidi Library, MS 966.

ing numbers. *al-Muṭawwal* (#930–933) *Sharḥ al-Muṭawwal* (#934), *Ḥāshiyat Mullāzādah ʿalā al-Muṭawwal* (#935), *Ḥāshiyat Mullā ʿAbd Allāh ʿalā al-Khiṭābī* (#937), *Talkhīṣ al-Miftāḥ fī al-maʿānī wa-al-bayān* (#948), *Talkhīṣ al-Miftāḥ* (#949–951), *Sharḥ al-Talkhīṣ* (#952–954), *Mukhtaṣar al-Maʿānī wa-al-bayān* (#955–959), *Sharḥ al-Mukhtaṣar lil-Saʿd al-Taftāzānī* (#960 and #961), *Adhhān al-adhkiyāʾ Sharḥ al-Talkhīṣ* (#962), *Ḥāshiya ʿalā al-Talkhīṣ* (#965), *Kitāb fī ʿilm al-maʿānī* (#968), *Kitāb fī al-Maʿānī wa-al-bayān* (#970 and #971), *Kitāb al-Mukhtaṣar* (#972), *Khizānat al-adab wa-ghāyat al-ʿarab* (#973), *Taḥrīr al-Taḥbīr fī ʿilm al-badīʿ Ṣināʿat al-shiʿr wa-al-nathr wa-bayān iʿjāz al-Qurʾān* (#982), *Fatḥ munazzil al-mathānī bi-sharḥ aqṣā al-amānī* (#990), *Sharḥ al-Kāfī al-badīʿ al-musammā bi-al-natāʾij* (#991), *Mukhtaṣar al-Mukātabāt al-badīʿa* (#1003), *al-Shifā fī badīʿ al-iktifā* (#1004), *al-Durar al-madrūza sharḥ al-Arjūza* (#1005), *Sharḥ Naẓm al-istiʿāra* (#1057), *Majmūʿ yashtamil ʿalā Sharḥ al-Istiʿāra li-ʿIṣām wa-ḥawāshī ʿalayh* (#1058), *Matn al-Samarqandiyya fī al-istiʿārāt farāʾid al-fawāʾid li-taḥqīq maʿānī al-istiʿārāt* (#1059), *Kitāb bi-ʿilm al-istiʿārāt* (#1665) and *Kitāb Zahr al-rabīʿ fī shawāhid al-badīʿ* (#1689) by Muḥammad b. ʿAbd Allāh b. Qurqumāz (d. 883/1478).

The principles of jurisprudence is the second most represented discipline in the section. The titles are not clustered but rather dispersed throughout the section. Seventeen titles regarding the principle of jurisprudence were recorded in the section. These are *Ḥāshiyat al-Sharīf fī al-uṣūl* (#936), *Tahdhīb al-Uṣūl, Tahdhīb al-Uṣūl ilā ʿilm al-uṣūl* (#938, #939 and #1012), *Kitāb fī ʿIlm al-uṣūl* (#941 and #944), *Kitāb fī ʿIlm al-uṣūl* (#942), *Sharḥ al-manār* (#943 and #1034), *Ḥāshiya ʿalā al-Mukhtaṣār lil-Jurjānī* (#963 and #964), *Minhāj al-wuṣūl ilā ʿilm al-uṣūl* (#967), *Khabāyā al-zawāyā* (#989), *Safīnat al-najāt* (#1012), *Minhāj al-uṣūl minhāj al-wuṣūl ilā ʿilm al-uṣūl lil-Bayḍāwī* (#1033), and *al-Tahdhīb* [*al-manṭiq wa-al-kalām*] (#1036 and #1038).

Titles dealing with *ādāb* in the section are the most difficult to identify since they may equally be identified as works in other fields of knowledge. There are twenty-eight titles regarding *ādāb*.[11] These are *Majmūʿa fī al-adab* (#974), *Majmūʿa fī al-adab* (#975), *Thamarāt al-awrāq fī al-muḥāḍarāt* (#976) by Ibn Ḥijja (d. 837/1434), *Rawḍat al-faṣāḥa* (#977) by al-Rāzī (d. 666/1268), *Kitāb fī ʿilm al-adab* (#978), *Thimār al-qulūb fī al-muḍāf wa-al-mansūb* (#979) by al-Thaʿālibī (d. 429/1038), *Sarḥ al-ʿuyūn fī Sharḥ Risālat Ibn Zaydūn* (#980) by Ibn Nubāta al-Miṣrī (d. 768/1366), *Risālat al-adab* (#983), *Sharḥ Qaṣīdat al-adab* (#985), *Qalaʾid al-ʿiqyān* (#986), *Badāyiʾ al-badāyiʿ* (#987), *Maṭlaʿ al-fawāʾid wa-majmaʿ al-farāʾid* (#988) by Ibn Nubātah al-Miṣrī (d. 768/1366), *Yatīmat Ibn al-Muqaffaʿ* (#992) by Ibn al-Muqaffaʿ (d. 142/759), *Ḥalabat al-kumayt* (#997) by al-Nawājī al-Qāhirī (d. 859/1455), *Ghurar al-maʿānī wa-al-nukat Sharḥ al-Maqāmāt* (#1006) by Abū ʿAbbās al-Sharīshī (d. 619/1222), *al-Hafawāt al-nādira wa-al-saqatāt al-bādirah* (#1008) by al-Ṣābī (d. 480/1088), *Majmūʿ laṭīf fī kull maʿnā ẓarīf* (#1010), *al-Majmūʿa al-laṭīfa* (#1011), *Mukātabāt al-Khwārizmī* (#1013, #1018) by al-Ṭabarī al-Khwarizmī (d. 383/993), *Kitāb Murāsalāt badīʿ al-inshāʾ wa-al-ṣifāt fī al-mukātabāt wa-al-murāsalāt* (#1014) by Zayn al-Dīn Marʿī b. Yūsuf al-Karmī (d. 1033/1624), *Rawḍat al-qulūb wa-nuzhat al-maḥbūb* (#1015) by al-Shayzarī (d. 589/1193?), *Kitāb al-muraṣṣaʿ fī al-kitābāt wa-al-iḍāfāt* (#1017) by Ibn al-Athīr (d. 606/1210), *Tarḥ al-mudr li-ḥall al-laʾālī wa-al-durar* (#1019) by al-Shirbīnī (d. 1098/1687), *Murāsalāt Zayn al-ʿĀbidīn al-Ṣiddīqī* (#1020) by al-ʿUbaydī (d. 1091/1680), [*Kitāb*] *Nasīm al-ṣibā* (#1023) by Abū Muḥammad Badr al-Dīn al-Ḥasan al-Dimashqī al-Ḥalabī (d. 779/1377), *Tahdhīb al-uṣūl* (#1045) by Khalīl b. Kaykaldī (d. 761/1359) and *Majmūʾ yashtamil ʿalā Sharḥ al-istiʿāra li-ʿiṣām wa-ḥawāshī ʿalayh* (#1058) by ʿIṣām al-Dīn Ibrāhīm al-Isfarāyīnī (d. 945/1538).

I will examine in that part of the chapter whether the *adab* section of the Jazzār library inventory represents canonical works. The inventory, for instance, surprisingly, does not have any copy

11 By adding seven titles recorded in the supplement, the number turns out to be thirty-five.

of the canonical bibliographic text *Kashf al-Ẓunūn* by Ḥajji Khalīfa known as Kātib Çelebi (d. 1657). Does the inventory include the canonical works for each field of knowledge? This analysis will help us understand how unique or generic this library was compared to other manuscript collections.[12]

1.1 Balāgha

Whether a library is designed for the use of *madrasa* students or not, all Islamic manuscript collections or libraries contain a significant collection of *balāgha* and related fields. The Jazzār library is no exception to this general observation. The section of the inventory has some canonical *balāgha* texts.

The chart below shows that three works and their commentaries occupy a large proportion of all thirty-nine *balāgha* titles. These are *Talkhīṣ al-miftāḥ* by Khaṭīb al-Qazwīnī (d. 739/1338), which is a commentary on the *al-balāgha* parts of al-Sakkākī's (d. 626/1229) *Miftāḥ al-ʿulūm*, *al-Muṭawwal* by al-Taftāzānī (d. 792/1390), a commentary on *Talkhīṣ al-Miftāḥ*, and *al-Mukhtaṣar* [*al-Maʿānī*] by al-Taftāzānī (d. 792/1390). These three texts are also canonical *al-balāgha* works throughout the history of the *madrasa* curriculum. Necmettin Kızılkaya portrays one of the curricula implemented in the Ottoman *madrasa*s according to the anonymous *Kawākib-i sabʿa risālesi* penned in 1155/1741. He itemises the main texts of *balāgha*: al-Sakkākī's *Miftāḥ al-ʿulūm*, al-Qazwīnī's *al-Talkhīs*, al-Taftāzānī's *al-Sharḥ al-Talkhīs* and *al-Sharḥ al-Muṭawwal*, and al-Jurjānī's *Dalāʾil al-iʿjāz* and *Asrār al-balāgha*. Occasionally, in some *madrasas*, *Īḍāḥ al-maʿānī* by al-Qazwīnī and *Alfiyya lil-maʿanī wa-al-Bayān* by al-Qabāqibī (d. 850/1446) were also studied.[13]

The section has four copies of *Talkhīṣ al-Miftāḥ* (#948–951), four commentaries (*Sharḥ al-Talkhīṣ*) (#952–954 and #962) and two annotations (*ḥashiya*) (#963 and #937) on it. On the other hand, one can find four copies of *al-Muṭawwal* (#930–933), one commentary (#934) and one annotation (#935) on *al-Muṭawwal*. The third work in the section with more than one copy and commentary or annotation is *al-Mukhtaṣar*. The book has six copies (#955–959 and #972) and two commentaries (#960 and #961). Therefore, twenty-four titles of the *balāgha*, more than half of the totality, are related to works by al-Qazwīnī and al-Taftāzānī.

One of the most popular texts on the metaphor (*istiʿāra*)[14] was penned by Abū al-Qāsim b. Abī Bakr al-Laythī al-Samarqandī (d. 888/1483), *Matn al-Samarqandiyya fī al-istiʿārāt farāʾid al-fawāʾid li-taḥqīq maʿānī al-istiʿārāt*, found in almost all manuscript collections. The Jazzār inventory also has this canonical work (#1059). Numerous scholars wrote commentaries and annotations on al-Samarqandī's text, which is also known as *Farāʾid al-fawāʾid*, *al-Farīda* and *Risāla al-istiʿāra*.

In addition to these canonical works by prominent authors, the inventory does not identify the author's name for some other titles about *maʿānī*, *bayān* and *badīʿ*: *Kitāb fī ʿilm al-maʿānī* (#968), *Kitāb fī al-maʿānī wa-al-bayān* (#970) and *Kitāb fī al-maʿānī wa-al-bayān* (#971).

To conclude, the *balāgha* part of the *al-maʿānī wa-al-bayān wa-al-ādāb wa-al-uṣūl wa-al-ʿarūḍ* section in the inventory of the Jazzār library, though a small collection, includes canonical works which make it a representative one. Nevertheless, the section does not have *Miftāḥ al-ʿulūm* by Abū Yaʿqūb al-Sakkākī (d. 626/1229), which is the source text of most *balāgha* works included in the *balāgha* section.[15]

12 For now, I will limit my exploration of representation to only the *al-balāgha* and *al-adab* sections of the inventory.

13 Kızılkaya, "From Means to Goal", 35–37.

14 While the term initially means borrowing one meaning to transfer it to another based on analogy, it is generally translated as 'metaphor' in English. I think 'metaphor' means exactly '*majāz*' in Arabic, as both denote conveying meaning from one side to another. See, for instance, el-Rouayheb, "al-Isfarāyīnī, ʿIṣām al-Dīn".

15 The reason might be just an access issue: Other texts were available on the market, whereas *Miftāḥ al-ʿUlūm* was not, for the time being.

TABLE 19.1 *al-Balāgha* Works Listed in the Jazzār Library

Number	Title	Author
[930]	*al-Muṭawwal*	Sa'd al-Dīn Mas'ūd al-Taftāzānī (d. 792/1390)
[931]	*al-Muṭawwal*	Sa'd al-Dīn Mas'ūd al-Taftāzānī (d. 792/1390)
[932]	*al-Muṭawwal*	Sa'd al-Dīn Mas'ūd al-Taftāzānī (d. 792/1390)
[933]	*al-Muṭawwal*	Sa'd al-Dīn Mas'ūd al-Taftāzānī (d. 792/1390)
[934]	*Sharḥ al-Muṭawwal*	More than one probable author.
[935]	*Ḥāshiya Mullāzādah 'alā al-Muṭawwal*	Mullāzādah Niẓām al-Dīn Aḥmad b. 'Uthmān al-Khiṭā'ī (d. 901/1495)
[937]	*Ḥāshiya Mullā 'Abd Allāh al-Hiṭāyī*	Mullā 'Abd Allāh al-Khiṭāyī (d. 901/1495)
[948]	*al-Talkhīṣ al-Miftāḥ fī al-ma'ānī wa-al-bayān*	Khāṭīb al-Qazwīnī (d. 739/1338)
[949]	*al-Talkhīṣ al-Miftāḥ*	Khāṭīb al-Qazwīnī (d. 739/1338)
[950]	*al-Talkhīṣ al-Miftāḥ*	Khāṭīb al-Qazwīnī (d. 739/1338)
[951]	*al-Talkhīṣ al-Miftāḥ*	Khāṭīb al-Qazwīnī (d. 739/1338)
[952]	*Sharḥ al-Talkhīṣ*	More than one probable author.
[953]	*Sharḥ al-Talkhīṣ*	More than one probable author.
[954]	*Sharḥ al-Talkhīṣ lil-Subkī*	Aḥmad b. 'Alī 'Abd al-Kāfī al-Subkī (d. 773/1372)
[955]	*Mukhtaṣar al-Ma'ānī wa-al-bayān*	Sa'd al-Dīn Mas'ūd al-Taftāzānī (d. 792/1390)
[956]	*Mukhtaṣar*	Sa'd al-Dīn Mas'ūd al-Taftāzānī (d. 792/1390)
[957]	*Mukhtaṣar*	Sa'd al-Dīn Mas'ūd al-Taftāzānī (d. 792/1390)
[958]	*Mukhtaṣar*	Sa'd al-Dīn Mas'ūd al-Taftāzānī (d. 792/1390)
[959]	*Mukhtaṣar*	Sa'd al-Dīn Mas'ūd al-Taftāzānī (d. 792/1390)
[960]	*Sharḥ al-Mukhtaṣar*	Sa'd al-Dīn Mas'ūd al-Taftāzānī (d. 792/1390)
[961]	*Sharḥ al-Mukhtaṣar*	Sa'd al-Dīn Mas'ūd al-Taftāzānī (d. 792/1390)
[962]	*Azhān al-Azkiyā Sharḥ al-Talkhīṣ*	Unidentified
[965]	*Ḥāshiya 'alā al-Talkhīṣ*	More than one probable author.
[968]	*Kitāb fī 'Ilm al-Ma'ānī*	Unidentified
[970]	*Kitāb fī al-ma'ānī wa-al-bayān*	Unidentified
[971]	*Kitāb fī al-ma'ānī wa-al-bayān*	Unidentified
[972]	*Kitāb al-Mukhtaṣar*	Sa'd al-Dīn Mas'ūd al-Taftāzānī (d. 792/1390)
[973]	*Khizānat al-Adab [wa-Ghāyat al-'Arab]*	Ibn Ḥijja (d. 837/1434)
[982]	*Taḥrīr al-Taḥbīr fī ṣinā'at al-shi'r wa-al-nathr wa-bayān i'jāz al-Qur'ān*	Abū Muḥammad Zakī al-Dīn 'Abd al-'Aẓīm al-Miṣrī (d. 654/1256)
[990]	*[Fatḥ munazzil mathānī bi] Sharḥ Aqṣā al-amānī*	Zakariyyā al-Anṣārī (d. 926/1520)
[991]	*Sharḥ Kāfī al-badī' al-musammā bi-al-Natā'ij [al-Natā'ij al-ilāhiyya fī sharḥ Kāfiyat al-badī'iyya]*	Abū al-Maḥāsin Ṣafī al-Dīn 'Abd al-Azīz b. Sarāyā b. 'Alī al-Ḥillī (d. 749/1348)
[1003]	*Mukhtaṣar al-Mukātabāt al-badī'a [fīmā yuktab min Umūr sharī'a]*	Muḥammad b. 'Abd al-Raḥmān Ibn al-Ṣayrafī (d. 13th century)
[1004]	*al-Shifā' fī al-badī' al-iktifā*	Shams al-Dīn Muḥammad b. Ḥasan b. 'Alī b. 'Uthmān al-Nawājī al-Qāhirī (d. 859/1455)

TABLE 19.1 *al-Balāgha* Works Listed in the Jazzār Library (*cont.*)

Number	Title	Author
[1005]	*al-Durar al-madrūza sharḥ al-Arjūza*	Abū ʿAbd Allāh Jalāl al-Dīn al-Anṣārī al-Maḥallī (d. 864/1459)
[1057]	*Sharḥ Naẓm al-istiʿāra*	Abū Saʿd Zayn al-Dīn Manṣūr al-Ṭablawī (d. 1014/1606)
[1058]	*Majmūʾ yashtamil ʿalā sharḥ al-Istiʿāra li-ʿIṣām wa-Ḥawāshī ʿalayh*	Unidentified
[1059]	*Matn al-Samarqandī fī al-istiʿārāt Farāʾid al-fawāʾid li-taḥqīq maʿānī al-Iistiʿārāt*	Abū al-Qāsim b. Abī Bakr al-Laythī al-Samarqandī (d. 888/1483)
[1665]	*Kitāb bi-ʿilm al-istiʿārāt*	Unidentified
[1689]	*Kitāb Zahr al-rabīʿ fī shawāhid al-badīʿ*	Muḥammad b. ʿAbd Allāh b. Qurqumāz (d. 883/1478)

The section does not itemise works according to any apparent criteria. It begins with *al-Muṭawwal*, its commentaries and annotations, then comes *Talkhīṣ al-Miftāḥ* without *Miftāḥ al-ʿulūm* itself. As their texts are almost the same, there should be no difference in the importance attached to them by the library's founder or his librarians.

1.2 Ādāb

One of the most controversial terms in intellectual Islamicate history is *adab*. Although the term is ancient and derived from the Arabic root *ʾ-d-b* (manner, habit), its employment in the classification of sciences is relatively recent. According to the entry written by Charles Pellat in the *Encyclopedia Iranica, adab* consists of three main categories: a) parenetic *adab*, which consists of ethical writings; b) cultural *adab*, works compiled for the benefit of the upper classes; and c) training or occupational *adab*, consisted of handbooks for the ruling, intellectual, and professional classes.[16] Those three areas denote ethics, culture and crafts. It is generally accepted that the *adab* writings began in the Abbasid era to treat bureaucrats and officers in writing. It then enlarged its scope to include ethics and guides for rulers or princes in administration. Thus, according to Pellat, the term has been employed for politeness, good manners, breeding and humanity. In another sense, *adab* comprises *belles lettres*, humanities and literature. In conclusion, politeness and refinement, as well as rules of conduct and culture, are the central notions of *adab*. Pellat argues that it opposed poetry (*shiʿr*), which is not the case in the modern sense of literature, *belles lettres*.

The *ādāb* section of the inventory of the Jazzār library contains thirty-five titles, including seven added from other sections of the inventory. In the following, I will compare the *ādāb* section of the inventory to adjacent and contemporary libraries: al-ʿAẓm Library in Damascus, al-Dūrikī Library in Aleppo and Abū al-Dhahab Library in Cairo. Regarding the ʿAẓm Library, there is no unique section devoted to *Ādāb*, but *adab* and history were recorded in one single section under the same title: *Kutub Tārīkh wa-al-Ādāb* (from number 274 to 363).[17] There are two book lists pertaining to the Dūrikī Library, one prepared by the librarian (contains 24 titles) and one reconstructed by Said Aljoumani (contains 181 titles), who analysed the library. According to the list prepared by the li-

16 Pellat, "ADAB II Adab in Arabic Literature".

17 Aljoumani, "Masrad Kutub Madrasa", 16, 47–53.

brarian, *adab* and history books were classified under the same title, similar to the ʿAẓm Library, whereas Aljoumani preferred to use *al-Lugha wa-al-Adab* as the title of the section. The latter one contains miscellanies, syntax, grammar, prosody, collections of poems, rhetoric, *al-maqāmāt* and *al-amthāl*.[18] The Abū al-Dhahab Library contains 650 manuscripts, most of which are on general jurisprudence. The library has a surprisingly small *adab* section, called *Kutub al-Ādāb*, which includes only two books: *Risālat Samarqandī* and *Risālat Masʿūd*.[19] Yet, these are not all the *adab* titles listed in the library, but they are rather itemised under other headings. To conclude, *adab* books were located under different sections using diverse headings even in temporally, geographically and culturally adjacent libraries.

One of the most remarkable characteristics of the *ādāb* section of the Jazzār library is that many titles contain generic words, such as *majmūʿa*, *kitāb* or *risāla*, which makes it almost impossible to identify their authors. Those titles *Majmūʿa fī al-adab* (#974), *Majmūʿa fī al-adab* (#975), *Majmūʿ laṭīf fī kull maʿnā ẓarīf* (#1010) and *al-Majmūʿa al-laṭīfa* (#1011) begin with the derivations of *majmuʿ*, whereas *Kitāb fī ʿIlm al-adab* (#978) and *ʿAn Kitāb Sharḥ al-Maqāmāt lil-Shaykh al-Zaynī* (#1634) contain *kitāb* in their title. Besides, *Risāla fī ādāb al-baḥth* (#946, 947), *Sharḥ al-ʿUyūn fī sharḥ Risālat Ibn Zaydūn* (#980), *Risālat al-Adab* (#983), *Murāsalāt Zayn al-ʿĀbidīn al-Ṣiddīqī* (#1020), and *Murāsalāt Abī al-ʿAlāʾ* (#1056) have derivations of *risāla* in their titles. Most of these titles are identifiable, among them *Murāsalāt Zayn al-ʿĀbidīn al-Ṣiddīqī* (#1020) by al-ʿUbaydī (d. 1091/1680) and *Murāsalāt Abī al-ʿAlāʾ* (#1056) by Abū al-ʿAlāʾ al-Maʿarrī (d. 449/1057). But the *Kitāb Sharḥ al-Maqāmāt* [*al-Ḥaririyya*] has more than one possible author because many scholars wrote commentaries on the *Maqāmāt*. *Badāyiʾ al-badāyiʾ* (#987) is unidentifiable, but the scribe probably miscopied the name of the manuscript because ʿAlī b. Ẓāfir (d. 613/1216) wrote a text called *Badāyiʾ al-badāyiḥ* which should be the one we look for.

Some titles in the inventory are well-known, especially those written by Abū Manṣūr al-Thaʿālibī (d. 429/1038), Ibn al-Muqaffaʿ (d. 142/759), Ibn Nubāta al-Miṣrī (d. 768/1366) and Muḥammad b. Mūsā al-Damīrī (d. 808/1405). Furthermore, the inventory does not represent some critical titles for an *adab* section. *Kalīla wa-Dimna* by Ibn al-Muqaffaʿ (d. 142/759), for example, who, according to some, is the founder of *adab* literature, is not included in that section. The works such as *Adab al-kātib* and *ʿUyūn al-akhbār* by Ibn Qutayba (d. 276/889) are also not represented in the section, just as one of the masterpieces, the *Maqāmāt* by Hamadānī (d. 398/1008), is not either.

2 Prominent Authors

Some authors are represented by more than one title in the inventory. I will portray those prominent authors and their works to characterise the *adab* section. Saʿd al-Dīn Masʿūd al-Taftāzānī (d. 792/1390) is the most representative author of the section, appearing in fifteen titles. Four of those occurrences are related to *al-Muṭawwal*, eight to *Mukhtaṣar*, two to *Tahdhīb* [*al-Manṭiq wa-al-Kalām*] and one to *al-Maqāṣid*. Sayyid Sharīf al-Jurjānī (d. 816/1413) is another prominent author in the section; his name is related to seven titles: *Sharḥ al-Muṭawwal*, *al-Uṣūl*, *al-Mukhtaṣār* (twice), *al-Talkhīṣ* and *Sharḥ al-Mawāqif* (twice). A geographical approach to Sayyid Sharīf al-Jurjānī demonstrates that he is from Gorgan, a city in modern Iran. Another scholar from one of the cities located in modern Iran, Nishābūr, is Abū Isḥāq ʿIṣām al-Dīn Ibrāhīm al-Isfarāyīnī (d. 945/1538), who has four occurrences among titles of the section: *Sharḥ al-Muṭawwal*, *Sharḥ al-Talkhīṣ* (twice) and *al-Lubb*. Nishābūr is a city in Khorāsān.

Abū al-Qāsim b. Abī Bakr al-Laythī al-Samarqandī (d. 888/1483) has three appearances re-

18 Aljoumani, *Maktaba Madrasiyya*, 48, 49.
19 Ibrāhīm, “Makataba ʿUthmāniyya”, 34.

lated to *Sharḥ al-Muṭawwal*, *Ḥāshiya ʿalā al-Talkhīṣ* and *Matn al-Samarqandī fī al-istiʿārāt* [*farāʾid al-fawāʾid li-taḥqīq maʿānī al-istiʿārāt*] while another al-Samarqandī, Shams al-Dīn Muḥammad b. Ashraf al-Ḥusaynī al-Samarqandī (d. 702/1303) also has three occurrences, all of them related to *Kitāb fī ʿIlm al-baḥth*. As their name implies, they are from Samarqand,[20] in Uzbekistan. Therefore, in terms of geography, Khorāsān is the most prominent area of the *adab* section because al-Taftāzānī, al-Jurjānī, al-Isfarāyīnī, al-Laythī al-Samarqandī and al-Ḥusaynī al-Samarqandī penned thirty-two out of 138 titles.

The section includes four copies of *al-Talkhīṣ al-Miftāḥ* by Khaṭīb al-Qazwīnī (d. 739/1338). Therefore, although it is only one work, al-Qazwīnī has four appearances. He was from Qazvīn, now a city in the Province of Qazvin, Iran. Another renowned scholar of Islamic sciences is al-Qāḍī Bayḍāwī (d. 685/1286),[21] who has four manuscripts in the *adab* section of the inventory: two copies of *Minhāj al-uṣūl* [*Minhāj al-wuṣūl ilā ʿilm al-uṣūl*] *li-Bayḍāwī*, *al-Awwal min al-Lubb* and *Ṭawāliʿ al-anwār li-Bayḍāwī*. Al-Qāḍī Bayḍāwī is from the well-known city of Shirāz, Iran. Adding those four titles from Qazvin and another four from Shirāz to thirty-two makes up forty books. In conclusion, forty books out of 138 were penned by authors from Greater Khorasan.

3 Old Titles Listed in the Section

One of the questions in the analysis of any collection is: Which texts are the oldest? The analysis is necessarily based on the death dates of the probable authors. The oldest author who penned one of the titles listed in this section was born in 142/759, whereas the youngest died in 1196/1782. Therefore, the period of the dates of writing the titles in the current section is 759–1782, which is relatively extensive.

Yatīmat Ibn Muqaffaʿ by Ibn al-Muqaffaʿ (d. 142/759), listed in the inventory number #992, seems to be the oldest title.[22] The original name of the title is *al-Durra al-yatīma* [*fī ṭāʿat al-mulūk*], in which the author relates the importance of keeping up with the ancients to make use of their knowledge, the habits and behaviours of viziers and rulers, manners, and characteristics of the true friend.[23] The second and third oldest texts are probably *Muqaddima fī fann al-ʿarūḍ* [*wa-al-qawāfī*] (#1027) and *Kitāb fī ʿilm al-ʿarūḍ* (#1028), which are the same work and it is highly probable that they were written by Khalīl b. Aḥmad, Abū ʿAbd al-Raḥmān al-Khalīl al-Farāhīdī (d. 175/791). As the title may belong to other authors, I could not identify any work under that name. Nevertheless, it is not sure that it is the work penned by Khalīl b. Aḥmad.

Kitāb al-Ukar (#1047) by Thābit b. Qurra al-Ḥarrānī (d. 288/901) is another possible old title in the section. Because it is unclear whether this is the original work, a copy or a commentary on it, the argument relies upon the possibility that it is the work written by al-Ḥarrānī. Otherwise, the date of the text will change.

Another possible early-dated text is *al-Lumaʿ* (#969). Two possibilities occur for this title: *al-Lumaʿ* by Abū Ḥasan al-Ashʿarī (d. 324/935–936) on rational theology and *al-Lumaʿ* by Abū Isḥāq al-Shirāzī (d. 476/1083) on the principles of jurisprudence. Provided al-Ashʿarī penned it, the text is one of the oldest in the entire inventory.

20 Samarqand is also a part of (historical) Greater Khorasan, which encompasses different regions from modern Afghanistan, Iran, Turkmenistan, Tajikistan, Uzbekistan, Kyrgyzstan and Kazakhstan.

21 He is famous for his Qurʾanic commentary. For details, see Walid A. Saleh's Chapter 13 in this volume.

22 Since manuscripts in this section are not extant, in most cases, the dates still need to be determined if it is unclear whether the manuscript was an original text written by the author or a commentary, annotation or simply another copy of the original text.

23 Durmuş, "Ibnü'l-Mukaffa", 133.

4 Conclusion

The section called *al-maʿānī wa-al-bayān wa-al-ādāb wa-al-uṣūl wa-al-ʿarūḍ* in the inventory of the Jazzār library comprises 132 titles and eight supplementary titles related to the *adab* and *balāgha*, which were registered in other sections. The first question in analysing the section was: What is the rationale behind gathering all these different sciences under the same heading? My tentative answer to the question is that *ādāb* and *uṣūl* are terms used to provide the right way of doing any craft, science or skill, which serve as the glue that binds them all together.

The two most represented sciences in the section are *balāgha* and *ādāb*. Thirty-nine titles (along with two in the supplement) represent the first, whereas the second has thirty-five (along with seven in the supplement). Furthermore, the principle of jurisprudence (*uṣūl al-fiqh*) has sixteen titles. The succession of the titles in the section does not have a logical connection; for instance, the section begins with titles about eloquence, continues with the principles of jurisprudence, and follows the art of disputation between #930 and #945.

I chose two sciences to scrutinise the representativeness of the section: *balāgha* and *ādāb*. The first comprises the well-known works *Talkhīṣ al-Miftāḥ*, *al-Muṭawwal* and *Mukhtaṣar*, which are famous commentaries and annotations on *Miftāḥ al-ʿulūm*. What is curious about the *balāgha* science is that the original work, which is *Miftāḥ al-ʿulūm*, is not available in the section. One of the most noteworthy characteristics of the *ādāb* books is that many titles contain generic words, such as *majmūʿa*, *kitāb* or *risāla*, which makes it almost impossible to identify their authors. Nevertheless, the holdings of the library on *ādāb* contain some famous titles by al-Thaʿālibī, al-Miṣrī and al-Damīrī. On the other hand, *Kalīla wa-Dimna* by Ibn al-Muqaffaʿ, *Adab al-kātib* and *ʿUyūn al-akhbār* by Ibn Qutayba, and *al-Maqāmāt* by Hamadānī are not part of the library's holdings.

Most of the authors of works on eloquence, such as Saʿd al-Dīn Masʿūd al-Taftāzānī, Sayyid Sharīf al-Jurjānī, Abū Isḥāq ʿIṣām al-Dīn Ibrāhīm al-Isfarāyīnī, Abū al-Qāsim b. Abī Bakr al-Laythī al-Samarqandī, Shams al-Dīn Muḥammad b. Ashraf al-Ḥusaynī al-Samarqandī, Khāṭib al-Qazwīnī and al-Qāḍī Bayḍāvī, were from Gorgan, Nishābūr, Samarqand, Qazvīn and Shirāz whereas most of the authors of *ādāb* titles were from modern Egypt, Saudi Arabia, Syria, North Africa, as their attribution (*nisba*), for example, 'Miṣrī', 'Qāhirī', 'Ḥijāzī', 'Dimashqī' and 'Maghribī', demonstrates.

The period of the writing of the titles ranges from ca. 142/759 to ca. 1196/1782. The oldest title, provided the author himself penned it, is *Yatīmat Ibn Muqaffaʿ* by Ibn al-Muqaffaʿ, written before 142/759.

Bibliography

Açıl, Berat. "Akl-ı Selimden Zevk-i Selime: 'Edebiyat' Kelimesinin İlk Kullanımı ve Anlamı." *İnsan ve Toplum Dergisi* 5, no. 10 (2015): 151–166.

Açıl, Berat. "Fazıl Ahmed Paşa Koleksiyonu ve İlimler Tasnifi." *darulfunun ilahiyat* 3, no. 1 (2023): 129–152. DOI: 10.26650/di.2022.34.2.1324985

Aljoumani, Said. "Masrad Kutub Madrasat Muḥammad Başa al-ʿAẓm: Nashr wa-Dirāsat." *Majallat Maʿhad al-Makhṭūṭāt alʿArabiyya* 61, no. 2 (2017): 10–73.

Aljoumani, Said. *Maktaba Madrasiyya fī Ḥalab Nihāyat al-ʿAhd al-ʿUthmānī al-Daftar al-Mujaddad li-Kutub Waqf ʿUtmān Pasha al-Dūrikī*. Beirut, 2019.

Arıcı, Mustakim. "Başlangıçtan 19. Yüzyıla İslam Ahlak Düşüncesine Bütüncül Bir Bakış: Konu-Problem (*Mevḍūʿ-Mesāʾil*) Ayrımı Temelli Bir Literatür Tasnifi." *Ankara Üniversitesi İlahiyat Fakültesi Dergisi* 63, no. 1 (2022): 81–120.

Burak, Guy. "On the Order of the Sciences He Who Wants to Learn Them." In *A Handbook and Reader of Ottoman Arabic*, edited by Esther-Miriam Wagner, 39–42. Cambridge, 2021.

Durmuş, İsmail. "Ibnü'l-Mukaffa." In *Türkiye Diyanet Vakfı İslam Ansiklopedisi* (*Encyclopaedia of Islam*). Ankara.

Hämeen-Anttila, Jaakko. "Adab a) Arabic, early developments." In *EI* (*Encyclopaedia of Islam*), Third Edition.

https://referenceworks.brill.com/display/entries/EI3O/COM-24178.xml?rskey=gkICta&result=6 (accessed 2 February 2023).

Ibrāhīm, ʿAbd al-Laṭīf. "Makataba ʿUthmāniyya: Dirāsa Naqdiyya wa-Nashr li-Rāṣid al-Maktaba." *Majallat Kulliyyāt al-Ādāb* xx, no. 2 (1958): 1–35.

Kızılkaya, Necmettin. "From Means to Goal: Auxiliary Disciplines in the Ottoman *Madrasa* Curriculum." In *A Handbook and Reader of Ottoman Arabic*, edited by Esther-Miriam Wagner, 23–38. Cambridge, 2021.

Mukhliṣ, ʿAbd Allāh. "Kitāb Rawdat al-Faṣāḥah." *Majallat al-Majmaʿ al-ʿIlmī al-ʿArabī bi-Dimashq* 22, no. 5 (1947): 418–426.

Mukhliṣ, ʿAbd Allāh. "Kitāb Taḥrīr al-Taḥbīr fī ʿIlm Badīʿ." *Majallat al-Majmaʿ al-ʿIlmī al-ʿArabī bi-Dimashq* 22, no. 6 (1947): 524–531.

Pellat, Charles. "ADAB II Adab in Arabic Literature." in *Encyclopedia Iranica*. http://iranicaonline.org/articles/adab-ii-arabic-lit (accessed 2 February 2023).

El-Rouayheb, Khaled, "al-Isfarāyīnī, ʿIṣām al-Dīn." *EI* (*Encyclopaedia of Islam*), Third Edition. https://referenceworks.brillonline.com/entries/encyclopaedia-of-islam-3/al-isfarayini-isam-al-din-COM_35720?s.num=1&s.rows=20&s.mode=DEFAULT&s.f.s2_parent=encyclopaedia-of-islam-3&s.start=0&s.q=istiara (accessed 14 March 2024).

Sezer, Yavuz. "The Architecture of Bibliophilia: Eighteenth-Century Ottoman Libraries." PhD Diss., Massachusetts Institute of Technology, 2016.

The al-maʿānī wa-al-bayān wa-al-ādāb wa-al-uṣūl wa-al-ʿarūḍ *Books*

[930] ***al-Muṭawwal***, AUTHOR: Saʿd al-Dīn Masʿūd al-Taftāzānī (d. 792/1390), EDITION: Aḥmad b. Ṣāliḥ al-Sudays, Riyadh, Maktabat al-Rushd 2019.

[931] ***al-Muṭawwal***, see #930.

[932] ***al-Muṭawwal***, see #930.

[933] ***al-Muṭawwal***, see #930.

[934] ***Sharḥ al-Muṭawwal***, AUTHOR: There are numerous authors for this work. To itemise a few of them: Abū Isḥāq ʿIṣām al-Dīn Ibrāhīm al-Isfarāyīnī (d. 945/1538), Sayyid Sharīf al-Jurjānī (d. 816/1413), Ḥasan b. Muḥammad Shāh al-Fanārī (d. 886/1482) and Abū al-Qāsim b. Abī Bakr al-Laythī al-Samarqandī (d. 888/1483).

[935] ***Ḥāshiyat Mullāzādah ʿalā al-Muṭawwal***, AUTHOR: Mullāzādah Niẓām al-Dīn Aḥmad b. ʿUthmān al-Khiṭāʾī (d. 901/1495).

[936] ***Ḥāshiyat al-Sharīf fī al-uṣūl***. There are two possibilities in identifying this work: 1) *Ḥāshiyya ʿalā al-Talwīḥ*, AUTHOR: al-Sayyid al-Sharīf al-Jurjānī (d. 816/1413), and 2) *Ḥāshiyya ʿalā Sharḥ Mukhtaṣar al-Muntahā*, AUTHOR: al-Sayyid al-Sharīf al-Jurjānī (d. 816/1413).

[937] ***Ḥāshiyat Mullā ʿAbd Allāh ʿalā* al-Khiṭāʾī**, AUTHOR: Mullāzāda Niẓām al-Dīn ʿUthmān b. ʿAbd Allāh al-Khiṭāʾī (d. 901/1495).

[938] ***Tahdhīb al-uṣūl***, *Tahdhīb al-Uṣūl ilā ʿilm al-uṣūl*, AUTHOR: Jamāl al-Dīn al-Ḥasan b. Yūsuf b. ʿAlī Ibn Muṭahhar al-Ḥillī (d. 726/1325), EDITION: Sayyid Muḥammad Ḥusayn, London, Muʾassasat Imam Ali, 2001.

[939] ***Tahdhīb al-uṣūl***, see #938.

[940] ***Multaqaṭ min Kitāb al-Tahdhīb***, *Multaqaṭ Tahdhīb al-Lugha*, AUTHOR: Abū al-Qāsim al-Zamakhsharī (d. 538/1144).

[941] ***Kitāb fī ʿilm al-uṣūl***, AUTHOR: There are numerous potential authors for this commentary. Ibn Malak (d. 821/1418) is the first scholar to be remembered. Some of the others are as follows: Abū ʿAbd Allāh Nāṣir al-Dīn Muḥammad b. Aḥmad b. ʿAbd al-ʿAzīz al-Qunawī al-Dimashqī (d. 764/1363), Khaṭṭāb b. Abī al-Qāsim al-Qaraḥiṣārī (d. 717/1317–1318) and ʿAbd Allāh b. Muḥammad b. al-Khabbāz (d. 692/1292–1293). EDITION: *Sharḥ al-Manār fī Uṣūl al-Fiqh* [li-Ibn Malak], Ilyas Kaplan, Beirut/Istanbul, Dār Ibn Ḥazm/Irshad Kitabevi, 2014.

[942] ***Kitāb Mīrzājān***. Though the name *kitāb* is anonymous to identify which work of the author was meant, it should be one of his works on *al-balāgha*. He authored works such as *Ḥāshiya ʿalā al-Muṭawwal*, *Ḥāshiya ʿalā Talkhīṣ al-Miftāḥ* and *Ḥāshiya ʿalā Ḥāshiyat al-Khitāʾī Mukhtaṣar al-Maʿānī*, AUTHOR: Mīrzā-

jān Ḥabīb Allāh b. ʿAbd Allāh al-Shirāzī (d. 941/1585).

[943] ***Sharḥ al-Manār***, AUTHOR: There are numerous potential authors for this commentary. Ibn Malak (d. 821/1418) is the first scholar to be remembered. Some of the others are as follows: Abū ʿAbd Allāh Nāṣir al-Dīn Muḥammad b. Aḥmad b. ʿAbd al-Azīz al-Qunawī al-Dimashqī (d. 764/1363), Khaṭṭāb b. Abī al-Qāsim al-Qaraḥiṣārī (d. 717/1317–1318) and ʿAbd Allāh b. Muḥammad b. al-Khabbāz (d. 692/1292–1293). EDITION: *Sharḥ al-Manār fī Uṣūl al-Fiqh* li-İbn Malak, Ilyas Kaplan, Beirut/Istanbul, Dār Ibn Ḥazm/Irshad Kitabevi, 2014.

[944] ***Kitāb fī ʿilm al-uṣūl***, see #941.

[945] ***Kitāb fī ʿilm al-baḥth lil-Samarqandī wa-maʿahu Ādāb al-mawlawī***, AUTHOR: Shams al-Dīn Muḥammad b. Ashraf al-Ḥusaynī al-Samarqandī (d. 702/1303).

[946] ***Risāla fī ādāb al-baḥth***, AUTHOR: Shams al-Dīn Muḥammad b. Ashraf al-Ḥusaynī al-Samarqandī (d. 702/1303).

[947] ***Risāla fī ādāb al-baḥth***, see #946.

[948] ***Talkhīṣ al-Miftāḥ fī al-maʿānī wa-al-bayān***, AUTHOR: al-Khaṭīb al-Qazwīnī (d. 739/1338), EDITION: ʿAbd al-Raḥmān al-Barqūqī, Qahira, 1932.

[949] ***Talkhīṣ al-Miftāḥ***, see #948.

[950] ***Talkhīṣ al-Miftāḥ***, see #948.

[951] ***Talkhīṣ al-Miftāḥ***, see #948.

[952] ***Sharḥ al-Talkhīṣ***, AUTHOR: Many scholars are potential authors for this work, such as Muḥammad b. al-Muwaffaq al-Qayṣarī (d. 761/1359–1360), Muḥammad b. ʿUthmān b. Muḥammad al-Zawzanī (d. 792/1389–1390), Akmal al-Dīn Muḥammad b. Maḥmūd b. Aḥmad al-Bābartī (d. 786/1384) and Abū Isḥāq ʿIṣām al-Dīn Ibrāhīm al-Isfarāyīnī (d. 945/1538), EDITION: [for that of Bābartī], Ramaḍān Ṣūfiyya, Ṭarāblus, al-Mansha' al-ʿĀmm li-Nashr wa-Tawziʿ, 1983.

[953] ***Sharḥ al-Talkhīṣ***, see #952.

[954] ***Sharḥ al-Talkhīṣ lil-Subkī***, AUTHOR: Abū Ḥāmid Bahā' al-Dīn Aḥmad b. ʿAlī ʿAbd al-Kāfī al-Subkī (d. 773/1372).

[955] ***Mukhtaṣar al-Maʿānī wa-al-bayān***, AUTHOR: Saʿd al-Dīn Masʿūd al-Taftāzānī (d. 792/1390), EDITION: Maktabat al-Bushrā, Karachi/Pakistan, 2010.

[956] ***Mukhtaṣar***, see #955.

[957] ***Mukhtaṣar***, see #955.

[958] ***Mukhtaṣar***, see #955.

[959] ***Mukhtaṣar***, see #955.

[960] ***Sharḥ al-Mukhtaṣar lil-Saʿd al-Taftāzānī***, AUTHOR: Saʿd al-Dīn Masʿūd al-Taftāzānī (d. 792/1390), EDITION: Ghulām ʿAlī Muḥammadī al-Bamyānī, *Durūs al-Balāgha: Sharḥ Mukhtaṣar al-Maʿānī lil-Taftāzānī*, Beirut, 2008.

[961] ***Sharḥ al-Mukhtaṣar***, see #960.

[962] ***Adhhān al-adhkiyā' Sharḥ al-Talkhīṣ***, Unidentified.

[963] ***Ḥāshiya ʿalā al-Mukhtaṣār lil-Jurjānī***, AUTHOR: al-Sayyid al-Sharīf al-Jurjānī (d. 816/1413). Two possibilities occur for this item: it is either ***Ḥāshiya ʿalā Sharḥ al-Mukhtaṣār al-muntahā***, an annotation on al-Ījī or ***al-Dībāj al-mudhhab***, an original work, both by al-Sayyid al-Sharīf al-Jurjānī.

[964] ***Ḥāshiya ʿalā al-Mukhtaṣār*** [*al-Muntahā*] ***lil-Jurjānī***, see #963.

[965] ***Ḥāshiya ʿalā al-Talkhīṣ***, AUTHOR: A few scholars are probable authors of this work. The most probable one is al-Sayyid al-Sharīf al-Jurjānī (d. 816/1413), while others, such as Mīrzājān Ḥabīb Allāh b. ʿAbd Allāh al-Shirāzī (d. 941/1585), Abū al-Qāsim b. Abī Bakr al-Laythī al-Samarqandī (d. 888/1483) and ʿUthmān Faḍlī al-Atpazarī/Osmân Fazlî Atpazarı (d. 1102/1691) are possible. As we do not have manuscripts from the *ādāb* section of the Jazzār library at hand, it is impossible to identify which one of the four scholars penned this manuscript.

[966] ***Sharḥ al-Miṣbāḥ***, AUTHOR: The original work *Miṣbāḥ* was written by Abū al-Fatḥ Burhān al-Dīn Nāṣir al-Muṭarrizī (d. 610/1213) and more than fifty commentaries were written on it. The most famous one is *al-Ḍaw' Sharḥ al-Miṣbāḥ* by Tāj al-Dīn Muḥammad b. Muḥammad al-Isfarāyīnī (d. 684/1285).

[967] *Minhāj al-wuṣūl ilā ʿIlm al-Uṣūl*, AUTHOR: al-Qāḍī al-Bayḍāwī (d. 685/1286), Zayn al-Dīn ʿAbd al-Raḥīm b. Ḥusayn al-ʿIrāqī, Risāla Publishing, Damascus/Beirut, 2013.

[968] ***Kitāb fī ʿilm al-maʿānī***. Unidentified.

[969] ***al-Lumaʿ***, AUTHOR: Two possible authors occur for this work, the first one is Abū Ḥasan al-Ashʿarī (d. 324/935–936) on rational theology and the second one is Abū Isḥāq al-Shirāzī (d. 476/1083) on the principles of jurisprudence. As this part of the inventory contains *al-balāgha* and principles of jurisprudence works, the name of the work is probably *al-Lumaʿ fī Uṣūl al-Fiqh* by al-Shirāzī. EDITION: Yūsuf ʿAbd al-Raḥmān al-Marʿashlī, Beirut, 1985.

[970] ***Kitāb fī al-maʿānī wa-al-bayān***. Unidentified.

[971] ***Kitāb fī al-maʿānī wa-al-bayān***, see #970.

[972] ***Kitāb al-Mukhtaṣar***, see #955.

[973] ***Khizānat al-adab*** *wa-Ghāyat al-Arab*, AUTHOR: Ibn Ḥijja (d. 837/1434), EDITION: Qahira, 1304.

[974] ***Majmūʿa fī al-adab***. Unidentified.

[975] ***Majmūʿa fī al-adab***, see #974.

[976] ***Thamarāt al-awrāq*** *fī al-Muḥāḍarāt*, AUTHOR: Ibn Ḥijja (d. 837/1434), EDITION: Muḥammad Abū al-Faḍl Ibrāhīm, Qahira, 1971.

[977] ***Rawḍat al-faṣāḥa***, AUTHOR: Muḥammad b. Abū Bakr al-Rāzī (d. 666/1268), EDITION: Abdullah Kızılcık, Amman, 2005. This manuscript was preserved in the Jazzār library, Acre, until 1947. ʿAbd Allāh Mukhliṣ saw and described it.[24]

[978] ***Kitāb fī ʿilm al-adab***. Unidentified.

[979] ***Thimār al-qulūb*** *fī al-muḍāf wa-al-mansūb*, AUTHOR: Abū Manṣūr al-Thaʿālibī (d. 429/1038), EDITION: Muḥammad Abū al-Faḍl Ibrāhīm, Qahira, 1965.

[980] ***Sharḥ al-ʿuyūn*** *fī Sharḥ Risālat Ibn Zaydūn*, AUTHOR: Ibn Nubāta al-Miṣrī (d. 768/1366), EDITION: Muḥammad Abū al-Faḍl Ibrāhīm, Qahira, 1964. It is the commentary on the ironic epistle transmitted from the Caliph Mustakfī-bi-llāh's daughter by Ibn Zaydūn. See https://islamansiklopedisi.org.tr/ibn-nubate-el-misri.

[981] ***Maʿānī al-akhlāq***. Unidentified.

[982] ***Taḥrīr al-taḥbīr*** *fī ʿIlm al-Badīʿ Ṣināʿat al-Shiʿr wa-al-Nathr wa-Bayān Iʿjāz al-Qurʾān*, AUTHOR: Ibn Abī Iṣbaʿ, Abū Muḥammad Zakī al-Dīn ʿAbd al-ʿAẓīm al-Miṣrī (d. 654/1256), EDITION: Ḥifnī Muḥammad Sharaf, Qahira, 1963. This manuscript was in the Jazzār library, Acre until 1947. ʿAbd Allāh Mukhliṣ saw and described it.[25] See https://islamansiklopedisi.org.tr/ibn-ebul-isba

[983] ***Risālat al-Adab***. Unidentified.

[984] ***Al-Luʾluʾ al-naẓīm fī*** *[Rawm]* ***al-taʿallum wa-al-taʿlīm***, AUTHOR: Zakariyā al-Anṣārī (d. 926/1520), EDITION: ʿAbd Allāh Nadhīr Aḥmad, Beirut, 1998.

[985] ***Sharḥ Qaṣīdat al-adab***. Unidentified.

[986] ***Qalaʾid al-ʿiqyān***, AUTHOR: There are two possibilities for the work's author: 1) The author is Marʿī b. Yūsuf (d. 1033/1624), thus the name of the work is *Qalāʾid al-Iqyān fī Faḍāʾil Mulūk Āl ʿUthmān*, or 2) the name of the author is Abū Naṣr al-Fatḥ b. Muḥammad b. ʿUbayd Allāh b. Khāqān b. ʿAbd Allāh al-Qaysī al-Ishbīlī (d. 529/1134) and the name of the work is *Qalāʾid al-ʿIqyān fī Maḥāsin al-Ruʾasā wa-al-Quḍāt wa-al-Kuttāb wa-al-Aʿyān*, EDITION: H. Peres, Algiers, 1946.

[987] ***Badāyiʾ al-badāyiʾ***, AUTHOR: I could not find any work under that name. The most probable outcome is *Badāyiʾ al-Badāyiḥ* by ʿAlī b. Ẓāfir (d. 613/1216), EDITION: Muḥammad Abū al-Faḍl Ibrāhīm, Qahira, 1970.

[988] ***Matlaʿ al-fawāʾid*** *wa-Majmaʿ al-Farāʾid*, AUTHOR: Ibn Nubāta al-Miṣrī (d. 768/1366), EDITION: ʿUmar Mūsā Bāshā, Dimashq, 1972.

[989] ***Khabāyā al-zawāyā***, AUTHOR: Abū ʿAbd Allāb Badr al-Dīn al-Zarkashī (d. 794/1392), EDITION: Ayman Ṣāliḥ Shaʿbān, Beirut, 1996.

24 Mukhliṣ, "Kitāb Rawḍat al-Faṣāḥa".

25 Mukhliṣ, "Kitāb Taḥrīr al-Taḥbīr fī ʿIlm Badīʿ".

[990] *Fatḥ munzil al-mathānī bi-**Sharḥ Aqṣā al-amānī***, AUTHOR: Zakariyā al-Anṣārī (d. 926/1520), EDITION: Ḥamzā al-Damīrdāsh Zaghlūl, Qahira, 1988.

[991] ***Sharḥ al-Kāfī al-badīʿ al-musammā bi-al-Natāʾij***, AUTHOR: Abū al-Maḥāsin Ṣafī al-Dīn ʿAbd al-Azīz b. Sarāyā b. ʿAlī al-Ḥillī (d. 749/1348), EDITION: Nasīb Nashāwī, Dimashq, 1983.

[992] ***Yatīmat Ibn al-Muqaffaʿ***, AUTHOR: Ibn al-Muqaffaʿ (d. 142/759), EDITION: al-Amīr Shakib Arslan, Dār al-Muktasib, Dimashq, 2014.

[993] ***Ghurar al-Dalāʾil wa-al-āyāt***, AUTHOR: Yūsuf b. Nāṣir b. Muḥammad al-Mashhadī al-Najafī (d. 727/1327).

[994] ***Barāʿat al-tawassul***. Unidentified.

[995] ***Mā Yuktab maqṣūran wa-mamdūdan***, AUTHOR: This is a generic name for the literature on Arabic words that end with *alif maqṣūra* and *alif mamdūda*. See https://islamansiklopedisi.org.tr/maksur-ve-memdud. The most famous work was written by Abū Bakr Muḥammad al-Ḥasan b. Durayd al-Azdī al-Baṣrī (d. 321/933) in the form of a *qaṣīda* under the name of *Qaṣīda fī Maʿrifat al-Maqṣūr wa-al-Mamdūd*, EDITION: Muḥammad Badr al-Dīn al-ʿAlawī, Qahira, 1949.

[996] ***Kitāb al-Marj al-naḍir***, AUTHOR: al-Sharīf Ṣalāḥ al-Dīn al-Asyūṭī (d. 859/1454–1455).

[997] ***Ḥalabat al-kumayt***, AUTHOR: Shams al-Dīn Muḥammad b. Ḥasan b. ʿAlī b. ʿUthmān al-Nawājī al-Qāhirī (d. 859/1455), EDITION: ʿAbd al-Qādir ʿAllām, Qahira, 1938.

[998] ***Fihrist al-Nadīm***, AUTHOR: Muḥammad b. Isḥāq al-Nadīm (d. 990), EDITION: Gustav Flügel, Johannes Roediger and August Mueller, Leipzig, 1871–1872; edited by Ramazan Şeşen, Istanbul, 2019, MANUSCRIPT: Dublin, Chester Beatty Library, Ar. 3315, https://viewer.cbl.ie/viewer/image/Ar_3315/13/

[999] ***al-Mushtarik waḍʿan*** *wa-al-Muftariq (Mukhtalif) Ṣuqʿan*, AUTHOR: Abū ʿAbd Allāh Shihāb al-Dīn Yāqūt b. ʿAbd Allāh al-Ḥamawī al-Baghdādī al-Rūmī (d. 626/1229), EDITION: F. Wüstenfeld, Göttingen, 1946.

[1000] ***Majmūʿa min ʿulūm shattā***. Unidentified.

[1001] *al-Awwal min **al-Lubb***, AUTHOR: The nature of the work is unidentifiable since many titles contain *al-Lubb*. I will itemise just titles about grammar, *al-adab* or *al-balāgha* because the part of the section of the inventory lists works related to these sciences: *Lubb al-Albāb fī ʿIlm al-Iʿrāb* by al-Qāḍī al-Bayḍāwī (d. 685/1286), Abū Isḥāq ʿIṣām al-Dīn Ibrāhīm al-Isfarāyīnī (d. 945/1538), or *Lubb al-Ādāb* by Abū Manṣūr al-Thaʿālibī (d. 429/1038) are probable titles, but some other works may also be the intended one.

[1002] ***al-Maqālāt al-muhdhiba***. Unidentified.

[1003] ***Mukhtaṣar al-Mukātabāt al-badīʿa***, AUTHOR: Muḥammad b. ʿAbd al-Raḥmān Ibn al-Ṣayrafī (d. 13th century), MANUSCRIPT: Jerusalem, Khalidi Library, MS 966, https://www.vhmml.org/readingRoom/view/509463

[1004] ***al-Shifāʾ fī badīʿ al-iktifā***, AUTHOR: Shams al-Dīn Muḥammad b. Ḥasan b. ʿAlī b. ʿUthmān al-Nawājī al-Qāhirī (d. 859/1455), EDITION: Maḥmūd Ḥasan Abū Nājī, Beirut, 1983.

[1005] ***al-Durar al-madrūza Sharḥ al-Arjūza***, AUTHOR: Manṣūr b. ʿAlī al-Maḥallī al-Suṭūḥī, al-Azharī (d. 1066/1656), EDITION: Zakaria Tonani, al-Jouf, 2020.

[1006] ***Ghurar al-maʿānī wa-al-nukat Sharḥ al-Maqāmāt***, AUTHOR: Abū ʿAbbās al-Sharīshī (d. 619/1222), EDITION: Muḥammad Abū al-Faḍl Ibrāhīm, Beirut, 1992.

[1007] ***Zahr al-ādāb*** *wa-thamar al-albāb*, AUTHOR: Abū Isḥāq al-Ḥuṣrī (d. 413/1022), EDITION: ʿAlī Muḥammad al-Bijāwī, Qahira, 1969.

[1008] ***al-Hafawāt al-nādira*** *wa-al-Saqatāt al-Bādirah*, AUTHOR: Abū al-Ḥasan Muḥammad b. Hilāl b. Muḥassin al-Ṣābī (d. 480/1088).

[1009] ***Kitāb al-Nuzha al-wajīza***. Unidentified.

[1010] ***Majmūʿ laṭīfa fī kull maʿnā Ẓarīf***. Unidentified.

[1011] ***al-Majmūʿa al-laṭīfa***. Unidentified.

[1012] ***Safīnat al-najāt***, AUTHOR: Mullā Muḥsin Muḥammad b. Shāh Murtaḍā b. Shāh Maḥmūd Kāshānī (d. 1090/1679).

[1013] ***Mukātabāt al-Khwārizmī*** *Rasāʾil* or *Dīwān al-*

Rasā'il, AUTHOR: Abū Bakr Jamāl al-Dīn al-Ṭabarī al-Khwarizmī (d. 383/993), EDITION: Nasīb Wahībah Ḥazīn, Beirut, 1970.

[1014] ***Kitāb Murāsalāt** Badīʿ al-Inshā' wa-al-Ṣifāt fī al-Mukātabāt wa-al-Murāsalāt*, AUTHOR: Zayn al-Dīn Marʿī b. Yūsuf al-Karmī (d. 1033/1624).

[1015] ***Rawḍat al-qulūb wa-nuzhat al-maḥbūb***, AUTHOR: ʿAbd al-Raḥmān al-Shayzarī (d. 589/1193?), EDITION: George J. Kanazi, Wiesbaden, 2003.

[1016] ***Mukhtār Qalā'id al-ʿaqīm***. Unidentified.

[1017] ***Kitāb al-Muraṣṣaʿ fī al-kitābāt wa-al-iḍāfāt** al-Muraṣṣaʿ fī al-Ābā ' wa-al-Ummahāt wa-al-Banīn wa-al-Banāt wa-al-Adhwā ' wa-al-dhawāt*, AUTHOR: Majd al-Dīn Ibn al-Athīr (d. 606/1210), EDITION: Christian Friedrich Seybold, Weimar, 1896; Fahmī Saʿd, Beirut, 1992.

[1018] ***Rasā'il Abī Bakr al-Khwārizmī** Dīwān al-Rasa'il*, see #1013.

[1019] ***Tarḥ al-madr li-ḥall al-la'ālī wa-al-durar***, AUTHOR: Yūsuf b. Muḥammad al-Shirbīnī (d. 1098/1687), EDITION: Muḥammad Khayr Ramaḍān Yūsuf, Dār Ibn Ḥazm, Beirut, 2003.

[1020] ***Murāsalāt Zayn al-ʿĀbidīn al-Ṣiddīqī***, most probably *Riyāḍ al-ʿārifīn fī murāsalāt al-ustādh Muḥammad Zayn al-ʿĀbidīn*, AUTHOR: Ibrāhīm b. ʿĀmir al-ʿUbaydī (d. 1091/1680).

[1021] ***Khulāṣat Taḥqīq al-ẓunūn** fī al-shurūḥ wa-al-mutūn*, AUTHOR: Muḥammad b. Muṣṭafā b. Kamāl al-Dīn b. ʿAlī al-Bakrī (d. 1196/1782).

[1022] ***Musḥaf al-Kashf***. Unidentified.

[1023] [***Kitāb***] ***Nasīm al-ṣibā** fī funūn al-adab al-qadīm wa-al-maqāmā al-adabiyya*, AUTHOR: Abū Muḥammad Badr al-Dīn al-Ḥasan al-Dimashqī al-Ḥalabī (d. 779/1377), EDITION: Maṭbaʿa al-Jawānib, Qsṭanṭiniyya, 1302/1885.

[1024] ***al-Khazrajiyya fī ʿilm al-ʿarūḍ***, AUTHOR: ʿAbd Allāh b. Muḥammad al-Khazrajī (d. 626/1229), EDITION: Ph. Guadagnoli, *Breves arabicae linguae instituones*, Rome 1642.

[1025] ***Sharḥ al-Khazrajiyya***. Unidentified. Approximately thirty people authored such a text, which is unidentifiable from the information provided in the inventory.

[1026] ***Sharḥ al-Khazrajiyya***, see #1025.

[1027] ***Muqaddima fī fann al-ʿarūḍ** wa-al-qawāfī*, AUTHOR: Khalīl b. Aḥmad, Abū ʿAbd al-Raḥmān al-Khalīl al-Farāhīdī (d. 175/791).

[1028] ***Kitāb fī ʿilm al-ʿarūḍ***, AUTHOR: Khalīl b. Aḥmad, Abū ʿAbd al-Raḥmān al-Khalīl al-Farāhīdī (d. 175/791).

[1029] ***Sharḥ al-Andalusiyya***, AUTHOR: Muḥsin al-Qayṣarī (d. 761/1360).

[1030] ***al-Maqṣad al-wāfī** fī al-ʿarūḍ wa-al-qawāfī*, AUTHOR: Abū Bakr Muḥyī al-Dīn al-Ḥusaynī al-Ṭabarī.

[1031] ***al-Tahdhīb fi al-uṣūl** Tahdhīb al-Uṣūl ilā ʿilm al-uṣūl*, see #939.

[1032] ***Sharḥ al-Mawāqif***, AUTHOR: al-Sayyid al-Sharīf al-Jurjānī (d. 816/1413), EDITION: Maḥmūd ʿUmar Dimyātī, Dār al-Kutub al-ʿIlmiyya, Beirut, 1998.

[1033] ***Minhāj al-uṣūl** Minhāj al-Wuṣūl ilā ʿIlm al-Uṣūl **lil-Bayḍāwī***, AUTHOR: al-Qāḍī al-Bayḍāwī (d. 685/1286), EDITION: Shaʿbān Muḥammad Ismāʿīl, Dār Ibn Ḥazm, Beirut, 2008.

[1034] ***Sharḥ al-Manār***, see #943.

[1035] ***Naẓm al-Tahdhīb***. Unidentified.

[1036] (Probably) ***al-Tahdhīb*** [*al-Manṭiq wa-al-Kalām*], AUTHOR: Saʿd al-Dīn Masʿūd al-Taftāzānī (d. 792/1390), EDITION: Qahira, 1912.

[1037] ***Ḥāshiyat Mīrzājān ʿalā al-Ṭawāliʿ***, AUTHOR: Mīrzājān Ḥabīb Allāh b. ʿAbd Allāh al-Shirāzī (d. 941/1585).

[1038] (Probably) ***al-Tahdhīb*** [*al-Manṭiq wa-al-Kalām*], see #1036.

[1039] ***Ḥāshiya ʿalā al-Tahdhīb***. Unidentified. There are approximately fifty commentaries on the work, which makes it impossible to identify the author of this title.

[1040] ***Sharḥ Ṭawāliʿ al-anwār***. Unidentified. There are about ten commentaries on that work, which makes it impossible to identify the author of this title.

[1041] ***Sharḥ al-Tahdhīb***. Unidentified. There are approximately fifty commentaries on the work, making it impossible to identify the author of this title.

[1042] ***Ṭawāliʿ al-anwār lil-Bayḍāwī***, AUTHOR: al-

Qāḍī al-Bayḍāwī (d. 685/1286), EDITION: ʿAbbās Sulaymān, Beirut, 1991.

[1043] ***Lawāmiʿ al-naẓar** fī Taḥqīq Maʿānī al-Mukhtaṣar*, AUTHOR: Aḥmad b. Yaʿqūb b. al-Wāllālī (d. 1128/1716), EDITION: Ibrahim Safri, Brill, 2022.

[1044] ***Sharḥ al-Mawāqif***, see #1032.

[1045] ***Tahdhīb al-uṣūl** [fī Aḥādīth al-Rusūl] Nāqiṣ al-Ākhir*, Abū Saʿīd Ṣalāḥ al-Dīn Khalīl b. Kaykaldī (d. 761/1359).

[1046] ***Minhāj** [**Manāhij**] **al-yaqīn** fī uṣūl al-Dīn*, AUTHOR: Ibn al-Muṭahhar al-Ḥillī, al-Ḥasan b. Yūsuf (d. 726/1325), EDITION: Yaʿqub al-Jaʿfarī, Qom, 1415/1994–1995.

[1047] ***Kitāb al-Ukar***, AUTHOR: Thābit b. Qurra al-Ḥarrānī (d. 288/901).

[1048] ***Sharḥ al-Ishārāt** [wa-al-Tanbīhāt]*, AUTHOR: Though there are many commentaries on *al-Ishārāt*, the most famous one, which is also the unique one that has the title *Sharḥ al-Ishārā*, was penned by Fakhr al-Dīn al-Rāzī (d. 606/1210).

[1049] *Lawāmiʿ al-asrār fī **Sharḥ al-Maṭāliʿ** al-anwār*, AUTHOR: Though there are many commentaries on *Maṭāliʿ*, the most famous one was authored by Quṭb al-Dīn al-Rāzī (d. 766/1365).

[1050] *al-Juzʾ min **al-Maqāṣid***, AUTHOR: Saʿd al-Dīn al-Taftāzānī (d. 792/1390), EDITION: ʿAbd al-Raḥmān ʿUmayra, Beirut, 1989.

[1051] ***Jāmiʿ al-tadqīq***. Unidentified.

[1052] ***Maṭāliʿ al-anẓar** ʿalā Ṭawāliʿ al-Anwār*, AUTHOR: Maḥmūd b. ʿAbd al-Raḥmān al-Iṣfahānī (d. 749/1349).

[1053] *Lawāmiʿ al-asrār fī **Sharḥ al-Maṭāliʿ** al-anwār*, see #1049.

[1054] ***Sharḥ** Umm **al-barāhīn wa-maʿahu Rasāʾil***, AUTHOR: This should be one of the commentaries on the *Umm al-barāhīn* by Abū ʿAbd Allāh al-Sanūsī (d. 895/1490). Two commentaries among them have more copies than others: 1) Muḥammad b. ʿUmar al-Tilimsānī (d. 897/1492) and 2) Muḥammad b. Manṣūr al-Hudhudī (d. 895/1490).

[1055] ***Sharḥ al-Tajrīd, al-Jawhar al-naḍīḍ***, AUTHOR: Jamāl al-Dīn Ḥasan, Ibn Muṭahhar al-Ḥillī (d. 726/1325), EDITION: Muhsin Bidarfar, Tehran 1384/2005–2006.

[1056] ***Murāsalāt Abī al-ʿAlāʾ***, AUTHOR: Though I could not find a manuscript with this title, Abū al-ʿAlāʾ al-Maʿarrī (d. 449/1057) has numerous *risālas*. Therefore, it is highly probable that he penned this work.

[1057] ***Sharḥ Naẓm al-istiʿāra***, AUTHOR: Abu Saʿd Zayn al-Dīn Manṣūr al-Ṭablawī (d. 1014/1606).

[1058] ***Majmūʾ yashtamil ʿalā Sharḥ al-Istiʿāra li-ʿIṣām wa-ḥawāshī ʿalayh***, AUTHOR: The miscellany comprises the commentary by ʿIṣām al-Dīn Ibrāhīm al-Isfarāyīnī (d. 945/1538) on *al-Istiʿāra* by al-Samarqandī and some other annotations.

[1059] ***Matn al-Samarqandiyya fī al-istiʿārāt** Farāʾid al-Fawāʾid li-Taḥqīq Maʿānī al-Istiʿārāt*, AUTHOR: Abū al-Qāsim b. Abī Bakr al-Laythī al-Samarqandī (d. 888/1483), EDITION: Abderrezzak Lacheref, *La Samarhkandya: Petit traite de rhetorique arabe, Alger, 1905.*

[1060] ***Khuṭab Jumʿa***, AUTHOR: (Probably) Ibn Nubāta al-Khaṭīb (d. 374/984). Nevertheless, there were some other probable authors.

[1061] ***Khuṭbat al-Kusūf***. Unidentified.

Works of adab *from the provenanced sections of the inventory*

Works taken from the library of al-Sayyid Yaḥyā Efendī b. al-Sayyid Muḥammad al-Ṭībī of Jaffa in 1218/1803

[526] ***Kitāb Ḥayāt al-ḥayawān***, AUTHOR: Muḥammad b. Mūsā al-Damīrī (d. 808/1405), EDITION: A.S.G., Jayakar, 1906, London, Luzac. https://archive.org/details/addamrsaytalayaoodamgoog

[580] ***Kitāb Qalamiyyat Mawlānā Muḥammad Afandī, Shaykh al-Ḥaram***, AUTHOR: Mawlānā Muḥammad Efendi, Shaykh al-Ḥaram (d. ?)

[589] ***Kitāb al-Murqiṣ wa-al-muṭrib** ʿUnwān al-Murqiṣāt wa-al-Muṭribāt*, AUTHOR: Ibn Saʿīd al-Maghribī (d. 685/1286), EDITION: ʿAbd al-Qādir Mahdād, Algeria, 1942.

[590] ***Kitāb Sharḥ al-Alfāẓ al-lughawiyya wa-al-maqāmāt al-Ḥarīriyya** Sharḥ mā fī al-Maqāmāt al-Ḥarīriyya min al-Alfaẓ al-Lughawiyya*, AUTHOR:

Muḥibb al-Dīn Abī al-Baqā ʿAbd Allāh b. Ḥusayn al-ʿUkbarī (d. 616/1219), EDITION: Muḥammad Rajab Dīb, Beirut, 1992.

Works taken from the libraries of al-Shaykh ʿAlī al-Rashīdī and al-Shaykh Muḥammad Wakīlkharaj in 1216/1801

[1634] ʿAn ***Kitāb Sharḥ al-Maqāmāt lil-Shaykh al-Zaynī***, AUTHOR: Numerous possible authors.

[1665] ***Kitāb bi-ʿilm al-istiʿārāt***. Unidentified.

[1689] ***Kitāb Zahr al-rabīʿ fī Shawāhid al-badīʿ***, AUTHOR: Muḥammad b. ʿAbd Allāh b. Qurqumāz (d. 883/1478).

Work classified in the history section

[1365] ***al-Durar al-manẓūma min al-nukat wa-al-ishārāt al-mafhūma***, AUTHOR: Shihāb al-Dīn Aḥmad b. Muḥammad b. ʿAlī al-Ḥijāzī (d. 875/1470).

CHAPTER 20

Logic in the Jazzār Collection (*manṭiq*)

Asad Q. Ahmed

The Logic section of the Jazzār library consists of several works considered to be elementary and intermediate in the training of a scholar in the discipline. The vast majority of the works are post-Avicennan, with the base/handbook texts issuing from the seventh/thirteenth century. The former category includes works such as Athīr al-Dīn al-Abharī's (d. 663/1265) *Īsāghūjī*, and Najm al-Dīn al-Kātibī's (675/1276) *Shamsiyya* would fall in the latter category. More advanced works, such as Sirāj al-Dīn al-Urmawī's (682/1283) *Maṭāliʿ*, are not represented in this library, nor, indeed, is there a presence of Jalāl al-Dīn al-Dawānī's (d. 908/1502) contribution to the field, something that is rather unexpected given the regional importance of his commentary on Saʿd al-Dīn al-Taftāzānī's (793/1390) *Tahdhīb*. This absence, among others noted below, might suggest that the intellectual sphere of the collection is probably North African. Some of the second-order commentaries on the *Shamsiyya* mentioned in the list were actually more advanced engagements, but their intertextual links can only be verified based on the study of the actual manuscripts. Beyond this general trend, a work by Avicenna is found in the list. It often served as a point of reference for the study of later texts. On occasion, the list may indicate strange cataloguing choices. It appears, for example, that the commentary by Mullā Jāmī (d. 898/1492) is actually on a rather well-known work of grammar, via the commentarial intermediary of ʿAḍud al-Dīn al-Ījī (756/1355). But this cannot be verified based on the list alone. Perhaps a more suitable option is that the commentary by Jāmī is on al-Ījī's *Risālā waḍʿiyya*, a work on semantic theory; but the popular commentary on this work was by Abū al-Qāsim al-Samarqandī (ca. 888/1483), with Jāmī's work receiving limited attention. The logic of the inclusion of the former possibility in this section, if it is not by error, may tell us something about the conception of disciplinary boundaries. Overall, this appears to be a basic and relatively minimal collection of recognisable works in the field. Further investigation into the marginalia and points of origin may shed light on how these works were used and precisely which topics were of interest to the patrons.

The history of the emergence and development of logic in the Arabo-Islamic tradition has been explored in various publications; thus, only a brief statement is suitable for this article.[1] The study of the discipline has its roots in the major translation project of the ʿAbbāsids (r. 132/750–656/1258). Initially, work in logic appealed to texts in Syriac and Pahlavi as a mediating layer; but this was quickly replaced by a focus on Aristotelian texts. By the middle of the third/ninth century, the entire *Organon* of Aristotle was available in Arabic translation. By the end of this same century, epitomes and overviews had been produced, further translation activities initiated and an investment in the work of Galen (216 CE) was pronounced. The increasingly exclusive inclination towards Aristotle picked up speed in the fourth/tenth century, often seen as a continuation of the commentarial practices of Late Antiquity, in the work of such scholars as Abū Naṣr al-Fārābī (d. 339/950). In the next phase, Fārābīan Aristotelianism was challenged in the magisterial work of Avicenna (d. 428/1037); this became the logic of the East.

1 Street, "Arabic Logic"; Street, "Kātibī"; Street, "Logic"; El-Rouayheb, "Arabic Logic"; El-Rouayheb, *Development*; El-Rouayheb, "Transformation"; Strobino, "Ibn Sina"; Ahmed, "Logic".

While a tradition of Aristotelian logic continued to flourish in North Africa and Iberia, it is Avicenna's contributions and syntheses that became the focal point of attention for a lot of the rest of the Islamic world. But just as Aristotle had been challenged and replaced by Avicenna, so the latter's contributions were critically assessed in the two centuries following his death. The dialectical spaces of diachronic contention ultimately resulted in the seventh/thirteenth-century handbooks that became the mainstay of the *madrasa* tradition. These base texts of the seventh/thirteenth century, some of their gateway commentaries, and other occasional base texts emerging out of the dialectics and critiques of the latter two constituted the foundation of logical training in the Islamic East, encompassing the Ottoman, Safavid and Mughal worlds. It is these three general types of works that continued to receive rich commentarial attention until the advent of modernity.[2] Unsurprisingly, it is some of these same works that appear in the list of the Jazzār Library, although some texts suggest a distinctly north African orientation.

A major methodological issue that one faces in writing about the Jazzār collection is one's reliance on the list alone. As I note below, a good number of works in the list have no authorial attribution; this is especially true of commentaries, where works often appear as *Sharḥ x*. In such cases, I have assumed that the allusion is to the most recognisable gateway commentary on the base text. However, if this assumption is incorrect, then much is lost in our understanding of the intentions and uses of the collection. A related issue is that significant work in the field of logic during the post-classical period (ca. 1200–1900 CE) was done in the form of marginal commentaries, and the latter are often embedded within a text without attribution. A work, for example, may be advertised as a commentary by Quṭb al-Dīn al-Taḥtānī (766/1365) on the *Shamsiyya* of al-Kātibī; yet, the full scope of the substantive aspects of the specific manuscript can only be evaluated based on the copious marginalia scattered throughout the pages. It is often within the lines of these marginalia that the living oral and written modes of the text's usage by the community of scholars and readers is revealed. Since I do not have access to the manuscripts, it is impossible to judge what the ultimate function of a work in the collection might be. In other words, it may be the case that, although the collection may be said to contain elementary works, their *Sitz im Leben* is lost to us. Marginalia may highlight a robust and sophisticated engagement with advanced features of logic.[3]

The logic section of the library of Aḥmad Pāshā al-Jazzār (d. 1804) is comparable to similar collections from this period and region. The relative quantity of logic works is minimal and the titles are generally those used in the elementary and intermediate levels of training in the discipline. The collection does not appear to have been invested in accumulating rare works, innovative critical pieces, or items across the historical and geographical range of logical studies in the Islamic tradition. Although the study of logic, indeed, constituted an important part of the training of students in the eighteenth century Ottoman world, the Jazzār and other similar libraries generally do not reflect this state of affairs. The ʿUthmān Pāshā al-Dūrikī library in Aleppo, for example, that consists of 1200 titles, contains only five distinct works on logic.[4] Similarly, the Mullā ʿUthmān al-Kurdī collection in Damascus comprised 462 titles, but had only seven works on logic.[5] We may also compare the inventory of titles in the Topkapi Palace

2 For further on theories of commentarial production, see Ahmed, *Palimpsests*. In this latter work, further details about the development of this tradition of logic in the South Asian landscape are also provided. See especially 26–36 for a broad historical overview of the works of logic relevant to South Asia and a sketch of the history of their passage to the region. Additional details are found in Ahmed, "Logic".

3 See Ahmed, *Palimpsests*.

4 Aljoumani, "Maktaba", 99–101.

5 Aljoumani, "Tārīkh maktabat al-Mullā ʿUthmān al-Kurdī", 232–234.

book treasury in Istanbul that was commissioned by the Ottoman sultan Bāyezīd II in 908/1501–1502. As with the collections noted above, so here the section on logic appears towards the end of the list and contains only 116 titles devoted to logic and dialectics. Insofar as the order may reflect a hierarchy of the sciences in terms of their nobility, the status of logic appears to be rather low. However, given what is generally known about the Ottoman systems of education, this order may concern the status of the various disciplines within the classification of the sciences based on their subject matters; it need not suggest that the value of logic as a necessary instrument for other sciences had declined or that it was not considered to be central to the training of students. The case is similar with the list at hand: manuscripts concerned with the transmitted religious sciences (exegesis, Prophetic Sayings, law, and so on) appear first and in considerably greater quantities in the Jazzār collection. There are only forty-seven entries for the discipline of logic, with several, such as the *Īsāghūjī* (three of the base texts and another five to six of its commentaries, depending on attribution), *Shamsiyya* (two entries of five, if the reference to *Taṣdīqāt* refers to the second part of the work) and their commentaries (seven and eight respectively, depending on attribution), represented by more than one copy. Again, this observation should not necessarily lead one to conclude that the study of logic had declined.[6]

Works of logic were ordered in accordance with their level of difficulty in the training of students. The manuscripts in the Jazzār collection appear to be listed without consideration of this pedagogical aspect. Manuscripts of the same or related work, however, are generally listed together. The manuscripts are mostly listed in abbreviated form (*Matn al-Shamsiyya* for *al-Risāla al-Shamsiyya, Sharḥ al-Shamsiyya* for *Taḥrīr al-qawāʿid al-manṭiqiyya fī sharḥ al-Risāla al-Shamsiyya*, assuming that this is the commentary in question, *Ḥāshiya ʿalā al-Shamsiyya* for *Ḥāshiya ʿalā Sharḥ al-Quṭb lil-Shamsiyya*, assuming that this is the gloss by al-Sayyid al-Jurjānī (816/1413) on al-Taḥtānī on the *Shamsiyya*), and the author of the work is generally not identified. This does not pose a problem in a number of cases, since the works with the abbreviated titles are rather well-known; in other cases, especially pertaining to commentaries—as in *Sharḥ al-Shamsiyya*—one may assume that the reference is to the most famous gateway commentarial engagement with the work. In a number of other cases, however, the work cannot be identified on the basis of the entry. The list, for example, includes *Majmūʿ fī al-manṭiq, Rasāʾil fī al-manṭiq* and *Kitāb manṭiq*. Where the authors are mentioned, they are identified in abbreviated form. Examples include al-Rāzī (for Quṭb al-Dīn al-Taḥtānī al-Rāzī), ʿIṣām (for ʿIṣām al-Dīn Ibrāhīm Isfarāyinī [943/1536–1537]) and al-Fenārī (for Meḥmed Fenārī [834/1431]).

Extended logic works often tended to elicit independent treatises devoted to the problemata they have engaged. With one possible exception, the collection at hand does not include such works. By and large, the list consists of works that are classified universally as those belonging to the discipline of logic. Some exceptions to this rule may well be justified. It includes, for example, one work on dialectics (*Sharḥ al-ʿAḍud*, assuming this is a reference to ʿAḍud al-Dīn al-Ījī's [756/1355] brief work on *ādāb al-baḥth*, in three entries), a discipline that was often grouped together with logic; it also includes a work on law (*Sharḥ al-Mukhtaṣar*, assuming this is a reference to Ibn Ḥājib's [646/1249] *Mukhtaṣar al-Muntahā*, two entries), whose opening chapter included logic and was often cited in works in the latter discipline.[7] Finally, the list

6 For an analysis of the logic works in the Topkapi Palace Library, see El-Rouayheb, "Books on Logic", 891–906.

7 The reference may well be to Muḥammad b. Yūsuf al-Sanūsī's (d. 895/1490) *Mukhtaṣar al-manṭiq*, on which the author wrote a self-commentary. This likely possibility would further allow us to group this collection within the ambit of a North African intellectual sphere, as opposed to an eastern one. I thank Hadel Jarada for bringing this

also includes a summa of philosophy (the *Shifāʾ* of Avicenna) and the arbitration of Avicenna's *Ishārāt* and Naṣīr al-Dīn al-Ṭūsī's (672/1274) commentary by al-Taḥtānī. The list mentions this work as *Muḥākamāt al-Shifāʾ*, but this is certainly an error.

Regarding the field of logic, one may argue that the collection resembles that of the Topkapi Palace library but on a much smaller scale; it is also far more limited than the collections of major libraries of South Asia, such as those of the Khuda Bakhsh Library (Patna), the Raza Library (Rampur) and the Maulana Abul Kalam Azad Arabic Persian Research Institute (Tonk); and the possible inclusion of a work by Ibn ʿArafa and/or Sanūsī suggests a further North African orientation. The libraries in the case of South Asia reflect a system of education, the Nizāmī system of training, wherein a large number of logic works were included. As a living tradition, commentaries and glosses on various standard works of logic that were produced in South Asia were also included in the training, and these are found in large numbers in these collections. Multivolume catalogues often contain an entire volume devoted to logic, reflecting both the importance of the study of logic in the region and the strength of the investment of various networks of scholars in its perpetuation. Unless they are not advertised and are folded within the margins of the manuscripts, no work in the Jazzār collection reflects the engagement of local or regional scholars.

There do not appear to be any works on logic that precede Avicenna in the Jazzār collection; this feature is similar to the Topkapı collection, which contains only two pre-Avicennan works. In the Topkapi collection, a few post-Avicennan logic summae, such as *al-Baṣāʾir al-nāṣiriyya, Kashf al-asrār* and *al-Manṭiq al-kabīr*, are represented; the Jazzār Library does not contain any such works. Similar to the former, the latter contains one philosophical summa: the *Shifāʾ* of Avicenna, presumably because it includes the discipline of logic. This latter work often served as a point of reference for resolving logical aporiae in the later tradition. Again, the Topkapi has several works in this category. The latter also contains numerous treatises on specific topics in the discipline of logic, including investigations of the fourth figure syllogism and several such treatises by al-Taḥtānī. The Jazzār collection has only two such items (*Risāla fī al-manṭiq* and *Rasāʾil fī al-manṭiq*); their contents cannot be verified. There is another manuscript entitled *Risāla lil-Rāzī*, and this may well be al-Tahtānī. Finally, similar to the Topkapi collection, the bulk of the logic works in the Jazzār Library are handbooks on logic from the thirteenth century; and the majority of these are either introductory (the *Īsāghūjī* of al-Abharī) or intermediate (the *Shamsiyya* of al-Kātibī). Commentaries on these works, including those of al-Fenārī (for the former) and of al-Taḥtānī (for the latter), are also listed. This much is not surprising, given what I have noted above regarding the career of logic after Avicenna. Most of the commentaries, however, do not have authorial attributions in the list. Other than these works, the Jazzār logic collection includes an untitled work by ʿIṣām al-Din Ibrāhīm Isfarāyinī,[8] a gloss by al-Jurjānī (perhaps on Taḥtānī on the *Shamsiyya*), a commentary on the *Mukhtaṣar* (very likely the jurisprudence work, *Mukhtaṣar al-muntahā* of Ibn Ḥajib that included a logic part, although this may well be a reference to the *Mukhtaṣar* of Ibn ʿArafa or al-Sanūsī, on which see above) and some other minor works, most of which cannot be identified by the list alone.

The works not included in the library can also tell us something about the collector's intentions. The Jazzār library, for example, like the Topkapı Palace Library, does not include any work on

possibility to my attention. Another likelihood is that the reference is to a logic work by Ibn ʿArafa al-Warghamī (d. 803/1401), on which al-Sanūsī wrote a commentary. This would, again, allow us to shift our gaze to North Africa. See El-Rouayheb, *Development*, 16, 121, 127.

8 The candidates include a gloss on al-Taḥtānī on the *Shamsiyya*, a commentary on al-Taftāzānī's *Tahdhīb* and a treatise on logical relations that obtain between contradictories. See El-Rouayheb, *Development*, 109–110, for a fuller list.

logic by al-Dawānī or al-Taftāzānī. The *Tahdhīb al-manṭiq* by the latter and its commentary by the former had already become quite important as part of Ottoman scholarship in the seventeenth century. It is found, for example, in the Aleppo Library and the Jaffa Library, along with commentaries and glosses.[9] Al-Dawānī's commentary on the *Tahdhīb*, similar to al-Urmawī's *Maṭāliʿ* (along with its commentaries), which is also missing from the list, was considered part of the advanced training of the student in this subject. Such works are found in substantial numbers in Iranian and South Asian libraries.

Unless the marginalia tell us otherwise, it is safe to conclude from the inclusions and exclusions that the library was meant to contain only introductory and intermediate works on logic that were taught in Ottoman colleges. Since we cannot yet study the actual manuscripts, it is unclear whether these introductory works were studied as points of departure for fuller arguments in the marginalia. Such writing would indicate the nature of the engagements with a given text that can often be intertextual and more advanced, despite the elementary or intermediate nature of a base text. That the library should mainly contain handbooks and commentaries on them makes sense, given that it was part of the *madrasa* system and also intended for public benefit; its books were endowed for the use of those seeking knowledge. It does not appear that this particular library's collection in the discipline of logic served in the same capacity as the collections of a number of South Asian and Iranian libraries, where logic works on some of the most subtle subjects and from a range of authors and levels abound. The Jazzār collection is rather similar to that of the Ottoman Topkapi Palace Library in terms of what it includes, and distinct from other regional libraries, such as the Aleppo and Jaffa Libraries, in terms of what it excludes. It may also manifest a distinct North African orientation if the surmise that a particular work should be attributed to Ibn ʿArafa and/or al-Sanūsī is correct.

9 See El-Rouayheb, "Books"; Aljoumani, "Maktaba"; ʿAṭāʾ Allāh, *Fihris*.

Bibliography

Ahmed, Asad Q. "Logic in the Khayrābādī School of India." In *Law and Tradition in Classical Islamic Thought: Studies in Honor of Professor Hossein Modarressi*, edited by Michael Cook, Najam Haider, Intisar Rabb and Asma Sayeed, 227–245. New York, 2013.

Ahmed, Asad Q. *Palimpsests of Themselves: Logic and Commentary in Postclassical Muslim South Asia*. Oakland, 2022.

Aljoumani, Said. *Maktaba madrasiyya fī Ḥalab Nihāyat al-ʿAhd al-ʿUthmānī: al-Daftar al-Mujaddad li-kutub waqf ʿUthmān Bāshā al-Dūrikī*. Beirut, 2019.

Aljoumani, Said. "Tārīkh maktabat al-Mullā ʿUthmān al-Kurdī bi-Dimashq iʿtimādan ʿalā khawārij makhṭūṭātihā." *Journal of the Institute of Arabic Manuscripts* 65, no. 1 (2021): 210–260.

ʿAṭā Allāh, Maḥmūd ʿAlī. *Fihris makhṭūṭāt al-maktaba al-islāmiyya fī Yāfā*. ʿAmmān, 1984.

El-Rouayheb, Khaled. "Arabic Logic after Avicenna." In *The Cambridge Companion to Medieval Logic*, edited by Catarina Dutilh-Novaes and Stephen Read, 67–93. Cambridge, 2016.

El Rouayheb, Khaled. "The Transformation of Eastern Arabic Logic in the Fourteenth and Fifteenth Centuries." In *In the House of Understanding: Histories in Memory of Kamal Salibi*, edited by Abdul Rahim Abu Husayn, Tarif Khalidi and Suleiman A. Mourad, 389–404. Beirut, 2017.

El-Rouayheb, Khaled. "Books on Logic (Manṭiq) and Dialectics (Jadal)." In *Treasures of Knowledge: An Inventory of the Ottoman Palace Library (1502/3–1503/4)*, edited by Gülru Necipoğlu, Cemal Kafadar and Cornell H. Fleischer, 1: 891–906. Leiden, 2019.

El-Rouayheb, Khaled. *The Development of Arabic Logic (1200–1800)*. Basel, 2019.

Street, Tony. "Arabic Logic." In *Greek, Indian and Arabic Logic*, edited by Dov M. Gabbay and John Woods, 523–596. *Vol. 1 of Handbook of the History of Logic*. Amsterdam, 2004.

Street, Tony. "Logic." In *The Cambridge Companion to Arabic Philosophy*, edited by Peter Adamson and Richard C. Taylor, 247–265. Cambridge, 2004.

Street, Tony. "Kātibī (d. 1277), Taḥtānī (d. 1365), and the Shamsiyya." In *The Oxford Handbook of Islamic Philosophy, edited by Khaled El-Rouayheb and Sabine Schmidtke*, 348–374. New York, 2016.

Strobino, Riccardo. "Ibn Sina's Logic." In *Stanford Encyclopedia of Philosophy. Stanford University, 1997–*. Article published August 15, 2018. https://plato.stanford.edu/archives/fall2018/entries/ibn-sina-logic/.

Logic Section—Kutub ʿilm al-manṭiq

[1062] ***Matn al-Shamsiyya***, AUTHOR: Najm al-Dīn al-Kātibī (d. 675/1276), EDITION: Istanbul, 1287/1870.

[1063] ***Sharḥ al-Shamsiyya***, AUTHOR: Quṭb al-Dīn al-Taḥtānī (d. 766/1365), EDITION: Istanbul, 1325/1907. The author is not mentioned in the inventory, but I have indicated al-Taḥtānī as his is the most widely read commentary on Kātibī's *Shamsiyya*.

[1064] ***Sharḥ al-Shamsiyya***, see #1063.

[1065] ***Sharḥ al-Shamsiyya***, see #1063.

[1066] ***Sharḥ al-Shamsiyya***, see #1063.

[1067] ***Sharḥ al-Shamsiyya***, see #1063.

[1068] ***Sharḥ al-Shamsiyya***, see #1063.

[1069] ***Matn al-Shamsiyya***, see #1062.

[1070] ***Ḥāshiya ʿalā al-Shamsiyya***, AUTHOR: al-Sayyid al-Jurjānī (d. 816/1413), EDITION: Cairo: Muṣṭafā al-Bābī al-Ḥalabī, 1948.

[1071] ***Taṣdīqāt***, AUTHOR: Najm al-Dīn al-Kātibī (675/1276), EDITION: Istanbul, 1287/1870. This is probably a reference to the second part of the *Shamsiyya* above #1062.

[1072] ***Taṣdīqāt***, see #1071.

[1073] ***Taṣdīqāt***, see #1071.

[1074] ***Sharḥ al-Aḍud li-Mullā Jāmī***. AUTHOR: Nūr al-Dīn Jāmī (d. 898/1492), EDITION: Paradigma Akademi, Çanakkale, 2021. This is probably Jāmī's commentary on ʿAḍud al-Dīn al-Ījī's *al-Risāla fī al-waḍʿ*.

[1075] ***Sharḥ al-ʿAḍud***, see #1074.

[1076] ***Sharḥ al-ʿAḍud***, see #1074.

[1077] ***Al-Shifāʾ li-Ibn Sīnā***, AUTHOR: Abū ʿAlī Ibn Sīnā, EDITION: Organisme General des Imprimeries Gouvernementales, 1964. I take this to be a reference to the logic of the *Syllogism* of *al-Shifāʾ*.

[1078] ***Muḥākamāt al-Shifāʾ***, AUTHOR: Quṭb al-Dīn al-Taḥtānī (d. 766/1365), EDITION: Tehran: Maṭbaʿat al-Ḥaydarī, 1377–1379/1958–1959. I take this to be the famous *Muḥākamāt* of al-Taḥtānī on the *Ishārāt* (not the *Shifāʾ* of Ibn Sīnā) and its commentary by Naṣīr al-Dīn al-Ṭūsī.

[1079] ***Kitāb fī al-manṭiq***.

[1080] ***Fawāʾid kalāmiyya manṭiqiyya***.

[1081] ***ʿIlm manṭiq***.

[1082] ***Majmūʿa min ʿilm al-manṭiq***.

[1083] ***Risāla fī al-manṭiq***.

[1084] ***Risāla lil-Rāzī***. AUTHOR: Quṭb al-Dīn al-Taḥtānī (d. 766/1365), EDITION: Istanbul: Türkiye Yazma Eserler Kurumu, Başkanlığı, 2013. I am assuming that this is the *Risāla fī taḥqīq al-kulliyyāt*.

[1085] ***Kitāb manṭiq***.

[1086] ***Kitāb min al-manṭiq***.

[1087] ***Taʾlīf li-ʿIṣām***, AUTHOR: ʿIṣām al-Dīn Ibrāhīm Isfarāyinī (943/1536–1537).

[1088] ***Sharḥ al-Rāzī***, AUTHOR: Quṭb al-Dīn al-Taḥtānī (d. 766/1365), EDITION: Istanbul, 1325/1907. I take this to be the same as #1063.

[1089] ***Majmūʿ fī al-manṭiq***.

[1090] ***Rasāʾil fī al-manṭiq***.

[1091] ***Sharḥ al-Mukhtaṣar***, AUTHOR: Muḥammad b. Yūsuf al-Sanūsī's (d. 895/1490), EDITION: Cairo, 1292/1875.

[1092] ***Ḥāshiya***.

[1093] ***Ḥāshiyat al-Fanārī***, AUTHOR: Meḥmed Fenārī (d. 834/1431), EDITION: Istanbul, 1294/1877. I take this to be al-Fanārī's commentary on al-Abharī's *Īsāghūjī*.

[1094] ***Ḥāshiya fī al-manṭiq***.

[1095] ***Ḥāshiya ʿalā al-Taṣdīqāt***, AUTHOR: al-Sayyid al-Jurjānī (d. 816/1413), EDITION: Cairo: Muṣṭafā al-Bābī al-Ḥalabī, 1948. I assume this is a gloss on the second part of #1063.

[1096] ***Ḥāshiyat al-Sayyid***, see #1095.

[1097] ***Ḥāshiya fī al-manṭiq***.

[1098] ***Ḥāshiyat al-Khayālī***, AUTHOR: Aḥmad b. Mūsā al-Khayālī (fl. /9th/15th). I am not aware of a gloss by Khayālī on a work of logic.

[1099] ***Ḥāshiyat Mullā ʿAbd al-Ghafūr***, AUTHOR: ʿAbd al-Ghafūr Lārī (d. 912/1506), EDITION: Istanbul, 1308/1890–1891. I am assuming that this is the author, given that Jāmī has appeared in the list (see #1074) and that Lārī was Jāmī's major commentator and disciple. The gloss in question may be on Jāmī's commentary on Ibn al-Ḥājib's *Kāfiya*, but this is a work on grammar.

[1100] ***Sharḥ al-Mukhtaṣar***, see #1091.

[1101] ***Īsāghūjī***, AUTHOR: Athīr al-Dīn al-Abharī (d. 663/1265), EDITION: Beirut: Dār al-Dhakhāʾir, 2015.

[1102] ***Īsāghūjī***, see #1101.

[1103] ***Īsāghūjī***, see #1101.

[1104] ***Sharḥ Īsāghūjī***. This work has many commentaries, therefore, it is difficult to determine to which one this title refers.

[1105] ***Sharḥ Īsāghūjī***, see #1104.

[1106] ***Sharḥ Īsāghūjī***, see #1104.

[1107] ***Sharḥ Īsāghūjī***, see #1104.

[1108] ***Īsāghūjī***, see #1101.

CHAPTER 21

The Poetry Section (*al-dawāwīn wa-al-qaṣāʾid*): Pedagogy and Devotional Piety

Khalil Sawan

The section entitled 'Odes and Poetry Collections' (*kutub al-dawāwīn wa-al-qaṣāʾid*) in the Jazzār library inventory is a showcase of the Arabic poetic canon with an Ottoman flavour.[1] It is made up of 110 entries and includes an assortment of classic poems and collections from the pre-Islamic through the caliphal periods; well-known poets from the Saljuq, Hamdanid, Ayyubid and Mamluk periods; and standard panegyrics of the Prophet and commentaries on them. The section prominently includes the poetry of the Sufi masters Ibn al-ʿArabī and Ibn al-Fāriḍ, both beloved in the Turkish-speaking Ottoman world, along with the entire poetic corpus of the eighteenth-century Damascene Sufi, ʿAbd al-Ghanī al-Nābulusī. The poetry section, thus, is representative of its time and place. It acknowledges a corpus of classical poetry up till the eighteenth century, when the library came into being, while exhibiting a specific Ottoman preference for certain Sufi poets, as displayed by the arrangement of titles in the list.

Two trends emerge within this general arc. The more obvious of the two is the pedagogical dimension of this *madrasa* library. The collection includes copies of standard titles offered in college *curricula*; a fact that is further evidenced by the number of copies found in the inventory, arguably for the use of students.

The second trend has to do with the doctrine of *al-nūr al-Muḥammadī* (or Muḥammmadan Light), its connection to the Ottoman-period veneration of the Prophet, and to the very name of the Jazzār *madrasa*-mosque complex: al-Nūr Aḥmadiyya (The Light of Aḥmad). I will argue that the collection's focus on panegyrics to the Prophet is not only for educational purposes. Consonant with other chapters of the inventory, especially the *ḥadīth* section, the poetry collection is about devotion to the Prophet and veneration of his *persona*.[2] However, the poetry section zooms in on a specific doctrine of devotion. The panegyrics to the Prophet, combined with the poetry of the main expounders of the doctrine of Muḥammadan Light, point to the creedal position of the library within the wider Ottoman intellectual landscape. In the context of the onslaught of the Wahhābī anti-Sufi menace, whose doctrines echoed the Kādızādeli puritanical movement from the previous century, the poetry collection is a defence of a classic Ottoman position and piety. It cannot be a simple coincidence that al-Jazzār chose a name almost identical to this doctrine for his complex. Some see the nomenclature of the complex as a deliberate attempt to echo contemporary Ottoman imperial architecture in Istanbul.[3] Here, I further argue that the name, the Light of Aḥmad, represents an embrace of the doctrine of Muḥammadan Light, while also exalting the governor, Aḥmad Pasha al-Jazzār. It brings the pasha a step closer to realis-

1 I would like to express my sincere gratitude to Dana Sajdi, who helped me develop my ideas in academic prose. Our brainstorming sessions and her patient, repeated edits were crucial for the final product. I thank Sharon Grosso for her general support and assistance in the editing and translation.

2 Chapter 15 by Garett Davidson.

3 See the editors' *Introduction* to this volume, which relates the Nūr Aḥmadiyya to the Nurosmaniyye in Istanbul.

ing the status of the Messiah (*al-mahdī*), according to apocalyptic prophecies that were being propagated at the time.

1 The Order of the Canon

The arrangement of the poetry section in the library inventory reveals a hierarchical order based on the poet or poem's prestige at the time, which was bibliographic practice in premodern Islamic libraries.[4] The opening of the poetry section with the name Ibn al-ʿArabī (#1133) is indicative. Ibn al-ʿArabī was initially underappreciated in Damascus, where the Sufi master died and was buried, but given political and cultural currency upon the Ottoman conquest of the city. His prophecies foretold Sultan Selīm's (d. 926/1520) conquest of Bilād al-Shām. Having adopted Ibn al-ʿArabī as a patron saint of the Ottoman House, the sultan built a mausoleum complex for the Sufi master in Damascus.[5] The poetry section, in other words, begins by announcing allegiance to the Ottomans, and, I will later argue, to a specific Ottoman doctrinal position.

The order of the poetry section seems to have been conceived in three consecutive, if rough, subsections that are arranged in descending order of authority and prestige. The first subsection is made up of Sufi poetry and panegyrics to the Prophet. The middle subsection is a display of Arabic 'classics' from pre-Islamic times through the Mamluk period. The last is an assortment of collections, not all of which are *dīwān*s proper. It includes anthologies of homoerotic poetry (#1219 and #1224), a *dīwān* on musicology (*ʿilm al-mūsīqā*) (#1233), and unidentified miscellanies and collections (*majmūʿ*, *majmūʿa*, *safīna*: #1221, #1227, #1229, #1236, #1237, #1239 and #1241).

Along with Ibn al-ʿArabī, poems and poetry collections by two other famous Sufis, Ibn al-Fāriḍ, whose work appears in multiple copies (#1134, #1135, #1136 and #1137), and the celebrated Levantine Sufi ʿAbd al-Ghanī al-Nābulusī, whose work recurs in the section (#1138, #1139 and #1140), occupy the first part of the list. Immediately following this Sufi triad, and strikingly occupying a lower position on the list, is the topic of the Prophet Muḥammad. The first subsection includes one of the two most famous panegyrics to him: *Bānat Suʿād* (Suʿād is Gone, #1141 and #1142). Multiple copies and a large number of accompanying commentaries listed immediately after the poem (#1143–1171) suggest that *Bānat Suʿād* was probably used for educational purposes. This same subsection, somewhat unexpectedly, also includes the collection of *Majnūn Laylā* (The Mad Lover of Laylā, #1156) and three copies of Abū al-ʿAlāʾ al-Maʿarrī's *dīwān* (#1158, #1159 and #1160, respectively). The poetry collection of *Majnūn Laylā* by the first/seventh-century poet Qays b. al-Mulawwaḥ, which is dedicated in ardent, chaste love for Laylā, is considered exemplary in the Arabic-speaking world, and its inclusion in this first subsection is notable. This high regard for *Majnūn Laylā* may be an indication of its popularity in its Persian and Turkish translations.[6] Moreover, its inclusion in the Sufi poetry part of the broader poetry collection might be explained by the mystical dimensions that were attached to later adaptations of the poem, especially in its non-Arabic versions.[7]

The second subsection in the poetry collection is a list of the 'top-of-the-charts' of Arabic poetry, starting with nine copies of al-Mutanabbī's *dīwān*.[8] This subsection includes the most famous poets from every period, which, for the sake of conve-

4 For example, the arrangement of subjects in the inventory of the Sultan Beyazid II's palace library also suggests a 'general sense of rank'. El-Rouayheb, "Books on Logic (Manṭiq) and Dialectics (Jadal)", 891.

5 Akkach, "The Eye of Reflection", 80–81.

6 Pellat et al., "Madjnūn Laylā".

7 Ibid. I am unable to explain the inclusion of the *dīwān* of Abū al-ʿAlāʾ al-Maʿarrī (#1185—#1160) in this section.

8 It is not unusual in premodern library inventories for subsections to begin with the title of the work with the highest number of copies. See Qutbuddin, "Books on Arabic Philology and Literature", 615.

nience, I will rearrange here in a roughly chronological order. From the pre-Islamic and early Islamic periods, the subsection includes the *dīwāns* of Imru' al-Qays (#1175) and Hassān b. Thābit (#1204). The Umayyad period is represented by al-Akhṭal (#1198). The Abbasid period is represented by Abū Tammām's *dīwān* (#1172–1174) and his *dīwān al-ḥamāsa* (#1185 and #1186); and the *dīwāns* of Ibn al-Rūmī (#1183) and Kushājim (#1189). From the Hamdanid court, we encounter the aforementioned al-Mutanabbī (#1163–1171) and Abū Firās al-Ḥamadānī's *dīwān* (#1176); from the Ayyubid period, the *dīwāns* of al-Bahā' Zuhayr (#1177) and Ibn 'Unayn (#1194); and from the Mamluk period, the *dīwāns* of Burhān al-Dīn al-Qīrāṭī (#1182), Ṣafī al-Dīn al-Ḥillī (#1184), Ibrāhīm al-Mi'mār and *Dīwān al-ṣabāba* written by Shihāb al-Dīn Ibn Abī Ḥajala (#1180 and #1181). Al-Nābulusī's poetry (#1139, #1140, #1150 and #1187) represents the Ottoman period.

The third and final subsection of the poetry collection consists of single poems and several types of anthologies that were popular and entertaining, almost all of them composed in the post-caliphal period. Al-Ṭughrā'ī's *Lāmiyyat al-'Ajam* (the Ode of the Persians in L, #1213) is a poem that evokes the pre-Islamic classic al-Shanfarā's (d. sixth century) *Lāmiyyat al-'Arab* (the Ode of the Arabs in L).[9] The poem has nothing to do with Persian, but denotes 'foreignness' due to the poet's use of foreign and unusual vocabulary.[10] Its rich vocabulary, in addition to its moralising nature, made it appropriate for educational purposes, which might explain the numerous commentaries on it found in the library inventory.[11] Two collections of homoerotic epigrams are represented in *Marāti' al-ghizlān fī waṣf al-ḥisān min al-ghilmān* (The Gazelle's Pastures Regarding the Description of Beautiful Youth, #1219) and *al-Ḥusn al-ṣarīḥ fī mi'at malīḥ* (The Barefaced Beauty of One Hundred Good-looking Boys, #1224). The former of these two consists of two thousand Ayyubid and Mamluk epigrams and is considered 'the most comprehensive collection of love epigrams ever produced'.[12]

Some of the anthologies included in this section are not authored entirely in verse, though they are not devoid of poetry. Ibn Hibat Allāh al-Iṣfahānī's *Aṭbāq al-dhahab* (Platters of Gold, #1232), a book of aphorisms imitating al-Zamakhshari's (d. 538/1144) similarly titled *Aṭwāq al-dhahab* (Necklaces of Gold), is predominantly a prose work. Its moralising, exhortative tone explains its location close to *Lāmiyyat al-'Ajam*. Al-Tha'ālibī's *al-Kināya wa-al-ta'rīḍ* (Book of Hints and Allusion, #1225), an anthology of figures of speech and another book in the poetry section that is a prose composition.[13] Another work by al-Tha'ālibī, *Nathr al-naẓm wa-ḥall al-'aqd* (#1188) is identified as a *dīwān*; it is listed in the second section, even though it also consists of poetry and prose. The same author's famous *Yatīmat al-dahr wa-maḥāsin ahl al-'aṣr* (#1220), an anthology survey of poetry and prose of the entire Islamic world, appears in the last section along with other anthologies.[14]

The third subsection of the poetry list also includes a set of generic titles that the inventory scribe does not identify. They are listed with various labels, including *dīwān* (#1215, #1216, #1217 and #1218); *majmū'/majmū'a* (miscellanies, #1221, #1227, #1236 and #1237); *safīna* (anthology, #1229);[15] *kitāb* (book, #1235 and #1240); *qaṣīda* (ode, #1228); *shi'r/ash'ār* (verse, #1222, #1223, #1227 and #1229); *ṭuraf* (anecdotes #1226); *fawā'id* (benefits/beneficial notes/advice, #1241); and *rasā'il* (letters/epistles #1221). These unidentifiable entries make up around ten per cent of the poetry section inventory.

9 Loop, "Arabic Poetry as Teaching Material", 234.
10 Hillenbrand, "al-Ṭughrā'ī", 783.
11 Loop, "Arabic Poetry as Teaching Material", 233–236.

12 Bauer, "Al-Nawājī", 329.
13 Orfali, *The Anthologist's Art*, 32.
14 The anthology also appears in the history section. See Chapter 22 by Dana Sajdi.
15 A *safīna* is 'a book which is wider than it is long, an oblong booklet; songbook; a collection of songs; an album of calligraphy by professional copyists for the leisured classes'. Kazimirski, *Dictionnaire*, 660. Cited and translated in Reynolds, "Lost Virgins Found", 75.

Given the hierarchical clustering, in which poetry about the Prophet takes primacy, there are some conspicuous absences: Prophetic *mawlids*, odes that celebrate the nativity of Muḥammad, and the famous panegyric *al-Burdā* (the Mantle) composed by Sharaf al-Dīn al-Būṣīrī (d. 694–696/1294–1297). This type of devotional poetry, which was popular and widespread during the time, is not represented in the poetry section. It turns out, however, that 'the missing texts' are not entirely absent from the larger library inventory. One finds five *mawlid* manuscripts and two copies of *al-Burdā* listed in the *ḥadīth* section (#201, #202, #203, #318, #326, and #236, #279, respectively). The classification of *mawlids* and *al-Burdā* in the *ḥadīth* section seems to be an intentional commission by the scribe or the librarian who categorised the books. The *ḥadīth* section is not exclusively limited to works of and related to *ḥadīth*. Many texts and compositions that are related to the Prophet, including devotional poetry and even the standard biographies of Muḥammad, are found there.[16] The complementarity between the *ḥadīth* and poetry sections is noteworthy.

The overall content of the poetry collection is quite standard and canonical. It includes classics as well as more popular literature with a clear order of status, beginning with Sufi poetry and panegyrics to Muḥammad, then Arabic classic poets and, lastly, collections for more general entertainment, the kind which might have been enjoyed at literary salons, and untitled *dīwāns* and anthologies.[17]

2 Cultivating Students at al-Nūr Aḥmadiyya

Although poetry itself was not a main subject in *madrasa* curricula, it was necessary for the general cultivation of the future *ʿulamāʾ*.[18] Poetry was no longer the purview of professional poets at royal courts by the Mamluk period, but a primary means of communication for a growing class of scholars.[19] Poetry books have always had their place in endowed libraries; as early as the thirteenth century, the Ashrafiyya library, for example, housed a strikingly large corpus of poetry books.[20] In addition to its purpose for the cultivation of students, poetry exemplified the proper use of language and good rhetoric. The poetry corpus served these purposes at al-Nūr Aḥmadiyya *madrasa*.

While it is hard—if not impossible—to definitively draw out al-Jazzār's college curriculum from its library collection, it is clear that the poetry collection was used, at least partially, for teaching purposes. In addition to the variety of Arabic *dīwāns* that students had the opportunity to peruse, the number of copies of certain works may indicate the demand and frequency of these works' use, presumably by teachers and students.[21] The profusion of explanatory commentaries (*shurūḥ*) on some works may also be a sign that these were standard works used for students' reading and comprehension.[22] In this section, I will try to point out the pedagogical facet of our *madrasa*'s poetry collection as indicated by *multiples*, whether the number of repeat copies and/or of commentaries on certain titles.

The *dīwān* of al-Mutanabbī was clearly the most frequently used. With eight copies, the title has by

16 See Chapter 15 by Garett Davidson.

17 The poetry section in the library significantly features famous poets and poems of the pre-Islamic and earlier Islamic periods. This suggests that poetry classics were preserved in libraries such as al-Jazzār's rather than rediscovered by scholars at the turn of the nineteenth century (El Shamsy, *Rediscovering the Islamic Classics*). The featuring of poetry classics in our library opens the door for a further exploration of the historical changes that were taking place in the nineteenth century.

18 Bauer, "Shāʿir", 718.

19 Bauer, "Mamluk Literature", 108–111.

20 Hirschler, *Medieval Damascus*.

21 This line of argument is followed by Qutbuddin, "Books on Arabic Philology and Literature", 607.

22 Again, Qutbuddin argues that such commentaries 'points to a readership interested in learning language-based skills from preferred commentaries on specific texts [or poems] by a handful of favorite authors [or poets]'. Ibid., 609.

far the most copies in the poetry inventory (#1163, #1164, #1165, #1166, #1167, #1168, #1169 and #1170). It is followed by one commentary (#1171) whose author is not mentioned. Al-Mutanabbī's *dīwān* appears in the Arabic section of the royal library of Beyazid II, a library that was also partially assembled for educational purposes.[23] Other classic *dīwāns* also appear more than once. There are two copies of the *dīwān* of Ibn al-Fāriḍ (#1134 and #1135); three copies of both Abū al-ʿAlāʾ al-Maʿarrī and Abū Tammām (#1158–1160, and #1172–1173, respectively); two copies of both al-Bahāʾ Zuhayr and Imruʾ al-Qays (#1177, #1178, and #1175 respectively). There are also two copies of Abū Tammām's *Dīwān al-ḥamāsa* (#1185 and #1186).

Perhaps more indicative of the pedagogical value of any one work is the number of explanatory commentaries that appear alongside it in the collection. The wildly popular panegyric of the Prophet *Bānat Suʿād* mentioned above, which itself appears twice (#1141 and #1142), is accompanied by four commentaries (#1143, #1144, #1145 and #1146), only one of which is identified by its author (#1147). Similarly, *Lāmiyyat al-ʿAjam* (#1213), famous for its use of unusual vocabulary, appears along with four commentaries (#1209, #1210, #1211 and #1212), none of which bears their author's name. Unlike other educational corpora that point to 'preferred commentaries,' our list does not show any preference for specific commentaries or commentators.[24] The majority of the commentaries listed in the poetry section remain unidentified. Only two of the nineteen commentaries in the collection appear with the commentators' names: *Sharḥ bānat Suʿād* by Ibn Hisham (#1145) and *Sharḥ al-badīʿiyyāt* by Ibn Ḥijja (#1162).

Attesting to their fame and use for teaching purposes, the odes *Bānat Suʿād* and *Lāmiyyat al-ʿAjam* mentioned previously appear in their so-called '*takhmīs*' versions. *Takhmīs*, which became popular in the Mamluk period, is a form of poetic amplification and thematic enhancement written by a later poet-commentator. The commentator adds three hemistichs to each original verse, turning the ode into a five-hemistich verse instead of two.[25] The inclusion of the entire 'apparatus' surrounding these two poems—the original poems, commentaries and further enhancements—shows their importance for didactic use. Though not represented with the same vigour, Ibn al-Fāriḍ's *dīwān* appears twice in the collection (#1134 and #1135) along with two commentaries (#1136 and #1137).

The collection includes commentaries on *dīwāns* and individual poems that themselves do not appear as separate titles in the poetry section, only their commentaries. Of course, the original texts, even if they do not appear as individual entries, are included in these commentaries. Thus, the appearance of the commentary alone seems like a pragmatic decision to get straight to the purpose: teaching. Most of these titles are significant for their sound rhetoric and edifying content, making them ideal for educational purposes. Examples of commentaries on entire collections include one on the poems of Ibn Zuhayr (#1554), the composer of *Bānat Suʿād*, and another on the *muʿallaqāt*, the pre-Islamic 'suspended odes' (#1238), among which Imruʾ al-Qays appears individually. Additionally, the inventory includes commentaries on separate poems, such as Ibn al-Fāriḍ's Ode in Yā (*Sharḥ al-yāʾiyya*, #1147), al-Ṣafaḍī's Ode in Tā (*Sharḥ tāʾiyyat al-Ṣafaḍī*, #1214) and an ode by a certain Abū al-Fatḥ (*Sharḥ tāʾiyyat Abū al-Fatḥ*, #1228).

The poetry collection at al-Nūr Aḥmadiyya *madrasa* allowed students to acquire a well-rounded education in poetry. The collection provides an introduction to the entire Arabic canon and a deeper exploration of individual odes and collections of individual poets from various time periods. The tension, however, between the teaching corpus as reconstructed based on the num-

23 Ibid.
24 Ibid., 607.
25 Kennedy, "Takhmīs".

ber of copies and commentaries, on the one hand, and the arrangement of the works, on the other, is striking. This tension helps to bring out a doctrinal stance.

It is notable that three works whose numerous copies or commentaries signify a considerable pedagogical value—the poem *Bānat Suʿād* and its commentaries, the *dīwān* of al-Mutanabbī and its commentary, and *Lāmiyyat al-ʿAjam* and its commentaries—while united in their didactic purpose, appear in different parts of the inventory regarding the three subsections I outlined above. *Bānat Suʿād*, being a work about the Prophet and an ode that Muḥammad himself listened to, appears in the first subsection, along with Sufi works by Ibn al-ʿArabī and Ibn al-Fāriḍ; al-Mutanabbī's work appears in the second subsection along with the classics of Arabic poetry; and the *Lāmiyya* appears in the third and last subsection with the least prestigious and numerous unidentified works.

Moreover, while Ibn al-ʿArabī crowns the poetry inventory, the collection includes only three entries related to his work. Beyond the initial opening entry, his *dīwān* and a commentary on it appear later down the list (#1152 and 1153, respectively). The relative scant appearance of the works of Ibn al-ʿArabī, in contrast to its position as the inaugural volume, shows us that the collection served two different purposes: one is educational, but the other is political. As I will show below, the poetry collection may be a reflection of, and even a response to, the specific political moment when certain doctrines and Sufi practices were under attack.

3 For the Love of the Prophet

It is expected in a college where future generations of *ʿulamāʾ* were meant to be trained that the Prophet, the first Muslim, would be the exemplar for the cultivation of students in poetry beyond their instruction in *ḥadīth* or his official biographies. Encomia to the Prophet and accompanying commentaries pervade the poetry section, despite the absences mentioned above, which are found in the *ḥadīth* section.

In addition to the foregoing discussion of the educational purposes of *Bānat Suʿād* and commentaries thereon, its position early in the list opens the way for other panegyric works. *Bānat Suʿād* provides what other encomia cannot: a direct connection to the Prophet. The Arabic literary tradition insists that *Bānat Suʿād* was recited in the presence of the Prophet himself. Accordingly, its many copies, commentaries and *takhmīs* connected the poetry collection directly to the person of the Prophet.

While al-Būṣīrī's *al-Burda* was placed in the *ḥadīth* section, the poem appears in an anonymous *takhmīs* in the poetry section (#1151). The transmission of *al-Burda* within a *takhmīs*, an enhancing outer text, was the standard context through which the poem was presented.[26] Similar to *Bānat Suʿād*, al-Būṣīrī's poem was also known as *al-Burda* in reference to the mantle of the Prophet.[27] However, al-Būṣīrī's *al-Burda* acquired more devotional fame during the Mamluk and Ottoman periods than its antecedent *Bānat Suʿād*, a fact that explains its higher position and placement in the *ḥadīth* section.

In addition to these two famous panegyrics, the early Islamic *Bānat Suʿād* and its Mamluk twin, the poetry section includes anthologies of devotional poetry related to the Prophet, such as *Ahnā al-manāʾiḥ li-asnā al-madāʾiḥ* (The Most Pleasant Grants for the Most Sublime Panegyrics) by Shihāb al-Dīn Abī al-Thanāʾ al-Ḥalabī (d. 725/1325) (#1148); *Nafḥat al-qabūl fī madḥ al-Nabī al-Rasūl* (The Southerly Breeze in Praising the Prophet) by ʿAbd al-Ghanī al-Nābulusī (d. 1143/1731)(#1150); and *Arāʾis al-afkār fī madāʾiḥ al-Mukhtār* (The Best Ideas in the Praise of the Chosen One) by Abū al-ʿAbbās Ibn ʿAbd al-Ḥayy al-Ḥalabī (d. 1120/1708–1709)(#1234).

26 Kennedy, "Takhmīs".

27 Homerin, "Al-Būṣīrī".

The focus on the Prophet in the poetry section is also illustrated by the inclusion of two entries related to the genre of *badīʿiyya*. This is a type of panegyric to the Prophet that is composed to display various types of figures of speech, or *badīʿ*.[28] *Badīʿiyya*s, thus, are well-suited for educational purposes given their thematic content and rhetorical displays.

The first of the two entries related to *badīʿiyya*s is 'Ibn al-Ḥijja's Commentary on the *Badīʿiyya*s' (#1162). This is probably Ibn Ḥijja al-Ḥamawī's famous commentary, whose official title is *Khizānat al-adab* (The Repository of Cultivation). This work includes a discussion of and commentary on various panegyrics, including the author's own, separately entitled *Taqdīm Abū Bakr* (The Precedence of Abū Bakr).[29] The purpose of al-Ḥamawī's *Khizāna* is to demonstrate the superiority of his *badīʿiyya* over the others discussed in the work. One of the *badīʿiyya*s that Ibn Ḥijja dismisses is *Badiʿiyyat al-ʿumyān* (The *Badīʿiyya* of the Blind), so-called in reference to its composer's blindness. Composed by Ibn Jābir al-Andalusī, it is the second entry related to the *badīʿiyya* genre in the collection (#1161).

Featuring poems and anthologies about the Prophet in a time when the veneration of his person had come under attack is not an exceptional event. If poetry is used for language education and general cultivation, then one would expect to find the Prophet's example and attributes in this context. However, the volume of this textual material about the Prophet is striking and may have something to do with another observation about the presentation of the Prophet in the section.

4 Muḥammadan Light in al-Nūr Aḥmadiyya

The veneration of the Prophet for education and edification purposes in any Islamic library is *not*, in and of itself, worthy of comment. However, in the case of al-Nūr Aḥmadiyya, the significant presence of the Prophet in devotional poetry—encomia, anthologies, *badīʿiyyāt* and *burda*s—alongside the works of prominent Sufis, is striking. This preponderance of devotional poetry may be understood within the specific context of the late eighteenth-century Ottoman Levant.

The most immediate context is, of course, the eruption of Wahhābism. The Wahhābī attacks on Sufism and Sufi practices, along with their disruption of the Ḥajj, made them a primary enemy of al-Jazzār himself. Wahhābism echoed the principles and arguments of an earlier movement, that of the seventeenth century Kadızadelis. While the Kadızadeli discourse remained confined in the seventeenth and early eighteenth centuries, the Wahhābī threat materialised into violent confrontations with al-Jazzār during the late eighteenth century.

Both current Wahhābī thought and earlier Kadızadeli arguments jeopardised central tenets of Sufi thought, including the doctrine of *al-nūr al-muḥammadī* or Muḥammadan Light.[30] The doctrine itself is associated with the very three figures whose names crown the poetry section: Ibn al-ʿArabī, Ibn al-Fāriḍ and, given the Levantine context, ʿAbd al-Ghanī al-Nābulusī. The poetry of this last local Sufi and scholar is noticeably recurrent throughout the poetry section (#1138, #1139, #1140, #1150 and #1187). His works also appear prominently in the history, *ḥadīth* and law (*fiqh*) sections.

The idea of an essential association between the Prophet and light is as early as Islam itself, and is even expressed in the sixth-century poetry of Hassān b. Thābit (listed in the inventory, #1204).[31]

28 Van Gelder, "Badīʿiyya".

29 According to Van Gelder, the title *Taqdīm Abū Bakr* refers not so much to the first Rightly-Guided Caliph of that name but to the author himself. Ibid.

30 Akkach, *Intimate Invocations*, 6–7.

31 On the poetry of Ḥassān Ibn Thābit, see Schim-

Light represented the primordial essence of the Prophet that preceded and succeeded his historical *persona*. It was Ibn al-ʿArabī, the thirteenth-century 'Great Shaykh' and later the patron saint of the Ottoman House, who systematised this association into a concept: 'the Essence of Muḥammad' (*al-ḥaqīqa al-muḥamadiyya*).[32] Ibn al-Fāriḍ was among the first Sufi poets to express the concept of Muḥammadan Light in verse.[33] The Light of Muḥammad, then, became a central tenet and the basis of a range of ritual objects and practices all over the Ottoman world.[34] The understanding of the luminous essence of the Prophet that preceded and superseded his historical role was at the heart of a certain kind of Ottoman piety, centred around devotion to the Prophet, a *pietas ottomanica*.[35]

The poetry section of the Jazzār library seems to be a confirmation of this 'classical' Ottoman piety. It confirms the idea of a transcendent Muḥammadan Light, which had been challenged by the Kadızadelis in the seventeenth century. For the Kadızadelis, Ibn al-ʿArabī's thought was so problematic that it was presented as a 'test of orthodoxy'. Those who followed Ibn al-ʿArabī, accepted him as an authority or even recited his verse were considered outright heretics.[36] Our poetry section, as I have shown, proudly brandishes Ibn al-ʿArabī.

The Wahhābīs of Arabia posed a similar challenge in the eighteenth century. The movement rendered blasphemous any allusion to the manifestation of the Prophet, including his light.[37] Thus, the inclusion of Ibn al-ʿArabī and Ibn al-Fāriḍ, the expounders of Muḥammadan Light, in our collection situates our library, doctrinally and intellectually, in opposition to Wahhābism. In addition to Ibn al-ʿArabī and Ibn al-Fāriḍ, the poetry collection insistently mentions a local Sufi and defender of Muḥammadan light: ʿAbd al-Ghanī al-Nābulusī. This eighteenth-century Damascene Sufi-scholar was one of the most important later propagators of Muḥammadan Light.[38] He believed that *eloquence* and *clarity* were direct effects of this blessed light.[39] Furthermore, the Sufi posited himself as an 'heir' to the 'Muḥammadan inheritance', and presented himself as a 'new locus of manifestation of al-Nūr al-Muḥammadī'.[40] In other words, our library does not only present the Muḥammadan Light as a primary message, but is pervaded by the utterances of the person who claimed to be the embodiment of the message itself.

In light of the poetry section's insistence on Muḥammadan Light, how does one reconcile the emphasis on the Sufis mentioned previously in the poetry section with the fact that the source and inspirational text for the Kadızadelis is found in the very same library inventory? Indeed, two copies of Taqī al-Dīn Birgivī Meḥmed Efendī's (d. 981/1573), *al-Ṭarīqa al-muḥammadiyya* 'Muḥammadan Way', the text that the Kadızadelis took as their primer, are found in the *ḥadīth* section (#238 and #282).

The inclusion of Birgivī's *Ṭarīqa* in the library is not, in and of itself, an espousal of the Kadızadeli agenda, despite the accustomed association of the text with the movement. Birgivī's works generally focused on a kind of sober quotidian piety.[41] Although he did attack some practices and rituals often associated with Sufism as innovations (*bidʿa*/*bidaʿ*), he himself did not intend the kind of zealotry that was later exhibited

mel, *And Muhammad Is His Messenger*, 124; on early-Islamic ideas about and manifestations of Muḥammadan Light, Ibid., 124–126; Rubin, "Pre-Existence and Light"; and Sajdi, "Muḥammad's Luminous Nativity", forthcoming.

32 Schimmel, *And Muhammad Is His Messenger*, 132.

33 Ibid.

34 Gruber, *The Praiseworthy One*, 252–309; Hagen, "Pietas Ottomanica", 21.

35 Hagen, "Pietas Ottomanica".

36 Zilfi, *The Politics of Piety*, 136.

37 Algar, *Wahhabism*, 1.

38 Pagani, "The Reality and Image of the Prophet", 503.

39 Ibid., 515.

40 Ibid., 516.

41 Ivanyi, *Virtue, Piety and the Law*, 110–111.

by the Kadızadelis.[42] According to one modern historian, Birgivī '[u]nlike his avid readers in the years to come, was [himself] a product of the glory years of the Ottoman state'.[43] The same Ottoman scholars who were critical of the Kadızadelis continued to respect Birgivī and understood his *al-Ṭarīqa* as a 'valuable work the intellectual integrity of which ought to be preserved'.[44] Even those Ottoman sultans who rejected Kadızadeli commentaries on *al-Ṭarīqa al-muḥammadiyya* appreciated the work itself.[45] In other words, although the Kadızadelis' appropriation of Birgivī's text threatened the doctrine of Muḥammadan Light, Birgivī and his *al-Ṭarīqa al-muḥammadiyya* remained separate from the Kadızadelis in the minds of many of Ottoman intellectuals. For some later Ottomans, Birgivī's work represented an attempt at reform during the 'glory days' of the Ottoman Empire and, as such, was a classic. Given *al-Ṭarīqa al-muḥammadiyya*'s classic status and its focus on the Prophet, the library inventory scribe found it appropriate to place it in the *ḥadīth* section along with other devotional literature related to the first Muslim.

Birgivī's text notwithstanding, the *ḥadīth* section, as mentioned earlier, seems to complement our section in its general and specific message. Let me return to the example of the five texts of *mawlid*, a verse form that celebrates the nativity of Muḥammad. While the particular texts remain unidentified, if we take ʿAbd al-Ghanī al-Nābulusī's works as an example, his *mawlid*s are anchored in the idea of Muḥammadan Light.[46]

Although the poetry section does not reference the Wahhābīs or the Kadızadelis,[47] the works of Ibn al-ʿArabī, Ibn al-Fāriḍ and, most especially, al-Nābulusī represent an affirmation of a classical Ottoman piety and a continued insistence on the doctrine of Muḥammadan Light. This point is especially relevant since the patron of the library himself, Aḥmad Pasha al-Jazzār, in his capacity as governor of Damascus and leader of the Ḥajj, engaged in direct battles with the Wahhābīs.[48] Thus, it is only expected that al-Jazzār, or whoever chose the books for the library, would feature al-Nābulusī's work so prominently as an intellectual and ideological reference and anchor.

5 Conclusion: The Pasha's Light?

The panegyrics that were written in praise of al-Jazzār, the patron of the collection, are absent from our inventory's rather expansive poetry section. One such panegyric was written upon Napoleon's failure in the siege of Acre, which occurred before the library inventory was written. Entitled *Tārīkh ḥiṣār ʿAkka* (The History of the Siege of Acre), the poem highlights al-Jazzār's heroic role.[49] The absence of this and other panegyrics may be due to the fact that not enough time had lapsed for their inclusion. Or, perhaps, the library's curator did not want to dilute the educational purpose of the library.

The absence of the acknowledgement of al-Jazzār's military prowess in verse makes the library's general message bolder. I have shown how the poetry section is a celebration of the Light of Muḥammad. Given that Aḥmad is merely another name for Muḥammad, calling the college and the library 'The Light of Aḥmad' (*al-nūr aḥmadiyya*) reveals an intention to strike a synonymous relationship with the Light of Muḥammad (*al-nūr al-muḥammadī*). In other words, al-Jazzār's college and library complex seems to claim a Muḥam-

42 Zilfi, *The Politics of Piety*, 59.
43 Ibid., 144.
44 Cavusoglu, "The Kadızadeli Movement", 6–8.
45 Ibid., 6.
46 Pagani, "The Reality and Image of the Prophet", 503.
47 It is important to note that one of al-Nābulusī's legal works, *Sharḥ al-dalalāt*, appears in the *fiqh* section of our library (#474). This work explicitly converses with the Wahhābīs and argues against their prohibition of listening to music and musical instruments.
48 For a detailed account of al-Jazzār's service as ʾamīr al-Ḥajj, see Güler, *Cezzar Ahmed Paşa*, 127–164.
49 Ibn Budayr, *Tārīkh Ḥiṣār ʿAkka*, Princeton, Princeton University, Garrett no. 96H.

madan inheritance in the person of al-Jazzār. This proposition was a crucial prerequisite for al-Jazzār to claim the position of 'the Awaited Guided One' (*al-mahdī al-muntaẓar*), a status that was chronicled in the pasha's biographies.[50]

One of al-Jazzār's biographies, written by ʿAbd al-Razzāq al-Bīṭār in his biographical dictionary *Ḥilyat al-bashar fī tārīkh al-qarn al-thālith ʿashar*, provides a direct link between al-Jazzār's messianic claims and the prophecies of Ibn al-ʿArabī. In *Ḥilyat al-bashar*, al-Bīṭār reports that Ibn al-ʿArabī spoke of al-Jazzār in his *magnum opus al-Futūḥāt al-makkiyya* (Meccan Revelations).[51] Of the hundreds of revelations in *al-Futūḥāt*, each of which occupies a chapter, only one addresses the theme of the *mahdī* and affirms the necessity of a vizier to execute the mission of the Imām.[52] The author further discusses the indispensability of both the Imām and the vizier in a manner that emphasises their *unity*. Put differently, the line in Ibn al-ʿArabī's revelation that differentiates the *mahdī* from his vizier is blurry.

The *mahdī* and his viziers, according to Ibn al-ʿArabī, are at the centre of governance. Governance is based on the two figures equally. More importantly, one cannot exist without the other. In his revelation, Ibn al-ʿArabī's depiction of the *mahdī*, is portrayed in verse:[53]

He is the Guided Master from the House of Aḥmad;
He is the severe sword when he kills
He is the sun that melts away every sorrow (cloud) and darkness (oppression);
He is a monsoon downpour in his bounty.[54]

The traits described in these verses are strikingly similar to the perceptions of al-Jazzār. He is seen as a brutal fighter, as shown by his *sobriquet* 'the Butcher', and a generous benefactor, as shown by his charitable works and money gifts. But, our (originally Christian) Bosnian governor who found in Ibn al-ʿArabī's prophecy an inspiration for, or vindication of, his severity and generosity, still required a direct connection to 'the House of Aḥmad' to fulfill the prophecy. The prophecies surrounding al-Jazzār seem to have effected a desired and intentional association with Muḥammad. While al-Jazzār was unable to claim a blood connection with the Prophet, he was able to attach himself to the Muḥammadan Essence (*al-ḥaqīqa al-muḥammadiyya*).

The poetry section in al-Jazzār's library is not only an educational collection; it serves to preserve a classical Levantine Ottoman creed and piety that centres around the Prophet by affirming the idea of Muḥammadan Light. These beliefs had come under attack in the seventeenth and eighteenth centuries by Kadızadelis and the Wahhābīs, respectively. In preserving this doctrine, the library provides the intellectual support and arsenal necessary for al-Jazzār to fight his enemies in Arabia. At the same time, that arsenal is employed as a means for self-aggrandisement. The Light of Aḥmad shines through the shelves that propagate Muḥammadan Light.

50 Al-Zayyānī, *al-Turjumāna*, 259. See the editors' *Introduction*, Chapter 4 by Feras Krimsti, Chapter 22 by Dana Sajdi and Chapter 24 by Liana Saif for a more detailed account of al-Jazzār's biographies.

51 Al-Bīṭār, *Ḥilyat al-bashar*, 129. A similar prophecy is found in the chronicle of the nineteenth century Ottoman historian Cabi Ömer Efendi. In it, the chronicler mentions another Ibn al-ʿArabī prophecy found in al-Shajara al-Nuʿmāniyya in connection with al-Jazzār. Cabi, *Cabi Tarihi*, 1, 84. I thank Guy Burak for this reference.

52 Ibn al-ʿArabī, *al-Futūḥāt al-makkiyya*, 50.

53 Ibid., 52.

54 *Huwa-al-sayyidu al-mahdiyyu min ʿāl Aḥmad / huwa-al-ṣārimu al-hindiyyu ḥīna yubīdu/*
Huwa-al-shamsu yajlū kulla ghammin wa-ẓulmatin / huwa-al-wābilu al-wasmiyyu ḥīna yajūdu

Bibliography

Akkach, Samer. *Intimate Invocations: Al-Ghazzī's Biography of ʾAbd al-Ghanī al-Nābulusī (1641–1731)*. Leiden/Boston, 2012.

Akkach, Samer. "The Eye of Reflection: Al-Nabulusi's Spatial Interpretation of Ibn ʿArabi's Tomb." *Muqarnas Online* 32, no. 1 (2015): 79–95.

Algar, Hamid. *Wahhabism: A Critical Essay*. Oneonta, 2002.

Bauer, Thomas. "Mamluk Literature: Misunderstandings and New Approaches." *Mamluk Studies Review* 9, no. 2 (2005): 10532.

Bauer, Thomas. "Al-Nawājī." In *Essays in Arabic Literary Biography 1350–1850*, edited by Joseph E. Lowry and Devin J. Stewart, 321–331. Weisbaden, 2009.

Bauer, Thomas. "S̲h̲āʿir." In *Encyclopaedia of Islam New Edition Online (EI-2 English)*, edited by P. Bearman. Leiden, 2012. DOI: https://doi.org/10.1163/1573-3912_islam_COM_1447

Al-Bīṭār, ʿAbd al-Razzāq. *Ḥilyat al-bashar fī tārīkh al-qarn al-thālith ʿashar*, edited by Muḥammad Bahjat al-Bīṭar. Beirut, 1993.

Cabi, Ömer Efendi, *Cabi tarihi veya Tarih-i Sultan Selim-i salis ve Mahmud-ı sani*. 2 vols. Edited by Mehmet Ali Beyhan. Ankara, 2003.

Cavusoglu, Semiramis. "The Kadizadeli Movement: An Attempt of Şeriʿat-minded Reform in the Ottoman Empire." Ph.D diss, Princeton University, 1990.

El Shamsy, Ahmed. *Rediscovering the Islamic Classics: How Editors and Print Culture Transformed an Intellectual Tradition*. Princeton, 2020.

Güler, Mustafa. *Cezzar Ahmed Paşa ve Akka Savunmasi*. Istanbul, 2013.

Gruber, Christiane. *The Praiseworthy One: The Prophet Muhammad In Islamic Texts and Images*. Indiana, 2018.

Hagen, Gottfried. "Pietas Ottomanica: The House of ʿOs̲mān and the Prophet Muḥammad." In *The Presence of the Prophet in Early Modern and Contemporary Islam*, edited by Rachida Chih, David Jordan and Stefan Reichmuth, 21–43. Volume 2, *Heirs of the Prophet: Authority and Power*. 3 vols. Leiden/Boston, 2022.

Hillenbrand, C. "Al-Ṭughrāʾī." In *Encyclopedia of Arabic Literature*, edited by Julie Meisami and Paul Starkey, II, 783. London/New York, 1998.

Hirschler, Konrad. *Medieval Damascus: Plurality and Diversity in an Arabic Library: The Ashrafiya Library Catalogue*. Edinburgh, 2016.

Homerin, Th Emil. "Al-Būṣīrī." In *Encyclopaedia of Islam Three Online*, edited by K. Fleet, G. Krämer, D. Matringe, J. Nawas and D.J. Stewart. Leiden, 2010. DOI: https://doi.org/10.1163/1573-3912_ei3_COM_23124

Ibn al-ʿArabī, Muḥyī al-Dīn. *Al-Futūḥāt al-makkiyya*, edited by Aḥmad Shams al-Dīn. 9 vols. Beirut, 2011.

Ibn Budayr, *Tārīkh Ḥiṣār ʿAkka*, Princeton, Princeton University Library, Garrett no. 96H.

Ivanyi, Katharina Anna. "*Virtue, Piety and the Law: A Study of Birgivī Meḥmed Efendī's* al-Ṭarīqa al-Muḥammadiyya." Ph.D diss, Princeton University, 2012.

Kazimirski, de Biberstein. *Dictionnaire Arabe-Français*. Paris, 1860.

Kennedy, P.F. "Tak̲h̲mīs." In *Encyclopaedia of Islam New Edition Online (EI-2 English)*, edited by P. Bearman. Leiden, 2012. DOI: https://doi.org/10.1163/1573-3912_islam_SIM_7332

Loop, Jan. "Arabic Poetry as Teaching Material in Early Modern Grammars and Textbooks." In *The Teaching and Learning of Arabic in Early Modern Europe*, edited by Jan Loop, Alastair Hamilton and Charles Burnett, 230–251. Leiden/Boston, 2017.

Orfali, Bilal. *The Anthologist's Art: Abū Manṣūr al-Thaʿālibī and His Yatīmat al-Dahr*. Leiden/Boston, 2016.

Pagani, Samuela. "The Reality and Image of the Prophet According to the Theologian and Poet ʿAbd Al-Ghanī al-Nābulusī." In *The Presence of the Prophet in Early Modern and Contemporary Islam*, edited by Denis Gril, Stefan Reichmuth and Dilek Sarmis, 501–534. Volume 1, *The Prophet Between Doctrine, Literature and Arts: Historical Legacies and Their Unfolding*. 3 vols. Leiden/Boston, 2022.

Pellat, Ch, J.T.P. de Bruijn, B. Flemming and J.A. Haywood. "Mad̲j̲nūn Laylā." In *Encyclopaedia of Islam New Edition Online (EI-2 English)*, edited by P. Bearman. Leiden, 2012. DOI: https://doi.org/10.1163/1573-3912_islam_COM_0608

Qutbuddin, Tahera. "Books on Arabic Philology and

Literature: A Teaching Collection Focused on Religious Learning and the State Chancery." In *Treasures of Knowledge: An Inventory of the Ottoman Palace Library (1502/3–1503/4)*, I, 607–634. Leiden/Boston, 2019.

Reynolds, Dwight. "Lost Virgins Found: The Arabic Songbook Genre and an Early North African Exemplar." *Quaderni Di Studi Arabi* 7 (2012): 69–105.

El-Rouayheb, Khaled. "Books on Logic (Manṭiq) and Dialectics (Jadal)." In *Treasures of Knowledge: An Inventory of the Ottoman Palace Library (1502/3–1503/4)*, edited by Gülru Necipoğlu, Cemal Kafadar and Cornell H. Fleischer, I, 891–906. Leiden/Boston, 2019.

Rubin, Uri. "Pre-existence and Light: Aspects of the Concept of Nūr Muḥammad." In *Muhammad the Prophet and Arabia*. Franham, 2011.

Sajdi, Dana. "Muḥammad's Luminous Nativity." Forthcoming.

Schimmel, Annemarie. *And Muhammad Is His Messenger: The Veneration of the Prophet in Islamic Piety*. Chapel Hill, 1985.

Van Gelder, Geert Jan. "Badīʿiyya." In *Encyclopaedia of Islam Three Online*, edited by K. Fleet, G. Krämer, D. Matringe, J. Nawas and D.J. Stewart. Leiden, 2009. DOI: https://doi.org/10.1163/1573-3912_ei3_COM_23309

al-Zayyānī, Abū al-Qāsim Muḥammad. *al-Turjumāna al-kubrā fī akhbār al-maʿmūr barran wa-baḥran*, edited by ʿAbd al-Karīm al-Fīlālī. 2nd ed. Rabat: Dār Nashr al-Maʿrifa, 1991.

Zilfi, Madeline C. *The Politics of Piety: The Ottoman Ulema in the Postclassical Age (1600–1800)*. Minneapolis, 1988.

Odes and Poetry Collections

Note: All references to Ḥājjī Khalīfa, *KẒ*; al-Ziriklī, *Aʿlām*; and Muḥammad Khalīl al-Murādī, *Silk al-Durar* (SD) are accessed via al-Makataba al-Shāmila, vers. 3.48, online access https://shamela.ws/, accessed Jan 2023. I am grateful to Elif Sezer-Aydınlı for her help in the initial stages of transcription, transliteration, and research.

[1133] ***Dīwān Muḥyī al-Dīn Ibn al-ʿArabī*** (d. 638/1240), AUTHOR: Muḥyī al-Dīn Ibn al-ʿArabī (d. 638/1240), EDITION: Cairo: Bulāq, 1850. There are several *dīwān*s attributed to Ibn al-ʿArabī. Several well-known poems are not included in the Būlāq edition.

[1134] ***Dīwān ʿUmar Ibn al-Fāriḍ***, AUTHOR: ʿUmar Ibn al-Fāriḍ (d. 632/1235), EDITION: Giuseppe Scattolin, Cairo: al-Maʿhad al-ʿIlmī al-Faransī lil-Āthār al-Sharqiyya, 2004.

[1135] ***Dīwān ʿUmar Ibn al-Fāriḍ***, see #1134.

[1136] ***Sharḥ dīwān ʿUmar Ibn al-Fāriḍ***, unidentified. At least two commentaries were written on Ibn al-Fāriḍ's *dīwān* before the nineteenth century. The first is by ʿAbd al-Ghanī al-Nābulusī (d. 1143/1731), *Kashf al-sirr al-ghāmiḍ fī sharḥ Dīwān Ibn al-Fāriḍ*, EDITION: Khālid al-Zarʿī, Damascus: Dār Nīnawā, 2017; and the second is by Badr al-Dīn al-Būrīnī (d. 1024/1615), *al-Baḥr al-fāʾiḍ fī sharḥ Dīwān Ibn al-Fāriḍ*, Cairo, Dār al-Kutub al-Qawmiyya, 676 Taymūr; and al-Būrīnī, *al-Baḥr al-fāʾiḍ*, Leipzig, Leipzig University Library, Vollers 536. Only the latter is mentioned by Hajjī Khalīfa, *KẒ*, 1:767.

[1137] ***Sharḥ dīwān ʿUmar Ibn al-Fāriḍ***, see #1136.

[1138] ***Dīwān ʿAbd al-Ghanī al-Nābulusī***, AUTHOR: ʿAbd al-Ghanī al-Nābulusī (d. 1143/1731), unidentified, cf #1140, see #1150 and #1187. Al-Nābulusī's poetry has been collected in several *dīwan*s making it difficult to identify the entry.

[1139] ***Dīwān al-ghazal li-ʿAbd al-Ghanī al-Nābulusī***, AUTHOR: ʿAbd al-Ghanī al-Nābulusī (d. 1143/1731). This title probably refers to the fourth part of *Dīwān al-Dawāwīn* (see #1187) which is also known as *Khamrat Bābil wa-ghināʾ al-balābil*, mentioned by al-Murādī among al-Nābulusī's works (al-Murādī, *SD*, 3, 34). The *dīwān* appears in print under a different title: *Burj Bābil wa-shadw al-balābil*. EDITION: Aḥmad al-Jundī, Damascus: Dār al-Maʿrifa, 1988.

[1140] ***Dīwān al-ghazal ʿAbd al-Ghanī al-Nābulusī***, see #1139.

[1141] ***Bānat Suʿād** wa-**Alfiyyāt al-ʿIrāqī***, AUTHORS: Kaʿb b. Zuhayr (d. first/seventh century) and Abū al-Faḍl Zayn al-Dīn ʿAbd al-Raḥmān al-ʿIrāqī (d. 806/1404), EDITION: for *Bānat Suʿād*: see #1142. For *Alfiyyāt al-ʿIrāqī*, also known as *al-Tabṣira wa-al-Tadhkira fī ʿIlm al-Ḥadīth*:

Al-ʿArabī al-Dāʾiz al-Firyaṭī, Riyadh: Dār al-Minhāj, 2005.

[1142] ***Bānat Suʿād***, AUTHOR: Kaʿb b. Zuhayr (d. first/seventh century), EDITION: Mufīd Qamḥiyya, Riyadh: Dār al-Shawwāf, and Jeddah: Dār al-Maṭbūʿāt al-Ḥadītha, 1989. This poem was edited and published as a part of Kaʿb b. Zuhayr's *dīwān*. I could not find a separate critical edition in print.

[1143] ***Sharḥ bānat Suʿād***, unidentified. There are many commentaries on *Bānat Suʿād* such as that of Ibn Hishām (see #1146); al-Khaṭīb al-Tibrīzī (d. 502/1109), EDITION: Fakhr al-Dīn Qabāwa, Cairo: Dār al-Salām, 2022; and Ibn Ḥijja al-Ḥamawī (d. 837/1434), EDITION: ʿAlī Ḥusayn al-Bawwāb, Riyadh: Dār al-Maʿārif, 2011.

[1144] ***Sharḥ bānat Suʿād***, unidentified, see #1143.

[1145] ***Sharḥ bānat Suʿād li-Ibn Hishām***, AUTHOR: ʿAbd Allāh b. Yūsuf Ibn Hishām (d. 213/828 or 218/833), EDITION: Ignatius Guidi, Lipsiae: Typis F.A. Brockhaus, 1871.

[1146] ***Sharḥ bānat Suʿād***, unidentified, see #1143.

[1147] ***Sharḥ al-yāʾiyya li-ʿUmar Ibn al-Fāriḍ***, unidentified. Ibn al-Fāriḍ composed several *yāʾiyyas* in his *dīwān*, but the longest and most famous, which begins with *ʿsāʾiq al-aẓʿān yaṭwī al-bīd ṭayy*ʾ (O' Caravan guide, crossing the desert), is the one known as *Yāʾiyyat Ibn al-Fāriḍ*, on which al-Suyūti wrote a commentary: *al-Barq al-wāmiḍ fī sharḥ yāʾiyyat Ibn al-Fāriḍ*. See: Al-Suyūti, *al-Barq al-wāmiḍ fī sharḥ yāʾiyyat Ibn al-Fāriḍ*, Cairo: Dār al-Kutub wa-al-Wathāʾiq al-Qawmiyya, 2011.

[1148] ***Ahnā al-manāʾiḥ li-asnā al-madāʾiḥ***, AUTHOR: al-Qāḍī Shihāb al-Dīn Abī al-Thanāʾ Maḥmūd b. Salmān b. Fahd al-Ḥalabī (d. 725/1325), EDITION: Maḥmūd b. Salmān b. Fahd and Alī Fahmī b. Rifāʿa al-Ṭahṭāwī, Cairo: Maṭbaʿat Jarīdat al-Shūrī, 1916. MANUSCRIPT: Dublin, Chester Beatty Library, AR. 3310.

[1149] *Qiṭʿa min* ***al-Hamziyya***, unidentified. The entry title is too generic. However, its placement early in the list within the category of panegyrics to the Prophet strongly suggests that the entry may refer to Sharaf al-Dīn Muḥammad b. Saʿīd b. Ḥammād al-Būṣīrī's (d. 694–696/1294–1297) famous *Hamziyya*, also known as *Qaṣīdat Umm al-Qurā fī madḥ Khayr al-Warā*. EDITION: Muḥammad al-Shādhilī al-Nayfar, Gaza: Wāḥat Āl al-Bayt li-Iḥyāʾ al-Turāth wa-al-ʿUlūm.

[1150] ***Nafḥat al-qabūl fī madḥ al-Nabī al-Rasūl***, AUTHOR: ʿAbd al-Ghanī al-Nābulusī (d. 1143/1731), EDITION: Firdaws Nūr ʿAlī Ḥusayn, Cairo: Dār al-Fikr al-ʿArabī, 1999. This *dīwān* is the second part of al-Nābulusī's *Dīwān al-Dawāwīn* (cf. #1187).

[1151] ***Takhmīs al-burda***, unidentified. The entry title is too vague. The author of the *takhmīs*, a form of poetical amplification that involves adding three hemistichs to each verse (*bayt*) of a poem, is not mentioned. Given that al-Būṣīrī's poem, *al-Burda* (The Mantle), enjoyed more than 80 such *takhmīs*es in the various Islamicate languages, it is probable that this entry may be one of those. However, one cannot dismiss the possibility of this being in reference to Kaʿb b. Zuhayr's *Bānat Suʿād*. (Kennedy, P.F., "Takhmīs", *EI2*. Accessed 08 January 2023).

[1152] ***Dīwān Muhyī al-Dīn Ibn al-ʿArabī***, see #1133.

[1153] ***Sharḥ qaṣāʾid Muhyī al-Dīn Ibn al-ʿArabī***, unidentified.

[1154] ***Sharḥ qaṣāʾid Ibn Zuhayr***, unidentified. Several scholars commented on Ibn Zuhayr's (d. first/seventh century) *dīwān*. One of the earliest compilers of and commentors on Ibn Zuhayr's poetry is Abū Saʿīd al-Ḥasan al-Sukkarī (d. 275/888). EDITION: *Sharḥ Dīwān Kaʿb b. Zuhayr*, ʿAbbās ʿAbd al-Qādir, Cairo: Dār al-Kutub al-Miṣriyya, 1950.

[1155] ***Sharḥ qaṣāʾid al-Munfarija***, AUTHOR: unidentified. *Al-qaṣīda al-munfarija* or *qaṣīdat al-faraj baʿd al-shidda* (poem on 'relief after difficulty') is a genre of poetry that begins with a promise of resolution to crisis or difficult circumstances. Historically, this genre was not limited to poetry, but several poems known as *al-munfarija* acquired canonical status and attracted commentators. Hajjī Khalīfa mentions a *munfarija* composed by Abū al-Ḥasan ʿAlī b. Khalīl al-Miṣrī al-Zāhid, who was known as al-Marṣafī (Hajjī Khalīfa, *KẒ*, 2: 369). Another *munfarija* is sometimes attributed to Abū Ḥāmid al-Ghazzālī (Brockelmann/Lameer (trans.), GAL I, 274.), but one of the most famous is the *munfarija* attributed to Yūsuf b. Muḥammad al-Tawzarī, who is known as Ibn al-Naḥwī. Ibn al-Naḥwī's *munfarija* attracted numerous commentators. Several commentaries on ibn al-Naḥwī's *munfarija*, one of which was written in Ottoman, are listed in *Kashf al-Ẓunūn* (Hajjī Khalīfa, KẒ, 2:346). The entry title above suggests that the book is a commentary, an anthology or a collection of *munfarija* poems, but it is impossible to identify since neither the commentator nor the poets are mentioned.

[1156] ***Dīwān Majnūn Laylā***, AUTHOR: Qays b. al-Mulawwaḥ (d. c. 68/688), EDITION: ʿAbd al-Sātir Aḥmad Farrāj, Cairo: Maktabat Maṣr, 1979.

[1157] ***Dīwān al-Shushtarī***, AUTHOR: ʿAlī b. ʿAbd Allāh al-Shushtarī (d. 668/1269), EDITION: Muḥammad al-ʿAdlūnī al-Idrīsī/Saʿīd Abū al-Fuyūḍ, Casablanca: Dār al-Thaqāfa, 2008.

[1158] ***Dīwān Abī al-ʿAlāʾ al-Maʿarrī***, AUTHOR: Abū al ʿAlāʾ al-Maʿarrī (d. 449/1058), unidentified. Al-Maʿarrī's poetry is collected in two known *dīwān*s: *Luzūm mā lā yalzam*, EDITION: ʿAzīz Zand, Cairo: Maṭbaʿat al-Maḥrūsa, 1891–1895; and *Saqṭ al-Zand*, EDITION: Yaḥyā Tibrīzī, Cairo: al-Maṭbaʿa al-Iʿlāmiyya: 1886.

[1159] ***Dīwān Abī al-ʿAlāʾ al-Maʿarrī***, see #1158.

[1160] ***Dīwān Abī al-ʿAlāʾ al-Maʿarrī***, see #1158.

[1161] *Qaṣāʾid fī madḥ khayr al-warā,* ***Badīʿiyyāt al-ʿumyān***, AUTHOR: Muḥammad b. Aḥmad b. Jābir al-Andalusī (d. 780/1378), EDITION: ʿAbd Allāh Mukhliṣ, Cairo: al-Maṭbaʿa al-Salafiyya, 1929–1930.

[1162] ***Sharḥ al-Badīʿiyyāt li-Ibn Ḥijja***, AUTHOR: Ibn Ḥijja Taqiyy al-Dīn b. Alī b. ʿAbd Allāh al-Ḥamawī al-Azrārī (d. 837/1434). The title hints at the author's commentary on his own *badīʿiyya*, known as *Khizānat al-adab wa-ghāyat al-arab*. In this commentary here, Ibn Ḥijja criticizes several other *badīʿiyyas* to show the superiority of his own. EDITION: Beirut: Dār wa-Maktabat al-Hilāl, 2004.

[1163] ***Dīwān Abī al-Ṭayyib al-Mutanabbī***, AUTHOR: Abū al-Ṭayyib Aḥmad b. al-Ḥusayn al-Mutanabbī (d. 354/965), EDITION: Friedrich Dieterici, Berlin: E.S. Mittler, 1861. One of the library's *Dīwān al-*Mutanabbī manuscripts is now to be found at al-Azhar library in Cairo. MANUSCRIPT: Cairo, al-Azhar Library, MS 22783.

[1164] ***Dīwān al-Mutanabbī***, see #1163.

[1165] ***Dīwān al-Mutanabbī***, see #1163.

[1166] ***Dīwān al-Mutanabbī***, see #1163.

[1167] ***Dīwān al-Mutanabbī***, see #1163.

[1168] ***Dīwān al-Mutanabbī***, see #1163.

[1169] ***Dīwān al-Mutanabbī***, see #1163.

[1170] ***Dīwān al-Mutanabbī***, see #1163.

[1171] ***Sharḥ Dīwān Abī al-Ṭayyib al-Mutanabbī,*** *al-juzʾ al-thānī*, unidentified. The commentaries on al-Mutanabbī's *dīwān* are too numerous to list here. Ḥajjī Khalīfa mentions some. See Hajjī Khalīfa, *KẒ*, 1:809.

[1172] ***Dīwān Abī Tammām***, AUTHOR: Abū Tammām Ḥabīb b. Aws al-Ṭāʾī (d. 231/845 or 232/846), EDITION: Muḥyī al-Dīn al-Khayyāṭ, Damascus: 1900.

[1173] ***Dīwān Abī Tammām***, see #1172.

[1174] ***Dīwān Abī Tammām***, see #1172.

[1175] ***Dīwān Imruʾ al-Qays***, AUTHOR: Imruʾ al-Qays (d. c. 550 A.D), EDITION: Muḥammad Abū al-Faḍl Ibrāhīm, Cairo: Dār al-Maʿārif, 1958.

[1176] ***Dīwān Abī Firās***, AUTHOR: Abū Firās al-Ḥamdānī (d. 357/968), EDITION: Sāmī al-Dahhān, Damascus: Institut Francais de Damas, 1944.

[1177] ***Dīwān al-Bahāʾ Zuhayr***, AUTHOR: Bahāʾ al-Dīn Zuhayr b. Muḥammad (d. 656/1258), EDITION: Muḥammad Abū al-Faḍl Ibrāhīm/Muḥammad Ṭāhir al-Jabalāwī, Cairo: Dār al-Maʿārif, 1982.

[1178] ***Dīwān al-Bahāʾ Zuhayr***, see #1177.

[1179] ***Dīwān Ibn Nubāta***, AUTHOR: Abū Bakr Jamāl al-Dīn Muḥammad Ibn Nubāta al-Miṣrī

(d. 768/1366), EDITION: Muḥammad al-Qalqīlī, Cairo: Maṭbaʿat al-Tamaddun, 1905.

[1180] ***Dīwān al-Ṣabāba***, AUTHOR: Shihāb al-Dīn Aḥmad b. Yaḥyā Ibn Abī Ḥajala (d. 776/1375), EDITION: Cairo: al-Maṭbaʿa al-Adabiyya, 1899–1900.

[1181] ***Dīwān al-Ṣabāba***, see #1180.

[1182] ***Dīwān al-Qīrāṭī***, AUTHOR: Ibrāhīm b. ʿAbd Allāh b. Muḥammad b. ʿAskar al-Ṭāʾī, known as Burhān al-Dīn al-Qīrāṭī (d. 781/1381). The poet's *dīwān* is entitled *Maṭlaʿ al-nayyirayn* (Where the Sun and Moon Rise), and it is mentioned by al-Ziriklī, *Aʿlām*, 1:49. However, I was not able to find a critical edition.

[1183] ***Dīwān Ibn al-Rūmī***, AUTHOR: Ibn al-Rūmī (d. 283/896), EDITION: Ḥusayn Naṣṣār, Cairo: Dār al-Kutub wa-al-Wathāʾiq al-Qawmiyya, 2003. The *dīwān* of Ibn al-Rūmī is enormous and never received a dependable critical edition. The current edition is not comprehensive, despite the editor's assertions to the contrary.

[1184] ***Dīwān Ṣafī al-Dīn al-Ḥillī***, AUTHOR: Ṣafī al-Dīn ʿAbd al-ʿAzīz b. Sarāya al-Ḥillī (d. c. 750/1349), EDITION: Damascus: Maṭbaʿat Ḥabīb Afandī Khālid, 1880.

[1185] ***Dīwān al-Ḥamāsa***, AUTHOR: Abū Tammām Ḥabīb b. Aws al-Ṭāʾī (d. 231/845 or 232/846), EDITION: Aḥmad Ḥasan Basaj, Beirut: Dār al-Kutub al-ʿIlmiyya, 1998.

[1186] ***Dīwān al-Ḥamāsa***, see #1185.

[1187] ***Dīwān al-Dawāwīn***, AUTHOR: ʿAbd al-Ghanī al-Nābulusī (d. 1143/1731). This *dīwān* consists of four poetry collections, each of which is a separate *dīwān*. It was carefully compiled by the poet in order to convey his spiritual achievement through its structure. Two parts of *Dīwān al-dawāwīn* are found individually in the library inventory: *Khamrat Bābil wa-ghināʿ al-balābil* (see #1139, #1140), and *Nafḥat al-qabūl fī madḥat al-Nabī al-Rasūl* (#1150). One of the library's manuscripts, now in Imam Mohammad Ibn Saud Islamic University, contains three diwans/parts of *Dīwān al-dawāwīn*. It is not *Nafḥat al-qabūl* (#1150) on its own, but it does not include the first *dīwān*/part of *Dīwān al-dawāwīn* (#1187) either. This manuscript might have been complete and listed under *Dīwān al-dawāwīn* (this entry), or might also be the *dīwān* listed under the title *Dīwān ʿAbd al-Ghanī al-Nābulusī* (#1138). MANUSCRIPT: Riyad, Imam Mohammad Ibn Saud Islamic University, MS 1094.

[1188] ***Dīwān Nathr al-naẓm wa-ḥall al-ʿaqd***, AUTHOR: ʿAbd al-Malik b. Muḥammad al-Thaʿālibī (d. 429/1038): EDITION: Damascus: Maṭbaʿat al-Wilāya al-Jalīla, 1883. Despite referring to it as a *dīwān*, this work is not a *dīwān*. It is, however, loaded with poetry which might explain its name and place in the library. It seems that a *dīwān*, according to the scribe, refers to a book of poetry even if it was not strictly a *dīwān*.

[1189] ***Dīwān Kushājim***, AUTHOR: Abū al-Fatḥ Maḥmūd b. al-Ḥusayn Kushājim (d. 350/961 or 360/971), EDITION: Muḥammad Ḥasan al-Shāfiʿī, Beirut: Dār al-Kutub al-ʿIlmiyya, 1998.

[1190] ***Dīwān Ibn Ḥajar***, unidentified. The *dīwān* listed in this entry is either that of the pre-Islamic poet Aws b. Ḥajar Abū Shurayḥ al-Tamīmī (sixth century), EDITION: Muḥammad Yūsuf Najm, Beirut: Dār Bayrūt lil-Ṭibāʿa wa-al-Nashr, 1980, or that of Shihāb al-Dīn Abū al-Faḍl Aḥmad Ibn Ḥajar al-Asqalānī, EDITION: Firdaws Nūr Alī Ḥusayn, Cairo: Dār al-Faḍīla, 2000.

[1191] ***Dīwān Ibn Kīwān***, AUTHOR: Aḥmad b. Ḥusayn b. Muṣṭafā Ibn Kīwān (d. 1033/1624), also known as al-Kīwānī, EDITION: ʿAbd al-Qādir Ibn ʿUmar Nabhān, Damascus: al-Maṭbaʿa al-Ḥanafiyya, 1884.

[1192] ***Dīwān Ibn Kīwān***, see #1191.

[1193] ***Dīwān al-Dūkānī***, unidentified. I could not find any poet called al-Dūkānī, but al-Murādī mentions an eighteenth-century Moroccan scholar, Qāsim al-Dūkālī (d. 1120/1708), who resided in Damascus (al-Murādī, *SD*, 4:9). Being a near-contemporary of al-Jazzār, al-Dūkālī's works may have made it to the al-Jazzār library, however, none of the works by al-Dūkālī available qualifies as a book of collected poetry. The entry might also refer to a *dīwān* of Muḥammad b. ʿAlī b. ʿAbd al-Wāḥid al-Dūkālī (d. 763/1361) who, according to al-Zirikli, 'had good poetry'. See al-Ziriklī, *Aʿlām*, 6:286.

[1194] ***Dīwān Ibn ʿUnayn***, AUTHOR: Muḥammad b. Naṣr Abū al-Maḥāsin Sharaf al-Dīn Ibn ʿUnayn (d. 630/1233), EDITION: Khalīl Mardam Bayk, Damascus: al-Majmaʿ al-ʿIlmī al-ʿArabī, 1946.

[1195] ***Dīwān Abī al-ʿAbbās***, unidentified. The entry is too generic given the abbreviation of the author's name to Abū al-ʿAbbās. There were several poets who shared this name. Among them are Abū al-ʿAbbās al-Ḥalabī whose *dīwān*, *ʿArāʾis al-afkār*, is listed in the inventory (see #1234). Another such poet is Abū al-ʿAbbās Fakhr al-Dīn who is also known as Ibn Luqmān. The latter was a student of al-Bahāʾ Zuhayr, whose *dīwān* is also found in the library inventory (see #1177, #1178). See al-Ziriklī, *Aʿlām*, 1:58. A third option might be Abū al-ʿAbbās ʿAbd Allāh b. al-Muʿtazz (d. 296/909).

[1196] ***Dīwān Ibn al-Ḥaddād***, AUTHOR: Muḥammad b. Aḥmad b. ʿUthmān, Ibn al-Ḥaddād (d. 480/1086–1087), EDITION: Yūsuf ʿAlī Ṭawīl, Beirut: Dār al-Kutub al-ʿIlmiyya, 1990.

[1197] ***Dīwān Jawhar al-naḍḍār***, unidentified.

[1198] ***Dīwān al-Akhṭal***, AUTHOR: Abū Mālik Ghiyāth b. Ghawth al-Akhṭal (d. 92/710), EDITION: Fakhr al-Dīn Qabāwa, Damascus: Dār al-Fikr, 1971.

[1199] ***Dīwān al-Bākharzī***, AUTHOR: Abū al-Ḥasan ʿAlī b. al-Ḥasan b. ʿAlī b. Abū al-Ṭayyib al-Bākharzī (d. 476/1075). EDITION: Muḥammad al-Tunjī, Benghazi: al-Jāmiʿa al-Lībiyya, 1973.

[1200] ***Dīwān al-Saʿāda***, unidentified. The author may be Aḥmad Shamsī Pāshā (d. 988/1580), whose Ottoman Turkish *Dīwān ʿUnwān al-Saʿāda* is in Damascus, National al-Asad Library, MS 10026.

[1201] ***Dīwān al-Mubarrad***, unidentified. The author may be Abū al-Abbās Muḥammad b. Yazīd al-Mubarrad (d. 285/898). Although a known poet, there is no surviving record of a *dīwān* attributed to him. Al-Mubarrad's most famous work, *al-Kāmil*, is an anthology of poetry and prose, EDITION: Ibrāhīm al-Daljamūnī al-Azharī, Cairo: al-Maṭbaʿa al-Azhariyya, 1920.

[1202] ***Dīwān Najdiyyāt***, AUTHOR: Abū al-Muẓaffar Muḥammad b. Aḥmad al-Abyawardī (d. 507/1113–1114). The work, which has not received a critical edition, is also known as *al-Najdiyyāt fī al-nasab*. See Hajjī Khalīfa, KẒ, 2:1930.

[1203] ***Dīwān ʿAlī Ibn al-Ḥusayn***, unidentified. The entry title is too vague, and there is no existing record of a poet under the name ʿAlī Ibn al-Ḥusayn. The author's name suggests a filial relation to al-Ḥusayn, the grandson of the Prophet and the third Shīʿī *imam*. However, al-Ḥusayn's eldest son, ʿAlī al-Akbar, was not known as a poet. The youngest son, Zayn al-ʿĀbidīn, was indeed a poet whose verse was collected under the title *Dīwān al-Sajjād*, EDITION: Mājid b. Aḥmad al-ʿAtiyya, Beirut: Muʾassasat al-Aʿlamī lil-maṭbūʿāt, 2002.

[1204] ***Dīwān Ibn Thābit***, AUTHOR: Ḥassān Ibn Thābit (d. 40/659 or before that year, or 50/669, or 54/673), EDITION: Tunis: Maṭbaʿat al-Dawla al-Tūnisiyya, 1864–1865.

[1205] ***Dīwān al-Ḥāfiẓ al-Shīrāzī***, AUTHOR: al-Ḥāfiẓ al-Shīrāzī (d. c. 792/1390), EDITION: Parvīz Nātil Khānlarī, Tehran: 1939–1942. This work is in Persian.

[1206] ***Dīwān al-Kaydānī***, unidentified.

[1207] ***Dīwān al-Miʿmār al-Adīb***, AUTHOR: Jamāl al-Dīn Ibrāhīm al-Miʿmār (d. 749/1348–1349), EDITION: Thomas Bauer, Anke Osigus, Hakan Özkan, Baden-Baden: Ergon Verlag, 2018.

[1208] ***Takhmīs Lāmiyyat al-ʿajam maʿ takhmīs Bānāt Suʿād***, unidentified. Hajjī Khalīfa mentions two poets who composed *takhmīs*es on *Lāmiyyat al-ʿajam*: Abū Jaʿfar al-Baghdādī (d.?) and Shihāb al-Dīn Aḥmad al-Andalusī (d. 739/1938–1939) (KẒ, 2:1537). As for *Bānat Suʿād*, Ḥājjī Khalīfa mentions two *takhmīs*es on the poem. One is by Muḥammad b. Shaʿbān al-Qurashī (d.?) and the other by al-Kisāʿī (d. 189/805) (KẒ, 2:1329).

[1209] ***Sharḥ Lāmiyyat al-ʿajam***, unidentified. This *lāmiyya* was subject to many interpretations, commentaries, and sequels to said commentaries. The most famous commentators are Abū al-Baqā' al-Akbarī (d. 616/1219–1220), ʿAlī b. Qāsim al-Ṭabarī (d. 683/1284–1284) and Khalīl b. Aybak al-Ṣafadī (d. 764/1363), (Ḥājjī Khalīfa, *KẒ*, 2:1537). Later commentators include al-Suyūṭī (d. 911/1505). EDITION: Aḥmad Alī Ḥasan, Cairo: Maktabat al-Ādāb, no date.

[1210] ***Sharḥ Lāmiyyat al-ʿajam***, see #1209.

[1211] ***Sharḥ Lāmiyyat al-ʿajam***, see #1209.

[1212] ***Sharḥ Lāmiyyat al-ʿajam wa-yalīhā Lāmiyyat Ibn al-Wardī***, unidentified. For *Sharḥ Lāmiyyat al-ʿajam*, see #1209. *Lāmiyyat Ibn al-Wardī*, composed by Sarāj al-Dīn ʿUmar b. Muẓaffar Zayn al-Dīn Ibn al-Wardī al-Kindī al-Maʿarrī (d. 749/1348–1349), carries the title *Naṣīḥat al-ikhwān wa-murshidat al-khillān fī al-mawāʿiẓ wa-al-ḥikam* (Advice to Brothers and Guide to Friends in Exemplary Lessons and Wisdoms), EDITION: Kamāl al-Dīn al-Adhamī, Cairo: al-Maṭbaʿa al-Maḥmūdiyya, 1932.

[1213] ***Lāmiyyat al-ʿajam***, AUTHOR: Ḥusayn b. Alī al-Ṭughrāʾī (d. 515/1121), EDITION: ʿAlī Jawād al-Ṭāhir, Baghdad: Dār al-ʿĀnī, 1962.

[1214] ***Sharḥ Tāʾiyyat al-Ṣafadī***, unidentified. ʿAbd al-Bāqī Ibn Ḥabīb al-Ṣafadī's (d.?) *tāʾiyya* is entitled *Salk al-ʿayn wa-idhhāb al-ghayn* (The Insertion of the Letter *ʿAyn* and the Omission of the Letter *Ghayn*). Hajjī Khalīfa mentions two commentaries on the poem: ʿUlwān b. ʿAtiyya al-Ḥalabī (d. 922/1516–1517) and ʿAbd al-Raḥmān b. Muḥammad al-Qarāmī (d.?) (KẒ, 2:997). A manuscript copy of a third commentary written by Shihāb al-Dīn Aḥmad b. Khalīl al-Subkī (d. 1032/1622–1623) can be found in al-Azhar University's collection (Al-Subkī, *Sharḥ al-Subkī ʿalā Tāʾiyyat al-Ṣafadī*, Cairo, Al-Azhariyya 97992), but I was not able to consult it.

[1215] ***Dīwān*** *nāqis al-awwal wa-al-ākhir*, unidentified.

[1216] ***Dīwān***, unidentified.

[1217] ***Dīwān***, unidentified.

[1218] ***Dīwān***, unidentified.

[1219] ***Marātiʿ al-ghizlān***, AUTHOR: Shams al-Dīn Muḥammad b. Ḥasan al-Nawāji (d. 859/1455). The full title of the work is: *Marātiʿ al-ghizlān fī waṣf al-ghilmān al-ḥisān* (The Gazelle's Pastures Regarding the Description of Beautiful Youth). A manuscript copy is at Princeton University Library, Garrett Collection, MS Nr. 14L.

[1220] ***Maḥāsin al-aṣr***, unidentified. The title is probably in reference to *Yatīmat al-dahr wa-maḥasin ahl al-ʿaṣr* (The Rarity of the Age and the Best of the Poets of the Time). AUTHOR: ʿAbd al-Malik b. Muḥammad al-Thaʿālibī (d. 429/1038), EDITION: Damascus: al-Maṭbaʿa al-Ḥanafiyya, 1885. The work is not a *dīwān* but an anthology of verse by the top poets of the period; it is listed in the History Section. Similarly, *al-Kināya wa-al-taʿrīḍ* (Periphrasis and Antonomasia) by the same author is listed in this section (cf. #1225).

[1221] ***Majmuʿ dīwān wa-rasāʾil***, unidentified. A collection of poetry anthologies and treatises. This entry might refer to a collection of treatises that was described by ʿAbd Allāh Mukhliṣ. The manuscript is now lost, but its description can still be found. See: Mukhliṣ, ʿAbd Allāh. *"Majmūʿat ʾashʿār muṣaʿʿabat al-mabānī mughmaḍat al-maʿānī,"* in *Majallat al-Majmaʿ al-ʿilmī al-ʿArabī bi-Dimashq*, v. 21, 11–12. Damascus: 1946.

[1222] ***Ashʿār wa-qaṣāʾid*** *nāqis al-awwal*, unidentified. Verse and odes with a missing first part.

[1223] ***al-Ikhtiyār fī maḥāsin al-ashʿār***, unidentified. Selections of the best of poetry.

[1224] ***al-Ḥusn al-ṣarīḥ fī māʾat malīḥ***, AUTHOR: Ṣalāḥ al-Dīn Khalīl ibn Aybak al-Ṣafadī (d. 764/1363), EDITION: Aḥmad Fawzī al-Hayb, Damascus: Dār Saʿd al-Dīn, 2003–2004.

[1225] ***al-Kināya wa-al-taʿrīḍ***, AUTHOR: ʿAbd al-Malik Ibn Muḥammad al-Thaʿālibī (d. 429/1038), EDITION: Muwaffaq Fawzī al-Jabr, Damascus: Dār al-Ḥikma, 1994. Also known as *al-Nihāya fī fann al-kināya*, the work is about poetry but is not a *dīwān*.

[1226] ***Ṭarāʾif al-ṭuraf***, AUTHOR: al-Ḥusayn b. Muḥammad b. ʿAbd al-Wahhāb al-Ḥārithī al-Bāriʿ al-Baghdādī (d. 524/1129–1130), EDITION: Hilāl Nājī, Beirut: ʿĀlam al-Kutub lil-Ṭibāʿa, 1998.

[1227] ***Majmūʿat shiʿr min kalām al-udabāʾ***, unidentified. A collection of poetry by some literati.

[1228] ***Sharḥ qaṣīdat al-Shaykh Abī al-Fatḥ***, unidentified. There are at least three poets known as Abū al-Fatḥ: Abū al-Fatḥ al-Bustī (d. 401/1010–1011), Abū al-Fatḥ al-Dumyāṭī (d. 553/1158–1159) and Abū al-Fatḥ al-Iskandarī (d. 567/1171–1172) (Ḥajjī Khalīfa, *KẒ*, 1:772, 1:772, and 1:923, respectively). Given these possibilities, it is hard to identify the commentary. It is noteworthy that the *dīwān* of al-Iskandarī, the last of these poets mentioned, may be the same as entry #1231 in the library inventory.

[1229] ***Safīnat ashʿār***, unidentified. A notebook with various poetry.

[1230] ***Dīwān li-baʿḍ al-shuʿarāʾ***, unidentified. A collection of verse by some poets.

[1231] *Al-thānī min* ***Rawḍat al-azhār***, unidentified. Ibn Qalāqis al-Iskandarī, Abū al-Fatḥ (d. 567/1171–1172), or of *Rawḍat al-azhār wa-ḥadīqat al-ashʿār*, AUTHOR: Ṣalāḥ al-Dīn Muḥammad Ibn Shākir al-Kutubī (d. 764/1362–1363). Both *dīwān*s are mentioned by Ḥajjī khalīfa, *KẒ*, 1:923. There are no critical editions of either.

[1232] ***Aṭbāq al-dhahab***. AUTHOR: ʿAbd al-Muʾmin b. Hibat Allāh al-Iṣfahānī (d. 600/1204). EDITION: Yūsuf al-Nabhānī, Beirut: al-Maṭbaʿa al-Adabiyya, 1891–1892.

[1233] ***Dīwān fī ʿilm al-mūsīqā***, unidentified. A collection of poetry on the science of music.

[1234] ***Arāʾis al-afkār fī madāʾiḥ al-Mukhtār***. AUTHOR: Abū al-ʿAbbās Aḥmad Ibn ʿAbd al-Ḥayy al-Ḥalabī (d. 1120 / 1708–1709), EDITION: Muḥammad Ḥamza al-Kittānī, Beirut: Dār al-Kutub al-ʿIlmiyya, 2007.

[1235] ***Kitāb al-majmaʿa***, unidentified.

[1236] ***Majmūʿat shiʿr***, unidentified. A miscellany of poetry.

[1237] ***Majmūʿat shiʿr***, unidentified. A miscellany of poetry.

[1238] ***Sharḥ al-muʿallaqāt***, unidentified. It is not possible to identify this commentary on the *muʿallaqāt*, the famous pre-Islamic 'suspended' odes, since numerous such commentaries survive.

[1239] ***Majmūʿat shiʿr***, unidentified. A miscellany of poetry.

[1240] ***Kitāb maqṣūrat al-Ghazzī***, unidentified. Although many poets carrying the name al-Ghazzī (of Gaza) have composed *maqṣūra*s, it is likely that this entry refers to *ʿIqd al-shawāhid fī al-ḥikam al-shawārid* by Najm al-Dīn al-Ghazzī (d. 1061/1651), who was famous throughout the Ottoman Levant. A manuscript copy is in Cairo, Dār al-Kutub, Shiʿr Taymūr 1081.

[1241] ***Majmūʿat ashʿār wa-fawāʾid***, unidentified. A miscellany of poems and useful verse.

Works of Poetry from the provenanced sections of the inventory

Works taken from the library of al-Sayyid Yaḥyā Efendī b. al-Sayyid Muḥammad al-Ṭībī of Jaffa in 1218/1803

[578] ***Kitāb Dīwān lil-Shihab Aḥmad al-Manṣūrī***, AUTHOR: Aḥmad b. Muḥammad b. ʿAlī Shihāb al-Dīn al-Manṣūrī (d. 887/1482) also known as Ibn al-Hāʾim. See al-Ziriklī, *Aʿlām*, 1:231.

CHAPTER 22

The Pasha's New Clothes: The History Section (*tārīkh*)

Dana Sajdi

Abū al-Qāsim al-Zayyānī (d. 1249/1833), a Moroccan scholar, ambassador and court secretary, met al-Jazzār in Mecca during one Ḥajj season.[1] The scholar had the nerve to write that al-Jazzār, the Ottoman Governor of the Provinces of Sidon and Damascus, and the leader of the Levantine Pilgrimage Caravan, who would soon repulse Napoleon's army from Acre, was simply 'an idiot'.[2] Al-Zayyānī was so brazen as to have written this after al-Jazzār had hosted him and fed him a meal that he had personally cooked and later gifted him a handsome sum.[3] Had al-Jazzār known of the scholar's imminent insolence, he might well have executed the ungrateful al-Zayyānī on the spot. After all, al-Jazzār had boasted to his guest of having just killed seven bookkeepers on suspicion of money mishandling.[4] 'The Butcher' wore his *sobriquet* proudly. In his mind, he was the evil-people slayer, a reputation that he seemed to cultivate vigorously.

The governor had invited the scholar to make a case. He appropriately chose a scholarly method in his attempt to persuade. It involved an 'old book' of demonstrably historical import that he retrieved from his personal bookcase.[5] The book contained a word puzzle whose solution required expert literary and mathematical knowledge: the science of letters. The pasha dared the scholar to solve the word riddle and the latter, expectedly, rose to the challenge. The puzzle's solution resulted in the sentence, '[...] al-Jazzār is the Awaited Guided One who possesses the East and the West (of the Islamic lands)'![6] Our governor, then, was making a claim of Messianic proportions. Not one to be fooled, al-Zayyānī saw that the governor's claim was unreasonable and subsequently judged him to be a fool. To us, al-Jazzār's use of a book to make the case for his claim is remarkable. The pasha employed a historical-literary book for the purpose of *haute couture* self-fashioning.

---

1 Immense gratitude goes to the editors of this collection, who individually offered help or relevant information at various points during the research and writing; to Elif Sezer-Aydınlı, for taking a stab at the initial transcription and transliteration of the book list and for getting the research process started; to Feras Krimsti, who has been generous with his information and sources; to Anton Shammas, whose questions always inspire and who offered hitherto unknown relevant literary works; to my student, Khalil Sawan, who helped me in comparing library catalogues; to Zina Jardaneh for attempting to assist me in reaching al-Najah University, to Sami Hijjawi, the Mayor of Nablus, who succeeded in that, and to Samah Qandeel, Adel Thaher and Khaldieh Samara who received me warmly at al-Najah University Library. I also thank the audiences at talks I gave at the Michael E. Marmura Lectures in Arabic Studies, Hearing Palestine, and the Seminar in Ottoman and Turkish Studies at the University of Toronto (October 28, 2022); at Readings in the Khalidiyya, Center for Palestine Studies, Columbia University (November 3, 2022); at Farouk Mustafa Memorial Friday Lecture Series, University of Chicago (January 27, 2023); and at the Department of History, University of California, Santa Barbara (April 17, 2023). Jim'cim, as usual, read the last draft and fixed my random punctuation.

2 al-Zayyānī, *al-Turjumāna*, 257–263, here 258. I am ever so grateful to Feras Krimsti for locating this source and allowing me to use it. The encounter between al-Zayyānī and al-Jazzār, according to Krimsti's calculations, must have taken place before al-Jazzār succeeded in defending Acre against Napoleon's armies in 1799.

3 Ibid., 260, 263.

4 Ibid., 260–261.

5 Ibid., 259–260.

6 *'Hādhā huwa-al-mahdī al-muntaẓar al-ladhī yamluku al-Mashriq wa-al-Maghrib,'* Ibid., 259. Given our knowledge of al-Jazzār's pursuit and destruction of the Shīʿī Mitwālis in Lebanon-Palestine, it is striking that he would employ or appropriate the figure of *al-mahdī*, which has a special resonance in Shīʿīsm.

Books and scholars are a theme in the Jazzār biography and contemporary news. The work that al-Jazzār brandished at al-Zayyānī in Mecca is similar in import to another mentioned by the nineteenth-century Damascene historian, ʿAbd al-Razzāq al-Bayṭār (d. 1335/1916). The latter's vociferously hateful biography of al-Jazzār states that 'a reckless [author], who has been misguided by God [...] composed a *book* in which he claimed that he [al-Jazzār] was a Renewer'.[7] More outlandish is an associate of the pasha who alleged that al-Jazzār was prophesied by the Great Master Ibn al-ʿArabī (d. 638/1240) in his *book, al-Futūḥāt al-makiyya*, Meccan Revelations. Even as far away as Istanbul, and this time in Ottoman Turkish, the local historian Cabi Ömer (d. 1229/1814) narrates a similar story about al-Jazzār's claim and its association with an *epistle* attributed to the same Ibn al-ʿArabī.[8] It is not so much al-Jazzār's messianic assertion that interests me, although this theme is salient in several other chapters in this book.[9] My curiosity lies in al-Jazzār's use and mobilization of books and epistles to proffer discursive scaffolding for the image that he desired to project to the world.

It is with the thought that al-Jazzār was cognizant of the image-making power of books that I approach the seemingly haphazard collection of titles listed in the 'section on the science of history' (*qism ʿilm al-tārīkh*). Whether al-Jazzār personally chose or read the books or if he had designated brokers or buyers to gather the collection remains unknown. I propose, however, that the history section was carefully curated. A modern historian has already observed a deliberateness in the choice of titles in the history section. But this observation was based on the fact of the low number of repeated titles.[10] I go further by suggesting that the conclusion about curation can be reached not only negatively, in the *absence* of too many repeated titles, but also positively, in the content of the books, their assemblage as a group and their presentation in the library inventory.

I should mention at the outset that the depth of curation of the history section as displayed by both the content of the works and their deliberate arrangement in the list, differs significantly from some sections of the inventory and shares some attributes with a few others. The content of the history section, for example, stands in sharp contrast to the law segment, which seems to have been assembled due to the availability of books in the market and without any deliberate curation.[11] However, similar to our section, the *ḥadīth* collection displays, at least in parts, a purposeful arrangement in the list connoting a hierarchy of value.[12] Similarly, the poetry section also reveals purpose in its content and arrangement.[13] Finally, the richness of the section on medicine, which does not conform to the library's purportedly pedagogical function, is similar to our collection in that it discloses an inclination to 'conspicuous consumption'.[14]

The collection of history books in the Jazzār library is neither standard nor canonical. It seems to have been purposefully put together to convey courtly refinement in royal style, comprehensively represent varied Muslim lives of local and imperial significance and, most importantly, project an image of the patron as a heroic warrior *and* a just ruler. All of this is executed, not merely abstractly, but evidently informed by al-Jazzār's own history and career. The collection references

7 *'Mujaddid'*, al-Bayṭār, *Ḥilyat al-bashar*, 127–132, at 130. My emphasis. Al-Bayṭār further informs us that another man with 'familiarity with some of the sciences' socialised with the elite of Damascus and got into an argument while advocating for al-Jazzār. His rage at their opposition was such that 'the hair of his moustache rose up like obelisks'; Ibid., 130. I thank Feras Krimsti for bringing this mention to my attention.

8 Cabi, *Cabi tarihi*, I, 84. I thank Guy Burak for this reference.

9 See the Chapters of Feras Krimsti (4), Liana Saif (24) and Khalil Sawan (21).

10 Güler, *Cezzar*, 190. The author argues that the pasha personally collected the books.

11 See Ahmed El Shamsy's Chapter 16.

12 See Garrett Davidson's Chapter 15.

13 See Khalil Sawan's Chapter 21.

14 See Deborah Schlein's Chapter 23.

Egypt, where the patron began his career as the 'butcher' hero; acknowledges the Levant, where he achieved pasha-hood; and looks to Istanbul, in whose chronicles and documents al-Jazzār appeared, and whose sultans he simultaneously emulated and challenged. Furthermore, the collection links al-Jazzār's military achievements to a heroic Ottoman past and contemporary Ottoman strategies.

Our section, thus, exceeds the aim of satisfying the curriculum of a local *madrasa* or the interests of readers of a provincial public library. It is a disproportionately ambitious attempt to project the image of al-Jazzār as a sword-brandishing conqueror and a mace-bearing sovereign, while elevating marginal Acre to the levels of venerable Cairo and glorious Istanbul. History, in our library inventory, is especially crafted to fit our Bosnian adventurer by a master tailor, whoever this curator might have been. The Pasha emerges through the collection with new clothes.

1 A Vanity Collection

The core collection in the category of history contains 148 entries. These are a part of an original collection that was surveyed in 1215/1800. Six additional related entries came later from confiscated libraries (the titles #515, #526, #543, #579, #599 and #1650 are part of a survey dated 1218/1803; and #1685 from a different survey dated 1216/1801).[15] I will distinguish between these two categories by calling the former the 'core collection' and the latter 'later acquisitions' throughout this essay when relevant. All in all, the collection constitutes 8.7 percent of the library, making the history list one of the larger sections in the library, preceded by the *ḥadīth*, law, grammar and Sufism sections at 14.4, 12.5, 11.3 and 9.9 per cent, respectively.

Discounting thirty-four entries representing repeated titles in the core collection, the history list constitutes 115 individual titles. Of these, twenty titles remain unidentified. Some of these have definite titles but are mysterious to me: for example, *Rawḍat al-akhbār*, the Garden of Reports (#1344). Others have such generic titles that, in the absence of their authors' identities, remain too difficult to locate: for example, *Kashf al-asrār*, the Revelation of Secrets (#1358). A few of these unidentified works seem to have eluded even the inventory author, who gave them general, non-committal descriptions: *Tārīkh nāqiṣ al-awwal*, for example, 'a history with a missing introduction' (#1370). But not all is lost in this cluster of unknown works. Some enigmatic titles are still indicative of the subjects and genres, for example, *Tārīkh al-awliyā'*, the History of Saints (#1253), or *Dhayl siyar Turkī*, 'a sequel to biographies/epics in Turkish' (#1389). Such titles allow us a fair degree of generalisation about the collection's attributes.

From my point of view as a student of Arabic Mamluk and Ottoman historiography of the Levant, at first sight, the history collection seems shockingly random. Arabo-Islamic historiography is traditionally defined through two main genres: the chronicle, in which past and contemporary events are recorded and organised around the passage of time; and biography, including hagiography (*manāqib*) and individual *vitae* (*tarjama*), which may appear as individual biographies in standalone works or as parts of larger biographical dictionaries (*ṭabaqāt*). Less than half of our collection represents titles that conform to the discipline of history in this narrower definition. It includes about twenty chronicles, twenty-five biographical works, and a single titleless entry on historiography. This last entry, *kitāb fī 'ilm al-tārīkh*, 'a book on historiography', is not found in the core collection but in later acquisitions (#599). Add to those a few works of topographical nature that have customarily been viewed as part and parcel of history, such as al-Maqrīzī's famous *al-Khiṭaṭ*, the Scheme (of Cairo) (#1308 and #1309) and al-Badrī's *Maḥāsin al-Shām*, the Beauties of the Levant. The latter title appears twice in the core collection (#1314 and #1315) and once in the later acquisitions (#579).

15 See Said Aljoumani's Chapter 2.

The rest of the history inventory includes topics either adjacent to the discipline or entirely non-historical. The section includes some of the most famous geographical, cosmographical and zoological works of quasi-historical nature,[16] such as al-Qazwīnī's *'Ajā'ib al-makhlūqāt*, the Wonders of Creation (#1298) and *Āthār al-Bilād*, the Monuments of Nations (#1335); Ibn al-Wardī's *Kharīdat al-'ajā'ib*, the Pearl of Wonders (#1299); and al-Damīrī's *Ḥayāt al-ḥayawān*, the Life of Animals. Al-Damīrī's work appears all of eight times and includes both the longer version of the work and its abbreviated counterpart (#1285–1291, and #526 in later additions). These popular titles are usually associated with the royal, the courtly and the refined, and often come in luscious, illustrated copies, the type commissioned by and gifted to rulers.[17]

Decidedly non-historical works include poetry anthologies (#1295, #1296, #1311, #1316 and #1365); the Egyptian al-Shirbīnī's wonderful satire of rural life (#1395); a work on *jinn* (#1347); works on ethics, such as al-Sha'rānī's advice to Sufi seekers (#1267), and a Turkish translation of al-'Aṭṭār's Persian-language *Manṭiq al-ṭayr*, the Conference of the Birds (#139); an epistle on war management (#1379); a copy of an endowment document (#1372); and six different works in the genre of Mirrors of Princes. Together, these last works impressively represent almost every single title of the genre written in the Arabic language and will be discussed below.

The variety of topics and genres that exceed the discipline of history in the section brings to mind the Arabic proverb: 'a flower from every meadow'.[18] It shows a diversity of topics, genres and fields echoing other categories in the inventory, most conspicuously, the *ḥadīth* section.[19] However, the history collection does not constitute a random assortment of wildflowers. The range of titles together demarcates a larger humanities field, indeed, a humanist's paradise, demonstrating elevated taste and a courtly profile that may be intended to bolster al-Jazzār's image. The heroic and royal contours of this image will be explained below. However, the point here is for us to see how the eclectic nature of the history section is of an elective sort. It seeks a certain representativeness and comprehensiveness, the sort that places Acre on the map of the Islamic world, while linking its regional context to its wider imperial world.

The history collection, thus, is far vaster than any history curriculum that students of the religious sciences might have needed in their course of study at al-Nūr al-Aḥmadī *madrasa*. Its audience is neither the student nor the accidental or intended individual reader of a specific book. This is a profoundly curated collection that stood for more than the sum of its parts. Similar to the collection on medicine in the inventory, the history collection is meant to impress those *who might hear about it as a collection*.[20] As such, its audience is not only its immediate users and readers, be they students, scholars, or occasional readers in the library in Acre, but scholars and dignitaries, rulers and princes, and the refined and cultivated wherever they might be. This is primarily a vanity collection, but I will show later that a small part of it had a practical purpose.

2 Brimming with Life: The Biographical Dimension

Biographical literature dominates in the narrower historical part of the core collection. There are about nineteen life stories. Several hagiographies open the history section (#1247–1251). If we consider travelogues as self-biographies written in mobility, the selection includes several such autobiographies (for example, #1258–1259 and #1293 in

16 These kinds of works are listed separately from history in the royal library of Bāyezīd II. See Emiralioğlu, 'Books on the Wonders of Creation'.

17 Especially al-Qazwīnī. See Berlekamp, *Wonder*.

18 *'min kulli rawḍin zahra'*.

19 See Garrett Davidson's Chapter 15.

20 See Deborah Schlein's Chapter 23.

the core collection; and #543 in the later acquisitions). There is one individual *vita* of an influential scholar (#1257). There are also encounters several biographies of celebrated rulers (for example, #1374). The section concludes with popular epics narrating the lives of heroic warriors (for example, #1383).

In addition to individual biographies, the inventory includes eleven biographical dictionaries. In as much as anthologies of poets and poetry, of which the collection lists six, celebrate the lives and achievements of poets as a collectivity between the two covers of a book, they serve a function similar to that of biographical dictionaries (#1296, #1312, #1316, #1294 and #1356). Furthermore, when we consider the chronicles in the inventory, many of them focus on collectivities of rulers, for example, *al-Durra al-saniyya*, the Resplendent Pearl, tackles the history of the Abbasids (#1360); *al-Nuzha al-saniyya*, the Splendid Picnic, (#1349) treats the caliphs and rulers of Egypt and so does *Mawrid al-laṭāfa*, the Source of Refinement (#1313); and *Tārīkh salāṭīn Āl ʿUthmān*, the History of the Sultans of the Ottoman House (#1323), belongs to a large cluster of authored and anonymous chronicles that deal with the lives of Ottoman sultans. The history collection, thus, brims with life.

The heart of the history section of our inventory is the memorialisation and celebration of Muslim lives. Indeed, one could even suggest that biography motivates the history core collection, which literally opens and, except for the last few titles, closes with life stories. The reader may follow the procession of such titles in our list between #1247–1255 and #1348–1394 (with some interruptions).

At this point, I need to digress to address the issue of title arrangement. Our general list is arranged by science or field/topic, similar to the case of some surviving library catalogues.[21] The topic progression in our inventory aligns with a certain etiquette regarding the arrangement of *physical* books. Social *decorum* required that holier topics be placed on top and, of course, crowned by the Qurʾān. The less holy the topic, the lower the book was placed in the stacking order. Within the same topic/discipline, books were to be arranged by the prestige of their authors. Finally, a mitigating circumstance in that prestige-determined arrangement is the size of the book: larger books were to be placed under smaller ones.[22] While we have no idea if our general inventory mirrored the actual physical arrangement of the books in the library, the author of our inventory seems to have followed a certain prestige-determined etiquette.

Within the history section, the prestige principle does not apply to the status of the authors of the books of the collection. Instead, as we shall see, it had a lot to do with the *metier* or social role of the individuals and groups that were the subject of the books. In this regard, if one recognises biographies as gates into and out of the history section, a clear pattern emerges, one that directs the reader's eye of the inventory from one category of lives to another.

The biographical dimension is a deliberate offering, a conscious presentation of representative lives. It showcases varied individual figures and groups hailing from every significant tranche of Islamic society. The history section opens with the lives of the holy, and proceeds to those of the pious and knowledgeable, then to cultural producers, on to rulers and statesmen, and ends with the lives of heroic warriors. Like an open hand fan or an arranged deck of cards, the section organises and displays people through their *vitae* in a procession-like manner. This arrangement is not strict and often interrupted. However, it does not veer off too far and the procession of individuals and groups resumes. Equally importantly, lurking behind the arrangement of the procession is a careful admission of the sovereignty of and attestation of loyalty to the Ottomans, on the one hand, and a simultaneous demonstration of fidelity to local affiliations and proclivities, on the other.

21 Aljoumani, "al-Fahāris", 19–20.

22 al-Murādī, *ʿArf al-bashām*, 14–17, at 17.

The first two titles in the history section are biographies of the 'Great Imām' (#1247 and #1248). The proper name of the subject is unnecessary because the figure is too famous and well-revered. He is none other than the eponymous founder of the legal rite of the Ottoman state, Abū Ḥanīfa (d. 150/767). The next entry (#1249) is the biography of al-Imām al-Shāfiʿī (d. 204/850), who is the counterpart of Abū Ḥanīfa for the Shafiʿī *madhhab*, to which the overwhelming majority of Muslims in Syria and Egypt belonged. Thus, the first three entries immediately announce the Islamic order under the aegis of the Ottoman House along with an acknowledgement of local affiliation.

The next group of hagiographies are similarly attentive to the provincial and the imperial, but the arrangement turns from the lives of *imāms* to a celebration of saints: the hagiography of ʿAbd al-Qādir al-Kīlanī (or al-Jīlānī, d. 561/1166, #1250), which is followed by that of Aḥmad al-Rifāʿī (d. 578/1183, #1251). These two saints are the eponymous founders of Sufi orders that were predominantly popular in the Arabic-speaking world. Immediately thereafter, the list turns to the imperial, to the virtues of the Companion of the Prophet, Abū Ayyūb al-Anṣārī (d. 52/672, #1255), the patron saint of Islamic Constantinople. The saint meant little to local Levantines, but his death during the Muslim siege of the Byzantine city provided a principal founding myth for the Ottomans upon their conquest of the city many centuries later. A few titles down the inventory, several works by the same author bring us back to the Levant and to the eighteenth century: the travelogues of the local celebrity saint, the Damascene scholar ʿAbd al-Ghanī al-Nābulusī (#1258–1260).

From holy individuals, the inventory takes us to holy collectives as memorialised in biographical dictionaries. The first of these might be the classic biographical dictionary of Sufis by the highly influential Egyptian scholar and Sufi, al-Shaʿrānī, which appears twice consecutively (#1261 and #1262). These particular entries carry the subtitle of al-Shaʿrānī's work, *Ṭabaqāt al-akhyār*, *Vetae* of the Select, rather than its main title, *lawāqiḥ al-anwār*, Fecundating Lights. The same work and a variation of it appear again, attesting to the work's popularity (#1264 in the core collection, and #1685 from the later acquisitions).

Thereafter, the inventory proceeds from the holy to the pious; to biographical dictionaries featuring the lives of the hard-working knowledge producers, the *ʿulamāʾ*. Strikingly, the first we encounter is authored by the Damascene Shams al-Dīn Ibn Ṭūlūn devoted to exceptional scholars of a specific affiliation, not those belonging to the majority Shāfiʿī rite, but their Ḥanafī counterparts (#1263). This work is rare and conspicuous in its presence in the library. Much later down the list, we come across another significant biographical work written by an Arabic-speaking Ḥanafī celebrating his *madhhab* colleagues: al-Tamīmī's *al-Ṭabaqāt al-saniyya*, Glorious *Vitae* (#1353). Taken together, these two dictionaries have been posited as responses to the attempt by Ottoman Turkish-speaking scholars to attach the royal dynasty to Ḥanafism and establish specific doctrinal positions preferred by imperial authorities.[23] Ibn Ṭūlūn's sixteenth-century composition is more contrarian and attempts to affirm local doctrinal articulations, while al-Tamīmī's seventeenth-century counterpart effects a reconciliation and harmonizes local with imperial views.[24] If Ibn Ṭūlūn's biographical dictionary is notably present in the inventory, the classic Ottoman Ḥanafī biographical dictionary, *al-Shaqāʾiq al-nuʿmāniyya*, the Anemones, by Taşköprüzade (d. 968/1561), to which the works by Ibn Ṭūlūn and al-Tamīmī mentioned previously are seen as reactions, is conspicuously absent from our collection.[25]

To return to the procession as exhibited in the list, Ibn Ṭūlūn's local response to Ottoman Ḥanafism is balanced out a brief two entries later with 'the Great Dictionary of the Shāfiʿīs' by al-Subkī (#1265). Thus, after reminding the reader of

23 Burak, *Second Formation*, 102–117.
24 Ibid.
25 Ibid., 94–100.

the imperial order, local loyalties are affirmed and Shāfiʿī scholars are given their due.

Moving down the inventory, the arrangement turns from specific affiliations towards the more general. The next biographical dictionary in the list casts a wide net. It is the voluminous and ambitious dictionary celebrating the lives of Muslim elites who have achieved excellence in various domains: Ibn Khallikān's *Wafayāt al-aʿyān*, Obituaries of the Elite. This work appears another eight times in the list making it the title most recurring in the history section (#1277–1284 and #1345).

Strikingly, the list omits many of the dictionaries that were written successively by Syrians throughout the Ottoman period. The works by Najm al-Dīn al-Ghazzī (1061/1570), Muḥammad al-ʿUrḍī (d. 1071/1661) and Khalīl al-Murādī (1206–1791) do not appear in the list.[26] Even the pre-Ottoman foundational work of Abū al-Qāsim Ibn ʿAsākir (571/1176) is nowhere to be found in the collection, a most glaring absence.[27] A little further down the list, we encounter only two Ottoman-period Syrian biographical dictionaries, those of al-Muḥibbī (#1292) and al-Būrīnī (#1322). Much further down, al-Khaṭīb al-Baghdādī's famous biographical work on Baghdad appears in the inventory. However, the work is incomplete and appears in seemingly random parts (#1332–1334). The seeming arbitrariness could have something to do with the voluminous nature of the work, which rarely got copied in its entirety. Alternatively, these volumes could have been included accidentally, perhaps through looting or confiscations.

It is clear that al-Jazzār, or his book buyer, did not intend to showcase Syrian talent and achievement *per se*. Rather, the first part of the inventory is a carefully chosen and neatly displayed presentation of lives, well-lived and deserving of adulation. Simultaneously, the arrangement displays an acknowledgment of the realities of the local and imperial, while striking a balance between them: one eye on the Levant and Egypt and another towards Istanbul.

The next group of biographical works of collectivities may fall outside the bounds of the genre of biographical dictionary in its strictest definition, however, they serve a similar function. These are anthologies of poets and of poetry. As such, they still fit within the list's arrangement and procession sequence and take the reader out of the domain of the holy and the pious into the space of the court and the pastime of the refined. Al-Thaʿālibī's *Yatīmat al-dahr*, the Unique Pearl, which appears in its varying titles three times (#1295, #1296 and #1303) is the most famous among these.

But, before we follow the list's progression, which begins to exit the domain of collectives in society to enter the domain of polity and the state, there are two mysterious titles that are possibly biographical works and noteworthy. If entry #1304 is, indeed, a part of the famous biographical dictionary by al-Ḥurr al-ʿĀmilī, then even Shīʿī scholars are represented in this overwhelmingly Sunnī collection. Of course, one immediately wonders whether this work arrived into our collection as a consequence of al-Jazzār's famed looting and destruction of the libraries of the Mitwālīs of Jabal ʿĀmil.[28]

Another title that is mysterious due to its abbreviation is *al-Mustaẓraf*. If this is actually the work authored by al-Suyūṭī, *al-Mustaẓraf min akhbār al-jawārī*, the Most Graceful News of Concubines, then the reader is presented with yet another collectivity. In as much as the book is of anecdotes on articulate and skilful concubines, it is akin

26 al-Ghazzī, *Luṭf*; al-Būrīnī, *Tarājim*; al-ʿUrḍī, *Maʿādin*; al-Murādī, *Silk*.

27 Ibn ʿAsākir, *Tārīkh*. This work was very popular in the Mamluk period, as attested by audition certificates left on manuscripts. See Hirschler, 'Reading Certificates', 80–81. And though public readings of this work may have waned overtime, the authority of the work as *the* canonical history of Damascus continued unabated. See Sajdi, "Ibn ʿAsākir's Children".

28 Winter, *Shiʿites*, 121 and note 10; Makkī, *al-Ḥaraka*, 40–42. See the Introduction and the Chapters 16 by Ahmed El Shamsy and 13 by Walid Saleh.

to a biographical dictionary of cultivated, albeit unfree, women. But since the title appears four times (#1269–1272), it may refer to the more popular work: al-Ibhīshī's *al-Mustaṭraf min kulli fannin mustaẓraf*, the Ultimate in Every Delightful Art. This latter is a popular compendium of *adab* and is often mistakenly referred to as an *al-Mustaẓraf* instead of *al-Mustaṭraf*. The work is also a good accompaniment to *Yatīmat al-dahr*, the dictionary of poets mentioned earlier and which also appears several times in the collection.

This history collection that is full of life stories of men, however, does not include any of the standard biographies of the most important Muslim: The Prophet Muḥammad. It turns out that this is not an omission because biographies of the Prophet are plentifully represented in our inventory, but they are categorised under a different section: the *ḥadīth* segment.[29]

There is, however, one chronicle within the history section of which a large part is reserved to the Prophet's life. The Quinquepartite History (*Tārīkh al-Khamīs* #1325) is written by al-Diyārbakrī, who is a later compiler. The preference for this particular title may be due to the fact that it was written in the Ottoman period, thus, privileging an Ottoman rendition of the life of Muḥammad.[30]

The history collection is impressively comprehensive and representative. It carefully includes the holy, the scholarly, both Sunnī and Shīʿī, the excellent and the literary. It is a snapshot of Islamic society and the location of social groups within it. Even animals are represented. Al-Damīrī's famous 'Life of Animals' is a zoological compendium describing the varieties of animals, which are arranged in alphabetical order (#1285–1291 and #526). This 'biographical dictionary of animals' is the most recurring title along with the most general and comprehensive biographical dictionary of (Muslim) humans in the inventory, that of Ibn Khallikān. Our collection, thus, is not parochial or even provincial. Instead, this is a collection of (ideal) Muslims. It constitutes flowers from every meadow of life bound together on the shelves of one provincial library. Yet, these are not the only lives represented in the collection. We have yet to meet epic heroes.

3 The Heroic Profile: In the Image of al-Jazzār?

We are still processing following the inventory's progression. I alert the reader that in the previous discussion, the numbers corresponding to the book listing have mostly remained in the #1200s zone, with a few titles in #1300s. Most of the titles within the latter come before #1350 (such as #1303, #1304, #1322, #1325, and #1332–1334). However, once the reader enters securely into the #1300s part of the list, they will encounter the genre of chronicles. Among these, we come across a few representing the rich tradition of chronicle production in pre-Ottoman Syria and Egypt, such as those of al-Suyūṭī (#1305), Ibn Taghribirdī (#1313) Ibn al-Athīr (#1326), Ibn Shiḥna (#1339), Abū Shāma (#1342) and al-Dawadārī (#1360). We find another group of chronicles with a common theme in the same zone. These have to wait till later. For now, I wish to tackle some of those works found in the second half of the #1300s of the list.

Several chronicles that fall in the #1370s and #1380s number zone focus on the Eastern Islamic lands and two on Yemen. This is, I will show, almost literally a puzzle. We can only begin to solve it if we think less of the geographies covered by the chronicles and consider the individual actors, that is, the lives presented in these books. The group of chronicles presents us with figures who had spectacular careers, for good or evil. Furthermore, though presented in disparate, discrete works, the heroic lives

29 According to Garrett Davidson's Chapter 15 in this book, the biographies of the Prophet are the 'single most popular genre in the "*al-ḥadīth al-sharīf*" section of the inventory'. Also, see Said Aljoumani's Chapter 2 on the misplacement of titles in the inventory.

30 It should be noted that there is one work of the popular genre on the stories of biblical prophets (*siyar al-anbiyāʾ*), al-Thaʿlabī's *Nafāʾis*, #1320.

offered in these works are sometimes thoroughly intertwined. Let us put the pieces together.

In one chronicle, we meet a most unlikely figure in a library in the Levant: Jalāl al-Dīn Mankūbirtī (d. 628/1231) (#1374). He was the last of the Khwarezmshahs, who had heroically stood up to the Mongol world conqueror, Cengiz Khan (d. 624/1227). In another chronicle, we read about the other Mongol world conqueror, Taymūr (d. 807/1705), who captured Ottoman territories, took Sultan Bāyezīd I (d. 805/1403) prisoner and wreaked havoc on Syria (#1321). Later in the list, the reader chances upon Murad II (d. 855/1451), the Ottoman warrior sultan who began the reconquest of the territories lost to Taymūr (#1373). And later down the list, and in a slightly different genre, we meet the heroic warrior Seyyid Baṭṭāl Gazi (d. 1st/8th century), after whom the same Murad II styled himself as a frontier-warrior, a *gazi* (#1378). A few entries later, we meet none other than Baṭṭāl's (supposed) mother, 'the Woman of Noble Resolve', the princess warrior, Dhāt al-Himma (#1383–1386). Baṭṭāl and Dhāt al-Himma, similar to al-Anṣārī, whose hagiography was listed earlier, are figures that satisfy a certain archetype. They are early Muslim heroes who fought against the Byzantines and both Baṭṭāl and al-Anṣārī served as foundational figures that legitimised Ottoman territorial expansion and conquest. The last piece of the puzzle that completes the picture is the appearance of Mehmet, the Conqueror of Constantinople (d. 886/1481), in a biographical sketch that may have been written by the famous Ottoman historian, Tursun Bey (#1375). This series of chronicles constitute a mosaic of heroic and interrelated lives, in which the Ottoman imperium emerges triumphant. We will see below that they provide a model for al-Jazzār's military career.

There are several other warrior-heroes that appear in the same zone of the history section. Two of them are not intertwined in the manner of the lives presented above, however, they form juxtapositions or counterpoints. This nexus takes place in the unexpected geography of Yemen. The celebrated chronicle, *al-Barq al-yamānī*, Yemeni Lightning, covers the Ottoman conquest of the region. It specifically highlights the military exploits of the statesman and vizier Koca Sinan (d. 1004/1596) (#1369).[31] The other chronicle that is related to Yemen is an odd inclusion in an evidently pro-Ottoman collection. *Tuḥfat al-asmāʿ*, the Audience's Gift, is about the career of al-Mutawakkil Ismāʿīl (d. 1087/1676), the Zaydī *imām* whose rule in Yemen marked the largest territorial expansion for the Shīʿī regime and marked the end of Ottoman presence in the region (#1361).[32] The only possible explanation for the selection of a work so inimical to the Ottomans is the martial and heroic attributes of the subject of the chronicle.

Indeed, almost all the figures that appear in the last part of the history section, some of whom were enemies, were all warrior rulers and founding statesmen. They were *not* routinised sovereigns, who operated in well-established state structures. Instead, they were fighters, splendid winners or honourable losers; history-makers whose hands were dirty with the bow and arrow and whose swords dripped with the blood of the enemies. In short, the biographies presented in the chronicles and epics reflect a systematic attempt to assemble a heroic profile.

The constitution of the final part of the history section, which includes biographies of rulers and epic heroes, is interesting and deserves a short digression. The combination of historical works and epics reveals an intrinsic connection between what we consider today to be distinct categories: history vs. legend. Although popular epics are listed at the very end of the section in acknowledgement of their generic specificity, the list's progression towards them after the biographies of warrior rulers guides us to see the two genres as

31 A Syrian commentary on this chronicle also appears on the list. It is al-Manīnī's *al-Fatḥ al-wahbī*, #1352.

32 Other warriors who appear in the inventory are the founder of the Ghaznavid regime, Sebügtekin (d. 287/997) (#1346) and ʿAntara b. Shaddād, the pre-Islamic black warrior (#1394).

bearing a similar historical import. The *vitae* of legendary warriors seem like a natural thematic extension of the lives of rulers as historical as Taymūr or Mehmet the Conqueror. In the mind of the curator of the collection, therefore, Baṭṭāl seems to be as real as Sultan Murad II. Given the clarity of the logic presented in the progression, there is no need to make remarks about the inclusion of such popular works written in a quasi-vernacular language in a high-brow book collection. In the minds of contemporaries, these genres, while distinguishable, were of similar value.

But to return to our larger argument, this dramatic, war-laden cluster of histories would not have been of much use to *madrasa* students or scholars of the religious sciences. These carefully curated works in a vanity collection serve to mirror the adventurous career of al-Jazzār himself with all the travails, intrigues and battles that his life involved. This life is echoed in the reception of al-Jazzār as shown in another chapter in this book.[33] Indeed, the pasha's heroic deeds did not go unnoticed in Istanbul. One extant work about al-Jazzār is evocatively entitled *Gazânâme-i Cezzâr Gazi el-Hacı Ahmed Paşa*, The Book of Battles of the Warrior, the Pilgrim Aḥmad Pasha al-Jazzār, written by a certain Resmi Mustafa Efendi.[34] The work recounts al-Jazzār's war against Napoleon. The description of al-Jazzār as a *gazi* is mirrored in the other 'Books of Battles' found in the collection, namely, those of Baṭṭāl and Sultan Murad II.

The history collection's heroic profile clearly proffers symbolism understandable to both local and imperial audiences. It significantly constructs an Ottoman heroic genealogy into which al-Jazzār can insert himself. The collection, therefore, hearkens back to the Ottoman past, but, as we shall soon see, it also shows an engagement with the Ottoman present.

33 See Feras Krimsti's Chapter 4.

34 Istanbul, Süleymaniye Library, Haci Mahmut Efendi 4910. Cited in Uyar, "Said", 23–24.

4 Royal Pretensions

Stories of frontier fighters, adventurous conquerors and valiant founders are one aspect of the history section. Other parts, especially the chronicles that do not focus on individual figures and the large collection of the Mirrors for Princes give the impression that al-Jazzār wanted to convey a sense of established, legitimate, even royal authority. The drama of battle is balanced out by courtly routine and ceremonial.

Within the zone of the #1300s, falling mostly before the #1370s, a motley group of chronicles do not treat individual heroes or specific biographies of rulers, but entire Islamic regimes: the ʿAbbāsids (#1360), the Buyids (#1382), the Saljūqs (#1336), the Zengids and Ayyūbids (#1342), the rulers of Egypt in two separate histories (#1305 and #1349) and, of course, the Ottomans in two different titles (#1323 and #1329). Add to these al-Maqqarī's history of al-Andalus, *Nafḥ al-ṭīb*, the Profusion of Fragrance, which appears early on and for all of three times (#1301, #1302 and #1307). The only common denominator for this motley group of works is the focus on regimes and dynasties successful and long-lasting enough to earn their separate historical treatments.

But the opener of the chronicle zone appears before we reach the #1300s: a book that appears as a complete work all of five times (#1273–1276 and 1367). This work is not about a particular individual or regime, but a comprehensive universal history. Written by al-Qaramānī, this work is one of the later comprehensive histories, which covers 'the state of the children of ʿUthmān, may God preserve them till the end of time'.[35] This history treats Ottoman rule copiously and generously within a larger Islamic firmament.[36] It also has the distinct quality of being written by a contemporary loyal to

35 al-Qaramānī, *Akhbār al-duwal*, III, 5.

36 Ibid., III, 5–90. The treatment of the Ottomans occupies a large space in this 3 volume printed work that also tackles non-Islamic polities.

the Ottomans, who also was a Damascene. One can only conclude that the repeated appearance of this particular work, regardless of its virtue as a comprehensive world history, could be seen as another acknowledgment of Ottoman sovereignty emanating from Syria. Yet, this is not abject subjecthood, but simply an acknowledgment of Levantine existence within an Ottoman cosmology. As to how the locality or the location of al-Jazzār in Acre is constituted, it is presented as no less of a royal court.

One of the most striking features of our collection is the selection of works that appealed to rulers' souls and conscience. This is expressed in the presence of the most courtly of genres: Mirrors for Princes. Our inventory includes almost all of the works written in Arabic in this genre, which are dispersed throughout the history collection. The core collection includes Ibn ʿArabshāh's *Fākihat al-khulafāʾ*, the Amusement of Caliphs, (#1297); al-Siqillī's *Sulwān al-muṭāʿ*, the Solace of the Sovereign (#1318); al-Ṭurtushī's *Sirāj al-mulūk*, the Light of Kings (#1351) and al-Ghazzalī's or al-Māwardī's *Naṣīḥat al-mulūk*, Advice to Kings (#1354). The inventory also lists the *Hümâyûn-nâme*, the Book of Royals (#1391), which is the Turkish translation of the fables of *Kalīla wa-Dimna*. The title *al-Tibr al-masbūk*, Purified Gold (#1340) appears on the list and may be the same as al-Ghazzālī's book just mentioned listed under its main title. Furthermore, *al-Aḥkām al-ṣultāniyya*, the Laws of Governance (#1650) by either al-Māwardī or Abū Yaʿlā is found in the later acquisitions.

This large collection of advice literature is too systematic and comprehensive to have been assembled due to availability in the market or random looting of local libraries. Nor is this intentional assortment meant for students, scholars or the average Acre resident. This is yet another deliberate effort to project a royal image. In contrast to the dramatic, heroic and legendary aspects of some of the chronicles in our collection, this other part of the cluster is about routinised power and just rule carefully crafted within an Ottoman dominion. Al-Jazzār and/or his book buyer wanted to demonstrate the pasha's poise and sagacity, in addition to his spectacular martial qualities. We will see below how the authorship of a particular kind of Mirrors of Princes texts became standard practice by the chancery officers and historians of the Ottoman court in the seventeenth and eighteenth centuries and how the library reflects this intellectual trend.

To be fair to al-Jazzār, his megalomania and attested bad temper and violence notwithstanding, he was both a formidable warrior and an indefatigable institution builder. His massive endowment of public amenities, including our library, still defines the old city of Acre to this very day.[37]

5 Gilt and Print: Connections to the Ottoman House

Bolstering the image of genteel sovereignty and royal panache is the material state of some books described in the inventory. I had mentioned earlier that some of the cosmographical and geographical works similar to those that are found in our collection often appear illustrated, especially those works that include maps. The scribe of the inventory is silent about the state of the embellishment of these particular works. However, the list includes seven entries that are described as gilt (*mudhahhab*).[38] Not surprisingly, three of these have to do with Ottoman royalty and confirm the curated aspect of the history section as a legacy collection and the pasha's connection to the Ottoman court. Two works listed as printed (*ṭabʿ*) rather than handwritten are also inconsonant with the rest of the history collection in material terms. These are also linked to with the Ottoman court. Along with another title in the collection, these

37 Muḥaybish, "Mujammaʿ al-Jazzār", 23–27.

38 For the details, follow the numbers in Said Aljoumani's edition of the inventory in Part IV. In addition to those listed below, the biography of Taymūr (#1321) mentioned above and 'a sequel to epics in Turkish' (#1389) are described as gilded.

printed books show an actual, practical connection with the imperial centre.

The most striking of the three gilt works mentioned is the biography of Sultan Mehmet the Conqueror. I have assumed that the work as found in our inventory and entitled in Arabic *Manāqib Abū al-Fatḥ Sulṭān Muḥammad Khān*, the Virtues of the Conqueror Sultan Muḥammad Khān (#1375), is the same as, or a translation of, the Turkish biography *Târîh-i Ebü'l-Feth*, the History of the Conqueror, written by Tursun Bey. If my conjecture is correct, then this is an astounding find. Tursun Bey's work, apparently, only became famous in the modern period. Prior to the nineteenth century, it had remained limited to Ottoman court libraries, of which only four manuscripts survive today.[39] How did al-Jazzār manage to get his hands on this work? Was it commissioned? Was it gifted? Is it a work similar to the one in the royal library and translated into Arabic upon al-Jazzār's request? None of these questions can be answered in the absence of the physical manuscript. However, if this is, indeed, Tursun Bey's work, the presence of the book in our Acre library may indicate the beginning of the trend of the work's wider reception. At the very least, the presence of the work indicates our pasha's admiration for and identification with the famous sultan.

Of the two other gilded codices that are related to Ottoman royalty is *Tārīkh Āl 'Uthmān*, the History of the Ottoman House (#1324), which is described as 'gilt, externally and internally', is one of the two other gilded codices that are related to Ottoman royalty.[40] This work, as mentioned earlier, remains only broadly identified since it belongs to a group of several such histories bearing the same title. The other work, similarly gilt inside and out and related to the Ottomans, is Osmanzâde Ahmed Tâ'ib's early eighteenth-century collection of biographies of sultans, *Hadîkatü'l-mulûk*, the Garden of Kings (#1329). Whether these lavish books about Ottoman royalty were gifted to or commissioned by al-Jazzār remains unknown. However, the fact of their presence in the library, especially as luxury items, only serves to acknowledge a close connection to the Ottoman house, at least, formally.

Further evidence of the deep involvement with the Ottoman court has to do with printed words in the history inventory, of which only two examples appear. Both are eighteenth-century chronicles penned by the Ottoman official court historians, or *vaka'anüvis*es, Subhî Mehmed Efendi and İzzî Sülayman Efendi, who were near contemporaries of al-Jazzār (#1392 and #1393). The contemporary nature of these printed chronicles, which relayed daily events at the imperial palace, allows one to think of them as royal court newspapers. Thus, the presence of these 'dailies' in Acre is akin to a White House newsletter dispatch to, say, the Governor of Massachusetts. There are, however, more connections to the court and with the Ottoman Turkish historiography of the period, which these two printed court histories belie. In order to reveal al-Jazzār's enmeshment in the politics and intellectual culture of the centre through books, I must digress to offer a historical and historiographical context.

The position of official court historian, whose incumbents were usually drawn from the chancery offices, was instituted in the eighteenth century. Before and throughout that century, many bureaucrats and chancery officers were also engaged in the writing of moralistic *nasihatname*s, Advice Books. Reminiscent of the Mirrors of Princes genre, these advice books and epistles attempted to address the crises that had befallen the empire and give sage council to the ruler.[41] A general modern *reformist* trend ensued and culminated in the late eighteenth century in the *Nizam-i Cedid* or the New Order under the auspices of Sultan Selim III (d. 1222/1807). The reformist wave found

39 Markiewicz, *The Crisis of Kingship*, 193. I thank Guy Burak for alerting me to this reference.

40 '*mudhahhab ẓāhiran wa-bāṭinan*'.

41 Abou Hadj, "Ottoman Nasihatname"; Lewis, "Ottoman Observers"; Howard, "Ottoman Historiography".

its full expression intellectually and historiographically in the work of 'the first of the modern Ottomans,' the court historian, Vasıf Ahmed Efendi (d. 1221/1806).[42] Although the New Order met with a mutinous end, one of the best performances of its new military corps was demonstrated in the defence of Acre against Napoleon under the leadership of our al-Jazzār.[43]

Within this context of reformist intellectual ideas and a new military order, it is notable that our collection shows some signs of the time. Decidedly traditionalist (rather than modern reformist), Canikli Ali Pasha's epistle on war management *tedbîr-i cedîd-i nâdir*, A Rare New Arrangement, appears in our collection (#1379). This epistle is considered one of the last examples of the *nasihatname* genre.[44] Strikingly, Canikli Ali was not a courtier, but similar to al-Jazzār, a provincial governor who used his epistle to negotiate with the centre.[45] This epistle is comparable and similar in import to a text that al-Jazzār himself wrote, *Niẓâmnâme-i Mıṣır*, The Regulation of Egypt, for which Canikli's epistle could have served as inspiration.[46]

Al-Jazzār's text, written in 1199/1785, which a modern historian dubbed as an 'intelligence report', was composed upon the High Porte's request. This was not meant to be a public document and is expectedly absent from our collection.[47] In it, al-Jazzār mobilises all of his experience in Egypt to describe its topography and conditions and mount a military plan for its conquest and retention. Of course, al-Jazzār offers himself as the obvious candidate to execute the plan and govern Egypt. The pasha's *Niẓâmnâme-i Mıṣır*, thus, was also a negotiation. Its effect in Istanbul was serious enough to have warranted a detailed description in the court chronicle of none other than the Vasıf Ahmed Efendi mentioned previously. Furthermore, al-Jazzār's plan was apparently followed to the letter, but not his offer to be governor of Egypt.[48]

If the gilt codices in the collection flaunt loyalty to royalty, the printed chronicles in addition to Canikli's war treatise reveal Acre's actual connections to and negotiations with the imperial centre. A few contemporary titles serve to reflect practical involvements with Istanbul within this vanity collection of titles, a large part of which were composed in the pre-Ottoman period.

6 The Pasha's Trodden Lands: Egypt and Syria

If the three gilt codices mentioned above show the respect due to the imperial sovereign, another two gilt books show knowledge of, even intimacy with, lands that were well-trodden by our Pasha. One of the works is a representation of the Levant, where al-Jazzār ruled for thirty years and sometimes in more than one province simultaneously, and where he would eventually defeat Napoleon. Al-Badrī's *Nuzhat al-anām fī maḥāsin al-Shām*, the Picnic of Humankind in the Beauties of the Levant (#1314) is a celebration of the verdant beauty of Syria and was a popular work in the region. Interestingly, the inventory author notes that the book is gilt 'with a new gilded binding'. Given the popularity of the book in the Levant, one wonders if this was an old (perhaps even looted) copy that was restored upon its acquisition.

42 Menchinger, *Modern Ottomans*.
43 Shaw, "Ottoman Military Reform", 302.
44 Sariyannis, *Ottoman*, 359.
45 Aksan, "Canikli".
46 Cezzar, *Egypt*. I thank Feras Krimsti for mentioning the book to me. While comparing the epistles is beyond the scope of this paper, they seem to echo each other. Sariyannis' discussion of Canikli's epistle brings out issues that are articulated in Kemp's article on al-Jazzār's epistle, such as the focus on non-military matters, the mobilisation of personal experiences of the authors and self-promotion. (Sariyannis, *Ottoman*, 345, 354–358; Kemp, "Eighteenth-century").
47 Kemp, "Eighteenth-century". On this work by al-Jazzār, see Feras Krimsti's Chapter 4.
48 See the editor Shaw's comment in Cezzar, *Egypt*, 8.

The other gilt topography is of the place where al-Jazzār seasoned his sword and proudly acquired his *sobriquet*: Egypt. This is represented by none other than the famed al-Maqrīzī's loving and vivid portrayal of Cairo (#1309). The reader will remember that al-Jazzār had shown off his knowledge of the topography of Egypt in his *Nizâmnâme-i Mıṣır*. Could al-Jazzār have taken a special interest in al-Maqrīzī's *Khiṭaṭ* for a utilitarian purpose? Perhaps so, but the work is famous beyond any practical application and, hence, is collectible regardless.

Whatever al-Maqrīzī meant to al-Jazzār, another title in our collection brings our survey of the history section full circle. Ibn al-Nadīm's *Fihrist* (#998), one of the oldest surviving manuscripts of one of the oldest 'bibliographies' in Islamic history is found among the titles in the library inventory under a different section.[49] This bibliographical book in a precious manuscript which was once owned by al-Maqrīzī himself could not have arrived in this collection accidentally. This manuscript once possessed by al-Maqrīzī seems to have been intentionally procured to be placed in the same collection alongside al-Maqrīzī's own work.

7 Conclusion: Acre Between Cairo and Istanbul

The history section of the library inventory of the al-Nūr Aḥmadīyya *madrasa* is neither canonical nor educational. It showcases neither the famous Egyptian and Levantine Arabic historiographical tradition nor its Ottoman-Turkish counterpart. And though the library's content shows an overlap with royal, provincial and *madrasa* libraries, prior and contemporary to it, no systematic patterns of shared titles emerge.[50] This eclectic collection is carefully curated to suit a specific political and cultural moment when Ottoman provincial governors were active 'partners of the empire' rather than the sultan's obedient servants.[51] It is a time when an adventurer such as al-Jazzār, who literally appeared in different guises throughout his variously rebellious and conformist career,[52] could claim a new *persona* and attire that transcended that of a local provincial vizier.

History on the bookshelves of Acre is less about past events and more a celebration of Muslim lives. It is a memorialisation of the variety of groups in their diverse spiritual, religious, social, military and political roles, on both the provincial and imperial levels. It is also a presentation of the eventful lives of warriors, heroes and conquerors and the felicitous guardianship and institutionalised sagacity of royals. And as soon as the image of the Ottoman, whether the conqueror or the royal, is projected in loyalty, it is immediately employed as a mirror to reflect al-Jazzār's career and aspirations. The collection, therefore, is relentlessly contrapuntal or filled with juxtapositions. Evidence of loyalty to the imperium and larger realm is offset by self-promotion and a sense of intimacy with, even proprietorship over, Egypt and the Levant. History as conceived by al-Jazzār or his broker, is a vanity exhibit whose reputation as a collection mattered as much as, if not more than, any reader's appreciation of the books therein.

49 See Berat Acıl's Chapter 19.

50 I compared the holdings of our library with the published catalogues of various institutions. The number of shared titles are indicated in the following list: al-Ashrafiyya Madrasa in Damascus, thirteenth-fifteenth centuries, 14; Bāyezīd II's royal library in Istanbul, sixteenth century, 22; al-ʿUthmāniyya al-Riḍāʾiyya Madrasa in Aleppo, eighteenth century, 13; al-Rifāʿiyya of Damascus, eighteenth and nineteenth centuries, 17; and Abū al-Dhahab in Cairo, eighteenth century, 8. See Hirschler, *Medieval Damascus*; Necipoğlu et al., *Treasures of Knowledge*; Aljoumani, "Tārīkh maktabat al-Mullā ʿUthmān al-Kurdī"; "Qalamos" for "Sammlung Refaiya" shorturl.at/eBR28, accessed November 14, 2023; Ibrāhīm, "Maktaba ʿuthmāniyya", respectively. I thank Said Aljoumani for sharing his unpublished work with me.

51 Yaycioğlu, *Partners*.

52 Al-Jazzār escaped a difficult situation in disguise. He once donned the attire of a Maghribi and another of an Armenian; Philipp, *Acre*, 51.

The sole document (as opposed to a literary text) that appears in the history section of the library inventory is a copy of an endowment text of the mosque-*madrasa* complex of the fifteenth-century Mamluk ruler al-Ashraf Barsbāy. This beautiful architectural structure is extant and still graces the skyline of Cairo today. Its purposes are similar to those of al-Jazzār's complex in Acre, making it probable that Cairo, where al-Jazzār began his political and military career, was a source of inspiration. But our Acre complex is decidedly Ottoman in style, with few peers in Palestine. It seems to be intentionally resonant of a near contemporary sultanic counterpart in Istanbul: the Nuruosmaniye.[53] Even the nomenclature is strikingly similar. The Nūr Aḥmadī or 'the Light of Praiseworthiness', therefore, served to connect Cairo with Istanbul by way of Acre. It is also the Light of Aḥmad, the 'idiotic pretender'—to paraphrase al-Zayyānī—who, indeed, turned out to be the Awaited Saviour from an impending French Empire. The pasha understood that military prowess needed to be enhanced through the propagandist potential of culture and the power of books. Through the library, the pasha raised Acre as a stage from which he showed off his new clothes.

53 See the editors' introduction and Muḥaybish, "Mujamma' al-Jazzār", 24.

Bibliography

Abou Hadj, Rifaat. "The Ottoman Nisihatname as a Discourse over 'Morality'." In *Mélanges Professeur Robert Mantran*, edited by Abdeljelil Temimi, 17–30. Zaghouan, 1988.

Aksan, Virginia. "Canikli Ali Paşa (d. 1785): A Provincial Portrait in Loyalty and Disloyalty." In *Popular Protest and Political Participation in the Ottoman Empire Studies in Honor of Suraiya Faroqhi*, edited by Eleni Gara, M. Eldem Kabadayı, and Christopher K. Neumann, 211–224. Istanbul, 2011.

Aljoumani, Sa'īd Ḍāmin. "al-Fahāris al-makhṭūṭa lil-maktabāt al-islāmiyya." *Turāthiyyāt* XIV, no. 7 (July 2009): 9–75.

Aljoumani, Said. "Tārīkh maktabat al-Mullā 'Uthmān al-Kurdī bi-Dimashq i'timādan 'alā khawārij makhṭūṭātihā." *Journal of the Institute of Arabic Manuscripts* 65, no. 1 (2021): 210–260.

al-Bayṭār, 'Abd al-Razzāq. *Ḥilyat al-bashar fī tārīkh al-qarn al-thālith 'ashar*, edited by Muḥammad Bahjat al-Bayṭār. Beirut, 1993.

Berlekamp, Persis. *Wonder, Image, and Cosmos in Medieval Islam*. New Haven, 2011.

Burak, Guy. *The Second Formation of Islamic Law: The Ḥanafī School in the Early Modern Ottoman Empire*. Cambridge, 2015.

al-Būrīnī, al-Ḥasan b. Muḥammad. *Tarājim al-a'yān min abnā' al-zamān*. Damascus, 1959.

Cabi, Ömer Efendi, *Cabi tarihi veya Tarih-i Sultan Selim-i salis ve Mahmud-ı sani*. 2 vols. Edited by Mehmet Ali Beyhan. Ankara, 2003

Cezzar, Ahmed. *Egypt in the Eighteenth Century: Nizâm-name-i Mısır of Cezzâr Aḥmed Pasha*, edited and translated by Stanford J. Shaw. Cambridge, 1964.

Emiralioğlu, Pınar. "Books on the Wonders of Creation and Geography in 'Atufi's Inventory." In *Treasures of Knowledge: An Inventory of the Ottoman Palace Library (1502/3–1503/4)*, edited by Gülru Necipoğlu, Cemal Kafadar and Cornell H. Fleischer, I, 597–606. Boston/Leiden, 2019.

al-Ghazzī, Najm al-Dīn Muḥammad. *Luṭf al-samar wa-qaṭf al-thamar min tarājim a'yān al-ṭabaqa al-ūlā min al-qarn al-ḥādī 'ashar*, edited by Maḥmūd Shaykh. Damascus, 1981.

Güler, Mustafa. *Cezzar Ahmed Paşa ve Akka Savunması*. Istanbul, 2013.

Hirschler, Konrad. "Reading Certificate (Sama'at) as a Prosopographical Source: Cultural and Social Practices of an Elite Family in Zangid and Ayyubid Damascus." In *Manuscript Notes as Documentary Sources*, edited by Andreas Görke and Konrad Hirschler, 73–92. Beirut, 2011.

Hirschler, Konrad. *Medieval Damascus: Plurality and Diversity in an Arabic Library, The Ashrafiyya Library Catalogue*. Edinburgh, 2016.

Howard, Douglas A. "Ottoman Historiography and the Literature of 'Decline' of the Sixteenth and Seventeenth Centuries." *Journal of Asian History* XXII, no. 1 (1988): 52–77.

Ibn al-ʿArabī, Muḥyī al-Dīn. *al-Futūḥāt al-makiyya*, edited by ʿUthmān Yaḥyā and revised by Ibrāhīm Madkūr, 14 vols. Cairo: al-Hayʾa al-Miṣriyya al-ʿĀmma lil-Kitāb, 1972.

Ibn ʿAsākir, Abū al-Qāsim ʿAlī. *Tārīkh madīnat Dimashq: wa-dhikr faḍlihā wa-tasmīyat man ḥallahā min al-amāthil aw ijtāza bi-nawāḥīhā min wāridīhā wa-ahlihā*, edited by Ṣalāḥ al-Dīn al-Munajjid et al. 80 vols. Damascus: Maṭbūʿāt al-Majmaʿ al-ʿIlmī al-ʿArabī, 1951.

Ibrāhīm, ʿAbd al-Laṭīf. "Maktaba ʿuthmāniyya: dirāsa naqdiyya wa-nashr li-raṣīd al-maktaba." In *Dirāsāt fī al-kutub wa-al-maktabāt al-islāmiyya*, 1–16. Cairo, 1962.

Kemp, Percy. "An Eighteenth-century Turkish Intelligence Report." *International Journal of Middle East Studies* XVI, no. 4 (1983): 497–506.

Lewis, Bernard. "Ottoman Observers of Ottoman Decline." *Islamic Studies* I, no. 1 (1963): 71–78.

Makkī, Muḥammad Kāẓim, *al-Ḥaraka al-fikriyya wa'l-adabiyya fī Jabal ʿĀmil*. Beirut, 1982.

Markiewicz, Christopher. *The Crisis of Kingship in Late Medieval Islam: Persian Emigres and the Making of Ottoman Sovereignty*. Cambridge, 2019.

Menchinger, Ethan A. *The First of the Modern Ottomans: The Intellectual History of Ahmed Vasıf*. Cambridge, 2017.

Muḥaybish, Ghassān Mūsā. "Mujammaʿ al-Jazzār al-khayrī fī ʿAkkā." MA Thesis, al-Quds University, 1996.

al-Murādī, Muḥammad Khalīl. *Silk al-durar fī aʿyān al-qarn al-thānī ʿashar*, edited by Muḥammad ʿAbd al-Qādir Shāhīn. Beirut, 1997.

al-Murādī, Muḥammad Khalīl. *ʿArf al-Bashām fī man waliya fatwā Domashq al-Shām*, edited by Muḥammad Muṭīʿ al-Hāfiẓ and Riyāḍ ʿAbd al-Ḥamīd Murād. Damascus/Beirut, 1988.

Mustafa, Resmi. *Gazânâme-i Cezzâr Gazi el-Hacı Ahmed Paşa*. Istanbul, Süleymaniye Library, Haci Mahmut Efendi 4910.

Necipoğlu, Gülru, Cemal Kafadar and Cornell H. Fleischer (eds). *Treasures of Knowledge: An Inventory of the Ottoman Palace Library (1502/3–1503/4)*. 2 vols. Boston/Leiden, 2019.

Philipp, Thomas. *Acre: The Rise and Fall of a Palestinian City, 1730–1831*. New York, 2001.

"Qalamos." https://www.qalamos.net/content/index.xed. Accessed November 14, 2022.

al-Qaramānī, Aḥmad b. Yūsuf. *Akhbār al-duwal wa-āthār al-uwal fī al-tārīkh*, edited by Aḥmad Ḥuṭayṭ and Fahmī Saʿd. Beirut, 1992.

Sajdi, Dana. "Ibn ʿAsakir's Children: Monumental Representations of Damascus until the 18th Century." In *Ibn ʿAsakir's Influence in Arabic Historiography*, edited S. Judd and J. Schneider, 30–63. Leiden, 2017.

Sariyannis, Marinos (with a contribution by Ekin Tuşalp-Atiyas). *A History of Ottoman Political Thought up to the Early Nineteenth Century*. Leiden, 2019.

Shaw, Stanford J. "The Origins of Ottoman Military Reforms: The Nizam-ı Cedid Army of Sultan Selim III." *The Journal of Modern History* XXXVII, no. 3 (1965): 291–306.

"ʿUmar b. al-Muẓaffar Abū al-Ḥafs Ibn al-Wardī (d. 1457 Ad?): Kharīdat al-ʿajaʾib wa-farīdat al-gharāʾib." Christie's, Accessed November 14, 2022. https://www.christies.com/en/lot/lot-5422255.

al-ʿUrḍī, Muḥammad b. ʿUmar. *Maʿādin al-dhahab fī al-aʿyān al-musharrafa bi-him Ḥalab*, edited by Muḥammad Tūnjī. Damascus, 1987.

Uyar, Yeşim Karaca. "Said Efendi'nin Vasf-ı Cezzar Ahmed Paşa: Adlı Eserinin Transkripsiyonu ve Değerlendirilmesi." PhD diss., Afyon Kocatepe University, 2009.

Winter, Stefan. *The Shiites of Lebanon under Ottoman Rule, 1516–1788*. Cambridge, 2010.

Yaycioğlu, Ali. *Partners of the Empire: The Crisis of the Ottoman Order in the Age of Revolutions*. Stanford, 2016.

al-Zayyānī, Abū al-Qāsim Muḥammad. *al-Turjumāna al-kubrā fī akhbār al-maʿmūr barran wa-baḥran*, edited by ʿAbd al-Karīm al-Fīlālī. 2nd ed. Rabat: Dār Nashr al-Maʿrifa, 1991.

The History Books

Note: All references to Ḥājjī Khalīfa *KẒ*; Kaḥḥāla, *MM*; and al-Ziriklī, *Aʿlām* are through al-Maktaba al-Shāmila al-Ḥadītha, vers. 3.48. https://shamela.ws, accessed August 2022.

I am grateful to Elif Sezer-Aydınlı for help in the initial stages of transcription, transliteration and research.

[1247] ***Tarjamat al-Imām al-Aʿẓam***, see #1248. None of the many biographies of al-Imām al-Aʿẓam, that is, the eponymous founder of the Ḥanafī *madhhab*, Abū Ḥanīfa (d. 150/767) bears this title.

[1248] ***Manāqib al-Imām al-Aʿẓam***, AUTHOR: Abū al-Muʾayyad al-Muwaffaq b. Abī al-Makkī (d. 568/1172) and Muḥammad b. Muḥammad al-Kardarī (d. 827/1424), EDITION: Hyderabad: Majlis Dāʾirat al-Maʿārif al-Niẓāmiyya, 1987. There are more than ten works of *manāqib* of varying titles devoted to Abū Ḥanīfa (Ḥājjī Khalīfa, *KẒ*, 2:838–839). The reason for my preference for al-Makkī and al-Kardarī's work is because it bears exactly the same title as the entry here, see Brockelmann and Lameer [trans.], *GAL*, *Supp*. II: 328–329.

[1249] ***Manāqib al-Imām al-Shāfiʿī***, AUTHOR: Fakhr al-Dīn al-Rāzī (d. 606/1209), EDITION: Aḥmad Ḥijāzi al-Saqqā, Cairo: al-Maktaba al-Azhariyya lil-Turāth, 2008. There are more than thirteen works of *manāqib* of varying titles devoted to al-Shāfiʿī, (Ḥājjī Khalīfa, *KẒ*, 2:840). The edition by al-Rāzī is popularly known by the entry title. Al-Rāzī's original title is *Irshād al-ṭālibīn ilā al-manhaj al-qawīm*.

[1250] ***Manāqib ʿAbd al-Qādir al-Kīlanī***, AUTHOR: Quṭb al-Dīn Mūsā b. Muḥammad al-Yūnīnī (d. 726/1326). The entry title appears as *Manāqib sayyidī ʿAbd al-Qādir al-Kīlānī*. While there are several other hagiographies of the saint ʿAbd al-Qādir al-Kīlānī (variously known as al-Jīlānī), al-Yūnīnī's work bears the title closest to that of the entry. However, there does not seem to be an extant copy of al-Yūnīnī's book. See al-Ziriklī, *Aʿlām*, 4:47; and Ḥājjī Khalīfa, *KẒ*, I: 719, I:747, I: 933, and II:853.

[1251] ***Bahjat** al-Shaykh Aḥmad **al-Rifāʿī***, AUTHOR: Anonymous. There are many hagiographies devoted to the saint Aḥmad al-Rifāʿī (d. 578/1183), see, for example, al-Ziriklī, *Aʿlām*, I:174, 3:805, and III:814. However, one work that al-Ziriklī cites is a manuscript that bears almost exactly the same title as that of our inventory entry. The work is by an unknown author and lodged in Berlin, Staatsbibliothek, Petermann 346. It is worth noting that the term '*bahja*' has been noted to be used interchangeably with a saint's hagiography. See ʿAbd al-Karīm Anīs, Bayān al-qaṣd fī qawli-him: bahjat al-Rifāʿī, *al-Alūka al-Thaqāfiyya*, 30/10/2014, Accessed 12 August 2022. https://www.alukah.net/culture/0/77824.

[1252] ***Manāqib al-aʾima al-akhyār al-musammā bi-Tuḥfat al-abrār***, unidentified. The book has proven impossible to locate for the popularity of the various terms in the title. *Tuhfat al-abrār* is a title for a work by al-Suyūṭī (d. 911/1505), but it is not about the virtues of *imāms* as indicated by our entry title. See Brocklemann and Lameer [trans.], *GAL*, *Supp* III-ii for *tuḥfat al-abrār*, 563, and for *manāqib al-akhyār*, 279, 364, 401, and 435.

[1253] ***Tārīkh al-awliyāʾ***, unidentified. The title, 'the History of Saints', is too generic to locate.

[1254] ***Manāqib al-aʾimma** al-arbaʿa*, AUTHOR: Muḥammad b. al-Ṭayyib al-Bāqillānī (d. 403/1013), EDITION: Samīra Farḥāt, Beirut: Dār al-Muntakhab al-ʿArabī, 2002.

[1255] ***Manāqib Abī Ayyūb al-Anṣārī***, unidentified. Ḥājjī Khalīfa mentions a biographical dictionary of Sufi saints by al-Sirāj Ibn al-Mulaqqin, noting that it commences with the biography of the companion Abū Ayyūb al-Anṣārī (d. 51/674). See Ḥājjī Khalīfa, *KẒ*, II:109–106. The only work devoted to al-Anṣārī seems to have been written too late to have been included in this library: ʿAbd al-Ḥafīẓ b. ʿUthmān al-Qārī, *Jalāʾ al-qulūb wa-kashf al-kurūb bi-manāqib Abī Ayyūb*, Istanbul, 1881. See al-Baghdādī, *ĪM*, I:364.

[1256] ***al-Iqtiṣād fī marātib al-ijtihād***, AUTHOR: Muḥammad b. Abī al-Ḥusayn al-Ṣiddīqī (d. 994/1586), MS: Princeton University Library, Garrett Islamic Manuscripts 19, 97^b to 100^b. This is an epistle of a few folios in a collection of epistles by al-Bakrī. It seems too short to qualify as a 'book' in the inventory.

[1257] ***Tarjamat Shaykh al-Islām Quṭb al-Awliyāʾ al-kirām Muḥyī al-Dīn al-Nawawī***, AUTHOR: Muḥammad b. ʿAbd al-Raḥmān al-Sakhāwī (d. 902/1497), MANUSCRIPT: Beirut, the Library of Zuhayr Muṣṭafā al-Shawīsh al-Ḥusaynī. The entry title appears as *Tarjamat Shaykh al-Islām*, which apparently is a biography of the famous jurist and *ḥadīth* scholar, Muḥyī al-Dīn al-Nawawī (d. 676/1277).

[1258] ***al-Ḥadra al-unsiyya fī al-riḥla al-qudsiyya***, AUTHOR: ʿAbd al-Ghanī al-Nābulusī (d. 1050/1731), EDITION: Akram Ḥasan al-ʿUlabī, Beirut: al-Maṣādir, 1990.

[1259] *al-Ḥaqīqa wa-al-majāz fī riḥlat Bilād al-Shām wa-al-Ḥijāz*, AUTHOR: ʿAbd al-Ghanī al-Nābulusī (d. 1050/1731), EDITION: Aḥmad ʿAbd al-Majīd Huraydī, Cairo: al-Hayʾa al-Miṣriyya al-ʿĀmma lil-Kitāb, 1986. The entry title in the inventory appears as ***al-Riḥla al-kubrā***, the Great Journey, which is the alternative title for this work. See Elizabeth Siriyyeh, The Mystical Journeys of ʿAbd al-Ghanī al-Nābulusī, *Die Welts des Islams* XXV (1985), 84–96.

[1260] *Ḥullat al-dhahab al-ibrīz fi* ***riḥlat*** *Baʿalbak wa-* ***al-Biqāʿ*** *al-ʿazīz*, AUTHOR: ʿAbd al-Ghanī al-Nābulusī (d. 1050/1731), EDITION: *Riḥlatān ilā Lubnān*, Ṣalāḥ al-Dīn al-Munajjid and Stefan Wild, Beirut: al-Maʿhad al-Almānī lil-Abḥāth al-Sharqiyya, 1979.

[1261] *Lawāqiḥ al-anwār fī* ***ṭabaqāt al-akhyār***, AUTHOR: ʿAbd al-Wahhāb al-Shaʿrānī (d. 973/1565), EDITION: Cairo: al-Maṭbaʿa al-ʿĀmira al-ʿUthmāniyya, 1898. The entry title is *Ṭabaqāt al-akhyār*. While many Arabic book titles carry the term '*al-akhyār*' (see, for example, Kaḥḥala, *MM*, 12:168 and 1:221; and Ḥajji Khalīfa, *KẒ*, 2:838), al-Shaʿrānī's is the only obvious biographical work (*ṭabaqāt*) that includes the term. The work is also known as al-Shaʿrānī's *al-Ṭabaqāt al-kubrā*. Entry #1264 no. 2 may be the sequel to this work.

[1262] ***Ṭabaqāt al-akhyār***, see #1261 and cf. #1264

[1263] ***al-Ghuraf al-ʿaliyya fī ṭabaqāt*** *mutaʾakhkhirī* ***al-Ḥanafiyya***, AUTHOR: Shams al-Dīn Ibn Ṭūlūn (d. 953/1546), EDITION: ʿAbd Allāh b. ʿAbd al-ʿAzīz Shabrāwī, Cairo: Dār al-Risāla lil-Nashr wa-al-Tawzīʿ, 2021. The entry title appears as ***Ṭabaqāt al-Ḥanafiyya al-musammā bi-al-Ghuraf al-ʿaliyya***.

[1264] EITHER 1. *Lawāqiḥ al-anwār fī* ***ṭabaqāt*** *al-akhyār, al-juzʾ al-thānī*, see #1261, AUTHOR: ʿAbd al-Wahhāb **al-Shaʿrānī** (d. 973/1565) OR 2. *Lawāqiḥ al-anwār al-qudsiyya fī manāqib al-ʿulamāʾ wa-al-ṣūfiyya* (*al-Ṭabaqāt al-ṣughrā*), cf. #1261, AUTHOR: ʿAbd al-Wahhāb **al-Shaʿrānī** (d. 973/1565), EDITION: Aḥmad ʿAbd al-Raḥīm al-Sāyiḥ and Hiba Taqfīq ʿAlī, Cairo: Maktabat al-Thaqāfa al-Dīniyya, 2005.

[1265] ***Ṭabaqāt*** *al-Shāfiʿiyya al-kubrā*, AUTHOR: Tāj al-Dīn **al-Subkī** (d. 771/1355), EDITION: 6 vols., Muṣṭafā ʿAbd al-Qādir Aḥmad ʿAtā, Beirut: Dār al-Kutub al-ʿIlmiyya, 1999.

[1266] ***Tārīkh al-ʿulamāʾ***, unidentified. 'The History of the Scholars' is too generic a title to locate.

[1267] ***Irshād al-ṭālibīn*** *ilā* ***marātib al-ʿulamāʾ al-ʿāmilīn***, AUTHOR: ʿAbd al-Wahhāb al-Shaʿrānī (d. 973/1565), MANUSCRIPT: Tokyo, University of Tokyo, Daiber Collection II, 76. The entry title appears as *Marātib al-ʿulamāʾ al-āʿmilīn al-musamā bi-irshād al-ṭālibīn*.

[1268] ***Mubāʿith al-irtiḥāl ilā maḥall shadd al-riḥal***, AUTHOR: Anonymous. This is an unpublished work related to the *ḥadīth*: 'travel for pilgrimage is to be performed to three destinations: the Holy Mosque [in Mecca], this mosque of mine [in Medina], and al-Aqṣā Mosque [Jerusalem]' (See al-Mawsūʿa al-Ḥadīthiyya, https://dorar.net/hadith/sharh/140827). A manuscript copy attests to the completion of the work in 1154/1741. The information is provided by the book's copiest, Muṣṭafā al-Baylūnī who completed the copy in 1195/1780 in Acre. In other words, our entry may point to the same as that copied by al-Baylūnī and ended up in the library of the Iraqi historian ʿAbbās al-ʿAzzāwī (d. 1391/1971). See Usāma Nāṣir and Ẓamyāʾ ʿAbbās, "Makhṭūṭāt ʿAbbās al-ʿAzzāwi: al-qism al-thānī, al-tārīkh wa-al-tarājim wa-al-siyar," *al-Mawrid* XIV, no. 1 (1985): 177–186 at 186. I thank Said Aljoumani for locating this reference.

[1269] EITHER 1. ***al-Mustaẓraf*** *min akhbār al-jawārī*, AUTHOR: Jalāl al-Dīn al-Suyūṭī (d. 911/1505), EDITION: Ṣalāḥ al-Dīn al-Munajjid, Beirut: Dār al-Kitāb al-Jadīd, 1963; OR 2. *al-Mustaṭraf fī kulli fannin* ***mustaẓraf***, AUTHOR: Muḥammad b. Aḥmad al-Ibhīshī (d. 852/1446), EDITION: 2 vols., Ibrāhīm Aḥdab, Cairo: Maṭbaʿat Aḥmad al-Bābī al-Ḥalabī, 1896. While the title entry, *al-Mustaẓraf*, should take us to al-Suyūṭī's work given that the term appears in the main title of his work, al-Ibhīshī's compendium of arts is much too famous to ignore though the term occurs in the subtitle and is sometimes popularly known by the same term.

[1270] ***al-Mustaẓraf***, see #1269.

[1271] Ibid.

[1272] Ibid.

[1273] *Akhbār al-duwal wa-āthār al-uwal fī al-****tārīkh***, AUTHOR: Aḥmad b. Yūsuf **al-Qaramānī** (d. 1019/1611), EDITION: 3 vols., Fahmī Saʿd and Aḥmad Ḥuṭayṭ, Beirut: ʿĀlam al-Kutub, 1992. The entry title appears as *Tārīkh al-Qaramānī* (the History of al-Qaramānī). This is one of two history works by the author. See Brockelmann and Lameer [trans.], *GAL* 2:388, and Shākir Muṣṭafā, *al-Tārīkh al-ʿarabī wa-al-muʾarrikhūn: dirāsa fī taṭawwur ʿilm al-tārīkh wa-maʿrifat rijāli-hi fī al-islām*, 4 vols. Beirut 1978–1993, II:226–227. The less famous of the two works is a biography of the ascetic Ibrāhīm b. Adham (c. 165/782), of which there is only one extant copy. Thus, I settled on his more famous work for this entry.

[1274] ***Tārīkh al-Qaramānī***, see #1273.

[1275] Ibid.

[1276] Ibid.

[1277] *Wafayāt al-aʿyān wa-anbāʾ abnāʾ al-zamān*, see #1345. AUTHOR: Shams al-Dīn **Ibn Khallikān** (d. 681/1282), EDITION: 8 vols., Iḥsān ʿAbbās, Wadād al-Qāḍī, and ʿIzz al-Dīn ʿUmar Aḥmad Mūsā, Beirut: Dār ṣādir, 1978. The entry title appears as ***Tārīkh Ibn Khallikān***, the History of Ibn Khallikān.

[1278] ***Tārīkh*** **[Ibn]** ***Khallikān***, see #1277.

[1279] Ibid.

[1280] Ibid.

[1281] *Min* ***Tārīkh Ibn Khallikān***, *al-juzʾ al-awwal*, see #1277.

[1282] *Min* ***Tārīkh Ibn Khallikān***, *juzʾ*, see #1277.

[1283] *Min* ***Tārīkh Ibn Khallikān***, *al-juzʾ al-awwal*, see #1277 MANUSCRIPT: Princeton University Library, Garrett Islamic Manuscripts 3415Y. Said Aljoumani believes that this is the entry that represents the Princeton manuscript and not entry #1282, which includes the same title. The conclusion is based on the dimensions of the Princeton manuscript, 15.3 × 20.8 cm, which is closer to the eighth format, the size specified for this entry.

[1284] Ibid.

[1285] ***Ḥayāt al-ḥayawān***, AUTHOR: Muḥammad b. Mūsā al-Damīrī (d. 808/1405), EDITION: 4 vols, Ibrāhīm Ṣāliḥ, Damascus: Dār al-Bashāʾir, 2005. This work comes in three different recensions of different lengths. Only the longest recension is printed.

[1286] ***Ḥayāt al-ḥayawān al-ṣughrā***, see #1285.

[1287] *Min* ***Ḥayāt al-ḥayawān***, *al-juzʾ al-awwal*, see #1285.

[1288] Ibid.

[1289] ***Ḥayāt al-ḥayawān***, *nāqiṣ al-awwal*, see #1285.

[1290] *Min* ***Ḥayāt al-ḥayawān***, *al-juzʾ al-thānī*, see #1285, AUTHOR: Muḥammad b. Mūsā al-Damīrī (d. 808/1405), MANUSCRIPT: Nablus, al-Najah University Library, NL 250213 (?). Al-Najah Library does not have a public catalogue rendering the call numbers confusing. Because the said Nablus manuscript contains the second part of *Ḥayāt al-ḥayawān*, it could correspond to either #1289, which is 'missing the first part', or #1291, which is explicitly marked as 'the second part'. I am grateful to Benedikt Reier for explaining the issue.

[1291] *Min* ***Ḥayāt al-ḥayawān***, *al-juzʾ al-thānī*, see #1285 and the note for #1291, AUTHOR: Muḥammad b. Mūsā al-Damīrī (d. 808/1405), MANU-

SCRIPT: Nablus, al-Najah University Library, NL 250213 (?).

[1292] *Khulāṣat al-athar fī aʿyān al-qarn al-ḥādī ʿashar*, AUTHOR: Muḥammad Amīn b. Faḍl Allāh **al-Muḥibbī** (d. 1111/1699), EDITION: 4 vols., Muḥammad Ḥasan Ismāʿīl, Beirut: Dār al-Kutub al-ʿIlmiyya, 2005. The entry title appears as ***Tārīkh al-Muḥibbī***, the History of al-Muḥibbī. This is the only known history the author composed.

[1293] EITHER 1. *Ḥadī al-aẓʿān al-najdiyya ilā al-Diyār al-Miṣriyya*, AUTHOR: **Muḥibb al-Dīn** b. Taqī al-Dīn al-Ḥamawī (d. 981/1573), EDITION: Muḥammad ʿAdnān al-Bakhīt, Muʿta (Jordan): ʿImādat al-Baḥth al-ʿIlmī wa-al-Dirāsāt al-ʿUlyā, 1993; OR 2. *Bawādī al-dumūʿ al-ʿandmiyya bi-wadī al-Diyār al-Rūmiyya*, AUTHOR: **Muḥibb al-Dīn** b. Taqī al-Dīn al-Ḥamawī (d. 981/1573), EDITION: ʿAbd al-Sattār Ḥajj Ḥāmid, Beirut: Dār al-Kutub al-ʿIlmiyya, 2018. The entry title appears as ***Riḥlat Muḥibb al-Dīn al-Qāḍī*** (the Journey of Muḥibb al-Dīn al-Qāḍī). The author wrote two travelogues, one to Egypt and the other to Istanbul. See al-Ziriklī, *al-Aʿlām*, V:282.

[1294] ***Sulāfat al-dahr fī maḥāsin ahl al-ʿaṣr***, AUTHOR: ʿAlī b. Aḥmad Ibn Maʿṣūm (d. 1119/1707), EDITION: 2 vols., Maḥmūd Khalaf al-Bādī, Damascus: Dār Kinān lil Ṭibāʿa wa-al-Nashr wa-al-Tawzīʿ, 2009.

[1295] ***Yatīmat al-dahr fī shuʿarāʾ al-ʿaṣr***, see #1296, AUTHOR: ʿAbd al-Malik b. Muḥammad al-Thaʿālibī (d. 429/1039), EDITION: 4 vols., Damascus: al-Maṭbaʿa al-Ḥanafiyya, 1885. This is the same work as #1296, but appears under a slightly different title. The fact was confirmed in a private communication with Bilal Orfali, author of *the Anthologist's Art: Abū Manṣūr al-Thaʿālibī and his* Yatīmat al-dahr, Leiden/Boston, 2016.

[1296] ***Yatīmat al-dahr fī maḥāsin ahl al-ʿaṣr***, see #1295, AUTHOR: ʿAbd al-Malik b. Muḥammad al-Thaʿālibī (d. 429/1039), EDITION: 4 vols., Muḥyī al-Dīn ʿAbd al-Ḥamīd, Cairo: al-Maktaba al-Tijāriyya, 1956.

[1297] ***Fākihat al-khulafāʾ*** *wa-mufākahat al-ẓurafāʾ*, AUTHOR: Aḥmad b. Muḥammad Ibn ʿArabshāh (d. 854/1450), EDITION: Cairo: Būlāq, 1874.

[1298] ***ʿAjāʾib al-makhlūqāt*** *wa-gharāʾib al-mawjūdāt*, AUTHOR: Zakariyyā b. Muḥammad al-Qāzwīnī (d. 682/1283), EDITION: Fārūq Saʿd, Beirut: Dār al-Āfāq al-Jadīda, 1983.

[1299] ***Kharīdat al-ʿajāʾib***, AUTHOR: Zayn al-Dīn ʿUmar b. al-Muẓaffar Ibn al-Wardī (d. 749/1349), EDITION: Anwar Maḥmūd Zinātī, Cairo: Maktabat al-Thaqāfa al-Islāmiyya, 2008.

[1300] ***Kharīdat al-ʿajāʾib***, *nāqisat al-awwal* see #1299.

[1301] ***Nafḥ al-ṭīb*** *min ghuṣn al-Andalus al-raṭīb wa-dhikr wazīrihā Lisān al-Dīn Ibn al-Khaṭīb*, AUTHOR: Aḥmad b. Muḥammad al-Maqqarī (d. 1041/1632), EDITION: 11 vols., Maryam Qāsim Ṭawīl and Yūsuf ʿAlī Ṭawīl, Beirut: Dār al-Kutub al-ʿIlmiyya, 1995.

[1302] ***Nafḥ al-ṭīb*** *min ghuṣn al-Andalus al-raṭīb wa-dhikr wazīrihā Lisān al-Dīn Ibn al-Khaṭīb*, see #1301.

[1303] ***Yatīmat al-dahr fī maḥāsin ahl al-ʿaṣr***, see #1295.

[1304] ***Tadhkirat al-mutabaḥḥirīn fī al-ʿulamāʾ al-mutaʾakhkhirīn***, AUTHOR: al-Ḥurr al-ʿĀmilī (d. 1104/1693), EDITION: 2 vols., Aḥmad Ḥusaynī, Baghdad: Maktabat al-Andalus, 1965–1966. This is probably the larger part of al-Ḥurr al-ʿĀmilī's *Amal al-Āmil*, which bears the same title as that of our entry as expressly mentioned by the author (see the cited edition, I:3).

[1305] ***Ḥusn al-muḥāḍara fī akhbār Miṣr wa-al-Qāhira***, AUTHOR: Jalāl al-Dīn al-Suyūṭī (d. 911/1505), EDITION: 2 vols., Muḥammad Abū al-Faḍl Ibrāhīm, Cairo: Maṭbaʿat al-Bābī al-Ḥalabī, 1904.

[1306] ***Ḥusn al-muḥāḍara fī akhbār Miṣr wa-al-Qāhira***, see #1305.

[1307] ***Nafḥ al-ṭīb*** *min ghuṣn al-Andalus al-raṭīb wa-dhikr wazīrihā Lisān al-Dīn Ibn al-Khaṭīb*, see #1301.

[1308] *al-Mawāʿiẓ wa-al-iʿtibār bi-dhikr* ***al-khiṭaṭ*** *wa-al-āthār*, AUTHOR: Taqī al-Dīn **al-Maqrīzī** (d. 845/1442), EDITION: 7 vols., Ayman Fuʾād al-Sayyid, London: Muʾassasat al-Furqān, 2013.

[1309] *al-Mawāʿiẓ wa-al-iʿtibār bi-dhikr* ***al-khiṭaṭ*** *wa-al-āthār, al-juz' al-thānī*, see #1308. Said Aljoumani notes that this is not the Princeton University Library, Garrett Islamic Manuscripts 3516Y because the entry qualifies the work as 'the second volume'. By contrast, the Princeton manuscript is of 'the first half of the work'. (https://catalog.princeton.edu/catalog/9954371983506421#viewer-container).

[1310] ***Tārikh mawāqiʿ Miṣr,*** *nāqiṣ al-awwal*, unidentified. Translated as 'the History of the Events of Egypt'. There are too many histories of Egypt that might include the title *waqāʾiʿ* (events) for me to pin down a specific title. See Ḥājji Khalīfa's delightful entry on the histories of Egypt, *KẒ*, 1:303–305.

[1311] ***Thamarāt al-awrāq***, AUTHOR: Ibn Ḥijja al-Ḥamawī (d. 837/1434), EDITION: Muḥammad Abū al-Faḍl Ibrāhīm, Cairo: Maktabat al-Khānjī, 1971.

[1312] EITHER 1. ***Qalāʾid*** *al-jumān fī al-taʿrīf bi-qabāʾil ʿarab al-zamān*, (see also #1338) AUTHOR: Aḥmad b. ʿAlī al-Qalqashandī (d. 821/1418), EDITION: Ibrāhīm al-Ibyārī, Cairo: Dār al-Kutub al-Ḥadītha, 1963; OR 2. ***Qalāʾid*** *al-jumān fī farāʾid shuʿarāʾ hādhā al-zamān*, AUTHOR: Ibn al-Shaʿʿār al-Mawṣilī (d. 654/1256), EDITION: 7 vols., Fuad Sezgin and Māzin ʿAmawī, Frankfurt: Maʿhad Tārīkh al-ʿUlūm al-ʿArabiyya wa-al-Islāmiyya, 1990. The entry title appears as *qalāʾid al-jamāl.*

[1313] ***Mawrid al-laṭāfa*** *fī man waliya al-ṣalṭana wa-al-khilāfa*, AUTHOR: Abū al-Maḥāsin Yūsuf Ibn Taghribirdī (d. 874/1470), EDITION: Nabīl Muḥammad ʿAbd al-ʿAzīz Aḥmad, Cairo: Dār al-Kutub al-Miṣriyya, 1997.

[1314] *Nuzhat al-anām fī* ***maḥāsin al-Shām***, AUTHOR: Abū al-Baqāʾ b. Muḥammad al-Badrī (d. 894/1488), EDITION: Ṣāliḥ Ibrāhīm, Damascus: Dār al-Bashāʾir, 2006.

[1315] ***Nuzhat al-anām fī mahāsin al-Shām***, see #1314.

[1316] ***Dumyat al-qaṣr*** *wa-ʿuṣrat ahl al-ʿaṣr, mukhtaṣara*, AUTHOR: ʿAlī b. al-Ḥasan al-Bākharzī (d. 467/1075), EDITION: Muḥammad Rāghib al-Ṭabbākh, Aleppo: al-Maṭbaʿa al-ʿIlmiyya, 1930.

[1317] ***Sāniḥāt dumā al-qaṣr*** *fī muṭāraḥāt banī al-ʿaṣr*, AUTHOR: Abū al-Maʿālī Darwīsh Muḥammad b. Aḥmad al-Ṭālawī (d. 1014/1606), EDITION: 2 vols., Muḥammad Mursī al-Khūlī, Beirut: ʿĀlam al-Kutub, 1983.

[1318] ***Sulwān al-muṭāʿ*** *fī ʿudwān al-atbāʿ*, AUTHOR: Muḥammad Ibn Ẓafar al-Ṣiqillī (d. 565/1172), EDITION: Muḥammad Aḥmad Damaj, Beirut: Muʾassasat ʿIzz al-Dīn, 1995.

[1319] ***Ḥullat al-dhahab al-ibrīz*** *fī riḥlat Baʿalbak wa-al-Biqāʿ al-ʿazīz*, see #1260.

[1320] ***Nafāʾis al-ʿarāʾis***, AUTHOR: Aḥmad b. Muḥammad al-Thaʿlabī (d. 427/1035), EDITION: Cairo: Maṭbaʿat al-Bābī al-Ḥalabī, 1954. The more well-known title of this work, which is also the title of the edition cited here, is slightly different than the entry title and is *Arāʾis al-majālis fī qiṣaṣ al-anbiyāʾ*. However, there are several extant manuscripts of the same work that bear the same title as our entry, *nafāʾis al-ʿarāʾis*. See Brockelmann and Lameer (trans), *GAL Supp. 1*, 610.

[1321] ***ʿAjāʾib al-maqdūr*** *fī nawāʾib Taymūr*, AUTHOR: Aḥmad b. Muḥammad Ibn ʿArabshāh (d. 854/1450), EDITION: ʿAlī Muḥammad ʿUmar, Cairo: The Anglo-Egyptian Library, 1979.

[1322] *Tarājim al-aʿyān min abnāʾ al-zamān*, AUTHOR: Ḥasan b. Muḥammad **Būrīnī** (d. 1024/1615), EDITION: Ṣalāḥ al-Dīn al-Munajjid, Damascus: Maṭbaʿat al-Taraqqī, 1963. The entry title appears as *Tārīkh al-Būrīnī*, the History of al-Būrīnī. *Tarājim al-aʿyān* is al-Burīnī's only, albeit influential, historical work.

[1323] ***Tārīkh Āl ʿUthmān***, unidentified. The difficulty in identifying this entry, the History of the Ottoman House, is due to the existence of many works on the subject, both authored and anonymous, with similar titles. See, Abdülkader Özcan, 'Tevârih-i Âl-i-Osmân' *TDVIA*, https://islamansiklopedisi.org.tr/tevarih-i-al-i-osman. Accessed August, 2022.

[1324] ***Tārīkh Āl ʿUthmān***, see #1323.

[1325] ***Tārīkh al-khamīs*** *fī aḥwāl anfas nafīs*, AUTHOR: Ḥusayn b. Muḥammad al-Diyārbakrī (d. 996/1558), EDITION: 2 vols., Cairo: al-Maṭbaʿa al-Wahbiyya, 1866. The entry title appears as *Tārīkh al-khamīs al-musammā bi-al-jawhar al-nafīs*, whose subtitle varies from the edition cited. That said, the phrase *Tārīkh al-khamīs* in the main title is unique enough to allow us certainty regarding the identification.

[1326] *al-Kāmil bi-al-**tārīkh***, AUTHOR: ʿIzz al-Dīn **Ibn al-Athīr** (d. 630/1233), EDITION: 10 vols., ʿUmar ʿAbd al-Salām Tadmurī, Beirut: Dār al-Kitāb al-ʿArabī, 1997.

[1327] ***Ḥall al-ʿurā fī Umm al-Qurā***. Despite the abundance of titles that include the term 'Umm al-Qurā', that is, Mecca, I was unable to locate this work. See Muḥammad al-Ḥabīb al-Hayla, *al-Tārīkh wa-al-muʾarrikhūn bi-Makka fī al-qarn al-thālith al-hijrī ilā al-qarn al-thālith ʿashar*. London 1994. I thank Harry Munt for introducing me to al-Hayla's work.

[1328] ***Ḥadīqat al-zawrāʾ*** *fī sīrat al-wuzarāʾ*, AUTHOR: ʿAbd al-Raḥmān al-Suwaydī (d. 1200/1761), EDITION: Ṣafāʾ al-Khulūṣī, Baghdad: Maṭbaʿat al-Zaʿīm, 1962.

[1329] ***Hadîkatü'l-mulûk***, AUTHOR: Osmanzâde Ahmed Tâ'ib (d. 1136/1724), MS: Istanbul, Süleymaniye Library, Esad Efendi, 2245. See Abdülkadir Özcan, 'Osmanzâde Ahmed Tâ'ib,' *TDVIA* (https://islamansiklopedisi.org.tr/osmanzade-ahmed-taib. Accessed January 14, 2023).

[1330] ***Tārīkh Amīn al-Dawla***, unidentified. Could this 'history of Amīn al-Dawla' have been the composition of Amīn al-Dawla Muslim b. Maḥmūd al-Shayzarī *circa* 622/1225? The formal title of Amīn al-Dawla's work is *Jamharat al-Islām dhāt al-nathr wa-al-lisān*. It is an anthology of poetry composed by Muslim poets and arranged by topic. See Brockelmann and Lameer (trans.), *GAL I*, 262. Strictly speaking, this is not a historical work. Alternatively, this could be a scribal error in which *amīn* is written for *yamīn*. In the latter case, this could be a duplicate of entry #1346.

[1331] ***Futūḥ al-Shām***, *al-awwal*, AUTHOR: Muḥammad b. ʿUmar al-Wāqidī (d. 207/823), EDITION: 2 vols., Beirut: Dār al-Kutub al-ʿIlmiyya, 1997. The entry title appears as *Futūḥāt al-Shām*.

[1332] *Min **Tarīkh** Baghdād, al-juzʾ al-khāmis*, AUTHOR: **al-Khaṭīb** al-Baghdādī (d. 463/1071), EDITION: 10 vols., Cairo: Maktabat al-Khānjī, 1931. The entry title appears as *min Tārīkh al-Khaṭīb*, from the history of al-Khaṭīb.

[1333] *Min **Tarīkh** Baghdād, al-juzʾ al-thānī*, see #1332.

[1334] *Min **Tarīkh** Baghdād, al-juzʾ al-ḥādī ʿashar*, see #1332.

[1335] ***Āthār al-bilād wa-akhbār al-ʿibād***, AUTHOR: Zakariyyā b. Muḥammad al-Qazwīnī (d. 682/1283), EDITION: Beirut: Dār Ṣādir, 1960.

[1336] ***Akhbār al-dawla*** *al-Saljūqiyya*, AUTHOR: Anonymous (d. thirteenth century CE), EDITION: Muḥammad Iqbāl, Lahore: The University of Punjab, 1933. Albeit an anonymous composition, this work includes large portions of Ṣadr al-Dīn al-Ḥusaynī's now lost *Zubdat al-tawārīkh*. See Clifford Edmund Bosworth, *The History of the Seljuq State: A Translation and Commentary of Akhbar al-Dawla al-Saljuqiyya*, London 2010, 4–5.

[1337] ***Nihāyat al-arab fī maʿrifat qabāʾil al-ʿarab***, AUTHOR: Aḥmad b. ʿAlī al-Qalqashandī (d. 821/1418), EDITION: Ibrāhīm al-Ibyārī, Cairo: Dār al-Kutub al-Islāmiyya, 1980.

[1338] ***Nihāyat al-arab*** *fī funūn al-adab* Cf. #1337, AUTHOR: Shihāb al-Dīn al-Nuwayrī (d. 1333/733), EDITION: 33 vols., Mufīd Qumayḥa et al., Beirut: Dār al-Kutub al-ʿIlmiyya, 2004. The similarity of the main title of this entry to the previous one may lead one to conclude that it is the same work. However, al-Nuwayrī's encyclopedia is too famous to exclude as a possibility especially because its content fits in the history collection.

[1339] *Nuzhat **al-nawāẓir** fī rawḍ al-manaẓir*, AUTHOR: Abū al-Faḍl b. Abī al-Walīd Ibn al-Shiḥna (d. 890/1485). The title entry is *Nahjat al-nawāẓir*. The first term of the main title is obviously a scribal error. The book title and its authorship have been the subject of much debate. Al-Ziriklī (*al-Aʿlām*, VII:51–52) and Kaḥḥāla (*MM*, IV:258) do not give the issue much attention. It has finally been established that it is the same famous work known as *al-Durr al-muntakhab fī taʾrīkh mamlakat Ḥalab*, ed. Joseph Sarkīs, Beirut, 1909. See Anne-Marie Eddé, Ibn al-Shiḥna, *EI3*.

[1340] EITHER 1. ***al-Tibr al-masbūk** fī dhayl al-Sulūk*, AUTHOR: 1. Shams al-Dīn Muḥammad al-Sakhāwī (d. 902/1497), EDITION: Cairo: Maktabat Kulliyat al-Azhar, 1900. OR 2. ***al-Tibr al-masbūk** fī naṣīhat al-mulūk*, see #1354, AUTHOR: Abū Ḥāmid al-Ghazzālī (d. 505/1111), EDITION: Aḥmad Shams al-Dīn, Beirut: Dār al-Kutub al-ʿIlmiyya, 2008. Two famous works, a chronicle by al-Sakhāwī and a mirror for princes by al-Ghazzālī, share this title. Since both genres are well-represented in this collection, there is not sufficient evidence to exclude either.

[1341] ***Sharḥ risālat Ibn ʿAbdūn***, AUTHOR: Unknown commentator on a work by Ibn ʿAbdūn al-Ishbīlī (d. after 542/1147), EDITION (of the *Risāla*): É. Lèvi-Provençal, Cairo: al-Maʿhad al-ʿIlmī al-Firansī lil-Āthār al-Sharqiyya, 1955. Ibn ʿAbdūn's epistle is in the field of market inspection, *risāla fī al-qaḍāʾ wa-al-ḥisba*.

[1342] EITHER 1. ***al-Rawḍatayn fī akhbār al-dawlatayn** al-Nūriyya wa-al-Ṣalāḥiyya*, AUTHOR: Shihāb al-Dīn ʿAbd al-Raḥmān Abū Shāma (d. 665/1268), EDITION: 5 vols., Ibrāhīm Zaybaq, Beirut: Muʾassasat al-Risāla, 1997. OR 2. ***al-Rawḍatayn fī akhbār** Bani Būya wa-al-Ḥamdāniyyīn*, AUTHOR: Muḥammad b. Ḥasan b. ʿAlī Āl Shukr al-ʿĀmilī (d. 1207/1792). This latter work does not seem to have survived, perhaps due to al-Jazzār's actions. In his biography of the scholar Muḥammad al-Āmilī, ʿAbd al-Amīn al-Ḥusaynī al-Najafī expressly mentions that al-Jazzār killed the scholar and stole his books, see al-Najafī, *Shuhadāʾ al-faḍīla*, Beirut, 1983, 272–273; and Kaḥḥāla, IX:202–203. I thank Said Aljoumani for alerting me to this reference.

[1343] ***Musayyir al-tārīkh***, AUTHOR: Abū al-Qāsim b. al-Munjib al-Ṣayrafī (d. 542/1147), EDITION: ʿAbd al-ʿAzīz ʿAbd al-Raḥmān Saʿd, Beirut: al-Dār al-ʿArabiyya lil-ʿUlūm, 2013.

[1344] ***Rawḍat al-akhbār***, unidentified. Brockelmann presents us with five titles that include the phrase *Rawḍat al-akhbār*, *GAL*, *Supp* III-ii, 582. Three of these are of historical import and, curiously, two have to do with Yemen: 1. *Rawḍat al-akhbār wa-bahjat al-asmār* by the Ismāʿīlī *dāʿī* Idrīs ʿImād al-Dīn al-Makramī (d. 872/1369), which is a history of the Ṭayyibī community in Yemen; 2. *Rawḍat al-akhbār wa-nuzhat al-asmār fī ḥawādith Yaman al-kibār fī al-huṣūn wa-al-amṣār* by Idrīs b. Ḥusayn al-Anf (d. second half of the ninth century CE) is a history of the Ṭāhirī order in Yemen (see, Brockelmann and Lameer [trans.], *GAL*, *Supp*, II: 247); and 3. *Rawḍat al-akhbār fī siyar al-nabī wa-al-āl wa-al-aṣḥāb* by Jamāl al-Dīn ʿAṭāʾ Allāh al-Shīrāzī (d. 803/1400). I do not have sufficient evidence to argue for any one of the three works.

[1345] ***Wafayāt al-aʿyān** wa-anbāʾ abnāʾ al-zamān*, see #1277. AUTHOR: Aḥmad b. Muḥammad Ibn Khallikān (d. 681/1282), EDITION: 8 vols., Iḥsān ʿAbbās, Beirut: Dār Ṣādir, 1972.

[1346] ***Kitāb** al-tarīkh **al-yamīnī** fī akhbār dawlat al-malik Yamīn al-Dawla*, AUTHOR: Muḥammad b. ʿAbd al-Jabbār al-ʿUtbī (d. 431/1040), EDITION: Maḥfūẓ Abī Bakr Ibn Maʿtūma, Cairo: Maktabat al-Thaqāfa al-Dīniyya, 2014.

[1347] ***Laqṭ al-marjān** fī aḥkām al-jānn*, AUTHOR: Jalāl al-Dīn al-Suyūṭī (d. 911/1505), EDITION: Khālid ʿAbd al-Fattāḥ Shibl, Cairo: Maktabat al-Turāth al-Islāmī, 1989. This title is an oddity in this history collection. See the occult sciences section.

[1348] ***Kunūz al-dhahab** fī tārīkh Ḥalab, al-awwal*, AUTHOR: Muwaffaq al-Dīn Ṣibṭ Ibn al-ʿAjamī (d. 884/1480), EDITION: 2 vols., Fāliḥ al-Bakūr and Shawqī Shaʿth, Aleppo: Dār al-Qalam, 1996–1997. The entry title is *Kanz al-dhahab*.

[1349] ***al-Nuzha al-saniyya** fi akhbār al-khulafāʾ wa-al-mulūk al-Miṣriyya*, AUTHOR: al-Ḥasan b. Ḥusayn Ibn al-Ṭūlūnī (d. 909/1503), EDITION: Muḥammad Kamāl al-Dīn ʿIzz al-Dīn ʿAlī, Cairo: ʿĀlam al-Kutub, 1988.

[1350] ***Akhbār al-aʿyān**, nāqiṣ al-awwal*, unidentified. This could not possibly be the biographical dictionary composed by the nineteenth-century scholar Tannūs al-Shidyāq which bears the same title.

[1351] ***Sirāj al-mulūk**, nāqiṣ al-awwal*, AUTHOR: Muḥammad b. al-Walīd al-Ṭurṭūshī (d. 520/1126), EDITION: Cairo: Maṭbaʿat Būlaq, 1872–1873.

[1352] *al-Fatḥ **al-wahbī** fī sharḥ tārīkh Abī **al-Naṣr** al-ʿUtbī*, AUTHOR: Aḥmad al-Manīnī (d. 1172/1759), EDITION: Cairo: al-Maṭbāʿa al-Wahbiyya, 1870. The entry title appears as *al-Naṣr al-wahbī*. Despite the variance of titles, al-Manīnī's work fame and influence in the Ottoman Levant makes it a probable candidate for this collection.

[1353] *al-**Ṭabaqāt** al-saniyya fī tarājim al-ḥanafiyya, al-thānī*, AUTHOR: Taqī al-Dīn **al-Tamīmī** al-Dārī (d. 1010/1601), MANUSCRIPT: Berlin, Staatsbibliothek, Landberg 9. The entry title appears as *Ṭabaqāt al-Tamīmī*, the biographical dictionary of al-Tamīmī.

[1354] *al-Tibr al-masbūk fī **Naṣīḥat al-mulūk***, see #1340. EITHER 1. AUTHOR: Abū Ḥāmid al-Ghazzālī (d. 505/1111), OR 2. ***Naṣīḥat al-mulūk***, AUTHOR: Alī b. Muḥammad al-Māwardī (d. 450/1058), EDITION: Muḥammad Jāthim al-Ḥadīthī, Baghdad: Dār al-Shu'ūn al-Thaqāfiyya al-ʿĀmma, 1986.

[1355] ***al-Firq al-mu'dhin bi-al-ṭarab** fī al-farq bayna al-ʿAjam wa-al-ʿArab*, AUTHOR: Muṣṭafā b. Kamāl al-Dīn al-Bakrī (d. 1162/1749), EDITION: Muḥammad ʿAbd al-Salām Muḥammad Iswīsī, Beirut: Dār al-Kutub al-ʿIlmiyya, 2020.

[1356] ***Nafḥat al-majlūb** fī thimār al-qulūb min al-muḍāf wa-al-majlūb*, AUTHOR: Anonymous. This seems to be an abridgement of al-Thaʿālibī's *thimār al-qulūb*. See Ḥājjī Khalīfa, KẒ I:523 and Edward Granville Browne, *A Hand-List of the Muhammadan Manuscripts Including All These Written in the Arabic Characters Preserved in the Library of the University of Cambridge*, Cambridge 1900, 239.

[1357] ***al-Ishārāt ilā amākin al-ziyārāt***, AUTHOR: ʿUthmān b. Aḥmad Ibn al-Ḥawrānī (d. 1000/1592), EDITION: Aḥmad al-Faḍl Ibrāhīm ʿĪd, Damascus: Wizārat al-iʿlām al-Sūriyya, 1998.

[1358] ***Kashf al-asrār***, unidentified. Ḥajjī Khalīfa cites numerous books with the phrase *kashf al-asrār*, the revelation of secrets, in their titles, KẒ, II:1485–1487. Of those, two are possibly of historical import. The first by al-Khaṭīb al-Baghdādī, for which I cannot find an extant manuscript (KẒ, II:1846). The second is *kashf al-asrār fī maʿrifat al-sāda al-akhyār* by a certain Aḥmad b. Ḥasan al-Bulqīnī (KẒ, II:1486). There is another work authored by Aḥmad b. al-ʿImād al-Aqfahsī (d. 808/1464) and is entitled (according to Ḥajjī Khalīfa), *Kashf al-asrār fī mā tasallaṭa fī-hi al-Dawādār Yashbak* (*sic*, I suspect the proper subtitle is *Yashbak al-Dawadār* since it is the correct name of the official and rhymes appropriately with the main title). See, Ḥājjī Khalīfa, KẒ, II: 1486.

[1359] ***Tanbīh al-ṭālib** wa-irshād al-dāris fīmā bi-Dimashq min al-jawāmiʿ wa-al-madāris*, AUTHOR: ʿAbd al-Qādir b. Muḥammad al-Nuʿaymī (d. 927/1521), EDITION: 2 vols., Jaʿfar Ḥasanī, Cairo: Maktabat al-Thaqāfa al-Dīniyya, 1988.

[1360] ***al-Durra al-saniyya** fī akhbār al-Dawla al-ʿAbbāsiyya*, AUTHOR: Abū Bakr b. ʿAbd Allāh b. Aybak al-Dawadārī (d. 713/1313), EDITION: Dortothea Krawulsky, Cairo: al-Maʿhad al-Almānī lil-Āthār, 1992. There seems to be no standalone work with the title *al-durra al-saniyya*. However, this is a famous individual part in Ibn al-Dawādarī's universal chronicle, *Kanz al-durar wa-jāmiʿ al-ghurar*. Its size and value are attested by the fact that this particular part received a critical edition and was published separately.

[1361] ***Tuḥfat** al-asmā' wa-al-abṣār bi-mā fī al-sīra al-mutawakkiliyya min gharā'ib al-akhbār*, AUTHOR: al-Muṭṭahir b. Muḥammad b. Aḥmad al-Jarmūzī (d. 1077/1667), EDITION: 2 vols., ʿAbd al-Ḥakīm b. ʿAbd al-Majīd al-Hajarī, Sanaa: Dār al-Imām Zayd Ibn ʿAlī al-Thaqāfiyya, 2002. The entry title appears as *tuḥfat al-samā* (*sic*).

[1362] ***Tārīkh Ibn Abī al-Majd** naẓm nāqiṣ al-awwal*, unidentified. The only author with the name Ibn Abī Majd that I was able to locate is ʿImād al-Dīn Abū Bakr Ibn Abī al-Majd al-Ḥanbalī (d. 804/1410). His work is an abridgment of Jamāl al-Dīn al-Mizzī's (d. 714/1341) *Tahdhīb al-kamāl fī asmā' al-rijāl*, a biographical work that is, however, not in verse (*naẓm*). See Brockelmann and Lameer [trans.], GAL, *Supp* II: 625. Or could this be one of the works of the famous Sufi poet, Abū al-Majd Majdūd b. Ādam al-Sanā'ī (d. 526/1131)? Sanā'ī is one of the first poets to compose *mathnawī* verse for which al-ʿAṭṭār was later also famous. Although Sanā'ī's work is decidedly non-historical and does not fit squarely in this collection, the presence of al-ʿAṭṭār's *Manṭiq al-Ṭayr* in the cluster makes the presence of the former possible. See #1390.

[1363] ***Jawāhir al-ḥikam*** *wa-tawārīkh al-umam wa-siyar mulūk al-ʿarab wa-al-ʿajam*, AUTHOR: ʿAbd Allāh b. ʿAllān Ibn Razīn (d. 623/1226). This work does not seem to have survived. Kaḥḥala, *MM*, 6:40.

[1364] ***al-Ghurar*** *mial-khaṣā'iṣ* ***al-wāḍiḥa*** *wa-ʿurar al-naqāyiṣ al-fāḍiḥa*, AUTHOR: Muḥammad b. Ibrāhīm al-Kutubī (al-Waṭwāṭ) (d. 718/1318), EDITION: Ibrāhīm Shams al-Dīn, Beirut: Dār al-Kutub al-ʿIlmiyya, 2008. This is the closest title match that I could find for the entry. The content of al-Kutubī's work, which is on ethics, fits relatively well within the genre of Mirrors for Princes.

[1365] ***al-Durar al-manẓūmā min al-nukat wa-al-ishārāt al-mafhūma***, AUTHOR: Shihāb al-Dīn b.ʿAlī al-Ḥijāzi (d. 875/1471). Please see the *Adab* section for this work.

[1366] *al-Futūḥ, al-awwal*, AUTHOR: Aḥmad **Ibn Aʿtham al-Kindī** al-Kūfī (d. 314/927?), MANUSCRIPT: Dublin, Chester Beatty Library, Ar. 3272. The entry title appears as ***min tārīkh Ibn Aʿtham al-Kindī***, 'from the history of Ibn Aʿtham al-Kindī'.

[1367] *Akhbār al-duwal wa-* ***āthār al-uwal*** *fī al-tārīkh, al-awwal*, see #1273. The entry title appears as ***Āthar al-dawla wa-al-akhbār***.

[1368] ***ʿIqd al-Qurāsh?***, *al-thānī*, unidentified.

[1369] ***al-Barq al-yamānī*** *fī al-fatḥ al-ʿuthmānī*, AUTHOR: Quṭb al-Dīn Muḥammad b. Aḥmad al-Nahrawālī (d. 990/1583), MANUSCRIPT: London, The British Library, Or. 1183.

[1370] ***Tārīkh*** *nāqiṣ al-awwal wa-al-ākhir*, unidentified.

[1371] ***Majmūʿat Saʿd al-Dīn***. Could this refer to a collection owned by a certain Saʿd al-Dīn rather than the name of an author?

[1372] ***Waqf al-Malik al-Ashraf bi-al-Qāhira***, AUTHOR: anonymous. MANUSCRIPT: Cairo, Ministry of Islamic Endowments Library, 209 / 2398. This is a copy of an endowment deed related to the construction of the famous Mosque-*Madrasa* complex by the Mamluk ruler al-Ashraf Sayf al-Dīn Barsbāy (d. 841/1438) in Cairo.

[1373] *Gazavât-ı* ***Sultân Murâd b. Mehemmed Hân***, AUTHOR: Anonymous (d. 15th century CE), EDITION: Halil Inalcik and Mevlud Oguz, Istanbul: Yeditepe, 2019. The entry title appears as *Tārīkh Sulṭān Murād Khān*. Given the absence of the Arabic definite article before '*sulṭān*', I assume that the title is in Ottoman Turkish. The anonymous work cited is the sole work exclusively devoted to the biography of Murad II. Other biographies of the sultan appear in general histories of the Ottoman House.

[1374] *Sīrat al-sulṭān Jalāl al-Dīn al-Mankubirtī al-Khawārizmī*, AUTHOR: Muḥammad b. Aḥmad al-Nasawī (d. 647/1249), EDITION: Ḥamdī Ḥāfiẓ, Cairo: Dār al-Fikr al-ʿArabī, 1953. The entry title appears as *Tārīkh Khawārizm Shāh*.

[1375] *Târîh-i* ***Ebü'l-Feth***, AUTHOR: Tursun Bey (d. fl. 896/1491), EDITION: A. Mertol Tulum, Istanbul: Baha Matbaası, 1977. The entry title appears as *Manāqib Abū al-Fatḥ Sulṭān Muḥammad Khān*.

[1376] ***Tārīkh*** [*Faransī?*] ***li-ʿajā'ib al-qudra***, unidentified.

[1377] ***Tārīkh al-Furs***, unidentified.

[1378] ***Baṭṭâlnâme***, AUTHOR: Anonymous, EDITION: 3 vols., Necati Demir and Mehmet Dursun Erdem, Ankara: Hece Yayınları, 2006. The entry title appears as ***Manāqib al-Sayyīd Baṭṭāl bi-al-Turkī***.

[1379] ***Tedbîr-i cedîd-i*** *nâdir*, AUTHOR: Canikli Hacı Ali Paşa (d. 1199/1785), EDITION: Yücel Özkaya, *Tarih Araştırmaları Dergesi* XII (1969): 119–191.

The entry title appears as ***Tedbîrnâma cedîd.*** I surmised that this is the epistle by al-Jazzār's fellow Ottoman governor and contemporary Aḥmad Basha al-Jāniklī. The same epistle appears under the title *Tedbîrü'l Ġazavât*. This is a military-administrative mirror for princes. See S. Çolak, Canikli Ali Paşan'ın 'Tedbîr-i Nizâm-i Memleket' Adli Risâlesinde Reâyânın Durumuna Dair Tespit ve Öneriler, *Atatürk Üniversitesi Sosyal Bilimler Enstitüsü Dergisi* 12 (2): 163–173. I thank Berat Açıl for help in locating this title.

[1380] *Zubad al-ʿulūm wa-ṣāḥib* ***al-manṭūq wa-al-mafhūm***, AUTHOR: Yūsuf b. Ḥasan Ibn al-Mibrad (d. 909/1503), EDITION: ʿAbd al-Allāh b. Ḥusayn al-Mūjān, Jiddah: Markaz al-Kawn, 2010.

[1381] ***Tārīkh*** *nāqiṣ al-awwal*, unidentified.

[1382] ***Tajārub al-umam***, *al-awwal*, AUTHOR: Aḥmad b. Muḥammad Ibn Miskawayh (d. 421/1030), EDITION: 4 vols., H.F. Amedroz and David Samuel Margoliouth, Baghdad: Maktabat al-Muthannā, 1914–1916.

[1383] ***Sīrat Dilhimma*** (*Dhāt al-Himma*), *al-awwal*, AUTHOR: Anonymous, EDITION: 4 vols, Cairo, 1909.

[1384] ***Sīrat Dilhimma*** (*Dhāt al-Himma*), *al-awwal*, see #1383.

[1385] ***Sīrat Dilhimma*** (*Dhāt al-Himma*), *al-ʿāshir*, see #1383.

[1386] ***Dilhimma*** (*Dhāt al-Himma*), *al-sābiʿ wa-al-ishrūn*, see #1383.

[1387] ***Min baʿd siyar al-awwalīn***, unidentified.

[1388] ***Kitāb al-tanbīh ʿalā makārim Yaḥyā al-Barmakī***, The written lore on the famous Abbasid vizieral family, the Barmakīs, is vast. However, I was not able to locate an exclusive biography/*manāqib* devoted to Yaḥyā al-Barmakī (190/805). Jalīl al-ʿAtiyya identifies about thirteen works about the family, see his *Akhbār al-Barāmika*. Beirut: Dār al-Talīʿa lil-Ṭibāʿa wa-al-Nashr, 2006, 9–11.

[1389] ***Dhayl siyar Turkī***, unidentified.

[1390] ***Mantik-u tayr***, AUTHOR: Ferîdüddin Attâr (d. fl. 618/1221), probably translated into Turkish by Gülşehri (14th century), Edition: *Gülşehri-nin Mantikut-tayrı*, Yavuz Kemal. Ankara: Kırşehir Valılığı Kültür yayınları, 2007 EDITION: S.Z. Javādī, Pul (Iran): Nashr-i Khallāq bā hamkārī-i Intishārāt-i Pul, 2012. Please see the *adab* section.

[1391] ***Hümâyûnnâme***, AUTHOR: Alâeddin Ali Çelebi (d. 950/1543), EDITION: Tuncay Bülbül, Ankara: Türkiye Bilimler Akademisi, 2017.

[1392] *Subhî* ***Târîhi***, AUTHOR: **Subhî** Mehmed **Efendi** (d. 1182/1769), EDITION: Istanbul: Matbaa-i Âmire 1784. The entry title is *Tārīkh Subḥī Afandī ṭabʿ turkī*, 'The history of Subḥī Afandī, printed, in Turkish'. The work was first printed and published along with two other chronicles under the title *Târîh-i Sâmi, Şâkir ve Subhî*.

[1393] ***Târîh turkī***, AUTHOR: **İzzî Sülayman Efendi** (d. 1168/1755), EDITION: Istanbul: Matbaa-i Âmire 1784–1785. The entry title appears as ***Tārīkh turkī ṭabʿ Iṣtanbūl li-ʿIzzī Sulaymān Afandī***, 'a Turkish-language history by ʿIzzī Sulaymān Afandī printed in Istanbul'.

[1394] ***Sīrat al-ʿAntar***, *qiṭʿa*, AUTHOR: Anonymous, EDITION: Jumāna Yaḥyā Kaʿkī, Beirut: Dār al-Fikr al-ʿArabī, 2002.

[1395] *Hazẓ al-Quḥūf bi-Sharḥ qaṣīd* ***Abī Shādūf*** *nāqis al-awwal*, AUTHOR: Yūsuf b. Muḥammad al-Shirbīnī (d. fl. 1098/1698), EDITION: Cairo: Būlāq, 1858.

Works of History from the provenanced sections of the inventory

Works taken from the library of al-Sayyid Yaḥyā Efendī b. al-Sayyid Muḥammad al-Ṭībī of Jaffa in 1218/1803

[515] ***Kharīdat al-ʿajāʾib***, see #1299.

[526] ***Ḥayāt al-ḥayawān***, see #1285.

[543] ***al-Uns al-jalīl fī tārīkh al-Quds wa-al-Khalīl***, AUTHOR: Mujīr al-Dīn al-ʿUlaymī (d. 928/1522), EDITION: 2 vols., ʿAdnān Yūsuf ʿAbd al-Majīd Nubāta, Hebron: Maktabat Dandīs, 1999.

[579] ***Maḥāsin al-Shām***, see #1314.

[599] ***Kitāb fī ʿilm al-tārīkh***, unidentified. This book 'on the science of history' could be any of the following works on historiography: Muḥam-

mad b. Ibrāhīm al-Ījī (d. 840/1436), *Tuḥfat al-faqīr ilā ṣāḥib al-sarīr fī ʿilm al-tawārīkh*; Muḥyi al-Dīn al-Kāfiyajī (d. 879/1474), *al-Mukhtaṣar fī ʿilm al-tārīkh*; al-Suyūṭī (d. 911/1505), *al-Shamārīkh fī ʿilm al-tārīkh*; al-Sakhāwī (d. 902/1497); *al-iʿlān bi-al-tawbīkh li-man dhamma al-tārīkh*. See Franz Rosenthal, *A History of Muslim Historiography*, Leiden 1968, 30–42, and 201–259.

Works taken from the libraries of al-Shaykh ʿAlī al-Rashīdī and al-Shaykh Muḥammad Wakīlkharaj in 1216/1801

[1650] EITHER 1. ***al-Aḥkām al-sulṭāniyya***, AUTHOR: ʿAlī b. Muḥammad al-Māwardī (d. 450/1058), EDITION: Muḥammad Badr al-Dīn al-Naʿsānī al-Ḥalabī, Cairo: Maktabat al-Khānjī, 1909; OR 2. ***al-Aḥkām al-sulṭāniyya***, AUTHOR: Abū Yaʿlā Muḥammad Ibn al-Farrāʾ (d. 458/1066), EDITION: Muḥammad Ḥāmid al-Fiqī, Cairo: Maṭbaʿat al-Bābī al-Jalabī, 1987. The title entry is preceded by *ʿan kitāb*, ʿfrom the book ofʾ.

[1685] ***Kitāb Lawāqiḥ al-anwār al-qudsiyya fī manāqib al-ʿulamāʾ wa-al-ṣūfiyya***, see #1264 no. 2.

CHAPTER 23

Amassing Medicine (*ṭibb*): Selections from an Ottoman Governor's Medical Collection

Deborah Schlein

Deep into the inventory of Aḥmad Pasha al-Jazzār's (d. 1219/1804) library, its compiler has dedicated two pages to the section of *kutub ʿilm al-ṭibb*, the science of medicine.[1] This list consisting of a total of forty-nine entries is one of the smallest sections of the inventory, making it clear that medicine was not the main focus of al-Jazzār's library.[2] Yet, these works, as well as those related to medicine found elsewhere in the inventory, suggest an interest in and knowledge of both medical texts and their place in the canon of elite, intellectual and even practical knowledge. What follows here is an examination of those entries, particularly in comparison to the contents of other library inventories in the region, and an exploration of possible reasons for why such a collection was amassed.

Medicine is a science and an art primarily requiring knowledge of medical theory and capability in practice. As Benedikt Reier explains, while 'medical training did not follow a fixed curriculum during this time', three different educational approaches could be followed to acquire this knowledge: 'theoretical study with a medical expert, training with a practising physician in an apprentice-like relationship, or autodidactic training'.[3] As of yet, there appears to be no evidence that Aḥmad Pasha al-Jazzār was ever a medical student or practitioner himself, but his ownership of these medical titles sheds light on an awareness of medical knowledge integral to the human experience, with medicine being embedded into the very fabric of society.[4] It also follows a pattern that Boris Liebrenz has pointed out: the majority of identifiable owners of medical manuscripts were not medical practitioners, but were more often legal and religious scholars.[5] To know how to heal oneself ensures longevity, health and, also importantly, a more successful career. A knowledge of medicine and its application in the eighteenth-century Ottoman world was considered both a prestigious and lucrative field.[6] Keeping medical texts, even if they did not read them, probably lent the owners of these works an air of respectability and intelligence. And the Jazzār library is not the only collection to include medical texts alongside *ḥadīth*, *fiqh* and histories.

1 The Medical Collection

In addition to the forty-nine entries of Arabic medical titles listed under *ʿilm al-ṭibb*, there are also four Prophetic medicine titles (*al-ṭibb al-nabawī*) in the *ḥadīth* section, five books re-

1 Library inventory, Vakıflar Genel Müdürlüğü (Ankara), Defter 1626, 62–63 of a total of 80 pages.

2 Smaller sections include *manṭiq* (47 titles) and dream interpretation (5 titles), as well as the section on the Qur'an (24 titles). Library inventory, Vakıflar Genel Müdürlüğü (Ankara), Defter 1626, forty-eight to fifty (*manṭiq*), fifty-five (dream interpretation) and fourteen to fifteen (Qur'an).

3 Reier, "Bibliophilia in Ottoman Aleppo", 483.

4 Shefer, "An Ottoman Physician", 103.

5 Liebrenz, "The Social History of Surgery", 40.

6 B. Harun Küçük explains that 'being unhealthy [...] made men incapable of carrying out their duties and of acting in a refined manner', a viewpoint expounded upon by Ibn Sallūm (d. 1669), himself an Ottoman physician who wrote medical works largely related to new European or Paracelsian medicine. Küçük, "New Medicine", 235.

lated to medicine in the section of works 'taken' (*ma'khūdha*) from the library of al-Sayyid Yaḥyā Efendī b. al-Sayyid Muḥammad al-Ṭībī of Jaffa in 1218/1803, and two books 'taken' from the libraries of al-Shaykh ʿAlī al-Rashīdī and al-Shaykh Muḥammad Wakīlkharaj in 1216/1801.[7] The medical section alone in al-Jazzār's library inventory, with a total of 1707 entries, constitutes 2.9 per cent of all the entries, and when we add these other eleven entries, this comes to 3.5 per cent of the total inventory. These percentages are very slightly above the medical compositions of two eighteenth-century Damascus libraries. Said Aljoumani has written about both Muḥammad Pasha al-ʿAẓm's (d. 1197/1783) collection and that of Mullā ʿUthmān al-Kurdī (fl. c. 1204/1789). Muḥammad Pasha al-ʿAẓm, the governor of Damascus, held a library collection with an inventory of 457 entries. Nine of those entries were listed under the heading of *ṭibb*, and one Prophetic medicine title was listed under *ḥadīth*, making the medically related composition of this library inventory 2.2 percent of the total inventory.[8] Similarly, Aljoumani's work in tracing the books of Mullā ʿUthmān al-Kurdī's library in Damascus notes 479 titles, eleven of which are related to medicine, constituting 2.3 per cent of the collection thus far.[9] Al-Jazzār governed in Sidon and Damascus in the latter half of the eighteenth century, and his decision to endow a *waqf* that included a library and add to that library a medical section that ultimately constituted at least 2.9 per cent of the entries in his inventory makes his library comparable to those of his regional, Ottoman counterparts.[10]

2 The Medical Titles: Known Texts

Al-Jazzār was governor of Sidon district beginning in 1775, during which time he moved his capital to Acre where he established his library, thus, he had ample reason to look the part of his educated status, both to his peers and to those he governed.[11] His collections in *ḥadīth* (189 entries), *fiqh* (more than 200), *nawḥ* (189), *tawḥīd* and *taṣawwuf* (well above 100), and history (148) speak to the importance and priority of these subjects.[12] Yet, this library was not meant to serve solely the interests of al-Jazzār, at least outwardly. The opening paragraph of the inventory stipulates that the library was a part of the *madrasa* complex, endowed and intended for the public benefit.[13] It is, therefore, possible that these works were amassed for the

7 Library inventory, Vakıflar Genel Müdürlüğü (Ankara), Defter 1626, twenty-four (*ḥadīth* section: #299, #300, #301 and #302), thirty-one to thirty-two (books from Sayyid Yaḥyā Efendī section: #549, #557, #583, #584 and #591) and seventy (books from al-Shaykh ʿAlī al-Rashīdī and al-Shaykh Muḥammad Wakīlkharaj: #1636 and #1641).

8 Aljoumani, "Masrad Kutub", 60–61 (#445–453), 33 (#84, *al-Ṭibb al-nabawī lil-Suyūṭī*).

9 Aljoumani lays out 479 entries in a table of works in Mullā ʿUthmān al-Kurdī's library. This number differs from the 462 manuscripts of the collection noted in Aljoumani's article. The percentage quoted above is based on the 479 entries in the table. Additionally, Aljoumani notes in his article on al-Kurdī's library that the titles he explicitly identifies as medicine are older, with authors such as Galen (d. ca. 216 CE), Ibn al-Nafīs (d. 687/1288), Muḥammad b. ʿUmar al-Badhdādī, Ibn al-ʿAdīm ʿUmar b. Aḥmad (d. 660/1262) and Ibn Ḥajar al-ʿAsqalānī (d. 852/1449). In Aljoumani's table, these are lines 185, 181, 182, 470 and 183 respectively, and we learn of other medically relevant titles from this table, noted here by line. Two medical texts have an unknown author (lines 184 and 469). There is one text on pharmacy (180), one text on nutrition (229), one text on Prophetic medicine (line 275), and one text on spiritual and religious treatment (209). Aljoumani, "Qāʿidāt Bayānāt Maktabat"; Aljoumani, "Tārīkh Maktabat al-Mullā", 232, 235.

10 A third Ottoman bibliophile and bureaucrat, Cārullah Efendī (d. 1151/1738), owned only six medical titles out of 3500 works, which he began collecting after 1698. Usluer, "Carullah Efendi'nin", 306–310.

11 Al-Jazzār was governor of Damascus in 1783, 1790–1795, 1798 and 1803. Safi, "al-Jazzār, Aḥmad Pasha", 57.

12 Library inventory, Vakıflar Genel Müdürlüğü (Ankara), Defter 1626, 19–24 (*ḥadīth*), 25–30 (*fiqh*), 37–43 (*nawḥ*), 33–37 (*tawḥīd* and *taṣawwuf*) and 55–60 (history).

13 (*nafʿ ʿamīm*) public benefit: this translation thanks to a reading by and discussion with Guy Burak. Library inventory, Vakıflar Genel Müdürlüğü (Ankara), Defter 1626, 24.

general edification of its users, broadly defined, who would benefit from the collection both as an educational good within the *madrasa* and a public good. Thus, similar to Ottoman Sultan Bāyezīd II's (r. 886–918/1481–1512) library, the collection was canonical and meant to be used, through reading, teaching and general study.[14] This is made apparent in the inventory, which lists many titles that were reputable and informative. The canonical nature of these texts is easy to spot in the medical section, with the most well-known titles appearing first.[15]

No text is more canonical for *ṭibb* than Ibn Sīnā's (d. 428/1037) medical encyclopaedia *al-Qānūn fī al-ṭibb*, and the first four entries of the library inventory remind us of that: "*al-Qānūn li-Ibn Sīnā*" (#1423), "*Min fann qānūn li-Ibn Sīnā*" (#1424), "*Min al-qānūn li-Ibn Sīnā*" (#1425) and "*Min al-qānūn li-Ibn Sīnā juzʾ awwal*" (#1426). Additionally, about twenty entries down the list, there is one more edition of the words of the *Qānūn*: "*Majmūʿa min kalām Ibn Sīnā min al-qānūn*" (#1444).[16] Orlin Sabev observes that, predominantly in the eighteenth and nineteenth centuries, 'the most popular title on medicine housed by public Ottoman libraries was *al-Qānūn fī al-ṭibb* by Ibn Sīnā'.[17] This is unsurprising given the pride of place Ibn Sīnā's *Qānūn* holds in the study of medicine from the medieval to the early modern periods across the Islamic world.[18] Al-Jazzār's collection of *Qānūn* entries is even more revelatory about the importance of this text and his own wealth because the very first entry, "*al-Qānūn li-Ibn Sīnā*" (#1423), is noted to be a printed copy described by the inventory compiler as *khaṭṭ ṭabʿ*.[19] Boris Liebrenz describes the 1593 Medici Press printing of Ibn Sīnā's *Canon* as widely used in eighteenth-century Greater Syria, and Benedict Reier points to a copy of a European printing of the *Qānūn* held by al-Taqāwī (d. 1061/1650–1651) in seventeenth-century Aleppo as possibly the first example of the region's reception of Arabic titles printed in Europe. Thus, precedent for owning and wanting to own a copy of this printed work was evident in the region where al-Jazzār's library inventory was compiled.[20] Starting the medical section of the inventory with multiple copies of Ibn Sīnā's *Qānūn*, including a printed work, therefore, seems to point towards an awareness on the part of the inventory compiler that this text is where foundational knowledge of *ṭibb* begins in both medical and library circles.

Additionally, two products of the *Qānūn* commentary tradition, which built on this foundational source, can also be found in this list: *al-Mūjaz (fī al-ṭibb)* (#1462) by Ibn al-Nafīs (d. 687/1288) and *al-Mughnī fī ṭibb sharḥ al-mūjaz* (#1430) by Sadīd al-Dīn al-Kāzarūnī (d. 758/1357).[21] This abridgment of the *Qānūn* and commentary on the abridgment continued the tradition of engaging with foundational medical sources and, in al-Jazzār's inventory, represent their solid impact and reputation centuries after they were written.

The second title recorded at the top of the medical section is noted with just as many entries. Dāʾūd b. ʿUmar al-Anṭākī's (d. 1008/1599) medical encyclopaedia *Tadhkirat ūlī al-albāb wa-al-jāmiʿ lil-*

14 The inventory of Bāyezīd II's library, housed at Topkapı Palace in Istanbul, was written by one Khayr al-Dīn Khidr ʿAtūfī (d. 1541) in 909/1503–1504. Varlık, "Books on Medicine", 52–58.

15 In Bāyezīd II's library inventory, the compiler ʿAtūfī adheres to somewhat of a hierarchical arrangement with more well-known and reputable titles noted at the beginning. Varlık, "Books on Medicine", 532.

16 Library inventory, Vakıflar Genel Müdürlüğü (Ankara), Defter 1626, 62.

17 Sabev, "Medical Books in Private and Public", 620.

18 Ibn Sīnā's Qānūn is considered to be 'the most influential of all medieval Islamic medical encyclopedias'. Pormann/Savage-Smith, *Medieval Islamic Medicine*, 49, 24.

19 Library inventory, Vakıflar Genel Müdürlüğü (Ankara), Defter 1626, 62.

20 Liebrenz, "From Leipzig to Damascus", 331; Reier, "Bibliophilia in Ottoman Aleppo", 491.

21 For Ibn Sīnā, his *Qānūn*, and its many commentaries, see Kâtip Çelebi, *Kashf al-ẓunūn*, IV, 496–501, entry 9354; Aljoumani, *Maktabat Madrasat fī Ḥalab*, footnote 633, 133; Brockelmann, *GAL*, I, 589–590, 598; Ibn Abī Uṣaybiʿa, *ʿUyūn al-anbāʾ*, 11.13. Library inventory, Vakıflar Genel Müdürlüğü (Ankara), Defter 1626, 63, 62.

ʿajab al-ʿujāb takes up the next three entries following those of the *Qānun*—*Tadhkirat Dāʾūd* (#1427), *Tadhkirat Dāʾūd* (#1428) and *Dhayl tadhkirat Dāʾūd* (#1429)—with *al-Juzʾ al-awwal min tadhkirat Dāʾūd* (#1454) listed about fifteen entries later and one more version of the text, *Kitāb ṣaghīr min tadhkirat Dāʾūd* (#583), found in the list of books taken from al-Sayyid Yaḥyā Efendī b. al-Sayyid Muḥammad al-Ṭībī of Jaffa in 1218/1803.[22] Born in Antioch, Dāʾūd al-Anṭākī lived and wrote in Cairo and Damascus more than five centuries after Ibn Sīnā lived.[23] As a well-known physician of the sixteenth century, his *Tadhkira* was one of the most famous medical texts during the Ottoman period.[24] Sabev emphasises in his "Medical Books in Private and Public Ottoman Libraries", the words of Ottoman writer Saçaklızāde Mehmed b. Ebū Bekir el-Maraşī (d. 1150/1737), who states that the study of medicine was necessary due to the abundance of disease in cities and every Muslim should, therefore, own a copy of al-Anṭākī's *Tadhkira*.[25] Thus, the fame and importance of this text led to the ownership of numerous copies of it, with al-Jazzār's collection including more than one copy of al-Anṭākī's work probably because it was already highly collected in the Ottoman world due to it being viewed as a wealth of useful medical knowledge.[26]

Unsurprisingly, this approach to collecting the most well-known texts of the field is found in the collections of other Ottoman libraries. Whether one was a medical practitioner or not, a library that contained medical titles often held the most reputable sources deemed useful, and owning such well-known titles lent an air of authority to the collector as well. Table 23.1, below, lists eleven collections in addition to that of al-Jazzār. Ten of these collections are Ottoman, with the last one listed covering Ottoman public libraries as a whole, as gathered by Sabev. The first collection after al-Jazzār's column, the Ashrafīya, is Ayyubid (1171–1260) and is included for pre-Ottoman background. These collections are largely located in *Bilād al-Shām*, or Greater Syria, with the exception of a few Ottoman libraries in Istanbul and a group of public libraries situated across the empire. The titles above—the *Qānūn*, the *Mūjaz*, the *Mughnī* and al-Anṭākī's *Tadhkira*—are in this table, as are four other titles found in singular entries in the inventory of the Jazzār library.

Kitāb ḥāwī Ilyās fī ʿilm al-tadāwī (#1459) is a medical reference work that was written by Najm al-Dīn Maḥmūd b. Ḍiyāʾ al-Dīn Ilyās al-Shīrāzī (d. 730/1330). It contains five sections on ailments, fevers, illnesses affecting specific body parts, simple and complex drugs.[27] Found in medical, imperial and public Ottoman libraries as *Kitāb ḥāwī fī ʿilm al-tadāwī*, with reference to Ilyās as the author, this text had appeal across collections. The two largely medical libraries of Aleppo—al-Taqāwī's (d. 1061/1650–1651) seventeenth-century collection (inventory compiled in 1039/1629) and the eighteenth-century Shukrī Ārūtīn family library belonging to the Maronite physician Ḥannā al-Ṭabīb—held copies, demonstrating the book's reputable status amongst physicians.[28] In addition to being included in Bāyezīd II's library register, eight copies of the text were also found in public Ottoman libraries dating from the eighteenth and nineteenth centuries.[29] Its popularity reached

22 Library inventory, Vakıflar Genel Müdürlüğü (Ankara), Defter 1626, 62, 63, 32.

23 İhsanoğlu, *Osmanlı Tıbbi Bilimler Literatürü Tarihi*, 197. Brockelmann, *GAL*, II, 478.

24 İhsanoğlu, *Osmanlı Tıbbi Bilimler Literatürü Tarihi*, XIV. Kâtip Çelebi, *Kashf al-ẓunūn*, II, 260–261, entry 2811.

25 Saçaklızade's text was *Tartīb al-ʿUlūm*. Sabev, "Medical Books in Private and Public", 615.

26 Varlık notes that titles appearing multiple times in Bāyezīd II's inventory probably indicated that the works were essential to medical knowledge. Varlık, "Books on Medicine", 531.

27 Kâtip Çelebi, *Kashf al-ẓunūn*, III, 11–12, entry 4385; Brockelmann, *GAL*, supplement 2, 298–299.

28 Reier, "Bibliophilia in Ottoman Aleppo", MS no. 61 (503), MS no. 98 (506). Krimsti, "Unpublished Table of Medical Books", Gotha, Ms. Orient. A 1943.

29 Eight copies found across twenty-two Ottoman public library collections. Sabev, "Medical Books in Private and Public", 622.

such heights that it was translated into Turkish as *Macma' al-Mucarrabat fi'l-Tibb* or *Tarcamat al-Havi fi 'Ilm al-Tadavi* by Ahmed b. Bali Fakih (fl. 10/14th century).[30] Such a collection and reception history meant that many copies of this work were produced, and, when amassing a medical collection, it is, therefore, no surprise that this title was included in the Jazzār library inventory.

Tadhkirat kaḥḥālīn, called *Kitāb fī 'ilm al-ṭibb al-musammā bi-tadhkirat al-kaḥḥālīn* (#1439) in the inventory, is a textbook on ophthalmology written by 'Alī b. 'Īsā al-Kaḥḥāl (d. after 400/1009). Arranged anatomically, the text contains three chapters that describe common diseases of the eye and their treatment.[31] *Tadhkirat kaḥḥālīn*'s reception history and popularity are evident as it spans inclusion in library inventories from that of the thirteenth-century Ashrafiyya library in Damascus (later moved to Istanbul), to the eighteenth-century library register of the Hagia Sophia, and the various Ottoman public libraries of the eighteenth and nineteenth centuries.[32] Between these centuries, medical practitioners felt the text useful enough to add to their own collections, as noted in the inventory of a private medical library in Ottoman Aleppo. Benedikt Reier's article on the medical library of al-Taqāwī also includes a photo he took of the medical practitioner Ibn Ḥamza's library inventory, which was compiled in 1665 1666 and written after that of al-Taqāwī in the same notebook.[33] The inventory lists *Tadhkirat kaḥḥālīn* second from the end of its penultimate line, noting its author to be 'Alī b. 'Īsā.[34] Thus, alongside public libraries and older collections, medical libraries also held *Tadhkirat kaḥḥālīn*. The text's relevance to specialised medical libraries and more general collections demonstrates both its importance and relative ubiquity, thus, its inclusion in the Jazzār library inventory is unsurprising.

Two other texts found in the medical section of the Jazzār library inventory show up in Ottoman-era library collections. *Kitāb al-wuṣla ilā al-ḥabīb (fī waṣf al-ṭayyibāt wal-ṭīb)* (#1441) gives details for the preparation of foodstuffs, perfumes, drinks and cures, and was written by 'Umar b. Aḥmad b. al-'Adīm (d. 660/1262).[35] *Jirāb al-mujarrabāt* (#1455), according to Reier, could be *Jirāb al-mujarrabāt wa-khizānat al-aṭṭibā'*, a transcription of Abū Bakr Muḥammad b. Zakarīyā al-Rāzī's (d. 311/923) case notes with his patients.[36] Both of these works are listed in the seventeenth-century inventory for al-Taqāwī's medically focused collection in Aleppo. While *Kitāb al-wuṣla ilā al-ḥabīb* is additionally part of Bāyezīd II's inventory in Istanbul, both texts also show up in eighteenth-century Ottoman collections in Greater Syria. Mulla 'Uthmān al-Kurdī (fl. c. 1204/1789) in Damascus owned a copy of *Kitāb al-wuṣla ilā al-ḥabīb*, and the eighteenth-century Shukrī Ārūtīn family library in Aleppo held a copy of *Jirāb al-mujarrabāt*.[37] Ownership of

30 İhsanoğlu, *Osmanlı Tıbbi Bilimler Literatürü Tarihi*, 188.

31 Ibn Abī Uṣaybi'a, *'Uyūn al-anbā' fī ṭabaqāt al-aṭibbā'*, 10.5; Ullmann, *Medizin*, 208–209.

32 The Ashrafiyya library was transferred to Istanbul in the sixteenth century. Hirschler, *Medieval Damascus*, 46, 181, Entry no. 274; Aya Sofya's Defter. 2/Fihrist 1 (CD 19380)—YAZMAFIHRIST 25-1, f. 122ª, entry 2; Sabev, "Medical Books in Private and Public", 622. A copy of *Tadhkirat al-Kaḥḥālīn* (Tübingen Ma VI 138) was also included in the private library of Aḥmad al-Rabbāṭ (fl. 18th and 19th centuries) in Syria. See Liebrenz, "The Library of Aḥmad al-Rabbāṭ", 31.

33 I am incredibly grateful to Benedikt Reier for including this photo in his article. It offers yet another window into seventeenth-century book collecting in Aleppo. Reier, "Bibliophilia in Ottoman Aleppo", 496.

34 Ibid., 496.

35 (Kamāl al-Dīn) 'Umar b. Aḥmad b. al-'Adīm. Kâtip Çelebi, *Kashf al-ẓunūn*, I, 191, entry 234; Brockelmann, GAL, supplement 1, 904.

36 There is a copy of *Jirāb al-mujarrabāt* at the Wellcome Library in London, MS Arabic 81, which has been digitised: https://wellcomecollection.org/works/xwak6jte. According to Brockelmann (GAL), the author could be Abū 'Abdallāh Muḥammad b. Yaḥyā b. Abī Ṭālib b. Aḥmad. MS no. 96. Reier, "Bibliophilia in Ottoman Aleppo", 506; Brockelmann, GAL, supplement 2, 1041.

37 MS no. 138, Varlık, "Books on Medicine", 544; Aljoumani, "Qā'idāt Bayānāt Maktabat", list no. 470 = MS no. 3259 in the National Library in Damascus. Krimsti, "Unpublished Table of Medical Books", Gotha, Ms. Orient. A 1965.

TABLE 23.1 Libraries and Shared Medical Titles

Title (in al-Jazzār's inventory, 1806, Acre)[a]	Ashrafīya, 1270s, Damascus[b]	Bayazid II, 1503–1504, Istanbul[c]	al-Taqāwī, inventory written in 1629, Aleppo[d]	Ibn Ḥamza, inventory written in 1665–1666, Aleppo[e]	Muḥammad Pasha al-ʿAẓam, d. 1783, Damascus[f]
al-Qānūn fī al-ṭibb, Ibn Sīnā (d. 428/1037), #1423–1426, #1444	2 copies (no. 861, f. 257[a] of inventory, p. 262; no. 1477, f. 267[b] of inventory, p. 398)	9 copies (55, 64–70, 72)	6 copies (no. 40, 41, 45, 46, 47, 48	2 copies (first title in first line of inventory)	1 copy (453, p. 60)
al-Mūjaz, Ibn al-Nafīs (d. 687/1288), #1462		6 in Arabic (96–100, 102), 2 in Persian translation (101, 103)	1 copy (no. 90)	1 copy (second to last title in third line)	
al-Mughnī fī ṭibb sharḥ al-mūjaz, Sadīd al-Dīn al-Kāzarūnī (d. 758/1357), #1430			4 copies (no. 103 - 3 copies, no. 107)		
Tadhkirat Dāʾud; Dāʾud b. ʿUmar al-Anṭākī (d. 1008/1599), #1427, #1428, #1429, #1454, #0583				1 copy (fourth title in first line)	3 copies (448 - two copies, 449; p. 60)
Kitāb ḥāwī Ilyās fī ʿilm al-tadāwī; Najm al-Dīn Maḥmūd b. Ḍiyāʾ al-Dīn Ilyās al-Shīrāzī (d. 730/1330), #1459		3 copies (52–54)	2 copies - (no. 61, 98)		
Kitāb fī ʿilm al-ṭibb al-musammā bi-tadhkirat al-Kaḥḥālīn; ʿAlī b. ʾIsā al-Kaḥḥāl (d. after 400/1009), #1439	1 copy (no. 274, f. 250[a] of inventory, p. 181)			1 copy (second-to-last title in penultimate line)	
Kitāb al-wuṣla ilā al-ḥabīb (fī waṣf al-ṭayyibāt wal-ṭīb), ʿUmar b. Aḥmad b. al-ʿAdīm (d. 660/1262), #1441		1 copy (138)	1 copy (no. 89)		
Jirāb al-Mujarrabāt, maybe al-Rāzī (d. 311/923), #1455			1 copy (no. 96)		

a. Library inventory, Vakıflar Genel Müdürlüğü (Ankara), Defter 1626; b. Hirschler., Medieval Damascus; c. Varlık, "Books on Medicine," in Treasures of Knowledge; d. Reier, "Bibliophilia in Ottoman Aleppo"; e. Reier, "Bibliophilia in Ottoman Aleppo," 496; f. al-Joumani, "Masrad Kutub Madrasat Muḥammad Bāshā al-ʿAẓam";

Mullā ʿUthmān al-Kurdī, fl. 1789, Damascus[g]	Shukrī Ārūtīn (Ḥannā al-Ṭabīb's) family library, Aleppo, 18th century[h]	Ragıp Paşa's (d. 1176/1763) inventory, Istanbul, 18th century[i]	Hagia Sophia inventory, Istanbul, 18th century[j]	Khālidīya, register: 1201/1787, library made public: 1900, Jerusalem[k]	Public Ottoman Libraries, largely 18th and 19th centuries[l]
	1 copy (Gotha, Ms. Orient. A 1913)	f. 20^{b}, first text in line one	f. 118^{a}, 3 copies (entries 2, 3, and 4 on the page)		26 copies in 22 collections (p. 621)
1 copy (no. 181 in list, no. 3146ت in the National Library in Damascus)	1 copy (Gotha, Ms. Orient. A 1921)	f. 20^{b}, third text in line eight	f. 121^{b}, 2 copies (entries 12 and 13 on the page)		17 copies in Arabic 22 collections,1 in Persian (p. 621)
	1 copy (Gotha, Ms. Orient. A 1925)		f. 120^{b}, 2 copies, (entries 11 and 12 on the page)		24 copies across 22 collections, but this includes other commentaries on the Mūjaz (al-Aqsarāʾī d. 791/1389; al-Kirmānī d. 842/1438–1439; el-Emşātī d. 902/1496; al-Qazvīnī d. 928/1522; Şihabeddin el-İci) (p. 621)
		f. 20^{b}, first text in line four	f. 122^{a}, 1 copy, (entry 1 on the page)	2 copies (MS 283 formerly MS 3959, MS 306 formerly MS 3958)	13 copies in 22 collections (p. 623)
	1 copy (Gotha, Ms. Orient. A 1943)				8 copies in 22 collections (p. 622)
			f. 122^{a}, 1 copy (entry 2) and 1 copy of the Persian translation (entry 3 on the page)		3 copies in 22 collections (p. 622)
1 copy (no. 470 in list, no. 3259 in the National Library in Damascus)					
	1 copy (Gotha, Ms. Orient. A 1965)				

g. al-Joumani, "Qāʿidāt Bayānāt Maktabat al-Mullā ʿUthmān al-Kurdī bi-Dimashq (ḥayy 1204 H/1789 M)," unpublished; h. Feras Krimsti's unpublished table of medical books in the Shukrī Ārūtīn family library; i. Ragıp Paşa library inventory, RAGIPPASA4111; j. Aya Sofya's Defter. 2/Fihrist 1 (CD 19380)—YAZMAFIHRIST25-1; k. Khālidī Library collection, Virtual Hill Museum and Manuscript Library https://www.vhmml.org/dataPortal; l. Sabev, "Medical Books in Private and Public Ottoman Libraries"

these two texts—one on preparations that could enhance health and the other a record of medical case studies—would prepare the reader for a better understanding of health and health management, skills a physician would need and subjects that would enhance any medical collection, whether it was held in a physician's library or not.

3 Other Medical texts in the Inventory: Known and Less So

The eight titles above, comprising sixteen entries in the inventory of al-Jazzār's library, make up over a quarter of the medical entries (60, with 49 of those entries in the medical section). Some of the other titles are also identifiable, such as *al-Tuḥfa al-Jāmiʿa (li-mufradāt al-ṭibb al-nāfiʿa)* (#1456), written by Abū Zakariyyāʾ ʿImād al-Dīn Yaḥyā b. Abī Bakr al-ʿĀmirī al-Tihāmī al-Ḥanafī (d. 893/1488) and noted in the inventory's medical section. Additionally, *Rawḍat al-ʿiṭr* (#1641), a pharmacopeia by Muḥammad b. Maḥmūd b. Ḥājī al-Shīrwānī (d. after 855/1451), is listed in the section of books taken from the libraries of al-Shaykh ʿAlī al-Rashīdī and al-Shaykh Muḥammad Wakīlkharaj in 1216/1801.[38] The latter was also included in the eighteenth-century Shukrī Ārūtīn family library in Aleppo belonging to the physician Ḥannā al-Ṭabīb.[39]

Perhaps the most intriguing identifiable entry of the group is #1451: *Bahr al-jawāhir fī al-ṭibb lil-Harawī*. This text, written by the Persian physician Muḥammad b. Yūsuf al-Harawī in 924/1518, is a medical lexicon that covers anatomical and pathological terms as well as medicinal substances and remedies.[40] Written in Arabic, it often also contains Persian explanations of the various terms it defines.[41] Its full title is *Bahr al-jawāhir fī taḥqīq al-muṣṭalaḥāt al-ṭibbiyya min al-ʿarabiyya wa-al-lāṭīniyya wa-al-yūnāniyya*, noting the linguistic foundations from which the medical terms and information came.[42] Al-Harawī explains early on in the text that he referred to a multitude of medical sources for his work on this lexicon, including the *Qānūn* and its commentaries as well as the *Mūjaz* and its commentaries, sources that are also found in the Jazzār library inventory. When he did not find what he needed, he discussed medical terms 'with learned physicians and experienced scholars'.[43] While the texts come first in the hierarchy of source material, oral knowledge, such as practical knowledge, is considered by al-Harawī to be useful for the production of his lexicon.[44] It is where he was when writing this work and speaking to knowledgeable and practising medical scholars that makes the inclusion of this text in al-Jazzār's inventory so interesting. Al-Harawī wrote *Baḥr al-Jawāhir* in Herat, in what was at the time Safavid Iran, and is now located in Afghanistan. He visited India and included Ayurvedic terms in his lexicon alongside some Persian explanations.[45] The Persianate and South Asian environments he inhabited and in which he carried out this work give his *Baḥr al-jawāhir* a distinctly non-Ottoman flavour. None of the Ottoman library registers consulted for

38 Library inventory, Vakıflar Genel Müdürlüğü (Ankara), Defter 1626, 63, 70; *al-Tuḥfa al-Jāmiʿa*: Brockelmann, GAL, supplement 2, 225; *Rawḍat al-ʿiṭr*: Kâtip Çelebi, *Kashf al-ẓunūn*, III, 504, entry 6657; İhsanoğlu, *Osmanlı Tıbbi Bilimler Literatürü Tarihi*, 42, 46. Called *ʿan Rawḍat al-ʿiṭr (liʾan yartāḍ al-ʿaṭṭār)* by Brockelmann, GAL, supplement 2, 327.

39 Krimsti, "Unpublished Table of Medical Books", Gotha, Ms. Orient. A 2015.

40 Iskandar, "Jawāhir al-lugha wa-Baḥr al-Jawāhir", 331, 334; National Library of Medicine, *A Shelflist of Islamic Medical Manuscripts*, 71.

41 Savage-Smith, *Bodleian*, MS Ouseley 174, 444; Ullmann, *Medizin*, 237, footnote 4.

42 al-Harawī, *Baḥr al-jawāhir fī taḥqīq al-muṣṭalaḥāt al-ṭibbīyah min al-ʿArabīyah wa-al-Lāṭīnīyah wa-al-Yūnānīyah*, Princeton University Library, Islamic Manuscripts, Third Series, No. 769.

43 Iskandar, "Jawāhir al-lugha wa-Baḥr al-Jawāhir", 334; al-Harawī, Baḥr al-jawāhir, Edited byʿAbd al-Majīd Mawlavī, 2.

44 Hamza, "Vernacular Languages and Invisible Labor in Ṭibb", 136.

45 Langermann, "The Chapter on Rasāyana", 148, 150.

this chapter list the text.[46] Thus, it does make one wonder, why did he include this particular work? Finding the copy of *Baḥr al-jawāhir* originally held in the Jazzār library may lead to clues that can help answer this question, but until that happens, we can only guess.

What is left of the medical entries are generically named works and titles in disciplines that could loosely be related to medicine. The compiler of the Jazzār library inventory often gave generic titles to works he probably did not recognise, such as one of the entries in the law section simply entitled 'a book on Ḥanafī *fiqh*'.[47] He did note the authors of some of these generic titles in the medicine section. These include *Risāla lil-shaykh al-ra'īs Abī 'Alī Ibn Sīnā* (#1448) and *Kitāb fī 'ilm al-ṭibb li-Abī al-Ḥazm*, which could be a work on medicine written by 'Alā' al-Dīn 'Alī b. Abi al-Ḥazm al-Qarashī (#1449), also known as Ibn al-Nafīs (d. 687/1288).[48] But most of the other generic titles had no other identifying information. Five entries were simply titled *Kitāb fī 'ilm al-ṭibb* (#1440, #1442, #1460, #1468 and #1469), and the compiler recorded other variations of this title in the medical section as well: *Kitāb ṭibb* (#1457) and *Kitāb fī al-ṭibb* (#1464).[49]

Most of the works that were connected to disciplines loosely associated with medicine were also generically titled, though one or two retained relatively specific titles. *Azhār al-Afkār* (*fī jawāhir al-aḥjār*) (#1460), written by Aḥmad b. Yūsuf al-Tīfāshī (d. 651/1253), and *Filāḥat al-basātīn* (#1463) were recorded near the end of the medical section of the inventory.[50] They belong, respectively, to the disciplines of gemstones and agriculture, more specifically horticulture. These two fields are also deemed part of the medical corpus in the inventory of Bāyezīd II's library, which contains an entry for *Azhār al-Afkār* and places entries related to these disciplines, as well as food and poisons, at the end of the medical section, just as the inventory compiler does for al-Jazzār.[51]

Similarly, works on horses and horsemanship are also included in the medical section of the Jazzār library inventory. Five titles on the topic (#1434–1438) are listed a few entries below the two most well-known medical texts in the inventory—Ibn Sīnā's *Qānūn* (#1423–1426) and al-Anṭakī's *Tadhkira* (#1427–1429).[52] The compiler describes

46 This is a pattern slightly opposite to that on which Christopher Bahl sheds light in his Chapter 18 on the grammar texts of the Jazzār library inventory in this current volume. Where the South Asian-inflected *Baḥr al-Jawāhir* is listed here but in no other Ottoman libraries, imperial or provincial, under review in this current chapter, Bahl explains that commentaries produced in South Asia on famous, Arabic grammatical texts were found in other Ottoman libraries. He traces Muḥammad al-Damāmīnī's (d. 827/1424) *Tuḥfat al-gharīb*, which builds on Ibn Hishām's fourteenth-century definitive grammatical treatise *Mughnī al-labīb*, to twenty-six copies in Istanbul's Suleymaniye collections. Yet, what complicates this is that while al-Damamini's commentary is nowhere to be found in the Jazzār library inventory, demonstrating that this South Asian-influenced work did not make it to al-Jazzār's collections, Ibn Hishām's *Mughnī al-labīb* is listed (#741–746) there. Thus, the beginning of this particular textual tradition, in its definitive starting point, is made part of the collection, but later commentaries, such as al-Damāmīnī's South Asian-influenced *Tuḥfat al-gharīb*, are not. See Christopher Bahl's Chapter 18 in this volume.

47 *Kitāb fiqh Ḥanafī*, #441, Library inventory, Vakıflar Genel Müdürlüğü (Ankara), Defter 1626, 27. Sabev also points out that the inheritance inventories of private Ottoman collections often referred to books by general expressions, such as *Kitāb fī al-ṭibb* or *Risāla fī al-ṭibb*. Sabev, "Medical Books in Private and Public", 624.

48 Library inventory, Vakıflar Genel Müdürlüğü (Ankara), Defter 1626, 62; Kâtip Çelebi, *Kashf al-ẓunūn*, IV, 10, entry 7397; Fancy, *Science and Religion in Mamluk Egypt*, 1.

49 Library inventory, Vakıflar Genel Müdürlüğü (Ankara), Defter 1626, 62–63.

50 Ibid., 63.

51 In addition to being listed in the inventory for Bāyezīd II's library, *Azhār al-Afkar* is also listed twice (entries 3 and 7) the inventory of the Aya Sofya, in Istanbul. Entry 308a; Varlık, "Books on Medicine", 553, 531; Shopov, "Books on Agriculture" 557; Aya Sofya's Defter. 2/Fihrist 1 (CD 19380)—YAZMAFIHRIST 25-1, f. 123a.

52 *Kitāb fī al-khayl* (#1434), *Kitāb mu'ālijat al-khayl wa-ghayrihā* (#1435), *Kitāb fī al-khayl* (#1436), *Kitāb al-*

one of these—*Kitāb fī al-khayl* (#1434)—as an elite copy with pictures, probably paintings, of horses. Other libraries, such as that of Bāyezīd II, held books on horses, though they were not included in the medical section of his inventory.[53] Both the thirteenth-century inventory of the Ashrafiyya in Damascus and the Khālidiyya in Jerusalem, which became a public library in 1900 but has an inventory that can be dated to 1201/1787, held multiple books on horses and horsemanship, demonstrating that horse manuals were deemed both worthy of elite ownership and of interest to their readers.[54]

The inclusion of titles of different kinds of practice, for example, horsemanship and agriculture, alongside medical works, which also require an understanding of practice in their application, may shed light on the very organisation of the inventory itself. It is apparent from the work of my colleagues in this volume that other sections in this inventory contain title entries that do not exactly fit their subject definitions either. In fact, the inventory compiler seems to have been working with rather expansive definitions of a number of subjects. Garrett Davidson notes, for example, that the *ḥadīth* section includes not only strictly defined works in this category covering the traditions of the Prophet Muḥammad, but also includes any text in the collection that is related to the Prophet.[55] The history section of the Jazzār library inventory, which Dana Sajdi cogently argues is carefully curated, also contains titles on cosmography, geography, zoology and poetry. These same titles show up in Bāyezīd II's inventory as well, though, in this case, not in the history section but instead listed apart from history.[56]

In terms of the medical section specifically, al-Jazzār seems to have been no physician and, though we know little about his inventory compiler, it does not appear that this person was a specialist in medicine either. It is possible, therefore, that these works were included in the medical section, like they were in the inventory of Bāyezīd II's library, simply because their practical nature was deemed a match with medical works, though they themselves were not medical in scope.

Focusing specifically on the medical section and taking this theory a step further, we can also ask why, if the practicality of these texts was judged to be a match to medicine as a craft, were occult texts excluded from this section and listed in their own group (#1472–552), a group in itself that contains other practical fields, such as astrology, astronomy, arithmetic and geometry, that were applied to everyday life and seen to affect or describe the natural world.[57] Spiritual approaches to medical practice have a long history of connection in the Islamic world. Liana Saif points to the connections between that spiritual aetiology and human pathology in her work on medicine and magic in medieval Islam, making occult works a prime foundation for medical application and clarifying an understanding of these works as practical in their own right.[58] Yet, these were not included in the medical section, forcing the reader to consider the place of occult works in the inventory. In fact, a kind of answer comes to us in the very order of

khayl (#1437) and *Kitāb al-khayl* (#1438). Library inventory, Vakıflar Genel Müdürlüğü (Ankara), Defter 1626, 62.

53 Varlık, "Books on Medicine", 554.

54 There are fifteen entries on horses in the Ashrafiyya inventory. Their inventory numbers are 31 (p. 150), 95, (p. 159), 359 (p. 194), 361 and 367 (p. 195), 374 (p. 196), 510 (p. 214), 704 (p. 240), 1142[b] (p. 304), 1175[b] (p. 313), 1208[b] (p. 325), 1221[a] (p. 330), 1226e (p. 333), 1243c (p. 342) and 1297[a] (p. 361). Hirschler, *Medieval Damascus*. Khālidī Library manuscripts catalogued by the Hill Museum and Manuscript Library on their virtual catalogue—https://www.vhmml.org/dataPortal *Kitāb fī ʿilm firāsat al-khayl*, MS 791, AKDI 01929 0791; *Surūr al-fuʾad bi-al-ṣafināt al-jīyād fī maʿarifat al-khayl wa-asmāʾihā*, MS 731, AKDI 01928 0731. On the Khālidī Library, see Chapter 7 in this volume (Hirschler) and Chapter 2 (Aljoumani).

55 See Garrett Davidson's Chapter 15 in this volume.

56 See Dana Sajdi's Chapter 22 in this volume.

57 *Kutub ʿilm al-falak wa-al-al-hayʾa wa-al-ḥarf wa-al-rūḥānī wa-al-raml wa-al-handasa wa-al-ḥisāb wa-al-kīmīyāʾ*, Library inventory, Vakıflar Genel Müdürlüğü (Ankara), Defter 1626, 64–67.

58 Saif, "Between Medicine and Magic", 314.

the inventory. While these disciplines were not included in the medical section, they do come right after it in the Jazzār library inventory. Thus, even though they are separated, it would appear the compiler was aware that they should be near each other, since their very practice is often connected in the understanding of human health and, more broadly, the effects of these disciplines on the natural world.

4 Prophetic Medicine

One genre of medical text that is included in the inventory of al-Jazzār's library but not found in the medical section is Prophetic medicine, or *al-ṭibb al-nabawī*, which focused on *ḥadīth* that offered medical advice in terms of disease prevention, suggested treatments and dietary rules. As Garrett Davidson also notes, four of these titles are found in the *ḥadīth* section—*al-Aḥkām al-nabawiyya fī ṣināʿat al-ṭibbiyya* (#299), two copies of a work simply titled *Kitāb ṭibb nabawī* (#300 and #301), and *al-Raḥma fī al-ṭibb wa-al-ḥikma* (#302).[59] This last title is one that was used by at least two authors for their works, so, this copy of *al-Raḥma fī al-ṭibb wa-al-ḥikma* could have been written by the Yemeni physician Muḥammad al-Mahdawī ibn ʿAlī ibn Ibrāhīm al-Ṣanawbarī (d. 815/1412) or Jalāl al-Dīn al-Suyūṭī (d. 911/1505), the Egyptian *ḥadīth* scholar and historian.[60] If it is al-Ṣanawbarī's version, it matches up with three copies of this same text that were held in the private Rifāʿiyya library in late Ottoman Damascus.[61] Benedikt Reier also notes that al-Taqāwī's 1629 inventory for his collection in Aleppo includes an entry for a work of the same title, ascribed to an author by the name of Abū Jaʿfar Aḥmad al-Qayrawānī, but this is more likely to be al-Ṣanawbarī's work as well.[62] Thus, with regional interest in the version by al-Ṣanawbarī, and the entries in the Jazzār library inventory often reflecting those regional collecting practices, there is ample reason for manuscript #302 in the inventory to be al-Ṣanawbarī's version of *al-Raḥma fī al-ṭibb wa-al-ḥikma*.

Two other Prophetic medicine titles are found outside of the medical section of the Jazzār library inventory. Taken from (one of) the libraries of al-Shaykh ʿAlī al-Rashīdī and al-Shaykh Muḥammad Wakīlkharaj in 1216/1801, *ʿan Kitāb Mukhtaṣar bi-al-ṭibb al-nabawī* (#1636) is more of a general title related to Prophetic medicine, with no ascribed author.[63] But *Kitāb Aḥkām al-nabawiyya fī ṣināʿat al-ṭibbiyya* (#549), located in the section of books taken from the library of al-Sayyid Yaḥyā Efendī b. al-Sayyid Muḥammad al-Ṭībī of Jaffa in 1218/1803, has a sibling in the *ḥadīth* section, *al-Aḥkām al-nabawiyya fī ṣināʿat al-ṭibbiyya* (#299), and is more identifiable.[64] Written by ʿAlī b. ʿAbd al-Karīm b. Ṭarkhān al-Ḥamawī (d. 720/1320), the work is considered part of the *arbaʿīn* literature due to its quoting of forty *ḥadīth*s on specific diseases and prevention of illness and another forty *ḥadīth*s on curing methods. Irmeli Perho's description of the text notes that the author follows this with eighty-three simple drugs and foodstuffs supported by both medical and non-medical *ḥadīth*, using the six standard *ḥadīth* collections as his source material.[65] This title is also listed in the inventory for al-Taqāwī's seventeenth-century Aleppo collection.[66]

59 See Garrett Davidson's Chapter 15 in this volume on *ḥadīth*

60 Brockelmann, GAL, II, 242; Ullmann, *Die medizin im Islam*, 188; Al-Ṣanawbarī's version is often confused with al-Suyūṭī's version of the text. Brockelmann, GAL, supplement 2, 252; Perho, *The Prophet's Medicine*, 59, 61.

61 Vollers 758, Vollers 759, and Vollers 767, Rifāʿiyya library, https://www.qalamos.net/receive/MyMssWork_work_00000844. Accessed 5 August 2023.

62 MS 72.1, see footnote 85 in Reier, *Bibliophilia in Ottoman Aleppo*, 504.

63 Library inventory, Vakıflar Genel Müdürlüğü (Ankara), Defter 1626, 70.

64 Library inventory, Vakıflar Genel Müdürlüğü (Ankara), Defter 1626, 24 (*ḥadīth* section: #299), 31 (books from Sayyid Yaḥyā Efendī section: #549).

65 Perho, *The Prophet's Medicine*, 57.

66 MS no. 108, Reier, *Bibliophilia in Ottoman Aleppo*, 508.

While the two titles above were included in the sections related to books that were taken from other collections, the four titles in the *ḥadīth* section were placed there and not in the medicine section. The inventory compiler chose to keep the four Prophetic medicine titles in the section pertaining to *ḥadīth*, suggesting a hierarchy of subjects. He considered these texts to be related to the Prophet first and medicine second. As most works of Prophetic medicine were written by *ḥadīth* scholars and not medical practitioners, the decision to keep them in the *ḥadīth* section was probably made based on the focus of those who wrote them.[67] Al-Jazzār's inventory compiler is not alone in doing this for library collection lists. The register for Muḥammad Pasha al-ʿAẓm's (d. 1197/1783) library in Damascus also separates medical and Prophetic medicine texts. While al-Suyūṭī's *al-Ṭibb al-nabawī* is located early on in his library inventory in the *ḥadīth* section, the nine medical texts in the collection are not listed until near the end of the register, under *kutub ʿilm al-ṭibb*.[68] Thus, there is an acknowledgment of text as *ḥadīth* first, even when it focuses on medicine, for both these inventories. Conversely, the Prophetic medicine titles in Bāyezīd II's inventory are included in the medical section. In fact, they are the first few texts noted in this section, and they include works written by ʿAtūfī, the compiler, himself.[69] It is probably due to the fact that ʿAtūfī wrote such works as *Kitāb rawḍ al-insān fī al-ṭibb al-nabawī* (Bāyezīd, #2a) that he places Prophetic medicine at the beginning of this inventory's medical section. ʿAtūfī had special interests in medicine, unlike the compiler of the Jazzār library inventory and that of Muḥammad Pasha al-ʿAẓm. He was probably trained at the hospital in Amasya, and was a physician who wrote two works on Prophetic medicine and one on preventative medicine.[70] Thus, he had ample reason to include Prophetic medicine in the medical section of Bāyezīd II's collection inventory, but the inventory compiler for al-Jazzār's library, without such apparent invested interests in *ṭibb*, placed titles of Prophetic medicine in the *ḥadīth* section, similar to other inventory compilers of the time.

5 Medical Gaps

It is clear from studying the inventory that well-known texts were central to the Jazzār library collection. This begs the question of what could be missing. The forty-nine entries in the medical section and the other eleven entries with titles related to medicine are all Arabic titles. There are sections later on in the inventory for Persian (22) and Turkish works (56), but none of these are medical in subject matter.[71] Two texts in the Arabic medical section invite questions pertaining to language, however, I have not been able to identify them. It would seem that *Kitāb fī ʿilm al-ṭibb li-Ṭahmāz al-ʿAjam* (#1458) could be written by a Persian writer, with *ʿajam* indicating his non-Arab status and Ṭahmāz possibly being the Arabic form of Ṭahmāsb/p.[72] The second text in question is called *Kitāb fī ʿilm al-ṭibb Turkī* (#1443) and, given its generic title, similar to that of Ṭahmāz al-ʿAjam, we have little to go on for identification except that it was either originally written in Turkish or possibly written by someone who was Turkish.[73]

67 Reier, *Bibliophilia in Ottoman Aleppo*, 488.

68 Aljoumani, "Masrad Kutub Madrasat", 33 (#84, *al-Ṭibb al-Nabawī lil-Suyūṭī*), 60–61 (#445–453).

69 Varlık, "Books on Medicine", 554.

70 Ibid., 527.

71 Library inventory, Vakıflar Genel Müdürlüğü (Ankara), Defter 1626, Persian Books—67–68, Turkish Books—68–70.

72 *ʿAjam* could be non-Arab or non-Arabic speaking, but also has overtones of 'barbarian', so one wonders if that overtone applies here, since the text was included in the medical section of Arabic entries. It probably means non-Arab for this text, since it is written in Arabic. Clarke, *Accommodating Outsiders*, 53. Library inventory, Vakıflar Genel Müdürlüğü (Ankara), Defter 1626, 63.

73 Library inventory, Vakıflar Genel Müdürlüğü (Ankara), Defter 1626, 62.

Given that there are no, or hardly any, Persian or Turkish medical texts in the inventory, what would we expect to see if the Jazzār library had included them? A choice Persian medical text found in Ottoman collections would be *Zakhīra-i Khvārazmshāhī*, by Zayn al-Dīn Ismāʿīl b. Ḥasan al-Jurjānī (d. 531/1136). Bāyezīd II's library holds two copies of this Persian medical encyclopaedia, and twenty copies of the text were traced to Ottoman public libraries largely dating from the eighteenth and nineteenth centuries.[74] Yet, even with these precedents, Persian medical works were clearly not the focus in the Jazzār library inventory.

More central to his Turkish connections, al-Jazzār, as an Ottoman governor, would have also had access to information about Ottoman Turkish medical works. Had this been a focus of his collection, the works of Jalāl al-Dīn Khidr b. ʿAlī, also known as Hacı Paşa (d. ca. 820/1417), would have been a prime option. Hacı Paşa was a court physician for the Aydınid ruler Fakhr al-Dīn ʿIsā Bey (r. ca. 1360–ca. 1389–1391), as well as a *qāḍī* and *madrasa* teacher. He wrote at least seven medical works in Arabic and in Turkish, and these texts essentially distilled, updated and localised what Sara Nur Yildiz calls Avicennan medicine, making medical texts more accessible for fourteenth-century Anatolia.[75] Reflecting this, one of his Arabic works, *Shifāʾ al-asqām wa-dawāʾ al-ālām*, was nicknamed *Kānūn-i Hacı Paşa* after its association with Ibn Sīnā.[76] As Yildiz notes, copies of this text produced by his own student, Yūsuf b. Muḥammed b, ʿOsmān, show up in both eighteenth-century inventories of the Aya Sofya and Ragıp Paşa, both collections based in Istanbul.[77] One other library inventory in the Ottoman centre, that of Bāyezīd II, also includes this title.[78] In the latter's same imperial collection, Bāyezīd II also held Hacı Paşa's Turkish *Kitāb al-Tashīl fī al-ṭibb*, which appears in the inventory over 200 entries after three of his Arabic medical works.[79]

More locally nearby, the nineteenth-century inventory of ʿUthmān Bāshā al-Dūrikī in Aleppo lists the same titles as those above—two entries of the Arabic *Shifāʾ al-asqām wa-dawāʾ al-ālām* dating from 1170/1756–1757, as well as a *mukhtaṣar* of the text, and one entry for Hacı Paşa's Turkish *Tashīl fī al-ṭibb* (dated 1009/1600–1601).[80] But this is the only regional collection inventory of those studied for this chapter that listed any of Hacı Paşa's works. Prior to ʿUthmān Bāshā al-Dūrikī's inventory, neither the eighteenth-century collection of the Shukrī Ārūtīn family nor the two seventeenth-century inventories of al-Taqāwī or Ibn Ḥamza included his titles. All three of these, similar to al-Dūrikī's collection, were located in Damascus. Much closer to Acre, the eighteenth-century collections of Mullā ʿUthmān al-Kurdī and Muḥammad Pasha al-ʿAẓm also contained no works by Hacı Paşa. Thus, while there is some evidence that Hacı Paşa's texts were collected closer to Acre, the prevailing pattern appears to be that it was more common for these works to appear in the Ottoman centre.

As neither Hacı Paşa's Turkish nor his Arabic works are listed in al-Jazzār's library inventory, and no identifiable Turkish medical works appear in the inventory either, this and the regional patterns of collection when it came to Hacı Paşa's texts lead

74 *Zakhīra-i Khvārazmshāhī*, MS no. 4, Varlık, "Books on Medicine", 537; Sabev, "Medical Books in Private and Public", 624, 622.

75 Yildiz, "From Cairo to Ayasuluk", 264, 292.

76 İhsanoğlu, *Osmanlı Tıbbi Bilimler Literatürü Tarihi*, 28.

77 MS. Süleymaniye, Ayasofya no. 3667 (copied in Ayasuluk but undated) and MS. Süleymaniye, Ragıp Paşa no. 956, dated to 789/1387–1388. Yildiz, "From Cairo to Ayasuluk", 276.

78 MS no. 8 *Kitāb al-Shifāʾ al-asqām wa-dawāʾ al-ālām*, Varlık, "Books on Medicine", 537.

79 MS no. 223 *Kitāb al-Tashīl fī al-ṭibb*, Varlık, "Books on Medicine", 548. MS no. 8 *Kitāb al-Shifāʾ al-asqām wa-dawāʾ al-ālām*, MS no. 9 *Kitāb al-Taʿlīm fī ʿilm al-ṭibb*, MS no. 10 *Kitāb al-Farīda fī dhikr al-aghdhīya*, Varlık, "Books on Medicine", 537.

80 MSS no. 15745 and 15746 *Shifāʾ al-asqām wa-dawāʾ al-ālām*, MS no. 2ت15787 *Mukhtaṣar Shifāʾ al-asqām wa-dawāʾ al-ālām*, MS no. 15876 *Tashīl fī al-ṭibb*. Aljoumani, *Maktaba madrasiya*, 350, 355, 360.

us to the conclusion that Turkish medical texts, similar to Persian ones, were probably not highly collected by al-Jazzār's contemporaries nearby or those who came before them. It is from these possible conclusions that we may see the Jazzār library inventory as possibly emulating regional collecting practices rather than those of the Ottoman imperial centre in Istanbul, at least for the medical section.

Similar to the broad scope of missing medical texts in languages not in Arabic, the Jazzār library inventory also lacks the very Greek foundations of works such as Ibn Sīnā's *Qānūn*. The textual traditions and medical theory that the *Qānūn* informed have their foundations in Hippocratic and, more so, Galenic works, many of which were translated by Ḥunayn b. Isḥāq (d. 260/873).[81] Public Ottoman libraries held copies of these works, as did Bāyezīd II's library, and so did private medical libraries in Aleppo.[82] Al-Taqāwī's 1629 inventory notes two Arabic works each ascribed to Galen (d. ca. 216 CE) and Hippocrates (d. ca. 370 BCE).[83] The eighteenth-century Shukrī Ārūtīn family library of Ḥannā al-Ṭabīb held a copy of *Kitāb al-aʿḍāʾ al-alīma li-Jālīnūs*.[84] But no references to Galen, Hippocrates or even Ḥunayn show up in the entries of al-Jazzār's medical section.

Further missing genres can be defined by contemporaneous events and movements. New developments in seventeenth- and eighteenth-century Ottoman medicine might be expected to appear in the medical entries of the inventory, but none of these titles are identifiable there. Such texts would have been related to European medicine and its transmission in the Ottoman Empire, particularly regarding Paracelsus (d. 1541) and what was called *ṭıbb-ı cedīd*, or new medicine. Paracelsus and his experimental chemistry in medicine focused on utilising mineral acids, inorganic salts and alchemical procedures in remedy production.[85] Efforts to benefit from this new and European medicine started selectively in the seventeenth century and were originally carried out through translation.[86] Ṣāliḥ b. Naṣrallāh b. Sallūm al-Ḥalabī, who served as chief physician under Meḥmed IV (r. 1058–1099/1648–1687), wrote *al-Ṭibb al-jadīd al-kimyāwī alladhī ikhtaraʿahu Barākilsūs* in 1655 as part four of his *Ghāyat al-itqān fī tadbīr badan al-insān*, and this "New chemical medicine invented by Paracelsus" was Ibn Sallūm's shortened Arabic translations of works by European followers of Paracelsus.[87] While Paracelsus was a factor in Ibn Sallūm's work, many of his treatises took theoretical inspiration from earlier Arabic medical sources, such as Dāʾūd al-Anṭākī's (d. 1008/1599) texts and Quṭb al-Dīn al-Shīrāzī's (d. 710/1311) commentary on Ibn Sīnā's (d. 428/1037) *Qānūn*, so his approach to Paracelsian medicine had mixed foundations and influences.[88] At its heart and into the eighteenth century, *ṭıbb-ı cedīd* was a revival of medieval Arabic medicine and an introduction of new remedies and diseases not encountered in previous centuries, such as in Ibn Sallūm's own medical works.[89] Though it was ultimately not suc-

81 Pormann/Savage-Smith, *Medieval Islamic Medicine*, 19, 25.

82 Sabev, "Medical Books in Private and Public", 624; Varlık, "Books on Medicine", 529–530.

83 MS no. 66 *Sharḥ Fuṣūl Buqrāṭ*, al-Jālīnūs (Galen), Translated by Ḥunayn; MS no. 83 *al-Tashrīḥ al-kabīr* (*al-Tashrīḥ al-ḥayawān al-ḥayy*), al-Jālīnūs (Galen); MS no. 74 *Fuṣūl*, Buqrāṭ (Hippocrates); MS no. 86; *Kitāb fī-l-bayṭara*, Buqrāṭ (Hippocrates) veterinary medicine. Reier, "Bibliophilia in Ottoman Aleppo", 503–505.

84 Krimsti, "Unpublished Table of Medical Books", Gotha, Ms. Orient. A 1901.

85 Ibid., 620. Pormann/Savage-Smith, *Medieval Islamic Medicine*, 171.

86 İhsanoğlu, *Osmanlı Tıbbi Bilimler Literatürü Tarihi*, XV.

87 The three Europeans Ibn Sallūm translated are Johann Jacob Wecker (d. 1586), a physician who wrote on medicine and alchemy, Oswald Croll (d. 1609), who was a professor of medicine and personal physician to Rudolph II von Habsburg (r. 1576–1612), and Daniel Sennert (d. 1637), who was a professor of medicine who tried to blend humoral and Paracelsian medicine. Shefer, "An Ottoman Physician", 102, 108, 109.

88 Pormann/Savage-Smith, *Medieval Islamic Medicine*, 171.

89 Ibn Sallūm described new types of sicknesses for the

cessful in the Ottoman Empire as a new medical system, with most physicians, particularly in the Ottoman provinces, being more content with Ibn Sīnā's *Qānūn*, it did spur many debates and writings, and later progressions of Paracelsus were added to the oeuvre of new medicine in Arabic and Turkish.[90]

These works appeared in some Ottoman collections, including the libraries of two physicians in Aleppo. The eighteenth-century Shukrī Ārūtīn family library belonging to the Maronite physician Ḥannā al-Ṭabīb held one copy of Ibn Sallūm's famous work on the new chemical medicine—*Kitāb al-ṭibb al-jadīd al-kimīyāʾī alladhī ikhtaraʿahu Barāklūsūs*.[91] Ibn Ḥamza's inventory of his book collection in Aleppo, which he compiled in 1665–1666 in the same notebook that contains al-Taqāwī's inventory, also lists a text related to Paracelsus. The third entry from the end of the penultimate line in Ibn Ḥamza's list is *Kimīyāʾ al-ṭibb*, ascribed to Barākulsūs.[92] Therefore, Ottoman collectors outside of Istanbul were certainly adding works with connections to Paracelsian medicine to their collections, even if the Jazzār library inventory did not reflect this.

Lastly, one other medical genre is conspicuously absent from al-Jazzār's library inventory that responds directly to what is happening in the contemporaneous, eighteenth-century environment: plague texts. Many plague treatises were considered to be vernacular works themselves, and, as Nükhet Varlık explains, such works began to appear in the Ottoman Empire primarily composed in Arabic in the early fifteenth century and were later translated into vernacular Ottoman Turkish beginning in the second half of the sixteenth century.[93] Waves of the Second Plague Pandemic, which began in the fourteenth century, continued into the eighteenth and nineteenth centuries in the region, affecting Ottoman communities.[94] In fact, Feras Krimsti notes that in 1762, Rufāʾīl of the Shukrī Ārūtīn family in Aleppo, seems to have succumbed to plague himself.[95] With this centuries-long experience with plague, the Ottoman state enacted its own policies of urban hygiene organisation and burial practice regulations, putting in place movement restrictions, outbreak monitoring and, eventually, quarantine practices. Begun in the eighteenth century, these public health measures were carried out by the imperial Ottoman bureaucracy all in an attempt to curtail plague's deadly effects.[96]

With this constant looming threat of plague, it is easy to understand why plague treatises were produced: as with all medicine, ailments affected everyone, no matter who they were. Knowledgeable physicians who were aware of plague patterns were necessary for the health of all members of society, and the need to learn how to identify and handle such an ailment inspired textual production on plague. Bāyezīd II's library inventory contains two Arabic texts on plague, referred to as *ṭāʿūn*: a generically titled *Risāla fī al-ṭāʿūn* and an autographed copy of al-Tūnisī's (15th century) *Kitāb al-ṭibb fī tadbīr al-musāfirīn wa-maraḍ al-ṭāʿūn*, produced in 1493.[97] Similarly, in eighteenth-century Damascus, Mullā ʿUthmān al-Kurdī's (fl. c. 1204/1789) library also held at least two texts on plague. These were *Kitāb fī al-ṭāʿūn*, or *Badhl al-māʿūn fī faḍl al-ṭāʿūn*, by Ibn Ḥajar al-ʿAsqalānī (d. 852/1449) and *Masʾala fī al-ḥadīth anna al-ṭāʿūn wakhaza ikhwānakum min al-jinn wa-abyā nuẓi-*

first time in Arabic, including scurvy and anaemia. Küçük, "New Medicine", 235; Shefer, "An Ottoman Physician", 108.

90 Turkish translations of these works include those produced by the Ottoman physician Ḥasan Efendi (fl. 1132/1720). Küçük, "New Medicine", 229, 226, 222; Shefer, "An Ottoman Physician", 122.

91 Krimsti, "Unpublished Table of Medical Books", Gotha, Ms. Orient. A 1941.

92 Reier, "Bibliophilia in Ottoman Aleppo", 496.

93 Varlık, "Between Local and Universal", 180, 183.

94 Ibid., 177. Varlık, *Plague and Empire*, 292.

95 Krimsti, "The Lives and Afterlives", 199.

96 Varlık, *Plague and Empire*, 246; Shefer-Messonsohn, "Health and Medical Services", 159.

97 MS no. 254 and MS no. 257, respectively. Varlık, "Books on Medicine", 550.

mat fī al-ṭāʿūn, by al-Suyūṭī (d. 911/1505).[98] This last text could also reasonably be designated as *ḥadīth* if the titles were organised in an inventory, demonstrating that all approaches to understanding and handling plague were taken in the written tradition.[99]

Yet, all of these works are earlier Arabic texts and, in the case of Mullā ʿUthmān al-Kurdī (fl. c. 1204/1789), neither of the works on plague that he owned were contemporaneous to or even near his own lifetime. While it is the case that writings on plague were still produced after the sixteenth century, there were far fewer Ottoman writers producing works on the topic in the seventeenth and eighteenth centuries, and even their texts circulated mostly in courtly and academic circles, as Birsen Bulmuş explains.[100] In the case of later Arabic works on plague, Michael Dols identifies three texts. Niʿmatallāh al-Jazāʾirī (d. 1112/1700) adds suggested remedies at the end of his *Kitāb maskin al-shujun fī ḥukm al-firār min al-ṭāʿūn*, which explores the justification for fleeing plague. ʿAbd al-Muʿṭī al-Saḥalāwī's *Risāla taṭhīr Ahl al-Islām bi-ṭaʿn wa-ṭāʿūn al-ʿāmm*, reporting on the plague of 1124–1125/1712–1713, also notes medical treatments, superstitions and a brief history of the plague. And a *Risāla fī al-ṭāʿūn* was written by one Ḥayātī Zadah Muṣṭafā Fayḍī in the early eighteenth century.[101] Therefore, it is not for a lack of texts or lack of plague that the Jazzār library inventory does not include plague treatises.

6 Conclusion

Representing someone with wide-ranging interests, a position of elite status and the wealth to go with it, al-Jazzār's library collection included works on sixteen different subjects, from *fiqh* and *ḥadīth*, to grammar, literature and poetry, and medicine and occult sciences.[102] There is clearly an element of conspicuous consumption here in book owning, with books being seen as valuable and prestigious, as well as reflections of their owner's intellectual interests and dynamism, as Feras Krimsti explains of eighteenth-century book owning in Aleppo.[103] In addition to this, al-Jazzār's elite status is also reflected in the library he endowed alongside the book collection it housed, thus, ensuring the collection could be of use to readers more broadly was probably of some importance. This is also a possible reason why the library inventory included medical encyclopaedias, such as al-Anṭākī's *Tadhkira*, Ibn Sīnā's *Qānūn*, and the commentaries related to it and not Arabic translations of Galen or Hippocrates, because known use and practicality, alongside reputation, may have been more important for the library collection than the very theory that is synthesised in these works.

Al-Jazzār's establishment of his library followed a pattern that Krimsti notes takes place in the Ottoman provinces as well as the imperial centre—that of powerful bureaucrats endowing public libraries in the eighteenth century.[104] The library being part of the *madrasa* complex that was meant to be for the public benefit implies that al-Jazzār probably wanted to ensure that those who frequented his library found its contents useful.[105] In terms of the medical titles, some of the most well-known, reputable sources were made available through this collection.[106] Others, though not

98 List no. 183 and no. 259 (MS no. 3862ت 12 in the National Library in Damascus), respectively. Aljoumani, "Qāʿidāt Bayānāt Maktabat".
99 In addition to *ḥadīth*, occult and astral magid\c was also advocated for in later plague treatises in the Ottoman realm. Bulmuş, *Plague, Quarantines and Geopolitics*, 68.
100 Ibid., 40.
101 Dols, *The Black Death in the Middle East*, 335.
102 Library inventory, Vakıflar Genel Müdürlüğü (Ankara), Defter 1626, 71.
103 Krimsti, "The Lives and Afterlives", 210.
104 Ibid., 213.
105 Library inventory, Vakıflar Genel Müdürlüğü (Ankara), Defter 1626, 24.
106 Original dates or periods of production for the thirty-five identifiable titles and/or authors dated from the ninth to at least the seventeenth centuries, with no period of Arabic medical text production in that range of centuries ignored in al-Jazzār's collection. The cen-

identifiable to us due to the more generic titles assigned to them by the inventory compiler, may have helped to give context and practical information for the reader interested in medical knowledge.

The most likely reason the Jazzār library inventory included certain medical texts and not others, well-known broader texts and not treatises on specific medical ailments or contemporaneous medical movements, appears to be, at least in part, because the act of collecting was led less by specific needs of a medical scholar, which neither he nor his inventory compiler appear to have been, but rather more by regional collection strategies when it came to medical sources, a kind of passive collection curation based on availability. Of the sixty entries in the library inventory that can be classified in some way as medical, at least thirty-five of them are identifiable either by their titles or, at the very least, by their specific subjects or authors.

Ultimately, it is striking that as the collection of a non-physician, the Jazzār library inventory included the medical titles that it did and excluded those that were more often a part of libraries at the Ottoman centre in Istanbul. How these medical titles were amassed specifically is not apparent, but it is probable that local collection practices and medical manuscript production patterns influenced what was available and, therefore, deemed worthy of collection by whoever made collection decisions, whether that was al-Jazzār himself, his inventory compiler or others. However this collection of medical titles came to be within the broader Jazzār library inventory, one can imagine conversations between learned physicians, booksellers and whoever acquired these books taking place, after which a copy of a *Qānūn* here or a *Tadhkirat kaḥḥālīn* there was procured for the collection.[107] From there, the medical section of Aḥmad Pasha al-Jazzār's (d. 1219/1804) library grew.

turies of medical text production with the most representation were the fifth/eleventh century with eight titles, the seventh/thirteenth century with at least five and possibly up to eight titles, and the tenth/sixteenth century with at least six if not seven titles.

107 I would like to thank Guy Burak for this imagery. Conversations about how these titles could have been acquired led to this imagined possibility.

Bibliography

Aljoumani, Said. "Masrad Kutub Madrasat Muḥammad Bāshā al-ʿAẓm." *Majallat Maʿhad al-Makhṭuṭāt al-ʿArabiyya* 21, *al-juzʾ* 2 (2017): 10–73.

Aljoumani, Said. *Maktaba madrasiya fī Ḥalab Nihāyat al-ʿAhd al-ʿUthmānī: al-Daftar al-Mujaddad li-kutub waqf ʿUthmān Bāshā al-Dūrikī*. Beirut, 2019.

Aljoumani, Said. "Tārīkh Maktabat al-Mullā ʿUthmān al-Kurdī Iʿtimādan ʿalā Khawārij Makhṭūṭātihā." *Majallat Maʿhad al-Makhṭuṭāt al-ʿArabiyya* 25, *al-juzʾ* 1 (2021): 210–260.

Aljoumani, Said. "Qāʿidāt Bayānāt Maktabat al-Mullā ʿUthmān al-Kurdī bi-Dimashq (ḥayy 1204 H/1789 M)," unpublished.

Aya Sofya's Defter. 2/Fihrist 1 (CD 19380)—YAZMAFIHRIST 25-1.

Brockelmann, Carl. *Geschichte Der Arabischen Litteratur* (*GAL*). Leiden, 1996.

Bulmuş, Birsen. *Plague, Quarantines and Geopolitics in the Ottoman Empire*. Edinburgh, 2012.

Clarke, Nicola. *The Muslim Conquest of Iberia: Medieval Arabic Narratives*. London/New York, 2012.

Dols, Michael. *The Black Death in the Middle East*. Princcton, 2019.

Dubler, C.E. "Diyusḳuridīs." In *Encyclopaedia of Islam*, Second Edition, edited by P. Bearman, Th. Bianquis, C.E. Bosworth, E. van Donzel and W.P. Heinrichs. Published Online 2012. http://dx.doi.org.ezproxy.princeton.edu/10.1163/1573-3912_islam_SIM_1884 Accessed 22 January 2023.

Fancy, Nahyan. *Science and Religion in Mamluk Egypt: Ibn al-Nafīs, Pulmonary Transit, and Bodily Resurrection*. London/New York, 2013.

Hamza, Shireen. "Vernacular Languages and Invisible Labor." Osiris 37, 1 (2022): 115–138.

al-Harawī, *Baḥr al-jawāhir taḥqīq al-muṣṭalaḥāt al-ṭibbiyya min al-ʿArabiyya wa-al-Lāṭīniyya wa-al-Yūnāniyya*, Princeton University Library, Islamic Manuscripts, Third Series, No. 769.

al-Harawī, Muḥammad ibn Yūsuf. *Baḥr al-jawāhir fī taḥqīq al-muṣṭalaḥāt al-ṭibbiyya min al-ʿArabiyya wa-al-Lāṭīniyya wa-al-Yūnāniyya*, edited by ʿAbd al-Majīd Mawlavī. Calcutta, 1830. Early Arabic Printed Books-BL: Science and History, link.gale.com/apps/doc/GQIROH373293482/EAPB?u=prin77918&sid=galemarc&xid=548d5c7a&pg=1.

Hirschler, Konrad. *Medieval Damascus: Plurality and Diversity in an Arabic Library: The Ashrafiya Library Catalogue*. Edinburgh, 2016.

İhsanoğlu, Ekmeleddin. *Osmanlı Tıbbi Bilimler Literatürü Tarihi =: History of the Literature of Medical Sciences During the Ottoman Period*. İstanbul, 2008.

Iskandar, A.Z. "Jawahir al-lugha wa-Bahr al-jawahir: muʿjaman mukhtalifan lil-tabib Muhammad ibn Yusuf al-Harawi." *al-Mashriq* 57, fasc. 3 (1963): 331–334.

Al-Jazzār's Library inventory, Vakıflar Genel Müdürlüğü (Ankara), Defter 1626.

(*Jirāb al-Mujjarrabāt*), London, Wellcome Library, MS Arabic 81.

Kaḥāla, ʿUmar Riḍā. *Muʿjam al-Muʾallifīn*. Beirut, 2006.

Kâtip Çelebi (Ḥājī Khalīfa). *Kashf al-ẓunūn ʿan asāmī al-kutub wa-al-funūn; Lexicon Bibliographicum et Encyclopædicum a Mustafa ben Abdallah Katib Chelebi dicto et nomine Ḥaji Khalfa celebrato compositum*, edited by Gustav Flügel, translated by Gustav Flügel and Richard Bentley, 1837. Early Arabic Printed Books-BL: Literature, Grammar, Language, Catalogues and Periodicals, tinyurl.gale.com/tinyurl/EPE951.

Krimsti, Feras. "The Lives and Afterlives of the Library of the Maronite Physician Ḥannā al-Ṭabīb (c. 1702–1775) from Aleppo." *Journal of Islamic Manuscripts* 9 (2018): 190–217.

Krimsti, Feras. Unpublished Table of Medical Books in the Shukrī Ārūtīn Family Library.

Küçük, B. Harun. "New Medicine and the Ḥikmet-i Ṭabīʿiyye Problematic in Eighteenth-century Istanbul." In *Texts in Transit in the Medieval Mediterranean*, edited by Y. Tzvi Langermann and Robert G. Morrison, 222–242. University Park, PA, 2016.

Langermann, Tzvi. "The Chapter on Rasāyana (Medications for Rejuvenation) in Miʿrāj al-duʿā', a Shiʿite Text from the 12th/18th Century," *Intellectual history of the Islamicate world*. 6, no. 1–2 (2018): 144–183.

Liebrenz, Boris. "The Library of Aḥmad al-Rabbāṭ. Books and their Audience in 12th to 13th/18th to 19th Century Syria." In *Marginal Perspectives on Early Modern Ottoman Culture: Missionaries, Travelers, Bookserllers*, edited by Ralf Elger and Ute Pietruschka, 17–59. Halle, 2013.

Liebrenz, Boris. "The Social History of Surgery in Ottoman Syria: Documentary Evidence From Eighteenth-Century Hamah," *Turkish Historical Review* 5 (2014) 32–58.

Liebrenz, Boris. "From Leipzig to Damascus: Wetzstein as a Broker of Arabic Prints in Syria." In *Manuscripts, Politics and Oriental Studies: Life and Collections of Johann Gottfried Wetzstein (1815–1905) in Context*, edited by Boris Liebrenz and Christoph Rauch, 323–345. Leiden, 2019.

Meyerhof, Max. "Mediaeval Jewish Physicians in the Near East, from Arabic Sources," *Isis* 2 (1938) 432–460.

National Library of Medicine, *A Shelflist of Islamic Medical Manuscripts at the National Library of Medicine*, Bethesda, Maryland, 1996.

Perho, Irmeli. *The Prophet's Medicine: A Creation of the Muslim Traditionalist Scholars*. Helsinki, 1995.

Pormann, Peter and Emilie Savage-Smith. *Medieval Islamic Medicine*. Washington, DC, 2007.

Rabin, C. "Ibn Jamīʿ on the Skeleton." In *Science, Medicine, and History: Essays on the Evolution of Scientific Thought and Medical Practice Written in Honour of Charles Singer*, edited by E.A. Underwood, 177–202, London/New York, 1953.

Ragıp Paşa's library inventory, MS Istanbul, Süleymaniye Library, RAGIPPASA4111.

Reier, Benedikt. "Bibliophilia in Ottoman Aleppo: Muḥammad Al-Taqawī and His Medical Library." *Der Islam: Zeitschrift für Geschichte und Kultur des islamischen Orients* 98, no. 2 (2021): 473–515.

Riddle, J.M. "Die Dioskurides-Erklärung des Ibn al-Baiṭār." *Medical History* 37, no. 1 (1993): 108–109.

Sabev, Orlin. "Medical Books in Private and Public Ottoman Libraries." In *Uluslararası Tıp Tarihi Kongresi Bildiri Kitabı, 1–6 EYLUL 2002/September 2002 = Pro-*

ceedings on the 38th International Congress on the History of Medicine, 2, no. 38 (2005): 615–628.
Safi, Khaled. "al-Jazzār, Aḥmad Pasha," In *The Encyclopedia of Islam Three*, edited by Kate Fleet, Gudrun Krämer, Denis Matringe, John Nawas and Everett Rowson, 56–58. Leiden, 2020.
Saif, Liana. "Between Medicine and Magic: Spiritual Aetiology and Therapeutics in Medieval Islam." In *Demons and Illness from Antiquity to the Early Modern Period*, edited by Siam Bhayro and Catherine Rider, 313–338. Leiden, 2017.
Savage-Smith, Emilie, *A New Catalogue of Arabic Manuscripts In the Bodleian Library, University of Oxford. Volume I, Medicine*. Oxford, 2011.
Shefer, Miri. "An Ottoman Physician and His Social and Intellectual Milieu: The Case of Salih Bin Nasrallah Ibn Sallum." *Studia Islamica* 106, no. 1 (2011): 102–123.
Shefer-Messonsohn, Miri. "Health and Medical Services in Ottoman Eretz Israel." In *Medicine from Biblical Canaan to Modern Israel*, edited by Stuart Stanton and Kenneth Collins, 151–167. London/Chicago, 2021.
Shopov, Aleksandar. "'Books on Agriculture (al-filāḥa) Pertaining to Medical Science' and Ottoman Agricultural Science and Practice around 1500." In *Treasures of Knowledge: An Inventory of the Ottoman Palace Library (1502/3–1503/4)*, Volume 1: Essays, edited by Gülru Necipoğlu, Cemal Kafadar and Cornell H. Fleischer, 557–568. Leiden/Boston, 2019.
Ullmann, Manfred. *Die medizin im Islam*. Leiden/Köln, 1970.
Ibn Abī Uṣaybiʿa, *ʿUyūn al-anbāʾ fī ṭabaqāt al-aṭibbāʾ*, The Best Accounts of the Classes of Physicians (Edition), edited by E. Savage-Smith, S. Swain and G.J. van Gelder. Brill's Scholarly Edition of A Literary History of Medicine. Leiden, 2020. https://doi.org/10.1163/37704_0668IbnAbiUsaibia.Tabaqatalatibba.lhom-ed-arai. Arabic edition. Accessed online 18 January 2022.
Usluer, Fatih. "Carullah Efendi'nin Cifir ve Tıp İlimlerine Dair Kitapları." In *Osmanlı Kitap Kültürü: Cârullah Efendi Kütüphanesi ve Derkenar Notları*, 297–312. Ankara, 2015.
Varlık, Nükhet. "Books on Medicine: Medical Knowledge at Work." In *Treasures of Knowledge: An Inventory of the Ottoman Palace Library (1502/3–1503/4)*, Volume 1: Essays, edited by Gülru Necipoğlu, Cemal Kafadar and Cornell H. Fleischer, 527–555. Leiden/Boston, 2019.
Varlık, Nükhet. "Between Local and Universal: Translating Knowledge in Early Modern Ottoman Plague Treaties." In *Knowledge in Translation: Global Patterns of Scientific Exchange, 1000–1800 CE*, edited by Patrick Manning and Abigail Owen, 177–190. Pittsburgh, 2018.
Varlik, Nükhet, *Plague and Empire In the Early Modern Mediterranean World: The Ottoman Experience, 1347–1600*. Cambridge, 2015.
Virtual Hill Museum and Manuscript Library, Khalidī Library collection, https://www.vhmml.org/dataPortal.
Yildiz, Sara Nur. "From Cairo to Ayasuluk: Hacı Paşa and the Transmission of Islamic Learning to Western Anatolia in the Late 14th Century." Journal of Islamic Studies 25, no. 3 (September 2014): 263–297.

The Medicine Books

[1423] ***al-Qānūn fī al-ṭibb li-Ibn Sīnā***, AUTHOR: Abū ʿAlī al-Ḥusayn **Ibn Sīnā** (d. 428/1037), EDITION: Beirut: Nūbilīs, 2006.[108]

[1424] ***Min fann al-Qānūn fī al-ṭibb li-Ibn Sīnā***, AUTHOR: Abū ʿAlī al-Ḥusayn **Ibn Sīnā** (d. 428/1037), EDITION: Beirut: Nūbilīs, 2006.

[1425] ***Min al-Qānūn fī al-ṭibb li-Ibn Sīnā***, AUTHOR: Abū ʿAlī al-Ḥusayn **Ibn Sīnā** (d. 428/1037), EDITION: Beirut: Nūbilīs, 2006.

[1426] ***Min al-Qānūn fī al-ṭibb li-Ibn Sīnā**, al-juzʾ al-awwal*, AUTHOR: Abū ʿAlī al-Ḥusayn **Ibn Sīnā** (d. 428/1037), EDITION: Beirut: Nūbilīs, 2006.

[1427] ***Tadhkirat Dāʾūd** ūlī al-albāb wa-al-jāmiʿ lil-ʿajab al-ʿujāb*, AUTHOR: **Dāʾūd** b. ʿUmar al-Anṭākī's (d. 1008/1599), EDITION: Beirut: Dār al-Fikr, 1996.[109]

[1428] ***Tadhkirat Dāʾūd***, see #1427

[1429] ***Dhayl Tadhkirat Dāʾūd***, see #1427

108 Kâtip Çelebi, *Kashf al-ẓunūn*, IV, 496, entry 9354. Brockelmann, *GAL*, I, 597.

109 Kâtip Çelebi, *Kashf al-ẓunūn*, II, 260–261, entry 2811. İhsanoğlu, *Osmanlı Tıbbi Bilimler Literatürü Tarihi*, 197; Brockelmann, *GAL*, II, 478.

[1430] ***al-Mughnī fī ṭibb sharḥ al-mūjaz***, AUTHOR: Sadīd al-Dīn al-Kāzarūnī (wrote text in 745/1344), EDITION: Hyderabad: Muʿīn Dakkan, 1937.[110]

[1431] ***Maʿnī*** (*Mughnī*) ***al-ṭabīb wa-ʿumdat al-arīb***, AUTHOR: Abī ʿAbdullah Muḥammad al-Zubaydī (d. 612/1214), MANUSCRIPT: Qatar, National Library, HC.MS.00211.[111]

[1432] ***al-Jāmiʿ fī al-ṭibb***—either ***al-Jāmiʿ fī al-ṭibb*** *fī al-adwīya al-mufrada*, AUTHOR: Abū Jaʿfar Aḥmad al-Ghāfiqī (d. 560/1165), EDITION: Jbeil, Lebanon: Dār wa-Maktabat Bīblīyūn, 2005,[112] or ***Jāmiʿ*** *mufradāt al-adwīya wa-al-aghdīya*, also known as ***al-Jāmiʿ fī al-ṭibb***, AUTHOR: Ibn al-Bayṭār (d. 646/1248), EDITION: 4 vols, Baghdad: Maktabat al-Muthannā, 1960–1969.[113]

[1433] ***al-Jāmiʿ fī al-ṭibb***, see #1432

[1434] ***Kitāb fī al-khayl***. Unidentified.

[1435] ***Kitāb muʿālajāt al-khayl wa-ghayrihā***. Unidentified.

[1436] ***Kitāb fī al-khayl***. Unidentified.

[1437] ***Kitāb al-khayl***. Unidentified.

[1438] ***Kitāb al-khayl***. Unidentified.

[1439] ***Kitāb fī ʿilm al-ṭibb al-musammā bi-tadhkirat al-kaḥḥālīn***, AUTHOR: ʿAlī b. ʿIsā al-Kaḥḥāl (d. after 400/1009), EDITION: Hyderabad: Maṭbaʿat Majlis Dāʾiratul Maʿārifil Osmānīya, 1964.

[1440] ***Kitāb fī ʿilm al-ṭibb***. Unidentified.

[1441] ***Kitāb al-wuṣla ilā al-ḥabīb*** *fī waṣf al-ṭayyibāt wal-ṭīb*, AUTHOR: ʿUmar b. Aḥmad b. al-ʿAdīm (d. 660/1262), EDITION: 2 vols, Aleppo, Jāmiʿat Ḥalab, Maʿhad al-Turāth al-ʿIlmī al-ʿArabī, 1986–1988.

[1442] ***Kitāb fī ʿilm al-ṭibb***. Unidentified.

[1443] ***Kitāb fī ʿilm al-ṭibb turkī***. Unidentified.

[1444] ***Majmūʿa min kalām Ibn Sīnā min al-Qānūn*** *fī al-ṭibb*, see #1423

[1445] ***Risālat al-Rāzī ṭibb***, possibly ***Risāla*** *fī al-ṭibb*, AUTHOR: Abū Bakr Muḥammad b. Zakariyyā **al-Rāzī** (d. ca. 313/925), EDITION: not found, but title listed in Bāyezīd II's library inventory.[114]

[1446] ***Ghunyat al-marām fī maʿrifat al-ramī bi-al-sihām***. Unidentified.

[1447] ***Durrat al-ghawwāṣ fī maʿrifat al-khawāṣṣ***. Unidentified, but could be ***Durrat al-ghawwāṣ*** *ʿalā al-manāfiʿ wa-**al-khawāṣṣ***, AUTHOR: Abū al-Ḥasan ʿAlī b. ʿĪsā b. ʿAlī al-Mutaṭabbib, during the reign of al-Muʿtamid (r. 256–279/870–892), EDITION: not found.[115]

[1448] ***Risālat lil-Shaykh al-Raʾīs Abī ʿAlī b. Sīnā***, AUTHOR: Abū ʿAlī al-Ḥusayn **Ibn Sīnā** (d. 428/1037), unidentified[116]

[1449] ***Kitab fī ʿilm al-ṭibb li-Abī al-Ḥazm***, unidentified text, but author could be AUTHOR: ʿAlāʾ al-Dīn Abū al-Ḥasan ʿAlī Ibn **Abī al-Ḥazm** al-Qarashī, better known as Ibn al-Nafīs (d. 687/1288).[117]

110 Kâtip Çelebi, *Kashf al-ẓunūn*, IV, 499, entry 9354; Brockelmann, *GAL*, I, 598.

111 This manuscript is the only one of the entries in the medical section that has been located thus far. I would have liked to have studied the marginal notes written in this manuscript to ascertain the reception of the work and use these notes to place the manuscript within a context of medical study and practice, especially if these notations contained points about a practice outside of what the text says. However, most of the marginal notes are written in Armenian, a language I do not read, and these notes probably signify later ownership and reception after that of al-Jazzār. While there are two major marginal notations written in Arabic (f. 70^{a} and f. 137^{a}), both of these notes are more citational in nature, citing other medical scholars, such as Galen, and, therefore, giving us no clues about contemporary medical practices written in the margins in response to this text.

112 Brockelmann, *GAL*, supplement 1, 891; MS no. 91, Reier, "Bibliophilia in Ottoman Aleppo", 506.

113 Brockelmann, *GAL*, I, 648; MS no. 97, Reier, "Bibliophilia in Ottoman Aleppo", 506; Kâtip Çelebi, *Kashf al-ẓunūn*, V, 353, entry 11278.

114 MS no. 17^{b} and MS no. 27^{b}, Varlık, "Books on Medicine", 538, 539.

115 Brockelmann, *GAL*, supplement 1, 417; Vollers 770, Rifāʿiyya library, https://www.qalamos.net/receive/DE15Book_manuscript_00015102. Accessed 5 August 2023.

116 According to Ibn Abī Uṣaybiʿa, there are at least twenty-six *risālas* written by Ibn Sīnā, so this could be any one of those *risālas*. *ʿUyūn al-anbāʾ fī ṭabaqāt al-aṭibbāʾ*, II.13.3.2.

117 Kâtip Çelebi, *Kashf al-ẓunūn*, IV 10, entry 7397; Fancy, *Science and Religion in Mamluk Egypt*, 1.

[1450] ***Kitāb fī ʿilm al-ṭibb***. Unidentified.

[1451] ***Baḥr al-jawāhir fī al-ṭibb****/taḥqīq al-muṣṭalaḥāt al-ṭibbiyya min al-ʿArabiyya wa-al-Lāṭīniyya wa-al-Yūnāniyya* ***lil-Harawī***, AUTHOR: Muḥammad b. Yūsuf **al-Harawī**, (fl. ca. 924/1518), EDITION: Qum: Intishārāt Jalāl al-Dīn, 2009.

[1452] ***Ghāyat al-Irshād***, could be ***Ghāyat al-Irshād*** *ilā maʿrifat aḥkām al-ḥayawān wa-al-nabāt wa-al-jamād*, AUTHOR: ʿAbd al-Raʾūf Muḥammad b. Tāj al-ʿĀrifīn b. ʿAlī b. Zayn al-ʿĀbidīn al-Ḥaddādī al-Munāwī al-Shāfiʿī (d. 1031/1621), EDITION: Cairo: al-Maktaba al-Azharīya lil-Turāth, 2006.[118]

[1453] ***Khaṣāʾiṣ al-ḥashāʾish li-Ibn Bayṭār***, AUTHOR: Abū Muḥammad ʿAlī b. Aḥmad Ḍiyāʾ al-Dīn al-Mālaqī **Ibn al-Bayṭār (d. 646/1248)**, possible EDITION: Göttingen: Vanderhoeck and Ruprecht, 1991.[119]

[1454] *al-Juzʾ al-awwal min* ***tadhkirat Dāʾūd*** *ūlī al-albāb wa-al-jāmiʿ lil-ʿajab al-ʿujāb*, see #1427

[1455] ***Jirāb*** ***al-mujarrabāt*** *wa-khizānat al-aṭṭibāʾ*, AUTHOR: anonymous on behalf of Abū Bakr Muḥammad b. Zakarīyā al-Rāzī's (d. 311/923) or by Abū ʿAbdallāh Muḥammad b. Yaḥyā b. Abī Ṭālib b. Aḥmad, EDITION: Alexandria: Dār al-Wafāʾ li-Dunyā al-Ṭibāʿa wa-al-Nashr, 2006.[120]

[1456] ***al-Tuḥfa al-jāmiʿa*** *li-mufradāt al-ṭibb al-nāfiʿa*, AUTHOR: Abū Zakariyyāʾ ʿImād al-Dīn Yaḥyā b. Abī Bakr al-ʿĀmirī al-Tihāmī al-Ḥanafī (d. 893/1488), EDITION: Tanta, Egypt: Dār al-Nābigha lil-Nashr wa-al-Tawzīʿ, 2019.[121]

[1457] ***Kitāb ṭibb***. Unidentified.

[1458] ***Kitāb fī ʿilm al-ṭibb li-Ṭahmāz al-ʿajam***, AUTHOR: **Ṭahmāz al-ʿajam**, unidentified.

[1459] ***Kitāb ḥāwī Ilyās fī ʿilm al-tadāwī***, AUTHOR: Najm al-Dīn Maḥmūd b. Ḍiyāʾ al-Dīn **Ilyās** al-Shīrāzī (d. 730/1330), EDITION: Beirut: Dār al-Kutub al-ʿIlmīya, 2001.[122]

[1460] ***Azhār al-afkār*** *fī jawāhir al-aḥjār*, AUTHOR: Shihāb al-Dīn Abū al-ʿAbbās Aḥmad b. Yūsuf al-Tīfāshī (d. 651/1253), EDITION: Cairo: al-Hayʾa al-Miṣriyya al-ʿāmma lil-Kitāb, 1977.[123]

[1461] ***Sharḥ al-mukhtaṣar fī al-ṭibb***. Unidentified.

[1462] ***al-Mūjaz*** *fī al-ṭibb*, AUTHOR: ʿAlāʾ al-Dīn Abū al-Ḥasan ʿAlī Ibn **Abī al-Ḥazm** al-Qarashī, better known as Ibn al-Nafīs (d. 687/1288), EDITION: Cairo: al-Majlis al-Aʿlā lil-Shuʾūn al-Islāmiyya, 2001.[124]

[1463] ***Filāḥat al-basātīn***. Unidentified.

[1464] ***Kitāb fī al-ṭibb***. Unidentified.

[1465] ***Intikhāb al-iqti(ḍ)āb ʿalā ṭarīq al-masʾala wa-radd al-jawāb***, AUTHOR: Abū Naṣr b. al-Masīḥī (d. 590/1194), EDITION: not found.[125]

[1466] ***Al-Lamḥa*** *al-ʿafīfa* ***fī al-ṭibb***, AUTHOR: al-ʿAfīf b. Abī Saʿd b. Abī Surūr al-Sāwī al-Isrāʾīlī b. ʿAmīr al-Dawla, EDITION: not found.[126]

118 Brockelmann, *GAL*, II, 393–395.

119 Ibn Abī Uṣaybiʿa lists Ibn al-Bayṭār's works, one of which is entitled *Sharḥ adwīyat kitāb Dīyasqūrīdus*. This could be the book the inventory compiler is referring to in entry [1454], as one of the titles of the Arabic translation of Dioscorides' *De materia medica* was *Kitāb al-ḥashāʾish*. The edition listed here is Dietrich Albert, Die Dioskurides-Erklärung des Ibn al-Baiṭār, Göttingen: Vanderhoeck and Ruprecht, 1991, as noted in J.M. Riddle's book review, "Die Dioskurides-Erklärung des Ibn al-Baiṭār". Ibn Abī Uṣaybiʿa, *ʿUyūn al-anbāʾ fī ṭabaqāt al-aṭibbāʾ*, 14.58; Dubler, "Diyusḳuridīs".

120 According to Benedikt Reier, the title could be a transcription of Abū Bakr Muḥammad b. Zakarīyā al-Rāzī's (d. 311/923) case notes with his patients. There is a copy of *Jirāb al-mujarrabāt* at the Wellcome Library in London, MS Arabic 81, which has been digitised: https://wellcomecollection.org/works/xwak6jte. According to Brockelmann (*GAL*), the author could be Abū ʿAbdallāh Muḥammad b. Yaḥyā b. Abī Ṭālib b. Aḥmad. Reier, "Bibliophilia in Ottoman Aleppo", 506; Brockelmann, *GAL*, supplement 2, 1041.

121 Brockelmann, *GAL*, supplement 2, 225–226.

122 Kâtip Çelebi, *Kashf al-ẓunūn*, III, 11–12, entry 4385; Brockelmann, *GAL*, supplement 2, 298–299.

123 Kâtip Çelebi, *Kashf al-ẓunūn*, I, 261, entry 542; Brockelmann, *GAL*, I, 652.

124 Kâtip Çelebi, *Kashf al-ẓunūn*, IV, 10, entry 7397; Brockelmann, *GAL*, supplement 1, 825, 899.

125 Abū Naṣr b. al-Masīḥī is Abū Naṣr Saʿīd b. Abī al-Khayr ʿĪsā b. al-Masīḥī, and Ibn Abī Uṣaybiʿa relates that he had two texts: 1) Kitāb al-Iqtiḍāb ʿalā ṭarīq al-masʾala wa-al-jawāb fī al-ṭibb and Kitīb Intikhāb al-Iqtiḍāb. 10.76.1 and 10.76.4. Kaḥāla, *Muʿjam al-Muʾallifīn*, IV, 132.

126 No death date found. Kâtip Çelebi, *Kashf al-ẓunūn*, V, 329–330, entry 11168; Brockelmann, *GAL*, supplement 1,

[1467] *Ṭibb ʿilm al-abdān*. Unidentified.

[1468] *Kitāb fī ʿilm al-ṭibb*. Unidentified.

[1469] *Kitāb fī ʿilm al-ṭibb*. Unidentified.

[1470] *Majmūʿa min kalām al-ḥukamāʾ*. Unidentified.

[1471] *Kitāb al-ṭibb nāqis al-awwal wa-al-akhir*. Unidentified.

Works of Medicine from the Provenanced Sections of the Inventory

Works taken from the library of al-Sayyid Yaḥyā Efendī b. al-Sayyid Muḥammad al-Ṭībī of Jaffa in 1218/1803

[549] *Kitāb al-aḥkām al-nabawiyya fī al-ṣināʿa al-ṭibbiyya*, AUTHOR: ʿAlī b. ʿAbd al-Karīm b. Ṭarkhān al-Ḥamawī (d. 720/1320), EDITION: Beirut: Dār al-Fikr, 2004.[127]

[557] *Kitāb al-irshād fī ṣināʿat al-ṭibb*, could be *al-Irshād fī maṣāliḥ al-anfus wa-al-ajsād*, AUTHOR: Hibatullah b. Zayn b. Jumayʿ (d. 594/1198), EDITION: not found.[128]

[583] *Kitāb ṣaghīr min tadhkirat Dāʾūd*, see #1427

[584] *Kitāb ṣaghīr fī al-ṭibb*. Unidentified.

[591] *Kitāb ghunyat al-miḥtāj li-adillat al-ikhtilāj*. Unidentified.

Works taken from the libraries of al-Shaykh ʿAlī al-Rashīdī and al-Shaykh Muḥammad Wakīlkharaj in 1216/1801

[1636] *ʿAn kitāb mukhtaṣar bi-al-ṭibb al-nabawī*. Unidentified.

[1641] *ʿAn rawḍat al-ʿiṭr fī al-ṭibb*, AUTHOR: Muḥammad b. Maḥmūd b. Ḥājī al-Shīrwānī (d. after 855/1451), EDITION: not found.[129]

Works of Medicine from the *Ḥadīth* Section of the Inventory

[299] *al-Aḥkām al-nabawiyya fī al-ṣināʿa al-ṭibbiyya*, AUTHOR: ʿAlī b. ʿAbd al-Karīm b. Ṭarkhān al-Ḥamawī (d. 720/1320), EDITION: Beirut: Dār al-Fikr, 2004.[130]

[300] *Kitāb ṭibb nabawī*. Unidentified.

[301] *Kitāb ṭibb nabawī*. Unidentified.

[302] *al-Raḥma fī al-ṭibb wa-al-ḥikma*, probably AUTHOR: Muḥammad al-Mahdī b. ʿAlī ibn Ibrāhīm al-Ṣanawbarī (d. 815/1412), EDITION: Cairo: Maṭbaʿat Dār al-Kutub al-ʿArabīya al-Kubrā, 1908.[131] Could be: *al-Raḥma fī al-ṭibb wa-al-ḥikma*, AUTHOR: Jalāl al-Dīn al-Suyūṭī (d. 911/1505), EDITION: Cairo: ʿAbd al-Ḥamīd Aḥmad Ḥanafī, 1938.[132]

898; Savage-Smith, *Bodleian*, entry 79, 355. Meyerhof, "Mediaeval Jewish Physicians", 458.

127 Perho, *The Prophet's Medicine*, 57. Same work as #299.

128 Ibn Abī Uṣaybiʿa, *ʿUyūn al-anbāʾ fī ṭabaqāt al-aṭibbāʾ*, 14.32.5, footnote 34; Ullmann, *Medizin im Islam*, 164. While no published edition was located, a translation of a section of the work exists: Rabin, "Ibn Jamīʿ on the Skeleton".

129 Kâtip Çelebi, *Kashf al-ẓunūn*, III, 504, entry 6657; İhsanoğlu, *Osmanlı Tıbbi Bilimler Literatürü Tarihi*, 42, 46; Krimsti, "Unpublished Table of Medical Books",—Gotha, Ms. Orient. A 2015.

130 Perho, *The Prophet's Medicine*, 57. Same work as #549.

131 Brockelmann, *GAL*, II, 242, supplement 2, 252; Ullmann, *Die medizin im Islam*, 188. İhsanoğlu, *Osmanlı Tıbbi Bilimler Literatürü Tarihi*, CXXII.

132 Al-Ṣanawbarī's version is often confused with al-Suyūṭī's version of the text. Ullmann, *Die medizin im Islam*, 188; Perho, *The Prophet's Medicine*, 59, 61.

CHAPTER 24

The Occult Sciences

Liana Saif

In *Ḥilyat al-bashar fī tārīkh al-qarn al-thālith ʿashar*, ʿAbd al-Razzāq al-Bīṭār portrays Murtaḍā al-Zabīdī (1145–1205/1732–1790), author of *Tāj al-ʿArūs*, as a man of immense wisdom, spiritual insights and high intellect, whose oeuvre had a deep impact on the intellectual and spiritual landscapes of Egypt, Maghreb and beyond. People from the Maghreb considered their journey to Egypt futile if they had not visited him. If any of them received a piece of writing from him, they would keep it as an amulet (*tamīma*). He was even known to give visitors amulets (*tamāʾim*) and *ruqā* (protective objects and texts). Al-Bīṭār also relates that al-Zabīdī sent Aḥmad Pāshā al-Jazzār a letter telling him that he is

> the awaited Mahdi and that greatness awaits him. This was received in him [al-Jazzār] as truth due to the inclination of souls toward wishful thinking (*li mayl al-nufūs ilā al-amānī*), and he kept this letter among his charms and amulets (*al-aḥrāz wa-al-tamāʾim*) in the protective necklace (*ḥijāb*) that he wore.[1]

1 The Messianic Aspirations of al-Jazzār

In the context of al-Jazzār's messianic aspirations, I analyse the eighty-one titles in the inventory of al-Jazzār's library under the subheading 'Books on the celestial science (*al-falak*), astronomy, (*al-hayʾa*), the [science of] letter[s], the spiritual [science], geomancy, geometry, arithmetic, and alchemy'. That itineraries of prominent figures included meeting al-Jazzār is evident from the stop Muḥammad ibn ʿAbd al-Wahhāb Ibn ʿUthmān al-Miknāsī makes in Acre. The Moroccan diplomat was on a diplomatic mission to Istanbul in 1201/1787, during the reign of Sultan ʿAbd al-Ḥāmid, which was followed by the Hajj pilgrimage, returning to Morocco after a *riḥla* of almost three years.[2] By analysing the content of the inventory's section on the occult and astral sciences, I highlight the strategic value of occult knowledge in validating political aspirations. I highlight what al-Bīṭār's anecdote alludes to, namely, that scholars, Sufis and occultists formed a network, from the Maghreb through Egypt to Syria, that was accessible to the political elite, forming what can be called a 'cultural retinue', and, in this case, that of Aḥmad Pāshā al-Jazzār.

Al-Jabartī records in his *ʿAjāʾib al-āthār* that al-Jazzār once declared 'I am the Awaited One, I am the Aḥmad mentioned in the *jafr* writings (*jufūr*) who rises between two palaces. Many of those who claim to be able to interpret, have interpreted for him dreams, significations, codes, and signs'.[3] This also testifies to the presence of occultists in his retinue. This intersection of the occult, the messianic and the political is, of course, not an anomaly. The occult sciences have long been instrumentalised for exercising and maintaining physical and metaphysical control over domains, peoples and resources.[4] An interesting Ot-

1 al-Bīṭār, *Ḥilyat al-bashar*, 1497, 1504. I am grateful to Garrett A. Davidson for sharing this reference with me.

2 Editors, "Ibn ʿUthmān al-Miknāsī", *Encyclopaedia of Islam*; al-Miknāsī, *Riḥlat al-Miknāsī*, 288.

3 al-Jabartī, *ʿAjāʾib al-āthār*, 508–510. I am grateful to Firas Krimsti for alerting me to this reference.

4 For this in the Ottoman context, see Fleischer, "Ancient Wisdom and New Sciences", 231–243; Şen, Reading the Stars, 557–608; Şen, Practicing Astral Magic, 66–88.

© LIANA SAIF, 2025 | DOI:10.1163/9789004720527_026

toman example of the embeddedness of the occult in the political aspirations of Sufis was studied by Hasan Karatas. Following the death of Mehmed II in 1481, there was a conflict between two Sufi orders over ascendancy in Constantinople: namely, Sheikh Vefa of Istanbul (d. 896/1491) and Celebi Halife of Amasya (d. 899/1494). According to the hagiographical sources, Sheik Vefa created a protective *vefk* (a square amulet) for the most powerful member of his political faction. Nevertheless, Çelebi Halife was able to establish his Sufi order in Constantinople thanks to his reputation in the mastery of occult sciences.[5]

Prophecy and apocalyptic political investments were a means for non-Muslim communities to confront Muslim control in the eighteenth century. The first of two letters studied by David Cook contains a Christin Arabic prophecy, embedded in *Tārīkh al-shām* by the priest Mikhāʾīl Burayk al-Dimashqī, written by the governor of Astrakhan to the head official in the city of Moscow.[6] It is concerned with two strange old men who arrived in Astrakhan, 'shouting, and saying that the heavens were very angry because of the plethora of sins and the great evil happening among the Christians'. They escape imprisonment, leaving behind a prophecy announcing that before the Second Coming of Christ in 1783, the city of Constantinople and the King ʿUthmān will be taken in the year 1762. The prophecy also tells that: 'in the year 1765 signs will appear in the heavens above and portents on the earth below, and a cowardly man will rise, [...] In the year 1767, commanders will arise, and iniquitous rulers, and there will be a terrible, frightening occurrence between them, man to man like wild animals'.[7] The second text analysed by Cook is found in *Mukhtaṣar tārīkh jabal Lubnān* by Father Augustine Ṭanūs al-Khūrī, datable to the period of the Napoleonic invasion of Egypt and Palestine in 1798–1799. Using the format of *jafr*, the author mentions the astrological context of the coming destruction:

> Beware of the crossing of Egypt, while Syria is gone from it. During this time Mars, and above it the Sun, will enter Gemini, and Sagittarius and Mars will descend. This is the clear proof, pointing the way [...] The rulers are immoral, the viziers are merchants, the subjects wolves and dogs, the viziers sitting drunken, the learned ones disputing and being deceitful, the light cloudy, clarity muddy, the king heedless, and the vizier inattentive.[8]

As such, al-Jazzār-as-messiah corresponds to the mood of diverse communities in the region, which the library with its *malḥama* and *jafr* literature informs and substantiates.

Furthermore, al-Jazzār himself was a subject of prophecies; for example, in the chronicle by the early-19th-century Ottoman historian Cabi:

> Cezzar Ahmed Paşa was one of the ağas of the inner court (Enderun) of the deceased honourable formerly [known] as Hekimzade, the former vizier Ali Paşa [...] He arrived in Egypt with the aforementioned Paşa [...] One day, while Ahmed Paşa was in a neighbourhood, one of the powerful [officials] called him: 'Come over here', three people said: 'Look, my son Ahmed Ağa, you are the *jīm* that the Greatest Shaykh (Ibn al-ʿArabī) wrote about and alluded to [in his *al-Shajara al-Nuʿmāniyya*].' One of them held his nose and the other two held their ears, and said: 'This so-called Sublime State [the Ottoman state] is the state of Muḥammad (*Devlet-i Muḥammadiyya*) [...]. Whoever betrays this state, betrays the Prophet and religion and will be quickly punished soon. You are a man of a degree lower than sultans [but] higher than viziers.

5 Karatas, "The City as a Historical Actor", 112.

6 Cook, "Two Christian Arabic Prophecies", 67. I am grateful to Feras Krimsti for pointing out this work and providing the text.

7 Ibid., 69–70.

8 Ibid., 73–74.

But be loyal to the Muḥammadan State and do not fear anyone.'[9]

The upheavals described by these texts depict a scene of political Messianic competition. This is the context within which we should understand al-Jazzār's statement addressed to the Druze who according to him 'took Jupiter and [the angel] Hārūt as your creed and religion; you have distanced yourself from the clear word of truth [that is, the Qur'an]'.[10] This is not merely a condemnation of 'superstition' and illicit practices—even if superficially it was instrumentalised as such—but more an encapsulation of al-Jazzār's awareness of the occult artillery of the Druze. Al-Jazzār himself is reputed to have 'used' jinn his assault on rebels from among his mamluk soldiers.[11]

The interplay between esotericism/messianism and politics in what was seen as a battle, occult as much as physical, can be observed in the narrative concerning the extremity of al-Jazzār's brutality and the nature of the alliances he made. Al-Bīṭār writes in *Ḥilyat al-bashar* that when al-Jazzār was appointed the governor of Damascus, his violence increased in extremity, executing many notable figures of Damascus, including 'Abd al Raḥmān Afandī al-Murādī, Mufti of the Ḥanafīs, and As'ad Afandī al-Maḥāsinī, also Mufti of the Ḥanafīs. These are figures of 'legalism' and the 'exoteric'. Al Bīṭār juxtaposes this with al-Jazzār's alliance with the Kurds:

He even invented various types of torture instruments with the help of a group of Kurds, and they aided him in his oppression of the people until corruption spread throughout the lands. They affirmed his claims that he was the 'Renewer of the Age'. Indeed, he and they were repelled and detested. Their leader was a man who claimed to be a Sufi, asserting that the greatest sheikh in his *Meccan Revelations* had informed about him. They claimed that killing and plundering, and all they did, were not forbidden but permissible. This notion became widespread about them until they declared the scholars of their time as disbelievers for rejecting their claims. Some reckless individuals, led astray by Allah despite their knowledge, authored a book in which they claimed to be the Renewer. Among his associates was a man named 'Abd al-Wahhāb, who had knowledge in some sciences. He sent him to Damascus along with a group of torturers and soldiers.[12]

The Kurds, the 'Other', reputed for the esoteric and occult, validate al-Jazzār's messianic aspirations, enabling him to overturn 'orthodoxy' itself by embracing esoteric thinking and occult practice.

In light of the context analysed so far, it is not surprising that the Jazzār library contains a substantial section on the magical, divinatory and astrological sciences. It is reflective of the way al-Jazzār mobilised the occult for the attainment of power. Similar to many libraries in Ottoman Syria, Palestine and Iraq of the same period, the bulk of the collection comprised religious books and language sciences.[13] Besides medicine, which has its own subheading, the natural sciences and the occult sciences are grouped together. Regarding the occult sciences, the largest number of titles belong to the subject of the astral sciences (astrology and astronomy), followed by magic and divination (geomancy, *malḥama, zāyirja, qur'a* and *jafr*) (see table 24.1). Al-Jazzār's library inventory provides an opportunity to observe the importance placed on the occult sciences in the eighteenth century.

9 Cabi, *Cabi Ta'rihi*, 84. I am grateful to Guy Burak for this reference and translation.

10 al-Shihābī, *Lubnān fī 'ahd al-umarā' al-Shihābīyīn*, 170.

11 al-Jabartī, *'Ajā'ib al-āthār*, III, 509–510.

12 al-Bīṭār, *Ḥilyat al-bashar*, 128–129.

13 al-Asali, "The Libraries of Ottoman Jerusalem", 285.

TABLE 24.1 Thematic distribution of the titles in the Occult Sciences section of the Jazzār library

Occult sciences	Number of titles Total: 76
Magic, including the science of letters, 'spiritual' magic, *khawāṣṣ* and others	18
Divination:	Total: 11
Geomancy	2
Malḥama	2
Zāyirja	4
Qurʿa	1
Jafr	2
Alchemy	6
Astrology	9
Astronomy:	Total: 32
Zīj	4
Others	28

2 Divination and Dream Interpretation

According to al-Bīṭār in his *Ḥilyat al-bashar*, al-Jazzār was so elated by al-Zabīdī's aforementioned letter that he made it into an amulet, about which he would only 'confide in some of his visitors who claim to have knowledge of *jafr* and *zāyirjāt*'.[14] This anecdote suggests that the volumes in the inventory on the science of letters and various divinatory arts may have been given to al-Jazzār by practitioners who visited him, especially when we consider that one copy of *Shams al-maʿārif al-kubrā* is noted in the inventory as being a gift from a Moroccan. *Jafr*, which is represented by two books, is a political-eschatological divinatory practice originally associated with the Shīʿī Imams, especially ʿAlī ibn Abī Ṭālib, which later came to refer to a range of millenarian divinatory practices correlated with the science of letters and divine names.[15] The inventory includes two *malḥamas* which are a literary genre devoted to political-eschatological predictions, such as the *Malḥamat Daniyāl* ('Apocalypse of Daniel').[16]

Geomancy is another divinatory art represented in the inventory. It is a form of knowledge which is deemed to have been revealed to the Prophet Idrīs and, in some texts, to the Prophet Daniel. Authors often cite the following *ḥadīth* to argue for geomancy's legitimacy: 'Among the prophets, one used to draw lines if [the lines of] whosoever were in keeping with his lines, it was right'.[17] It was also associated with the Indian Sage Ṭumṭum al-Hindī whose teachings were transmitted to Khalaf al-Barbarī (d. 17/634) and then to a series of disciples reaching Abū ʿAbd Allāh Muḥammad ibn ʿUthmān al-Zanātī (fl. before 1230), who was from the Berber tribe of Zanāta which thrived in the Maghreb. Another important author on geomancy is Ibn Maḥfūf who probably lived in Syria or Egypt before 1266 and whose treatise was translated into Latin. Shaykh Aḥmad ibn ʿAlī ibn Zunbul al-Rammāl (d. after 960/1552) was a notable Ottoman geomancer born in Mahalla in Delta circa 1500, who also happened to be the dream interpreter of Maḥmūd Pasha.[18]

14 al-Bīṭār, *Ḥilyat al-bashar*, 1504.

15 Gardiner, "Jafr"; Coulon, *La magie islamique*, 848.

16 Gardiner, "Jafr"; Fahd, "Malḥama"; Fahd, *La divination arabe*, 408–409; This work seems to have circulated widely among different religious groups during the eighteenth century. Georg Graf mentions copies in Syriac and Karshuni in the first volume of his *Geschichte der christlichen arabischen Literatur*, see Graf, *Geschichte der christlichen arabischen Literatur*, I, 216. Two copies of the work are preserved today in the National Library of Israel; one of those copies was owned by a priest from Ramla (Ms. AP Ar. 121) in the second half of the eighteenth century, and the other one is Ms. Ar. 279. One can also find the *Malḥama* in the Sbath collection in Aleppo (today in the Fondation Georges et Mathilde Salem, Sbath 1085). This copy once also belonged to a Maronite priest. I am grateful to Firas Krimsti for drawing my attention to these manuscripts.

17 Al-Nīsābūrī, *Ṣaḥīḥ*, Book 5, 7, 33, I, 243.

18 Saif, "Magic and Divination", 428–429; Lory, "Geomancy, Divination and Islam", 452–466.

Oneiromancy, or dream interpretation, is a divinatory science that is given its own subheading, containing five titles, four of which are designated as *Tafsīr Ibn Shāhīn* [#1243–1246], which could refer to *Ishārāt fī ʿilm al-ʿibārāt* by Khalīl ibn Shāhīn al-Ẓāhirī (813–873/1410–1468), the Mamluk statesman, courtier and learned man. He also authored the *Kitāb al-Kawkab al-munīr fī uṣūl al-taʿbīr* ('The Book of the Shining Star on the Principles of Dream Interpretation').[19]

Its relationship to the occult sciences can be gleaned from works on the classification of the sciences. Ibn Sīnā classifies dream interpretation as a secondary natural science, including medicine, astrology, physiognomy, talismanry, *nīranjs*, alchemy and dream interpretation, which pertains to 'the knowledge of the unseen' (*ʿilm al-ghayb*).[20] Ḥājjī Khalifa uses Ibn Sīnā's definition and classification, so does Tashköprüzāda (d. 968/1561) in his *Miftāḥ al-saʿāda wa-miṣbāḥ al-siyāda* ('The Key to Happiness and the Land of Lordship'), stressing that the skill instrumentalises the 'rational soul' (*fiʿl al-nafs al-nāṭiqa*).[21] Al-Ḥasan ibn Masʿūd al-Yūsī (1040–1102/1630–1691), the Maghrebi Sufi, theologian and logician, in his classification of knowledge, lists medicine, veterinary medicine, physiognomy, dream interpretation, astrology, magic, science of talismans, lettrist magic (*al-sīmiyāʾ*), alchemy and agriculture under the natural science (*al-ʿilm al-ṭabīʿī*).[22] In such classifications, the occult sciences and dream interpretation share the naturalistic frameworks through which they were understood. Ibn Khaldūn explains in his *Muqaddima* that dream interpretation instrumentalises the 'heart's spirit' which is the vessel of the rational soul. Nevertheless, he gives it an explicit religious sense: 'this is one of the *sharʿī* (religious/permissible) sciences' verified by the story of Joseph and the *ḥadīth* that states: 'a true "prophetic dream" (*ruʾyā ṣāliḥa*) is 1/46th of prophecy'.[23] Al-Ghazālī even describes dream interpretation as a 'wondrous secret among the secrets of the heart',[24] while Ibn Shāhīn himself stresses the legitimacy of dream interpretation as the only 'science of secrets' that complies with the *sharīʿa*.[25] This position is informed by a long tradition that has placed dream interpretation as a 'natural science', while, at the same time, ascribes a religious and esoteric significance to it due to the privilege it is given as a mark of a piety, especially among the Sufis, and prophetic ability, as in the case of the Prophet Joseph.[26] This ambiguity of dream interpretation explains the fact that, in the case of the Jazzār Library, titles for dream interpretation are separated from the section on the natural and occult sciences, and this suggests that dream interpretation is seen by the Jazzār cultural retinue as akin to the religious sciences.

3 *Shams al-Maʿārif* (*al-kubrā* and Others) and Magic in the Seventeenth and Eighteenth Centuries

The prominence of al-Būnī, particularly *Shams al-maʿārif* (*al-kubrā* especially) is indicative of its

19 Fahd, *La divination arabe*, 351–352.
20 Ibn Sīnā, "al-Risāla fī aqsām al-ʿulūm al-ʿaqliyya", 104–105, 110–111.
21 Ṭashköprüzāde, *Miftāḥ al-saʿāda*, I, 301–302, 311–312, 340–346; Ḥājjī Khalīfa, *Kashf al-ẓunūn*, I, 11–18.
22 Stearns, *Revealed Sciences*, 85–86.
23 Ibn Khaldūn, *Muqaddima*, 459–460.
24 Al-Ghazālī, *Iḥyāʾ ʿulūm al-dīn*, V, 92–93.
25 Loiseau, "Ibn Shāhīn al-Ẓāhirī".
26 'O Joseph, the man of truth! Explain to us (the dream) of seven fat cows whom seven lean ones were devouring, and of seven green ears of corn, and (seven) others dry, that I may return to the people, and that they may know.' (Joseph) said: 'For seven consecutive years, you shall sow as usual and that (the harvest) which you reap you shall leave in ears, (all)—except a little of it which you may eat. Then will come after that seven hard (years), which will devour what you have laid by in advance for them, (all) except a little of that which you have guarded (stored). Then thereafter will come a year in which people will have abundant rain and in which they will press (wine and oil).' Q. 12, 43–49. See Kinberg, "Dreams"; Abuali, "Dreams and Visions", 1–29; Fahd, *La Divination arabe*, 247–317.

centrality in the canon of occult sciences among eighteenth-century cultural milieus. We find three copies of *Shams al-maʿārif al-kubrā* and three copies of *Khafiyat Aflāṭūn* (see #1487), two of which are from Shaykh ʿAbd al-Raḥmān, the Hanafi imam, in the inventory of the *madrasa* of ʿUthmān Bāshā al-Dūrikī in Aleppo. We also find other works attributed to al-Būnī under the titles *al-Ghāya al-quṣwā fī asrār al-ḥurūf wa-al-asmā'*, *Risāla fī al-rūḥāniyyāt* and *Khātam Sulaymān*.[27] The prevalence of *Shams al-maʿārif* and the science of letters in earlier major libraries can also be seen in the inventory of the holdings of the Topkapı Palace book treasury in Istanbul, commissioned by the Ottoman sultan Bāyezīd II from his royal librarian ʿAtufı in the year 908 (1502–1503) and transcribed in a clean copy in 909 (1503–1504).[28] Regarding the *Shams al-maʿārif al-kubrā*, Noah Gardiner writes in his study of Aḥmad al-Būnī:

Shams al-maʿārif al-kubrā is a lengthy, talisman-laden, quasi-encyclopædic work on the occult sciences that is replete with texts on alchemy, astrology, geomancy, the science of letters, and other topics that could be gathered under the broad heading of 'occult sciences'. It is in fact an amalgamation of bits and pieces of some of al-Būnī's authentic works with texts by other authors. In the manuscripts surveyed for this project, there were no copies of it dated to earlier than the eleventh/seventeenth century, and in my view it is likely a product of that century or the latter part of the preceding one. The Kubrā was quite popular judging from the number of surviving copies reproduced in lithograph in the nineteenth century, and has been continuously in print in a series of non-scholarly editions, mostly emanating from Cairo and Beirut, since around the turn of the twentieth century.[29]

This leads Gardiner to conclude that the work probably originated in the seventeenth century and that the designation '*al-kubrā*' appears in the same century.[30] '*Al-ṣughrā*' was applied to various shorter al-Būnian or pseudo-Būnian texts.[31]

To understand the place of al-Būnī's texts in the context of the Jazzār library it is important to look closer at knowledge transmission and Sufism in the seventeenth and eighteenth century. Challenging the narrative of intellectual staleness of these centuries, Khaled El-Rouyaheb argues that we can no longer limit our scholarly attention to 'studies of popular chroniclers, Sufi diarists, and popularizers of medical or occult knowledge' although their study is 'most welcome'; however, his own objective is to present a narrative that restores 'a legitimate place for the study of the ideas, issues, and controversies that preoccupied the "academics" of the period'.[32] This is responding to the erroneous view that the era is marked by 'unthinking scholarly imitation (*taqlīd*), crude Sufi pantheism, and syncretic and idolatrous popular religious practices' to which the occult sciences are associated.[33] However, it is as Albrecht Hofheinz stresses, we cannot understand eighteenth-century intellectual culture without considering:

that (a) the Sufi tradition, in particular in the form of a piety centred on the Prophet Muḥammad, provided a unique combination of emotional experience and intellectual teachings that facilitated the

27 Aljoumani, *Maktaba madrasiyya fī Ḥalab*, 84, 130, 192, 314, 362. This library contains similar texts on alchemy, geomancy, astrology and the science of letters and divine names.

28 Burak, "The Section on Prayers", 347–348; Gardiner, "Books on Occult Sciences", 735–752; Liebrenz, "The Sciences in Two Private Libraries", 787–797.

29 Gardiner, "Esotericism in a Manuscript Culture", *passim*; Coulon, *La magie islamique*, 477–497.

30 Gardiner, "Esotericism in a Manuscript Culture", 16.

31 Ibid., 32.

32 el-Rouyaheb, *Islamic Intellectual History*, 3.

33 el-Rouyaheb, *Islamic Intellectual History*, 2, fn 3: a view perpetuated by the rhetoric of Muslim reformers, such as Muḥammad ʿAbduh (d. 1905), Muḥammad Rashīd Riḍā (d. 1935), and Muḥammad Iqbāl (d. 1938).

increasing internalisation of norms taught by Islamic authorities; and that (b) pietist reform movements since the eighteenth century were essential agents in spreading this understanding of what Islam means on an unprecedented scale, leading to a growing number of individual believers gaining a measure of autonomy from the old authorities.[34]

In the context of the Maghreb, Justin Stearns highlights the trend of knowledge transmission characterised by a synthesis between Ashʿarī theology and mostly Shādhilī Sufism, adding:

The occult sciences feature in these taxonomies not as an exception or a contrast category, but as an accepted part of the natural sciences. Even as this point bears emphasizing due to current narratives that undermine the rationality of the occult, it is also true that it can be difficult to precisely delineate the line between licit and illicit invocations of occult powers. The difference between a prayer and a spell is the addressee—God or jinn—not the form or mechanism with which it is carried out (e.g., talisman, letters, magic square).[35]

Nevertheless, in elevating the knowledge production of the intellectual elite, el-Rouyaheb inadvertently puts to the fore the fuzziness of the line between Sufism, the occult sciences and elite scholarship. Focusing on the rational sciences and logic, el-Rouyaheb shows that the intellectual scene of Cairo was invigorated by incoming scholars from the Maghreb. He analyses the place of Aḥmad ibn ʿAbd al-Munʿim al-Damanhūrī (1101–1192/1689–1778), the prolific Islamic scholar of Egypt, in that scene. He was engaged in disciplines such as logic, rhetoric, rational theology, Qur'an recitation, law, medicine, anatomy, mirrors for princes, arithmetic and the occult sciences. Al-Damanhūrī was initiated into the Shādhilī Sufi order and became Rector of al-Azhar College (*Shaykh al-Azhar*) in 1768.[36] The Moroccan polymath Muḥammad ibn Sulaymān al-Rūdānī (1037–1094/1628–1683), initiated into the Shādhilī order, was also a prominent teacher of logic and especially astronomy in the Hijaz. He was described as follows:

His knowledge of *ḥadīth* and *uṣūl* [again, theology or jurisprudence or both] is unequalled by anyone we have met. As for the science of belles-lettres (*adab*), he is the ultimate authority. In the philosophical sciences—logic, physics, and metaphysics—he was the teacher whose knowledge could not be acquired through natural means. And he was proficient in the sciences of mathematics: Euclid, astronomy, geometry, Almagest, calculus, algebra, arithmetic, cartography, harmony, and geodesy. His knowledge of these fields was unique, other scholars knowing only the preliminaries of these sciences rather than the advanced issues [...]. In the occult sciences such as divination, magic squares, numerology and alchemy he was skilled to the utmost.[37]

As Stearns shows, Muḥammad ibn al-Ṭayyib al-Qādirī (d. 1187/1773) focuses largely, but not exclusively, on Maghrebi scholars of the seventeenth and eighteenth centuries in his *Nashr al-Mathānī*, and gives the biographies of 843 scholars, fifty-eight of whom were masters of the rational or natural sciences, especially logic, followed by time-keeping and medicine, with a few striking examples of scholars who were known for their mastery of the occult sciences, such as the properties of letters, letter magic or magical squares.[38]

Many such Sufi scholars seem to be acquainted with *Shams al-maʿārif*. Abū ʿAbd Allāh Muḥammad ibn Saʿīd al-Mirghitī (d. 1089/1678), for example, studied astrology and numerology (*al-*

34 Hofheinz, "The Islamic Eighteenth Century", 238.
35 Stearns, *Revealed Sciences*, 98.
36 el-Rouyaheb, *Islamic Intellectual History*, 136.
37 Ibid., 165.
38 Stearns, *Revealed Sciences*, 80.

tarqīm), as well as the lettrist magic via the al-Būnian *Shams al-maʿarif*. Al-Mirghitī, himself, was the author of several books on magic.[39] Another major figure that reaffirms the place of al-Būnī and the occult sciences in the intellectual milieus of the seventeenth century and the impact of the Maghrebi scene in particular is Aḥmad al-Maqarrī al-Tilimsānī (d. 1041/1632), author of *Nafḥ al-tīb fi ghuṣn al-Andalus al-raṭīb*, who resided at the Zāwiya Dilā'iyya and was interested in the occult sciences.[40] We find a poem by the Andalusian ʿUmar al-Zajjāl addressing his shaykh in *Nafḥ al-ṭīb*, asking to be given the *ijāza* (formal permission to transmit a text) for several works including *Shams al-maʿārif* 'about whose authorship I asked every man', reflecting the ambiguity concerning the authorship of the *Shams*.[41]

Closer to our Aḥmadiyya library, lettrist magic in greater Syria and Palestine constituted a practice whereby scholarly-religious verification and common concerns intersect. The use of talismans is ubiquitous across all social levels, often undertaken by Sufis. Khālid al-Naqshbandī (d. 1827), one of the most influential Sufis of his generation, had the ability to deprive his enemies of their sanity or scatter them with a single withering glance. In other contexts, we encounter Abū Bakr al-Dusūqī (d. 1779), a Sufi from Damascus, specialised in prescriptions for the sick, who swore by the efficacy of his treatments. Ayyūb al-Khalwatī (d. 1660), a Damascene Sufi, purportedly wrote a talisman for villagers who reported that jinn had been stoning their huts at night. He instructed them to soak it, and then sprinkle the mixture of water and ink around their fields.[42]

In addition to lettrist magic, some titles in the inventory probably belong to a non-Lettrist Judeo-Islamic tradition. These are three volumes with the same generic title: *Kitāb rūḥānī*, and a fourth, *al-Hidāya al-rūḥānī*. *Al-ʿilm rūḥānī* has been used since the twelfth century to refer to magic centred around the adjuration of angels and binding jinn. In the context of eighteenth- and nineteenth-century Syria and Palestine, as James Grehan shows, the Jewish community of Jerusalem referred to rabbis who used magical writings and scripture and other practices to solve community issues.[43] On the local level, Jewish magical practices and Islamic ones must have intermingled historically. Mediaeval Jewish magic—before the Kabbalah—as Gideon Bohak specifies, spans from third century BCE to the seventh century CE, with its connections to and continuations of late antique Egyptian, Palestinian and Babylonian practices. This is magic practiced by Jews in Palestine and its closest neighbours, from present-day Egypt to Syria and Turkey, 'for Jewish and non-Jewish clients, and as borrowed from them by non-Jews', as attested by sources such as the Cairo genizah. This magic extensively utilises magic words, *charactêres*, (in Aramaic, *kalaqṭiraia*, and in Arabic *khalqaṭriyyāt*), the Hebrew alphabet, demon subjugation formulae and angelic adjurations, extensive use of the Name of God and the names of angels and demons. This was facilitated by the Arabic versions of influential Jewish texts, such as *Sefer ha-Razim, Harba de Moshe* and the *Testament of Solomon*, with the first being especially influential.[44] It is important to emphasise that following the twelfth century, many elements of this non-Lettrist Judeo-Islamic magical tradition, including the angelic and demonic regimentation and the major place accorded to divine and angelic names, were incorporated into the Sufi-Lettrist tradition from the thirteenth century. From the mid-fourteenth century, the occult sciences were increasingly 'mathematicized' and simultaneously 'sanctified' by the Sufi and millenarian frameworks through which they were legitimated by figures such as Ibn al-ʿArabī, al-Būnī, and members of

39 Ibid., 80, 104.
40 el-Rouyaheb, *Islamic Intellectual History*, 154–155.
41 al-Tilmisānī, *Nafḥ aṭ-ṭīb*, V, 45.
42 Grehan, *Twilight of the Saints*, 81, 150–153.
43 Ibid., 154.
44 Saif, "The 'Sanctification' of Arabic Hermeticism", forthcoming.

the self-identifying neo-Ikhwān al-Ṣafāʾ, including ʿAbd al-Raḥmān al-Bisṭāmī. In this process, the science of letters and divine names were classified as one of the mathematical sciences and one of the sciences of *walāya* (sainthood or sacral power).[45]

4 Conclusion

Occult practices in the eighteenth century permeated all sections of Islamic societies through the exchange of knowledge and texts between the intellectual, spiritual and political elites. The inventory of the al-Aḥmadiyya Library is a valuable source for gauging the relevance of the occult sciences to the cultural retinue of Aḥmad Pasha al-Jazzār, who is reported to have carried amulets. Taking centre stage is al-Būnī's *Shams al-maʿārif*, three copies thereof that are complemented by a number of treatises on the science of letters and lettrist magic which include a volume of *Shams al- maʿārif* gifted to al-Jazzār by a mysterious Maghrebi. Al-Jazzār did not only wear amulets for protection, as many would have done, but his engagement was also much deeper. As attested by the *jafr* and *malḥama* literature, in addition to astrological and magical texts, and confirmed by the historical sources at our disposal, it is clear that the occult and divinatory inventory at the al-Aḥmadiyya library reflects al-Jazzār's mobilisation of the occult sciences and messianic discourse for his political and military missions. This was enabled by a network of Sufis and occultists—from Maghreb through Egypt to Syria and Palestine—who were part of al-Jazzār's cultural retinue and who probably capitalised on the region's messianic anxieties. The library presents the physical and metaphysical control that he sought and, most significantly, the global approach with which such a library ought to be studied.

45 Burak, "The Section on Prayers", 342; Melvin-Koushki, "Powers of One", 127–199.

A more systematic study of the occult and esoteric holdings of Islamicate libraries and the development of occult-scientific canons is needed to substantiate the argument of this present chapter. Such studies would help us to explore the ways in which shifts in the epistemological frameworks that underlie the occult sciences are reflected in personal and public libraries, rendering inventories valuable tools to understanding boundary work involved in the development and acquisition of occult knowledge and practice.

Bibliography

Abuali, Eyad. "Dreams and Visions as Diagnosis in Medieval Sufism: The Emergence of Kubrawī Oneirology." *Journal of Sufi Studies* 8, no. 1 (2020): 1–29.

Aljoumani, Said. *Maktaba madrasiyya fī Ḥalab Nihāyat al-ʿAhd al-ʿUthmānī: al-Daftar al-Mujaddad li-kutub waqf ʿUthmān Bāshā al-Dūrikī*. Beirut, 2019.

al-Asali, Kamal J. "The Libraries of Ottoman Jerusalem." In *Ottoman Jerusalem: The Living City: 1517–1917*, edited by Sylvia Auld and Robert Hillenbrand, 2 vols, 285–290. London, 2000.

al-Baghdādī, Ismāʿīl Bāshā. *Hidāyat al-ʿārifīn*. 2 vols. Tehran, 1951.

al-Bīṭār, ʿAbd al-Razzāq. *Ḥilyat al-bashar fī tārīkh al-qarn al-thālith ʿashar*, edited by Muḥammad al-Bīṭār. Beirut, 1993.

Burak, Guy. "The Section on Prayers, Invocations, Unique Qualities of the Qurʾan, and Magic Squares in the Palace Library Inventory." In *Treasures of Knowledge: An Inventory of the Ottoman Palace Library (1502/3–1503/4)*, edited by Gülru Necipoğlu, Cemal Kafadar and Cornell H. Fleischer. Leiden, 2019.

Cabi Ömer Efendi. *Cabi Ta'rihi veya Ta'rih-i Sultan Selim-i salis ve Mahmud-ı sani*, edited by Mehmet Ali Beyhan, 2 vols. Ankara, 2003.

Chahanovich, W. Sasson. "Ottoman Eschatological Esotericism: Introducing *Jafr* in Ps. Ibn al-ʿArabī's *The Tree of Nuʿmān (al-Shajarah al-nuʿmāniyyah)*." *Correspondences* 7, no. 1 (2019): 61–108.

Cook, David. "Two Christian Arabic Prophecies of Liber-

ation from Muslim Rule from the Late 18th Century." *Oriens Christianus* 84 (2000): 66–76.
Coulon, Jean-Charles. "La magie islamique et le 'corpus bunianum' au Moyen Âge." PhD diss., Université Paris IV—Sorbonne, 2013.
Coulon, Jean-Charles. "Building al-Būnī's Legend: The Figure of al-Būnī through ʿAbd al-Raḥmān al-Bisṭāmī's Shams al-āfāq." *Journal of Sufi Studies* 5, no. 1 (2016): 1–26.
Editors. "Ibn ʿUthmān al-Miknāsī." *Encyclopaedia of Islam Two. Online: https://referenceworks.brill.com/display/entries/EIEO/SIM-8677.xml.*
Fahd, Toufic. "Malḥama." *Encyclopaedia of Islam.* 2nd edition. Leiden, 2012.
Fahd, Toufic. *La divination arabe. Études religieuses, sociologiques et folkloriques sur le milieu natif de l'Islam.* Leiden, 1966.
Fleischer, Cornell H. "Ancient Wisdom and New Sciences: Prophecies at the Ottoman Court in the Fifteenth and Early Sixteenth Centuries." In *Falnama: The Book of Omens*, edited by Massumeh Farhad and Serpil Bağcı, 231–243. Washington DC, 2009.
Gardiner, Noah. "Jafr." *Encyclopaedia of Islam Three.* Online: https://referenceworks.brill.com/display/db/ei30
Gardiner, Noah. "Esotericism in a Manuscript Culture: Aḥmad al-Būnī and His Readers through the Mamlūk Period." PhD diss., University of Michigan, 2014.
Gardiner, Noah. "Books on Occult Sciences." In: *Treasures of Knowledge: An Inventory of the Ottoman Palace Library (1502/3–1503/4)*, edited by Gülru Necipoğlu, Cemal Kafadar and Cornell H. Fleischer, 735–752. Leiden, 2019.
Gardiner, Noah. "The Occult Encyclopedism of ʿAbd al-Raḥmān Bisṭāmī." *Mamluk Studies Review* 20 (2017): 25–27.
Al-Ghazāli, Abū Ḥāmid. *Ihyā' ʿulūm al-dīn*, 10 vols. Jeddah, 2011.
Graf, Georg. *Geschichte der christlichen arabischen Literatur.* 5 vols. Città del Vaticano, 1944.
Grehan, James. *Twilight of the Saints: Everyday Religion in Ottoman Syria and Palestine.* New York, 2014.
Ḥājjī Khalīfa. *Kashf al-ẓunūn*, edited by Şerafettin Yaltqaya and Rifʿat al-Kilīsī, 2 vols. Beirut: Dār iḥyā' al-turāth al-adabī, n.d.
Hofheinz, Albrecht. "The Islamic Eighteenth Century: A View from the Edge." In *Islam in der Moderne, Moderne im Islam*, edited by Florian Zemmin, Johannes Stephan and Monica Corrado, 234–253. Leiden, 2018.
Ibn Khaldūn. al-*Muqqadima*, edited by Darwīsh al-Juwaydī. Beirut: al-Maktaba al-ʿaṣriyya, 1995.
Ibn Sīnā. "al-Risāla fī aqsām al-ʿulūm al-ʿaqliyya." In *Tisʿ rasā'il fī al-ḥikma wa-al-ṭabīʿiyyāt*, 104–116. Cairo: Dār al-ʿarab, n.d.
Iskandar, A.Z. *A Descriptive List of Arabic Manuscripts on Medicine.* Leiden, 1984.
al-Jabartī, ʿAbd al-Raḥmān. *ʿAjā'ib al-āthār fī al-tarājim wa-al-akhbār.* edited by ʿAbd al-Raḥīm ʿAbd al-Raḥīm, 4 vols. Cairo: Dār al-kutub 1998.
Karatas, Hasan. "The City as a Historical Actor: The Urbanization and Ottomanization of the Halvetiye Sufi Order by the City of Amasya in the Fifteenth and Sixteenth Centuries." PhD diss., University of California, Berkeley, 2011.
Kinberg, Leah. "Dreams." *Encyclopaedia of Islam Three.* Online: https://referenceworks.brill.com/display/db/ei30
Liebrenz, Boris. "The Sciences in Two Private Libraries from Ottoman Syria." In *Routledge Handbook on the Sciences in Islamicate Societies*, edited by Peter Barker, Sonja Brentjes and Rana Brenjes, 787–797. London, 2023.
Loiseau, Julien. "Ibn Shāhīn al-Ẓāhirī." *Encyclopaedia of Islam Three.* Online: https://referenceworks.brill.com/display/db/ei30
Lory, Pierre. "Geomancy, Divination and Islam." In *Magic in Malta: Sellem Bin al-Sheikh Mansur and the Roman Inquisition, 1605*, edited by Alexander Mallett, Catherine Rider and Dionisius Agius, 452–466. Leiden, 2022.
Melvin-Koushki, Matthew. "Powers of One: The Mathematicialization of the Occult Sciences in the High Persianate Tradition." *Intellectual History of the Islamicate World* 5 (2017): 127–199.
al-Miknāsī, Ibn ʿUthmān. *Riḥlat al-Miknāsī: Iḥrāz al-muʿallā wa-l-raqīb fī ḥajj bayt Allāh al-ḥarām*, edited by Muḥammad Būkubūṭ. Beirut: al-Mu'assasa al-ʿarabiyya lil-dirāsāt wa-al-nashr, 2003.
Al-Nīsābūrī. *Saḥīḥ*, 2 vols. Riyadh: Dār ṭība, 2006.

Ragep, Sally P. "al-Djaghmīnī." *Encyclopaedia of Islam*. 2nd edition. Leiden, 2012.

al-Rouyaheb, Khaled. *Islamic Intellectual History in the Seventeenth Century: Scholarly Currents in the Ottoman Empire and the Maghreb*. Cambridge, 2015.

Saif, Liana. "Magic and Divination, Lost in Translation: A Cairene in a Maltese Inquisition." In *Magic in Malta: Sellem Bin al-Sheikh Mansur and the Roman Inquisition, 1605*, edited by Alexander Mallett, Catherine Rider and Dionisius Agius, 420–451. Leiden, 2022.

Saif, Liana. "The 'Sanctification' of Arabic Hermeticism via Jewish Magic: The Case of al-Sakkākī's (1160–1229) *al-Kitāb al-Shāmil fī al-baḥr al-kāmil*." forthcoming.

al-Shihābī, Ḥaydar Aḥmad. *Lubnān fī ʿahd al-umarāʾ al-Shihābīyīn*, edited by Asad Rustom Beirut, 1933.

Şen, A. Tunç. "Reading the Stars at the Ottoman Court: Bāyezīd II (r. 886/1481–918/1512) and His Celestial Interests." *Arabica* 64 (2017): 557–608.

Şen, A. Tunç. "Practicing Astral Magic in Sixteenth-century Ottoman Istanbul. A Treatise on Talismans Attributed to Ibn Kemāl (d. 1534)." *Magic, Ritual, and Witchcraft* (Spring 2017): 66–88.

Stearns, Justin. *Revealed Sciences: The Natural Sciences in Islam in Seventeenth-century Morocco*. Cambridge, 2021.

Ṭashköprüzāde. *Miftāḥ al-saʿāda wa-miṣbāḥ al-siyāda*, 3 vols. Beirut, 1985.

al-Tilimsānī, Aḥmad ibn Muḥammad al-Maqqarī. *Nafḥ aṭ-ṭīb min ghuṣn al-Andalus al-raṭīb*, edited by Iḥsān ʿAbbās. 7 vols. Beirut: Dār Ṣāder, 1997.

Witkam, Jan Just. "Gazing at the Sun: Remarks on the Egyptian Magician al-Būnī and his Work." In *O ye Gentlemen: Arabic Studies on Science and Literary Culture*, edited by Arnoud Vroloijk and Jan Hogendijk, 183–200. Leiden, 2007.

al-Zabīdī, Muḥammad Murtaḍā. *Tāj al-ʿArūs*. 20 vols. Beirut, 2011.

The Natural, Mathematical, Celestial, and Occult Sciences Books, in Addition to Interpretation of Dreams

Titles under the section 'On the celestial science (ʿilm al-falak), astronomy (ʿilm al-hayʾa), [the science of] Letter[s] (al-ḥarf), the spiritual [science] (al-rūḥānī), geomancy, geometry, arithmetic and alchemy'

[1472] ***Shams al-maʿārif al-kubrā***, AUTHOR: falsely attributed to the Sufi and lettrist Aḥmad al-Būnī (d. ca. 1225). See #1552 and #1675.

[1473] ***Shams al-maʿārif al-ṣughrā***, AUTHOR: falsely attributed to Aḥmad al-Būnī. See #1472, #1552 and #1675.

[1474] ***Shams al-āfāq***, full title: *Shams al-āfāq fī ʿilm al-ḥurūf wa-al-awfāq*, AUTHOR: Sufi and lettrist ʿAbd al-Raḥmān al-Bisṭāmī (d. 858/1454), which 'established al-Būnī as the premier authority in the science of letters'.[46]

[1475] ***al-Hidāya rūḥānī*** (on spirits), unidentified, generic title.

[1476] ***Kitāb rūḥānī*** (on spirits), unidentified, generic title.

[1477] ***Kitāb rūḥānī*** (on spirits), unidentified, generic title.

[1478] ***Kitāb rūḥānī*** (on spirits), unidentified, generic title.

[1479] ***Kitāb khawāṣṣ*** (on occult properties), unidentified, generic title.

[1480] ***Al-Lumʿa al-nūrāniyya sharḥ al-shajara al-nuʿmāniyya***. AUTHOR: falsely attributed to Ṣadr al-Dīn al-Qunawī (d. 673/1274). This is a commentary on *al-Shajara al-nuʿmāniyya* which is a late sixteenth/early seventeenth-century commentary on pseudo-Ibn al-ʿArabī's *al-Shajara al-nuʿmāniyya fī al-dawla al-ʿuthmāniyya*, belonging to *jafr* literature.[47]

[1481] ***jafr***, identified as belonging to al-Jazzār's library. MANUSCRIPT: Süleymaniye Manuscript Library, Pertevniyal V. Sultan 759.

46 Coulon, "Building al-Būnī's Legend", 1–26; Gardiner, "The Occult Encyclopedism", 25–27.

47 Chahanovich, "Ottoman Eschatological Esotericism".

[1482] ***Kitāb aqlām mukhtalifa*** (on different scripts), unidentified, generic title.

[1483] ***Kitāb zāyirja***, unidentified, generic title.

[1484] ***Majmūʿ fī al-zāyirja*** (a collection on *zāyirja*), unidentified, generic title.

[1485] ***Kitāb qurʿa***, unidentified, generic title.

[1486] ***Kitāb fī ʿilm al-ḥarf known as al-Kashf***, AUTHOR: Aḥmad al-Būnī. This is *Kitāb al-Kashf fī ʿilm al-ḥarf*, MANUSCRIPT: Wellcome Collection, MS Arabic 256.

[1487] ***Shamsiyyat Aflāṭūn***. This could be referring to the popular magical text known as *Khāfiyat Aflāṭūn*,[48] which Ḥājjī Khalīfa classifies under the subheading 'The Science of Letters and Names'.[49]

[1488] ***Kitāb Zāyirja al-Sabtiyya***, AUTHOR: Abū al-ʿAbbās al-Sabtī (d. 721/1321), described by Ḥājjī Khalīfa as the chief of Sufis in Marrakesh and to whom the entire science of the *zāyirja* is attributed, MANUSCRIPT: Institute of Arabic Manuscripts, 58/26.

[1489] ***al-Shumūs al-muḍīʾa***, unidentified.

[1490] ***Jahān-nāmah***, AUTHOR: Kātib Çelebi's (1017–1068/1609–1657), originally written in Ottoman Turkish in 1065/1654, EDITION: Kātib Çelebi, *An Ottoman Cosmography: Translation of Cihânnümâ*, edited by Gottfried Hagen and Robert Dankoff, translated by Ferenc Csirkés, John Curry and Gary Leiser. Leiden: Brill, 2021.

[1491] ***Rawḍat al-azhār fī ʿilm al-awfāq***, possibly ***Rawḍat al-azhār fī ʿilm waqt al-layl wa-al-nahār***, AUTHOR: ʿAbd al-Raḥmān al-Jādirī (fl. 747/1341).

[1492] ***Kitāb zāyirja***, unidentified, generic title.

[1493] ***Mawāqiʿ al-nujūm***, AUTHOR: Ibn al-ʿArabī (558–638/1164–1240), MANUSCRIPT: Jerusalem, NLI, Ms. AP Ar. 177.

[1494] ***Gharīb al-funūn***, unidentified.

[1495] ***Barāʿat al-istihlāl fīmā yataʿallaq bi-al-shahr wa-al-hilāl***, AUTHOR: ʿAbd al-Raḥmān ibn ʿĪsā al-Murshidī, imam and mufti of the Ḥaram (975–1037/1567–1628), MANUSCRIPT: Süleymaniye Manuscript Library, Fatih 3694.

[1496] ***Kitāb zīj***, unidentified, generic title.

[1497] ***Irshād al-ḥāʾir fī maʿrifat rasm khuṭūṭ al-dāʾir***, AUTHOR: Abū al-ʿAbbās Shihāb al-Dīn Aḥmad ibn Zayn al-Dīn Rajab ibn Tubayghā al-Atābakī, known as al-Majdī or Ibn al-Majdī (d. 850/1447). He was a renowned and prominent mathematician, geometrician and astronomer, who served as the timekeeper of the al-Azhar Mosque.[50]

[1498] ***Kitāb malḥama***, unidentified, generic title.

[1499] ***Kitāb Natījat aḥkām al-mīqāt***, unidentified, unidentified.

[1500] ***Kitāb ʿilm al-falak, majmūʿ fīhi jadāwil*** (on the celestial sphere, collection with tables), unidentified, generic title.

[1501] ***Risāla fī al-mīqāt wa-huwa-majmūʿ fī ʿilm al-falak*** (an epistle on time-keeping and it is a collection on the science of the celestial sphere), unidentified, generic title.

[1502] ***Kitāb al-malḥama***, unidentified, generic title.

[1503] ***Kitāb al-Falakiyyāt lil-Ṭūsī***, AUTHOR: Nāṣir al-Dīn al-Ṭūsī (d. 672/1274). I am not aware of this title among al-Ṭūsī's works.

[1504] ***Kitāb ajzāʾ min al-falakiyyāt***, partial version of ***Kitāb al-Falakiyyāt lil-Ṭūsī*** #1503.

[1505] ***Kitāb Tashrīḥ al-aflāk***, AUTHOR: Bahāʾ al-Dīn Muḥammad ibn Ḥusayn al-ʿĀmilī (d. 1030/1621), MANUSCRIPT: Wellcome Collection, MS Arabic 376.

[1506] ***Aḥkām qirānat al-kawākib***, AUTHOR: Abū Maʿshar al-Balkhī.

[1507] ***Dustūr al-ʿamal***, unidentified.

[1508] ***Kitāb Abū Maʿshar***, AUTHOR: Abū Maʿshar al-Balkhī. Could be a reference to his influential text *Kitāb al-Madkhal al-kabīr ilā ʿilm aḥkām al-nujūm*, or the abridged version of *Kitāb al-Madkhal al-kabīr*, EDITION: *The Great Introduction to Astrology by Abū Maʿshar*, edited by

48 Leiden University Library, Or. 123, 8ʳ to 13ᵛ. Princeton University Library, Garrett Islamic Manuscripts 548, and 549.

49 Ḥājjī Khalīfa, *Kashf al-Ẓunūn*, I: 653.

50 Ibid., I: 64, under "ilm aritmāṭīqī'.

Keiji Yamamoto and Charles Burnett, 2 vols., Leiden: Brill, 2019.

[1509] ***Kitāb Majmūʿ Abū Maʿshar***, AUTHOR: Abū Maʿshar. Possibly a collection of his teachings. See #1508.

[1510] ***Kitāb Natījat aḥkām al-mīqāt***, unidentified.

[1511] ***Risālat al-Aṣṭurnūmiyā***. AUTHOR: not mentioned. This is possibly the epistle on astronomy by Ikhwān al-Ṣafāʾ, which forms the third epistle of *Rasāʾil Ikhwān al-Ṣafāʾ*, EDITION: On *'Astronomia': An Arabic Critical Edition and English Translation of Epistle* 3, edited and translated by F. Jamil Ragep and Taro Mimura, Oxford University Press, in association with the Institute of Ismaili Studies, 2015.

[1512] ***Rūznāma***, (an almanac), unidentified, a generic title.

[1513] ***Rūznāma maʿfalakiyyāt*** (an almanac with celestial matters), unidentified, a generic title.

[1514] ***Kitāb al-hayʾa al-musammā bi-al-Nīshābūrī***, unidentified.

[1515] ***Ishārāt min al-ḥikma*** (philosophical allusions), unidentified, a generic title.

[1516] ***Ḥāshiyat Mawlānā Zādeh***, possibly referring to *Ḥāshiyat Mawlānā Zādeh fī al-ḥikma*. Ismāʿīl Bāshā al-Baghdādī (1839–1920), in his *Hidāyat al-ʿārifīn*—attributes *Ḥāshiya ʿalā sharḥ Mawlānā Zādeh li-hidāyat al-ḥikma* to Imām-Zādeh al-Barsawī also known as Imām Zādeh al-Ḥanafī (d. 977/1569), who is also author of *Mafātiḥ al-jinān fī sharḥ shirʿat al-islām* ('The Keys to Heaven in Explanation of the Law of Islam'). Ḥājjī Khalīfa mentions that Mawlā Mūsā ibn Maḥmūd, known as Zādeh al-Rūmī, has written *A Ḥāshiya ʿalā sharḥ Mawlānā Zādeh*. MANUSCRIPT: Maktabat al-awqāf bi-Ḥalab, 3531/2119 (5).[51]

[1517] ***al-Fatḥiyya fī al-hayʾa***, AUTHOR: ʿAlī ibn Muḥammad al-Qūshjī al-Samarqandī (d. 879/1475) theologian, mathematician, and astronomer, who was a central contributor to the development of the observation programme for the *zīj* of Ulugh Beg. MANUSCRIPT: British Library, IO Islamic 3758, 1^a to 49^b.

[1518] ***Kitāb min ʿilm al-handasa*** (a book on geometry), unidentified, a generic title.

[1519] ***Kitāb fī ʿilm al-hayʾa*** (a book on astronomy), unidentified, a generic title.

[1520] ***Kitāb handasa nāqiṣ*** (an incomplete book on geometry), unidentified, a generic title.

[1521] ***Kitāb baʿḍ suʾālāt li-man yurīd al-handasa*** (a book with some questions to whomever seeks [the study of] geometry), unidentified, generic title.

[1522] ***Kitāb Bidāyat al-ḥikma***, unidentified, unidentified.

[1523] ***Kitāb Sharḥ fī ʿilm al-hayʾa wa-huwa Sharḥ al-Jighmīnī***, a commentary on *al-Mulakhkhaṣ fī ʿilm al-hayʾa* by Maḥmūd ibn Muḥammad ibn ʿUmar al-Jaghmīnī al-Khawārizmī (fl. 13th century).[52]

[1524] ***Kitāb Sharḥ fī ʿilm al-hayʾa***, see #1523.

[1525] ***Kitāb al-Mulakhkhaṣ fī ʿilm al-hayʾa***, AUTHOR: Maḥmūd ibn Muḥammad ibn ʿUmar al-Jaghmīnī al-Khawārizmī. See #1523 and #1524.

[1526] ***Kitāb min ʿilm al-hayʾa*** (a book on astronomy), unidentified, a generic title.

[1527] ***Kitāb al-Mulakhkhaṣ fī ʿilm al-hayʾa***, see #1523–1525.

[1528] ***Maṣāriʿ al-maṣāriʿ***, AUTHOR: Naṣr al-Dīn al-Ṭūṣī, EDITION: Fayṣal Badīl ʿAwn, Cairo: Dār al-thaqāfa, ND.

[1529] ***Kitāb nawādir al-falāsifa***, AUTHOR: Ḥunayn ibn Isḥāq (d. 260/874).

[1530] ***Kitāb fī ʿilm al-hayʾa*** (a book on astronomy), unidentified, a generic title.

[1531] ***Kitāb al-Mulakhkhaṣ fī ʿilm al-hayʾa***, see #1523–1525 and #1527.

[1532] ***Majmūʿ rasāʾil fī ʿilm al-ṭabīʿiyyāt*** (a collection of epistles on the natural sciences), unidentified.

---

51 Ḥājjī Khalīfa, *Kashf al-Ẓunūn*, II, 2029–2030.

52 Ragep, Al-Djaghmīnī; Ṭashköprüzāde, I, 349. See British Library, Add MS 23398, 66^b to 86^a. A commentary by ʿAlī ibn Muḥammad al-Jirjānī is found in British Library, Add MS 23398, 2^a to 65^b. Another one by Mūsā ibn Muḥammad Qāḍī-zādah can be accessed here https://catalog.hathitrust.org/Record/002641690.

[1533] *Ṭāliʿ al-mawlūd ʿalā qawāʿid al-furs*, unidentified.

[1534] ***Kitāb Qabs al-anwār***, AUTHOR: in MS King Saud 3586, the name of the author is given as Abū al-Ḥajjāj Yūsuf ibn ʿAlī ibn Aḥmad ibn Muḥammad al-Nadūrī al-Maghrebī. This manuscript ends with a reference to *Jafr Ibn ʿArabī* in relation to the subject of rulership and viziers. It is listed by Ḥājjī Khalīfa under *ʿilm al-ḥurūf wa-al-asmāʾ*.[53]

[1535] ***Kitāb raml*** (a book on geomancy), unidentified, a generic title.

[1536] ***Kitāb raml*** (a book on geomancy), unidentified, a generic title.

[1537] ***Sharḥ Khulāṣat al-ḥisāb***. This is a commentary on *Khulāṣat al-ḥisāb* by Bahāʾ al-Dīn al-ʿĀmilī, MANUSCRIPT: Süleymaniye Manuscript Library, Fatih 3446. See #1538

[1538] ***Kitāb Khulāṣat al-ḥisāb*** by Bahāʾ al-Dīn al-ʿĀmilī, see #1537.

[1539] ***Sharḥ Khulāṣat al-ḥisāb***, see #1537 and #1538.

[1540] ***Kitāb fī ʿilm al-ḥisāb*** (a book on arithmetic), unidentified, a generic title.

[1541] ***Kitāb fī ʿilm al-ḥisāb, Sharḥ al-khulāṣa***, see #1537–1540.

[1542] ***al-Miṣbāḥ fī ʿilm al-muftāḥ fī al-kīmiyāʾ***, AUTHOR: Aydamir ibn ʿAbd Allāh al-Jildakī (d. 743/ 1342).

[1543] ***Risāla fī ʿilm al-kīmiyāʾ***, unidentified.

[1544] ***Kitāb fī al-ḥajar al-mukarram*** (a book on the noble [philosopher's] stone), unidentified, generic title.

[1545] ***Muqaddima fī ʿilm al-kīmiyāʾ*** (an introduction to the science of alchemy), unidentified, generic title.

[1546] ***al-Miṣbāḥ fī ʿilm al-muftāḥ fī al-kīmiyāʾ***, see #1542.

[1547] ***al-Miṣbāḥ fī ʿilm al-muftāḥ fī al-kīmiyāʾ***, see #1542 and #1546.

[1548] ***Kitāb min ʿulūm shattā*** (a book on various sciences), unidentified, a generic title.

[1549] ***ṭāliʿ*** (a natal chart), unidentified, generic title.

[1550] ***rūznama maʿ mīqāt*** (almanac with timekeeping calendar), unidentified, generic title.

[1551] ***al-Sakhāwiyya***. This is likely to be *al-Risāla al-Sakhāwiyya fī al-ḥisāb*, AUTHOR: ʿAbd al-Qādir ibn ʿAlī al-Sakhāwī, MANUSCRIPT: Mhinni El Barouni Library, EAP1216/1/1/2/59.[54]

[1552] ***Shams al-maʿārif al-kubrā***, AUTHOR: Aḥmad al-Būnī. It is noted in the inventory as 'a gift to his Excellency by a Maghrebi man'. See #1472 and 1675.

Works of the Occult Sciences from the provenanced sections of the inventory

Works taken from the library of al-Sayyid Yaḥyā Efendī b. al-Sayyid Muḥammad al-Ṭībī of Jaffa in 1218/1803

[555] ***Kitāb Mawālīd al-rijāl wa-al-nisāʾ***, AUTHOR: pseudo-Abū Maʿshar al-Balkhī (171–271/787–886). A popular astro-magical work. MANUSCRIPT: Süleymaniye Manuscript Library, Esad Efendi 2003; Wellcome, WMS Arabic 499, 617, and 884.

[574] ***Kitāb fī al-aʿdād wa-ʿilm al-ḥisāb*** (a book on numbers an arithmetic), unidentified, generic title.

Works taken from the libraries of al-Shaykh ʿAlī al-Rashīdī and al-Shaykh Muḥammad Wakīlkharaj in 1216/1801

[1635] ***Kitāb al-Durr al-naẓīm bi-ʿilm al-aḥkām wa-al-taqwīm***, possibly the astrological and timekeeping text known as *al-Durr al-naẓīm fī tashīl al-taqwīm*, AUTHOR: Muḥammad ibn Maʿrūf, MANUSCRIPT: King Saud University, MS 4848.

[1644] ***Shumūs al-anwār wa-kunūz al-asrār***, possibly *Shumūs al-anwār wa-kunūz al-asrār al-kubrā*, AUTHOR: Ibn al-Ḥajj Muḥammad ibn Muḥammad al-Fāsī al-Tilimsānī mentioned by Ismāʿīl

53 Ḥājjī Khalīfa, *Kashf al-Ẓunūn*, I, 657.

54 Digitised by the British Library here: https://eap.bl.uk/archive-file/EAP1216-1-1-2-59

Bāshā al-Baghdādī in *Hidāyat al-ʿārifīn*.[55] This work is concerned with the science of letters and divine names.

[1656] ***Risāla fī ʿulūm al-kawākib wa-intiqāl al-marātib*** (an epistle on the science of the stars—astrology—and their movement of planetary ranks), unidentified.

[1659] ***Kitāb al-Madkhal al-kabīr***, see #1508 and #1509.

[1675] ***Shams al-maʿārif al-kubrā***, see #1472 and #1552.

[1680] ***Risāla fī sharḥ al-zāyirja*** (an epistle dedicated to a commentary on the *zāyirja*), unidentified, generic title.

[1684] ***Kitāb al-Zīj***, AUTHOR: Damascene astronomer and mathematician Ibn al-Shāṭir's (704–777/1304–1375).

[1686] ***Kitāb fī ʿilm al-nujūm*** (a book on astrology), unidentified, generic title.

[1687] ***Kitab Zubd al-lumʿa fī ḥall al-kawākib al-sabʿa***. A work known as *Kitāb al-lumʿa fī ḥall al-kawākib al-sabʿa* is attributed to Shihāb al-Dīn Aḥmad ibn Ghulām Allāh al-Rīshī (d. 836/1432). See Harvard University, Houghton Library, MS Arab 249. In MS Staatsbibliothek Berlin, Landberg 801, we find this title for a commentary on the zīj of Ibn Shāṭir. Another commentary on this text is written by Muḥammad ibn Muṣṭafā al-Khudarī (d. 1287/1870) called *Sharḥ al-lumʿa fī ḥall al-kawākib* can be accessed here https://babel.hathitrust.org/cgi/pt?id=mdp.39015081446968&seq=6.

[1688] ***Kitāb iqtirānāt al-kawākib*** (a book on planetary aspects), unidentified.

[1690] ***Kitāb Ijtimāʿ al-shaml fī maʿrifat ʿilm al-raml***, AUTHOR: Muḥammad ibn Aḥmad ibn Ḥasan (fl. 883/1478), MANUSCRIPT: Dublin, Chester Beatty Library, Ar. 3120.

[1691] ***Kitāb Zīj al-durr al-yatīm***, AUTHOR: Egyptian astrologer and imam of *al-Mashhad al-Ḥusaynī* of Cairo ʿAbd al-Munʿim al-Nabtītī al-Ḥanafī (d. 1084/1673), MANUSCRIPT: Ambrosiana Library, MS 80.[56]

[1692] ***Fatḥ al-malik al-majīd***, AUTHOR: Abū al-ʿAbbās Aḥmad al-Dayrabī.[57] *Fatḥ al-malik al-majīd li-nafʿ al-ʿabīd* is concerned with *khawāṣṣ al-Qurʾān* (the properties of the verses of the Qurʾān). Although this genre is not exclusively 'occult', elements, such as astrological elections, creation of talismans and amulets, and invocations, were integrated into some literature, including *Tartīrb al-daʿawāt* attributed to Aḥmad al-Būnī.[58] Another text mentioned by al-Jabartī authored by al-Dayrabī is an epistle 'concerned with the seven planets, the good hours (astrological elections), striking with high and low mandals' in addition to invocations and a 'tablet of life and death'. EDITION: Abū al-ʿAbbās Aḥmad al-Dayrabī, *Mujarrabāt al-Daybarī: Fatḥ al-malik al-majīd li-nafʿ al-ʿabīd* (Cairo: Maktabat al-jumhūriyya al-ʿarabiyya, ND).

[1693] ***Durrat al-āfāq fī ʿilm al-ḥurūf wa-al-awfāq***, AUTHOR: ʿAbd al-Raḥmān al-Bisṭāmī, author of *Shams al-āfāq* which the inventory also lists (see #1474), MANUSCRIPT: Dublin, Chester Beatty Library, Ar. 4491, Ar. 4892.

[1697] ***Natījat al-afkār fī aʿmāl al-layl wa-al-nahār***. AUTHOR: Shams al-Dīn Muḥammad ibn Muḥammad al-Lādhiqī, See, Gotha Research Library, Ms. Orient A 1399; MANUSCRIPT: Maktabat Baladiyyat Iskandariyya, MS 8708.[59]

[1698] ***Kitāb [...] al-tanjīm*** (a book on astrology), unidentified.

[1699] ***Kitāb al-zīj fī al-mīqāt*** (a book of zīj on timekeeping), unidentified.

55 al-Baghdādī, *Hidāyat al-ʿārifīn*, II, 149; Iskandar, *A Descriptive List*, 37.

56 Muḥammad Murtaḍā al-Zabīdī, *Tāj al-ʿArūs*, III, 145.

57 ʿAbd al-Raḥmān al-Jabartī, ʿAjāʾib al-āthār fī al-tarājim wa-al-akhbār, I, 274–275.

58 Witkam, "Gazing at the Sun", 187–190.

59 Another manuscript can be accessed here https://babel.hathitrust.org/cgi/pt?id=mdp.39015081446851&view=1up&seq=40.

[1703] ***Kitāb Sharḥ al-khātim al-muthallath wa-al-Ghazālī.*** Ḥājjī Khalīfa lists a text known as *al-Durr al-manẓūm fī al-sirr al-maktūm* attributed to al-Ghazālī 'known as the seal (*khatm*) al-Ghazālī', adding that it was commented on (*sharaḥahu*) al-Ṭulayṭilī, naming it *Mustawjibāt al-maḥāmid fī sharḥ khatm Abī Ḥāmid.* Its author is probably al-Ṭulayṭilī Abū 'Abdallāh Muḥammad ibn Ibrāhīm ibn Shiqq al-Layl al-Ṭulayṭilī (d. 445/1053) author of a *Kitāb al-Karāmāt wa-barāhīn al-ṣaliḥīn*, according to Ḥajjī Khalīfa.[60]

Occult works under 'Persian Books'

[1599] ***Kitāb fī sirr al-ḥurūf*** (a book on the secret of letters), unidentified, generic title.

The Interpretation of Dreams Books

[1242] First part of ***Tafsīr Ibn Shāhīn***. *al-Ishārāt fī 'ilm al-'Ibārāt*, AUTHOR: Ibn Shāhīn al-Ẓāhiry, Khalīl (d. 873/1468).

[1243] First part of ***Ta'bīr Ibn Shāhīn***, see #1242.

[1244] Second part of ***Tafsīr Ibn Shāhīn***, see #1242.

[1245] Second part of ***Tafsīr Ibn Shāhīn***, see #1242.

[1246] ***Kitāb Ta'bīr nāqiṣ al-awwal***, (a book of dream interpretation missing the first part), unidentified, generic title.

60 Ḥājjī Khalīfa, *Kashf al-Ẓunūn*, I, 735.

CHAPTER 25

A Language-oriented Approach: The Section on Persian and Turkish Books

Berat Açıl

The inventory of the Aḥmad Pasha al-Jazzār library categorises its manuscripts under thematic headings, as shown in the previous chapters. However, two sections stand out: those for Persian and Turkish books.[1] This raises the question of why Persian and Turkish titles were not classified thematically. Was the unique characteristic of these titles the languages in which they were written? Was their principal feature being non-Arabic titles? Considering the library was established in Acre, a city with primarily Arabic-speaking inhabitants, it is necessary to explain why it has Persian and Turkish books.

The library was established in a multilingual Empire, thus, Acre and Damascus were not only inhabited by Arabic speakers. Among their inhabitants were native speakers of Persian, Turkish, Kurdish, and other languages spoken and written across the empire. Moreover, some Arab scholars both spoke and used Persian and Turkish in Greater Syria (*bilād al-Shām*). This phenomenon is observed in a recent study by Theodore S. Beers, who argues that Arabic literati knew Persian in seventeenth-century Damascus, where Persian could be learned.[2] Moreover, al-Murādī provides many examples of multilingual scholars in his book *Silk al-Durar*, a biographical work on prominent eighteenth-century Arab scholars, for instance, Ibrāhīm b. Ṣari Ḥaydar al-Dimashqī reads both Turkish and Persian.[3] Shākir al-ʿUmarī, known as Ibn ʿAbd al-Hādī al-Ḥanafī al-Dimashqī, had excellent writing skills in Arabic and Turkish,[4] while a certain ʿAbd al-Raḥmān b. Jaʿfar, famous as al-Kurdī, spoke four languages: Arabic, Persian, Turkish and Kurdish.[5] ʿAbd al-Fattāḥ b. Muḥammad issued *fatwas* in Arabic and Turkish, whereas al-Sayyid ʿAbd al-Qādir b. al-Kaylānī was also conversant in Persian and Turkish.[6] Similarly, al-Sayyid Muḥammad al-Murādī[7] knew three languages: Arabic, Persian and Turkish, as did his father Murād al-Murādī[8] and Muṣṭafā al-Safarjalānī.[9] Michael Winter also argues that bilingualism was not rare in Damascus, Aleppo and Cairo (the latter fewer than the first two), in the seventeenth and the eighteenth centuries. Using al-Ghazzī, al-Muḥibbī and al-Murādī, biographies including scholars from the sixteenth to the eighteenth centuries, the author argues, 'A not insignificant number of the Damascus élite, definitely including not only bureaucrats but ʿulamaʾ as well, were fluent in Arabic and Turkish.'[10] Therefore, the existence of the Turkish and Persian sections in

1 I am indebted to the editors of this volume for their insightful recommendations, comments and corrections. I thank Nimet İpek and Isa Uğurlu for their help searching Persian and Turkish titles. The database provided by ISAM called 'Türkiye Kütüphaneleri Kataloğu' (http://ktp.isam.org.tr) and the website of Türkiye Yazma Eserler Kurumu Başkanlığı (https://portal.yek.gov.tr) were frequently used when searching the titles.

2 Beers, "Paths Crossing in Damascus", 239.

3 Al-Murādī, *Silk al-Durar*, I, 8.

4 Ibid., II, 183.

5 Ibid., II, 291–292. It is apparent that ʿAbd al-Raḥmān b. Jaʿfar was not Arab but Kurdish since al-Murādī mentioned Kurdish as the language of his 'people' (*qawm*).

6 Ibid., III, 46.

7 Ibid., IV, 114.

8 Ibid., IV, 129.

9 Ibid., IV, 209–210.

10 Winter, "Cultural Ties", 189.

DOI:10.1163/9789004720527_027

the library's inventory located in Acre, inhabited to some extent by essentially Arabic speakers, is plausible.

Another reason the library contains Turkish and Persian manuscripts might have something to do with Ottoman ruling elites, such as al-Jazzār himself, who principally used Turkish and then learned Persian and Arabic during their first education, as I will discuss later. Therefore, the library was also built to serve these rulers.

The Persian and Turkish sections of the Jazzār library inventory are language-oriented, and the number of titles is small; I will, therefore, examine them in a single chapter. The Persian section of the inventory of Jazzār library includes twenty-two titles, whereas the Turkish section covers fifty-six. Persian titles comprise Sufi-oriented poetic books and Persian-Turkish dictionaries. The Ottomans (Rūmīs) used Persian books related to Sufi poetry to improve their Persian language skills, which is still valid in modern Turkey. The Turkish titles include Turkish rewritings, translations, commentaries of Arabic books and original works used in the *madrasa* curriculum,[11] such as rational theology, recitation of the Qur'an, exegesis of the Qur'an, sayings of the Prophet Muḥammad, jurisprudence, *taṣawwuf*, catechism, dictionaries, together with manuals regarding military, political and administrative manners. Therefore, Turkish books of the inventory have practical and functional uses. I will divide the chapter into two parts: the analysis of Persian titles in the first part and Turkish titles in the second. Before that I will review and problematise Turkish and Persian books briefly in the other sections.

Classifying Turkish and Persian books does not mean that all Turkish and Persian manuscripts in the inventory are recorded in these two sections. Such titles also found their way into other sections. Two books from the history section, for instance, are written in Turkish. One is called *Tārīkh Turkī* (#1393) by İzzî Süleymân Efendi (d. 1168/1755). The second history book was written by Subhî Mehmed Efendi (d. 1182/1769), who is known as *Ṣubḥī Tārīkhi* (#1392).[12]

The inventory contains some Persian titles which could have been classified under the Persian book section. The manuscript recorded as *Tafsīr Fārisī* (#57)[13] in the Qur'anic commentary section might have been in Persian. It seems that the scribe of the inventory wanted the manuscript to be in this section because of its content. Another manuscript (#700) is about the names of Allāh, classified under *taṣawwuf and tawḥīd*.[14] Similarly, *Kitāb Lugha Fārisī* (#1621) is categorised under Turkish books because it is a Turkish-Persian or Persian-Turkish dictionary. *Dīwān al-Ḥāfiz al-Shīrāzī* (#1205) by al-Ḥāfiz al-Shīrāzī (d. c. 792/1390) is by nature in Persian, but is located in the poetry (*dawāwīn wa-qaṣā'id*) section.[15] *Bahr al-jawāhir fī al-ṭibb lil-Harawī* (#1451) by Muḥammad b. Yūsuf al-Harawī, though written in Arabic, contains some Persian explanations of the terms.[16] Deborah Schlein, in Chapter 23 on medicine, states that '*Kitāb fī ʿilm al-ṭibb li-Ṭahmāz al-ʿAjam* (#1458) could have been written by a Persian writer, with *ʿajam* indicating his non-Arab status and Ṭahmāz possibly being the Arabic form of Ṭahmāsb/p.'

Language-oriented classification of the titles was not unique to the Jazzār library inventory. One might come across a similar classification in the libraries adjacent to Acre. Among them is the eighteenth-century library founded by ʿUthmān Pasha al-Dūrikī in Aleppo. The inventory of al-Dūrikī library records Turkish and Persian titles under the title *kutub al-lugha al-Turkiyya*. The Jazzār library inventory records Turkish and Persian titles separately, but al-Dūrikī's inventory prefers

11 For a short list and discussion on auxiliary disciplines, see Kızılkaya, "From Means to Goal".

12 See Dana Sajdi's Chapter 22 in this volume.
13 See Walid Salih's Chapter 13 in this volume.
14 See Hadel Jarada's Chapter 17 in this volume.
15 See Khalil Sawan's Chapter 21 in this volume.
16 See Deborah Schlein's Chapter 23 in this volume.

to cover them under the same title.[17] The inventory also has some Turkish books in other sections, similar to the Jazzār library, such as Qurʾanic commentaries[18] and dictionaries. The ʿAẓm Library of Damascus contains only three non-Arabic titles: two Persian and one Turkish.[19] Another library that might be compared to the Jazzār Library in terms of how it treats Turkish and Persian titles is the library of the Egyptian governor Muḥammad Bey Abū al-Dhahab in Cairo. In that inventory, the language was not considered a criterion for classifying titles. Besides, the language of each title was not specified in the inventory.[20]

In conclusion, classifying titles according to their languages seems quite rare in the Arabic-speaking provinces of the empire and having a dedicated section to Persian and Turkish appears to be a particular feature of the Jazzār Library.

1 Persian Books

It is not apparent why the scribe chose to have a separate heading for Persian books since the titles listed in this section could have been assigned to other sections, such as *qaṣāʾid*, poetry and *ādāb*, according to their thematic content. Persian books contain two types of titles: *taṣawwuf*-related books and dictionaries. The first group includes sixteen titles, generally Sufi-related poetic works, while the second group comprises six dictionaries. Sufi poetic books may eventually be divided into two groups: The first comprises Sufi poems by well-known poets and commentaries on them; the second consists of poetic works by famous Sufi masters.[21]

The first Persian title in the inventory of al-Jazzār Library is *al-Mathnawī al-Maʿnawī* (*Mathnavī-i Maʿnavī* in Persian) by Mawlānā Jalāl al-Dīn al-Rūmī (d. 672/1273), one of the well-known, if not the most famous, of Muslim authors of the thirteenth century. He founded the Sufi order, called the Mawlaviyya (or Mevleviye, in Turkish) after his name.[22] The *al-Mathnavī al-Maʿnavī* is the main text read in that Sufi order/network until today. Although it is written in Persian, it was circulated and consumed in the Ottoman lands more than in the Persian-speaking territories. *Mathnavī* has also become the name of a genre in Ottoman and modern Turkish literature. *Mathnavī* could often refer to either Rūmī's work or the genre, including in modern Turkish. Many translations of the work, commentaries on it, dictionaries dedicated to it, recensions and collections of excerpts from the *Mathnavī-i Maʿnavī* have been penned throughout time and passed down after Rūmī's death. In that sense, it is one of the most influential texts written in Islamic history.

The Jazzār library inventory includes five manuscripts of the *Mathnavī-i Maʿnavī*. The first entry in the list (#1553) contains the full name of the work, whereas the remaining four (#1554, #1555, #1556 and #1557) are titled *al-Mathnawī* by the scribe, assuming that the reader will know it is Rūmī's. The function of the text was twofold: pedagogically, to teach the Mavlavī order and, at the same time, to let students improve their Persian language skills. The pedagogical function was implemented in Mavlavī lodges called *Mevlevīkhāne* in Turkish. According to Kātib Çelebi, almost all big cities inhabited mostly by Arab people, such as Aleppo,[23] Damascus,[24] Hama, Homs, Tripoli,[25]

17 Aljoumani, *Maktaba Madrasiyya*, 108–112.
18 Aljoumani, *Maktaba Madrasiyya*, 75, 102.
19 Aljoumani, "Masrad Kutub Madrasa", 18.
20 Ibrāhīm, "Makataba ʿUthmāniyya", 1–35.
21 Murat Umut İnan conducted research on how Ottomans read and used Persian classics, specifically Persian poetry. See İnan, "Ottoman Reading Persian Classics", 160–181.
22 For an introduction to al-Rūmī, see Ritter/Bausani, "Djalāl al-Dīn Rūmī"; and the Mavlaviyya, see Öngören, "Mevlânâ Celâleddîn-i Rûmî", 441–448; Yazıcı et al., "Mawlawiyya"; Tanrıkorur, "Mevleviyye", 468–475.
23 Küçük, "Halep Mevlevihanesi", 78, 80, 81, 89.
24 Küçük, "Suriye'de İki Mevlevihane", 288, 290, 312, 313.
25 De Jong, "The Takīya of the Mawlawiyya in Tripolis", 92, 94; Glassen, "Trablusşam Mevlevihanesi", 28.

Latakia, Jerusalem,[26] Medina, Mecca, Cairo, Baghdad, Mosul and Kirkuk, housed a Mavlavī lodge.[27]

Jāmiʿ al-Āyāt Sharḥ al-Abyāt (#1567) by Ismāʿīl Rüsūḫī Anḳaravī (d. 1041/1631) is a well-known commentary on the *Mathnavī-i Maʿnavī*. Anḳaravī was among the most prominent commentators of al-Rūmī in the Ottoman Empire, a fame that earned him the title 'the commentator' (*shāriḥ*).[28] This book could be considered as a commentary on *Mathnavī*, because Anḳaravī explains verses of the Qur'an and sayings of the Prophet Muḥammad as well as some problematic couplets in Arabic used in *Mathnavī* to make the book understandable for all readers. Thus, it is, in a way, a guide to reading and understanding the *Mathnavī* in a 'correct' way.

In addition, the inventory of the Jazzār library contains books by three luminary Persian poets: Saʿdī-i Shirāzī (d. 691/1292), Khvāja Shams al-Dīn Muḥammad al-Ḥāfiẓ al-Shirāzī (d. 792/1390) and Niẓāmī-i Ganjavī, Abū Muḥammad Jamāl al-Dīn Ilyās b. Yūsuf b. Zakī (d. 611/1214). They are, according to many literary historians of Persian literature, among the most influential poets of all times.[29]

Saʿdī-i Shirāzī is famous for his *Gulistān* and *Bustān*, both of which were used to teach students Persian. There are numerous translations and commentaries of *Gulistān* and *Bustān*, which is a sign of their fame and influence. The section has two copies of *Sharḥ-i Gulistān* (#1562 and #1563), a commentary on Saʿdī-i Shirāzī's masterpiece *Gulistān*. However, it is impossible to identify these titles with certainty, although it is probably the commentary written by Sūdī-i Bosnevī (d. 1007/1599) because of its popularity among Ottoman (Rūmī) readers. The section also includes a certain *Kitāb-i Bustān* (#1564). Even though the name of the author of *Kitāb-i Bustān* was not mentioned, it is most probably the famous *Bustān* authored by Saʿdī-i Shirāzī, his second masterpiece. What is of interest here is that the inventory has *Bustān*, but two commentaries on *Gulistān* instead of the book itself. There should be no need to have a separate copy of the Gulistān as the famous commentators of the *Gulistān* and *Bustān*, such as Bosnevī, Şemʿī (d. 1011/1602–1603) and Sūdī (d. 1007/1599), included the original text of *Gulistān* and *Bustān* in their commentaries.[30]

Dīwān al-Ḥāfiẓ al-Shirāzī (#1565 and #1566) is doubtlessly the famous *Dīvān* by Khvāja Shams al-Dīn Muḥammad al-Ḥāfiẓ al-Shirāzī (d. 792/1390). The first copy was registered as *Dīvān al-Ḥāfiẓ al-Shirāzī*, whereas the second one was recorded as *Dīwān al-Ḥāfiẓ*. Ḥāfiẓ is, according to many, the most significant poet in the Persian literary tradition, and his Dīvān *al-Ḥāfiẓ al-Shirāzī* has numerous copies all around the world. Thus, it is natural that this small Persian collection has two copies of his *Dīvān*.

Another prominent Persian poet is Niẓāmī-i Ganjavī, Abū Muḥammad Jamāl al-Dīn Ilyās b. Yūsuf b. Zakī (d. 611/1214), known by his *khamsa* (five *mathnavī*s). The inventory describes the manuscript as the summary of the *Khamsa*, *Khulāṣat al-Khamsa* (#1571), without any qualifications. Although many other poets have written *khamsa*s, the work most probably refers to Niẓāmī-i Ganjavī's work (albeit he never authored the work, most recensions are collections made on his behalf). Since all these titles were monuments of Persian eloquence, they are listed in this section. Besides, they are listed for pedagogical use.

As argued above, the uttermost feature of those books for the scribe who compiled the inventory is that they are written in Persian. *Manẓūm bi-al-Fārisī* (#1570) could be any verse book written

26 Tütüncü, "Kudüs Mevlevîhânesi Tarihi ve Mimarisi", 701.

27 Kreiser, "Evliya Çelebi ve Başka".

28 For his life and works, see Yazıcı, "Ismāʿīl Rusūkh al-Dīn Ismāʿīl b. Aḥmad al-Anḳarawī"; Yetik, "Ankaravî, İsmâil Rusûhî", 211–213.

29 For the authors in question, see, respectively, Davis, "Saʿdī"; Çiçekler, "Saʿdî-i Şîrâzî", 405–407; Wickens, "Ḥāfiẓ"; Yazıcı, "Hâfız-ı Şîrâzî", 103–106; Chelkowski, "Niẓāmī Gandjawī"; Kanar, "Nizâmî-i Gencevî", 183–185.

30 For the biographies and works of them, see Burrill, "Sūdī"; Aruçi, "Sûdî Bosnevî", 466; de Bruijn, "Shemʿī"; Öztürk, "Şemʿî", 503–504.

in Persian. Similarly, *Zī al-Fārisī* (#1572), similar to *Manẓūm bi-al-Fārisī*, was an unidentifiable versed work written in Persian. The work *Risāla-i Tawḥīd bi-al-Fārisī* (#1561) is unidentifiable. It is a treatise on theology (*Tawḥīd*) written in Persian. According to the bibliographic sources, several authors could have penned such theological treatises.

Similarly, the work referred to in the inventory as *Salmān al-Fārisī* (#1568) is unidentifiable. The famous companion of the Prophet Muḥammad, Salmān al-Fārisī, did not author any books as far as we can tell from the recorded literary tradition.[31] Nevertheless, *Masā'il al-Ruhbān* and *Kitāb Ḥadīth Cāthīlīk* were attributed to him in some sources.[32] It should be one of these titles providing the scribe registers the name of the book or the author correctly.

It is not easy to find out if there is any book absent in this list compared to other libraries because it is hard to find any section devoted to Persian manuscripts in other libraries in *bilād al-Shām*.

The remaining titles in the Persian books section are dictionaries used primarily in the Ottoman *madrasas* and literary circles. Though poets, scholars and non-specialists of every age could use bilingual dictionaries for different purposes, they are used mainly as pedagogical tools to teach pupils Persian.

The first dictionary mentioned in the inventory is *Tuḥfe-i Shāhidī*, a well-known Persian-Turkish dictionary used in the Ottoman Empire. This title indicates that Turkish speakers were among the audiences of the library (or at least passed through the city and left their copy) because only a person who can read Turkish in Acre might use this dictionary; the governor or his librarians followed a well-established pattern, as the book was among the primary texts used in the *madrasa* curriculum in core lands of the empire (and beyond) throughout the Ottoman period.

The inventory of the Jazzār library lists three copies of *Tuḥfe-i Shāhidī*.[33] The first two of them were recorded as *Shāhidī* (#1558 and #1559), whereas the full name of the book, *Tuḥfe-i Shāhidī*, was used for the third one (#1560). Numerous commentaries were written on *Tuḥfe-i Shāhidī* in the Ottoman era.[34] The inventory includes a commentary on this dictionary (#1574), *Sharḥ al-Shāhidī*. The scribe has used the Arabic compound noun instead of the Persian *iẓāfat* in recording the name of the commentary, which shows the interchangeable use of languages by the scribe in the inventory and the multilingual character of eighteenth-century Acre.

Some other Persian-Turkish or Turkish-Persian dictionaries exist in the Persian books section of the inventory. The first one, *Kitāb-ı Niʿmetullāh, Türkī* (#1569), was compiled to help students learn Persian. Two dictionaries, including this title, were written in the sixteenth and seventeenth centuries by Niʿmetullāh b. Aḥmed b. Mübārek el-Rūmī (d. 969/1561) and Bursalı Nakibzāde Niʿmetī (d. 1060/1650), respectively.[35] The second dictionary held at the library is another unidentifiable Turkish-Persian dictionary (#1573), referred to as *Lughat-i Türkī-Fārisī*.

The most critical absence in the inventory regarding the Persian-Turkish dictionaries is *Tuḥfe-i Vehbī*, the well-known work by Sünbül-zāde Meḥmed Efendi (d. 1224/1809), written in 1197/1782. The *Tuḥfe* was such a popular dictionary in the

31 For the legend of Salmān al-Fārisī, see Vida, "Salmān al-Fārisī"; Hatiboğlu, "Selmân-ı Fârisî", 441–443.

32 This is a *ḥadīth* argued to be transmitted by Salmān al-Fārisī. Cāthīlīk is a Christian priest according to the *ḥadīth*. See http://shiaonlinelibrary.com/ _4050/الكتب نفس-الرحمن-في-فضائل-سلمان-ميرزا-حسين-النوري-الطبرسي الصفحة/_223#top, 236, 489–512.

33 See the library inventory, Vakıflar Genel Müdürlüğü (Ankara), Defter 1626, Persian Books 64.

34 For an introduction to İbrāhīm Şāhidī, the author of Tuḥfe-i Şāhidī, see Çıpan, "İbrâhim Şâhidî", 273–274. For commentaries written on İbrāhīm Şāhidī's Tuḥfe, see Öz, *Tuhfe-i Şâhidî Şerhleri*.

35 See Berthels, "Niʿmat Allāh b. Aḥmad"; Niʿmetullāh Aḥmed, *Lugat-i Niʿmetu'llâh*; Mehtap Erdoğan, "Niʿmetî". For the latter, also see Top, "Bursalı Şâir Nakîbzâde Niʿmetî", 280–287.

Ottoman era that it has more than four hundred copies in the manuscript libraries in Turkey.[36] Even if it is a fact that *Tuḥfe-i Vehbī* imitated a previous work penned by Şāhidī Ahmed Dede, which was generated and used for educational purposes, its widespread use critically had an impact on the use of Şāhidī's work from the late eighteenth century onwards.[37]

In conclusion, the titles in the Persian section of the inventory demonstrate characteristics of the Ottoman writerly culture, and, in all likelihood, the audience of this section consisted of essentially Turkish speakers. It is reasonable to argue that the books in the inventory were used for educational purposes in Ottoman scholarly circles, and the collection itself is designed to be part of an Ottoman(ised) library, as indicated in Chapter 1 by Açıl, İpek and Burak in this volume.[38]

2 Turkish Books

The inventory of the Jazzār library includes fifty-six Turkish books, most unidentifiable because the scribe registered them by generic names. Those titles are related to diverse subject matters from rational theology, recitation of the Qur'an, exegesis of the Qur'an, sayings of the Prophet Muḥammad, jurisprudence, *taṣawwuf*, many genres of literature in verse and prose, laws regarding military (*ḳānūn-nāme*), political and social regulations, manuals of Islamic faith, worship and catechisms (*'ilm al-ḥāl*), and a dictionary. Therefore, this is a Turkish miniature of a complete *madrasa* library seen throughout the Ottoman Empire, especially regarding the classification of the sciences.

Similar to the Persian titles, the scribe, in most cases, provides just the theme and the language of books. This implies that what is essential to him or the prospective user(s) in registering the texts is not the name of the authors but the theme and the language alone. This is yet another reminder that the inventory was not a library catalogue in the modern sense. Instead, it should be arranged as a reminder for the scribe, the library's administrator or the founder, Aḥmad Pasha al-Jazzār, because he would identify a book by knowing its theme and language. This feature of the inventory might also indicate that the scribe of the original inventory was probably not proficient enough in Turkish to provide all the details.

2.1 *Identified Authors*

Though most of the authors remain unknown because of the scribe's method of registering the items, some well-known authors of the titles in the inventory could still be identified. Some of those authors are identifiable by their book's title, though, in some cases, this may turn out to be quite challenging. Twenty-six of fifty-six titles are identifiable with high probability and subdivided into three categories: *taṣawwuf*-related titles, dictionaries and miscellanea.

Taḳiyüddīn Meḥmed Birgivī (d. 981/1573), one of the most influential Ottoman scholars of his time and in the centuries following his death,[39] is represented by six books in the inventory. The only book by Birgivī registered by its name in the Turkish books section is his *Vaṣiyyet-nāme* (#1614), a famous catechism (*'ilm al-ḥāl*), which highly influenced Ottoman culture. Numerous commentaries were written on the work.[40] The remaining five books were registered just as *Birgili* (#1591, #1592, #1593, #1594 and #1595). The scribe did not mention the names of the books in these entries. Although the author penned numerous books, he

36 See search result for *Tuḥfe-i Vehbī* at https://portal.yek.gov.tr/works/search/full?key=tuhfe-i+vehbi&search_key_type=3&search_form_type=ALL_FIELDS.

37 Björkman/Burrill, "Sünbül-Zāde Wehbī"; Kuru, "Sünbülzâde Vehbî", TDVIA, 40–141.

38 See Açıl, İpek and Burak's Chapter 1 in this volume for the characteristics of the Jazzār library.

39 For more on Birgivī Mehmed, see Küfrevî, "Birgewī"; Yüksel, "Birgivî".

40 See Kaylı, "A Critical Study of Birgivi Mehmed Efendi's", 146–255.

was famous for three works: *Vaṣiyyet-nāme, ʿIlm-i Ḥāl* and *Tarīḳat ül-Muḥammadiyye*. As can be seen above, entry #1614 refers to the catechistic work. The rest of the entries may be additional copies of the work, as the *Ṭarīḳat ül-Muḥammadiyye* (*al-Ṭarīqa al-Muḥammadiyya*) appears elsewhere in the inventory.

Another famous author is Aḥmed-i Bīcān (d. 870/1466) of the Yazıcızāde family, a renowned scholar, Sufi, translator and prose writer.[41] His name was registered in the inventory (#1602) instead of the book title. It is well-known that some books were known by their authors' reputations in the Islamic manuscript tradition, as in the Ottoman Empire. But this is not the case with Aḥmed-i Bīcān because he has more than one masterpiece (among his best-known works, one can list *Envār ül-ʿĀşıḳīn, Dürr-i Meknūn* and *ʿAcāʾib ül-Makhlūḳāt*). This record proves the comments above that some inventory titles serve as a reminder because the scribe or the library founder already knew which of Aḥmed-i Bīcān's books they owned and the insufficient knowledge of Turkish of the original scribe. The title meant in the inventory might be a *taṣawwuf*-related one because Aḥmed-i Bīcān was famous for his *taṣawwuf* works, such as *Envār ül-ʿĀşıḳīn, Dürr-i Meknūn* or *ʿAcāʾib ül-Makhlūḳāt*.[42]

Entries #1589, #1599 and #1615 contain titles related to *taṣawwuf*. The first one is registered under the name *Tercemet ül-Geylānī*. Although it is not apparent, it might be a translation of the work by the Sufi master ʿAbdülḳādir el-Geylānī (d. 561/1166) by Ismail Kemal Ümmî (d. 1475),[43] known as *Tercüme-i ʿAbdülḳādir el-Geylānī*. *Kitāb fī Sırr ül-Ḥurūf* (#1599) is unidentifiable by the name registered, but another famous Sufi author, Ismāʿīl Haḳḳı Bursevī (d. 1137/1725),[44] penned a book called *Kitāb fī Esrār ül-Ḥurūf*, which is most probably the title meant by the scribe. The book by Bursevī is about the numeric, lettrist equivalent of the Arabic letters (*abjad*). The last Sufi text among the Turkish titles is *Mecmūʿ ul-Leṭāʾif* (#1615). Though the name *Leṭāʾif* might be a generic one, with the plural form of *laṭīfe*, ʿIsmāʿīl Rüsūḫī Ankaravī (d. 1041/1631) authored a book called *Mecmūʿat ül-Leṭāʾif ve Maṭmūret ül-Maʿārif*. The intention of the scribe in using the *Mecmūʿ ul-Leṭāʾif* might be this title, even though it could not be ascertained.

Though, at first glance, it seems like a political title, *Kitāb fīʾl-Khilāfet* (#1590) is also a *taṣawwuf*-related book because a work *Cevāhir-i Tāc-ı Khilāfet* by the famous Sufi Ṣalāḥuddīn al-ʿUşşāḳī (d. 1197/1783) under this name could not be identified.[45] Therefore, it is not a title concerning the political caliphate in general but an interpretation of the role of the caliphate in the Sufi Ottoman discourse.

Arabic-Turkish and Persian-Turkish dictionaries find their place in Turkish books. Among them is the well-known Arabic-Turkish dictionary *Akhterī-i Kebīr* by Akhterī, Musliḥüddīn Muṣṭafā (d. 968/1560–1561), registered as *Tercümān ül-Akhterī* (#1629).[46] Another Arabic-Turkish dictionary was recorded under the name *Türkī ve ʿArabī* (#1627). It is probably a Turkish-Arabic dictionary, which is unidentifiable as it is unknown whether it is in verse or prose. *Kitāb-ı Ibn Feriştā* (#1613) is also an Arabic-Turkish dictionary by ʿAbdül-laṭīf ibn Melek (d. after 1418).[47] The dictionary has numerous copies, known as *Ferişteoğlu* in Turkish. The last dictionary was recorded as *Tercümān, Türkī* (#1628), which is unidentifiable.

41 See Ménage, "Bīdjān"; Çelebioğlu, "Ahmed Bîcan", 49–51.

42 Though *ʿAcāʾib ül-Makhlūḳāt*, at first glance, is about Islamic cosmography, it is a cosmography interpreted and narrated by a Sūfī author.

43 For his biography and works, see Ünver, "Kemâl Ümmî", 229–230.

44 For a long introductive entry on this prolific Sufi author, see Namlı et al., "İsmâil Hakkı Bursevî", 102–110; Kut, "Ismāʿīl Ḥaḳḳī".

45 Semih Ceyhan, "Salâhî Efendi", 17–19.

46 Hulusi Kılıç, "Ahterî", 184–185.

47 For *Ferişteoğlu*, see Akün, "Firishte-Oghlu"; Baktır, "İbn Melek", 175–176.

Kitāb-ı Ibn Ferişṭā, as Guy Burak quoted from Saçaklızāde, was one of the dictionaries used in the order of the sciences for a person who wanted to be a scholar in the Ottoman *madrasa* system. Burak, who argues that Saçaklızāde was 'aware of the different linguistic backgrounds of the students across the Empire',[48] translated an excerpt from the well-known book *Tartīb al-ʿUlūm* by Saçaklızāde (d. 1732–1733) on the order of sciences when learning them. In this passage, the author wrote about *Ibn Ferişṭā* as follows:

Then, he should be ordered to study the entire Qurʾān. Then, he should be ordered to study and memorise *Lughat Ibn Firishta*. After having studied *Lughat Ibn Firishta*, be he young or mature, he should be ordered to study the science of morphology (*ṣarf*), then grammar (*naḥw*), then [jurisprudential] practical rulings (*ʿilm al-aḥkām*), then logic, the disputation (*munāẓara*), then theology (*kalām*), then rhetoric (*maʿānī*), then the fundamentals of jurisprudence and the jurisprudence.[49]

According to Saçaklızāde, non-Arabic speakers must memorise the dictionary to promote their education in Islamic sciences. This may explain why the scribe recorded *Kitāb-ı Ibn Ferişṭā* in the Turkish section since it was principally intended to be used by non-Arabic speakers, in this case, Turkish speakers.

One remarkable fact about those dictionaries is that the scribe uses the term *Tercümān* (literally 'translator') to mean dictionary (*lugha*). This should be a figurative (*mecāzī*) use of language, because dictionaries help people understand what is said or written, just as translators do, and they are also apparatuses for learning Arabic.

The third subcategory of Turkish books is unidentifiable titles in terms of their contents. Nevertheless, it seems they were used to fulfil the various needs of different readers, from how to recite the Qur'an to how to act appropriately regarding law and administrative issues.

Particular *Tecvīd* works were recorded (#1582, #1583 and #1584) without mentioning any names related to the book or the author. In earlier centuries, before the establishment of the Jazzār library, many books or booklets regarding the Holy Qur'an were written because reciting the Holy Qur'an correctly was a crucial issue among Muslims.[50] The most famous book called *Tecvīd* was *Ḳarabaş Tecvīdi* by Şeykh ʿAbdürraḥmān Karabaşī (904/1498).[51] Therefore, it is highly probable that the *Tecvīd* implied is *Ḳarabaş Tecvīdi*. Three copies of the *Tecvīd* might indicate a need to learn how to recite the Holy Qur'an and an educational goal pursued at the library.

There are titles related to reports to make the sultan understand how to regulate defects in governmental issues. *Tedbīr-i Cedīd-nāme* has two copies in the inventory in consecutive numbers (#1600 and #1601). Although the authors were unspecified in the list, there are two probable authors: Dağıstanlı ʿAlī Paşa (d. 1194/1780) and Canikli ʿAlī Paşa (d. 1199/1785), whose works are known as *Tedbīr-i Cedīd-i Nādir*.[52] *Ādāb ül-Mülūk* (#1618), which is probably *Rebīʿ ül-Mülk ve Adâbü Sülūk il-Mülūk* by Pertevī ʿAlī Efendi (d. 1076/1665), is also this kind of text used to advise the sultan against disorders.[53] Another title which might be treated

48 Burak, "On the Order of the Sciences", 39.

49 Burak, "On the Order of the Sciences", 40.

50 As Shady Nasser states in Chapter 14 in this volume, 'Qirāʾat and tajwīd, had been already fixed, standardized, and institutionalised' which facilitates reciting the Qu'ran accordingly.

51 Şeykh ʿAbd al-Raḥmān Karabaşī's biography has not yet been studied. For his famous work, see ʿAbd al-Raḥmān Karabaşī, *Tecvīd-i Karabaş*. For a study on Ottoman Tecvīds written in verse and prose, see Gökdemir, "Genel Hatlarıyla Osmanlı Tecvid Eserleri".

52 For a comprehensive study on the latter, see Özkaya, "Canikli Ali Paşa"; Karagöz, *Canikli Ali Paşa*. Also see Lewis, "Djānīkli Ḥadjdji ʿAlī Pasha". Yücel Özkaya proves convincingly that Dağıstanlı ʿAlī Paşa had not authored this work. See Özkaya, "Canikli Ali Paşa'nın Risalesi 'Tedâbirü'l-Gazavât'".

53 Pertevî Ali Efendi, *Rebîü'l-Mülk ve Âdâbü Sülûki'l-Mülûk*.

as bureaucratic writing is a kind of briefing by Ḳoca Rāġıp Paşa (d. 1176/1763)[54] to summarise the issues to bring to the sultan's attention. Thus, the title *Telkhīṣāt, Türkī* (#1623) should be this work by Koca Rāġıp Paşa. Another possible author for the same title is Ḳoçi Bey (d. ca. 1650),[55] who has a work called *Telkhīsāt* that contains advice for the sultan. These titles were especially crucial for Acre and the *bilād al-Shām*, where Aḥmad Pasha al-Jazzār wanted to rule and govern.[56]

Behcet ül-Futuvvā (#1598) is unidentifiable, but a well-known *fatwa*-collection by Şeykhulislām ʿAbdullāh Efendi (d. 1156/1743) called *Behcet ül-Fetāvā* exists.[57] Though it is unclear, having a *fatwa*-collection by a şeykhulislām in a library established in a city far from the capital is plausible. The title *Taḳvīm* (#1608) is ambiguous because it is unclear which theme and authors were meant by the scribe. There are four possible titles and authors for this entry: 1. Aḥmed-i Dāʿī (d. 824/1421), *Terceme-i Sī Faṣl fīʾl-Taḳvīm*;[58] 2. Vaḥyī (d. 960/1519–1520), *Taḳvīm*;[59] 3. Bahāyī, Ḥasan Çelebi (d. 1660), *Taḳvīm ül-Ḳavīm*;[60] and 4. Kātib Çelebi (d. 1067/1657), *Taḳvīm ül-Tevārīkh*.[61] The same argument is valid for the *Mecmūʿa-i Dīvān* (#1603) because there are six possible manuscript entries found in the libraries.[62] The title *Mecmaʿ ul-Cevāhir* (#1609) has two probable authors according to modern manuscript library catalogues: Süleymaniye Library, Hacı Mahmud Efendi 4493, Ḥasan Naṣūḥ b. el-Bosnevī (d.?), or Süleymaniye Library, Reşid Efendi 845, Cemālī (d.?).

2.2 *Unidentified, Generic Titles*

Thirty out of fifty-six Turkish manuscripts are unidentified because they were registered so generically that an observer needs help understanding what the scribe or the founder meant. Nevertheless, I will categorise these unidentified titles in terms of the generic names attributed to them. Some of those titles are recorded as just *Risāle, Türkī or Türkiyye*, as is the case with entries #1610, #1616, #1619 and #1630 while some others are recorded as *Kitāb, Türkī* (see entries #1606, #1607 and #1622). The term *risāle* denotes treatises in Turkish, which means these texts are not book-length. It is specified that some books were in verse: entry #1596 was a *mes̱nevī*, #1597 a *ḳaṣīde* whose content is also mentioned, #1605 as are several rhymed works (#1611 and #1626). The title in #1624 was registered as *Mecmūʿa-i Türkī*, which is unidentified because it is unclear what kind of miscellany it was. Another manuscript recorded as *Mes̱nevī-i Türkī* (#1596) is also unidentifiable because it is impossible to specify the author.

Most titles related to religious (*şerʿī*) sciences are unidentifiable because the scribe only mentions their subject matter and, in some cases, the language, Turkish, was specified: *Kitāb-ı Aḳīde* (#1576), *Miʿrāc, Türkī* (#1577), *Aḳāʾid, Türkī* (#1578), *Ḳavāʿid ül-Īmān* (#1579), *Ḥadīs̱, Türkī* (#1580), *Tefsīr, Türkī* (#1581), *Şerḥ-i Fıḳh* (#1588), *Kitāb-ı Taṣrīf* (#1620), *Kitāb-ı Lugha, Fārisī* (#1621)[63] and *Tekmīl Şerīʿat* (#1625). They are about rational theology, the ascension mirage of the Prophet Muḥammad, Qu'ranic commentary, jurisprudence, Ara-

54 Franz Babinger, "Rāghib Pasha"; Aydıner, "Râgıb Paşa", 403–406.

55 Colin Imber, "Ḳoči Beg"; Akün, "Koçi Bey", 143–148.

56 For 'the image-making power of books' of which Aḥmad Pasha al-Jazzār was aware and, thus, implemented through his library inventory, see Dana Sajdi's Chapter 22 in this volume.

57 For brief information on the şeykhulislām in question and his fatwa-collection, see İpşirli, "Abdullah Efendi, Yenişehirli", 100–101; Özel, "Behcetü'l-Fetâvâ", 346.

58 İz, "Dāʿī"; Kut, "Ahmed-i Dâî", 56–58.

59 Köksal, "Vahyî". Also see Ekinci, "Klasik Türk Edebiyatında Mizahî Takvimler".

60 Ramazan Ekinci, "Bahâyî, Küfrî, Hasan Çelebi".

61 Gökyay, "Kātib Čelebi"; Gökyay, "Kâtib Çelebi", 36–40.

62 Those six items are: 1. Süleymaniye Hasib Efendi 478, *Mecmūʿa-i Dīvān-ı Makhṭūmī* by *Makhṭūmī* Vāḥid (d. 1145/1732–1733); 2, 3, 4 and 5. Süleymaniye İzmirli İ. Hakkı 3399, Edirne BAD. 2357, Edirne BAD. 2365, and Edirne BAD. 2367, *Mecmūʿa-i Dīvān*; 6. Zeytinoğlu 333; *Dīvān Mecmūʿası*.

63 This title seems to be in Persian. It is classified under Turkish books since it is a Persian-Turkish or Turkish-Persian dictionary.

bic morphology, (probably) Turkish-Persian dictionary, and *sharīʿa*, Islamic canonical law in general.

A certain *Taʿbīr-nāme* (#1604) might be a dream interpretation that was very popular in the Ottoman Empire.[64] More than one hundred manuscript copies of Turkish *Taʿbīr-nāme*s are preserved in manuscript libraries in Turkey.[65] They have a Sufistic tone in their style and way of interpretation. Nevertheless, it is unidentifiable which *Taʿbīr-nāme* was meant by the scribe. The same is true for the *Ḳānūn-nāme* (#1617), because it is unclear to which genre it belongs. It may be a book on the laws regarding land and general state rules as *Fātiḥ Ḳānūn-nāmesi*, and so on. Hundreds of entries came up when searching by name, *Ḳānūn-nāme*. The title *Muḥyī ül-Emvāt* (#1612) seems to be the name of a book, but I could not find a manuscript with this name. Another possibility is that it is a book regulating or reforming the rules on goods.

One of the essential books in the inventory is *Şurūṭ ül-Ṣalāt*, which has three copies (#1585, #1586, and #1587). *Şurūṭ ül-Ṣalāt* is a branch of jurisprudence, being a kind of catechism related to issues on faith, praying and ablution. Works in this genre were penned in both verse and prose. Manuscript libraries include numerous copies of the *Şurūṭ ül-Ṣalāt*, most of them are in Arabic. Most of the Turkish *Şurūṭ ül-Ṣalāt* manuscripts are somehow translations of or commentaries to Arabic *Şurūṭ ül-Ṣalāt* whether it is stated in the text or not. Therefore, which author the scribe meant is unidentifiable.

The last title I want to elaborate on is *Enʿām-ı Şerīf* (#1575). Turkish manuscript libraries are full of *Enʿām-ı Şerīf*s because they were widely copied and used in the Ottoman era. This kind of manuscript allows worshippers to recite the Holy Qu'ran at a given time because it comprises divided parts. Around the year 1500, another format of the Qur'an gradually developed in Ottoman Turkey. It consisted of selected chapters of the Qur'an in one volume. After the eighteenth century, these works became known as *enʿam-ı şerif* in Turkish as they usually began with the sixth chapter of the Qur'an, *sura al-Anʿām* (The Cattle), often preceded by the first sura, *al-Fātiḥa* (the Opening).[66]

Therefore, this title arguably indicates how deeply the profile of the Jazzār library was embedded in Ottoman writerly culture.

Since this section is not a common one comparing other inventories or libraries located in *bilād al-shām*, it is impossible to identify the expected or absent titles in this section. The inventory contains titles that Turkish-speaking or Turkish-reading audiences and rulers sent to Acre by the central government might require or want to read.

3 Conclusion(s)

The Jazzār library was founded in the eighteenth century in Acre, where the language of communication was principally Arabic. Nevertheless, Turkish, Persian and Kurdish were among the other languages used daily in Acre. Although the language used in the library's inventory was Arabic and most of the books were written in Arabic, there were also some Turkish and Persian books in the library. Because of that phenomenon, the inventory categorised all titles in terms of their themes except Turkish and Persian books. These two sections were organised based on their languages.

Persian books comprise two main groups of works: Sufi poetry and dictionaries. In the Ottoman context, Sufi poetry and Persian-Turkish dictionaries were used for educational purposes; examining the titles recorded in the inventory, it is apparent that these titles are no exception to this rule. An-

64 See Liana Saif's Chapter 24 in this volume.

65 Abdurrahman Otugüzel itemises 106 manuscripts preserved in Turkish Libraries. See Otugüzel "Tabir-nâme", 5–22.

66 Rettig, "The Rise of the Enʿam", 185; Bain, "The En'an-ı Şerif".

other remarkable feature of Sufi poetry-related titles in the list is that they are either written by Ottoman poets or Persian Sufi poets who were well-known in the scholarly circles of the imperial centres and well beyond.

The identified Turkish books comprise *taṣawwuf*-related titles, dictionaries and miscellanea, whereas it is not easy to classify unidentified titles. Unidentified Turkish titles were recorded so generically that one can only understand the theme and language of the work from the register. It seems that what is essential regarding these titles for the scribe is their themes and language. Another possible interpretation is that the scribe needs to have adequate Turkish knowledge to include the relevant information about the work.

Although the implied addressees of the library were Turkish-speaking users, it is evident that the scribe of the inventory needs to know the traditional customs of preparing inventories valid in the Ottoman capital sufficiently.

Bibliography

ʿAbd al-Raḥmān Karabaşī, Şeykh. *Tecvīd-i Karabaş*. İstanbul 1863.

Akün, Ömer Faruk. "Firishte-Oghlu." In *EI* (***Encyclopaedia of Islam New Edition Online*** [***EI-2 English***]). Second Edition, 143–148. http://dx.doi.org/10.1163/1573-3912_islam_SIM_2379 (accessed 23 February 2023).

Akün, Ömer Faruk. "Koçi Bey." In *Türkiye Diyanet Vakfi İslam Ansiklopedisi* (*Encyclopaedia of Islam*), 143–148. Ankara.

Aljoumani, Said. "Masrad Kutub Madrasa Muḥammad Başa al-ʿAẓm: Nashr wa-Dirāsa." *Majalla Maʿhad al-Makhṭūṭāt al-ʿArabiyya* XXI, no. 2 (2017): 10–73.

Aljoumani, Said. *Maktaba madrasiyya fī Ḥalab Nihāyat al-ʿAhd al-ʿUthmānī: al-Daftar al-Mujaddad li-kutub waqf ʿUthmān Bāshā al-Dūrikī*. Beirut, 2019.

Aruçi, Muhammed. "Sûdî Bosnevî." In *Türkiye Diyanet Vakfi İslam Ansiklopedisi* (*Encyclopaedia of Islam*), 466. Istanbul.

Aydıner, Mesut. "Râgıb Paşa." In *Türkiye Diyanet Vakfi İslam Ansiklopedisi* (*Encyclopaedia of Islam*), 403–406. Ankara.

Babinger, Franz. "Rāghib Pasha." In *EI* (***Encyclopaedia of Islam New Edition Online*** [***EI-2 English***]). Second Edition. http://dx.doi.org/10.1163/1573-3912_islam_SIM_6189 (accessed 23 February 2023).

Bain, Alexandra. "The En'am-ı Şerif: Sacred Text and Images in a Late Ottoman Prayer Book." *Archivum Ottomanicum* 19 (2001): 213–238.

Baktır, Mustafa. "İbn Melek." In *Türkiye Diyanet Vakfi İslam Ansiklopedisi* (*Encyclopaedia of Islam*), 175–176. Ankara.

Beers, Theodore S. "Paths Crossing in Damascus: Familiarity with Persian among Eleventh/Seventeenth-Century Arabic Literati." *Philological Encounters* 7/3–4 (2022): 238–267.

Berthels, E. "Niʿmat Allāh b. Aḥmad." In *EI* (***Encyclopaedia of Islam New Edition Online*** [***EI-2 English***]). Second Edition. http://dx.doi.org/10.1163/1573-3912_islam_SIM_5914 (accessed 23 February 2023).

Björkman, W. and Burrill, Kathleen. "Sünbül-Zāde Wehbī." In *EI* (***Encyclopaedia of Islam New Edition Online*** [***EI-2 English***]). https://doi.org/10.1163/9789004206106_eifo_COM_1122 (accessed 23 February 2023).

Burak, Guy. "On the Order of the Sciences He Who Wants to Learn Them." In *A Handbook and Reader of Ottoman Arabic*, edited by Esther-Miriam Wagner, 39–42. Cambridge, 2021.

Burrill, Kathleen. "Sūdī." In *EI* (***Encyclopaedia of Islam New Edition Online*** [***EI-2 English***]). Second Edition. http://dx.doi.org/10.1163/1573-3912_islam_SIM_7121 (accessed 23 February 2023).

Ceyhan, Semih. "Salâhî Efendi." In *Türkiye Diyanet Vakfi İslam Ansiklopedisi* (*Encyclopaedia of Islam*), 17–19. Ankara.

Chelkowski, P. "Niẓāmī Gandjawī." In *EI* (***Encyclopaedia of Islam New Edition Online*** [***EI-2 English***]). Second Edition. http://dx.doi.org/10.1163/1573-3912_islam_SIM_5948 (accessed 23 February 2023).

Çelebioğlu, Âmil. "Ahmed Bîcan." In *Türkiye Diyanet Vakfi İslam Ansiklopedisi* (*Encyclopaedia of Islam*), 49–51. Ankara.

Çıpan, Mustafa. "İbrâhim Şâhidî." In *Türkiye Diyanet Vakfi İslam Ansiklopedisi* (*Encyclopaedia of Islam*), 273–274. Ankara.

Çiçekler, Mustafa. "Saʿdî-i Şîrâzî." In *Türkiye Diyanet Vakfı İslam Ansiklopedisi* (*Encyclopaedia of Islam*), 405–407. Ankara.

Davis, R. "Saʿdī." In *EI* (***Encyclopaedia of Islam New Edition Online*** [***EI-2 English***]). Second Edition. http://dx.doi.org/10.1163/1573-3912_islam_SIM_6416 (accessed 23 February 2023).

De Bruijn, J.T.P. "Shemʿī." In *EI* (***Encyclopaedia of Islam New Edition Online*** [***EI-2 English***]). Second Edition. http://dx.doi.org/10.1163/1573-3912_islam_SIM_6910 (accessed 23 February 2023).

De Jong, Frederich. "The Takīya of the Mawlawiyya in Tripolis." *Osmanlı Araştırmaları* XIV (1994): 91–100.

Ekinci, Ramazan. "Bahâyî, Küfrî, Hasan Çelebi." https://teis.yesevi.edu.tr/madde-detay/bahayi-kufri-hasan-celebi (accessed 23 February 2023).

Ekinci, Ramazan. "Klasik Türk Edebiyatında Mizahî Takvimler." *Divan Edebiyatı Araştırmaları Dergisi* 17 (2016): 55–90.

Erdoğan, Mehtap. "Niʿmetî." https://teis.yesevi.edu.tr/madde-detay/nimeti (accessed 23 February 2023).

Glassen, Erika. "Trablusşam Mevlevihanesi". *Türkiyat Araştırmaları Dergisi* 2, no. 2 (1996): 27–29.

Gökdemir, Ahmet. "Genel Hatlarıyla Osmanlı Tecvid Eserleri." In *Osmanlı Tecvîd Risâleleri*, edited by Ahmet Gökdemir, 9–24. Ankara, 2020.

Gökyay, Orhan Şaik. "Kātib Čelebi." In *EI* (***Encyclopaedia of Islam New Edition Online*** [***EI-2 English***]). Second Edition. http://dx.doi.org/10.1163/1573-3912_islam_COM_0467 (accessed 25 February 2023).

Gökyay, Orhan Şaik. "Kâtib Çelebi." In *Türkiye Diyanet Vakfı İslam Ansiklopedisi* (*Encyclopaedia of Islam*), 36–40. Ankara.

Hatiboğlu, İbrahim. "Selmân-ı Fârisî." In *Türkiye Diyanet Vakfı İslam Ansiklopedisi* (*Encyclopaedia of Islam*), 441–443. Ankara.

İnan, Murat Umut. "Ottoman Reading Persian Classics: Readers and Reading in the Ottoman Empire." In *The Edinburgh History of Reading: Early Readers*, edited by Mary Hammond, 160–181. Edinburgh, 2020.

Ibrāhīm, ʿAbd al-Laṭīf. "Makataba ʿUthmāniyya: Dirāsat Nakqdiyyat wa-Nashr li-Rāṣid al-Maktaba." *Majallat Kulliyyat al-Ādāb* XX, no. 2 (1958): 1–35.

Imber, Colin. "Ḳoči Beg." In *EI* (***Encyclopaedia of Islam New Edition Online*** [***EI-2 English***]). Second Edition. http://dx.doi.org/10.1163/1573-3912_islam_SIM_4421 (accessed 23 February 2023).

İpşirli, Mehmet. "Abdullah Efendi, Yenişehirli." *Türkiye Diyanet Vakfı İslam Ansiklopedisi* (*Encyclopaedia of Islam*), 100–101. Ankara.

İz, Fahir. "Dāʿī." In *EI* (***Encyclopaedia of Islam New Edition Online*** [***EI-2 English***]). Second Edition. http://dx.doi.org/10.1163/1573-3912_islam_SIM_1669 (accessed 25 February 2023).

Kanar, Mehmet. "Nizâmî-i Gencevî." In *Türkiye Diyanet Vakfı İslam Ansiklopedisi* (*Encyclopaedia of Islam*), 183–185. Ankara.

Karagöz, Rıza. *Canikli Ali Paşa*. Ankara, 2003.

Kaylı, Ahmet. "A Critical Study of Birgivi Mehmed Efendi's (d. 981/1573) Works and Their Dissemination in Manuscript Form." MA Thesis. Boğaziçi University, 2010.

Kılıç, Hulusi. "Ahterî." In *Türkiye Diyanet Vakfı İslam Ansiklopedisi* (*Encyclopaedia of Islam*), 184–185. Ankara.

Kızılkaya, Necmettin. "From Means to Goal: Auxiliary Disciplines in the Ottoman *Madrasa* Curriculum." In *A Handbook and Reader of Ottoman Arabic*, edited by Esther-Miriam Wagner, 23–38. Cambridge, 2021.

Kuru, Selim Sırrı. "Sünbülzâde Vehbî." In *Türkiye Diyanet Vakfı İslam Ansiklopedisi* (*Encyclopaedia of Islam*), 140–141. Istanbul.

Köksal, Mehmet Fatih. "Vahyî." https://teis.yesevi.edu.tr/madde-detay/vahyi (accessed 23 February 2023).

Kreiser, Klaus. "Evliya Çelebi ve Başka Kaynaklara Göre Arap Âleminin Doğusundaki Büyük Şehirlerde Mevlevihaneler." Trs. Semih Tezcan. *Osmanlı Araştırmaları XIV* (1994): 101–115.

Kut, Günay. "Ahmed-i Dâî." In *Türkiye Diyanet Vakfı İslam Ansiklopedisi* (*Encyclopaedia of Islam*), 56–58. Ankara.

Kut, Günay. "Ismāʿīl Ḥaḳḳī." In *EI* (***Encyclopaedia of Islam New Edition Online*** [***EI-2 English***]). Second Edition. http://dx.doi.org/10.1163/1573-3912_islam_SIM_3655 (accessed 23 February 2023).

Küfrevî, Kasım. "Birgewī." In *EI* (***Encyclopaedia of Islam New Edition Online*** [***EI-2 English***]). Second Edition. http://dx.doi.org/10.1163/1573-3912_islam_SIM_1434 (accessed 23 February 2023).

Küçük, Sezai. "Halep Mevlevîhânesi." *İlam Araştırma Dergisi* 3, no. 2 (1998): 73–106.

Küçük, Sezai. "Suriye'de İki Mevlevihane: Halep ve Şam Mevlevihaneleri." In *Birinci Uluslararası Mevlânâ, Mesnevî ve Mevlevîhâneler Sempozyumu Bildirileri (19–21 Aralık 2001-Manisa Mevlevîhânesi)*, edited by Emrehan Küey, 283–316. Manisa, 2002.

Lewis, B. "D̲j̲ānīklī Ḥādjdjī ʿAlī Pasha." In EI (***Encyclopaedia of Islam New Edition Online [EI-2 English]***). Second Edition. http://dx.doi.org/10.1163/1573-3912_islam_SIM_1994 (accessed 23 February 2023).

Ménage, V.L. "Bīd̲j̲ān." In EI (***Encyclopaedia of Islam New Edition Online [EI-2 English]***). Second Edition. http://dx.doi.org/10.1163/1573-3912_islam_SIM_1395 (accessed 23 February 2023).

Al-Murādī, Abū al-Faḍl Muḥammad Khalīl b. ʿAlī. *Silk al-Durar fī Aʿyān al-Qarn al-Thānī ʿAshar*, 4 vol. Beirut 1988.

Namlı, Ali, Murat Yurtsever and Yusuf Şevki Yavuz—Cağfer Karadaş. "İsmâil Hakkı Bursevî." *Türkiye Diyanet Vakfı İslam Ansiklopedisi (Encyclopaedia of Islam)*, 102–110. Ankara.

Niʿmetullāh Aḥmed. *Lugat-i Niʿmetuʾllâh*. Prepared by Adnan İnce. Ankara 2015.

Otugüzel, Abdurrahman. "Tabir-nâme: Tabir-nâme-i İbn-i Sîrîn-i Âfâkî (Giriş-Metin-Sözlük-Tıpkıbasım)." MA Thesis, Karadeniz Teknik Üniversitesi, 2018.

Öngören, Reşat. "Mevlânâ Celâleddîn-i Rûmî." In *Türkiye Diyanet Vakfı İslam Ansiklopedisi (Encyclopaedia of Islam)*, 441–448. Ankara.

Öz, Yusuf. *Tuhfe i Şâhidî Şerhleri*. Konya, 1999.

Özel, Ahmet. "Behcetü'l-Fetâvâ." In *Türkiye Diyanet Vakfı İslam Ansiklopedisi (Encyclopaedia of Islam)*, 346. Ankara.

Özkaya, Yücel. "Canikli Ali Paşa." *Belleten* XXXVI, no. 144 (1972): 483–525.

Özkaya, Yücel. "Canikli Ali Paşa'nın Risalesi 'Tedâbirü'l-Gazavât.'" *Tarih Araştırmaları Dergisi* 12 (1969): 119–191.

Öztürk, Şeyda. "Şemʿî." In *Türkiye Diyanet Vakfı İslam Ansiklopedisi (Encyclopaedia of Islam)*. Ankara

Pertevî Ali Efendi. *Rebîü'l-Mülk ve Âdâbü Sülûki'l-Mülûk*. Prepared by Kayhan Atik, 503–504. Ankara 2017.

Rettig, Simon. "The Rise of the Enʿam: Manuscripts of Selections of Suras in the Early Sixteenth-Century Ottoman Empire." in *The World Illuminated: Form and Function of Qurʾanic Manuscripts from the Seventh to Seventeenth Century*, edited by Simon Rettig and Sana Mirza, 185–212. Washington, 2023.

Ritter, H. and A. Bausani, "D̲j̲alāl al-Dīn Rūmī." In EI (***Encyclopaedia of Islam New Edition Online [EI-2 English]***). Second Edition. http://dx.doi.org/10.1163/1573-3912_islam_COM_0177 (accessed 23 February 2023).

Tanrıkorur, Barihüda. "Mevleviyye." In *Türkiye Diyanet Vakfı İslam Ansiklopedisi (Encyclopaedia of Islam)*, 468–475. Ankara.

Top, Yılmaz. "Bursalı Şâir Nakîb-zâde Niʿmetî (ö. 1060?) Efendi ve Onun Süleymaniye Kütüphanesi Esad Efendi Koleksiyonu 3424 Numarada Kayıtlı Mecmûʿa-i Kasâʾid adlı Şiir Mecmuasının Muhtevası." *Türk Kültürü İncelemeleri Dergisi* 31 (2014): 265–348.

Tütüncü, Mehmet. "Kudüs Mevlevîhânesi Tarihi ve Mimarisi." In *Uluslarası Düşünce ve Sanatta Mevlânâ Sempozyumu Bildirileri*, 699–723. Çanakkale, 2006.

Ünver, İsmail. "Kemâl Ümmî." In *Türkiye Diyanet Vakfı İslam Ansiklopedisi (Encyclopaedia of Islam)*, 229–230. Ankara.

Vida, G. Levi Della. "Salmān al-Fārisī." In EI (***Encyclopaedia of Islam New Edition Online [EI-2 English]***). Second Edition. http://dx.doi.org/10.1163/1573-3912_islam_DUM_3129 (accessed 23 February 2023).

Wickens, G.M. "Ḥāfiẓ." In EI (***Encyclopaedia of Islam New Edition Online [EI-2 English]***). Second Edition. http://dx.doi.org/10.1163/1573-3912_islam_SIM_2613 (accessed 23 February 2023).

Winter, Michael. "Cultural Ties between Istanbul and Ottoman Cairo." In *Frontiers of Ottoman Studies, vol. 1: State, Province and the West*, edited by Colin Imber and Keiko Kiyatoki, 187–202. London, 2005.

Yazıcı, Tahsin. "Hâfız-ı Şîrâzî." In *Türkiye Diyanet Vakfı İslam Ansiklopedisi (Encyclopaedia of Islam)*, 103–106. Ankara.

Yazıcı, Tahsin. "Ismāʿīl Rusūkh al-Dīn Ismāʿīl b. Aḥmad al-Anḳarawī." In EI (***Encyclopaedia of Islam New Edition Online [EI-2 English]***). Second Edition. http://dx.doi.org/10.1163/1573-3912_islam_SIM_3652 (accessed 23 February 2023).

Yazıcı, Tahsin, D.S. Margoliouth and F. de Jong. "Mawlawiyya." In EI (***Encyclopaedia of Islam New Edition

Online [*EI-2 English*]). Second Edition. http://dx.doi.org/10.1163/1573-3912_islam_COM_071 (accessed 23 February 2023).

Yetik, Erhan. "Ankaravî, İsmâil Rusûhî." In *Türkiye Diyanet Vakfı İslam Ansiklopedisi* (*Encyclopaedia of Islam*), 211–213. Ankara.

Yüksel, Emrullah. "Birgivî." In *Türkiye Diyanet Vakfı İslam Ansiklopedisi* (*Encyclopaedia of Islam*), 191–194. Ankara.

The Persian Books

[1553] ***al-Mathnawī al-Maʿnawī***, AUTHOR: Mawlānā Jalāl al-Dīn al-Rūmī (d. 672/1273), EDITION: R. Nicholson, London, 1925–1940; Jawid Mojaddedi, Oxford: Oxford University Press, 2004; Derya Örs, Hicabi Kırlangıç, İstanbul: YEK, 2015.

[1554] ***al-Mathnawī***, see #1553.

[1555] ***al-Mathnawī***, see #1553.

[1556] ***al-Mathnawī***, see #1553.

[1557] ***al-Mathnawī***, see #1553.

[1558] ***Shāhidī***, [most probably *Tuḥfe-i Şāhidī*], AUTHOR: Ibrāhīm Shāhidī (d. 957/1550), EDITION: Ahmad Hilmi İmamoğlu, Muğla: Muğla Üniversitesi, 2005.

[1559] ***Shāhidī***, see #1558.

[1560] ***Tuḥfa-e Shāhidī***, see #1559.

[1561] ***Risāla-e Tawḥīd bi-al-Fārisī***, AUTHOR: Some catalogues include manuscripts on that issue but have not been confirmed yet. Those are 1. *Risāla fī Iʿrāb Kalimat al-Tawḥīd*, by Nūr al-Dīn ʿAbd al-Raḥmān al-Jāmī (d. 898/1492) [Istanbul: Süleymaniye Manuscript Library, Esad Efendi, MSS 3712, 37–39]; 2. *Risāla fī al-Tawhīd wa-al-Kufr wa al-Ilḥād*, by ʿAbd al-ʿAzīz b. Muḥammad al-Nasafī (d. 700/1300) [Istanbul: Süleymaniye Manuscript Library, Şehid Ali Paşa, MSS 1381, 164–169]; and 3. *Risāla fī al-Tawhīd al-Bārī* by Abū ʿAbd Allāh Muḥammad b. al-Ḥanafī al-Shirāzī [Kastamonu, KHK260/04, 19^{b}–29^{b}].

[1562] ***Sharḥ-e Gulistān***, AUTHOR: Though there are many commentaries on *Gulistān* by Saʿdī, the manuscript meant in the inventory is by Surūrī (d. 969/1562).

[1563] ***Sharḥ-e Gulistān***, see #1562.

[1564] ***Kitāb-e Bustān***, [most probably *Bostān*], AUTHOR: Saʿdī Shirāzī (d. 691/1292), EDITION: *Kulliyāt-i Saʿdī*, M. Ali Furūghī-ʿAbdulazīm Karīb, Tahran, 1351/1932; Schlechta-Wassehrd, Wien, 1852.

[1565] ***Dīwān ül-Ḥāfiẓ ül-Shirāzī***, AUTHOR: Khāja Shams al-Dīn Muḥammad al-Ḥāfiẓ al-Shirāzī (d. 792/1390), EDITION: Abdulbaki Gölpınarlı, İstanbul: İş Bankası, 2011; Paul Smith, Melbourne: New Humanity Books, 1986.

[1566] ***Dīwān al-Ḥāfiẓ***, see #1565.

[1567] ***Jāmiʿ al-Āyāt Sharḥ al-Ābyāt***, AUTHOR: Ismāʿīl Rusūkhī Anḳarawī (d. 1041/1631). Istanbul, Süleymaniye Manuscript Library, Mihrişah Sultan, 181.

[1568] ***Salmān al-Fārisī***, AUTHOR: Two titles are attributed to Salmān al-Fārisī (d. 36/656). 1. *Masāʾil al-Ruhbān* (Antalya Akseki Halk Kütüphanesi 306, 181^{r}–182^{v}), and 2. *Kitāb Ḥadīth Cāthīlīk* (see DIA 15, 39; shiaonlinelibrary.com (http://shiaonlinelibrary.com/الكتب/4050_نفس-الرحمن-في-فضائل-سلمان-ميرزا-حسين-النوري-الطبرسي/الصفحة_223#top) 236, 489–512).

[1569] ***Kitāb-e Niʿmatullāh***, *Turkī*, AUTHOR: There were two "Niʿmetullāh" who penned Persian-Turkish dictionaries. It is not apparent which one of these is meant. 1. Niʿmetullāh b. Aḥmed b. Mubārak al-Rūmī (d. 969/1561), EDITION: Adnan İnce, *Niʿmetullâh Ahmed Lügat-ı Niʿmetullâh*, Ankara: TDK, 2015; 2. Bursalı Nakibzāde Niʿmetī (d. 1060/1650), EDITION: Neslihan Gören, "Bursalı Nakibzâde Niʿmetî'nin 'Tuhfe-i Niʿmetî' Adlı Farsça-Türkçe Manzum Sözlüğü: Metin-İnceleme," MA Thesis, Istanbul, 2016.

[1570] ***Manẓūm** bi-al-Fārisī*. Unidentified.

[1571] ***Khulāṣat al-Khamsa***, AUTHOR: Though many authors have *Khamsa*s in Persian, the most famous one is penned by Niẓāmī-e Kūnjaūī, Abū Muḥammad Jamāl al-Dīn Ilyās b. Yūsuf b. Zakī (d. 611/1214). Someone after his death should have gathered his *mas̱navīs* under this name because he has not done it alone.

[1572] ***Zī al-Fārisī***. Unidentified.

[1573] ***Lugha Turkī-Fārisī***, AUTHOR: Most likely a Turkish-Persian dictionary, but not easy to define which one it is.

[1574] ***Sharḥ al-Shāhidī***, AUTHOR: There are numerous *sharḥ*s of *Shāhidī*'s dictionary in Arabic, Turkish and Persian. Besides, because of the nature of the work, one cannot determine in which language the commentary was written. Thus, the title remains unidentifiable.

The Turkish Books

[1575] ***Enʿām-ı Şerīf***, see #1640, (ʿulūm al-Qurʾan).

[1576] ***Kitāb-ı ʿAḳīda***, *Turkī*, AUTHOR: It is unidentifiable because it is a generic name. It is impossible to define which *aḳāʾid* is implied.

[1577] ***Miʿrāj***, *Turkī*, AUTHOR: It is unidentifiable because it is a generic name. It is impossible to define which *miʿrāc* is implied.

[1578] ***ʿAḳāʾid***, *Turkī*, AUTHOR: It is unidentifiable because it is a generic name. It is impossible to define which *aḳāʾid* is implied.

[1579] ***Qawāʿid ül-Īmān***. Unidentified.

[1580] ***Ḥadīth***, *Turkī*, AUTHOR: It is unidentifiable because it is a generic name. It is impossible to define which *fiḳh* is implied.

[1581] ***Tafsīr***, *Turkī*, AUTHOR: It is unidentifiable because it is a generic name. It is impossible to define which *fiḳh* is implied.

[1582] ***Tajwīd***, AUTHOR: It is unidentifiable because it is a generic name. Nevertheless, the most famous work was the *Ḳarabaş Tecvīdi* by Shaykh ʿAbdurraḥmān Ḳarabaşī (904/1498), EDITION: Dersaadet, 1330/1912.

[1583] ***Tajwīd***, see #1582.

[1584] ***Tajwīd***, see #1582.

[1585] ***Shurūṭ ül-ṣalāt***, AUTHOR: It is unidentifiable because numerous manuscripts used this title.

[1586] ***Shurūṭ ül-ṣalāt***, see #1585.

[1587] ***Shurūṭ ül-ṣalāt***, see #1585.

[1588] ***Sharḥ-i fiqh***, AUTHOR: It is unidentifiable because it is a generic name.

[1589] ***Tarjamat ül-Geylānī***, AUTHOR: It should be a translation related to ʿAbdulqādir al-Geylānī (d. 561/1166). Those are probable titles: 1. *Tercume-i ʿAbdulqādir al-Geylānī* probably by İsmail Kamal Ummî (d. 1475), including al-Kaylānī's warriors. (Süleymaniye Library, Serez 1799); *Terceme-i Risāle-i ʿAbdülḳādir el-Geylānī* (Süleymaniye Library, Laleli 1370/1).

[1590] ***Kitāb fī al-Khilāfa*** *Jawāhir Tāj al-Khilāfa*, *Turkī*, AUTHOR: Ṣalāḥuddīn al-ʿUshshāqī (d. 1197/1793), EDITION: Semih Ceyhan, *Islam Araştırmaları Dergisi* 25 (2011).

[1591] ***Birgili*** al-Ṭarīqa al-*Muḥammadiyya*, *ʿIlm-i Ḥāl*, *Vaṣiyyet-nāme*, AUTHOR: Taḳiyuddīn Meḥmed Birgivī (d. 981/1573), EDITION: The work implied is unidentifiable.

[1592] ***Birgili***, see #1591.

[1593] ***Birgili***, see #1591.

[1594] ***Birgili***, see #1591.

[1595] ***Birgili***, see #1591.

[1596] ***Mathnawī***, *Turkī*. Unidentified.

[1597] ***Qaṣīda fī beshārat ummatihi***. Unidentified.

[1598] ***Bahjat ül-Fatwa***, [*Bahjat ül-Fatawa*], AUTHOR: A title under the name of Behcet al-Futuvvā is unidentifiable; it is most probably *Behcet ül-Fetāvā* by Şeykhulislām ʿAbdullāh Efendi (d. 1156/1743), EDITION: Süleyman Kaya et al., *Abdullah Yenishehrî, Behcetü'l-Fetāvā*, Klasik Yayınları, Istanbul, 2012; Hilmar Flügel, *Fetwa-und Siyar*, Wiesbaden, 1978.

[1599] ***Kitāb fī sirr al-ḥurūf***, [*Kitāb fī Asrār al-Ḥurūf*], *Turkī*, AUTHOR: *Kitāb fī Sırr al-Ḥurūf* is unidentifiable but the famous Sufi author Burscvī penned a book called *Kitāb fī Asrār al-Ḥurūf* on the numeric equivalent of the Arabic letters (abjad). AUTHOR: Ismāʿīl Haqqı Bursawī (d. 1137/1735).

[1600] ***Tadbīr-i Jadīd Nāmeh***, AUTHOR: Two probable authors occur for this title. 1. Daghıstanlı Ali Pasha (d. 1194/1780), *Tedbīr-i Cedīd-i Nādir*, 2. Canikli Ali Paşa (d. 1199/1785), *Tedbīr-i Cedīd-i Nādir*, EDITION: Yücel Özkaya.

[1601] ***Tadbīr-i Jadīd Nāmeh***, see #1600.

[1602] ***Aḥmed-i Bījān***, AUTHOR: Aḥmed-i Bījān has seven famous works; thus, it is not easy to identify which one was meant by the scribe. 1. *Anwār ül-ʿĀshiqīn*, EDITION: Abdullah Uğur, Cambridge, 2019; 2. *Durr-i Maknūn*, EDITION: Ahmet Demirtaş, Istanbul, 2009; Kaptein La-ban, 2007; 3. *ʿAjāʾib ül-Makhlūqāt*, EDITION: Mustafa Erkan, Istanbul, 2014; 4. *Būstān ül-Ḥaqāyıq*, EDITION: Bülent Yorulmaz, 1970; 5. *Jawāhir nāmeh*, EDITION: Serdal Kara, 2016; 6. *Rūḥ ül-Arwāh*, EDITION: Siyabend Ebem, 2014; 7. *Kitāb ül-Muntahā al-Mushtahā ʿalā al-Fuṣūṣ*.

[1603] ***Majmūʿat-ı Dīwān***. Unidentified. Nevertheless, six possible records occur. 1. *Majmūʿat-ı Dīwān Makhṭūmī* by Makhṭūmī Wāḥid (d. 1145/1732–1733) [Süleymaniye Hasib Efendi 478], 2, 3, 4, 5. Four *Majmūʿat-ı Dīwān* (Süleymaniye İzmirli İ. Hakkı 3399, Edirne BAD. 2357, Edirne BAD. 2365, and Edirne BAD. 2367), 6. *Dīwān-ı Majmūʿat*, (Zeytinoğlu 333).

[1604] ***Taʿbīr nāmeh***, *Turkī*, AUTHOR: Unidentifiable because numerous (more than twenty) authors penned the work.

[1605] ***Manẓūma***, *Turkī*. Unidentified.

[1606] ***Kitāb***, *Turkī*. Unidentified.

[1607] ***Kitāb***, *Turkī*. Unidentified.

[1608] ***Taḳwīm***, AUTHOR: Four possible authors occur for this title. 1. Aḥmad Dāʿī (d. 824/1421), *Terceme-i Sī Faṣl fīʾl-Taḳvīm*, EDITION: Emre Kundakçı, Istanbul, 2021; 2. Vaḥyī (d. 960/1519–1520), *Taḳwīm*, EDITION: Ramazan Ekinci, 2016; 3. Bahāyī, Ḥasan Çelebi (d. 1660), *Taḳwīm al-Qawīm*, EDITION: Ramazan Ekinci, 2016; 4. Kâtib Çelebi (d. 1067/1657), *Taqwīm al-Tawārīkh*, EDITION: M. Tayyip Gökbilgin, Ankara, 1991.

[1609] ***Majmaʿ ül-jawāhir***, AUTHOR: Two names seem to pen works under that name. 1. Ḥasan Naṣūḥ b. al-Būsnawī (Süleymaniye Library, Hacı Mahmud Efendi 4493) and Cemālī (Süleymaniye Library, Reşid Efendi 845).

[1610] ***Risāla Turkiyya***. Unidentified.

[1611] ***Kitāb al-musammā bi-Nawḥat al-mushtāq***, *naẓm Turkī*. Unidentified.

[1612] ***Muḥyī ül-amwāt*** [Iḥyāu al-amwāt?]. Unidentified.

[1613] ***Kitāb-ı Ibn Firishtā***, AUTHOR: ʿAbdullaṭīf ibn Malak (d. after 1418), EDITION: Cemal Muhtar, Istanbul, 1993.

[1614] ***Waṣiyyat nāmeh***, AUTHOR: Taqiyuddīn Muḥmmad Birjiūī (d. 981/1573), EDITION: Mūsa Duman, Istanbul, 2000.

[1615] ***Majmūʿ ül-Laṭāʾif***, AUTHOR: If *al-Leṭāʾif* is not a generic name, ʿIsmāʿīl Rusūḥī Anḳarawī (d. 1041/1631) has a work called *Majmūʿ al-Laṭāʾif wa-Maṭmūrat al-Maʿārif*, EDITION: Ayşe Gültekin, PhD. Thesis, Selçuk Üniversitesi, 2006.

[1616] ***ʿAlā al-Sharīʿa***, *Risāla, Turkī*. Unidentified.

[1617] ***Ḳānūn nāmeh***. Unidentified.

[1618] ***Ādāb ül-Mulūk*** [*Rabīʿ al-Mulk wa-Adāb Sulūk al-Mulūk*], AUTHOR: Pertevī ʿAlī Efendi (d. 1076/1665), EDITION: Kayhan Atik, Berikan Yayınevi, Ankara, 2017.

[1619] ***Risāla Turkī***, AUTHOR: It should be a book in an unidentifiable Turkish booklet.

[1620] ***Kitāb-ı Taṣrīf***, *Turkī*, AUTHOR: It should be a grammar in Turkish on Arabic, Persian or even Turkish.

[1621] ***Kitāb-ı Lugha***, *Fārisī*, AUTHOR: It is probably a Persian-Turkish dictionary.

[1622] ***Kitāb***, *Turkī*. Unidentified.

[1623] ***Talkhīṣāt***, *Turkī*, AUTHOR: Two possible authors occur for a title including this name: 1. *Talkhīṣāt*, Ḳoçi Bey (d. ca. 1650) [Süleymaniye, Hüsrev Paşa 296]; 2. *Telkhīsāt wa-Munshaʾāt or Telkhīsāt* [*Ḳoca*] *Rāġıp* [*Pasha*], Ḳoca Rāġıp Pasha (d. 1176/1763).

[1624] ***Majmūʿa***, *Turkī*. Unidentified.

[1625] ***Takmīl Sharīʿa***.

[1626] ***Kitāb***, *Turkī*, *Manẓūm*, *nāqıs*, AUTHOR: It is an incomplete manuscript containing Turkish verses, but unidentifiable which one was meant.

[1627] ***Turkī wa-ʿArabī***, AUTHOR: It is probably an Arabic-Turkish dictionary, just like *al-Akhterī*, but it is unidentifiable from this specification.

[1628] ***Turjumān***, *Turkī*, AUTHOR: It should be a dictionary, but it is unidentifiable which one was meant.

[1629] ***Turjumān al-Akhtarī*** [*Akhtarī Kabīr*], AUTHOR: Akhtarī, Musliḥüddīn Muṣṭafā (d. 968/1560–1561), EDITION: Ali Bey Matbaası, 1292/1875, Istanbul.

[1630] ***Risāla***, *Turkī*. Unidentified.

Edition of the Inventory

Said Aljoumani

1 الرموز المستخدمة في التحقيق

﴿ ﴾ لتمييز آي القرآن الكريم

[ ] ترقيم الصفحات حسب الأصل، أو لإضافة كلمة أو حرف يقتضيهما السياق

[...] فراغ في الأصل، أو كلمة لم تُقرأ

[؟] كلمة مشكوكٌ في قراءتها

2 بيان الكتب التي كانت موجودة في كتب خانة جامع النّور أحمديَّة بعكا[1]

[14] ﴿إنَّه من سليمان وإنه بسم الله الرحمن الرحيم﴾[2]

الحمد لله مُنزِّل الكتب السماويّة القديمة في علمه، ومُوصِل مُحبيه[3] إلى تدبّر أحكامها، بحكمه أوضح لنا حكمة أزليّة، وأفاض علينا[4] أبحر مدده بمنحٍ أحمديّة، والصلوة والسلام على أكمل إمام [في][5] البدء والختام سيدنا ومولانا محمد، وأحمدُ المبعوث على المنهج الأحمد، المُنبئ بأحكام الصّمد، بمعجز آياته ودُرّها النظيم ﴿قلْ هو نبأ عظيم﴾[6]، وعلى آله وأصحابه وأتباعه وأحبابه نجوم الهدى، والثواقب للعدا أبداً سرمداً وبعد: فهذه صحائف حسنة [و][7] لطائف مستحسنة أشرق أفق سمائها بأسماء الكتب النورانيّة المكنونة بمدرسة جامع النور الأحمديّة بعكا المحميّة من كل بليّة، فكان ﴿فيها كتب قيّمة﴾[8] بالشريعة[9] والحقيقة

1 العنوان مُستقى من نهاية هذا البيان، تُنظر الورقة (72).

2 القرآن الكريم، سورة النمل، الآية 30.

3 في الأصل: محببيه.

4 في الأصل: عليهنا.

5 إضافة يقتضيها السياق.

6 القرآن الكريم، سورة ص، الآية 67.

7 إضافة يقتضيها السياق.

8 القرآن الكريم، سورة البيّنة، الآية رقم 3.

9 في الأصل باالشريعة.

© SAID ALJOUMANI, 2025 | DOI:10.1163/9789004720527_028

مُعَلّمة، قد وقفها لوجه مولاه العليم ابتغاءً لمرضاته تعالى بحصول النفع العميم، المنصور المؤيد والمسعود المؤبّد ناصر الملّة والدين محيي ملّة سيد المرسلين بالفتح[10] المُبين المشهور في العالمين ﴿ذلك فضل الله يؤتيه من يشاء والله ذو الفضل العظيم﴾[11] ألا وهو الوزير الشهير والبدر المنير ناشر ألوية العدل والأمان وباسط أكف الفضل والإحسان بلا امتنان، المحفوف بعناية الملك الرحمن، منحه الله من الخير ما يشاء ويختار، سيدنا ومولانا الحاج أحمد باشا الجزّار، وشرط أطال الله بالصحّة حيواته وجمَّل بالنصر والسعادة أوقاته وأحسن ختامه وأناته البديعة، وأعلى في دار المثوبة درجاته الرفيعة، أن لا تُخرَج هذه الكتب التي وقفها بمدرسة جامعه النور الأحمدي المذكور خارج الجامع المنور اللامع بل تبقى داخله وفي طبقاته حين المطالعة فيها وتأمل خوافيها حفظاً لها وصيانة فمن حفظها حفظه الله وصانه حيث إنها مال الله تعالى جلّت قدرته وتعالت[12] عظمته ﴿فمن بدله بعدما سمعه فإنما إثمه على الذين يبدلونه إنَّ الله سميع عليم﴾.[13] وصلى الله على سيدنا محمد النبي الأمي وعلى آله وصحبه أجمعين وسلم والحمد لله رب العالمين.

3 مصاحف شريفة

-1 مصحف شريف تام بخط إسلامبول عالٍ[14] مُذَهّب قطع الربع مُحيَّر[15] مُجَلَّد جلد1.
-2 مصحف شريف تام بخط عجم وتذهيب عجم عالٍ قطع كامل مُجَلَّد جلد1.
-3 مصحف شريف تام بخط ريحاني[16] مُذَهّب بتذهيب الغرب[17] قطع كامل مُجَلَّد جلد1.
-4 مصحف شريف تام بخط إستانبول عالٍ وتذهيب إستانبول قطع الثُّمن مُجَلَّد جلد1.

10 في الأصل باالفتح.

11 القرآن الكريم، سورة الجمعة، الآية رقم 4.

12 في الأصل: تعالى.

13 القرآن الكريم، سورة البقرة، الآية 181.

14 المقصود: أن الناسخ خطاطٌ محترف.

15 المقصود: أن الورقَ تعرضَ لقصِّ أطرافه فنقص عن الحدِّ المعياريّ لقطعه الأصليّ؛ فأصبحَ بين منزلتين (بين الكامل والنصف/ أو بين النصف والربع/ أو بين الربع والثمن). أو أنَّه صُنع أصلا من قطع غير البغدادي الكامل.

16 الخط الريحاني: هو خط يشبه الخط الديواني ولكن حروفه متشابكة ومتداخلة. ينظر بنبين، أحمد وطوبي، مصطفى، معجم مصطلحات المخطوط العربي، 149.

17 يقصد بلاد المغرب العربي (ليبيا، تونس، الجزائر، المغرب).

-5 مصحف شريف تام بخط النسخ عال مُجَدْوَل[18] بإكليل[19] قطع كامل مُجَلَّد جلد1.

-6 مصحف شريف تام بخط ريحاني مُجَدْوَل بإكليل قطع كامل مُجَلَّد جلد1.

-7 مصحف شريف قديم على هامشه قراءات[20] بخط نسخ وسط[21]، قطع الربع مجلَّد جلد1.

-8 مصحف شريف بخط نسخ وسط، مُجَدْوَل بإكليل، قطع كامل، مُجَلَّد، جلد1.

-9 مصحف شريف قديم بخط نسخ وسط مُهَمَّش[22]، قطع الربع مُحَيَّر بجلد جلد1.

-10 مصحف شريف قديم بخط نسخ وسط مُجَدْوَل بأحمر، قطع الثمن واسع[23] بجلد جلد1.

-11 مصحف شريف بخط نسخ وسط، مُجَدْوَل بأحمر قطع الثمن واسع مُجَلَّد جلد1.

-12 مصحف شريف بخط نسخ وسط بلا جدول، قطع كامل بجلد جلد1.

-13 مصحف شريف بخط نسخ وسط مُجَدْوَل بأحمر قطع النصف بجلد جلد1.

-14 مصحف شريف وسط[24] مُجَدْوَل بأحمر قطع النصف مُحَيَّر، بجلد جلد1.

-15 مصحف شريف بخط مصري مُجَدْوَل بأحمر قطع كامل بجلد جلد1.

-16 مصحف شريف بخط نسخ وسط قطع كامل بجلد جلد1.

-17 مصحف شريف بخط مصري قطع الربع واسع بجلد جلد1.

-18 نصف مصحف قديم كُهْنا[25] بخطوط مختلفة جلد1.

-19 ربع مصحف شريف بخط مصري قطع الربع بجلد جلد1.

-20 ربع[26] مصحف شريف بخط نسخ وسط عتيق كهنا بجلد جلد1.

---

18 المقصود: أن النصّ مؤطَّر.

19 الإكليل: "كل ما احتفَ بالشيء من جوانبه فهو إكليل". ينظر ابن منظور، لسان العرب، 3919. والإكليل: "شبه عِصابة مُزيّنة بالجوهر". ابن منظور، لسان العرب، 3920. وبناءً عليه فإنَّ المقصود بمُجَدْوَل بإكليل: أنَّ النصَّ محاط بإطار مزخرف مُزيّن بأشكال هندسية أو نباتية، بخلاف الإطار الساذج من دون أية حلية، الذي سيعبر عنه بمُجَدْوَل فقط، أو مُجَدْوَل بأحمر أي أنَّ لون الإطار أحمر.

20 في الأصل: قراءت.

21 المقصود: أن مستوى خط الناسخ متوسط، وهو دون العالي.

22 المقصود: أنَّ على هوامشه قيود (تفسير، أو حاشية، أو شرح لبعض الكلمات ... إلخ).

23 ربما يقصد أنّ عرض الورقة زاد عن الحدِّ المعياري، وهذا يحدث إذا ما تُرِك فرخ الورق كما خرج من الورّاقة/ المصنع ولم يُشذبه المُجلِّد.

24 نسي أن يذكر نوع الخط.

25 كُهْنا: تعني قديم، عتيق باللسان الفارسي، كسرائي، شاكر. قاموس فارسي—عربي (فرهنك فارسي—عربي). بيروت: الدار العربية للموسوعات، 2014. ص 405. وفعلاً نجد هذه الكلمة تتكرر في الفهرس مع الكتب العتيقة. وهذا المصطلح كان مستخدماً في سجلات المحكمة الشرعية بيافا مع بيان التركات سنة 1216هـ، السجل رقم 2، الورقات 45، 74، 115. الورقة 126. السجل رقم 1، الورقة 55- 56. ولكنه كان يُرسم (كهنه).

26 في الأصل: رابع.

-21 رَبْعة شريفة ثلاثون جزواً بخط إستانبول عالٍ قطع النصف مُحيَّر بجلود حُمر جديدة نُمرو1.[27]

ربعة شر[يفة] ثلا[ثون جزواً][28]

[15] -22 ربعة شريفة ثلاثون جزواً بخط نسخ وسط مُجَدْوَل بإكليل قطع الثمن بجلود خضر أطلس[29] منقوش نُمرو1.

-23 ربعة شريفة ثلاثون جزواً بخط ريحاني قديم قطع النصف مُحيَّر بجلود حمر قديمة نمرو1.

-24 ربعة شريفة عشرة أجزاء تحوي مصحفاً شريفاً تاماً بخطٍ مصري قطع النصف مُحيَّر بجلود قديمة نمرو1.

حسابه[30] نُمرو[31] 24 قطعاً أربعة وعشرون لا غير.

4 كتب التفسير الشريفة

-25 تفسير ابن عباس بخط نسخ عالٍ مُذَهَّب ظاهراً وباطناً قطع كامل مُجَلَّد بظرف[32] جلد1.

-26 الدّر المنثور أجزاء أربعة تام بخط مصري قطع كامل بجلود وظروف جلد4، فقط أربعة.

-27 البيضاوي تام بخط نسخ مُذَهَّب قطع كامل مُحيَّر مُجَلَّد بلا ظرف جلد1.

-28 بيضاوي تام بخط نسخ مُجَدْوَل بأحمر قطع كامل مُجَلَّد بلا ظرف جلد1.

-29 بيضاوي تام بخط نسخ مصري قطع النصف مُحيَّر مُجَلَّد بظرف جلد1.

-30 من البيضاوي أجزاء أربعة تام بخط مصري مُجَدْوَل بأحمر وأزرق قطع الربع بجلود وظروف جلد4، فقط أربعة.

-31 من البيضاوي أجزاء أربعة بخط مصري قطع الربع بجلود وظروف جلد4، فقط أربعة.

-32 جلالين بخط نسخ عالٍ مُذَهَّب قطع الربع مُجَلَّد بظرف مُذَهَّب جلد1.

-33 جلالين منخرم الوسط بخط مصري قطع الربع مُجَلَّد بظرف جلد1.

-34 أبو السعود تام بخط تعليق مُذَهَّب قطع كامل مُحيَّر مُجَلَّد بظرف جلد1.

-35 أبو السعود بخط نسخ قطع كامل مُجَلَّد بظرف جلد1.

-36 أبو السعود ناقص من الأول إلى آخر سورة هود بخط مصري قطع كامل مُجَلَّد بظرف جلد 1.

-37 أبو السعود ناقص من سورة يوسف إلى الآخر بخط مصري قطع كامل مُجَلَّد بظرف جلد1.

27 نمرو: رقم أو عدد، يُنظر أحمد رضا، معجم متن اللغة، بيروت، دار الحياة، 1958، ج1، ص 115. وهي مأخوذة عن نمرو الإيطالية، يُنظر محمد رواس قلعجي ، وحامد صادق قنيبي، معجم لغة الفقهاء، بيروت، دار النفائس، 1988، ص 20.

28 تعقيبة في الهامش الأيسر السفلي.

29 ربما كانت أجزاء هذه الربعة، مُبطَنة بحريرٍ أطلس منقوش.

30 في الأصل: حسا. وهي مختصر حسابه، وسيستخدم هذا الاختصار في جميع مواطن الإحصاء في الفهرس.

31 أي عدد.

32 المقصود أنَّ الكتاب محفوظ ضمن ظرفٍ، وقد يكون هذا الظرف مصنوعاً من الورق المقوى، أو من القماش.

-38 الخازن بخط نسخ وسط مُجْدوَل بأحمر قطع كامل مُجلَّد بظرف جلد1.

-39 تفسير الطبري تام ثمانية أجزاء بخط مصري قطع كامل بجلود حمر بلا ظروف جلد8، فقط ثمانية.[33]

-40 مجمع البيان تام بخط نسخ قطع كامل مُجلَّد بظرف جلد1.

-41 الأول والثاني من مجمع البيان بخط[34] ناقص الأول قطع النصف مُجلَّد بلا ظرف جلد1.

-42 الخامس من مجمع البيان بخط مصري قطع كامل مُجلَّد بظرف أخضر جلد1.

-43 النصف الأول من البغوي بخط مصري قطع كامل مُجلَّد بلا ظرف جلد1.

-44 من البغوي جزآن الأول تفسير سورة البقرة والثاني من آل عمران إلى آخر الأنعام بخط ريحاني، أحبار وألوان، قطع كامل جلدين بظرفين جلد2، فقط اثنان.[35]

-45 النصف الأول من الكشاف بخط تعليق قطع كامل مُجلَّد بلا ظرف جلد1[36]

-46 النصف الثاني من الكشاف بخط نسخ قطع كامل مُجلَّد بلا ظرف جلد1.

-47 النصف الثاني من الكشاف بخط مصري قطع النصف مُحيَّر مُجلَّد بلا ظرف جلد1.

-48 تفسير[37] النصف الأول بخط مصري قطع الربع مُجلَّد بلا ظرف جلد1.

-49 تفسير سورة يس بخط نسخ جديد مُجلَّد قطع الربع بلا ظرف ومعه شرح الاستغفار بخط تعليق وغير ذلك، جلد1.

-50 تفسير ﴿إنَّ أول بيت﴾ ويليه رسالة بخط مصري قطع الربع مُجلَّد بظرف جلد1.

-51 تفسير البيضاوي بخط مصري قطع النصف مُجلَّد بلا ظرف جلد1.

-52 تفسير ماء الحيوة بخط نسخ قطع النصف مُجلَّد بلا ظرف جلد1. [16]

-53 تفسير غريب القرآن بخط مصري قطع الربع مُحيَّر مُجلَّد بلا ظرف جلد1.

-54 تفسير النصف الأخير لابن الجوزي بخط نسخ عالٍ مُذَهّب قطع الربع مُجلَّد بظرف جلد1.

-55 تفسير الفاتحة والبقرة ونصف آل عمران بخط مصري قطع الربع مُجلَّد بظرف جلد1.

-56 غرر الفوائد تفسير بعض آيات بخط مصري قطع النصف مُجلَّد بلا ظرف جلد1.

---

33 جامع البيان في تأويل القرآن، أو تفسير الطبري. لابن جرير الطبري، محمد بن جرير (ت 310هـ/ 923م). أحد هذه الأجزاء محفوظ اليوم في الرياض، مركز الملك فيصل للبحوث والدراسات الإسلاميَّة، برقم 100.

34 نسي أن يحدد نوع الخط.

35 الجزء الأول من هذه النسخة محفوظ في دبلن، مكتبة تشستربيتي برقم Ar. 3268

36 هذه النسخة كانت موجودة في المكتبة الإسلاميَّة بيافا برقم (180) حسب فهرس محمود عطالله، ومصورتها على الرابط الآتي:
https://manuscripts.najah.edu/node/217?page=1
ولكنها الآن موجودة في مؤسسة إحياء التراث والبحوث الإسلاميَّة، بأبي ديس في القدس، رقم المخطوط (301/ 2)، حسب فهرس مخطوطات فلسطين المصورة، ج5، 72.

37 لم يحدد عنوان الكتاب.

-57 تفسير فارسي بخط تعليق عالٍ مُذَهّب قطع نصف التلخيص مُجلَّد بظرف جلد1.

-58 من السّراج المنير الأول والثاني والثالث والرابع بخط مصري قطع كامل بجلود وظروف جلد4، فقط أربعة.

-59 إعراب القرآن للعكبري بخط مصري عتيق قطع النصف مُحيَّر مُجلَّد بظرف جلد1.

-60 خواص القرآن نسختين بخط مصري مُجلَّدين بلا ظروف جلد2، فقط اثنان.

-61 إعراب القرآن ابن النحاس بخط مصري مُحيَّر الربع مُجلَّد بظرف جلد1.[38]

-62 حاشية شيخي زاده على البيضاوي بخط مصري مُجَدْوَل بأحمر قطع كامل مُحيَّر مُجلَّد بظرف جلد1.

-63 حاشية عصام على البيضاوي بخط نسخ قطع النصف طويل[39] مُحيَّر مُجلَّد بلا ظرف جلد1.

-64 حاشية بهاء الدين العاملي على البيضاوي بخط تعليق قطع الربع مُحيَّر مُجلَّد بظرف جلد1.

-65 حاشية على الكشاف بخط مصري قطع كامل مُجَدْوَل بأحمر مُجلَّد بظرف جديد جلد1.

-66 حاشية على خطبة الكشاف للزمخشري بخط نسخ قطع الربع مُحيَّر مُجلَّد بظرف جلد1.

-67 حاشية على تفسير سورة الأعراف[40] بخط تعليق قطع الربع مُجلَّد بظرف جلد1.

-68 حاشية تقديم البسملة على الحمدلة بخط نسخ قطع الثمن مُجلَّد بظرف جلد1.

-69 حاشية على تفسير سورة النبأ بخط تعليق قطع الربع مُجلَّد بظرف جلد1.[41]

-70 جزؤ أول من حاشية العماد على الكشاف بخط مصري قطع النصف مُحيَّر مُجلَّد بظرف جلد1.

-71 حاشية على جزؤ ثالث من تلخيص الكشاف ناقص الأول عتيق بخط مصري قطع النصف مُحيَّر مُجلَّد بظرف جلد1.

-72 جزؤ عاشر من تفسير مجمع البيان بخط نسخ قطع النصف مُجلَّد بلا ظرف جلد1.

-73 حاشية على تفسير سورة المنافقون بخط مصري قطع الربع مُجلَّد بلا ظرف جلد1.

-74 خواص القرآن بخط مصري عتيق ناقص الأول قطع الربع مُحيَّر مُجلَّد بلا ظرف جلد1.

-75 مختصر في إعراب بعض سور من القرآن العظيم بخط مصري قطع الربع مُجلَّد بلا ظرف جلد1.

-76 الدر النظيم في فضل القرآن العظيم بخط نسخ قطع الثمن مُجلَّد بلا ظرف جلد1.

38 هي غير النسخة المحفوظة اليوم في مكتبة جامع النور أحمديَّة بعكا رقم 6، وصورتها في المكتبة البريطانية برقم EAP399/1/46
https://eap.bl.uk/archive-file/EAP399-1-46
لإنها الجزء الثاني فقط، وقطعها مُحيَّر النصف، وليس مُحيَّر الربع.

39 أغلب الظن أن فرخ الورق طوي من جانبه الأقصر (العرض)، وليس من جانبه الأطول (الطول)، فأصبح شكل الكتاب متطاولاً.

40 هناك عملان، الأول لزكريا بن بيرم الأنقروي (ت 1001هـ/ 1593م)، يُنظر نويهض، عادل، معجم المفسرين من صدر الإسلام وحتى العصر الحاضر، ج 1، 196. والثاني للكهنوي ملا غلام نقشبند بن عطاء الله (ت 1126هـ/ 1714م). يُنظر الفهرس الشامل، علوم القرآن: مخطوطات التفسير وعلومه، ج2، 747.

41 حاشية الأنطاكي أو حاشية على الجزء الثلاثين من تفسير القرآن الكريم، الأنطاكي مصطفى بن حسن (ت 1100هـ/ 1689م). وهذه النسخة محفوظة في مكتبة وزارة الأوقاف المصرية برقم 3018.

-77 مجموعة أولها فضائل القرآن العظيم[42] ويليها عشرة رسائل بخط مصري قطع الثمن مُجَلَّد بلا ظرف جلد1.

-78 حمائل[43] بخط مصري قطع الثمن بلا ظرف جلد1.

-79 ذهاب ليل الشكوك في معنى قوله تعالى ﴿إن الملوك﴾ بخط مصري قطع الربع مُجَلَّد بلا ظرف جلد1.

-80 شرح آية الإسراء بخط مصري قطع الربع مُجَلَّد بلا ظرف جلد1.[44]

كتب علم القراءات[45]

[17]

5 [كتب علم القراءات[46]]

-81 الإتقان[47] في علوم القرآن بخط مصري قطع كامل مُجَدْوَل بأحمر مُجَلَّد بظرف جلد1.[48]

-82 حجج القرآن بخط نسخ قطع النصف مُحَيَّر مُجَلَّد بظرف جلد1.

-83 منتهى الأماني والمسرات في علوم القراءات[49] بخط مصري مُجَلَّد بلا ظرف جلد1.

-84 لطائف الإشارات بخط مصري قطع الربع مُجَلَّد بلا ظرف جلد1.

-85 بدائع البرهان في علوم القرآن بخط مصري مُجَلَّد بلا ظرف جلد1.

-86 الأول من لطائف الإشارات بخط مصري قطع النصف عتيق مُجَلَّد بلا ظرف جلد1.

-87 ذكر وقوفات القرآن بخط مصري قطع الربع مُحَيَّر مُجَلَّد بظرف جلد1.

---

42 يُنظر الفهرس الشامل، علوم القرآن: مخطوطات التفسير وعلومه، ج2، 1215- 1216.

43 وهي التمائم والتعويذات التي استُخدِمَت فيها آيات من القرآن وسوره. يُنظر:
Burak, Guy. "The Section on Prayers, Invocations, Unique Qualities of the Qur'an, and Magic Squares in the Palace Library Inventory," in Treasures of Knowledge: An Inventory of the Ottoman Palace Library (1502/3–1503/4).

44 عدد مجلدات كتب التفسير الشريفة هو 77، ولكنه لم يسجلها هنا.

45 في الأصل: القرات. تعقيبة في الهامش الأيسر السفلي.

46 في الأصل القرات.

47 في الأصل: التقان. وهو لجلال الدين السيوطي (ت 911هـ/ 1505م).

48 هذا الوصف الببليوغرافي ينطبق على النسخة المحفوظة في المكتبة الخالدية بالقدس برقم AKDI 00073 0586
https://w3id.org/vhmml/readingRoom/view/508759
وليس على النسخة المحفوظة حالياً في مكتبة جامع النور أحمديَّة بعكا رقم 4، وصورتها في المكتبة البريطانية رقم EAP399/1/50
https://eap.bl.uk/archive-file/EAP399-1-50
لأن هذه النسخة غير مُجَدْوَلة بأحمر.

49 في الأصل: القرات.

88- تقريب النشر في القراءات[50] العشر بخط مصري قطع الربع مُجلَّد بظرف جلد1.

89- النشر في القراءات[51] العشر بخط مصري قطع الربع مُجلَّد بلا ظرف وهو الجزؤ الثاني[52] جلد1.

90- التيسير لابن الجوزي بخط مصري قطع الربع مُجلَّد بظرف جلد1.

91- ترتيب زيبا بخط مصري قطع الربع مُجلَّد بلا ظرف جلد1.[53]

92- شاطبية بخط نسخ قطع كامل مُجْدَوَل بأحمر مُجلَّد بلا ظرف جلد1.

93- شاطبية بخط نسخ مُجْدَوَل بأحمر قطع الربع مُجلَّد بظرف جلد1.

94- شاطبية بخط نسخ قطع النصف مُحيَّر عتيق مُجلَّد بظرف جلد1.

95- شاطبية بخط نسخ قطع الربع مُجلَّد بلا ظرف جلد1.

96- شاطبية بخط مصري مُجْدَوَل بأحمر قطع الثمن عتيق بلا جلد ولا ظرف جلد1.

97- شرح الشاطبية بخط مصري قطع الربع مُجلَّد بظرف جلد1.

98- شرح الشاطبية بخط مصري قطع الربع مُجلَّد بلا ظرف جلد1.

99- شرح الشاطبية بخط مصري قطع النصف مُجلَّد بظرف جلد1.

100- شرح الشاطبية بخط مصري قطع الربع مُجلَّد بلا ظرف جلد1.

101- شرح الشاطبية بخط مصري قطع الربع مُجلَّد بلا ظرف جلد1.

102- قراءة[54] حفص من طريق الشاطبية بخط مصري قطع الربع مُجلَّد بلا ظرف جلد1.

103- مأخذ الخلاف من شاطبية بخط مصري قطع الربع مُجلَّد بظرف جلد1.

104- التحفة في حل مشكلات الشاطبية بخط نسخ مُجلَّد بلا ظرف جلد1.

105- متن الجزرية نسختين بخط مصري قطع الربع مُجلَّدين بلا ظرف جلد2، فقط اثنان.

106- متن الجزرية بخط مصري قطع الربع مُجلَّد بظرف جلد1.

107- مجموع أدلة متن الجزرية بخط مصري قطع الربع مُجلَّد بلا ظرف جلد1.

108- شرح الجزرية لتلميذ المصنف بخط مصري قطع الثمن عتيق مُجلَّد بلا ظرف جلد1.

109- الفوائد المسعدية في حل المقدمة الجزرية بخط مصري قطع الربع مُجلَّد بظرف جلد1.

110- البديع فيما رسم في معرفة التاء والهاء والواو والياء في المصحف بخط مصري قطع الثمن مُجلَّد بظرف جلد1.

111- مقدمة في وقف حمزة وهشام بخط مصري قطع الربع مُجلَّد بلا ظرف جلد1. [18]

50 في الأصل: القرأت.

51 في الأصل القرات.

52 في الأصل: وهو الجزؤ والثاني.

53 هذه النسخة محفوظة في المكتبة الأزهرية، برقم 874.

54 في الأصل: قرأة.

-112 المسائل والأجوبة جزؤين بخط مصري قطع الربع مُجلَّدين بظرفين جلد2، فقط اثنان.

-113 المقصد لتلخيص المرشد بخط مصري قطع الربع مُجلَّد بلا ظرف جلد1.

-114 كتاب الشمعة بخط مصري قطع الربع مجلَّد بلا ظرف جلد1.

-115 كتاب التتمة بخط مصري قطع الربع مُحيَّر مُجلَّد بلا ظرف جلد1.

-116 العنوان بخط مصري قطع الربع مُجلَّد بلا ظرف جلد1.

-117 بغية المستفيد بخط مصري قطع الثمن مُجلَّد بلا ظرف جلد1.

-118 قرة العين بخط نسخ قطع الربع مُجلَّد بلا ظرف جلد1.

-119 إرشاد الطلبة إلى شواهد الطيبة بخط مصري قطع الربع واسع مُجلَّد بلا ظرف جلد1.[55]

-120 اللؤلؤ المكنون بخط مصري قطع الربع مُجلَّد بلا ظرف جلد1.

-121 عمدة العرفان بخط مصري قطع الربع مُجلَّد واسع بلا ظرف جلد1.

-122 متن في تكملة العشرة ومعه الجزرية بخط مصري قطع الربع مُجلَّد بلا ظرف جلد1.

-123 تجويد القواعد المقررة بخط مصري قطع الربع مُجلَّد بلا ظرف جلد1.

-124 زبدة البيان بخط نسخ قطع النصف مُحيَّر مُجلَّد بظرف جلد1.

-125 كتاب التنبيه بخط مصري قطع الربع واسع مُجلَّد بظرف جلد1.

-126 رسالة إجازة في علم القراءات[56] بخط مصري قطع الثمن مُجلَّد بلا ظرف جلد1.

-127 رسالة في جمع أوجه التكبير بخط نسخ قطع ربع مُجلَّد بلا ظرف جلد1.

-128 رسالة في جمع أوجه التكبير بخط نسخ قطع[57] مُجلَّد بلا ظرف جلد1.

-129 رسالة في بيان تصحيح المعتمد بخط نسخ قطع الثمن مُجلَّد بلا ظرف جلد1.

-130 رسالة أوجه التكبير بخط مصري قطع الربع مُجلَّد بلا ظرف جلد1.

-131 إنشاد الشريد بخط مصري قطع الربع واسع مُجلَّد بلا ظرف جلد1.

-132 إجازة في القراءات[58] العشرة من طريق الشاطبية بخط مصري قطع الربع مُجلَّد بلا ظرف جلد1.

-133 رسالة في علم التجويد بخط مصري قطع الربع مُجلَّد بلا ظرف جلد1.

-134 رسالة في جمع أوجه التكبير بخط مصري قطع الربع مُجلَّد بلا ظرف جلد1.

-135 الدرر اللوامع بخط نسخ قطع الربع مُجلَّد بلا ظرف جلد1.

---

55 وهذه النسخة محفوظة اليوم في مكتبة جامعة الإمام محمد بن سعود الإسلاميَّة بالرياض، برقم 979.

56 في الأصل: القرأت. العمل عبارة عن إجازة تُمنح لمن حفظ القرآن بمختلف طرق التلاوة.

57 نسي أن يحدد القطع.

58 في الأصل: القرأت.

136- إجازة في القراءات[59] العشرة بخط مصري قطع الربع مُجَلَّد بلا ظرف جلد1.

137- شرح أرجوزة مشكلات القرآن بخط مصري قطع الربع مُجَلَّد بلا ظرف جلد1.

138- حصن القارئ في اختلاف المقارئ بخط مصري قطع الربع مُجَلَّد بلا ظرف جلد1.

139- رسالة نظم مخارج الحروف بخط مصري قطع الربع مُجَلَّد بلا ظرف جلد1.

140- متن الجزرية بخط نسخ قطع الثمن مُجَلَّد بلا ظرف جلد1.

حسابه نمرو 62 فقط اثنين وستين لا غير

كتب الحديث الشريف[60]

[19] 6 كتب الحديث الشريف

141- بخاري شريف تام أجزاء ثلاثون في صندوق ومع فهرست1، بخط نسخ قطع الربع مُجَدْوَل بإكليل بجلود حمر جديدة جلد31. فقط واحد وثلاثون.

142- بخاري شريف تام بخط مصري عالٍ مجدول بأحمر ولازورد قطع كامل بجلد مُذَهَّب وظرف جلد1.

143- السابع من صحيح البخاري بخط ريحاني قطع الربع مُجَلَّد عتيق الورق والجلد جلد1.

144- الأول من القسطلاني ناقص الأول المسمى بالساري شرح صحائح البخاري بخط مصري جديد قطع كامل مُجَلَّد بلا ظرف جلد1.

145- الأول والثالث من القسطلاني شرح البخاري بخط مصري قطع كامل مُجَلَّد جديد بلا ظرف جلد2، فقط اثنان.

146- الرابع من القسطلاني شرح البخاري المعبر عنه بتفسير أبي ذر غلطاً بخط مصري قطع كامل جديد مُجَلَّد بلا ظرف جلد1.

147- الثاني من فتح الباري شرح البخاري بخط مصري قطع كامل مُجَلَّد بظرف جلد1.

148- الخامس من فتح الباري شرح البخاري بخط مصري قطع الربع مُجَلَّد بظرف جلد1.

149- الثاني من فتح الباري شرح صحيح البخاري بخط مصري قطع النصف مُحَيَّر مُجَلَّد بظرف جلد1.

150- الرابع عشر من فتح الباري شرح صحيح البخاري بخط مصري قطع الربع مُجَلَّد بظرف جلد1.[61]

151- شرح مختصر البخاري للأجهوري بخط مصري قطع الربع مُجَلَّد بظرف جلد1.

152- الثاني من صحيح مسلم بخط ريحاني قطع الربع واسع مُجَلَّد بظرف جلد1.

153- الثاني من صحيح مسلم بخط مصري قطع النصف مُجَلَّد بظرف جلد1.

---

59 في الأصل: القرأت.

60 تعقيبة في الهامش الأيسر السفلي.

61 هذه النسخة محفوظة في مكتبة جامعة النجاح بنابلس رقم (NL 211508) https://manuscripts.najah.edu/node/594?page=2

154- الثاني من شر[ح] البخاري للكرماني بخط مصري قطع النصف مُحيَّر مُجَلَّد بظرف جلد1.

155- شفا شريف بخط تعليق عالٍ مُذَهَّب ظاهراً وباطناً قطع الربع مُجَلَّد بظرف جلد1.

156- شفا شريف بخط نسخ عالٍ مُذَهَّب ظاهراً وباطناً قطع الربع مُجَلَّد بظرف جلد1.

157- شفا شريف بخط مصري قطع الربع مُجَلَّد بظرف جلد1.

158- شفا شريف بخط تعليق عالٍ مُذَهَّب قطع الربع مُجَلَّد بظرف جلد1.

159- شفا شريف بخط مصري مُحَشًّى قطع النصف قديم مُجَلَّد بلا ظرف جلد1.

160- شفا شريف بخط نسخ مُجَدْوَل بأحمر قطع الربع مُحيَّر مُجَلَّد بلا ظرف جلد1.

161- شمائل شريفة بخط ريحاني مُجَدْوَل بأحمر قطع الربع مُجَلَّد بظرف جلد1.

162- الأول والثاني من جامع الحافظ الترمذي بخط مصر[ي] قطع الربع مُجَلَّدين بظرفين جلد2، فقط اثنان.

163- الجامع الصغير بخط مصري قطع الربع مُجَلَّد بظرف جلد1.

164- متن الأربعين حديثاً بخط ريحاني قطع الثمن مُذَهَّب مُجَلَّد بلا ظرف جلد1.

165- متن الأربعين حديثاً بخط نسخ قطع الثمن مُجَلَّد عتيق بلا ظرف جلد1.

166- متن الأربعين حديثاً بخط مصري قطع الربع مُجَلَّد بلا ظرف جلد1.

167- متن الأربعين حديثاً بخط مصري قطع الربع مُجَلَّد بظرف جلد1.

168- متن الأربعين حديثاً ومختصر البخاري وشرح الجزرية[62] بخط مصري قطع الربع مُجَلَّد بظرف جلد1. [20]

169- متن الأربعين حديثاً بخط مغربي قطع الثمن مُجَلَّد بلا ظرف جلد1.

170- المواهب اللدنية بخط مصري جديد قطع الربع بجلد أحمر بلا ظرف جلد1.

171- الأول من المواهب اللدنية بخط مصري قطع الربع مُجَلَّد بلا ظرف جلد1.

172- المصابيح بخط مصري مُهَمَّش قطع الربع مُجَلَّد بلا ظرف جلد1.

173- شرح المشارق بخط مصري قطع الربع[63] مُجَلَّد بظرف جلد1.

174- شرعة الإسلام بخط نسخ مُهَمَّشة قطع الربع مُجَلَّد بظرف جلد1.

175- الإشاعة بخط مصري قطع الربع مُجَلَّد بظرف جلد1.

176- الإشاعة بخط مصري قطع الثمن مُجَلَّد بلا ظرف جلد1.

177- الصواعق المحرقة بخط مصري قطع الربع مُجَلَّد بظرف جلد1.

178- النهاية في غريب الحديث بخط مصري قطع كامل مُجَلَّد بظرف جلد1.

179- الأول والثاني من سيرة الحلبي بخط مصري قطع الربع مُجَلَّدين بلا ظرف جلد2، فقط اثنان.

180- جزؤين من سيرة الحلبي بخط مصري قطع الربع مُجَلَّدين بظرف وبلا ظرف جلد2، فقط اثنان.

---

62 للمقدمة الجزرية في علم التجويد شروح كثيرة. يُنظر خليفة، كشف الظنون، ج2، 1799.

63 في الأصل: الرابع. مبارق الأزهار في شرح مشارق الأنوار. لابن ملك، عبد اللطيف بن عبد العزيز (ت 801هـ/ 1398م).

-181 جزؤين من سيرة الحلبي ناقص الأول بخط مصري قطع الربع مُجَلَّد بظرف جلد1.

-182 قطع من سيرة الحلبي ناقص الأول بخط مصري قطع كامل مُجَلَّد بلا بظرف جلد1.

-183 الصواعق المحرقة بخط مصري قطع الربع مُجَلَّد بلا ظرف جلد1.

-184 توضيح ما خفا من ألفاظ الشفا بخط مصري قطع الربع مُحَيَّر مُجَلَّد بظرف جلد1.

-185 خلاصة الأخبار في ذكر النبي المختار صلى الله عليه وسلم بخط مصري قطع الربع مُجَلَّد بظرف جلد1.

-186 الإشراف في فضائل الأشراف بخط مصري قطع الربع مُجَلَّد بظرف جلد1.[64]

-187 مطالع المسرات بخط مصري قطع الربع مُجَلَّد بظرف جلد1.

-188 مطالع المسرات بخط مصري مُجَدْوَل بأحمر قطع الربع مُجَلَّد بلا ظرف جلد1.

-189 الخلاصة في معرفة الحديث بخط تعليق عالٍ قطع النصف مُحَيَّر مُجَلَّد بظرف جلد1.[65]

-190 مطالع المسرات بخط مصري مُجَلَّد مُجَدْوَل بأحمر بلا ظرف جلد1.

-191 الإشاعة في أشراط الساعة بخط نسخ قطع الربع مُجَلَّد بظرف جلد1.

-192 التذكار بأطيب الأذكار بخط نسخ قطع الربع مُحَيَّر مُجَلَّد بظرف جلد1.

-193 البيان والتوضيح تراجم رجال الحديث بخط مصري قطع الربع مُجَلَّد عتيق بظرف جلد1.[66]

-194 الأذكار بخط نسخ عالٍ مُجَدْوَل بإكليل مُذَهَّب الجلد قطع الربع واسع مُجَلَّد بظرف جلد1.

الأذكار بخط مصري قطع الثمن مُجَلَّد بلا ظرف جلد1.[67]

[21] -195 الأذكار بخط مصري قطع الثمن مُجَلَّد بلا ظرف جلد1.

-196 الأذكار بخط مصري قطع الربع مُجَلَّد بظرف جلد1.

-197 الأذكار بخط مصري قطع النصف مُجَلَّد بلا ظرف جلد1.

-198 شرح الأربعين للمصري ناقص الآخر بخط مصري قطع الربع مُجَلَّد بظرف جلد1.

-199 شرح الأربعين بخط نسخ مُجَدْوَل بأحمر قطع الربع مُحَيَّر مُجَلَّد بلا ظرف جلد1.

-200 شرح الأربعين للعاملي بخط مصري مُجَدْوَل بأحمر قطع الربع مُجَلَّد بظرف جلد1.

-201 مولد شريف ويليه رسائل بخط مصري قطع الثمن مُجَلَّد بظرف جلد1.

-202 مولد شريف لابن حجر بخط مصري قطع الربع مُجَلَّد بظرف جلد1.

---

64 للسمهودي، إبراهيم الحسيني (حي 963هـ/ 1555م). هذه النسخة محفوظة في المكتبة الخالدية بالقدس. الرقم AKDI 01699 1125 https://w3id.org/vhmml/readingRoom/view/510065

65 للطيبي، الحسين بن محمد (ت 743هـ/ 1342م). هذه النسخة محفوظة في مكتبة جامعة القديس يوسف ببيروت برقم USJ 2 00214 https://www.vhmml.org/readingRoom/view/129045

66 هذه النسخة محفوظة في مكتبة الجامعة الأمريكية ببيروت برقم AUB MS 920.05 I65bA

67 تعقيبة في الهامش الأيسر السفلي.

203- مولد شريف ويليه رسائل بخط مصري قطع الربع مُجَلَّد بلا ظرف جلد1.

204- سيرة النبي علية الصلوة والسلام بخط مصري قطع الربع مُجَلَّد بلا ظرف جلد1.

205- الزواجر بخط مصري قطع الربع واسع بجلد مذهب وظرف جلد1.

206- مسند أبي نعيم بخط ريحاني قطع النصف مُحيَّر مُجَلَّد بلا ظرف جلد1.

207- الإصابة في أسماء الصحابة بخط مصري قطع كامل مُجَلَّد بظرف جلد1.

208- الإحياء للغزالي خمسة أجزاء بخط ريحاني قطع النصف مُجَلَّد بلا ظرف جلد5، فقط خمسة.

209- شرح نخبة الفكر في مصطلح أهل الأثر بخط مصري قطع الربع مُجَلَّد بظرف جلد1.

210- الدراية في الحديث بخط تعليق قطع الثمن مُجَلَّد عتيق بلا ظرف جلد1.

211- البدور السافرة بخط ريحاني قطع الربع مُجَلَّد بظرف جلد1.

212- الدرة الفاخرة في علوم الآخرة بخط [...][68] قطع الربع مُجَلَّد بظرف جلد1.[69]

213- مطالع المسرات بخط نسخ قطع الربع مُجَلَّد بظرف جلد1.

214- الحصن الحصين بخط نسخ عالٍ مُجَدْوَل بإكليل مُهَمَّش قطع الربع مُجَلَّد بظرف جلد1.

215- شرح الحصن الحصين بخط مصري مُجَدْوَل بأحمر قطع الربع مُجَلَّد بظرف جلد1.[70]

216- أحاديث الكشاف بخط نسخ قطع النصف مُحيَّر مُجَدْوَل بأحمر مُجَلَّد بظرف جلد1.

217- ربيع الأبرار للزمخشري بخط مصري مُجَدْوَل بأحمر قطع كامل مُجَلَّد بلا ظرف جلد1.

218- شرح الهمزية لابن حجر بخط مصري مُجَدْوَل بأحمر قطع الربع مُجَلَّد بظرف جزوين جلد2، فقط اثنان.

219- شرح الهمزية لابن حجر بخط مصري قطع الربع مُجَلَّد بلا ظرف جلد1.

220- شرح المحيّا بخط مصري قطع الربع مُجَلَّد بظرف جلد1.

---

68 فراغ في الأصل بمقدار كلمة. للغزالي، محمد بن محمد (ت 505هـ/ 1111م).

69 أعتقد أنَّ هذه هي النسخة المحفوظة في مكتبة جامعة لايبزيغ برقم Vollers 118، وليس النسخة المكررة تحت الرقم 1629. لأنه لا يوجد عليها تملك للشيخ علي الرشيدي، أو للشيخ محمد وكيلخرج.

https://www.refaiya.uni-leipzig.de/receive/RefaiyaBook_islamhs_00000015?&page=vollers_118_003.jpg&derivate=RefaiyaBook_derivate_00000181&zoom=3&x=0&y=0&tosize=screen&maximized=true&rotation=0

70 أغلب الظن أن المقصود هو الحرز الثمين للحصن الحصين. للملا علي القاري، علي بن سلطان محمد (ت 1014هـ/ 1606م). وأنها النسخة المحفوظة في المكتبة الوطنية بالقدس برقم Ms. AP Ar. 258، وعلى الرغم من أن خاتم الوقف مطموس إلا أن سبب ترجيح هذه النسخة هو تتطابقها إلى حدٍ كبير مع الوصف البيبليوغرافي المعطى عنها من حيث قطع الورق، أي قطع الربع المحيّر (15.5 x 21.5سم) ، ومن حيث الجدولة بالأحمر. يُضاف إلى ذلك أن الحدود الرئيسة للخاتم مرئية بوضوح، وحجم الخاتم متطابق مع حجم خاتم الجزار (4 x 4.3 سم) .ومساحة الجزء السفلي للخاتم أيضا متطابقة مع مثيلتها في خاتم الجزار، أي 1 سم. نشكر الباحث (Vincent Engelhardt) الذي اكتشف هذه المخطوطة وقدم البيانات عن الخاتم.

https://www.nli.org.il/he/manuscripts/NNL_ALEPH003484093/NLI#$FL197324931

221- حاشية على الترغيب لبرهان الدين المحدث بخط مصري قطع الربع مُجلَّد بظرف جلد1.[71]

222- كتاب أدعية وأحاديث بخط مصري قطع الربع مُجلَّد بظرف جلد1.

223- كتاب المعجزات الباهرة بخط مصري قطع الربع بظرف جلد1.

224- المنجم في المعجم للسيوطي بخط مصري قطع الربع مُجلَّد بظرف جلد1.

225- المجالس[72] الشامية في المواعظ الرومية بخط مصري قطع الربع مُجْدْوَل بأحمر مُجلَّد بظرف جلد1.

226- فضائل آل البيت بخط نسخ قطع الثمن مُجلَّد بظرف جلد1.

227- كتاب في بيان الأحاديث و[الخواص؟] ويليه عشرة رسائل بخط مصري قطع الربع مُجلَّد بظرف جلد1.

228- الفوز العظيم بخط مصري قطع الربع مُجلَّد بظرف جلد1. [22]

229- سدرة المنتهى بخط مصري قطع الربع مُجلَّد بظرف جلد1.

230- بهجة النفوس بخط مصري قطع الربع مُجلَّد بظرف جلد1.

231- صفحة آل البيت بخط نسخ جديد مُجْدْوَل بأحمر قطع الربع مُحيَّر بجلد مُذَهَّب بلا ظرف جلد1.

232- كتاب نوع من الأحاديث بخط نسخ مصري قطع النصف مُجلَّد بظرف جلد1.

233- اختيار الأولَى في شرح حديث اختصم الملأ الأعلى بخط مصري قطع الربع مُجلَّد بظرف جلد1.

234- كتاب أسماء الرواة بخط مصري نسخ قطع الثمن مُجلَّد بظرف جلد1.

235- كتاب وِرْد السحر وصلوات البكري[73] قدّس سرّه بخط نسخ قطع الربع مُجلَّد بظرف جلد1.

236- شرح البرء لابن مرزوق بخط مصري مُجْدْوَل بأحمر قطع كامل مُجلَّد بلا ظرف جلد1.

237- دلائل النبوة بخط مصري قطع النصف مُجلَّد عتيق بلا ظرف جلد1.

238- الطريقة المحمدية بخط نسخ جديد مُهمَّش مُجْدْوَل بأحمر قطع الربع مُحيَّر مُجلَّد بلا ظرف جلد1.

239- كتاب أحاديث شريفة وإجازات صريحة بخط مصري قطع الربع مُجلَّد بظرف جلد1.

240- كتاب النفحات السنية بخط تعليق مُجْدْوَل بأحمر قطع الربع مُجلَّد بظرف جلد1.

241- كتاب شجرة نسب النبي صلى الله عليه وسلم بخط ريحاني ونسخ ألوان مختلفة قطع كامل مُجلَّد بلا ظرف جلد1.

242- الروح بخط نسخ جديد قطع الربع مُجلَّد بلا ظرف جلد1.

243- البركة في فضل السعي والحركة بخط مصري قطع الربع مُجلَّد بلا ظرف جلد1.

244- اللطف بخط نسخ عالي مُجْدْوَل بإكليل قطع الربع مُجلَّد بظرف جلد1.

245- كتاب العظمة بخط نسخ مصر[ي] قطع الربع مُذَهَّب ظاهراً وباطناً مُجلَّد بلا ظرف جلد1.

71 عجالة الإملاء المتيسرة من التذنيب على ما وقع للحافظ المنذري من الوهم في كتاب الترغيب والترهيب. لبرهان الدين الحلبي، إبراهيم بن محمد بن محمود الناجي (ت 900هـ/ 1495م). وهذه النسخة محفوظة في المكتبة البريطانية. London, British Library, Or. 4706

72 في الأصل: «المجالسة».

73 في الأصل: وصلوات لكبرى.

246- كتاب تعلم الفروسية بخط نسخ قطع النصف مُحيَّر مُجلَّد بلا ظرف جلد1.

247- رياض الجنة بخط مصري قطع الربع مُجلَّد بظرف جلد1.

248- خير البشر بخط مصري قطع الربع مُجلَّد بظرف جلد1.

249- الفوائد في الصلة والعوائد بخط مصري قطع الربع مُجلَّد بظرف جلد1.

250- عين العلم مختصر الإحياء[74] بخط تعليق مُجدْوَل بأحمر قطع الربع مُجلَّد بلا ظرف جلد1.

251- رياض أهل الجنة بخط مصري قطع الربع مُجلَّد بلا ظرف جلد1.

252- رياض الصالحين[75] بخط مصري قطع النصف مُحيَّر مُجلَّد بلا ظرف جلد1.

253- نزهة المشتاق بخط مصري قطع الربع مُجلَّد بظرف جلد1.

254- صيغ صلوات على النبي صلى الله عليه وسلم بخط مغربي قطع النصف مُجلَّد بلا ظرف جلد1.

255- حيوة القلوب بخط تعليق قطع النصف مُجلَّد بلا ظرف جلد1.

256- حلية الخاقاني بخط تعليق تركي قطع الثمن مُجلَّد بظرف جلد1.

257- نفحات العوارف وهي قطعة من المواهب بخط مصري قطع الربع مُجلَّد بلا ظرف جلد1.

258- الدر المنظم بخط نسخ مُجدْوَل بأحمر قطع الربع مُجلَّد بظرف جلد1.

259- سلوة الكئيب بوفاة الحبيب بخط مصري قطع الربع مُجلَّد بظرف جلد1.

260- أسماء أهل بدر وغير ذلك بخط نسخ عالٍ مُذَهَّب ظاهراً وباطناً قطع الربع مُحيَّر مُجلَّد بلا ظرف جلد1.

عقيلة وهمزية.[76]

261- عقيلة وهمزية ومواهب ورسائل بخط مصري قطع الربع مُجلَّد بظرف جلد1. [23]

262- كنز الأسرار بخط مصري قطع كامل مُجلَّد بظرف جلد1.

263- روضة العلماء بخط نسخ قطع كامل مُجلَّد بظرف جلد1.

264- اللباب[77] للسيوطي بخط مصري قطع الربع مُجلَّد بلا ظرف جلد1.

265- الدر المستطاب بخط نسخ قطع الربع مُجلَّد بلا ظرف جلد1.

266- مطلع النيرين بخط التعليق قطع الربع طويل مُجلَّد بلا ظرف جلد1.

267- كتاب في مدح النبي صلى الله عليه وسلم بخط مصري قطع الربع مُجلَّد بظرف جلد1.

268- كتاب في فضل آل البيت والصحابة بخط ريحاني قطع الربع مُجلَّد بظرف جلد1.

269- كنز الادخار بخط نسخ مُجدْوَل بأحمر قطع الثمن مُجلَّد بلا ظرف جلد1.

---

74 في الأصل: الأحياء.

75 في الأصل: الحصالحين.

76 تعقيبة في الهامش الأيسر السفلي.

77 في الأصل: لاالباب.

-270 حصول الرفق بخط مصري قطع الربع مُجَلَّد بلا ظرف جلد1.

-271 منتهى العقول بخط مصري قطع الربع مُجَلَّد بظرف جلد1.

-272 تسلية الحزين بموت البنين بخط مصري قطع الربع مُجَلَّد بظرف جلد1.

-273 فوائد الصلوة على النبي صلى الله عليه وسلم بخط مصري قطع الربع مُجَلَّدين بلا ظرف جلد2، فقط اثنان.

-274 الفوائد في الصلة والعوائد بخط مصري قطع الربع مُجَلَّد بلا ظرف جلد1.

-275 نزهة الأبصار بخط مصري قطع الربع مُجَلَّد بظرف جلد1.

-276 من الروض الأنف الأول والثاني بخط مصري قطع كامل مُجَلَّدين بلا ظرف جلد2[78]، فقط اثنان.

-277 معارج النبوة بخط فارسي تعليق قطع كامل مُجَلَّد بظرف جلد1.

-278 فضل الجَلَد بوفاة الولد بخط مصري قطع الربع مُجَلَّد بظرف جلد1.

-279 شرح البرءة بخط مصري قطع الربع مُجَلَّد بظرف جلد1.

-280 الرياض الأنيقة بخط نسخ قطع الربع مُجَلَّد بظرف جلد1.

-281 ثبت محمد بن الطيب المدني للأحاديث المسلسلة بخط النسخ قطع الربع مُجَلَّد بلا ظرف جلد1.

-282 الطريقة المحمدية[79] بخط نسخ قطع الربع مُجَلَّد بلا ظرف جلد1.

-283 مشكل الصحيحين[80] بخط مصري قطع[81] مُجَلَّد عتيق بلا ظرف جلد1.

-284 دلائل الخيرات بخط مصري قطع الثمن مُجَلَّد قديم بلا ظرف جلد1.

-285 الأرج في الفرج بخط مصري قطع الربع مُجَلَّد بظرف جلد1.

-286 فوائد الآيات بخط مصري قطع الربع مُجَلَّد بظرف جلد1.

-287 الوسائل إلى معرفة الأوائل بخط مصري قطع الربع مُجَلَّد بلا ظرف جلد1.

-288 كيمياء[82] السعادة بخط مصري نسخ قطع الثمن مُجَلَّد بلا ظرف جلد1.

-289 الفرج بخط مصري قطع الثمن كَهْنا مُجَلَّد بلا ظرف جلد1.

-290 حلية الأبرار للنووي بخط مصري كَهْنا قطع النصف مُجَلَّد بلا ظرف جلد1.

-291 مراصد المطالع بخط مصري قطع الثمن مُجَلَّد بلا ظرف جلد1.

-292 سلوان المصاب بفرقة الأحباب بخط مصري مُجَدْوَل بأحمر قطع الربع مُجَلَّد بلا ظرف جلد1.

---

78 الروض الأنف أو شرح السيرة النبوية لابن هشام. للسهيلي، عبد الرحمن بن عبد الله (ت 581هـ/ 1185م). وهذه النسخة محفوظة في مكتبة تشستربيتي برقم Ar. 3294

79 في الأصل: الحمدية. يُنظر (238).

80 في الأصل: الصحين.

81 نسي تحديد القطع.

82 في الأصل: كيماء.

293- كتاب طيب الكلام بخط نسخ[83] قطع الربع مُجلَّد بظرف جلد1.

294- كتاب المهرجان بخط مصري قطع الربع مُجلَّد بظرف جلد1.

295- وصية يزيد بن الحكم بخط نسخ ممحو قطع الربع واسع مُجلَّد بظرف جلد1.

296- كتاب فضائل الشهور بخط تعليق قطع النصف مُحيَّر مُجلَّد بظرف جلد1.

297- الرسالة[84] الوجيزة بخط نسخ قطع الثمن ناقصة الأول جلد1. [24]

298- كتاب للعيني ومعراج الأجهوري[85] بخط نسخ قطع الربع مُجلَّد بظرف[86] جلد1.

299- الأحكام النبوية في الصناعة الطبية بخط مصري قطع الربع مُجلَّد بظرف جلد1.

300- كتاب طب نبوي بخط ريحاني قطع النصف مُجلَّد بلا ظرف جلد1.

301- كتاب طب نبوي بخط مصري قطع الربع مُجلَّد بظرف جلد1.

302- الرحمة في الطب والحكمة بخط نسخ قطع الربع مُجلَّد بظرف جلد1.

303- مجموع حديث بخط مصري قطع الربع مُجلَّد بظرف جلد1.

304- مجموع رسائل للعلامة الأثري المعروف بابن عقيلة المكي وفي أوله ثبت بخط نسخ قطع الربع مُجلَّد بظرف جلد1.

305- مجموع فيه كتاب كشف الأسرار ورسائل ثلاثة بخطوط[87] قطع الثمن مُجلَّد بظرف جلد1.

306- مجموع رسائل بخط مصري قطع الربع مُجلَّد بظرف جلد1.

307- مجموع فوائد ورسائل بخط مصري قطع الربع مُجلَّد عتيق بلا ظرف جلد1.

308- مجموع فضائل الشهور بخط مصري قطع الربع مُجلَّد بظرف جلد1.

309- مجموع فوائد بخط تركي قطع الثمن بظرف جلد1.

310- مجموع يشتمل على[88] ثلاثة رسائل الوصف الذميم والقول السديد وفضل الكلاب بخط مصري قطع الربع مُجلَّد بظرف جلد1.

311- بشر[ى] الكئيب في لقاء الحبيب بخط مصري قطع الربع مُجلَّد بظرف جلد1.[89]

312- كتاب أدعية وأذكار بخط نسخ قطع الثمن مُجلَّد بلا ظرف جلد1.

313- سيرة الأنبياء لعبد العزيز بخط نسخ قطع الربع مُجلَّد بظرف جلد1.

83 نسخ: مكررة في الأصل.

84 في الأصل: رسالة.

85 النور الوهاج في الكلام على الإسراء والمعراج. للأجهوري، علي بن زين العابدين بن محمد (ت 1066هـ/ 1655م).

86 في الأصل: ظرف.

87 هكذا في الأصل، وربما نسي كتابة كلمة "مختلفة".

88 في الأصل: علا.

89 هذه النسخة محفوظة في المكتبة الأزهرية برقم 83318، وهي عبارة عن مخطوط متعدد النصوص للجلال السيوطي، عبد الرحمن بن أبي بكر (ت 911هـ/ 1505م).

314- الأول من نهج البلاغة بخط مصري قطع كامل مُجَلَّد جديد بظرف جلد1.

315- الثالث والرابع والخامس من نهج البلاغة في جلد واحد بخط مصري قطع كامل مُجَلَّد بظرف جلد1.

316- السابع من شرح نهج البلاغة بخط مصري قطع النصف مُحيَّر مُجَلَّد بظرف جلد1.

317- السادس عشر من نهج البلاغة إلى العشرين بخط مصري قطع كامل مُجَلَّد بظرف جلد1.

318- مولد النبي صلى الله عليه وسلم بخط مصري قطع الربع مُجَلَّد بلا ظرف جلد1.

319- حمايلي شريف بخط نسخ قطع الثمن مُجَلَّد بلا ظرف جلد1.

320- البرهان في علامات مهدي آخر الزمان بخط مصري قطع الربع مُجَلَّد بلا ظرف جلد1.

321- مسائل عبد الله بن سلام بخط نسخ قطع الربع مُجَلَّد بلا ظرف جلد1.

322- الدرة المنيفة في السيرة الشريفة نظماً بخط مصري قطع الثمن بلا ظرف جلد1.

323- مسائل الراهب والرهبان بخط مصري قطع الربع مُجَلَّد بلا ظرف جلد1.[90]

324- الأربعين حديثا النووية بخط مصري قطع الربع مُجَلَّد بلا ظرف جلد1.

325- النفحة السنية من بعض الأحاديث القدسية بخط قطع الربع مُجَلَّد بلا ظرف جلد1.

326- مولد النبي صلى الله عليه وسلم بخط مصري قطع الربع واسع مُجَلَّد بلا ظرف جلد1.

327- مقدمة في نزول سيدنا عيسى عليه الصلاة والسلام بخط نسخ قطع الربع مُجَلَّد بلا ظرف جلد1.

328- معراج النبي صلى الله عليه وسلم بخط نسخ قطع الربع مُجَلَّد بلا ظرف جلد1.

329- معراج النبي صلى الله عليه وسلم للغيطي بخط مصري قطع الربع مُجَلَّد بلا ظرف جلد1.

330- أشرف الوسائل في أجوبة السائل نظماً بخط مصري قطع الثمن مُجَلَّد بلا ظرف جلد1.

حسابه نُمرو 231 فقط مائتين واحد وثلاثين

كتب الفقه الشريف[91]

[25] 7 كتب الفقه الشريف

331- الدرر والغرر بخط نسخ مصري مُجَدْوَل بأحمر مُهَمَّش قطع كامل مُجَلَّد بظرف جلد1.

332- الهداية بخط تعليق عالٍ مُهَمَّش مُذَهَّب ظاهراً وباطناً قطع الربع مُحيَّر مُجَلَّد بظرف جلد1.

333- من الهداية بخط مصري مُهَمَّش قطع كامل وهو الجزؤ الثاني مُجَلَّد بظرف جلد1.

334- جزؤ ثامن من[92] شرح الهداية بخط نسخ قطع النصف مُجَلَّد بلا ظرف جلد1.

90 منه نسخة في مركز الملك فيصل للبحوث والدراسات الإسلامية، رقم 02819-5.

91 تعقيبة في الهامش الأيسر السفلي.

92 في الأصل: حرف الجر من مكرر.

- 335 أجزاء أربعة من شرح الهداية بخط مصري قطع كامل بجلود بلا ظروف جلد4، فقط أربعة.
- 336 كنز الدقائق بخط نسخ مُهَمَّش قطع كامل مُحيَّر مُجلَّد بلا ظرف جلد1.
- 337 كنز الدقائق بخط مصري قطع الربع مُجلَّد بظرف جلد1.
- 338 شرح الكنز[93] لملا مسكين بخط مصري قطع الثمن مُجلَّد بلا ظرف جلد1.
- 339 شرح الكنز لملا مسكين بخط مصري قطع الربع واسع مُجلَّد بظرف جلد1.
- 340 شرح الكنز للعيني بخط مصري قطع النصف مُحيَّر مُجلَّد بظرف جلد1.
- 341 شرح الكنز وهو البحر الرائق بخط نسخ مصري مُهَمَّش مُجدْوَل بأحمر قطع كامل مُجلَّد بلا ظرف جلد1.
- 342 من شرح الكنز[94] المسمى بالبحر الرائق أجزاء ستة بخط مصري مُجلَّدين بلا ظرف جلد6، فقط ستة.[95]
- 343 الأول من شرح الهداية بخط مصري قطع كامل مُجلَّد بلا ظرف جلد1.
- 344 ملتقى الأبحر بخط نسخ مُهَمَّش قطع الربع مُجلَّد بظرف جلد1.
- 345 ملتقى الأبحر نسختين بخط تعليق قطع الربع مُجلَّدين بظرفين جلد2، فقط اثنان.
- 346 ملتقى الأبحر ناقص بخط تعليق قطع الربع مُجلَّد بظرف جلد1.
- 347 تنوير الأبصار بخط مصري قطع الربع مُجلَّد بظرف جلد1.
- 348 من شرح الكنز[96] للزيلعي أجزاء أربعة بخط مصري قطع[97] كامل مُجلَّدين بظروف جلد 4، فقط أربعة.
- 349 مجمع البحرين بخط مصري قطع الربع مُجلَّد بظرف جلد1.
- 350 شرح مجمع البحرين بخط مصري قطع النصف مُحيَّر مُجلَّد بظرف جلد1.
- 351 شرح الوهبانية بخط مصري قطع النصف مُجلَّد بلا ظرف جلد1.
- 352 الأشباه والنظائر بخط مصري قطع الربع مُجلَّد بظرف جلد1.
- 353 الوقاية بخط مصري قطع الربع مُجلَّد بظرف جلد1.
- 354 شرح الوقاية لابن كمال باشا بخط مصري قطع الربع مُجلَّد بظرف جلد1.
- 355 نور الإيضاح بخط مصري قطع الثمن مُجلَّد عتيق بلا ظرف جلد1.
- 356 نور الإيضاح بخط مصري قطع الربع عتيق غائب الخط مُجلَّد بلا ظرف جلد1.
- 357 صدر الشريعة بخط مصري مُهَمَّش قطع الربع مُجلَّد بظرف جلد1.

- 93 في الأصل: اكنز.
- 94 في الأصل: اكنز.
- 95 منه الجزء الثالث كان محفوظا في مكتبة جامع النور أحمديَّة بعكا برقم 9 حسب فهرس عطا الله سنة 1983م، ولكنه خرج من المكتبة فلم تصوره المكتبة البريطانية بمشروعها بين سنتي 2010- 2012م. أي أن هذا المخطوط خرج من المكتبة بين سنتي 1983- 2012م.
- 96 في الأصل: اكنز.
- 97 في الأصل: كلمة قطع مكررة.

358- نور الإيضاح بخط مصري قطع الربع مُجلَّد بلا ظرف جلد1.

359- القدوري بخط مصري عتيق قطع الربع مُجلَّد بظرف جلد1.

360- القدوري بخط مصري عتيق قطع الربع مُجلَّد بظرف جلد1.

361- شرح نور الإيضاح لأبي[98] السعود بخط مصري قطع النصف مُحيَّر مُجلَّد بظرف جلد1.

362- منية المصلي بخط مصري قطع الربع مُجلَّد بظرف جلد1.

363- منية المصلي بخط مصري عتيق قطع الربع مُجلَّد بلا ظرف جلد1.

364- شرح منية المصلي بخط مصري قطع الربع واسع مُجلَّد بلا ظرف جلد1. [26]

365- شرح منية المصلي بخط مصري قطع الربع مُجلَّد بظرف جلد1.

366- شرح منية المصلي الكبير للحلبي بخط مصري قطع كامل مُجلَّد بظرف جلد1.

367- شرح منية المصلي جزؤين بخط تعليق مُذَهَّب ظاهراً وباطناً قطع الربع الأول والثاني مُجلَّدين بظرفين جلد2، فقط اثنان.

368- شرح منية المصلي بخط مصري قطع الربع مُجلَّد بظرف جلد1.

369- شرح منية المصلي لإبراهيم الحلبي بخط مصري قطع الربع مُجلَّد بظرف جلد1.

370- شرح منية المصلي ناقص الأول بخط مصري قطع الربع مُجلَّد بظرف جلد1.

371- الذخائر الأشرفية في ألغاز الحنفية بخط مصري مُجلَّد بظرف جلد1.

372- عنوان الشرف بخط نسخ قطع الربع مُجلَّد بظرف لابن المقري جلد1.

373- عنوان الشرف للمقري بخط مصري قطع الربع مُجلَّد بظرف جلد1.

374- عنوان الشرف بخط نسخ قطع الربع مُجلَّد بلا ظرف جلد1.

375- الميزان بخط مصري قطع كامل مُجلَّد بلا ظرف جلد1.

376- شرعة الإسلام بخط نسخ قطع الربع مُجلَّد عتيق بلا ظرف جلد1.

377- جمع الجوامع أصول مخروم بخط مصري قطع الربع مُجلَّد بظرف جلد1.[99]

378- شرح جمع الجوامع للعيني بخط مصري قطع الربع مُجلَّد بظرف جلد1.

379- المغني[100] في أصول الفقه بخط تعليق مهمَّش قطع الربع مُجلَّد بظرف جلد1.

---

98 في الأصل: أبي السعود.

99 للجلال السيوطي، عبد الرحمن بن أبي بكر (ت 911هـ/1505م). وليس لتاج الدين السبكي (ت 771هـ/ 1370م). المحفوظ في مكتبة جامع النور أحمديَّة بعكا الجزء الرابع، وحسب فهرس محمود عطالله رقم 2، ولكن قَطْعَه الكامل مُحيَّر وليس الربع، وصورته في المكتبة البريطانية برقم EAP399/1/27

https://eap.bl.uk/archive-file/EAP399-1-27

والجزء الثالث بحسب فهرس عطالله رقم1، قطعه الكامل محيَّر، وصورته في المكتبة البريطانية برقم EAP399/1/52

https://eap.bl.uk/archive-file/EAP399-1-52

100 في الأصل: المعني.

380- المختار نسختين بخط مصري قطع الربع مُجلَّدين بظرفين جلد2، فقط اثنان.

381- المختار على فضائل الأعمال بخط مصري قطع الربع مُجلَّد بظرف جلد1.

382- شرح منظومة ابن وهبان بخط مصري قطع الربع مُجلَّد بظرف جلد1.

383- منهاج بخط نسخ عالٍ مُجدْوَل بإكليل قطع النصف مُجلَّد بظرف جلد1.

384- المنهاج بخط مصري قطع النصف مُجلَّد عتيق بلا ظرف جلد1.

385- منهاج ناقص الأول والآخر بخط مصري قطع كامل مُجلَّد بظرف جلد1.

386- من المنهاج جزؤ تاسع بخط مصري قطع النصف مُجلَّد بظرف جلد1.

387- من شرح المنهاج جزؤ ثالث بخط مصري قطع النصف مُجلَّد بظرف جلد1.

388- من شرح المنهاج جزؤ ثالث بخط مصري قطع كامل مُجلَّد بظرف جلد1.

389- الصيد والذبائح بخط مصري قطع النصف مُجلَّد بظرف جلد1.

390- مقدمة أبي[101] الليث بخط مصري قطع الربع مُجلَّد بظرف جلد1.

391- شرح المقدمة بخط مصري قطع الثمن مُجلَّد بظرف جلد1.

392- أساس الصالحين بخط ريحاني قطع الربع مُجلَّد بظرف جلد1.

393- الكسب[102] بخط مصري قطع الربع مُجلَّد بظرف جلد1.

394- تعليقات مهمة نسختين بخط نسخ قطع الربع مُجلَّد بظرف جلد2، فقط اثنان.

395- الإحرام في رفع اليدين عند تكبيرة الإحرام بخط ريحاني قطع الربع مُجلَّد بظرف جلد1.

396- ردع الراغب عن الجمع في صلاة الرغائب بخط مصري قطع الربع مُجلَّد بظرف جلد1.

397- رد الطاعن لأبي حنيفة تأليف الغزالي بخط مصري مُجلَّد بظرف جلد1.

398- في أسماء النكاح بخط مصري قطع الربع مُجلَّد بظرف جلد1.

399- شرح الدرة المنيفة بخط مصري قطع الربع مُجلَّد بظرف جلد1.

خلاصة المذهب جلد1.[103]

[27] 400- خلاصة المذهب بخط نسخ مُهمَّش قطع الربع مُحيَّر مُجلَّد بظرف جلد1.

401- الجزء الأول من المنهاج بخط مصري قطع الربع مُجلَّد بظرف جلد1.

402- البيوع والرهائن بخط مصري قطع النصف مُحيَّر مُجلَّد بظرف جلد1.

403- الثاني من الوافي بخط نسخ قطع كامل مُجلَّد بظرف جلد1.

404- الأحكام في معرفة الحلال والحرام بخط مصري قطع كامل مُجلَّد بظرف جلد1.

101 في الأصل أبو.

102 في الأصل: الكشب.

103 تعقيبة في الهامش الأيسر السفلي.

405- الرد على أبي[104] بكر الخطيب فيما ذكر في تاريخه في ترجمة الإمام سراج الأمة أبي حنيفة رضي الله عنه بخط ريحاني قطع الربع مُجلَّد بظرف جلد1.

406- أجزاء خمسة فقه شافعي[105] بخط مصري قطع كامل بجلود وظروف جلد5، فقط خمسة.

407- أحكام من الفقه شافعي جزوين بخط مصري قطع النصف مُجلَّدين بظرفين جلد2، فقط اثنان.

408- في بيان أحكام الأوقاف والصدقات بخط نسخ قطع النصف مُجلَّد بظرف جلد1.

409- الثاني من الخطيب الشربيني على أبي شجاع بخط نسخ مصري قطع الربع مُجلَّد بظرف جلد1.

410- قواعد الأحكام بخط نسخ مُهمَّش قطع كامل مُجلَّد بظرف جلد1.

411- مناسك الحج بخط مصري قطع الثمن مُجلَّد بظرف جلد1.

412- مناسك الحج بخط نسخ قطع الربع[106] مُجلَّد بظرف جلد1.

413- مناسك الحج بخط نسخ قطع الثمن مُجلَّد بلا ظرف جلد1.

414- مناسك الحج لملا علي القاري بالتركي قطع الثمن مُجلَّد بظرف جلد1.

415- أول وثاني من المهمات قطع كامل مُجلَّدين بظرفين بخط مصري جلد2، فقط اثنان.

416- الرابع من المهمات بخط مصري قطع كامل مُحيَّر مُجلَّد بظرف جلد1.[107]

417- تحرير الأحكام بخط نسخ قطع كامل مُجلَّد بظرف جلد1.

418- من الرملي الأول والثاني والثالث بخط مصري قطع الربع واسع مُجلَّدين بلا ظرف جلد3، فقط ثلاثة.

419- فقه شافعي بخط مصري قطع الربع مُجلَّد بظرف جلد1.

420- متن الغزنوي بخط مصري قطع الربع مُجلَّد بلا ظرف جلد1.

421- إرشاد الأذهان إلى الأحكام بخط نسخ مُجلَّد قطع كامل بظرف جلد1.

422- درر البحار لأحمد ابن حنبل رضي الله تعالى عنه بخط مصري قطع الربع مُجلَّد بظرف جلد1.

423- الثالث من المهذب للشيرازي بخط مصري قطع الربع مُجلَّد بظرف جلد1.

424- كتاب العشرة بخط نسخ قطع النصف مُجلَّد بظرف جلد1.

425- فقه شافعي بخط مصري قطع النصف مُحيَّر مُجلَّد بظرف جلد1.

426- الأحكام في فقه الشافعي بخط مصري قطع كامل مُحيَّر مُجلَّد بظرف جلد1.

427- المسائل اللطيفة في الخلاف بين الشافعي وأبي حنيفة بخط مصري قطع الربع مُجلَّد بظرف جلد1.

---

104 في الأصل: أبو.

105 في الأصل: شامي.

106 في الأصل: الرابع.

107 هذه النسخة محفوظة في المكتبة الوطنية بالقدس برقم Ms. AP Ar. 290
https://www.nli.org.il/en/manuscripts/NNL_ALEPH003484125/NLI#$FL168501979

428- شرح منظومة ابن العماد في الطعام بخط مصري قطع الربع مُجلَّد بظرف جلد1.

429- الإرشاد و[النظرين؟[108]] بخط نسخ قطع الربع مُجلَّد بظرف جلد1.

430- المختار بخط تعليق مُهمَّش قطع الربع مُجلَّد بظرف جلد1.

431- النهي عن ارتكاب المحارم بخط نسخ قطع الربع مُحيَّر مُجلَّد بظرف جلد1.

432- من الفقه الشافعي بخط مصري قطع الربع كبير مُجلَّد بظرف جلد1.

433- خلاصة الفتاوى بخط نسخ قطع كامل مُجلَّد بلا ظرف جلد1.

434- خلاصة الفتاوى للرافعي بخط مصري قطع كامل مُجلَّد بظرف جلد1.

435- فتاوى علي أفندي بخط مصري قطع النصف مُجلَّد بظرف في المذهب[109] الحنفي جلد1.

فتاوى البدر الرشيد.[110]

28] فارغة.

29] 436- فتاوى البدر الرشيد بخط نسخ قطع الربع مُجلَّد بظرف جلد1.

437- الثاني من الوسيط شرح المهذب بخط مصري قطع الربع مُجلَّد بظرف جلد1.

438- شرح الجامع الصغير للرازي بخط مصري قطع الربع مُحيَّر مُجلَّد بلا ظرف جلد1.[111]

439- فقه حنفي معلوم بخط تعليق قطع كامل بظرف جلد1.

440- قطعتين من الفقه[112] الحنفي بخط تعليق قطع الربع بجلدين وظرفين جلد2، فقط اثنان.

441- كتاب فقه حنفي بخط مصري قطع النصف مُجلَّد بظرف جلد1.

442- فقه حنفي بخط مصري قطع النصف مُجلَّد بظرف جلد1.

443- فقه حنفي ناقص بخط تعليق كامل مُجلَّد بظرف جلد1.

444- تكملة البحر للطوري قطع الربع بخط نسخ مُجلَّد بلا ظرف جلد1.

445- قطعة من الفقه الحنفي[113] بخط نسخ قطع الثمن مُجلَّد بظرف جلد1.

446- كتاب من أصول الفقه بخط نسخ قطع الربع مُحيَّر طويل مُجلَّد جلد1.

447- من الفقه الشافعي بخط مصري قطع كامل مُجلَّد بظرف جلد1.

448- ألفاظ الكفر بخط مصري قطع الربع مُجلَّد بظرف جلد1.

---

108 هكذا في الأصل ولم أهتد للمقصود.

109 في الأصل: مذهب.

110 تعقيبة في الهامش الأيسر السفلي. مع أنّ هذا ليس مكان التعقيبة، إلا أنه وضعها هنا لأنَّ ظهر الورقة فارغ، ولتبيان أنَّه لا يوجد نقص في المدخلات حيث نجد هذا المدخل هو بداية الصفحة [29].

111 لحسام الدين الرازي (ت 598هـ/ 1201م). هذه النسخة محفوظة في مكتبة تشستربيتي برقم Ar. 3316

112 في الأصل: فقه.

113 في الأصل: حنفي.

449- متن الزبد بخط نسخ قطع الربع مُحيَّر مُجلَّد عتيق بلا ظرف جلد1.

450- متن الزبد، وشرح الستين مسألة، بخط مصري قطع الثمن مُجلَّد عتيق بلا ظرف جلد1.

451- الإقناع بخط نسخ مصري قطع الربع مُجلَّد بلا ظرف جلد1.

452- تحرير المقال بخط نسخ مصري قطع الربع مُجلَّد بلا ظرف جلد1.

453- مقدمة الغزنوي بخط مصري قطع الثمن مُجلَّد عتيق بلا ظرف جلد1.

454- تلخيص الجامع للخلاطي بخط نسخ قطع النصف مُحيَّر مُجلَّد بلا ظرف جلد1.

455- سيف القضاة على البغاة بخط نسخ قطع الربع مُجلَّد بلا ظرف جلد1.

456- غاية المراد بخط مصري قطع الربع مُجلَّد بلا ظرف جلد1.

457- بغية الألباب بخط مصري قطع الربع مُجلَّد بظرف جلد1.

458- الفرائض والوصايا بخط مصري قطع الربع مُجلَّد بلا ظرف جلد1.

459- شروط الصلوة بخط مصري قطع الربع مُجلَّد بلا ظرف جلد1.

460- الجواهر بخط تعليق قطع الربع مُجلَّد بلا ظرف جلد1.

461- شروط الصلوة بخط ريحاني قطع الربع مُجلَّد بلا ظرف جلد1.

462- جامع الدرر بخط مصري قطع الثمن مُجلَّد بظرف جلد1.

463- كتاب فقه على مذهب الإمام الأعظم بخط نسخ قطع مُحيَّر النصف مُجلَّد بظرف جلد1.

464- شرح النقاية بخط مصري قطع الربع مُجلَّد بظرف جلد1.

465- الثاني من شرح الحاوي بخط مصري قطع النصف بظرف جلد1.

466- شرح التوضيح بخط نسخ قطع الربع مُجلَّد بظرف جلد1.

467- مختصر عنوان الأدلة للأئمة الأربعة بخط مصري قطع الربع مُجلَّد بلا ظرف جلد1.

468- معين الحكام بخط مصري قطع الربع مُحيَّر مُجلَّد بلا ظرف جلد1.

469- المنخول[114] بخط مصري قطع الربع مُجلَّد بظرف جلد1.

470- الراية بخطوط شتى قطع النصف مُجلَّد بظرف جلد1.

471- تشنيف الأسماع بخط مصري قطع الربع مُحيَّر مُجلَّد بظرف جلد1.

472- المختصر في الأحكام بخط نسخ مُحيَّر النصف مُجلَّد بظرف جلد1. [30]

473- الدراية بخط تعليق مُهمَّش قطع كامل مُجلَّد بظرف جلد1.

474- إيضاح الدلالات بخط نسخ قطع الربع مُجلَّد جديد بلا ظرف جلد1.

475- شرح البهجة بخط مصري قطع النصف مُجلَّد بظرف جلد1.

476- أحكام الصغار بخط نسخ قطع الربع مُجلَّد بلا ظرف جلد1.

---

114 في الأصل: المتحول.

477- تحفة الطلاب بخط مصري قطع الربع واسع مُجَلَّد بلا ظرف جلد1.

478- شرح الكبائر بخط نسخ تركي قطع الربع مُحَيَّر طويل مُجَلَّد بلا ظرف جلد1.

479- الثاني من شرح القواعد بخط مصري قطع الربع مُجَلَّد عتيق بلا ظرف جلد1.

480- الثاني من المستصفى بخط مصري قطع النصف مُجَلَّد بلا ظرف جلد1.

481- شرح الأخستكي بخط نسخ قطع النصف مُجَلَّد بلا ظرف جلد1.

482- الأول والثاني والثالث من مدارك الأحكام بخط تعليق قطع النصف مُجَلَّد بلا ظرف جلد1.

483- الجواهر الزكية بخط مصري قطع الربع مُجَلَّد بظرف جلد1.

484- شرح الوصية للإمام الأعظم بخط تعليق قطع الربع مُجَلَّد بظرف جلد1.

485- مجموعة رسائل، وعظ وفقه وفرائض، بخط نسخ قطع الربع مُجَلَّد بظرف مُذَهَّب جلد1.

486- حاشية على إرشاد الأذهان[115] بخط تعليق قطع الثمن مُجَلَّد عتيق بلا ظرف جلد1.

487- حاشية البرماوي بخط مصري قطع الربع مُجَلَّد عتيق بلا ظرف جلد1.

488- حاشية اللمعة في الفقه بخط تعليق قطع الربع مُجَلَّد بلا ظرف جلد1.

489- جمع المناسك بخط تعليق قطع النصف مُجَلَّد أخضر بلا ظرف جلد1.

490- الأول والثاني من تحفة الحريص شرح التلخيص بخط نسخ قطع النصف مُجَلَّدين بلا ظرف جلد2، فقط اثنان.

491- المقاصد السنية بخط[116] مصري قطع الربع مُجَلَّد بظرف جلد1.

492- الوجوه والنظائر بخط مصري قطع الربع واسع مُجَلَّد بظرف جلد1.[117]

493- المنحة البقاعية بخط مصري قطع الربع مُجَلَّد بلا ظرف جلد1.

494- تحفة الرائض في علم الفرائض بخط مصري قطع الربع مُجَلَّد بظرف جلد1.

495- كتاب في علم الفرائض بخط نسخ قطع الثمن طويل مُجَلَّد بظرف جلد1.

496- شرح الإيجاز في الفرائض للكرماني[118] بخط مصري قطع الربع مُجَلَّد بظرف جلد1.

497- شرح المختصر للعضد في أصول الفقه بخط تعليق قطع الربع بلا ظرف جلد1.

498- جزؤ من المسالك بخط مصري قطع الربع مُجَلَّد عتيق بلا ظرف جلد1.

499- شرح جمع الجوامع بخط مصري قطع الربع مُجَلَّد بظرف جلد1.

500- وصية الإمام الأعظم بخط مصري عتيق قطع الربع مُجَلَّد بلا ظرف جلد1.

115 في الأصل الأزمان.

116 في الأصل: مكرر بخط بخط.

117 الوجوه والنظائر في القرآن. لهارون بن موسى الأزدي الأعور (ت 170هـ/ 786م). هذه النسخة محفوظة في مكتبة تشستر بيتي برقم 3334. ولكنها في علم التفسير وليس في علم الفقه.

118 في الأصل: لكرماني.

-501 عنوان الشرف قطع النصف مُجَلَّد بظرف جلد1.

-502 الثاني من منتهى المطلب لابن حنبل بخط مصري قطع كامل مُجَلَّد بلا ظرف جلد1.

-503 وقفية الشيخ السيد محمود بن الشيخ السيد محمد النقشبندي بخط نسخ قطع الربع مُجَلَّد بلا ظرف جلد1.

-504 شرح الرحبية فرائض بخط مصري قطع الربع مُجَلَّد بلا ظرف جلد1.

-505 متن الستين مسألة بخط نسخ قطع الثمن مُجَلَّد بلا ظرف جلد1.

-506 شرح الرملي الكبير على الستين مسألة بخط مصري قطع الربع مُجَلَّد بظرف جلد1.

-507 مناسك الحج على مذهب الإمام الأعظم أبي حنيفة رضي الله تعالى عنه وأمدنا به بخط نسخ قطع الثمن مُجَلَّد بلا ظرف جلد1.

-508 متن العشماوية على مذهب سيدنا مالك بن أنس رضي الله تعالى عنه وأمدنا به بخط مصري قطع الثمن مُجَلَّد بلا ظرف جلد1.

[31] 8 **عن بيان عدد الكتب المأخوذة من السيد يحيى أفندي ابن السيد محمد الطيبي بيافا كما مرقوم أدناه في 23 ص[119] سنة 1218 وذلك[120] موجود بهم بعض كتب.**

-509 كتاب كنوز الحقائق نُمرو1.

-510 عن رسالة روح القدس نُمرو1.

-511 كتب الأول من صفة الصفوة نُمرو1.

-512 كتاب سبب نزول القرآن نُمرو1.

-513 كتاب عنقاء مغرب نُمرو1.

-514 كتاب تسهيل السبيل نُمرو1.

-515 كتاب خريدة[121] العجائب نُمرو1.

-516 كتاب أشرف الوسائل نُمرو1.

-517 كتاب الصحاح باللغة قطع الكامل مُذَهَّب نُمرو1.

-518 كتاب رفع الكساء نُمرو1.

-519 كتاب شرح المنظومة المسماة بالفرائد[122] السنية نسخ حنفي نُمرو1.

---

119 أي شهر صفر.

120 في الأصل: وذالك.

121 في الأصل: جريدة.

122 في الأصل: المسما باالفرائض.

-520 كتاب البخاري مُجَلَّد مذهب قطع الكامل نُمرو2، فقط اثنان.

-521 كتاب معالم التنزيل في تفسير القرآن مُجَلَّد نُمرو2، فقط اثنان.

-522 كتاب اللغة مُذَهَّب [مخلوج؟[123]] نُمرو2.

-523 كتاب تفسير البيضاوي قطع ربع نُمرو1.

-524 كتاب شرح منية المصلي نُمرو1.

-525 كتاب جلال الدين ابن كمال الدين السيوطي الشافعي في نزول القرآن ومواقفه نُمرو1.

-526 كتاب حياة[124] الحيوان نُمرو1.

-527 كتاب تاج اللغة بالعربية[125] مُجَلَّد نُمرو1.

-528 كتاب الجامع البهي في دعوة النبي نُمرو1.

-529 كتاب قطع الكامل في صفات النبي صلى الله عليه وسلم نُمرو1.

-530 كتاب لطائف المعارف فيما لمواسم العام[126] من الوظائف[127] مُجَلَّد نُمرو1.

-531 كتاب آكام[128] المرجان في أحكام الجان نُمرو1.

-532 كتاب دعوة الفصول نُمرو1.

-533 كتاب تفسير القرآن الجليلي نُمرو1.

-534 كتاب في التوحيد نُمرو1.

-535 كتاب جواهر النصوص في حل كلمات نُمرو1.

-536 كتاب العهود الكبيرة للشعراني نُمرو1.

-537 كتاب نزهة القلوب تفسير القرآن نُمرو1.

-538 كتاب الإمام الغزنوي نُمرو1.

-539 كتاب الجزء الثاني من تفسير الجليلي نُمرو1.

-540 كتاب شرح الأربعين للنووي نُمرو1.

-541 كتاب شرح الهداية نُمرو1.

-542 كتاب القول المحبوب فيما تغفر به الذنوب نُمرو1.

---

123 الخلاج: ضربٌ من البُرود المخطَّطة، البستاني، محيط المحيط، 246. ربما يقصد أن الكتاب مُغلَّف بهذا النوع من النسيج.

124 في الأصل: حيات.

125 في الأصل: باالعربية.

126 في الأصل: العامرة.

127 في الأصل: الوضائق.

128 في الأصل: كام.

-543 كتاب الأنس الجليل في تاريخ القدس والخليل نُمرو1.

-544 كتاب الدرر والغرر جزء نُمرو2، فقط جزآن.[129]

-545 كتاب مشتمل على أربعة عشر علماً أولها أصول الدين نُمرو1.

-546 كتاب السبعيات للهمداني نُمرو1.

-547 كتاب شرح الحكم في التصوف نُمرو1.

-548 كتاب نفخة الصور ونفحة[130] الزهور في الكلام على أبيات قبضة النور نُمرو1.

-549 كتاب الأحكام النبوية في الصناعة الطبية[131] نُمرو1.

-550 كتاب فضائل يوم الجمعة وتفسير آيات نُمرو1.

-551 كتاب الروح إلى ابن القيم نُمرو1.

-552 كتاب غاية الرشاد في أحاديث البلاد نُمرو1.[132]

-553 كتاب فقه حنفي إلى إبراهيم الحلبي نُمرو1.

-554 كتاب حل الرموز نُمرو1.

-555 كتاب مواليد الرجال والنساء نُمرو1.

-556 كتاب منهاج العابد نُمرو1.

[32] -557 كتاب الإرشاد في صناعة الطب نُمرو17.

-558 كتاب شرح الأربعين إلى ابن حجر نُمرو1.

-559 كتاب المختار للقنوي نُمرو1.

-560 كتاب السادات للشيخ عنوان نُمرو1.

-561 كتاب فتاوى[133] شيخ الإسلام نُمرو1.

-562 كتاب التنوير[134] في إسقاط التدبير نُمرو1.

-563 كتاب آداب المريد نُمرو1.

---

129 لا يمكن أن تكون هي النسخة المحفوظة في مكتبة جامعة برينستون Garrett no. 3959Y، وعنوانها "درر الفوائد وغرر الفوائد على شرحي القواعد".

https://catalog.princeton.edu/catalog/9962685333506421

لإنها موقوفة على المكتبة سنة 1196هـ، بينما الدرر والغرر المذكورة هنا دخلت المكتبة سنة 1218هـ.

130 في الأصل: والنغشية.

131 في الأصل: أحكام النبوية في صناعة الطبية.

132 منها نسخة في المكتبة الوطنية بالقدس.

https://www.nli.org.il/en/manuscripts/NNL_ALEPH003033183/NLI#$FL168226778

133 في الأصل: فتاوة.

134 في الأصل: التنور.

564- كتاب عقدة لسان البياني نُمرو1.

565- كتاب وِرد الصبح شيخ السبكي نُمرو1.

566- كتاب الجواهر شرح الرجابية نُمرو1.

567- كتاب كشف الأسرار عما يخفى[135] عن الأفكار نُمرو1.

568- كتاب الفتاوى[136] للشيخ ابن نجم الدين المصري نُمرو1.

569- كتاب شرح الألفية لابن هشام[137] نُمرو1.

570- كتاب في الأحاديث الموضوعة صغير نُمرو1.

571- كتاب تفسير القرآن قطع الكامل من أول سورة سبأ مُجلَّد نُمرو1.

572- كتاب مسالك الحنفا في الصلاة على المصطفى للقسطلاني نُمرو1.

573- نبذة من كتاب الروح لابن القيم نُمرو1.

574- كتاب في الأعداد وعلم الحساب نُمرو1.

575- عن كتاب مستخلص الحقائق للسمرقندي[138] نُمرو1.

576- كتاب بلغة الغواص والأكوان إلى معدن الإخلاص في معرفة الإنسان نُمرو1.

577- كتاب الدرة المضية في معرفة طريقة الصوفية[139] نُمرو1.

578- كتاب ديوان للشهاب أحمد المنصوري نُمرو1.

579- كتاب محاسن الشام نُمرو1.

580- كتاب قلمية مولانا محمد أفندي شيخ الحرم نُمرو1.

581- كتاب تلخيص المفتاح للغزنوي نُمرو1.

582- كتاب منخرم من الأولانية نُمرو1.

583- كتاب صغير من تذكرة داود نُمرو1.

584- كتاب صغير في الطب نُمرو1.

585- كتاب كشف الغيوم نُمرو1.

586- كتاب في التورع نُمرو1.

---

135 في الأصل: يحفى.

136 في الأصل: الفتاوة.

137 في الأصل: الشام.

138 في الأصل: الاسمرقندي.

139 في الأصل: الصفية.

-587 كتاب حاشية الأشباه والنظائر[140] نُمرو1.

-588 كتاب شرح الشفا للقاضي عياض نُمرو1.

-589 كتاب المرقص والمطرب نُمرو1.

-590 كتاب شرح الألفاظ اللغوية والمقامات الحريرية نُمرو1.

-591 كتاب غنية المحتاج لأدلة الاختلاج نُمرو1.

-592 كتاب فقه رايح[141] أوله رايح نُمرو1.

-593 جملة أوراق منخرمة من داخل محفظة نُمرو1.

-594 كتاب الجزء الثاني من تفسير الجلالين نُمرو1.

-595 كتاب في أحوال القرآن على أبواب، تنوف على خمسمائة وستين باباً[142] نُمرو1.

-596 كتاب الفتاوى[143] المحمدية في فقه الحنفية نُمرو1.

-597 عن الجزء السادس من الزيلعي نُمرو1.

-598 عن رسالة التوحيد مع جملة رسائل نُمرو1.

-599 كتاب في علم التاريخ نُمرو1.

يكون كامل كتب السيد يحيى نُمرو 96[144] فقط ستة وتسعون جزءاً.[145]

حسابه نُمرو 203 فقط مائتين وثلاثة لا غير.

[33] 9 كتب التوحيد والتصوف

-600 شرح جوهرة التوحيد نسختين بخط مصري قطع الربع مُجَلَّدين بظرفين أحمر وأصفر جلد2، فقط اثنان.

-601 شرح الجوهرة بخط مصري قطع الربع مُجَلَّد بظرف تأليف ابن عبد السلام جلد1.[146]

-602 الأول من شرح جوهرة التوحيد الكبير بخط مصري قطع الربع مُجَلَّد بظرف جلد1.

-603 شرح جوهرة التوحيد المسمى بهداية[147] المريد بخط نسخ مصري قطع الربع مُجَلَّد بظرف جلد1.

---

140 في الأصل: النضائر.

141 ضُرب عليها في الأصل.

142 في الأصل: وستون باب.

143 في الأصل: فتاوة.

144 الصواب: 95.

145 في الأصل: جزء.

146 هكذا في الأصل: "ابن عبد السلام". وأغلب الظن أنَّ الصواب: "ابنه عبد السلام".

147 في الأصل: لهداية.

604- كتاب أصول توحيد بخط تعليق قطع النصف مُحيَّر مُجلَّد بظرف جلد1.

605- أم البراهين بخط مصري قطع الربع مُجلَّد بظرف جلد1.

606- شرح أم البراهين بخط نسخ قطع الربع مُجلَّد عتيق بلا ظرف جلد1.

607- السنوسية[148] ومعها غيرها بخط مصري وغيره قطع الربع بجلود داخل ظرف جلد1.

608- متن السنوسية بخط مصري قطع الثمن بظرف جلد1.

609- شرح العقائد للنيسابوري بخط نسخ قطع الربع مُجلَّد بظرف جلد1.

610- شرح عقيدة الشيباني بخط مصري قطع الربع بجلود ثلاثة وظروف جلد3، فقط ثلاثة.

611- شرح العقائد بخط مصري قطع الربع مُجلَّد بظرف جلد1.

612- تجريد العقائد نسختين بخط نسخ قطع النصف وقطع الربع بجلدين وظرفين جلد2، فقط اثنان.

613- شرح عقيدة الأجهوري بخط مصري قطع الربع مُجلَّد بظرف جلد1.

614- شرح العقائد بخط نسخ مُهمَّش قطع الربع مُجلَّد بظرف جلد1.

615- شرح عقيدة الأجهوري بخط مصري قطع الربع مُجلَّد بلا ظرف جلد1.

616- شرح السنوسية بخط مصري قطع الربع واسع مُجلَّد بظرف جلد1.

617- شرح السنوسية للتلمساني بخط مصري قطع الربع مُجلَّد بظرف جلد1.

618- شرح القصيدة المقريَّة بخط نسخ قطع الربع مُجلَّد بلا ظرف جلد1.

619- الصحف الإلهية بخط نسخ قطع الربع مُجلَّد بظرف جلد1.

620- المنقذ من الضلالة بخط ريحاني قطع الربع مُجلَّد بظرف جلد1.

621- إضاءة الدجنة بخط مغربي مُجْدَوَل بإكليل قطع الربع بظرف جلد1.

622- كتاب في التوحيد بخط مصري ناقص الأول قطع الربع مُجلَّد بلا ظرف جلد1.

623- مفتاح الفلاح ناقص الأول بخط نسخ قطع الربع مُجلَّد بظرف جلد1.

624- خلاصة بحر الحقائق بخط نسخ قطع الربع مُجلَّد بظرف جلد1.

625- رسالة في التوحيد للغزالي بخط نسخ قطع الثمن مُجلَّد بظرف جلد1.

626- رسالة في التوحيد للغزالي بخط مصري قطع الربع مُحيَّر مُجلَّد بظرف جلد1.

627- عنوان التحقيق بخط نسخ قطع الربع مُجلَّد بظرف جلد1.

628- المعاونة والمظاهرة بخط مصري قطع الربع مُجلَّد بظرف جلد1.

629- المنقذ من الضلالة بخط مصري قطع الربع مُجلَّد بظرف جلد1.

630- السيف المسلول ومعه رسالة بخط نسخ قطع الثمن مُجلَّد بظرف جلد1. [34]

631- الملل والنحل بخط مصري قطع الربع مُجلَّد بلا ظرف جلد1.

148 في الأصل: النوسية.

632- الملل والنحل بخط مصري قطع النصف مُجلَّد بظرف جلد1.

633- تشييد الأركان بخط مصري ومعه رسالتين قطع الربع مُجلَّد بظرف جلد1.

634- اليواقيت والجواهر في عقائد السادة الأكابر بخط نسخ مُجْدَوَل بأحمر قطع النصف مُجلَّد بظرف جلد1.

635- اليواقيت والجواهر بخط نسخ مُجْدَوَل بأحمر قطع النصف مُجلَّد بلا ظرف جلد1.

636- تأسيس القواعد بخط مصري قطع الربع مُجلَّد بظرف جلد1.

637- سعد الدين على العضد بخط تعليق قطع النصف مُحيَّر مُجلَّد بظرف جلد1.[149]

638- حاشية إلياس على العقائد بخط نسخ قطع الثمن مُجلَّد بظرف جلد1.

639- حاشية في العقائد بخط تعليق قطع الربع مُجلَّد بظرف جلد1.

640- حاشية على الجوهرة بخط مصري قطع الربع مُجلَّد بظرف جلد1.

641- حاشية على أم البراهين بخط مصري قطع الربع مُجلَّد بلا ظرف جلد1.

642- حاشية الجرجاني بخط مصري قطع الربع مُجلَّد بظرف جلد1.

642/أ- شرح القصيدة المقريَّة بخط نسخ قطع الربع مُجلَّد بظرف جلد1.

642/ب- الرسالة القدرية بخط نسخ قطع الربع مُجلَّد بظرف مُجلَّد1.

642/ج- شرح فصوص الحكم بخط نسخ قطع الربع مُجلَّد بلا ظرف جلد1.

643- البيان المقبول في رد السول بخط سيدي مؤلفه عبد الغني النابلسي قدس سره قطع الثمن مُجلَّد بلا ظرف جلد1.

644- العقد والتوحيد كتاب الكافي بخط نسخ قطع النصف مُحيَّر بلا ظرف جلد1.

645- مجموع في التوحيد بخط مغربي قطع الربع مُجلَّد بلا ظرف جلد1.

646- كتاب الكشف والتبيين ومعه غيره بخط مصري قطع الثمن مُجلَّد بظرف جلد1.

647- الكشف والبيان بخط مصري قطع الربع مُجلَّد بلا ظرف جلد1.

648- شرح الفصوص بخط تعليق قطع الثمن مُجلَّد بظرف جلد1.

649- شرح الفصوص بخط نسخ مُجْدَوَل بأحمر قطع النصف مُجلَّد بلا ظرف جلد1.

650- رسائل الشيخ يحيى[150] الدين بخط نسخ قطع الربع مُجلَّد بلا ظرف جلد1.

651- الفتوحات المكية بخط نسخ قطع كامل 4 بظرف مُجْدَوَلة بإكليل جلد4، فقط أربعة.

652- الفتوحات المكية بخط مصري قطع كامل مُجلَّد بلا ظرف جلد1.

653- قطعة من الفتوحات المكية بخط مصري قطع الربع مُجلَّد بلا ظرف جلد1.

654- مختصر الإحياء وسلوان المطاع بخط مصري قطع النصف مُحيَّر مُجلَّد بظرف جلد1.

149 حاشية السعد التفتازاني على شرح العضد على مختصر ابن الحاجب. للسعد التفتازاني، مسعود بن عمر (ت 793هـ/ 1390م). هذه النسخة محفوظة في مكتبة الحرم المكي، رقم 1499.

150 هكذا في الأصل وربما يقصد محيي الدين.

655- الإنسان الكامل بخط ريحاني قطع الربع مُجَلَّد بلا ظرف جلد1.

656- المنن للشعراني بخط مصري قطع النصف مُجَلَّد بلا ظرف جلد1.

مقامات الخواص.[151]

[35] 657- مقامات الخواص بخط مصري قطع الربع مُجَلَّد بلا ظرف جلد1.

658- الرسالة القشيرية جزؤين بخط مصري قطع الربع مُجَلَّدين بظرف وبلا ظرف جلد2، فقط اثنان.

659- الرسالة القشيرية بخط نسخ قطع الربع واسع مُجَلَّد بظرف جلد1.

660- الرسالة القدسية بخط مغربي قطع الربع مُجَلَّد بظرف جلد1.

661- تصوف جزؤين بخط مصري قطع الربع مُجَلَّدين بظرفين جلد2، فقط اثنان.

662- موازين الرجال بخط مصري قطع الربع مُجَلَّدين بظرفين جلد2، فقط اثنان.

663- كشف الحجاب والران بخط مصري قطع الربع مُجَلَّد بظرف جلد1.

664- كشف الحجاب والران بخط مصري قطع الربع مُجَلَّد بلا ظرف جلد1.

665- رياض الصالحين بخط مصري قطع النصف مُجَلَّد بلا ظرف جلد1.

666- التنوير في إسقاط التدبير بخط نسخ قطع الربع مُجَلَّد بظرف جلد1.

667- التنوير في إسقاط التدبير بخط مصري قطع الربع مُجَلَّد بلا ظرف جلد1.

668- التنوير في إسقاط التدبير بخط مصري قطع الربع مُجَلَّد بلا ظرف جلد1.

669- بستان العارفين بخط مصري قطع الربع مُجَلَّد بظرف أصفر جلد1.

670- بستان الزاهدين بخط مصري قطع الربع مُجَلَّد بظرف جلد1.

671- زبدة الوصول بخط نسخ قطع الربع مُجَلَّد بظرف جلد1.

672- الكبريت الأحمر للشعراني بخط نسخ قطع الربع مُجَلَّد بلا ظرف جلد1.

673- شرح أسماء الله الحسنى بخط مغربي قطع الربع واسع مُجَلَّد بظرف ومعه رسائل ثلاثة جلد1.

674- شرح أسماء الله الحسنى للقونوي بخط مصري قطع الربع واسع مُجَلَّد بظرف جلد1.

675- شرح الحكم بخط مصري قطع الربع مُجَلَّد بظرف جلد1.

676- اغتنام الفوائد بخط مصري قطع الربع مُجَلَّد بلا ظرف جلد1.

677- منهاج العابدين بخط نسخ قطع النصف مُجَلَّد بلا ظرف جلد1.

678- بهجة الرسائل بخط مصري قطع الربع مُجَلَّد بظرف جلد1.

679- حلية أهل الفضل والكمال بخط مصري قطع الربع مُجَلَّد بظرف جلد1.

680- خواص الدمياطية بخط مغربي قطع الربع مُجَلَّد بلا ظرف جلد1.

681- قوانين حكم الإشراق بخط مصري قطع الربع مُجَلَّد بظرف جلد1.

---

151 تعقيبة في الهامش الأيسر السفلي.

682- التدبيرات الإلهية[152] بخط نسخ مُجَدْوَل بأحمر قطع الربع مُجلَّد بلا ظرف جلد1.

683- الفتح الرباني بخط مصري قطع الربع بلا ظرف جلد1.

684- الرسالة الرسلانية لسيدي الشيخ عبد الغني النابلسي قدس سره بخط مصري قطع الربع بلا ظرف جلد1.

685- مجموع رسائل تصوف بخط مصري مُحيَّر النصف مُجلَّد بلا ظرف جلد1.

686- شرح الرسالة الشناوية لسيدي عبد الغني النابلسي قدس سره بخط نسخ قطع الربع مُجلَّد بلا ظرف جلد1.

687- المشاهد القدسية لسيدي محيي الدين [ابن] عربي قدس سره بخط نسخ قطع الربع مُجلَّد بلا ظرف جلد1. [36]

688- الوصايا للشيخ الأكبر بخط تعليق قطع الربع مُجلَّد بظرف جلد1.

689- إجازات أهل طريق بخط مصري قطع الربع عتيق بلا ظرف جلد1.

690- كنز العرش بخط نسخ قطع الثمن مُجلَّد بلا ظرف جلد1.

691- المنهج الحنيف بخط نسخ مُجَدْوَل بأحمر قطع الربع مُجلَّد بلا ظرف جلد1.

692- رسالة النقشبندية[153] بخط مصري قطع الثمن مُجلَّد بلا ظرف جلد1.

693- مفاتيح الكنوز بخط مصري مُجلَّد بظرف جلد1.

694- تذكرة السائر بخط مصري مُجلَّد بظرف جلد1.

695- دلائل التحقيق بخط مصري مُجلَّد بلا ظرف جلد1.

696- طهارة القلوب بخط مصري قطع الربع مُجلَّد بلا ظرف جلد1.

697- رسالة في علم النفس بخط مصري قطع الربع بلا ظرف جلد1.

698- المنجيات السبع مع أوراد بخط نسخ قطع الربع مُجلَّد بلا ظرف جلد1.

699- شرح أسماء [الله] الحسنى بخط مصري قطع النصف بظرف جلد1.

700- معاني أسماء الله الحسنى باللغة الفارسية بخط نسخ قطع النصف مُحيَّر مُجلَّد بظرف جلد1.

701- نور العين[154] بخط مصري قطع الربع مُجلَّد بلا ظرف جلد1.

702- قمع النفوس بخط مصري قطع الربع مُجلَّد بظرف جلد1.

703- الفرق الضالة والناجية بخط نسخ قطع الربع مُجلَّد بظرف جلد1.

704- القول الجلي في ذكر العلي بخط مصري قطع الثمن مُجلَّد بظرف جلد1.

705- تحفة الأريب في الرد على أهل الصليب بخط مصري قطع الربع مُجلَّد بلا ظرف جلد1.

706- الروض الفائق بخط ريحاني قطع النصف مُجلَّد بلا ظرف جلد1.

707- زاد المريد بخط مصري قطع الربع مُجلَّد بظرف جلد1.

---

152 في الأصل: تدبيرات الآلهية.

153 في الأصل: النقش بنديه.

154 في الأصل: نور الين.

-708 السير والسلوك بخط نسخ قطع الربع مُجَلَّد بلا ظرف جلد1.

-709 الفقه الأكبر بخط مصري مُجَلَّد بلا ظرف جلد1.

-710 الموارد الإلهية[155] ومعها رسائل بخط مصري قطع الربع مُجَلَّد بظرف جلد1.

-711 التنوير بخط مصري قطع الربع مُجَلَّد بظرف جلد1.

-712 علم الكمون والبروز بخط مصري قطع الربع مُجَلَّد بظرف جلد1.

-713 مصطلحات القوم بخط مغربي قطع الربع مُجَلَّد بظرف جلد1.

-714 كتاب النزهة الفكرية بخط مصري قطع الثمن مُجَلَّد بظرف جلد1.[156]

-715 درة الغواص في أوهام الخواص بخط مصري قطع الربع مُجَلَّد بظرف جلد1.

-716 أسرار السرور بخط مصري قطع الربع مُجَلَّد بظرف جلد1.

-717 لواقح الأنوار للشيخ الأكبر بخط مصري قطع الربع مُجَلَّد بظرف جلد1.

-718 تذكرة الإعداد ليوم المعاد بخط مصري قطع النصف مُجَلَّد بظرف جلد1.[157]

-719 محاضرة الأوائل بخط نسخ قطع الربع مُجَلَّد بلا ظرف جلد1.

الجواهر للشعراني بخط تعليق قطع الربع واسع.[158]

[37] -720 الجواهر للشعراني بخط تعليق قطع الربع واسع مُجَلَّد بظرف جلد1.

-721 مجموعة أدعية وأوراد بخط نسخ قطع الربع مُجَلَّد بلا ظرف جلد1.

-722 دعاء الجوشن بخط مصري قطع الثمن مُجَلَّد بلا ظرف جلد1.

-723 ورد الشيخ عبد الغني النابلسي قدس سره بخط مصري قطع الثمن مُجَلَّد بلا ظرف جلد1.

-724 أوراد مولانا بخط نسخ قطع الثمن مُجَلَّد بلا ظرف جلد1.

-725 شرح الدور الأعلى للداموني بخط مصري قطع الربع مُجَلَّد بلا ظرف جلد1.

-726 أوراد لمنلا علي القاري بخط نسخ قطع الربع مُحيَّر مُجَلَّد بظرف جلد1.

-727 ورد السَّحَر بخط نسخ مُجَدْوَل بأحمر قطع الربع بلا ظرف جلد1.

-728 شرح ورد السَّحَر بخط مصري قطع الربع مُجَلَّد بظرف جلد1.

-729 أدعية وأوراد بخط مصري قطع الربع مُجَلَّد بلا ظرف جلد1.

-730 شرح حزب النووي بخط مصري قطع الربع مُجَلَّد بلا ظرف جلد1.

-731 شرح الدور الأعلى بخط مصري قطع الربع واسع مُجَلَّد بظرف جلد1.

---

155 في الأصل: الهية.

156 لم اهتدِ للمقصود.

157 للصنهاجي، خليل بن هارون (ت 826هـ/ 1423م). هذه النسخة محفوظة في مكتبة تشستربيتي برقم Ar. 3236

158 تعقيبة في الهامش الأيسر السفلي.

-732 شرح الدور الأعلى[159] بخط مصري قطع الربع واسع مُجلَّد بلا ظرف جلد1.

-733 دعاء بالتركي قطع الثمن مُجلَّد بلا ظرف جلد1.

-734 متن السنوسية بخط نسخ قطع الثمن مُجلَّد بلا ظرف جلد1.

-735 مختصر السنوسية بخط مصري قطع الثمن مُجلَّد بلا ظرف جلد1.

-736 نظم العقيدة بخط نسخ مُجدْوَل بأحمر قطع الربع مُجلَّد بلا ظرف جلد1.

-737 متن السنوسية بخط نسخ قطع الربع مُجلَّد بلا ظرف جلد1.

-738 شرح أم البراهين بخط مصري قطع الربع مُجلَّد بلا ظرف جلد1.

-739 السير والسلوك بخط مصري قطع الربع واسع مُجلَّد بلا ظرف جلد1.

-740 عنقاء مغرب في معرفة ختم الأولياء، وشمس المغرب بخط نسخ قطع الربع مُحيَّر مُجلَّد بلا ظرف جلد1.

حسابه نُمرِو 154 فقط مائة وأربعة وخمسين.

10 كتب النحو

-741 مغني اللبيب بخط نسخ مُهمَّش قطع النصف[160] مُجلَّد بلا ظرف جلد1.

-742 مغني اللبيب بخط تعليق مصري قطع الربع مُجلَّد بظرف جلد1.

-743 مغني اللبيب بخط مصري قطع النصف مُحيَّر مُجلَّد بظرف جلد1.

-744 مغني اللبيب بخط ريحاني قديم مُجلَّد بلا ظرف جلد1.

-745 مغني اللبيب منخرم من أوله بخط مصري مُهمَّش قطع الربع مُجلَّد بظرف جلد1.

-746 مغني اللبيب منخرم الأول بخط نسخ قطع الربع مُجلَّد بظرف جلد1.

-747 التصريح شرح التوضيح بخط مصري قطع الربع جديد مُجلَّد بظرف جلد1.

-748 التصريح بخط مصري قطع الربع جديد مُجلَّد بظرف جلد1.

-749 التصريح ناقص الأول بخط مصري قطع النصف مُجلَّد بلا ظرف جلد1.

[38] -750 التسهيل لأبي حيان بخط نسخ قديم أجزاء سبعة قطع النصف بجلود وظروف جلد7، فقط سبعة.[161]

-751 متن الألفية بخط نسخ قطع الثمن مُجلَّد بلا ظرف جلد1.

---

159 في الأصل: الدرر أعلا. يُنظر (728).

160 في الأصل: نصف.

161 العنوان بهذا الشكل خاطئ، والصواب هو: التذييل والتكميل في شرح التسهيل، أو شرح تسهيل الفوائد وتكميل المقاصد لابن مالك. لأبي حيان النحوي، محمد بن يوسف (ت 745هـ/ 1344م). الجزء الخامس منه محفوظ في مكتبة تشستربيتي برقم Ar. 3342، والأجزاء (1، 3، 4، 7). محفوظة في دار الكتب المصرية تحت الرقم (6016 هـ).

752- متن الألفية بخط مصري قطع الربع مُجَلَّد بلا ظرف جلد1.

753- متن الألفية عتيق بخط مصري قطع الربع مُجَلَّد كَهْنا بلا ظرف جلد1.

754- متن الألفية بخط نسخ مُهَمَّش قطع الربع مُجَلَّد بظرف جلد1.

755- شرح الألفية لابن عقيل بخط مصري قطع الربع مُجَلَّد بظرف جلد1.

756- الخلاصة الألفية بخط نسخ قطع الربع مُحَيَّر مُجَلَّد بظرف جلد1.

757- شرح الخلاصة الألفية للكردي بخط مصري قطع الربع واسع مُجَلَّد بظرف جلد1.

758- شرح الألفية بخط نسخ مُجَدْوَل بإكليل قطع الربع مُجَلَّد بظرف جلد1.

759- شرح الألفية بخط مصري قطع النصف مُحَيَّر[162] مُجَلَّد بظرف جلد1.[163]

760- شرح الألفية بخط مصري قطع النصف مُحَيَّر مُجَلَّد بظرف جلد1.

761- شرح الألفية لابن الناظم بخط مصري قطع الربع مُجَلَّد بظرف جلد1.[164]

762- شرح الألفية بخط نسخ مُهَمَّش قطع النصف مُحَيَّر مُجَلَّد بظرف جلد1.

763- شرح الألفية بخط مصري قطع النصف مُحَيَّر مُجَلَّد بلا ظرف جلد1.

764- شرح الألفية بخط نسخ مُجَدْوَل بأحمر قطع الربع مُجَلَّد بظرف جلد1.

765- شرح الألفية بخط مصري قطع الربع مُحَيَّر مُجَلَّد بلا ظرف جلد1.

766- شرح الألفية بخط مصري عتيق قطع الربع مُجَلَّد بلا ظرف جلد1.

767- شرح الألفية ناقص الأول بخط تعليق قطع الثمن مُجَلَّد بلا ظرف جلد1.

768- شرح الألفية بخط مصري قطع الربع مُجَلَّد بظرف جلد1.

769- شرح الألفية للسيوطي بخط مصري قطع الربع مُجَلَّد بظرف جلد1.[165]

770- شرح الألفية بخط مصري قطع الربع مُجَلَّد بظرف جلد1.

771- شرح الألفية ناقص بخط مصري قطع الربع مُجَلَّد بلا ظرف جلد1.

162 مضروبٌ عليها في الأصل.

163 إحدى النسخ (762، 763، 766، 768، 769، 771، 773). هي المحفوظة في مكتبة وزارة الأوقاف المصرية برقم 4490، وهي شرح الألفية للمكودي، عبد الرحمن بن علي (ت 808هـ/ 1405م).

164 أغلب الظن أن هذه هي النسخة المحفوظة اليوم في مكتبة جامع النور أحمديّة بعكا، وصورتها في المكتبة البريطانية برقم EAP399/1/30
https://eap.bl.uk/archive-file/EAP399-1-30
تنظر دراسة سماح حجاب وفهرسها الذي وضعته للمكتبة سنة 2022، دراسة غير منشورة، الكتّاب رقم 48.
Samah Hijab, *Al-Ahmadiyya school of Acre Collection of Manuscripts*, End term Paper History of Science in Islamicate Societies MA Intellectual Encounters of the Islamicate World Freie Universität Berlin.

165 البهجة المرضية في شرح الألفية. للسيوطي، جلال الدين (ت 909هـ/ 1505م).

772- حل مشكلات الألفية بخط مصري مُجْدْوَل[166] بأحمر قطع الربع مُجلَّد بظرف جلد1.

773- إعراب الألفية للشيخ خالد بخط مصري مُجْدْوَل بأحمر قطع النصف مُجلَّد بظرف جلد1.

774- إعراب الألفية بخط نسخ قطع الربع مُجلَّد بظرف جلد1.

775- شرح اللباب بخط مصري قطع الربع مُحيَّر ~~قطع الربع~~[167] مُجلَّد بظرف جلد1.

776- شرح اللباب بخط مصري قطع الربع مُحيَّر مُجلَّد بظرف جلد1.

777- شرح اللباب بخط تعليق قطع النصف مُحيَّر مُجلَّد بظرف جلد1.[168]

778- لب اللباب بخط مصري قطع الربع مُجلَّد بظرف جلد1.

779- شرح الخلاصة بخط نسخ قطع الربع طويل مُجلَّد بظرف جلد1.

780- خلاصة الإعراب بخط تعليق مُجلَّد قطع الربع بظرف جلد1.

781- شرح الشواهد بخط مصري قطع الربع مُجلَّد بظرف جلد1.

782- شرح الشواهد بخط نسخ قطع الربع مُجلَّد بلا ظرف جلد1.

الشواهد.[169]

[39] 783- الشواهد للعيني بخط مصري قطع الربع مُجلَّد بظرف جلد1.

784- شرح الشواهد بخط تعليق قطع الربع طويل مُجلَّد بظرف جلد1.

785- شرح الشواهد للعيني بخط مصري قطع الربع مُجلَّد بظرف جلد1.

786- شرح الشواهد للعيني بخط نسخ قطع الربع مُجلَّد بظرف جلد1.

787- شواهد القَطر بخط نسخ قطع الربع مُجلَّد بظرف جلد1.

788- شرح اللباب بخط تعليق قطع النصف مُجلَّد بظرف جلد1.

789- الدرة المضيئة شرح الألفية بخط مصري قطع النصف مُجلَّد بظرف جلد1.

790- شرح القواعد بخط مصري عتيق قطع الربع مُجلَّد بلا ظرف جلد1.

791- الإعراب عن قواعد الإعراب بخط نسخ مُهمَّش قطع كامل مُجلَّد بظرف جلد1.

792- مجموع قواعد الإعراب بخط مصري قطع الثمن مُجلَّد بظرف جلد1.

793- المرشد شرح الإرشاد بخط مصري قطع الربع مُجلَّد بظرف جلد1.

---

166 في الأصل: مجلدول.

167 مضروب عليها في الأصل.

168 شرح اللباب في علم الإعراب. للسيرافي، محمد بن مسعود (حي 712هـ/ 1312م). هذه النسخة محفوظة في المكتبة الوطنية بالقدس برقم Ms. AP Ar. 410، وسبب ترجيحها على سابقتيها هو حجمها (25 x 17سم) أي من قطع النصف محيَّر وليس الربع.
https://www.nli.org.il/en/manuscripts/NNL_ALEPH003484244/NLI#$FL184645166

169 تعقيبة في الهامش الأيسر السفلي.

794- البسيط والجامع المحيط بخط نسخ قطع النصف مُحيَّر مُجلَّد بظرف جلد1.

795- موصل الطلاب إلى قواعد الإعراب بخط نسخ قطع الربع مُجلَّد بظرف جلد1.

796- موصل الطلاب إلى قواعد الإعراب بخط مصري قطع الثمن مُجلَّد بلا ظرف جلد1.

797- شرح القواعد بخط نسخ قطع الربع مُحيَّر مُجلَّد بظرف جلد1.

798- الشذور لابن هشام بخط مصري قطع الربع مُجلَّد بظرف جلد1.

799- الشذور بخط نسخ قطع الربع مُجلَّد بظرف جلد1.

800- شرح الشذور بخط مصري جديد مُجدْوَل بأحمر قطع الربع مُجلَّد بظرف جلد1.

801- شرح الشذور بخط مصري قطع الربع مُجلَّد بظرف جلد1.[170]

802- شرح قطر الندا بخط مصري قطع الربع مُجلَّد بظرف جلد1.

803- شرح القطر للفاكهي بخط نسخ قطع الربع مُجلَّد بظرف جلد1.

804- شرح القطر بخط مصري قطع الربع مُجلَّد بظرف جلد1.

805- شرح القطر بخط مصري عتيق قطع الربع مُجلَّد بظرف جلد1.

806- شرح القطر بخط نسخ قطع الثمن مُجلَّد بظرف جلد1.

807- شرح القطر بخط نسخ قطع الربع مُجلَّد بلا ظرف جلد1.

808- شرح القطر بخط مصري عتيق قطع الربع مُجلَّد بلا بظرف جلد1.

809- شرح القطر لابن هشام بخط مصري عتيق قطع الربع مُجلَّد بظرف جلد1.

810- شرح القطر لابن هشام بخط مصري قطع الربع مُجلَّد بلا ظرف جلد1.

811- متن الكافية والشافية بخط مصري قطع الثمن مُجلَّد بظرف جلد1.

812- كافية بخط[171] نسخ قطع الربع مُحيَّر مُجلَّد بظرف جلد1.

813- متن الكافية بخط تعليق مُجدْوَل بأحمر قطع الثمن مُجلَّد بظرف جلد1.

814- متن الكافية وعوامل بخط نسخ مُهمَّش قطع الربع مُحيَّر مُجلَّد بظرف جلد1.

815- متن الكافية بخط نسخ قطع الثمن مُجلَّد بظرف جلد1.

816- شرح الكافية بخط تعليق قطع الربع مُجلَّد بظرف جلد1. [40]

817- شرح الكافية بخط نسخ قطع النصف مُحيَّر مُجلَّد بظرف جلد1.

818- شرح الكافية بخط تعليق مُهمَّش قطع الربع مُجلَّد بظرف جلد1.

---

170 ربما هي النسخة التي كانت محفوظة في مكتبة جامع النور أحمديَّة بعكا برقم 40 /2 حسب فهرس عطا الله، وهي ضمن المخطوط المجموع رقم 2. ولكنها فقدت من المكتبة في الفترة ما بين 1983- 2012. وربما تكون النسخة رقم (894). ويُنظر ما سجل مع شرح الشافية رقم (1113).

171 في الأصل: بخط بخط.

-819 شرح الكافية بخط مصري قطع الربع مُجلَّد بظرف جلد1.

-820 شرح الكافية بخط تعليق قطع الربع مُجلَّد بظرف جلد1.

-821 شرح الكافية بخط مصري قطع الربع مُحيَّر مُجلَّد بظرف جلد1.

-822 شرح الكافية بخط تعليق مُهمَّش قطع الربع مُجلَّد بظرف جلد1.

-823 شرح الكافية بخط مصري قطع الربع مُجلَّد بظرف جلد1.

-824 شرح الكافية لملا جامي بخط تعليق مُهمَّش قطع الربع طويل مُجلَّد بظرف جلد1.

-825 شرح الكافية بخط نسخ قطع كامل مُجلَّد بظرف جلد1.

-826 شرح الكافية بخط مصري قطع الربع طويل مُجلَّد بظرف جلد1.

-827 شرح الكافية بخط تعليق قطع الربع مُجلَّد بظرف جلد1.

-828 شرح الكافية بخط نسخ مُهمَّش قطع النصف مُحيَّر مُجلَّد بظرف جلد1.

-829 حل مشكلات الكافية بخط نسخ مُهمَّش قطع الربع مُجلَّد بظرف جلد1.

-830 حل مشكلات الكافية بخط[172] قطع الربع مُجلَّد بظرف جلد1.

-831 الفوائد الوافية في حل الكافية بخط نسخ مُهمَّش قطع الربع مُجلَّد بظرف جلد1.

-832 المصباح في النحو بخط نسخ مُهمَّش عتيق قطع الربع مُجلَّد بظرف جلد1.

-833 المصباح في النحو بخط تعليق قطع الربع مُجلَّد بظرف جلد1.

-834 المصباح والضوء بخط مصري قطع الربع واسع مُجلَّد بظرف جلد1.

-835 شرح المصباح بخط تعليق قطع الثمن مُجلَّد بظرف جلد1.

-836 أسرار العربية بخط مصري قطع الربع مُحيَّر مُجلَّد بظرف جلد1.

-837 شرح نتيجة ابن الحاجب بخط نسخ قطع النصف مُحيَّر مُجلَّد بظرف جلد1.

-838 فوائد حسن الكرماني بخط نسخ مُهمَّش قطع النصف مُحيَّر مُجلَّد بظرف جلد1.

-839 الأنموذج بخط مصري عتيق قطع الربع مُجلَّد بلا ظرف جلد1.

-840 الفوائد الإلهية[173] بخط نسخ قطع الثمن مُجلَّد بظرف جلد1.

-841 شرح الإظهار المسمى بنتائج الأفكار بخط مصري قطع الربع مُجلَّد بلا ظرف جلد1.

-842 شرح الشمسية في النحو بخط مصري قطع الربع مُجلَّد بظرف جلد1.

-843 شرح الكلام بخط نسخ مُجدْوَل بأحمر وأسود قطع[174] بجلد مُذَهَّب وظرف جلد1.

-844 ألغاز نحوية بخط مصري قطع الربع مُجلَّد بظرف جلد1.

172 نسي تحديد نوع الخط.

173 في الأصل: آلهية.

174 نسي تحديد نوع القطع.

845- إعراب ديباجة المصباح بخط مصري قطع الربع مُجَلَّد بظرف جلد1.

846- شرح القطر للحريري بخط نسخ قطع الربع مُجَلَّد بظرف جلد1.

847- توجيه اللمع بخط نسخ عتيق قطع النصف مُحَيَّر مُجَلَّد بظرف جلد1.

848- المعرب في النحو بخط نسخ قطع الربع مُجَلَّد بظرف جلد1.[175]

مصنفات ابن هشام.[176]

849- مصنفات ابن هشام بخط نسخ قطع النصف مُجَلَّد بظرف جلد1. [41]

850- الانتصاف[177] بخط نسخ عتيق مُحَيَّر النصف مُجَلَّد بظرف جلد1.

851- الطوالع بخط نسخ مُهَمَّش قطع الثمن مُجَلَّد بظرف جلد1.

852- شرح كبير متوسط ناقص الأول بخط مصري قطع النصف مُجَلَّد بظرف جلد1.

853- شرح الورقات وغيره بخط مصري قطع الربع مُجَلَّد بظرف جلد1.

854- قلادة الجواهرية بخط نسخ قطع الربع مُجَلَّد بظرف جلد1.

855- صنعة الإعراب بخط نسخ عتيق قطع الربع مُجَلَّد بظرف جلد1.

856- السِّراج المنير بخط نسخ قطع النصف مُحَيَّر مُجَلَّد بظرف جلد1.

857- تحفة الإخوان بخط تعليق قطع الثمن مُجَلَّد بلا ظرف جلد1.

858- السِّفر الأول من إعراب شعر[178] قطع كامل بخط نسخ مُجَلَّد بظرف جلد1.

859- إعراب الألفية بخط مصري قطع الربع مُجَلَّد بظرف جلد1.

860- مجموعة كتب في علم العربية بخط تعليق قطع الربع مُجَلَّد بلا ظرف جلد1.

861- الافتتاح في علم النحو بخط تعليق قطع الربع مُجَلَّد بظرف جلد1.

862- كتاب الضوء بخط تعليق قطع الربع مُجَلَّد بظرف جلد1.

863- شرح الوسيط بخط نسخ قطع الربع مُجَلَّد بظرف جلد1.

864- شرح الإرشاد بخط مصري قطع الربع مُجَلَّد بظرف جلد1.

865- كتاب التهذيب بخط مصري قطع الربع واسع مُجَلَّد بظرف جلد1.

175 للجزائري، نعمة الله بن عبد الله الحسيني (1112هـ/ 1701م). هذه النسخة محفوظة اليوم في مكتبة جامع النور أحمديَّة بعكا برقم 34 حسب فهرس عطالله، وصورتها في المكتبة البريطانية برقم EAP399/1/2

https://eap.bl.uk/archive-file/EAP399-1-2

تنظر دراسة سماح حجاب Samah Hijab وفهرسها الذي وضعته للمكتبة سنة 2022، دراسة غير منشورة، الكتاب رقم 12.

176 تعقيبة في الهامش الأيسر السفلي.

177 هكذا في الأصل.

178 في الأصل لشعر.

866- شرح المقدمة بخط تعليق قطع النصف مُجلَّد بظرف جلد1.

867- ثمار القلوب في المضاف والمنسوب بخط نسخ قطع النصف مُجلَّد بظرف جلد1.

868- ملحة الإعراب بخط نسخ قطع الثمن مُجلَّد بلا ظرف جلد1.

869- معرب العوامل بخط مصري قطع الربع مُجلَّد بظرف جلد1.

870- شرح الأزهرية للشيخ خالد بخط نسخ قطع الربع مُجلَّد بلا ظرف جلد1.

871- شرح الأزهرية بخط مصري قطع الربع مُجلَّد بظرف جلد1.

872- عوامل بخط نسخ عالٍ مُذَهَّب قطع الربع مُجلَّد بلا ظرف جلد1.

873- العوامل الجديدة بخط نسخ قطع الربع مُجلَّد بلا ظرف جلد1.

874- شرح العوامل في النحو بخط تعليق قطع الربع مُجلَّد بظرف جلد1.

875- عوامل بخط تعليق مُجلَّد بظرف جلد1.

876- حاشية على شرح الألفية بخط مصري قطع الربع واسع مُجلَّد بظرف جلد1.

877- حاشية على الأشموني[179] للحفناوي الجزء الثاني بخط مصري قطع النصف مُجلَّد بظرف جلد1.

878- حاشية على شرح ملا جامي بخط نسخ قطع الثمن مُجلَّد بظرف جلد1.

879- حاشية في علم النحو بخط نسخ قطع الربع مُحيَّر مُجلَّد بظرف جلد1.

880- حاشية على الكافية بخط تعليق قطع الثمن مُجلَّد بظرف جلد1.

881- حاشية على الكافية بخط تعليق مُهمَّش قطع الربع مُجلَّد بظرف جلد1.

[42] 882- حاشية على الكافية بخط مصري قطع الثمن مُجلَّد بظرف جلد1.

883- حاشية عصام على ملا جامي بخط تعليق قطع الربع مُجلَّد بظرف جلد1.

884- حاشية الشيخ عبد المعطي بخط مصري قطع الربع مُجلَّد بظرف جلد1.

885- حاشية الشنواني على القَطر بخط مصري قطع الربع مُجلَّد بظرف جلد1.

886- حاشية على شرح المطالع بخط تعليق قطع الثمن مُجلَّد بظرف جلد1.

887- حاشية عصام على ملا جامي بخط تعليق عظيم قطع الربع طويل مُجلَّد بظرف جلد1.

888- حاشية الزرقاني بخط مصري قطع الربع مُجلَّد بظرف جلد1.

889- حاشية في الاشتقاق بخط نسخ قطع النصف مُحيَّر مُجلَّد بظرف جلد1.

890- كتاب في علم العربية بخط نسخ قطع الربع مُحيَّر مُجلَّد بظرف جلد1.

891- كتاب نحو لأبي حيان وهو شرح الملحة بخط نسخ عتيق قطع الربع مُجلَّد بظرف جلد1.

892- كتاب في علم النحو منخرم الأول بخط نسخ قطع النصف مُحيَّر مُجلَّد بظرف جلد1.

---

179 في الأصل: الأشخوني.

893- كتاب في علم النحو وهو شرح الشذور بخط مصري قطع الربع مُجلَّد بظرف جلد1.[180]

894- حاشية على شرح الخلاصة بخط تعليق قطع الربع مُجلَّد بظرف جلد1.

895- حاشية في علم النحو بخط مصري قطع الربع مُجلَّد بظرف جلد1.

896- مجموع حواشي لابن عبد البر بخط مصري قطع الربع مُجلَّد بظرف جلد1.

897- مجموع في علم النحو بخط نسخ قطع الربع مُجلَّد بظرف جلد1.

898- كتاب النحو بخط تعليق قطع الربع مُجلَّد بظرف جلد1.

899- كتاب في النحو للسيد علي بخط تعليق مُجَدْوَل بأحمر قطع الربع مُجلَّد بظرف جلد1.

900- كتاب في النحو بخط مصري عتيق قطع الربع مُجلَّد بلا ظرف جلد1.

901- الجزء الأول من حاشية الحفناوي على الأشموني بخط مصري قطع الربع مُجلَّد بظرف جلد1.

902- حاشية على الألفية بخط مصري قطع الثمن مُجلَّد بظرف جلد1.[181]

903- كتاب في النحو قطع الربع مُجلَّد عتيق بلا ظرف جلد1.

904- كتاب نحو منخرم الأول بخط مصري قطع الربع واسع مُجلَّد بظرف جلد1.

905- كتاب نحو منخرم الأول والآخر بخط نسخ قطع الربع طويل مُجلَّد بظرف جلد1.

906- كتاب نحو منخرم الأول والآخر بخط نسخ مُهمَّش قطع الربع مُجلَّد بظرف جلد1.

907- كتاب نحو منخرم الأول بخط مصري قطع الثمن مُجلَّد بلا ظرف جلد1.

908- كتاب نحو ناقص الأول بخط نسخ قطع الثمن مُجلَّد بلا ظرف جلد1.

909- متن الأجرومية[182] وشرح الأزهرية بخط مصري قطع الربع مُجلَّد بلا ظرف جلد1.

910- إعراب الأجرومية بخط مصري قطع الربع مُجلَّد بلا ظرف جلد1.

911- شرح الأجرومية بخط مصري قطع الربع مُجلَّد بلا ظرف جلد1.

912- شرح الأجرومية بخط مصري قطع الثمن مُجلَّد بظرف جلد1. [43]

913- شرح الأجرومية بخط ريحاني قطع الربع مُحيَّر مُجلَّد بلا ظرف جلد1.

914- شرح الأجرومية بخط مصري قطع الثمن مُجلَّد بظرف جلد1.

915- شرح الأجرومية بخط مصري قطع الربع مُجلَّد بظرف جلد1.

---

180 شرح شذور الذهب في معرفة كلام العرب. لابن هشام الأنصاري، عبد الله بن يوسف (ت 761هـ/ 1360م). ربما هي النسخة التي كانت محفوظة في مكتبة جامع النور أحمدية بعكا برقم 40 /2 حسب فهرس محمود عطا الله، وهي ضمن المجموع رقم 2. ولكنها فقدت من المكتبة في الفترة ما بين 1983- 2012. وربما تكون النسخة رقم (801). أو ربما تكون نسخة أخرى مستقلة كانت في المكتبة.

181 يصعب القول: إنها النسخة المحفوظة اليوم في مكتبة جامع النور أحمدية بعكا برقم 64 حسب فهرس محمود عطا الله، وفهرس سماح حجاب Samah Hijab الكتاب رقم 53. لأنَّ أبعادها 21 × 15 سم، أي أنها من قطع الربع وليس الثمن.

182 في الأصل: أجرومية.

-916 شرح الأجرومية بخط مصري قطع الربع مُجلَّد بظرف جلد1.

-917 شرح الأجرومية بخط مصري قطع النصف مُحيَّر مُجلَّد بظرف جلد1.

-918 شرح الأجرومية للشنواني بخط مصري قطع الربع مُجلَّد بظرف جلد1.

-919 شرح الأجرومية بخط مصري قطع الثمن مُجلَّد بظرف جلد1.

-920 شرح الأجرومية بخط مصري قطع الربع مُجلَّد بظرف جلد1.

-921 شرح الأجرومية للحريري بخط نسخ عتيق قطع الربع واسع مُجلَّد بظرف جلد1.

-922 شرح الأجرومية بخط مصري عتيق قطع الربع مُجلَّد بلا ظرف جلد1.

-923 ألفية ابن مالك بخط نسخ قطع الربع مُجلَّد بلا ظرف جلد1.

-924 شرح الشواهد الكبرى للعيني ناقص الآخر بخط نسخ قطع النصف مُجلَّد بلا ظرف جلد1.

-925 الألغاز النحوية بخط مصري قطع الربع مُجلَّد بلا ظرف جلد1.

-926 متن الأجرومية بخط نسخ قطع الربع مُجلَّد بلا ظرف جلد1.

-927 متن الأجرومية بخط نسخ قطع الربع مُجلَّد بلا ظرف جلد1.

-928 شرح الأجرومية للشيخ خالد بخط نسخ قطع الربع مُجلَّد بلا ظرف جلد1

-929 شرح الأجرومية ناقص الآخر بخط نسخ قطع الثمن مُجلَّد بلا ظرف جلد1.

حسابه نُمِرو 195 فقط مائة وخمس وتسعين لا غير.

11 كتب المعاني والبيان والآداب والأصول والعروض.

-930 المطول بخط نسخ قطع كامل مُجلَّد بظرف جلد1.

-931 المطول بخط نسخ قطع النصف مُجلَّد بظرف جلد1.

-932 المطول بخط مصري قطع النصف مُجلَّد بظرف جلد1.

-933 المطول بخط نسخ قطع النصف طويل مُحيَّر مُجلَّد بظرف جلد1.

-934 شرح المطول بخط تعليق قطع الربع مُحيَّر طويل مُجلَّد بظرف جلد1.

-935 حاشية ملا زاده على المطول بخط تعليق قطع الثمن مُجلَّد بظرف جلد1.

[44] -936 حاشية الشريف في الأصول بخط تعليق قطع الربع مُجلَّد بظرف جلد1.

-937 حاشية ملا عبد الله على الخطائي بخط نسخ قطع الثمن مُجلَّد بظرف جلد1.

-938 تهذيب الأصول بخط نسخ قطع النصف مُجلَّد بظرف جلد1.

-939 تهذيب الأصول بخط مصري قطع الربع مُجلَّد بظرف جلد1.

-940 ملتقط من كتاب التهذيب بخط نسخ قطع الربع بلا ظرف جلد1.

-941 كتاب في علم الأصول بخط نسخ قطع الربع مُجلَّد بظرف جلد1.

942- كتاب ميرزاجان بخط تعليق قطع الربع مُجَلَّد بظرف جلد1.

943- شرح المنار بخط ريحاني قطع كامل مُجَلَّد بظرف جلد1.

944- كتاب في علم الأصول بخط مصري قطع الربع مُجَلَّد بظرف جلد1.

945- كتاب في علم البحث للسمرقندي ومعه[183] آداب المولوي بخط نسخ قطع الربع مُجَلَّد بظرف جلد1.

946- رسالة في آداب البحث بخط مصري قطع الربع مُجَلَّد بظرف جلد1.

947- رسالة في آداب البحث بخط مصري قطع الربع مُجَلَّد بظرف جلد1.

948- تلخيص المفتاح[184] في المعاني والبيان بخط مصري قطع الربع مُجَلَّد بظرف جلد1.

949- تلخيص المفتاح بخط مصري قطع الربع مُجَلَّد بلا ظرف جلد1.

950- تلخيص المفتاح بخط مصري قطع الربع مُجَلَّد بظرف جلد1.

951- تلخيص المفتاح بخط تعليق عتيق قطع النصف مُحَيَّر طويل كَهْنا مُجَلَّد بلا ظرف جلد1.

952- شرح التلخيص بخط تعليق قطع النصف مُحَيَّر مُجَلَّد بلا ظرف جلد1.

953- شرح التلخيص بخط تعليق قطع الربع مُجَلَّد بظرف جلد1.

954- شرح التلخيص للسبكي بخط مصري قطع النصف مُحَيَّر مُجَلَّد بظرف جلد1.

955- مختصر المعاني والبيان بخط تعليق قطع الربع مُجَلَّد بظرف جلد1.

956- مختصر بخط تعليق قطع الربع مُجَلَّد بظرف جلد1.

957- مختصر بخط تعليق قطع الربع مُجَلَّد بظرف جلد1.

958- مختصر بخط نسخ قطع الربع مُجَلَّد بلا ظرف جلد1.

959- مختصر بخط تعليق عتيق قطع الربع مُجَلَّد بلا ظرف جلد1.

960- شرح المختصر للسعد التفتازاني بخط نسخ قطع الربع مُجَلَّد بظرف جلد1.

961- شرح المختصر بخط تعليق قطع كامل مُحَيَّر مُجَلَّد بظرف جلد1.

962- أذهان الأذكياء شرح التلخيص بخط نسخ قطع النصف مُحَيَّر مُجَلَّد بظرف جلد1.

963- حاشية على المختصر للجرجاني بخط تعليق قطع الثمن مُجَلَّد بظرف جلد1. [45]

964- حاشية على المختصر للجرجاني بخط تعليق قطع الربع مُجَلَّد بظرف جلد1.

965- حاشية على التلخيص بخط نسخ قطع الربع مُحَيَّر طويل مُجَلَّد بظرف جلد1.

966- شرح المصباح بخط نسخ قطع الربع مُجَلَّد بظرف جلد1.

967- منهاج الوصول بخط مصري قطع كامل مُجَلَّد بظرف جلد1.

968- كتاب في علم المعاني بخط مصري قطع الربع مُجَلَّد بلا ظرف جلد1.

183 في الأصل: ومع.

184 في الأصل: المفتاحي.

969- اللمع بخط مصري قطع الربع مُجلَّد بظرف جلد1.

970- كتاب في المعاني والبيان بخط تعليق قطع النصف طويل مُجلَّد بظرف جلد1.

971- كتاب في المعاني والبيان بخط تعليق قطع النصف طويل مُجلَّد بظرف جلد1.

972- كتاب المختصر بخط تعليق قطع الربع مُجلَّد بظرف جلد1.

973- خزانة الأدب بخط مصري قطع النصف مُحيَّر مُجلَّد بظرف جلد1.

974- مجموعة في الأدب بخط مصري قطع الربع مُجلَّد بظرف جلد1.

975- مجموعة في الأدب بخط نسخ قطع الربع مُجلَّد بظرف جلد1.

976- ثمرات الأوراق بخط مصري قطع الربع مُجلَّد بظرف جلد1.

977- روضة الفصاحة بخط نسخ قطع الربع مُجلَّد بظرف جلد1.[185]

978- كتاب في علم الأدب بخط ريحاني قطع الربع مُجلَّد بظرف ناقص الأول والآخر جلد1.

979- ثمار القلوب بخط مصري ناقص الآخر قطع الربع مُجلَّد بظرف جلد1.

980- شرح العيون بخط مصري قطع الربع واسع مُجلَّد بظرف جلد1.[186]

981- معاني الأخلاق بخط مصري قطع الربع مُجلَّد بلا ظرف جلد1.

982- تحرير التحبير بخط[187] قطع الربع مُحيَّر مُجلَّد بلا ظرف جلد1.[188]

983- رسالة الأدب بخط نسخ قطع الربع مُجلَّد بلا ظرف جلد1.

984- اللؤلؤ النظيم في التعلم والتعليم بخط مصري قطع الثمن مُجلَّد بظرف جلد1.

985- شرح قصيدة الأدب بخط مصري قطع الربع مُجلَّد بظرف جلد1.

986- قلائد العقيان بخط مصري قطع الربع مُجلَّد بلا ظرف جلد1.

987- بدائع البدائع بخط نسخ قطع الثمن مُجلَّد بلا ظرف جلد1.

988- مطلع الفوائد بخط مصري قطع الربع مُجلَّد بظرف جلد1.

---

185 كانت هذه النسخة موجودة في مكتبة جامع النور أحمديّة بعكا حتى سنة 1947م، ثم فُقِدت، فقد شاهدها هناك عبد الله مخلص ووصفها. ينظر عبد الله مخلص، كتاب روضة الفصاحة، مجلة المجمع العلمي العربي بدمشق، مج 22، ع 9- 10 (أيلول وتشرين الأول 1947). 418- 426. محمد خالد كلاب، المخطوطات العربية في فلسطين، دعوة للإنقاذ ودعوة للتواصل. بيروت: دار النوادر، 2014، 93.

186 هكذا في الأصل: شرح العيون، وربما يقصد: سرح العيون في شرح رسالة ابن زيدون لابن نباتة، محمد بن محمد (ت 768هـ/1366م).

187 نسي تحديد نوع الخط.

188 كانت هذه النسخة موجودة في مكتبة جامع النور أحمديّة بعكا حتى سنة 1947م، ثم فُقِدت، فقد شاهدها هناك عبد الله مخلص ووصفها. ينظر عبد الله مخلص، كتاب تحرير التحبير في علم البديع، مجلة المجمع العلمي العربي بدمشق، مج22، ع 11- 12 (تشرين الثاني وكانون الأول 1947). 524- 531. محمد خالد كلاب، المخطوطات العربية في فلسطين، دعوة للإنقاذ ودعوة للتواصل. بيروت: دار النوادر، 2014، 93. وكان شاهد هذه النسخة الشيخ طاهر الجزائري في ربيع الأول سنة (1316هـ/1898م). ينظر الجزائري، طاهر بن صالح، دفتر منوعات، مخطوطة المكتبة الوطنية بدمشق، رقم 11728، الورقة 4ب.

989- خبايا الزوايا بخط مصري قطع الربع مُجلَّد بلا ظرف جلد1.

[46] 990- شرح أقصى الأماني بخط مصري قطع الربع مُجلَّد بظرف جلد1.

991- شرح الكافي البديع المسمى بالنتائج بخط مصري قطع الثمن مُجلَّد بظرف جلد1.

992- يتيمة ابن المقفع بخط ريحاني قطع الثمن مُجلَّد بظرف جلد1.

993- غرر الدلائل والآيات بخط مصري قطع الربع مُجلَّد بلا ظرف جلد1.

994- براعة التوسل بخط مصري قطع الربع مُجلَّد بظرف جلد1.

995- ما يُكتب مقصوراً وممدوداً بخط مصري قطع الربع مُجلَّد بلا ظرف جلد1.

996- كتاب المرج النضر بخط نسخ قطع النصف مُحيَّر مُجلَّد بلا ظرف جلد1.

997- حلبة الكميت بخط نسخ النصف مُحيَّر مُجلَّد بلا ظرف جلد1.

998- فهرسة النديم بخط مصري مُحيَّر النصف مُجلَّد بلا ظرف جلد1.[189]

999- المشترك وضعاً بخط مصري قطع الربع مُجلَّد بلا ظرف جلد1.

1000- مجموعة من علوم شتى بخط مصري قطع الثمن مُجلَّد بظرف جلد1.

1001- الأول من اللب بخط نسخ قطع كامل مُحيَّر مُجلَّد بظرف جلد1.

1002- المقالات المهذبة بخط مصري قطع الربع مُجلَّد بظرف جلد1.

1003- مختصر المكاتبات[190] البديعة بخط ريحاني قطع الربع مُجلَّد بظرف جلد1.[191]

1004- الشفا في بديع الاكتفا بخط مصري قطع الربع مُجلَّد بظرف جلد1.

1005- الدرر المدروزة شرح الأرجوزة[192] بخط مصري قطع الربع مُحيَّر مُجلَّد بظرف جلد1.

1006- غرر المعاني والنكت شرح المقامات بخط مصري مُحيَّر النصف مُجلَّد بلا ظرف جلد1.

1007- زهر الآداب بخط مصري قطع الربع مُجلَّد بظرف جلد1.

1008- الهفوات النادرة بخط مصري قطع الربع مُجلَّد بظرف جلد1.

---

189 هذه النسخة محفوظة في مكتبة تشستربيتي برقم Ar. 3315
https://viewer.cbl.ie/viewer/image/Ar_3315/13/

190 في الأصل: مكاتبات.

191 لابن الصيرفي، محمد بن عبد الرحمن (ق 7هـ/ 13م). هذه النسخة محفوظة في المكتبة الخالدية بالقدس. AKDI 00966 0700
https://w3id.org/vhmml/readingRoom/view/509463
وهي الرسالة الأولى ضمن مخطوط مجموع، فيه عمل آخر بخط الناسخ نفسه. لم نستطع تحديد عنوانه نخرم في أوله، ولكن موضوعه في علم الشروط، إذ يقدم صوراً لعقود نكاح ومقاسمة وإقطاع ووقف. وهذا رابطه
https://www.vhmml.org/readingRoom/view/509464

192 في الأصل: الدرر الفروزة في شرح الأجوزة. ربما يقصد الدرر المدروزة شرح الأرجوزة. للمحلي السطوحي، منصور بن علي (ت 1066هـ/ 1656م).

1009- كتاب النزهة الوجيزة بخط نسخ قطع الربع طويل مُجَلَّد بظرف جلد1.

1010- مجموع لطيف في كل معنى ظريف بخط تعليق مُجَلَّد بلا ظرف جلد1.

1011- المجموعة اللطيفة بخط مصري قطع الربع مُجَلَّد بظرف جلد1.

1012- سفينة النجاة بخط مصري قطع الثمن مُجَلَّد بظرف جلد1.

1013- مكاتبات الخوارزمي بخط نسخ قطع الربع مُجَلَّد بظرف جلد1.

1014- كتاب مراسلات بخط الربع مُجَلَّد بظرف جلد1.

1015- روضة القلوب ونزهة المحبوب بخط مصري قطع الربع مُجَلَّد بظرف جلد1.

1016- مختار قلائد العقيم[193] بخط مصري قطع الربع بظرف جلد1.

[47] 1017- كتاب المرصع في الكتابات والإضافات بخط مصري قطع الربع مُجَلَّد بلا ظرف جلد1.

1018- رسائل أبي بكر الخوارزمي بخط نسخ قطع النصف مُحيَّر مُجَلَّد بلا ظرف جلد1.

1019- طرح المدر لحل اللآلئ والدرر بخط نسخ قطع الربع مُجَلَّد بلا ظرف جلد1.

1020- مراسلات زين العابدين الصديقي بخط نسخ قطع الربع مُجَلَّد بظرف جلد1.

1021- خلاصة تحقيق الظنون بخط مؤلفه ابن البكري نسخ قطع كامل بجلد مُذَهَّب وظرف جلد1.

1022- مصحف الكشف بخط مصري قطع الربع مُجَلَّد بظرف جلد1.

1023- نسيم الصبا بخط مصري قطع الربع مُجَلَّد عتيق بلا ظرف جلد1.

1024- الخزرجية في علم العروض بخط تعليق قطع الربع مُجَلَّد بظرف جلد1.

1025- شرح الخزرجية بخط مصري قطع الربع مُحيَّر مُجَلَّد بلا ظرف جلد1.

1026- شرح الخزرجية بخط مصري قطع الربع مُجَلَّد بظرف جلد1.

1027- مقدمة في فن العروض بخط مصري قطع الثمن مُجَلَّد بظرف جلد1.

1028- كتاب في علم العروض بخط مصري قطع الثمن مُجَلَّد بظرف جلد1.

1029- شرح الأندلسية بخط مصري قطع الربع مُجَلَّد بظرف جلد1.

1030- المقصد الوافي بخط مصري عتيق قطع الثمن مُجَلَّد بظرف جلد1.

1031- التهذيب في الأصول بخط مصري قطع الربع مُجَلَّد بظرف جلد1.

1032- شرح المواقف بخط مصري قطع الربع مُجَلَّد بظرف جلد1.

1033- منهاج الأصول للبيضاوي بخط تعليق قطع الربع مُجَلَّد بظرف جلد1.

1034- شرح المنار بخط مصري قطع الربع مُجَلَّد بظرف جلد1.

1035- نظم التهذيب بخط مصري قطع الربع مُجَلَّد بظرف جلد1.

1036- التهذيب بخط تعليق قطع الثمن كبير مُجَلَّد بلا ظرف جلد1.

---

193 هكذا في الأصل.

-1037 حاشية ميرزاجان على الطوالع بخط تعليق قطع الثمن كبير مُجلَّد بظرف جلد1.

-1038 التهذيب بخط نسخ قطع الربع مُجلَّد بظرف جلد1.

-1039 حاشية على التهذيب بخط مصري قطع الربع مُجلَّد بظرف جلد1.

-1040 شرح طوالع الأنوار بخط نسخ قطع الربع كبير مُجلَّد بظرف جلد1.

-1041 شرح التهذيب بخط مصري قطع الربع مُجلَّد بظرف جلد1.

-1042 طوالع الأنوار للبيضاوي بخط تعليق قطع الربع مُجلَّد بظرف جلد1.

-1043 لوامع النظر بخط مصري قطع الربع كبير مُجلَّد بظرف جلد1.

[48] -1044 شرح المواقف بخط نسخ قطع النصف مُجلَّد بظرف جلد1.

-1045 تهذيب الأصول ناقص الآخر بخط مصري قطع الربع مُجلَّد بلا ظرف جلد1.

-1046 منهاج اليقين بخط مصري قطع الربع مُجلَّد بظرف جلد1.

-1047 كتاب الأكر بخط تعليق قطع الربع طويل مُجلَّد بظرف جلد1.

-1048 شرح الإشارات بخط نسخ قطع النصف مُحيَّر مُجلَّد بظرف جلد1.

-1049 شرح المطالع بخط تعليق قطع الربع مُجلَّد بظرف جلد1.

-1050 الجزؤ من المقاصد بخط نسخ قطع الربع كبير مُجلَّد بظرف جلد1.

-1051 جامع التدقيق بخط مصري قطع النصف مُجلَّد بظرف جلد1.

-1052 مطالع الأنظار بخط تعليق قطع النصف مُحيَّر مُجلَّد بلا ظرف جلد1.

-1053 شرح المطالع بخط تعليق قطع الربع مُجلَّد بظرف جلد1.

-1054 شرح البراهين ومعه رسائل بخط مصري قطع الربع مُجلَّد بظرف جلد1.

-1055 شرح التجريد الجوهر النضيد[194] بخط تعليق قطع الربع مُجلَّد بظرف جلد1.

-1056 مراسلات أبي العلاء بخط مصري قطع الربع مُجلَّد بلا ظرف جلد1.

-1057 شرح نظم الاستعارة بخط نسخ مُجَدْوَل بإكليل قطع النصف مُحيَّر طويل مُجلَّد بلا ظرف جلد1.

-1058 مجموع يشتمل على شرح الاستعارة لعصام وحواشٍ[195] عليه بخط نسخ قطع الربع مُجلَّد بظرف جلد1.

-1059 متن السمرقندية[196] في الاستعارات بخط مصري قطع الربع مُجلَّد بلا ظرف جلد1.

-1060 خطب جمعة بخط مصري قطع الثمن مُجلَّد بلا ظرف جلد1.

-1061 خطبة الكسوف بخط مصري قطع الثمن مُجلَّد بلا ظرف جلد1.

حسابه نُمرِو 132 فقطماية واثنتين وثلاثين لا غير.

194 في الأصل: النقيض.

195 في الأصل: حواشي.

196 في الأصل: السمرقندي.

12 كتب علم المنطق

1062- متن الشمسية بخط نسخ قطع الربع مُجلَّد بظرف جلد1.

1063- شرح الشمسية بخط تعليق قطع الربع مُحيَّر مُجلَّد بظرف جلد1.

1064- شرح الشمسية بخط نسخ قطع الربع مُحيَّر مُجلَّد بظرف جلد1.

1065- شرح الشمسية بخط مصري قطع الربع مُحيَّر مُجلَّد بظرف جلد1.

1066- شرح الشمسية بخط مصري قطع الربع مُجلَّد بظرف جلد1.

1067- شرح الشمسية بخط مصري قطع الربع مُجلَّد بظرف جلد1.

1068- شرح الشمسية بخط مصري قطع الربع مُجلَّد بلا ظرف جلد1. [49]

1069- متن الشمسية بخط نسخ قطع الربع مُجلَّد بظرف جلد1.

1070- حاشية على الشمسية بخط مصري قطع الثمن مُجلَّد بظرف جلد1.

1071- تصديقات بخط تعليق قطع الربع مُحيَّر مُجلَّد بظرف جلد1.

1072- تصديقات بخط مصري قطع الربع مُجلَّد بظرف جلد1.

1073- تصديقات بخط تعليق قطع الثمن مُجلَّد بظرف جلد1.

1074- شرح العضد لملا جامي بخط تعليق قطع الربع مُجلَّد بظرف جلد1.

1075- شرح العضد بخط نسخ قطع الربع مُحيَّر مُجلَّد بظرف جلد1.

1076- شرح العضد بخط مصري قطع الربع مُحيَّر مُجلَّد بظرف جلد1.

1077- الشفا لابن سينا بخط تعليق قطع النصف مُجلَّد بظرف جلد1.

1078- محاكمات الشفا بخط تعليق قطع النصف طويل مُجلَّد بظرف جلد1.

1079- كتاب في المنطق بخط تعليق قطع النصف طويل مُجلَّد بظرف جلد1.

1080- فوائد كلامية منطقية بخط مصري قطع الربع مُجلَّد بظرف جلد1.

1081- علم منطق بخط مصري قطع الربع مُجلَّد بظرف جلد1.

1082- مجموعة من علم المنطق بخط نسخ قطع الثمن مُجلَّد بظرف جلد1.

1083- رسالة في المنطق ومعها النقاية وتحفة الظرف وشرح تعريف التورية بخط مصري قطع الربع مُجلَّد بظرف جلد1.

1084- رسالة للرازي بخط نسخ قطع الربع مُجلَّد بظرف جلد1.

1085- كتاب منطق ناقص الأول بخط نسخ مُجلَّد بلا ظرف جلد1.

1086- كتاب من المنطق بخط مصري قطع الربع مُجلَّد بظرف جلد1.

1087- تأليف لعصام بخط تعليق قطع الربع مُحيَّر مُجلَّد بظرف جلد1.

1088- شرح الرازي بخط نسخ قطع الثمن كبير مُجلَّد بظرف جلد1.

1089- مجموع في المنطق بخط تعليق قطع الربع كبير مُجلَّد بلا ظرف جلد1.

1090- رسائل في المنطق بخط مصري قطع الربع مُجلَّد بلا ظرف جلد1.

1091- شرح المختصر بخط نسخ قطع الربع كبير مُجلَّد بظرف جلد1.

1092- حاشية بخط نسخ قطع الثمن مُجلَّد بظرف جلد1. 50]

1093- حاشية الفناري بخط نسخ قطع الربع مُجلَّد بظرف جلد1.

1094- حاشية في المنطق بخط تعليق قطع النصف مُحيَّر طويل مُجلَّد بظرف جلد1.

1095- حاشية على التصديقات بخط تعليق قطع الربع مُجلَّد بظرف جلد1.

1096- حاشية السيد بخط تعليق قطع الربع طويل مُجلَّد بلا ظرف جلد1.

1097- حاشية في المنطق بخط تعليق قطع الربع مُجلَّد بظرف جلد1.

1098- حاشية الخيالي بخط تعليق قطع الربع مُجلَّد بظرف جلد1.

1099- حاشية ملا عبد الغفور بخط تعليق قطع الربع طويل مُجلَّد بظرف جلد1.

1100- شرح المختصر بخط مصري قطع الربع مُجلَّد بظرف جلد1.

1101- إيساغوجي بخط نسخ قطع الثمن مُجلَّد بظرف جلد1.

1102- إيساغوجي ومعه شافية بخط تعليق قطع الربع مُجلَّد بظرف جلد1.

1103- إيساغوجي بخط تعليق قطع الربع مُجلَّد بظرف جلد1.

1104- شرح إيساغوجي بخط نسخ قطع الربع مُجلَّد بظرف جلد1.

1105- شرح إيساغوجي بخط مصري قطع الثمن مُجلَّد بظرف جلد1.

1106- شرح إيساغوجي قطع الربع مُحيَّر مُجلَّد بظرف جلد1.

1107- شرح إيساغوجي بخط مصري قطع الربع مُجلَّد بظرف جلد1.

1108- إيساغوجي بخط تعليق قطع الربع مُحيَّر مُجلَّد بلا ظرف جلد1.

حسابه نُمرِو 47 فقط سبعة وأربعين لا غيره.

13 كتب علم الصرف

1109- الشافية بخط مصري قطع الربع مُجلَّد بظرف جلد1.

1110- شرح الشافية بخط نسخ مُهمَّش قطع الربع مُحيَّر مُجلَّد بظرف جلد1.[197]

197 للجاربردي، أحمد بن الحسين (ت 746هـ/ 1346م). أغلب الظن أنها النسخة المحفوظة اليوم في مكتبة جامع النور أحمديَّة بعكا برقم 40 /1 حسب فهرس عطا الله، وهي ضمن المخطوط المجموع رقم (2). وصورته في المكتبة البريطانية برقم EAP399/1/34

https://eap.bl.uk/archive-file/EAP399-1-34

هذا المخطوط المجموع يضم رسالتين هما: (شرح الشافية/ في علم الصرف، وشرح شذور الذهب في معرفة كلام العرب/ في علم النحو). ولكن

1111- شرح الشافية بخط نسخ قطع الربع مُجلَّد بلا ظرف جلد1.

1112- المفتاح بخط مصري قطع الربع مُحيَّر مُجلَّد عتيق بظرف جلد1.

1113- شرح العزي بخط مصري قطع الربع مُجلَّد بظرف جلد1.

1114- شرح المراح بخط مصري قطع النصف مُجلَّد بظرف جلد1.

1115- شرح المقصود لسعد الدين بخط مصري قطع الربع مُجلَّد بظرف جلد1.

1116- شرح المقصود للتفتازي[198] بخط مصري قطع الربع واسع مُجلَّد بظرف جلد1.

1117- شرح المقصود للتفتازي[199] بخط مصري قطع الربع واسع مُجلَّد بظرف جلد1.

1118- أمثلة صرف بخط نسخ مُهَمَّش قطع الربع مُجلَّد بلا ظرف جلد1. [51]

1119- المناهج الكافية بخط مصري قطع الربع مُجلَّد بظرف جلد1.

1120- جاربردي بخط نسخ مُهَمَّش قطع كامل مُجلَّد بظرف جلد1.

1121- كتاب في علم الصرف بخط تعليق مُهَمَّش قطع الربع مُجلَّد بظرف جلد1.

1122- كتاب العيون وعزى بخط نسخ قطع الربع مُجلَّد بظرف جلد1.

1123- مجموع في علم الصرف بخط نسخ قطع الربع مُجلَّد بظرف جلد1.

1124- كتاب في علم التصريف بخط نسخ قطع الربع مُحيَّر مُجلَّد بظرف جلد1.

1125- كتاب في التصريف بخط نسخ قطع الربع مُجلَّد بظرف جلد1.

1126- كتاب تصريف بخط مصري قطع الثمن مُجلَّد بظرف جلد1.

1127- كتاب تصريف بخط مصري قطع الثمن مُجلَّد بظرف جلد1.

1128- رسالة في التصريف ناقصة الأول بخط تعليق قطع الربع مُجلَّد بظرف جلد1.

1129- كتاب صرف بخط نسخ قطع الربع مُجلَّد بظرف جلد1.

1130- كتاب في الصرف بخط تعليق قطع الربع مُجلَّد بظرف جلد1.

في (بيان الكتب) لدينا عملان مستقلان لشرح الشافية (1111، 1112)، وثلاثة أعمال مستقلة لشرح الشذور (800، 801، 894). ولا يوجد في (بيان الكتب) مخطوط مجموع يضم العملين سوية، وبناءً عليه يُمكن افتراض أنَّه في وقت لاحق، بعد كتابة (بيان الكتب)، تمَّ دمج أحد شرحي الشافيّة، مع أحد شروح الشذور في مخطوط مجموع واحد هو المخطوط المجموع رقم (2)، هذا أمرٌ، والآمرُ الآخر أننا نجد العملين في المخطوط المجموع الذي صوَّره محمود علي عطا الله في مطلع الثمانينات، بينما نجد أن المخطوط المجموع نفسه فقدَ بعض الأوراق بما فيها مقدمة رسالة شرح الشذور في التصوير الذي قامت به المكتبة البريطانية سنة (2010م)، أي أنَّ هناك أوراقاً فُقِدت من المخطوط المجموع رقم (2) في الفترة ما بين (1982- 2010م). ينظر فهرس سماح حجاب Samah Hijab الكتاب رقم 16.

198 هكذا في الأصل، والصواب: للتفتازاني.

199 هكذا في الأصل، والصواب: للتفتازاني.

1131- تصريف العزي وتلخيص المفتاح بخط نسخ قطع الربع مُجَلَّد بظرف جلد1.

1132- أمثلة بخط نسخ قطع الثمن مُجَلَّد بلا ظرف جلد1.

حسابه نُمِرو 24 فقط أربعة وعشرين لا غير.

14 كتب الدواوين والقصائد

1133- ديوان سيدي محي الدين ابن العربي قدس سره بخط نسخ قطع الربع كبير مُجَلَّد بلا ظرف جلد1.

1134- ديوان سيدي عمر ابن الفارض قدس سره بخط مصري قطع الربع مُجَلَّد بظرف جلد1.

1135- ديوان سيدي عمر ابن الفارض قدس سره بخط نسخ قطع الربع مُجَلَّد بظرف جلد1.

1136- شرح ديوان سيدي عمر بن الفارض بخط مصري قطع الربع مُجَلَّد بظرف جلد1.

1137- شرح ديوان سيدي عمر ابن الفارض بخط مصري قطع الربع مُجَلَّد بظرف جلد1.

1138- ديوان سيدي عبد الغني النابلسي قدس سره بخط مصري قطع النصف مُحَيَّر مُجَلَّد بظرف جلد1.

1139- ديوان الغزل لسيدي عبد الغني النابلسي قدس سره بخط مصري قطع الربع مُحَيَّر بلا ظرف جلد1.

1140- ديوان الغزل لسيدي عبد الغني النابلسي قدس سره بخط نسخ قطع الثمن مُجَلَّد بظرف جلد1.

1141- بانت سعاد وألفية العراقي بخط تعليق قطع الربع مُجَلَّد بظرف جلد1.

1142- بانت سعاد بخط نسخ قطع الربع مُجَلَّد بظرف جلد1.

1143- شرح بانت سعاد بخط مصري قطع الثمن مُجَلَّد بظرف جلد1.

1144- شرح بانت سعاد بخط نسخ قطع الربع مُجَلَّد بظرف جلد1.

[52] 1145- شرح بانت سعاد لابن هشام بخط مصري قطع الربع مُجَلَّد بلا ظرف جلد1.

1146- شرح بانت سعاد بخط مصري قطع الربع مُجَلَّد بظرف جلد1.

1147- شرح اليائية لسيدي عمر ابن الفارض قدس سره بخط مصري قطع الربع مُجَلَّد بظرف جلد1.

1148- أهنى المنائح[200] لأسنى المدائح بخط ريحاني قطع الربع مُجَلَّد بظرف جلد1.[201]

1149- قطعة من الهمزية بخط مصري قطع الربع مُجَلَّد بظرف جلد1.

1150- نفحة[202] القبول في مدح النبي الرسول صلى الله تعالى عليه وسلم قطع الثمن مُجَلَّد بلا ظرف جلد1.

1151- تخميس البردة بخط نسخ قطع الربع مُجَلَّد بلا ظرف جلد1.

1152- ديوان سيدي محي الدين ابن العربي بخط مصري قطع الربع مُجَلَّد بظرف جلد1.

---

200 في الأصل: المنائج.

201 لشهاب الدين أبي الثناء محمود بن سلمان بن فهد (ت 725هـ/ 1325م)، هذه النسخة محفوظة في مكتبة تشستربيتي برقم Ar. 3310

202 في الأصل: نفخة.

1153- شرح قصائد سيدي محي الدين ابن العربي بخط نسخ قطع الربع مُجَلَّد بظرف جلد1.

1154- شرح قصيدة ابن زهير بخط مصري قطع الربع مُجَلَّد بظرف جلد1.

1155- شرح قصيدة المنفرجة بخط مصري قطع الربع مُجَلَّد بظرف جلد1.

1156- ديوان مجنون ليلى بخط تعليق قطع الثمن مُجَلَّد بظرف جلد1.

1157- ديوان الششتري بخط مصري قطع الربع مُجَلَّد بظرف جلد1.

1158- ديوان أبي العلاء المعري بخط مصري قطع كامل مُجَلَّد بلا ظرف جلد1.

1159- ديوان أبي العلاء المعري بخط نسخ مُجَدْوَل بأحمر قطع الربع مُجَلَّد بظرف جلد1.

1160- ديوان أبي العلاء المعري بخط مصري قطع الربع مُجَلَّد بظرف جلد1.

1161- قصائد في مدح خير الورى صلى الله عليه وسلم وهي بديعية العميان بخط مصري قطع الربع مُجَلَّد بظرف جلد1.

1162- شرح البديعيات لابن حجة جلدين قطع النصف وقطع الربع مُجَلَّدين بظرفين جلد2، فقط اثنان.

1163- ديوان أبي الطيب المتنبي بخط نسخ مُجَدْوَل بأحمر قطع الربع مُجَلَّد بظرف جلد1.[203]

1164- ديوان المتنبي بخط مصري قطع الربع واسع مُجَلَّد بظرف جلد1.

1165- ديوان المتنبي بخط مصري قطع الربع واسع مُجَلَّد بظرف جلد1.

1166- ديوان المتنبي بخط نسخ مُجَدْوَل بأحمر قطع النصف مُحيَّر طويل مُجَلَّد بظرف جلد1.

1167- ديوان المتنبي بخط مصري قطع الربع مُجَلَّد بظرف جلد1.

1168- ديوان المتنبي بخط مصري قطع الربع مُجَلَّد بظرف جلد1.

1169- ديوان المتنبي بخط نسخ قطع الربع مُحيَّر مُجَلَّد بظرف جلد1.

1170- ديوان المتنبي بخط ريحاني قطع النصف مُجَلَّد بظرف جلد1.

1171- شرح ديوان أبي الطيب المتنبي وهو الجزؤ الثاني منه بخط مصري قطع الربع مُجَلَّد بظرف جلد1.

1172- ديوان أبي تمام بخط مصري قطع الربع واسع بلا ظرف جلد1.

1173- ديوان أبي تمام بخط تعليق قطع الثمن مُجَلَّد بلا ظرف جلد1.

1174- ديوان أبي تمام بخط مصري مُجَدْوَل بأحمر قطع النصف مُجَلَّد بلا ظرف جلد1.

ديوان امرئ القيس جلد1.[204]

[53] 1175- ديوان امرئ القيس بخط مصري قطع الربع مُجَلَّد بظرف جلد1.

1176- ديوان أبي فراس بخط [...][205] قطع الربع مُجَلَّد بظرف جلد1.

203 لأبي الطيب المتنبي، أحمد بن الحسين (ت 354هـ/ 965م). هذه النسخة محفوظة في المكتبة الأزهرية برقم 22783. لأن أبعادها 15×22.5 سم، فهي أقرب إلى قطع الربع من قطع النصف محيَّر طويل، كما أنها مُجَدْوَلة بأحمر، وبالتالي ليست النسخة رقم 1166.

204 تعقيبة في الهامش الأيسر السفلي.

205 فراغ في الأصل بمقدار كلمة.

1177- ديوان البهاء زهير بخط تعليق قطع الربع مُجَلَّد بلا ظرف جلد1.

1178- ديوان البهاء زهير بخط مصري قطع الربع مُجَلَّد بظرف جلد1.

1179- ديوان ابن نباتة بخط نسخ قطع النصف مُجَلَّد بظرف جلد1.

1180- ديوان الصبابة بخط نسخ قطع الربع مُجَلَّد بلا ظرف جلد1.

1181- ديوان الصبابة بخط مصري قطع الربع مُجَلَّد بظرف جلد1.

1182- ديوان القيراطي بخط مصري قطع النصف مُجَلَّد بلا ظرف جلد1.

1183- ديوان ابن الرومي بخط مصري قطع الربع مُجَلَّد بلا ظرف جلد1.

1184- ديوان صفي الدين الحلي بخط نسخ قطع الربع مُجَلَّد بلا ظرف جلد1.

1185- ديوان الحماسة بخط ريحاني قطع النصف مُجَلَّد بلا ظرف جلد1.

1186- ديوان الحماسة بخط ريحاني قطع الربع مُجَلَّد بظرف جلد1.

1187- ديوان الدواوين بخط مصري قطع الربع مُجَلَّد بظرف جلد1.[206]

1188- ديوان نثر النظم وحل العقد بخط نسخ قطع مُجَلَّد بلا ظرف جلد1.

1189- ديوان كشاجم بخط مصري قطع الربع مُجَلَّد بظرف جلد1.

1190- ديوان ابن حجر بخط نسخ قطع الربع مُجَلَّد بلا ظرف جلد1.

1191- ديوان ابن كيوان بخط نسخ مُجَدْوَل بأحمر قطع الربع مُجَلَّد بلا ظرف جلد1.

1192- ديوان ابن كيوان بخط مصري قطع الربع مُجَلَّد بظرف جلد1.

1193- ديوان الدوكاني بخط ريحاني قطع الربع واسع مُجَلَّد بظرف جلد1.

1194- ديوان ابن عنين بخط ريحاني قطع النصف مُحَيَّر مُجَلَّد بظرف جلد1.

1195- ديوان أبي العباس بخط مصري قطع الربع مُجَلَّد بظرف جلد1.

1196- ديوان ابن الحداد بخط مغربي عتيق قطع النصف مُحَيَّر مُجَلَّد بظرف جلد1.

1197- ديوان جوهر النضار بخط مصري قطع الربع مُجَلَّد بظرف جلد1.

1198- ديوان الأخطل بخط مغربي قطع الربع واسع مُجَلَّد بظرف جلد1.

1199- ديوان الباخرزي بخط ريحاني عتيق قطع النصف مُحَيَّر مُجَلَّد بظرف جلد1.

1200- ديوان السعادة بخط مصري قطع الربع مُجَلَّد بظرف جلد1.

1201- ديوان المبرد بخط نسخ قطع النصف مُحَيَّر مُجَلَّد بظرف جلد1.

1202- ديوان نجديات بخط نسخ مُهَمَّش قطع النصف مُجَلَّد بظرف جلد1.

1203- ديوان علي ابن الحسين بخط نسخ قطع الربع مُجَلَّد بظرف جلد1

---

206 للنابلسي، عبد الغني بن إسماعيل (ت 1143هـ/ 1731م). المجلد الثاني من هذه النسخة محفوظة في مكتبة جامعة الإمام محمد بن سعود الإسلاميَّة، رقم (م 1094).

1204- ديوان ابن ثابت بخط نسخ قطع الثمن مُجلَّد بظرف جلد1.

1205- ديوان الحافظ الشيرازي بخط تعليق قطع الربع مُجلَّد بلا ظرف جلد1. [54

1206- ديوان الكيداني بخط نسخ قطع الربع مُجلَّد بلا ظرف جلد1.

1207- ديوان المعمار الأديب بخط نسخ قطع الربع مُجلَّد بظرف جلد1.

1208- تخميس لامية العجم مع تخميس بانت سعاد بخط مصري قطع الربع مُجلَّد بظرف جلد1.

1209- شرح لامية العجم بخط مصري قطع الربع مُجلَّد بظرف جلد1.

1210- شرح لامية العجم بخط نسخ قطع الربع مُجلَّد بلا ظرف جلد1.

1211- شرح لامية العجم بخط مصري قطع الربع مُحيَّر مُجلَّد بظرف جلد1.

1212- شرح لامية العجم ويليها لامية ابن الوردي بخط مصري قطع الربع بظرف جلد1.

1213- لامية العجم بخط مصري قطع الثمن مُجلَّد بظرف جلد1.

1214- شرح تائية الصفدي بخط مصري قطع الربع مُجلَّد بظرف جلد1.

1215- ديوان بخط مصري ناقص الأول والآخر قطع الربع مُجلَّد بلا ظرف جلد1.

1216- ديوان بخط مصري قطع النصف مُجلَّد بظرف جلد1.

1217- ديوان بخط مصري عتيق قطع الربع مُجلَّد بلا ظرف جلد1.

1218- ديوان بخط مصري عتيق قطع[207] مُجلَّد بلا ظرف جلد1.

1219- مراتع الغزلان بخط مصري قطع الربع مُجلَّد بلا ظرف جلد1.

1220- محاسن العصر بخط نسخ قطع الربع طويل مُجدْوَل بأحمر مُجلَّد بظرف جلد1.

1221- مجموع ديوان ورسائل بخط نسخ قطع الربع واسع مُجدْوَل بأحمر مُجلَّد بظرف جلد1.

1222- أشعار وقصائد ناقص الأول بخط مصري قطع الربع مُجلَّد بظرف جلد1.

1223- الاختيار في محاسن الأشعار بخط مصري عتيق قطع الربع مُجلَّد بظرف جلد1.

1224- الحسن الصريح في مائة مليح بخط مصري قطع الربع مُجلَّد بظرف جلد1.

1225- الكناية والتعريض بخط نسخ قطع الربع مُجلَّد بظرف جلد1.

1226- طرائف الطُّرَف بخط نسخ قطع الربع مُحيَّر مُجلَّد بلا ظرف جلد1.

1227- مجموعة شعر من كلام الأدباء بخط نسخ جديد قطع الربع مُجلَّد بلا ظرف جلد1.

1228- شرح قصيدة الشيخ أبي الفتح بخط نسخ قطع الربع مُجلَّد بظرف جلد1.

1229- سفينة أشعار بخط نسخ مُجلَّد بلا ظرف جلد1.

1230- ديوان لبعض الشعراء ناقص الأول بخط مصري قطع الربع مُجلَّد بظرف جلد1.

1231- الثاني من روضة الأزهار بخط مصري قطع الربع مُجلَّد بلا ظرف جلد1.

---

207 نسي تحديد القطع.

1232- أطباق الذهب بخط نسخ قطع الربع مُحيَّر مُجَلَّد بلا ظرف جلد1.

1233- ديوان في علم الموسيقى[208] بخط نسخ قطع الربع مُجَلَّد بظرف جلد1.

1234- عرائس الأفكار بخط مصري قطع الربع مُجَلَّد بلا ظرف جلد1.

كتاب المجمعة جلد1.[209]

[55] 1235- كتاب المجمعة بخط تعليق قطع الربع مُجَلَّد بظرف جلد1.

1236- مجموعة شعر بخط مصري قطع النصف مُحيَّر مُجَلَّد بلا ظرف جلد1.

1237- مجموعة شعر بخط مصري قطع النصف طويل مُجَلَّد بلا ظرف قديم جلد1.

1238- شرح المعلقات بخط مصري قطع الربع مُجَلَّد بلا ظرف جلد1.

1239- مجموعة شعر بخط تعليق عالٍ قطع الربع مُجَلَّد بلا ظرف جلد1.

1240- كتاب مقصورة الغزي بخط نسخ قطع الربع مُجَلَّد بلا ظرف جلد1.

1241- مجموعة أشعار وفوائد بخطوط[210] قطع الثمن مُجَلَّد بظرف جلد1.[211]

حسابه نُمرو 113 مائة وثلاثة عشر لا غير.[212]

15 كتب تعبير الرؤيا

1242- الأول من تفسير ابن شاهين بخط مصري قطع الربع مُجَلَّد بظرف جلد1.

1243- الأول من تعبير ابن شاهين بخط مصري قطع الربع مُجَلَّد بظرف جلد1.

1244- الثاني من تعبير ابن شاهين بخط مصري قطع الربع مُجَلَّد بظرف جلد1.

1245- الثاني من ابن شاهين بخط مصري قطع الربع مُجَلَّد بظرف جلد1.

1246- كتاب تعبير ناقص الأول والآخر بخط مصري قطع الربع مُجَلَّد بلا ظرف جلد1.

حسابه نُمرو 5 فقط خمسة لا غير

---

208 في الأصل: المويسقى.

209 تعقيبة في الهامش الأيسر السفلي.

210 ربما نسي كتابة كلمة "مختلفة".

211 يغلب على الظن أن هذه النسخة كانت موجودة في مكتبة جامع النور أحمديّة بعكا حتى سنة 1946م، ثم فُقِدت. لإنها تتقاطع مع النسخة التي شاهدها هناك عبد الله مخلص ووصفها. ينظر عبد الله مخلص، مجموعة أشعار مصعبة المباني مغمضة المعاني، مجلة المجمع العلمي العربي بدمشق، مج21، ع 11- 12 (تشرين الثاني وكانون الأول 1946). 544- 547.

212 الصواب: 110 مجلدات.

16 كتب علم التاريخ

1247- ترجمة الإمام الأعظم بخط نسخ قطع الربع مُجلَّد بلا ظرف جلد1.

1248- مناقب الإمام الأعظم بخط تركي قطع الربع مُجلَّد بظرف جلد1.

1249- مناقب الإمام الشافعي بخط مصري قطع النصف مُجلَّد بلا ظرف جلد1.

1250- مناقب سيدي عبد القادر الكيلاني قدس سره بخط تركي قطع الربع مُجلَّد بلا ظرف جلد1.

1251- بهجة سيدي الرفاعي قدس سره بخط مصري قطع الربع مُجلَّد بظرف جلد1.

1252- مناقب الأئمة الأخيار المسمى بتحفة الأبرار بخط نسخ قطع النصف مُجلَّد بظرف جلد1.

1253- تاريخ الأولياء بخط مصري مُجلَّد بلا ظرف جلد1.

1254- مناقب الأئمة بخط نسخ قطع الربع واسع مُجلَّد بلا ظرف جلد1.

1255- مناقب أبي أيوب الأنصاري بخط نسخ قطع الربع مُجلَّد عتيق بلا ظرف جلد1.

[56] 1256- الاقتصاد في مراتب الاجتهاد بخط مصري قطع الربع مُجلَّد بظرف جلد1.

1257- ترجمة شيخ الإسلام بخط مصري قطع الربع مُجلَّد بظرف جلد1.[213]

1258- الحضرة الأنسية في الرحلة القدسية لسيدي عبد الغني النابلسي قدس سره بخط نسخ قطع الربع مُجلَّد بظرف جلد1.

1259- الرحلة الكبرى لسيدي عبد الغني النابلسي قدس سره بخط نسخ قطع الربع مُجلَّد بظرف جلد1.

1260- رحلة البقاع[214] لسيدي عبد الغني النابلسي قدس سره بخط نسخ مُجدْوَل بأحمر قطع الربع مُجلَّد بلا ظرف جلد1.

1261- طبقات الأخيار بخط مصري قطع الربع مُجلَّد بلا ظرف جلد1.

1262- طبقات الأخيار بخط نسخ قطع النصف مُحيَّر مُجلَّد بلا ظرف جلد1.

1263- طبقات الحنفية المسماة بالغرف العلية بخط مصري قطع الربع مُجلَّد بظرف جلد1.

1264- طبقات الشعراني الجزء الثاني بخط مصري قطع الربع مُجلَّد بظرف جلد1.

1265- طبقات السبكي بخط نسخ مُجدْوَل بأحمر قطع كامل مُجلَّد بظرف جلد1.

1266- تاريخ العلماء بخط ريحاني قطع النصف مُجلَّد بظرف جلد1.

1267- مراتب العلماء العاملين المسمى بإرشاد[215] الطالبين بخط مصري قطع الربع مُجلَّد بظرف جلد1.[216]

1268- مباعث الارتحال إلى محل شد الرحال بخط مصري مُجدْوَل بأحمر قطع النصف مُجلَّد بظرف جلد1.

---

213 ترجمة شيخ الإسلام قطب الأولياء الكرام محيي الدين النووي. للسخاوي، محمد بن عبد الرحمن (ت 902هـ / 1497م). وهذه النسخة محفوظة اليوم في مكتبة زهير مصطفى الشاويش الحسيني.

214 في الأصل: البقا.

215 في الأصل: بإرشاد.

216 للشعراني، عبد الوهاب (ت 973هـ/ 1565م). هذه النسخة محفوظة في معهد دراسات الثقافة الشرقية بجامعة طوكيو برقم [2148] Ms.76 http://ricasdb.ioc.u-tokyo.ac.jp/daiber/db_ShowImg.php?ms=76&txtno=&size=S&page=2

-1269 المستظرف بخط مصري قطع كامل مُجَلَّد بظرف جلد1.

-1270 المستظرف بخط مصري قطع كامل مُجَلَّد بظرف جلد1.

-1271 من المستظرف الجزء[217] الأول بخط مصري قطع الربع مُجَلَّد بظرف جلد1.

-1272 من المستظرف الجزء[218] الأول بخط مصري قطع الربع مُجَلَّد بظرف جلد1.

-1273 تاريخ القرماني بخط نسخ قطع الربع مُجَلَّد بظرف جلد1.

-1274 تاريخ القرماني بخط مصري قطع كامل مُجَلَّد بظرف جلد1.

-1275 تاريخ القرماني بخط مصري قطع كامل مُجَلَّد بلا ظرف جلد1.

-1276 تاريخ القرماني بخط مصري قطع الربع مُجَلَّد بلا ظرف جلد1.

-1277 تاريخ ابن خلكان بخط مصري قطع كامل مُجَلَّد بلا ظرف جلد1.

-1278 تاريخ [ابن] خلكان بخط مصري قطع كامل مُجَلَّد بلا ظرف جلد1.

-1279 تاريخ ابن خلكان بخط مصري قطع كامل مُجَلَّد بظرف جلد1.

-1280 تاريخ ابن خلكان بخط مصري قطع النصف مُجَلَّد بلا ظرف جلد1.

-1281 من تاريخ ابن خلكان الجزؤ الأول بخط مصري قطع كامل مُجَلَّد بظرف جلد1.

-1282 من تاريخ ابن خلكان جزء بخط نسخ قطع النصف مُجَلَّد بظرف جلد1.

من تاريخ ابن خلكان جلد1.[219]

[57] -1283 من تاريخ ابن خلكان الجزؤ الأول بخط مصري قطع الربع مُجَلَّد بلا ظرف جلد1.[220]

-1284 من تاريخ ابن خلكان الجزؤ الثاني بخط مصري قطع الربع مُجَلَّد بلا ظرف جلد1.

-1285 حيوة الحيوان بخط مصري قطع [...][221] مُجَلَّد بظرف جلد1.

-1286 حيوة الحيوان الصغرى بخط مصري قطع[...][222] مُجَلَّد بلا ظرف جلد1.

-1287 من حيوة الحيوان الجزؤ[223] الأول بخط مصري قطع كامل مُجَلَّد بظرف جلد1.

---

217 في الأصل: جزء.

218 في الأصل: جزء.

219 تعقيبة في الهامش الأيسر السفلي.

220 أعتقد أنّ هذه هي النسخة المحفوظة في مكتبة جامعة برينستون برقم Garrett 3415Y. لأنَّ أبعادها 20,8×15,3 cm، فهي أقرب إلى قطع الربع، وبالتالي ليست النسخة المكررة بالرقم (1282) ذات القطع الكامل.
https://catalog.princeton.edu/catalog/9951702863506421

221 فراغ في الأصل بمقدار كلمة.

222 فراغ في الأصل بمقدار كلمة.

223 في الأصل: جزؤ.

1288- من حيوة الحيوان الجزؤ[224] الأول بخط مصري عتيق مُجَلَّد بلا ظرف جلد1.

1289- حيوة الحيوان ناقص الأول بخط مصري قطع كامل مُجَلَّد بظرف جلد1.

1290- من حيوة الحيوان الجزؤ[225] الثاني بخط مصري قطع النصف مُحَيَّر مُجَلَّد عتيق بلا ظرف جلد1.[226]

1291- من حيوة الحيوان الجزؤ[227] الثاني بخط مصري قطع كامل مُجَلَّد بظرف جلد1.

1292- تاريخ المحبي بخط مصري قطع كامل مُجَدْوَل بأحمر مُجَلَّد بظرف جلد1.

1293- رحلة محب[228] الدين القاضي بخط مصري قطع الربع مُجَلَّد بظرف جلد1.

1294- سلافة الدهر في محاسن أهل العصر قطع الربع مُجَلَّد بظرف جلد1.

1295- يتيمة الدهر في شعراء العصر بخط نسخ قطع النصف مُحَيَّر مُجَلَّد بلا ظرف جلد1.

1296- يتيمة الدهر في محاسن أهل العصر بخط نسخ قطع الربع مُجَلَّد بظرف جلد1.

1297- فاكهة الخلفاء بخط نسخ قطع الربع مُجَلَّد بظرف جلد1.

1298- عجائب المخلوقات بخط تعليق تركي قطع مُجَلَّد بلا ظرف جلد1.

1299- خريدة العجائب بخط مصري قطع الربع مُجَلَّد بظرف جلد1.

1300- خريدة العجائب ناقصة الأول بخط نسخ قطع الربع مُجَلَّد بلا ظرف جلد1.

1301- نفح الطيب بخط مصري مُجَدْوَل[229] بأحمر قطع كامل مُجَلَّد بلا ظرف جلد1.

1302- نفح الطيب بخط نسخ قطع النصف الجزؤ[230] الثاني مُجَلَّد بلا ظرف جلد1.

1303- يتيمة الدهر في محاسن أهل العصر بخط مصري قطع الربع مُجَلَّد بظرف جلد1.

1304- تذكرة المتبحرين في العلماء المتأخرين بخط مصري قطع الربع مُجَلَّد بظرف جلد1.

1305- حسن المحاضرة في أخبار مصر والقاهرة[231] بخط مصري قطع كامل مُجَلَّد بلا ظرف جلد1.

224 في الأصل: جزؤ.

225 في الأصل: جزؤ.

226 هذه النسخة محفوظة في مكتبة جامعة النجاح بنابلس برقم (NL 250213)، وقد فهرست هناك خطأً ككتاب في التاريخ.

https://manuscripts.najah.edu/node/739

لأنها الجزء الثاني من الكتاب، ولأن أبعادها تتطابق مع قطع النصف، وليس مع قطع الكامل كما في النسخة رقم (1292).

227 في الأصل: جزؤ.

228 في الأصل: المحب.

229 في الأصل: مجلدول.

230 في الأصل: جزؤ.

231 في الأصل: في الأخبار المصر القاهرة.

1306- حسن المحاضرة في أخبار مصر والقاهرة[232] بخط مصري قطع[233] مُجَلَّد بظرف جلد1.

1307- نفح الطيب بخط نسخ مُحَيَّر الكامل مُجَلَّد بظرف جلد1.

1308- الخطط للمقريزي بخط نسخ قطع كامل مُجَلَّد بلا ظرف جلد1.

1309- الخطط للمقريزي الجزؤ[234] الثاني بخط نسخ مُجَدْوَل بذهب مُحَيَّر النصف بظرف جلد1.[235]

1310- تاريخ مواقع مصر ناقص الأول بخط مصري قطع كامل مُجَلَّد بظرف جلد1.

1311- ثمرا ت[236] الأوراق بخط مصري قطع الربع مُجَلَّد بظرف جلد1.

1312- قلائد الجمال[237] بخط نسخ قطع الربع مُجَلَّد بظرف جلد1.

[58] 1313- مورد اللطافة بخط مصري قطع الربع مُجَلَّد بظرف جلد1.

1314- محاسن الشام بخط نسخ مُذَهَّب قطع الربع بجلد مُذَهَّب جديد بلا ظرف جلد1.

1315- نزهة الأنام في محاسن الشام بخط نسخ قطع الربع بظرف جلد1.

1316- دمية القصر مختصرة بخط تعليق مُجَدْوَل بأحمر مُحَيَّر النصف مُجَلَّد بلا ظرف جلد1.

1317- سانحات دمى القصر بخط نسخ قطع الربع مُجَلَّد بظرف جلد1.

1318- سلوان المطاع بخط نسخ قطع الربع مُجَلَّد بلا ظرف جلد1.

1319- حلة الذهب الإبريز[238] بخط مصري قطع الربع مُجَلَّد أحمر بلا ظرف جلد1.

1320- نفائس العرائس بخط مصري قطع الربع مُجَلَّد بلا ظرف جلد1.

1321- عجائب المقدور بخط نسخ مُذَهَّب ظاهراً وباطناً قطع الربع مُجَلَّد بظرف جلد1.

1322- تاريخ البوريني بخط نسخ عالٍ قطع النصف مُجَلَّد بظرف جلد1.

1323- تاريخ آل عثمان بخط مصري قطع الربع مُجَلَّد بلا ظرف جلد1.

1324- تاريخ آل عثمان بخط نسخ تركي مُذَهَّب ظاهراً وباطناً قطع الربع مُجَلَّد بلا ظرف جلد1.

1325- تاريخ الخميس المسمى بالجوهر النفيس بخط نسخ قطع الربع مُجَلَّد بلا ظرف جلد1.

1326- تاريخ ابن الأثير[239] بخط نسخ مُجَدْوَل بأحمر قطع النصف مُجَلَّد بلا ظرف جلد1.

---

232 في الأصل: في الأخبار مصر القاهرة.

233 نسي تحديد القطع.

234 في الأصل: جزؤ.

235 هي غير النسخة المحفوظة في مكتبة جامعة برينستون برقم Garrett 3516Y. لأنها النصف الأول وليست الجزء الثاني.
https://catalog.princeton.edu/catalog/9954371983506421#viewer-container

236 في الأصل: ثمراة.

237 هكذا في الأصل، وربما المقصود: قلائد الجمان.

238 في الأصل: الإبرين.

239 في الأصل: الأسير.

1327- حل العرى[240] في أم القرى بخط مصري قطع الربع مُجلَّد بظرف جلد1.

1328- حديقة الزوراء بخط نسخ قطع الربع مُجلَّد بلا ظرف جلد1.

1329- حديقة الملوك بخط نسخ تركي مُذَهَّب ظاهراً وباطناً قطع الربع مُجلَّد بظرف جلد1.

1330- تاريخ أمين الدولة بخط ريحاني قطع النصف مُجلَّد بلا ظرف جلد1.

1331- الأول من فتوحات الشام بخط مصري عتيق قطع الربع مُجلَّد بظرف جلد1.

1332- من تاريخ الخطيب الجزؤ[241] الخامس بخط مصري قطع الربع مُجلَّد بلا ظرف جلد1.

1333- من تاريخ الخطيب الجزؤ[242] الثاني بخط مصري قطع الربع مُجلَّد بلا ظرف جلد1.

1334- من تاريخ الخطيب الجزؤ[243] الحادي عشر بخط مصري قطع الربع مُجلَّد بلا ظرف جلد1.

1335- آثار البلاد وأخبار العباد بخط مصري قطع كامل مُجلَّد بلا ظرف جلد1.

1336- أخبار الدولة بخط نسخ قطع النصف مُجلَّد بلا ظرف جلد1.

1337- نهاية الأرب في معرفة قبائل العرب[244] بخط مصري قطع الربع مُجلَّد بظرف جلد1.

1338- نهاية الأرب بخط مصري قطع النصف مُحيَّر مُجلَّد بلا ظرف جلد1.

1339- نهجة النواظر بخط مصري قطع الربع مُحيَّر مُجلَّد بلا ظرف جلد1.

1340- التبر المسبوك بخط مصري قطع كامل مُحيَّر مُجلَّد بظرف جلد1.

1341- شرح رسالة ابن عبدون بخط مصري قطع الربع مُجلَّد بظرف جلد1.

1342- الروضتين في أخبار[245] الدولتين بخط نسخ قطع الربع مُجلَّد بلا ظرف جلد1.

[59] 1343- مُسيّر[246] التاريخ بخط مصري قطع الربع مُجلَّد بظرف جلد1.

1344- روضة الأخبار بخط مصري قطع الربع مُجلَّد بظرف جلد1.

1345- وفيات[247] الأعيان بخط نسخ قطع كامل مُجلَّد بظرف جلد1.

1346- كتاب اليميني بخط نسخ قطع الربع مُجلَّد بظرف جلد1.

1347- لقط المرجان بخط مصري قطع الربع مُجلَّد بظرف جلد1.

1348- الأول من كنز الذهب بخط مصري قطع الربع واسع مُجلَّد بظرف جلد1.

---

240 في الأصل: العرا.

241 في الأصل: جزؤ.

242 في الأصل: جزؤ.

243 في الأصل: جزؤ.

244 في الأصل: في المعرفة القبائل العرب.

245 في الأصل: الأخبار.

246 في الأصل: مشير.

247 في الأصل: وافيات.

1349- النزهة السنية بخط مصري قطع الربع مُجَلَّد بظرف جلد1.

1350- أخبار الأعيان ناقص الأول بخط مصري قطع كامل مُجَلَّد بلا ظرف جلد1.

1351- سراج الملوك ناقص الأول بخط مصري قطع النصف مُجَلَّد عتيق بلا ظرف جلد1.

1352- النصر الوهبي بخط تعليق قطع كامل مُجَلَّد بظرف جلد1.

1353- الثاني من طبقات التميمي[248] بخط نسخ قطع الربع مُجَلَّد بظرف جلد1.[249]

1354- نصيحة الملوك بخط مصري قطع الربع مُجَلَّد بلا ظرف جلد1.

1355- الفرق المؤذن بالطرب[250] بخط نسخ قطع الربع مُجَلَّد بظرف جلد1.

1356- نفحة المجلوب بخط تعليق قطع الربع مُجَلَّد بظرف جلد1.

1357- الإشارات إلى أماكن الزيارات بخط مصري قطع الربع مُجَلَّد جلد1.

1358- كشف الأسرار بخط مصري قطع الربع مُجَلَّد بظرف جلد1.

1359- تنبيه الطالب بخط تعليق قطع الربع مُجَلَّد بظرف جلد1.

1360- الدرة السنية بخط تعليق قطع الثمن مُجَلَّد بلا ظرف جلد1.

1361- تحفة السما بخط مصري قطع الربع مُجَلَّد بظرف جلد1.

1362- تاريخ ابن أبي المجد نظم ناقص الأول بخط مصري قطع الربع مُجَلَّد بظرف جلد1.

1363- جواهر الحكم بخط مصري قطع الربع مُحيَّر مُجَلَّد بظرف جلد1.

1364- الغرر الواضحة بخط مصري قطع النصف مُحيَّر مُجَلَّد بظرف جلد1.

1365- الدرر المنظومة من النكت والإشارات المفهومة[251] بخط مصري قطع الربع مُجَلَّد بلا ظرف جلد1.

1366- الأول من تاريخ[252] ابن أعثم[253] الكندي بخط مصري قطع كامل مُجَلَّد بظرف جلد1.[254]

1367- آثار الدولة والأخبار الأول بخط نسخ مُجَدْوَل بأحمر قطع الربع مُجَلَّد بلا ظرف جلد1.

1368- الثاني من عقد [القراش؟] بخط ريحاني قطع الربع مُجَلَّد بظرف جلد1.

---

248 في الأصل: التيمي.

249 هذه النسخة محفوظ في مكتبة الدولة ببرلين برقم Landberg 9
https://digital.staatsbibliothek-berlin.de/werkansicht/?PPN=PPN74130158X&PHYSID=PHYS_0007

250 في الأصل: بطرب.

251 في الأصل: مفهومة.

252 في الأصل: التاريخ.

253 في الأصل: عثم.

254 لابن اعثم، أحمد بن عثمان الكندي الكوفي (ت 314هـ/ 927م). هذه النسخة محفوظة في مكتبة تشستربيتي برقم Ar. 3272 ، ومن الراجح أنَّها خرجت من مكتبة الجزَّار سنة (1929م)، عن طريق إبراهام يهودا. يُنظر فصل الدكتور كونراد هيرشلر.

1369- البرق اليماني بخط مصري قطع الربع مُجَلَّد بظرف جلد1.[255]

1370- تاريخ ناقص الأول والآخر بخط مصري قطع الربع مُجَلَّد بظرف جلد1.

1371- مجموعة سعد الدين بخط مصري قطع الربع مُجَلَّد بظرف جلد1.

1372- وقف الملك[256] الأشرف بالقاهرة بخط مصري قطع الربع مُجَلَّد بظرف جلد1.[257]

1373- تاريخ سلطان مراد خان بخط مصري قطع الربع مُجَلَّد بظرف جلد1. [60]

1374- تاريخ خوارزم شاه بخط نسخ قطع الربع مُجَلَّد بلا ظرف جلد1.

1375- مناقب أبو الفتح سلطان محمد خان بخط نسخ قطع النصف مُحيَّر مُذَهَّب مُجَلَّد جلد1.

1376- تاريخ [فرنسي؟] لعجائب القدرة بخط تعليق في صور مختلفة الأشكال قطع كامل التلخيص مذهب مُجَلَّد بلا ظرف جلد1.

1377- تاريخ الفرس بخط مصري قطع الربع مُجَلَّد بظرف جلد1.

1378- مناقب السيد بطال بالتركي قطع الربع مُجَلَّد بلا ظرف جلد1.

1379- تدبير نامه جديد بخط رقعة التركي قطع الربع مُجَلَّد بلا ظرف جلد1.

1380- المنطوق والمفهوم بخط مصري قطع الربع مُجَلَّد بلا ظرف جلد1.

1381- تاريخ ناقص الأول بخط مصري قطع النصف مُجَلَّد بظرف جلد1.

1382- الأول من تجارب[258] الأمم بخط مصري قطع النصف مُجَلَّد بلا ظرف جلد1.

1383- الأول من سيرة الدهمه[259] بخط مصري قطع الربع مُجَلَّد بظرف جلد1.

1384- الأول من سيرة الدهمه بخط مصري قطع الربع بلا ظرف جلد1.

1385- العاشر من سيرة الدهمه بخط مصري قطع الربع مُجَلَّد بظرف عتيق جلد1.

1386- السابع والعشرون من الدهمه بخط مصري قطع الربع مُجَلَّد بظرف جلد1.

1387- من بعض سير الأولين بخط [...][260] قطع الربع مُجَلَّد بظرف جلد1.

1388- كتاب التنبيه على مكارم يحيى البرمكي بخطوط قطع الربع مُجَلَّد بظرف جلد1.

1389- ذيل سير تركي بخط تعليق قطع الربع بظرف مذهب جلد1.

1390- منطق الطير بخط تعليق تركي مُجَدْوَل بأحمر قطع الثمن مُجَلَّد بلا ظرف جلد1.

1391- همايون نامه بخط تعليق تركي مذهب قطع الربع مُجَلَّد بلا ظرف جلد1.

---

255 للنهرواني، قطب الدين محمد بن أحمد (ت 990هـ/ 1583م). هذه النسخة محفوظة في المكتبة البريطانية برقم، Or. 1183

256 في الأصل: ملك.

257 هذه النسخة محفوظة في مكتبة وزارة الأوقاف المصرية، برقم 2398 / 209.

258 في الأصل: تجاريب.

259 هكذا في الأصل، والراجح أنه يقصد "سيرة دَلهمه والبطال".

260 فراغ في الأصل بمقدار كلمة.

1392- تاريخ صبحي أفندي طبع تركي قطع كامل مُجلَّدين بظرفين جلد2، فقط اثنان لا غير. 1 أخذه شريف أفندي خواجكان.[261]

1393- تاريخ تركي طبع إستانبول لعزي سليمان أفندي قطع كامل مُجلَّدين بظرف وبلا ظرف جلد2، فقط اثنان لا غير.

1394- قطعة من سيرة العنتر بخط مصري قطع الربع مُجلَّد بظرف جلد1.

1395- أبو شادوف ناقص الأول بخط مصري قطع الربع مُجلَّد بظرف جلد1.

حسابه نُمرو 151 فقط مائة وواحد وخمسين لا غيره. 1 الذي أخذه شريف أفندي، 150.

17 كتب علم اللغة

1396- قاموس بخط نسخ مُجدْوَل بإكليل قطع كامل مُجلَّد بظرف جلد1.

1397- قاموس بخط نسخ قطع كامل مُحيَّر مُجدْوَل بإكليل بظرف جلد1.

1398- قاموس بخط نسخ قطع كامل مُجدْوَل بأحمر بظرف جلد1.

[61] 1399- قاموس بخط نسخ قطع كامل مُحيَّر مُجلَّد بظرف جلد1.

1400- قاموس بخط نسخ قطع كامل مُجلَّد بظرف جلد1.

1401- قاموس بخط نسخ قطع النصف مُحيَّر مُجلَّد بظرف جلد1.

1402- قاموس بخط مصري قطع النصف مُحيَّر مُجلَّد بظرف جلد1.

1403- من شرح القاموس الجزؤ[262] الأول للمناوي بخط مصري مُجدْوَل بأحمر قطع كامل مُجلَّد بلا ظرف جلد1.

1404- من شرح القاموس جزؤ ثاني بخط مصري مُجدْوَل بأحمر قطع كامل مُجلَّد بلا ظرف جلد1.

1405- الصحاح بخط نسخ مُجدْوَل بإكليل قطع كامل مُجلَّد بظرف جلد1.

1406- الصحاح بخط نسخ قطع النصف التلخيص مُجلَّد بظرف جلد1.

1407- مختار الصحاح بخط تعليق قطع الربع مُجلَّد بظرف جلد1.

1408- التوقيف على مهمات التعريف بخط مصري قطع الربع مُجلَّد بظرف جلد1.

1409- النظام الغريب بخط مصري قطع الربع مُجلَّد بظرف جلد1.

1410- المضاعف من اللغة بخط نسخ قطع الربع مُجلَّد بظرف جلد1.

1411- السامي في الأسامي بخط ريحاني قطع النصف مُحيَّر مُجلَّد بظرف جلد1.

261 خواجكان ديوان همايون: إحدى الرتب الملكيَّة أو الإداريَّة. يُنظر بيرم، محمد الهادي، الرتب الملكية في الدولة العلية، مجلة المقتطف، ع 9 (يونيو 1894)، 591- 594، هنا الصفحة 594؛ بيرم، محمد الهادي، الرتب العلمية في الدولة العلية، مجلة المقتطف، ع 7 (أبريل 1894). 445- 449، هنا الصفحة 448.

262 في الأصل: جزؤ.

1412- السامي في الأسامي بخط ريحاني قطع النصف مُحيَّر مُجلَّد عتيق بظرف جلد1.

1413- الدر النثير بخط نسخ قطع كامل مُحيَّر مُجلَّد بظرف جلد1.

1414- الوجيز بخط تعليق قطع النصف مُحيَّر مُجلَّد بظرف جلد1.

1415- المعرب على حروف المعجم بخط ريحاني قطع الربع مُجلَّد بلا ظرف جلد1.

1416- فقه اللغة بخط نسخ قطع الربع مُحيَّر مُجلَّد بظرف جلد1.

1417- شرح الكافية في اللغة بخط نسخ قطع النصف مُجلَّد بظرف جلد1.

1418- الثاني من النهاية بخط نسخ مُجدْوَل بإكليل قطع النصف مُجلَّد جلد1.

1419- قطعة من القرطبي في اللغة[263] ناقص بخط ريحاني قطع النصف مُجلَّد بلا ظرف جلد1.

1420- الثاني من لسان العرب لغة ناقص الأول بخط مصري ربع مُحيَّر مُجلَّد بظرف جلد1.

1421- كتاب من اللغة[264] بخط مصري ناقص الأول قطع النصف مُجلَّد بظرف جلد1.

1422- كتاب منتخب في علم اللغة تركي بخط نسخ قطع الربع مُجلَّد بظرف جلد1.

حسابه نِمرو 27 فقط سبعة وعشرين لا غير.

[62] 18 كتب علم الطب

1423- القانون لابن سينا بخط طبع قطع كامل مُجلَّد بلا ظرف جلد1.

1424- من فن القانون لابن سينا بخط نسخ قطع النصف مُحيَّر مُجلَّد بظرف جلد1.

1425- من القانون لابن سينا بخط مصري مُجدْوَل بأحمر قطع الربع مُجلَّد بظرف جلد1.

1426- من القانون لابن سينا الجزؤ الأول[265] بخط نسخ مُجدْوَل بإكليل قطع الربع مُجلَّد بظرف جلد1.

1427- تذكرة داود بخط مصري قطع كامل مُجلَّد بلا ظرف جلد1.

1428- تذكرة داود بخط مصري قطع النصف مُجلَّد بظرف جلد1.

1429- ذيل تذكرة داود بخط مصري قطع النصف مُجلَّد بظرف جلد1.

1430- المغني في الطب شرح الموجز بخط مصري قطع كامل مُجلَّد بظرف جلد1.

1431- مغني[266] الطبيب وعمدة الأريب بخط مصري قطع الربع مُجلَّد بظرف جلد1.[267]

---

263 في الأصل: للغة.

264 في الأصل: الغة.

265 في الأصل: جزؤ أول.

266 في الأصل: معنى.

267 للزبيدي، محمد بن احمد بن يوسف (ت 612هـ/ 1214م). هذه النسخة محفوظة في مكتبة قطر الوطنية برقم HC.MS.00211

1432- الجامع في الطب بخط نسخ قطع النصف مُحيَّر مُجلَّد بظرف جلد1.

1433- الجامع في الطب بخط نسخ قطع النصف مُحيَّر مُجلَّد بظرف جلد1.

1434- كتاب في الخيل بخط نسخ عالٍ فيه صور الخيل قطع نصف التلخيص مُجلَّد بلا ظرف جلد1.

1435- كتاب معالجات الخيل وغيرها بخط مصري قطع الثمن مُجلَّد بظرف جلد1.

1436- كتاب في الخيل بخط نسخ مُجَدْوَل بأحمر قطع الربع مُحيَّر مُجلَّد بظرف جلد1.

1437- كتاب الخيل بخط مصري قطع الربع مُجلَّد بظرف جلد1.

1438- كتاب الخيل بخط نسخ ريحاني قطع النصف مُحيَّر مُجلَّد بظرف جلد1.

1439- كتاب في علم الطب المسمى بتذكرة الكحالين بخط مصري[268] تعليق قطع الربع مُجلَّد بظرف جلد1.

1440- كتاب في علم الطب بخط نسخ مجدل بأحمر قطع كامل مُجلَّد بلا ظرف جلد1.

1441- كتاب الوصلة إلى الحبيب بخط نسخ قطع الربع مُجلَّد بظرف جلد1.

1442- كتاب في علم الطب بخط نسخ قطع الربع واسع مُجلَّد بظرف جلد1.

1443- كتاب في علم الطب تركي قطع الربع مُجلَّد بظرف جلد1.

1444- مجموع من كلام ابن سينا من القانون بخط نسخ قطع [...][269] مُجلَّد بظرف جلد1.

1445- رسالة الرازي طب بخط مصري قطع الربع مُجلَّد بظرف جلد1.

1446- غنية المرام في معرفة الرمي بالسهام بخط نسخ قطع الربع مُجلَّد بلا ظرف جلد1.

1447- درة الغواص في معرفة الخواص بخط مصري قطع الربع مُجلَّد بلا ظرف جلد1.

1448- رسالة للشيخ الرئيس أبي علي ابن سينا بخط تعليق قطع الربع مُجلَّد بظرف جلد1.

1449- كتاب في علم الطب لأبي الحزم بخط مصري قطع الربع مُجلَّد بظرف جلد1.

[63] 1450- كتاب في علم الطب بخط نسخ قطع الربع مُحيَّر مُجلَّد بظرف جلد1.

1451- بحر الجواهر في الطب للهروي بخط نسخ قطع الربع مُجلَّد بظرف جلد1.

1452- غاية الإرشاد بخط مصري قطع الربع مُجلَّد بظرف جلد1.

1453- خصائص الحشائش لابن البيطار بخط نسخ قطع النصف مُحيَّر مُجلَّد بلا ظرف جلد1.

1454- الجزؤ الأول من تذكرة داود بخط مصري قطع النصف مُجلَّد بظرف جلد1.

1455- جراب المجربات بخط نسخ قطع الثمن مُجلَّد بلا ظرف جلد1.

1456- التحفة الجامعة بخط نسخ قطع الربع مُجلَّد بلا ظرف جلد1.

1457- كتاب طب بخط نسخ قطع الربع مُجلَّد بلا ظرف جلد1.

---

268 مضروب عليها في الأصل.

269 فراغ في الأصل بمقدار كلمة.

1458- كتاب في علم الطب لطهماز العجم بخط تعليق قطع الربع مُجَلَّد بظرف جلد1.

1459- كتاب حاوي إلياس في علم التداوي بخط تعليق قطع النصف مُحَيَّر مُجَلَّد بظرف جلد1.

1460- أزهار الأفكار بخط ريحاني قطع النصف مُحَيَّر مُجَلَّد بلا ظرف جلد1.

1461- شرح المختصر في الطب بخط مصري قطع الربع واسع مُجَلَّد بظرف جلد1.

1462- الموجز بخط مصري قطع الربع مُجَلَّد بظرف جلد1.

1463- فلاحة البساتين بخط نسخ قطع الربع مُجَلَّد بلا ظرف جلد1.

1464- كتاب في الطب بخط مصري قطع الربع مُجَلَّد بلا ظرف جلد1.

1465- انتخاب الاقتضاب[270] على طريق المسألة ورد الجواب بخط نسخ قطع الثمن مُجَلَّد بظرف جلد1.

1466- اللمحة في الطب بخط مصري قطع الثمن مُجَلَّد بلا ظرف جلد1.

1467- طب علم الأبدان بخط نسخ قطع الربع مُحَيَّر مُجَلَّد بظرف جلد1.

1468- كتاب في علم الطب بخط تعليق قطع الربع مُجَلَّد بظرف جلد1.

1469- كتاب في علم الطب بخط مصري قطع النصف مُجَلَّد بلا ظرف جلد1.

1470- مجموع من كلام الحكماء بخط مصري قطع الربع مُجَلَّد بظرف جلد1.

1471- كتاب الطب ناقص الأول والآخر بخط نسخ قطع كامل مُجَلَّد بلا ظرف جلد1.

حسابه نُمرِو 49 فقط ~~لا غير~~[271] تسعة وأربعين لا غير.

[64] 19 كتب علم الفلك والهيئة والحرف والروحاني والرمل والهندسة والحساب والكيمياء[272]

1472- شمس المعارف الكبرى بخط نسخ مُذَهَّب قطع كامل مُجَلَّد بظرف جلد1.

1473- شمس المعارف الصغرى بخط مصري قطع الربع مُجَلَّد بظرف جلد1.

1474- شمس الآفاق بخط نسخ قطع النصف مُحَيَّر مُجَلَّد بظرف جلد1.

1475- الهداية روحاني بخط مصري قطع الثمن مُجَلَّد بلا ظرف جلد1.

1476- كتاب روحاني بخط نسخ قطع الربع مُجَلَّد قديم بلا ظرف جلد1.

1477- كتاب روحاني بخطوط مُشَكَّلة قطع الربع مُجَلَّد جديد بلا ظرف جلد1.

1478- كتاب روحاني خطوط قطع الربع مُحَيَّر مُجَلَّد بلا ظرف جلد1.

1479- كتاب الخواص بخط مصري قطع الربع مُجَلَّد بلا ظرف جلد1.

---

270 في الأصل الاقتصاب.

271 مضروب عليها في الأصل.

272 في الأصل: الكيماء.

1480- اللمعة النورانية شرح الشجرة النعمانية بخط نسخ قطع الربع مُجَلَّد بلا ظرف جلد1.

1481- جفر بخط نسخ قطع الربع مُجَلَّد بظرف جلد1.[273]

1482- كتاب أقلام مختلفة بخط نسخ قطع الربع مُجَلَّد بلا ظرف جلد1.

1483- كتاب زايرجا بخط نسخ قطع النصف عريض مُجَلَّد بلا ظرف جلد1.

1484- مجموع في الزايرجا بخط نسخ قطع الربع مُجَلَّد بلا ظرف جلد1.

1485- كتاب قرعة بخط مصري قطع النصف مُحيَّر مُجَلَّد بلا ظرف جلد1.

1486- كتاب في علم الحرف اسمه الكشف ومعه غيره بخط نسخ قطع الربع مُجَلَّد بظرف جلد1.

1487- شمسية أفلاطون بخط نسخ قطع الربع مُجَلَّد بلا ظرف جلد1.

1488- كتاب زايرجا السبتية بخط نسخ قطع الربع مُجَلَّد بظرف جلد1.

1489- الشموس المضيئة بخط مصري قطع الربع مُجَلَّد بظرف جلد1.

1490- جهان نامه قطع كامل مُحيَّر طبع إسلامبول مُجَلَّد بلا ظرف جلد1.

1491- روضة الأزهار في علم الأوفاق بخط نسخ قطع الربع مُجَلَّد بظرف جلد1.

1492- كتاب زايرجا بخط مصري قطع الربع مُجَلَّد بظرف جلد1.

1493- مواقع النجوم للشيخ الأكبر قدس سره بخط نسخ قطع الثمن مُجَلَّد بلا ظرف جلد1.[274]

1494- كتاب ملقَّب بغريب الفنون فلك بخط مصري قطع الربع مُجَلَّد بظرف جلد1.

1495- براعة الاستهلال فيما يتعلق بالشهر والهلال بخط مصري قطع الربع مُجَلَّد بلا ظرف جلد1.

1496- كتاب زيج بخط مصري قطع الربع مُجَلَّد بلا ظرف جلد1.

1497- إرشاد الحائر في معرفة رسم خطوط فضل الدائر بخط مصري قطع الربع مُجَلَّد بظرف جلد1.

1498- كتاب ملحمة بخط نسخ قطع الربع مُجَلَّد بلا ظرف جلد1.

1499- كتاب نتيجة[275] أحكام الميقات بخط مصري قطع الربع مُجَلَّد بظرف جلد1. [65]

1500- كتاب في علم الفلك مجموع أمثلة فيه جداول بخط نسخ قطع الربع مُجَلَّد بظرف جلد1.

1501- رسالة في الميقات وهو مجموع في علم الفلك بخط نسخ قطع الربع مُجَلَّد بظرف جلد1.

---

273 هذه النسخة محفوظة اليوم في المكتبة السليمانية برقم 759.

274 لابن العربي (638هـ/ 1240م). لا يمكن أن تكون هي النسخة المحفوظة في المكتبة الوطنية بالقدس برقم Ms. AP Ar. 177، أولاً لأن الخاتم مطموس، وثانياً لأن القياس المتري لهذه النسخة هو (18×13.5cm)، أي أنها من قطع الربع محيَّر وليست من قطع الثمن، وثالثاً لأن خطها فارسي وليس نسخاً.

https://www.nli.org.il/he/manuscripts/NNL_ALEPH003484012/NLI#$FL154166987

275 في الأصل: النتيجة.

-1502 كتاب الملحمة بخط مصري قطع الثمن واسع مُجَلَّد بظرف جلد1.

-1503 كتاب الفلكيات للخواجة الطوسي بخط طبع قطع كامل مُجَلَّد بظرف جلد1.

-1504 كتاب أجزاء من الفلكيات وغيره بخط مصري قطع الربع مُجَلَّد بظرف جلد1.

-1505 كتاب تشريح الأفلاك بخط مصري قطع الثمن مُجَلَّد بلا ظرف جلد1.

-1506 أحكام قرانات الكواكب بخط نسخ قطع الثمن طويل مُجَلَّد بلا ظرف جلد1.

-1507 دستور العمل بخط تركي قطع الربع مُحَيَّر مُجَلَّد بظرف جلد1.

-1508 كتاب مجموع أحكام أبو معشر بخط مصري قطع الربع مُجَلَّد بلا ظرف جلد1.

-1509 كتاب أبو معشر البلخي بخط مصري قطع الربع مُجَلَّد بظرف جلد1.

-1510 كتاب النتيجة في علم الميقات بخط نسخ قطع الربع مُجَلَّد بظرف جلد1.

-1511 رسالة الإصطرنوميا[276] بخط نسخ قطع الربع مُجَلَّد بظرف جلد1.

-1512 روزنامه مُذَهَّب بخط إسلامبولي تركي قطع الربع مُجَلَّد بلا ظرف جلد1.

-1513 روزنامه مع الفلكيات بخط مصري قطع الربع طويل مُجَلَّد بظرف جلد1.

-1514 كتاب الهيئة المسمى بالنيشابوري بخط تعليق قطع الربع مُجَلَّد بظرف جلد1.

-1515 إشارات من الحكمة فلسفة بخط تعليق قطع الربع مُحَيَّر مُجَلَّد بظرف جلد1.

-1516 حاشية مولانا زاده بخط تعليق قطع الربع مُجَلَّد بظرف جلد1.

-1517 الفتحية في الهيئة بخط نسخ قطع الربع مُجَلَّد بظرف جلد1.

-1518 كتاب من علم الهندسة بخط نسخ قطع الربع طويل واسع[277] مُجَلَّد بظرف جلد1.

-1519 كتاب [في][278] علم الهيئة بخط نسخ مُهَمَّش قطع الربع مُحَيَّر مُجَلَّد بظرف جلد1.

-1520 كتاب هندسة ناقص الأول بخط تعليق قطع الربع مُحَيَّر طويل مُجَلَّد بلا ظرف جلد1.

-1521 كتاب بعض سؤالات لمن يريد الهندسة بخط نسخ قطع الربع واسع مُجَلَّد بظرف جلد1.

-1522 كتاب بداية الحكمة بخط تعليق قطع الثمن واسع مُجَلَّد بظرف جلد1.

-1523 كتاب شرح في علم الهيئة وهو شرح الجغميني بخط نسخ قطع الربع مُجَلَّد بظرف جلد1. [66]

-1524 كتاب شرح المختصر المسمى بالملخص في الهيئة بخط نسخ قطع الربع مُجَلَّد بظرف جلد1.

-1525 كتاب ملخص من علم الهيئة بخط نسخ قطع الربع مُجَلَّد بظرف جلد1.

---

276 في الأصل الإضطرنوميا.

277 إذا صحَّ ما فهمناه من معنى طويل، من أن الورق طوي من جانبه الأقصر فأصبح متطاولاً، يُنظر الكتاب رقم (63)، وصحَّ ما فهمناه من معنى واسع من أن فرخ الورق لم يُشذب فزاد عرضه عن الحدّ المعياري، يُنظر الكتاب رقم (10). فيمكن القول عن هذا المصطلح (واسع طويل) بأن فرخ الورق لم يُشذب وبقي على مقاسه الذي خرج به من الورّاقة/ المصنع، وأنه طُويَ من جانبه الأقصر.

278 إضافة يقتضيها السياق.

1526- كتاب من علم الهيئة بخط تعليق قطع الربع مُحيَّر مُجلَّد بظرف جلد1.

1527- كتاب الملخص في علم الهيئة بخط[279] قطع الربع مُجلَّد بظرف جلد1.

1528- مصارع المصارع ومعه رسالة في الفلسفة[280] بخط نسخ قطع الربع مُجلَّد بظرف جلد1.

1529- كتاب نوادر الفلاسفة بخط مصري قطع الربع مُجلَّد بظرف جلد1.

1530- كتاب في علم الهيئة بخط تعليق قطع الربع مُجلَّد بظرف جلد1.

1531- كتاب الملخص في علم الهيئة وهو شرح الجغميني بخط مصري قطع الربع مُجلَّد بظرف جلد1.

1532- مجموع رسائل في علم الطبيعيات فلك بخط مصري مُهمَّش قطع الربع مُجلَّد بظرف جلد1.

1533- طالع المولود على قواعد[281] الفرس بخط تركي قطع الربع مُجلَّد بلا ظرف جلد1.

1534- كتاب قبس الأنوار بخط نسخ قطع الربع مُجلَّد بلا ظرف جلد1.

1535- كتاب رمل بخط نسخ قطع النصف مُجلَّد قديم بلا ظرف جلد1.

1536- كتاب رمل بخط نسخ قطع الربع مُجلَّد بلا ظرف جلد1.

1537- شرح خلاصة الحساب بخط نسخ قطع الربع مُجلَّد بلا ظرف جلد1.

1538- كتاب خلاصة الحساب بخط نسخ وتعليق قطع الربع طويل مُجلَّد بظرف جلد1.

1539- شرح خلاصة الحساب بخط نسخ قطع الربع مُحيَّر مُجلَّد بظرف جلد1.

1540- كتاب في علم الحساب بخط مصري قطع الثمن مُجلَّد بلا ظرف جلد1.

1541- كتاب في علم الحساب شرح الخلاصة بخط مصري قطع الربع مُجلَّد بظرف جلد1.

1542- المصباح في علم المفتاح في الكيمياء بخط نسخ قطع الربع مُجلَّد بظرف جلد1.

1543- رسالة في علم الكيمياء بخط مصري قطع الربع طويل مُجلَّد بظرف جلد1.

1544- كتاب في الحجر المكرّم بخط تعليق قطع الربع مُحيَّر مُجلَّد بظرف جلد1.

1545- مقدمة في علم الكيمياء بخط نسخ قطع الربع مُجلَّد بظرف جلد1.

1546- المصباح في علم المفتاح ناقص الأول بخط مصري قطع الربع مُجلَّد بلا ظرف جلد1.

1547- كتاب المصباح بخط مصري قطع الربع مُجلَّد بلا ظرف جلد1. [67]

1548- كتاب من علوم شتى بخط مصري قطع الربع مُجلَّد بظرف جلد1.

1549- طولع بالتركي لسنة 1189 بخط نسخ مُجدْوَل بإكليل قطع الربع مُجلَّد بلا ظرف جلد1.

1550- روزنامه مع ميقات بخط نسخ تركي مُذَهّب قطع الربع مُجلَّد بلا ظرف جلد1.

279 نسي تحديد نوع الخط.

280 في الأصل: فلسفة.

281 في الأصل: قوائد.

1551- السخاوية بخط نسخ قطع الربع مُجَلَّد بلا ظرف جلد1.

1552- كتاب شمس المعارف الكبرى هدية إلى سعادته من رجل مغربي مُجَلَّد من غير ظرف جلد1.

حسابه نُمِرو 80 فقط ثمانين لا غيره. 1 جدّ هدية من مغربي 81.

20 كتب الفارسي

1553- المثنوي المعنوي بخط تعليق مُذَهَّب قطع كامل مُجَلَّد بلا ظرف جلد1.

1554- المثنوي بخط ~~مصري~~[282] تعليق مذهب قطع الربع مُجَلَّد بلا ظرف جلد1.

1555- المثنوي بخط تعليق قطع الربع مُجَلَّد بظرف جلد1.

1556- المثنوي بخط تعليق قطع الربع مُجَلَّد بظرف جلد1.

1557- المثنوي ناقص الأول بخط تعليق قطع الربع واسع مُجَلَّد بظرف جلد1.

1558- شاهدي بخط نسخ قطع الربع مُجَلَّد بلا ظرف جلد1.

1559- شاهدي بخط تعليق قطع الربع مُجَلَّد بلا ظرف جلد1.

1560- تحفة شاهدي بخط نسخ قطع الربع مُجَلَّد بلا ظرف جلد1.

1561- رسالة توحيد بالفارسي بخط تعليق قطع الربع مُجَلَّد بظرف جلد1.

1562- شرح كلستان بخط تعليق قطع الربع مُجَلَّد بظرف جلد1.

1563- شرح كلستان بخط تعليق قطع الربع مُجَلَّد بظرف جلد1.[283]

1564- كتاب بستان بخط نسخ قطع الربع مُجَلَّد بظرف جلد1.

1565- ديوان الحافظ الشيرازي بخط تعليق قطع الثمن مُجَلَّد بلا ظرف جلد1.

1566- ديوان الحافظ بخط تعليق تعليق قطع الربع مُحَيَّر مُجَلَّد بلا ظرف جلد1.

1567- جامع الآيات شرح الأبيات بخط تعليق قطع الربع مُجَلَّد بلا ظرف جلد1.

1568- سلمان الفارسي بخط تعليق قطع الثمن مُجَلَّد بلا ظرف جلد1.

1569- كتاب نعمة الله تركي بخط تعليق قطع الربع مُجَلَّد بظرف جلد1.

1570- منظوم بالفارسي بخط تركي قطع الربع مُجَلَّد بظرف جلد1.

[68] 1571- خلاصة الخمسة بخط تعليق قطع الربع مُجَلَّد بظرف جلد1.

1572- زي الفارسي مجموع بخط تعليق قطع الربع مُحَيَّر مُجَلَّد بلا ظرف جلد1.

1573- لغة تركي فارسي بخط نسخ قطع الثمن مُجَلَّد بظرف جلد1.

---

282 مضروب عليها في الأصل.

283 إحدى هاتين النسختين، كانت معروضة في مزاد Antiquariat Inlibris Gilhofer Nfg. GmbH في شهر حزيران 2023م.

1574- شرح الشاهدي بخط نسخ قطع الربع واسع مُجلَّد بلا ظرف جلد1.
حسابه نُمرو 22 فقط اثنين وعشرين لا غيره.

21 كتب التركي

1575- أنعام شريف[284] بخط نسخ قطع الربع مُجلَّد بلا ظرف جلد1.
1576- كتاب عقيدة تركي بخط نسخ قطع الربع مُجلَّد بظرف جلد1.
1577- معراج تركي بخط عادة قطع الثمن مُجلَّد بظرف جلد1.
1578- عقائد تركي بخط نسخ قطع الربع مُجلَّد بظرف جلد1.
1579- قواعد الإيمان قطع الثمن بخط [...][285] مُجلَّد بظرف جلد1.
1580- حديث تركي بخط نسخ وتعليق قطع الربع عتيق مُجلَّد بلا ظرف جلد1.
1581- تفسير تركي بخط تركي قطع الربع مُجلَّد بلا ظرف جلد1.
1582- تجويد بخط مصري قطع الثمن مُجلَّد بظرف جلد1.
1583- تجويد بخط نسخ قطع الثمن مُجلَّد بظرف جلد1.
1584- تجويد بخط مصري قطع الثمن مُجلَّد بظرف جلد1.
1585- شروط الصلاة بخط نسخ قطع الثمن مُجلَّد بظرف جلد1.
1586- شروط الصلاة بخط نسخ قطع الربع مُجلَّد بظرف جلد1.
1587- شروط الصلاة بخط نسخ قطع الربع مُجلَّد بظرف جلد1.
1588- شرح فقه بخط نسخ قطع الربع مُجلَّد بظرف جلد1.
1589- ترجمة الكيلاني بخط نسخ قطع الربع مُجلَّد بلا ظرف جلد1.
1590- كتاب في الخلافة تركي ناقص قطع الربع مُجلَّد بلا ظرف جلد1.
1591- بركلي بخط نسخ عالٍ مُذَهَّب قطع الربع مُجلَّد بلا ظرف جلد1.
1592- بركلي بخط نسخ قطع الثمن مُجلَّد بظرف جلد1.
1593- بركلي بخط نسخ قطع الثمن مُجلَّد بظرف جلد1. [69]

284 هذه نسخة مستقلة من سورة الأنعام. كان هذا تقليدًا عثمانيًا جديدًا. لمزيد من التفاصيل حول هذا النوع من الكتيبات يُنظر: Rettig, Simon. "The Rise of the Enʿam: Manuscripts of Selections of Suras in the Early Sixteenth-Century Ottoman Empire," in *The Word Illuminated: Form and Function of Qur'anic Manuscripts from the Seventh to the Seventeenth Century*, ed. Simon Rettig and Sana Mirza (Washington, D.C.: Smithsonian Scholarly Press, 2023), 185–212.

285 فراغ في الأصل بمقدار كلمة.

-1594 بركلي بخط نسخ قطع الربع مُجلَّد بلا ظرف جلد1.

-1595 بركلي بخط مصري قطع الربع مُجلَّد بلا ظرف جلد1.

-1596 مثنوي تركي بخط قطع النصف مُجلَّد بلا ظرف جلد1.

-1597 قصيدة في بشارة أمته بخط عربي قطع الربع مُجلَّد بلا ظرف جلد1.

-1598 بهجة الفتوة بخط تعليق مذهب قطع النصف مُجلَّد بظرف جلد1.

-1599 كتاب في سر الحروف تركي بخط نسخ قطع الربع مُجلَّد بظرف جلد1.

-1600 تدبير جديد نامه بخط نسخ قطع الثمن مُجلَّد بظرف جلد1.

-1601 تدبير جديد نامه بخط نسخ قطع الثمن مُجلَّد بظرف جلد1.

-1602 أحمد بيجان بخط نسخ قطع النصف مُجلَّد بلا ظرف جلد1.

-1603 مجموعة ديوان بخط تعليق قطع الربع مُجلَّد بظرف جلد1.

-1604 تعبير نامة تركي بخط نسخ قطع الربع مُجلَّد بلا ظرف جلد1.

-1605 منظومة تركي بخط نسخ قطع الثمن مُجلَّد بلا ظرف جلد1.

-1606 كتاب تركي بخط تركي قطع الربع مُجلَّد بلا ظرف جلد1.

-1607 كتاب تركي بخط [...][286] قطع الربع مُجلَّد بظرف جلد1.

-1608 تقويم بخط نسخ عالٍ مُذَهَّب قطع الربع مُجلَّد بلا ظرف جلد1.

-1609 مجمع الجواهر بخط نسخ قطع الربع مُجلَّد بلا ظرف جلد1.

-1610 رسالة تركية بخط عادة قطع الربع مُجلَّد بظرف جلد1.

-1611 كتاب المسمى بنوحة المشتاق نظم تركي بخط نسخ قطع الربع مُجلَّد بلا ظرف جلد1.

-1612 محيي الأموات بخط نسخ قطع الربع مُجلَّد بظرف جلد1.

-1613 كتاب ابن فرشتا بخط نسخ قطع الربع مُجلَّد بظرف جلد1.

-1614 وصية نامه بخط نسخ قطع الربع مُجلَّد بلا ظرف جلد1.

-1615 مجموع اللطائف بخط نسخ قطع الربع مُجلَّد بلا ظرف جلد1.

-1616 على الشريعة رسالة تركي بخط نسخ قطع الربع مُجلَّد بظرف جلد1.

-1617 قانون نامه بخط تعليق قطع الربع مُحيَّر مُجلَّد بظرف جلد1.

-1618 آداب الملوك بخط تعليق عالٍ مُذَهَّب قطع الربع مُحيَّر مُجلَّد بظرف جلد1.

-1619 رسالة تركي بخط نسخ قطع الربع مُجلَّد بظرف جلد1.

[70] -1620 كتاب تصريف تركي بخط نسخ قطع الثمن مُجلَّد بظرف جلد1.

-1621 كتاب لغة فارسي بخط نسخ قطع الربع مُجلَّد بظرف جلد1.

---

286 فراغ في الأصل بمقدار كلمة.

1622- كتاب تركي وعظ بخط نسخ قطع الربع مُجَلَّد بلا ظرف جلد1.

1623- تلخيصات تركي بخط نسخ قطع الربع مُجَلَّد بلا ظرف جلد1.

1624- مجموعة تركي بخط نسخ قطع الربع مُجَلَّد بظرف جلد1.

1625- تكميل شريعة بخط العادة قطع الربع مُجَلَّد بلا ظرف جلد1.

1626- كتاب تركي منظوم ناقص قطع الربع مُجَلَّد بلا ظرف جلد1.

1627- تركي وعربي بخط تعليق قطع الربع مُجَلَّد بلا ظرف جلد1.

1628- ترجمان تركي قطع الربع مُجَلَّد بظرف جلد1.

1629- ترجمان الأختري تركي وعربي قطع كامل مُجَلَّد بلا ظرف جلد1.

1630- رسالة تركي وهي معراج نظم بخط تعليق قطع الربع مُجَلَّد بلا ظرف جلد1.

حسابه نُمِرو 56 فقط ستة وخمسين لا غير.

22 عن بيان الكتب[287] المأخوذة من الشيخ علي الرشيدي ومن الشيخ محمد وكيلخرج[288] وكان ذلك في 17 ص[289] سنة 1216

1631- عن كتاب الدرة[290] الفاخرة في علم أهل الآخرة قطع الثمن مُجَلَّد1.

1632- عن كتاب الوعظ والنصيحة خط نسخ قطع الثمن جلد1.

1633- عن كتاب الأذكار للنووي[291] قطع الربع خط نسخ جلد1.

1634- عن كتاب شرح المقامات للشيخ الزيني قطع النصف كامل خط مصري جلد1.

1635- عن كتاب الدر النظيم بعلم الأحكام والتقويم قطع الربع خط نسخ جلد1.

1636- عن كتاب مختصر بالطب النبوي قطع الربع مُحيَّر جلد1.

1637- عن كتاب الجزؤ[292] الثاني مستخلص الحقائق شرح كنز الدقائق قطع الربع خط مصري جلد1.

1638- عن كتاب شرح مقصود من الصرف خط تعليق قطع الربع جلد1.

1639- عن كتاب المولود [... ...] الشيخ [محمود] نجم الدين قطع الربع خط مصري مُجَدْوَل مذهب جلد1.

1640- عن أنعام شريف قطع الربع مُحيَّر خط مصري جلد1.

287 في الأصل: كتب.

288 وكيل خرج: مصطلح كان يُطلق في العهد العثماني للدلالة على شخص يُشرف على الإنفاق، وهو متولي المؤونة داخل كل بلوك (وحدة) من بلوكات الجيش الإنكشاري. ينظر حلاق، حسان وصباغ، عباس، المعجم الجامع، 231–232.

289 أي شهر صفر.

290 في الأصل: درة.

291 في الأصل: النوري.

292 في الأصل: جزؤ.

1641- عن روضة العطر خط نسخ قطع الربع جلد1.

1642- عن كتاب فقه شرح لأبي شجاع قطع الربع مُجَدْوَل بأحمر مصري جلد1.

1643- عن كتاب الجزؤ[293] الثاني من حاشية الشيخ على الشريفين قطع الربع جلد1.

1644- عن شموس الأنوار وكنوز الأسرار خط مصري قطع النصف مُحيَّر جلد1.

1645- عن قواعد التوحيد خط تعليق عال قطع الربع جلد1.

1646- عن كتاب الحامدية قطع الربع مُجَلَّداً1.

1647- عن شرح إعراب خط مصري قطع الربع جلد1.

1648- عن كتاب الشيخ خالد على الأجرومية خط مصري سقيم قطع الربع جلد1.

1649- عن الفوائد[294] المرضية في شرح قصيدة اللامية[295] قطع الربع جلد1.

1650- عن كتاب الأحكام[296] السلطانية قطع الربع جلد1.

1651- عن كتاب فقه ناقص قطع النصف جلد نُمِرو1.

1652- عن كتاب متعلق في حديث خط نسخ قطع الربع جلد1.

1653- عن كتاب مجموعة من جواهر العلوم المكتوم خط نسخ قطع الثمن جلد1.

1654- عن كتاب خطبة [الاثنين؟] قطع الربع جلد1.

كتاب تأليف على حرف التاء.[297]

[71] 1655- كتاب تأليف على حرف التاء[298] خط مصري قطع الربع جلد1.

1656- رسالة في علوم الكواكب وانتقال المراتب قطع الربع من غير جلد1.

1657- كتاب في أسماء الجنة خط تعليق من غير جلد نُمِرو1.

1658- البدر[299] المنير خط مصري قطع الربع جلد1.

1659- كتاب المدخل في أحكام النجوم قطع الربع جلد1.

1660- كتاب المناسخات لابن الهائم[300] خط مصري قطع الربع جلد1.

1661- علم الإعراب قطع الربع خط مصري جلد1.

---

293 في الأصل: جزؤ.

294 في الأصل: فوائد.

295 في الأصل: الامية.

296 في الأصل: لأحكام.

297 تعقيبة في الهامش الأيسر السفلي.

298 ويمكن أن تُقرأ (الباء، الثاء، الياء).

299 في الأصل: بدر.

300 في الأصل: الماسخات لان الهائمي.

1662- مسائل فقهية قطع الربع جلد1.

1663- اقتحام البحة اللآلي قطع الربع خط مصري جلد1.

1664- الفوائح المسكية في الفواتح المكية[301] قطع الربع مُجَلَّد جلد1.

1665- كتاب بعلم الاستعارات قطع الربع جلد1.

1666- شرح ألفية ابن مالك قطع الربع جلد1.

1667- كتاب منهج الطلاب في الطهارة قطع الربع مُجَلَّد جلد1.

1668- مصحف شريف خط نسخ قطع الربع مُجَلَّد بظرف [قديم؟] أحمد يمق [قرينة؟] نُمرو1.

1669- رسالة خط نسخ قطع الربع جلد1.

1670- كتاب جامعة الطرقات في قسمة المحاصات والموزع من التركات قطع الثمن جلد1.

1671- رسالة على النحو خط سقيم جلد1.

1672- كتاب أوراد ودعاء خط نسخ قطع الربع جلد1.

23 تابع الكتب التي[302] من وكيلخرج والرشيدي

1673- كتاب النخبة للعلامة ابن حجر من غير جلد نُمرو1.

1674- كتاب الجوامع البهية شروح الأربعين النووية[303] خط مصري قطع الربع جلد1.

1675- شمس المعارف الكبرى جزوين مُجَلَّدين قطع النصف خط مصري جلد1.

1676- كتاب في طريق المولوية[304] للشيخ عبد الغني[305] النابلسي خط تعليق قطع الربع جلد1.

1677- رسالة اللمعة الشمسية على التحفة القدسية[306] خط سقيم من غير جلد قطعة1.

1678- كتاب فقه شافعي قطع الربع خط مصري جلد1.

1679- قطع [الشراع/ الشرائح؟] من اللغة السريانية إلى الألفاظ العربية[307] خط مصري قطع الربع جلد1.

---

301 في الأصل: فتوايح المسكية في فواتح المكية.

302 في الأصل: الذي.

303 في الأصل النورية. وهو غير الجواهر البهية في شرح الأربعين النووية. لمحمد الشبشيري. المحفوظ في جامعة برينستون برقم Garrett 2996Y،
https://catalog.princeton.edu/catalog/9952531493506421
فنسخة برينستون موقوفة على المكتبة سنة 1197هـ، بينما النسخة المذكورة هنا دخلت المكتبة سنة 1216هـ.

304 في الأصل: المولاوية.

305 في الأصل: للشيخ علي.

306 في الأصل: رسالة لامية الشمسية على تحفة القدسية.

307 في الأصل: من لغات السرنانية.

1680- رسالة في شرح الزايرجا قطع الربع جلد نُمِرو1.

1681- كتاب كسوفات الأدلاء في الكسوفات قطع الربع جلد1.

1682- حاشية الشيخ الإمام[308] الشربيني قطع الربع من غير جلد قطع نُمِرو1.

1683- كتاب التبيان في إعراب القرآن خط نسخ قطع الربع جلد1.

1684- كتاب الزيج لابن الشاطر قطع النصف مُحَيَّر جلد1.

1685- كتاب لواقح الأنوار القدسية في مناقب العلماء والصوفية[309] قطع النصف خط مصري جلد1.

1686- كتاب في علم النجوم أوله[310] ناقص وآخره ناقص قطع الربع مُحَيَّر جلد1.

1687- كتاب زبد اللمعة في حل الكواكب السبعة[311] قطع الربع جلد1.

1688- كتاب اقترانات الكواكب قطع الربع خط مصري جلد1.

1689- كتاب زهر الربيع في شواهد البديع قطع الثمن مطاول[312] خط مصري جلد1.

1690- كتاب اجتماع الشمل في معرفة علم الرمل[313] قطع الربع مُجَلَّد جلد1.

1691- كتاب زيج الدر اليتيم قطع الربع جلد1.

1692- كتاب فالله فتح الملك المجيد قطع الربع جلد1.

1693- كتاب درة الآفاق في علم الحروف والأوفاق[314] قطع الربع جلد1.

1694- رسالة مزج الصلاة[315] خط مصري جلد نُمِرو1.

1695- كتاب معرفة الأدلاء في معرفة أصول التواريخ المستعملة قطع الربع بظرف جلد1.

1696- كتاب منحة السلوك في شرح[316] تحفة الملوك قطع الربع خط مصري بظرف جلد1.

[72] 1697- كتاب نتيجة الأفكار في أعمال الليل والنهار قطع الربع مُحَيَّر جلد1.

1698- كتاب [...] التنجيم قطع [الثمن؟] جلد1.

1699- كتاب الزيج في الميقات قطع الربع مُجَلَّد جلد1.

1700- كتاب الإشارة في تغيير الأحكام قطع الربع جلد1.

---

308 في الأصل: الإيمام.

309 في الأصل: لوائح أنوار القدسية في مناقب العلماء والصرفية.

310 في الأصل: أولها.

311 في الأصل: زبد اللمعة في حل الكواكب السيف.

312 هكذا في الأصل: ويقصد متطاول. ينظر تفسير طويل.

313 في الأصل: علم الرمع.

314 في الأصل: درة الأقات في علم الحروف والأقات.

315 في الأصل: الصلا.

316 في الأصل: شرع.

1701- كتاب فتح الرحمن مجموعة قطع الربع خط مصري جلد1.

1702- رسالة منافع القرآن من غير جلد قطعة1.

1703- كتاب شرح الخاتم[317] المثلث والغزالي قطع الثمن جلد1.

1704- رسالة في الصرف مقدار عشرة أوراق نُمرو1.

1705- كتاب رسالة شرح الشيخ الأ[...] على الفتح القدسي من غير جلد قطعة نُمرو1.

1706- رحلة الطالبين خط مصري قطع الربع جلد1.[318]

بيان كامل الكتب أجمعها، الموجودة في الكتب خانة الشريفة الكائنة بجامع النور الأحمدي بعكا المحمية كما يأتي تفصيله أدناه علماً بعلم. وكان ذلك في اليوم التاسع من شهر جمادى الأولى لسنة خمسة عشر ومائتين وألف من الهجرة النبوية على صاحبها أفضل الصلاة وأزكى التحية سنة 1215 وتُسلَّم جميع هذه الكتب المُسَطَّرة المذكورة لسليمان أفندي ناظر كتبخانة المذكورة وأمينها

عدة	
24	مصاحف شريف
77	تفاسير شريفة
62	قراءات[319]
231	حديث شريف
203	[الفقه الشريف]
597	[المجموع]
154	تصوف وتوحيد
195	نحو
132	معاني وبيان وأصول وعروض واستعارات
47	المنطق
24	صرف
1149	[المجموع]
113	دواوين وقصائد
5	تعبير رؤية

317 في الأصل: شرع خاتم.

318 عدد المجلدات المأخوذة منهما 76 مجلداً.

319 في الأصل: قرأت.

151 تواريخ

27 لغة

1445 [المجموع]

49 طب

80 فلك هيئة وحرف وروحاني ورمل وهندسة وحساب وكيمياء

22 فارسي

56 تركي

1652[320][المجموع]

صحَّ جمع جميع الكتب المحررة أعلاه وهو ألف وستمائة واثنان وخمسون كتاباً فقط لا غـ[ـير]

تحريراً في اليوم التاسع من شهر جمادى الأولى لسنة خمسة عشر ومائتين وألف سنة 1215

"واقف مشار إليهك مهريله ممهور ورود ايدن دفترى ذيلنه حرمين شريفين محاسبه سيكه قيد اولنمه سى محلنه إيصال اولنمق ا چون رد اولنه ديو صادر اولان فرمان شريف موجبنجه عينيله قيد اولنوب رد اولنمغله اش بو محله شرح ويريلدى في غره م سنه ١٢٢١".[321]

320 الصواب: 1649 مجلداً، وإذا ما أضفنا المأخوذ من مكتبة يحيى بن محمد الطيبي 95 مجلداً، ومن مكتبتي علي الرشيدي ومحمد وكيلخرج 76 مجلداً، يصبح المجموع 1820 مجلداً.

321 قامت الباحثة Nimet Ipek بقراءة هذين السطرين وترجمتهما من اللغة العثمانية، فلها كل الشكر والتقدير.

Facsimile of the Inventory

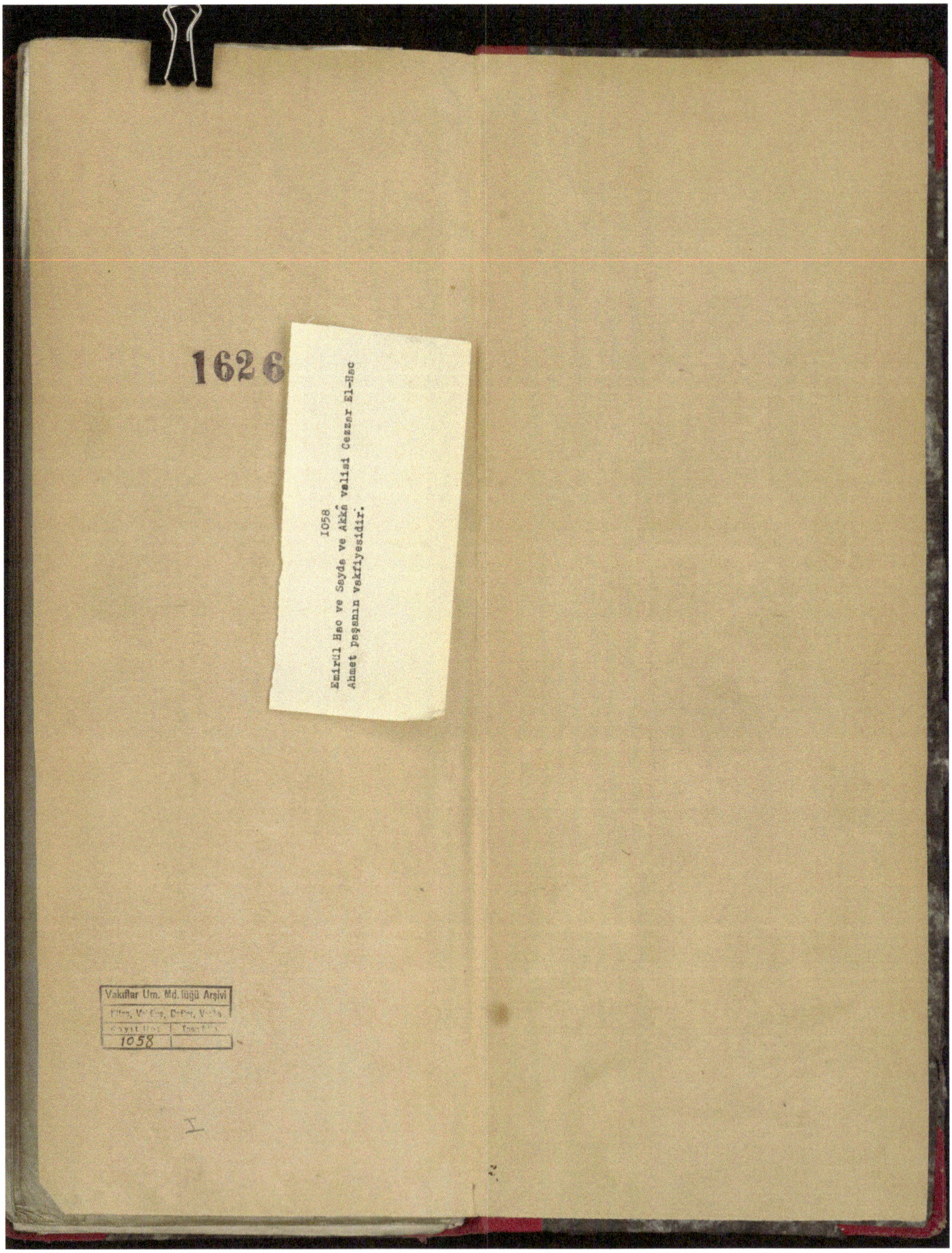
1626
I058
Emirül Hac ve Sayda ve Akkâ valisi Cezzar El-Hac
Ahmet paşanın vakfiyesidir.
Vakıflar Um. Md.lüğü Arşivi
1058

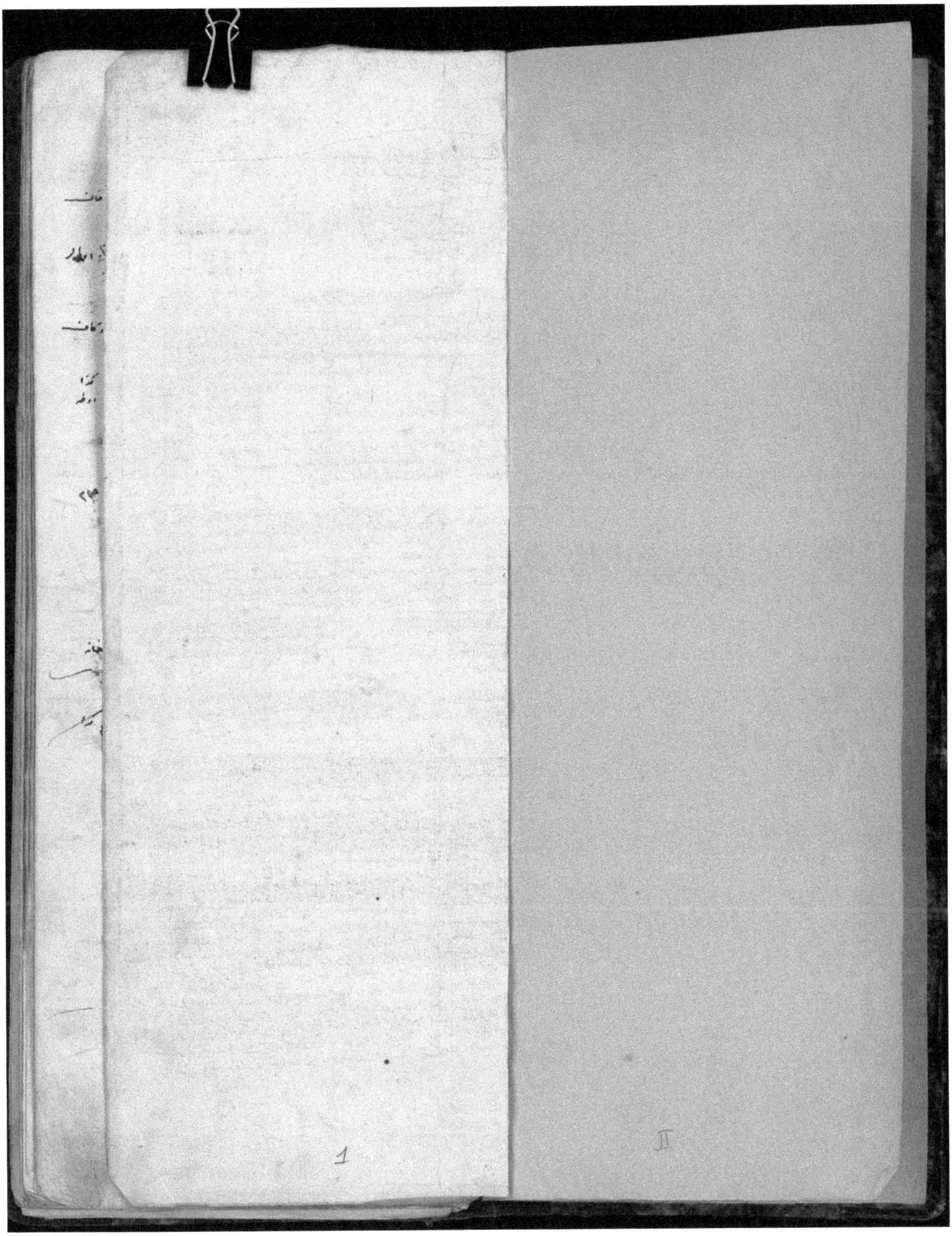

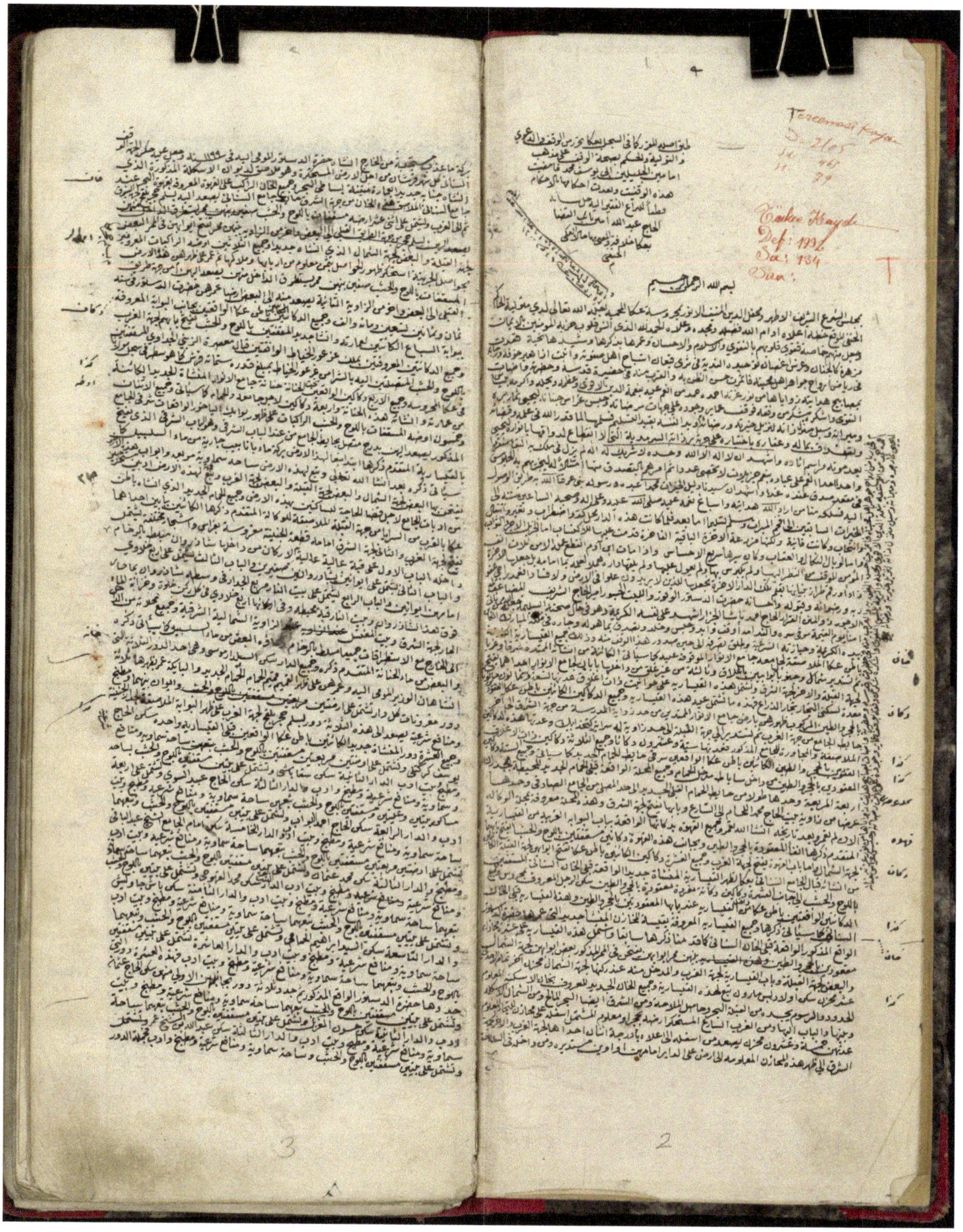
بسم الله الرحمن الرحيم

3

2

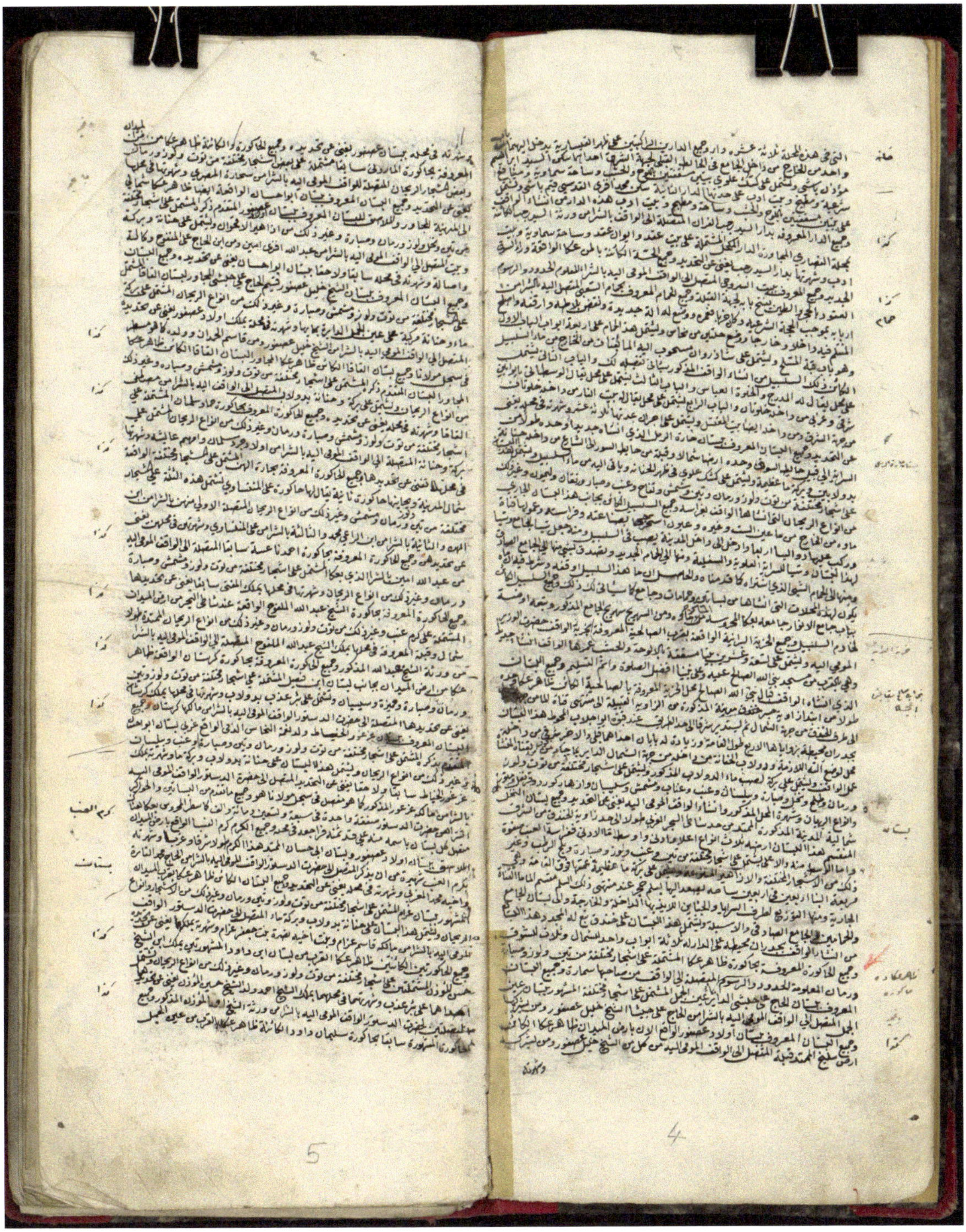

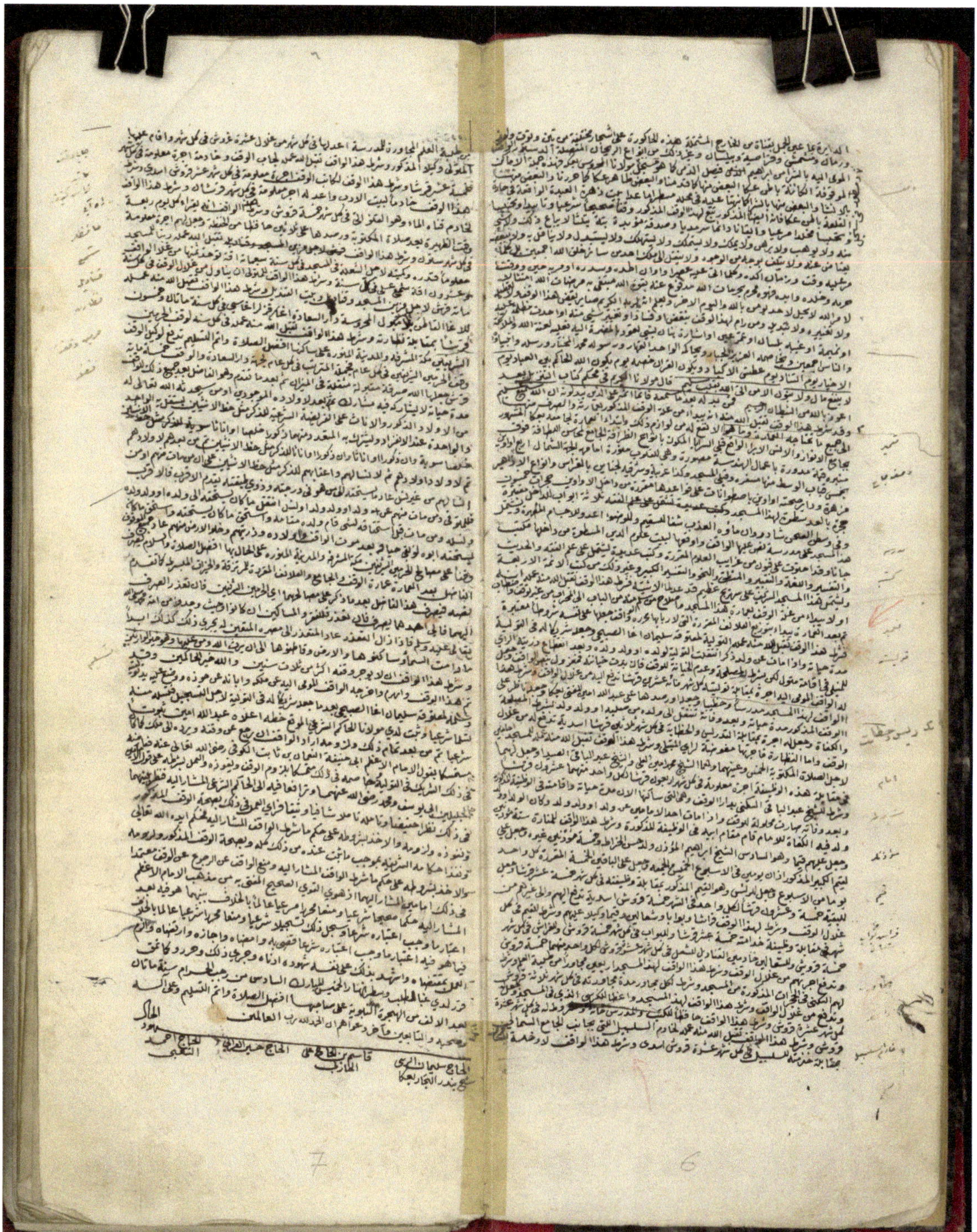

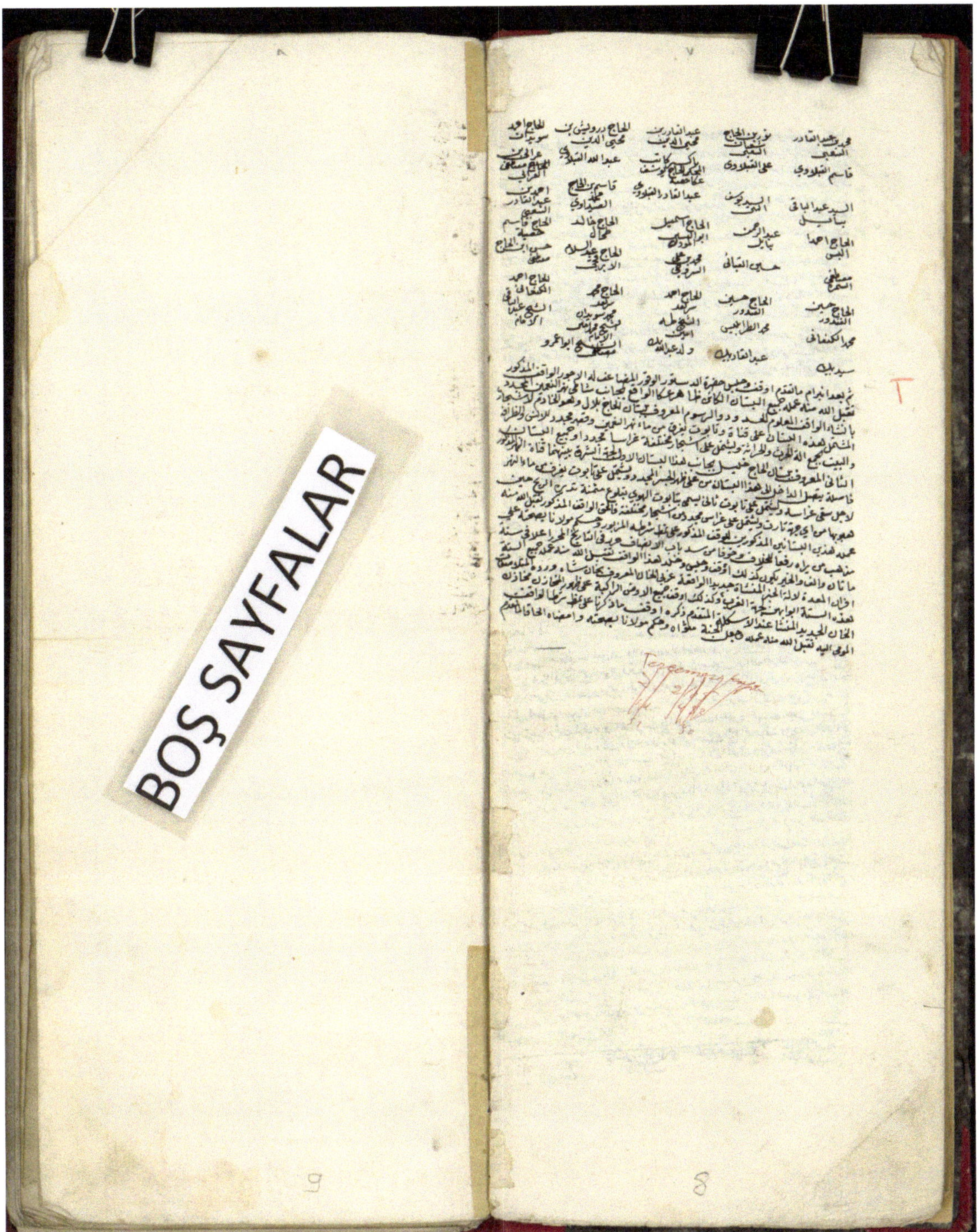
BOŞ SAYFALAR

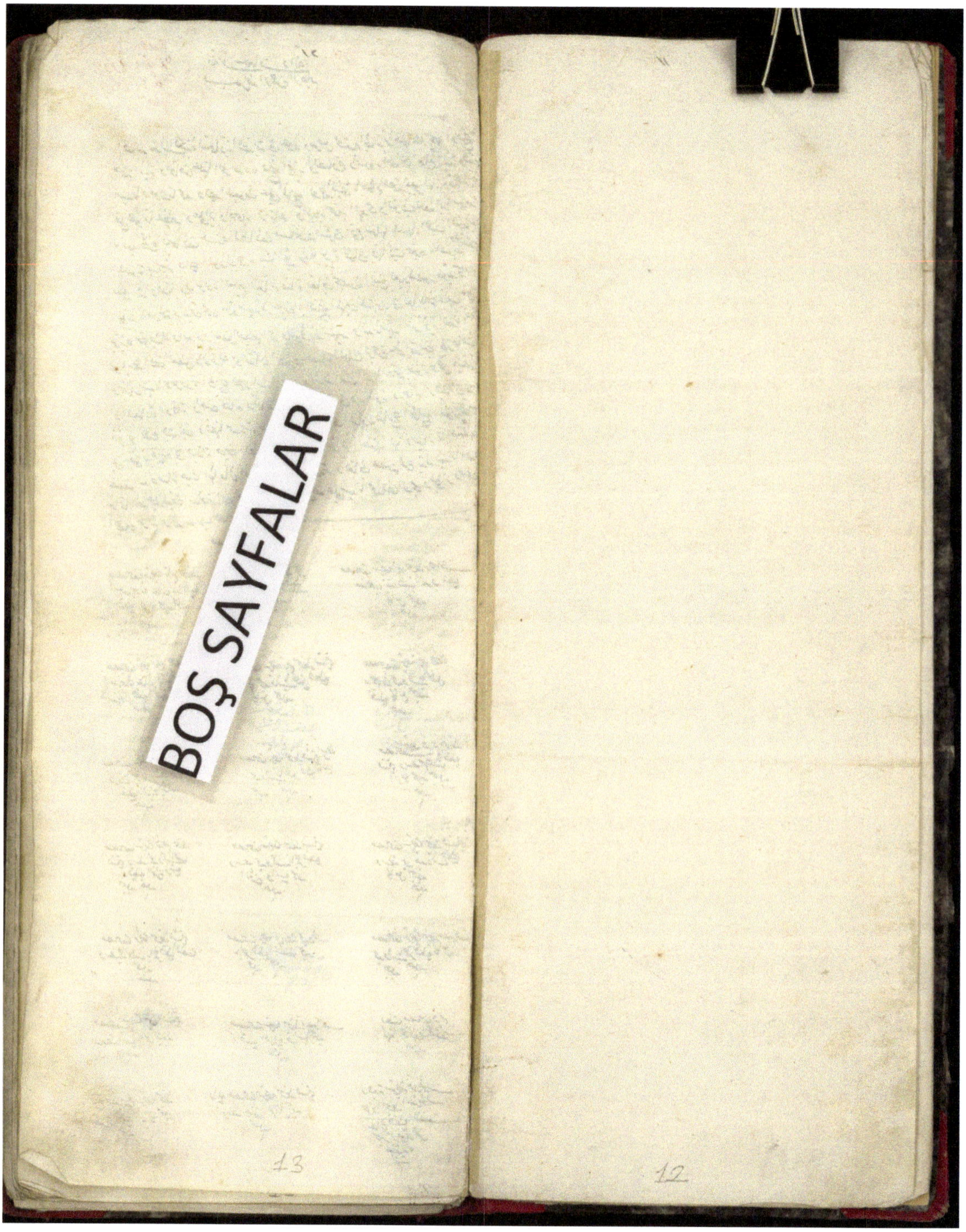
BOŞ SAYFALAR
13
12

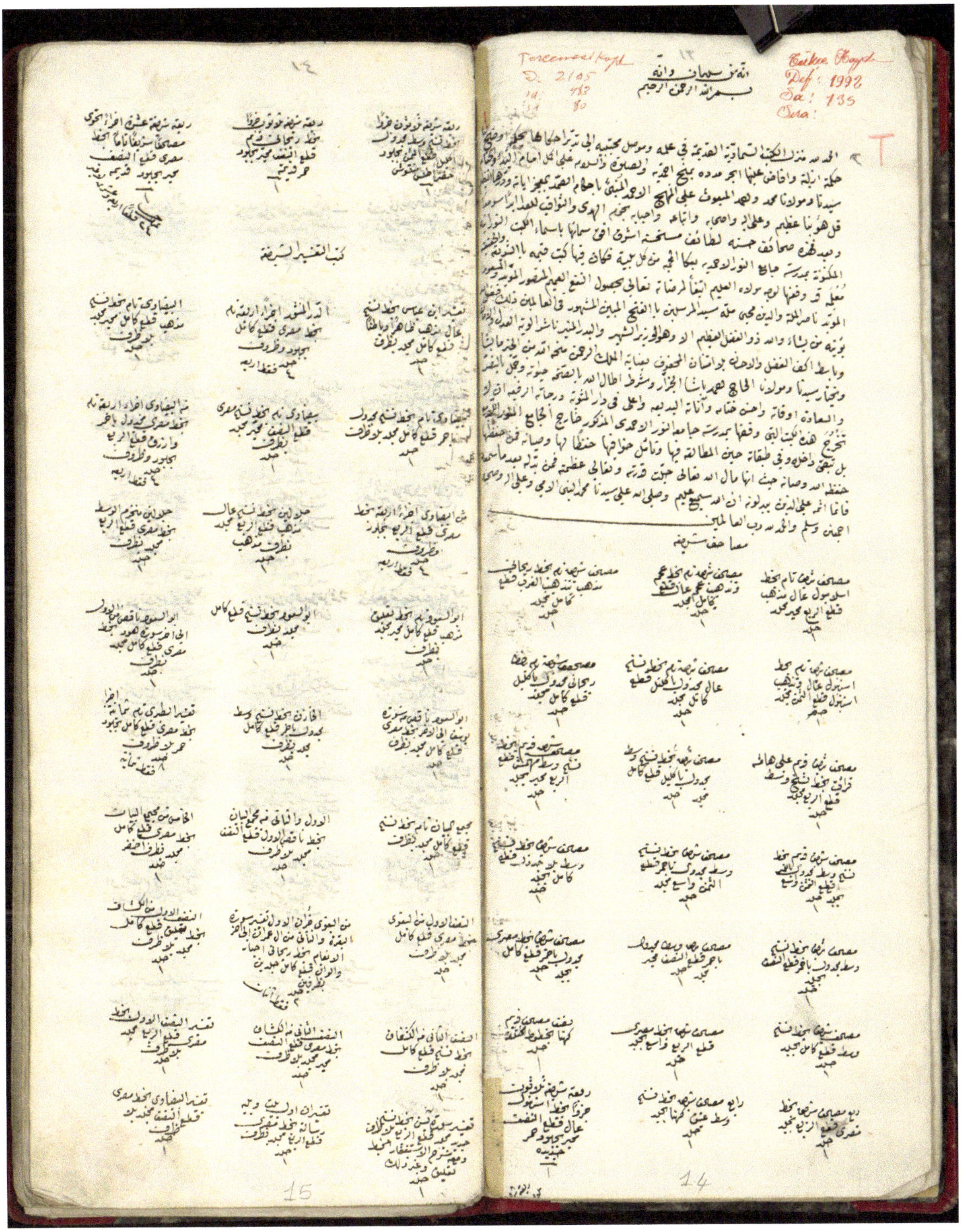

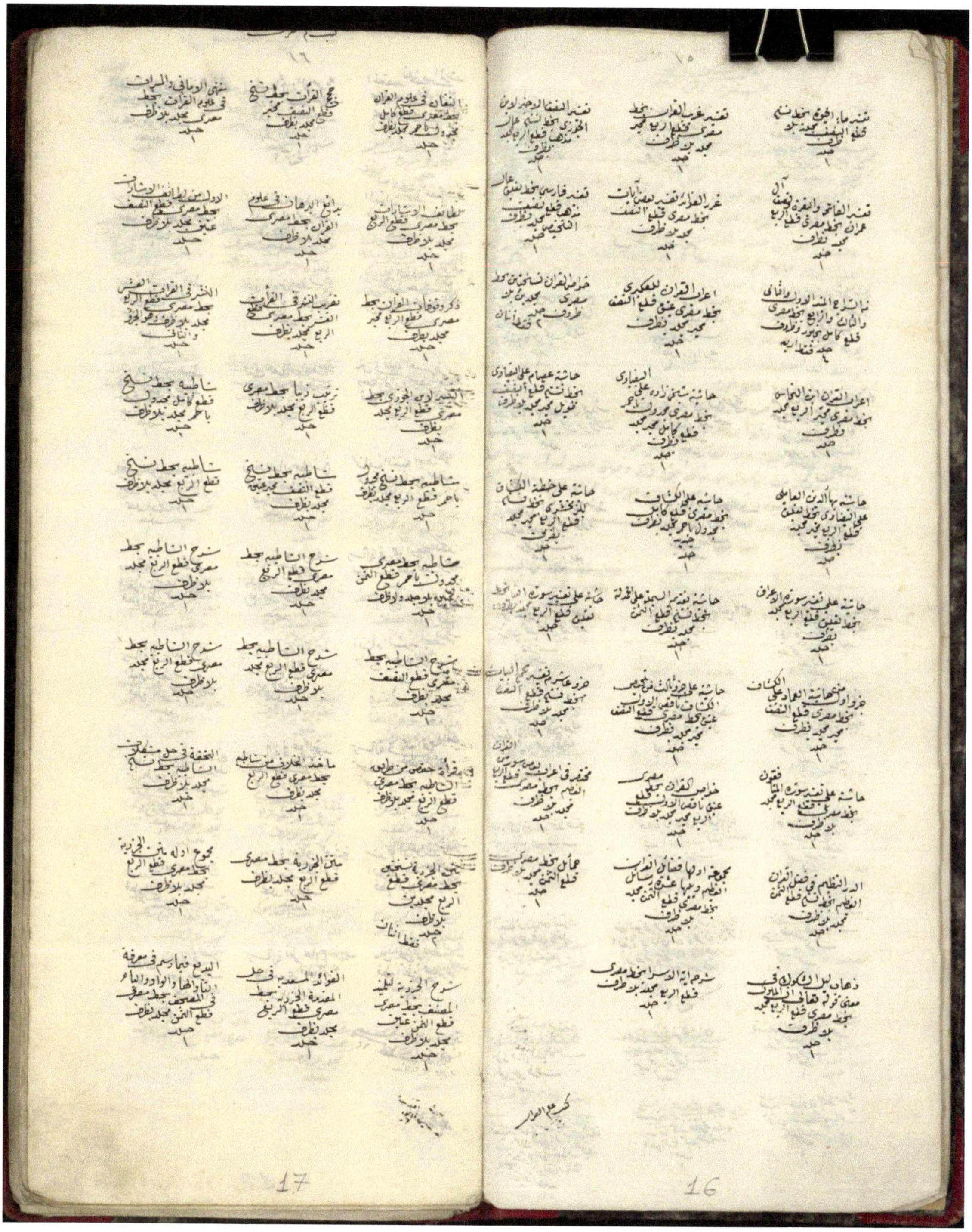

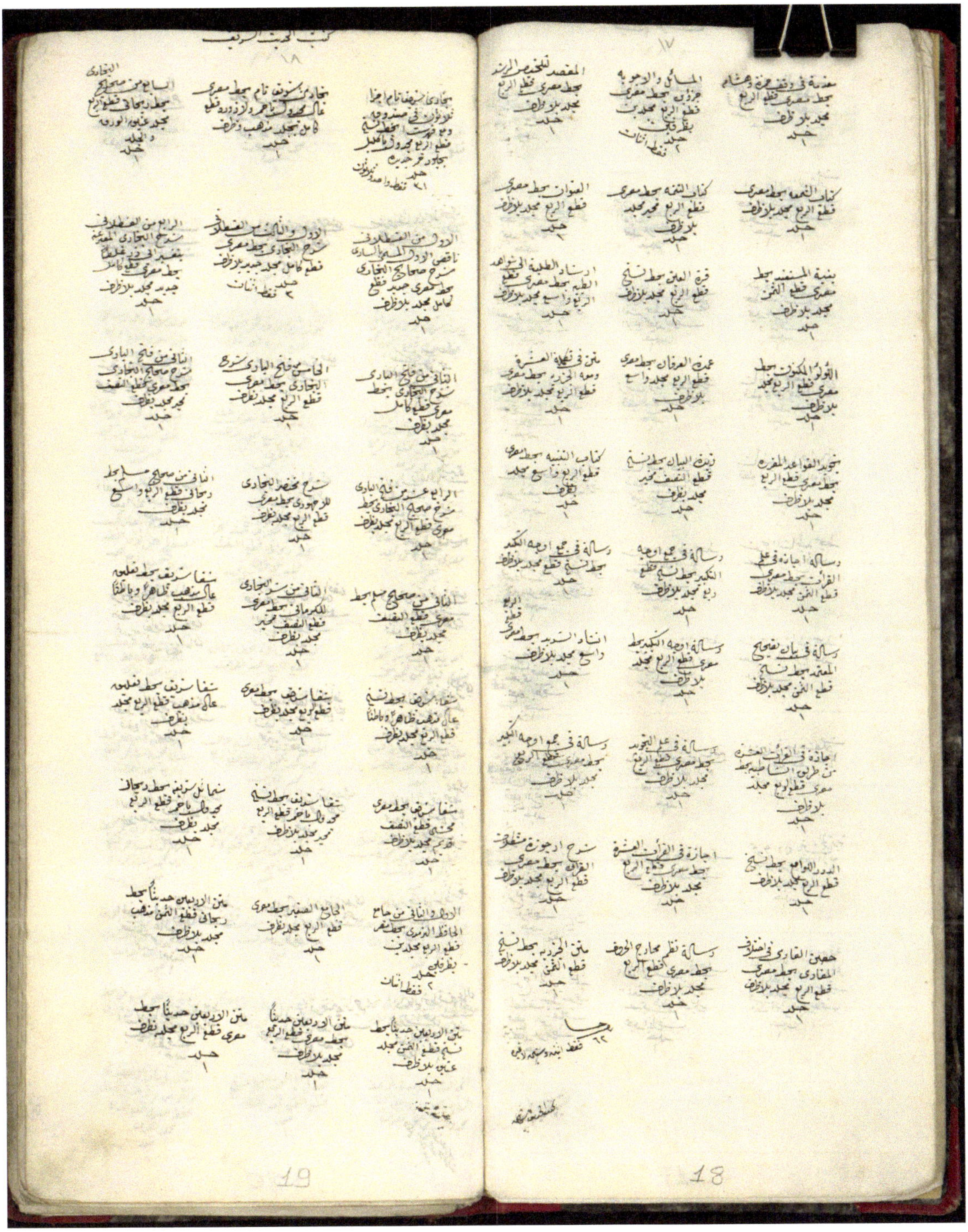

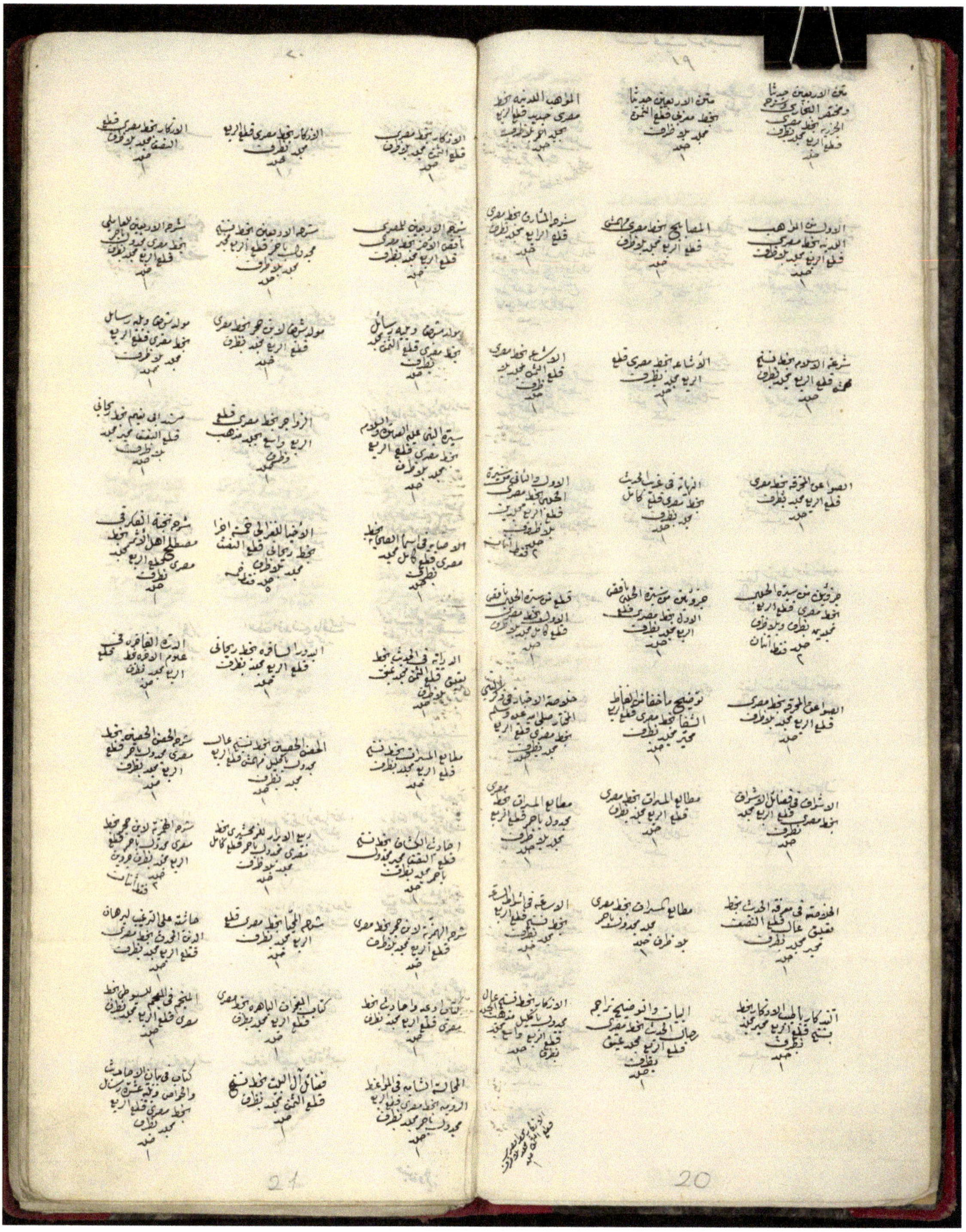

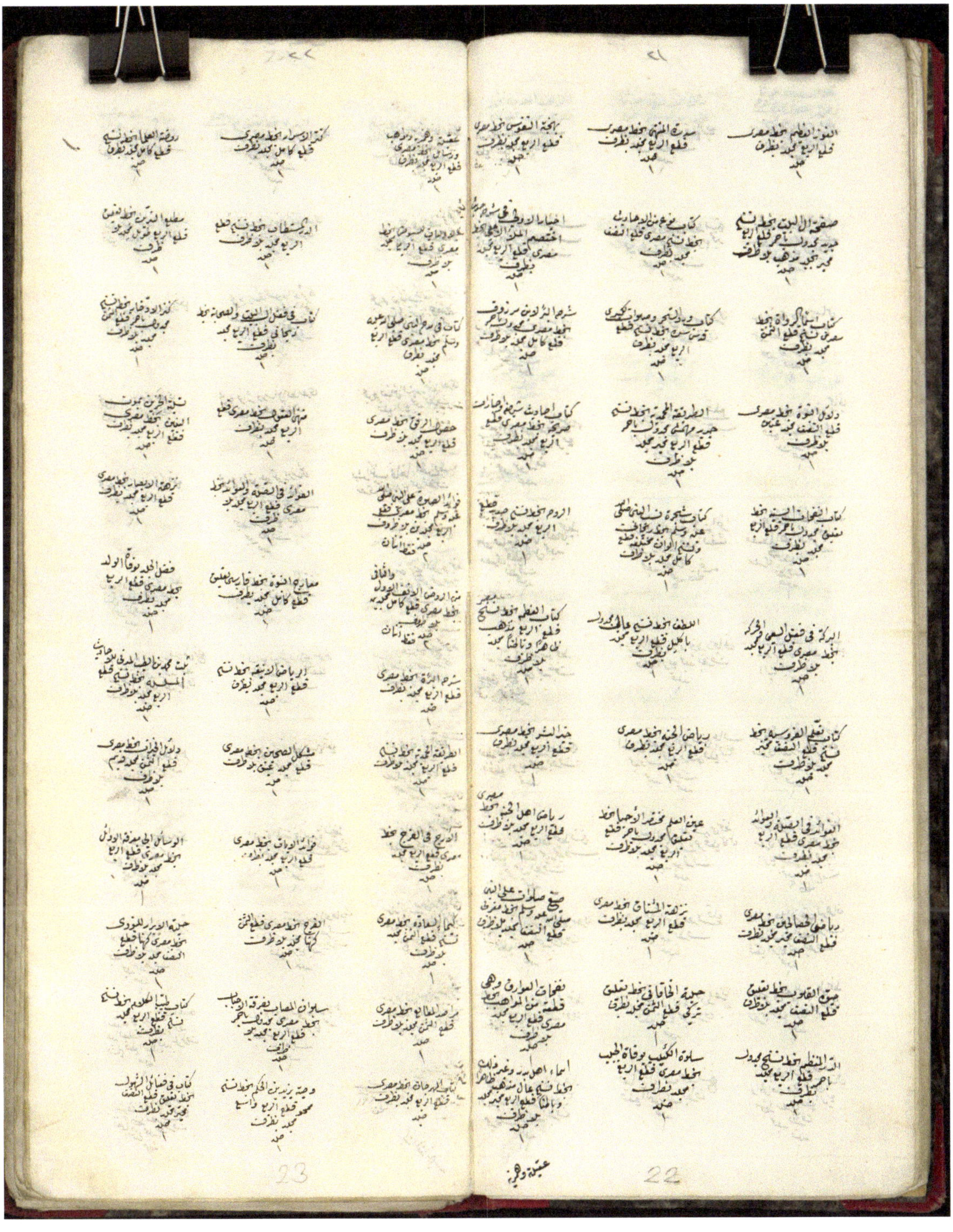

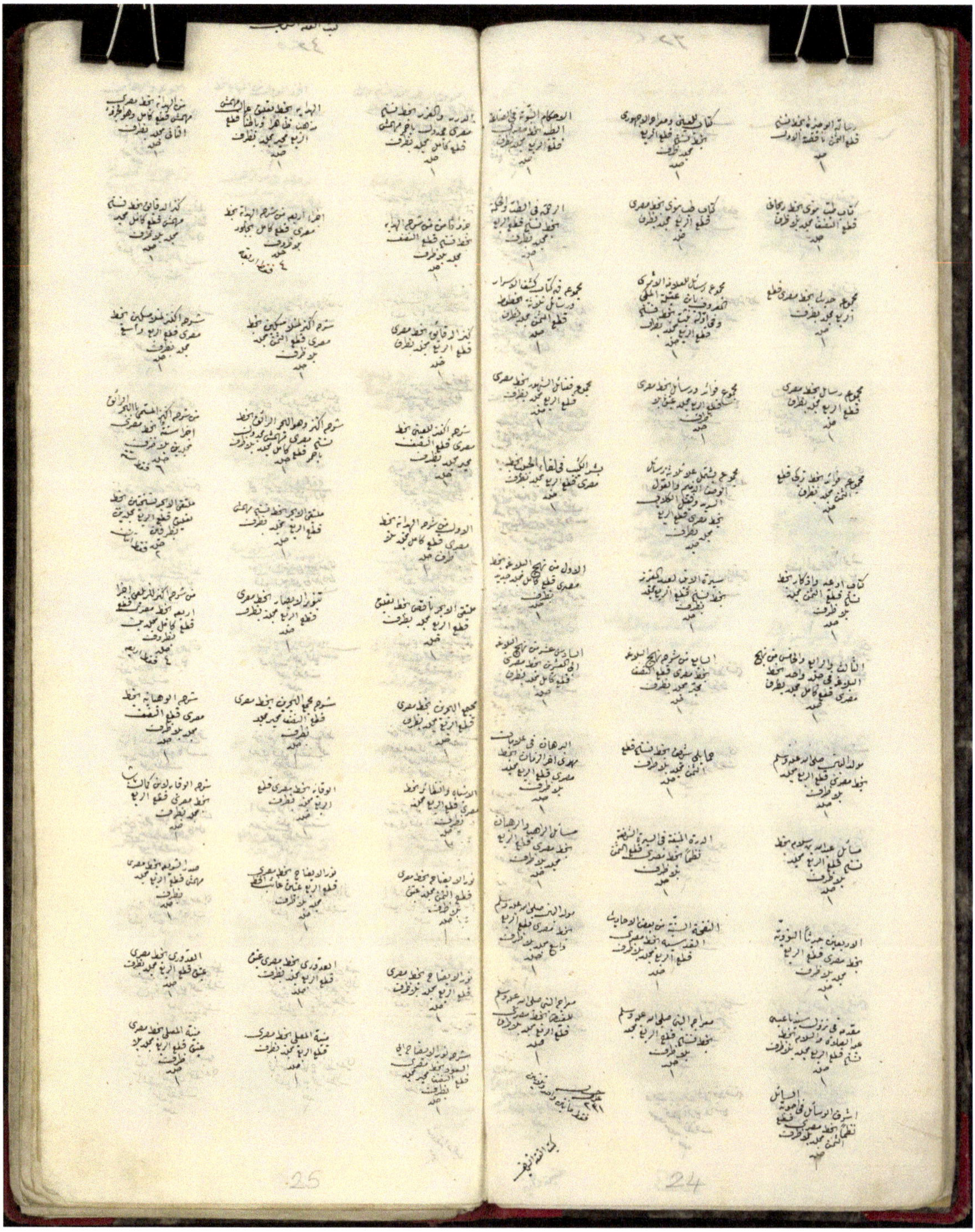

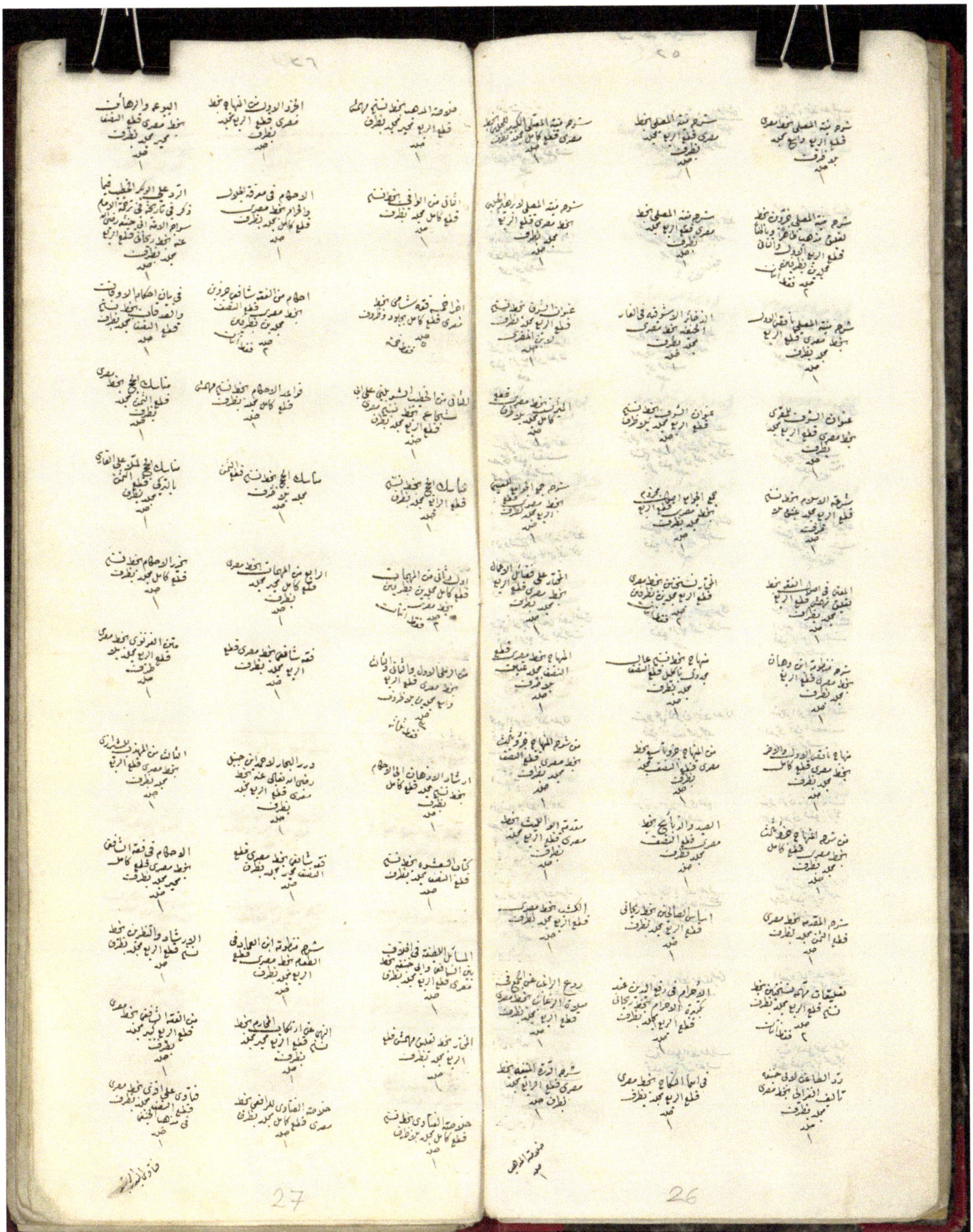

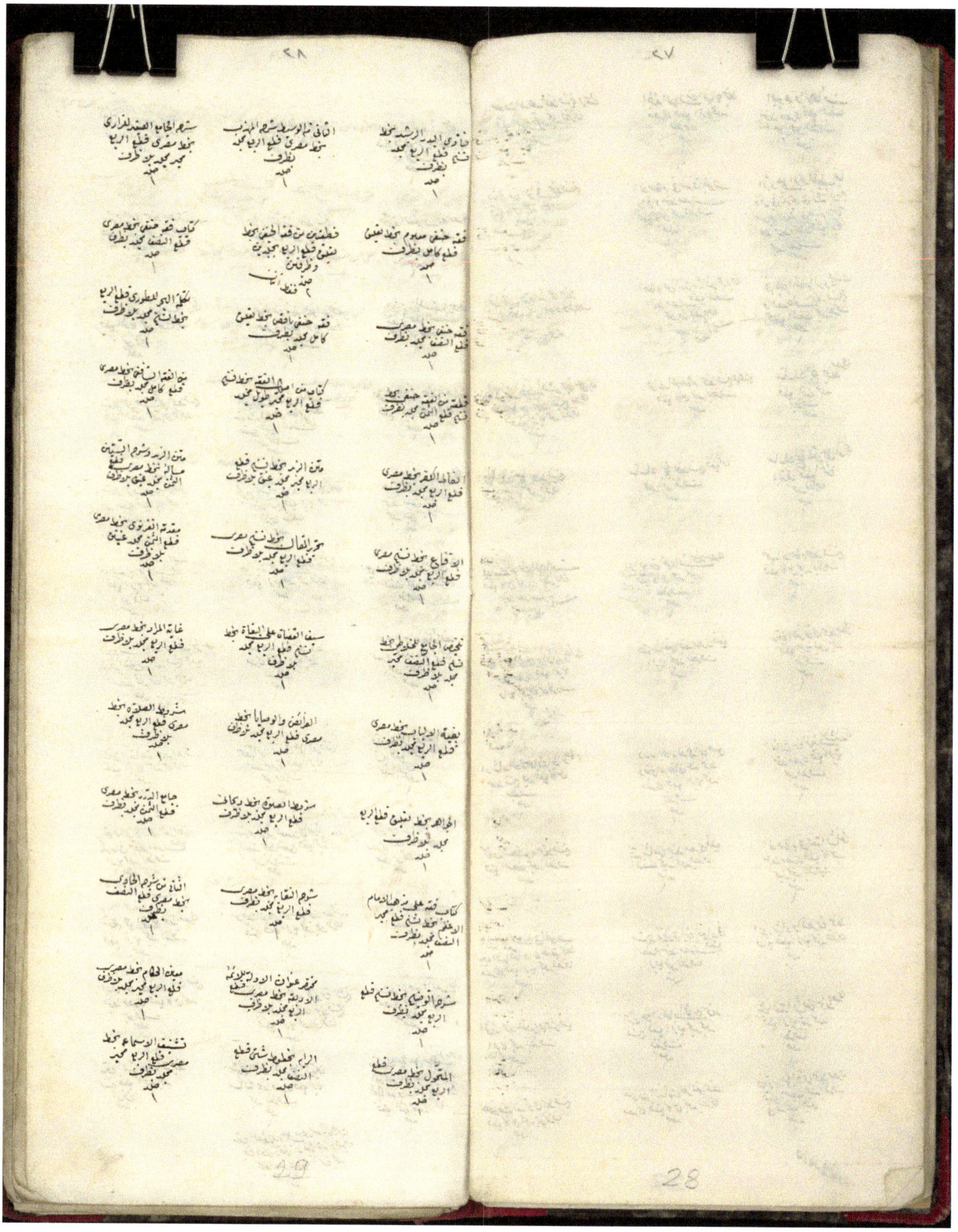

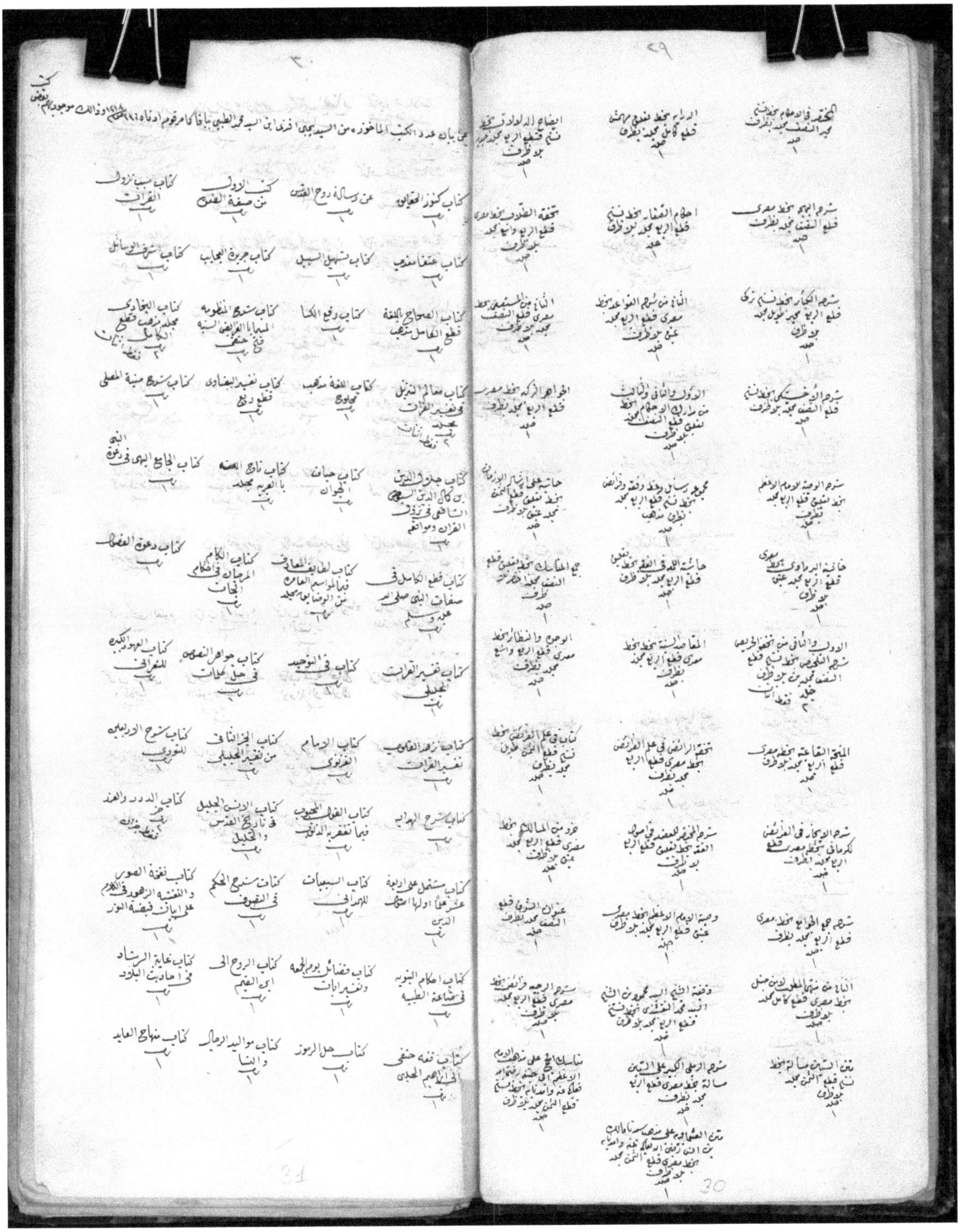

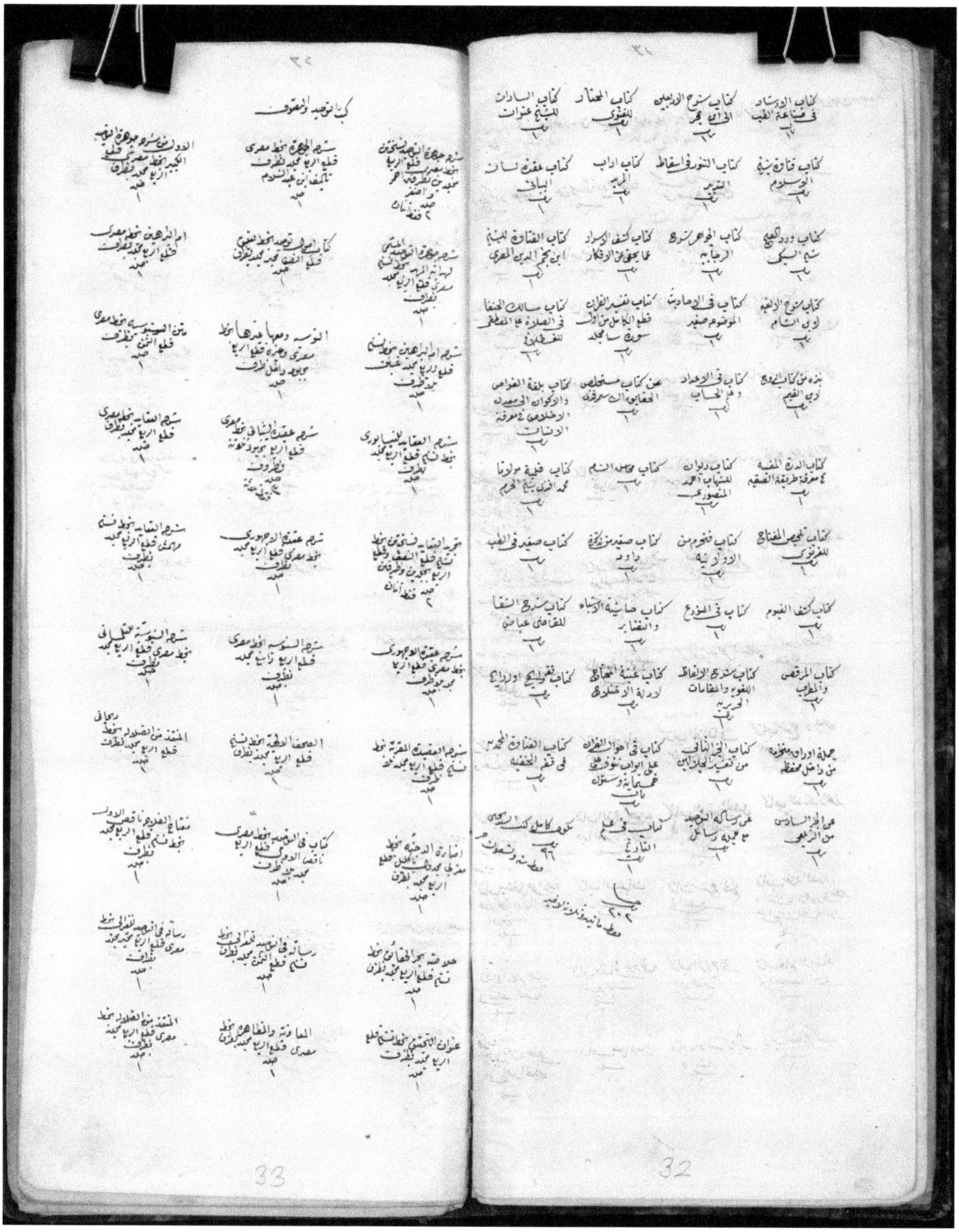

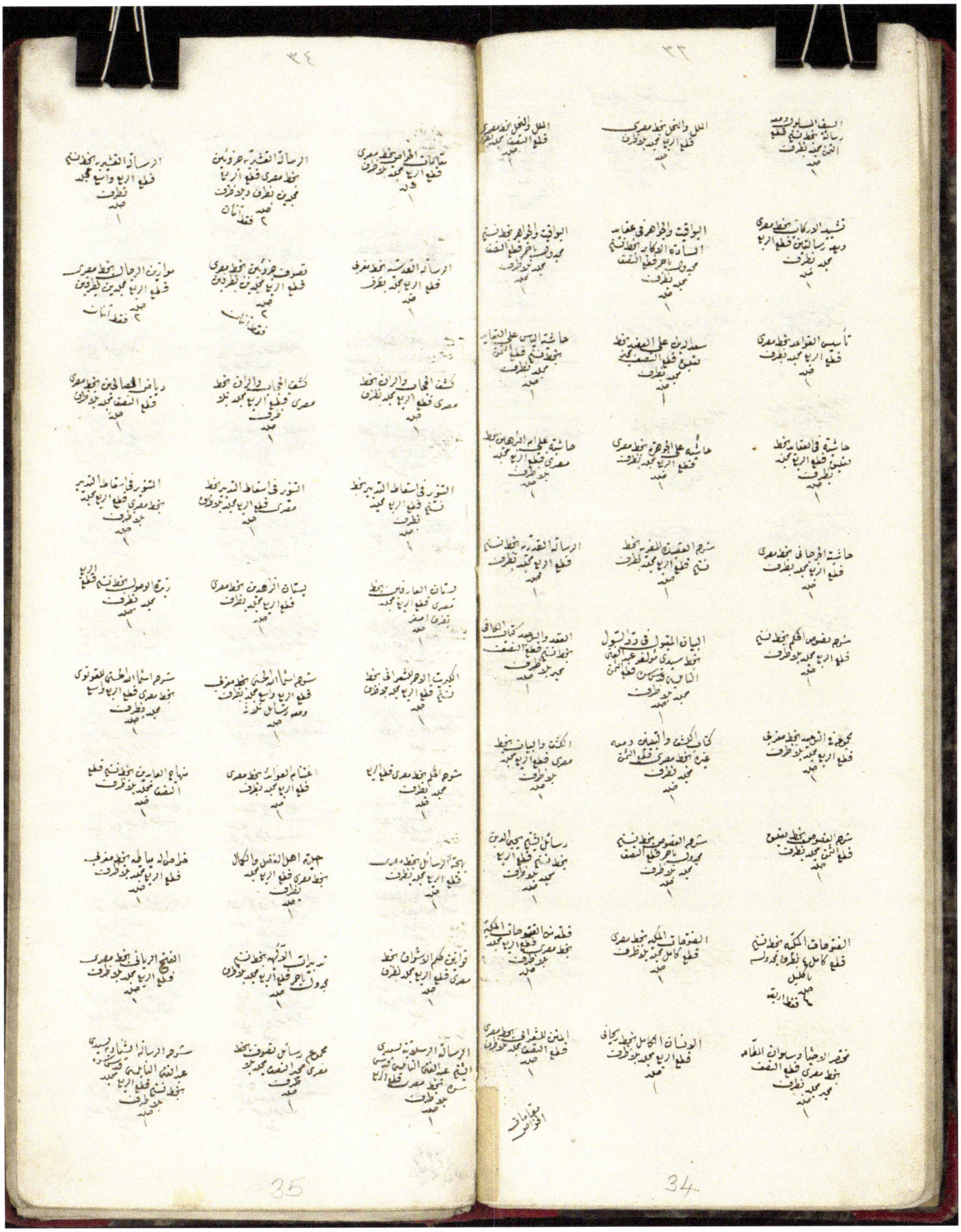

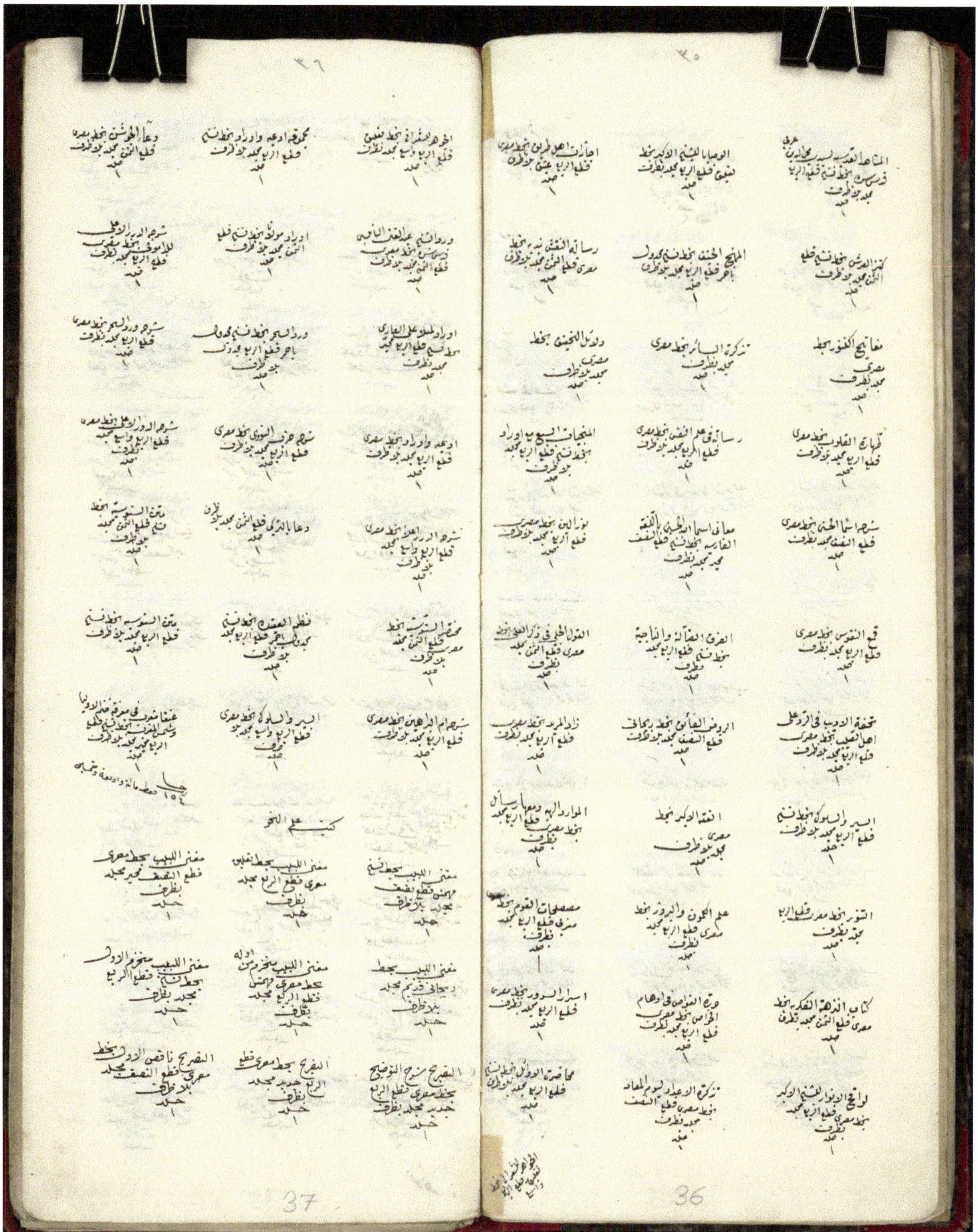

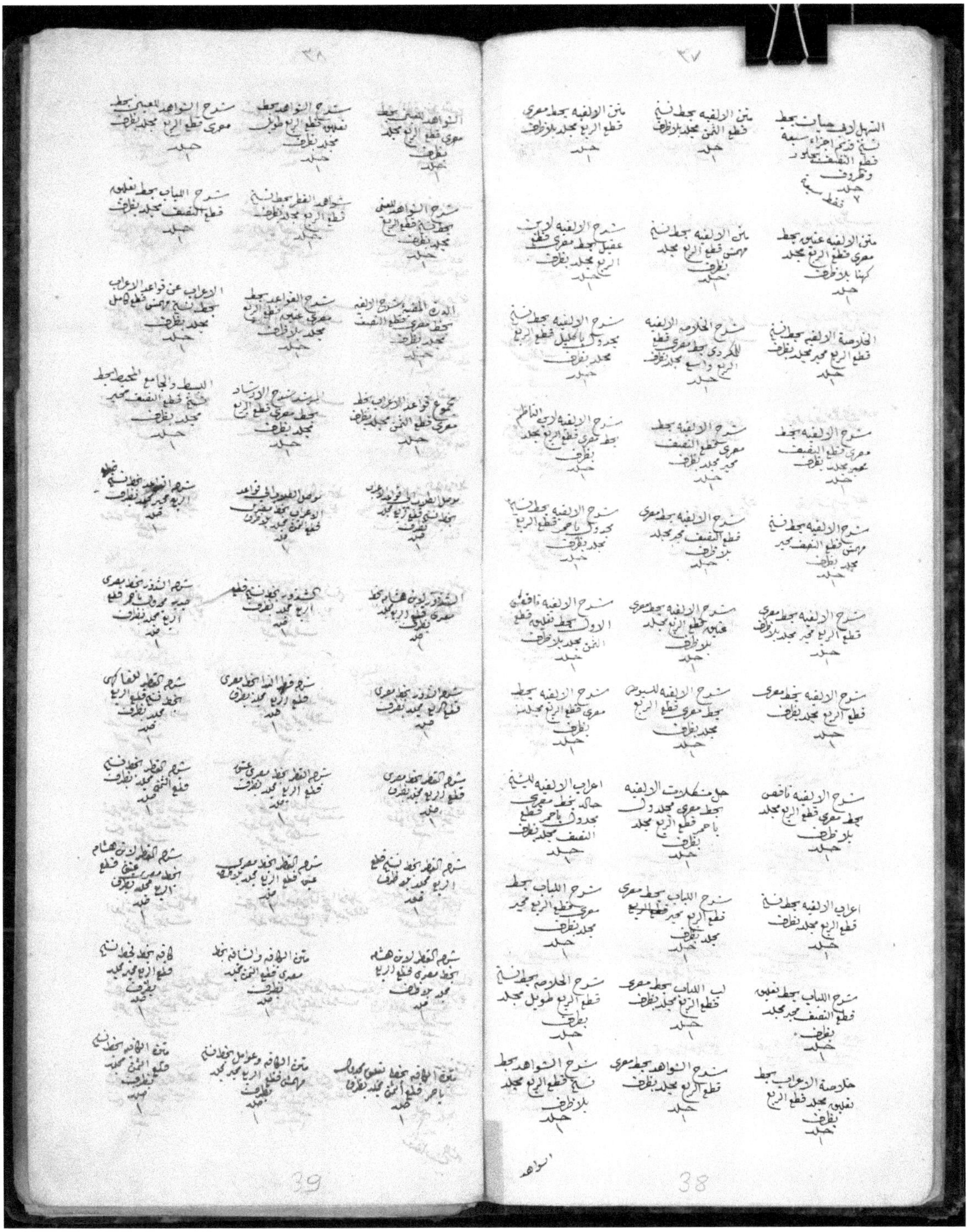

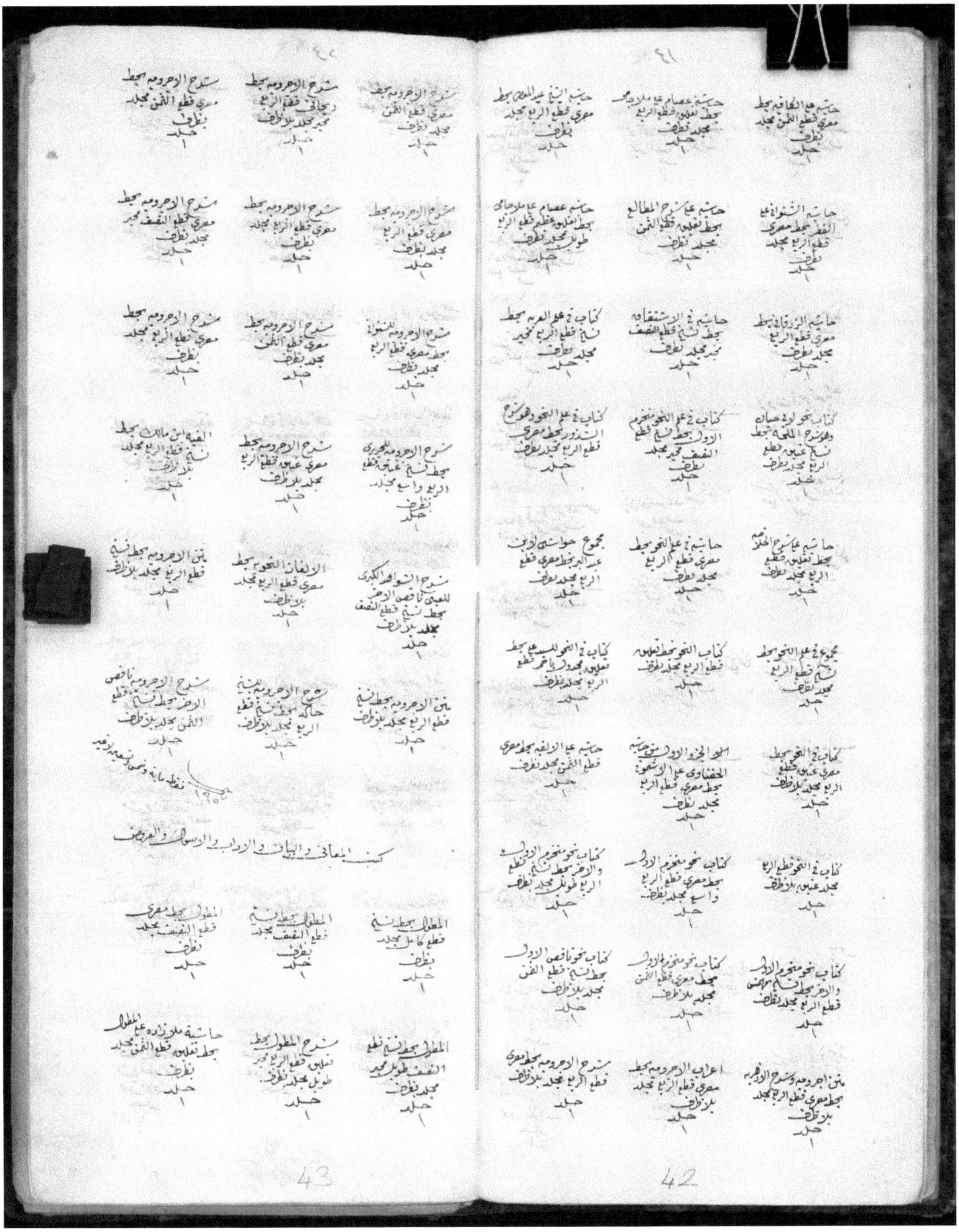

٤١

حاشيه على الكافيه بخط مصري قطع الثمن مجلد بظرف جلد ١

حاشيه عصام على ملا جامي بخط تعليق قطع الربع مجلد بظرف جلد ١

حاشيه الشيخ عبد المعطي بخط مصري قطع الربع مجلد بظرف جلد ١

حاشيه الشنواني على القطر بخط مصري قطع الربع مجلد بظرف جلد ١

حاشيه على شرح المطالع بخط تعليق قطع الثمن مجلد بظرف جلد ١

حاشيه عصام على ملا جامي بخط تعليق عظيم قطع الربع طويل مجلد بظرف جلد ١

حاشيه الزرقاني بخط مصري قطع الربع مجلد بظرف جلد ١

حاشيه في الاشتقاق بخط نسخ قطع النصف كبير مجلد بظرف جلد ١

كتاب في علم العربيه بخط نسخ قطع الربع كبير مجلد بظرف جلد ١

كتاب نحو لابن صايغ وهو شرح الملحه بخط نسخ عتيق قطع الربع مجلد بظرف جلد ١

كتاب في علم النحو مخروم الاول بخط نسخ قطع النصف كبير مجلد بظرف جلد ١

كتاب في علم النحو وهو شرح الشذور بخط مصري قطع الربع مجلد بظرف جلد ١

حاشيه على شرح الحلاصه بخط تعليق قطع الربع مجلد بظرف جلد ١

حاشيه في علم النحو بخط مصري قطع الربع مجلد بظرف جلد ١

مجموع حواشي لابن عبد البر بخط مصري قطع الربع مجلد بظرف جلد ١

مجموع في علم النحو بخط نسخ قطع الربع مجلد بظرف جلد ١

كتاب النحو بخط تعليق قطع الربع مجلد بظرف جلد ١

كتاب في النحو للسيد علي بخط تعليق مجدول باحمر قطع الربع مجلد بظرف جلد ١

كتاب في النحو بخط مصري عتيق قطع الربع مجلد بلا ظرف جلد ١

الجزء الاول من حاشيه الحفناوي على الاشموني بخط مصري قطع الربع مجلد بظرف جلد ١

حاشيه على الالفيه بخط مصري قطع الثمن مجلد بظرف جلد ١

كتاب في النحو قطع الربع مجلد عتيق بلا ظرف جلد ١

كتاب نحو مخروم الاول بخط مصري قطع الربع واسع مجلد بظرف جلد ١

كتاب نحو مخروم الاول والاخر بخط نسخ قطع الربع طويل مجلد بظرف جلد ١

كتاب نحو مخروم الاول والاخر بخط نسخ مهمل قطع الربع مجلد بظرف جلد ١

كتاب نحو مخروم الاول بخط مصري قطع الثمن مجلد بلا ظرف جلد ١

كتاب نحو ناقص الاول بخط نسخ قطع الثمن مجلد بلا ظرف جلد ١

متن اجروميه وشرح الازهريه بخط مصري قطع الربع مجلد بلا ظرف جلد ١

اعراب الاجروميه بخط مصري قطع الربع مجلد بلا ظرف جلد ١

شرح الاجروميه بخط مصري قطع الربع مجلد بلا ظرف جلد ١

42

٤٢

شرح الاجروميه بخط مصري قطع الثمن مجلد بظرف جلد ١

شرح الاجروميه بخط رجاني قطع الربع كبير مجلد بلا ظرف جلد ١

شرح الاجروميه بخط مصري قطع الثمن مجلد بظرف جلد ١

شرح الاجروميه بخط مصري قطع الربع مجلد بظرف جلد ١

شرح الاجروميه بخط مصري قطع الربع مجلد بظرف جلد ١

شرح الاجروميه بخط مصري قطع النصف كبير مجلد بظرف جلد ١

شرح الاجروميه للشنواني بخط مصري قطع الربع مجلد بظرف جلد ١

شرح الاجروميه بخط مصري قطع الثمن مجلد بظرف جلد ١

شرح الاجروميه بخط مصري قطع الربع مجلد بظرف جلد ١

شرح الاجروميه للجبري بخط نسخ عتيق قطع الربع واسع مجلد بظرف جلد ١

شرح الاجروميه بخط مصري عتيق قطع الربع مجلد بلا ظرف جلد ١

الفيه ابن مالك بخط نسخ قطع الربع مجلد بلا ظرف جلد ١

شرح الشواهد الكبرى للعيني ناقص الاخر بخط نسخ قطع النصف مجلد بلا ظرف جلد ١

الالغاز النحويه بخط مصري قطع الربع مجلد بلا ظرف جلد ١

متن الاجروميه بخط نسخ قطع الربع مجلد بلا ظرف جلد ١

متن الاجروميه بخط نسخ قطع الربع مجلد بلا ظرف جلد ١

شرح الاجروميه للشيخ خالد بخط نسخ قطع الربع مجلد بلا ظرف جلد ١

شرح الاجروميه ناقص الاخر بخط نسخ قطع الثمن مجلد بلا ظرف جلد ١

فقط مايه وخمس وتسعين لا غير ١٩٥

كتب المعاني والبيان والاداب والادب والعروض

المطول بخط نسخ قطع كامل مجلد بظرف جلد ١

المطول بخط نسخ قطع النصف مجلد بظرف جلد ١

المطول بخط مصري قطع النصف مجلد بظرف جلد ١

المطول بخط نسخ قطع النصف طويل كبير مجلد بظرف جلد ١

شرح المطول بخط تعليق قطع الربع كبير طويل مجلد بظرف جلد ١

حاشية ملا زاده على المطول بخط تعليق قطع الثمن مجلد بظرف جلد ١

43

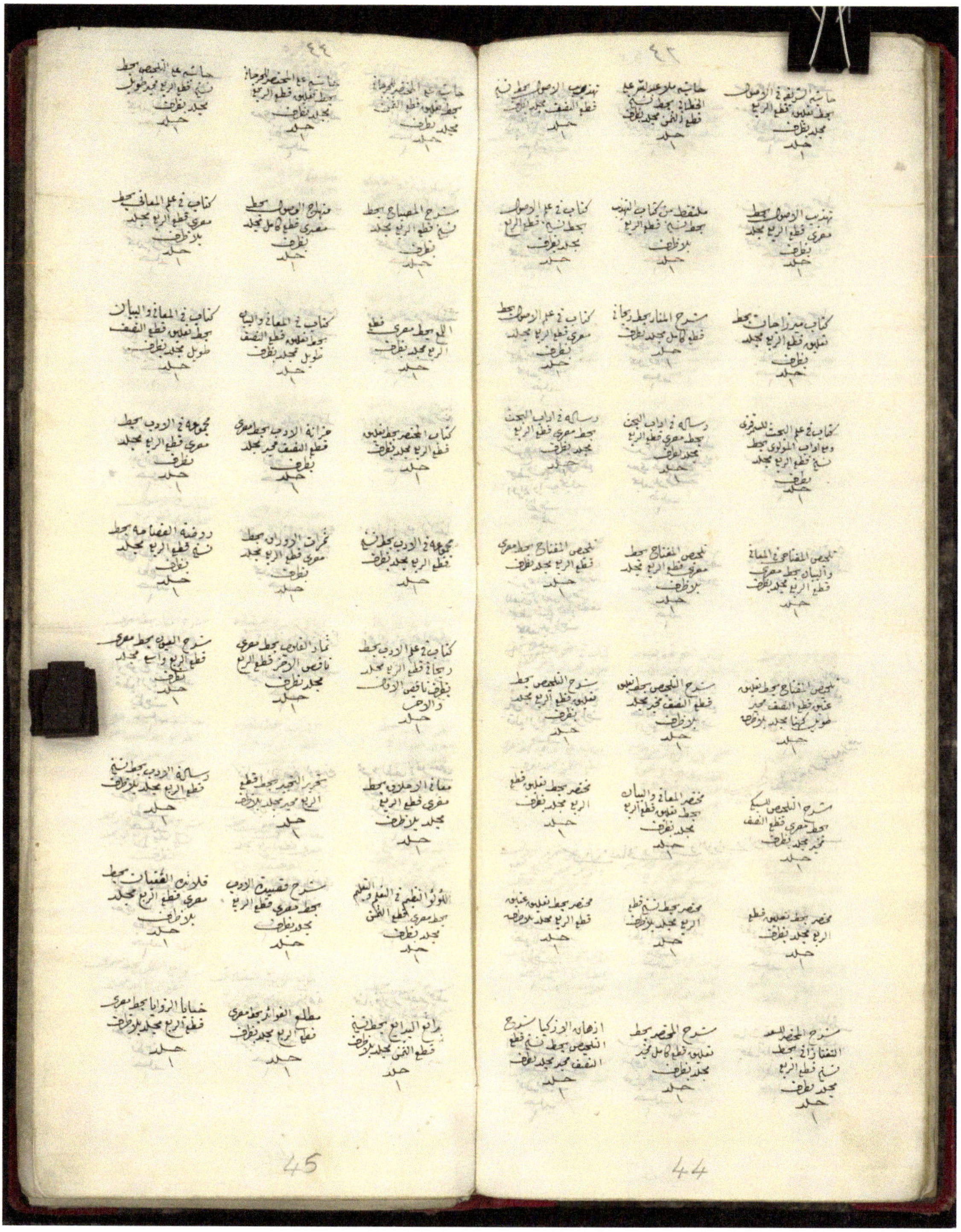

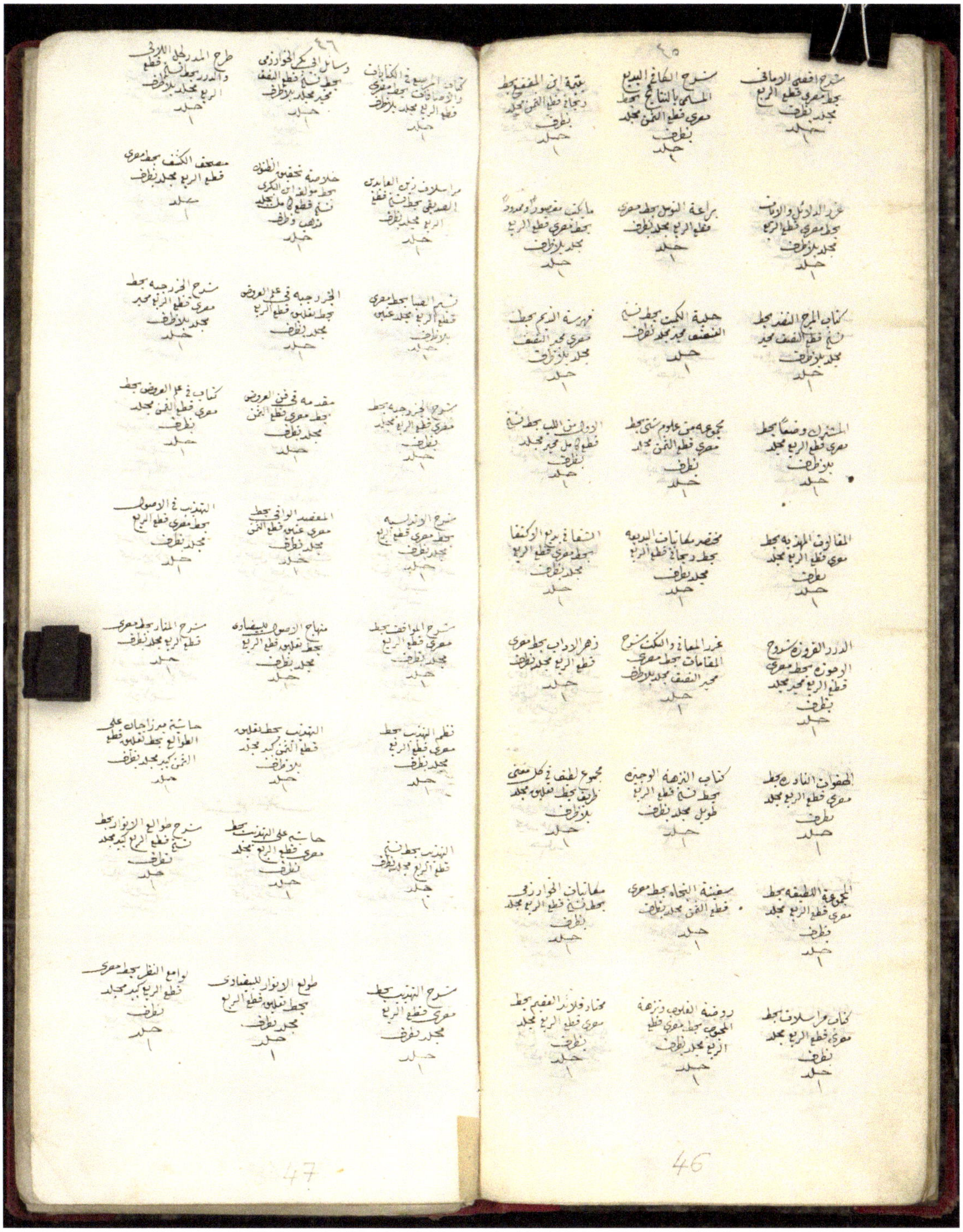
٤٥

شرح اقصى الاماني بخط معري قطع الربع مجلد بظرف جلد ١

شرح الكافي البديع المسمى بالنتائج بخط معري قطع الثمن مجلد بظرف جلد ٢

يتيمة ابن المقفع بخط دبجاني قطع الثمن مجلد بظرف جلد ١

غرر الدلائل والايات بخط معري قطع الربع مجلد بلا ظرف جلد ١

براعة النوس بخط معري قطع الربع مجلد بظرف جلد ١

ما كتب مقصوراً وممدوداً بخط معري قطع الربع مجلد بلا ظرف جلد ١

كتاب المرج النضر بخط نسخ قطع النصف مجيد مجلد بلا ظرف جلد ١

حلية الكميت بخط نسخ النصف مجيد مجلد بظرف جلد ١

فهرسة الديم بخط معري مجيد النصف مجلد بلا ظرف جلد ١

المشترك وضعاً بخط معري قطع الربع مجلد بلا ظرف جلد ١

مجموعه من علوم شتى بخط معري قطع الثمن مجلد بظرف جلد ١

الدر من اللب بخط نسخ قطع الكامل مجيد مجلد بظرف جلد ١

المقاوف المهذبه بخط معري قطع الربع مجلد بظرف جلد ١

مختصر مكاتبات البديعه بخط دبجاني قطع الربع مجلد بظرف جلد ١

الشفا في بديع الاكتفا بخط معري قطع الربع مجلد بظرف جلد ١

الدرر الفروزه شرح الارجوزه بخط معري قطع الربع مجيد مجلد بظرف جلد ١

غرر المعاني والنكت شرح المقامات بخط معري مجيد النصف مجلد بلا ظرف جلد ١

زهر الاداب بخط معري قطع الربع مجلد بظرف جلد ١

الصفوات النادح بخط معري قطع الربع مجلد بظرف جلد ١

كتاب النزهة الوجيزه بخط نسخ قطع الربع طويل مجلد بظرف جلد ١

مجموع لطيف في كل معنى ظريف بخط تعليق مجلد بلا ظرف جلد ١

المجموعة اللطيفه بخط معري قطع الربع مجلد بظرف جلد ١

سفينة النجاه بخط معري قطع الثمن مجلد بظرف جلد ١

مكاتبات الخوارزمي بخط نسخ قطع الربع مجلد بظرف جلد ١

كتاب مراسلات بخط معري قطع الربع مجلد بظرف جلد ١

روضة القلوب ونزهة المحبوب بخط معري قطع الربع مجلد بظرف جلد ١

مختار قلائد العقيان بخط معري قطع الربع مجلد بظرف جلد ١

46

٤٦

كتاب اسجع الكنايات والاصطلاحات بخط معري قطع الربع مجلد بلا ظرف جلد ١

رسائل ابي بكر الخوارزمي بخط نسخ قطع النصف مجيد مجلد بلا ظرف جلد ١

طرح المدرك على اللالي والدرر بخط نسخ قطع الربع مجلد بلا ظرف جلد ١

مراسلات زين العابدين الصديقي بخط نسخ قطع الربع مجلد بظرف جلد ١

خلاصة تحقيق الظنون بخط مؤلفها ابن البكري نسخ قطع الكامل مجلد مذهب وظرف جلد ١

مصحف الكشف بخط معري قطع الربع مجلد بظرف جلد ١

نسيم الصبا بخط معري قطع الربع مجلد عتيق بلا ظرف جلد ١

الخزرجيه في علم العروض بخط تعليق قطع الربع مجلد بظرف جلد ١

شرح الخزرجيه بخط معري قطع الربع مجيد مجلد بلا ظرف جلد ١

شرح الخزرجيه بخط معري قطع الربع مجلد بظرف جلد ١

مقدمه في فن العروض بخط معري قطع الثمن مجلد بظرف جلد ١

كتاب في علم العروض بخط معري قطع الثمن مجلد بظرف جلد ١

شرح الاندلسيه بخط معري قطع الربع مجلد بظرف جلد ١

المقصد الوافي بخط معري عتيق قطع الثمن مجلد بظرف جلد ١

التهذيب في الاصول بخط معري قطع الربع مجلد بظرف جلد ١

شرح المواقف بخط معري قطع الربع مجلد بظرف جلد ١

منهاج الاصول للبيضاوي بخط تعليق قطع الربع مجلد بظرف جلد ١

شرح المنار بخط معري قطع الربع مجلد بظرف جلد ١

نظم التهذيب بخط معري قطع الربع مجلد بظرف جلد ١

التهذيب بخط تعليق قطع الثمن كبير مجلد بلا ظرف جلد ١

حاشية ميرزاجان على الطوالع بخط تعليق قطع الثمن كبير مجلد بظرف جلد ١

التهذيب بخط نسخ قطع الربع مجلد بظرف جلد ١

حاشيه على التهذيب بخط معري قطع الربع مجلد بظرف جلد ١

شرح طوالع الانوار بخط نسخ قطع الربع كبير مجلد بظرف جلد ١

شرح التهذيب بخط معري قطع الربع مجلد بظرف جلد ١

طوالع الانوار للبيضاوي بخط تعليق قطع الربع مجلد بظرف جلد ١

لوامع النظر بخط معري قطع الربع كبير مجلد بظرف جلد ١

47

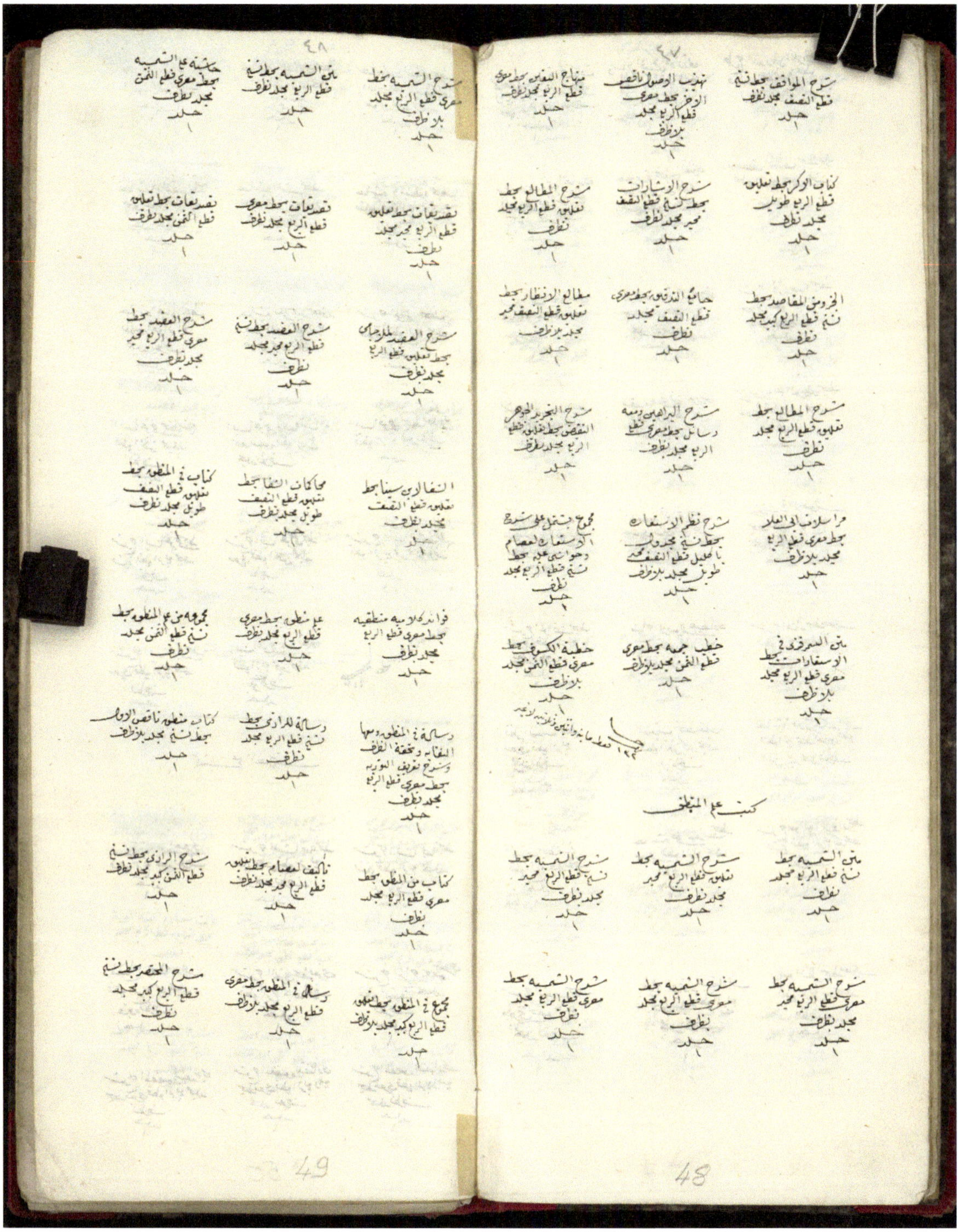

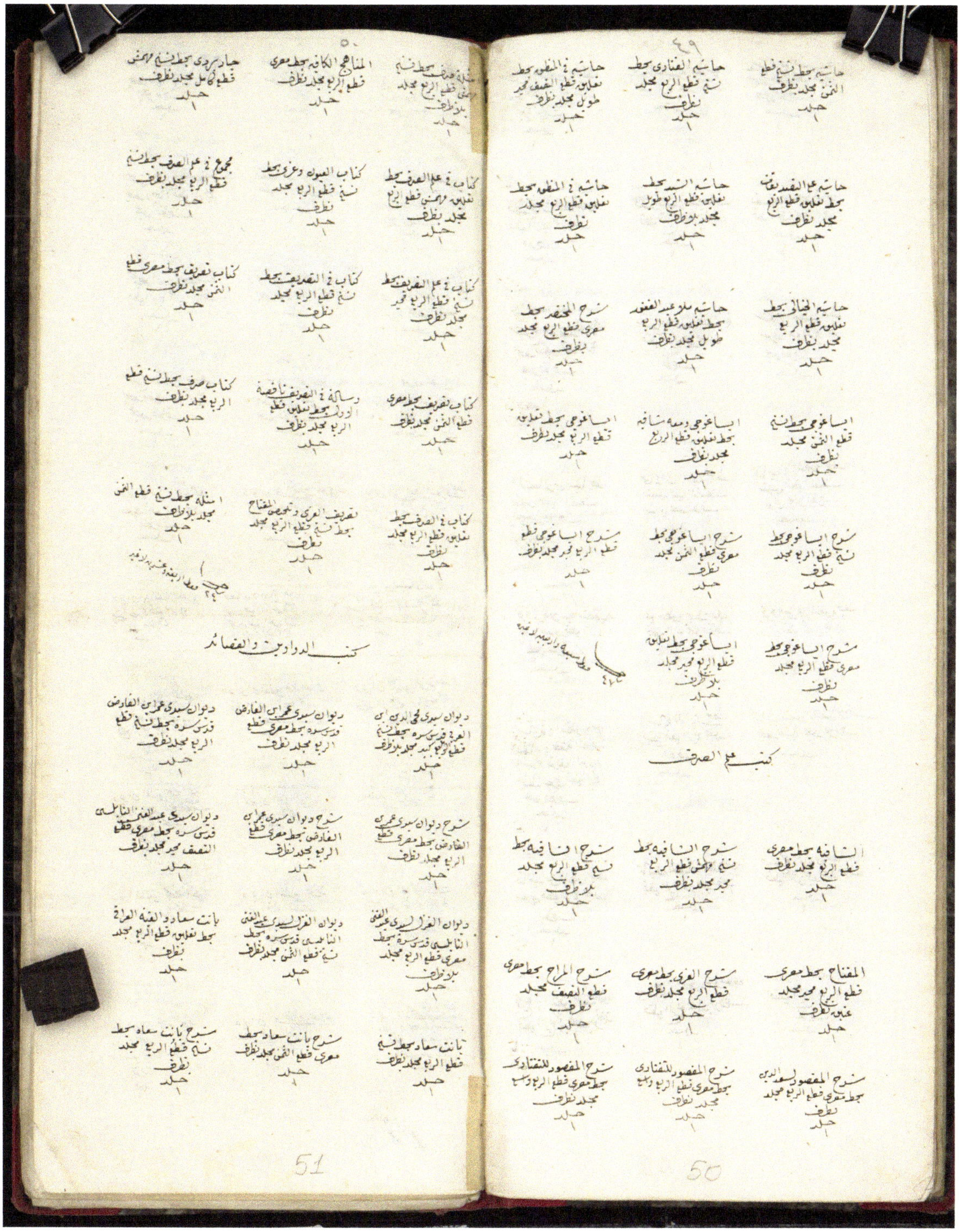

٤٩

حاشيه بخط نسخ قطع الثمن مجلد بظرف جلد ١

حاشيه الفنارى بخط نسخ قطع الربع مجلد بظرف جلد ١

حاشيه في المطول بخط تعليق قطع النصف مجيد طويل مجلد بظرف جلد ١

حاشيه على [illegible] بخط تعليق قطع الربع مجلد بظرف جلد ١

حاشيه السيد بخط تعليق قطع الربع طويل مجلد بظرف جلد ١

حاشيه في المطول بخط تعليق قطع الربع مجلد بظرف جلد ١

حاشيه الخيالي بخط تعليق قطع الربع مجلد بظرف جلد ١

حاشيه ملا عبد الغفور بخط تعليق قطع الربع طويل مجلد بظرف جلد ١

شرح المختصر بخط معري قطع الربع مجلد بظرف جلد ١

ايساغوجي بخط نسخ قطع الثمن مجلد بظرف جلد ١

ايساغوجي ومعه شافيه بخط تعليق قطع الربع مجلد بظرف جلد ١

ايساغوجي بخط تعليق قطع الربع مجلد بظرف جلد ١

شرح ايساغوجي بخط نسخ قطع الربع مجلد بظرف جلد ١

شرح ايساغوجي بخط معري قطع الثمن مجلد بظرف جلد ١

شرح ايساغوجي قطع الربع مجيد مجلد بظرف جلد ١

شرح ايساغوجي بخط معري قطع الربع مجلد بظرف جلد ١

ايساغوجي بخط تعليق قطع الربع مجيد مجلد بلا ظرف جلد ١

٤٧ [illegible] سبعه واربعين لا غير

كتب علم الصرف

الشافيه بخط معري قطع الربع مجلد بظرف جلد ١

شرح الشافيه بخط نسخ محشي قطع الربع مجيد مجلد بظرف جلد ١

شرح الشافيه بخط نسخ قطع الربع مجلد بلا ظرف جلد ١

المفتاح بخط معري قطع الربع مجيد مجلد عتيق بظرف جلد ١

شرح العزي بخط معري قطع الربع مجلد بظرف جلد ١

شرح المراح بخط معري قطع النصف مجلد بظرف جلد ١

شرح المقصود لسعد الدين بخط معري قطع الربع مجلد بظرف جلد ١

شرح المقصود للتفتازاني بخط معري قطع الربع وسيع مجلد بظرف جلد ١

شرح المقصود للتفتازاني بخط معري قطع الربع وسيع مجلد بظرف جلد ١

50

٥٠

[illegible] صرف بخط نسخ قطع الربع مجلد بلا ظرف جلد ١

المناهج الكافيه بخط معري قطع الربع مجلد بظرف جلد ١

چاربردي بخط نسخ محشي قطع كامل مجلد بظرف جلد ١

كتاب في علم الصرف بخط تعليق محشي قطع الربع مجلد بظرف جلد ١

كتاب العيون وغيره بخط نسخ قطع الربع مجلد بظرف جلد ١

مجموع في علم الصرف بخط نسخ قطع الربع مجلد بظرف جلد ١

كتاب في علم التصريف بخط نسخ قطع الربع مجيد مجلد بظرف جلد ١

كتاب في التصريف بخط نسخ قطع الربع مجلد بظرف جلد ١

كتاب تصريف بخط معري قطع الثمن مجلد بظرف جلد ١

كتاب تصريف بخط معري قطع الثمن مجلد بظرف جلد ١

رسالة في التصريف ناقصه اوراق بخط تعليق قطع الربع مجلد بظرف جلد ١

كتاب صرف بخط نسخ قطع الربع مجلد بظرف جلد ١

كتاب في الصرف بخط تعليق قطع الربع مجلد بظرف جلد ١

تصريف العزي وتخميس المفتاح بخط نسخ قطع الربع مجلد بظرف جلد ١

امثله بخط نسخ قطع الثمن مجلد بلا ظرف جلد ١

٢٤ [illegible] اربعه وعشرين لا غير

كتب الدواوين والقصائد

ديوان سيدي محي الدين ابن العربي قدس سره بخط نسخ قطع الربع كبير مجلد بلا ظرف جلد ١

ديوان سيدي عمر ابن الفارض قدس سره بخط معري قطع الربع مجلد بظرف جلد ١

ديوان سيدي عمر ابن الفارض قدس سره بخط نسخ قطع الربع مجلد بظرف جلد ١

شرح ديوان سيدي عمر ابن الفارض بخط معري قطع الربع مجلد بظرف جلد ١

شرح ديوان سيدي عمر ابن الفارض بخط معري قطع الربع مجلد بظرف جلد ١

ديوان سيدي عبد الغني النابلسي قدس سره بخط معري قطع النصف مجيد مجلد بظرف جلد ١

ديوان الغزل لسيدي عبد الغني النابلسي قدس سره بخط معري قطع الربع مجلد بلا ظرف جلد ١

ديوان الغزل لسيدي عبد الغني النابلسي قدس سره بخط نسخ قطع الثمن مجلد بظرف جلد ١

بانت سعاد والفيه العراقي بخط تعليق قطع الربع مجلد بظرف جلد ١

بانت سعاد بخط نسخ قطع الربع مجلد بظرف جلد ١

شرح بانت سعاد بخط معري قطع الثمن مجلد بظرف جلد ١

شرح بانت سعاد بخط نسخ قطع الربع مجلد بظرف جلد ١

51

٥١

شرح بانت سعاد لابن هشام بخط مصري قطع الربع مجلد بلا ظرف جلد ١
شرح بانت سعاد بخط مصري قطع الربع مجلد نظرف جلد ١
شرح اليائية لسيدي عمر ابن الفارض قدس سره بخط مصري قطع الربع مجلد نظرف جلد ١

أهنى المنائح في أسنى المدائح بخط ريحاني قطع الربع مجلد نظرف جلد ١
قطعة من الهمزية بخط مصري قطع الربع مجلد نظرف جلد ١
نفحة القبول في مدح النبي الرسول صلى الله عليه وسلم قطع الثمن مجلد بلا ظرف جلد ١

تخميس البردة بخط نسخ قطع الربع مجلد بلا ظرف جلد ١
ديوان سيدي محي الدين بن العربي بخط مصري قطع الربع مجلد نظرف جلد ١
شرح قصائد سيدي محي الدين ابن العربي بخط نسخ قطع الربع مجلد نظرف جلد ١

شرح قصيدة ابن زهير بخط مصري قطع الربع مجلد نظرف جلد ١
شرح قصيدة المنفرجة بخط مصري قطع الربع مجلد نظرف جلد ١
ديوان مجنون ليلى بخط تعليق قطع الثمن مجلد نظرف جلد ١

ديوان الششتري بخط مصري قطع الربع مجلد نظرف جلد ١
ديوان أبي العلا المعري بخط مصري قطع كامل مجلد بلا ظرف جلد ١
ديوان أبي العلا المعري بخط نسخ مجدول بالأحمر قطع الربع مجلد نظرف جلد ١

ديوان أبي العلا المعري بخط مصري قطع الربع مجلد بظرف جلد ١
قصائد في مدح خير الورى صلى الله عليه وسلم وهي بديعية العميان بخط مصري قطع الربع مجلد نظرف جلد ١
شرح البديعيات لابن حجة جلدين قطع النصف وقطع الربع مجلد بين بظرف وبلا جلد ٢ قطعة اثنان

ديوان أبي الطيب المتنبي بخط نسخ مجدول بالأحمر قطع الربع مجلد بظرف جلد ١
ديوان المتنبي بخط مصري قطع الربع واسع مجلد نظرف جلد ١
ديوان المتنبي بخط مصري قطع الربع واسع مجلد نظرف جلد ١

ديوان المتنبي بخط نسخ مجدول بالأحمر قطع النصف مجزء طويل مجلد نظرف جلد ١
ديوان المتنبي بخط مصري قطع الربع مجلد بظرف جلد ١
ديوان المتنبي بخط مصري قطع الربع مجلد بظرف جلد ١

ديوا المتنبي بخط نسخ قطع الربع مجزء مجلد بظرف جلد ١
ديوان المتنبي بخط ريحاني قطع النصف مجلد بظرف جلد ١
شرح ديوان أبي الطيب المتنبي وهو الجزء الثاني منه بخط مصري قطع الربع مجلد بظرف جلد ١

ديوان أبي تمام بخط مصري قطع الربع واسع مجلد بلا ظرف جلد ١
ديوان أبي تمام بخط تعليق قطع الثمن مجلد بلا ظرف جلد ١
ديوان أبي تمام بخط مصري مجدول بالأحمر قطع النصف مجلد بلا ظرف جلد ١

ديوان امرئ القيس جلد ١

52

٥٢

ديوان امرئ القيس بخط مصري قطع الربع مجلد بظرف جلد ١
ديوان أبي فراس بخط قطع الربع مجلد بظرف جلد ١
ديوان البهاء زهير بخط تعليق قطع الربع مجلد بلا ظرف جلد ١

ديوان البهاء زهير بخط مصري قطع الربع مجلد بظرف جلد ١
ديوان ابن نباتة بخط نسخ قطع النصف مجلد بظرف جلد ١
ديوان الصبابة بخط نسخ قطع الربع مجلد بلا ظرف جلد ١

ديوان الصبابة بخط مصري قطع الربع مجلد بظرف جلد ١
ديوان القيراطي بخط مصري قطع النصف مجلد بلا ظرف جلد ١
ديوان ابن الرومي بخط مصري قطع الربع مجلد بلا ظرف جلد ١

ديوان صفي الدين الحلي بخط نسخ قطع الربع مجلد بلا ظرف جلد ١
ديوان الحماسة بخط ريحاني قطع النصف مجلد بلا ظرف جلد ١
ديوان الحماسة بخط ريحاني قطع الربع مجلد بظرف جلد ١

ديوان الدواوين بخط مصري قطع الربع مجلد بظرف جلد ١
ديوان نثر النظم وحل العقد بخط نسخ قطع مجلد بلا ظرف جلد ١
ديوان كشاجم بخط مصري قطع الربع مجلد بظرف جلد ١

ديوان ابن حجة بخط نسخ قطع الربع مجلد بلا ظرف جلد ١
ديوان ابن كيوان بخط نسخ مجدول بالأحمر قطع الربع مجلد بلا ظرف جلد ١
ديوان ابن كيوان بخط مصري قطع الربع مجلد بظرف جلد ١

ديوان الدوكالي بخط ريحاني قطع الربع واسع مجلد بظرف جلد ١
ديوان ابن عنين بخط ريحاني قطع النصف مجزء مجلد بظرف جلد ١
ديوان أبي العباس بخط مصري قطع الربع مجلد بظرف جلد ١

ديوان ابن الحداد بخط مغربي عتيق قطع النصف مجزء مجلد بظرف جلد ١
ديوان جوهر النضار بخط مصري قطع الربع مجلد بظرف جلد ١
ديوان الأخطل بخط مغربي قطع الربع واسع مجلد بظرف جلد ١

ديوان الباخرزي بخط ريحاني عتيق قطع النصف مجزء مجلد بظرف جلد ١
ديوان السعادة بخط مصري قطع الربع مجلد بظرف جلد ١
ديوان المبرد بخط نسخ قطع النصف مجزء مجلد بظرف جلد ١

ديوان بخديات بخط نسخ مهمش قطع النصف مجلد بظرف جلد ١
ديوان علي ابن الحسين بخط نسخ قطع الربع مجلد بظرف جلد ١
ديوان ابن نباتة بخط نسخ قطع الثمن مجلد بظرف جلد ١

53

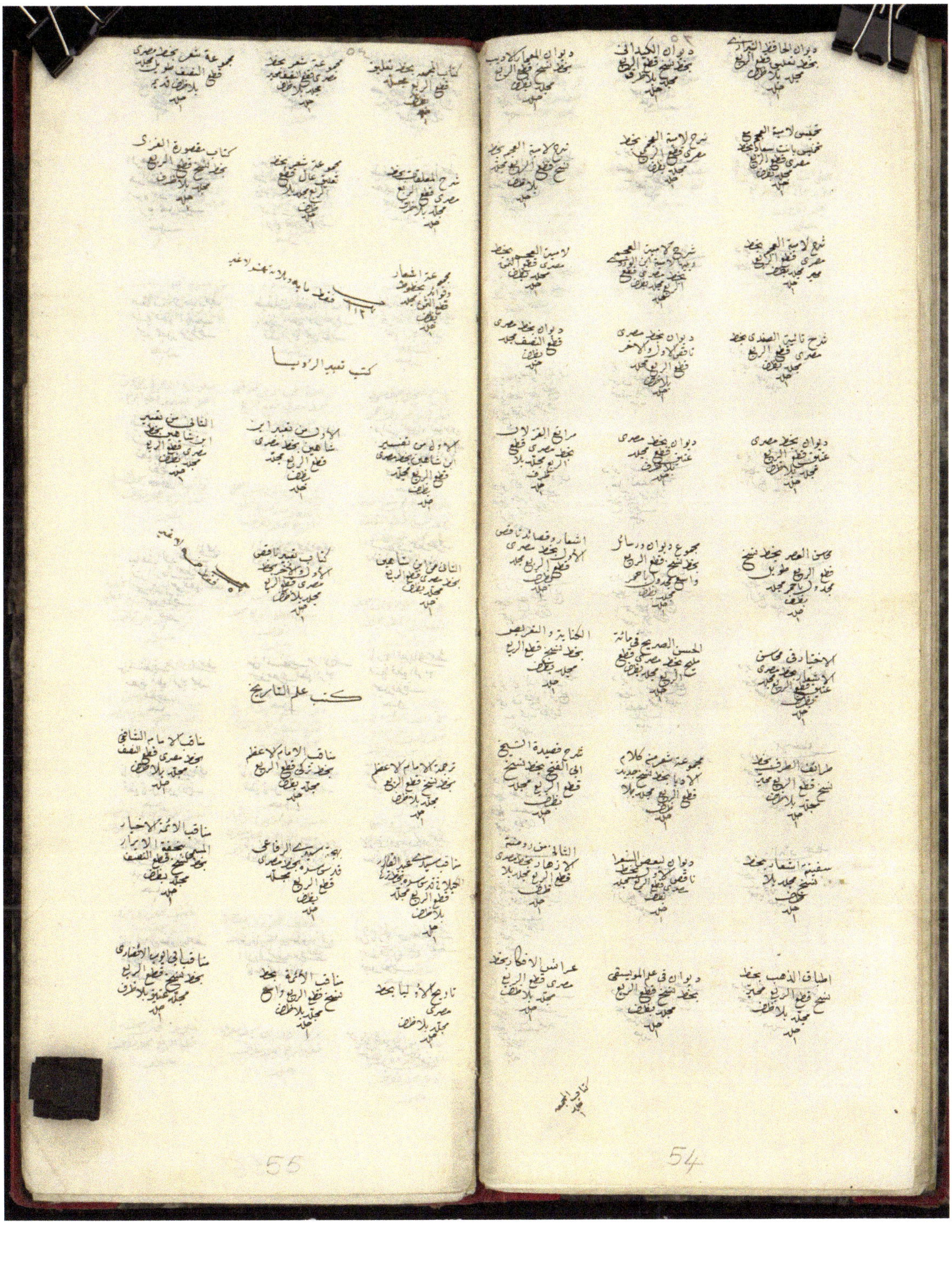
كتب تعبير الرؤيا

كتب علم التاريخ

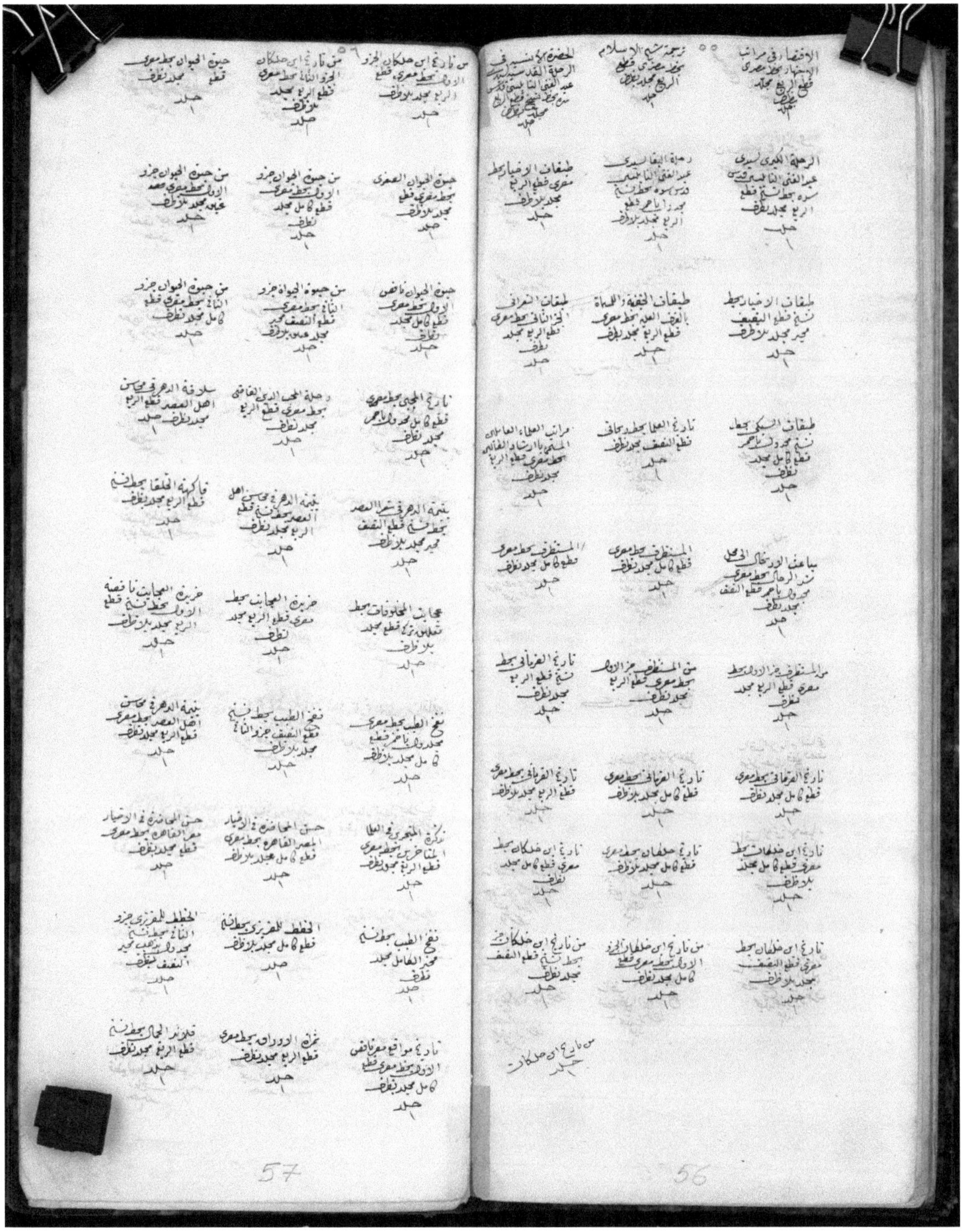
57
56

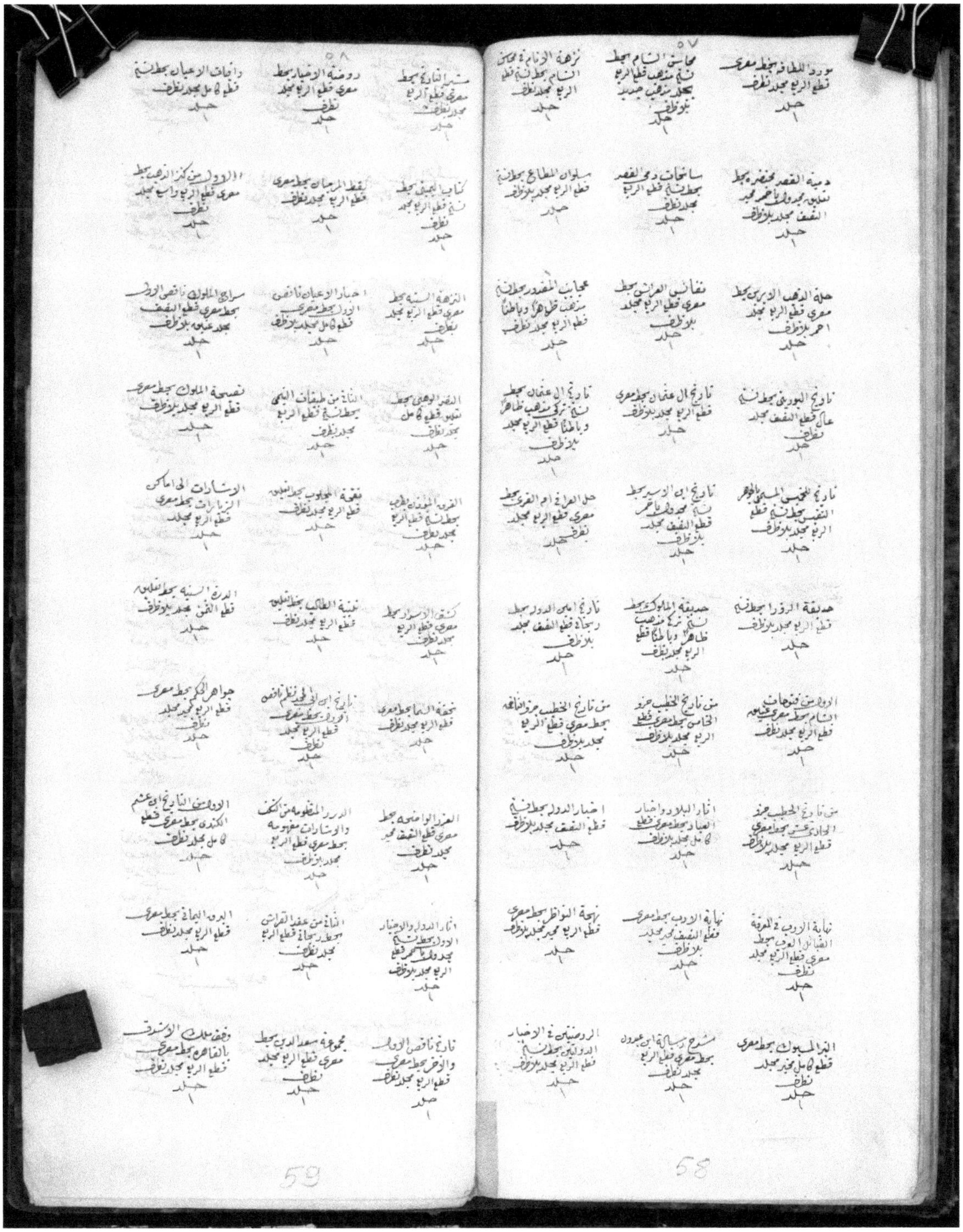

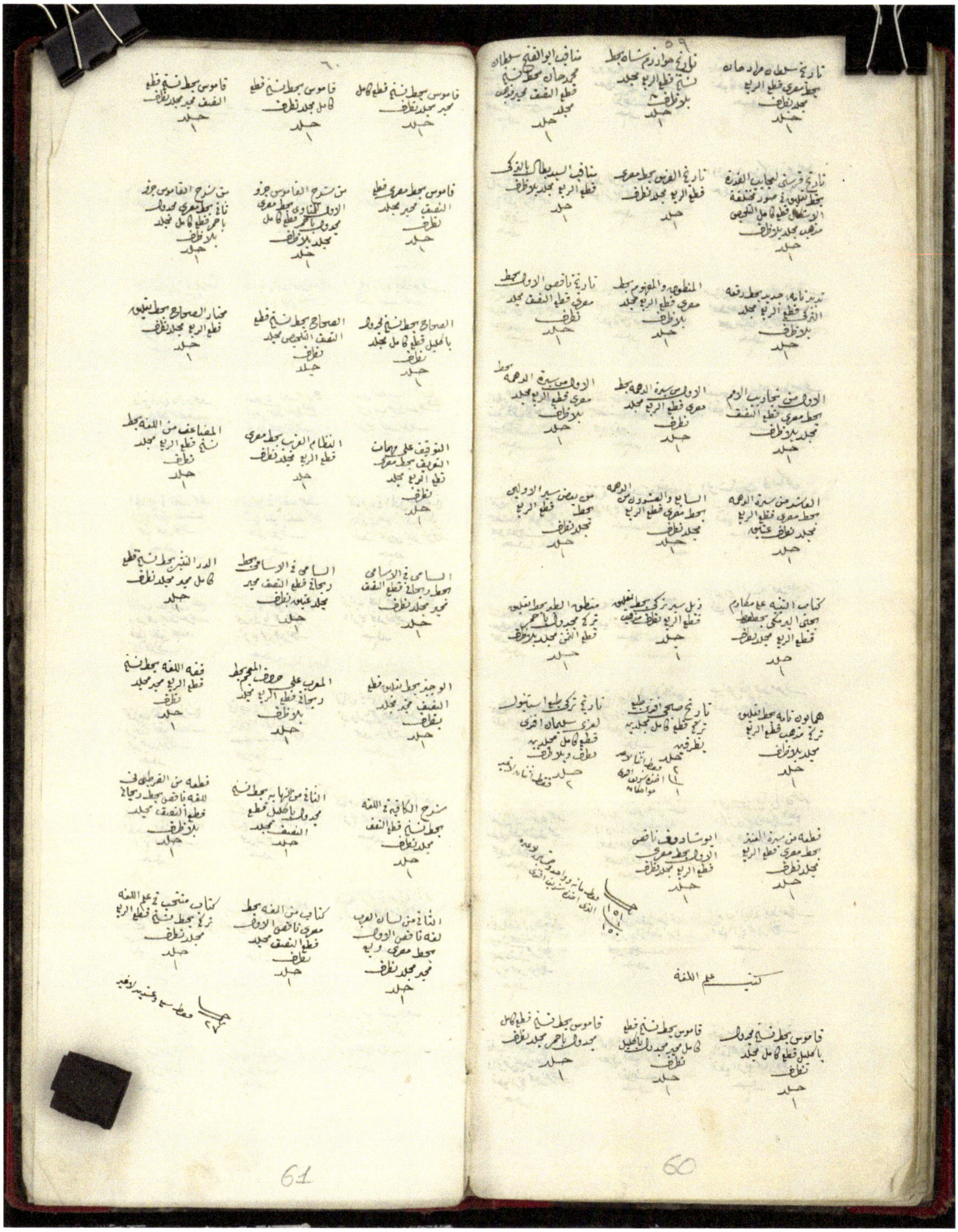

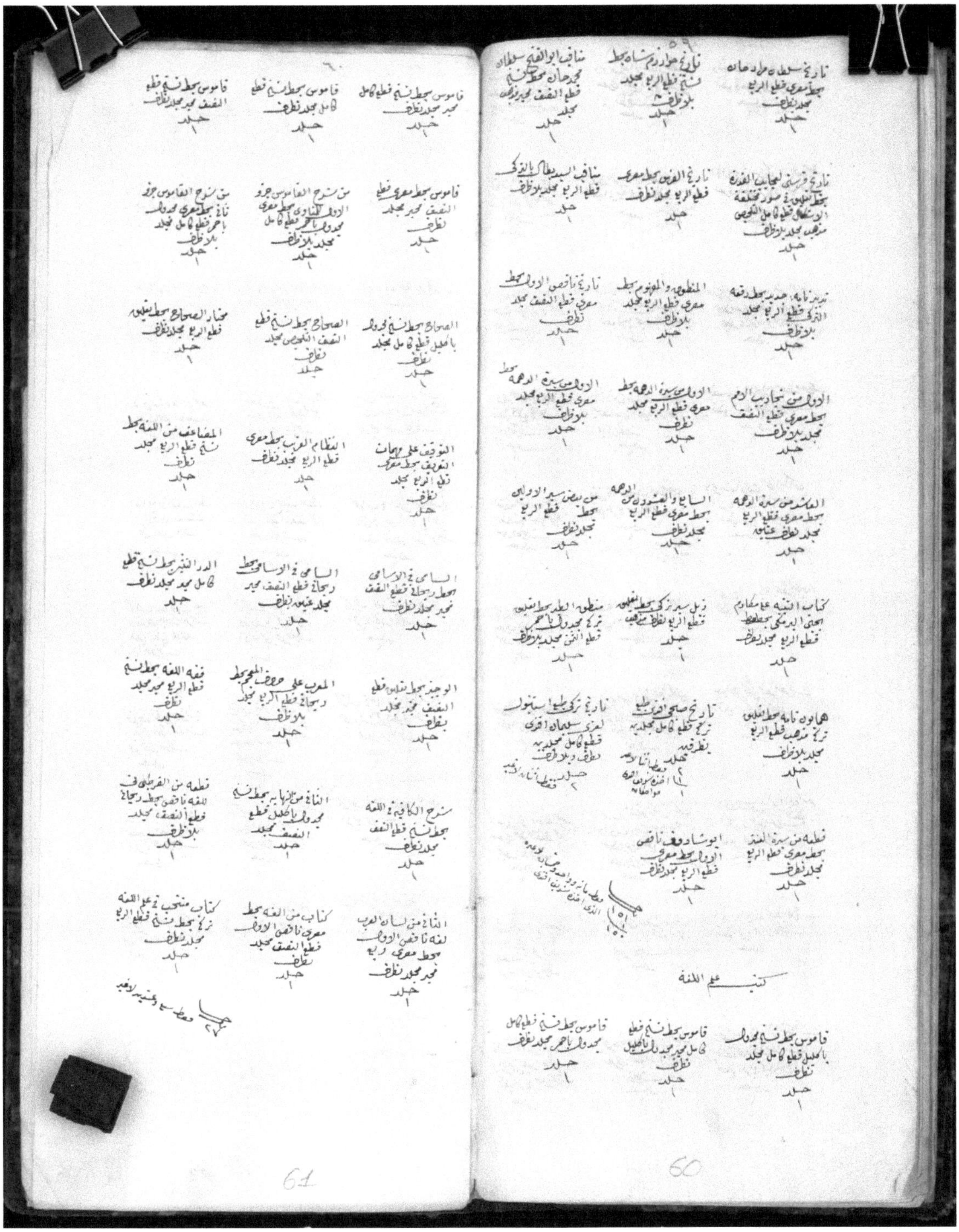

كتب علم اللغة

قاموس بخط نسخ مجدول بالذهب قطع كامل مجلد نظيف
جلد
١

قاموس بخط نسخ قطع كامل مجدول بالذهب مجلد نظيف
جلد
١

قاموس بخط نسخ قطع كامل مجدول باحمر مجلد نظيف
جلد
١

60

61

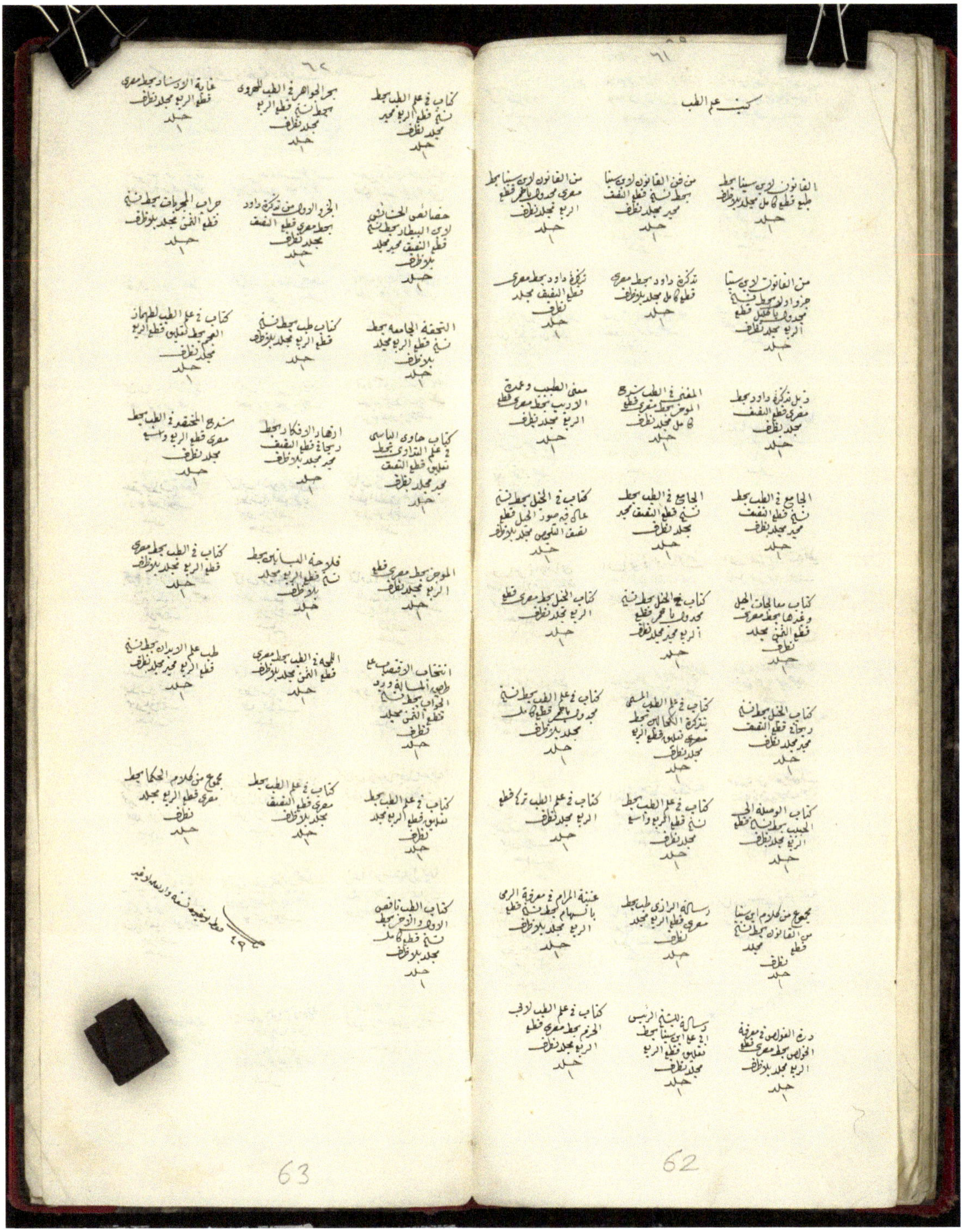
٦١
كتب علم الطب
القانون لابن سينا بخط طبع قطع كامل مجلد بلا ظرف جلد ١
من فن القانون لابن سينا بخط نسخ قطع النصف مجيد مجلد نظاف جلد ١
من القانون لابن سينا بخط معري مجدول بالاحمر قطع الربع مجلد نظاف جلد ١
من القانون لابن سينا جزو اول بخط فارسي مجدول بالكحل قطع الربع مجلد نظاف جلد ١
تذكرة داود بخط معري قطع كامل مجلد بلا ظرف جلد ١
تذكرة داود بخط معري قطع النصف مجلد نظاف جلد ١
ذيل تذكرة داود بخط معري قطع النصف مجلد نظاف جلد ١
المغني في الطب شرح الموجز بخط معري قطع كامل مجلد نظاف جلد ١
مغني الطبيب وعمدة الاديب بخط معري قطع الربع مجلد نظاف جلد ١
الجامع في الطب بخط نسخ قطع النصف مجيد مجلد نظاف جلد ١
الجامع في الطب بخط نسخ قطع النصف مجيد مجلد نظاف جلد ١
كتاب في الخيل بخط نسخ عالي فيه صور الخيل قطع نصف التلميس مجلد بلا ظرف جلد ١
كتاب معالجات الخيل وغيرها بخط معري قطع الثمن مجلد نظاف جلد ١
كتاب في الخيل بخط نسخ مجدول بالاحمر قطع الربع مجيد مجلد نظاف جلد ١
كتاب الخيل بخط معري قطع الربع مجلد نظاف جلد ١
كتاب الخيل بخط نسخ ديباجة قطع النصف مجيد مجلد نظاف جلد ١
كتاب في علم الطب المسمى بتذكرة الكحالين بخط معري تعليق قطع الربع مجلد نظاف جلد ١
كتاب في علم الطب بخط نسخ مجدول بالاحمر قطع كامل مجلد بلا ظرف جلد ١
كتاب الوصلة الى الحبيب بخط نسخ قطع الربع مجلد نظاف جلد ١
كتاب في علم الطب بخط نسخ قطع الربع واسع مجلد نظاف جلد ١
كتاب في علم الطب تركي قطع الربع مجلد نظاف جلد ١
مجموع من كلام ابن سينا من القانون بخط نسخ قطع مجلد نظاف جلد ١
رسالة الرازي طب بخط معري قطع الربع مجلد نظاف جلد ١
غنية المرام في معرفة الرمي بالسهام بخط نسخ قطع الربع مجلد بلا ظرف جلد ١
درة الغواص في معرفة الخواص بخط معري قطع الربع مجلد بلا ظرف جلد ١
رسالة للشيخ الرئيس ابي علي ابن سينا بخط تعليق قطع الربع مجلد نظاف جلد ١
كتاب في علم الطب لابي الحزم بخط معري قطع الربع مجلد نظاف جلد ١
62
٦٢
كتاب في علم الطب بخط نسخ قطع الربع مجيد مجلد نظاف جلد ١
بحر الجواهر في الطب الهروي بخط نسخ قطع الربع مجلد نظاف جلد ١
غاية الارشاد بخط معري قطع الربع مجلد نظاف جلد ١
خصائص الحشائش لابن البيطار بخط نسخ قطع النصف مجيد مجلد بلا ظرف جلد ١
الجزو الاول من تذكرة داود بخط معري قطع النصف مجلد نظاف جلد ١
جراب المجربات بخط نسخ قطع الثمن مجلد بلا ظرف جلد ١
التحفة الجامعة بخط نسخ قطع الربع مجلد بلا ظرف جلد ١
كتاب طب بخط نسخ قطع الربع مجلد بلا ظرف جلد ١
كتاب في علم الطب لطهماز العجم بخط تعليق قطع الربع مجلد نظاف جلد ١
كتاب حاوي الاساسي في علم التداوي بخط تعليق قطع النصف مجيد مجلد نظاف جلد ١
ازهار الافكار بخط ديباجة قطع النصف مجيد مجلد بلا ظرف جلد ١
شرح المختصر في الطب بخط معري قطع الربع واسع مجلد نظاف جلد ١
الموجز بخط معري قطع الربع مجلد نظاف جلد ١
فلاحة البابلي بخط نسخ قطع الربع مجلد بلا ظرف جلد ١
كتاب في الطب بخط معري قطع الربع مجلد بلا ظرف جلد ١
انتخاب الاقتضاب على طريقة المسالة ورد الجواب بخط نسخ قطع الثمن مجلد نظاف جلد ١
اللمحة في الطب بخط معري قطع الثمن مجلد بلا ظرف جلد ١
طب علم الابدان بخط نسخ قطع الربع مجيد مجلد نظاف جلد ١
كتاب في علم الطب بخط تعليق قطع الربع مجلد نظاف جلد ١
كتاب في علم الطب بخط معري قطع النصف مجلد بلا ظرف جلد ١
مجموع من كلام الحكما بخط معري قطع الربع مجلد نظاف جلد ١
كتاب الطب ناقص الاول والاخر بخط نسخ قطع كامل مجلد بلا ظرف جلد ١
صح ٤٢
63

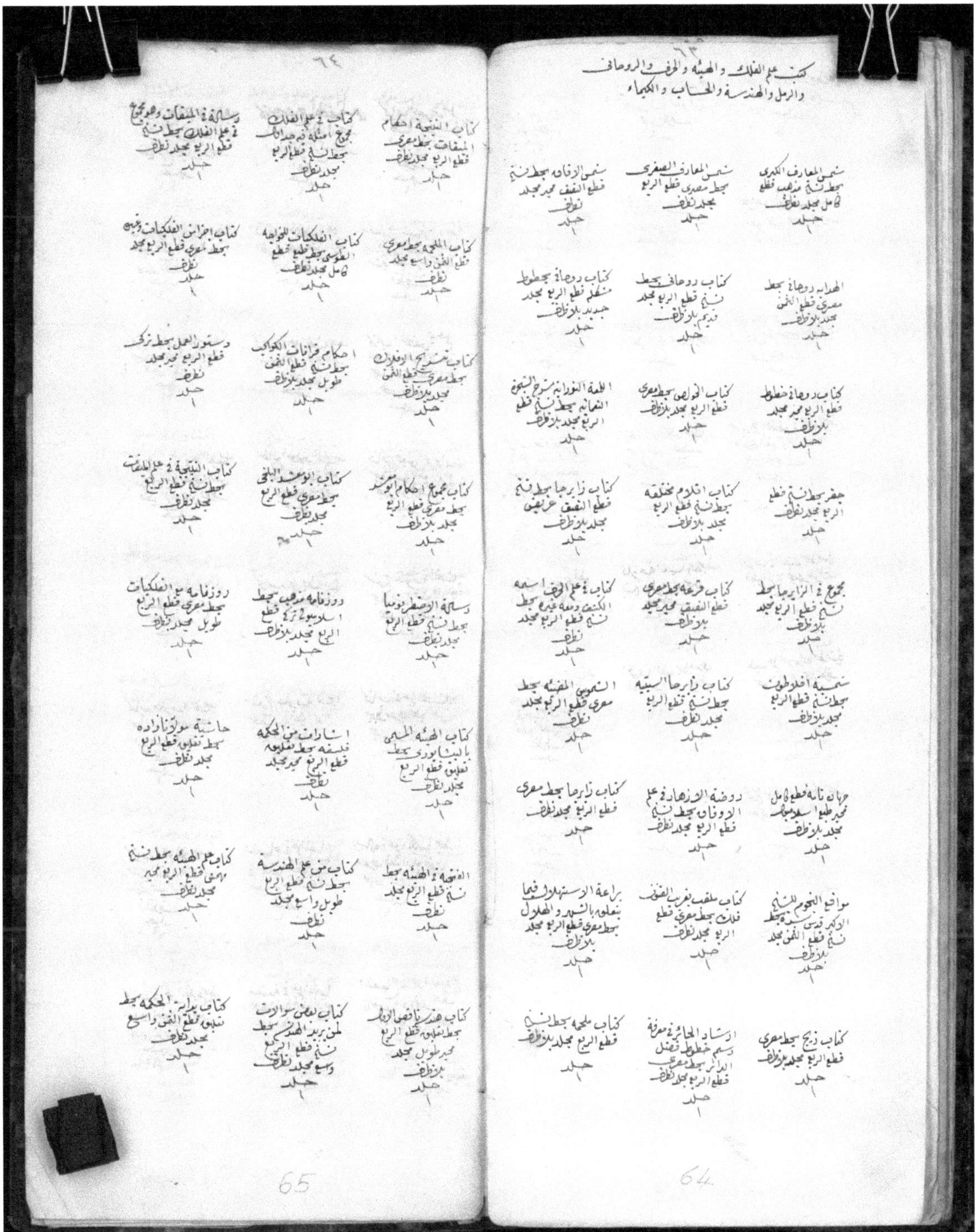
كتب علم الفلك والهيئة والحرف والروحاني
والرمل والهندسة والحساب والكيمياء

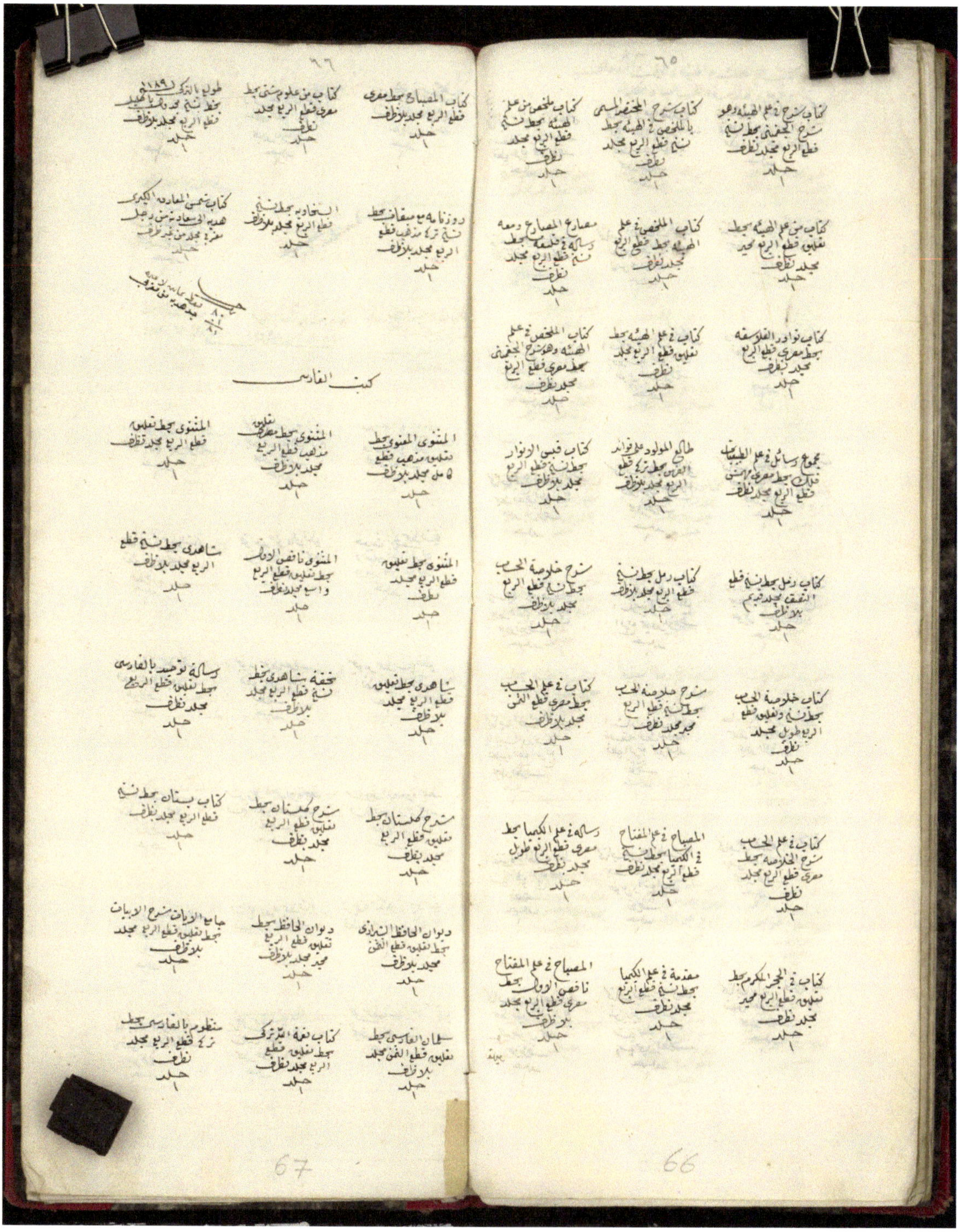

٦٥

كتاب شرح في علم الهيئة وهو شرح الجغميني بخط نسخ قطع الربع مجلد نظيف جلد ١

كتاب شرح المختصر المسمى بالملخص في الهيئة بخط نسخ قطع الربع مجلد نظيف جلد ١

كتاب ملخص من علم الهيئة بخط نسخ قطع الربع مجلد نظيف جلد ١

كتاب من علم الهيئة بخط تعليق قطع الربع جديد مجلد نظيف جلد ١

كتاب الملخص في علم الهيئة بخط قطع الربع مجلد نظيف جلد ١

مصارع المصارع ومعه رسالة في قلعة بخط نسخ قطع الربع مجلد نظيف جلد ١

كتاب نوادر الفلاسفة بخط معري قطع الربع مجلد نظيف جلد ١

كتاب في علم الهيئة بخط تعليق قطع الربع مجلد نظيف جلد ١

كتاب الملخص في علم الهيئة وهو شرح الجغميني بخط معري قطع الربع مجلد نظيف جلد ١

مجموع رسائل في علم الطب [illegible] فلك بخط معري والنسخ قطع الربع مجلد نظيف جلد ١

طالع المولود على فوائد الفرس بخط تركي قطع الربع مجلد بلا ظرف جلد ١

كتاب قبس الأنوار بخط نسخ قطع الربع مجلد بلا ظرف جلد ١

كتاب رمل بخط نسخ قطع النصف مجلد قديم بلا ظرف جلد ١

كتاب رمل بخط نسخ قطع الربع مجلد بلا ظرف جلد ١

شرح خلاصة الحساب بخط نسخ قطع الربع مجلد بلا ظرف جلد ١

كتاب خلاصة الحساب بخط نسخ وتعليق قطع الربع طويل مجلد نظيف جلد ١

شرح خلاصة الحساب بخط نسخ قطع الربع مجلد مجلد نظيف جلد ١

كتاب في علم الحساب بخط معري قطع الثمن مجلد بلا ظرف جلد ١

كتاب في علم الحساب شرح الخلاصة بخط معري قطع الربع مجلد نظيف جلد ١

المصباح في علم المفتاح في الكيميا بخط نسخ قطع الربع مجلد نظيف جلد ١

رسالة في علم الكيميا بخط معري قطع الربع طويل مجلد نظيف جلد ١

كتاب في الحجر المكرم بخط تعليق قطع الربع جديد مجلد نظيف جلد ١

مقدمة في علم الكيميا بخط نسخ قطع الربع مجلد نظيف جلد ١

المصباح في علم المفتاح ناقص الأوراق بخط معري قطع الربع مجلد بلا ظرف جلد ١

66

٦٦

كتاب المصباح بخط معري قطع الربع مجلد بلا ظرف جلد ١

كتاب من علوم شتى بخط معري قطع الربع مجلد نظيف جلد ١

طوالع بالتركي ١٨٩ بخط نسخ جديد [illegible] قطع الربع مجلد بلا ظرف جلد ١

روزنامه مع مسقات بخط نسخ تركي مذهب قطع الربع مجلد بلا ظرف جلد ١

السخاويه بخط نسخ قطع الربع مجلد بلا ظرف جلد ١

كتاب شمس المعارف الكبرى هدية إلى سعادة [illegible] مجلد من غير ظرف جلد ١

٨٠ ١ ٨١

كتب الفارسي

المثنوي المعنوي بخط تعليق مذهب قطع كامل مجلد بلا ظرف جلد ١

المثنوي بخط معري تعليق مذهب قطع الربع مجلد بلا ظرف جلد ١

المثنوي بخط تعليق قطع الربع مجلد نظيف جلد ١

المثنوي بخط تعليق قطع الربع مجلد نظيف جلد ١

المثنوي ناقص الأوراق بخط تعليق قطع الربع واسع مجلد نظيف جلد ١

شاهدي بخط نسخ قطع الربع مجلد بلا ظرف جلد ١

شاهدي بخط تعليق قطع الربع مجلد بلا ظرف جلد ١

تحفة شاهدي بخط نسخ قطع الربع مجلد بلا ظرف جلد ١

رسالة توحيد بالفارسي بخط تعليق قطع الربع مجلد نظيف جلد ١

شرح گلستان بخط تعليق قطع الربع مجلد نظيف جلد ١

شرح گلستان بخط تعليق قطع الربع مجلد نظيف جلد ١

كتاب بستان بخط نسخ قطع الربع مجلد نظيف جلد ١

ديوان الحافظ الشيرازي بخط تعليق قطع الثمن مجلد بلا ظرف جلد ١

ديوان الحافظ بخط تعليق قطع الربع مجلد مجلد بلا ظرف جلد ١

جامع الأبيات شرح الأبيات بخط تعليق قطع الربع مجلد بلا ظرف جلد ١

سلمان الفارسي بخط تعليق قطع الثمن مجلد بلا ظرف جلد ١

كتاب لغة إلى تركي بخط تعليق قطع الربع مجلد نظيف جلد ١

منظوم بالفارسي بخط تركي قطع الربع مجلد نظيف جلد ١

67

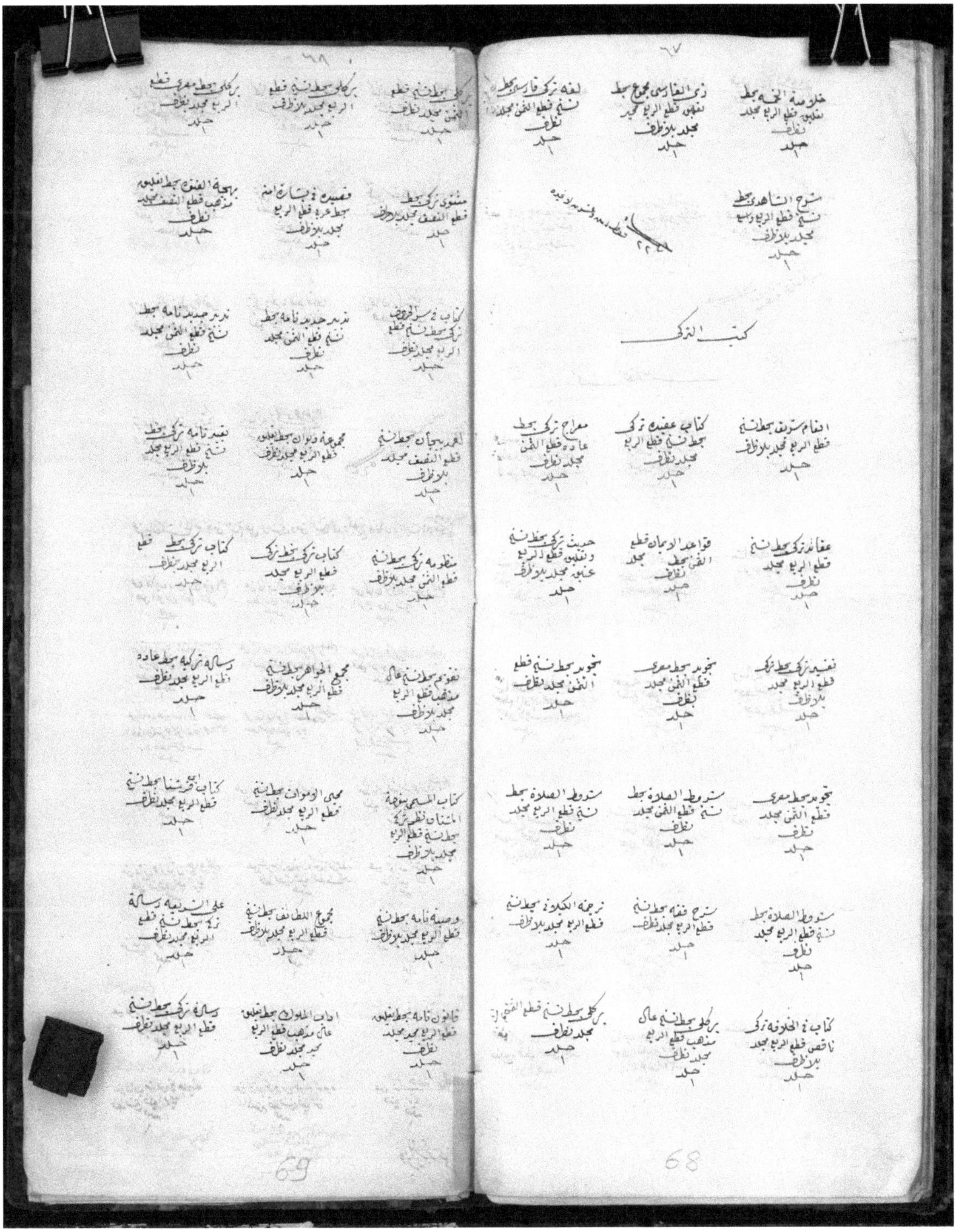
خلوصة الخمسه بخط تعليق قطع الربع مجلد نظاف
جلد ١
ذى الفارسى مجموع بخط تعليق قطع الربع مجلد بلا ظرف
جلد ١
لغة تركى فارسى بخط نسخ قطع الثمن مجلد نظاف
جلد ١
شرح الشاهدى بخط نسخ قطع الربع مجلد بلا ظرف
جلد ١
كتب التركى

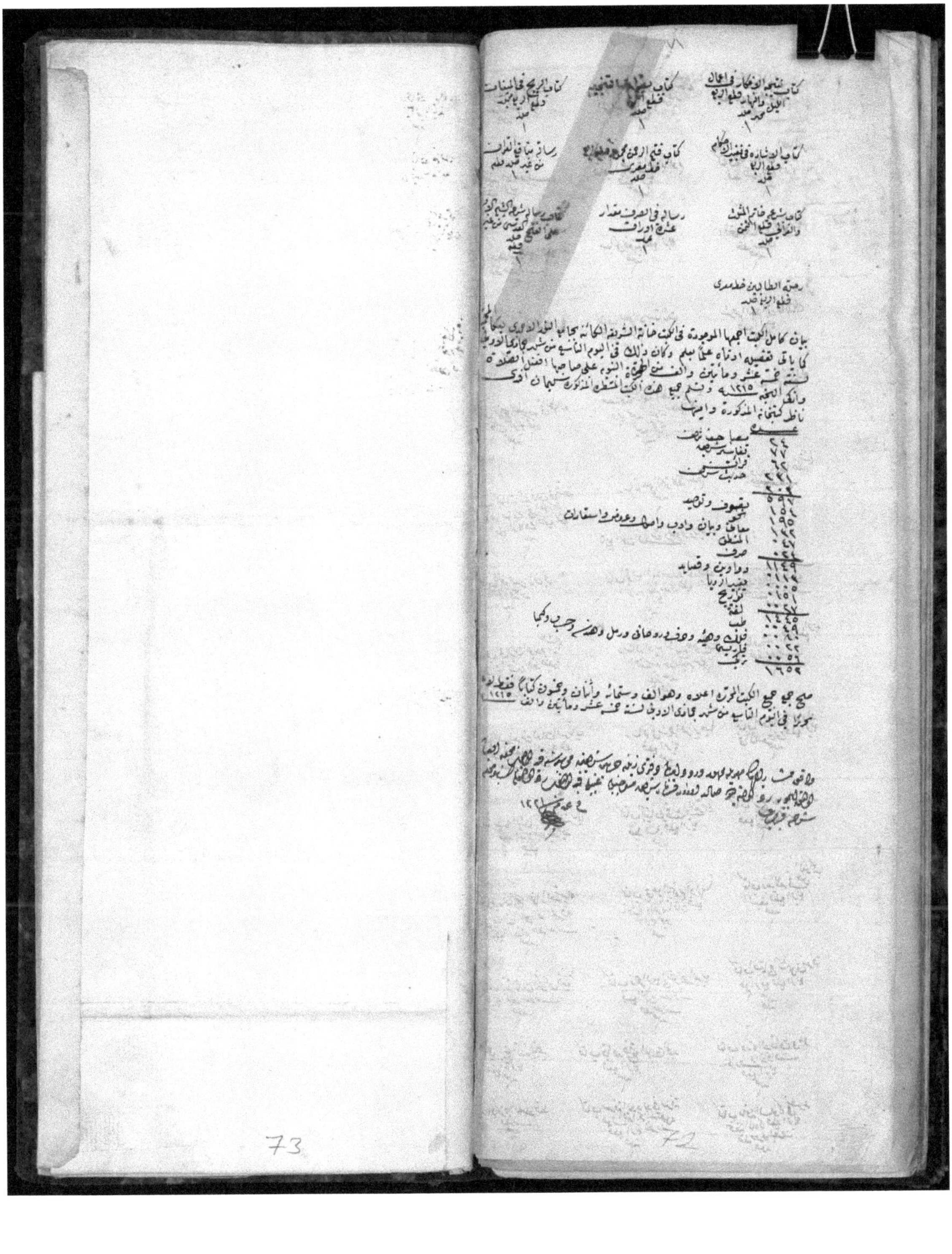

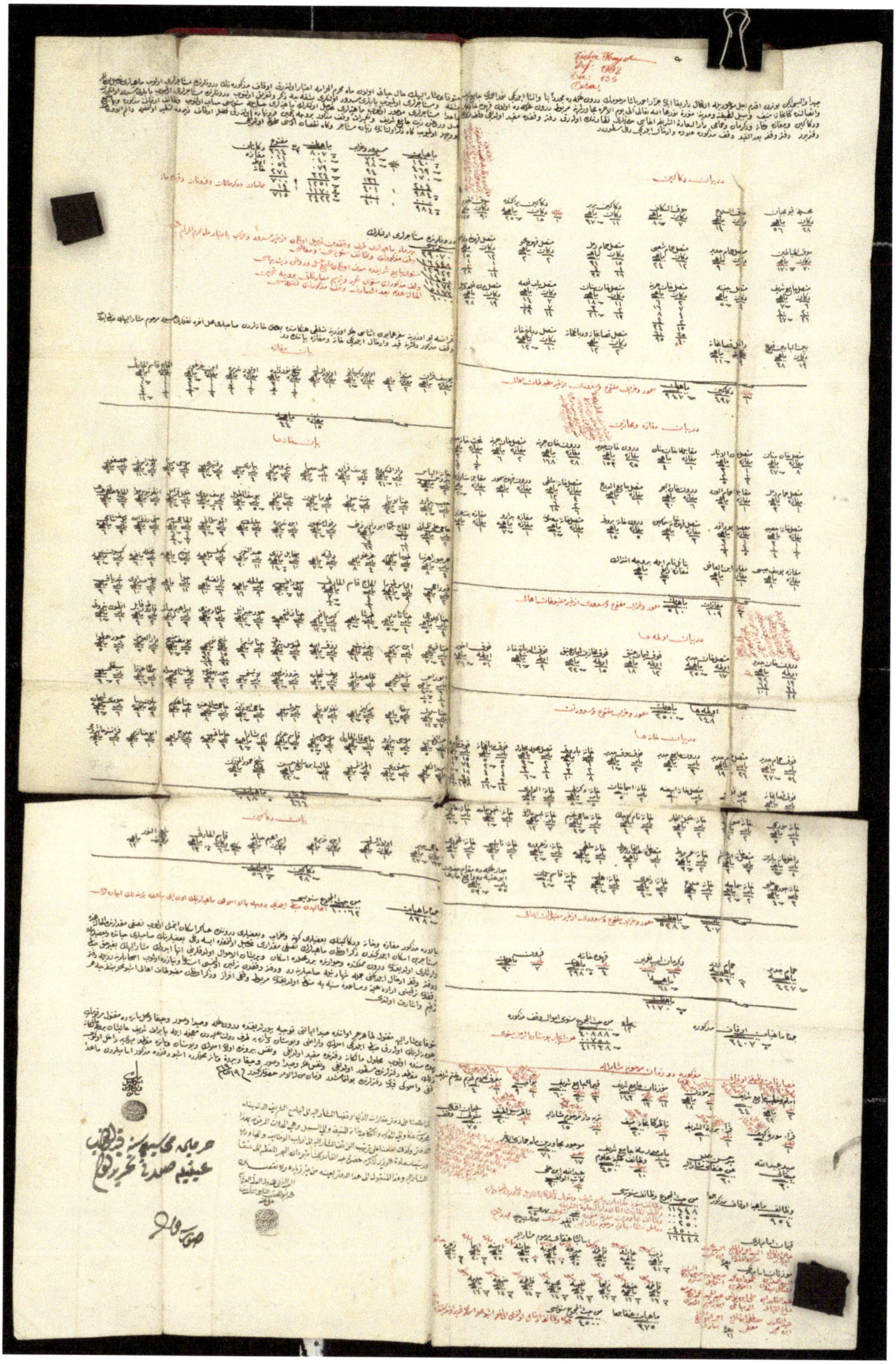

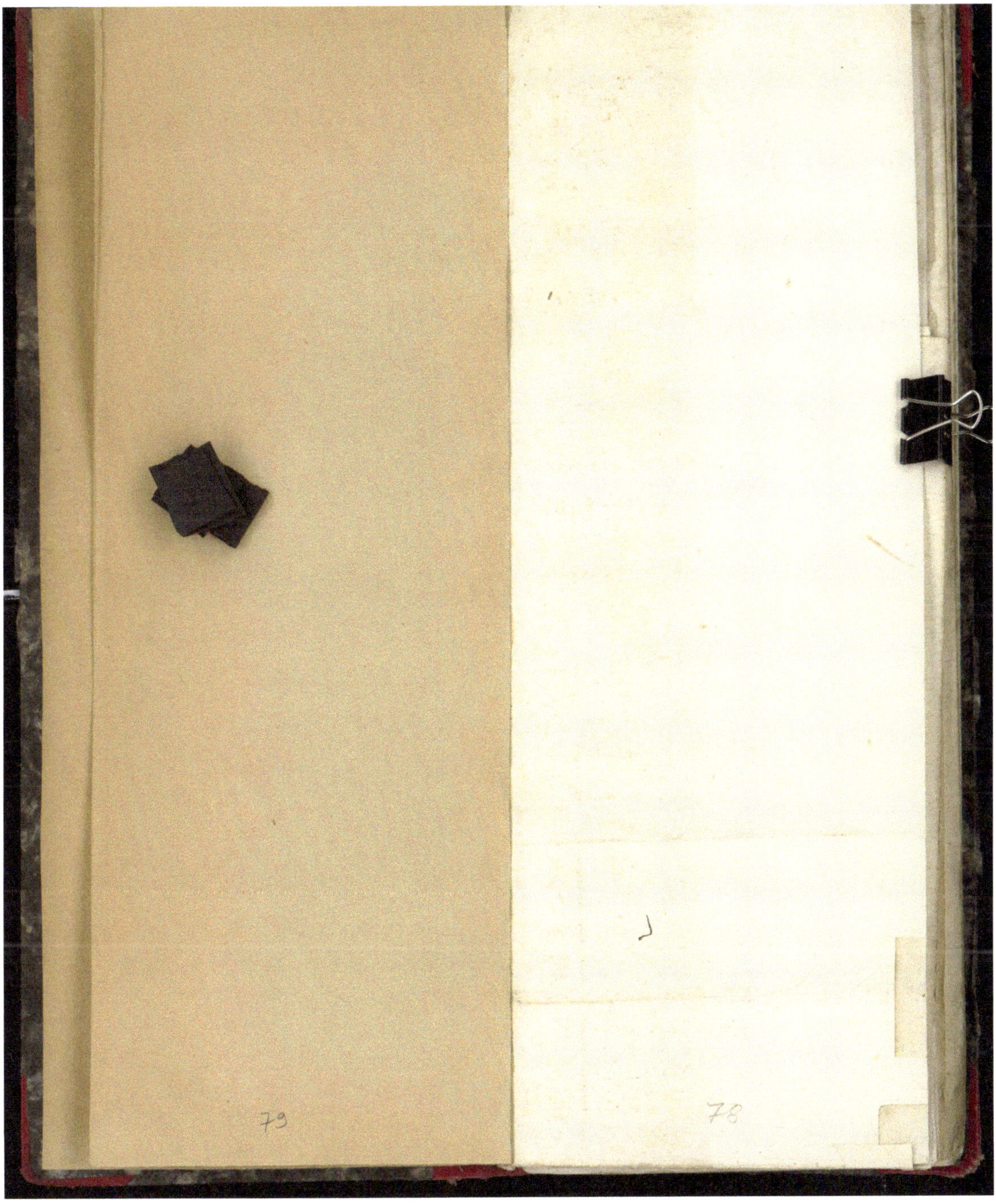
79
78

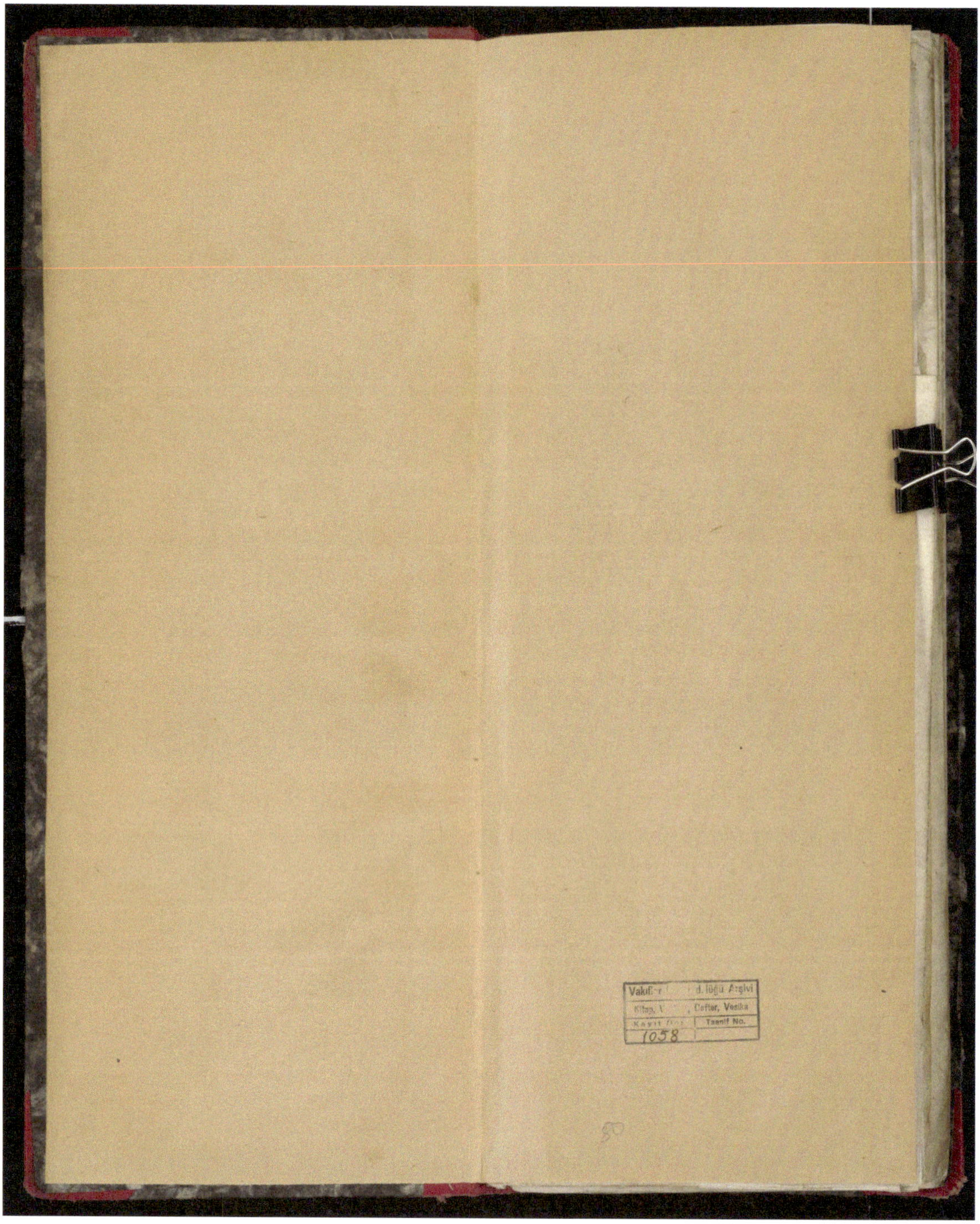
d.lüğü Arşivi
Defter, Vesika
Tasnif No.
1058

Index of the Inventory's Book Titles

Numbers refer to the entry number in the inventory.

آثار البلاد وأخبار العباد (1335)

آداب المريد (563)

آداب المولوي (945)

آكام المرجان في أحكام الجان (531)

إتحاف المريد بجوهرة التوحيد (601)

الإتقان في علوم القرآن (81)

إجازات أهل الطريق (689)

إجازة في القراءات العشرة (136)

إجازة في القراءات العشرة من طريق الشاطبية (132)

إجازة في علم القراءات (126)

اجتماع الشمل في معرفة علم الرمل (1690)

أجوبة أربعين مسألة من المسائل المشكلة في القراءات (137)

أجوبة المسائل المشكلات في علم القراءات (112)

الإحرام في رفع اليدين عند تكبيرة الإحرام (395)

الأحكام السلطانية (1650)

أحكام من الفقه الشافعي (406، 407، 419، 425، 426، 432، 447)

الأحكام النبوية في الصناعة الطبية (299، 549)

أحوال القرآن على أبواب تنوف على خمسمائة وستين باباً (595)

إحياء علوم الدين (208)

أخبار الدول وآثار الأول (1273، 1274، 1275، 1276، 1367)

أخبار الدولة (1336)

اختيار الأولَى في شرح حديث اختصم الملأ الأعلى (233)

الاختيار في محاسن الأشعار (1223)

أدعية وأحاديث (222)

الأذكار (194، 195، 196، 197)

الأذكار للنووي (1633)

أذهان الأذكياء شرح التلخيص (962)

الأربعين النووية من كلام خير البرية (324)

الأرج في الفرج (285)

الأرجوزة في الأجوبة عن المسائل المذكورة (137)

أرجوزة في مشكلات القرآن (137)

إرشاد الأذهان في أحكام الإيمان (421)

إرشاد الحائر في معرفة رسم خطوط فضل الدائر (1497)

إرشاد الساري لشرح صحيح البخاري (144، 145، 146)

إرشاد الطلبة الى شواهد الطيبة (119)

إرشاد العقل السليم إلى مزايا الكتاب الكريم (34، 35، 36، 37)

إرشاد المريد لجوهرة التوحيد (601)

الإرشاد في صناعة الطب (557)

الإرشاد والنظرين (429)

أزهار الأفكار في جواهر الأحجار (1460)

أساس الصالحين (392)

أسباب نزول القرآن (512)

أسرار السرور بالوصول الى عين النور (716)

أسرار العربية (836)

أسماء الجنة (1657)

أسماء أهل بدر ومناقبهم وفضائلهم (260)

الإشارات إلى أماكن الزيارات (1357)

الإشارات في علم العبارات (1242، 1243، 1244، 1245)

إشارات من الحكمة (1515)

الإشارة في تغيير الأحكام (1700)

الإشاعة في أشراط الساعة (175، 176، 191)

الأشباه والنظائر (352)

الإشراف في فضائل الأشراف (186)

أشرف الوسائل إلى فهم الشمائل (516)

أشرف الوسائل في أجوبة السائل (330)

الإصابة في تميز الصحابة (207)

الإصطرنوميا (1511)

أصول التوحيد (604)

أصول الفقه (446)

إضاءة الدجنة في عقائد أهل السنة (621)

أطباق الذهب (1232)

إظهار صدق المودة في شرح قصيدة البردة (236، 279)

إعراب الأجرومية (910)

إعراب القرآن وتبيين مافيه من النحو وذكر القراءات التي تحتاج إلى ذكر مافيها من العربيَّة (61)

إعراب ديباجة المصباح (845)

بداية الحكمة (1522)
بدائع البدائع (987)
بدائع البرهان في علوم القرآن (85)
البدر المنير (1658)
البدور السافرة في امور الآخرة (211)
بديع الإنشاء والصفات في المكاتبات والمراسلات (1014)
البديع في معرفة ما رسم في مصحف عثمان (110)
بديعية العميان (1164)
براعة الاستهلال فيما يتعلق بالشهر والهلال (1495)
براعة التوسل (994)
البرق الوامض في شرح يائية ابن الفارض (1147)
البرق اليماني (1369)
البركة في فضل السعي والحركة (243)
البرهان في علامات مهدي آخر الزمان (320)
بستان الزاهدين (670)
بستان العارفين (669)
البسيط والجامع المحيط (794)
بشرى الكئيب في لقاء الحبيب (311)
بعض سؤالات لمن يريد الهندسة (1521)
بغية الألباب في شرح غنية الطلاب (457)
بغية المستفيد في علم التجويد (117)
بلغة الغواص في الأكوان إلى معدن الإخلاص في معرفة الإنسان (576)
بلوغ القصد والمنى في خواص أسماء الله الحسنى (680)
بهجة الرسائل (678)
بهجة الفتوة (1598)
البهجة المرضية في شرح الألفية (769)
بهجة النفوس (230)
بهجة سيدي الرفاعي (1251)
بيان المعاني في شرح عقيدة الشيباني (610)
البيان المقبول في رد السول (643)
البيان والتوضيح لمن أخرج له في الصحيح وقد مُسَّ بضرب من التجريح (193)
البيوع والرهائن (402)
تاج اللغة وصحاح العربية (517، 527، 1405، 1406)
تاريخ [فرنسي؟] لعجائب القدرة (1376)
تاريخ ابن أبي المجد (1362)
إعراب شعر (858)
الإعراب عن قواعد الإعراب (791)
اغتنام الفوائد في التنبيه على معاني قواعد العقائد للغزالي (676)
الافتتاح في شرح المصباح للمطرزي (861)
الإفصاح في أسماء النكاح (398)
اقتحام البحة اللآلي في شرح منفرجة الغزالي (1663)
اقترانات الكواكب في البروج الاثني عشر وما يلحق بذلك (1688)
الاقتصاد في مراتب الاجتهاد (1256)
الإقناع في حل ألفاظ أبي شجاع (209، 451، 1642)
الألغاز النحوية (844، 925)
ألفاظ الكفر (448)
ألفية ابن مالك (751، 752، 753، 754، 923)
ألفية العراقي (1141)
أم البراهين (605، 607، 608، 734، 737)
أم القرى في مدح خير الورى (261، 1149)
أمالي المرتضى (56)
أمثلة صرف (1118)
إملاء ما منَّ به الرحمن من وجوه الإعراب والقراءات في جميع القرآن (59)
انتخاب الاقتضاب على طريق المسألة ورد الجواب (1465)
الانتصاف (850)
الأنس الجليل في تاريخ القدس والخليل (543)
إنسان العيون في سيرة الأمين المأمون (179، 180، 181، 182)
الإنسان الكامل في معرفة الأواخر والأوائل (655)
إنشاد الشريد في ضوال القصيد (131)
أنعام شريف (1575، 1640)
الأنموذج (839)
أنوار التنزيل وأسرار التأويل (27، 28، 29، 30، 31، 51، 523)
أهنى المنائح لأسنى المدائح (1148)
أوراد مولانا (724)
أوضح المسالك الى ألفية ابن مالك (569)
إيساغوجي (1101، 1102، 1103، 1108)
إيضاح الدلالات في سماع الآلات (474)
الإيضاح شرح الإصلاح لمتن الوقاية وشرحها (354)
بحر الجواهر في المصطلحات الطبية من العربية واللاتينية واليونانية (1451)
البحر الرائق شرح كنز الدقائق (341، 342)

تحفة الطلاب بشرح تحرير تنقيح اللباب (477)
تحفة الظرف (1083)
تحفة المريد لمقدمة علم التجويد (108)
تحفة شاهدي (1558، 1559، 1560)
تخميس البردة (1151، 1208)
تخميس لامية العجم (1208)
تدبير جديد نامه (1379، 1600، 1601)
التدبيرات الإلهية في إصلاح المملكة الإنسانية (682)
التذكار في أطيب الأذكار (192)
تذكرة الأريب في تفسير الغريب (54)
تذكرة الإعداد ليوم المعاد (718)
تذكرة أولي الألباب والجامع للعجب العجاب (583، 1427، 1428، 1454)
تذكرة داود الأنطاكي (583، 1427، 1428، 1454)
تذكرة السائر (694)
تذكرة الكحالين (1439)
تذكرة المتبحرين في ترجمة سائر العلماء المتأخرين (1304)
تراجم الأعيان من أبناء الزمان (1322)
ترتيب زيبا (91)
ترجمان الأختري (1629)
ترجمة الإمام الأعظم (1247)
ترجمة شيخ الإسلام قطب الأولياء الكرام محيي الدين النووي (1257)
تسلية الحزين بموت البنين (272)
تسهيل السبيل (514)
تشريح الأفلاك (1505)
تشنيف الأسماع بحكم الحركة في الذكر والسماع (471)
تشييد الأركان من ليس في الإمكان أبدع مما كان (633)
التصديقات (1071، 1072، 1073)
التصريح بمضمون التوضيح (747، 748، 749)
تصريف العزي (1131)
تعبير نامة تركي (1604)
تعليق وجيز في تدوين علم الكمون والبروز (712)
تعليقات (394)
تفسير ابن عباس (25)
تفسير أبي السعود (34، 35، 36، 37)
تفسير إنَّ أول بيت (50)
تاريخ ابن أعثم الكندي (1366)
تاريخ آل عثمان (1323، 1324)
تاريخ أمين الدولة (1330)
تاريخ الأولياء (1253)
تاريخ السلطان محمد الفاتح (1375)
تاريخ العلماء (1266)
تاريخ الفرس (1377)
تاريخ بغداد (1332، 1333، 1334)
تاريخ سلطان مراد خان (1373)
تاريخ صبحي أفندي (1392)
تاريخ مواقع مصر (1310)
تأسيس القواعد والأصول وتحصيل الفوائد لذوي الوصول في التصوف (636)
تأليف على حرف التاء (1655)
التبر المسبوك فى ذيل السلوك (1340)
التبر المسبوك في نصيحة الملوك (1354)
التبيان في إعراب القرآن (59، 1683)
تبيين الحقائق شرح كنز الدقائق (348)
التتمة في القراءات الثلاثة الأئمة (115)
تجارب الأمم وتعاقب الهمم (1382)
تجريد العقائد (612)
تحرير الأحكام الشرعية على مذهب الإمامية (417)
تحرير التحبير (982)
تحرير الطرق والروايات في بعض الآيات من طريق طيبة النشر في القراءات العشر (119)
تحرير الكلام في القيام عند ذكر مولد خير الأنام (202)
تحرير المقال (452)
تحفة الإخوان (857)
تحفة الإخوان في الخلف بين الشاطبية والعنوان (104)
تحفة الأريب في الرد على أهل الصليب (705)
تحفة الأسماع والأبصار بما في السيرة المتوكلية من الأخبار (1361)
تحفة الأشراف بكشف غوامض الكشاف ودرر الأصداف في حل عقد الكشاف (70)
تحفة الأنام في الوقف على الهمز لحمزة وهشام (111)
التحفة الجامعة لمفردات الطب النافعة (1456)
تحفة الحريص شرح التلخيص (490)
تحفة الرائض في علم الفرائض (494)

ثمرات الأوراق في المحاضرات (976، 1311)
جامع الآيات في شرح ما وقع في كتاب المثنوى من الآيات والأحاديث والأبيات (1567)
جامع أحكام الصفار (476)
الجامع البهي في دعوة النبي (528)
جامع البيان في تأويل القرآن (39)
جامع التدقيق (1051)
جامع الدرر (462)
الجامع الصغير من حديث البشير النذير (163)
الجامع الكبير (162)
الجامع في الطب (1432، 1433)
جامعة الطرقات في قسمة المحاصات والموزع من التركات (1670)
جراب المجربات وخزانة الأطباء (1455)
جفر (1481)
جمع الجوامع (377)
جمع المناسك ونفع الناسك (489)
جهان نامه (1490)
الجوامع البهية شروح الأربعين النووية (1674)
الجواهر (460)
جواهر تاج الخلافة (1590)
جواهر الحكم وتواريخ الأمم وسير ملوك العرب والعجم (1363)
الجواهر الزكية في حل ألفاظ العشماوية للعشماوي (483)
الجواهر شرح الرجابية (566)
جواهر العلوم المكتوم (1653)
جواهر النصوص في حل كلمات الفصوص (535)
الجواهر النفيسة في شرح الدرة المنيفة (399)
الجواهر والدرر الصغرى من كلام سيدي علي الخواص (720)
الجوهر النضيد في شرح منطق التجريد (1055)
حادي الأظعان النجدية إلى الديار المصرية (1293)
حاشية الأشباه والنظائر (587)
حاشية الأنطاكي (69)
حاشية البرماوي على شرح محمد سبط المارديني على الرحبية (487)
حاشية بهاء الدين العاملي على البيضاوي (64)
حاشية الجرجاني على شرح السعد التفتازاني على العقائد النسفية (642)
حاشية خيالي على شرح العقائد (1098)
تفسير البغوي (43، 44)
تفسير البيضاوي (27، 28، 29، 30، 31، 51)
تفسير الجلالين (32، 33، 533، 539، 594)
تفسير الخازن (38)
تفسير الطبري (39)
تفسير سورة يس (49)
تفسير غريب القرآن (53، 537)
تفسير الفاتحة والبقرة ونصف آل عمران (55)
تفسير فارسي (57)
تفسير ماء الحياة (52)
تفضيل عقد الفوائد بتكميل قيد الشرائد (351، 382)
تقريب النشر في القراءات العشر (88)
تقويم (1608)
تكملة البحر الرائق (444)
تكميل شريعة (1625)
تلخيص البيان في علامات مهدي آخر الزمان (320)
تلخيص الجامع الكبير (454)
تلخيص المفتاح في المعاني والبيان للسكاكي (948، 949، 950، 951، 1131)
تلخيص المفتاح للغزنوي (581)
تلخيصات راغب باشا في الإنشاء (1623)
تمرين الطلاب في صناعة الإعراب (773، 774، 859)
تنبيه الطالب وإرشاد الدارس فيما في دمشق من الجوامع والمدارس (1359)
التنبيه على حدوث التصحيف (125)
التنبيه على مكارم يحيى البرمكي (1388)
تنوير الأبصار وجامع البحار (347)
التنوير في إسقاط التدبير (562، 666، 667، 668، 711)
التهذيب (1036، 1038)
تهذيب الأصول إلى علم الوصول (938، 939، 1031، 1045)
تهذيب اللغة (865)
توجيه اللمع (847)
توضيح ما خفى من ألفاظ الشفا (184)
التوقيف على مهمات التعريف (1408)
تيسير البيان في تفسير القرآن (90)
ثبت محمد بن الطيب المدني للأحاديث المسلسلة (281)
ثمار القلوب في المضاف والمنسوب (867، 979)

حاشية في العقائد (639)
حاشية في علم النحو (879، 895)
حاشية ملا زاده على المطول (938)
حاشية ملا عبد الغفور (1099)
حاشية ملا عبد الله على الخطائي (937)
الحاوي شرح مختصر المزني (465)
الحاوي في علم التداوي (1459)
حجج القرآن (82)
الحجر المكرّم (1544)
حديقة الزوراء في سيرة الوزراء في تاريخ بغداد (1328)
حديقة الملوك (1329)
حرز الأماني ووجه التهاني (92، 93، 94، 95، 96)
الحرز الثمين للحصن الحصين (215)
الحسن الصريح في مائة مليح (1224)
حسن المحاضرة في أخبار مصر والقاهرة (1305، 1306)
الحصن الحصين من كلام سيد المرسلين (214)
حصن القارئ في اختلاف المقارئ (138)
حصول الرفق بأصول الرزق (270)
الحضرة الأنسية في الرحلة القدسية (1258)
الحقيقة والمجاز فى رحلة بلاد الشام ومصر والحجاز (1259)
حل الرموز (554)
حل العرى في أم القرى (1327)
حل مشكلات الألفية (772)
حلبة الكميت (997)
حلة الذهب الإبريز في رحلة بعلبك والبقاع العزيز (1260، 1319)
حلية الأبرار وشعار الأخيار في تلخيص الدعوات والأذكار المستحبة في الليل والنهار (290)
حلية أهل الفضل والكمال باتصال الأسانيد بكمل الرجال (679)
حلية الخاقاني (256)
حمائل (78، 319)
حياة الحيوان (526، 1285، 12886، 1287، 1288، 1289، 1290، 1291)
حياة القلوب (255)
خبايا الزوايا (989)
خريدة العجائب وفريدة الغرائب (515، 1299، 1300)
خزانة الأدب (973)
الخزرجية (1024)
حاشية السعد التفتازاني على شرح العضد على مختصر ابن الحاجب (637)
حاشية السيد على شرح الشمسية للقطب على التصديقات (1096)
حاشية الشيخ الإمام الشربيني (1682)
حاشية شيخ زاده على أنوار التنزيل وأسرار التأويل (62)
حاشية الشيخ عبد المعطي (884)
حاشية الشيخ على الشريفين (1643)
حاشية الكوراني على شرح التفتازاني للعقائد النسفية (638)
حاشية عصام الدين على أنوار التنزيل وأسرار التأويل (63)
حاشية عصام على ملا جامي (883، 887)
حاشية على إرشاد الأذهان (486)
حاشية على الألفية (902)
حاشية على أم البراهين للسنوسي (641)
حاشية على التصديقات (1095)
حاشية على تفسير سورة الأعراف (67)
حاشية على تفسير سورة المنافقون (73)
حاشية على تفسير سورة النبأ (69)
حاشية على التلخيص (965)
حاشية على التهذيب (1039)
حاشية على الجزء الثالث من تلخيص الكشاف (71)
حاشية على الجوهرة (640)
حاشية على الكافية (880، 881، 882)
حاشية على الكشاف (65)
حاشية على المختصر للجرجاني (963، 964)
حاشية على المطول (942، 1037)
حاشية على خطبة الكشاف (66)
حاشية على شرح الأشموني في ألفية ابن مالك (877، 901)
حاشية على شرح الألفية (876)
حاشية على شرح الخلاصة (894)
حاشية على شرح الرسالة الشمسية للقطب التحتاني الرازي (1070)
حاشية على شرح مختصر منتهى السول والأمل في علمي الأصول والجدل لعضد الدين الإيجي (936)
حاشية على شرح المطالع (886)
حاشية على شرح ملا جامي (878)
حاشية على قواعد الإعراب لابن هشام في النحو (888)
حاشية على هداية الحكمة (1516)
حاشية في الاشتقاق (889)

درة الغواص في أوهام الخواص (715)
الدرة الفاخرة في علوم الآخرة (212، 1631)
الدرة الفريدة في شرح العقيدة السنوسية (617)
الدرة المضية في شرح الألفية (761، 789)
الدرة المضية في قراءات الأئمة الثلاثة المرضية (122)
الدرة المضية في معرفة طريقة الصوفية (577)
الدرة المنيفة في السيرة الشريفة (322)
الدرة اليتيمة في آداب الملوك (992)
دستور العمل (1507)
دعاء الجوشن (722)
دعاء كنز العرش (690)
دعوة الفصول (532)
دلائل التحقيق (695)
دلائل الخيرات وشوارق الأنوار بذكر الصلاة على النبي المختار (284)
دلائل النبوة ومعرفة أحوال صاحب الشريعة (237)
دليل الهدى شرح مجيب الندا (846)
دمية القصر وعصرة أهل العصر (1316)
ديوان ابن حجر (1190)
ديوان ابن الحداد (1196)
ديوان ابن الرومي (1183)
ديوان ابن عنين (1194)
ديوان ابن كيوان (1191، 1192)
ديوان ابن المعمار الأديب (1207)
ديوان ابن نباتة (1179)
ديوان أبي تمام (1172، 1173، 1174)
ديوان أبي الطيب المتنبي (1163، 1164، 1165، 1166، 1167، 1168، 1169، 1170)
ديوان أبي العباس عبد الله ابن المعتز (1195)
ديوان أبي العلاء المعري (1158، 1159، 1160)
ديوان أبي فراس (1176)
ديوان الأخطل (1198)
ديوان امرئ القيس (1175)
ديوان الباخرزي (1199)
ديوان البهاء زهير (1177، 1178)
ديوان جوهر النضار (1197)
ديوان الحافظ الشيرازي (1205، 1565، 1566)
ديوان حسان بن ثابت (1204)
خصائص الحشائش (1453)
خطب جمعة (1060)
خطبة [الاثنين؟] (1654)
خطبة الكسوف (1061)
خلاصة الأثر في أعيان القرن الحادي عشر (1292)
خلاصة الأخبار في سيرة النبي المختار (185)
خلاصة الإعراب (780)
الخلاصة الألفية (751، 752، 753، 754، 923)
خلاصة بحر الحقائق (624)
خلاصة تحقيق الظنون في الشروح والمتون (1021)
خلاصة الحساب (1538)
خلاصة الخمسة (1571)
خلاصة الفتاوى (433، 434)
خلاصة المذهب (400)
الخلاصة في معرفة الحديث (189)
خمرة الحان ورنة الألحان شرح رسالة الشيخ أرسلان (684)
الخميس في أحوال أنفس نفيس (1325)
خواص الدمياطية وشرحها (680)
خواص القرآن العظيم (60، 74)
خير البِشَر بخير البشر (248)
الدر المستطاب في موافقات عمر بن الخطاب وأبي بكر وعلي أبي تراب وترجمتهم مع عدة من الأصحاب (265)
الدر المنثور في التفسير بالمأثور (26)
الدر المنظم في مولد النبي المعظم (258)
الدر النثير (1413)
الدر النظيم بعلم الأحكام والتقويم (1635)
الدر النظيم في فضل القرآن العظيم (76)
الدراية في الحديث (210)
الدراية لأحكام الرعاية (473)
درر البحار (422)
درر الكلام في مسائل عبد الله بن سلام لنبينا عليه أفضل الصلاة وأتم السلام (321)
الدرر اللوامع في أصل مقرأ الإمام نافع (135)
الدرر المدروزة شرح الأرجوزة (1005)
الدرر والغرر (331، 544)
درة الآفاق في علم الحروف والأوفاق (1693)
الدرّة السنية في أخبار الدولة العباسية (1360)

رسالة الرازي (1445)
رسالة في آداب البحث (946، 947)
رسالة في الميقات (1501)
رسالة في بيان تصحيح المعتمد (129)
رسالة في شرح الزايرجا (1680)
رسالة في علم التجويد (133)
رسالة في علم النفس (697)
رسالة في علوم الكواكب وانتقال المراتب (1656)
رسالة في معرفة ما يتعلق بجميع أوجه التكبير في القراءات العشر (127، 128، 130، 134)
الرسالة القدرية (642/ب)
الرسالة القدسية بأدلتها البرهانية (625، 626، 660)
الرسالة القشيرية (658، 659)
رسالة للرازي (1084)
رسالة للشيخ الرئيس أبي علي ابن سينا (1448)
رسالة نظم مخارج الحروف (139)
الرسالة النقشبندية (692)
الرسالة الوجيزة (297)
رسائل ابن عقيلة الأثري (304)
رسائل أبي بكر الخوارزمي (1013، 1018)
رسائل أبي العلاء (1056)
رسائل الشيخ محيي الدين ابن العربي (650)
رفع الكساء عن عبارة البيضاوي في سورة النساء (518)
رمز الحقائق في شرح كنز الدقائق (340)
روح القدس في محاسبة النفس (510)
روزنامه (1512، 1513، 1550)
الروض الفائق في المواعظ والرقائق (706)
روضة الأخبار (1344)
روضة الأزهار (1231)
روضة الأزهار في علم الأوفاق (1491)
الروضة البهية في شرح اللمعة الدمشقيَّة (488)
روضة العطر (1641)
روضة العلماء (263)
روضة الفصاحة (977)
روضة القلوب ونزهة المحبوب (1015)
الروضتين في أخبار الدولتين (1342)
الرياض الأنيقة في شرح أسماء خير الخليقة (280)
ديوان الحماسة (1185، 1186)
ديوان الدكالي (1193)
ديوان الدواوين (1187)
ديوان الدواوين وريحانة الرياحين في تجليات الحق المبين (1150)
ديوان الششتري (1157)
ديوان الشهاب أحمد بن الهائم المنصوري (578)
ديوان الصبابة لأهل العشق والكآبة (1180، 1181)
ديوان صفي الدين الحلي (1184)
ديوان عبد الغني النابلسي (1138)
ديوان علي ابن الحسين (1203)
ديوان عمر ابن الفارض (1134، 1135)
ديوان عنوان السعادة (1200)
ديوان الغزل المترجم بلسان المعاني الأدبية عن حضرة الأزل المسمى بخمرة بابل وغناء البلابل (1139، 1140)
ديوان في علم الموسيقى (1233)
ديوان القيراطي (1182)
ديوان كشاجم (1189)
ديوان الكيداني (1206)
ديوان المبرد (1201)
ديوان مجنون ليلى (1156)
ديوان محي الدين ابن العربي (1133، 1152)
ديوان نثر النظم وحل العقد (1188)
ديوان نجديات (1202)
الذخائر الأشرفية في ألغاز الحنفية (371)
ذكر وقوفات القرآن (87)
ذهاب ليل الشكوك في معنى قوله تعالى ﴿إن الملوك﴾ (79)
ذيل تذكرة داود (1429)
الرامزة في علمي العروض والقافية (1024)
ربيع الأبرار ونصوص الأخبار (217)
ربيع الملوك في آداب سلوك الملوك (1618)
رحلة الطالبين (1706)
الرحمة في الطب والحكمة (302)
رد الطاعن لأبي حنيفة (397)
الرد على أبي بكر الخطيب (405)
ردع الراغب عن الجمع في صلاة الرغائب (396)
رسالة أسماء الرواة (234)
رسالة الأدب (983)

سنن الترمذي (162)
السنوسية (605، 607، 608، 734، 737)
سير الأولين (1387)
السير والسلوك الى ملك الملوك (708، 739)
سيرة الأنبياء لعبد العزيز (313)
السيرة الحلبية (179، 180، 181، 182)
سيرة دَلهمه والبطال (1383، 1384، 1385، 1386)
سيرة السلطان جلال الدين الخوارزمي (1374)
سيرة عنترة (1394)
سيرة النبي علية الصلاة والسلام (204)
سيف القضاة على البغاة (455)
السيف المسلول (630)
الشاطبية (92، 93، 94، 95، 96)
الشافية (1109)
شباك المناسخات (1660)
شجرة نسب النبي صلى الله عليه وسلم (241)
شذور الذهب في معرفة كلام العرب (798، 899)
شرح آية الإسراء (80)
شرح إساغوجي (1104، 1105، 1106، 1107)
شرح أسماء الله الحسنى (673، 674، 699)
شرح الأجرومية (911، 912، 913، 914، 915، 916، 917، 919، 920، 922، 929)
شرح الأجرومية للشنواني (919)
شرح الأخستكي (481)
شرح الأربعين حديثاً (198، 199، 200)
شرح الأربعين للنووي (540)
شرح الإرشاد (864)
شرح الأزهرية للشيخ خالد (870، 871، 909)
شرح الإشارات (1048)
شرح الألفاظ اللغوية والمقامات الحريرية (590)
شرح الألفية (758، 759، 760، 762، 763، 764، 765، 766، 767، 768، 770، 771، 779)
شرح ألفية ابن مالك (1666)
شرح الألفية لابن عقيل (755)
شرح أم البراهين (606، 616، 617، 738)
شرح الأندلسية (1029)
شرح الإيجاز في الفرائض للكرماني (496)
رياض أهل الجنة في آثار أهل السنّة (251)
رياض الجنة في آثار أهل السنة (247)
رياض الصالحين من كلام سيد المرسلين (252، 665)
رياض العارفين في مراسلات الاستاذ محمد زين العابدين البكري (1020)
زاد المريد (707)
زايرجا السبتية (1488)
زبد العلوم وصاحب المنطوق والمفهوم (1380)
زبد اللمعة في حل الكواكب السبعة (1687)
زبدة البيان (124)
زبدة الوصول إلى علم الأصول (671)
زهر الآداب وثمر الألباب (1007)
زهر الربيع في شواهد البديع (1689)
الزواجر (205)
زي الفارسي (1572)
زيج ابن الشاطر (1684)
زيج الدر اليتيم (1691)
الزيج في الميقات (1699)
السادات للشيخ عنوان (560)
السامي في لغة الأسامي (1411، 1412)
سانحات دمى القصر في مطارحات بني العصر (1317)
السبعيات في عد البريات (545)
السخاوية (1551)
سدرة المنتهى (229)
سراج الملوك (1351)
السِّراج المنير (856)
السراج المنير في الإعانة على معرفة بعض معاني كلام ربنا الحكيم الخبير (58)
سرح العيون في شرح رسالة ابن زيدون (980)
سفينة النجاة (1012)
سلافة العصر في محاسن أهل العصر (1294)
سلك اللآلي في شرح مثلث أبي حامد الغزالي (1703)
سلمان الفارسي (1568)
سلوان المصاب بفرقة الأحباب (292)
سلوان المطاع في عدوان الاتباع (654، 1318)
سلوة الكئيب بوفاة الحبيب (259)
السمرقندية (1059)

شرح الشذور (800، 801)
شرح شذور الذهب في معرفة كلام العرب (893)
شرح الشفا للقاضي عياض (588)
شرح الشمسية في المنطق (1063، 1064، 1065، 1066، 1067، 1068، 1088)
شرح الشمسية في النحو (842)
شرح الشواهد الكبير (781، 782، 785، 786)
شرح طوالع الأنوار (1040)
شرح العقائد للنيسابوري (609)
شرح العقائد النسفية (611، 614)
شرح العزي (1113)
شرح عقيدة الأجهوري (613، 615)
شرح على مختصر السنوسي (1091، 1100)
شرح العوامل البركوي (874)
شرح الفتح القدسي (1705)
شرح فصوص الحكم (642/ج، 648، 649)
شرح القاموس المحيط للمناوي (1403، 1404)
شرح قصائد محي الدين ابن العربي (1153)
شرح قصيدة الشيخ أبي الفتح (1228)
شرح القصيدة المقرّية (618، 642/أ)
شرح قصيدة المنفرجة (1155)
شرح قطر الندى (802، 803، 804، 805، 806، 807، 808، 809، 810)
شرح القواعد (790، 797، 1647)
شرح قواعد الأحكام (479)
شرح الكافية (816، 817، 818، 819، 820، 821، 822، 823، 825، 826، 827، 828، 1417)
شرح الكبائر (478)
شرح الكلام (843)
شرح كلستان (1562، 1563)
شرح كنز الدقائق لمنلا مسكين (338، 339)
شرح لامية العجم (12092، 1210، 1211، 1212)
شرح اللباب في علم الإعراب (775، 776، 777، 788)
شرح مجمع البحرين (350)
شرح المحيا (220)
شرح مختصر الجامع الصحيح لابن أبي جمرة (151)
شرح المختصر في الطب (1461)
شرح بانت سعاد (1143، 1144، 1145، 1146)
شرح بديعية تقديم أبي بكر (1162)
شرح البراهين (1054)
شرح البسملة والحمدلة (68)
شرح بهجة النفوس وعنايتها بمعرفة ما لها وما عليها لابن أبي جمرة (151)
شرح تائية الصفدي (1214)
شرح تحفة الشاهدي (1574)
شرح تسهيل الفوائد وتكميل المقاصد لابن مالك (750)
شرح تعريف التورية (1083)
شرح التلخيص (952، 953)
شرح التهذيب (1044)
شرح التوضيح (466)
شرح الجامع الصغير (438)
شرح الجزرية (168)
شرح جمع الجوامع للعيني (378، 499)
شرح جوهرة التوحيد (600، 602، 603)
شرح حزب النووي (730)
شرح الحكم العطائية (547، 675)
شرح الخزرجية (1025، 1026)
شرح خلاصة الحساب (1537، 1539، 1541)
شرح دلائل الخيرات للجزولي (187، 188، 190، 213)
شرح الدور الأعلى للداموني (725، 731، 732)
شرح ديوان أبي الطيب المتنبي (1171)
شرح ديوان عمر ابن الفارض (1136، 1137)
شرح ديوان كعب بن زهير (1154)
شرح الرحبية (504)
شرح رسالة ابن عبدون (1341)
شرح رسالة الاستعارة لعصام الأسفراييني (1058)
شرح الرسالة الرسلانية (684)
شرح الرسالة الشناوية (686)
شرح الرسالة العضدية (1074، 1075، 1076)
شرح رسالة في آداب البحث (945)
شرح الستين مسألة (450، 506)
شرح الشاطبية (97، 98، 99، 100، 101)
شرح الشافية (1110، 1111،)
شرح الشافية للجاربردي (1120)

شمس المعارف ولطائف العوارف في علم الحروف والخواص (1472، 1552، 1675)
الشمسية (1062، 1069)
شمسية أفلاطون (1487)
الشمعة المُضيَّة بنشر قراءات السبعة المرضيَّة (114)
شموس الأنوار وكنوز الأسرار (1644)
الشموس المضيئة (1489)
شواهد الخرائد في مختصر الشواهد (783، 924)
شواهد القَطر (787)
الصحاح في اللغة (517، 527، 1405، 1406)
الصحف الإلهية (619)
صحيح البخاري (141، 142، 143، 520)
صحيح مسلم (152، 153)
صدر الشريعة (357)
صفات النبي صلى الله عليه وسلم (529)
صفة الصفوة (511)
صفحة آل البيت (231)
صنعة الإعراب (855)
الصواعق المحرقة في الرد على أهل البدع والضلال والزندقة (177، 183)
الصيد والذبائح (389)
صيغ صلوات على النبي صلى الله عليه وسلم (254)
ضوء المصباح (834، 862)
ضوء المصباح في شرح نور الإيضاح (361)
الضياء الشمسي على الفتح القدسي أو شرح ورد السحر (728)
طالع المولود على قواعد الفرس (1533)
طب علم الأبدان (1467)
طبقات التميمي (1353)
طبقات الشافعية الكبرى (1265)
طرائف الطُّرَف (1226)
طرح المدر لحل اللآلئ والدرر (1019)
الطريقة المحمدية والسيرة الأحمدية (238، 282، 1591، 1592، 1593، 1594، 1595)
طهارة القلوب والخضوع لعلام الغيوب (696)
الطوالع (851)
طوالع الأنوار (1042)
طولع بالتركي لسنة 1189 (1549)
شرح المختصر للسعد التفتازاني (960، 961)
شرح مختصر منتهى السول والأمل لابن الحاجب (497)
شرح المراح (1114)
شرح المصباح (835، 966)
شرح المطول (934)
شرح المعلقات (1238)
شرح المقاصد (1115، 1116، 1117)
شرح المقامات للشيخ الزيني (1634)
شرح المقدمة الآجرومية (928، 1648)
شرح مقدمة أبي الليث السمرقندي (391)
شرح المقدمة الأزهرية في علم العربية (866)
شرح مقصود من الصرف (1638)
شرح الملخص في علم الهيئة (1523)
شرح الملخص للجغميني في علم الهيئة (1524)
شرح المنار (943، 1034)
شرح المنظومة الوهبانية (351، 382)
شرح المنهاج (387، 388)
شرح منية المصلي (364، 365، 367، 368، 370، 524)
شرح المواقف (1032، 1044)
شرح النقاية (464)
شرح الهداية (334، 335، 343، 541)
شرح الورقات (853)
شرح الوسيط (863)
شرح الوصية للإمام الأعظم (484)
شرح نتيجة ابن الحاجب (837)
شرح نخبة الفكر (209)
شرح نظم الاستعارة (1057)
شرح نهج البلاغة (316)
شرعة الإسلام (174، 376)
شروط الصلاة (459، 461، 1585، 1586، 1587)
الشفا بتعريف حقوق المصطفى (155، 156، 157، 158، 159، 160)
الشفا في بديع الاكتفا (1004)
الشفا لابن سينا (1077)
شمائل الترمذي (161)
الشمائل النبوية والخصال المصطفوية (161)
شمس الآفاق في علم الحروف والأوفاق (1474)
شمس المعارف الصغرى (1473)

طيب الكلام بفوائد السلام (293)
عجالة الإملاء المتيسرة من التذنيب على ما وقع للحافظ المنذري من الوهم في كتاب الترغيب والترهيب (221)
عجالة خاصة الأحباب في خلاصة مناقب الآل والأصحاب (268)
عجائب المخلوقات وغرائب الموجودات (1298)
عجائب المقدور في نوائب تيمور (1321)
عرائس الأفكار في مدائح المختار (1234)
عروس الأفراح في شرح تلخيص المفتاح (954)
العشرة الكاملة في عشرة مسائل من أصول الفقه (424)
عقد [القراش؟] (1368)
عقد الدرر واللآلي في فضائل الشهور والأيام والليالي (296، 308)
العقد والتوحيد كتاب الكافي (644)
عقدة لسان البياني (564)
العقود اللؤلؤية في طريق السادة المولوية (1676)
العقيدة الصغرى (605، 607، 608، 734، 737)
عقيلة أتراب القصائد في أسنى المقاصد (261)
علم الأدوار في أحكام النجوم (1508، 1509)
على الشريعة (1616)
عمدة العرفان في وجوه القرآن (121)
عنقاء مغرب في معرفة ختم الأولياء وشمس المغرب (513، 740)
عنوان التحقيق (627)
عنوان الشرف الوافي في الفقه والنحو والتاريخ والعروض والقوافي (372، 373، 374، 501)
عنوان المرقصات والمطربات (589)
العنوان في القراءات السبع (116)
العهود الكبيرة (536، 717)
العوامل الجديدة (873)
العوامل المائة (872، 875)
عين العلم وزين الحلم في اختصار إحياء العلوم للغزالي (250، 654)
عيون أخبار الأعيان ممن مضى في سالف العصور والأزمان (1350)
غاية الإرشاد إلى معرفة أحكام الحيوان والنبات والجماد (1452)
غاية الرشاد في أحاديث البلاد (552)
غاية المراد في شرح نكت الإرشاد (456)
الغرر البهية في شرح البهجة الوردية (475)
غرر الخصائص الواضحة وعرر النقائص الفاضحة (1364)
غرر الدلائل والآيات (993)
غرر الفوائد ودرر القلائد (56)
غرر المعاني والنكت شرح المقامات (1006)
الغرف العلية في تراجم متأخري الحنفية (1263)
غريب الفنون فلك (1494)
غزوات سيد بطال غازي (1378)
غنية المتملي في شرح منية المصلي (366)
غنية المحتاج لأدلة الاختلاج (591)
غنية المرام في معرفة الرمي بالسهام (1446)
الغواص على المنافع والخواص (1447)
فاكهة الخلفاء ومفاكهة الظرفاء (1297)
فتاوى البدر الرشيد (436)
الفتاوى الحامدية (1646)
الفتاوى المحمدية في فقه الحنفية (596)
فتاوى شيخ الإسلام (561)
فتاوى علي أفندي (435)
الفتاوى للشيخ ابن نجم الدين المصري (568)
فتح الباري بشرح صحيح البخاري (147، 148، 149، 150)
فتح الجواد بشرح منظومة ابن العماد للأقفهسي (428)
الفتح الرباني والفيض الرحماني (683)
فتح الرحمن (1701)
الفتح القدسي والكشف الأنسي والمنهج القريب إلى لقاء الحبيب (235)
الفتح المبين لشرح الأربعين (558)
فتح الملك المجيد المؤلَّف لنفع العبيد وقمع كلِّ جبارٍ عنيد (1692)
فتح منزل المثاني بشرح أقصى الأماني في علم البيان والبديع والمعاني (990)
الفتح الوهبي في شرح تاريخ أبي النصر العتبي (1352)
الفتحية في الأعمال الجيبية (1517)
فتوحات الشام (1331)
الفتوحات المكية في الأسرار المالكية (651، 652، 653)
فرائد القلائد في مختصر شرح الشواهد (783، 924)
الفرائض والوصايا (458)
الفرج (289)
الفرق الضالة والناجية (703)
الفرق المؤذن بالطرب في الفرق بين العجم والعرب (1355)
فضائل آل البيت (226)
فضائل القرآن العظيم (77)
فضائل يوم الجمعة وتفسير آيات (550)

فضل الجلد عند فقد الولد (278)
فضل الكلاب على كثير ممن لبس الثياب (310)
الفقه الأكبر (709)
فقه حنفي (439، 440، 441، 442، 443، 445، 463)
فقه اللغة (1416)
فلاحة البساتين (1463)
الفلكيات (1503، 1504)
فهرسة النديم (998)
الفوائح المسكية في الفواتح المكية (1664)
فوائد الآيات (286)
الفوائد الإلهية (840)
فوائد حسن الكرماني (838)
الفوائد السمية في شرح الفرائد السنية (519)
فوائد الصلوة على النبي صلى الله عليه وسلم (273)
الفوائد الضيائية بحل مشكلات الشافية (824، 829، 830، 831)
الفوائد الفنارية على الرسالة الأثيرية (1093)
الفوائد في الصلة والعوائد (249، 274)
فوائد كلامية منطقية (1080)
الفوائد المرضية في شرح القصيدة اللامية (1649)
الفوائد المسعدية في حل المقدمة الجزرية (109)
الفوز العظيم (228)
في بيان أحكام الأوقاف والصدقات (408)
القاموس المحيط والقابوس الوسيط الجامع لما ذهب من كلام العرب شماطيط (1396، 1397، 1398، 1399، 1400، 1401، 1402)
القانون في الطب (1423، 1424، 1425، 1426، 1444)
قانون نامه (1617)
قبس الأنوار (1534)
قراءة حفص من طريق الشاطبية (102)
قرانات الكواكب في البروج الاثني عشر وما يلحق بذلك (1506)
قرة العين في الفتح والإمالة بين اللفظين (118)
قصيدة بانت سعاد (1141، 1142)
قصيدة البردة (1141، 1142)
القصيدة الرائية (261)
قصيدة في بشارة أمته (1597)
القصيدة الهمزية (261، 1149)
قطع [الشراع/ الشرائح؟] من اللغة السريانية إلى الألفاظ العربية (1679)
قلادة الجواهرية (854)
قلائد الجمان (1312)
قلائد العقيان في محاسن الأعيان (986)
قلمية مولانا محمد أفندي شيخ الحرم (580)
قمع النفوس ورقية المأيوس (702)
قواعد الأحكام في معرفة الحلال والحرام (404)
قواعد الإيمان (1579)
القواعد البقرية (123)
قواعد التوحيد (1645)
قواعد الحكام (410)
القواعد المقررة والفوائد المحررة (123)
قوانين حكم الإشراق الى كل الصوفية بجميع الآفاق (681)
القول الجلي في ذكر العلي (704)
القول السديد (310)
القول المحبوب فيما تغفر به الذنوب (542)
الكافي الشاف من تخريج أحاديث الكشاف (216)
كافية ابن الحاجب (812، 813، 814، 815)
الكافية الشافية (811)
الكامل بالتاريخ (1326)
الكبريت الأحمر في علوم الشيخ الأكبر (672)
كتاب ابن فرشتا (1613)
كتاب أحاديث شريفة وإجازات صريحة (239)
كتاب أدعية وأذكار (312)
كتاب أقلام مختلفة (1482)
كتاب الأكر (1047)
كتاب بستان (1564)
كتاب تعلم الفروسية (246)
كتاب الخواص (1479)
كتاب الروح (242، 551، 573)
كتاب زيج (1496)
كتاب العظمة (245)
كتاب العيون (1122)
كتاب في أسرار الحروف (1599)
كتاب في بيان الأحاديث والخواص (227)
كتاب في الحيل (1434، 1436، 1437، 1438)
كتاب في علم الطب لطهماز العجم (1458)
كتاب في علم المعاني (968، 970، 971)

لطائف الإشارات لفنون العبارات في القراءات الأربع عشرة (86)
لطائف المعارف فيما لمواسم العام من الوظائف (530)
لطائف المنن والأخلاق في بيان وجوب التحدث بنعمة الله على الإطلاق (656)
لغة نعمة الله (1569)
لقط المرجان في أخبار الجان (1347)
اللمحة العفيفية في الطب (1466)
اللمع في أصول الفقه (969)
اللمعة الشمسية على التحفة القدسية (1677)
اللمعة النورانية شرح الشجرة النعمانية (1480)
لواقح الأنوار في طبقات الأخيار (1261، 1262، 1264)
لواقح الأنوار القدسية في بيان العهود المحمدية (536، 717)
لواقح الأنوار القدسية في مناقب العلماء والصوفية (1685)
لوامع الأسرار في شرح مطالع الأنوار (1049، 1053)
لوامع النظر في تحقيق معاني المختصر (1043)
اللؤلؤ المكنون في جمع الأوجه من: سورة الكوثر إلى قوله سبحانه وتعالى: ﴿ وأولئك هم المفلحون ﴾ (120)
اللؤلؤ النظيم في روم التعلم والتعليم (984)
ما يُكتب مقصوراً وممدوداً (995)
مأخذ الخلاف من الشاطبية (103)
مبارق الأزهار في شرح مشارق الأنوار (173)
مباعث الارتحال إلى شد الرحال (1268)
متن الأربعين حديثاً (164، 165، 166، 167، 168، 169)
متن الزبد (449، 450)
متن الستين مسألة (505)
متن العشماوية على مذهب سيدنا مالك بن أنس (508)
المثنوي المعنوي (1553، 1554، 1555، 1556، 1557، 1596)
المجالس الشامية في المواعظ الرومية (225)
مجمع البحرين وملتقى النهرين (349)
مجمع البيان لعلوم القرآن (40، 41، 42، 72)
مجمع الجواهر (1609)
مجموع حواشي لابن عبد البر (896)
مجموع في علم النحو (897)
مجموع اللطائف (1615)
مجموعة أدعية وأوراد (721، 729)
مجموعة في الأدب (974، 975)
مجيب الندى إلى شرح قطر الندى (803)
كتاب في مدح النبي صلى الله عليه وسلم (267)
كتاب في النحو للسيد علي (899)
كتاب قرعة (1485)
كتاب اللطف (244)
كتاب اللغة (522)
كتاب المجمعة (1235)
كتاب الملحمة (1498، 1502)
كتاب المهرجان (294)
كتاب نحو لأبي حيان وهو شرح الملحة (891)
كتاب نوع من الأحاديث (232)
كتاب الهيئة المسمى بالنيشابوري (1514)
الكسب (393)
كسوفات الأدلاء في الكسوفات (1681)
الكشاف عن حقائق التنزيل وعيون الأقاويل في وجوه التأويل (45، 46، 47)
كشف الأسرار (305، 1358)
كشف الأسرار عما خفي عن الأفكار (567)
كشف الحجاب والران عن وجه أسئلة الجان (663، 664)
كشف الغيوم (585)
الكشف في علم الحروف (1486)
الكشف والبيان (647)
الكشف والتبيين عن غرور الخلق أجمعين (646)
الكناية والتعريض (1225)
كنز الادخار (269)
كنز الأسرار (262)
كنز الدقائق (336، 337)
كنز الذهب (1348)
كنوز الحقائق في حديث خير الخلائق (509)
الكواكب الدراري في شرح صحيح البخاري (154)
كيمياء السعادة (288)
اللآلئ السنية في شرح الآجرومية (921)
لامية العجم (1213)
لب اللباب في تحرير الأنساب (264)
لب اللباب في علم الإعراب (778، 1001)
لباب التأويل في معاني التنزيل (38)
لباب النقول في أسباب النزول (525)
لسان العرب (1420)

مستخلص الحقائق في شرح كنز الدقائق (575، 1637)
المستصفى (480)
المستظرف من أخبار الجواري (1269، 1270، 1271، 1272)
المسلك المتقسط في المنسك المتوسط (411، 412، 413، 414)
مسند أبي نعيم (206)
مُسيّر التاريخ (1343)
مشارق الأنوار القدسية في بيان العهود المحمدية (536، 717)
المشاهد القدسية (687)
المشترك وضعاً والمفترق صقعاً (999)
مشتهى العقول في منتهى النقول (271)
مشكل الصحيحين وكشف النقاب عما روى الشيخان للأصحاب (283)
مصابيح الجامع (172)
مصابيح السنة (172)
مصارع المصارع (1528)
المصباح في النحو (832، 833، 834)
المصباح في علم المفتاح في الكيمياء (1542، 1546، 1547)
مصحف الكشف (1022)
مصطلحات القوم (713)
مصنفات ابن هشام (849)
المضاعف من اللغة (1410)
مطالع الأنظار في شرح طوالع الأنوار (1052)
مطالع المسرات بجلاء دلائل الخيرات (187، 188، 190، 213)
المطلب التام السوي على حزب الإمام النووي (730)
المطلب الروي على حزب الإمام النووي (730)
مطلع الفوائد (988)
مطلع النيرين في الحديث (266)
المطول (930، 931، 932، 933)
معارج النبوة في مدارج الفتوة (277)
معالجات الخيل (1435)
معالم التنزيل (43، 44، 521)
معاني الأخلاق (981)
معاني أسماء الله الحسنى (700)
المعاونة والمظاهرة (628)
المعجزات الباهرة والكمالات الظاهرة (223)
معراج النبي صلى الله عليه وسلم (328، 329، 1577، 1630)
المعرب على حروف المعجم (1415)
محاسن الشام (579)
محاسن العصر (1220)
محاضرة الأوائل ومسامرة الأواخر (719)
المحاكمات في شرح الإشارات (1078)
محيي الأموات (1612)
المختار (380، 430)
مختار الصحاح (1407)
المختار على فضائل الأعمال (381)
مختار قلائد العقيم (1016)
المختار للقنوي (559)
مختصر بالطب النبوي (1636)
مختصر البخاري (168)
مختصر السنوسية (735)
مختصر عنوان الأدلة للأئمة الأربعة (467)
مختصر غنية المتملي في شرح منية المصلي (369)
المختصر في الأحكام (472)
مختصر في إعراب بعض سور من القرآن العظيم (75)
مختصر القدوري (359، 360)
مختصر المرشد في الوقف والابتداء (113)
مختصر المعاني والبيان (955، 956، 957، 958، 959، 972)
مختصر المكاتبات البديعة (1003)
مدارك الأحكام في شرح شرائع الإسلام (482)
المدخل في أحكام النجوم (1659)
مراتب العلماء العاملين المسمى بإرشاد الطالبين (1267)
مراتع الغزلان في وصف الحسان من الغلمان (1219)
مراسلات أبي العلاء (1056)
مراصد المطالع الطالع في تناسب المطالع والمقاطع (291)
المرج النضر والأرج العطر (996)
المرشد شرح الإرشاد (793)
المرصع في الكنايات والإضافات (1017)
المرقص والمطرب في أخبار أهل المغرب (589)
مزج الصلاة (1694)
المسالك (498)
مسالك الحنفا إلى مشارع الصلاة على النبي المصطفى (572)
مسائل الراهب والرهبان (323)
المسائل اللطيفة في الخلاف بين الشافعي وأبي حنيفة (427)
مسائل عبد الله بن سلام مع النبي صلى الله عليه وسلم (321)

من الروض الأنف (276)
مناسك الحج على مذهب الإمام الأعظم أبي حنيفة (507)
منافع القرآن (1702)
مناقب أبي أيوب الأنصاري (1255)
مناقب الإمام الأعظم (1248)
مناقب الإمام الشافعي (1249)
مناقب الأئمة (1254)
مناقب الأئمة الأخيار المسمى بتحفة الأبرار (1252)
مناقب عبد القادر الكيلاني (1250، 1589)
المناهج الكافية في شرح الشافية (1119)
منتخب في علم اللغة (1422)
منتهى العقول في منتهى النقول (271)
منتهى المطلب في تحقيق المذهب (502)
المنجم في المعجم (224)
المنجيات السبع (698)
المنح المكية في شرح الهمزية (218، 219)
المنحة البقاعية بشرح التحفة القدسية (493)
منحة السلوك في شرح تحفة الملوك (1696)
المنخول من تعليقات الأصول (469)
منطق الطير (1390)
المنقذ من الضلالة على شرح عقيدة الرسالة (620، 629)
المنهج الحنيف في معنى اسمه تعالى اللطيف و ما قيل فيه من الخواص و التصريف (691)
منهاج الطالبين وعمدة المفتين (383، 384، 385، 386، 401)
منهج الطلاب (1667)
منهاج العابد المتقي ومعراج السالك المرتقي (556)
منهاج العابدين إلى الجنة (677)
منهاج الوصول إلى علم الأصول (967، 1033)
منهاج اليقين (1046)
منية المصلي وغنية المبتدي (362، 363)
المهذب (423)
المهمات (415، 416)
الموارد الإلهية (710)
موازين الرجال القاصرين عن حال المشائخ (662)
موازين القاصرين في معرفة الأولياء أو إرشاد السالكين (662)
المواعظ والاعتبار في ذكر الخطط والآثار (1308، 1309)
مواقع النجوم للشيخ الأكبر (1493)
معرب العوامل الجديدة للبركوي (869)
المعرب في النحو (848)
معرفة الأدلاء في معرفة أصول التواريخ المستعملة (1695)
معين الحكام فيما تردد بين الخصمين من الأحكام (468)
المغني شرح الموجز في الطب (1430)
مغني الطبيب وعمدة الأريب (1431)
المغني في أصول الفقه (379)
مغني اللبيب عن كتب الأعاريب (741، 742، 743، 744، 745، 746)
مغني المستفتي عن سؤال المفتي (1646)
مفاتيح الكنوز (693)
مفتاح الفلاح (623)
المفتاح في الصرف (1112)
مفردات القرآن (53، 537)
المقاصد (1050)
المقاصد السنيَّة بشرح السراجيَّة للحنفية (491)
المقاصد النحوية (781، 782، 783، 786)
المقالات المهذبة (1002)
مقامات الخواص (657)
مقدمة أبي الليث السمرقندي (390)
المقدمة الأجرومية (909، 926، 927)
المقدمة الجزرية (105، 106، 107، 122، 140)
مقدمة الغزنوي (420، 453، 538)
مقدمة في أحكام التجويد (117)
مقدمة في علم الكيمياء (1545)
مقدمة في الكلام على البسملة والحمدلة (68)
مقدمة في فن العروض (1027)
مقدمة في نزول سيدنا عيسى عليه الصلاة والسلام (327)
مقدمة في وقف حمزة وهشام (111)
المقصد لتلخيص مافي المرشد (113)
المقصد الوافي شرح الكافي في علمى العروض والقوافي (1030)
مقصورة الغزي (1240)
ملتقط تهذيب اللغة (940)
ملتقى الأبحر (344، 345، 346، 553)
ملحة الإعراب (868)
ملخص في الهئية البسيطة (1525، 1527، 1531)
الملل والنحل (631، 632)
الملمع شرح النعت المرصع بالمجنس المسجع (726)

النقاية (1083)
نهاية الأرب في معرفة قبائل العرب (1337، 1338)
نهاية المحتاج إلى شرح المنهاج (418)
النهاية في غريب الحديث (178، 1418)
نهج البلاغة (314، 315، 317)
النهي عن ارتكاب المحارم (431)
نوادر الفلاسفة (1529)
نوحة المشتاق (1611)
نور الإيضاح ونجاة الأرواح (355، 356، 358)
نور العين وعين النور (701)
النور الوهاج في الكلام على الإسراء والمعراج (298)
الهداية (332، 333)
الهداية روحاني (1475)
هداية المريد إلى جوهرة التوحيد (603)
هداية مجيب الندا إلى شرح قطر الندى (885)
هز القحوف بشرح قصيدة أبي شادوف (1395)
الهفوات النادرة من المغفلين الملحوظين والسقطات البادرة من المغفلين المحظوظين (1008)
همايون نامه (1391)
الوافي في الفقه على مذهب الإمام الأعظم أبي حنيفة النعمان (403)
الوجوه والنظائر في القرآن (492)
الوجيز (1414)
ورد السَّحَر (235، 727)
ورد الشيخ عبد الغني النابلسي (723)
وِرد الصبح شيخ السبكي (565)
الوسائل إلى معرفة الأوائل (287)
الوسيط شرح المهذب (437)
الوصايا الأكبرية (688)
الوصف الذميم في فعل اللئيم (310)
الوصلة إلى الحبيب في وصف الطيبات والطيب (1441)
وصية الإمام الأعظم لأبي يوسف (500)
وصية نامه (1614)
وصية يزيد بن الحكم (295)
الوعظ والنصيحة (1632)
وفيات الأعيان وأنباء أبناء الزمان (1277، 1278، 1279، 1280، 1281، 1282، 1283، 1284، 1345)
مواليد الرجال والنساء (555)
المواهب اللدنية بالمنح المحمدية (170، 171، 261)
الموجز لابن النفيس (1462)
مورد اللطافة فيمن ولي السلطنة والخلافة (1313)
موصل الطلاب إلى قواعد الإعراب (795، 796)
موقد الأذهان وموقظ الوسنان (844، 925)
مولد شريف (201، 203)
مولد النبي صلى الله عليه وسلم (318، 326)
الميزان الكبرى (375)
نتائج الأفكار في شرح الإظهار (841)
نتائج الألمعية في شرح الكافيه البديعية (991)
نتيجة أحكام الميقات (1499، 1510)
نتيجة الأفكار في أعمال الليل والنهار (1697)
نخبة الفكر في مصطلح أهل الأثر (1673)
نزهة الأبصار في الحديث (275)
نزهة الأنام في محاسن الشام (1314، 1315)
النزهة السنية في أخبار الخلفاء والملوك المصرية (1349)
النزهة الفكرية (714)
نزهة القلوب تفسير القرآن (53، 537)
نزهة المشتاق (253)
نزهة النظر في توضيح نخبة الفكر في مصطلح أهل الأثر (209)
نزهة النواظر في روض المناظر (1339)
النزهة الوجيزة (1009)
نسيم الصبا (1023)
النشر في القراءات العشر (89)
نصب الراية لأحاديث الهداية (470)
النظام الغريب (1409)
نظم التهذيب (1035)
نظم العقيدة (736)
نفائس العرائس ونزهه العيون والمجالس (1320)
نفح الطيب من غصن الأندلس الرطيب (1301، 1302، 1307)
النفحات السنية (240)
نفحات العوارف (257)
النفحة السنية (325)
نفحة القبول في مدحة الرسول (1150)
نفحة المجلوب من ثمار القلوب في المضاف والمنسوب (1356)
نفخة الصور ونفحة الزهور شرح نظم قبضة النور (548)

يتيمة الدهر في محاسن أهل العصر (1295، 1296، 1303)
يميني في تاريخ يمين الدولة محمود بن سبكتكين (1346)
اليواقيت والجواهر في بيان عقائد الأكابر (634، 635)
وقاية الرواية في مسائل الهداية (353)
وقف الملك الأشرف بالقاهرة (1372)
وقفية الشيخ السيد محمود بن الشيخ السيد محمد النقشبندي (503)

List of Identified al-Jazzār Manuscripts and Their Current Location

This list is also available at the Research Data Repository of Universität Hamburg where the al-Jazzār Library Project will keep updating it (https://doi.org/10.25592/uhhfdm.14178).

No.	Place	Library	Class mark	Title	Author	Inventory no.	Seal	Statement[1]
1	Acre	al-Jazzār Mosque	MS 1 EAP399/1/52	جمع الجوامع، ج3	السيوطي	377?	lost	
2	Acre	al-Jazzār Mosque	MS 2 EAP399/1/27	جمع الجوامع، ج4	السيوطي	377?	lost[2]	
3	Acre	al-Jazzār Mosque	MS 6 EAP399/1/46	الثاني من إعراب القرآن	ابن النحاس	61?	circular	1196
4	Acre	al-Jazzār Mosque	MS 9[3] not EAP[4]	البحر الرائق شرح الكنز، ج3	ابن نجيم	342		
5	Acre	al-Jazzār Mosque	MS 21 EAP399/1/3	المهمات في شرح الرافعي والروضة	الإسنوي	JnIB[5]	oval	1196
6	Acre	al-Jazzār Mosque	MS 25 not EAP	الكامل في اللغة	المبرد	JnIB		
7	Acre	al-Jazzār Mosque	MS 33 not EAP	مسالك الأفهام إلى تنقيح شرائع الإسلام	زين الدين العاملي	JnIB		
8	Acre	al-Jazzār Mosque	MS 34 EAP399/1/2	معرب في النحو	ابن عبد الله الجزائري	848		1197
9	Acre	al-Jazzār Mosque	MS 37 EAP399/1/14	الوسيلة في الحساب	أحمد ابن الهائم	JnIB	circular	
10	Acre	al-Jazzār Mosque	MS 40/1 EAP399/1/34	شرح الشافية	الجاربردي	1110	oval	1196
11	Acre	al-Jazzār Mosque	MS 47 EAP399/1/42	خالص التلخيص	الشهرزوري	JnIB		
12	Acre	al-Jazzār Mosque	MS 51 EAP399/1/30	شرح الألفية (احتمال)	ابن الناظم	761?		
13	Acre	al-Jazzār Mosque	MS 64 not EAP	حاشية على الألفية	محمد العثماني	902?		

1 Hijrī year.
2 'Lost': explicit statement in the manuscript that the seal was lost when the manuscript was rebound.
3 Class marks in the Jazzār Mosque Library according to ʿAṭāʾ Allāh, *Fihris ʿAkkā*, 1983.
4 EAP: British Library, Endangered Archives Project, https://eap.bl.uk/collection/EAP399-1 (accessed 2 January 2023).
5 JnIB: al-Jazzār non-inventory book, that is, a book that clearly belonged to the Jazzār library, but is not mentioned in 1221/1806 inventory (see Chapter 7).

(*cont.*)

No.	Place	Library	Class mark	Title	Author	Inventory no.	Seal	Statement
14	Acre	al-Jazzār Mosque	MS 67 EAP399/1/45	مختصر تنبيه الأنام	عبد الجليل المرادي	JnIB	lost	
15	Beirut	American University	MS 920.05 I65bA	البيان والتوضيح	احمد العراقي	193		
16	Beirut	Université Saint-Joseph	HMML[6] no. USJ200214	الخلاصة في معرفة الحديث	الحسين الطيبي	189	circular	1197
17	Beirut	Zuhayr al-Shāwīsh Library		ترجمة شيخ الإسلام	السخاوي	1257	circular	
18	Berlin	Staatsbibliothek	Landberg 9	الطبقات السنية	تقي الدين التميمي	1353	circular	1197
19	Cairo	al-Azhar	MS 22783	ديوان المتنبي	أبو الطيب المتنبي	1163	oval	1197
20	Cairo	al-Azhar	MS 83318	مجموع رسائل	السيوطي	311	circular	1197
21	Cairo	al-Azhar	MS 85307	ترتيب زيبا	الواردداري	91		
22	Cairo	al-Azhar	MS 91135	زبدة الأصول	بهاء الدين العاملي	JnIB	circular	1197
23	Cairo	Dār al-kutub	6016h	التذييل والتكميل ، ج3، 4	أبو حيان الأندلسي	750	circular	1196
24	Cairo	Dār al-kutub	Taymur, Muṣṭalaḥ al-ḥadīth 97	مجموع إجازات			oval	1199
25	Cairo	Ministry of Islamic Endowments	MS 209/ 2398	وقف الملك الأشرف		1372	illeg.	
26	Cairo	Ministry of Islamic Endowments	MS 3018	فوائد و تعليقات على سورة النبأ من تفسير البيضاوي	مصطفى بن حسن الإنطاكي	69	oval	
27	Cairo	Ministry of Islamic Endowments	MS 4490	شرح الألفية	المكودي	759–770?[7]	oval	1197
28	Damascus	al-Majmaʿ al-ʾilmī	MS 44	حاشية السامسوني	السامسوني	JnIB	oval	1197
29	Damascus	National al-Asad Library	MS 219	وقاية الرواية	برهان الشريعة	353		
30	Damascus	National al-Asad Library	MS 11008					

6 HMML: Hill Museum and Manuscript Library.
7 Likely candidates are 759, 760, 763, 765, 766, 768 and 770.

(*cont.*)

No.	Place	Library	Class mark	Title	Author	Inventory no.	Seal	Statement
31	Damascus	National al-Asad Library	MS 11144	جامع البيان	الطبري	39		
32	Damascus	National al-Asad Library	MS 16925	بديع الشباب في شرح مقدمة الإعراب	عمر بن صالح بن عبد الصمد الرومي		Oval	1196
33	Dublin	Chester Beatty	Ar. 3236	تذكرة الإعداد ليوم المعاد	الصنهاجي	718	oval	
34	Dublin	Chester Beatty	Ar. 3268	معالم التنزيل، ج1	البغوي	44		
35	Dublin	Chester Beatty	Ar. 3272	الفتوح	أبن أعثم الكوفي	1366	circular	1197
36	Dublin	Chester Beatty	Ar. 3294	الروض الأنف الباسم	عبد الرحمان السهيلي	276	circular	
37	Dublin	Chester Beatty	Ar. 3310	أهنى المنائح	ابن فهد	1148	circular	
38	Dublin	Chester Beatty	Ar. 3315	الفهرست	النديم	998	circular	No date
39	Dublin	Chester Beatty	Ar. 3316	شرح الجامع الصغير	علي بن مكي الرازي	438	circular	
40	Dublin	Chester Beatty	Ar. 3334	الوجوه والنظائر	هارون بن موسى الأزدي الأعور	492	circular	1197
41	Dublin	Chester Beatty	Ar. 3342	التذييل والتكميل، ج5	أبو حيان الأندلسي	750	oval	1196
42	Istanbul	Süleymaniye	Pertevniyal V.S. 759	كتاب الجفر		1481	oval	
43	Istanbul	Süleymaniye	Kemankes 21	جواهر التفسير لتحفة الأمير	الملا حسين الكاشفي	57?	circular	1205
44	Istanbul	Süleymaniye	Yazma Bağışlar 766	تحفة الباري على صحيح البخاري	زكريا بن محمد الأنصاري	JnIB		1197
45	Jaffa	al-Maktaba al-Islāmiyya	MS 86[8]	كتاب سيبويه	سيبويه	JnIB	oval	1196
46	Jerusalem (Abu Dis)	The Center for Heritage Revival and Islamic Research	301/2[9]	النصف الأول من الكشاف	الزمخشري	45	circular	1196
47	Jerusalem	Is'āf al-Nashāshībī	MS 115	الفتاوى الأمينية	أمين الدين محمد المصري	561?	circular	
48	Jerusalem	Khalidi	MS 73	الإتقان في علوم القرآن	السيوطي	81	circular	1205
49	Jerusalem	Khalidi	MS 966	مختصر المكاتبات البديعة	محمد ابن الصيرفي	1003	illeg.	
50	Jerusalem	Khalidi	MS 1060	الفتوحات المكية	ابن العربي	656		

8 Class mark according to 'Aṭā' Allāh, *Fihris Yāfā*, 1984; accessed via Nablus, al-Najāḥ University Library website, MS 467.

9 Class mark according to Afaneh et al., *Fihris makhṭūṭāt Filasṭīn al-muṣawwara*, V, 72; formerly Jaffa: MS 52 ('Aṭā' Allāh, Fihris Yāfā, 1984) microfilm on Nablus, al-Najāḥ University Library website.

(*cont.*)

No.	Place	Library	Class mark	Title	Author	Inventory no.	Seal	Statement
51	Jerusalem	Khalidi	MS 1699	الإشراف على فضل الأشراف	إبراهيم الحسيني السمهودي	186	circular	1197
52	Jerusalem	National Library of Israel	Ms. AP Ar. 177	مواقع النجوم	ابن العربي	1493	illeg.	illeg.
53	Jerusalem	National Library of Israel	Ms. AP Ar. 258	الحرز الثمين	الملا علي القاري	215	illeg.	illeg.
54	Jerusalem	National Library of Israel	Ms. AP Ar. 261	مختصر شرح الحنفية	منلا خسرو		oval	
55	Jerusalem	National Library of Israel	Ms. AP Ar. 290	المهمات في شرح الرافعي والروضة ج4	الإسنوي	416	circular	1196
56	Jerusalem	National Library of Israel	Ms. AP Ar. 410	شرح اللباب في علم الإعراب	محمد بن مسعود	777	circular	
57	Jerusalem	National Library of Israel	Ms. Temp. Ar. 186.1	المنح المكية في شرح الهمزية	ابن حجر الهيتمي	218		
58	Leipzig	Universitäts-bibliothek	Vollers 118	الدرة الفاخرة	أبو حامد الغزالي	212	oval	
59	London	British Library	Or. 1183	البرق اليماني	قطب الدين محمد النهروالي	1369	circular	
60	London	British Library	Or. 1206	ديوان جرير	جرير	1215–1218?	oval	1197
61	London	British Library	Or. 4706	عجالة الإملاء	برهان الدين إبراهيم الناجي	221	circular	1199
62	Mecca	al-Ḥaram al-Makkī	MS 1499	حاشية على شرح العضد	السعد التفتازاني	637	circular	1197
63	Nablus	al-Najāḥ University	NL 211508[10]	فتح الباري	ابن حجر العسقلاني	150	circular	
64	Nablus	al-Najāḥ University	NL 250213	حياة الحيوان، ج2	الدميري	1290 or 1291	oval	No date
65	Princeton	University Library	Garrett 2996Y	الجواهر البهية / شرح المعراج/ السبعيات	الشبشيري/ نجم الدين الغيطي/ محمد الهمذاني	JnIB	circular	
66	Princeton	University Library	Garrett 3415Y	وفيات الأعيان	ابن خلكان	1283	circular	

10 We use, on advice from the library, the barcode number for al-Najāḥ University Library.

(*cont.*)

No.	Place	Library	Class mark	Title	Author	Inventory no.	Seal	Statement
67	Princeton	University Library	Garrett 3516Y	الخطط	المقريزي	JnIB	circular	
68	Princeton	University Library	Garrett 3959Y	درر الفرائد وغرر الفوائد	محمد بن علي الحرفوشي	JnIB	circular	
69	Princeton	University Library	Garrett 4691Y	مجموع		JnIB	circular	
70	Princeton	University Library	Garrett 5157Y	جمع النهاية	عبد الله ابن أبي جمرة	168?	oval	
71	Qatar	National Library	HC.MS.00211	مغني الطبيب وعمدة الأريب	محمد الزبيدي	1431	oval	1197
72	Qatar	National Library	HC.MS.00495	الزروع	فسطوس بن اسكور اسكينه	JnIB	oval	1201
73	Riyadh	Imam Mohammad Ibn Saud Islamic University	MS 979	إرشاد الطلبة الى شواهد الطيبة	علي بن سليمان المنصوري	119	circular	
74	Riyadh	Imam Mohammad Ibn Saud Islamic University	MS 1094	ديوان الدواوين	عبد الغني النابلسي	1187	circular	
75	Riyadh	King Faisal Center	MS 100	تفسير الطبري	ابن جرير الطبري	39		
76	Shinqit, Mauritania	Collection of Ahl Ḥabat	MS 9/96[11]	الموشح في شرح الكافية	محمد بن أبي بكر الخبيصي	816 or 828		
77	Tokio	University Library	Daiber Collection II, 76	إرشاد الطالبين إلى مراتب العلماء العاملين	عبد الوهاب الشعراني	1267		1196 or 1197?
78	'Paris book'[12]			شرح كلستان	سروري	1562 or 1563	circular	illeg.

11 Based on Baffioni, *Catalogue des Manuscrits*, 227.

12 Offered by Antiquariat Inlibris (Vienna), Catalogue *37th Antiquaria Ludwigsburg* (15–17 June 2023), no. 18: https://inlibris.com/item/bn60713/?catalogue=102466 (accessed 19 June 2023). For the term 'Paris book', see the *Introduction* of this book.

Bibliography

Afaneh, Hosam El Din (ʿAfāna, Ḥusām al-Dīn) et al. *Fihris makhṭūṭāt Filasṭīn al-muṣawwara*. 5 vols. Jerusalem: Wizārat al-awqāf wa-al-shuʾūn al-dīnīya, Muʾasassat iḥyāʾ al-turāth wa-al-buḥūth al-islāmiyya, 2000–2012.

ʿAṭāʾ Allāh, Maḥmūd ʿAlī. *Fihris makhṭūṭāt al-Maktaba al-Aḥmadiyya fī ʿAkkā*. 1983.

ʿAṭāʾ Allāh, Maḥmūd ʿAlī. *Fihris makhṭūṭāt al-Maktaba al-Islamiyya fī Yāfā*. 1984.

Baffioni, Carmela. *Catalogue des Manuscrits. Fondation Ahel Habott de Chinguetti*. Siena, 2006.